SECOND EDITION

AMERICAN MUSIC

A Panorama

Daniel Kingman

SCHIRMER BOOKS
A Division of Macmillan, Inc.
NEW YORK

Collier Macmillan Publishers
LONDON

Acknowledgments for quoted material are on pp. 661–662, which constitute a continuation of the copyright page.

Schirmer Books
A Division of Macmillan, Inc.
866 Third Avenue, New York, N. Y. 10022

Collier Macmillan Canada, Inc.

Library of Congress Catalog Card Number: 89-34119

Printed in the United States of America

printing number
2 3 4 5 6 7 8 9 10

Library of Congress Cataloging-in-Publication Data

Kingman, Daniel.
American music : a panorama / Daniel Kingman.—2nd ed.
p. cm.
ISBN 0-02-873370-3
1. Music—United States—History and criticism. I. Title.
ML200.K55 1990
780′.973—dc20

89-34119
CIP
MN

To Louise

The *panorama* was a popular form of didactic art in the larger frontier cities of America in the mid-1800s. It was an exhibition of the painter's art done on a mammoth scale. A huge canvas, twenty feet high or more, would slowly pass before the assembled audience, moving, scroll-like, from one large roll to another. The paying spectators would see vast scenes unrolling before their eyes in a sort of primitive motion picture—battle scenes, or the course of the Mississippi River between two points. Often this was done to the accompaniment of music.

CONTENTS

PART SIX Classical Music 411

PREFACE

ONCE more this preface begins, as did that of the first edition, with the most important person of all to a writer: the reader. An author usually has a rather clear and persistent image of the reader for whom he or she is writing. For myself, I have always envisioned the ideal reader of this book as someone who has somewhere picked up a lively interest in some kind of American music—be it blues or bluegrass, Cage, Coltrane, or Copland—and whose desire to find out more about *that* has led to engagement, bit by bit, through the interconnectedness of things, with the whole subject. The reader I have in mind need not be musically trained, though there is no doubt that the musician will read with a more experienced and penetrating grasp. But the occasional technical term has been used only when it seemed unavoidable, and I have tried to accompany it in most cases with a brief explanatory word or phrase. An active, open mind and an inquiring spirit—these I have regarded throughout as the only real essentials in a reader.

This work had its genesis, many years ago, in little more than an awakened enthusiasm for the music of my native land, an enthusiasm that manifested itself modestly enough at first in the inclusion of a few lectures on American music in the context of a general introductory course. My involvement came, by progressive stages, to embrace all of our varied musics, with the growing conviction that no aspect of our music should or *could* be excluded without maiming our perception of the whole teeming panorama. By this time an entire course had evolved, at a time when few such courses were offered, and when comprehensive writing on the whole subject of American music was rather narrow, and was not adequately informed by a sense of the vastness, variety, and grandeur of the scene to be surveyed. The appearance in 1955 of the first edition of Gilbert Chase's *America's Music* was a welcome departure in this regard.

It is interesting to note some of the landmarks along the path of a lengthening perspective of American music. Looking over my very early notes, for example, I find Charles Ives and John Alden Carpenter treated together. It made a certain sense at the time; they were nearly exact contemporaries, and both were businessmen-composers—heirs, it seemed, of a distinctly American tradition of amateur composers who earned their daily bread in some occupation entirely apart from music. The tradition can be traced all the way back to William Billings and his fellow Yankee tunesmiths; it exists no more. It does not diminish Carpenter's place in American music to see from a later vantage point that he was a talented mannerist with a rather narrow range, while Ives, with all the unevenness of his vast output, was a true pioneer.

Similar siftings and reassessments go on continuously among those of us who have a passionate interest in American music. As I prepared the revision of a book whose first edition has had a reception kind enough to justify its reincarnation in a second, I became ever more aware of and impressed by the phenomenal activity in the field, in which there has been literally an explosion of knowledge in the past decade or so. Projects of research, recording, and publication (both of the music itself and of sound analytical and biographical works) are going forward at an ever-increasing rate, and more and more scholars and writers seem drawn to the subject.

An author's preface is not the place for an extended list of resources, but a mere sampling of the evidence of a burgeoning interest in American music scholarship would not be out of place:

We now have a comprehensive four-volume reference work in *The New Grove Dictionary of American Music* (1986); this may well be regarded as a supplementary resource for every chapter in this book, and for every subject.

A fascinating and unique inventory of source materials for future research has been compiled in the *Resources of American Music History* (1981)—a handy volume in case, for example, you want to know what relics of American music may be tucked away in the Town Library of Peterborough, New Hampshire, the Tuolumne County Museum in California, or the Historical Society of Adams County, Nebraska; or if you are curious about the whereabouts of a hundred boxes of the papers of Mark Blitzstein, or eight thousand published orchestrations for circus band!

In the field of recording, the comprehensive *Recorded Anthology of American Music* put out by New World Records has reached at the time of writing 164 LPs. And following the death of the veteran producer, archivist, and enthusiast Moses Asch, the vast and seminal Folkways library of recordings has taken a new lease on life, safe in the arms of the Smithsonian Institution, which also continues its own series of important annotated issues.

Facsimile reprints let us see in their original published form the songs of Stephen Foster, or *The Indian Princess*, an opera on the subject of Pocahontas (1808), or the florid exuberances of Anthony Philip Heinrich's *The Dawning of Music in Kentucky, or The Pleasures of Harmony in the Solitudes of Nature*, of 1820. More and more authoritative and annotated editions in modern notation and format are also appearing.

Scholarly organizations and their publications and conferences are a valuable forum for sharing the fruits of research across the whole spectrum of American music, and for reviewing the ever-increasing flood of new books and recordings. The Sonneck Society for American Music holds annual conferences, and publishes both *American Music* (quarterly) and the *Sonneck Society Bulletin* (triannually). The Institute for Studies in American Music at Brooklyn

College of the City University of New York publishes a growing list of monographs and a semiannual *Newsletter*.

All this is stimulating, but it complicates the task of the generalist who must still try to make some sense out of the panorama for his readers. Having mapped this panorama initially in the first edition, I have taken another hard look at that map, reorienting here and there, filling in more detail where needed, and extending the range into the 1980s. But I have not altered the fundamental organization of the book; I have still rejected a traditional chronological-historical approach to the whole subject, and have maintained an ordering that reflects my view of American music as a number of more or less distinct but parallel streams. Of these streams, some are narrow, some broad, some at times have nearly dried up, some at times have overflowed their banks, spilling into one another, interpenetrating, merging, diverging again. Both the terrain and my own perception of it have changed in the past decade, but the metaphor still remains, for me, a sufficiently useful and compelling one.

From my vantage point near the end of the 1980s, I think I can still make out six such streams, though I have changed their labels a little. To the six sections devoted to these streams I have added a seventh, to call attention to what is more than ever an important characteristic of American music—a regionalism that defies absorption and homogenization, and a diversity that calls into question the concept of the "melting pot."

The question of balance in the allotment of the limited space available in a single-volume work inevitably arises. In order to give this book the character I believe it should have, several concerns, sometimes competing, have entered into decisions regarding space. The dominant concern, of course, has been, as it must be, the relative importance of the music itself, however difficult this may be to assess, and however widely individual assessments may vary.

This, however, has not been the sole concern. For example, since this book is designed to be used in teaching, the varying degrees of experience and background students bring to various kinds of American music has been taken into account. This led to a somewhat fuller and more detailed exposition of our twentieth-century fine-art or "classical" music than some critics would have liked, and to the adoption in Chapter 16 of an approach deliberately planned to move in stages from easily accessible and attractive twentieth-century works, especially those with extramusical associations, to works requiring a bit more preparation and experience.

A more important concern in the allocation of space, however, has been my conviction that the fullest and most rewarding understanding of American music is gained by seeing it in the context of American history and society. For example, the extended consideration of the minstrel show in Chapter 11, of the songs of Stephen Foster and of the later ragtime songs in Chapter 12, of the career of Thomas ("Blind Tom") Bethune in Chapter 15, and of bebop and the succeeding "black nationalism" in Chapter 14 all bear on the troublesome and inescapable American question of the relations between the races.

It is also of vital concern, in my opinion, to view American music in the context of *ideas*—of our various competing and evolving notions about art, and what it should be and how it should function. This conviction has influenced the treatment of many subjects in the book. Charles Ives has been given extensive space in Chapter 17 not only on account of his music, but because of the ideas he raises about (among other things) the negative aspects of professionalism, as well as the very nature of music itself—ideas that are further explored at some length in Chapter 18. Nineteenth-century men and women such as Anthony Philip Heinrich, William Fry, George Frederick Bristow, and even non-musicians such as John Sullivan Dwight, Richard Storrs Willis, and Margaret Fuller, have been given space in Chapter 15 on account of the issue of musical "Americanism" they raised—an issue that is still alive today. The career and ideas of Arthur Farwell are given space in the same chapter because of the democratic ideals implicit in his ambitious productions, and the implications of his pioneering publishing venture, the Wa-Wan Press. (He wanted *quality*, as he perceived it, and he wanted it for the *masses*—a dual objective that is not without certain potential contradictions.)

I am not unmindful of some imbalances in the content and length of individual chapters. In the late 1980s I am content to let stand the statement about the contemporary fine art scene that is made by placing the topic "Beyond Modernism" in a short independent chapter, and the emphasis and even encouragement that having a separate Chapter 20 gives to our *regional*, as well as ethnic, diversity. In the 1990s, should there be a third edition, perhaps these imbalances will be ameliorated—or replaced by others. In the meantime, I am prepared, on their account, to accept with good grace any accusations of eccentricity.

Whatever reservations, then, one may have about this way of mapping the terrain (and I freely confess to having some of my own), it can at least be said that each stream consists of a considerable and important body of music waiting to be known. Once the enthusiast has gotten to know the music, he can discard the categories or rearrange the music into his own. Nor are the boundaries always sharp. There are ambiguous composers and ambiguous pieces that could fit almost as well in one category as in another. Was John Philip Sousa primarily an entertainer or a "serious" musician? William Billings was one of a "school" of composers and his contemporaries wrote almost nothing but sacred music. Yet he is sometimes regarded as our first popular composer; his "Chester," at least, was indisputably the hit song of the American Revolution. And what of Leadbelly's "Goodnight Irene"? Leadbelly himself came into prominence as a folk singer, but this song—certainly not traditional—made the hit parade as a popular song. The thoughtful student can add many more examples. Rather than being exceptions, they prove the rule that American music is broadly interrelated, unpredictable, and defiant of categories.

Nevertheless, on a practical level organization is indispensable, and this particular ordering of the subject maintains what I regard as an important characteristic—a flexibility that allows the reader to use any of the six parts as a point of departure for an exploration of the whole subject. For example, those who feel most at home with folk or ethnic music, or hold the view that this is the key to our musical culture, will naturally begin with Part One, but will be able to go on from there to explore our folk-based popular music in Part Three, trace the folk influence in our native religious music in Part Two, and then observe its use as a basis for some of our classical music in Part Six.

But the study of American music could begin equally well with jazz (Part

Five), then proceed to a treatment of its roots as discernible in the music treated in Chapters 2, 6, and 8, and finally note its relation to our classical music in Part Six.

Religion has played an important role in the formation of American character and culture. A study of our native religious music in Part Two, and in Chapter 2 of Part One, could be followed by a study of both its echo and its antithesis as observable in blues, country music, and rock (Part Three), and in jazz (Part Five).

For many, rock has been the first point of contact with American music. From this starting point, this visceral form could be traced to its roots in Chapters 7 and 8; to its near relation, urban folk music, in Chapter 4; via jazz-rock to Part Five; or via contemporary "art rock" to the avant-garde classical music in Chapter 18; and so ever onward.

The vast popular music of the "Broadway galaxy" (Broadway, Hollywood, and Tin Pan Alley, of Part Four) has been for many their primary contact with American music, and could well serve as a point of departure, as could also our vigorous tradition of classical music, which has produced many works of wide appeal.

Wherever one should choose to begin, in other words, one can find, if my intentions have been to any degree realized, not only a substantial treatment of that subject but also an invitation to relate it to all other parts of the whole.

There is always a question, in a book about music, as to how much strictly biographical information to include. We can never deny the fact that it is *individuals* that make all the difference in music, and that their lives are part of its history, and are therefore never wholly irrelevant and are often fascinating. But the panorama is so vast, and the number of musicians, even quite important ones, is so great, that limits had to be placed somewhere. The reader will not find, then, an obligatory paragraph of biography for each composer mentioned. Some biographical material is indeed included where it seemed to shed light either on the nature of the music itself, on the milieu from which it came, or on some aspect of American music that goes beyond the career of a single individual. I offer this explanation to readers who may not find enough herein to satisfy their curiosity about a particular American musician, and I hope that they will have access to a reference work such as the single-volume *Baker's Biographical Dictionary*, edited by Nicolas Slonimsky (not limited to American musicians); to *The Encyclopedia of American Music*, edited by Edward Jablonski: for the modern period, to the *Dictionary of Contemporary Music*, edited by John Vinton (again not limited to Americans); or, for all periods, to the more detailed four-volume *New Grove Dictionary of American Music*, edited by H. Wiley Hitchcock and Stanley Sadie.

Musical examples have been used rather profusely in certain chapters, where they seem to be practical and particularly essential. They should enhance the text for the individual reader who can read music; in the lecture hall or classroom the teacher may play or sing such examples as are relevant. Songs and song excerpts have been pitched for comfortable singing.

When listening to vocal music, it always deepens ones perception of it to have the text available. Since it has not been possible, for reasons of space, to include as many vocal music texts as would have been ideal, I urgently recommend that the listener or the teacher make the effort necessary to have the text available in some form. Sources have been indicated where it was not possible to print the full text.

It is not usual to call special attention to endnotes, but I have reasons for most earnestly advising readers that they are in this case far from perfunctory. In addition to the usual and obligatory documentation of sources, they serve two further and even more important functions. First, the recorded examples cited are nearly indispensable illustrations of the points being made. Furthermore, the wealth of recorded material cited, especially in archival collections such as those issued by New World and Smithsonian, includes annotations that make it possible, where there is sufficient interest and initiative, to assemble musical illustrations that go into more detail than the scope of this book allows.

Second, the notes often provide additional background, references, and relevant "asides," beyond what could be incorporated into the text itself, thus opening up avenues of further exploration for the interested reader.

The reading lists at the end of each chapter are quite selective and include only those works that are apt to be readily available, are eminently readable in their own right, and are important to any further investigation of the topics treated in the chapter. Some non-music books are there because of their value in furnishing background. Musical biographies are numerous, and very uneven in quality and value. For lack of space I have in principle excluded them, except for a few that illuminate a period or a milieu especially well. Basic biographical information is readily available in the sources indicated above.

Listening to the music under discussion is of course indispensable. Live performances would be ideal, but recordings are a nearly obligatory substitute for immediate first acquaintance. Discography dates rapidly; furthermore, it is unnecessary in some areas, and more or less arbitrary in others. For the individual chapters the lists of suggested recordings are as extensive as it seems useful to have them. In areas in which there are good anthologies that are likely to be found in most institutional record libraries—areas such as folk music, country music, and jazz, for example—many of the musical examples have been chosen for the reader's convenience on the basis of their availability in these collections. The basis of the Listening lists is the LP record, which is still the basic medium for most libraries, even though it is true that by the 1990s discographies in books of this kind will have to reflect the rapid displacement of the LP by the compact disc and the cassette.

Since this book is an open-ended introduction to the subject, the suggestions for projects at the end of each chapter are to be considered an integral part of it. They are intended to give the student an opportunity to investigate further, on her or his own, many different aspects of American music. Even a tiny scrap of knowledge that one discovers, with a little effort, for oneself becomes a cherished corner of the whole subject—forever one's own, in a sense. It will be seen that the projects vary rather widely in the extent of work they involve and in the amount of musical background they presuppose, although the number of those calling for some knowledge of music has been kept to a minimum. This range is designed to allow for as much flexibility as possible in the use of individual projects. Furthermore, they are merely suggestions; the imaginative teacher and the inventive student can come up with many more, along similar or different lines. It will be noted that in nature and format the projects are by no means confined to the conventional "paper." I remember with pleasure how one student learned a group of sixteenth-century psalm tunes, set words from the Bay Psalm Book to them, added a simple, tasteful modal guitar accompaniment, and sang them for the class. The historical anachronism involved was a minor consideration as compared with the value of experiencing these old tunes as living music. (Needless to say, a similar project found its way into a list in this book.) I would be pleased to hear from students and teachers who have been innovative in this regard. The substance of what this book attempts to offer is not confined to the material in the chapters themselves. For the reader with the curiosity of an inquiring mind, the suggestions for projects, supported in many cases by the suggestions for further reading, offer many more avenues of approach to American music. It is for precisely that sort of reader, whether he or she happens to answer to the name of student, teacher, or simply enthusiast, that I like to feel this work was written.

Those who attempt to scan a panorama as vast as that of American music, and bring its diverse parts together somehow for the reader, are heavily dependent on, and indebted to, the specialists who delve deeply and with skill, knowledge, and integrity into the individual subjects that make up the whole. I have of course drawn on many printed sources, which I have tried to acknowledge in the body of the text or in the notes. In addition, I would like here to acknowledge the personal assistance and advice by many of my colleagues in American music, and to mention especially Joaquín Fernández in Hispanic-American music, Kate Van Winkle Keller in eighteenth-century secular tunes and dances, LeRoy Larson and Philip Nusbaum in Scandinavian-American music, and Brenda Marie Osbey in the Creole music of Louisiana.

Finally, it is a pleasure to thank Nancy Nerenberg and all the friendly and helpful people at the Copy Shack, who dealt not only competently but cheerfully with the photocopying complexities involved in the second edition. Last, and not least, do I take this opportunity express deep appreciation to my wife, Louise, for the sacrifices she has made (of which postponing too many good hikes in the Sierra constitutes only a small but significant part), and the help, understanding, and encouragement she has given in the long course of the preparation not only of the original edition, but of this revision as well.

Photo by David Gahr

PART ONE

Folk and Ethnic Musics

A SCANNING of the vast panorama of American music can begin nowhere more logically than with our folk and ethnic musics. America's music, throughout its broad spectrum, is so relatively new as to have remained closer to folk sources for its sustenance than is the case in almost any other country. The professional sector of our musical life has never gone very long without returning to refresh and revitalize itself at the fount of folk culture. Masterpieces as diverse as *Porgy and Bess* and *Appalachian Spring* bear witness to this, as do large amounts of music in popular culture, from Dan Emmett to Bob Dylan and Paul Simon.

Yet this very closeness of our music to its roots is attended by a paradox. There is probably no other country in the world in which the soil of folk culture has been so thoroughly broken up, and either eroded away or rendered sterile. Not only have the all-pervasive media spread commercial urban music thoroughly, but they have put music largely into the hands of the professional entertainer. Continuous and extensive migration has broken down isolation and emasculated regional character. And affluence, spectacular in comparison to the rest of the world, has put the appliances and products of the media into the hands of virtually everyone, so that the need or desire to make one's own music has lessened or disappeared.

So it would appear that the rich humus of folklore has provided us with nourishment but proved to be fragile as well. Yet the realization of its fragility has made us more aware of its value and encouraged us to make great efforts to conserve it. And our folk and ethnic musics do live on in the space age—perhaps because, faced with the formidable challenge to human values and human scale posed by technology, and with the disorientations of an unstable world, we have come to realize our need for the sense of continuity that a living connection with the past provides, and at the same time the benefits of keeping alive, through adaptation to the world we live in, an oral tradition that is simple, direct, and unflinchingly honest in its expression.

1

The British-American Tradition

AMERICAN culture, during the course of an evolution spanning more than four centuries, has been subjected to a greater variety of ethnic and folk influences than has that of any other country. An ethnic music existed among the sparse inhabitants of the continent before the transoceanic migrations of historic times began. With these migrations have come musical traditions from four other continents, in continuing waves. Chapters 1 and 2 treat the two dominant strains of American folk music—those whose preeminent influence in our culture is undeniable. These are the ones whose origins can be found in the British Isles and in black Africa.

The British-American strain is best epitomized in the ballad. There are songs, hymns, and dance tunes to be dealt with as well, of course; but it is the ballad that has been the main vehicle of the tradition, that most typifies it, and that has attracted the most serious attention from both scholars and folk singers.

Since ballad singing has been going on since the Middle Ages, we are not dealing with a phenomenon that can be limited to any single historical period. Ballads may be very old; some bear clear traces of their medieval origin, while some hint of origins still older. Or they may be very young; on the fair assumption that ballad making is not dead, it is possible that today, somewhere, there is being fashioned or refashioned a piece that will eventually be recognized as a traditional ballad, or a variant of one.

As an introduction to this vast body of folk literature, you might try to hear several different versions of a single traditional ballad. "Barbara Allen," the most popular in America (possibly because it was printed in so many songbooks in the nineteenth century), would be a good one to start looking for.

You might be fortunate enough to hear the song in person from several singers: professionals, amateur folk enthusiasts, or just friends or acquaintances. This is the folk way. But if this is not possible, there is the medium of recordings.[1]

"Barbara Allen" has traveled far and wide. The Library of Congress Archive of American Folk Song contained, as of 1962, 243 transcribed versions of this ballad, picked up from twenty-seven states, from Maine to Florida to California. In addition to a wide geographical range, you will become aware of a wide range in styles of presentation. Your search might yield versions that range all the way from a field recording of the unadorned performance of a solitary singer, who learned the song from oral tradition, to a full commercial production number with studio orchestra and choral background. You will thus acquire a sense of both the pervasiveness and the durability of the traditional ballad. This done, it will be time to examine more closely some of its characteristics.

Some Marks of the Ballad

A good story well told is one of the delights of human intercourse. If we add to this the power of a good tune to fix story and mood in the memory, and to this the hand-rubbed luster that any well-worn object has received from loving generations of its possessors, we have the essential ingredients of the ballad.

"A story sung—preferably from memory": this will do as the beginning of a definition. It is also metered and rhymed, though with innocent inexactitude. The casualness of the traditional ballad in both meter and rhyme is illustrated in the following charmingly wayward stanza:

They gave to her the nutmeg,
  And they gave to her the ginger;
But she gave to them a far better thing,
  The seven gold rings off her fingers.

We must not expect of the true ballad of the folk the discipline of literary poetry. By way of rounding off the definition, we can note as an unvarying feature of the ballad that all its many verses (each usually four lines in length) are sung to the same tune.

The ballad has roots, many of which go deep. When we hear Pete Seeger sing of the plucky girl who cleverly turns the tables on a habitual murderer and pushes *him* into the sea to drown, we are hearing a tale that has been sung in varying versions by the Danish, Swedish, Norwegian, Icelandic, German, Polish, Magyar, Italian, Spanish, and Portuguese folk, and a tale that has its analogy in a story from Hebrew scripture. When Woody Guthrie sings "The Gypsy Davy,"[2] his version sounds very much at home on the western plains, but this ballad is at least as old as the attempt by king and parliament to expel the gypsies from Scotland about the time of Shakespeare.

What the ballad offers us is drama—drama as unfolded by a solitary singer. It is drama often of extraordinary terseness and condensation. The main points of the mournful tale of "Barbara Allen," for example, may be set out in eight or nine verses. Usually the characters are not given any introduction, or it may be a very cursory one ("a lady in the North Countrie"; "a wooer out of the West"), and time and place are described in the barest terms (" 'Twas in the lovely month of May"; "the land where the grass grows green"). Prior events leading up to the climactic action are rarely set forth. The poet Thomas Gray characterized this terseness by saying that the ballad "begins in the fifth act of the play."

Description is lean, or lacking entirely. Occasionally it may be very telling, as:

> She glistened and glittered and proudly she walked
> The streets on the banks of the sea.

Often, however, it is rendered in the conventionalized language of the cliché phrase ("milk-white steed"; "lily-white hand"). These phrases may wander freely from one ballad to another.

Altogether, the way of the ballad is to leave a great deal to the imagination of the hearer, who is thus free to fill in scenes and events with extraordinary vividness. Jean Ritchie, a well-known folk singer from the Appalachians, tells of the impression made on her as a child by these scenes, which were fleshed out in her imagination as she heard the ballads:

> The song itself seemed unreal and far, far way, telling dreamily of Fair Ellender and Lord Thomas and courts and processions, love and death, but the people my half-closed eyes saw were alive and beautiful. Fair Ellender rode slowly by on her snow-white horse, her hair like long strands of silver and her face like milk in the moonlight. Then came her waiting maids, dressed all in green, and holding their heads high and proud. There was Lord Thomas, tall and brave with his sword shining in his hand, there the wedding folk around the table.[3]

Oral Tradition and the Ballad Texts

A folk song is an organic whole, consisting of words, a tune, and a way of singing. It is incomplete without any one of the three. For purposes of further study, however, we must consider each element in turn. We shall begin with the element that first attracted the attention of literary men and scholars, and that can most easily be grasped by the general reader—the words.

It is an accepted criterion of folk music that it not rely on print, but be transmitted and preserved simply by being sung or played. This is what is meant by oral tradition, and it has a significance, when we think about it, far beyond that of simply a technical definition. What is committed to the reservoir of memory is intimate to us and has importance in our lives. Most of us can remember the strong impression made on us in childhood by a song that someone close to us sang from memory. "By heart" is not a gratuitous or accidental phrase. We don't properly sing a folk song until we have lived with it long, handled its imagery, and allowed its meaning to resonate within us. By this time memorizing has become incidental. Only then do we project it fully.

Charles Seeger mentions the "luminous quality" that characterizes true ballad singing, which is often possessed not only by the exceptionally talented but even by ordinary carriers of the tradition.[4]

The Forces of Change

It is generally agreed that traditional folk singers do not intentionally alter a song. But there are many things about oral transmission that make changes inevitable—that lead, in other words, to the production of variants. Since the processes as well as the products of oral change may be fascinating, let us look at just a few. Simple forgetting is a constant factor. The change it works may be minor and may not affect the ballad to any essential degree, since something almost equally suitable may be substituted for what is forgotten. If from one singer we hear "When the flowers they were blooming" and from another "When red buds they were swellin'," the precise image has changed but the general evocation of spring remains. Or if some element is left out entirely, it may be very incidental and sufficiently far removed from what has been called the "emotional core," or very essence, of the ballad to make no great difference. But when major portions—the entire ending or the whole narrative context, for example—are forgotten, the whole point of the ballad may be changed.

The tendency to "localize" both the place names and the names of characters in the narratives is another obvious source of change. The "Oxford girl" easily becomes the "Knoxville girl" or even the "Waco girl."[5] Similarly, conventionalized descriptions may change; the "milk-white steed" becomes, more appropriately in the West, the "buckskin horse."

A misunderstanding of elements of language as the ballad ages is an interesting source of change. Difficult or ambiguous words, or words and phrases no longer in current usage, are very vulnerable to change. An older version of "The Gypsy Laddie," still retaining aspects of the supernatural, says of the gypsy band that as they saw the lady "They coost their glamourie owre her." A presumably later and obviously garbled version says of the gypsies at this point that "They called their grandmother over"! Not only has the word *glamourie* ("glamour") been misunderstood, but its older meaning as an actual spell to be cast over someone has been lost, to the impoverishment of the ballad.

Misunderstanding of older words and phrases has produced especially interesting results in the refrains, or burdens, of the ballads. "Juniper, gentian, and rosemary"; "Savory, sage, rosemary, and thyme"—in this age of renewed interest in the use of herbs it is surprising that these names should ever have been misunderstood or forgotten. But behold what the loss of their meaning has wrought with the passage of time. The first phrase appears transmuted into girls' names—"Jennifer gentle, and Rosemaree"—and the second has undergone a bewildering array of transformations. Some of these, gleaned from Bronson's fifty-five versions of this ballad (known variously as "The Elfin Knight," "Scarborough Fair," or "The Lovers' Tasks," among other names),[6] are here arranged in approximate order of increasing distance from the pure "plant" refrain:

Save rosemary and thyme.
Rose Mary in time.
Rose de Marian Time.
Every rose grows merry in time.
Every leaf grows many a time.
So sav'ry was said come marry in time.
Whilst every grove rings with a merry antine.
Green grows the merry antine.[7]

In each of these one can sense an attempt to be faithful to the *sound* of what was heard but not understood, and at the same time in many cases to make some kind of new sense out of it.

Refrains make a particularly interesting study in themselves. Some refrains that now consist completely of nonsense syllables may be descended from phrases that once had meaning, even as incantations of some sort. But this is speculative. In any case, even if they have lost all "meaning" in the usual sense (if they ever had any), or any direct connection with the story, they cannot be eliminated without damaging the ballads artistically. This sense of their effect on both the mood and the pace of the narrative has kept them an integral part of many ballads. The effect of the refrain is cumulative, evocative, almost hypnotic. As Evelyn Wells has written, "One's interest is held by a singer who, with every other line, pauses for the refrain; the tale is dignified by the interruptions. Suspense mounts, and mounts rhythmically, with the regular recurrences of the refrain. The tempo of the tale is steadied, its stride evened."[8]

Finally, a kind of censorship, conscicus or unconscious, may operate to make changes in the ballad. Folk singers will naturally be selective in the themes, images, or elements of the story that they "remember" according to their own moral or aesthetic standards or those of their society, and whether or not this is done at a conscious level is not of great significance. In certain instances sexual themes are muted, or avoided entirely, as are references to nakedness, but this is not very common. Far more consistent and interesting are changes that reflect an altered framework of reality as the legacy is passed to succeeding generations. References to the supernatural are very common in older versions. These tend to disappear in more recent ones, especially in the transplantation to the New World. This often impoverishes the ballad from a poetic or imaginative standpoint, for the loss of the supernatural dimension is not usually compensated for by a corresponding gain in depth of insight into human nature.[9]

What happens to old ballads, then, is very like what happens to old buildings. None survive the passage of time intact. Some, of exceptional strength, may have only a few stones replaced here and there. In some, a ruined or lost wing may be replaced by an entirely new part, so that the outlines of the whole are drastically altered. Of others, only a wall or a piece of foundation remains—an inscrutable fragment that no longer makes sense in our world and has to be relegated to fantasy. Still others may be dismantled entirely, and their stones scattered; later the keen observer may happen to notice a cornerstone, or a piece of an arch, that has been appropriated by builders of a later age, so that out of their new work bits of the old project curiously here and there as strange and unaccountable anachronisms.

Print and the Ballad

The oral tradition—human memory as the conservator and the human voice as the "publisher"—has been stressed here at some length. Among folklorists, oral transmission still retains its preeminence as the *ideal* medium of folk song, and whether a ballad can be found to be in oral tradition is still regarded as a valid test of its "folkness," regardless of its origins. But print has long had a hand in ballad conservation and dissemination, and more recently so have other media such as recordings. So intertwined for centuries have been the printed and oral traditions that the notion of a "pure" oral tradition, existing uninterruptedly for generations, aloof from the contaminating populism or professionalism of printed media, is a myth with no more relation to actuality than the romantic but discredited notion of the spontaneous "communal creation" of ballads.[10] The facts are, first, that a ballad, however it may have changed over time, was originally the product of a single individual (who can even be identified in some cases); and, second, that the older it is, the more likely it is to have been in and out of print over the course of its history. Furthermore, it is likely that its printed versions have had an influence both on the state in which it exists today and on its geographical distribution. For example, when multiple versions of a ballad recovered from oral tradition are strikingly similar in their details, this usually points to the preexistence, at some point, of a printed version.

The "broadside" (a cheap printed version of a ballad—the words only, without the music— on a single sheet) and the "songster" (a small collection of such texts, also cheaply printed, for popular sale) have long figured in ballad history, both here and in the British Isles. Broadside ballads were usually hastily written (using existing material liberally) by hack writers for quick sale to capitalize on current and public events, such as hangings. (Many "last words" of condemned criminals found their way into ballads.)[11] Broadsides were published in America right up to the end of the nineteenth century, and in rural areas the tradition was still alive in the twentieth. James W. Day was a blind Kentucky musician who used the pseudonym Jilson Setters. He told of writing a ballad about a convicted murderer named Simpson Bush, which Setters took to the hanging. He recalled: "I had my pockets plum full of my song-ballet that I had made up about Bush and that a printer had run off for me on a little hand press at the county seat. I sold every one I had."[12] The "broadside" was brought up to date in terms of media during the famous Scopes trial of 1925, when sixty thousand phonograph recordings of a ballad on the subject were sold on the steps of the courthouse in Dayton, Tennessee, while the trial was going on.[13]

The ephemeral, topical nature of the "broadside" ballads, as well as their routinely inferior literary qualities, have caused scholars to distinguish them from "traditional" ballads, which are epitomized in the canon of those collected and edited in the late nineteenth century by Harvard professor Francis James Child.[14] But the fact is that even some of the Child ballads, as they are called, may well have originated in print.

Three examples of the interaction between print and sound media on the one hand and oral tradition on the other will close our brief consideration of this complex and fascinating subject. In 1839 there were published some verses by the Reverend Edwin Chapin on the subject of the death at sea of a young man. The verses were titled "The Ocean Burial," and they began with the line, repeated often, "O! bury me not in the deep, deep sea." The poem was set to music and published in 1850. The "ocean" version was later recovered from oral tradition in New England, but the ballad became far better known in its western (and generally improved) adaptation as "The Dying Cowboy," beginning with the words "Oh bury me not on the lone prairie."[15] In 1862 William Shakespeare ("Will") Hays wrote a Civil War song, "The Drummer Boy of Shiloh," about the death in battle of a young drummer. It quickly became one of the "hit" songs of the war.* While war ballads usually have a shorter life span than other types, "The Drummer Boy of Shiloh" appeared in songsters (an intermediate step to oral tradition) in New York and Texas in the 1870s, and it was recovered in this century from oral tradition in the Appalachians, in the Ozarks, and in Utah.[16] Finally, in 1925 Polk Brockman, an early country-music talent scout, heard of a cave death in Kentucky and wired the Reverend Andrew Jenkins in Atlanta, in effect "ordering" a song on the subject, for which he paid him $25, plus another $25 to make a recording of it, which became popular. This was the origin of the ballad "Floyd Collins," which was later collected from oral tradition in Virginia, North Carolina, Tennessee, Kentucky, New York, and Utah.[17]

Imported Versus Native Ballads

Before leaving the subject of the ballad texts, it will be useful to treat briefly the question of whether there has grown up a body of truly *native* ballads, and if so in what ways they differ essentially from those imported from England, Scotland, and Ireland, however much the latter may have been adapted. The answer to the first question is that there is indeed a body of native ballads, naturally much younger than the imported ones. Malcolm Laws identifies only a scant number from Colonial and Revolutionary times ("Springfield Mountain" being the best known) and relatively few from either the early nineteenth or the twentieth centuries. He has concluded that the latter part of the nineteenth century—a time of expansion and conquest, of both the wilderness and its inhabitants—produced the greatest number of our native ballads still in circulation.[18] It was a time recent enough so that its *events* and its *ambience* are not too remote to be identified with, and not so recent that urbanization and industrialization had supplanted ballad making with the products of Tin Pan Alley.

Whereas the Child ballads, even in adaptation, have not entirely concealed their "archaic style and medieval atmosphere" (part of their charm for twentieth-century singers, no doubt), the native ballads have more "realistic immediacy." Native ballads in many cases have known authors, and they are much more apt to be based on actual occurrences, even though assigning an exact time and place to the events may present nearly insoluble, if fascinating,

* See Chapter 12 for more about this and other Civil War songs.

problems. (The search for the factual basis of the railroad ballad "Casey Jones" and the lumberjack ballad "The Jam on Gerry's Rock" are cases in point.) Finally, in contrast to the older British ballads, American ballads tend to be more about occupations—railroading ("The Wreck of Old 97"), cowboys ("Little Joe the Wrangler"), lumberjacks ("The Jam on Gerry's Rock"), sailors ("The Bigler's Crew"), and even criminals ("Jesse James")—and frequently involve fatal physical disasters ("The Avondale Disaster," "The Titanic") or a more or less journalistic recounting of murders and executions ("Pearl Bryan," "Little Omie Wise," "John Hardy") rather than dwelling on more psychic, introverted, or pathological themes such as supernatural phenomena, fatal jealousy, or incest. Native ballads are characterized by a more subjective, sympathetic approach to their heroes or heroines—an approach that leads both to sentimentality and to a tendency to moralize (though not to the extent that afflicted the commercial popular song of the same era, as we shall see in Chapter 12). Laws finds in the American ballad evidence of a "tender humanity toward all who are faced with tragedy," and concludes that "Native balladry may be rugged and colorful or commonplace and sentimental; much of it may be inept, some even illiterate, but above all it shows compassion, neighborliness, and concern for other men's misfortunes."[19]

Oral Tradition and the Music of the Ballads

It is somewhat unfortunate that the early attention given to ballads was directed almost exclusively to their texts. Early collectors and scholars were, for the most part, not musicians, and were neither sensitive to the tunes nor equipped to record or study them. Indeed, "the ballad as literature" is still a dominant theme, and in fact has been more prevalent in America than in England. The imbalance of this one-sided approach is being redressed, and it should be a function of a book on American music to lend a hand in this process.

To be sure, for the person not skilled in music and just becoming interested in ballads, the words are certainly their most approachable element. The story, and its embodiment in language, is the very core of the ballad. Most folk music the world over is closely wedded to words. But it is also true that it is simply not possible to gain any true idea of a ballad separated from its music. The words alone, abstracted in print as we find them in books, can impart only the dimmest notion of the effect of the same ballad sung—just as a reprint in black and white must fail to convey the depth, color, nuances, and mood of the original oil painting. Many traditional singers, it is interesting to note, find themselves unable to recall the words of a folk song apart from the music, or the music apart from the words.

Tune Variation

Tunes are subject to the same organic processes of change wrought by oral tradition that operate on the words, and these also produce tune variants—sometimes in great numbers. How does the tune of "Barbara Allen" go? It all depends on who is singing it. Examples 1–1 and 1–2 are two versions recovered from traditional singing. They are quite different. Each is representative of a large group of tunes that has dozens of variants. Example 1–1 was recorded in West Liberty, Kentucky, in 1937.

Example 1–1

Transcription by the author

It was early in the month of May,
When the May-buds they were a-swelling,
Sweet William on his death-bed lay
For the love of Barbara Allen.

Example 1–2 is from Tennessee, as sung for the Library of Congress Archive collection in 1936.

Example 1–2

Transcription by the author

'Twas in the lovely month of May
The flowers all were bloomin'.
Sweet William on his death-bed lay
For the love of Barbry Allen.[20]

Interestingly enough, the tune most commonly printed in popular collections, and thus the one most frequently encountered in commercial arrangements and professional performances, is not to be found in traditional sources at all. It apparently derives from a version of the ballad first printed in England in 1839 (Example 1–3).

Example 1–3

In Scarlet town where I was born,
  There was a fair maid dwelling,
Made every youth cry, Well away,
  And her name was Barb'ra Allen.

As must be clear by now, it is not that folk singers try to be different, or original. But time, memory, and geography operate on music as well as on words, and no ballad is apt to have only a single tune indissolubly wedded to it. Yet neither is any given tune always exclusively associated with only one ballad. Charles Seeger puts it both accurately and colorfully when he writes that "both spouses are frequently unfaithful to their common-law kind of union." Yet he does attest to "a permanence of a sort not lightly to be regarded."[21]

Tune Sources

Where do the tunes come from? In folk music this is usually very difficult to answer with certainty. It is easier in cases in which a tune from a known source, or by a known composer, goes over into the oral tradition for a long enough period to acquire the characteristics of folk music, including the production of variants. But this takes a long time, and it happens very rarely. Most tunes associated with the ballads can be definitely traced only as far back as the nineteenth century, though a few are traceable as far as the seventeenth. This is not to say, however, that some do not exhibit characteristics of far greater antiquity. Paying attention to tune *characteristics,* rather than note-for-note identity, makes it possible to trace a tune's family back much farther. Bertrand Bronson[22] has shown in a number of cases, for example, the relation between tunes of the traditional ballads and sections of medieval plainchant. While it is not possible to claim on the basis of this relation that the ballad tunes were derived directly from the chants of the Roman Catholic Church that were in use during the Middle Ages, it does show that certain tune prototypes, or tune *shapes,* have been a part of our musical heritage for a thousand years or more. Some tune types have proven to be extremely durable, with the ability to travel far and outlive any number of different word settings.

Tune Scales

Whether the tunes of many of the ballads as we know them are really very old or not, many of them *sound* archaic, particularly those coming from the Appalachians. Their antique flavor is based in part on a free concept of rhythm; they don't appear to us to keep "strict time." Of course, this is related to the fact that traditionally they are sung without accompaniment; but a good deal of this antique flavor can be attributed to the scales on which they are based. Many use five-tone or six-tone scales, or else seven-tone scales that conform to the older *modes* instead of to our more modern major and minor scales. You may encounter, in descriptions of folk tunes, the Greek names assigned to the modes during the Middle Ages: Dorian, Phrygian, Lydian, Mixolydian, Aeolian, and Ionian. These modal scales are also being used in our time in some of the more esoteric and folk-influenced jazz and rock. A full explanation of the use of five-tone, six-tone, and modal seven-tone scales in folk music is beyond the scope of this book,[23] but if you have access to any keyboard you can acquire a rudimentary knowledge of the scale material of Anglo-American folk music (and, indeed, most of the world's folk music) by some exploratory playing using the white keys only. If you resist the gravitational attraction that more conventional music has given to the note C (you will have to know or learn the letter names of the keys), you will begin to get a feel for the greater freedom of choice as regards a *final* tone that is characteristic of folk music. A fairly common mode in this music, for example, is the Dorian, which, on the white notes, uses the scale in Example 1–4, with D as final.

Example 1–4

Example 1–5 is a ballad tune collected in Maine that is in the Dorian mode.

Example 1–5

I'll tell you of a false-hearted knight
  Who courted a lady gay,
And all that he wanted of this pretty fair maid
  Was to take her sweet life away.

The finals of the other modes (still using just the white notes) are: Phrygian, E; Lydian, F; Mixolydian, G; Aeolian (equivalent to our natural minor scale), A; Ionian (equivalent in material, if not in its usage, to our familiar major scale), C. Not all these modes, however, are used in Anglo-American folk music with anything like equal frequency; the Lydian and Phrygian are very rare indeed.

Very common in folk music are various hexatonic (six-tone) and pentatonic (five-tone) scales. These scales can also be played on the white notes alone; indeed their sound, as used in folk music, is very similar to that of the full seven-tone modal scales, with the omission of one or two tones. The first two versions of "Barbara Allen" (Examples 1–1 and 1–2) are both pentatonic. The first uses the scale shown in Example 1–6. (The notes at each end of the

Example 1–6

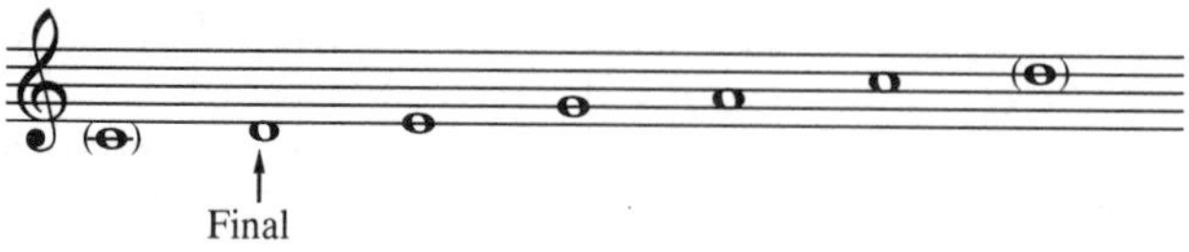

examples do not add new tones to the scale, but merely extend the range by duplicating scale notes an octave higher or lower.) The second uses Example 1-7. It can be shown that these scales are both versions of the same prototypical

Example 1–7

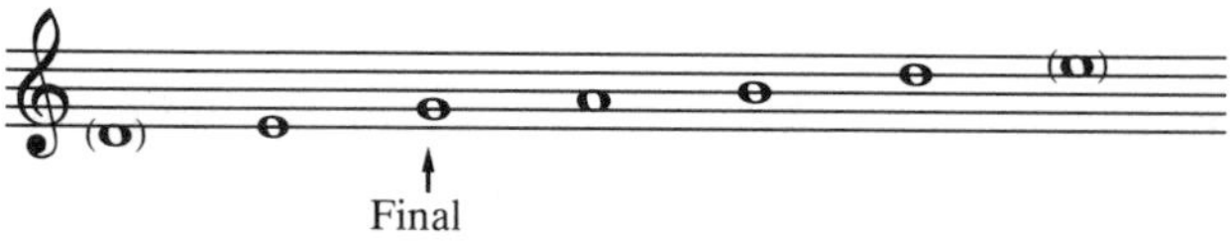

pentatonic scale. This scale (which can also be produced by playing just the *black* keys on the keyboard) is extremely widespread in its use. The number and geographical distribution of tunes that are pentatonic (or very nearly so) is surprising. Our music has received this legacy from many sources: native American Indian tunes, African tunes, tunes from central Europe, from Scotland, and from the Orient. It has also been adopted, perhaps unconsciously, by writers of popular songs when they are composing in a vernacular or quasi-folk idiom. As an example, the first two phrases of two of Stephen Foster's best-known songs, "Old Folks at Home" and "Oh, Susannah," are purely pentatonic.

Instruments and Ballad Singing

Today we seldom hear folk songs unaccompanied, and it may be surprising to learn that traditionally they were usually sung without accompanying instruments. In the southern highlands, for example, there was both an instrumental and a vocal tradition, but they were apparently kept separate for the most part. The fiddle was originally the most common instrument in most parts of rural America, but very seldom was it used to accompany folk songs; its usual role, as we shall see, was to provide music for dancing. Three instruments that have since become associated with folk songs, in the approximate order in which they were introduced into tradition, are the dulcimer, the banjo, and the guitar.

The addition of instrumental accompaniment to the medium of purely vocal folk music operates to change that music in very fundamental ways. In the first place, all instruments except the winds (which are the most closely related to the human voice) lend themselves to a manner of playing that is rather strongly marked rhythmically—that is, there is usually a very discernible "beat." This tends to make the formerly free-flowing vocal line more rhythmic, but at the same time more rigid. Accompaniment also has a strong impact on harmony. Instruments like the guitar tend to become, especially in the hands of the modestly skilled, fundamentally harmonic—that is, used to produce chords only. Furthermore, the number of chords at the command of the casual player is not great, so that the accompaniment comes to consist of those very few chords (basically three: the tonic, subdominant, and dominant)* that have become fundamental to Western cultivated music since the dissolution of the old modes. This has naturally tended to force the old tunes into a new and rather limited harmonic mold—or to force the replacement of the old tunes by newer ones conceived in the new mold. The result has been the suppression, almost to the point of extinction, of the older tunes, with their rich, varied, and strange-sounding modality.[24]

Singing Style as an Integral Part of Folk Song

Finally, we cannot leave the music of the ballads without treating the third vital ingredient of the ballad as mentioned earlier: a *way* of singing. Just as the printed text of a ballad is deficient without the music, so even the addition of printed music fails to convey the whole of the ballad, in that it cannot indicate the manner in which it is sung. Musical notation is a highly useful convention, but it is most useful in dealing with music that has evolved around a written tradition (such as fine-art music), and which has only one authoritative version—that of the composer. Notation is least adequate when dealing with music highly dependent upon oral tradition. Of the six American musics dealt with in the first six parts of this book, the one in which print bears the least relationship to the actuality of the sound is folk music. The tone quality and inflections of the voice, the way a singer embellishes a tune, the way rhythm and pitch are subtly varied—these are all part of the song.[25] There is here, as in the case of words and notes alone, much latitude for individual variation, but there are also rather widely accepted conventions of singing style within folk communities.[26] Sound recordings have become indispensable for the preservation, propagation, and study of this aspect of folk song.

Folk Music in the Hands of the Professional Singer

How has folk music fared in the hands of the professional singer or entertainer? It depends, of course, upon your point of view. A short answer would probably be, Not as badly as might be thought. But to understand the situation more fully, we must at least consider briefly the distinction between the traditional folk singer and the professional. Traditional singers are themselves part of the

* In other words, the chords of C, F, and G in C major.

tradition. They have learned the songs from it, their memory constitutes the reservoir of this tradition, and through their singing it is not only enjoyed by the community but transmitted to others of that community and preserved. Traditional singers may happen to *become* professional, if they are sufficiently talented, but the role of the professional is quite different. Professionals, for whom singing becomes a livelihood, must reach a larger audience—a vastly larger audience, in fact, if they are to survive—and must of course please and entertain that audience. They must therefore make their songs as attractive as they can to those who do not belong to its tradition, and who may know little or nothing about that tradition. In doing so they may find it necessary to make changes, large or small, that compromise the tradition somewhat. It has been said that professionals must think not only of *what* they are singing but of *how* they are singing it. Personal traits, interpretative or "expressive" idiosyncrasies that may have begun as a way to help put the piece across, become trademarks of his or her style, so that we may be hearing more of the singer than the song.

But professionals have positive contributions to make as well. They may stimulate interest in, and thus help to preserve, traditional music that would otherwise be lost. They bring to their performances a proven degree of musical talent inherently greater than that of the average "carrier" of the tradition. The best professionals, those knowledgeable in the field of ballads and sensitive to their values, will seek out many different versions, listen to many traditional singers, and choose and collate from the versions those elements of text and music that are artistically the most satisfying. Further, their renditions are not going to be marred by the lapses of memory that mutilate many a ballad in the hands of traditional singers. All in all, it should be appreciated that the contributions of both the traditional singer and the professional are significant, but that their roles are distinct, and that this distinction should be kept in mind in listening to either one.

The Ballad Today and Its Contributions

Some students speak of the fifteenth century as the ideal "ballad age." Others point to a flowering of the ballad in the eighteenth century. Certainly it cannot be said that our time is in any sense a golden age of the ballad. Yet we now know that the ballad lives, whereas a short time ago it was thought to be dying. Not only does it live, but it has managed to color the music and poetry of our own time. The revival of the cultivation of folk music over the past quarter-century has not only kept the ballad from disappearing forever but has allowed its style and outlook to permeate our popular musical-poetic life—resulting in the creation of a whole new genre of popular song, vast and uneven in quality, to be sure, but reflecting at its best the common touch, the poignancy, the unflinching observation of life, and the touches of poetic realism that place it far above the trite mediocrity of the run-of-the-mill popular song of a generation ago. This new enrichment bears witness in no small measure to the influence of the traditional ballad and those qualities that have given it such a long life.

Lyrical Songs, Play-Party Games, and Fiddle Tunes

Following the paths of the ballad takes us far and wide, and offers ample material for a fascinating study in and of itself, but if we are to gain a fuller picture of Anglo-American folk music as a whole, it will need some rounding out.

First of all, it may naturally be asked whether there are not other folk songs besides the ballads. Indeed, there are. In fact, the term "folk song" is sometimes used in *contradistinction* to the term "ballad": that is, a song that is *not* narrative, but primarily lyrical, is often what is meant, strictly, by a folk song. The distinction, of course, is not always easy to make. Among the most strikingly beautiful lyrical folk songs are love songs such as "Black Is the Color of My True Love's Hair."

Another type of Anglo-American folk song occupies a peculiar ground somewhere between the ballad and the fiddle tune (discussed next). These are songs that became widely used for a form of organized dancing called the *play-party,* and so became known as play-party games or play-party songs. They have their origin in the prohibition, in some religious traditions, against dancing as such, but especially against the use of the fiddle, considered a sinful instrument of the devil. At the play-party, originally, there was neither fiddle nor orchestra, so that the participants made their own music by singing, with spectators clapping hands and stamping feet.[27] Among the more familiar play-party songs are: "Skip to My Lou" (*Lou,* from Scotch usage, is a word used to mean "love" or "sweetheart"); "Going to Boston"; "Charlie's Sweet" (the Scotch heritage is found here again in the reference to Bonnie Prince Charlie and the eighteenth-century Stuart uprising); "Loupy Lou" (or "Looby Lou"); and "Get Along Home, Cindy." Some of these songs, such as "Old Dan Tucker" and "Buffalo Gals," show an interesting derivation from blackface minstrel songs.

Many of the play-party songs are also found as fiddle tunes: "Old Joe Clark," "Sally Goodin," and "Old Dan Tucker," for example. There is considerable overlapping between the vocal and instrumental traditions in this type of song. It may be treated as a song with instrumental accompaniment or a dance tune to which verses of the song are simply sung intermittently.[28] Many phrases of the texts make it clear that the songs, regardless of their origin, have for a long time been associated with dancing:

> One hand in the hopper and the other in the sack,
> Ladies step forward and the gents fall back.
>
> Corn-stalk fiddle and shoe-string bow,
> Come down gals on Cotton Eyed Joe.
>
> Blackeyed Susie, sitting in a corner,
>   She's a pretty girl, 'pon my honor.
> Hey pretty little blackeyed Susie,
>   Hop up, pretty little blackeyed Susie.
>
> Shake that little foot, Sally Ann. . . .
>
> Fly all around, my pretty little Pink . . .[29]

Finally, we come to the fiddle tunes themselves. There is probably no form of rural homespun music so indelibly associated in the popular mind with the American folk scene as the familiar "hoedown." The fiddle, in spite of religious prejudices against it in some quarters, was long the dominant instrument in the "country" music of rural white America. Indeed, the violin as an instrument to accompany dancing has had a long history in Europe, where it retains its popularity and dominance in folk dance to this day, especially in Scandinavia. "Violin" and "fiddle" are usually used as contrasting terms to describe the contrasting uses to which the same instrument is put in the fine-art and folk traditions, respectively. Interestingly enough, both words come from the same root.

Fiddle Tune Types and Sources

What kinds of tunes are found in the repertory of the country fiddler? Most typical, of course, are the "hoedowns," or "breakdowns"—rapid dance tunes in duple meter,* relatives of the reels and hornpipes of the British Isles. The names and tunes of the most popular breakdowns are well known to any square-dance enthusiast or frequenter of fiddlers' contests: "Soldier's Joy," "Devil's Dream," "Leather Britches," "Wag'ner" ("Wagoner"), "Old Joe Clark," "Lost Indian," "Give the Fiddler a Dram," "Natchez Under the Hill," "Sourwood Mountain," and so on.[30] The term *breakdown* is but one illustration of the frequent exchange between the often-parallel musical traditions of blacks and whites that is characteristic of American music. It was a name used in the nineteenth century for any dance in African-American style, but especially those popular with white boatmen on the Ohio and the Mississippi.[31]

The jigs are there, too (called in some areas quadrilles)—lively tunes in 6/8 time like "The Irish Washerwoman"—but these are not actually very common. The waltz, a seemingly unlikely transplant from central Europe, has a somewhat surprising currency among country fiddlers. Less surprising are the occasional schottisches, with their characteristic dotted rhythms like those of the Scottish strathspey. More recently the fiddler's repertory, especially in the lowlands and in the West, has even come to include a few rags and blues.

The tunes come from a variety of sources. Since we earlier considered the ballad at some length, it would be appropriate to ask first whether there are any traditional ballad tunes that have been transformed into fiddle tunes. The answer is, Very few. Example 1–8 is an adaptation of a tune to "The Gypsy Laddie" (Child 200). The fiddle tune, as heard in Oklahoma, is given first, followed by the ballad tune in a variant recovered in Illinois (from *Some Representative Illinois Folk-Songs* by David Seneff McIntosh) but belonging to a group of such tunes prevalent from North Carolina to the lower Midwest. Both ballad and fiddle tune go by the common title "Black Jack Davy" (or "Davie").

* *Meter,* as a musical term, refers to the grouping of the strong pulses, or *beats.* Duple meter (of which the march is representative) has two beats in each measure, or bar; triple meter (of which the waltz is representative) has three. Other meters are quadruple, quintuple, and so on.

Example 1–8

Black Jack Davie came ridin' through the plain,
He sang so loud and clearly.
He made the green-wood around him sing,
To charm the heart of a lady,
To charm the heart of a lady.

The play-party songs as fiddle tunes have already been mentioned. Neither the ballad nor the folk song repertory has furnished the bulk of Anglo-American fiddle tunes, however; these have come more or less directly from the thriving body of reels and hornpipes used for dancing in the British Isles, and especially in Scotland.

Some individual tunes not in any of these categories may have interesting histories. For example, both "Jordan Is a Hard Road to Travel" and "Old Dan Tucker" (the latter already mentioned as a play-party song) were written by Dan Emmett for the professional minstrel stage. And the famous "Bonaparte's Retreat" is a kind of reminiscence of the Battle of Waterloo—possibly, as the solemn drone indicates, having reached the fiddle repertory by way of a bagpipe air.

Print and the Fiddle Tune

The complex intertwining of print and oral tradition that we have observed in the case of the ballad has also been at work with the fiddle tune. Despite many fiddlers' independence of, or honest aversion to, notated music ("Girl, they ain't no music to them tunes. You jes' play 'em."),[32] the fact is that fiddle tunes have been collected in written form, at first in manuscript and later to appear in published collections, since at least as far back as the early nineteenth century. While these collections may have begun as simple helps to memory on the part of fiddlers acquainted with notation, there is also evidence that some fiddlers themselves learned from written or printed sources. In the northern states, in fact, there was a stricter regard for print, and less of a tendency to produce variants, than was normal in the South. The manuscript collection of fiddle tunes made by the Long Island painter and fiddler William Sydney Mount in the 1840s is a significant example. At about the same time Elias Howe, a New England fiddler, published in 1840 *The Musician's Companion,* a collection of fiddle tunes which he sold from door to door. He published numerous and ever-larger collections over the next half-century, culminating in a joint venture with Sydney Ryan in 1883—*Ryan's Mammoth Collection of 1050 Jigs and Reels*. This was reissued by M. M. Cole in 1940 as *1000 Fiddle Tunes*. Sold initially through the Sears Roebuck stores across the nation, it has since become firmly established as the "fiddler's bible."

The relation of print to oral (or, to be more accurate, *aural*)* tradition is a complex one, and the existence of fiddle tunes in print has certainly not inhibited the production of variants, especially, as indicated above, in the South and West. Marion Thede, writing from her experience in Oklahoma, had this to say about the emergence of variants from aural tradition:

> I am inclined to the belief that fiddlers pick up a tune by hearing the general structure and then supplying a whole set of notes to their own fancy. After repeated tries, there finally emerges a fixed version only used by this one fiddler and perhaps his immediate family; even that is doubtful. Even in the same community, each fiddler comes out with his own personal way of playing a tune.[33]

The variants, therefore, even of very common tunes were staggeringly numerous, and were apt to differ so widely from each other as to constitute in some cases different tunes altogether. The detailed study of fiddle tunes and their variants has never been undertaken to the degree that it has been with the ballads, and probably it is too late now, in spite of the revivals, to study the traditional tunes to any extent. From phonograph recordings, however, and from the few really careful written transcriptions, we can form some idea of the process, and the profusion of variants in existence. Example 1–9 is in the form of three versions of an old reel called "Tom and Jerry." The first staff is from the famous *1000 Fiddle Tunes,* transposed with note values halved for purposes of comparison; the second staff is transcribed from a recording of 1951, and the third staff from the live performance of a fiddler in Oklahoma. It must be pointed out that these versions are closer together than many sets of variants that share a single title.

The Instruments

We have implied that although the violin and the "fiddle" are quite different instruments as far as usage is concerned, they are at least physically the same

* *Oral* is appropriate as a term referring to songs, or other items of folklore, disseminated by the human voice. The term *aural,* as referring to folklore learned by ear, is appropriate to all kinds of folk music, instrumental as well as vocal.

Example 1–9

(Example 1–9 Continued)

(Example 1–9 Continued)

instrument. Even this is not strictly true. The fiddler's instrument may be "store-bought," possibly from a mail-order house. (An old catalog lists "Our Amati Model Violin" for $7.25, while the "Special Stradivarius Model" sells for $9.25, the latter including bow, case, an extra set of strings, an instruction book, and a fingerboard chart.)[34] On the other hand, fiddles were often entirely homemade, out of any well-seasoned wood that was available, or they were in some cases reconstructed from parts of damaged violins.

The standard violin tuning in perfect fifths was used, but so were a number of variants as well, and for various reasons. To secure a low "drone" string, the G string was sometimes tuned down to an E or even a D; open strings were sometimes duplicated for resonance in a given key (the standard tuning for "Bonaparte's Retreat," for example, uses three D strings!); or more fourths, or even thirds, were introduced into the tuning to make possible the sounding of two strings in unison in a technique requiring very little shifting of the hand, and for the most part not using the little finger at all.

Such were (and are) the marvelous eccentricities and nonconformities of country fiddles and fiddlers. We can say "are" with a degree of assurance that would have seemed unfounded optimism as recently as the 1960s. The old-timers are leaving the scene, to be sure. But there is currently enough interest among younger performers to inspire reasonable confidence that the highly social and contagiously joyous art of country fiddling will not perish for some time to come.

Further Reading

General song collections, with expository notes

Lomax, Alan. *The Folk Songs of North America*. Garden City, NY: Doubleday, 1960.
This excellent broad collection surveys the entire field of American folk songs in the English language. The introduction and notes are especially valuable.

Lomax, John A. and Alan. *Folk Song U.S.A.* Music arrangements by Charles and Ruth Seeger. Reprint, New York: New American Library, 1975.

Sandburg, Carl. *The American Songbag*. New York: Harcourt Brace & World, 1927.
An early landmark collection by an American writer famous for his enthusiasm for folklore, song, and poetry. The notes have the Sandburg touch, and make good reading.

Specialized or regional song collections, mostly with expository notes

Barry, Phillips, Fannie H. Eckstrom, and Mary W. Smyth. *British Ballads from Maine*. New Haven: Yale University Press, 1929.

Belden, Henry Marvin. *Ballads and Songs Collected by the Missouri Folk-Lore Society*. 2d ed. Columbia: University of Missouri Press, 1955.

Cohen, Norm. *Long Steel Rail: The Railroad in American Folk Song*. Urbana: University of Illinois Press, 1981.

Cox, John Harrington. *Folk Songs of the South*. Cambridge, MA: Harvard University Press, 1925.

Davis, Arthur Kyle, Jr. *Traditional Ballads of Virginia*. Cambridge, MA: Harvard University Press, 1929.

Dunson, Josh, and Ethel Raim, eds. *Anthology of American Folk Music*. New York: Oak Publications, 1973.
This useful little book consists of transcriptions of material from old recordings which is included in the important record collection of the same title issued by Folkways (listed below). Commentary is included.

Eddy, Mary O. *Ballads and Songs from Ohio*. New York: J. J. Augustin, 1939.

Fife, Austin and Alta. *Cowboy and Western Songs: A Comprehensive Anthology*. New York: Clarkson N. Potter, 1969.

Green, Archie. *Only a Miner: Studies in Recorded Coal-Mining Songs*. Urbana: University of Illinois Press, 1972.

Lomax, John A. *Cowboy Songs and Other Frontier Ballads*. 2d ed. New York: Macmillan, 1916.

Moore, Ethel and Chauncey O. *Ballads and Folk Songs of the Southwest*. Norman: University of Oklahoma Press, 1964.
Extensive collection of songs recovered in Oklahoma, including many Child ballads.

Newell, William Wells. *Games and Songs of American Children*. Reprint, New York: Dover, 1963.
A reprint of the 2d edition (1903) of this important work published first in 1883.

Niles, John Jacob. *The Ballad Book of John Jacob Niles*. Boston, 1961. Paperback reprint, New York: Dover, 1970.

Ohrlin, Glenn. *The Hell-Bound Train: A Cowboy Songbook*. Urbana: University of Illinois Press, 1973.

Owens, William A. *Texas Folk Songs*. Dallas: SMU Press, 1976.

Randolph, Vance, and Floyd C. Shoemaker. *Ozark Folksongs*. 4 vols. Columbia: State Historical Society of Missouri, 1946–50.

Randolph, Vance. *Ozark Folksongs*. Edited and abridged by Norm Cohen. Urbana: University of Illinois Press, 1982.
A single-volume abridgement of this classic collection.

Ritchie, Jean. *Singing Family of the Cumberlands*. New York: Oak Publications, 1963.

Seeger, Mike, and John Cohen. *The Old-Time String Band Songbook*. Formerly published as *The New Lost City Ramblers Song Book*. New York: Oak Publications, 1976.
An important collection of transcriptions, with commentary, of songs popular in the 1920s and 1930s, from the repertory of the New Lost City Ramblers. Seventeen of the songs are on the album *The New Lost City Ramblers* (listed below).

Sharp, Cecil. *English Folk-Songs from the Southern Appalachians*. 2 vols. Edited by Maud Karpeles. London: Oxford University Press, 1932.
Not only is the collection a rich source of ballads and their variants in pure form from oral tradition, but the introduction is a valuable essay on both the folk and their songs.

Thorpe, N. Howard "Jack." *Songs of the Cowboys*. Reprint, New York: Bramhall House, 1966.
A pioneering collection, first published in 1908.

White, John I. *Git Along, Little Dogies: Songs and Songmakers of the American West*. Urbana: University of Illinois Press, 1975.

Wolfe, Charles K. *Folk and Country Music of Kentucky*. Lexington: University of Kentucky Press, 1985.

Primarily studies, with some complete ballads

Abrahams, Roger D., and George Foss. *Anglo-American Folksong Style*. Englewood Cliffs, NJ: Prentice-Hall, 1968.
A brief but comprehensive study dealing technically but lucidly and interestingly with all aspects of the subject.

Wells, Evelyn Kendrick. *The Ballad Tree*. New York: Ronald Press, 1950.
A broad and well-written study, ranging in scope through such topics as the supernatural elements in the ballads, the ballad's influence on literature, theories of the origins of the ballads, and biographical studies of Child and Sharp.

Studies of the ballads

Bronson, Bertrand Harris. *The Ballad as Song*. Berkeley: University of California Press, 1969.

———. "Folksong and the Modes," *Musical Quarterly*, vol. 32, no. 1 (January 1946).
An important treatise, of interest to those with some musical background. Reprinted in *The Ballad as Song*.

Coffin, Tristram. *The British Traditional Ballad in North America*. Philadelphia: American Folklore Society, 1950.

Laws, G. Malcolm, Jr. *American Balladry from British Broadsides*. Philadelphia: American Folklore Society, 1957.

———. *Native American Balladry*. Philadelphia: American Folklore Society, 1964.
A significant study of native balladry outside the Child canon, dealing with an area of American folk song indispensable to a comprehensive picture.

Wilgus, D. K. *Anglo-American Folksong Scholarship Since 1898*. New Brunswick, NJ: Rutgers University Press, 1959.
Indispensable for anyone interested in what has been going on in the study of the ballads here since Professor Child published the last volume of his crucially important collection.

Extensive, basic reference works on the ballads

Bronson, Bertrand Harris. *The Traditional Tunes of the Child Ballads*. 4 vols. Princeton, NJ: Princeton University Press, 1959–72.

Child, Francis James. *The English and Scottish Popular Ballads*. 5 vols. Boston, 1882–98. Paperback reprint, New York: Dover, 1965.

Fiddle tune collections, some with expository material

Bayard, Samuel P. *Hill Country Tunes*. Philadelphia: American Folklore Society, 1944.

Christeson, R. P. *The Old-Time Fiddler's Repertory*. Columbia: University of Missouri Press, 1973.
A finely printed practical collection of 245 tunes, collected (some from recordings, apparently) mostly in Missouri. Some expository material.

Ford, Ira. *Traditional Music of America*. New York: E.P. Dutton, 1940.

Thede, Marion. *The Fiddle Book*. New York: Oak Publications, 1967.
This excellent collection also contains a wealth of information, set forth in an interesting manner, and some fine pictures.

1000 Fiddle Tunes. Chicago: M. M. Cole, 1940–67.
The basic "fiddler's bible," an abridged edition of *Ryan's Mammoth Collection of 1050 Jigs and Reels* of 1883.

Listening

From the New World Recorded Anthology of American Music

I'm on My Journey Home: Vocal Styles and Resources in Folk Music. NW-223. Notes by Charles Wolfe.

That's My Rabbit, My Dog Caught It: Traditional Southern Instrumental Styles. NW-225. Notes by Mark Wilson.

Going Down the Valley: Vocal and Instrumental Styles in Folk Music from the South. NW-236. Notes by Norm Cohen.

Brave Boys: New England Traditions in Folk Music. NW-239. Notes by Sandy Paton.

Oh, My Little Darling: Folk Song Types. NW-245. Notes by Jon Pankake.

Old Mother Hippletoe: Rural and Urban Children's Songs. NW-291. Notes by Kate Rinzler.

From the Library of Congress Archive of American Folk Song (AAFS)

Selections, mostly of field recordings, from the vast archive of the Library of Congress, Music Division.

Anglo-American Ballads, ed. Alan Lomax. L-1.

Anglo-American Shanties, Lyric Songs, Dance Tunes, and Spirituals. L-2.

Anglo-American Ballads, ed. B. A. Botkin. L-7.

Play and Dance Songs and Tunes. L-9.
Contains a wealth of traditional tunes, played on dulcimer and banjo as well as fiddle.

Anglo-American Songs and Ballads, ed. Duncan Emrich. L-12, 14, 20, 21.

American Sea Songs and Shanties. L-26, L-27.

Cowboy Songs, Ballads, and Cattle Calls from Texas. L-28.

The Ballad Hunter, John A. Lomax (lectures with musical examples). L-49–53.

Versions and Variants of "Barbara Allen," ed. Charles Seeger. L-54.

Child Ballads Traditional in the United States, ed. Bertrand Bronson. L-57, L-58.

American Fiddle Tunes. L-62.

From Folkways/Smithsonian

Anthology of American Folk Music, vol. 1, *Ballads;* vol. 2, *Social Music;* vol. 3, *Songs*. Folkways 2951–53.
An important collection from early commercial recordings. Some of the pieces are transcribed in the identically titled book listed above.

Ballads and Songs of the Blue Ridge Mountains: Persistence and Change. Folkways: 3831

The Unfortunate Rake. Folkways FS-3805.
Twenty examples showing the metamorphosis of a single ballad.

Mountain Music of Kentucky. Folkways FA-2317
Includes four standard fiddle tunes, and some ballads and play-party songs, as well as more recent material.

Old Time Country Music by Mike Seeger. Folkways FA-2325.
Contemporary re-creations of older music, including several ballads, and the fiddle tune "Bonaparte's Retreat."

The New Lost City Ramblers. Folkways FA-2396.
Contemporary re-creations of older music, including some of the material in *The Old-Time String Band Songbook* (listed above).

Other

The Long Harvest. Argo: (Z) DA-66-75.
Ten LPs including forty-four ballads in numerous variants, sung by Ewan MacColl and Peggy Seeger, two eminent authorities close to the ballad tradition. There are extensive notes accompanying the complete printed texts. For those who have heard plenty of primi-

tive archival or field recordings the studio quality of these is a welcome change.

Old Time Ballads from the Southern Mountains. County 522.
From recordings of the 1920s.

The Old-Time Fiddler's Repertory. University of Missouri.

Songs of the Western Soil and *Fences, Barbed Wire, and Walls*. Kicking Mule 329 and 338.
Authentic modern re-creations of cowboy songs, ballads, and fiddle tunes by Horse Sense (John Nielson and Justin Bishop).

Steady as She Goes: Songs and Chanties from the Days of Commercial Sail. Collector Records 1928.

PROJECTS

1. Find an example of a traditional ballad sung by a present-day professional singer, and compare it with a version in a printed collection (either words or music, or both).

2. Find, by comparing recordings, an instance in which a professional singer has modeled his or her version of a traditional ballad on the performance of a traditional singer.

3. Find examples of popular music, especially folk-rock, which in your opinion show the influence of the ballad, and define this influence.

4. Find some traditional ballads in collections of folk music from your own region. (A few outstanding regional collections are listed in the "Further Reading" section accompanying this chapter. Libraries in your region will emphasize local collections.)

5. Make a collection and comparison of ballad refrains, noting the presence or absence of meaningless syllables, words, or phrases.

6. Find and record some piece of folklore (song, poem, story) that your family, friends, or acquaintances know from oral tradition.

7. Investigate the *localization* of names and places that occurs when ballads travel. If you have access to the services of a large library you might consult a doctoral thesis by W. Edson Richmond, "Place Names in the English and Scottish Popular Ballads and Their American Variants" (Ohio State University, 1947).

8. If you are familiar with another language and its culture, find an example of one of the traditional ballads (many of which are international) in this other language.

9. If you perform folk music, learn a traditional ballad and add it to your repertoire. You may feel it desirable to collate a version from several sources, as professionals often do; but invent or change *on your own* as little as possible.

10. If you are a musician familiar with the dulcimer and have access to one, use it to demonstrate the older modal scales by means of its various tunings. Useful in this regard is *The Dulcimer Book*, by Jean Ritchie (New York: Oak Publications, 1963).

2

The African-American Tradition

AFRICAN-American folk music has been not only a richly cultivated tradition in itself but one whose influence on American music generally has been both pervasive and critical. There is very little of our music, especially in the popular tradition, that has not been at least touched by it. Since it was really the first native music to be "discovered" and made known to Americans (and to the world) at large, it was for a time, during our first important wave of musical nationalism, considered to be almost our *only* folk music.

So vast and varied is African-American folk music that no single image is adequate to embrace it all. Instead, a number of vivid pictures are apt to flash before us, distinct yet sometimes blurring one into another. There is the picture of the slave at work, in the field or at the oars of a boat—and we think of field hollers, or the rhythmic chanting of work songs. There is the picture of the slave at rare moments of play—the slave quarters ringing with the sound of singing and dancing, to the accompaniment of homemade fiddles and banjos, and of clapping and stamping—and we think of breakdowns, banjo tunes, cakewalks. There is the picture of black folk improvising praise songs with deep meaning out of remembered strains of Dr. Watts's hymns, and pouring forth a "torrent of sacred harmony" in the meeting house or at the outdoor revival—and we think of spirituals. There is the picture of the strange, fierce, voodoo-flavored dances in Congo Square, New Orleans—and we think of "La Bamboula" and other Creole songs. In contrast, somewhat removed from folk music, is the picture of the black musician as an accomplished professional, much in demand as a fiddler at dances—and we think of the "Negro jigs" published in early collections. At a later time there is the picture of his rural heir, the itinerant minstrel with his most prized possession, his guitar, his "easy rider," slung around his neck, sometimes playing and singing at all-night parties for a few dollars—and we think of the blues. All, and more, are part of the panorama, and we cannot fuse them into a single convenient image.

African Music and Its Relation to Black Music in America

The fact that black people were brought to this continent from Africa in more or less continuous waves of forced migration over a period of some two hundred years raises a profound first question with regard to African-American music: To what extent is it African? This question is not new, nor does it belong only to the heightened racial consciousness that marked the third quarter of our century. It has fascinated students since the Civil War. In our own time, when ethnic studies has become a highly developed academic pursuit, and there is a growing awareness of "world music," a title such as "The Survival of African Music in America" has a contemporary ring: actually, it is the title of an article published in 1899.[1]

There is, as might be expected, a broad disparity in the relative strength and distribution of African survivals in the New World. They are strongest on the north and east coasts of South America, and in the islands of the Caribbean—areas of large plantations, with a high percentage of blacks in the population, where minimal attempts were made during slavery to control the activities of the blacks when not at work. (The Caribbean may be said to include, culturally, French-dominated Louisiana until this century.) In what is now the United States, African traits survived less vigorously, owing to the smaller ratio of blacks to whites, their more direct supervision by slave masters, their conversion in large numbers to Christianity, and the attempts to repress African customs by those who regarded them (especially the dancing, which was nearly inseparable from music in African culture) as lascivious, immoral, and pagan. Nevertheless, there is no doubt that African culture did survive in various forms, and was especially to be observed in the customary celebrations on special occasions. In the South under slavery Christmas and Easter were traditionally occasions for "jubilees," and before the mid-nineteenth century colorful public festivities such as 'Lection Day in New England (in May or June), Pinkster (which immediately followed Pentecost, or *Pinksteren* in Dutch) in New York, or the Sunday afternoon dancing in Congo Square in New Orleans were occasions that furnished ample evidence of the survival of African music and dance in antebellum America.[2]

One geographical area noted for its exceptional preservation of African music, language, and customs is that of the Sea Islands off the coast of Georgia and South Carolina. Here, in relative isolation, numbers of black people, often living in extreme poverty, retained Africanisms in music, speech, and customs well into this century. This area has been a rich mine for folklorists and anthropologists.[3]

While it is beyond the scope of this book to include a treatment of African music in any detail, certain outstanding traits can be noted that have marked correspondences with black music in America. Most obvious, and of the greatest importance, is the dominance of *rhythm*, manifested in a number of ways:

(1) a high development of what has been called the "metronome sense"—the sense of an inexorably steady pulse governing the music;[4] (2) the active enjoyment of a high degree of rhythmic complexity and diversity for its own sake; (3) the perception of music as largely a *kinetic* experience, practically inseparable from some form of bodily movement such as dancing; and (4) the corresponding dominance of percussion instruments. Other traits, having to do with musical form, are the use of short vocal phrases, repeated and varied, against a continuous rhythmic background, and the often-cited use of the call-and-response pattern.

To sum up the question of African influence, one could do worse than simply listen to two examples in juxtaposition. From many, you might choose first a piece of music in praise of a Yoruban chief, recorded in Nigeria, and then the famous ring-shout* "Run, Old Jeremiah," recorded in Louisiana.[5] You will not only hear embodied many of the traits previously mentioned, but will deepen your appreciation of African influence by direct experience and feeling.

Religious Folk Music: The Spiritual

The term *spiritual* (derived from a shortening of the New Testament phrase "spiritual songs") has been applied to two distinct but related bodies of folk music that began to flourish notably in the nineteenth century—one black and the other white. The African-American spiritual has antecedents extending far back into the history of the settlements of Europeans and Africans in North America, although clearly it could not have come into being without the conversion of significant numbers of slaves to Christianity. Before 1800 such conversion was greeted with widespread indifference or outright opposition by slaveholders.[6] The religious singing of blacks in Colonial times is unfortunately cloaked in an obscurity barely penetrated by a few contemporary observations.[7]

From New York in 1745:

> I have got our Clark [parish clerk] to raise a Psalm when their instruction is over, and I can scarce express the satisfaction I have in seeing 200 Negroes and White Persons with heart and voice glorifying their Maker.
>
> —Rev. Richard Charlton

From the southern colonies in the 1760s:

> My landlord tells me . . . they heard the Slaves at worship in their lodge, singing Psalms and Hymns in the evening, and again in the Morning, long before break of day. They are excellent singers, and long to get some of Dr. Watt's [sic] Psalms and Hymns, which I encourage them to hope for.
>
> —Rev. Wright

Again from the southern colonies, no date:

* The term "shout" has a dual meaning in referring to African-American religious observances: in addition to the common meaning of loud, vociferous vocal expression, it can also refer to bodily movement, or dance.

> I can hardly express the pleasure it affords me to turn to that part of the Gallery where they [the slaves] sit, and see so many of them with their Psalm or Hymn Books, turning to the part then sung, and assisting their fellows who are beginners, to find the place; and then all breaking out in a torrent of sacred harmony, enough to bear away the whole congregation to heaven.
>
> —Rev. Samuel Davies

Toward the end of the eighteenth century, the first independent black churches were established, and in 1801 the first hymnbook compiled for the use of a black congregation by a black man was printed in Philadelphia: *A Collection of Spiritual Songs and Hymns Selected from Various Authors by Richard Allen, African Minister*. (The collection contained words only, with no indication, unfortunately, of the tunes to be used.)[8]

After 1800 the evangelical movement that swept the South and the frontier resulted in widespread conversions of both blacks and whites. (The camp meetings of the period, and the emergence of the white spiritual along with the black, are described in Chapter 6.) It was probably during the period between the Kentucky Revival of 1801 and Emancipation that the great body of folk song that we know as the antebellum black spirituals took form and was disseminated throughout the slaveholding areas. The question of the spirituals' origin, and of whether the stronger influence in the popular religious song of the time was from white to black or from black to white, has been a subject of much controversy and will be addressed briefly below in discussing the music. What is clear is that African-American spirituals evolved as a body of folk song, in oral tradition, largely unnoticed at the time by the majority of white southerners, and virtually unknown outside the South until after the Civil War.

The Discovery, Publication, and Adaptation of Spirituals

The Civil War and its aftermath brought whites from the North, many of them abolitionists, into direct contact with black people for the first time. Even before the war's end, events such as the formation of black regiments fighting for the Union cause, and the famous "Port Royal experiment" (in which teachers and missionaries from the North were recruited to teach and supervise thousands of African-Americans on Carolina Sea Island plantations abandoned by white owners and overseers as a result of the Union blockade of the coast), began the process of acquainting northerners with the songs of the slaves. Written accounts appeared in northern periodicals, some with texts of spirituals, and before the end of 1861 there was published the first spiritual to appear in sheet music form—"The Song of the Contrabands: 'O Let My People Go' " (a highly conventionalized version of "Go Down Moses"). The next year more sensitive settings of two "Songs of the Freedmen of Port Royal, Collected and Arranged by Miss Lucy McKim" were published: these were "Poor Rosy, Poor Gal" and "Roll, Jordan Roll."[9] In 1867 Lucy McKim (later married to a son of the abolitionist William Lloyd Garrison) collaborated with William Allen and Charles Ware to publish the first collection of African-American spirituals in book form, *Slave Songs of the United States*. This justly famous collection includes a number of spirituals well known today, although some are more familiar in later variants. These include "Roll, Jordan, Roll," "Michael, Row the Boat Ashore," "Nobody Knows the Trouble I've Had," and "Good News, Member." There were also a number of secular songs, among them work songs ("Heave away, Heave away! I'd rather court a yellow gal than work for Henry Clay"—a song that later appeared frequently as an American fiddle tune, "Run, Nigger, Run") and a number of Louisiana Creole songs in patois French. Altogether a rather broad collection!

After the Civil War a number of schools and colleges were established in the South, under the auspices of the Freedmen's Bureau and various church and missionary groups, to begin the great task of educating the newly freed slaves. One of the first of these was Fisk University, in Nashville, Tennessee, founded by the American Missionary Association in 1866. Early on, when the inevitable financial problems arose, George L. White, the school's treasurer and music instructor, formed a chorus from the many fine singers among the students. After a period of intensive training and some successful local concerts, he took the singers on a daring tour of the northern states to raise money for the school. Although their programs consisted of a variety of songs (which at first did not even include spirituals), they soon found that it was the spirituals that were the most enthusiastically received. Even though most of the group's programs were given in churches, it was a long and hard struggle for them to escape the image and expectations set up in the popular mind by the minstrel show. When the chorus, which had by then adopted the famous name Jubilee Singers, sang in Henry Ward Beecher's Plymouth Church in Brooklyn, New York, the headline in the *New York Herald* read: "Beecher's Negro Minstrels: The Great Plymouth Preacher as an 'End Man'—a Full Troupe of Real Live Darkies in the Tabernacle of the Lord—Rollicking Choruses, but No Sand Shaking or Jig Dancing." Not all critical comment was as demeaning, however, for the singers and their songs were winning audiences and critics alike, and the Brooklyn concerts, under Beecher's aegis, proved to be a turning point. They went on for a successful tour of New England, and sang in Washington, DC, where they were greeted by President Grant. Subsequently a group of eight of the singers toured Europe with tremendous success. By the time the original troupe disbanded in Hamburg in 1878, the Jubilee Singers had, in seven years' work, raised $150,000 for Fisk University and, still more important, had pioneered in making the African-American spiritual widely known by musicians and public alike in this country and in Europe.

Of course the Fisk Jubilee Singers were not alone in this work. In 1873 the famous Hampton Singers, of the Hampton Institute in Virginia, were formed and began to tour. The tradition spread, and in this century, in addition to the continuing work of Fisk and Hampton, the choirs of Howard University and the Tuskegee Institute have become well known. In 1925 the first of a series of Hall Johnson Choirs was formed; as professional choirs, these groups have also furthered the tradition of choral spiritual singing. These are only a few among hundreds of examples.

Solo singers also performed spirituals. Although white soloists began including them in their programs in the 1920s, it was great black artists such as Roland Hayes, Paul Robeson, and Marian Anderson who sang them with the greatest effectiveness and meaning, and established their stature in the repertoire of solo song.

Thus the spiritual, in what might be termed its concert phase, was launched. It began almost at once to diverge from its folk phase. The concert spiritual, like the ballad in the hands of the professional folk singer, who was faced with the task of popularizing a folk form in a cultural milieu outside the original folk community, inevitably underwent adaptation and change. It was written down, harmonized, arranged, and usually (especially for the solo singer) provided with a piano accompaniment—all of these retaining the character of the original song to an extent that depended on the talent, background, and intent of the arranger. That the results preserved the spirit of the original as often as they did is attested by the impact that arranged spirituals continued to have when well performed, and is a tribute to the skill and integrity of such musicians as J. Rosamund Johnson, Hall Johnson, and R. Nathaniel Dett. The concert spiritual is, of course, perfectly valid music. The point to be aware of is that it should not be confused with African-American religious folk song as it originally existed, or as it has continued to exist down to our own time in the backwoods churches and camp meetings of the South.

The Words of the Spiritual

Not all African-American folk music is religious. Many people within the African-American community regard the blues as sinful music, and even if we view the condemnation as the product of a particular tradition of religious orthodoxy, we can also recognize that between the broad epic and moral connotations of "Go Down, Moses" and the self-centered eroticism of "The Black Snake Moan" there is indeed a great gulf fixed. Nevertheless, the lines of demarcation between sacred and secular are far from rigid. Thus, the Biblical imagery so pervasive in the spiritual may also appear in the work song:*

Well, God told Norah.
  Hammer, ring.
Well, God told Norah.
  Hammer, ring.
You is a-goin' in the timber.
  Hammer, ring.
You is a-goin' in the timber.
  Hammer, ring.

It may even occasionally crop up in the blues:

I went down in Death valley, nothin' but the
  tombstones and dry bones,
I went down in Death Valley, nothin' but the
  tombstones and dry bones,
That's where a poor man be, Lord, when I'm dead
  and gone.

* Dialect spelling is given as published by early folk song collectors.

Of greater significance is the all-encompassing view expressed in those songs commonly regarded as "spirituals." No image was either too humble or too intimately connected with daily life to be used.

Cryin' what kind o' shoes am dose you wear, . . .
Cryin' dese shoes I wear am de Gospel shoes, . . .

Mind out brother how you walk de cross,
  Wan'ta go to heaben when I die.
Yo' foot might slip-a an' yo' soul get-a los',
  O, wan'ta go to heaben when I die.

I know my robe's gwinter fit me well,
  I'm gwinter lay down my heavy load,
I tried it on at de gates of hell,
  I'm gwinter lay down my heavy load.

Loose horse in the valley
Aye
Who goin' t' ride 'im
Aye
Nothin' but the righteous
Aye, Lord
Time's a drawin' nigh.

If it be true—to quote another spiritual—that "He's got the whole world in His hands," then nothing in the whole range of human feeling is beyond inclusion. Of the wheel of Ezekiel it was sung:

There's 'ligion in the wheel
  Oh, my soul! . . .
There's moanin' in the wheel
  Oh, my soul! . . .
There's prayin' in the wheel
  Oh, my soul . . .
There's shoutin' in the wheel
  Oh, my soul! . . .
There's cryin' in the wheel
  Oh, my soul! . . .
There's laughin' in the wheel
  Oh, my soul . . .

Spirituals, as we know, have drawn deeply upon a thorough acquaintance with Biblical narrative and symbol, as dramatized through the generations by many a gifted and anonymous backwoods preacher. So immense is their number and range that they constitute *in toto* an epic re-creation, in folk fashion, of virtually the entire Bible, from Genesis:

He made the sun an' moon an' stars,
  To rule both day an' night;
He placed them in the firmament,
  An' told them to give light.
My God He is a Man—a Man of War,
My God He is a Man—a Man of War,
My God He is a Man—a Man of War,
  An' de Lawd God is His name.

to Revelation:

De Lord spoke to Gabriel,
  Fare you well, Fare you well;
Go look behin' de altar,
  Fare you well, Fare you well.
Take down de silvah trumpet,
  Fare you well, Fare you well.
Blow yo' trumpet Gabriel;
  Fare you well, Fare you well.

Instances abound of the vivid pictorial imagery brought to their subjects by anonymous black poets:

Dark clouds a-risin'!
Thunder-bolts a-bustin'!
Master Jesus comes a-ridin' by
With a rainbow on his shoulder.

It should be noted, however, that the generally assumed anonymity of the authors was not universal; the existence of individual African-American "bards" in the late nineteenth century has been documented. James Weldon Johnson, in his preface to *The Books of American Negro Spirituals*, describes "Singing" Johnson, who went from church to church making up, singing, and teaching new songs to the congregations.

No consideration of the texts of spirituals can be considered complete if it fails to treat the question of their relation to contemporary circumstances among the black people. It was once commonly believed that spirituals represented solely an otherworldly view; that they expressed the consolation that African-Americans found in religion for their intolerable worldly conditions, and that the promises and hopes referred only to life in the hereafter. There is considerable evidence to refute this concept, however, and arguments for a contrasting view, a view of spirituals' concrete relationship to contemporary conditions, began to be put forward a century ago by abolitionist writers and others.[10] In this view spirituals express (or cloak) in Biblical terms not only the wretchedness of slavery, but hopes and plans for an escape from its bondage in this life. This could come about either through northern intervention (thus "de Lord" could stand for a collective embodiment of "de Yankees") or through escape ("Steal away") to the North ("heab'n") or to Canada ("Canaan"). The secret meetings to which the faithful were called ("Go down in de lonesome valley") kept hope and morale alive, spread news, and laid plans. The yearning for a "home" encouraged by the colonization projects could be expressed as a reliance on the "old ship of Zion" that would "take us all home"—or even as the hope for a Moses who would smite and divide the broad waters ("Deep river") so that the slaves could miraculously pass over—back to Africa. The figure of Moses was quite naturally a very central one. The Israelites were the slaves, longing for deliverance; Pharaoh represented the slaveowners; Egypt (or alternatively Babylon) was the South and slavery. The famous "Go Down, Moses" hardly needs "translation" to see its relevance to the black people in slavery.

> When Israel was in Egypt's land,
>   Let my people go.
> Oppressed so hard they could not stand,
>   Let my people go.
>
> Go down, Moses,
>   'Way down in Egypt's land;
> Tell ole Pharaoh,
>   Let my people go.

There is evidence, indeed, that this interpretation of the spiritual was not lost on the slaveowners, especially in the uneasy years between the bloody Nat Turner revolt in Virginia in 1831 (Nat Turner himself, it should be remembered, had been a preacher) and the Civil War a generation later. References to freedom, and especially to escape and to vengeance on the slave beaters and betrayers, had to be more carefully veiled than ever. In South Carolina in 1862 slaves were jailed for singing "We'll Soon Be Free"—it was quite evident by then that the freedom sought was not just in the life *after* death.

The Music of the Spiritual

When we come to a description of the music of the spiritual, it is well to keep in mind that we are dealing with folk music, and that what we see in print cannot convey anything like the full effect of the music as sung. As William Francis Allen wrote in 1867,

> The best we can do, however, with paper and types, or even with voices, will convey but a faint shadow of the original. The voices of the colored people have a peculiar quality that nothing can imitate; and the intonations and delicate variations of even one singer cannot be reproduced on paper. And I despair of conveying any notion of the effect of a number singing together, especially in a complicated shout, like "I can't stay behind, my Lord," or "Turn, sinner, turn O!" There is no singing in *parts*, as we understand it, and yet no two appear to be singing the same thing—the leading singer starts the words of each verse, often improvising, and the others, who "base" him, as it is called, strike in with the refrain, or even join in the solo, when the words are familiar. When the "base" begins, the leader often stops, leaving the rest of his words to be guessed at, or it may be they are taken up by one of the other singers. And the "basers" themselves seem to follow their own whims, beginning when they please and leaving off when they please, striking an octave above or below (in case they have pitched the tune too low or too high), or hitting some other note that chords, so as to produce the

> effect of a marvelous complication and variety, and yet with the most perfect time, and rarely with any discord. And what makes it all the harder to unravel a thread of melody out of this strange network is that, like birds, they seem not infrequently to strike sounds that cannot be precisely represented by the gamut, and abound in "slides from one note to another, and turns and cadences not in articulated notes."[11]

This description tells us much about the singing, in fact. At least four distinct points are confirmed that will serve as an introductory description to the music as actually performed. First, the subtlety and variety of vocal delivery is noted: the "intonations and delicate variations," the "sounds that cannot be precisely represented by the gamut," the "slides from one note to another." Second, we are definitely reminded that this is communal singing; unlike the more solitary blues, it calls for the participation, the interaction, of a closely knit society of singers, all feeling the same impulsion to break into song. Third, though it is choral singing, there is usually a leader to whom the rest of the group responds, although these responses do not have the drilled rhythmic precision we are used to in performances of spirituals by trained choirs. And fourth, we are reminded of the important role of improvisation—the spur-of-the-moment variations wrought spontaneously by the singers. This is a trait particularly associated with black music. "No two African performances are identical," says A. M. Jones, and the description applies equally to American blues, American jazz, and the African-American spiritual, though we are not as accustomed to thinking of the latter in these terms.

Only one further observation, implicit in early descriptions, must be added to round out a fairly accurate picture of early spiritual singing in its folk phase. This is that there was in most cases no accompaniment by instruments. The use of piano, guitar, tambourine—even in some cases trumpet or trombone—was a later addition belonging more to gospel songs.

Mention has been made of the controversy over where the music of the spiritual came from. The details of the conflicting views held by scholars are readily available elsewhere, and will not be set forth here; they deal with such matters as the reliability of printed versions, the source of the call-and-response pattern (as seen in the frequent internal refrains and choruses), and the sources of the tunes themselves, as indicators of whether the direction of influence was white-to-black or black-to-white. In dealing with this question, it is enough to remind ourselves of a few important considerations. The first is that printed versions cannot give us accurate evidence of the age of a song that may have had a fairly long history in oral tradition. Even more important, notated versions cannot convey an adequate idea of what early spirituals actually sounded like, a point that was consistently made (as we have seen) by the very people who wrote them down. Therefore a comparison of printed versions is not a comparison of the actual music as it was sung. The second point to be kept in mind is that the first half of the nineteenth century was a formative period for both the white and the black spiritual, and that there was ample opportunity for mutual influence. Although rural and frontier camp meetings were segregated, they were nonetheless occasions on which blacks and whites assembled on as nearly equal terms as was possible at the time. Hymns with choruses did appear in print in white hymnody in the eighteenth century; nevertheless, it is entirely possible that the strong African call-and-response tradition had a significant influence on the evolution of the camp meeting songs sung by whites as well as blacks, and indeed on later gospel hymnody as well. In the matter of the melodies, it is indisputable that the tunes of many black spirituals have their counterparts in white-sung hymns and spirituals, a good number of which can even be traced to Great Britain. Given the long exposure of blacks to white sacred music, this is hardly surprising; nor does it minimize African-Americans' melodic invention or contribution, still less the undoubted Africanisms that pervaded the manner in which spirituals were sung. The most balanced view is probably that presented by John Garst in the importance he ascribes to the "mutual reinforcement" of characteristics shared by the two cultures in the evolution of the spiritual.[12]

The Survival of the Folk Spiritual

"The black masses have preserved the spirituals. Acculturated Negroes have generally neglected them unless they were edited." So wrote Miles Mark Fisher in 1953. We have already referred to the cleavage between the folk and the concert spiritual that began with the spread and popularization of African-American religious folk music after the Civil War. Folk spirituals have indeed survived in popular culture, and the description deduced from Allen's observation of 1867, quoted earlier, may be reviewed as a quite accurate description of rural spiritual singing as it has survived into our own time. Fortunately, some of this old-style singing was recorded in the 1930s and 1940s. It is probably best epitomized in the spirituals sung by Dock Reed and Vera Hall of Alabama. In "Look How They Done My Lord" and "Handwriting on the Wall," for example, we hear variants of traditional spirituals, which have been reproduced in printed collections, sung in a living folk context.[13] Call-and-response, in which the responder finishes the line begun by the caller (a practice described by Allen over a century ago), is beautifully illustrated, as is the rhythmic impulse or "metronome sense." We also hear in their singing the use of the variable, or ambiguous, third and seventh degrees of the scale*—a practice that does not, as is popularly assumed, belong exclusively to the blues.[14] "Move, Members, Move" and "My Name Has Been Written Down," by a family of singers, furnish fine examples of communal singing in the old style, with hand-clapping emphasizing the rhythmic pulse and drive of the music.[15]

To be aware of the larger context of the spiritual, you should experience an actual religious service, especially the sermon, during which members of the congregation, in their role as responders, become actual participants. Often then the intensity of feeling and participation finds outlet in musically intoned sounds, and the tones gradually accumulate into a kind of choral background. The preacher himself may break into song. If this cannot be experienced in person, the next best thing is to listen to recordings. A number of these sermons with responses were recorded and sold in the 1920s and have been reissued in anthologies.[16]

The spiritual, as one of our richest and most perennial funds of folk music, has provided material and inspiration for many subsequent forms. Though it

* See Examples 2-1 and 2-2 for illustrations.

is still cultivated to some extent in the old style as a folk form, it was inevitable that African-American religious music would over time reflect changing social and cultural patterns, and particularly the growth of popular music and a popular-music industry. The story of the emergence of gospel music, both black and white, is discussed in Chapter 6. From our present vantage point of folk music, it is possible and instructive to trace the gradual replacement of the older spiritual, the successive imprints of currently popular sounds on African-American religious music, and the trend in this century (in the sacred music of both races) toward professionalism and commercialism.

First, the arranged vocal quartet, singing in more or less "barbershop" style and harmony, appeared in the early decades of this century and is still important in gospel music today. Early quartets were often fostered by the same educational institutions, such as Fisk University and the Tuskegee Institute, that had played such an important part in popularizing the spiritual in the nineteenth century. Instrumental accompaniment of banjo, guitar, and later piano, with the addition on occasion of tambourine and even brass instruments, began to be used. This brought with it the same demands for simpler harmony and melody that we saw operating in the case of the Anglo-American ballad tunes. Some traditional spirituals were adapted to this accompaniment,[17] but for the most part they were replaced by the simpler tunes that were being turned out literally by the hundreds by professional religious songwriters. These tunes were invariably in the major mode, and got along for the most part, as did white hillbilly tunes, with only the three well-worn pedestrian harmonies of tonic, subdominant, and dominant.[18] But African-American religious song also began to reflect the blues (especially as regards form and harmony), as the singing of Bozie Sturdivant and others illustrates.[19] Jazz influences were evident as early as the 1920s, as some commercial recordings indicate.[20] (Perhaps, as has been said, the influence was really the other way around.) Finally, the heavier, boogie-related beat of rhythm-and-blues has been adopted by gospel music.[21] But always in the background of African-American religious music, at times obscured but neither eliminated nor forgotten, is the "mother lode" of the spiritual, fecund and inexhaustible.

Secular Folk Music

Early documentation and collection of secular music is scanty, for reasons already mentioned in discussing the spiritual, though we are apt to forget that the very first collection, *Slave Songs of the United States,* did include a good many secular songs. In the preface of this collection an unidentified "gentleman from Delaware" is quoted on the subject of the importance of secular music to any comprehensive view of African-American music:

> We must look among their non-religious songs for the purest specimens of negro minstrelsy. . . . Some of the best *pure negro* songs I have ever heard were those that used to be sung by the black stevedores, or perhaps the crew themselves, of the West India vessels, loading and unloading at the wharves in Philadelphia and Baltimore. I have stood for more than an hour, often, listening to them, as they

hoisted and lowered the hogsheads and boxes of their cargoes; one man taking the burden of the song (and the slack of the rope) and the others striking in with the chorus. They would sing in this way more than a dozen different songs in an hour. . . .

These were the work songs, which we shall return to at the end of the chapter. But there were other kinds as well. Let us take a brief look at some of them.

Cries, Calls, and Hollers

A kind of musical expression among black people that is at once primitive and evocative is found in the cries, calls, and hollers. Early observers here described these occasionally, and they can still be heard in Africa. Frederick Olmsted, reporting on a journey through the South in 1853, tells of being awakened in his railroad car in the middle of the night by a gang of black workmen enjoying a brief break around a fire.

> Suddenly one raised such a sound as I had never heard before, a long, loud, musical shout, rising, and falling, and breaking into falsetto, his voice ringing through the woods in the clear, frosty night air, like a bugle call. As he finished, the melody was caught up by another, then by several in chorus.[22]

These cries and calls—of the field, the levee, the track—were highly individualized expressions, for communication, for relieving loneliness, for giving vent to feelings, or simply for expressing the fact of one's existence. Their city counterparts, the street cries, were more utilitarian: they advertised goods and services. Both types have all but disappeared from their original setting. A few have been recorded.[23] Musically, they are florid, melismatic vocalizations, based on a single interval, a single chord, or a pentatonic or modal scale, with embellishing tones and often certain "blue" notes of variable pitch not capable of precise notation.

In fact, the embryonic blues scale is so apparent in some of these calls that it will be well to introduce its main features here. This will serve as a reminder of the close relation between some of these solitary, highly individualized calls and hollers and the primitive rural blues. For this purpose, it will be useful to examine two calls in some detail.[24] They are both cornfield hollers, or *arwhoolies;* these two are specifically songs sung at quitting time. The first may be notated (though only approximately!) as shown in Example 2–1. (Accidental signs over the notes indicate that the notation only approximates the sung pitch.) It will be noted that there are only three essential pitch areas; a high one (which may be called the *dominant*) on which nearly all the phrases begin; a low one (which may be called the *final*) on which they all end; and an important area a third above the final, a *mediant*. The first two are relatively stable in pitch, but the mediant is variable. It sometimes gives a definite impression of major (marked with a sharp); sometimes it sounds minor, and sometimes ambiguous (indeterminately in between major and minor). The area between the mediant and the dominant is used as a relatively inessential auxiliary-tone area. Careful listening will reveal that it is also subject to inflection, sometimes being so high as to sound like a flattened version of the dominant, a feature we shall have occasion to note again.

Example 2–1

Transcription by the author

The second call (Example 2–2) is more florid and more complex. It will be seen that the range is greater; most of the phrases start an octave above the final. The dominant is also present, and is an important tone. What is interesting to note is that the variable-pitch area is now found a third above the *dominant,* or a seventh above the final, the third above the final being here fairly stable. Again the fourth degree of the scale, also inflected, is used as a passing tone. The falsetto ornaments (shown in small notes) are not uncommon, and may have been what caused Olmsted to refer to this music as "Negro jodling" [yodeling].

Example 2–2

Transcription by the author

These two examples show the two areas of variable pitch in what has come to be known as the blues scale. If we make a composite of the pitch material of these two calls, adding additional tones to fill in the gaps, we have the complete blues scale in something resembling the form in which it is usually printed (Example 2–3).

It should be noted that both the variable (or ambiguous) third and the variable seventh (which is actually a variable third above the dominant, as we have seen) do not necessarily occur in every tune. There is, as we have said, also

Example 2–3

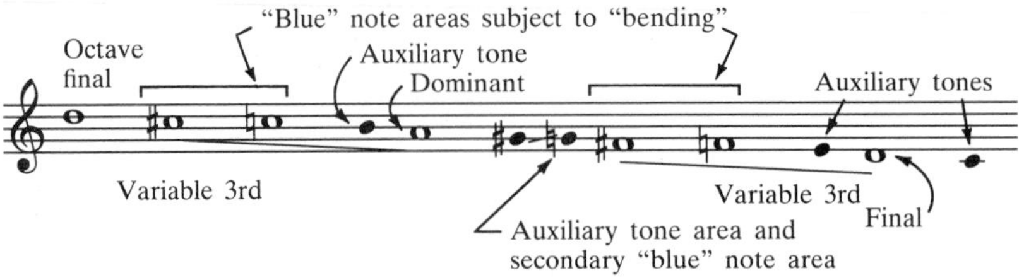

a tendency occasionally to inflect the dominant downward as well, giving rise to yet a third area of variable pitch, and an alternative interpretation of the raised fourth-degree passing-tone area.[25]

Playing this music on an instrument of fixed and equal temperament such as the piano gives a highly conventionalized and falsified impression of its subtly inflected and extremely fluid nature as performed by the voice, whether in spirituals, hollers, or blues. Thus our conventional concept of this variable-pitched scale is a somewhat mechanized and secondhand one.

Folk Blues

African-American cries, calls, and hollers were intensely personal expressions, and this is also one of the most important characteristics of the blues. When we listen to "I Don't Mind the Weather" or "Joe the Grinder,"[26] we realize how this kind of elemental song gradually approaches the rural blues in proportions, and in range and explicitness of expression. A further step would be represented by an extended holler such as the one beginning "Oh baby, what you want me to do?," captured in a field recording for the Library of Congress archive.[27] This is actually a primitive blues, albeit extremely rambling, improvisatory, and formless by "classic" blues standards. A less rambling song, in a rather tightly knit stanza form of four repeated lines, still unaccompanied, is the rather haunting and enigmatic "Another Man Done Gone," as sung by Vera Hall.[28]

Social changes and the blues

If these examples are only a few steps away from the barely articulate field holler, it is readily apparent that they are very large steps. Furthermore, they are steps that could have been possible only after Emancipation, and the turbulent developments that followed in its wake. The spiritual began life in slavery; the blues could only have evolved afterward. Amiri Baraka (formerly LeRoi Jones) calls attention to at least five aspects of the profoundly changed life of African-Americans in the South after the Civil War that made the evolution of the blues possible.

There was a new dimension of leisure—circumscribed for most by hard economic necessity, but nonetheless real, as the absence of the overseer's lash was real.

There was on small individual farms, for either owner, tenant farmer, or sharecropper, a new degree of solitude that encouraged the cultivation of individuality—hallmark of the blues. This, in contrast to the older tribal nature of black culture, both in Africa and under the enforced tribal conditions the common bond of slavery imposed, gave a new and uniquely American dimension to black life and thought.

There was the confrontation with an entirely new set of social and economic problems, not the least being the need for money.

There was, as a consequence of broader contacts and experiences, a much greater fluency in the American language and a greater range of expression in its use.

Finally, and probably most important, there was a new mobility. This in itself gave access to a broader range of experience. The mobility was forced in most cases by the relentless (and new) necessity of finding employment—much harder, as Baraka points out, for the men than for the women. But for a few persons mobility either was not forced or was accepted willingly. There developed a small class of footloose wanderers, and it is among this class that many of the early blues musicians were found—genuine itinerant minstrels, in the original medieval sense of the term. To this class belonged also, perforce, the blind street musicians who had gravitated to the larger cities; making street music was the prime means of livelihood and independence available to those with even a modicum of talent. Thus it happened that the blues were propagated by a class of musicians who were to a degree outcasts, even among their own race—rejected at least by its more settled and established members, especially the most devoutly religious, to whom the blues were "devil songs." The black author Richard Wright, going somewhat farther back in time and contrasting the origin of the spiritual with that of the blues, writes in his preface to Paul Oliver's *The Meaning of the Blues*:

> All American Negroes do not sing the blues. These songs are not the expression of the Negro people in America as a whole. I'd surmise that the spirituals, so dearly beloved of the Southern American Whites, came from those slaves who were closest to the Big Houses of the plantations where they caught vestiges of Christianity whiffed to them from the Southern Whites' cruder forms of Baptist or Methodist religions. If the plantations' house slaves were somewhat remote from Christianity, the field slaves were almost completely beyond the pale. And it was from them and their descendants that the devil songs called the blues came—that confounding triptych of the convict, the migrant, the rambler, the steel driver, the ditch digger, the roustabout, the pimp, the prostitute, the urban or rural illiterate outsider.[29]

It was perhaps inevitable, for a variety of reasons, that the prisons came to hold more than their share of bluesmen; many field recordings were made in the penitentiaries and prison farms of the South in the 1930s and 1940s, and some important blues singers were discovered there.

Blues texts and subjects

The subjects treated in the blues encompass a wide range. No area of commonly shared human experience is excluded. Some blues speak of a nameless depression.

Early this morning the blues came walking in my room.

Some are about work—

I worked all summer, yes, and all the fall
Going to spend Christmas in my overalls.

or the lack of it—

I'm goin' to Detroit, get myself a good job,
Tried to stay around here on this starvation farm.

Some sing of gambling—

Jack of Diamonds, you appear to be my friend
But gamblin' gonna be our end.

of crime, of the law, of prisons—

Judge gave me life this mornin' down on Parchman Farm;

of prostitution, of enslaving addiction, or of the necessity or the irresistible urge to move on—

When a woman gets the blues, she hangs her head and cries.
But when a man gets the blues, he flags a freight train and rides.

But the greatest number are in some way about the fundamental man-woman relationship. As the blues singer Robert Pete Williams said, "Love makes the blues. That's where it comes from."[30] The man-woman relationship is displayed in the blues in a great variety of aspects—from a comment on the power of a woman's attraction—

Well, a long, tall woman will make a preacher lay his Bible down

or the exhilaration of being in love—

Well, I feel all right and everything is okay.
Yes, I feel all right, everything is okay.
It's the love of my baby, oh, makes me feel this way.

to a scornful comment on infidelity—

High yeller, she'll kick you, that ain't all,
When you step out at night 'nother mule in your stall.

or the painful fact of separation—

My man left this morning, jest about half past four,
He left a note on his pillow, sayin' he couldn't use me no more.

or the most bitter rejection—

If I was cold and hungry, I wouldn't even ask you for bread,
I don't want you no more, if I'm on my dying bed.

Blues language is keen, apt, and colorful, if not grammatical, and is given to the use of irony, metaphor, and double entendre. No subject is off limits, and although broad social comment is foreign to such a personal medium, the blues poet finds a way to relate the most topical subject to an earthy metaphor with a telling phrase—

Uncle Sam ain't no woman, but he sure can take your man away.

Blues form

The form of the blues is often described as though it were invariably conventionalized. It should be kept in mind that the rural blues is often quite free in form. The sung portions do not always arrange themselves into three-line stanzas, but many consist of a varying number of lines, often quite unequal in length. The standard form—a line, repeated, followed by a different concluding line—should be considered, in the country blues, as a tendency only.

My mama told me before I left home,
My mama told me before I left home,
You better let them Jacksonville women alone.

It was perhaps first crystallized in the published blues that began appearing as early as 1912, and that certainly influenced subsequent blues performers. The foregoing example also illustrates a feature common to much folk poetry—a casual inexactitude of both rhythm and meter. As in many ballads, additional syllables in a line were simply crammed in.

The standard musical phrase is four bars long—hence the standard "12-bar blues" form. But in the case of the blues in its folk phase, single phrases could be four and a half, five, or seven bars long, with the singer beginning the next line whenever he or she felt like it (in the rural blues, it was almost invariably he). When there is instrumental accompaniment, which is nearly always, the sung line never takes up the whole musical "space," so to speak. The voice comes to its cadence about halfway through, and the phrase is always completed by an instrumental *break*. This paces the song, gives the singer time to think of the next line, and provides the opportunity for some more or less fancy and often highly individual instrumental playing. The blues is always introduced by an instrumental "warm-up," which may be the length of an entire stanza.

The music of the blues

The melodic material of the blues has already been set forth in the discussion of field hollers, and the two or three pitch areas in the scale that are prone to inflection have been pointed out. But a sense of clearly defined pitch may be further obscured by a wide variety of highly personalized vocal techniques. Samuel Charters has made the point, in his notes to *The Rural Blues*, that the prime object of the blues is to express emotion, not to tell a story. Therefore the words themselves are not as important as, for example, in the ballad. The blues may thus be shouted (a manner of delivery related to the primitive field holler, which has been taken over successively by "rhythm-and-blues" and rock 'n' roll). They may be hummed; they may be sung in falsetto, or with falsetto breaks; they may be sung with the gravelly tone of the false bass voice; they may be chanted in the manner of a recitative; they may even be spoken.[31] In the folk blues, words and even lines may be left unfinished. As for melodic contour, there are many individual variations, but the general tendency is to start the phrase high and proceed downward, ending with a dropping inflection, as in the two field hollers previously transcribed. This is a trait of much primitive music.

Blues harmony may consist simply of a single chord with embellishments.[32] (This rudimentary harmony is likely to be associated with guitar tunings in which all the strings are tuned to the notes of a single chord.) The more usual practice involves the use of the three principal chords of the key in a pattern that *tends* toward the standard blues plan:*

1st phrase	I	—	—	I^7
2d phrase	$IV^{(7)}$	—	I	—
3d phrase	V^7	(IV)	I	—

Sometimes more sophisticated embellishing harmonies are used, especially at the end of the second phrase and the beginning of the last. This practice shows the influence of European harmony, probably by way of ragtime, and is typical of blues harmony as used in jazz.

The elemental blues, related to field calls and hollers, was sung unaccompanied. But at some undefined early date, the guitar was adopted as the natural instrument for accompanying the individual sung laments and comments that were the blues. The pungent nasal twang of the banjo was ideal for the fast breakdowns, but died too quickly to furnish sustained support for the slower blues. The fiddle was not widely used among African-Americans in the lowlands and delta regions, where the blues grew up; it also was thin-toned and incapable of providing harmonic support. But the guitar, with its deeper-toned strings and greater resonance, proved ideal. It could provide harmony, rhythm, and, in the hands of an adept player, melody as well, for the warm-ups and the breaks. Skillful players developed their own individual sounds and techniques, elements of which could, by assiduous listening and imitation, be learned by others and so pass into general currency.

Sliding between tones was made possible by the use of the back of a knife

* In all such diagrams, each symbol represents one measure of music; a dash signifies a repetition of the same harmony. See also Chapter 14.

blade on the strings, or the broken top of a bottle (with the jagged edge annealed) worn on the little finger. This "bottleneck" style, perhaps suggested by the Hawaiian guitar, overrode the rigid tuning imposed by the frets and provided a flexibility that made it possible for a skillful performer to match the sliding and wailing of the voice. The playing of Robert Johnson, among many others, illustrates this.

Other instruments were used as auxiliaries to the ubiquitous guitar. The harmonica was fairly cheap and very portable, and this "blues harp" became, in the hands of virtuosos such as Sonny Terry, a very flexible and expressive instrument, capable of shadings and bendings that approached the subtlety of the voice. Improvised instruments were common. The jug served as a kind of substitute tuba; used as a resonator for the voice, it was also capable of the sliding tone. The washboard, fitted out with auxiliary metal pans and lids attached, was a whole rhythm section. The inverted washtub, with a piece of rope stretched between a hole through its center and a broom handle, was a substitute bass (and was a relative of the African earth bow). Jug bands and washboard bands incorporating these instruments were sometimes recorded commercially, so that their sounds have come down to us—along with those of present-day revivals.

The piano, basically an urban instrument and far from portable, probably did not figure largely in early rural blues. However, in the bars and bordellos of the cities and towns, professional entertainers were soon singing blues with piano accompaniment—a kind of accompaniment that evolved into boogie-woogie, a style very different from ragtime.

The blues story, including boogie-woogie, is continued in Chapter 8 as the story of a popular music evolving from folk roots. Admittedly it is difficult to draw a very precise line between the blues as folk music and the blues as essentially popular music, with professional entertainers catering to a "public" instead of casual music-makers performing within a closely knit community. But the distinction exists, nonetheless. Amiri Baraka has written:

> Socially, classic blues and the instrumental styles that went with it represented the Negro's entrance into the world of professional entertainment and the assumption of the psychological imperatives that must accompany such a phenomenon. . . . It was no longer strictly the group singing to ease their labors or the casual expression of personal deliberations on the world. It became a music that could be used to entertain others *formally*. The artisan, the professional blues singer, appeared; blues-singing no longer had to be merely a passionately felt avocation, it could now become a way of making a living. An external and sophisticated idea of performance had come to the blues, moving it past the casualness of the "folk" to the conditioned emotional gesture of the "public."[33]

It is at this real, if difficult to define, boundary that we take leave of the blues for the present.

Work Songs and Ballads

The blues, like the antecedent cries and hollers, were personal expressions that a lone singer might communicate to a few other sympathetic listeners, or simply sing to himself in his solitude. But there were other songs that, like spirituals, were communal, social songs.

The use of singing to coordinate and lighten physical work, acting as both stimulus and lifter of spirits, is practically universal among men who must engage in hard communal labor, on land or sea. Work songs were prevalent among black laborers during slavery; even spirituals could be used in this way, and some of the earliest collected songs (such as "Michael, Row the Boat Ashore") had this duality of function about them. After the Civil War, work songs were needed wherever gang labor was used, in moving cotton bales, cutting sugar cane, or chopping logs, and especially in the work of building railroads. There had to be a leader, of course; this called for a special skill involving not only a firsthand knowledge of the work and its pacing and a gift for timing, but the ability to infuse into the work the balm of rhythm and song. A few of the recordings we possess of genuine work songs communicate this sense of rhythm and spirit.[34] With increased mechanization, of course, the work song almost disappeared. The only conditions under which it survived, at least until a generation or so ago, were those that closely duplicated conditions under slavery—that is, in the prisons and on the work farms, where, indeed, practically all the field recordings of work songs were made.

The ballad and the work song are both social forms of music-making, though very dissimilar in function. However, the leader's need to prolong the work song to fit the task at hand often led to the adoption of the ballad, or storytelling, method, with its possibilities for improvisation and its indefinite proliferation of stanzas. Thus it is that many black work songs and ballads are related; indeed, this fact may suggest the circumstances in which some ballads, or at least some of their verses, were composed.

The ballad of John Henry, the steel driver, is probably the best known of all African-American ballads. So much attention has it attracted, as an important example of native folklore, that the ballad itself is the subject of two complete books. A hero-ballad, it also deals with the once-well-known occupation of hand-driving a steel drill to make a deep hole in solid rock for a blasting charge. The competition between mechanization and the "natural man" is an important feature in most versions of the ballad that have not been severely truncated. It is one of the few ballads that legend has attached to an actual event: the construction of the Big Bend Tunnel on the Chesapeake & Ohio Railroad near Hinton, West Virginia, in 1870–72. The ballad has been transmuted into both a work song and a blues.[35]

"John Henry" is an exception to the general truth that most African-American ballads are about murder and criminals. "Stagolee" ("Stackerlee") is the archetypal "bad man" and a "bully from his birth." "John Hardy" (traceable perhaps to a man of that name hanged for murder in 1890) has killed for the most capricious of reasons. The crimes are not condoned, and in most versions the murderers eventually pay with their lives. Nevertheless, there is in the telling of these tales—black or white—an unmistakable strain of admiration for their almost superhuman embodiments of evil and meanness, or a strain of sympathy for the fugitive and the prisoner. "Frankie and Albert" (more popularly known as "Frankie and Johnny") is on the other hand more of a domestic tragedy, and probably originated in a more urban milieu, perhaps even as a product of professional songmakers.

Students of the African-American ballad such as Malcolm Laws have pointed out the fecundity of invention that manifests itself in improvisation, and also (in contrast with white balladry) the greater emphasis on character and situation, rather than on events as such.[36] This observation may well serve as a fitting conclusion to our brief survey of African-American folk music, for it serves to underscore a trait the perceptive reader and listener will have noted time and again—the ability to evoke in the listener, by means of an intensely personal and emotional kind of expression, a unique and characteristic degree of empathy with both subject and singer.

Further Reading

Collections, with some expository notes

Allen, William Francis, Charles Pickard Ware, and Lucy McKim Garrison, eds. *Slave Songs of the United States*. New York, 1867. Reprinted since, most recently with piano accompaniments and guitar chords: ed. Irving Schlein, New York: Oak Publications, 1965.
A classic, of permanent importance as the first such collection published.

Dett, R. Nathaniel. *Religious Folk-Songs of the Negro, as Sung at Hampton Institute*. Hampton, VA, 1927. Reprint, New York: AMS Press, 1972.
This is the venerable Hampton Institute Collection, first published in 1874, as revised by one of Hampton's most famous choral directors and composers. As in the John Wesley Work collection listed below, most of the settings are for vocal quartet.

Grissom, Mary Allen. *The Negro Sings a New Heaven*. Chapel Hill, NC, 1930. Paperback reprint, New York: Dover, 1969.
Good collection of forty-five spirituals, with numerous stanzas of text included. The musical transcription is exceptionally carefully done, and probably comes as close as is reasonably possible to representing in print the way the songs are actually sung in the folk tradition.

Jackson, Bruce. *Wake up, Dead Man: Worksongs from Texas Prisons*. Cambridge, MA: Harvard University Press, 1972.

Johnson, James Weldon and J. Rosamund, eds. *The Books of American Negro Spirituals*. 2 vols. in 1. New York: Viking, 1940.
Originally issued as two books, the first in 1925, this is a standard collection. James Weldon Johnson was a novelist and poet, author of *God's Trombones (Seven Negro Sermons in Verse)*. His brother, J. Rosamund Johnson, made the piano arrangements.

Lomax, Alan. *The Folk Songs of North America*. Garden City, NY: Doubleday, 1960; paperback, 1975.
A fine general collection, as the title implies, with commentary.

Parrish, Lydia. *Slave Songs of the Georgia Sea Islands*. New York, 1942. Reprint, Hatboro, PA: Folklore Associates, 1965.
An important work by an amateur folklorist working in an area where much folklore, song, and speech survived into the mid-twentieth century. Includes some good photographs.

Work, John Wesley. *American Negro Songs and Spirituals*. New York: Bonanza, 1940.
Some 40 pages of commentary, followed by a collection of songs of all types, with a preponderance of spirituals—mostly arranged for vocal quartet.

Primarily studies, which include some complete songs

Charters, Samuel. *The Bluesmen*. New York: Oak Publications, 1967.

———. *Sweet as the Showers of Rain*. New York: Oak Publications, 1977.

These two titles constitute a two-volume expansion of the author's earlier *The Country Blues* (New York: Rinehart, 1959)

Courlander, Harold. *Negro Folk Music, U.S.A.* New York: Columbia University Press, 1963.
Includes forty-three complete songs.

Epstein, Dena J. *Sinful Tunes and Spirituals: Black Folk Music to the Civil War.* Urbana: University of Illinois Press, 1977.
A valuable study, with extensive citations from contemporary sources.

Jackson, George Pullen. *White and Negro Spirituals: Their Life Span and Kinship.* New York: Da Capo, 1975 (reprint of original 1944 ed.).
A well-documented study, but controversial in its conclusion that transmission of the material of spirituals was primarily from white to black. Includes a "tune comparative list" of 116 "melodies of white people paired with the same number of negro-sung variants." Dissenting views are presented by Epstein, Lovell, and Tallmadge in this reading list.

Katz, Bernard, ed. *The Social Implications of Early Negro Music in the United States.* New York: Arno, 1969.
A collection of important articles and excerpts from books, dating from 1862 to 1939, most of which include a generous number of examples.

Krehbiel, Henry Edward. *Afro-American Folksongs: A Study in Racial and National Music.* New York: Frederick Ungar, 1914; reprint, 1962.
An early musicological study, with examples to which piano accompaniments have been added, many by H. T. Burleigh. Includes African music, Creole music, and dances.

Scarborough, Dorothy. *On the Trail of Negro Folk-Songs.* Cambridge, MA, 1923. Reprint, Hatboro, PA: Folklore Associates, 1963.
A fine study, including a generous collection of ballads (including African-American versions of Child ballads), reels, children's songs, lullabies, work songs, and railroad songs, many of which have become well known.

Studies and background reading

Baraka, Amiri. *Blues People.* New York: Morrow, 1963
A perceptive social study of African-American music by a prominent black writer (known as LeRoi Jones when the book was first published). The first six chapters are applicable to folk music.

Bebey, Francis. *African Music: A People's Art.* Trans. from French by Josephine Bennett. Chicago: Chicago Review, 1975.

Charters, Samuel. Notes to *The Rural Blues,* Folkways RF 202.

———. Notes to *Roots of Black Music in America,* Folkways 2694.

Cook, Bruce. *Listen to the Blues.* New York: Scribner's, 1973.

Evans, David. *Big Road Blues: Tradition and Creativity in the Folk Blues.* New York: Da Capo, 1987.

Ferris, William, Jr. *Blues from the Delta.* New York: Da Capo, 1984 (reprint of 1979 ed.).

Herskovits, Melville. *The Myth of the Negro Past.* New York: Harper Bros., 1951.
A landmark work, the result of studies begun in the 1930s. Traces Africanisms in New World black culture, daily life, and religion; one chapter deals with language and the arts.

Jackson, Bruce. *The Negro and His Folklore in Nineteenth-Century Periodicals.* Austin: University of Texas Press, 1977.

Laws, G. Malcolm, Jr. *Native American Balladry.* Philadelphia: American Folklore Society, 1964.
This basic study, treating texts and subjects only, but with ample references to versions in print, has a section on African-American ballads.

Lovell, John, Jr. *Black Song: The Forge and the Flame.* New York: Macmillan, 1972.
A major comprehensive survey (686 pages long) of the spiritual. While no aspect is excluded, Lovell, a literary scholar, devotes his major attention to

the texts and to their social background and implications. The book becomes at times somewhat argumentative in its denial of white influence on the spiritual.

Nketia, Joseph. *The Music of Africa*. New York: W. W. Norton, 1974.

Odum, Howard, and Guy B. Johnson. *The Negro and His Songs*. Chapel Hill, NC, 1925. Reprint, Hatboro, PA: Folklore Associates, 1964.
A study of religious, social, and work songs. A rather exhaustive treatment of the texts, with many complete examples. No music.

Oliver, Paul. *The Story of the Blues*. Philadelphia: Chilton, 1969.
The first part of the book deals with the folk phase of the blues. There is an excellent collection of photographs.

———. *Savannah Syncopators*. Briarcliff Manor, NY: Stein & Day, 1970.
Subtitled *African Retentions in the Blues*, it is a provocative if somewhat tentative study. Oliver has not claimed that his work is conclusive. Others, however, including A. M. Jones, have also pointed out that the presence or absence of Islamic influence is a basic distinction in African music.

———. *The Meaning of the Blues*. New York: Macmillan, 1960; paperback ed., New York: Collier, 1963.
An exhaustive and perceptive study of blues subjects and the milieu of its people, in the form of an extensive commentary on 350 blues texts arranged according to subject. Most of the blues lines used as examples in this chapter are quoted in Oliver's work.

Olmsted, Frederick. *Journey in the Seaboard Slave States, with Remarks on Their Economy*. 1856. Reprint, New York: Negro University Press, 1969.

Ramsey, Frederic, Jr. *Been Here and Gone*. New Brunswick, NJ: Rutgers University Press, 1960.
Among the numerous photographic studies with commentary this is surely one of the best.

Roberts, John Storm. *Black Music of Two Worlds*. New York: Praeger, 1972.
This wide-ranging book covers Africa and the entire Western Hemisphere; most relevant to the United States are chapters 3 and 6.

Southern, Eileen. *The Music of Black Americans*. 2d ed. New York: W. W. Norton, 1983.
A comprehensive, indispensable study of the entire field.

——— (ed.). *Readings in Black American Music*. 2d ed. New York: W. W. Norton, 1983.
Excerpts from important source material ranging over the entire field.

Stearns, Marshall. *The Story of Jazz*. New York: Oxford University Press, 1956.
Early chapters deal with African influences, and their transplantation here, both directly and via the West Indies. Also discussed are the work song, the blues, and the spiritual.

Turner, Lorenzo. *Africanisms in the Gullah Dialect*. Chicago: University of Chicago Press, 1949.

Articles

Epstein, Dena J. "A White Origin for the Black Spiritual? An Invalid Theory and How It Grew," *American Music*, vol. 1, no. 2 (Summer 1983).

Evans, David. "African Elements in Twentieth Century U.S. Folk Music" in *Report of the Twelfth Congress: Berkeley, 1977*, ed. Daniel Heartz and Bonnie Wade (Philadelphia: American Musicological Society, 1981), pp. 54–66.

Garst, John F. "Mutual Reinforcement and the Origins of Spirituals," *American Music*, vol. 4, no. 4 (Winter 1986).
An objective evaluation and balancing of the opposing views of Jackson on the one hand and Tallmadge, Lovell, and Epstein on the other as to the black and white contributions to the spiritual.

Maultsby, Portia K. "West African Influences and Retentions in U.S. Black Music: A Sociocultural Study" in Irene Jackson, ed., *More Than Dancing: Essays on Afro-American Music and*

Musicians (Westport, CT: Greenwood, 1985).

Starks, George L., Jr. "Salt and Pepper in Your Shoe: Afro-American Song Tradition on the South Carolina Sea Islands" in Jackson *More Than Dancing*, above.

Tallmadge, William. "The Black in Jackson's White Spirituals," *The Black Perspective in Music*, no. 9 (1981).

Waterman, Richard Alan. "African Influence on the Music of the Americas" in Sol Tax, ed., *Acculturation in the Americas* (New York: Cooper Square, 1967), pp. 207–18.

See also the reading list for Chapter 8; there is unavoidable overlapping between African-American folk music and the blues.

Listening

African Music

Negro Folk Music of Africa and America, ed. Harold Courlander. Folkways 4500.
An excellent and far-ranging collection, edited by a noted authority.

Roots of Black Music in America: Some Correspondence Between the Music of the Slave Areas of West Africa, and the Music of the United States and the Caribbean, comp. and ed. Samuel Charters. Folkways 2694.
A highly interesting collection, juxtaposing, for example, African drumming with that of the early jazz drummer "Baby" Dodds. In listening to it, however, we must realize that the highly selective excerpts, brilliantly chosen for their often superficial resemblances, may blind us momentarily to the very fundamental differences between African and American black music.

Music of the Jos Plateau and Other Regions of Nigeria. Folkways 4321.

African Drums. Folkways 4502.

Africa South of the Sahara, comp. Harold Courlander, notes by Alan Merriam. Folkways 4503.

Religious Folk Music

From the Library of Congress Archive of American Folk Song (AAFS)

Afro-American Spirituals, Work Songs, and Ballads, ed. Alan Lomax. L-3.

Negro Religious Songs and Services, ed. B. A. Botkin. L-10.

Both these albums are valuable field recordings, with useful accompanying notes.

Other

Spirituals with Dock Reed and Vera Hall Ward. Folkways FA-2038.

Anthology of American Folk Music, vol. 2: *Social Music*. Folkways 2952.
The basic anthology consists of commercial recordings of folk music made in the 1920s and 1930s. The notes contain a great deal of information, including discography and bibliography. This volume includes sermons and early gospel songs.

An Introduction to Gospel Song, ed. Samuel Charters. Folkways RF-5.

History of Jazz, vol. 1: *The South*. Folkways 2801.

The Fisk Jubilee Singers. Folkways 2372.

Negro Folk Music of Alabama, vol. 2, ed. Harold Courlander. Folkways 4418.

Georgia Sea Island Songs, from the *Recorded Anthology of American Music*: NW-278.
A fine collection, with notes by Alan Lomax, who did the recording. Side 1 consists of spirituals.

Secular Folk Music

Cries, calls, and hollers

Negro Work Songs and Calls, ed. B. A. Botkin. AAFS: L-8.

Negro Blues and Hollers, ed. Marshall Stearns. AAFS: L-59.

Negro Folk Music of Alabama, vol. 1, ed. Harold Courlander. Folkways 4417.

Blues

Afro-American Blues and Game Songs, ed. Alan Lomax. AAFS: L-4.

Negro Blues and Hollers, ed. Marshall Stearns. AAFS: L-59.

History of Jazz, vol. 2: *The Blues.* Folkways 2802.

The Country Blues, vols. 1 and 2. ed. Samuel Charters. Folkways RF-1, RF-9.

The Rural Blues: A Study of the Vocal and Instrumental Resources, compiled and annotated by Samuel Charters. Folkways RF-202.

Anthology of American Folk Music, vol. 3. Folkways 2953.

The Jug Bands, ed. Samuel Charters. Folkways RF-6.

Roots of the Blues. NW-252. Notes by Alan Lomax.

Work songs and ballads

Negro Work Songs and Calls, ed. B. A. Botkin, AAFS: L-8.

Afro-American Spirituals, Work Songs, and Ballads, ed. Alan Lomax. AAFS: L-3.

Negro Prison Songs from the Mississippi State Penitentiary, collected and annotated by Alan Lomax. Tradition TLP-1020. Exceptionally fine recordings, with commentary, of prison work songs.

History of Jazz, vol. 1: *The South.* Folkways 2801.

Anthology of American Folk Music, vol. 1: *Ballads.* Folkways 2951.

Georgia Sea Island Songs. NW-278. See under Religious Folk Music, above. Side 2 consists of secular songs.

PROJECTS

1. Write a short paper on the South Carolina and Georgia Sea Islands as repositories of black folklore, speech, and song. Include whatever you can find out about conditions there today.

2. Review some of the significant studies that have been made of African survivals in American black music. Some of these are by Melville Herskovits, Alan Merriam, Harold Courlander, Richard Waterman, and Paul Oliver (*Savannah Syncopators*).

3. Make a brief study of the instruments used in African-American folk music.

4. Collect at least five quotations (other than those found in this chapter) from pre–Civil War writers bearing on the music, the musical aptitudes, and the musical practices of the slaves.

5. Prepare a two-part sketch map of West Africa and the Caribbean and the southeastern United States, showing the original locations of various African tribes and the areas in the New World where slaves from these tribes were settled. (Stearns, *The Story of Jazz,* may furnish a point of departure.)

6. Compare the Latin, Catholic-dominated colonial areas (Louisiana, Florida, Hispaniola, Cuba) and the British, Protestant-dominated ones (Barbados, Jamaica, and the rest of the mainland South) for the survival of African traits among blacks. (Refer to Stearns and at least one other source.)

7. Write a short paper on the influence of Isaac Watts (who never visited the United

States) on American hymnody and spirituals, black and white.

8. Write a short paper on the work and significance of the Fisk Jubilee Singers. (Locate if possible nineteenth-century works by Marsh and Pike in the bibliography of Katz, *Social Implications of Early Negro Music in the United States*.)

9. Write a short paper on textual themes in African-American spirituals, including the double meanings they contain. (John Lovell's article in Katz, and Sterling Brown, *Negro Poetry and Drama*, could serve as points of departure.)

10. Compare a traditional version of a spiritual (as found in an early collection such as Allen et al., *Slave Songs of the United States*) with a concert version as sung by a recitalist or a trained concert choir. Discuss the advantages and disadvantages of such concert arrangements.

11. If you are somewhat experienced in music, make a brief study of the similarities between the music of spirituals and that of the blues.

12. If you sing folk songs, learn two songs from the famous *Slave Songs of the United States*, using guitar or piano accompaniment if desired, and sing them for friends or the class. (See the reading list for this chapter for a modern edition with guitar chords and accompaniment added.)

13. Collect recorded examples of at least three different blues guitarist-singers. Describe and compare their original guitar techniques and styles, especially their treatment of the "breaks."

14. Collect recorded examples of blues illustrating at least four of the textual themes identified and treated in Paul Oliver, *The Meaning of the Blues*.

3

American Indian and Hispanic Traditions

IT is an irony inherent in our American experience that our oldest indigenous music—a music that has been heard here since prehistoric times—should be generally the most foreign to us. Except perhaps for Oriental music, no music has had less influence upon, or has proved more difficult to absorb into, our culture than the music of the American Indians.

There are two reasons for this. First, native American music is so different from European-derived music, both in sound and in function, that it may defy even understanding, much less assimilation, by non-Indians. Second, this music belongs to peoples that for too long were regarded by too many as being inferior, with little or nothing in their culture that the immigrant races could find of value. Even those Europeans who earliest took a sympathetic interest in American Indians, the Christian missionaries, most often viewed their music as "heathen," and strove (successfully in some cases) to replace it with the singing of psalms or Christian hymns. This prejudice has now largely disappeared, and we have entered an age in which other Americans are beginning to recognize and esteem the cultural achievements of America's first people, particularly their remarkable harmony with nature. The first difficulty, however, remains formidable. Much of the music is strange to non-Indian ears, unless the owners of those ears have had long and practiced acquaintance with it.

At the time of the first European exploration and colonization, it is estimated that some three million native people lived in North America, between one and two million of them north of what is now Mexico. The population consisted of a thousand different tribal units, each generally having its own language, belonging to one of approximately sixty language families.* The music of the North American Indians has many characteristics shared by all; this fact has given a limited validity to the concept of *generic*, or pan-Indian, music, as we shall see in due course. But there are significant distinctions as well—characteristics that can be identified more or less successfully with some eight roughly defined *culture areas*: Southeast, Northeast (both east of the Mississippi), Plains, Southwest (including most of California), Great Basin, Northwest Coast (from northern coastal California to and including coastal Alaska), Plateau (north of the Great Basin, between the Northwest Coast area and the Rocky Mountains), and North (Arctic and Sub-Arctic, including the Athapaskan and Inuit, or Eskimo, peoples).[1]

As we study Indian music, we must remember that we are dealing with the music of native societies that once were aboriginal cultures but are so no longer. In the 300-odd years during which the whites completed their westward advance across the continent, aboriginal Indian life was thoroughly disrupted—native societies were dispossessed and decimated by disease and warfare; some tribal groups were totally destroyed; most others were relocated or confined on reservations, where they were first treated as a conquered, subject population. As a consequence, large elements of aboriginal cultural ways, including some musical elements, disappeared—destroyed, discarded, lost, or altered beyond modern recognition. Under these conditions, one of the most remarkable things about American Indian musical culture is that a significant remnant of it has indeed survived.

Not only has it survived, but it has entered a new phase of cultivation, as we shall note in due course. It will therefore be necessary to treat native American music in two distinct, though related, aspects: first, what can be learned of it as an integral part of the culture of an aboriginal people; and second, Indian music as it exists today.

Music in Aboriginal Indian Life

There are two ways to view an artifact, tangible or intangible, that is the result of artistic endeavor. The first is as a thing of interest and beauty wholly in and of itself. The second is as something to be viewed in the complete context of the society that brought it forth, having essential meaning only in this context. The two are never absolutely separate: we experience every art object with some mixture of both. But the closer we get to art in the folk or primitive state, the more necessary it becomes to take into account the second view. While never abandoning the study and apprehension of a work of art intrinsically, we must give a much greater proportion of our effort to understanding what the lives of those who made the art were like, and what place and meaning it had for them. This is in no case more imperative than with the music of the Indian people.

* The cultural complexity resulting from the 25,000-year history of the aborigines in North America is illustrated by the fact that the language families are not necessarily identified or coincident with the culture areas, as defined below. The Navajo and Apache of the desert Southwest, for example, have a language related to that of the tribes of the far north of Canada and Alaska.

To non-Indian ears on first acquaintance, some Indian tribal music has instant appeal, but often much of it seems forbidding and aesthetically unpromising—strange, monotonous, even ugly. Whatever one's immediate reaction, however, it must be realized that the music was never created to be experienced in the essentially passive way in which we listen to music in the concert hall or on recordings. Even more than in the case of folk music, its ambience is its very essence. As Willard Rhodes has said: "Primitive music is so inextricably bound up in a larger complex, ceremonial or social, that it is practically non-existent out of its functional context."

Here is a condensation of a description of a Hopi ceremony that included music, as in fact do most Indian ceremonies:

> With a Hopi acquaintance I drove one July morning to Bakabi, to see the final ritual of the *Niman*. When I arrived in the village, I found that most of the Hopis had ascended to the line of roof tops, from which they could watch the ceremony in the plaza below. . . . The sky was cloudless and intensely blue. Sunshine flooded everything, illuminating the white walls of the houses along the plaza's farther side. . . . Soon a file of fifteen or twenty men came slowly into the plaza. . . . Each man's body, bare above the waist, was painted brown and marked with white symbols. Behind his right knee was fastened a rattle, made of a turtle shell. With each step that he took, the rattle gave out a hollow, muffled sound. In his right hand he carried a gourd rattle. . . . But the striking feature was the mask that each man wore. This covered his head completely and came down to his shoulders. The front was white and was inscribed with block-like figures, which suggested eyes, nose, and mouth. . . . Immediately, the ceremony began. With measured, rhythmic step the long single file moved slowly forward, in time with a subdued chant. . . . With every step the turtle-shell rattle fastened behind the right knee contributed its hollow accent, sometimes suddenly magnified when all the dancers in unison struck the right foot sharply against the ground. Now and then the gourd rattles were shaken for two or three seconds, giving a curious accompaniment of elevated sound in contrast to the low, chanting voices. . . . When it was all over, I came away with the feeling that I had witnessed an ancient rite that was rich in symbolism and impressive in its significance.[2]

Even if a recording of this music had been made, how much could it convey to us, abstracted from its context?

Music had not only an importance in Indian life greater than is general among musically sophisticated societies, but also a *concreteness* unknown to such societies. The abstraction "music" would have been an unfamiliar and useless concept; it was only "this song" that had meaning. The important thing about a song is not its *beauty* but its *efficacy*. Frances Densmore, one of the pioneering authorities on Indian music, has written: "The radical difference between the musical custom of the Indian and our own race is that, primarily, the Indians used song as a means of accomplishing definite results."[3] A recent incident illustrates the fact that this view of music is not totally dead even now. For a recent recording of gambling songs by the Yurok and Tolowa tribes of northern California, translations of the words could not be made because, it was explained, "to do so would put the songs' luck in jeopardy."[4]

The degree of concreteness with which Indian songs are viewed is further illustrated by the fact that in many cases they are treated as strictly personal possessions, which may be transmitted to others only by being sold or given away. One old man, after being persuaded to record a noted war song, said that he would not live long now that he had given away his most valuable possession. There is, in fact, a sense of tangible reality, of magical power, of "presence," in *all* manifestations of what we would term "art" among primitive peoples. In the nineteenth century, after an eastern artist had been among the Plains Indians sketching the buffalo, an old Indian complained to a white friend that there were no longer so many buffalo on their range—a white man had put a great number of them in a book and taken them away with him. Is this not indeed an expression of the same magic-imbued world view that inscribed on rocks and in caves those often remarkably impressionistic likenesses of beasts the hunters needed to kill? It is this world we must be prepared to enter if we would understand what music originally meant to our first people.

Let us return to Frances Densmore's perceptive introduction to her chapter entitled "Why Do Indians Sing?"

> Singing was not a trivial matter. . . . It was used in treating the sick, in securing success in war and the hunt, and in every undertaking which the Indian felt was beyond his power as an individual. An Indian said, "If a man is to do something more than human he must have more than human power." Song was essential to the putting forth of this "more than human power," and was used in connection with some prescribed action. . . . Thus it is seen that Indian music (both vocal and rhythmic instrumental) originally lay in the field of what we call religion.[5]

Music was thus a means of communication with what we would regard as the supernatural world—a world in which sun, moon, stars, lakes, rivers, mountains, and all animals each had an indwelling spirit (or, to use the Iroquois word, *orenda*) that the Indian could call upon in need, provided he possessed and used the right "medicine."

Songs of great power, sung chiefly by medicine men or women, would be used in communal ceremonies, and would be very carefully passed on in oral tradition. In the songs of the Navajo, for example, the need for extreme accuracy was (and is) crucial to their efficacy. There could also be new songs, belonging to men who had acquired them in the course of "vision quests"—self-imposed ordeals of courage and self-denial that were known among virtually all tribes in their aboriginal state. Lonely fasts, often carried out in locations and conditions of extreme discomfort and danger, and lasting as long as four days, would, when successful, result in what appeared as tangible communication with the spirit dwelling in some animal or some natural phenomenon. With the imparting of the vision (which identified the seeker forever afterward with the particular animal, if that was the apparent source) would often come what was received as a new song. These, then, were the "real" songs—the property either of individuals or of the tribe. A clear distinction was made in most tribes between these songs, which had inherent power, and other songs that were either borrowed from other tribes or were made up—consciously composed—and used to enhance various forms of recreation. In recent years, under the pressures of acculturation, the old songs have decreased in importance in the repertory of most tribes. Many that are known to have existed have been lost altogether.

The older ceremonial songs are heard in their purer form on the early recordings, sung often by old men whose memories stretch back to a time on the Plains and farther west when little acculturation had yet taken place. One example is from the Menominee, an Algonquian tribe which, at the time this song was collected in the late 1920s, was still living along the Menominee River in Wisconsin, in the same locality they had inhabited for at least three centuries, going back to the time when they were first encountered by the whites. Example 3–1, a dream song that was said to have power in healing the sick and was so used, was sung by Louis Pigeon, who had secured it as a boy. After fasting for two days, he saw two birds, a crow and a raven, who gave him the song.[6]

Example 3–1

Game songs are also present in the earliest collections. A favorite among many tribes was the moccasin game. The players were divided into two opposing sides. One side hid four small objects such as bullets or prune pits under four overturned moccasins; one of the objects was specially marked, and the point of the game was for the other side to guess under which moccasin the marked object lay. Wagers were often heavy, and assistants could be used to sing songs or otherwise bring luck. Example 3–2 is a Menominee moccasin game song.[7]

Another important class of songs were those used for healing. There were love songs as well—not, as in our popular culture, for the expression of sentimental feelings, but as "lucky" songs, to secure success in love through the invocation of magical power. Social dancing, with its own music, was originally relatively unimportant, though it has now become much more prevalent—one manifestation of the changes that have come over Indian life. Work songs exist, as for example the corn-grinding songs of the Southwest. So do narrative songs, especially among the Northwest Coast tribes. Neither work songs nor storytelling songs figure prominently in Indian repertory generally, however. Songs for other social functions exist: to welcome and bid farewell to guests (very elaborate along the northwestern coast); to honor warriors and chieftains; and to use in contests and other purely social ceremonies.

Example 3–2

Transcription by the author

Characteristics of Indian Music

Indian music is predominantly vocal; there is very little purely instrumental music. The singing is usually accompanied, however, by a drum or some sort of rattle, or both. The basic unit of the music is the song, which may last anywhere from less than a minute to several minutes. When the song accompanies dancing, as it very often does, there is a good deal of repetition; it is common to sing a song four times.

The scales used in Indian music are found generally to correspond to our familiar diatonic scale—that is, the basic scale structure available on the white keys of the piano. When fewer than the full seven tones to the octave are used, as is often the case, some form of the pentatonic scale (that obtainable on the black keys) is very common, as it is in much folk and primitive music the world over. The piano is mentioned here merely as a means of reference; it must be understood that Indian music, in intonation, only *approximates* the tuning implied in our notational system. There are subtle deviations in the qualities of certain intervals that are consistent in repeated renditions of the same song. Even microtones (intervals smaller than the smallest on the piano) are occasionally found. *Portamento,* or sliding from one pitch to another, is common, particularly a descending slide at the end of a phrase. Singing in other than the unison (or octave, if the women sing also) is extremely rare, though not unknown.

Indian instruments include drums, whistles, flutes, hand-shaken rattles, and ornaments worn by dancers (usually made of some type of shells), which produce a rhythmic kind of rattling during the dance. The drums range in size from small hand-held ones to quite large ones resting on the ground, or suspended between posts in the ground, and played by several people at once.

They are made in a variety of ways, and are even improvised from inverted baskets, washtubs or kettles covered with skin, or wooden boxes. Flutes are usually fashioned from some straight-grained wood or cane, but in the Southwest they can be made of clay. Rattles are nearly universal, are of many types, and usually have (or had) ritual significance.

The flute is almost uniquely associated with love songs, and these songs constitute almost the only use of purely instrumental music. Example 3–3 is a portion of a Sioux love song, as played on a flute.[8] Words can be put to the melodies so that they can also be sung, as this example sometimes is.

Example 3–3

Transcription by the author

The use of drums alone, without singing, is virtually unknown; this is in distinct contrast to African, and hence to West Indian, tradition. The rhythms of drum and rattle are simple, the impulses usually grouped in pairs in a relation that ranges from perfectly even pulses (Example 3–4) to those based on the triplet (Example 3–5). Very often it is somewhere in between. Longer songs may be divided into clearly defined sections, with definite tempo changes. The tempo of the drum, curiously, is sometimes independent of that of the voice.

Since the music is nearly all vocal, the question of the words arises.

Example 3–4

Example 3–5

Interestingly enough, the songs are very often not in the language of speech. *Vocables*—simple vocal sounds—often either are interpolated between actual words or replace them altogether. (The same tendency, in refrains, was noted in Anglo-American folk music.) To call these syllables meaningless is not quite correct; they may have private or ritual significance, or they may be sounds whose original meaning has been lost, either through changes in the language or because they were borrowed from other tribes. Whatever their origin, the vocables are not improvised, but belong to the given song and are reproduced with complete consistency.

Indian music has not proved incapable of assimilating certain aspects of non-Indian music. On occasion, the tunes of Christian hymns and white secular songs have been adopted.[9] English words have been used, with either Indian tunes or disguised white tunes. A "forty-nine song" is a particular kind of humorous, often derisive, song with English words. A recent rendition of the Rabbit Dance, a social dance of the northern Plains Indians, contains the following lines, in a parody of a white cowboy song.

> Hey, sweetheart, I always think of you.
> I wonder if you are alone tonight.
> I wonder if you are thinking of me.[10]

Indian Music and Acculturation

As we have noted, acculturation has gone on continuously since the first contacts with the white man. The French Huguenots were teaching the Florida Indians to sing psalms in the sixteenth century, and the Franciscans who traveled with the *conquistadores* in the seventeenth brought Spanish religious festivals and music to the Rio Grande Valley. The length of time that the Indians have been exposed to the white man's culture varies widely from area to area, of course. We know the least about aboriginal Indian music in the eastern United States, where the cultural pressures, and the dispossessions and dispersions, began earliest and were most severe. As a single example of a major uprooting, Indians from five tribes (the Choctaw, the Creek, the Cherokee, the Chickasaw, and the Seminole) were forced to move between 1830 and 1842 (in an episode known as the "Trail of Tears") from the southeastern states to an area west of the Mississippi known as the Indian Territory—and formally so designated until its admission to the Union as the state of Oklahoma in 1907.[11] After the Civil War, the western portion of the

Indian Territory became home for many Indians from the northern and central Plains as well. This kind of dislocation brought tribes from greatly separated regions into contact, and this contact marked the beginnings of the pan-Indian movement to which reference will be made later.

The Ghost Dance and the Peyote Cult

Two singular developments in the West since the encroachment of white civilization deserve mention, since they grew out of that cataclysm, directly or indirectly. The first of these was the spread of the Ghost Dance, with its accompanying music. Originating in the Great Basin area, the Ghost Dance cult represented a kind of messianic religious belief in the appearance of a savior and the expulsion of the white man, accompanied by the resurrection of dead Indian leaders and the return of the buffalo and of the old ways. In the 1880s the Ghost Dance spread rapidly, especially among Plains tribes. It was outlawed by the Bureau of Indian Affairs, and its repression by the United States Army culminated in the tragic massacre of Sioux Ghost Dance devotees at Wounded Knee in South Dakota in 1890. As an active cult and ritual, a vehicle of a fanatical hope, the Ghost Dance died out as rapidly as it had spread. Its songs persisted, however, and were recorded among Plains tribes as late as the 1940s. It was a pan-Indian cultural phenomenon; Ghost Dance songs of various tribes show similar characteristics, of Great Basin origin, that are often markedly different from those of their own indigenous tribal music.[12]

A second development, not unrelated to the rapid spread and decay of the Ghost Dance cult, has been the spread of the peyote cult (the Native American Church), based on the use of the hallucinogenic buttons of the peyote cactus. Originating apparently in pre-Columbian Mexico, it had spread northward into the Rio Grande and Gila River basins by the eighteenth century, where it was known among the Apache. The cult reached the Plains about 1870. Taking on there a somewhat different form, it became a group or community rite, with a well-defined ceremonial that incorporated some elements of Christian theology and symbolism. Its spread since then has been rather carefully documented, and is still going on; it reached some groups of the Navajo, and the Indians of Canada and Florida, in the mid-twentieth century. Singing is an integral part of the meetings at which the peyote buttons are consumed, and while any songs, including Christian hymns, may be used, special peyote songs have evolved.[13] The relation of the peyote cult to the vanished Ghost Dance, and to the severe upheaval to which the American Indians and their aboriginal culture generally have been subjected in the modern world, is summed up by David McAllester:

> The wide spread of the Ghost Dance must have contributed to the receptivity of the Indians to peyote. After the brief currency of the former the Indians were left with little sense of spiritual direction, although the conditions of radical change and insecurity that fostered the Ghost Dance were intensified after its collapse. . . . In place of resistance a philosophy of peaceful conciliation and escape rose. . . . The vision, all-important on the Plains, was made easily available by the use of the cactus.[14]

Outside Influences on Music Made by Indians

Indians themselves have absorbed and adopted outside influences in their music. We have already noted the adaptation of Christian hymns and secular songs, and the satirical "forty-nine songs," all of which involve the use of the English language. The greatest degree of integration of Indian and non-Indian elements in music and dance has taken place in the Southwest. Hispanic influence is evident in the *matachines* of New Mexico—pageants of dance and drama derived from quite old Spanish fiestas (possibly introduced by the Franciscans as early as the seventeenth century) which are associated with the Christian observances of Easter and Christmas.[15]

A more recent absorption, wholly in the secular domain, is represented by the popular dance music among the Papago, Pima, and Yaqui tribes in southern Arizona known as *waila*, or more popularly as "chicken scratch." Chicken scratch bands use combinations of such instruments as guitar, accordion, saxophone, and (non-Indian) drum set to play waltzes, two-steps, and polkas that show resemblances to Mexican *mariachi* music, Texas-Mexican *norteña* music, German band music, and even Louisiana *zydeco*.[16]

The State of Indian Music Today

Indian music today can best be described as a *renovated* art—that is, an art renewed in a way that consciously preserves tradition while adapting it in a manner that allows it to survive, and even thrive, in the conditions under which Indians live in the modern world.

The American Indian population, which had declined to half a million or less by the end of the nineteenth century, has begun again to grow at a rapid rate, and now numbers well over one million. Automobiles, radio, and television have ended the isolation of reservation life, and a large-scale movement of Indian people toward urban centers since the end of World War II has intensified cultural contact not only between Indians and whites but—most important for Indian music—between Indian people of different tribal traditions. It is important to recognize, then, that the indigenous and inherited culture of over one million native Americans is not dead. It is true that much of the older music has been irretrievably lost. Alan Merriam quotes a young Flathead musician, on being asked about the fact that the younger performers do not know the old songs: "Well, the old-timers are kickin' off fast, and that kind of song is gettin' to be old stuff nowadays."[17]

Twentieth-century influence is seen in an altered view of the *function* of music. While its religious function has by no means disappeared altogether, it coexists with both a recreational function and an entertainment function—music and dance in something resembling a concert situation, for a passive "audience" often of tourists. A group of professional or semiprofessional performers has grown up in response to this development—a development with ramifications in two directions. On the one hand, there is a tendency to preserve and extend a pan-Indian "cultural front," purveying a kind of "generic" Indian music. On the other, serious Indian musicians have the opportunity to function as composers, using Indian culture as a basis for the creation of individual works within, and with meaning for, the Indian community—an opportunity that did not exist in the older tribal society.

In spite of the pressures of professionalism and commercialization, music has been part of a serious movement of cultural *revival* since the 1950s. The intertribal *powwows* held annually on the Plains (especially in Oklahoma) are today primarily great social events, but they include the performance of songs and dances that maintain at least a certain amount of regional, if not tribal, identity and characteristics, and thus represent a return to tribal or regional particularism and a movement away from pan-Indianism in matters of culture.[18] The Crow Indians furnish an example of a tribe that has been particularly successful in maintaining its cultural identity. The fact that some groups, such as the Ponca Singers of Oklahoma, have become professionalized to the extent of traveling and performing regularly for pay at various powwows does not necessarily mean that they have corrupted or compromised Indian song itself, or even that they have blurred tribal or regional distinctions.

The movement of American Indians off the reservations and into the cities was given extra impetus in the 1950s by a Bureau of Indian Affairs program aimed at eventually abolishing the special status of the American Indians and eliminating the reservation system. This program has since been abandoned, but not all the Indians who were relocated returned to reservations, and there exist very sizable communities of American Indians not only in virtually every small city in the West, but in and around large urban areas, particularly Chicago, Denver, Los Angeles, and Oakland and the San Francisco Bay area. These urban Indian communities also regularly enjoy large social gatherings, at which Indian songs and dances are performed—in Los Angeles, for example, by such groups as the Los Angeles Northern Singers, made up of members of the Sioux, Arikara, Hidatsa, and Northern Arapaho tribes. At these gatherings, not only are the tribal songs and dances found to be flourishing, but along with the new emphasis on the social function of the music there are preserved unmistakable traces of the older attitude toward music as well. These can be seen, for example, in the custom of "sponsoring" an entertainment in honor of a person or event (which had its aboriginal counterpart in customs such as the *potlatch*), and in surviving manifestations of the concepts that certain songs are private possessions and that certain songs bring luck. This blending of the old and the new is, according to the *functionalist* view of folk art and folklore, both a ceaseless process and a perennial condition.

Iberian-Indian-African Traditions from the South

The surprising and baffling intricacies awaiting any one investigating music coming from "south of the border" (to use the shorthand term) can be traced ultimately to the fact that this music represents an extremely complex overlaying of cultures that resists simple characterization or explanation. There is not even a single all-inclusive name for this music: neither "Spanish" (nor "Hispanic") nor even the more general term "Latin" are adequate to represent accurately the whole; still less the narrower "Mexican," "Chicano," "Aztlán," "Afro-Caribbean," "Afro-Cuban," or "Puertorriqueño." In effect we are dealing with a blending of cultures from four continents—Central America and Mexico, South America, Europe (specifically the Iberian peninsula), and West Africa. Let us start our exploration of this complex subject with the impact of Spanish conquest and colonization on the Western Hemisphere.

The first European presence in America was that of the Spaniards. In the generation following Columbus's voyages, Spain, the foremost European power of the time, entered upon a period of phenomenal exploration and conquest. By the mid-sixteenth century the Spanish had begun extensive exploration by land and by sea from Florida to the northern California coast, and by the beginning of the seventeenth century the first attempts at colonization in what is the present area of the United States (many of which proved to be disastrous) had begun. Although Florida was the first point of contact, Spanish influence along the eastern coast of the Gulf of Mexico was not destined to be significant. In the Southwest, on the other hand, it was decisive. Beginning with the earliest missions and small colonial settlements in the upper Rio Grande Valley of New Mexico in the seventeenth century, and culminating with the high-water mark of Spanish penetration in the California mission period of the late eighteenth and nineteenth centuries, the foundation was laid for Hispanic influence, which is still of the greatest importance culturally in that part of the country, and which has been reinforced in all periods by almost continuous migrations from Mexico.

Hispanic-Derived Sacred Music from Mexico

The first musical influences were religious. Spanish sacred music reached the highest point of its development in the prosperous sixteenth century, rivaling in its excellence and in the intensity of its cultivation that of Rome itself. It was Spanish sacred music from that era that traveled with the *conquistadores*, and music was found to be one of the priests' most powerful tools for converting and teaching the Indians.* Before the end of the sixteenth century both vocal and instrumental music were intensively cultivated in Mexico, accompanied by the manufacture of musical instruments and the printing of music.

New Mexico

Because of its early penetration by both conquistadores and missionaries beginning in the 1540s, New Mexico is the area of the oldest sustained Hispanic influence in the United States. And because of its subsequent relative isolation (from the Re-Conquest after the Pueblo Revolt of the 1680s to the testing of the atomic bomb in the 1940s), especially in the valleys of the upper Rio Grande and Pecos River, this influence has until recently persisted with little interference. The opening of the Santa Fe Trail in 1821, and the conquest and annexation of the area by the United States in 1846–48 had little effect on life in the remote villages, much of which centered on their churches.

* A survival of this influence into the twentieth century has been cited earlier, in the matachines dance-drama among the Indians of New Mexico.

Not surprisingly, it is religious music that has the longest history of cultivation and preservation. Representative of this, and of particular antiquity and interest, is the music of *La Fraternidad Piadosa de Nuestro Padre Jesús Nazareno*, more familiarly known as *Los Hermanos Penitentes*, or simply *Los Penitentes*. This lay brotherhood, related to and now recognized by the Roman Catholic Church, is devoted to helping the poor and the sick in its small, isolated communities, and to observing forms of worship which, culminating in Holy Week, commemorate the Passion of Jesus through austere rites of penance. As one close student of the Brotherhood has written,

> Many Brotherhood rites formerly involved closely supervised expressions of a penitential spirit through self-flagellation, cross bearing, and other forms of mortification. Sometimes, in the past, a Brother was tied to a large cross during a short simulation of the Crucifixion on Good Friday. Unfortunately, these practices attracted undue attention from uncomprehending outsiders, and the Brothers were forced to alter their devotional patterns, becoming more secretive in order to protect their right to worship according to tradition.[19]

The precise origins of this tradition are obscure, though there was ample precedent for severe penitential practices in Spain from the fifteenth through the seventeenth centuries, and subsequently in Old Mexico. The Brotherhood itself has been linked to a thirteenth-century lay order of the Franciscans, who were the dominant religious influence in New Mexico for two and a half centuries. But the extreme isolation of the Spanish villages of northern New Mexico and southern Colorado, seldom visited by priests and all but ignored by the hierarchy of the Church, fostered a self-reliance in religious (as in all other) matters, and the lay "brothers of penance" assumed an important role in their communities which is still strong and in evidence today.

The most characteristic form of music cultivated by the Penitentes was the *alabado*, a religious folk song in free meter sung in unison. The alabado, whose currency is not limited to the Brotherhood, has indeed been called the "backbone of congregational singing since the 16th century" and has been and still is sung in Hispanic Catholic churches throughout the Southwest.[20] Its forebears are the medieval plainchant of the Catholic Church, and the cantillations of the Sephardic Jews of Spain and Portugal. Most of the alabados sung by the Penitentes are lengthy strophic songs commemorating aspects of the Passion of Christ, such as the Stations of the Cross, which are reenacted in pageant form. They are unaccompanied except by the florid improvised interjections of the *pito* (a homemade flute played only during Holy Week), which are said to represent the lamenting cries of the Virgin Mary. Occasionally the processions were accompanied by the sound of the *matracas*, a wooden ratchet that replaced the sound of the bells, which were traditionally silenced on Good Friday. Many of the alabados have been preserved, having been recorded around 1950 in their many variants from village to village.[21]

A more widespread form of religious folk song is that associated with the Christmas play *Los Pastores* (The Shepherds), and its prelude, *Las Posadas* (The Lodgings). They are related to the mystery plays, liturgical dramas prevalent in Europe from the ninth through the sixteenth centuries. Possibly written by the Franciscans in Mexico, they made their ways by separate routes to California, New Mexico, and Texas. *Las Posadas* and *Los Pastores* commemorate first Mary and Joseph seeking lodging, and then the shepherds coming to pay homage to the infant Jesus. Many versions of *Los Pastores* were also recorded in New Mexico around the middle of this century, and some have been painstakingly transcribed.[22] Today *Las Posadas*, partially because of the interest it has aroused among non-Hispanics, is more frequently cultivated than the longer and more involved *Los Pastores*.

California

A distant and attenuated echo of the greatness of Spanish church music belatedly reached California in the eighteenth century. It is now known that during the brief flourishing of the Franciscan missions in California from 1769 to their secularization beginning in 1834, there was a rather considerable musical culture. It embraced strictly liturgical music (at least some of which was probably composed there), as well as more informal and folklike hymns and alabados, and even secular songs and dances, performed for festive occasions. Both vocal and instrumental music were taught to the Indians, who made up the choirs and small orchestras. After the secularization of the missions and the departure of the Franciscan priests, such manuscripts as existed (consisting wholly of liturgical music) were destroyed or forgotten, and what little was preserved of a musical culture went over into oral tradition. Under the circumstances, it is remarkable that any survived; it is therefore rather surprising to come upon a remarkable photograph of the last Indian choir of Mission San Buenaventura, taken in 1860, with each of the Indians holding what appears to be a homemade instrument—a flute, for example, fashioned from an old gun barrel. That the singing of the Indian choirs survived even longer in some cases, without losing its intensity or meaning, is attested to by Robert Louis Stevenson's account of a festival at Mission San Carlos Borromeo (Carmel) in 1879: "I have never seen faces more vividly lit up with joy than the faces of these Indian singers. It was to them not only the worship of God, nor an act by which they recalled and commemorated better days, but was besides an exercise of culture, where all they knew of art and letters was united and expressed."[23] Some of the sacred music of the missions has now been recovered and recreated; many of the simple liturgical pieces have a naive charm that is quite distinctive.[24]

Secular Music from Mexico

Secular folk music from Latin America has been far more widespread and influential in our culture than has sacred music. To begin to understand the nature and sources of this music, it is important to realize that the *mestizo* folk culture of Latin America is everywhere a blend of Spanish, Indian, and African elements, the mix varying from region to region. African influence is strongest in the Caribbean (especially Cuba and Hispaniola), and in the Caribbean and Brazilian coastal areas of South America, though it is not to be discounted in Mexico itself.[25] The music from south of our borders has reached the United States in two strains that have much in common but are yet distinct, and by two routes. That which has come from Mexico is obviously of the greatest importance in the Southwest—in Texas, New Mexico, Colorado, Arizona, and California—but has penetrated farther north as well. The other strain, that from the Caribbean and South America, will be treated later.

An important point to note initially about the secular music that has come to this country from Mexico (as indeed from the rest of Latin America as well) is that dance and song are closely associated. Many kinds of music can be used for either. For example, the *corrido*[26] (or ballad) can be danced as well as sung, and the *huapango*, originally a dance from Veracruz, can also be sung. Dancing was a very important pastime from the earliest times in rural Hispanic communities, and there are numerous accounts of *bailes* (or dances) in the *salas* of the towns or villages of New Mexico, to the accompaniment of fiddle and guitar. Popular dances were *el valse* (the waltz), *la polca* (the polka), *el chotis* (the schottische), and *el cutilio* (the cotillion or square dance).[27]

A second point to observe about this music is the marks that other cultures have made on it, either here or in Mexico itself.[28] The mixture of Austrian, German, Czech, and Anglo-American influences can be seen in the types of dances cited above and in their names. We shall presently observe that the German influence in particular (its chief contributions being the polka and the button accordion) proved to be decisive, as the music of the border region evolved into an ethnically distinct and commercially viable product.

A third point to be realized is that it is often difficult to make a distinction between folk and popular in considering Mexican music in the United States. For one thing, many songs that were composed and disseminated as popular music in Mexico tended, when they came north, to become *de facto* folk songs. One example is "Canción mixteca," composed in Mexico by José Lópe Alavés; never very popular in Mexico, it has become a cherished song in oral tradition, especially among the present-day older generation of Mexican-Americans in the Southwest, probably because of its expression of nostalgic longing for the mother country.

Another source of confusion between folk and popular is the fact that, while genuine regional musics, as enjoyed by the mostly rural people in the highly differentiated parts of Mexico, have existed and continue to exist, they have been overshadowed by a kind of "generic" Mexican music, perpetuated as part of a professionalized "cultural front." This development is similar to, but much older than, that of the pan-Indian music described earlier in this chapter. In the 1880s, for example, during the Díaz regime, *orquestas típicas*, made up of professional musicians dressed in *charro*[29] costumes, were formed, and were supported by the government as a means of promoting Mexican culture abroad. Orquestas típicas toured the United States and Europe before the turn of the century, and since then such ensembles have been important, both as tourist attractions in the large Mexican cities and as exporters of "typical" Mexican music. This has become the function of the more recent trumpet mariachi ensembles. (Trumpet mariachis are distinct from the more traditional and folklike string mariachis; it is interesting to note that the trumpets, so strongly associated with our usual idea of mariachi music, were added only in the 1930s, when a more incisive sound was needed for radio broadcasting.) With the advent of broadcasting and recording, the production of popular music based on folk styles but performed by professional musicians began in Mexico City, in the same kind of development that produced "country music" from regional folk styles here.

Mariachi and Norteño Music: Two Instrumental Traditions

The result of this popularization and consequent standardization has been the emergence of two dominant types of instrumental ensemble, used to accompany either dancing or singing. One is the mariachi, which in its popular form consists of trumpets, violins, and guitars (two or three of each), and a guitarróne or bass guitar. The other is the *conjunto*, or ensemble, of the *musica norteña*. This more distinctively regional ensemble, coming from the lower Rio Grande Valley shared by Texas and the far northeastern part of Mexico (hence the adjective *norteña*, "northern"), consisted in its early stages of only the highly characteristic button accordion with an accompaniment of guitar or *bajo sexto* (a form of twelve-string guitar). Beginning in the 1950s, a saxophone was frequently added (often doubling the accordion in thirds, a typically Mexican device also used with voices and with mariachi trumpets), as well as a jazz-type drum set and a bass—more recently an electric one. The differences between mariachi music and musica norteña are not so much distinctions in repertory—they may perform the same songs or dances—but in their instrumentation and style of performance. Musica norteña most often has as its rhythmic basis either the "oom-pa oom-pa" of the adopted polka or the "oom-pa-pa oom-pa-pa" of the adopted waltz, while the mariachi ensemble is more apt to retain the complex rhythms and cross-rhythms of the Mexican *son*.*

Mariachi music attained considerable popularity north of the border after trumpets were added to the ensemble. With its rhythms and its trumpets in parallel thirds, it is often used as a kind of convenient symbol, or even caricature, of "Mexicanness." Norteño or conjunto music, on the other hand, is probably more widely popular among Mexican-Americans themselves. It evolved into a distinctive and regionally very influential style at the hands of accordionists such as Narciso Martinez ("El Huracán del Valle"), the singer-guitarist Lydia Mendoza, and groups such as Los Alegres de Terán. The music was spread throughout the Southwest by a more recent generation of performers, including the accordionist-singer Flaco Jiménez and the guitarist-singers Freddy Fender (Baldemar Huerta), Doug Sahm (an Anglo with the acquired name of Doug Saldaña), and José Maria De Leon ("Little Joe") Hernández. Acquiring political overtones to some degree, and associated with the ethnic pride and aspirations of Chicanos, music norteña has become identified throughout the West as Chicano music.[30]

Corrido and Canción

Of all the folk forms now popular, none is more distinctive or more interesting than the *corrido*. The Hispanic love of poetry, and especially the commemo-

* The most characteristic cross-rhythm of the *son* is the juxtaposition, either simultaneously or sequentially, of simple triple (3/4) and compound duple (6/8) meters. The traditional and very popular *son* "La Negra" is typical. It may be heard as recorded in Jalisco, Mexico, on *Mariachi Aguilas de Chapala* (Folkways 8870).

ration of people and events in poetry, here finds expression in what is still a vital tradition. The corrido is the modern equivalent of the folk ballad—a narrative strophic song. As distinguished from the older *romance,* of Spanish origin, it deals with actual people and events, often of immediate and topical concern, in an earthy, frank, and unembellished way. It had its origins in Mexico in the turbulent mid-nineteenth century, when it was often political and satirical. Corridos were cheaply printed as broadsides (words only), just like those found earlier in England and the United States.

The corrido of the southwestern United States is nearly as old as its Mexican forebear. An area rich in the production of corridos and other folklore has been the valley of the lower Rio Grande, from the two Laredos to the Gulf. A fertile valley in the midst of an arid plain, overlooked in early exploration and colonialization, largely ignored by Spain and Mexico, and spurned by the United States, it was inhabited by people of a fiercely independent spirit. When in 1836 Texas declared its independence of Mexico, the valley suddenly became a border area, and a period of unrest, oppression, and bloodshed began that was to last intermittently for nearly a century. Like many strife-torn border areas—that between England and Scotland, for example—it bred its heroes and its villains, and its ballads to commemorate them. An early corrido was "El Corrido de Kiansis," known in the border area by 1870. It describes the experiences and hardships of the Mexican *vaqueros* in the cattle drives of the late 1860s and early 1870s from Texas to the western terminus of the railroad in Kansas.

One of the most famous corridos, still sung today, is "El Corrido de Gregorio Cortez" (Example 3–6), based on an incident that took place in Karnes County, Texas, in 1902. The hero was a young Mexican who, having been falsely accused of horse stealing, shot and killed in self-defense the sheriff who had fatally wounded his brother. The corrido, in some twenty to thirty stanzas, goes on to trace Cortez's flight and capture, ending with the customary *despedida,* "Now with this I say farewell."

Example 3–6

Transcription by the author

En el con - da - do del Car - men mir -
-en lo que‿ha su - ce - di - do, Mu - rió‿el she - ri - fe ma-yor que
dan - do Ro - mán he - ri - do.

In Karnes County
Look what has happened;
The sheriff died,
Leaving Román badly wounded.[31]

This corrido shows the typical form of four-line rhymed stanzas, or *coplas*, each line customarily having eight syllables. The musical rhythm is simple, but rather characteristically irregular in its metrical structure. This combination of regular poetic form with irregular musical form is typical of Mexican-American music. Whether consciously contrived or not, it is a feature that enables the music to retain its interest through the repeated hearings inherent in the strophic form. The habitual singing in parallel thirds so typical of nearly all of this music is of uncertain origin, but it has been compared by John Donald Robb, authority on the folk music of New Mexico, with a medieval practice known as *gymel*.

In the corrido we encounter a ballad tradition still very much alive. Corridos are being composed and sung on topical events by amateurs and professionals alike. Many are recorded and issued in the common currency of popular music, the 45-rpm "single." Subjects of recent corridos have included the first Russian sputnik ("La Luna Rusa"); the murder of eight nurses in Chicago; the killings at the 1972 Olympic Games in Munich; and the assassinations of John Kennedy, Robert Kennedy,[32] and Martin Luther King. Since the 1970s there have been many corridos on César Chavez and Dolores Huerta and the farm labor movement in California. Example 3–7 is a typical modern corrido with words by Arnoldo Ramirez and music by his brother, Rafaél Ramirez; entitled "La Muerte de Martin Luther King" (The Death of Martin Luther King).[33]

Gentlemen, I am going to sing for you
About the glory of a valiant man,
Who, while trying to save his country,
Found death in his pathway.

A statesman in a time of violence,
A just man of valor,
He struggled for mankind, he taught,
  with mercy,
That all are created equal.

Oh dove of peace, you who fly
Wounded on an April Fourth,
Take with you in your beak the sad notice
Of the death of Martin Luther King.

(Translation by Joaquín Fernández)

The *canción* has been described as lyrical and often sentimental, in contrast to the narrative and even epic quality of the corrido. (A similar distinction was noted in Chapter 1 between the folk song and the ballad.) Nevertheless, it should be made clear that the term is used to cover a broad

Example 3–7

Transcription by the author

range of songs, of which songs about love are only one type. In the category of folk songs in oral tradition, Robb has printed ninety-two cancións from New Mexico alone, including such traditional songs as "Cielito Lindo" and "La Golondrina."[34] Two soldiers' songs are "La Cucaracha," of which there are many satirical parodies, and "La Adelita," extremely popular during the revolutionary period of 1910–20. Belonging to a large and variously defined category of songs are the *cancións rancheras*. According to one writer, "The term, 'canción ranchera' was coined to describe songs previously sung by peasants on the haciendas and now performed by professional singers as interludes between acts"—that is, in the nationalist theater in Mexico City, as part of the "country music revival" glorifying the peasantry after the Revolution of 1910.[35] The best-known survivor, generally considered an authentic traditional song, is "Allá en el Rancho Grande." As remnants of this tradition in the United States, Robb includes five in his collection from New Mexico; among them are "El Sombrerito," "Las Chaparreras," "El Toro Bravo," and "El Jabali."[36] In Mexico the ranchera, with its hybrid folk and professional origins, was cultivated after the advent of radio by singers and composers (most notably José Alfredo Jiménez) who moved from the country to the city; this paralleled the popularization and commercialization of country-and-western songs in the United States.

We conclude our consideration of folk music from Mexico with a canción of powerful significance to Chicanos in recent years, especially those in the farm worker movement in California. "De colores" (Example 3–8) is of undetermined origin; it appeared at least as early as the 1960s, as the farm worker movement gained strength and identity under the leadership of César Chavez, and it was certainly sung during the historic march from Delano to Sacramento in 1966. Though with its theme of harmony and unity it has been effective in organizing workers, it is not a militant song. Literal translation fails to convey the essence of the simple words, which invoke light, cōlor, and the harmony of nature, using the images of the colors of the fields in spring, the colors of birds that come from afar, and the colors that are seen in the rainbow. It has assumed the character of a deeply meaningful hymn—one of the functions of a true folk song.

Music from the Caribbean and South America

Mexican music reached the United States from a single, though richly varied, source. In contrast, music from the Caribbean and South America has come from areas as far away as Argentina and as close as Cuba, and from cultures reflecting individually unique mixtures of Spanish, Portuguese, and African influences. (All are in the final analysis importations to the Americas, since the influence of native Indian musics from these regions has been negligible.) The music has come by two routes. The first was overland through Mexico, where Caribbean musical styles were cultivated by Agustin Lara, Rafaél Hernández, Pérez Prado, and others before they crossed the border into the Southwest. The second was by sea, the main "ports of entry" having been New Orleans in the nineteenth century and New York City in the twentieth.

Latin-Derived Fashions in American Popular Music

There are two aspects to these importations. The first has been their impact on American popular music and dance, which can be only briefly touched on here. The "Latin tinge" in jazz, attributed to the presence of the *habanera* around the turn of the century, has been unmistakable, if insufficiently recognized and studied. (One author has found a "Spanish tinge" in ragtime and some blues as well.)[37] Thereafter, in the 1910s and 1920s, the rage of the *tango* (related

Example 3–8 DE COLORES

De co - lo - res, de co - lo - res se vis-ten los cam-pos en
la pri - ma - ve - ra; de co - lo - res, de co -
-lo - res son los pa - ja - ri - llos que vie - nen de fue - ra.
De co - lo - res, de co - lo - res es el ar - co i - ris qu
ve - mos lu - cir, y por e - so los gran-des a - mo - res de
mu - chos co - lo - res me gus - tan a mi, y por e - so los
gran-des a - mo - res de mu - chos co - lo - res me gus - tan a mi.

rhythmically to the habanera) arrived from Argentina by way of Paris! In the 1930s came the *rumba*, from the Cuban *son*, and after this the *samba* (Afro-Brazilian), the *mambo* (Afro-Cuban), the *chachachá* (Cuban), the *merengue* (Dominican), the *bossa nova* (Brazilian). Finally, the current name for "hot" Afro-Caribbean music (like the term *soul* as applied to black music, it indicates less a specific form or rhythm than a style) is *salsa* ("sauce"). These successive waves of popular Latin genres have been initiated mostly as professional musicians, steeped in their own traditions, moved into the arenas of American jazz or popular music (which included making recordings), bringing their traditional styles with them but adapting them to cater to broad popular taste. The careers of Xavier Cugat (a Spaniard brought up in Cuba, who came to New York at the age of twenty-one), Don Azpiazú, "Machito" (Frank Grillo), and Mario Bauza—all active in New York—illustrate this pattern.[38]

Indigenous Music of the Caribbean Immigrants

More relevant to the context of this chapter is the second aspect of the importation of Latin music to the United States, and that is its service to the Latin immigrants themselves, in their own lives and communities. As John Storm Roberts has explained,

> The presence of a large Latin community in New York—and later in other U.S. cities—provided a demand for authenticity, a place for musicians to play undiluted Latin styles, and, perhaps most important, a doorway for innovations from Cuba and other Latin countries.[39]

Roberts's point about the "doorway" has been discussed above; his point about the "demand for authenticity" also deserves attention. Just as Chicano music has become a symbol and focus of ethnic pride for those of Mexican descent in the Southwest, so has salsa performed the same function for those of Cuban and Puerto Rican origin in New York City. They illustrate, in the words of one writer, "the proclivity of people to seize on traditional cultural symbols as a definition of their own identity."[40] *

But Latino musicians are no different from other musicians in that they do not *automatically* "seize on traditional cultural symbols" in making their music; these must usually be learned, in one way or another. How does this learning take place? The Afro-Caribbean music played in New York is essentially a music played by ear and therefore aurally transmitted. But the personal contact between musicians that is traditionally associated with aural transmission has been to a considerable degree replaced by learning from records. (The same has been true in jazz from its very beginnings.) In this regard, it is interesting to note the role played by men such as René López and Andy González—who have large record collections and who are also effectively social and political historians, educators, impresarios, record producers, and even performers themselves—in educating other Latino musicians as to what their "traditional cultural symbols" are, their history, and the importance of their authenticity if they are to serve to "define their own identity."[41]

New York City has long been a magnet for immigration from the Caribbean, and its Latin populations make up small cities within the super-city. Immigration from Puerto Rico (ceded to the United States after the Spanish-American War and given commonwealth status in 1952) has been significant ever since United States citizenship was granted to Puerto Ricans in 1917, and it reached a peak in the 1940s and early 1950s. Immigration from Cuba has been less extensive, but an important ingredient in *la salsa* in New York City has been the presence of Cubans of the poorer classes, especially black Cubans who came to the United States before the Revolution of 1959.[42] Thus for two generations New York has echoed with the strongly flavored music of the Caribbean: the Spanish-derived forms of the *danza*, the *seis*, and the *aguinaldo*, and the African-influenced *bomba*, *rumba*, and music of the *lucumi* ritual (*santería*). A unique feature of Caribbean culture has always been its mixture

* Ethnologists have invented for this phenomenon, widespread and familiar in our time, the awkwardly clinical and dehumanized term "the new ethnicity."

of the African with the Hispanic. African influence is especially strong on the islands of Cuba and Hispaniola (the latter is divided between Haiti and the Dominican Republic), where the importation of slaves by the Spanish colonizers was particularly heavy and formed the basis for a sizable black population. The chief musical influence has been that of rhythm; the variety of drums and other percussion instruments, and the pervasiveness and complexity of the rhythmic underpinning, set Afro-Caribbean music apart from all other North American Hispanic music. The most African-sounding music in the United States can be heard in the playing of Afro-Cuban groups in New York.

The Rhythms of Caribbean Music

A basic ingredient of Afro-Caribbean rhythm is the *clave*, a rhythmic pattern whose constant repetitions unify the piece. At its simplest it is two measures in length, and consists in its skeletal form of five strokes distributed over the two measures either "2+3" (Example 3–9) or "3+2" (Example 3–10).

Example 3–9

Example 3–10

The clave as played on the instrument known as the *claves* (two hardwood sticks struck together) is a familiar sound in Latin music; but the clave is by no means invariably performed on that instrument, nor is it always clearly and overtly stated in its simplest form. What *is* invariably characteristic is the presence of a rhythmic ground (*tumbao*) built around the clave, and repeated (with subtle variations) throughout the piece. This ground (called by Singer the "pitch-timbre-rhythm complex") is traditionally executed, according to Singer, on two drums (the deeper *tumba* and the higher *segundo*), with the possible addition of maracas or claves along with a third drum, which is played in an improvisational way. In larger and more jazz-oriented ensembles, both the piano and the bass may take part in executing the tumbao.[43]

It may be said that Iberian-Afro-Indian music from the south has influenced what may be regarded as "mainstream" American music in ways far less superficial than the successive waves of popular Latin dance fashions. Two additional examples, in addition to what has already been cited, are illustrative. For one, the Afro-Caribbean influence on rock, especially in drumming, is clear and significant, in terms both of a repetitive ground as the rhythmic basis of the music and of the clearly duple division of the beat, as opposed to the "swing" beat of jazz.* (This opens up the possibility of earlier Afro-Caribbean influence on boogie-woogie as well.) And certainly some of the "minimalism" of fine-art music of the 1960s and 1970s, which will be discussed in Chapter 18, owes something to the same origins. The "Latin tinge," then, is an important, if largely unacknowledged, hue in much of our music.

Further Reading

American Indian Music

General

Burton, Frederick R. *American Primitive Music, with Special Attention to the Songs of the Ojibways.* Port Washington, NY: Kennikat, 1909. Reprint, 1969.
A work written from the standpoint of an older approach to the music, including the consideration of its "art value." It includes some songs arranged with piano accompaniment.

Curtis, Natalie (Natalie Curtis Burlin). *The Indians' Book.* New York: Harper Bros., 1907. Reprint, New York: Dover, 1968.
An important early work, illustrated with paintings and drawings by Indians. Includes a considerable number of song transcriptions.

Densmore, Frances. *The American Indians and Their Music.* New York: Women's Press, 1926.
An early comprehensive work by a pioneer researcher. It is supplemented by tribal studies listed below.

Herndon, Marcia. *Native American Music.* Norwood, PA: Norwood Editions, 1980.

Heth, Charlotte. *The Music of American Indians.* Los Angeles: University of California Selected Reports in Ethnomusicology, n.d.

Merriam, Alan P. *The Anthropology of Music.* Evanston, IL: Northwestern University Press, 1964.
An introduction to the whole subject of ethnomusicology.

Nettl, Bruno. *North American Indian Musical Styles.* Philadelphia: American Folklore Society, 1954.
An important brief study, somewhat technical, of regional characteristics. Includes some musical examples.

Representative regional studies, or works on special topics

Black Bear, Ben, Sr., and R. D. Theisz. *Songs and Dances of the Lakota.* Aberdeen, SD: North Plains Press, 1976.

Densmore, Frances. Except as noted, the following studies were published originally by the Bureau of American Ethnology of the Smithsonian Institution, and issued by the Government Printing Office, Washington, DC. They are now available in reprint editions from Da Capo Press, New York. Far more than mere transcriptions and analyses of melodies, they treat in considerable detail the customs, ceremonies, and legends of the tribes, thus forecasting the type of study Alan P. Merriam was to do nearly a half-century later. The transcriptions themselves are not as accurate in either rhythm or pitch as modern standards would require (insofar as can be determined by comparing them with the recordings from which they were presumably derived); perhaps understandably overinfluenced by European music, they are too rigid in notation, especially as regards rhythm.
Cheyenne and Arapaho Music. Los Angeles: Southwest Museum, 1936.
Chippewa Music. 2 vols. 1910–13.
Choctaw Music. 1943.
Music of the Maidu Indians. Los Angeles: Southwest Museum, 1958.
Mandan and Hidatsa Music. 1923.
Menominee Music. 1932.

* See Chapter 9, Example 9-3.

Nootka and Quileute Music. 1939.
Northern Ute Music. 1922.
Papago Music. 1929.
Pawnee Music. 1929.
Teton Sioux Music. 1918.
Yuman and Yaqui Music. 1932.

Frisbie, Charlotte H., ed. *Southwestern Indian Ritual Drama.* Albuquerque: University of New Mexico Press, 1980.

Hudson, Charles. *The Southeastern Indians.* Knoxville: University of Tennessee Press, 1972.

Kurath, Gertrude P. *Music and Dance of the Tewa Pueblos.* Santa Fe: Museum of New Mexico Press, 1970.
This modern study includes extensive transcriptions of music, diagrams of dance, and some photos.

La Barre, Weston. *The Peyote Cult.* Yale University Publications in Anthropology, no. 19. New Haven: Yale University Press, 1938.

McAllester, David P. *Indian Music in the Southwest.* Colorado Springs, CO: Taylor Museum, 1961.

———. *Peyote Music.* Viking Fund Publications in Anthropology, no. 13. New York: Viking, 1949.
This study includes music.

Merriam, Alan P. *Ethnomusicology of the Flathead Indians.* Chicago: Aldine, 1967.
The jacket description is accurate: "The first complete survey of the entire musical output of a people in its cultural context, exemplifying a new technique of musical analysis." This important work has helped to set new standards for research and writing in the field.

Mooney, James. *The Ghost Dance Religion.* Bureau of American Ethnology, Smithsonian Institution, 14th annual report, part 2, 1892–93.

Paige, Harry W. *Songs of the Teton Sioux.* Los Angeles: Westernlore Press, 1970.
A contemporary study, dealing with music in the lives of the Indians. No musical examples.

Rhodes, Willard. "Acculturation in North American Indian Music" in *Acculturation in the Americas.* Chicago: University of Chicago Press, 1952.

Hispanic Music

Studies that include music

Da Silva, Owen, O.F.M. *Mission Music of California.* Los Angeles: Warren Lewis, 1941.
A book of fine artistic quality, this presents a selection of liturgical music, and some useful expository information on the priest-musicians and on mission life as viewed by the Franciscans.

Hague, Eleanor. *Spanish-American Folk-Songs.* Lancaster, PA: American Folklore Society, 1917.
An old collection but available in many libraries; 100-odd songs, some from Mexico and Central and South America.

Paredes, Americo. *A Texas-Mexican Cancionero: Folksongs of the Lower Border.* Urbana: University of Illinois Press, 1976.

Rael, Juan B. *The New Mexican Alabado.* Palo Alto, CA: Stanford University Press, 1951. Reprint, New York: AMS Press, 1967.

Robb, John Donald. *Hispanic Folk Songs of New Mexico.* Albuquerque: University of New Mexico Press, 1954.
A valuable regional study by an eminent authority, with a representative sampling of music both sacred and secular.

———. *Hispanic Folk Music of New Mexico and the Southwest: A Self-Portrait of a People.* Norman: University of Oklahoma Press, 1980.
More extensive than his 1954 publication listed above, this is the major summary in published form of many years of collecting by this scholar. The anthology (891 pages) includes many types of music, sacred, secular, and instrumental, with informative notes on each type. The songs include texts and English translations.

Stark, Richard B. *Music of the Spanish Folk Plays in New Mexico.* Santa Fe: Mu-

seum of New Mexico Press, 1969.
Songs and texts of various versions of *Los Pastores* transcribed from recordings made between 1940 and 1968. Includes some songs from *Las Posadas* and from another folk play, *El Niño Perdido*.

Studies

Contreras, Maximiliano. *Crossing: A Comparative Analysis of the Mexicano, Mexican-American and Chicano.* San Pedro, CA: International Universities Press, 1983.

Dickey, Dan William. *The Kennedy Corridos: A Study of the Ballads of a Mexican American Hero.* Austin: University of Texas Press, 1978.

Henderson, Alice Corbin. *Brothers of Light: The Penitentes of the Southwest.* New York: Harcourt Brace, 1937. Reprint, Chicago: Rio Grande Press, 1962.
A sensitive eyewitness account of the rituals of this brotherhood during Holy Week, from a half-century ago, with illustrations by the author's husband, William Penhallow Henderson.

Geijerstam, Claes Af. *Popular Music in Mexico.* Albuquerque: University of New Mexico Press, 1976.
Since popular and folk music are so closely interrelated, this book provides indispensable background on the folk music of Mexico as well. Includes an appendix, "Border Music of the 1970s in the Southwestern United States," by Elizabeth H. Heist.

Lucero-White, Aurora. *The Folklore of New Mexico,* vol. 1. Santa Fe, NM: Seton Village Press, 1941.
A collection (words only) of romances and corridos, as well as tales, proverbs, and riddles.

Paredes, Americo. *"With his pistol in his hand."* Austin: University of Texas Press, 1958.
An extensive documentation of a ballad ("El Corrido de Gregorio Cortez") and its hero, which supplies valuable background information on the Texas-Mexico border country.

Peña, Manuel. *The Texas-Mexican Conjunto: History of a Working-Class Music.* Austin: University of Texas Press, 1985.

Ray, Sister Mary Dominic, O.P., and Joseph H. Engbeck, Jr. *Gloria Dei: The Story of California Mission Music.* State of California, Department of Parks and Recreation, n.d.
An informative illustrated booklet (24 pp.), with quotations from contemporary accounts.

Roberts, John Storm. *The Latin Tinge: The Impact of Latin American Music in the United States.* New York: Oxford University Press, 1979.
Deals with influences from all of Latin America; useful, even though the emphasis is on popular music. Relevant to Chapters 12 and 14 as well.

Tinker, Edward Larocque. *Corridos and Calaveras.* Austin: University of Texas Press, 1961.
Although this deals specifically with the corrido and related forms as found in Old Mexico, it is excellent background reading for the corrido as a genre. Especially fascinating are the reproductions of the old broadsides themselves, with their drawings by the famous artist José Guadalupe Posada, a forerunner of Rivera and Orozco. A delightful book, in a very artistic format.

Weigle, Marta. *Brothers of Light, Brothers of Blood: The Penitentes of the Southwest.* Albuquerque: University of New Mexico Press, 1976.
A well-documented, thorough, and sympathetic treatment of this brotherhood, counteracting the often exaggerated and sensational accounts that had appeared earlier.

Articles

From Latin American Music Review

Limon, José. "Texas-Mexican Popular Music and Dancing: Some Notes on History and Symbolic Process," vol. 4, no. 2 (Fall–Winter 1983).

Peña, Manuel. "Ritual Structure in a Chicano Dance," vol. 1, no. 1 (Spring–Summer 1980)

Singer, Roberta L. "Tradition and Innovation in Contemporary Latin Popular Music in New York City," vol. 4, no. 2 (Fall–Winter 1983).

Warkentin, Larry. "The Rise and Fall of Indian Music in the California Missions," vol. 2, no. 1 (Spring–Summer 1981).

From Aztlán: A Journal of Chicano Studies *(UCLA Chicano Studies Research Center)*

Gutiérrez, Ramon. "Unraveling America's Hispanic Past: Internal Stratification and Class Boundaries," vol. 17, no. 1 (Spring 1986).

Hurtado, Aída, and Carlos H. Arce "Mexicanos, Chicanos, Mexican-Americans, or Pochos . . . Qué somos?: The Impact of Nativity on Ethnic Labelling," vol. 17, no. 1 (Spring 1986).

Listening

American Indian Music

From the Library of Congress, Archive of American Folk Song (AAFS)

Edited by William Fenton, recorded 1941–45:
- *Songs from the Iroquois Longhouse.* L-6.
- *Seneca Songs from Coldspring Longhouse.* L-17.

Edited by Frances Densmore, recorded 1910–30:
- *Songs of the Chippewa.* L-22.
- *Songs of the Sioux.* L-23.
- *Songs of the Yuma, Cocopa, and Yaqui.* L-24.
- *Songs of the Pawnee and Northern Ute.* L-25.
- *Songs of the Papago.* L-31.
- *Songs of the Nootka and Quileute.* L-32.
- *Songs of the Menominee, Mandan, and Hidatsa.* L-33.

Edited by Willard Rhodes, *Music of the American Indian* series, recorded 1940–52:
- *Northwest (Puget Sound).* L-34.
- *Kiowa.* L-35.
- *Indian Songs of Today.* L-36
- *Delaware, Cherokee, Choctaw, Creek.* L-37.
- *Great Basin: Paiute, Washo, Ute, Bannock, Shoshone.* L-38.
- *Plains: Comanche, Cheyenne, Kiowa, Caddo, Wichita, Pawnee.* L-39.
- *Sioux.* L-40.
- *Navajo.* L-41.
- *Apache.* L-42.
- *Pueblo: Taos, San Ildefonso, Zuni, Hopi.* L-43.

From the New World Recorded Anthology of American Music

Songs of Earth, Water, Fire and Sky: Music of the American Indian. NW-246.
First and more general album, with excellent notes by Charlotte Heth.

Songs of Love, Luck, Animals, & Magic: Music of the Yurok and Tolowa Indians. NW-297.

Region: Northern California. Notes by Charlotte Heth.

Oku Shareh: Turtle Dance Songs of San Juan Pueblo. NW-301.
Region: Rio Grande Valley north of Santa Fe, New Mexico, the same as that covered in Kurath, *Music and Dance of the Tewa Pueblos* (cited above). Notes and text translation by Alfonso Ortiz.

Songs and Dances of the Eastern Indians from Medicine Spring & Allegany. NW-337.
Regions: Southeast, Cherokee and Creek (recorded in Oklahoma); Northeast, Seneca (Iroquois Confederacy), recorded at Allegany Reservation, Salamanca, New York. Notes by Charlotte Heth; unfortunately, as with most recent New World releases, the space for notes has been severely curtailed.

Powwow Songs: Music of the Plains Indians. NW-343.
Regions: northern and southern Plains, the latter mostly Oklahoma. Recorded in Oklahoma and Los Angeles. Notes, in limited space (see entry above), by Charlotte Heth.

From Folkways/Smithsonian

North American Indian and Eskimo Music. 2-LP set. 4541.

Cry from the Earth: Music of North American Indians. 37777.

Music of the Sioux and the Navajo. 4401.

Music of the American Indians of the Southwest. 4420.

Songs and Dances of the Flathead Indians, recorded by Alan Merriam. 4445.

The Promised Land: American Indian Songs of Lament and Protest. 37254.

Two other labels with extensive recordings of Indian music are Indian House and Canyon. As an example of acculturation, the following is cited:

"Chicken Scratch:" Popular Dance Music of the Indians of Southern Arizona. Canyon C-6085.

Hispanic Music

Caliente = Hot: Puerto Rican and Cuban Musical Expression in New York. NW-244.

California Mission Music, performed by the John Biggs Consort. Issued by the Regents of the University of California.
While too eclectic and polished to convey much of an idea of the actual sound of the music of the mission period, this recording surveys the field in its broadest sense with some very elegant performances.

Catholic Mission Music in California. From the *Music in America* series of the Society for the Preservation of the American Musical Heritage: MIA-96.
This older recording of mission music conveys in some ways a more authentic atmosphere, especially in the two alabados and the "Santo Dios."

Chicano Music All Day: El Trio Casindio and the Royal Chicano Air Force. Centro de Artistas Chicanos. Nonántzin C/S284.
The Chicano point of view as expressed in contemporary (1985) poems of artist-musicians José Montoya and Esteban Villa, set in an eclectic variety of styles.

Bahaman Songs, French Ballads and Dance Tunes, Spanish Religious Songs and Game Songs. AAFS: L-5.
Side 2 is especially interesting for its inclusion of six brief excerpts from religious folk plays, and a Mexican corrido as performed by a blind itinerant singer of Brownsville, Texas.

Dark and Light in Spanish New Mexico. NW-292.
Side 1 contains alabados associated with the Penitentes, including the pito or flute. Side 2 is devoted to dance music played by a noted New Mexican fiddler, including waltzes, cutilios (for square dancing), a polka, and a schottische.

José-Luis Orozco canta 160 Años del Corrido Mexicano y Chicano. Bilingual Media Productions JL-10.
A professionally sung anthology of cor-

ridos beginning with the nineteenth century and ending with corridos about César Chavez and Dolores Huerta and the farm labor struggle.

Old-Country Music in a New Land. NW-264.

Side 1 tracks 7 (a canción as sung and played by Lydia Mendoza and her family) and 8 (a polka representative of musica norteña) are relevant.

Spanish Folk Songs of New Mexico. Folkways 2204.

Peter Hurd recreates ranchera songs; texts included in notes.

Spanish and Mexican Folk Music of New Mexico. Folkways 4426.

Recorded and with notes by J. D. Robb.

Texas-Mexican Border Music: Una Historia de la Musica de la Frontera, issued by Arhoolie Records, 9003–07, 9011–13, 9016–21.

An extensive anthology on 14 LPs.

Taos recordings and publications

Taos Spanish Songs. Taos 22.

New Mexican Alabados. Taos 23.

Taos Matachines Music. Taos 24 and 25a.

Possibly hard to get outside south Texas

Corridos Famosos. Falcon FLP-2035.

Corridos y Tragedias del Siglo 20. 2 vols. Norteño 803 and 805.

El Corrido de Martin Luther King. Falcon FLP-2091.

PROJECTS

1. Select one American Indian tribe and listen to as much of its music as is available. (Try to work from a sample of at least fifteen songs.) Note the musical characteristics, and see to what extent they conform to, or differ from, the description of the area characteristics as given by Nettl in *North American Indian Musical Styles,* or in his article in the *New Grove Dictionary of American Music,* vol. 2, pp. 460ff.

2. The footnote on page 56 mentioned that Indian cultural areas and Indian language groups are far from coinciding. Investigate this fact, and present in a paper some of what it means in terms of the long history of the aboriginal peoples in North America before the coming of the Europeans.

3. If there is one in your vicinity, attend a powwow or other Indian gathering that includes singing, dancing, and games. In a paper assess the degree to which what you observed either reinforces or contradicts the impressions you have gotten of Indian music and culture from reading this chapter. Assess also the ways in which acculturation has taken place, and those areas in which it has *not* taken place.

4. Talk with some persons of Indian descent—at least two, if possible—about the current state of Indian culture from their point of view. Should it be preserved, and if so for what reasons? In what ways should the preservation of traditional ways compromise and adapt to modern society, and in what ways should it retain its distinctness and integrity?

5. Write an essay discussing what you, or what non-Indians in general, might have to learn from the way Indians traditionally used and regarded music.

6. Do some research into the curriculum of one or more Indian colleges (Navajo Community College, for example); try to determine the extent to which traditional Indian music is being studied and taught there.

7. Write a paper on one or two Indian composers of today—that is, composers as distinct from those who are primarily performers, or carriers of the older tradition.

8. If you are fluent in Spanish, transcribe and translate one or more corridos that are in current circulation on recordings. (Among other sources, they are available from Norteña Records, San Antonio,

Texas; and Arhoolie Records, El Cerrito, California.)

9. Investigate and describe in as much detail as you can the origin and characteristics of any specified number of the following Caribbean or South American–derived musical/dance forms: aguinaldo, bolero, bomba, bossa nova, bugalú, chachachá, danza, danzón, guaguancó, guajira, guaracha, habanera, mambo, mapayé, mixixe, merengue, pachanga, plena, rumba, samba, seis, son (Cuban), tango.

10. Investigate and describe in as much detail as you can the origin and characteristics of any specified number of the following Mexican musical/dance forms: fandango, huapango, jarabe, jota, malagueña, pasodoble, son (Mexican), son jarocho, zapateado.

11. If literature, and especially poetry, is your forte, investigate and describe the Spanish-derived *copla, décima,* and *romance,* and their relation to music in North America.

12. Write a paper on the state of Chicano music today, including a discography, and a list of poet-musicians active in Chicano circles. Two periodicals listed in the Further Reading section might be helpful.

4

Aspects of Folk Music in Twentieth-Century America

THE 1920s saw the irreversible onset of change for American folk music. Through the media of radio and recordings, urban popular music was brought to the "folk" (which at that time still rather clearly meant the rural people). It was then, too, that America's rural music, both black and white, was "discovered" by urban entrepreneurs. Not only was it being broadcast, but it was found commercially profitable to make recordings of it and sell them back to the folk. As we shall see in chapters 7 and 8, both white "hillbilly" music and rural African-American blues were first recorded in the 1920s, a development that had profound effects on both of these folk musics. It is interesting to note that one of the most important published collections of recordings documenting our folk music, the Folkways *Anthology of American Folk Music,* consists entirely of commercial recordings made in the 1920s and 1930s.

It was also true that increased industrialization and migration to the cities, spurred on subsequently by the depressed economic conditions of the 1930s and the war effort of the early 1940s, brought increased mobility to rural peoples, virtually did away with the isolation in which some sections of the country had existed, and worked irrevocable changes in folkways. These environmental changes were paralleled by changes in the way people thought about folk music. The distinctly "non-folk" intellectual awareness of folk music—as the expression of a vaguely defined spirit of a people, as a "cry for justice," as "art," or as artifact, to be collected and studied or else to be pressed into service for some specific purpose—began to replace the folk "unawareness" of it as something wholly integrated into daily life itself, and no more to be abstracted from it than the making of clothes or the building of fences (which have also become the objects of study as *folklore*). In other words, the singing of folk music has become, in our time, a much more self-conscious activity.

Americans' involvement with folk music has been taking place on what might be thought of as three more or less distinct levels during the past fifty years. (1) Folk music, urbanized and adapted, has been used for propaganda. (2) It has been popularized, for entertainment and profit, beyond the boundaries of any definable "folk community." (3) It has been collected and studied extensively by scholars, both amateur and professional, who have been hard at work to preserve the artifacts of traditions that they saw as disappearing with increasing rapidity. We shall here consider briefly each of these involvements in turn.

Folk Music As an Instrument of Persuasion

The use of folk music in the service of a cause is nothing new. John Powell, American composer and student of folk music, has called attention to an anecdote about the ingenuity and zeal of St. Aldhelm, seventh-century abbot of Malmesbury:

> According to this story, the Saint would station himself on a bridge in the guise of a gleeman and would collect an audience by singing popular songs. He would then gradually insert into his entertainment the words of the holy scriptures and so lead his hearers to salvation.[1]

From St. Aldhelm in the seventh century to the CIO labor organizer in the twentieth, the method is the same—adapting an already known and accepted song (or song *style*, in the case of newly composed songs) so as to transform it into an instrument of persuasion. The use of vernacular music as an adjunct to religion is perennial, as we shall see. Our present concern, however, is the association of folk music with social and political causes.

As John Greenway and others have documented, protest songs have been composed and sung here since Colonial times, mostly in the "broadside" tradition of printing the words only, to be sung to some preexisting and well-known tune.[2] An example of this, a piece called the "Junto Song" that satirized what was seen as British avarice in taxing the colonists, was published in *Holt's Journal* in 1775. It runs in part:

> 'Tis money makes the member vote,
> And sanctifies our ways;
> It makes the patriot turn his coat,
> And money we must raise.
>
> (Chorus)
> And a-taxing we will go,
> A-taxing we will go,
> A-taxing we will go.[3]

A lively tradition of propaganda songs continued right through the nineteenth and into the twentieth century, and Greenway cites many interesting examples. What was new about the period that began in the 1930s was not only the more conscious adoption of real folk tunes and a folk style, but the attempt to appropriate virtually an entire folk tradition in the service of social and political causes. As D. K. Wilgus has said, in describing this period,

> The recognition that "singing has a direct and reciprocal relation to social, economic, and political issues" has led to an equation of the "cry for justice" and folksong. . . . The use of folksong for political purposes is an old device: what is new is the use of the folk concept, the magic term *folk*.[4]

The "magic" inherent in the term *folk* has been described by R. Serge Denisoff as "Folk Consciousness."

> Folk Consciousness refers to an awareness of folk music which leads to its use in a foreign (urban) environment in the framework of social, economic, and political action. The addition of social and organizational themes to traditional tunes, the emulation of rural attire, and the idealization of folk singers as "people's artists" are all aspects of Folk Consciousness.[5]

Thus the *folk* became easily equated with the *proletariat* or, more specifically, with union members among the industrial workers. In terms of what activists in the thirties and forties hoped to accomplish by means of folk music, it meant the imposition of an essentially rural song tradition upon urban workers.

This movement had two main motivations. In the first place, as Denisoff[6] has documented extensively, it was in the 1930s that the Russian Bolshevik example of using indigenous folk music for propaganda purposes during and after the 1917 Revolution began to be urged upon American Communists, who had hitherto mostly used Soviet "agitprop" songs without much success. (A historian of the Southern Tenant Farmers Union, for example, reported that the "Internationale" just didn't go over with the sharecroppers.")

A second and far more important motivation for the adoption of rural folk music and folk style was the fact that—as northern labor organizers found when they went into the South to organize the mine and textile-mill workers—the tradition of folk singing, which was still vital in the rural South, was already at work providing songs to rally the workers in the bitter struggle. At the scene of the textile strike in Gastonia, North Carolina, in 1929 Ella May Wiggins, a ballad singer of some reputation, was singing songs like this adaptation of a hymn:

> Toiling on life's pilgrim pathway
> Wheresoever you may be,
> It will help you, fellow workers,
> If you will join the ILD.[7]

And in Harlan County, Kentucky, scene of violent labor disputes in the coal mines in 1931, Aunt Molly Jackson (born Mary Magdalene Garland; 1880–1960), a larger-than-life heroine who was midwife, doctor, union organizer, and ballad singer for the coal miners, and who had lost brother, husband, and son in the mines, was singing:

> I am a union woman,
> Just as brave as I can be.
> I do not like the bosses
> And the bosses don't like me.
>
> (Refrain)
> Join the CIO. Come join the CIO.
>
> I was raised in old Kentucky
> In Kentucky borned and bred,
> And when I joined the union,
> They called me a Rooshian Red.
>
> (Refrain)[8]

As Archie Green has said:

> In a sense, Piedmont mill villages and Cumberland mine camps became meeting grounds for the ideologies of Andrew Jackson and Karl Marx, Abraham Lincoln and Mikhail Bakunin. Few of the mill hands or coal miners were able to synthesize traditional and modern values into lasting literature, but some managed to compose folk-like songs which fused time-worn melodies with strange, revolutionary lyrics.[9]

Genesis of the "Urban Folk Song Movement"

When the union organizers and their supporters and chroniclers, such as John Dos Passos and Theodore Dreiser, returned to the North, they brought with them not only many of the songs but some of the singers as well, including Aunt Molly Jackson herself, who had been banished, in effect, from Kentucky. In New York's Coliseum in 1931 she sang for twenty-one thousand people:

> I was born and raised in old Kentucky;
> Molly Jackson is my name.
> I came up here to New York City,
> And I'm truly glad I came.
>
> I am soliciting for the poor Kentucky miners,
> For their children and their wives,
> Because the miners are all blacklisted
> I am compelled to save their lives.[10]

This importation of the southern rural folk song tradition, and of some of its singers, was the genesis of what has become known as the urban folk song movement. Its beginning was, in a sense, a transplantation of the rural South to Greenwich Village. In addition to singers from the Kentucky coal mining region, there were African-Americans associated with the blues tradition, such as Leadbelly, Josh White, Brownie McGhee, and Sonny Terry. Leadbelly

(Huddie Ledbetter, 1885–1949) was an interesting figure in the movement, though not typical. After a violent youth, he was discovered in a Louisiana prison by John and Alan Lomax, who secured his parole and brought him to New York. There he sang all sorts of songs from his vast repertoire, and added new ones based on his new experiences and appropriate to his new audiences, such as the "Bourgeois Blues":

> Me and my wife run all over town,
> Everywhere we'd go people would turn us down.
>
> Lawd, in the bourgeois town, hoo!
> The bourgeois town.
> I got the bourgeois blues,
> Gonna spread the news all around.[11]

Other musicians and writers who entered or passed through the somewhat amorphous orbit of New York left-wing circles in the 1930s and 1940s included men and women who became well known in the folk song movement but who could hardly be classified as "folk" in background, as the term was still understood then: the writer Millard Lampell, a graduate of the University of West Virginia; Earl Robinson, a classically trained musician and composer from the University of Washington; Bess Lomax, daughter and sister of two eminent folklorists; and Pete Seeger, son of a distinguished ethnomusicologist, who left Harvard in his sophomore year, committed to the social and political causes he worked to further through singing (his own songs as well as those of others) and playing his banjo.

Woody Guthrie

Woody Guthrie (1912–1967) was an exceptional and somewhat enigmatic figure in this circle. His Oklahoma background (he began early to sing and play at gatherings in Oklahoma and Texas) was certainly folk in any sense of the term. His complete absorption of his own heritage is evident in the many early recordings he made of traditional ballads and songs, both for commercial release and for the Library of Congress Archive—recordings that include "Buffalo Skinners," "John Henry," "Sourwood Mountain," "Cumberland Gap," and even the Child ballad "Gypsy Davy." "Pretty Boy Floyd," in the outlaw ballad tradition, was one of his own compositions. He early began to compose ballads and songs, something he did easily, naturally, compulsively, and with amazing fecundity. His preserved output, according to those who knew him, represents only a fraction of the songs he actually made up and sang.

As he began to move about the country, hoboing, working, barding, supporting in his own highly individualistic way various workers' causes as he found them, it can perhaps be said that he transcended the roots of the local tradition in which he had been brought up; but it is also true in a sense that he cut himself off from them, in his efforts to identify with a larger, more heterogeneous, and to an extent mythical, folk community. "So Long, It's Been Good to Know You" (originally a far more topical song about Dust Bowl life than its later popular form would indicate) and "Hard Travelin' " certainly have their roots in his personal experience. But they begin to show the effects of their separation from a definable folk community. The famous Dust Bowl Ballads were neither sung nor known by the migrant workers themselves who left the area for the West in the thirties. Songs like "I Ain't Got No Home in This World Anymore" and "Pastures of Plenty" show an increasing trend away from the specific and the individual—being applicable to many, they are about no *one*, and sung for no one group. Thus they lose some of the strength and validity of true folk song. This tendency reaches its ultimate conclusion in a song like "This Land Is Your Land." It is so broadly inclusive—"from California to the New York island,/ from the redwood forest to the Gulf Stream waters"—that it sacrifices altogether the concreteness of folk music; though as popular song it is so far above the run-of-the-mill patriotic ditty as to beggar comparison. The song conveys the feeling that Guthrie, at least, had *seen* the redwood forest and the Gulf Stream waters and the ribbon of highway and the golden valley–as indeed he had.

Guthrie's enormous talent, when brought to bear on a specific event, could produce a truly great song, through his faculty of making us sense at once the human dimension. "The Sinking of the *Reuben James*," about the seamen lost in the first American ship torpedoed in World War II, was probably the best ballad to come out of that conflict. Guthrie's intention, from which he could barely be restrained, of incorporating into the ballad the names of all ninety-five men who lost their lives, should ideally have been realized to make the ballad a true folk epic. As it was, another member of the Almanac Singers (discussed below) asked the question "What *were* their names?" and this furnished the song with its effective chorus. (The tune is an adaptation of the early country song "Wildwood Flower," made popular by the Carter Family.)[12]

He could even bring to life an event twenty years or so in the past. His unusual commission to produce a set of ballads and songs on the famous Sacco and Vanzetti case produced work that was uneven in quality and to an extent forced, but the best real ballad in the collection, "Suassos Lane," shows the true touch of the folk balladeer.[13]

Guthrie was at his best as a balladeer. In later years, anything was grist for his mill. Being so prolific, he naturally produced a great deal that was nearly worthless. He felt acutely his limitations, as well as the pressures of the mantle he found himself wearing. A man of shrewd intelligence and diverse talents (he read voluminously, was a very prolific writer apart from his songs, a painter, the confidant of a president of the United States), he was no simple "man of the soil"; yet he often found himself having to deny his own acute perceptions and conceal his intellect behind a mask of simplistic doggerel in trying to fulfill his most difficult job of all—which was largely thrust upon him—that of being a kind of universal "folk poet" of the common man. By nature more perceptive than much of his more mediocre writing would indicate, Guthrie was not immune to brooding over the effects on him of such labels as "the best folk ballad composer whose identity has ever been known" or a "rusty-voiced Homer." In a typically self-revealing outburst he said:

> I kick myself in the britches pretty hard some times. You dont hate me any worse than I do. You dont bawl me out any more than I do. Oh well, dam it all anyhow, I never really set my head on being a public figure. Its all what you mean when

> you say success. Most of the time success ain't much fun. Lots of times it takes a lot of posing and pretending.[14]

Charles Seeger writes sensitively of the changes wrought in the singers by the pressures of the situations in which they found themselves.

> Put, for example, any good "authentic," traditional singer before a microphone or on a platform before an audience not of its own kind and soon the peculiar requirements of the situation produce the typical traits of exhibitionism. To my personal observation, it took Molly Jackson only a few months to convert herself, when expedient, from a traditional singer, who seemed never to have given a thought to whether anyone liked or disliked her singing, into a shrewd observer of audience reaction, fixing individual listeners one after another with her gaze, smiling ingratiatingly, gesturing, dramatizing her performance. Leadbelly was already an astute handler of the non-folk by the time I met him. Woody Guthrie was another case, almost swamping his native talent in Greenwich Villagese.[15]

Pete Seeger, the Almanac Singers, and the End of the Guthrie-Seeger Era

It was Pete Seeger (b. 1919), the perennial survivor of many of its subsequent phases, whose ideas, energy, and dedication were crucial in leading the protest folk song movement through the decisive 1940s to the end of an era. Early in 1941 Seeger assembled a group of folk song enthusiasts then active in New York's left-wing (which at that time included Communist) circles, and formed a group called the Almanac Singers. This somewhat amorphous group included, at various times, Lee Hays, Peter Hawes, Millard Lampell, Josh White, Bess Lomax, Agnes Cunningham, and Arthur Stern. From time to time they were joined by Woody Guthrie. Their principal causes were support of the unions and opposition to war. Their story is an interesting one of a well-intentioned, somewhat idealistic enterprise that was doomed to failure. The intellectuals and the Communists, who constituted almost the only audience for folk music in the cities in the 1930s, did identify fervently with their concepts of the "folk" and of the uses of folk art, but the goal of singers such as the Almanacs, to transform industrial workers into singing militants by giving them a ready-made body of protest songs in folk style, was never to any significant degree realized. Pete Seeger later reflected: "Most union leaders could not see any connection between music and porkchops. . . . 'Which Side Are You On' was known in Greenwich Village, but not in a single miners' union local."[16] Far more popular with the workers were productions in the popular Broadway style such as the famous *Pins and Needles*, a phenomenally successful satirical revue staged by the New York garment workers' union in 1937.

Another factor that doomed the protest song movement after it had led a thriving existence in certain circles throughout the 1930s was its dogmatic attachment to the Communist Party line. The weakness of being thus tied to an institutionalized ideology (a legacy of the early thirties) became painfully apparent as the tragically inhumane machinations of World War II unfolded. The songs were at first anti-Fascist, and urged American intervention; the Spanish Civil War was the most important rallying cause, and "Los Quatros Generales" one of its best-known songs.

The four insurgent generals, mamita mia,
They tried to betray us.

Next Christmas holy evening, mamita mia,
They'll all be hanging.

Then in August 1939, with the signing of the Nazi-Soviet pact, the line became pacifist and noninterventionist:

Franklin, Oh Franklin, we don't want to go to war.
Franklin, Oh Franklin, we don't want to go to war.
We want to stay home.[17]

The sudden Nazi invasion of Russia in the summer of 1941 caused an immediate switch in the party line, which, according to Denisoff, "cut the Almanacs' repertoire in half. Anti-war songs were no longer appropriate now that German tanks thundered on Russian soil." After Pearl Harbor Pete Seeger, in a talking blues number, said,

So what I want is for you to give me a gun,
And we can hurry up and get the job done.[18]

The Almanac Singers, which in its heyday had become a somewhat large and changing stable of singers able to fill two or three simultaneous engagements, had ceased to exist as a group before the war's end. Its failure was an illustration of the pitfalls of trying to cloak a particular party line in the mantle of the folk.

After the war, Pete Seeger founded and ran People's Songs, Inc., as "an organization to make and send songs of labor and the American people throughout the land." During its three-year existence, which ended in 1949, it assembled a vast library of protest songs, encouraged and acted as a clearinghouse for the publication of new ones, taught classes in the "use of songs as a weapon," and published the *People's Song Bulletin*.

A parallel organization of performers, formed to promote and manage live performances of folk music, was People's Artists, Inc. A special vehicle for this was the "hootenanny," a gathering featuring well-known folk performers, introducing new ones, and emphasizing audience participation in the singing. But despite the continued success of the "hoots," the times were changing.

The 1950s marked a transition. In the prewar period the "folk entrepreneurs" had derived their organizational strength and their sense of direction and purpose from the labor unions and the political parties of the Old Left—in particular, the Communist Party. After the war, the labor unions, as they assumed more power and "establishment" status, became more disdainful of help from mere folk singers. And postwar disillusionment with and suspicion of Communism (and especially Stalinism) rose to a fever pitch and took extremist form in McCarthyism and the attendant blacklisting of performers. It had earlier shown an even uglier side in the shocking hatred and even physical violence inflicted on performers at a rally attended by Seeger and his family in Peekskill, New York, in 1949.[19]

A few stalwarts such as Seeger kept the movement alive, at least partly by broadening their material to include folk music that was not about politics. The Weavers (made up of Seeger, Ronnie Gilbert, Fred Hellerman, and Lee Hays) began a very successful career in 1950, with personal appearances and recordings of less overtly controversial material such as "Freight Train Blues," "Darling Cory," "Tzena, Tzena" (an Israeli soldiers' tune), "The Roving Kind," "So Long, It's Been Good to Know You" (Woody Guthrie's song with its Dust Bowl origins obscured), "The Midnight Special," and Leadbelly's popular "Goodnight, Irene." Bringing folk music successfully into the arena of popular music, the Weavers, in spite of a hiatus in their appearances when they were blacklisted in the early 1950s, were ultimately a major factor in bringing about the folk music revival of the late 1950s, to be described in due course. Another manifestation of the broader approach to folk song at the time was the reconstituting in 1950 of the old *People's Song Bulletin* of the 1940s as the new *Sing Out!*

Protest and Folk Song in the 1960s

When the protest folk song movement reemerged in the 1960s it presented a marked contrast to the movement of the thirties and forties—the era of Guthrie, the early Seeger, and the Almanacs. The old supportive organizations were no longer there; the political parties of the Old Left (Communist and Socialist) were out of the picture, and the labor unions, as indicated, had become conservative and, on environmental issues, even reactionary. Without this organizational support, the whole character of the movement had changed; in fact, as a single unidirectional movement it had ceased to exist. The emphasis in the new songs was no longer on "changing the system" (e.g., "destroying Capitalism"), but focused instead on specific issues. There was also a shift in the attitudes projected in the songs. What Denisoff has termed the "magnetic" song, which suggested concrete solutions or actions to be taken (such as joining a union), was replaced by what he has called the "rhetorical" song, which simply dramatized an issue. Seldom was a solution set forth, and the action to be taken, if any, was more likely to be on an individual, personal level, expressing a wide range of responses—from the bitterly destructive

Burn, baby, burn

to the transcendent

Let us wrap you in our warm and freedom love.

Audience participation, something Seeger excelled at evoking, was cultivated less.* Songs became longer, and often lacked the refrains that would allow an audience to sing along. Performances tended to focus more on the performer as soloist, and folk "stars" began to emerge.

* The major exception to this was in the "freedom songs" of the Civil Rights movement in the South, discussed below.

Bob Dylan

The career and work of Bob Dylan (Robert Zimmerman, b. 1941) illustrate dramatically how little the sixties and seventies resembled the thirties and forties. Dylan emerged into prominence from the same Greenwich Village milieu that had launched his idol Woody Guthrie before him into the role of protester and "folk poet." But the men, their backgrounds, and most of all their times, were vastly different, in ways that are worth considering if we are to understand their work in relation to the whole problem of folk music in our time.

First, the changed times that separated them are significantly indicated by the differences in their backgrounds. The hardships of Guthrie's early life were not self-imposed, whereas Dylan was a child of less stringent times and circumstances, who dropped out of college in Minnesota and went to New York to join the Greenwich Village scene. As a folk musician Guthrie never had consciously to adopt a style and never felt it necessary to change his style, and in fact there is no indication that he was ever much *aware* of such a thing as style. Dylan, coming along at a later and more self-conscious period for folk music, had already gone from rock 'n' roll to acoustic folk by the time he went to New York; he was to change his style, his sound, and his type of material many times thereafter. Because of Dylan's popularity and the force of his talent, each of his changes in the 1960s sent waves of influence through the folk and rock worlds. In the 1970s and 1980s, his continued shifts have attracted less notice.

Dylan's talents as a songwriter are great (as exemplified in such songs as "Mr. Tambourine Man")—probably at least as great as Guthrie's. Certainly he is a far more distinctive and original *musician*; Guthrie apparently found his tunes and accompaniments by a largely offhand and unconscious process, as he himself has hinted. As a folk musician, he was an appropriator and an adaptor. Dylan, on the other hand, was never really a folk musician, but a composer in (among others) a folklike style.

To put the work of both men in proper perspective, it must be realized that the majority of their songs can hardly be said to be in the realm of "social significance" at all; they deal with themes that are both more universal and more personal. Guthrie, essentially a balladeer rather than a writer of lyrical songs, was capable of using any event as the basis for a song. Dylan, more of a lyricist, tends to write songs that deal, like the majority of blues, with variants of the man-woman theme.

Dylan did create some memorable songs and ballads of protest, however, especially in his early career. Some are explicit as to the issues and belong more or less to the older tradition: "The Lonesome Death of Hattie Carroll" and "Seven Curses" (the corruption of justice); "Only a Pawn in Their Game" and "Oxford Town" (the machinations of racial prejudice); "Masters of War" and "With God on Our Side" (war); "Let Me Die in My Footsteps" (bomb shelters). He also produced some very realistic ballads that are not overt protest songs, in that the target, as a defiantly general human condition, is less readily assailable: "The Ballad of Hollis Brown" and "North Country Blues" (poverty). Others are more highly distilled and convey more generalized feelings about the future: "Blowin' in the Wind" and "The Times They Are A-Changin'."

But some, even among the early songs, begin to display that surrealistic kind of private imagery that marks much of the poetry and pseudo-poetry of the sixties and seventies, and is a sign of a distinct departure from the old tradition in the direction of the esoteric ("A Hard Rain's A-Gonna Fall"; "Subterranean Homesick Blues"). It was this trend that brought on the severe criticism of the old-line folk protestors.

Dylan has absorbed, most probably unconsciously, many influences. These are apparent even at his most esoteric, and they link at least his early works to the dominant roots of American folk music and folklore. Perhaps this partly explains his appeal, and his enthusiastic adoption, in the beginning, by those who felt a special attachment to folk music. His debt to African-American blues is readily apparent. Somewhat less obvious is his relationship to the Anglo-American ballad tradition and to the cultural milieu (including the religious) that nourished it. A few examples will suffice to draw attention to this. His "Girl of the North Country" is an offshoot of a perennial ballad. The tune of "Masters of War" is basically that of the haunting "Nottamun Town," a song from the Appalachians. The question-and-answer incipits to the stanzas of "A Hard Rain's A-Gonna Fall" are an adaptation of the "Lord Randall" form; and "Who Killed Davy Moore?" is a modern version of "Cock Robin," which, like many children's songs, has far older and more meaningful antecedents. "When the Ship Comes In" draws on the imagery of the revival spiritual, and "I Pity the Poor Immigrant" has the parallel construction of the Old Testament canticles.[20]

Dylan's adoption, in 1965, of the instrumentation, style, and approach of rock was at the time a subject of much controversy, as was his later move away from protest material and even toward an accommodation (as it was seen) with commercial country music, represented by his *Nashville Skyline* of 1969.

Broadside *Magazine, and the Younger Protest Singers in the North*

As an organ of the new topical song movement in the North (which then meant pretty much Greenwich Village), Pete Seeger and Malvina Reynolds started the periodical *Broadside* in 1962, to give new songwriters a chance to have their work published, and to include more topical material than *Sing Out!* (Bob Dylan's "Talking John Birch Society" appeared in *Broadside*'s first issue.) *Broadside* became, in association with Oak Publications and Folkways Records, what might be called the publishing and disseminating wing of the protest folk song movement. As such it was an important vehicle for such younger writers and performers of the 1960s as Phil Ochs, Tom Paxton, Peter La Farge, and Mark Spoelstra.

Freedom Songs, and the Civil Rights Movement in the South

For all the differences between the 1930s and the 1960s, there was an interesting parallel. In the thirties, as we have seen, labor sympathizers who went into the South to help organize the miners found a sturdy singing tradition already at work furnishing songs for the workers. In the early 1960s, protest folk singers from the North who went into the South at the time of the early Civil Rights struggle also found a southern tradition, in this case based on African-American religious singing, already furnishing songs for those engaged in marches, mass meetings, sit-ins, and prayer vigils, and for those in jails. Many of these songs reached deeply into a body of song (the spiritual) that had been rejected by educated urban African-Americans. Important groundwork in putting future Civil Rights workers in touch with this heritage was done by Guy Carawan at the Highlander Folk School in Monteagle, Tennessee, where he went as music director in 1959. As Carawan himself has written of the songs,

> The most important ones are the old, slow-paced spirituals and hymns (some in the minor mode) that sing of hope and determination, and the rhythmic jubilee spirituals and bright gospel songs that protest boldly and celebrate eventual victory. These are in the majority and usually have new or revised words to old tunes.[21]

Of these songs from an indigenous tradition "We Shall Overcome," based on the African-American church song "I'll Overcome Some Day," with words by the gospel hymnodist C. Albert Tindley, is the best known, and it is sung today all over the world.[22] From the same sources are "We Shall Not Be Moved" and the spirited "This Little Light of Mine," "I'm Gonna Sit at the Welcome Table," and "Ain't Gonna Let Nobody Turn Me Round." As an example of adaptation, an old gospel song "I Woke Up This Morning with My Mind Stayed on Jesus" became "Woke Up This Morning With My Mind on Freedom."[23]

After a visit to the South, the northern songwriter Tom Paxton communicated the following in a phone interview. It is worth quoting at some length because of the light it sheds on the differences between the topical songs of the North and the freedom songs of the South:

> There is an enormous difference musically between what they're doing and what we're doing. . . . I was tremendously moved by the music we heard down there, and the thing that knocked me out was that all those songs are what I call action songs. Songs to be sung in the thick of it with no need for guitars or microphones, or any of it because with the first bar sung by one man, they all know the song. . . . What we write are essentially musical editorials where, if you agree with me, you sing the chorus. But there the entire song, sometimes with only a few words being changed from verse to verse,[24] is sung right in the face of the cops and mobs and they're fantastic. Songs to be sung in jails. . . . Our songs might line up a little support and a little bread but their songs are right in the fight.[25]

Continuity and Change in Folk Style of Persuasion in the 1970s and 1980s

Several factors contributed to the fact that the writing and singing of protest songs no longer attracted the attention in the 1980s that it did in the 1960s. The popular folk song revival, which spread and popularized the protest song even as it diluted and commercialized it, was long over. With the end of the Vietnam War, and with the Civil Rights struggle assuming—in the minds of many—less of the dimension of crisis (in that it had moved from the streets and jails to the courts and legislative halls), the single big issues with the capacity to galvanize a significant portion of the public were replaced by issues that were far more diverse and complex. Quite a few of the veterans were still active, among them Sis Cunningham, Malvina Reynolds, Peter, Paul, and Mary, the perennial Pete Seeger, and the younger Tom Paxton and Arlo Guthrie (son of Woody). *Broadside* magazine continued gamely to publish, and a perusal of numbers from the late 1980s shows attention to a wide variety of issues, most of them outside this country. Central America, especially Nicaragua, was a frequent subject, as was South Africa and the struggle against apartheid. Domestic issues were exceedingly diverse: the many facets of the environmental problem, nuclear energy, women's rights, opposition to capital punishment, support for choice on the question of abortion, help for the aging and the disabled.

Songs promoting unity and solidarity among the *already committed* who are actually engaging in acts of protest or civil disobedience (e.g., Civil Rights demonstrations, farm labor marches, antinuclear sit-ins) are still and always will be effective sustainers of morale. Beyond that, the old-line hard-hitting protest song is probably being sung to a diminishing public. Today it appears, especially in the case of complex issues such as the environment, that reliable scientific research, painstaking legal work, and well-informed political pressure with as broad a base as possible are more effective than emotion-laden "outbursts of desperation."

Nevertheless, these outbursts, granted that they are often grossly exaggerated, crudely expressed, and simplistic, and are made only by the committed few, *can* express the gut concerns of the many. In that sense they are part of a long and healthy tradition of dissent that has contributed to the character of American culture and its music. And there is gold in the songs themselves, as the ephemeral dross is discarded: "We Shall Overcome" (from black hymnody), "So Long, It's Been Good to Know You" (Woody Guthrie), "Where Have All the Flowers Gone" (Pete Seeger), and "Blowin' in the Wind" (Bob Dylan) are as much a part now of our oral tradition as the songs of Stephen Foster or the favorites of Tin Pan Alley.

The Popularization of Folk Music

The milieu that fostered the more earnest aspects of protest and propaganda in urban folk song was the same milieu from which sprang another, somewhat unexpected phenomenon: folk music became, in the late 1950s and early 1960s, enormously popular. In terms of the protest content of folk music, this was paradoxical. Popular music, in order to *be* popular, must appeal to as many potential customers as possible; by its very nature, then, it should avoid material that is controversial or presents views seen as deviant by the broad mass of people, who support the very status quo that protest music is supposed to change. But certain forces operated to mitigate this paradox. Where actual protest songs did become popular, especially in "cover" versions by pop artists, the lyrics were sometimes altered.[26] And it is probable that a good deal of the time the general public either did not pay much attention to the words, or did not fully grasp their import. They simply found folk music—especially as purveyed by energetic and committed performers such as the Weavers or Peter, Paul, and Mary—a refreshing change from either Tin Pan Alley songs or rock 'n' roll. Thus we find Pete Seeger's accusatory indictment of war "Where Have All the Flowers Gone" on the Top Ten (though not without having undergone a subtle change), and Seeger's and Hays's "If I Had a Hammer," which was originally written for a benefit for Communist Party leaders on trial, entering oral tradition and the domain of children's summer camp songs!

Pete Seeger himself played an important, though at times reluctant and self-doubting, role in this popularization. The Almanacs had begun to achieve a promising degree of popularity before a combination of party-line shift and blacklisting truncated their career. The renaissance of approximately the same group as the Weavers in 1948, again on Seeger's initiative, met with considerable and unexpected success in the 1950s, as we have seen. From the Vanguard in Greenwich Village they went on to nationwide appearances and very successful recordings, culminating in *The Weavers at Carnegie Hall,* released in 1957. In addition, Seeger himself had a busy career as a solo performer, playing and singing a variety of folk and children's songs.

Other individual performers also contributed to the popularization of folk music, of whom two, Burl Ives (b. 1909) and Harry Belafonte (b. 1927) may be taken as typical. Ives was part of the Greenwich Village scene in the late 1930s and the 1940s, singing for leftist audiences and drawing praise from the Communist press of the period. Though invited, he did not join the Almanac Singers; he later disavowed left-wing associations and went on to a professional career both as a singer of folk songs and an actor. Harry Belafonte's career represents a somewhat different pattern. He interrupted a promising pop music career to study folk music, delving into the Library of Congress Archive, among other sources. He began a second career in Greenwich Village, from which milieu he went on to Hollywood, television, and films. Born in New York of West Indian parentage, he spent some formative years in Jamaica. Identified primarily with Calypso music (he did more than any other single performer to popularize it), he has successfully purveyed the music of other traditions as well, including spirituals.

A landmark in the popularization of folk music was the appearance in 1958 of a recording of a nineteenth-century North Carolina murder ballad, "Tom Dooley," by a young group called (because of the then-current Calypso craze) the Kingston Trio.[27] The trio had come to Greenwich Village from San Francisco, where it originated, performing in places like the hungry i and the Purple Onion. The recording was hugely successful, and led to an extensive career.

Another group to emerge from the New York folk scene was Peter, Paul, and Mary (Peter Yarrow, Noel Paul Stookey, and Mary Ellin Travers), who first recorded in 1962. Their career may be cited as evidence that even some of the professionally successful folk singers had not fully broken the link with social and political protest. In 1963 they recorded "Blowin' in the Wind," by fellow Greenwich Village alumnus Bob Dylan. That same year they sang for the August march on Washington in behalf of Civil Rights. In 1968 they campaigned for Eugene McCarthy, the Democratic nominee for president; this was just twenty years after the Almanacs had stumped for Henry Wallace.

In 1963 the high-water mark of the folk music "revival," as it has been called, was reached. That was the year of the memorable Civil Rights confrontations in the South, and of a somewhat revitalized and united folk singers' activist effort in support of the cause of southern blacks. It was also the year of the reconstitution, after a two-year hiatus, of the Newport (Rhode Island) Folk Festival. The festival drew tremendous crowds, and the performers represented a broad spectrum. Southern traditional music was represented by Clarence Ashley, Doc Watson, Maybelle Carter, and Jean Ritchie; protest music of the 1930s by Jim Garland; the southern Civil Rights movement by the Freedom Singers; the new topical song movement by Sam Hinton, Phil Ochs, and Tom Paxton; and finally, the "big drawers"—those singers who by then had achieved significant popularity, but who kept in their repertory a number of songs reflecting social concern—by Pete Seeger, Joan Baez, Bob Dylan, and Peter, Paul, and Mary.

If the mid-1960s marked the height of the folk music revival, then the folk festivals were surely the "camp meetings" of this revival. The social concerns of the period (mainly civil rights) seemed to create, at least temporarily, a folk-singing "community," and particularly at the early festivals a feeling of fervent, almost religious enthusiasm was generated. The cohesion of this "community" proved to be short-lived and illusory, however. For one thing, the ideological commitments, for those who saw *these* in folk music, were far more diffused, individualistic, and transitory than they had been in the thirties and forties. Then, too, with the new popularity of folk music had come an inevitable commercialism. If performers thought in terms of a career (whose rewards might be more attractive than ever before), they had to be very conscious of popularity charts, based on the sale of records and concert tickets. A "star system" rapidly evolved, which was completely foreign both to the very essence of folk music itself and to the ideals of the proletarian "folk movement" of the earlier period.

As for the mass audience represented by the popularity charts, its preoccupation with folk music was fleeting, and its exposure limited largely to the highly processed and commercially packaged article. Thus whatever mass audience folk music had in the 1950s and 1960s, it never viewed folk music as other than a branch of popular music—nor could it have been expected to. Having been introduced to "folk music" by groups such as the Kingston Trio, it drifted away with the coming of the Beatles.

The 1980s have given evidence of a quiet renaissance of interest in folk music. Unlike the popular surge of the late 1950s and early 1960s, it is not taking the country (and the media) by storm, but is manifested in the reappearance of folk festivals (of which the reconstituted "granddaddy" of them at Newport, Rhode Island, is only one), of coffeehouse concerts, and of additional folk programming on radio stations. So great is the variety of styles, traditions, and approaches represented that the term "folk music" has come to be replaced by a term that focuses on the one thing all the performers have in common—"acoustic music" (referring to the absence of electrified instruments). This music has not lost its persuasive aspect, but this is apt to be more evident as commentary (often humorous) on social conditions than as overtly political statement. *Broadside* magazine, which has tended to maintain its militant stance, is no longer representative of the entire folk scene, which includes such new talents as Bill Morrissey, Claudia Schmidt, and Greg Brown. As Christine Lavin has pointed out, "Most of the folk stuff being written is gentle, with some social satire—not nearly as political as it was." And Margaret Leighton, of Rounder Records, has said: "Many of the new singer/songwriters have more in common with the best of the new regional fiction writers than with traditional folk subjects."[28]

Modern Collecting, Study, and Thought in Folk Music

Any worthwhile assessment of folk music in relation to American life and culture must be based on understanding. Understanding is based on disciplined study, and disciplined study requires not only trained and experienced minds but a body of material faithfully and carefully collected and preserved. This is the third level at which Americans have been involved with folk music in our time.

It is beyond our scope to include a survey of folk song scholarship in America. Yet the reader should be aware that by now a vast amount of American folk music has been collected, and made available for study and re-creation. This is due to the labors of a broad range of workers in the field. Harvard professors Francis James Child and George Lyman Kittredge began the work and laid down the guidelines around the turn of the century (incidentally making Harvard a leading center for folk song study). But the work of collecting subsequently was pursued with enthusiasm by both amateurs and professionals in all corners of the country. Jack Thorp, an easterner turned cowboy, published in Estancia, New Mexico, the first edition of his *Songs of the Cowboys* in 1908, to be followed by John Lomax's *Cowboy Songs and Other Frontier Ballads* in 1910. Collecting was meanwhile going on in Missouri, in Michigan, in Nebraska, in Kentucky, in West Virginia. The English collector Cecil Sharp, building on the work of American enthusiasts, collected folk songs in the southern Appalachians in the summers of 1916–18. Roland Gray was collecting ballads among the Maine lumberjacks in the early 1920s, and George Korson concentrated on the anthracite-coal miners in Pennsylvania at about the same time. In the thirties John Lomax and his son Alan first took their electric recording machine into the back country and prisons of the Deep South, and made historic recordings of African-American work songs, field cries, ballads, and blues. John Greenway delved into the material collected by the New York–based People's Songs, Inc., interviewed many of the singers connected with that endeavor, and came up with *American Folksongs of Protest* in 1953. Mike Seeger has found and recorded many old-time musicians such as Dock Boggs, as well as perpetuating traditional styles in his own playing and with the New Lost City Ramblers. And central to all these endeavors, and functioning as a great national repository of folk music, is the monumental Archive of American Folk Song of the Library of Congress. This Archive, established as long ago as 1928, has represented the collective efforts of many workers, but those most closely associated with it in the public mind, and with good reason, have been the Lomaxes. Its collection consists mostly of recordings made in the field, but such diverse figures as Woody Guthrie and Jelly Roll Morton have been brought to the recording laboratory in Washington by Alan Lomax to record songs, instrumental pieces, and reminiscences for posterity. The Archive now has preserved more than 60,000 performances.

An additional resource, to which reference has been made many times in these first four chapters, is the large catalog of Folkways Records—2,200 albums characterized as "the greatest collection of folk music ever made available to the buying public." The entire enterprise was the work of a single man, Moses Asch—a Polish Jew who came to New York at the age of eight (his father was the writer Sholem Asch), who was "a lifelong Socialist—passionate, though nondoctrinaire," and a lifelong documenter of American speech and song. Folkways' monumental catalog—which includes American Indian music, jazz, blues, ragtime, mountain music, ballads, and electronic music, and preserves the voices of Eugene V. Debs, Booker T. Washington, W. E. B. Dubois, Margaret Mead, and Eleanor Roosevelt, alongside those of Leadbelly, Woody Guthrie, and Pete Seeger—has been taken over, since the death of Moses Asch, by the Smithsonian Institution.

These major sources, and many others, will become increasingly valuable as future students look ever more penetratingly at the varied phenomena of folk music in America—tracing its paths and finding out what it can tell us about ourselves and our ways.

Further Reading

Studies and Background Reading

Denisoff, R. Serge. *Sing Me a Song of Social Significance.* 2d ed. Bowling Green, OH: Bowling Green State University Press, 1983.
More a collection of articles than a unified book. In spite of its date, the second edition has very little material on anything past the mid-1970s, and the lack of an index limits its usefulness.

———. *Great Day Coming: Folk Music and the American Left.* Urbana: University of Illinois Press, 1971.
This short study is the most nearly comprehensive and objective study to date of this controversial topic.

Dunaway, David King. *How Can I Keep From Singing: Pete Seeger.* New York: McGraw-Hill, 1981.
An ample and objective account of the career—to date—of the one outstanding "survivor" in the folk protest scene. Mercurial but persistent, with stamina, dedication, and overall optimism matched by few, he has been part of that scene from the Guthrie era of the late 1930s to the present. The book therefore offers valuable firsthand insight into the entire procession of eras. A nearly complete discography is very useful.

Dunson, Josh. *Freedom in the Air: Song Movements of the Sixties.* New York: International Publishers, 1965.
A brief account, with examples of song words, of the second flourishing period of folk song as propaganda. Treats mainly the Civil Rights movement.

Greenway, John. *American Folksongs of Protest.* Philadelphia: University of Pennsylvania Press, 1953. Paperback reprint, New York: A. S. Barnes, 1960.
A rather detailed account of protest songs, especially those used in the labor movement. Many examples, including music.

Guthrie, Woody. *Bound for Glory.* New York: E. P. Dutton, 1943.

Autobiographical reminiscences, often of considerable poetic intensity, by one of the best-known authors and singers of the urban folk movement.

Jackson, Bruce, ed. *Folklore and Society.* Hatboro, PA: Folklore Associates, 1966.
This collection of essays in honor of folklorist B. A. Botkin includes excellent articles by Charles Seeger, Willard Rhodes, Richard Dorson, and Ellen Stekert.

Malone, Bill C. *Country Music, U.S.A.* Austin: University of Texas Press, 1968 and 1985. See chapter 4, both editions.

Noebel, David A. *The Marxist Minstrels: A Handbook on Communist Subversion of Music.* Tulsa, OK: American Christian College Press, 1974.
A rather shrill and alarmist expression of dissenting opinion on the urban folk movement, based on the obvious and continuing bias of some leading segments of it towards the extreme left, including Communism.

Reuss, Richard A. *A Woody Guthrie Bibliography, 1912–1967.* New York: Guthrie Children's Trust Fund, 1968.

Wilgus, D. K. *Anglo-American Folksong Scholarship Since 1898.* New Brunswick, NJ: Rutgers University Press, 1959.
A comprehensive survey and evaluation of the work of this century. As the work of an authoritative scholar treating subjects that are often still controversial, it is of great value. Includes a discography, useful even though out of date, and a very comprehensive bibliography.

See also the reading list for Chapters 1 and 2.

Song Collections

Some general collections, such as Alan Lomax's *The Folk Songs of North America* and Carl Sandburg's *The American Songbag* (see Chapter 1), have songs relevant to this chapter. Of the more specialized collections, the following should be mentioned:

American Folksong. Compiled by Woody Guthrie, edited by Moses Asch. New York: Oak Publications, 1961.

Greenway, *American Folksongs of Protest* (cited above).
Contains many complete songs, with music for a few.

Bob Dylan. New York: Warner Bros., 1974.

Hard-Hitting Songs for Hard-Hit People. Compiled by Alan Lomax, with notes by Woody Guthrie; music transcribed and edited by Pete Seeger. New York: Oak Publications, 1967.
Probably the best collection concentrating on the period of the 1930s. Illustrated with fine photographs made under the auspices of the Farm Security Administration by Walker Evans and others.

Songs of Work and Protest. Edited by Edith Fowke and Joe Glazer. New York: Dover, 1973.
This anthology of 100 songs includes a wide range of material, including songs from the eighteenth century, nineteenth-century abolitionist and labor songs, twentieth-century IWW songs, and many songs from the Almanacs and People's Songs, Inc.

We Shall Overcome: Songs of the Southern Freedom Movement. Compiled by Guy and Candie Carawan. New York: Oak Publications, 1963.
Songs of the Civil Rights movement, with commentary.

The Woody Guthrie Song Book. New York: Grosset & Dunlap, 1976.

Periodicals

Broadside (New York).
The leading publication for topical songs, its editorial policy is to include songs by a variety of writers, thus giving new writers a chance to be published. It was started in 1962 by Pete Seeger,

Malvina Reynolds, and Agnes Cunningham to serve this purpose, and to include more topical songs than the earlier *Sing Out!*

Sing Out! (Bethlehem, PA).
Founded in 1950, *Sing Out!* tends toward more traditional folk songs than does *Broadside*, and includes articles.

Articles

Bluestein, Gene. "Moses Asch, Documentor," *American Music*, vol. 5, no. 3 (Fall 1987).

Scherman, Tony. "The Many Voices of Moses Asch," *Smithsonian*, ca. 1987.

Yurchenko, Henrietta. "The Beginning of an Urban Folk-Song Movement in New York: A Memoir," *Sonneck Society Bulletin*, vol. 8, no. 2 (Summer 1987).
A brief, vivid account of this movement in New York in the 1930s, including firsthand impressions of Woody Guthrie, by one who participated in it.

Listening

General

Anthology of American Folk Music, 3 vols. Folkways 2951–53.

American Industrial Folksongs, ed. John Greenway. Riverside RLP-12-607.

American Industrial Ballads, Pete Seeger. Folkways FH-5251.

The Promised Land: American Indian Songs of Lament and Protest. 1981. Folkways FHS-37254.
Indian "message" music, in "an urban folksinging genre akin to Woody Guthrie."

Colonial

The Birth of Liberty. NW-276.

Pre-1930

The Songs of Joe Hill, Joe Glazer. Folkways 2039.

1930s and 1940s

Brother, Can You Spare a Dime?: American Song During the Great Depression. NW-270.
A broad cross-section of songs from both the popular and folk domains.

Songs of the Great Depression, New Lost City Ramblers. Folkways FH-5264.

Talking Union, Almanac Singers. Folkways FH-5285.

The Songs and Stories of Aunt Molly Jackson. Folkways 5457.

Aunt Molly Jackson, Library of Congress Recordings. Rounder 1002.

Dust Bowl Ballads, Woody Guthrie. Folkways FH-5212.

Hootenanny Tonight, Pete Seeger and others. Folkways FH-2511.

Hootenanny at Carnegie Hall, Almanac Singers. Folkways FH-2512.

Songs of Struggle and Protest, Pete Seeger. Folkways FH-5233.

Songs of the Lincoln Brigade, the Almanac Singers and Ernst Busch. Stinson SLP-52.
Songs of the Spanish Civil War.

Protest songs from the 1960s and beyond

Folkways/Smithsonian has, especially in its 5000 series, a large number of albums of songs from the Civil Rights movement, and songs printed in *Broadside*. Catalog available from Birch Tree Group Ltd.

We Shall Overcome, Pete Seeger. Columbia CL-2101.

All the News That's Fit To Sing, Phil Ochs. Elektra EKL-269.

Ain't That News, Tom Paxton. Elektra EKL-298.

Newport Folk Festival 1963. Vanguard 79148.

Newport Folk Festival 1964. Vanguard 79184.

Woody Guthrie

Woodie Guthrie: The Early Years. Everest 2088.

The Legendary Woody Guthrie. Everest 2058.

Woody Guthrie, Library of Congress Recordings, 2 vols. Elektra EKL-271, EKL-272.

Original Recordings Made by Woody Guthrie: 1940–1946. Warner Brothers BS-2999.

Ballads of Sacco and Vanzetti, Woody Guthrie. Folkways FH-5485.

See also the list for the 1930s and 1940s.

Bob Dylan

The Times They Are A-Changin', Bob Dylan. Columbia KCS-8905.

The Freewheelin' Bob Dylan. Columbia PC-8786.

The Popularization of Folk Music

The Weavers' Greatest Hits, 2 vols. Vanguard VSD-15, VSD-16.

The Weavers at Carnegie Hall. Vanguard 6533E.

Time to Think, Kingston Trio. Capitol ST-2011.

Harry Belafonte: Pure Gold. RCA ANL-1-0979-E.

Burl Ives' Greatest Hits. MCA 114.

Peter, Paul, and Mary. Warner Brothers 1449.

The Best of Peter, Paul, and Mary. Warner Brothers 2552.

The World of Pete Seeger, 2 LPs. Columbia CG-31949.

PROJECTS

1. Read Charles Seeger's thought-provoking article "The Folkness of the Non-Folk vs. the Non-Folkness of the Folk," in Jackson, *Folklore and Society.* Write a brief essay setting forth *your* interpretation of "folkness" and "non-folkness," drawing examples from the life and culture you see around you.

2. Make a study of the IWW (the "Wobblies") and their use of music. Consult, if possible, a copy of the *Red Song Book,* documenting where feasible the sources of the songs. Are they fundamentally European or American?

3. Write a brief paper on the U.S. Communist Party's views and attitudes towards music, and the uses of it advocated in various periods. (For a start, consult the bibliography in Denisoff, *Great Day Coming.*)

4. Write a brief paper on the Lincoln Battalion and its role in the Spanish Civil War, with special attention to the songs that came out of the conflict.

5. Do a brief essay on the "hootenanny"—the term itself and the social gathering to which it was applied. (You may wish to consult, among other sources, Peter Tamony's article in *Western Folklore*, July 1963.)

6. For many of his songs, Woody Guthrie used tunes that were already traditional. (Consult his own description of his methods in *Born to Win*.) Trace the tune sources of at least three such songs, comparing them with Guthrie's versions.

7. Try to document a local example of a topical song or a protest song being used at a meeting, rally, or other gathering. Analyze the song itself (trying to determine its source) and as much of the context of its usage as you can. Consider, for example: How well did the people seem to know it? Was it sung primarily to sway the uncommitted or to promote solidarity and raise morale among the cause's adherents?

8. Interview some people prominent in local labor unions, to find out the current state of labor songs and singing in the labor movement, and their views on what the role of singing either could or should be.

9. Analyze the body of songs in a year's issues of some topical song publication such as *Sing Out!* or *Broadside*. Consider (1) the number of topical subjects involved and the proportion of songs devoted to each; (2) the proportion of *magnetic* songs to *rhetorical*, as defined by Denisoff and alluded to in this chapter.

10. Compare a popularized version of a folk song with a traditional one, giving attention to tune, words, style of singing, and accompaniment. Include some conclusions and comments. (An example would be Simon and Garfunkel's "Scarborough Fair/Canticle" as compared with a traditional rendition of Child ballad 2—known by such titles as "The Elfin Knight" and "The Lover's Tasks"—from the Library of Congress Archive releases.)

11. Make a report on any recent "folk music festival," including such topics as the range of traditions represented; the proportion of what could be regarded as traditional folk singers to professional or popular singers of folk songs; any "stars" that were involved. What does the festival tell you about the state of folk music today?

Photo by Dorothea Lange

PART TWO

Popular Sacred Music

AMERICA is too young to have been able to nurture such highly cultivated worship music as is represented, for example, by the rich flowerings of Gregorian chant or the Lutheran cantata. Nor, the mere question of time aside, have the conditions been present that could produce such flowerings. With our broad spectrum of religious denominations, with our inbred distrust of the ecclesiastical organization and wealth that are indispensable for building a tradition of highly refined religious art, and with our increased secularization, the intensity of focus has been lacking here that in Europe, from the Middle Ages up to the time of the social and industrial revolutions, could put large resources of talent at the service of the Church, and produce, at the apex, a *Notre Dame Mass* or a *St. Matthew Passion*. Thus our output of what might be called cultivated religious music has been meager, and up to now mostly derivative.

At the relatively unconscious and unlearned level of folk, or near-folk, art, on the other hand, we have produced religious music that, in accord with its homely character, has become deeply embedded in the culture of a broad segment of our people. Thus, as is true of so much of our music, the most significant of our religious music is that which has remained closest to folk sources. Like popular music (and it *is* popular music in the sense of the large market it has had for a century and a half, and the commercial establishment that has grown up to serve this market), it draws its significance not primarily from its aesthetic value (though it would be narrow-minded to deny that this exists) but from its meaning in the lives of those who sing it, and from the response it evokes. Indeed, immediacy and depth of response, without the distancing of any art-consciousness, are part and parcel of the phenomena of both folk and popular art. Charles Ives, one of our greatest composers but also one of our greatest musical thinkers, pointed up in the epilogue to his *Essays Before a Sonata* the importance of this near-folk music to those whose music it is. He is speaking to the American composer, but his words have substance for anyone who would understand American music.

> The man "born down to Babbitt's Corners" may find a deep appeal in the simple but acute Gospel hymns of the New England "camp meetin' " of a generation or so ago. He finds in them—some of them—a vigor, a depth of feeling, a natural-soil rhythm, a sincerity—emphatic but inartistic—which, in spite of a vociferous sentimentality, carries him nearer the "Christ of the people" than does the *Te Deum* of the greatest cathedral. . . . [If] the Yankee can reflect the fervency with which "his gospels" were sung—the fervency of "Aunt Sarah," who scrubbed her life away for her brother's ten orphans, the fervency with which this woman, after a fourteen-hour work-day on the farm, would hitch up and drive five miles through the mud and rain to "prayer meetin'," her one articulate outlet for the fulness of her unselfish soul—if he can reflect the fervency of such a spirit, he may find there a local color that will do all the world good. If his music can but catch that spirit by being a part with itself, it will come somewhere near his ideal—and it will be American, too.

5

Religious Music in Early America

TWO rich native traditions of religious music in America have been the African-American spiritual on the one hand, and on the other a white quasi-folk tradition whose lineage can be traced from seventeenth-century psalm singing through the singing-school of the eighteenth century, and its descendants in the shape-note tradition of the South through the nineteenth and into the twentieth centuries. The Afro-American spiritual, as a predominantly folk form, has been treated in an earlier chapter. This chapter will deal with the development from psalm tune to singing-school, while also turning aside for a brief look at some worthy and fascinating music from the religious communities—such as the Moravians and the Shakers—that functioned as more or less self-sufficient "islands" in our midst.

Psalmody in America

Very probably the first musical sounds from the Old World that the aborigines heard in that part of the New that is now the United States were the sturdy psalm tunes sung by Protestant settlers and sailors. Lest this image be confined to the Pilgrims and Puritans of New England, it should be noted that French Huguenots were singing psalms from their psalter in Florida half a century before the landing of the English Separatists at Plymouth—and, before their massacre by the Spaniards, were teaching them to the friendly and receptive natives. At the other edge of the continent, the California Indians were fascinated by the psalm singing of Sir Francis Drake's men in 1579. When the first permanent settlements in Massachusetts were established, psalters were an important part of the few precious possessions brought over. Subsequently psalms were sung both by the Indians and by many of the blacks along the eastern seaboard, as taught by missionaries. Psalm tunes were the most important body of religious music in constant use throughout those colonies founded by the English and Dutch, almost until the time of the Revolution. They were subsequently largely replaced by the music of hymns, anthems, and fuging tunes, but many of the old psalm tunes have survived, and tune names such as "Toulon," "Windsor," "York," "Bristol," "Old 104th," "Old 112th," "Old 120th," and the famous "Old 100th" bespeak their presence in every major modern hymnal.

Calvinism and the Psalms

A glance at a map of Europe, together with some understanding of the situation there at the time of the Reformation, will make clear why it was the psalm tune, rather than the Lutheran chorale or the venerable and cultivated music of the Roman Catholic Church, that dominated our early religious music and left its mark on its development for three hundred years. It is beyond the scope of this book to fill in the background in any detail; suffice it to say that many of our earliest permanent settlers brought with them not only their psalters and their psalm tunes, but their pronounced aversion to state religion and temporal ecclesiastical hierarchy and power—all of which, to them, was summed up in one word: "popery." This was to have a profound effect on the development of American consciousness and culture.

Music in the Calvinist churches was rather severely limited to the unaccompanied unison singing of metrical versions of the psalms. This limitation can best be understood in the light of the ancient and ever-present dichotomy that exists, when it comes to the uses of music in worship, between the musician and the theologian. The musician wishes to use the utmost skill and craft, and give the music free rein; the theologian wishes to keep music simple and ensure its subordination to the worship itself. The controversy is nearly as old as the Christian Church itself, and the history of church music is the history of the swinging of the pendulum back and forth between the two positions. The Church recognized, as the Greeks had long before, the power of music over the human emotions. As two recent writers have aptly summarized the situation: "The Christian church has carried on a long, often fruitful relationship with music, governed, however, by the kind of uneasy truce man had struck with fire."[1] It so happened that in the sixteenth century the pendulum swung decisively to the side of strict control of music, in both the Roman Catholic Church and the new Reformed Church, but much more drastically and completely in the latter. In the Reformed Church, the new broom had no weight of musical tradition to encumber it. Psalm singing, then, was the product of a musical simplicity enforced on theological grounds.

Psalm Tunes and Psalters

With John Calvin's exhortation to psalm singing came the need for metered and rhymed versions of the psalms, and tunes to which they could be sung by entire congregations, and not by trained choirs. This need began to be met immediately, and Calvin's first psalter was published in Strasbourg in 1539, followed by the Geneva Psalter in 1551, whose musical editor was Louis Bourgeois. Bourgeois is credited with composing many of the tunes himself, including both "Old 100th" and "Old 124th," the ancestor of the modern "Toulon." The sixteenth century saw the establishment of two great bodies of sacred tunes, the Lutheran chorales and the psalmody of the Reformed Church. They share similar characteristics: they are easily singable tunes of fairly simple construction, with vestiges of the old modal scales already encountered in our study of folk music.

The psalm tunes, especially those of French origin, display a rhythmic variety in the arrangement of long and short notes that was typical of Renaissance music, especially that for dancing. This rhythmic variety was lost sight of as succeeding generations tended to flatten out the rhythm into the rather pedestrian versions of the tunes as we have come to know them, plodding along in notes of equal value. Compare, for instance, the original version of "Old 100th" (Example 5–1) with the version now commonly used (Example 5–2).

Example 5–1

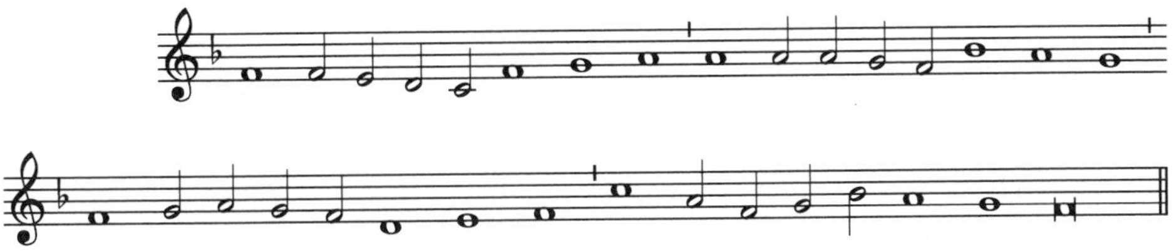

Example 5–2

Many of the tunes, especially when sung at a fairly lively pace, exhibit a kind of syncopation in relation to an implied steady pulse, as for example the version of Psalm 21 found in the Ainsworth Psalter (Example 5–3).

Example 5–3

That the psalms were not always performed slowly (at least outside of church) may be inferred from Shakespeare's oft-quoted allusion in *The Winter's Tale* to the Puritan who "sings psalms to hornepipes."

Of importance to America was the publication in 1612 in Amsterdam of a psalter in English for the use of the English Separatists who had taken refuge in Holland: *The Book of Psalmes: Englished both in Prose and Metre*. Henry Ainsworth, the compiler, incorporated into his work thirty-nine fine and varied melodies, mostly from French sources. It was the Ainsworth Psalter that the Separatists (or Pilgrims, as they came to be known) brought with them when they founded the Plymouth Colony in 1620, and they used it in a number of editions until this colony merged with the larger Massachusetts Bay Colony in 1692.[2]

The importance of psalm singing in the early Puritan colonies is attested to by the fact that the first book printed in what is now the United States was a newly translated, metered, and rhymed version of the psalms. *The Whole Booke of Psalmes Faithfully Translated into English Metre* was published in Boston in 1640, and from the Massachusetts Bay Colony it has acquired the nickname of the Bay Psalm Book. It contained no music (nor did any subsequent edition until the ninth of 1698); singers were referred to the two common English psalters of the day,those of Ravenscroft or Sternhold and Hopkins, for the tunes to be sung. The preface is scholarly, and the metered translations are literal, if somewhat rough as poetry. It was no mean achievement for a community of fewer than twenty thousand people that had established itself on the edge of the American wilderness scarcely more than a decade before. The motive of these scholars is revealed in characteristic words at the close of the preface:

> If therefore the verses are not always so smooth and elegant as some may desire or expect; let them consider that Gods Altar needs not our pollishings: Ex. 20. for wee have respected rather a plaine translation, then to smooth our verses with the sweetness of any paraphrase, and soe have attended Conscience rather than Elegance, fidelity rather than poetry, in translating the hebrew words into english language, and Davids poetry into english meetre; that soe wee may sing in Sion the Lords songs or prayse according to his owne will; untill hee take us from hence, and wipe away all our tears, & bid us enter into our masters joye to sing eternall Halleluiahs.

Two Divergent "Ways"

By the 1720s a hundred years of psalm singing in America had produced not one but two discernible traditions, simultaneous but widely divergent. They amounted to a written and an oral practice of singing. It is plain from accounts of the period that the oral practice, or "Usual Way," as it was called, had gained the upper hand. In the written practice, the tunes would be sung as they were notated in the psalm books of the time. But few in the congregations, especially in rural areas, could read music, and most had to rely on a combination of their own memory and the singing of a deacon or precentor who led them with a powerful voice. Since there was little to ensure the accuracy (to say nothing of the vocal ability) even of the precentor, it is plain that the stage was set for the evolution of a distinctly oral, or *folk,* practice; and this is exactly what the Usual Way was.

It meant, first, that the number of tunes in common usage shrank to a very few (five or six, by most accounts), and that even these few were imperfectly remembered, so that local variations would develop, and fragments of one tune would find their way into another. It also meant that the pace of the music became slower and more erratic. There are probably two reasons for this. In the first place, in any communal singing that is not strongly led there is a tendency for each singer to sing in his or her own tempo, and this inevitably leads to a slowing of the general tempo in accommodation to the slowest singers.

But the pace of the tunes (originally, as has been indicated, probably quite lively) was also slowed by another development—the practice of "lining out" the psalms, which called for a deacon, or the pastor himself, to recite each line before it was sung by the congregation. This hoary practice had its beginnings in England and Scotland, where it was prescribed by authorities as an antidote to the forgetting of the words on the part of the congregations, many of whose members could not read. In time it became an established practice, and then a cherished one, clung to tenaciously even when no longer needed as a prop to memory. Lining out was apparently introduced to American psalm and hymn singing at the end of the seventeenth century. It is important to note that, as we shall presently see, it is practiced still, especially in rural churches.

Lining out naturally interrupted the flow and momentum of the tune, which had to be started up anew with each phrase. This was a decisive factor in slowing the tempo. Just how slow it became in extreme cases is difficult to determine. Critics are apt to exaggerate, but one observer noted, "I myself have twice in one Note paused to take Breath."

The slowing down led to another development: the embellishment of the tunes in folk fashion with passing notes, slides, turns, and other devices—what one scholar has termed a "compensatory florid filling in"—perhaps by the more talented, inventive (and impatient) singers. The practice has been colorfully described (by those opposed to it) as consisting of "many Turnings of, or Flourishes with the Voice" or a "Tittering up and down." One observer counted as many as a hundred and fifty notes in a tune that, in its written version, consisted of thirty.

There was, at that time, no concept of "folk," "folklore," or "folk practice"; but there is no doubt that this is exactly what it was: a way of singing, understood and cherished in common by a community, unwritten, and passed from one generation to another as an oral tradition. It was more pronounced, of course, in rural areas, where it persisted longest. If we were to search for a modern equivalent, it would be precisely in the "backwoods" that something at least analogous to it could be found today, in the singing in rural churches, chiefly in the South now—among the blacks or the mountain whites.[3]

Opposition to the Usual Way on the part of a more musically literate portion of the populace grew more outspoken as time went on, and came to a head in the 1720s. Those who favored reform were, as always, much more articulate than the "folk," who were perfectly content to enjoy what they had always known, and even highly suspicious of anything new. It has been pointed out that almost the only descriptions we have of the Usual Way come from those who were highly critical of it. They objected to the practice of lining out ("praising God by Peace-meal," as one critic put it), and they castigated the incompetence of the deacons who performed it.[4] They opposed the slow tempo and the florid embellishments that resulted. They also wanted to enlarge the repertoire of tunes in common use. To replace the Usual Way they promoted what was called "Regular Singing."

Reform and Instruction

What the reformers, or proponents of Regular Singing, wanted to make happen could be accomplished only by teaching people to read music. This is exactly what they set out to do. Instruction books such as *An Introduction to the Singing of Psalm Tunes in a Plain and Easy Method* (Rev. John Tufts) and *The Grounds and Rules of Musick Explained, or An Introduction to the Art of Singing by Note* (Rev. Thomas Walter) appeared in the 1720s, and went through many editions. As intimated in their titles, these books represented only the first of a long series of assaults by American ingenuity on the perennial problem of how to make music easier for the uninitiated. From *An Introduction in a Plain and Easy Method* through *Ragtime in Ten Easy Lessons* this elusive goal has been pursued—often, as we shall see, with some success. Tuft's device for removing some of the difficulties of reading ordinary notation was to place on the five-line staff not the customary note symbols, but letters standing for the four solmization syllables (fa, sol, la, mi), which had long been in common use by then. As rendered by Tufts, the tune of "Old 100th" looked like Example 5–4. Tuft's system was never widely adopted, but a related and still more ingenious device of using notes of various *shapes* to stand for the syllables became very widespread in rural America in the next century, as we shall see.

Example 5–4

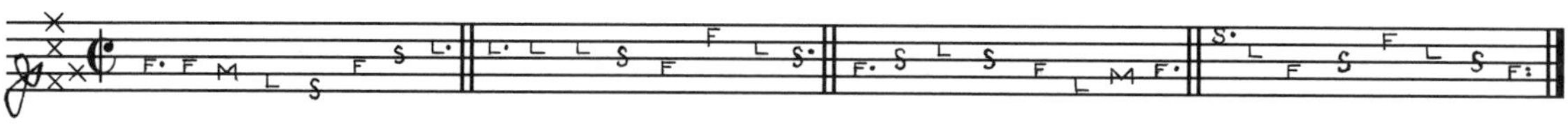

But no one has ever learned to perform music just by reading a book. The need for instruction by a "master," and for practicing together under his tutelage, produced one of the most important and pervasive musical (and social) institutions in our history—the singing-school.

The Singing-School Tradition

That uniquely American institution, the singing-school, may have had its beginnings in New England, but ultimately it spread far and wide. In the cities its descendants are represented by the numerous choral societies, great and small. In rural areas it retained its original characteristics longest; here, as a social as well as musical gathering, it brightened the routine of lives that were otherwise all too often harsh and dreary. The firm place and meaning of the singing-school in rural American life before this century can hardly be better attested to than by the following excerpt from the reminiscences, in folk verse form, of a pioneer woman writing of her life in Sangomon County, Illinois, in the mid-nineteenth century.

> We had so few things to give us pleasure
> The memories of such times I love to treasure.
> Our singing school, where we looked forward to meet
> Our beloved teacher, and his pupils to greet.
> Our singing books, few here now, ever saw
> The old patent notes, fa, sol, la, sol, fa, me, la.
> There were some good voices to lead the rest,
> All long since gone to the home of the blest.
> I seem to hear their voices now singing, loud and clear
> And almost feel their presence hovering near.

How the Singing Schools Worked

Organized instruction in singing by note was being offered in the colonies as early as 1719 (in Virginia). From the 1720s on, the movement gradually picked up momentum, and the period 1760 to 1800, encompassing the Revolution and the founding of the new nation, saw the greatest activity of the singing-school, especially in New England.

Just how did the singing-school function? There were many variations in the details, but basically it was a private venture, taught by an itinerant master. The school would be advertised in advance in the community, and subscriptions taken. There was usually a close relationship with the local church; sometimes the church would pay part of the cost of the school in return for the improvement of its choir. But the singing-school itself was not a denominational institution, and in fact the instruction did not always take place in the church; a room in a schoolhouse or local tavern was sometimes used. If the singing-master had published a tunebook the pupils would be expected to buy and use it, thus somewhat augmenting his income, which was seldom large.[5] The length of the term and the frequency of the meetings varied, of course, but two or three meetings a week for three months seems to have been common, at least in and around Boston.

As for the actual instruction, the solmization syllables (fa, sol, la, mi) were invariably taught as a basis for learning to sing the correct pitches, and the words of the pieces were not allowed to be sung until the syllables had been mastered. As an ingenious device for getting the tempo exact, homemade pendulums (of a length carefully specified) were recommended, and Billings gives the following directions for making them in the preface to his *Continental Harmony*:

> Make a pendulum of common thread well waxed, and instead of a bullet take a piece of heavy wood turned perfectly round, about the bigness of a pullet's egg, and rub them over, either with chalk, paint or white-wash, so that they may be seen plainly by candle-light.

(It was usually stipulated that the students bring their own candles.) At the close of the term, there was almost always a public concert, or "exhibition" (sometimes called a "singing lecture" if the minister or some other dignitary graced the occasion with an address on music). The pupils thus got a chance to show off what they had learned; the singing-master then moved on to another community.

Contemporary accounts show that the pupils were mostly young people. The importance of the singing-school as a social gathering has already been remarked; it seems, from the directions for the conduct of a singing-school that have survived, that the teacher's ability to keep order was at least as important as his ability to teach music—an observation that has a familiar ring in all periods. Yet, generally, there is little doubt that the singing-schools accomplished their objectives very well. After the term was over, one or more of the ablest pupils might start teaching themselves, or even try their hand at composing psalm settings, anthems, or fuging tunes.

The singing-schools had a great impact in raising the general level of musical literacy, in greatly expanding the repertory of music available, and, probably most important, in encouraging the development of native composers.

Billings of Boston and His Contemporaries

Not every singing-master became a composer, of course, but the number that did is substantial, and in fact the singing-school movement gave us our first school of indigenous American composers—who worked under the most fruitful conditions a composer can experience: writing music for which there is a clear demand and appreciation on the part of a well-defined public. This fruitful period for our first native composers did not last long—near-ideal conditions for art never do—but the productivity was intense (one scholar has termed it a "golden age"), for one authority has estimated that by 1800 there were over a thousand different compositions in print in American tunebooks, most of them by native composers.[6]

It should not be assumed, however, that teaching singing-schools and composing anthems was an occupation one could rely on as a sole source of livelihood. The singing-masters and composers were for the most part humble craftsmen, artisans, or small businessmen, who composed and taught in addition to plying their trades. They were among the first in the tradition of the American "amateur" composer—a tradition that, from William Billings to Charles Ives, has been such an important feature of American musical life, but has nearly disappeared in the past half-century. The names and trades of these "native pioneers," as Gilbert Chase has called them, read like a litany of eighteenth-century New England names and occupations, and perhaps helps to give the flavor of the singing-school movement in a way nothing else can: Supply Belcher, tavernkeeper; David Belknap, farmer and mechanic; William Billings, tanner; Amos Bull, storekeeper; Oliver Holden, carpenter; Jeremiah Ingalls, cooper; Jacob Kimball, lawyer; Abraham Maxim, farmer and schoolteacher; Justin Morgan, horse breeder; Daniel Read, storekeeper and maker of combs; Timothy Swan, hatter.[7]

William Billings (1746–1800), the best known among these, was also the most prolific, inventive, and enthusiastically dedicated. He was early apprenticed in the tanning trade, an occupation he pursued, except for brief intervals, throughout his life. But vocal music was his passion, which he indulged with indefatigable energy. In 1770, at the age of twenty-four, he published the first tunebook in America consisting entirely of music by a single composer: the famous *New-England Psalm-Singer* contained more than 120 compositions. In the next quarter-century he brought out five more books, whose titles give something of their flavor and usage: *The Singing Master's Assistant* (1778), *Music in Miniature* (1779), *The Psalm-Singer's Amusement* (1781), *The Suffolk Harmony* (1786), and *The Continental Harmony* (1794). All but one (*Music in Miniature*) consisted entirely of Billings's own compositions. They show an increasing mastery; he publicly deprecated some of the early compositions of *The New-England Psalm-Singer,* and consistently revised many of his own works in later publications. They also show an increasing tendency toward compositions of greater length, so that the later books contain fewer pieces.

He became quite well known in his time, and was certainly ranked as Boston's leading psalmodist. His fame spread outside New England; his works were performed in public concerts in Philadelphia, for example. Yet he was never able to give up his tanning trade permanently, and in fact records show him to have held down several civil posts in order to help make ends meet for himself and his family—posts such as Sealer of Leather for the city of Boston, and even jobs that had to do with keeping hogs off the streets, and keeping the streets clean in Boston's Eleventh Ward. He died in severe poverty.

Billings, a friend of Samuel Adams and Paul Revere, was an ardent patriot, and his patriotic song "Chester" (Example 5–5) was one of the most

Example 5–5

Original a fourth higher

Let ty - rants shake their i - ron rod,
And sla - v'ry clank her gall - ing chains;
We fear them not, we trust in God,
New Eng - land's God for - ev - er reigns.

popular songs of the Revolution. As a stirring tune it is worthy of being quoted—and sung. With its first stanza, it appeared in 1770 in *The New-England Psalm-Singer;* during the Revolution, further stanzas were added, with the names of five British generals, and the boast that "Their Vet'rans flee before our Youth,/ And Gen'rals yield to beardless Boys"—and it was in this form that it appeared in *The Singing Master's Assistant* of 1778.

Billings was a colorful and energetic writer of prose as well, as his salty, conversational, and sometimes lengthy prefaces to his tunebooks attest. His philosophical approach to music, as well as to politics, was one of independence and self-reliance. Oft-quoted statements of his—such as "Nature is the best Dictator"; "I don't think myself confin'd to any Rules for Composition laid down by any that went before me"; and "I think it best for every Composer to be his own Carver"—may, taken out of their own context and the context of his work, suggest a degree of rebellious iconoclasm far beyond Billings's actual intent, or what his works show. Nevertheless, he was among the first to sound here a note of independence that was more fully orchestrated half a century later by Emerson, and again a full century later by Charles Ives.

Perhaps the best summation of Billings as man and composer is contained in an entry in the diary of the Rev. William Bentley of Salem, made a few days after Billings's death. Bentley, one of America's best-educated men of his time, and a man of broad interests and accomplishments (Jefferson had thought of him for the presidency of the University of Virginia), moved in circles unfamiliar and even inaccessible to Billings. Nevertheless, his insight into Billings's work and importance moved him to write: "Many who have imitated have excelled him, but none of them had better original power. . . . He was a singular man, of moderate size, short of one leg, with one eye, without any address, & with an uncommon negligence of person. Still he spake & sung & thought as a man above the common abilities."*

Yankee Tunebooks by the Hundreds

Billings was but one among many. An examination of the singing-school period during its golden age gives an impression of tremendous activity and vitality. By 1810 about three hundred of the distinctive tunebooks, homely in appearance and typography, had been published. Their oblong shape gave rise to the terms "long boys" and "end-openers." The looks of their pages varied a great deal. The engraving could be clean and elegant, as in James Lyon's *Urania* (the first large-scale compilation, published in Philadelphia in 1761), or rather crude, as in Billings's *Psalm-Singer's Amusement*. The cheaper typesetting methods for music that were coming into use toward the end of the period produced the rather stiff appearance of Billings's later *Continental Harmony,* in which the staff lines come out as a series of dashes.

The titles of these old books tell us much. Some show the classical education or aspirations of their compilers: *Urania; Harmonia Americana.*

* The phrase "without any address" should not, despite his poverty, be taken as meaning that Billings was among the homeless. The phrase uses the word "address" in a sense now uncommon, and describes Billings as one who lacked either the capacity for "skillful management," or a tactful and cultivated manner of speaking, or possibly both.

Some of the titles show clearly the books' use and purpose: *The Musical Primer; The Easy Instructor, The Psalmodist's Assistant* (reminiscent of Billings's *Singing Master's Assistant*); *The Psalmodist's Companion; The Chorister's Companion*. Many bespeak their own locale: *The Massachusetts Compiler; The Vermont Harmony; The Harmony of Maine; The Worcester Collection of Sacred Harmony; The Essex Harmony*. The word "harmony" was widely used: *The American Harmony, The Northern Harmony; The Union Harmony; The Federal Harmony; The New England Harmony; The Christian Harmony;* and, as a final distillation, *The Harmony of Harmony*. To close the list, there appeared (with singular appropriateness to their environment) *The Rural Harmony* and *The Village Harmony*.

In view of their didactic purpose, most of the books begin with some sort of instruction in such rudiments of music as the scale or "gamut," the names of the pitches and their syllables, and an explanation of rhythmic values, followed sometimes by rudimentary vocal exercises, or "Lessons for tuning ye Voice." On occasion the introduction would be expanded by the inclusion of a kind of Socratic dialogue between "Master" and "Scholar"; Billings's voluble nature makes this section one of the longest (for example, in his *Continental Harmony*), and incidentally one of the most revealing and interesting, as he roams freely from technical musical questions to matters of performance practice and even to philosophical questions.[8]

The Music of the Tunebooks

What kind of pieces do we find in these tunebooks? The terms "psalmodist" and "psalm-singer" that appear in the titles must be understood as being applicable in the strict sense to only a limited proportion of the music. The venerable psalm tunes are well represented in some of the earlier collections (*Urania*, for example), but along with these appear the tunes for the short non-Scriptural *hymns* to original texts, and the larger and more ambitious *anthems*—more elaborate settings of Scriptural texts, adapted Scriptural texts, or original texts. It is evident that by this time hymnody had fairly well succeeded in replacing psalmody.

The *canon* (or *round*) does not appear frequently, although Billings has given us a beautiful example in his first publication, the justly famous "When Jesus Wept" (Example 5–6).[9]

Of particular interest are the famous *fuging tunes* (the term, though derived from *fugue*, was very possibly pronounced "fudging" in contemporary usage). The best simple description of the fuging tune is probably that of Alan Buechner, who writes of it as a piece that "begins like a hymn and ends like a round." It was the second section, or *fuge*, that was distinctive, with its rather informally constructed homespun imitative entrances of the voices. The fuging tune was very popular in its day: the effect of hearing the successive entrances coming from different parts of the U-shaped meeting-house gallery must have thrilled both singers and congregation alike. Billings describes these pieces as being "twenty times as powerful as the old slow tunes." Although he composed many himself, there were other composers of the time who favored them even more, and it has been found that over a thousand were published by 1810. The fuging tune later fell into disfavor among reformers of

Example 5–6

Original a major second higher

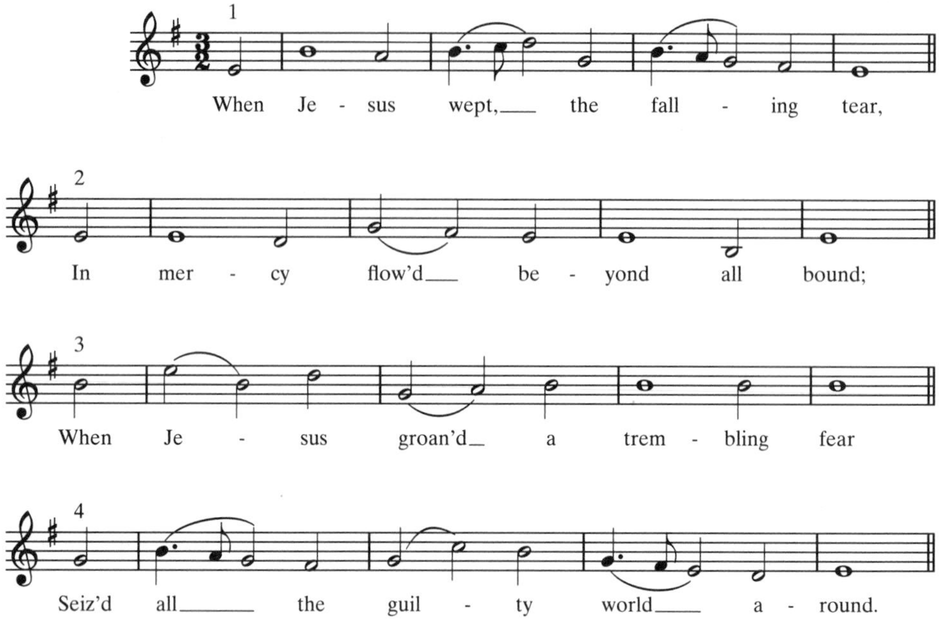
1
When Je - sus wept,___ the fall - ing tear,
2
In mer - cy flow'd___ be - yond all bound;
3
When Je - sus groan'd_ a trem - bling fear
4
Seiz'd all______ the guil - ty world____ a - round.

church music, who urged that it was both too crude and too lively as music for worship. But its appeal among the rural folk persisted, and fuging tunes in considerable numbers appear, as we shall see in the next chapter, in the shape-note songbooks of the nineteenth century.

A number of the larger anthems and set-pieces were written for specific occasions or observances—for Thanksgiving, for a Fast Day, for Ordination, for Christmas,[10] for Easter, for thanksgiving "after a victory," to commemorate the landing of the Pilgrims, and so on. Some were of a still more topical nature, as illustrated by Billings's famous "Lamentation Over Boston," a spirited paraphrase of Psalm 137 commemorating the British occupation of the city during the war. It begins:

> By the Rivers of Watertown we sat down & wept
> when we remembered thee—O Boston.
> As for our Friends Lord God of Heaven
> preserve them, defend them, deliver and
> restore them unto us again;
> For they that held them in Bondage
> Required of them to take up Arms against their Brethren.
> Forbid it Lord God that those who have
> sucked Bostonian Breasts should thirst for American
> Blood.[11]

The musical settings were practically all in the usual four parts: soprano (called "treble"), alto (called "counter"), tenor, and bass. In accordance with an already old practice, the melody was assigned not to the soprano but to the tenor. In actual performance, the distribution of parts among the voices was a matter of considerable flexibility; the tenor part could be sung (an octave higher, of course) by women as well as men, and the treble (an octave lower) by men as well as women. In the assignment of voices, it is evident that Billings himself preferred a somewhat "bottom-heavy" emphasis on the bass part, specifying "three or four deep voices suitable for the Bass to one for the upper parts." The bass part was also, as we shall see, often doubled on an instrument: a bass viol, cello, or bassoon.

The prejudice against instrumental music in the churches was strong, but instruments were gradually introduced before 1800 to support the voices. After the pitch pipe (to help the singers find the pitches) came the bass viol, though not without much controversy. (Churches using the "devil's fiddle" were branded as "cat-gut churches" at first.) Finally, the flute, clarinet, bassoon, and even the notorious violin (so much the secular instrument because of its use as an accompaniment to dancing) were admitted, and the small "gallery orchestra" evolved, being especially useful in churches that could not afford organs. Some pieces in the later nineteenth-century tunebooks even included, very occasionally, short sections for instruments alone, called "symphonies."

The End of an Era

By 1810, as McKay and Crawford have pointed out, a "reform" movement had successfully established a trend away from the native, unschooled, "innocent" art of the pioneer tradition, and toward the closer imitation of European models. Thus the first flourishing of indigenous musical art that America had experienced was pretty much over by then—at least in the cities.[12]

Much of the joy of the fuging tune and the anthem is felt most keenly by the singers themselves, and it cannot be too strongly emphasized that actually re-creating this music is by far the best way to understand and appreciate it. Fortunately, the availability of much of this music in modern editions, and its increasing popularity with church and amateur choirs, make it more accessible than at any time in the last century and a half. Hearing it sung is next best, and even through the thirdhand medium of recordings it is now possible to gain some experience of it; this, at least, is indispensable.[13]

Music Among Our Smaller Independent Sects

Conditions in America have been such as to nurture from the beginning, despite glaring episodes of intolerance and persecution, a lively tradition of religious independence and nonconformity. Many sects either have been transplanted to this country or have sprung up here, where, especially in the eighteenth and nineteenth centuries, they found the space necessary to provide the measure of isolation and self-sufficiency they so deeply desired. Not all of these numerous sects placed a particularly high value on music; some, like the Quakers, even abjured it. But there were a few to whom music was vitally important, and these sects cultivated music that often proved to be unique. The relatively small number of their adherents, as well as their relative isolation, has kept this music from significantly affecting the main development of American music. But they have contributed some vivid and irreplaceable patches to the quilt of a national music whose most salient characteristics are variety and nonconformity.

The Moravians

The most important of these sects musically was the Moravian Church, or *Unitas Fratrum,* to use the original name. It has had a venerable history, in both the Old and the New World. It was a pre-Reformation church, founded in what is now Czechoslovakia in the mid-fifteenth century by followers of the religious leader John Hus, who was burned as a heretic in 1415. Nearly exterminated during the bloody and disastrous Thirty Years' War of the seventeenth century, it emerged with new life in 1722, in exile from its native Bohemia and Moravia but under the protection of Count Nikolaus Ludwig von Zinzendorf of neighboring Saxony (in what is now East Germany). It was shortly after this that its history in the New World began, for the renewed *Unitas Fratrum* had a strong commitment to missionary work throughout the world. Its first mission on the mainland of the New World was established in Georgia in 1735. This was abandoned after five years, but meanwhile work was going on elsewhere, and an important settlement was founded at Bethlehem, Pennsylvania, in 1742, with others in North Carolina (Bethabara, Bethania, and Salem) beginning in 1753. Bethlehem and Salem (later incorporated into Winston-Salem) became—and remain—the two important centers of the Moravian Church in the United States.

Considering the Czech origin and early German influence on the Moravian Church, it is not surprising that music was a vital part of life for its adherents from the start. Hus himself encouraged congregational singing in the vernacular, and wrote and translated hymns. The *Unitas Fratrum* produced the first Protestant hymnal in 1501, a generation before Calvin's first psalter came into being, and the Moravians brought their rich musical tradition with them to America. The singing of hymns was an integral part of their daily life—in the family circle in the morning and evening, at work, or at the "love feasts," which were times of worship, fellowship, and song, where bread and drink were shared to the continuous accompaniment of music. Musical skills were taught and prized, and the cultivation of music even included the making of musical instruments. Not only did the Moravians perform the works of European composers of the day—Carl Friedrich Abel, Johann Stamitz, Joseph Haydn, as well as many obscure ones—but they produced a large share of their own music. Over thirty Moravian composers working in America have been identified. As in the case of the New England singing-school composers, these men were not professional musicians; most were ministers. The principal forms of music cultivated were the choral anthem, the solo song, and the hymn or *chorale,* the latter resembling very closely the Lutheran chorale. This music differed from that of the singing-school tradition in two important ways. First, it was more sophisticated musically, coming from a people who were much closer to the Germanic tradition that was the most advanced and dominant strain of European music of the time. (John Antes, for example, a Moravian composer and violinist, is said to have known Haydn and played in ensembles with him.)

Secondly, Moravian music was instrumental as well as vocal. The anthems and solo songs all had an orchestral accompaniment of strings, and a few winds were occasionally added. Almost all the music was religious, but a few examples of pure instrumental music have survived: string trios, string quintets, and a number of pieces for six wind instruments, ideal for informal outdoor music-making. The Collegium Musicum of Bethlehem may well have constituted the first symphony orchestra in the United States. Also famous were the trombone choirs, which played at funerals and on festive occasions. Their repertoire was mostly four-part chorales, often played—in the European tradition of "tower music"—from the church belfry. (One such performance was credited with repelling an attack by hostile Indians.)

By the mid-nineteenth century Moravian communities had become more secularized, tastes had changed, and the period of musical cultivation and creativity was largely over. The legacy of Moravian music was not rediscovered until the late 1930s in Bethlehem, and the 1950s in Winston-Salem.[14]

The Moravians furnish the most important example of a familiar phenomenon in the history of American music up until modern times: the more or less isolated, self-sufficient "pocket" of culture, relatively rich but destined to remain apart. In summarizing the Moravians' contribution, one eminent scholar has said: "Unfortunately for the history of American music, very little of this enormous quantity of music ever entered the stream of musical life in America."[15]

The Shakers

The most unusual of the sects to give much importance to music was the United Society of Believers in Christ's Second Appearing, commonly called the Shakers. The Society originated in the mid-eighteenth century as a kind of offshoot of Quakerism in the English Midlands, then in the throes of becoming industrialized. Its adherents were predominantly poor people who were attracted to its millennial teachings. Ann Lee, or "Mother Ann," as she came to be called, joined the Society in 1758 and soon became a dominant force in the movement. She and eight other members of the order came to America in 1774. In spite of persecution and imprisonment, by the time she died in 1784 eight Shaker communities had been established in New England and upstate New York. Their somewhat mystical teachings and practices included dedication to simplicity, humility, and service; communalism as regards property; equality of the sexes; celibacy; a reliance upon visions; and the importance of both song and dance in worship.

The order spread to the frontier during the first part of the nineteenth century (communities were founded in Kentucky, Ohio, and Indiana), where the spontaneity and abandoned fervor of its religious exercises accorded with the revivalism so prevalent there at the time. It reached its peak before the Civil War and declined afterwards; at this writing the only active religious community of Shakers left is at Sabbathday Lake, Maine.

The music of the Shakers represents, in all its aspects, a nearly pure folk art. Cut off by strict taboos in the beginning from almost all other music, the Believers had to evolve their own, out of improvisations and half-remembered scraps. For decades everything was in oral tradition; written music, which entailed the necessity of developing music reading, was not introduced until after 1800. In the early days, wordless songs were common; some of these obviously accompanied the movements and dancing of the fervent religious exercises.

Many songs were received in "visions"—a phenomenon also prevalent among the American Indians, as we have seen.[16] These vision songs often had texts comprised of meaningless syllables, in what were considered "unknown tongues." Some of the vision songs were said to be received from the spirits of people of other races—American Indians especially, but also Persians, Abyssinians, Hottentots, Laplanders, Eskimos, Chinese, and others. When the Shaker sisters and brothers became "instruments" of these spirits (who were seeking salvation) during a "manifestation," they would pantomime appropriate actions, such as Eskimos driving dogsleds. The "words" of one vision song, in an "unknown tongue," begin:

> O san-nisk-a-na nisk-a-na, haw, haw, haw,
>   fan-nick-a-na, haw, haw, haw.
> O san-nisk-a-na nisk-a-na yea se-ne-aw,
>   fan-a-na, nisk-a-na, haw, haw, haw.

Most Shaker singing was unharmonized and unaccompanied. Many of the songs used the primitive pentatonic scale, or the archaic modes, as described in Chapter 1. All these features identify the music closely with the folk tradition. As the repertory increased, it was inevitable that it be written down and then published. The first Shaker hymnal, *Millennial Praises,* was published in 1813. By this time, of course, borrowings and adaptations from other sources were quite evident; in particular the revivalism of the frontier had a considerable influence on the Shaker song repertory.

In concluding our consideration of the music of the Shakers, we cannot do better than to present two examples of this unique body of song, with the hope that, as with the other examples, they will be sung as well as looked at. The first, called "The Humble Heart" (Example 5–7), appeared in a hymnal from the New Lebanon, New York, community in 1822. It is a fine example of an old modal tune. The text (three of six verses are given) sets forth with rather felicitous imagery the Shaker philosophy.

Example 5–7

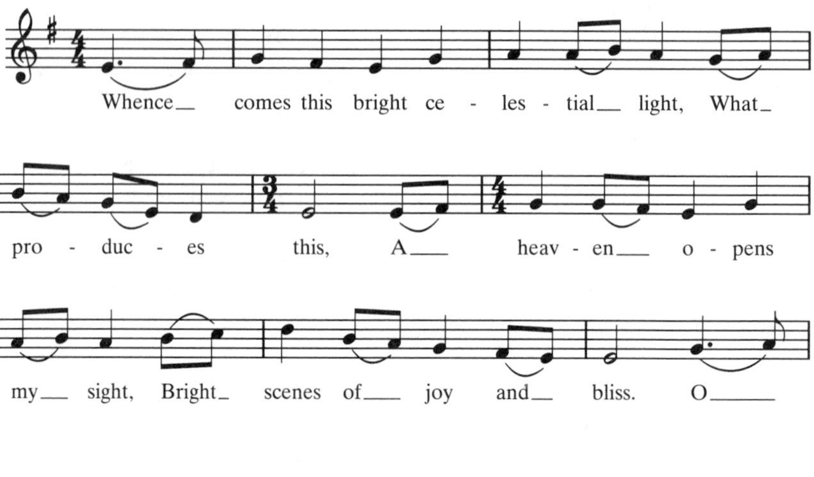

Lord Je - ho - vah_ art thou_ here. This_ light pro - claims_ thou
art, I_____ am___ in - deed, I'm___ al - ways
near Un - to the hum - ble heart.

Tall cedars fall before the wind,
The tempest breaks the oak,
While slender vines will bow and bend
And rise beneath the stroke.
I've chosen me one pleasant grove
And set my lovely vine,
Here in my vineyard I will rove,
The humble heart is mine.

Of all the fowls that beat the air
I've chose one little dove,
I've made her spotless white & fair,
The object of my love.
Her feathers are like purest gold,
With glory she does shine,
She is a beauty to behold,
Her humble heart is mine.[17]

One of the best known of all Shaker songs, both within the movement and without, is "Simple Gifts" (Example 5–8).[18] This song gives expression to the basic Shaker themes of simplicity and humility. In both words and music it stands as a consummate achievement of innocent religious art. Edward Deming Andrews, the uniquely qualified authority on Shaker music, dance, and ritual, has written: "Shaker ritualism was a true folk art." Elaborating further on its peculiar intensity, freedom, and imagery, he states:

> In no other way, in fact, could the restrained Shaker spirit find such freedom of expression. The Believer was disciplined to a precise and simplified functionalism in the crafts; in industry he followed strict routines and traditions; he was inhibited by the doctrinal taboos on recreation, reading, and intercourse with the world and the opposite sex; the normal sex impulses were suppressed by the great basic principle of the faith. But in songs and operations of worship the urge to play, to love, to create, found release in ways which revealed the very soul of the individual and the essential ethos of the sect.[19]

Example 5–8

'Tis the gift to be sim-ple, 'tis the gift to be free, 'Tis the
gift to come down where we ought to be, And when we find our-selves in the
place just right, 'Twill be in the val - ley of love and de-light. When true sim -
-pli - ci - ty is gained, To bow and to bend we shan't be a-sham'd, To
turn, turn will be our de-light, 'till by turn - ing, turn - ing we come round right.

Further Reading

Psalmody and the Singing-schools

Facsimile Editions

The following modern facsimile reprints of important old books are interesting and give us ready access to the only kinds of sources we have for an indispensable firsthand acquaintance with this music. Arranged in chronological order these are:

The Bay Psalm Book. Boston, 1640. Reprint, Chicago: University of Chicago Press, 1956.
The first book published in the United States—a new metrical translation of the psalms. Editions before the ninth, in 1698, contained no music.

Tufts, John. *An Introduction to the Singing of Psalm Tunes*. 5th ed. Boston, 1726. Reprint, Philadelphia: Musical Americana, 1954.
One of the earliest instruction books, using the four syllables (fa-so-la-mi) on the staff in place of conventional notes. The tunes are harmonized in three parts.

Lyon, James. *Urania*. Philadelphia, 1761. Reprint, New York: Da Capo, 1974.

Billings, William. *The Psalm-Singer's Amusement*. Boston, 1781. Reprint, New York: Da Capo, 1974.

———. *The Continental Harmony*. Boston, 1794. Reprint, Cambridge, MA: Harvard University Press, 1961, with an introduction by Hans Nathan.

Belcher, Supply. *The Harmony of Maine*. Boston, 1794. Reprint, New York: Da Capo. 1972.

Modern editions of music, including scholarly editions and anthologies

The Music of Henry Ainsworth's Psalter (Amsterdam, 1612). Edited by Lorraine Inserra and H. Wiley Hitchcock. I.S.A.M. Monograph no. 15. Institute for Studies in American Music, 1975.
Contains both facsimiles and transcriptions of all the thirty-nine tunes, with extensive commentary, and a table of the tune sources. This largely replaces the Pratt edition, below, which is out of print but is available in many libraries.

The Music of the Bay Psalm Book, 9th edition (1698). Edited by Richard G. Appel. I.S.A.M. Monograph no. 5. Brooklyn: Institute for Studies in American Music, 1975.
This contains both facsimiles and transcriptions in modern notation of the 11-page supplement to the 9th edition (the first to include music) of the Bay Psalm Book, preceded by a short commentary.

Billings, William. *The Complete Works of William Billings*. Boston: American Musicological Society and Colonial Society of Massachusetts, 1981.
A scholarly edition in four volumes with very extensive notes by the editor, Karl Kroeger.

Crawford, Richard A. *The Core Repertory of Early American Psalmody*. Recent Researches in American Music, vols 11 and 12. Madison, WI: A-R Editions, 1984.
A scholarly collection, with an extensive introduction, commentary and appendices, of the 101 sacred compositions most frequently printed in America between 1698 and 1810, thus exemplifying the basic concept of a "core repertory."

Marrocco, W. Thomas, and Harold Gleason, eds. *Music in America*. New York: W. W. Norton, 1964.
A basic anthology for American music up to the Civil War, with an excellent selection of psalm tunes and singing-school music. The notes are also valuable.

Pratt, Waldo Selden. *The Music of the Pilgrims*. Boston: Oliver Ditson, 1921.
Includes a transcription of the complete music of the Ainsworth Psalter, with excellent notes and a representative selection of texts. Though out of print, and superseded by the Inserra and Hitchcock edition listed above, it can still be found in many libraries.

In addition, many publishers with substantial sacred choral music catalogs now include editions of music from the New England singing-school tradition. An example is Concordia, of St. Louis, which has a rather extensive series, *Sacred Choral Music from Colonial America by William Billings*, with useful notes.

Studies, some with incidental musical examples

Barbour, J. Murray. *The Church Music of William Billings*. East Lansing: Michigan State University Press, 1960.
A thorough musicological study that has become a basic work for scholars, and is unlikely to be supplanted for some time.

Buechner, Alan C. Notes to the record album *The New England Harmony*. Folkways FA-2377 (1964).
This excellent 32-page booklet has much valuable information on the singing school tradition, on which the author wrote a doctoral dissertation at Harvard in 1960. The booklet is available separately from Folkways, although the record album is nearly indispensable as well.

Crawford, Richard A. *Andrew Law, American Psalmodist*. Evanston, IL: Northwestern University Press, 1968.

Daniel, Ralph T. *The Anthem in New England Before 1800*. Evanston, IL: Northwestern University Press, 1965.

Foote, Henry Wilder. *Three Centuries of American Hymnody*. Hamden, CT: Shoe String Press, 1940. Reprint, 1961. Chapters 1–5.

Lowens, Irving. *Music and Musicians in Early America*. New York: W. W. Norton, 1964. Chapters 2, 3, 8, 14, 18.
A collection of valuable articles by one

of the most eminent scholars in American music.

MacDougall, Hamilton C. *Early New England Psalmody*. Brattleboro, VT, 1940. Reprint, New York: Da Capo, 1969.

McKay, David P., and Richard Crawford. *William Billings of Boston: Eighteenth-Century Composer*. Princeton, NJ: Princeton University Press, 1975.
A fine and very readable addition to work in the field of the Yankee singing-school. It includes much valuable background information, including a complete survey of sacred music in New England to the time of Billings. It is now a basic work on Billings himself and his time.

Scholes, Percy A. *The Puritans and Music in England and New England*. Oxford, England: Clarendon Press, 1934. Reprint, New York: Russell & Russell, 1962.
A valuable and copiously documented treatise correcting the stereotype of the Puritans as being universally and implacably opposed to music, the fine arts in general, and the appreciation of beauty.

Stevenson, Robert. *Protestant Church Music in America*. New York: W. W. Norton, 1966. Paperback, 1970. Chapters 1, 2, 3, 7.
A brief but invaluable survey, written with a broad perspective of the subject by a noted scholar. Begins with the all-but-forgotten Huguenot settlements in Florida more than half a century before the landing of the Pilgrims. Excellent bibliography.

Articles

Murray, Sterling E. "Timothy Swan and Yankee Psalmody," *Musical Quarterly*, vol. 61, no. 3 (July 1975).

Osterhout, Paul R. "Note Reading and Regular Singing in Eighteenth-Century New England," *American Music*, vol. 4, no. 2 (Summer 1986).

Wolf, Edward C. "Two Divergent Traditions of German-American Hymnody in Maryland circa 1800," *American Music*, vol. 3, no. 3 (Fall 1985).

Our Smaller Independent Sects

The Moravians

The best source of information on Moravian music is the Moravian Music Foundation, Winston-Salem, NC. It issues lists of the published music, of which there is by now a considerable amount, from various publishers. The foundation has also to date issued seven short monographs, of which *The Moravian Contribution to American Music* (no. 1) and *A Moravian Music Sampler* (no. 7) are probably of the greatest general interest.

Two pamphlets useful for background information on the Moravians are:

Davis, Chester S. *Hidden Seed and Harvest: A History of the Moravians*. Winston-Salem, NC: Wachovia Historical Society, 1973.

Weinlick, John R. *The Moravian Church Through the Ages*. Bethlehem, PA, and Winston-Salem, NC: Comenius Press, 1966.

Also relevant is:

Marrocco and Gleason, *Music in America*, (see above). Chapter 3 includes six examples of Moravian music.

The Shakers

Andrews, Edward Deming. *The Gift to be Simple: Songs, Dances and Rituals of the American Shakers*. Locust Valley, NY, 1940. Reprint, New York: Dover, 1962.
A short study including seventy complete songs; a good introduction, now subordinate to Patterson (below) in the extensiveness of its coverage.

Hall, Roger L., ed. *The Happy Journey: Thirty-five Shaker Spirituals Compiled by*

Miss Clara Endicott Sears. Harvard, MA: Fruitlands Museums, 1982.

Patterson, Daniel W. *The Shaker Spiritual*. Princeton, NJ: Princeton University Press, 1979.
An extensive and definitive study of the music of the Shakers, based on the examination not only of printed sources, but of 798 manuscript collections from the various Shaker communities. Includes extensive commentary.

Listening

Early Psalmody

Early American Psalmody. The Margaret Dodd Singers. *Music in America* series: MIA-102.
Issued by the Society for the Preservation of the American Musical Heritage. Eight psalm tunes. Each tune is sung first in unison, with a precentor "setting the tune" for each line (i.e., singing it, in contrast with the more common practice of "lining out," which was a mere reading of each line). This is followed by harmonized versions from European sources. The performance is polished, with impeccable rhythm and ensemble —far too much so, in fact, to convey an idea of what congregational singing must have really been like in seventeenth-century New England.

Music of the Pilgrims. Haydn Society HSL-2068.
Side 1 presents nine psalms from the Ainsworth Psalter, interspersed with narration in the form of excerpts from Governor William Bradford's *Of Plimoth Plantation*. The performance, although too well drilled to be historically realistic, is spirited, and conveys well the lively rhythms of the old French tunes.

For a more realistic evocation of the "Usual Way" as it still exists in living tradition, listen to the singing on *The Gospel Ship*, NW-294, and "Amazing Grace" on *Mountain Music of Kentucky*, Folkways FA-2317.

The Usual Way of psalm singing persists to this day in the Free Church of Scotland, especially in the Outer Hebrides. This has been recorded in *Gaelic Psalmody Recital*, vols. 1 and 2 (cassette) produced by Lewis Recordings, Stornoway, Isle of Lewis, Scotland.

The Singing-School Tradition

Choral Music in Colonial America, University of Utah Chorale and Chorus. *Music in America* series: MIA-114.
Anthems by William Billings and Daniel Read. Credit is due to this early and worthy venture in re-creating this music. The performance is polished, anachronistic (for example, in its use of organ), and, unfortunately, dull.

The New England Harmony: A Collection of Early American Choral Music. Folkways FA-2377.
This excellent album of music recorded in the meeting house at Old Sturbridge Village, Massachusetts, in 1964, includes twenty-six pieces by Billings and his contemporaries. A medium-sized chorus of nonprofessional singers recruited from local church and school choirs is used, and this is surely indicative of the right way to perform this music. For instrumental accompaniment on a few of the pieces, a small re-creation of a "gallery orchestra" is used—five performances at most. The notes by Alan Buechner are excellent.

Make a Joyful Noise: Mainstreams and Backwaters of American Psalmody. NW-255.
Seventeen compositions by Billings and

his contemporaries; notes by Richard Crawford.

Vermont Harmony. Philo 1000.
Complete published works of Justin Morgan, and some by other Vermont composers of the late eighteenth century. The complete music for both this and Vermont 2 (below) is available from the producers, Philo Records.

Vermont Harmony 2. Philo 1038.

The Moravians

Music of the American Moravians, the Moravian Festival Chorus and Orchestra: Thor Johnson, conductor. Columbia Odyssey 32-16-0340.
An excellent "sampler" of solo, choral, and instrumental music.

American Colonial Instrumental Music. Folkways FH-5109.
Includes two string quintets by Johann Friedrich Peter, a Moravian.

The Flowering of Vocal Music in America, vol. 1: *The Moravians and Anthony Philip Heinrich*. NW-230.
Ten vocal selections, most with string orchestra; notes by Edward Berlin.

Vocal Music in Colonial America: The Moravians. MIA-98.
One of a series produced by the Society for the Preservation of the American Musical Heritage; out of print, but in many library collections.

The Shakers

Music of the Shakers. Folkways FH-5378.

Brave Boys: New England Traditions in Folk Music. NW-239.
Includes two Shaker songs.

Early Shaker Spirituals, Sung by Sister Mildred Barker and other members of the Sabbathday Lake community in Maine; notes by Daniel W. Patterson. Rounder 0078.

PROJECTS

1. Compare very succinctly the early musical traditions of the three major branches of the Reformation: the Reformed (Calvinist), the Lutheran, and the Anglican. Explain which had the most effect on early American music, and why.

2. If you like to sing folk songs, learn a psalm tune (from those reprinted in Marrocco and Gleason, *Music in America*, or from the Ainsworth Psalter as reproduced in Pratt, *The Music of the Pilgrims*, or any other authentic source); fit a psalm text of the same poetic meter to it from the Bay Psalm Book (or any other early translation); and add it to your repertoire. You may sacrifice historical authenticity to the extent of contriving a tasteful accompaniment to it on the guitar if you wish.

3. John Hus, John Calvin, Isaac Watts—none of these men were musicians, and none ever saw the New World, yet each had a definite influence on American music. Write a brief paper on any one of them, identifying him and tracing his influence.

4. Find three psalm tunes (*besides* "Old 100th"!) that are still in use and appear in modern hymn collections in this country. Find out as much as you can about the origins of the tunes, and in which early psalters they appeared. Find and consult early versions of the tunes if possible. (Most hymnals have a good index of composers and sources, which can help, as can the index of tune names. The *Hymnal of the Protestant Episcopal Church in the U.S.A.*, for example, is rather rich in tunes from the old psalters of the sixteenth and seventeenth centuries.)

5. If you read and write music, transcribe two psalm tunes from John Tufts, *An Introduction to the Singing of Psalm Tunes*, 5th ed., into regular musical notation. Sing or play the tunes (or have them sung or played) for the class, and explain Tuft's syllable system for learning music. (You can reproduce just the melody—"cantus"—or the entire three-part setting as Tufts arranged it.)

6. Read Williams Billings's prefaces to his *Continental Harmony*—both "To the several Teachers of MUSIC, in this and the adjacent States" and "A Commentary on the preceding Rules: by way of Dialogue, between Master and Scholar." Comment on what these treatises seem to say about Billings himself: his sense of humor, his ability and ingenuity as a teacher, and his views on music, especially vocal music.

7. Compile a biographical listing of at least five of the New England singing-school composers of the Colonial and Federal periods (besides Billings), listing their nonmusical occupations, some other biographical data, and some of their compositions.

8. Do an informal survey in your immediate area on the extent to which music of the New England singing-school composers is included in the repertoire of church choirs. (Much of it is now available in modern performing editions.) If it is being sung, arrange to hear some of it. If not, perhaps you know a choir director who would be sympathetic to introducing some.

9. Make a study of Hussite hymns (those of the pre-Reformation precursors of the Moravians), noting their relationship to those of the later Lutherans.

10. Investigate and trace the relationship between John Wesley, founder of Methodism, and the Moravians, especially with regard to church music.

11. Make a study of music in the Moravian church today, and to what extent the Moravians incorporate into present-day services the music of their heritage.

12. Investigate music among a small independent sect other than those treated in this chapter. Examples would be the Seventh-Day Baptists of the Ephrata Cloister, the Mennonites, or the followers of Johannes Kelpius (the "Hermit of the Wissahickon").

13. Make a brief study of German Pietism and its effect on the music of its time.

14. Make a study of Shaker handicraft. Compare its characteristics with those of Shaker music.

15. Assemble some accounts of Shaker community life and ritual as recorded by outsiders who visited them. Try to included references or accounts by some of their famous visitors, such as Lafayette, Horace Greeley, Walt Whitman, or William Dean Howells. Consult the bibliography in Andrews, *The Gift to Be Simple.*

6

Religious Music During and After the Time of Expansion

AMERICA's expansion, which can be said to have begun in earnest with the opening of the nineteenth century, manifested itself in two vitally significant directions at once: in the growth of our cities in size, complexity, and sophistication; and in the continuous rolling westward of our frontier. Both had profound effects on American thought, life, and art—including our indigenous religious music. We shall trace some of these developments in this chapter, exploring in the process the unique legacy of music—hymns, spiritual songs, and revival songs—that we have inherited from this tumultuous time of expansion and change. We shall end with an examination in some detail of gospel music, the twentieth-century heir to this populist tradition.

The Native Tradition Suppressed in the Urban East

With the growth of cities, many urban churchgoers became increasingly sophisticated. They were being made more acutely aware of European music by outspoken musicians, both native-born and immigrant, who if they were not trained in its conventions were at least aware of its more highly cultivated style, which they conceived as being more appropriate for worship. There developed, beginning about the turn of the century, what has been described as an "anti-American" sentiment regarding music. Though this may have been the first widespread expression of the conviction that America was culturally inferior to Europe, it was far from the last. (Emerson railed against this conviction in the mid-nineteenth century, and Ives in the early twentieth; it plagues us still in some quarters.)

Andrew Law, a university-educated Congregational minister who was a composer, singing-school teacher, and noted compiler of tunebooks, virtually led off the campaign, when, as early as 1794, he wrote that "American music is extremely faulty," and expressed regret that the products of native composers such as Billings "are actually preferred, and have taken a general run, to the great prejudice of much better music, produced even in this country, and almost to the utter exclusion of genuine European compositions."

The charge of being "unscientific" was leveled at American compositions, and tunebooks for urban consumption compiled after 1810 show a marked decrease in the number of American works they included, with a corresponding increase in European hymns and anthems, often by second-rate composers. The fuging tune especially was castigated. As an example, the Methodist Episcopal Church voiced mild disapproval even before 1800, stating in one publication: "We do not think that fuge-tunes are sinful, or improper to be used in private companies: but do not approve of their being used in our public congregations." In 1807 the preface of a new compilation characterized the fuging tunes as "those wild fugues, and rapid and confused movements, which have so long been the disgrace of congregational psalmody."[1]

Of European influences, the English was of course predominant, as represented not only by Handel but by such lesser lights as Samuel Arnold, William Croft, William Boyce, Martin Madan, and Robert Wainwright. The German-Austrian influence also began to loom with prophetic strength. There were those who defended the virtues of the homespun Yankee tunes and their composers; some of this music was even reprinted in special collections in Boston throughout the nineteenth century. But for the most part, at least in the cities, it was true that, as one observer wrote in 1848, "the good old days of New England music have passed away, and the singing-masters who compose and teach it, are known only in history as an extinct race."[2]

The Frontier and Rural America in the Nineteenth Century

That the music of the New Englanders was in fact far from extinct is now clear to us. As is often the case, in the rural areas the "old ways"—and the old music—were clung to tenaciously long after they had been replaced in the cities. And the frontier, southwestward into the long valleys of the Appalachians and beyond into the broad river valleys of the Ohio and the Tennessee, was an extension of rural America. We can follow the movement of the singing school tradition along these paths just by tracing the continued appearance of its odd oblong books of tunes. Moving out of Boston and Philadelphia, we find compilations being made in Harrisburg, Pennsylvania; in the Shenandoah Valley of Virginia; in Hamilton, Georgia; in Spartanburg, South Carolina; in Lexington, Kentucky; in Nashville, in Cincinnati, in St. Louis. The titles tell a story of both continuity and movement. As lineal descendants of *The New England Harmony* and *The Harmony of Maine*, we find *The Virginia Harmony, The Kentucky Harmony, the Knoxville Harmony, the Missouri Harmony, The Western Lyre, The Southern Harmony*, and, finally, the famous *Sacred Harp*. These books clearly revealed their ancestry—in their shape and appearance; in their prefatory introductions to the "Rudiments of Music"; in their continued use of the four solmization syllables (fa, sol, la, mi); in their hymns in three and four parts, with the melody buried in the middle of the texture in the tenor voice; and in their sprinkling of more ambitious anthems and fuging tunes. Pieces by Billings himself were almost invariably included; far from being "extinct," as the Boston editor lamented in the middle of the nineteenth century, William Billings and some of his contemporaries have turned out to be the most continuously performed composers in American history. Indeed, their music has already entered its third century.

The singing-schools continued to flourish in the nineteenth century, fulfilling their dual musical and social function much as they had done in New England in Colonial times. Later came the institution of annual gatherings, or "singings," some lasting two or three days, with "dinner on the grounds" a fixed feature.

Thus we see that the "old ways" did not die. Two important additions were made, however, as the native tradition moved out of the East into the South and West, One was the development of the famous shape notes, and the other was the infusion of the folk element into the music.

The Shape Notes

We have already noted the perennial attempts to simplify and speed up the process of teaching people to read music through various modifications of musical notation, beginning with John Tufts's system in Boston in the early eighteenth century (see Chapter 5). It has been pointed out that in this country these attempts have almost always been associated with religious music, for the encouragement and improvement of the democratic institution of congregational singing. There appeared in 1801 in a book by William Little and William Smith called, appropriately, *The Easy Instructor,* which introduced a simple but ingenious device that proved to be eminently practical. This consisted of the use of differently shaped notes for each of the four syllables then in use to indicate degrees of the scale. In the key of F major, for example, the scale with its syllables would look like Example 6–1. This system proved to be a successful blend of conventionality and novelty. The staff, with all its advantages of visual orientation, was preserved; key signatures and accidentals were provided for; and the troublesome problems inherent in inventing a new rhythmic notation were avoided, because the rhythmic values of the notes could still be rendered in the conventional way—only the shapes of the note heads were affected.

Example 6–1

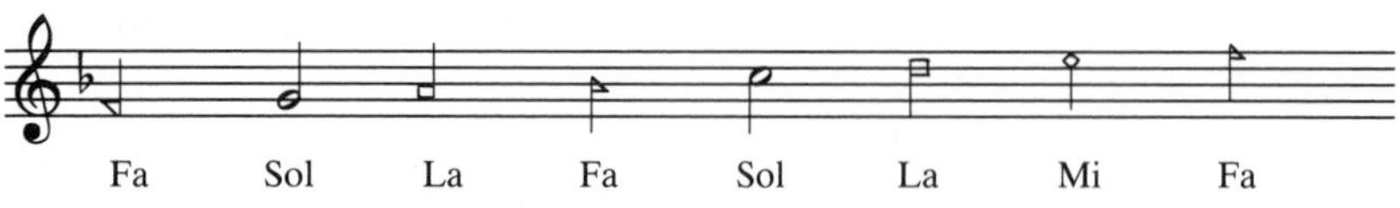

The device appears to have caught on rather quickly and well. *The Easy Instructor* was reissued in various editions (though its ownership changed hands) for thirty years; by the time it ceased publication there were at least eighteen other songbooks in print using the same device (many times that number, if one takes into account the numerous editions most of these books went through). In 1816, in an attempt to secure the protection that the short duration of copyrights in those days (fourteen years) failed to provide, the shape-note device was actually patented—hence the term "patent notes."

The Easy Instructor was first published in the urban East (Philadelphia). The shape-note method was so readily adopted by the compilers of the traditional rural songbooks, however, that the notation soon became associated exclusively with this tradition, and for reasons probably having largely to do with this association was in disfavor in urban circles of more "advanced" or "scientific" religious music. Thomas Hastings (of "Rock of Ages" fame) dubbed the shape notation "dunce notes." So it was that this quaint but practical device for learning to sing the pitches quickly and accurately became so indelibly associated with the rural tradition, and particularly with the South, that its vast literature—for so long all but unknown to outsiders—has taken on the name "southern shape-note hymnody."[3]

Infusion of the Folk Element

Another important development as this rural hymnody moved southwest at the beginning of the nineteenth century was a fresh infusion of the folk element into the tune collections. Folk or folkish tunes of Anglo-Celtic cast, given sacred words and spare, austere harmonic settings, were found in the new books, alongside the established hymn tunes, anthems, and fuging tunes. This had actually already begun in New England. Jeremiah Ingalls, for example, in his *Christian Harmony* (Vermont, 1805), put sacred words to what was plainly a rollicking dance tune from the fiddlers' repertory (Example 6–2). George Pullen Jackson, who has done more than anyone else to bring this music to light, has said of Ingalls's contribution: "The conviction is unavoidable, after singing these romping tunes, that Ingalls was a musical daredevil. It is evident that he was the first in this land to dare put between the covers of a book those capering songs which others had had the courage merely to sing."[4]

The "borrowing" of folk tunes to supply the needs of sacred music—"plundering the carnal lover"—is a venerable practice, of course. The great body of Lutheran chorale tunes, for example, contains its share of melodies that began life as folk or popular tunes, in some cases love songs.[5]

An influential publication in which many folk hymns, as these came to be called, made their first appearance was John Wyeth's *Repository of Sacred Music, Part II*, published in Harrisburg, Pennsylvania, in 1813. It was evidently produced to satisfy the demand and taste of those congregations, mostly Methodists and Baptists, who sang these folk hymns and who took part in the revivalism that was so memorable a feature of rural and frontier life in America at this time. Issuing from a town that lay in the path of southwestward migration, it was remarkably successful, since it was said to have sold 25,000 copies.

One tune that was designated as "new" in this collection was "Rockingham," which was reprinted in several later books. The version in Example 6–3

Example 6–2

Come_ we that love the_ Lord_ in - deed, Who_
are from sin and bond - age_ freed; Sub - mit to_ all the_
ways_ of_ God, and walk_ this_ nar - row_ hap - py road. Great_
tri - bu - la - tion_ you_ shall_ meet, But_ soon shall walk the
gold - en_ street, Tho' hell may_ rage and_ vent_ her_ spite, Yet
Christ_ will_ save_ his_ heart's de - light.

from *The Southern Harmony,* is interesting because of the compiler's attempt to approximate in notation, through the use of eighth notes and grace notes, the manner in which this tune was probably actually sung in oral tradition.

Example 6–3

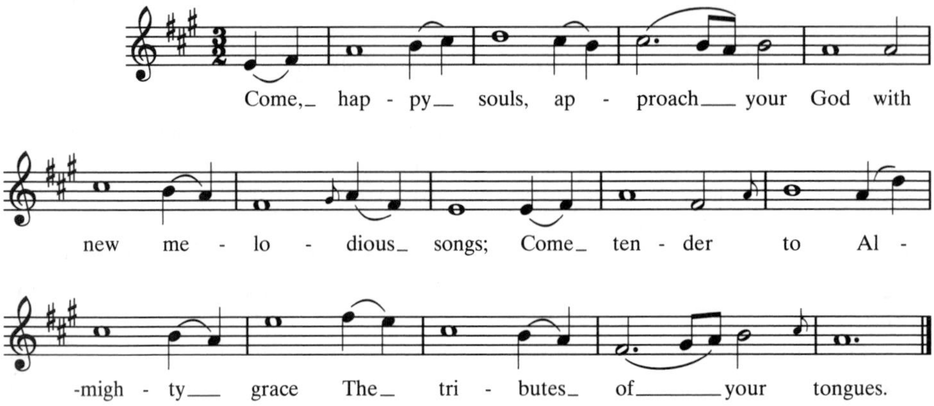
Come,_ hap - py_ souls, ap - proach_ your God with
new me - lo - dious_ songs; Come_ ten - der to Al -
-migh - ty_ grace The_ tri - butes_ of_ your tongues.

The procession of these books that followed in the next decades has already been alluded to. Nearly forty tunebooks, some in several editions, were published before the Civil War using the four-shape notation and including folk hymns. Of these, the two most influential were *The Southern Harmony* (1835), compiled by William ("Singin' Billy") Walker, of Spartanburg, South Carolina, and *The Sacred Harp* (1844), by Benjamin Franklin White and E. J. King, of Hamilton, Georgia. *The Sacred Harp,* which has gone through many editions and revisions, has outlasted all the others and has stayed in continuous use for almost a century and a half.

A folklike melody of unknown origin variously known as "Harmony Grove," "New Britain," "Redemption," "Symphony," or "Solon" appeared in shape-note hymnody at least as early as 1831 in *The Virginia Harmony,* with a text beginning

> There is a land of pure delight
> Where saints immortal reign.

It became far better known with the text that was later associated with it, which has given it the title by which we know it—"Amazing Grace" (Example 6–4).[6]

Example 6–4

Original a fourth higher

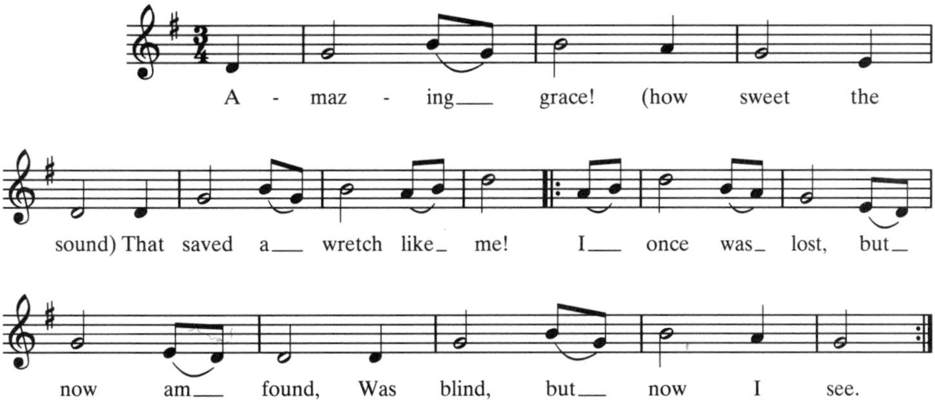

In certain cases the secular counterpart of a folk hymn can be identified. The modal tune in Example 6–5 was still called "Captain Kidd" when it was first printed in William Walker's *Southern Harmony* in 1835.

Example 6–5

Through all the world be - low, God is seen all a -
-round; Search__ hills and val - leys through, There he's found.
The grow - ing of the corn, The__ li - ly and the
thorn, The____ plea - sant and for - lorn, All de - clare God is
there, In the mea - dows drest in green, There he's seen.

The tune was originally associated with a broadside ballad composed on the occasion of the hanging of Captain Kidd for piracy in London in 1701. The first of at least nine verses runs as follows:

My name was Robert Kidd,
As I sailed, as I sailed,
My name was Robert Kidd,
As I sailed,
My name was Robert Kidd
And God's laws I did forbid,
And much wickedness I did,
As I sailed, as I sailed,
And much wickedness I did,
As I sailed.

Another aspect of the folkishness of these hymns as they appeared in the old tunebooks was the harmonic setting, which abounds in the austere open consonances (octaves, fifths, fourths). The voice leading often yokes two or more voices together in parallel movement at these intervals—a practice scrupulously avoided in academically "correct" harmony. The spare openness of the harmonic texture contributes as much as the modality of the tunes, to the distinctiveness of this music, which must be actually *heard* to establish any basis for its understanding. This style is nowhere better illustrated than in the three-voice setting of the famous folk hymn "Wondrous Love," as found in *The Southern Harmony* (Example 6–6.)[7]

Example 6–6

252
WONDROUS LOVE. 12, 9, 6, 6, 12, 9
Christopher.
What won-drous love is this, oh! my soul! oh! my soul! What won-drous love is this, oh! my soul! What won-drous love is this! That
caused the Lord of bliss, To bear the dread-ful curse for my soul, for my soul, To bear the dread-ful curse for my soul.

The fact is that this music is in some ways unlike any other music that was heard in the nineteenth century. It was almost as though the "primitive" musical craftsmen who harmonized the folk hymns, isolated to a considerable degree from the mainstream of cultivated music, were called upon to solve anew the problems of polyphonic music. The unique style that resulted from their solution resembles in some rather striking ways the church music of medieval Europe, with its primal reliance on the open consonances, the parallelism of its organum[8] (a kind of pre-counterpoint), and its basically polyphonic conception of musical texture as the simultaneous sounding of individual sung lines, rather than a succession of chords. It is also interesting to note that some American composers in the 1930s and 1940s, such as Aaron Copland and Virgil Thomson, writing at a time when American classical music had begun to find its own voice, would tend to adopt similarly lean textures and sounds.

Revivalism and the Camp Meeting

The successive waves of religious revivalism that have swept America since 1800 have had a decided impact on our indigenous religious music. This was most pronounced in the period of the expanding frontier before the Civil War, for it was on the frontier that revivalism nurtured its most striking manifestation: the camp meeting. The camp meeting in turn nurtured, for its own needs, one of our most distinctive forms of religious music: the revival spiritual. In order to understand the origin, nature, and function of the revival spiritual, it will be useful for a moment to turn our attention to the camp meeting itself, to see how it evolved and functioned and learn something of what it meant in the lives of the sincere believers who attended.

The Colonial South was far from being a devout society. The fundamentalist faith that later became so ingrained there was established as a result of two factors. One was the hardship of what amounted to a frontier existence throughout the antebellum South for the "plain folk" who made up the bulk of the population—mostly white subsistence farmers, who were continually forced to move and take up less arable land as the large slave-worked plantations spread into the fertile lowlands. This kind of existence bred a need for the reassurance and consolation that could be supplied by an evangelical religion—a religion that held out the promise in the hereafter of all the good that was so elusive and pitifully transient in the here-and-now. The other factor was the unremitting effort of the three most popular denominations after the Revolution: the Presbyterians, the Baptists, and the Methodists (the latter most especially, with their organized hierarchy and their corps of indefatigable circuit-riding preachers). These two factors set the stage for the Great Revival of the early nineteenth century.

At its beginning it was called the Kentucky Revival, for that state was its fertile seedbed. Of all the newly opened territories west of the Appalachians, Kentucky was the first to attract settlers, and it acted as a kind of staging area for those who were eventually to move on. By 1800 it was a "boom" state, having a greater population (over 200,000) than all the other states and territories outside the original thirteen colonies combined. It was about this time that revivalism in its most sensational form came to this raw frontier state.

The early camp meetings of the Kentucky revival were huge, chaotic, turbulent affairs. Many people traveled for days to get there. The famous camp meeting of August 1801 at Cane Ridge, in the gently rolling country of Bourbon County, northeast of Lexington, lasted six days, and estimates of the number in attendance ran between ten and twenty-five thousand. The preaching, praying, shouting, and singing went on day and night.

According to one of the many eyewitness accounts,

> The noise was like the roar of Niagara. The vast sea of human beings seemed to be agitated as if by a storm. I counted seven ministers, all preaching at one time, some on stumps, others in wagons, and one . . . was standing on a tree which had, in falling, lodged against . . . another. Some of the people were singing, others praying, some crying for mercy in the most piteous accents, while others were shouting most vociferously. . . . A strange supernatural power seemed to pervade the entire mass of mind there collected. . . . Soon after I left and went into the woods, and there I strove to rally and man up my courage.
>
> After some time I returned to the scene of excitement, the waves of which, if possible, had risen still higher. The same awfulness of feeling came over me. I stepped up on to a log, where I could have a better view of the surging sea of humanity. The scene that presented itself to my mind was indescribable. At one time I saw at least five hundred swept down in a moment as if a battery of a thousand guns had been opened upon them, and then immediately followed shrieks and shouts that rent the heavens.[9]

There was many a strange and disquieting sight to be viewed on the American frontier, and none more so at times than the camp meeting. But Cane

Ridge represented the extreme. Subsequently the camp meetings, particularly under the Methodists, whose specialty they became, were much more carefully planned and organized—the more so precisely on account of the excesses and debaucheries that stigmatized the earlier and more spontaneous ones. In spite of their undenied excesses, their emphasis on emotionalism, and the dubious significance of many of the "conversions," most careful observers now conclude that the positive influence of the camp meetings outweighed the negative. As Charles Johnson has summed it up, "Among all of the weapons forged by the West in its struggle against lawlessness and immorality, few were more successful than the frontier camp meeting. This socioreligious institution helped tame backwoods America."[10]

What began as the Kentucky Revival became the Great Revival, spreading like wildfire through Tennessee, the Carolinas, and Georgia. The first conflagration had pretty well subsided by 1805. But the camp meeting had become by this time a regular institution of religion in the South. After the Great Revival of 1800–1805 a subsequent wave appeared, beginning in the 1830s, which has been called the Millennial Excitement. This millennialism was accompanied by all the phenomena that had characterized the Great Revival: large camp meetings, conversions in great numbers, and every manifestation of religious hysteria. The old spirituals needed very little adapting to convey in very explicit terms the message that time was running out in which to seek salvation. After the 1840s, the excitement subsided; but revivalism, in urbanized form, has been periodically active right down to our own time. By the time of the Civil War, however, the heyday of the outdoor camp meeting, for a variety of reasons, was over.

The Revival Spiritual

Singing was a vital part of revivalism from the beginning—an effective opener to set the mood for an exhortation, an outlet for the emotionalism of the occasion, and a communal act into which one could pour all one's energies in fellowship with other believers. These have always been the functions of popular religious song. Another account of Cane Ridge tells of the powerful impulse of song: "The volume of song burst all bounds of guidance and control, and broke again and again from the throats of the people." Still another eyewitness reported that at the camp meetings the "falling down of multitudes, and their crying out . . . happened under the singing of Watts's Psalms and Hymns, more frequently than under the preaching of the word."[11] All agree that the singing was loud. "The immediate din was tremendous; at a hundred yards it was beautiful; at a distance of a half a mile it was magnificent."[12]

What was sung at the camp meetings? Since it was for so long a matter of purely oral tradition, evidence must be pieced together. The reference above to "Watts's Psalms and Hymns" refers to the words; certain hymns, and bits and pieces of hymns, of eighteenth-century English divines were much used. Tunes themselves were not written down and published until the 1840s, though pocket-sized "songsters" with just the words began to appear about 1805. There were several reasons why camp-meeting singing continued as an essentially oral tradition: anything in print was scarce on the frontier; few could have read the music, and many would not have been able even to read the words; in any case, many must have known at least portions of the tunes and words; probably the crowds often sang only the refrains or the choruses, which would have been easy to learn on the spot; and, finally, the degree of participation, physical as well as emotional, would have made it not only inconvenient but actually impossible to try to read songs out of a book at a spirited revival meeting.

From later collections that recorded what must have been current in oral tradition for some time, we can get a pretty good idea of the camp-meeting repertory. Given the requirements of revival song, we know what the hallmarks of the true revival spiritual were. The tunes had to be lively and easily learned. There was an almost unvarying reliance on the verse-chorus form; everyone could at least join in on the choruses, even if they didn't know the verses, or if the leader introduced unfamiliar ones or even made them up on the spot. A further development along the line of what has been called "text simplification," for the sake of mass participation, was the single-line refrain, interpolated after a couplet of original text or even after every line. With the crowds joining in on the refrains, this turned the singing into the familiar call-and-response pattern. Indoor church hymns could be transformed into revival spirituals by this process.

It is interesting to observe this at work in the case of one of the most popular hymn texts of the time. The original hymn "Canaan" by the English clergyman Samuel Stennett (1727–95) describes in Blakean imagery and language the beauties of heaven. The first of many verses runs:

> On Jordan's stormy banks I stand,
> And cast a wishful eye,
> To Canaan's fair and happy land,
> Where my possessions lie.
> O, the transporting rapturous scene,
> That rises to my sight!
> Sweet fields array'd in living green,
> And rivers of delight.

In the revival-song version shown in Example 6–7, only one couplet at a time is used, with a typical chorus added, spelling out in more homely language of action and urgency the conviction that the believer is actually *going* to the promised land so poetically described. The result is a spirited and popular revival spiritual that was first printed in William Walker's *Southern Harmony* in 1835.

A further stage in the "revivalizing" of this hymn is illustrated in Example 6–8, in which a one-line refrain is interpolated after every line of the text. Both the words and music of the refrain then become the basis for an added chorus. The whole appears in *The Revivalist* of 1868, set to a folkish tune that has acquired a decidedly Irish lilt.

George Pullen Jackson says of songs in this familiar pattern: "It is safe to guess that the basic text was sung by one person or a few, while everybody came in on the refrain and chorus." Speaking further of the basic text, usually composed of rhymed couplets, he points out how these couplets became

Example 6–7

Original a major third higher

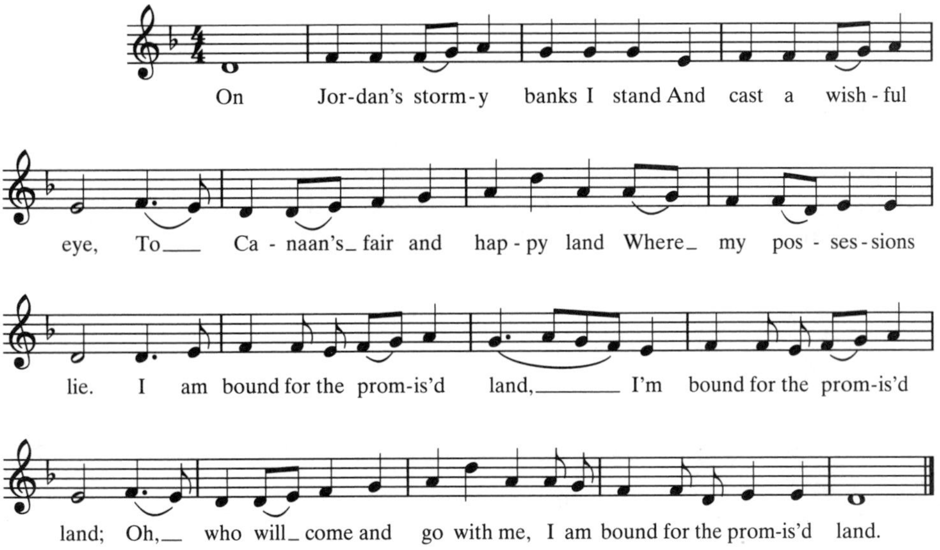
On Jor-dan's storm-y banks I stand And cast a wish-ful
eye, To___ Ca-naan's_ fair and hap-py land Where_ my pos-ses-sions
lie. I am bound for the prom-is'd land,________ I'm bound for the prom-is'd
land; Oh,__ who will_ come and go with me, I am bound for the prom-is'd land.

Example 6–8

Original a major second higher

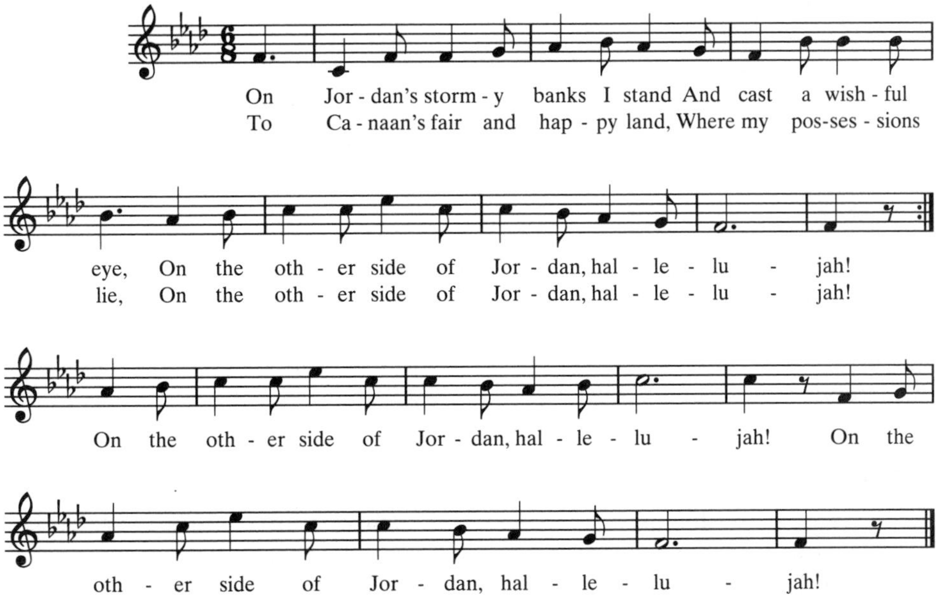
On Jor-dan's storm-y banks I stand And cast a wish-ful
To Ca-naan's fair and hap-py land, Where my pos-ses-sions
eye, On the oth-er side of Jor-dan, hal-le-lu-jah!
lie, On the oth-er side of Jor-dan, hal-le-lu-jah!
On the oth-er side of Jor-dan, hal-le-lu-jah! On the
oth-er side of Jor-dan, hal-le-lu-jah!

detached and took to "wandering"—turning up in various songs when and as needed. The same was true of entire "wandering choruses."[13]

We have noted in Chapter 2 that leader-and-chorus ("call-and-response") singing was a typical mode of performance among black people. The singing of the blacks at frontier camp meetings, even segregated as they were, may have had considerable influence on the verse-refrain form of the revival spiritual.[14]

Repetition was carried even further through the use of a form in which a single word is changed to make each new stanza, as can be seen in Example 6–9, from *The Social Harp* of 1855. According to Jackson, this spiritual was probably sung with "fathers" only in the first verse, then "mothers" in a second. Further multiplication of verses was easy, using "brothers," "sisters," "friends," "neighbors," and so on. This pattern was to persist in vernacular religious song, especially among African-Americans; it proved useful, as we have seen in Chapter 4, in the "freedom songs" of the Civil Rights movement of the 1960s—songs that were most often adaptations of old spirituals and hymns.

Example 6–9

Original a major third higher

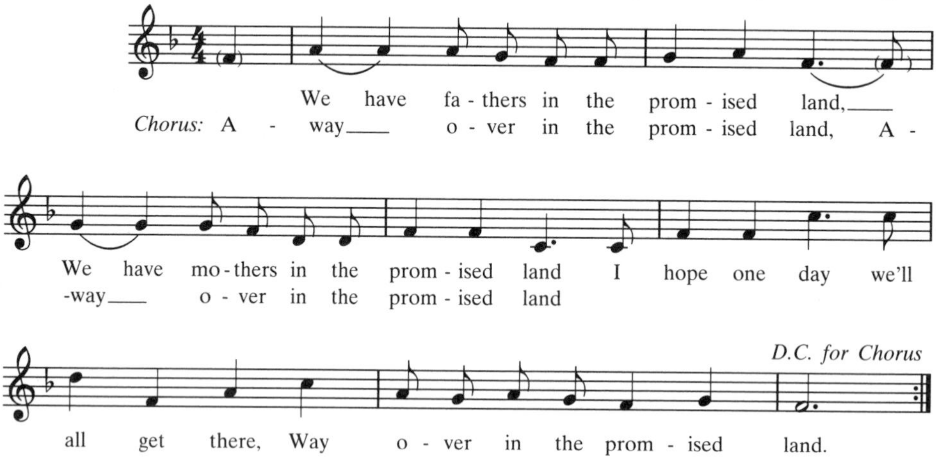

The revival spirituals (the definitive term, "revival spiritual songs," traces its lineage all the way back to Isaac Watts's *Hymns and Spiritual Songs* of 1709) were also distinguished by the style and content of their texts. These emphasized the basic themes of the prevailing theology—especially salvation, its attendant joys, and the glories of a heaven that was far removed from the present life. The examples already cited have been replete with expressions that pervade the spirituals: "promised land," "Canaan," "the other side of Jordan." Along with the descriptions of heaven and its joys is a dissatisfaction with this present life that is so pronounced as to amount at times to a rejection of the world and, if not actually a wish for death, at least a poignant anticipation of the joys and release from pain it would bring to the righteous saints who had been converted:

> Our bondage it shall end, by and by, by and by.
>
> I am a stranger here below.
>
> This world is not my home.

How blest the righteous when he dies!
How gently heaves the expiring breast
How mildly beams the closing eyes
When sinks a weary soul to rest.

Sweet home! Oh, when shall I get there?

Parallel Traditions: White and Black Spirituals

The African-American spiritual has been treated extensively in Chapter 2. That parallel traditions of these "spiritual songs" existed among blacks and whites is incontrovertible, as has been documented, for example, by George Pullen Jackson, who included in his *White and Negro Spirituals* a comparative list of 116 tunes from both. There is also considerable evidence that white rural hymnody—folk hymns and, especially, revival spirituals—furnished a great deal of raw material, at least, for African-American spirituals. John Lovell, Jr., the black author of an exhaustive work on the African-American spiritual, has written: "There is hardly any doubt that the Afro-American songmaker borrowed from the hymns he heard, and from the Biblical stories he picked up."

The instructive point to consider here is that the main opportunities for this transmission occurred not in the large slaveholding areas of the South, and not through the master-slave relationship, but precisely in those regions and under those conditions that nurtured the folk hymn and the revival spiritual among whites—in the uplands and on the frontier, among the plain folk and at the camp meeting. They would have reached the "black belt" of the lowland and tidewater South later on. The frontier, not hospitable to barriers of race or caste, represented perhaps the most democratic region in nineteenth-century America. The camp meeting, a frontier institution, was probably the site of as uninhibited a meeting of the races as could be encountered in that time. Many of the early camp-meeting preachers, such as Lorenzo Dow and Peter Cartwright, preached against slavery, and were in fact among our earliest abolitionists.

The parallelism and interaction of the black and white traditions has already been illustrated in Chapter 2, with a comparison between the familiar black spiritual "Go Down, Moses" and the white revival song "There Is a Rest Remains." A comparison of the white hymn "Roll Jordan" (Example 6–10) with the black spiritual "Roll, Jordan, Roll" (Example 6–11)[15] shows the differences as well as the parallels between the two traditions. Musically, the African-American spiritual has the more lively and supple rhythm, including some mild syncopation, and its chorus has a characteristic "blue note"—a flatted seventh. The text extracts the usable imagery of the hymn and makes it more immediate. The river—a powerful metaphor that in the white original was only a refrain—becomes an actual presence, something to hear.

The City and Urban Revivalism

The opening decades of the nineteenth century, as we have noted, witnessed the beginnings of a growing cultural cleavage between the city and the coun-

Example 6–10 ROLL JORDAN

Original a major second higher

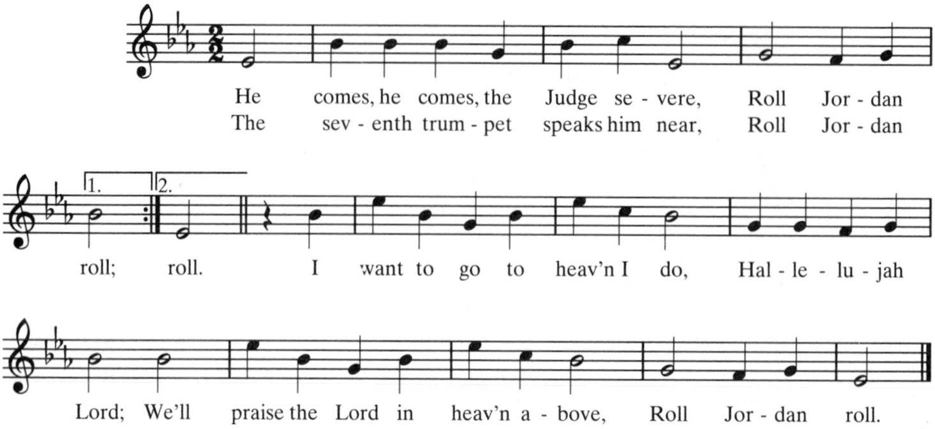
He comes, he comes, the Judge se - vere, Roll Jor - dan
The sev - enth trum - pet speaks him near, Roll Jor - dan
1. 2.
roll; roll. I want to go to heav'n I do, Hal - le - lu - jah
Lord; We'll praise the Lord in heav'n a - bove, Roll Jor - dan roll.

Example 6–11 ROLL, JORDAN, ROLL

Original a major second higher

O bro - thers, you ought t'have been there,
Yes, my___ Lord, A - sit-ting in the king-dom to hear Jor - dan
roll. Roll, Jor - dan roll, Roll, Jor - dan roll; I
want to go to heav-en when I die, to hear Jor - dan roll.

try. In cities such as Boston the products of our native school of church composers were progressively cast aside by those dedicated to what they saw as the improvement of church music, who naturally turned to Europe not only for "rules" as to what was correct, but also for actual tunes. The Boston Handel and Haydn Society was in the forefront of this movement, and its collection of church music, published first in 1822, was something of a landmark. It still had the shape and something of the look of the "long boys" that continued to flourish in the country; the tunes were still buried in the tenor voice; and there was the time-honored pedagogical preface, even incorporating the fa-sol-la-mi syllables. But the content was new. Gone were the fuging tunes; there was not a single piece by Billings, Ingalls, or Swan. Instead, there were European hymn tunes, as well as adapted tunes by Handel, Mozart, Haydn, and Beethoven,[16] complete with European *figured bass* (a shorthand device for indicating the harmony, of convenience to the organists who now nearly invariably accompanied choral and congregational singing in those churches wealthy enough to afford organs). Gone were all vestiges of the modal scales of folk music, and the minor mode itself, a favorite of the folk, was nearly banished; most tunes were in major keys and were harmonized with European correctness. The preface declared proudly that "gentlemen of taste and science in this country" went "to the fountains of Music in Europe" for refreshment, seeking material that would further their "purpose of improving the style of Church Music" and insuring "increasing refinement in the public taste." Thus began the growth in this country of a progressively greater cultural schism, not only between city and country, but between "highbrow" and "lowbrow." It was an inevitable development. Our age of artistic innocence was over.

The compiler of *The Boston Handel and Haydn Society Collection of Church Music,* whose "taste and science . . . well fitted him for the employment," was none other than Lowell Mason, whom we shall discuss more fully later on. He was at the time just under thirty. Throughout the next fifty years he was to dominate American urban church music with his phenomenal industry—as composer, adapter, and arranger of hymn tunes; as publisher of numerous collections of sacred music; as choral director; and as educator.

Nineteenth-century America's capacity to consume published collections of sacred music seems phenomenal for the time. Mason himself published more than twenty; his *Carmina Sacra* sold half a million copies. And he was far from working alone. We have already mentioned Thomas Hastings, who was so scornful of the shape notes: he composed six hundred hymns and more than a thousand hymn tunes, and published fifty volumes of music. William Bradbury published more than fifty collections, one of which sold over a quarter of a million copies. Of course sales of this magnitude netted sizable profits. Mason, who earned between $10,000 and $30,000 on his first compilation alone, is said to have made as much as $100,000 on a single volume later—a rather stark contrast to Billings, who, even with the help of his tanner's trade and several municipal posts, could not avert a virtual pauper's death.

The inexorable divergence between "highbrow" and "lowbrow" in American tastes after 1800 made no exception for religious music. There was also, by mid-century, a pronounced "layering" of denominations in social and economic terms. For the worship services of the urban churches that had a pronounced liturgical bent, coupled with a substantial tradition and an intellectual, even aesthetic, dimension to their appeal (Episcopal, Lutheran, Presbyterian to some degree, as well as Roman Catholic), a hymnody continued to develop along the lines Lowell Mason had established—cultivated and eclectic, selecting and adapting from a wide range of traditions. Any recent hymn book of these denominations (such as *The Hymnal of the Protestant Episcopal Church in the United States of America* [1940]) will illustrate this. Here medieval plainchant, Lutheran chorales, Calvinist psalm tunes, and melodies by classical and modern composers rub shoulders with American folk hymns such as "Kedron," from the tradition discussed earlier in this chapter.

On the other hand, after 1800 the broadly popular evangelical denominations and sects continued to demand a popular type of song, particularly for special occasions such as revival meetings, which incorporated many features of the old camp-meeting spiritual.

Urban Revivalism After the Civil War: The Moody-Sankey Era of Gospel Hymns

Hymn tunes have been called by Stevenson "pre-eminently the food of the common man." We have just seen that nineteenth-century America had a seemingly insatiable hunger for this food. In the period following the American Revolution, the demand for popular hymnody was met by drawing upon the wealth of folk music in the possession of the rural people, thereby creating the folk hymn. After the Civil War, folk music, no longer a very vital part of the lives of a now much larger and increasingly citified populace, could not be drawn upon to satisfy this demand, which had become enormous. Instead, it was met by a large number of hymn writers and composers, most of whom had only a modest amount of formal training but had an instinctive feel for what would best appeal to the great numbers of Christian believers, many of them new converts. These hymn writers and composers maintained a prodigious output of what have come to be known as gospel songs or gospel hymns. The production of these became especially copious after the revivalism of Dwight Moody and Ira Sankey swept the country beginning in 1875. In that year Sankey published, with P. P. Bliss, a volume called *Gospel Hymns*. This was followed by five sequels, culminating in *Gospel Hymns Nos. 1 to 6 Complete* in 1895, a compendium of more than seven hundred hymns and songs that typify the genre. As comprehensive as such a collection might seem, it represents only a fraction of the simple, homely songs and hymns produced.[17]

The models for these gospel songs[18] seem not to have come from the European-influenced collections of Mason and others; rather, their lineage was from the earlier camp-meeting song via the Sunday school songs for children that began to be published in mid-century. Their newer (for the time) and more optimistic stance is revealed in the titles of collections such as *Happy Voices, The Sunny Side,* and *Golden Chain.*

A new feature of revivalism was that singing the gospel became as important as preaching the gospel; therefore, to reach the masses the gospel hymn had to be of the utmost simplicity, governed by a conventionality that virtually amounted to a formula. With extremely rare exceptions, all the tunes were in the major mode, in contrast to the dour minor and modal tunes of the old rural folk hymns.[19] They were harmonized with the three most basic chords, embellished occasionally with some chromaticism in the style that has since become known as "barbershop harmony." The form is nearly always that of verse and chorus. The chorus is a feature that not only shows a direct descent from the earlier revival spiritual, but also relates the music to the commercial secular songs of Tin Pan Alley. This chorus often embodies a sort of polyphony even more rudimentary than that of the old fuging tunes; it imparts a similar "kick" to the second part of the hymn, and illustrates the perennial delight that the most naive manifestations of counterpoint have for the musically innocent. A chorus from a hymn with music by the renowned Ira Sankey himself (Example 6–12) illustrates this feature.[20]

Example 6–12

As this example shows, the music was usually written on two staves in four-part harmony. The tune was now on top, in the soprano: this made it more prominent for congregational singing. The four-part harmonizations were also eminently convenient for the mixed solo quartet of soprano, alto, tenor, and bass (often paid professionals) that was such a popular feature in churches from the Civil War on.

The words, as might be expected, show the same preoccupation with the central theme of salvation as did those of the revival spiritual, though there is less gloomy dwelling upon death and, with the increased cheerfulness that pervaded popular theology, a great deal more sentimentality. The intimate relation of many of these gospel songs to country music will be explored further in Chapter 7.

Despite the ephemeral nature of most of this gospel music, a few survivals, of enormous popularity and some distinction, have found their way into modern hymn collections. What is more important, they have become woven into America's musical consciousness, as Charles Ives shows when he quotes them so liberally in his works, and as other more recent composers like Virgil Thomson have demonstrated in their treatment and transformation of them. Perhaps a brief litany of nearly forgotten composers, with an even dozen of their hymn tunes, will serve to recall for us this heritage that an English writer has characterized as "at best . . . honestly flamboyant and redolent of the buoyancy of the civilization that created New York and Pittsburgh and

Chicago."[21] These composers and tunes are: P. P. Bliss, "Hold the Fort" ("for I am coming") and "Let the Lower Lights Be Burning"; William B. Bradbury, "Sweet Hour of Prayer," "He Leadeth Me," and "Just As I Am"; Robert Lowry, "Beautiful River" ("Shall we gather at the river?"), "Where Is My Boy Tonight?" and "I Need Thee Every Hour"; Charles C. Converse, "What a Friend We Have in Jesus"; George A. Minor, "Bringing in the Sheaves"; Simeon P. March, "Jesus, Lover of My Soul"; J. R. Sweney, "Beulah Land."

The Billy Sunday–Homer Rodeheaver Era: Further Popularization and Commercialization

In the last quarter of the nineteenth century, gospel hymnody had unquestionably become one of the most successful of all popular musics known up to that time. But in spite of massive sales of printed copies, there was little overt exploitation of the commercial aspects of the genre; Dwight Moody, for example, agreed to accept profits from the sales of the hymn books only when it was pointed out that they could be used to further his evangelistic enterprise, and Ira Sankey, their composer and compiler, derived no personal income from them. But after the turn of the century the situation changed perceptibly.

A new commercialism went hand in hand with a new popularization and even secularization of evangelical song. There was a greater emphasis on informality and entertainment in revival meetings; the piano replaced the old reed organ, and Homer Rodeheaver (associated for twenty years, from 1909 to 1929, with the evangelist Billy Sunday) added trombone solos to his singing and piano playing to liven up the proceedings. In mid-career Rodeheaver made full use of the new media of radio and recordings; he also published extensively, through the Rodeheaver Company of Winona Lake, Indiana. His *Christian Service Songs* (for which practical orchestrations were available) went through many editions. It included older traditional material (standard tunes by Handel, Mendelssohn, and the like, and by the Americans Mason and Root) but is best known for the popular sacred and semi-sacred songs that characterized the era, among them "Brighten the Corner Where You Are" (Charles Gabriel, 1913), "In the Garden" (C. Austin Miles, 1912), and "The Old Rugged Cross" (George Bernard, 1913).[22]

After a decline during the Depression era, urban revivalism again began attracting attention with the activities of Billy Graham. The music accompanying his meetings was conservative, with a return to the repertoire represented in the Moody-Sankey *Gospel Hymns*.[23] With the advent of television evangelism, the emphasis, as in the Sunday-Rodeheaver era, is again on entertainment, eclecticism, and commercialism.

Gospel Music After the Advent of Radio and Recordings

Following the course of jazz, blues, and country music, what Charles Wolfe has called "the fourth great genre of grass roots music"*—gospel music—entered

* It goes almost without saying that Wolfe was talking about grass roots music *from the South,* an area rich in musical traditions, both black and white, and the source of so much of our popular music. The first three—the secular genres of jazz, blues, and country music—will be treated in Chapters 13, 8, and 7 respectively.

the commercial arena of the radio and the phonograph in the mid-1920s, and was profoundly influenced by both media. In the sixty years since, two parallel traditions, black and white, have developed, both drawing to a significant degree on the same reservoir of nineteenth-century gospel hymnody, but each reacting in its own way to popular secular currents of the times—white gospel music to those of white country music, and black gospel music to those of jazz, blues, and rhythm-and-blues.

Southern White Gospel Music

Twentieth-century white gospel music in the South had its musical roots in the rural shape-note tradition described earlier and, instrumentally, in the folk music of that region. Its religious roots were in evangelical revivalism, and in the Holiness and Pentecostal[24] movements that around the turn of the century began to sweep across the whole country, taking root especially in the South, the Midwest, and California, where they made converts among the poor, both black and white. At first the musical fare in the white churches was that of the rather staid gospel hymns of the Moody-Sankey era, which began to reach rural southerners in shape-notes as early as 1890. (By that time the four-shape system, as preserved in *Southern Harmony* and *The Sacred Harp,* had largely given way to a seven-shape system, which had been introduced in the mid-nineteenth century and which persists in publications to this day.) Gospel hymns continued to appear in the late nineteenth-century in new collections, alongside earlier American hymns of the Lowell Mason vintage and still older European standard tunes. But by the 1920s, when radio and recordings had come on the scene, a new kind of gospel song was becoming more popular—a type more indigenous to the region, which reflected the influences of both secular country ("hillbilly") music and, to a certain extent, Tin Pan Alley. The texts emphasized more down-to-earth, homely, and even topical metaphors. As in secular country music and the blues, the train motive appeared in songs like "Life's Railway to Heaven," and "The Glory Train"—the latter with Jesus as "our great conductor" who "has been this way before." The faithful are admonished: "Get your ticket and be ready,/ For this train may come today . . . Have your baggage checked for glory,/ So you'll meet with no delay."

In "The Royal Telephone" of 1919 we find the chorus:

> Telephone to glory, O what joy divine!
> I can feel the current moving on the line;
> Built by God the Father for his loved and own,
> We may talk to Jesus thru this royal telephone.[25]

The texts tended to anticipate the joys of heaven, as in "Where We'll Never Grow Old" (1914), "When the Roll Is Called Up Yonder (I'll be there)" (1921), and "Can the Circle Be Unbroken" (ca. 1907). The stern warning, as in "What Would You Give in Exchange (for your soul?)" (1912) or "He Will Set Your Fields on Fire," became less common. There was more emphasis instead on the semi-sacred "message" song, which simply advocated cheerful optimism, as in the popular "Give the World a Smile," or indulged in sentimentality, as in "If I Could Hear My Mother Pray Again." (This latter trait is found in abundance in country music, as we shall see in the next chapter.)[26]

Musically, the melodic and harmonic vocabulary of twentieth-century white gospel music has been basically the same as that which had proven so workable and popular in the nineteenth century: simple tunes, all in the major mode, harmonized essentially with the three basic chords, with the very occasional accidentals associated with the embellishments of "barbershop" harmony. The verse-chorus form is nearly always used, with the chorus containing the kind of antiphonal "answering" effects already illustrated in Ira Sankey's "To Be There" (Example 6–12 above).

The principal musical differences between the urban gospel hymns of the nineteenth century and the Southern white gospel songs of the twentieth have been in the manner of their performance. In early recordings before much commercial influence was evident (and in more recent revivals of earlier styles), we hear the staid hymns of the Moody-Sankey era "ruralized" and "southernized" by being given an instrumental accompaniment of guitar, banjo, and mandolin (more rarely fiddle), with characteristic introductions and instrumental choruses.[27] The singing style in the early period was the same straight (vibrato-less), tense, and somewhat harsh tone, with sliding between pitches, that is familiar from recordings of southern folk music.

In its more commercial aspects, white gospel music showed the influence of popular music, with a trend toward enhancing its entertainment aspects. This was especially noticeable in the singing of the many male quartets that publishers sent out to churches and singing conventions to promote the sales of their songbooks. Recordings of the famous Stamps Quartet from the late 1920s show the addition of piano accompaniments that introduce ragtime figures in the breaks. The choruses sometimes indulged in tricky instrumental-like afterbeat effects (see below), and sometimes whole choruses were repeated with the voices imitating guitars and banjos ("boom-boom-boom-plink-boom-plink-boom-plink-boom-plink-boom-plink-a-plink-plink-plink"). Voice quality was modified from the old tense, straight folk style, but slides between notes were still prevalent. The popularity of bass soloists in gospel music, still apparent in 1980s recordings of male gospel groups, goes back to this period of the publishing-house quartets. In some instances the straight eighth notes of the written versions were performed unevenly, with the first of each pair lengthened, as in swing jazz (in the black gospel tradition, this was known as "gospelizing"). As Bill Malone has put it, "The gospel singers learned much of their four-part harmony from the shape-note singing schools, but they also picked up elements from the barbershop quartets, the black gospel quartets, and other popular quartets of their day."[28]

Example 6–13, from the chorus of "He Bore It All" (1926), shows the seven-shape notation, and the antiphonal afterbeat effects found in some of the popular-style professional quartet arrangements of the period.

The influence of the commercial process has been a major part of the story of gospel music in this century, both black and white. In white gospel music the process was under way by the turn of the century. Publishers such as James D. Vaughan of Lawrenceburg, Tennessee (long a leader in the field), whose business was to sell songbooks, found many ways to promote their wares. As Bill Malone has written, "Vaughan [a devout member of the Church of the

Example 6–13

Nazarene] and his gospel cohorts preached an otherworldly message, but they very astutely utilized the techniques of this world to popularize that vision."[29] A dominant publishing firm further west was Stamps-Baxter, of Dallas, which published numerous books of songs and hymns, and sponsored many of the publishing-house quartets that were described above. The powerful media of radio and recordings were of course taken full advantage of; in the 1920s, James D. Vaughan owned both a radio station (one of the first in Tennessee) and a record company, for which one of his quartets recorded as early as 1922.

Independent soloists and groups were also singing on the radio. Charlie D. Tillman, composer of "Old Time Religion" (a song associated more than any other in the popular mind with white gospel music) and "Life's Railway to Heaven," was among the first to broadcast this music, in 1922 in Atlanta; three years later he too was making recordings. Record companies, discovering the sales potential of secular hillbilly music and blues, were also looking for artists to record gospel music. J. Frank Smith and Smith's Sacred Singers and Ernest Phipps and his Holiness Singers, performing songs in circulation in the seven-shape-note repertory in the South, are two groups whose early recordings can be heard in archival collections today.[30]

Performers who already had a reputation for doing mostly secular songs and ballads also recorded some gospel songs—among them Bascomb Lamar Lunsford, Uncle Dave Macon, the Stoneman Family, the Carter Family, and the Stanley Brothers.[31] Since then virtually all country singers have included in their repertory, and recorded, some gospel songs.

In the face of a persistent trend toward the commercialization of white gospel music since the 1930s, a few groups continued to perform it with the traditional sound and spirit. One of these was a mixed quartet (originally a father, son, and two daughters) from Texas that had the somewhat misleading name of the Chuck Wagon Gang thrust upon them. From the late 1930s to the early 1970s, they achieved considerable and enduring popularity, on radio and recordings, singing mostly old songs, familiar from the seven-shape-note books, in a conservative manner to a simple guitar accompaniment; only in the late 1950s was an electric guitar sometimes substituted.[32] Somewhat later, in the 1960s and 1970s, the Blackwood Brothers were performing traditional gospel music. But by the 1960s, with the rewards of commercial success becoming ever larger, as could be seen by looking at the careers of successful country and rock groups, two distinct motivations for performing gospel music had emerged. As Malone puts it, "The sense of religious mission no doubt still burned brightly in the lives of many gospel singers, but an increasing number viewed the music as just another facet of popular music, or as an avenue for entrance into different kinds of performing careers."[33] The Oak Ridge Boys and the Statler Brothers typify the latter tendency; they eventually dropped gospel music for straight country pop.

In the 1980s popular commercial gospel groups such as the Florida Boys, a male quintet, most typically purvey a slick, studio-produced product, with a large pop/soft-rock backup group with drums and a mixture of electric and acoustic instruments, strangely at odds with the very conservative old-line evangelical message of the words. Their repertory, while mostly new, includes an occasional older song such as Tillman's "Life's Railway to Heaven," done in a very stylized evocation of the "old-time" way.[34]

Outside the gospel movement itself, some folk revivalists have taken a renewed interest in songs from the old seven-shape-note repertory, and it is not unusual to hear, in the old singing style, with string band accompaniment, songs like "The Lonesome Road," "Can the Circle Be Unbroken" (in its more recent variant, "Will the Circle Be Unbroken"), and of course the perennial "Amazing Grace."

Black Gospel Music: The Roots

African-American gospel music had its religious roots in the turn-of-the-century Holiness movement mentioned earlier. The Holiness sects are based on a highly personal, vivid, and emotional religious experience—an experience that involves, ultimately, possession by the Holy Spirit. This possession shows itself in emotionally charged expression and movement—moaning, singing, speaking in tongues, and dancing (the term "shout" can refer to a dance as well as a type of song).* This amazing and seemingly unbridled expression—the one and only outlet for pent-up emotions in the lives of the poor of both races, who made up the majority of adherents of the Holiness sects—elicited amusement and scorn from the world at large.[35] (The derogatory term "Holy Rollers" was frequently heard.) Since these believers were already among the outcasts of society, the contempt only strengthened the sense of community they felt in their worship. Though the Holiness and Pentecostal adherents were always in a minority numerically among church members, the freedom of expression that they encouraged, especially in music, had a special appeal and gave them, eventually, an influence disproportionate to their numbers. The singular fact is that it was just these scorned modes of worship, this rejected music of the disinherited, that ultimately came to influence not only a large segment of American religious music, white and black, but indirectly a great spectrum of our popular music as well.

We cannot go very far in understanding the conditions under which black gospel music developed unless we understand something of the role of the black preacher. W. E. B. Du Bois has said: "The Preacher is the most unique personality developed by the Negro on American soil. A leader, a politician, an orator, a 'boss,' an intriguer, an idealist—all these he is, and ever, too, the

* See Chapter 2.

center of a group of men, now twenty, now a thousand in number."[36] In the Holiness church, being a preacher did not require a degree or being ordained; what was demanded was that one have the combination of qualities enumerated by Du Bois, and that one feel the "call" to preach. An indispensable gift of the preacher was the ability to elicit a response from his congregation. As, in the course of his exhortation, the responses became more frequent and more intense, the sounds of preacher and congregation together gradually merged into song. Early recording entrepreneurs recorded many of these sermons-into-songs, in conditions not unlike those of the storefront churches where the actual services took place. It is estimated that over seven hundred "sermons" were recorded in the 1920s and early 1930s; Anthony Heilbut has called preachers "the best-selling religious artists of the 1920s."[37] Some preachers, such as the Rev. J. M. Gates and the Rev. F. W. McGee, were much in demand. The few recordings that are available in archival collections give at least some flavor of what the Sanctified services were like.[38]

The black Holiness churches welcomed the use of instruments. There were the characteristic percussion instruments (the tambourine, the triangle, and later the drums) as well as the guitar and its urban replacement, the piano. But the services often included, especially on the recordings of the 1920s, the highly "secular" instruments associated with jazz, especially the trombone. The music, in fact, often has the sound and feel of early jazz.[39] To conclude, however, that jazz influenced the music of the Sanctified churches is to get the picture as much backwards as forwards; they grew up together, and jazz may well owe nearly as much to the music of the Holiness churches as it does to the streets and brothels of New Orleans. One small clue is the fact that the traditional jazz standard "When the Saints Go Marching In" is actually a Sanctified "shout." Early gospel singers such as Ernestine Washington and the guitar-playing Rosetta Tharpe sang and recorded with jazz players and jazz bands.[40]

Black gospel music, unlike its white counterpart, was a music of the cities. Its roots can be found not only in what preachers and their congregations were doing in many humble storefront Holiness churches, but also in the music of many blind street evangelists. Of these Blind Willie Johnson (1902–50), a street singer in Dallas, was probably the best known and most influential. His "God Moves on the Water," one of many songs based on the sinking of the *Titanic* in 1912,[41] shows him to have been the religious counterpart, in terms of style and guitar technique, to blues singers such as Blind Lemon Jefferson.[42] In "John the Revelator," which Johnson recorded in 1930, his wife Angeline joins him in the rhythmic call-and-response chorus: "Well, who's that writin'?" "John the Revelator."[43] Memphis, world headquarters of the Church of God in Christ, the largest black Sanctified denomination, was a center for Sanctified music in the 1920s. If any further evidence is required of the influence of Sanctified singing on jazz, one need only listen to Elders McIntorsh and Edwards in "Since I Laid My Burden Down." Even more to the point is the singing of Sister Bessie Johnson, who together with Sister Melinda Taylor recorded "He Got Better Things for You" as the Memphis Sanctified Singers (1929). The growling, rasping vocal quality is exactly what jazz musicians were imitating on trumpet and trombone.[44]

The Methodist minister and composer Charles Albert Tindley (1851/

59–1933) has been called the "progenitor of black-American gospel music." In the first decade of the twentieth century he was writing songs in what became the prototypical form and style of gospel music—simple melodies and harmonies, in verse and chorus form. Among these were "I'll Overcome Some Day" of 1901 (the chorus of which entered, by a circuitous route, the Civil Rights struggle a half-century later as "We Shall Overcome"), "What Are They Doing in Heaven" of the same year (one of several songs to cross over into the white gospel tradition), "We'll Understand Better By and By" (1905), and "Stand by Me" (also 1905). The center of Tindley's work was Philadelphia, where he wrote songs for "new arrivals in the North who poured in daily, most of them poor and illiterate, and who valued highly the simple, direct, and emotional life style of which Tindley spoke."[45]

By the 1920s the gospel music indigenous to the Holiness churches was beginning to be introduced to other African-American denominations as well. Late nineteenth-century Holiness and Pentecostal hymnals eventually achieved rather wide circulation, and in 1921 the hymnal *Gospel Pearls* was introduced at the black National Baptist Convention. But the phenomenal growth of modern gospel music as it is known today did not begin until the 1930s.

Modern Black Gospel Music's First Phase: The 1930s, 1940s, and 1950s

The one person most responsible for the initial propagation of modern gospel music was Thomas A. Dorsey (b. 1899). After an early career as a blues singer, composer, and pianist—as "Georgia Tom" he had played and recorded blues with Ma Rainey and Tampa Red—he was first drawn to gospel music in 1921 (he had one song published in the hymnal *Gospel Pearls* of that year). For a while he continued to play and record blues, but from 1932 on he devoted himself wholly to the blues' sacred counterpart. It was in that year that he wrote his most famous song, "Precious Lord." Dorsey proved to be an indefatigable promoter, organizer, and manager, as well as composer, of gospel music. He published his own compositions, and went from church to church in Chicago, and later from city to city, with singers such as Sallie Martin and later Mahalia Jackson, performing and plugging gospel music. Dorsey published his songs not in book collections, as had been the case with popular sacred music up to this time, but rather (in the manner of Tin Pan Alley) as sheet music. In his capacity as organizer as well as composer, performer and promoter, he started with Sallie Martin the National Convention of Gospel Choirs and Choruses.

Thanks in part to Dorsey's promotional activity, the solo gospel singer began to assume more importance. During the first phase of modern gospel music (from the 1930s into the 1950s) it was women singers who dominated, just as in the 1920s female singers had dominated the classic urban blues. In fact, the two greatest influences on the first two generations of women gospel soloists were the music of the Holiness churches* and the singing of blues

* Of women singers prominent in the first three decades of gospel music Mahalia Jackson, Rosetta Tharpe, Marion Williams, and Ruth Davis either came out of Holiness backgrounds or were

singers like Ma Rainey and Bessie Smith. The "first generation" of singers included Roberta Martin (1907–69), who began as the pianist for Dorsey's chorus, Mahalia Jackson (1911–72), with whom Dorsey toured as pianist from the mid-1930s until around 1950, Willie Mae Ford Smith (b. 1906), and Sister Rosetta Tharpe (1915–73); the second included such singers as Clara Ward (1924–73), Marion Williams (b. 1927), Ruth Davis (1928–70), and Albertina Walker (b. 1930). These women developed distinctive styles that were individual blends of certain enduring characteristics of gospel singing: the bending of notes, the sliding into or between pitches, the bending of rhythms (in common with jazz singers), the repetition of syllables or words, the interpolation of extra words or exclamations, and a range of vocal effects that included shouting, falsetto, and a hoarse, rasping, or growling vocal quality.

In the beginning the basic accompanying instrument was the piano, played in a "gospel" style, which, quite unlike the accompaniments played for congregational hymn singing, owed a great deal to ragtime, stride piano, and other popular styles. Soon it was common to add bass and drums to the piano; in the 1950s the electric organ became an indispensable part of the ensemble. A small vocal group (mostly female, but occasionally including men) was frequently added, but the soloist tended to dominate; the vocal backup group merely added support, and reiterated key phrases of the soloist for emphasis. When gospel music began to enter the commercial arena with recordings, radio appearances, and tours, many soloists formed their own groups, such as the Roberta Martin Singers, the Davis Sisters, the Clara Ward Singers, and later the Caravans.

The above capsule description helps to define somewhat the traditional gospel group led by the female "diva," but the other type of group important in gospel music's first phase was the male ensemble—usually a quartet that sang unaccompanied, dressed in business suits. The unaccompanied male gospel quartet predated modern gospel music; early quartets in what Boyer has termed the "folk" phase, up until 1930, were built on the nineteenth-century tradition of the Fisk Jubilee Singers and others.[46] In the period 1930–45, termed by Boyer the "gospel" or "jubilee" period, groups adopted mannerisms from the more rhapsodic aspects of Holiness singing and from the rhythmic aspects of jazz; a characteristic number would start slowly, with florid improvisation, and then work up to a highly rhythmic ending. This period merged imperceptibly into Boyer's next phase, that of "sweet" gospel, in which a lead singer emerged as dominant, with the rest of the group forming a close harmony background and responding to the lead. Well known in this period were the Dixie Hummingbirds, the Blue Jay Singers, the Golden Gate Quartet, and the Soul Stirrers.[47]

Styles in Black Gospel Music Since Mid-Century

Since mid-century, and especially beginning in the 1970s, gospel music has evolved along two fairly distinct lines: "contemporary" and "traditional." Underneath the difference in style and sound, the basic distinction between the

---

strongly affected by the music, and Willie Mae Ford Smith joined a Holiness church in 1939, at the age of thirty-three.

two types lies in the way each regards its public. For "contemporary" gospel the public is an audience to be entertained, and perhaps soothed and comforted; for "traditional" gospel, it is a congregation to be charged with religious ecstasy.

Traditional gospel music, even on recordings, always conveys the ambience of an actual service. Even though the location may be Carnegie Hall (and it is much more apt to be an actual church) the congregation is palpably there, and participating. The "sermonette" before the song (an innovation evolved out of the old recorded preachers' sermons by Willie Mae Ford Smith, Dorothy Norwood, Inez Andrews, and other old-line gospel singers) or the pastor's exhortation is delivered over an instrumental background that merges into the next song. The instrumentation of piano, electric organ, electric guitar, electric bass, and drums is in the direct line of the tradition evolved since the 1930s. The choir, singing in an altogether homophonic texture, is an important element. Numbers now appear for chorus alone, representing a resurgence of actual choral singing in gospel music. More frequently the chorus is used for backing up the soloist, singing a verse or chorus of the song, or sometimes repeating short phrases, in the background, under the soloist's improvisation. The soloists tend to sing in a "hard gospel" style, highly charged emotionally. The fast numbers, driven by the accompaniment (all the instruments except the organ can be considered a rhythm section), are highly rhythmic and syncopated, and often incorporate handclapping.

The excerpt quoted in Example 6–14 from "Lord, Send Me Down a Blessing" by Willie Devone illustrates the *vamp,* a frequent device in traditional gospel music. After a 16-bar verse (not shown), the choir sings a chorus consisting of a 4-measure phrase followed by five repetitions, over which the soloist sings a free, melismatic* line (of which Example 6–14 shows merely a sample), amplifying and intensifying the message of the chorus. After another verse the vamp returns; this time it is sung eight times, followed by a 2-measure "tag" sung five times. The last time there is a ritard, and the piece ostensibly ends. But after the applause starts there is an immediate reprise, with seven more statements of the 4-bar vamp. The intensity and momentum built up by this means has to be heard (preferably live) to be appreciated.[48]

During the vamp the leader may go down and circulate among the congregation, and the congregation may respond to the highly charged emotional momentum established by the music and go into a "shout," dancing or moving rhythmically. In a live situation this may go on for as long as half an hour before leader and ensemble bring it to a close; recordings obviously must edit these vamps.

The slow numbers may build very gradually in force and momentum over a period of ten minutes or so, with the soloist again, as in the fast numbers, doing highly melismatic improvisations, which in the slower pieces involve a great many melismas, a good deal of word and phrase repetition, and an increasingly ecstatic manner of delivery. These numbers, like some extended blues, can develop overpowering emotional climaxes that may take several minutes to subside. For example, a recorded performance of "I Worship Thee,"

* A *melisma* is a group of notes sung to a single syllable.

Example 6–14

Transcription by the author

by John Kee, has the form A-B-Chorus-B-B-Chorus-Chorus. At the B verse's first appearance the soloist sings the following, with only three fairly short melismas, on the words "strong," "always," and "adore:"

> You taught me how to love all my enemies.
> In the midst of a storm, I'll be strooooong.
> And that's why my spirit will alwaaays be
>   free
> And I, I adore, I adoooore Thee.

On its third and last appearance the B verse is considerably extended, with word and phrase repetition and an interpolated phrase:

> Youuuu taught me how to love, you taught me how to love
>   all my enemies.
> In the midst of a storm I'll be strong.
> [Got to keep holding on, got to be stroooong]
> That's why my spirit, my spirit, my spirit will alwaaaays be free
>
> And I, I adore, I adoooore Thee.[49]

A leading figure in maintaining the continuity of traditional gospel music since the 1960s has been James Cleveland (b. 1932), whose background included apprenticeships with Thomas Dorsey (as a boy soprano) and Roberta Martin. His style, like that of other traditionalists such as Shirley Caesar, Dorothy Love Coates, and the Barrett Sisters, is basically that described above. In 1968 Cleveland founded the Gospel Music Workshop of America, devoted to the improvement of gospel choirs, which has become the largest organization in African-American church music.

Although there is a considerable overlap between "traditional" and "contemporary" gospel music, the latter tends to sound as if it is more at home in the concert hall than in church, and often more in the recording studio than either. The singing style and vocal quality of both soloists and choir tend to be smoother, more polished, and more "pop"-oriented, with less of the emotion-driven "edge" that characterizes traditional gospel singing. Solo cuts may have a soft-rock or soft-rhythm-and-blues background, with velvet-voiced studio backup singers replacing the incisive and committed voices of the historic gospel choir. Instrumentally there is a heavy reliance on a battery of electronic keyboards, and on studio electronic manipulation. Brass instruments and even a full orchestra augment or replace the basic piano-organ-drums sound of traditional gospel. Heilbut has summed it up in these words: "The eclecticism of 'contemporary gospel' derives from several sources: the academic training of many young choir directors; the example of the highly complex recording techniques of a Stevie Wonder or Michael Jackson; and the simple financial lure."[50]

In live performances and on live recordings, "audience" has replaced "congregation." Perhaps the trend toward multiracial concert audiences accounts in part for Boyer's

> observation that congregational response during many contemporary gospel concerts consists of smiling, soft weeping, and clapping, most often on a primary, rather than a secondary beat [i.e., shunning the "backbeat" so traditional in black music, both sacred and secular]; where a section of a song would have previously elicited a moan, shout, or vocal utterance, the audience response is only applause at concerts of contemporary gospel.[51]

Boyer goes on to note the loss of "participation" in contemporary gospel; a passive role has replaced the formerly active one.

Andraé Crouch, one of the leaders of contemporary gospel, goes so far in the lyrics of one of his songs as to disown gospel's roots in the worship of the Holiness churches:

> You don't have to jump no pews,
> Run down no aisles,
> No chills run down your spine;
> But you know that you've been born again.
> Don't you know my hands didn't shake,
> The earth didn't quake,
> No sparks fell from the sky;
> But I know that I've been born again.[52]

Secularization and Commercialization in African-American Gospel Music

The evolution of "contemporary" gospel style so briefly described above is only one manifestation of what has been happening to African-American gospel music since mid-century. It has experienced vastly increased acceptance and popularity on the one hand, and on the other, directly related to this, the tensions and divisions that inevitably result from growing commercialism.

Of course gospel music, both black and white, was commercialized as soon as the first record was made and sold (and with white gospel music the process had started even earlier, as we have seen, with southern publishers such as James D. Vaughan and Stamps-Baxter). But the pressures of change on the music itself, and on the singers and composers who made it, did not become significant until gospel music began to reach a much larger audience. Boyer notes that it was between 1945 and 1955 that black gospel music rose from the "shabby store-front churches" to extravaganzas "involving 15 to 20 artists or groups in a single concert lasting four to six hours." In 1957 the Newport Jazz Festival included Clara Ward and the Ward Singers, and the next year Mahalia Jackson sang there. By this time the concertgoing public was becoming aware of black gospel music. In 1961 two significant events occurred: Mahalia Jackson sang at one of John F. Kennedy's inauguration parties, and Clara Ward and the Ward Singers started singing in nightclubs. Mahalia Jackson's appearance symbolized the widespread acceptance of gospel music, Clara Ward's its secularization.

Secularizing gospel music means essentially taking it out of its context of worship and using it as entertainment. There are three aspects of this to be noted. The first is that of gospel singers themselves moving into secular venues. Rosetta Tharpe's style, as both singer and guitarist (she was raised in a Holiness church), easily incorporated jazz elements. She was singing with jazz bands in the 1940s, and as a recording artist with Decca she was the first gospel singer to gain nationwide recognition. The Ward Singers' nightclub debut in 1961 was by no means a totally new development: Tharpe, the Golden Gate Jubilee Quartet, and the Dixie Hummingbirds were already performing in New York's Cafe Society Downtown in the 1940s.

A second aspect is the secularizing of the material; "message" songs, expressing optimistic or altruistic sentiments but avoiding the words "God" or "Jesus," could be sung to a broader audience, and thus earn both popularity and money. Contemporary gospel has a tendency in this direction; "He Ain't Heavy (he's my brother)" is a recent example. However, it should also be noted that some gospel songs were either born with or acquired social or political "messages" having nothing to do with entertainment; "Move on Up a Little Higher," "Surely God Is Able (to carry you through)," "I'm Climbing Higher and Higher (and I won't come down)," all by the Rev. W. Herbert Brewster, and "How I Got Over" by Clara Ward, as sung during the Civil Rights struggle of the 1950s, carried more than religious implications, just as spirituals had before Emancipation.

A third aspect of the secularization of gospel music has been the "song exchange" between gospel and secular pop music, wherein pop songs could be "gospelized," and their popularity appropriated, merely by changing a word here and there. Thus "You're the Best Thing that Ever Happened to Me" could easily be changed into "Jesus Is the Best Thing that Ever Happened to Me"; "I Had a Talk with My Man Last Night" into "I Had a Talk with God Last Night."

The ease and frequency with which this secularization of gospel music took place is placed in clearer perspective if we remember two things. First, it has never been characteristic of African-American culture to make much of a distinction in style between sacred and secular music. Second, popular black religious music, and indeed popular black religion itself, has always had a worldly strain to it—the pressing earthly concerns of its congregations have been reflected in the homely, earthy images of its poetry. It has been pointed out that street life was very close to the storefront church.

With the sacred and the secular sharing much in common, the influence has flowed in the other direction as well. Beyond mere song exchange (Ray Charles, for example, has based several of his songs on gospel originals, including "I've Got a Woman," "Lonely Avenue," and "This Little Girl of Mine") there is the more fundamental influence that gospel performers have exerted on the style and sound of black secular music. This is most notable in rhythm-and-blues and in soul music, which is in some respects really secular gospel music, particularly in terms of the intense and ecstatic delivery of its singers. The rhythm-and-blues singer Little Richard, himself an off-and-on preacher, and the soul singer Aretha Franklin (whose father was a prolific recording preacher, and who was strongly influenced by Clara Ward), have both sung and recorded gospel songs, and gospel influence is also clear on such heavy soul performers as James Brown, Otis Redding, and B. B. King.

It would be a mistake to assume that gospel music, for all its popularity, represents the whole of black religious music. Influential black teachers have asked if gospel music is replacing the spiritual. They speak of the need to maintain the distinction, and to avoid simplistic assumptions, particularly on the part of whites, who, according to one writer, "assume gospel is representative of all black Christianity, that it *is* black culture."[53]

Gospel music today presents a pluralistic and largely decentralized picture. In its commercial aspect, as represented by contemporary gospel, it now accounts for a significant segment of the American popular music industry. At the grass roots level of church and community choirs, on the other hand, traditional gospel music is flourishing; ensembles such as the New Jerusalem Baptist Church Choir in Flint, Michigan, or the Sacramento Community Choir in California are giving live performances and producing "live" recordings that have a resounding authenticity. Gospel has become multiracial, and other Christian denominations, including such liturgically conservative ones as the Roman Catholic Church, have instituted gospel choirs, as have many colleges and universities. A network of teachers, workshops, and conventions (especially the large Gospel Music Workshop of America) is active in propagating and offering instruction in gospel music, not only in the United States but in other countries as well. Gospel music, following jazz and rock 'n' roll, may be the next in a long succession of exports of American popular music—all of which have stemmed from African-American roots.

Further Reading

Facsimile Editions of the Music

Wyeth, John. *Wyeth's Repository of Sacred Music, Part Second.* 2d ed. Harrisburg, PA, 1820. Reprint, New York: Da Capo, 1964.
The first shape-note publication to include folk hymns. This reprint edition has an excellent introduction by Irving Lowens.

Mason, Lowell. *The Boston Handel and Haydn Society Collection of Church Music.* Boston, 1822. Reprint, New York: Da Capo, 1973.
A landmark of the "better music" movement, this interesting book retains the form and appearance of the older books, but contains very little American music, and was the harbinger of a flood of later popular urban collections.

McCurry, John G. *The Social Harp.* Philadelphia, 1855. Reprint, Athens: University of Georgia Press, 1973.
One of the rarest of the shape-note books, reprinted with an extensive introduction by Daniel W. Patterson.

Walker, William. *The Southern Harmony.* Philadelphia, 1854. Reprint, Los Angeles: Promusicamericana, 1966.
The revised edition of this important shape-note publication, which appeared first in 1835.

White, B. F., and E. J. King. *The Sacred Harp.* 3d ed. Philadelphia, 1860. Reprint, Nashville, TN: Broadman, 1968.
This reprint of another very important shape-note publication includes George Pullen Jackson's essay "The Story of the Sacred Harp 1844–1944."

Sankey, Ira, et al. *Gospel Hymns Nos. 1 to 6 Complete.* New York, 1895. Reprint, New York: Da Capo, 1972.
A large and very representative collection of late nineteenth-century gospel hymns.

Anthologies

Marrocco, W. Thomas, and Harold Gleason, eds. *Music in America.* New York: W. W. Norton, 1964.
This basic anthology contains a small but fairly representative selection of shape-note music transcribed, with good notes. It has nothing past the Civil War.

Publications by George Pullen Jackson

These five volumes are basic to the study of the shape-note tradition, and of nineteenth-century popular rural hymnody in general. Together they contain over 900 tunes. They are listed in chronological order.

Jackson, George Pullen. *White Spirituals in the Southern Uplands.* Chapel Hill, NC, 1933. Paperback reprint, New York: Dover, 1965.
The basic history of the shape-note movement and its background. It includes the seven-shape branch. It also includes a listing, with initial-phrase quotations, of the eighty most popular tunes in the tradition.

———. *Spiritual Folk-Songs of Early America.* New York, 1937. Paperback reprint, New York: Dover, 1964.
This important collection has 250 complete tunes and texts, with sources and notes, and an extensive introduction. It is the basic annotated compendium of tunes and texts in the shape-note tradition.

———. *Down-East Spirituals and Others.* New York: J. J. Augustin, 1939; 2d ed. 1953.
A supplement to *Spiritual Folk-Songs,* presenting additional material that could not be included in the earlier publication, with some new material from

the Northeast (hence the title). There are 300 complete tunes and texts.

———. *White and Negro Spirituals: Their Life Span and Kinship*. New York, 1944. Reprint, New York: Da Capo, 1975.
This study further explores popular religious hymnody, including that of revivalist and millennial sects, and the relation of the black to the white spiritual. The core of it is a comparative tune list of 116 white and black spirituals, printed side by side. Some of the author's conclusions have aroused controversy, but the scholarship is sound and perceptive.

———. *Another Sheaf of White Spirituals*. Jacksonville: University of Florida Press, 1952.
Another supplement to *Spiritual Folk-Songs* and *Down-East Spirituals*, containing another 363 tunes. The foreword by Charles Seeger and the introduction by the author (including a unique map) are valuable.

Representative Twentieth-Century Song and Hymn Collections

Christian Service Songs. Compiled by Homer Rodeheaver et al. Winona Lake, IN: Rodeheaver Hall-Mack, 1939.
From the Billy Sunday era of urban revivalism; successor to the nineteenth-century *Gospel Hymns Nos. 1 to 6*.

Favorite Songs and Hymns. Compiled by Morris, Stamps, Baxter, and Combs. Dallas: Stamps-Baxter, 1939.
Printed in seven-shape notation, this is representative of the twentieth-century rural white gospel tradition in the South and West.

The Baptist Standard Hymnal. Edited by Mrs. A. M. Townsend. Nashville, TN: Townsend Press, 1973. Published by the Sunday School Publishing Board of the National Baptist Convention.
Standard hymnal used in black Baptist churches today; a large collection of 745 hymns, it encompasses a broad range of material from nineteenth- and twentieth-century gospel hymnody, including hymns from the Lowell Mason, George Frederick Root, Ira Sankey, Homer Rodeheaver, and Charles A. Tindley eras.

More recent collections that reflect to a greater degree the influence of gospel music in the various denominations are: *The New National Baptist Hymnal* (incorporating songs by Cleveland and Crouch); *Songs of Zion* (from the United Methodist Church); *Lift Every Voice* (from the Episcopal Church); and *Yes, Lord!* (from the Church of God in Christ, a black Holiness church).
In addition, gospel songs are being published in octavo and songbook form by many of the same companies that produce records. One of the largest publishers of black gospel music is Lexicon Music.

Studies on Nineteenth-Century Hymnody

Foote, Henry Wilder. *Three Centuries of American Hymnody*. Hamden, CT: Shoe String Press, 1940. Reprint, 1961. Chapters 6, 7, 8.

Jackson, George Pullen. *White Spirituals in the Southern Uplands* (cited above).

Lorenz, Ellen Jane. *Glory, Hallelujah! The Story of the Campmeeting Spiritual*. Nashville, TN: Abingdon, 1978.
Includes music and words for forty-eight "northern campmeeting spirituals."

Lowens, Irving. *Music and Musicians in Early America*. New York: W. W. Norton, 1964.
This collection of essays contains a detailed study of *Wyeth's Repository of Sacred Music, Part II*.

Stevenson, Robert. *Protestant Church Music in America*. New York: W. W. Norton, 1966. Paperback reprint, 1970.
In this brief but well-documented study, chapters 8 and 10 are relevant.

Studies on Twentieth-Century Gospel Music

Boyer, Horace Clarence. "A Comparative Analysis of Traditional and Contemporary Gospel Music" in *More Than Dancing,* ed. Irene V. Jackson. Westport, CT: Greenwood, 1985.

———. "Contemporary Gospel Music," *Black Perspectives in Music,* vol. 7, no. 2 (Spring 1979).

Heilbut, Tony. *The Gospel Sound.* New York: Simon & Schuster, 1971. The subject is black gospel music. While there is much information, mostly anecdotal, the book is press-agentish in tone and approach, and is not the kind of serious, well-documented study the subject deserves.

———. "The Secularization of Black Gospel Music" in *Folk Music and Modern Sound,* eds. William Ferris and Mary L. Hart. Jackson: University Press of Mississippi, 1982.

Jackson, Irene V. *Afro-American Religious Music: A Bibliography and Catalog of Gospel Music.* Westport, CT: Greenwood, 1979.

Malone, Bill C. *Country Music, U.S.A.* Rev. ed. Austin: University of Texas Press, 1985. While dealing primarily with secular music, it furnishes valuable background on rural white gospel music.

———. *Southern Music—American Music.* Lexington: University Press of Kentucky, 1979. This has more material specifically on gospel music than does *Country Music, U.S.A.*

Oliver, Paul. *Songsters and Saints: Vocal Traditions on Race Records.* Cambridge: Cambridge University Press, 1984. Well-documented and well-written study of blues and gospel recordings made in the late 1920s. See the Listening section below for recordings of the examples.

Warrick, Mancel, et al. *The Progress of Gospel Music: From Spirituals to Contemporary Gospel.* New York: Vantage, 1977.

Wolfe, Charles K. "Gospel Goes Uptown: White Gospel Music, 1945–1955" in *Folk Music and Modern Sound,* eds. William Ferris and Mary L. Hart. Jackson: University Press of Mississippi, 1982.

Historical and Religious Background

Anderson, Robert Mapes. *Vision of the Disinherited: The Making of American Pentecostalism.* New York: Oxford University Press, 1979.

Boles, John B. *The Great Revival, 1787–1805.* Lexington: University Press of Kentucky, 1972.

Bruce, Dickson D., Jr. *And They All Sang Hallelujah.* Knoxville: University of Tennessee Press, 1974.

Goodspeed, Rev. E. J. *A Full History of the Wonderful Career of Moody and Sankey in Great Britain and America.* New York, 1876. Reprint, New York: AMS Press, 1973.

Johnson, Charles A. *The Frontier Camp Meeting.* Dallas: SMU Press, 1955.

Levine, Lawrence W. *Black Culture and Black Consciousness.* New York: Oxford University Press, 1978.

Sizer, Sandra S. *Gospel Hymns and Social Religion: The Rhetoric of Nineteenth-Century Revivalism.* Philadelphia: Temple University Press, 1978.

Weisberger, Bernard A. *They Gathered at the River: The Story of the Great Revivalists and Their Impact upon Religion in America.* Boston: Little, Brown, 1958.

Listening

Nineteenth Century

White Spirituals from "The Sacred Harp." NW-205.
Twenty folk hymns, anthems, and fuging tunes as sung by the Alabama Sacred Harp Convention in 1959, with complete printed versions in shape-note notation for all the pieces. Remarks and prayers are included, and help convey the singers' feeling for the music, and for these annual "sings." Notes by Alan Lomax.

Sacred Harp Singing. AAFS: L-11.
This 1942 recording of the same convention as above includes nineteen pieces, only some of which are the same. Technically inferior to NW-205, but a fine documentary.

Old Harp Singers. Folkways 2356.
Made by the Old Harp Singers of eastern Tennessee, who belong to the seven-shape-note tradition.

The Gospel Ship: Baptist Hymns & White Spirituals from the Southern Mountains. NW-294. Notes by Alan Lomax.

Brighten the Corner Where You Are: Black and White Urban Hymnody. NW-224.
The first four tracks of side 2 are nineteenth-century urban gospel songs and hymns.

Where Home Is: Life in 19th-Century Cincinnati. NW-251.
Includes several evangelistic songs and a temperance song.

Twentieth century

The following anthologies consist mostly of old 78-rpm recordings documenting early gospel music.

An Introduction to Gospel Song. Folkways RF-5.
Black tradition only.

Country Gospel Song. Folkways RF-19.
Both black and white traditions.

Anthology of American Folk Music, vol. 2. Folkways 2952.
Both black and white traditions; includes four sermons.

The Asch Recordings, vol. 1. Folkways AA1/2.
Includes two cuts of the Gospel Keys (one of them Dorsey's "Precious Lord"), and two cuts of Ernestine Washington with Bunk Johnson's band.

Folk Song Types. NW-245.
Includes one track by an early white gospel group, Ernest Phipps and his Holiness Singers, and one *Sacred Harp* selection.

Brighten the Corner Where You Are: Black and White Urban Hymnody. NW-224.
A good anthology, with notes by Anthony Heilbut and Harry Eskew.

Favorite Gospel Songs. Folkways 2357.
A 1950s recording of older gospel material, much of it from the nineteenth-century Moody-Sankey tradition, and from the early twentieth-century seven-shape-note collections published by Vaughan, Stamps-Baxter, and others.

Chuck Wagon Gang. Columbia Historic Edition FC-40152.
Sixteen songs from 1936 to 1960 by this popular white gospel group.

Great Ladies of Gospel. Savoy SA 7095.
Sixteen tracks, on four sides; one each of almost all the important "divas" except Mahalia Jackson. Unfortunately lacks documentation.

Songsters and Saints. 2 vols. Matchbox 2001/2 and 2003/4.
Recordings accompanying and illustrating Paul Oliver's book of the same title.

Negro Religious Music. 3 vols. Blues Classics 17, 18, 19.

The Golden Age of Gospel Singing. Folklyric 9046.

Acapella Gospel Singing. Folklyric 9045.

Jubilee to Gospel. J.E.M.F. 108.

A large selection of gospel recordings, and an extensive catalog, is available from Down Home Music, Inc.

Two recommended recent albums are:

Sacramento Community Choir Live. Onyx R 3824.

Show Me the Way. The New Jerusalem Baptist Church Choir (of Flint, Michigan). Sound of Gospel Records, SoG-2D160.

As in popular music, quasi-anthologies are available in the form of reissues labeled "The Best of . . ." or ". . . 's Greatest Hits." Unfortunately, most such collections give little or no documentation as to the dates or personnel of the original recordings. Heilbut's *The Gospel Sound* has a fairly extensive discography.

PROJECTS

1. If you like to sing folk songs, learn two folk hymns from one of the nineteenth-century shape-note collections, and add them to your repertory. (The tenor, or next to the bottom line, has the tune.) Look up the tunes in Jackson, *Spiritual Folk-Songs of Early America,* and put together a brief commentary on the songs.

2. Try to find three folk hymns from the shape-note tradition that are included in present-day hymnals. As in project 1 above, find out what you can about the tunes and put together a brief commentary.

3. Try to find three revival spirituals in present-day hymnals. As in projects 1 and 2 above, find out what you can about the tunes and put together a brief commentary. The Lorenz book in the reading list may also be helpful.

4. Find out what you can about the present state of shape-note singing (sometimes called Sacred Harp singing, or Old Harp singing) in this country, especially in your area. If there are regular meetings, or "sings," attend one and write a descriptive commentary. (More and more such groups are being formed in various parts of the country. They can often be located through the evangelical churches.) If there is no such activity in your area, find out about sings and singing societies elsewhere, especially in the South (the Knoxville Old Harp Singers is a typical group).

5. Make a brief biographical study of at least four of the nineteenth-century shape-note songbook compilers, giving what data you can find and including a listing of their books.

6. Write a commentary on the theology and/or sociology implicit in the texts of either the revival spirituals or the later gospel songs. For the former, the Sizer book in the reading list may be helpful.

7. Write a brief paper comparing the camp meetings of the Kentucky Revival with the large outdoor rock festivals of the 1960s.

8. Investigate the relationships between the revival spirituals and some types of children's songs sung at summer camps and elsewhere. Look for relationships of form and of tune, and even for parodies of the words.

9. Make a study of Holiness or Pentecostal churches in your area, especially as regards their music.

10. Make a survey of religious music in the repertory of currently popular country-music stars, including types of songs and, if possible, their origin. To what extent has the "message" song superseded the overtly religious or gospel song? How does the situation now compare with that in the generation of Hank Williams, Sr.? Of the Carter Family?

11. Make a survey of "Christian music" in the urban churches today, with emphasis on your own area if you live in a city.

12. Using W.E.B. DuBois's description of

the African-American preacher in *Souls of Black Folk* as a point of departure, carry this into our own time by writing a paper on the social and political roles of the black preacher since mid-century. Has the relationship of preacher to congregation carried over into the relationship of speaker to audience? In what ways?

13. Make a survey of the hymns of Charles Albert Tindley, and the extent to which they are found in hymn collections of the past ten to fifteen years.

14. Make a study of the singing of any of the female "divas" of black gospel music mentioned in this chapter. Describe her vocal style as best you can; compare it with the singing of any of the female blues singers or soul singers.

15. Make a study of the music in the black churches in your area. How does it relate to the gospel music described in this chapter? What part do older hymns or spirituals play in the repertory? Are there differences in musical preferences between one denomination and another?

16. Listen to some examples of both "traditional" and "contemporary" gospel music. In an essay, make your own comparisons between them, evaluate what you see as the function of each, and conclude with a well-reasoned expression of your own preference.

17. Make a study of the hymn "Amazing Grace": its sources, its history, and an annotated discography of performances in both the white and the black traditions.

Photo courtesy of Southern Historical Collection, University of North Carolina

PART THREE

Three Prodigious Offspring of the Rural South

THE rural American South, in its isolation and its conservatism, fathered, like a patriarchal Abraham, two musical offspring, reared in private within its confines and long unknown outside. Like Isaac and the outcast Ishmael, son of the bondwoman, the country music of white people and the blues of black people are these two offspring—half-brothers, unlike in significant ways, yet sharing a patrimony and a native soil. As the prophecy runs, both have become in our time mighty musical nations with half a century of commercial success behind them. And the two nations, so long segregated, have been reunited in a third prodigious, electrified, urbanized offshoot: rock.

How did the South come to produce its Isaac and its Ishmael? What were the antecedents, musically and culturally? Are there certain enduring characteristics of both? These questions we shall attempt to explore, and we shall trace the two musics as they emerged from the isolation of folklore into the bright public arena of popular culture. For both assuredly come straight out of folk origins. Hardly better examples exist of forms of popular music whose characteristics so clearly derive from their cultural ambience than those furnished by country music and the blues.

And what of this ambience? The South, spelled with a capital S, seems to call up in the mind of most Americans more than simply a geographical area (that roughly coextensive with the states of the old Confederacy). If it is the land, it is also the people, the culture, the climate; further than this, it is a history, a lore, a habit of thinking, an aura, almost a mythology. It is not surprising that the South has constituted the largest and richest single reservoir of folklore we have.

Why should this be? Two key words have already been mentioned: isolation and conservatism. The isolation has been not only geographic (of the lowlands as well as the highlands) but also demographic—an isolation of the southern people, largely, from the greater mass of the American people. For once the frontier had passed through and moved on west, there was emigration from the South but little significant immigration to the South. And the conservatism, of course, owed a good deal to this isolation, but also to the almost exclusively agrarian economy; to the hierarchical (if not actually aristocratic) social and political structure; to the defensive attitude assumed almost monolithically by southern whites toward the institution of slavery and its equally problematic sequel, white supremacy; and, last but by no means least, to the prevailing orthodox religious modes of thought. Out of this soil, then, sprang the two most pervasive forms of rural music America has ever produced (or is ever likely to produce, so profoundly have cultural patterns altered) and, as a second generation, a citified but visceral amalgamation that has revolutionized popular music throughout the English-speaking world. In Chapters 7, 8, and 9 we shall take a closer look at each of them in turn.

7

Country Music

THE latent popularity of country, or "hillbilly," music,[1] fully revealed only after it had spread beyond its original geographical limits in the 1930s and 1940s, was one of the surprises of the century, at least to those who were generally supposed to be wise in such matters—that is, city-bred entrepreneurs and savants of popular culture. Its base of popularity was found not only in the rural South and, as might be expected, among its people who had emigrated to the cities and to other parts of the country, but also among rural white people elsewhere who had no cultural ties with the South at all. We are dealing, then, with the closest thing to a universal "people's music" that rural white Americans have had.[2]

Enduring Characteristics of the Music

Despite evolution and change, which have been as forcefully at work in country music as in any other, certain enduring characteristics have been consistently identified with it. The choice of instruments, the style of singing, the melody, and the harmony are all distinctive.

The Instruments

Country music, in the main, is music played on those stringed instruments that are easily portable. (Rarely homemade, they were readily obtainable in the early days from mail-order firms.) The dominant instrument in country music is unquestionably the *fiddle*. As the only stringed instrument capable of producing a sustained tone, it takes the lead, not only in the fiddle tunes intended for dancing (and it was long associated with dance music, both in America and in Europe) but in the long preludes and interludes in songs and ballads. The straight, penetrating, vibrato-less tone and the sliding up into the longer held notes are characteristic, and are akin to the way in which the human voice, too, is handled.

All the rest of the stringed instruments are plucked or strummed. The *mountain dulcimer* and the *autoharp* belong more to the folk origins of this music, and did not survive long into country music itself. The *banjo*, however (possibly acquired in the lowlands, through contact with the blacks and minstrelsy), became an early mainstay of country music, where it established itself as being useful for solos, for accompanying songs, and for furnishing both harmony and rhythm in small bands. In the second quarter of this century it was almost supplanted by the *guitar*, a somewhat more resonant instrument with a greater range, which took over the same functions. In the present era's revival of older styles the banjo has come into its own again, and its pungent tone in the hands of virtuosos has made it once more a lead instrument, even rivaling the fiddle in importance. The *mandolin* entered country music in the 1930s, being at first associated with Bill Monroe and subsequently with the whole style known as "bluegrass." With its thin but penetrating tone, the mandolin for a time also competed with the banjo for the lead parts.

Country music has not been immune to outside influences, and new instruments have tended to bring with them their own peculiar styles of playing. Thus the mandolin, long associated with the popular music of Italy, has brought to country music the rapid *tremolando* sustaining of long notes characteristic of the Italian manner of playing.[3] Another exotic addition to the hillbilly band came from the other direction—in fact, from as far west as Hawaii, probably by way of the Hawaiian bands that were so popular in this country in the early decades of this century. The Hawaiian *steel guitar*, with its sliding, wailing sound, was appropriated by country musicians as far back as the 1920s and 1930s. (Similar sliding effects were obtained by many early black blues guitarists, stopping the strings with broken bottles, or knife blades.) A guitar with a built-in resonator, which served to amplify the sound mechanically before the advent of the electric guitar, was known as the *Dobro*.[4]

The *string bass*, a much less portable instrument, came relatively late to country music, probably from the jazz band. Still later (and still less portable) additions have come with "rural electrification"; the steel guitar was the first to be electrically amplified, followed by the standard guitar and the string bass.

The Style of Singing

A characteristic manner of singing songs and ballads has remained fairly constant throughout the years, and is in fact one of the features that have stamped country music indelibly. A direct carryover from the folk singing of the rural South, it is typified, in its more traditional phase, by a high, nasal, and somewhat strained tone.[5] The "lonesome," impassive manner of delivery (which gives an impression of the singer's detachment from the hearers, though not from the song) is suited to the impersonality of the ballad tradition. The clear, vibrato-less tone so akin to that of the country fiddle also lends itself to the kind of vocal ornamentation familiar in this music: short slides and anticipatory flourishes heard in advance of the principal notes, especially in slow tunes.[6] This is distinctly folk practice.

This high, tense, rigid vocal quality was later modified somewhat, particularly under southwestern influence. A tendency for the voice to "break," as if under the stress of the song's emotions, was introduced as a more subjective style crept into the music, and as the audience, seen or unseen, began to be more of a factor in the delivery of the song.

A familiar vocal feature, particularly in lowland and western styles, was the yodel. It became associated with cowboy music, but it was first recorded by a singer from Georgia,[7] and probably comes from a combination of influences: black field hollers and blues; Mexican song; and possibly (representing still another exotic influence on country music!) the yodeling of Swiss singers who toured the Midwest in the nineteenth century.[8] Jimmie Rodgers popularized the yodel, through his series of "blue yodels," around 1930; it is seldom heard today except in specialty numbers deliberately evocative of some of the older railroad or cowboy songs.[9]

Essential to any consideration of vocal style is that utter sincerity of delivery without which country music is not genuine. This has been commented upon frequently by observers both within and outside the tradition. It too is a direct inheritance from folk origins. The impassive face, the often-closed eyes, the unashamed tear on the singer's cheek—these can be parodied and laughed at by sophisticates, but the sincerity and total immersion in the song and its subject of which they are only the visible manifestations is absolutely central to the meaning of country singing. Hank Williams expressed it vividly when asked about the success of country music:

> It can be explained in just one word: sincerity. When a hillbilly sings a crazy song, he feels crazy. When he sings, "I Laid My Mother Away," he sees her a-laying right there in the coffin. He sings more sincere than most entertainers because the hillbilly was raised rougher than most entertainers. You got to know a lot about hard work. You got to have smelt a lot of mule manure before you can sing like a hillbilly.[10]

Melody and Harmony

Sophistication of melody or harmony are not to be found, by and large, in country music. There are reasons for this. We have seen in Chapter 1 how the folk music of the ballad tradition that showed English and Scottish influence tended to preserve the old modal scales, with their attendant archaic-sounding melodic patterns. As country music sought to expand its public, and thus both to compete with and to be influenced by urban popular music, the old quaint and often hauntingly beautiful modal tunes began to lose favor. Singers brought up in the older tradition still sang them privately but were reluctant to record them, or sing them for "outsiders."[11] We have already investigated in Chapter 1 the process by which old tunes fell victims to the new practice of accompanying folk songs, chiefly on the guitar. Thus either the old tunes were greatly modified or else, most frequently, altogether new tunes were substituted—melodies that became inseparable from their accompaniment and therefore were tied to a harmonic framework of the utmost simplicity.

The melodies of two of the best-known songs in the repertoire will illustrate the harmonic vocabulary of most country-music tunes. Both imply the same three basic chords only; further, both tunes follow the outlines of their clearly implied harmonies. The first is "Wildwood Flower" (Example 7–1).[12]

Example 7–1

I V7 I
Oh, he taught me to love him and called_ me his flower
I V7 I
That was bloom-ing to cheer him through life's_ drea-ry hour;
I IV I
Oh, I long to see him and re - gret the dark hour, He's
I V7 I
gone and neg - lec - ted this pale__ wild-wood flower.

The tune of the second song, "Wabash Cannon Ball" (Example 7–2), follows its chord outlines even more faithfully; only seven tones in the entire tune do not belong to the prevailing chords.[13]

Though "Wildwood Flower" has been unmistakably a country song ever since the Carter Family recorded it in the 1920s, the melody can be traced to sources outside the rural South—in this case, as in many others, to a parlor song of the previous century. As the scholar D. K. Wilgus has said, "A good percentage of the lyric songs of the early hillbilly tradition seem to derive from the nineteenth century sentimental parlor song—and are often considerably improved in the process."[14] The parlor song (which will be dealt with in more detail in Chapter 12), with its melodies governed by these same simple harmonies, was extremely popular with amateur singers. Many of them were published, and therefore no doubt sung, with guitar accompaniment as an alternative to the piano; this early adaptation to the guitar must have made even easier their later passage into the repertoire of country musicians.[15]

In country music, as in folk music, tunes are freely borrowed and adapted to make new songs. The tune of "Wildwood Flower" became the basis for Woody Guthrie's "The Sinking of the *Reuben James*" (see Chapter 4); and "Wabash Cannon Ball" furnished the model for "Footprints in the Snow," a favorite among bluegrass performers. "I'm Thinking Tonight of My Blue Eyes"

Example 7–2

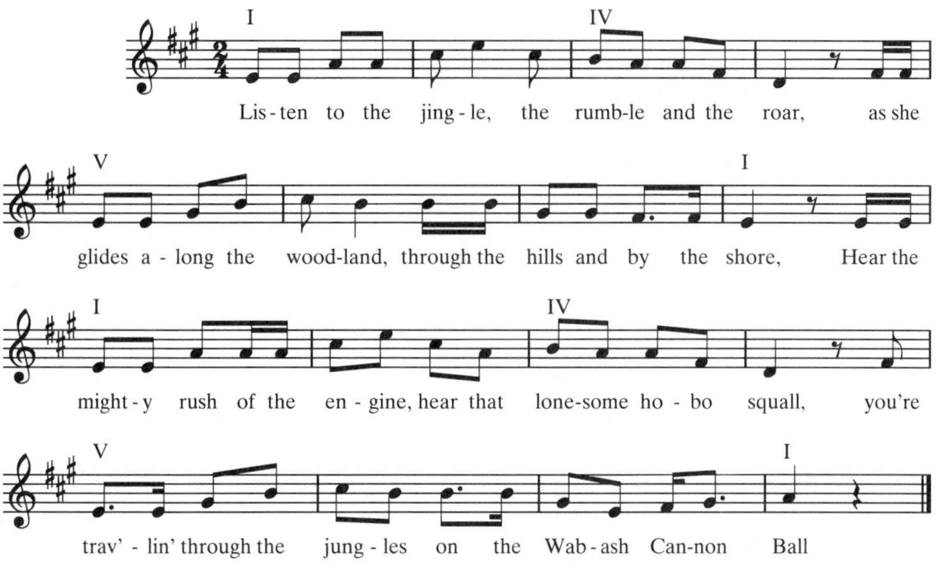
I
IV
Lis - ten to the jing - le, the rumb-le and the roar, as she
V
I
glides a - long the wood-land, through the hills and by the shore, Hear the
I
IV
might - y rush of the en - gine, hear that lone-some ho - bo squall, you're
V
I
trav' - lin' through the jung - les on the Wab - ash Can-non Ball

has become a kind of generic country music tune (though like many others it probably originated elsewhere). It was the basis for "Great Speckled Bird," made famous by Roy Acuff; for "It Wasn't God Who Made Honky-Tonk Angels," as sung by Kitty Wells; and for the translation of the latter into the Cajun song "Le cote farouche de la vic."[16]

An exception to the harmonic simplicity of conventional country music tunes is occasionally found in so-called "old-time" songs, some of which have been taken over into the bluegrass repertory. Here can be detected vestiges of the old modes discussed in Chapter 1. The most frequently encountered survivor is the Mixolydian mode, with its flatted seventh degree of the scale. It can be heard, for example, in the song "The Old Man at the Mill," as sung by Clarence Ashley (Example 7–3).[17]

Example 7–3

Same old man liv - in' at the mill, the mill turns a-round of its
own free will; one hand in the hop-per and the oth - er in the sack.
Ladi - es step for - ward and the gents fall back.

Here the flatted seventh is harmonized in a way that paradoxically sounds quite modern. That it can sound that way to our ears is due to the fact that popular music has, in a way, come full circle; new expanded and more eclectic harmonic practices have found ways to embrace the old modal scales, which thus have enjoyed a considerable revival in folk-oriented rock and even in jazz. The same Mixolydian survival can be heard in a ballad made famous by the Carter Family, "John Hardy."[18]

We cannot leave a consideration of the musical characteristics of country music without taking account of the influence of hillbilly music's half-brother, the African-American blues. There can be no doubt of the continuing musical exchange that went on between rural blacks and whites, especially in the lowlands. Many white country musicians, such as Dock Boggs and Jimmie Rodgers, learned much from black musicians in their formative years. Thus it was that musical characteristics of the blues went into the vocabulary of country music. The most evident influences were blues harmonies and blues intonation; the variable, sliding pitch of the third degree of the scale, for example, was a vocal effect that could very well be imitated on the fiddle. These influences were of course most evident in the actual blues numbers, designated as such. From very early times, these blues were a part of country music.

Enduring Characteristics of the Words

The words of songs and ballads, and their meaning for both performer and listener, are of paramount importance in country music, just as they are in folk music. They exhibit, furthermore, certain pervasive traits that have consistently characterized this genre through its half-century of change, and that may therefore be thought of as typical. Most significant are those having to do with fundamental attitudes and recurrent themes; less so, but nevertheless interesting, are characteristics such as the use of dialect and other regionalisms.

Fundamental Attitudes

Country music is steeped in a unique and somewhat paradoxical blend of realism and sentimentality. The realism reveals itself in a readiness to treat almost any human situation in song, and to deal unflinchingly with any aspect of life that genuinely touches the emotions. It shows up in extreme cases, for example, in the depicting of such grim scenes as the following:

> He went upstairs to make her hope
> And found her hanging on a rope.[19]

A later song, "Wreck on the Highway," updates this penchant for furnishing grisly details.[20] Such unsparing realism (a characteristic of the ballad tradition) contrasts strikingly with the conventionalized subject matter and treatment of most urban commercial song before 1950, and identifies country music as a progenitor of the subsequent "revolution" in American popular music.

Paradoxically, the obverse of this realism is a nearly universal tendency toward sentimentality—a sentimentality that may often strike one outside the tradition as excessive, and even on occasion tinged with self-pity.[21]

> Walking down this lonesome road,
> I'll travel while I cry
> If there's no letter in the mail,
> I'll bid this world goodbye.[22]

The traditional song "I'm a Man of Constant Sorrow" is almost a prototype of this attitude, pushed to the verge of exaggeration:

> I am a man of constant sorrow,
> I've seen trouble all my days.
> I bid farewell to old Kentucky,
> The place where I was borned and raised.
>
> . . . . . .
>
> You can bury me in some deep valley
> For many years where I may lay
> Then you may learn to love another
> While I am sleeping in my grave.[23]

The sentimentalizing of objects is common, especially in the "weepers" of the later, more commercial phase of country music, such as "Send Me the Pillow You Dream On." The pathetic fallacy is frequently encountered: objects in nature, or even inanimate artifacts, may be endowed with the capacity for human feelings and even the ability to manifest them visibly. The lyrics of Hank Williams's "I'm So Lonesome I Could Cry" are typical in this regard.

Perennial Themes

The subjects of country songs and ballads, while diverse, group themselves easily around certain perennial themes. One is love:

> Tell me that you love me, Katy Cline.
> Tell me that your love's as true as mine.[24]

Another is death:

> There's a little black train a-coming
> Fix all your business right;
> There's a little black train a-coming
> And it may be here tonight.[25]

Still another is religion:

> I am bound for that beautiful city
> My Lord has prepared for his own,
> Where all the redeemed of all ages
> Sing, "Glory!" around the white throne.[26]

And a fourth is nostalgia:

> There's a peaceful cottage there,
> A happy home so dear.
> My heart is longing for them day by day.[27]

Trains figure prominently in country music, as they do in blues:

> I'm riding on that New River train
> I'm riding on that New River train
> The same old train that brought me here
> Is going to carry me away.[28]

They were links with big cities and faraway places; they could put the overwhelming separation of distance between lovers, and they could overcome that separation. The railroad train and the life of the rambler were romanticized in rural thought. In recent times the truck and even the jet airplane have figured in country songs, but they have not seized the imagination with anything like the vivid intensity that the train has been able to evoke.

Songs about events were once an important part of country music, and any country singer worthy of the name could make up his own songs on important happenings of the day, local or national.

> Come all you fathers and mothers,
> And brothers, sisters too,
> I'll relate to you the history
> Of the Rowan County Crew.[29]

This trait shows clearly country music's relation to the earlier ballad tradition. And in fact a fine assortment of native ballads and near-ballads found their way into country music. Many songs and ballads collected by Cecil Sharp in the southern highlands in 1916–18 appear in country music recordings of the 1920s and 1930s, often with the typical instrumental accompaniment of fiddle, banjo, and guitar.[30] The ballad "John Hardy," already cited, was presumably based on an actual episode in 1894 that culminated in the execution of one John Hardy for murder in West Virginia. It was collected by Sharp in 1916, and was recorded commercially by the influential Carter Family in 1930.[31]

The ballad tradition was kept alive as event songs continued to be written. With the coming of commercialism, it became vital to hit the market as soon after the event as possible. A song based on General Douglas MacArthur's speech before Congress in 1951, after President Harry Truman removed him from command in Korea, was written and recorded within hours of the event, while a song on the assassination of Senator Huey Long of Louisiana in 1935 was written two years *before* his death—and was even sung to him by its author.[32] The growth of mass communications in our time has virtually stopped the production of event songs, but songs such as "White House Blues" (on the assassination of President William McKinley in 1901) or "The Louisiana Earthquake" are still sung by those interested in traditional country music.

Dialect and Other Regionalisms

The early country singers naturally retained not only their regional accent in their songs but their dialect as well, of which such usages as "a-going," "a-coming," "rise you up," and "yonders" may be given as samples. With the first wave of commercial success and the broadening of country music's public, there was a tendency (on the part of singers like Jimmie Rodgers, for example) to drop the dialect and substitute standard English. In more recent country music there are a few vernacular survivals, such as the well-nigh universal "ain't," and the dropping of the final *g*'s of the *-ing* suffix ("ramblin'," "cheatin' "), which have become virtual clichés. The loss of an authentic vernacular, together with the introduction of such devices as more sophisticated rhymes ("infatuation," "sensation," "imagination"), has introduced an artificial conventionality to latter-day country music, which has already lost many of its distinctive regional characteristics in the general process of commercial homogenization.

Commercial Beginnings: Early Recordings, Radio, and the First Stars

We first encounter country music proper as it emerged from the folk tradition into the professional and commercial realm of the popular tradition in the 1920s. Within the folk culture, some professionalism had begun to develop even before the "discovery" of this music by the outside world. The fiddler and the itinerant entertainer were familiar figures. Just as traveling minstrel bands furnished an apprenticeship for many black musicians who later became jazz performers, so more than a few white country musicians got their professional start as itinerant players and singers with the medicine shows that toured the rural South.[33] Thus there was no lack of performers, both singly and in groups, and ranging in ability from the mediocre to the highly proficient, who were on hand for the exposure that came in the 1920s.

Although commercial phonograph recording was established before the turn of the century, its application to jazz, blues, and hillbilly music did not come for another two decades, principally because recording executives either were only dimly aware that those genres existed or were unsure as to whether there was a market for such recordings. In view of later developments, this is somewhat ironic. When recording companies did move into the area of hillbilly music (camouflaging it at first under such names as "old-time music" or "old familiar tunes"),[34] they did so at least partly in response to growing competition from that other powerful new medium of the day, radio. Thus the roles of radio and phonograph recording in the dissemination and popularization of country music were elaborately intertwined from the start—and still are, as we shall see.

The account of two old-time fiddlers—one from Texas, dressed in cowboy clothes, and the other from Virginia, dressed in a Confederate uniform—showing up in 1922 at the offices of the Victor Company in New York, fresh from a reunion of Civil War veterans in Virginia, to record their music, is one to give a pleasant stir to the imagination.[35] It was one beginning, though not a commercially significant one. Another, more significant one was made the following year in Atlanta, when the Georgia moonshiner, circus barker, and political campaign performer Fiddlin' John Carson (who had recently become a locally popular radio performer) recorded "The Little Old Log Cabin in the Lane" and "The Old Hen Cackled and the Rooster's Going to Crow."[36] This recording proved to be phenomenally, and prophetically, successful—and the move to record hillbilly music was on. Recording companies made excursions into the South, set up temporary studios, and began recording country musicians by the score, either singly or in groups. In other cases the newfound artists were brought to New York to record. A few who were recorded in the twenties became famous—the stars of the ensuing period. These included Uncle Dave Macon (from Tennessee), the Carter Family (from Virginia), Gid Tanner and his Skillet Lickers (from Georgia), Vernon Dalhart (from Texas), and Jimmie Rodgers (from Mississippi).

Radio broadcasting, until then an amateur's plaything, suddenly came of age in the 1920s. As receiving sets came within the economic reach of more and more Americans, broadcasting stations appeared and multiplied, and with them grew the demand for performers to cater to the new invisible audience. Some stations in the South began almost immediately to broadcast country music by local musicians, most notably WSB, Atlanta, in 1922. In 1925 WSM in Nashville began a show, with two unpaid performers and without a commercial sponsor, that was to evolve into "Grand Ole Opry." The early radio programs, like the early recordings, presented a highly traditional country music, still close to its folk origins.[37] But its very popularity generated winds of change.

It is certainly not true that the radio and the phonograph record "created" country music. However, when a medium brings a particular genre into contact with a broader public, and transforms its performers into professionals whose success depends upon pleasing that larger public, changes are bound to be wrought. This was the situation in which country music found itself after its first wave of popularity and dissemination.

Of the five "stars" of early country music mentioned above, the first two are representative of performers who never essentially changed their style or material in order consciously to appeal to a larger audience. David Harrison ("Uncle Dave") Macon (1870–1952) got his professional start playing banjo and singing in vaudeville, and the basis of his style and repertory was his background in nineteenth-century minstrel, circus, and vaudeville songs and routines. Such versatility was typical of early country performers, and he also sang and recorded hymns and his own topical songs. He was a favorite performer on "Grand Ole Opry" from 1925 to 1952.[38] The Carter Family (A.P., Maybelle, and Sara) came from a Virginia mountain background. Their varied repertory (which included not only nineteenth-century parlor songs but also early Tin Pan Alley songs and gospel hymns, as well as ballads and other folk material) made them very influential, as did their distinctive sound and style, with Sara Carter playing autoharp, and Maybelle Carter playing the melody on the bass strings of the guitar and the harmony and rhythm on the upper strings.

The Skillet Lickers were a group whose nucleus (Gid Tanner, fiddler, and Riley Puckett, guitarist) got their start on the radio in Atlanta, and then, with two other Georgia musicians, began recording for Columbia in New York. Theirs was essentially a string band sound, dominated by two fiddles. In the beginning highly traditional in their repertoire, they later broadened it to include material from Tin Pan Alley, jazz, and popular music.[39]

Vernon Dalhart and Jimmie Rodgers, in contrast to Macon and the Carters, anticipated the commercial success of what eventually became known as country music, and consciously adapted their style and material for broader appeal. Vernon Dalhart (1883–1948; he was born Marion Try Slaughter, and like the later Conway Twitty he combined the names to two southern towns to create a stage name) was a trained singer who for a decade sang and recorded popular songs and light opera in and around New York before turning opportunistically to hillbilly music when he saw its commercial potential. The somewhat incongruous combination of his "stage" tenor voice, complete with vibrato, with his conscious traces of dialect ("sayin'," "warnin'," "willin' ") symbolized the entry of the professional entertainers into country music.[40]

Jimmie Rodgers (1897–1933) based his career on music he had actually grown up with, but he contributed enormously to the popularization of that music, and in the process wore a number of different country "hats."

The work of country music's first real "star" embodied many of the changes that were to come. Jimmie Rodgers, the "Singing Brakeman" of Meridian, Mississippi, had an extremely short career as a performing and recording artist. But in a mere six years (from his first trial recording in 1927 to his death in 1933) he recorded 111 songs, sold twenty million records, became internationally famous, and led country music into greener pastures than it had ever dreamed existed.

Rodgers recorded many types of songs: sentimental love songs, melancholy nostalgic songs, cowboy and railroad songs, white blues. Many he wrote himself, many were written for him; he was able to put across a great variety of material by the force of his sincerity and personality. His eclecticism was bound to lead him away somewhat from traditional country songs and traditional country style. He introduced the famous "blue yodel" into country music, and was really one of the first popular "crooners." With the advent of Jimmie Rodgers, the attention and emphasis in country music shifted to the solo singer.[41]

Rodgers's career marked the passage of country music into full-fledged commercialism. Yet it did not thereby cease to be a genuine "people's music," and some interesting interaction between the commercial country music of the thirties and what was held to be "folk music" shows how complex the relationship between the two had become after the advent of radio and recordings. We have already noted in Chapter 1 some of these interactions; as further reinforcement it can be noted that folklorists traveling through the South in the 1930s, in the first wave of collecting on behalf of the Library of Congress and others, "discovered" and collected songs that their singers had learned from the commercial recordings of Jimmie Rodgers!

Hillbilly music's native soil was the upland South, and this region furnished more musicians to be heard from in the 1930s and 1940s—musicians raised in the string band tradition. From this hill country came the Blue Sky Boys (Bill and Earl Bolick, from western North Carolina), the Delmore Brothers (Alton and Rabon, from northeastern Alabama), and, among the best known in this period, Roy Acuff (b. 1903 in eastern Tennessee). And from lowlands only slightly to the west (in west central Kentucky) came the Monroe Brothers, Bill and Charles. It is the music these performers produced—played with acoustic guitar, mandolin, fiddle, with the occasional string bass, steel guitar, dobro, or harmonica, and sung with a straight, unembellished vocal tone and unaffected regional accent—that has come to be unmistakably identified with the country music of the Southeast.[42] But meanwhile the West was being heard from.

The West: The Cowboy Image

America has long pursued a love affair with its own romantic conception of the West and the cowboy. The "western branch" of country music has played its part in the propagation of this romanticism. For just as the Southwest is in large degree a cultural extension of the South, so is "western" music an extension and adaptation of hillbilly music.

The link, of course, is Texas. Here the southern influence, especially in east Texas, is notably strong. The country was settled primarily by southern planters, and slavery and the raising of cotton flourished, along with southern religion, culture, and folklore. But Texas is also, as the song goes, "where the West begins." The dry and spacious topography, the open range and the raising and transporting of cattle to the new railroads, and ultimately the industrialization following the oil boom produced a distinctive Texan economy; while the influence of Mexican, Louisiana Cajun, and midwestern American culture distinguished Texas culturally from the old South.

Authentic Cowboy Music

There is a rich store of authentic cowboy and frontier songs that were actually sung in the old West. As Charlie Seemann has pointed out:

> Authentic traditional cowboy songs are occupational folk songs, as are songs of sailors, loggers and miners. They grew out of the day-to-day work experience and reflect the tasks and life of the working cowboy. In these songs we find a harsh realism as the cowboys deal with the business of herding cattle, the hardships and dangers of the drive, and the food and living conditions on the trail and in the cow camps.[43]

Many of these songs were adaptations of broadside ballads or nineteenth-century popular songs. It is some indication of the romantic interest in the West that they were among the first folk songs, after African-American spirituals, to be collected and published in the United States, antedating even the attention given to southern mountain songs.[44] Early singers like Jules Verne Allen and Harry "Haywire Mac" McClintock, who really *had* been cowboys, and Carl T. Sprague and Powder River Jack Lee, who learned songs at first hand from cowboys, made recordings of cowboy songs in the 1920s.[45] But the cowboy image did not loom large in American popular culture until the advent of western movies and the "singing cowboy."

The Cowboy Image on Records and Film

The "western" part of the trade designation "country-and-western" was added as cowboy life began to be romanticized, with stylized costumes, props, and settings. The western movie played a large role in this process. Ken Maynard was perhaps the first singing cowboy; he sang two traditional songs in *The Wagon Master* as early as 1929. The genre—and the image—was well launched in the 1930s. Jimmie Rodgers, already a star as the "Singing Brakeman" from Mississippi, adopted the ten-gallon hat, Texas as his home state, and the role of singing cowboy. Native Texans such as Gene Autry, Ernest Tubb, and Woodward Maurice "Tex" Ritter soon capitalized further on this image.* Rubye Blevins moved from her native Arkansas to California and became, as Patsy Montana, the first singing cowgirl. The Sons of the Pioneers, which included Leonard Slye (later Roy Rogers), was among the earliest singing groups.[46]

Thus the western image and motif became established in country music. But paradoxically, few actual cowboy songs went into its repertoire. The country music entertainer adopted cowboy dress (often in fancy and exaggerated form) and continued to sing country songs. It was the production of cowboy films in Hollywood that spurred the writing of popular songs based on western themes, as opposed to authentic cowboy songs. Thus it was that songs like "Tumbling Tumbleweeds" and "Cool Water," by Bob Nolan (a Canadian by birth), and "The Last Roundup," by Billy Hill (who was born and grew up in Boston), became prototypes of the "western" song—and enjoyed enormous popularity.

The West: Realism and Eclecticism

Honky-Tonk Music

The occupation of cowboy has not gone out of existence. The chronicling, in song, poem, and story, of the lives and traditions of real-life cowboys, as they have changed and adapted over the years, continues.[47] But the open range, with its freely roaming cows and cowboys, was largely fenced and gone by 1900, and the great cattle drives ended a century ago. A more realistic ambience of the West, particularly in Texas, has been for half a century that of small farm towns and oil-boom towns, of truck stops and taverns; its more realistic heroes and heroines the oil "boomers," the truck drivers, and their women. A new kind of "western" music evolved to fit this environment—the environment of the honky-tonk. The honky-tonk, which Malone has described as a "social institution," was a generic term for the neon-light-emblazoned bars, taverns, saloons, dance halls, ballrooms, and nightclubs that grew up, gener-

* Their background was the farm, rather than the range, but farm life has never been successfully romanticized in America.

ally on the outskirts of towns. The music evolved for this environment had to emphasize the louder and more incisive instruments; the steel guitar and bass were standard, and the distinctly urban piano began to appear. The use of amplified instruments in country music really began, as a matter of necessity, with honky-tonk music. In the absence of live performers—and Malone has pointed out that country musicians "found receptive audiences in the oil communities"—the music reached its consumers via the ubiquitous jukebox.

The music was no longer concerned with nostalgia for rural life, home, or family, nor with traditional religion or mores; it dealt with harsh realities, preeminently loneliness and infidelity ("slippin' around"). "I'll Get Along Somehow," "Walking the Floor Over You," and "Try Me One More Time" were typical of the early 1940s; in the period after World War II, the themes were continued in songs like "I'm So Lonesome I Could Cry," "There's a Poison in Your Heart," "The Wild Side of Life" (also known as "I Didn't Know God Made Honky-Tonk Angels"), and its "answer song," "It Wasn't God Who Made Honky-Tonk Angels." Texans have been the main purveyors of the honky-tonk style. The durable Ernest Tubb, whose career lasted from the 1930s to the 1980s, was the one most associated with the genre, but other Texans such as Floyd Tillman (born in neighboring Oklahoma but raised in Texas), Lefty Frizzell, Hank Thompson, and Ray Price carried it on in the 1950s, as has George Jones in the 1970s.[48] In the 1970s and 1980s the Austin, Texas, "outlaw" wing of country-and-western music reincarnated the honky-tonk sound, style, subject matter, and spirit.[49]

Hybridization with Jazz: Western Swing

Texas, at the crossroads of a variety of influences, was hospitable to bands that were more innovative and eclectic in their instrumentation and repertory than those of the more traditional Southeast. It is not surprising, then, that Texas was the locale where hybridization took place between country music and big band jazz (including pronounced blues elements). The introduction of such hitherto alien instruments as saxophones, drums, and later trumpets into the string band of fiddles, mandolins, and guitars began as early as the 1930s. Bob Wills, most closely associated with this development, started his famous Texas Playboys in 1934; by the early 1940s the popularity of this eclectic blending of styles and repertory allowed him to move the band's base of operations from Texas to California, from whence he toured and recorded extensively. The mix became known as "western swing," and other bandleaders such as Milton Brown, Spade Cooley, Tex Williams, and Hank Penny cultivated it as well. California, more than Texas, nurtured this hybrid genre; Bakersfield-born Merle Haggard, among others, has been responsible for its recent revival.[50]

Postwar Dissemination and Full-Scale Commercialization

The migrations and upheavals that attended both the Depression of the 1930s and the World War of the 1940s had the effect of spreading country music far beyond the provincial soil that had given it birth, dispersing its devotees to the cities and their suburbs, and to all parts of the country. This regional music thus acquired nationwide popularity, and became altered—de-regionalized—in the process. This set the stage for its full-scale commercialization in the decades that followed.

Mainstream Stars of the 1950s and 1960s

The term "mainstream" is easy to use but difficult to define. Its use here is prompted by the fact that the country music stars mentioned below clearly came out of, and continued to cultivate, what might be described as the dominant and most characteristic traditions of country music.

Of these, Alabama-born Hank Williams (1923–1953) probably shone the brightest and cast the longest shadow—all the more remarkably since his career, like that of Jimmie Rodgers twenty years earlier, was brief (essentially 1947–52). His band, the Drifting Cowboys,* had a traditional instrumentation of fiddle, guitars, steel guitar, bass, and occasional mandolin. His vocal style could be relaxed and rhythmic or highly intense, depending on his material, and his technique included such traditional effects as a modified yodel (as in "Lovesick Blues"), and an almost-sobbing break on emotion-laden songs (as in "I'm So Lonesome I Could Cry"). Many of his songs reflect both his own very troubled life, and country music's tendency (already mentioned) toward a sentimentality verging on self-pity. In spite of this, his range was broad. It is characteristic of country singers (as of blues and rock singers) that, unlike most of those in the fields of pop, jazz, or classical music, they write many of their own songs. Williams excelled in this regard; his memorable songs include "Your Cheatin' Heart," "Move It on Over," "Kaw-liga," "Honky-Tonkin'," and "Hey, Good Lookin'," as well as "I'm So Lonesome I Could Cry." Further evidence placing him in the mainstream of country musicians is the fact that he wrote and recorded religious songs, including his well-known "I Saw the Light," based on an earlier gospel song.[51]

Other lesser but still prominent stars who worked in a more or less traditional vein during country music's postwar surge of popularity were Hank Snow (Canadian-born, and known best for "I'm Moving On"), Johnny Cash (from Arkansas, basically traditional despite his early association with rockabilly, and his "high media visibility"), and Tennessee Ernie Ford (actually from Tennessee, and known for his performance of Merle Travis's "Sixteen Tons," and for his subsequent turn to gospel music). Of more recent popularity are Loretta Lynn (from Kentucky, known for her autobiographical song "Coal Miner's Daughter", whose title was borrowed for a book and a movie), and Merle Haggard (from Bakersfield, California, who came to prominence after his release from San Quentin prison in 1960, and has been known for his loyalty to both honky-tonk and western swing styles).

* The pervasiveness of the western image is seen in the name Williams gave his band, and the stylized cowboy costume he sometimes wore, despite the fact that he had virtually no cowboy songs in his repertory.

Rockabilly and a New Generation of Performers and Fans

The influence of African-American musical styles has never been absent from country music; blues have been in the repertory from the beginning, and the debt of the Delmore Brothers, Jimmie Davis, Jimmie Rodgers, Bob Wills, and many others to blues and jazz is clear. In the 1950s a few white performers then in their twenties (principally Carl Perkins, Elvis Presley, and Jerry Lee Lewis, and to a somewhat lesser extent Buddy Holly and Johnny Cash) began copying the material and style of black blues and rhythm-and-blues singers such as Arthur Crudup, Little Richard, and Otis Blackwell. The story of rock 'n' roll, and its subsequent evolution under the umbrella term "rock," is dealt with in a later chapter. But the nascent rock 'n' roll had a heavy impact on country music itself, splitting its constituency (many fans and performers alike left traditional country for rock, some to return later), and leaving its mark on Nashville and commercial country music, in the form of the rock beat, the electrification of the instruments, and the studio-produced sound.

The immediate progeny of this cross-fertilization was *rockabilly*—according to Gary Giddins, "an amalgamation of honky-tonk, country, blues, gospel, and boogie-woogie jack-hammered by white performers . . . [and] largely the creation of Sun Records, operated by Sam Phillips."[52] Its most representative performers were, as indicated above, Carl Perkins, Elvis Presley, and Jerry Lee Lewis. The mixture of ingredients in this music, which had such overwhelming appeal for youthful fans, is complex, as Giddins's summary indicates.* The persistent influence of rock on subsequent commercial country music (in the musical terms noted above) is attributable in large part to the historic background and tastes of many country fans who grew up in the rockabilly era of the 1950s and 1960s. On the other hand, a somewhat different, and largely urban, generation of youth brought up on the folk-rock of Bob Dylan were introduced to country music when Dylan visited it briefly in the late 1960s in the albums *John Wesley Harding* (1968) and *Nashville Skyline* (1969, with Johnny Cash).

Nashville and the Lure of Pop

After World War II, when country music became more than just a regional music, performers began, as Jimmie Rodgers had done a generation earlier, to seek to appeal to a broader audience. One of the first signs of this was the abandonment of the straight, tense, nasal singing style (a trait of its folk origins) that had characterized it. Eddy Arnold adopted a crooning pop style of singing as early as the 1940s. In the next decade Johnny Cash brought to rockabilly, and Jim Reeves to honky-tonk songs, deep baritone voices foreign to hillbilly music, while Patsy Cline was sounding far more like the female pop recording stars of the day (Kay Starr or Doris Day, for example) than like Sara Carter, Rose Maddox, or Kitty Wells.

The move toward pop music involved far more than singing style, however. The major changes had to do with the sound of the instrumental

* In connection with the gospel ingredient in rockabilly, it is interesting to note that both Presley and Lewis came out of Pentecostal (specifically Assembly of God) backgrounds.

accompaniment—changes that were primarily associated, for variety of reasons, with Nashville, Tennessee. Nashville had an early lead in establishing itself as a center for the commercial production and dissemination of country music, thanks to the presence there since 1925 of radio station WSM, and a "barn dance" program that came to be called "Grand Ole Opry." Recording began as a sideline in conjunction with the station in the 1940s. The availability of talent in the area, together with the increasing market for country music, caused major record companies to begin recording there instead of in New York or Chicago, and ultimately to establish their own studios in Nashville. Independent record companies also sprang up, and as more and more records were produced there the city acted like a magnet for performers from all over the South. The cycle of growth went on, and the combination of superbly equipped studios and an abundance of skilled engineers and versatile musicians available as session players led to the expansion of the Nashville recording industry to include all types of popular music. The city is also the home of a number of television studios, publishing houses, and booking agencies. The new Grand Ole Opry House is in the center of a huge amusement park. The film *Nashville* (1975) portrays the city as a modern Hollywood.

The "Nashville sound" was a product of versatile talent, up-to-date technology, and the lure of the pop market. Its characteristics, which began to be evident in the 1950s, include the regular use of drums (which, except in the jazz-hybrid "western swing," had been foreign to country music), electric bass (sometimes pounding out a fairly heavy beat reminiscent of rock or boogie), a background of strings (definitely violins and not country fiddles!), and the use of singers to provide an impersonal, anonymous kind of vocal backup (tightly disciplined gospel groups such as the Jordanaires were favorites for this). Studio techniques such as echo effects and overdubbing (adding material in later recording sessions) became and remain standard. A common device for sustaining interest in popular arrangements—raising the pitch a half step when material is repeated—was adopted in Nashville productions; easy for today's facile session players, it sounds oddly out of place in country music, which has its roots in traditional tonality and ways of playing the instruments.

The occasional whine of the steel guitar, the very occasional faint sound of a fiddle or banjo (often overdubbed), simple diatonic harmonies and melodies, and above all lyrics that still exude an inbred and ineradicable sentimentality—these are virtually all that remain to distinguish thoroughly "Nashvillized" country music from any other kind of "easy listening" fare.

Austin, Texas: "Outlaws" and Honky-Tonk

An alternative to the Nashville sound and concept is the neo-honky-tonk ("cosmic cowboy") music emanating from Texas, where honky-tonk began. Austin has a rather unique ambience that combines ranchers and cowboys with college students at the University of Texas. The now-legendary Threadgill's bar brought students and "rednecks" together in the 1960s, and the Armadillo World Headquarters (another club) in the 1970s added hippie culture to the mix. The result was that, in Bill Malone's words, "a musical culture emerged which enveloped them all, and one which reflected a curious combining of images and symbols: hippie, Texan, and, above all, cowboy

. . ."[53] The best-known country musician to be associated with the Austin musical scene is Willie Nelson (b. 1933). His high name-recognition, especially among the young, is due to the success of his appeal to the rock-hippie counterculture. After his move to Austin in 1972, his symbolic abandoning of the Stetson for a headband, earrings, and long hair, while he went on purveying a brand of uncomplicated, pre-Nashville honky-tonk music, ensured his appeal to the three constituencies Malone referred to: the hippie, the Texan, and the cowboy. The loosely defined "Outlaws" of Austin (of whom Waylon Jennings was the most conspicuous, but which included Nelson, Tompall Glaser, Bobby Bare, and David Allan Coe) consciously promoted an image (the "badman") which would appeal to both the counterculture and the cowboy; though the image was commercial hype, the music itself, as an alternative to the slick Nashville product, helped to preserve some of the integrity and identity of country music.[54]

Country Music's Identity Crisis: Crossovers and Superstars

The identity of country music is precisely what has been imperiled in the 1970s and 1980s. In the wake of its tremendous commercial success, the country music industry has, in Malone's words, "discovered that its best interests lie in the distribution of a package with clouded identity, possessing no regional traits . . . a music that is all things to all people . . . "[55] This is a capsule description of country pop, which reflects the music's "ambivalence about its rural past." As the music itself has become more bland and less regional, its performers have tended to move out and away from both the context and the material of country music. Tammy Wynette, Barbara Mandrell, and Dolly Parton have achieved superstar status in crossing over into pop styles, and into the media of television and movies. In the other direction, pop singers like Kenny Rogers have successfully crossed over and achieved a measure of identification as country singers—though exactly what that designation now means, and to whom, is no longer as clear as it once was, since the identity of the audience for country music has also undergone a considerable shift.

The Persistence and Revival of Traditional Styles

Bluegrass

The single strongest bastion of tradition of the music of the rural southeastern United States is bluegrass music. Yet bluegrass music as we know it today is scarcely forty years old. Its origins, well documented, are within the living memory of many, and many of its originators are still playing and singing. It is less a literal *revival* of an older style than it is a new, highly demanding, highly professional virtuoso style *based* on and evolved from the music of the old string bands and the singers who sang with them. In brief, the term "bluegrass" stands for an acoustic string band sound (fiddle, mandolin, banjo, guitar, and bass), and a singing style that stresses a high-pitched, straight tone. What has been repeatedly described as the "high, lonesome sound" is further enhanced by the choice of the "open-sounding" intervals of perfect fourths and fifths in the harmony parts in the choruses. There is also a pronounced blues influence, palpable not only in the presence of blues numbers in the repertory (including Bill Monroe's famous rendering of Jimmie Rodgers's "Muleskinner Blues," and even more in his "Rocky Road Blues"), but also in the frequent blues inflections in fiddle and banjo passages. Example 7–4, an approximation of an Earl Scruggs chorus for five-string banjo in "Earl's Breakdown," shows these inflections, as well as the blues chord in the third and eleventh bars, and the speeded-up ragtime rhythms.

Example 7–4

Transcription by the author

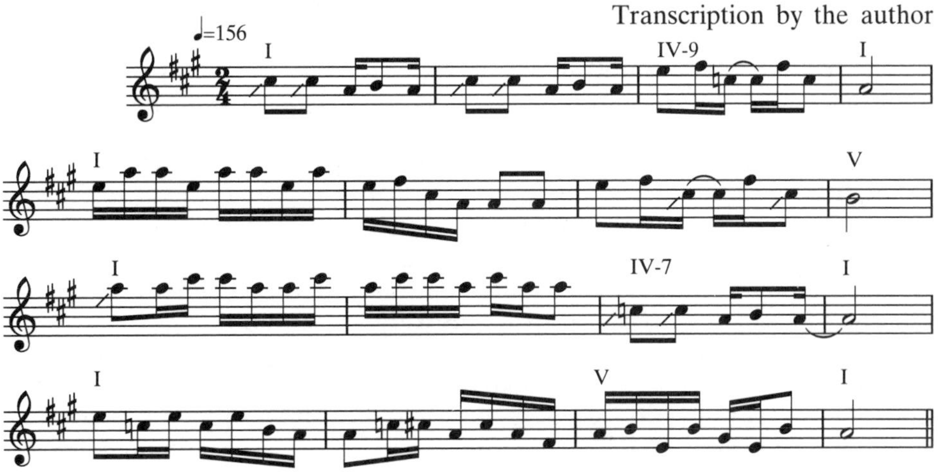

There are slow, mournful bluegrass songs, but its most characteristic tempo, in the popular conception, is fast—often breathtakingly so. Bluegrass shares with bebop jazz (a revitalization of jazz by virtuosos that actually evolved about the same time) the distinction of being the fastest vernacular music we have—pushed to its limits by phenomenal players.

We have noted that the beginnings of bluegrass music are well documented; and there is one man who, more than any other, was responsible for its evolution, and whose group, the Blue Grass Boys, gave it its name—Bill Monroe. Monroe is a gifted mandolin player, guitarist, and singer who began his professional career performing with his two brothers, and proceeded, with persistence and integrity, to develop a style that was true to the old-time music. Monroe (b. 1911) was not from the bluegrass country, but from further west in Kentucky. Nor did the style evolve there; it came into being slowly, by degrees, in Atlanta (where the Blue Grass Boys were first assembled) and in Nashville (where they became part of "Grand Ole Opry").

Monroe's high, clear singing style and his mandolin playing were important hallmarks of the genre, as was the reinstatement of the fiddle. But the most characteristic trademark of bluegrass in the popular mind is the incisive tone of the five-string banjo, played with virtuoso technique. The banjo had all but disappeared as a significant ingredient in country music by the 1940s, but it had a dramatic revival, in a picking style native to western North Carolina, as exemplified in the phenomenal playing of Earl Scruggs (b. 1924). Scruggs joined the Blue Grass Boys in 1945. His tenure with them was fairly brief; it is in the nature of professional careerdom that rising potential stars do not stay long with their mentors, but leave to form their own groups. But it was in the three short years when Scruggs and Monroe were playing together (along with three other outstanding performers, Lester Flatt, guitarist and singer, Chubby Wise, fiddler, and Howard Watts, bassist) that the "bluegrass sound" was essentially established. Flatt and Scruggs left in 1948 to form the Foggy Mountain Boys; they, the Stanley Brothers, the Lilly Brothers, Jim and Jesse McReynolds, Mac Wiseman, and Jimmy Martin, among others, continued the cultivation and evolution of bluegrass music.[56]

Bluegrass has for some time, possibly because of its strict loyalty to acoustic instruments, had an existence independent of the more mass-audience-oriented and ambivalent country music. But the style has also by this time spawned sub-styles, branching off in several directions. "Progressive" bluegrass (or "newgrass") has added drums, and applied bluegrass sounds and textures to a repertory that includes Stephen Foster, John Philip Sousa, Kurt Weill, Bob Dylan, urban ragtime, and songs from rock, Broadway, and Tin Pan Alley. The groups Country Gentlemen and Seldom Scene have been the most prominent in this expansion of the repertoire and scope of bluegrass. Seldom Scene has purveyed a smooth honky-tonk bluegrass (as in "Bottom of the Glass" of 1974), and the Osborne Brothers were already producing in the 1960s a kind of neo-bluegrass (as in "Rocky Top" of 1967), adding piano and drums, sophisticated harmonic progressions, and lyrics that, with their somewhat corny references to such stereotypical images as moonshine, were pseudo-hillbilly.[57] But traditional bluegrass flourishes as well, especially in the many summer festivals that have been taking place since the early 1960s and that encompass all the many styles the genre has produced.

Other Aspects of Traditionalism

Mike Seeger, John Cohen, and the New Lost City Ramblers took a different course in relation to traditional music—that of establishing a repertory ensemble which, among other things, would keep alive older styles and older songs, such as those that had hitherto survived only on recordings from the 1920s and 1930s. Their recordings for Folkways and their *New Lost City Ramblers Song Book* embodied this approach.[58] And groups such as Horse Sense (Justin Bishop and John Nielson) have specialized in researching and keeping alive traditional cowboy music.

In the year 1974 two interesting signposts appeared, in a sense pointing in opposite directions. "Grand Ole Opry" in Nashville moved from the historic Ryman Auditorium to its opulent new state-of-the-art home in Opryland. And Garrison Keillor, who had written a piece on "Grand Ole Opry" for the *New Yorker*, started his own radio show in St. Paul, "A Prairie Home Companion." This return to the format and feeling of old-time radio, with its audience becoming involved as part of the show, was partly satirical and partly serious. Over the thirteen years of its existence the program included jazz, ragtime, blues, gospel, ethnic music, and high school bands and choirs, as well as old-time country music and bluegrass, and the featured performers were consistently either older traditional musicians such as Ralph Stanley, mid-generation established stars such as Emmylou Harris, or younger performers such as Peter Strushko, who played and sang out of a genuine understanding of and love for the music they were re-creating. In spite of Keillor's gifts as a storyteller, the enormous popularity of the program could not have been due to him alone; it was an indication that an increasing number of people were growing tired of the slick, homogenized productions, hype, and packaging of the pop music industry (including country-pop), and responded to the freshness and the down-to-earth lack of pretension of a kind of music that had not been stripped of the flavor or the eccentricities of either the region or the culture from which it had come. It is significant that this recognition and response could come even from those whose own background was very different from that of a Ricky Skaggs, or whose chronological age was far removed from that of a Ralph Stanley or a Bill Monroe. It is in the nature of youth to seek innovation and change, but it has also been the young in great numbers, both performers and audience, who in our time have recognized the value of the traditional aspects of our culture, and have been enthusiastic in cultivating them and keeping them fresh.

Further Reading

Reference Works

Gentry, Linnell, ed. *A History and Encyclopedia of Country, Western, and Gospel Music.* 2d ed. Nashville, TN: Clairmont, 1969. 598 pp.
One of the earliest reference works; still useful for its anthology of periodical articles, 1908–68. Second part consists of short biographical entries.

Stambler, Irwin, and Grelun Landon. *The Encyclopedia of Folk, Country & Western Music.* 2d ed. New York: St. Martin's 1983. 902 pp.
Extensive entries of names and groups.

Collections of Music

Clifton, Bill, ed. *150 Old-Time Folk and Gospel Songs.* Burke, VA: Bluegrass Unlimited, ca. 1950.

Dunson, Josh, and Ethel Raim, eds. *Anthology of American Folk Music.* New York: Oak Publications, 1973.
Transcriptions from the Folkways 3-LP recorded anthology with the same title. Commentary and photographs are especially good. Includes blues and gospel music. This and the next entry constitute the basic anthologies in notation of old-time music, much of which has never been transcribed in this form.

Seeger, Mike, and John Cohen, eds. *The Old-Time String Band Songbook.* Formerly published as *The New Lost City Ramblers Song Book.* New York: Oak Publications, 1976.
An important collection of transcriptions from recordings of songs popular in the 1920s and 1930s. Documentation, commentary, and photographs make this especially valuable.

In addition, many of the folk music collections listed in Chapter 1 contain material that is relevant to early country music, especially the Appalachian collection of Cecil Sharp.

Studies

Artis, Bob. *Bluegrass.* New York; Hawthorn, 1975.

Cash, Wilbur J. *The Mind of the South.* New York: Knopf, 1941.

Green, Douglas B. *Country Roots: The Origins of Country Music.* New York: Hawthorn, 1976.

Malone, Bill C. *Country Music, U.S.A.* Rev. ed. Austin: University of Texas Press, 1985.
The best comprehensive work available on the subject; its revised edition has been updated, and is longer by 140 pages.

———. *Southern Music—American Music.* Lexington: University Press of Kentucky, 1979.
Shorter than *Country Music, U.S.A.*; covers more kinds of music, with more focus on the South.

Reid, Jan. *The Improbable Rise of Redneck Rock.* Austin, TX: Heidelberg, 1974.
A lively, personal, and informative account of the Austin scene.

Rosenberg, Neil V. *Bluegrass: A History.* Urbana: University of Illinois Press, 1987.

Shelton, Robert. *The Country Music Story: A Picture History of Country and Western Music.* Indianapolis: Bobbs-Merrill, 1966.
A book in popular style, profusely illustrated with photographs.

Wolfe, Charles K. *Grand Ole Opry: The Early Years, 1925–1935.* London: Old-Time Music, 1975.

———. *Tennessee Strings: The Story of Country Music in Tennessee.* Knoxville: University of Tennessee Press, 1977.
Regional in scope, this is well written and informative, especially on the story of Nashville.

Articles

Green, Archie. "Austin's Cosmic Cowboys: Words in Collision" in *"And Other Neighborly Names": Social Process and Cultural Image in Texas Folklore,;* Richard Bauman and Roger D. Abrahams, eds. Austin: University of Texas Press, 1981.

Lornell, Kip. "Early Country Music and the Mass Media in Roanoke, Virginia," *American Music,* vol. 5, no. 4 (Winter 1987).
Regional study of the kind needed to supplement one's understanding of any kind of American music.

Rosenberg, Neil V. "Image and Stereotype: Bluegrass Sound Tracks," *American Music,* vol 1, no. 3 (Fall 1983)

Listening

Anthologies

Basic

Anthology of American Folk Music. Folkways 2951–53. Edited by Harry Smith.
Eighty-four selections, on 6 LPs, of music from early recordings. Includes ballads, blues, gospel, and Cajun music as well as the old-time progenitors of country music.

The Smithsonian Collection of Classic Country Music. Edited by Bill Malone.
A comprehensive collection, on 8 LPs, from 1922 to 1975, with excellent documentation and notes.

From the New World Recorded Anthology of American Music

These four issues are briefer but valuable.

Country Music South and West. NW-287. Annotated by Douglas B. Green.
Country Music in the Modern Era: 1940's–1970's. NW-207. Annotated by William Ivey.
Hills & Home: Thirty Years of Bluegrass. NW-225. Annotated by Neil V. Rosenberg.
Back in the Saddle Again: American Cowboy Songs. NW-314 and 315. Annotated by Charlie Seemann.

From Folkways/Smithsonian

The catalog has many relevant issues, among which are the following:

Uncle Dave Macon. RF 51.
Dock Boggs, vols. 1 and 2. 2351 and 2392.
Mike Seeger: Old Time Country Music. 2325.
Old Time Music at Clarence Ashley's. 2355.
Tom Ashley and Tex Isley. 2350.
Mountain Music Bluegrass Style. 2318.
The New Lost City Ramblers, vols. 1–5, 2395–99.
The Country Gentlemen, vols. 1–3, 2409–11.

Commercial record companies frequently issues "anthologies" (unfortunately usually without documentation) of their stars, under such titles as "The Best of . . ." or " . . . 's Greatest Hits." Individual performers cannot be extensively represented in an anthology like that issued by Smithsonian; consequently, much material is available only in this form, including the Carter Family and Jimmie Rodgers (from RCA), Roy Acuff (from Columbia), Hank Williams (from MGM), and Ernest Tubb, Bob Wills, and Bill Monroe (from MCA).

PROJECTS

1. Interview a number of people, from varied backgrounds, on the subject of country music, with a view to ascertaining the degree of correlation (if any) between a like or dislike of country music and a basically rural or urban background and orientation. It may be well to play some recorded examples as part of the interview. Include yourself as one respondent if you like.
2. If you are a singer, especially of folk songs, learn two traditional country songs from the anthologies listed above or from other sources, and add them to your repertoire. Find out as much as you can about the songs.
3. Investigate the state of country music in your own area to determine whether there are live performances of it by local groups, professional or amateur, and what styles are favored. If there is a sizable public for this music, try to determine something about its makeup. If possible, interview some local performers.
4. Find additional examples of country songs on subjects illustrating at least four of the "perennial themes" treated in this chapter. Transcribe the texts, with your own commentary.
5. The qualities of *sincerity* and *authenticity* have been discussed as aspects of singing style in country music. These properties of a performer or a performance are not quantifiable or analyzable, but they are felt to be important (see Hank Williams's comment on p. 175 above). Are sincerity and authenticity the same thing in country music? Explore your own perceptions of these qualities by studying four or five performances by as many different country singers, covering a fairly broad chronological range. Give each a (necessarily subjective) "sincerity rating"

and/or "authenticity rating," and force yourself to examine your own subjective criteria by giving reasons for your ratings.

6. The point has been made that the tunes in country music either outline, or strongly imply, basically simple chords (expressed as I, IV, and V in the key). What other body of songs known to you has this property? If you have some musical background, contrast a country music melody with a sophisticated show tune or popular song of the 1930s or later, in which more complex harmonies, which are not implied in the melody itself, are nevertheless always associated with that melody.

7. Do a study contrasting rock lyrics with those of country music. In what ways are they similar (e.g. choice and range of subject matter, frankness in its treatment) and in what ways different (e.g. presence or absence of sentimentality, sophistication, use of consciously "poetic" imagery, etc.)?

8. If you are a movie buff, contrast the music of "westerns" in different periods; include the characteristics, context, and accompaniment of identifiable songs (if any), and the use and character of background music and/or theme music.

9. Compare the treatment of the man-woman relationship in a typical honky-tonk song of the 1940s with that of a typical popular song (Tin Pan Alley–Hit Parade type) of the same period.

10. Make the same comparison suggested in No. 9 above, using a 1970s or 1980s neo-honky-tonk song ("Outlaw" or "redneck," as exemplified by, say, Willie Nelson or Waylon Jennings) with a "mainstream pop" song of the last decade or so.

11. Make a study of current bluegrass styles, relating them to the prototypical style evolved by the Blue Grass Boys in the 1940s, as described in the chapter.

12. Make a study of bluegrass festivals, especially any that may take place in your area and that you could attend. Give attention to who the performers are, the repertory represented, the amount of amateur performance (formal or informal), the ambience, etc. Consult periodicals such as *Bluegrass Unlimited* and *Pickin'*.

8

Blues: From Country to City

IF country music has become a mighty (and a wealthy) nation, the blues has prospered and increased mightily also, and the range of its influence on our music has been even broader. How was it that the South's Ishmael, offspring of the bondwoman, came to occupy such a prominent place in our musical vernacular? That is what we shall explore in this chapter.

The cultural ambience of the rural South that spawned both country music and the blues has already been alluded to in the previous chapter. And as we noted in Chapter 2, in tracing the blues through its folk phase, it was a kind of music that, though belonging to a race that came to this continent in bondage, could not emerge until slavery itself was abolished. For the blues was neither a tribal nor a communal expression. It was (and is) the lament, the comment, often mocking or ironic, of the solitary individual, bereft of the support of tribe or close-knit society, facing *alone*, on personal terms, a hostile or indifferent world.

Yet long before our time the lament had become an entertainment, the solitary singer's comment had crystallized into a form that could be printed and sold, and the lone cry had become a commodity. It had become, in a word, popular music—even before the first recordings of it appeared.

But the legacy of its folk beginnings remained to characterize the blues indelibly: the way the voice is handled, the blues intonation, the range and treatment of its subjects, and, above all, the basic blues feeling that has its roots in a solitary experience and view of life. Those who were to become its professionals and its stars had, like their white hillbilly counterparts, served their apprenticeship in traveling tent shows and minstrel and medicine shows, or in playing and singing for all-night parties and dances, or even (as many blind singers did) in performing for passersby in front of country stores or on city streets.

Early Published Blues

It was inevitable that a type of music being sung and played in cities and small towns in the lowland South from the Piedmont to Texas should eventually find its way into print. This happened first in 1912, when by coincidence within a period of two months blues were published in St. Louis ("Baby Seals Blues"), Oklahoma City ("Dallas Blues"), and Memphis ("Memphis Blues"). "Memphis Blues" had been widely played in that city for three years before its publication, by the enterprising composer-bandleader who, more than any other early professional, was to promote the blues as popular music and bring it to a wide public—William C. Handy. Handy's early experiences with the performance and publication of these compositions are interestingly set forth in his autobiography, *Father of the Blues.* In the beginning, "Memphis Blues" netted him $50, with the real profits for years going to others. But Handy was to learn quickly. If the nickname "father of the blues" is something of an exaggeration (Bruce Cook has said that a more accurate one would be "rich uncle"),[1] his place in blues history is still important, and his ties with its roots are perfectly genuine.

What was the blues like by the time it was being composed and arranged for broad popular consumption? For one thing, of course, the musical form had to be extended. It came to include at least two strains (in verse-and-chorus relationship), and sometimes three. The three-phrase, 12-bar pattern with its usual harmonic plan (as outlined in Chapter 2) was standard for at least one of the strains and was sometimes used for all of them, but there were also strains cast in a more classical European 16-bar form. These early published blues, as a matter of fact, showed a mixture of influences. The blues elements were often quite attenuated, and the music was sometimes pure ragtime, with its more elaborate European harmonies, as in the second strain of Handy's "Memphis Blues." At times still other influences were evident; the best-known strain of the most famous blues of all, the "St. Louis Blues," is actually, as Handy wrote it, a 16-bar tango! As he notes in his autobiography, the effect of this tango rhythm—the "Spanish tinge" of which Jelly Roll Morton spoke—on black dancers for whom he played was not lost on the observant Mr. Handy, and he used it again in his "Beale Street Blues" and "Aunt Hagar's Children."

The relationship between the blues as published and the blues as sung by a steadily growing number of professional blues singers is an interesting one, and difficult to unravel. While each had its own public and its own standards of what was admissible in terms of subject matter and language, there was undoubtedly some mutual exchange of musical and textual ideas. As a case in point, W. C. Handy wrote both the words and music of a song he copyrighted and published in 1915, "The Hesitating Blues." The words are about a woman who stalls one suitor in the hope of marrying her absent, and hesitating, lover. The first verse sets forth the motif that runs through the song:

Hello Central, what's the matter with this line?
I want to talk to that High Brown of mine,
Tell me how long will I have to wait?
Please give me 298, why do you hesitate?[2]

In 1926 Gertrude "Ma" Rainey recorded "Sissy Blues," which deals frankly with a homosexual theme, and runs in part:

I dreamed last night I was far from harm,
Woke up and found my man in a sissy's arms.
Hello Central, it's bound to drive me wild,
Can I get through, or will I have to wait a while?[3]

The music is essentially that of the first part of Handy's blues. Although the Rainey recording was made eleven years after Handy published his blues, it is not possible to say for certain who borrowed from whom, since Ma Rainey (and others) had been singing the blues professionally for years before they were recorded. Handy made a practice of noting down folk phrases he heard here and there ("Goin' where the Southern cross' the Dog"; "Ma man's got a heart like a rock cast in de sea") and incorporating them into his songs. The "Hello Central" motive, in common enough currency, could have been used in a folk blues that Handy heard—or it could well have been the other way around.

More important than the question of mutual borrowing is a comparison of the two pieces themselves, for they illustrate the divergence that had already occurred between the earthy blues of the tent shows (which were later to become so popular on recordings) and the blues as cultivated and polished specifically for general public consumption. The published blues of Handy and others are more developed in form and use more sophisticated harmonies. The rhymes are more exact and the lyrics are facile, employing clever plays on words. But compared with the folk (and near-folk) blues, both words and music are apt to sound stilted and artificial. Though quoted perhaps somewhat unfairly out of context, an excerpt from the topical "Wall Street Blues" (published in 1929) illustrates the gulf that had already opened between the folk-derived blues and its commercial counterpart:

Never had the blues like the blues I'm blue with now,
Never had the blues like the blues I'm blue with now,
Oh, what I recall of the street called Wall and how!
Wailing Wall, Oh Jerusalem! There's one in New York too,
Where I got a whalin', now I'm ailin', Wailin' 'cause I'm blue.[4]

"Classic" City Blues

The blues as a more or less standardized form of popular music for a large public (mostly black, but with a growing white element) enjoyed what has been called its "classic" period from 1920, when the first recordings were made and sold, until the onset of the Depression in the early 1930s. It was a period of intense activity and popularity for the blues. Personal-appearance tours (mostly on vaudeville circuits) and nightclub appearances were a mainstay for the more popular blues singers, and there were some radio performances and even some films. But the principal medium for the propagation of the blues was the phonograph recording. Thousands of blues performances by hundreds of singers were recorded, and millions of copies sold. There was a parallel development, of course, in instrumental jazz, in white hillbilly music (as we have seen), and in the rural blues (as we shall presently note).

The period of the classic city blues was dominated by the female blues singer. Various reasons have been advanced for this, but the most likely ones have to do with the nature of show business at the time and the success of the women singers in tent and vaudeville shows. Unlike the folk blues—which, as we have seen in Chapter 2, encompassed a wide range of subjects—the classic blues were almost exclusively concerned with man-woman relations and were usually written from the woman's point of view. The treatment of sexual themes ranged from the frank earthiness of much of Ma Rainey's material to the kind of slick and smirking double entendre heard in the sleazier vaudeville shows—a type of lyric exploited in both city and country blues by record companies eager to bolster sales in the early years of the Depression, when the amazingly prosperous era of the classic blues was waning.

In view of the enormous popularity of blues recordings in the 1920s, it may seem strange that record companies were so skeptical at first about recording this music, but it was indeed regarded at the outset as a risky venture. The first singers recorded were not strictly blues singers at all, but professional entertainers with experience in cabaret and vaudeville singing in styles much like those of popular white singers. Mamie Smith made the famous first recording ("That Thing Called Love" and "You Can't Keep a Good Man Down") in 1920. After that record's promising success she recorded the famous "Crazy Blues," and the potential became unmistakable. Other professional black club and theater singers such as Lucille Hegamin and Edith Wilson recorded blues. Real blues singers in the southern tradition began to be recorded a few years later. Of these by far the best known and most influential were Ma Rainey (1886–1939) and Bessie Smith (1894–1937), both of whom began recording blues in 1923.

Ma Rainey's early career, though only sketchily known, deserves some attention because of the light it sheds on the milieu in which the classic blues evolved. She was born Gertrude Pridgett in Columbus, Georgia. Both her parents were in the minstrel-show business, and she herself was singing on the stage by the time she was fourteen. She acquired her familiar nickname "Ma" when, at age eighteen, she married William "Pa" Rainey, a minstrel performer, and they began touring with their song-and-dance routine. (She herself preferred to be called "Madame" Rainey.) Thus she had had more than twenty years of professional experience in touring circus, variety, and minstrel shows by the time she made her first blues recording. Of all the classic blues singers she remained closest to the vernacular blues tradition. She never sang professionally outside the South, except to make recordings in New York and Chicago during a four-year period that ended in 1928. By then, a recording executive is said to have expressed the opinion that Ma's "down-home" material had gone out of fashion. During this brief period she recorded with some of the leading jazz musicians, including Louis Armstrong and Fletcher Henderson, but also made blues recordings with a jug, kazoo, washboard, and banjo band of a kind traditional in the South. Significantly, her last recording, with just a banjo accompaniment, was a duet with Papa Charlie Jackson, who had been the first country blues singer to record.

By this time, blues form had become well standardized, and the conventional 12-bar harmonic and structural mold was almost invariable. As for the texts, Ma Rainey's material reflected to a certain extent the country blues range of subject matter, and went beyond the perennial types of man-woman themes to touch on poverty, alcoholism, prostitution, topical references ("Titanic Man Blues"), and even, as already indicated, homosexuality. Contemporary accounts and pictures indicate that she was a stocky, somewhat ugly woman, imbued with what must have been an imposing stage presence and an uncanny degree of what can best be described by that much-abused term "charisma." In her surviving recordings what we hear, dimly transmitted through primitive recording techniques, is a voice and a kind of singing devoid of the slightest trace of artificiality.[5]

Bessie Smith, born in Chattanooga, Tennessee, and fourteen years younger than Ma Rainey, began her career as the latter's protégée, though she declined to acknowledge this in later years. She and Ma Rainey began recording about the same time, but Bessie Smith eventually became far better known, and was undoubtedly a more gifted and versatile singer. She became identified wholly with the sophisticated city blues tradition, and her material was tailored largely for this market. She worked with the leading jazz musicians, and recorded with piano (with Fletcher Henderson, for example), with piano and one instrument (quite often with Joe Smith or Louis Armstrong playing muted blues cornet), with a small jazz combo, and even with choral background in some early "production numbers." Her mastery of the idiom and the forcefulness and directness of her delivery are undisputed. But Bessie Smith, too, was out of fashion by the time she made her last recordings in 1933, and the dissipation and sad deterioration of her life toward the end were all too indicative of what could happen to the brightest popular stars propelled into fame and fortune by the phenomenal activity of the recording industry during the prosperous twenties.[6]

Other singers in the classic blues tradition included Ida Cox, Bertha "Chippie" Hill, Clara Smith, Sippie Wallace, and Victoria Spivey, all of whom performed with major jazz musicians of the 1920s and 1930s. It was the day of the woman blues singers, and while there have been eminent black female popular singers since (Ella Fitzgerald, Billie Holiday, Sarah Vaughan, Aretha Franklin), none after the classic period has been so exclusively identified with the blues. The dominant role in blues singing has since passed largely to men.

Blues and Jazz

Most of the great female blues singers performed with jazz musicians, as we have seen. The blues had evolved structurally in such a way as to demand the complementing role of an answering voice (or instrument) at the end of each sung line. This manifestation of call-and-response is, in fact, a distinguishing feature of genuine blues. The solitary blues singer filled in his own breaks on his guitar; in the city blues the piano, and later the collaborating instrumentalist, took up this function. Joe Smith and Louis Armstrong participated in many recordings with the classic blues singers in the 1920s. An interesting example of distinctive jazz breaks provided by a small combo can be heard in Ma Rainey's "Countin' the Blues," in which each break in the three-line blues form is taken in turn by cornet, clarinet, and trombone.[7] These collaborations provide some of the finest moments in early jazz (Example 8–1).

Example 8–1 COUNTIN' THE BLUES (first of five verses)

Transcription by the author

So closely identified was jazz with the city blues at this time that "blues" and "jazz" were taken by some to be one and the same. They are, of course, separate and distinct traditions; their parallel development is a rather complex history of periodically strong influence and identification. While the rural blues was slowly taking shape, something like its urban counterpart was having a hand in the early formation of jazz. There were bands in New Orleans (and possibly in Memphis and other cities as well) playing music by 1900 that was called "blues." None of it was published, so far as we know, and if any of it was written down it has not survived. Since this was nearly two decades before phonograph recordings of such music were to be made, it is clear that we will never know what the blues played by these early bands sounded like. But the identification of blues with jazz remained exceptionally close through the classic blues period we have been examining. Then, in the 1930s, began a gradual divergence; the blues declined somewhat, and jazz evolved in other directions. While the blues as a harmonic and formal design can be heard in all ages of jazz, the blues references, as we advance through the so-called modern period, become increasingly attenuated. Recently, under the impact of the reenergized urban blues and the synthesis called "soul" music, jazz has been forcibly pulled back to a closer relation with its blues roots.

Three Examples

In form and feeling, the blues has never been wholly absent from jazz and may be said to be in fact one of its vital ingredients. By the time the recorded history of jazz began, the blues had come to signify a well-recognized form, a harmonic matrix, and a melodic genre that gave special emphasis of the "blue" degrees of the scale. Within this well-recognized set of boundaries, jazz produced in the ensuing decades thousands of blues, all of them variations in some respect on the "given" premises. The following survey of just three contrasting examples will give a rudimentary idea, at least, of the way in which purely instrumental jazz continued to be involved at various periods with the blues.

1. *"Dippermouth Blues"* (1923).[8] This is a clear and typical instrumental blues in New Orleans jazz style. After the short introduction there follow nine choruses in the basic 12-bar blues pattern.* Notice that the tempo is not a reliable factor in defining blues, which are not invariably slow.

2. *"Ko-ko"* (1940).[9] Here is instrumental blues on a very sophisticated level musically. The form is clear enough; after an 8-bar introduction there are seven choruses of regular 12-bar blues, followed by a coda of the same length as one chorus. But the mode (minor instead of the more usual major) makes it somewhat more distinctive, and the harmonies are much richer, subtler, and more complex than the ordinary blues chords.

3. *"Parker's Mood"* (1948).[10] This example, from a period of "modern" jazz characterized as having gotten away from the blues to a large extent, is an interesting and beautiful reinterpretation of it. It shows how the perennial forms that can be said to have become classic can be seen anew in each era through the temperaments of changing styles, and so become renewed. The small combo (alto saxophone, piano, bass, and drums) makes for the intimacy of expression of chamber music. There are just four choruses, with an introduction and short coda.

Boogie-Woogie

Boogie-woogie is a solo piano form, as is ragtime, essentially, but quite distinct from it in origin and style. Its progenitor and closest relative is the blues. Its

* For a more detailed discussion of this piece, see Chapter 14.

sound is unforgettable—a driving left hand with a hypnotically repeated pattern (the musical term for this, *ostinato*, is related to our word "obstinate"); the right hand often insisting equally obstinately on its own repeated figures; and, underlying all, blues form and harmony. It was spawned as piano entertainment in bars, nightclubs, and houses of prostitution. Generically, boogie-woogie was probably an adaptation of what blues singer-guitarists had been doing, with their intricate, ostinato-like accompaniments. It is significant as further evidence of the close relationship with the blues that the early boogie-woogie soloists would often sing along, or talk to their audience, while they were playing.

Boogie-woogie, transferred out of the environment of its origins, went through a period of short but intense popularity in the late 1930s. This is apt to obscure the fact that it is a much older phenomenon. Jelly Roll Morton has said that many piano performers in his early days (shortly after the turn of the century) played in what must have been something like this style of piano blues with heavy ostinato-like left hand. W. C. Handy mentions adopting and orchestrating for his group a type of piano music played in the bordellos of the Mississippi delta region around the turn of the century. It was called "boogie-house music."

There is a relationship between boogie-woogie and the big bands of the 1930s, especially in Kansas City, where the "jump" style was in many ways a translation of boogie idioms to the jazz band, just as the idioms of ragtime had been transferred to traditional jazz a generation earlier.

Although the craze for it subsided somewhat in the 1940s, boogie-woogie remained a potent musical style. With its driving ostinato and blues form, it was to emerge as a major influence on rock 'n' roll in the 1950s, as can be heard, for example, in the work of Jerry Lee Lewis.

Boogie-woogie's resources are limited. Nevertheless, within those limitations a considerable amount of variety is found—variety of tempos (not all boogie is fast), of left-hand patterns, and of general feeling. The famous "Honky-Tonk Train" (1937)[11] can be considered a prototype. The right hand here is quite complex rhythmically, and is at times strikingly independent of the steady left hand. Many boogie-woogie titles carry similar allusions to railroad trains, and it is probable that some boogie has its origin in a programmatic imitation of the sounds of trains. The same thing had been done on the guitar, and the sounds would certainly have been familiar to both itinerant piano players and blues singers. The work of Jimmy Yancey is especially noteworthy, in terms both of technical mastery and range of expression. Two final illustrations show contrasting aspects of boogie-woogie as played by Yancey: first, his hard-driving "Yancey Stomp," and second, his "How Long Blues," a rare marvel of almost classical restraint.[12]

Country Blues

The rural blues as a folk form has been examined in some detail in Chapter 2, and its characteristics noted. It remains here to chronicle its emergence as "country blues"—largely through the medium of recordings—into the realm of a popular music, and the changes wrought in the process. Recordings of city blues, which first appeared in 1920, were very successful, and as the business of selling records by mail grew it was realized that a large market existed among the black people of the rural South for recordings of their own country blues singers. (The market for white hillbilly music, it will be recalled, was discovered and began to be exploited about the same time.) It was 1924 before the first man who might be called a country blues singer made a recording. Papa Charlie Jackson was actually a minstrel- and medicine-show performer from New Orleans, and therefore was more a professional entertainer than a traditional country bluesman.* Jackson recorded his "Lawdy Lawdy Blues" in Chicago, and in the promotional material accompanying its release more emphasis was placed on the fact that it was a man singing the blues (at a time when most blues singers were women) than on its being rural blues. After an encouraging amount of commercial success, however, the search for country blues performers was on, and there soon followed recordings by singers from across the entire South, from Florida (Blind Blake) to Texas (Blind Lemon Jefferson). Although country blues singing was an almost exclusively male domain, the boundaries are never clear-cut, and there is a sense in which Ma Rainey, from Georgia, belongs here as well, since her background and singing owe almost as much to country as to city blues tradition.

For the earliest recordings, singers were brought to Chicago, where they worked in "studios" often primitive even by the standards of the time. But expeditions through the South with recording equipment were also undertaken, and new singers were discovered. Collecting and documenting country blues recordings from this period, as with other kinds of "race records" (the trade terms for several decades for recordings by black musicians intended for black audiences), has been fraught with difficulties. The engineering and production of the records were for the most part as cheap as the promotional material was crass, and usually little attempt was made to preserve the masters. With notable exceptions the blues singers themselves were exploited while being treated with disdain.

Charles Keil has identified three fairly distinct country blues areas, with corresponding styles. His outline, while admittedly an oversimplification, will serve as a preliminary guide.[13]

The Mississippi delta region is the most famous blues area, and the one most extensively documented in recordings, writings, and, more recently, photographic essays as well. It is represented, in the early phase, by such singers as Charlie Patton, Willie Brown, Son House, and Robert Johnson, and later by Bukka White, Muddy Waters (McKinley Morganfield), and John Lee Hooker. The style is characterized by a chordal guitar technique that Keil describes as having a "heavy" texture, and that is very reminiscent of boogie-woogie styles on the piano. It is with the delta blues also that the bottleneck technique, with its sliding effects, is most often associated. The vocal delivery is apt to be impassioned, with short phrases and utterances at times moaning,

* The parallel with Fiddlin' John Carson, the professional entertainer who had made the first substantially successful recording of hillbilly music the previous year, is interesting. See Chapter 7.

at times sliding in and out of falsetto, at times chanted without definite pitch, at times almost shouted, at times nearly inarticulate. This style, especially as cultivated by later delta blues singers, heavily influenced rock 'n' roll.[14]

Texas has produced a significant number of country blues singers, including Blind Lemon Jefferson, Texas Alexander, Mance Lipscomb, and Lightnin' Hopkins. The blues of this region, as typified by the very influential Jefferson, who recorded between 1924 and 1930, are characterized by longer vocal lines, delivered in a more relaxed vocal style. The guitar style is more open and less chordal, with emphasis on melody playing on a single string during the breaks.[15]

The southeastern seaboard and the southern highlands, an important source of white folk music, does not have as distinctive a blues tradition as does, say, the Mississippi delta. Nevertheless, this area has produced some individually significant performers, including Peg Leg Howell, Blind Willie McTell, Blind Blake, Blind Boy Fuller, Brownie McGhee, and the harmonica player Sonny Terry. Fuller and Terry, both from North Carolina, worked as a team, and after Fuller's death Terry found a new partner in Brownie McGhee. Terry and McGhee, probably the best-known bluesmen from this region, subsequently moved to New York for good, pursuing successful professional careers.[16]

Mention of McGhee and Terry brings us to what might be regarded as the final phase of the country blues: its absorption into the urban stream of popular music. This urbanization process was given some impetus, paradoxically enough, by a project designed to document and preserve important specimens of American folk music before they passed into oblivion—the archival recordings made for the Library of Congress in the 1930s and early 1940s. The project did indeed result in the recording of a large treasury of valuable folk material, as the references to it in this book have amply illustrated. But the interesting effect it had in addition was to help bring folk music, and the country blues in particular, to the attention of urban intellectuals at a crucial time—a time when the so-called urban folk movement, as we have seen in Chapter 4, was just getting under way. Leadbelly of Louisiana, Muddy Waters of Mississippi, and Sonny Terry of North Carolina were among those recorded, and all three later became successful professionals. Leadbelly's story, including his release from the Angola prison farm in Louisiana at the behest of folklorist John Lomax, and his subsequent professional career, has been alluded to in Chapter 4.[17]

By the 1950s, the country blues had achieved significant popularity not only in the urban North but in Europe as well, where personal-appearance tours were enormously successful. In addition to making recordings and touring, by 1960 country bluesmen had appeared in productions on Broadway (*Cat on a Hot Tin Roof, Finian's Rainbow*). Folk festivals such as the one at Newport, Rhode Island, featured some of the traditional country blues singers who survived into the 1960s and 1970s, most of whose styles and accompaniments had, with greater or less degrees of subtlety, adapted to the tastes and expectations of their wider, and younger, audiences.[18]

Urban Blues and "Soul" Music

We have characterized the blues as an offspring of the rural South. Paradoxically, there is nothing that epitomizes the harsher aspects of urban life, especially for blacks, better than the urban blues. Unlike white country music, the blues, except for the more or less self-conscious revival or cultivation of older styles, has actually become urban music. The heartwood of the blues is rural, but at the layer where it is continuing to add living tissue it is wholly of the city. Thus the blues, like the great mass of the black populace whose music it is, has made the move from country to city.

Amiri Baraka, in this *Blues People*, describes this phase in a perceptive chapter titled "The Blues Continuum." This continuum bespeaks an irreducible core of identity for the blues. The blues continuum is less easy to separate into movements than that of jazz (whose evolution has been at times very discontinuous). The thread of identity in this continuum is, of course, the singer. Thus the singing of B. B. King, for example, has far more in common with that of Blind Lemon Jefferson than does the playing of Miles Davis, say, with that of King Oliver.

Blues *accompaniment* has, of course, changed markedly with the times, and here especially the blues has reflected the pressures for change that attend any form of popular art. The guitar has remained in many cases as a kind of symbol of continuity with its rural forebear, but the progression toward urban blues and "soul" music has been one of increasing emphasis on instruments; there are more of them and, like the now-electrified guitar, they are louder. This in turn has affected vocal style. The modern blues singer has a microphone, of course, but the shouting style that southern Midwest blues singers like Joe Turner and Jimmy Rushing had to adopt to be heard, unamplified, over the big band sounds of, say, Kansas City, has remained as a characteristic of much blues singing today. As Baraka has put it,

> These Southwestern "shouters" and big blues bands had a large influence on Negro music everywhere. The shouter gave impetus to a kind of blues that developed around the cities in the late thirties called "rhythm and blues," which was largely huge rhythm units smashing away behind screaming blues singers.[19]

The symbolic distortion forced upon that most sensitive of all musical instruments, the human voice, by the stridency and abrasiveness of a stark urban milieu is summed up by Baraka:

> Blues had always been a vocal music . . . but now the human voice itself had to struggle, to scream, to be heard.[20]

Although small instrumental ensembles (and occasionally large ones, in the theaters) accompanied the classic female blues singers, the real move toward modern urban blues was associated with bluesmen and actually began, very probably, with the introduction of that quintessentially urban instrument, the piano, into the country blues ensemble. The combination of piano and guitar was used by the influential team of Leroy Carr and Scrapper Blackwell in the 1930s, and the piano almost invariably figured in Chicago blues recordings of the period. The style of piano playing, except for traces of ragtime, was, not surprisingly, essentially that of the blues-related boogie-woogie, with its heavy and incessant left-hand ostinatos clearly presaging the main features of rock 'n' roll. Also significant was the addition of drums to many of the Chicago groups, showing the close relation to jazz. But this was a curiously transitional period in the citification of the blues; some recordings still included such down-home instruments as the harmonica and even the washboard. The blues, just before World War II, had one foot in the city and one still in the country.[21]

After the war the blues band began to take on some of its modern characteristics. The most significant development was electrification. Aaron "T-Bone" Walker, a Texas singer-guitarist who had moved to the West Coast, led the way, having long used an electric guitar with his blues singing. Younger players quickly adopted it. Then came the electric bass, so well adapted to projecting with booming intensity the boogie-like bass patterns that could be produced on it with great facility. The electric organ was occasionally used, as was, ultimately, the electric piano. The dominant wind instrument was the saxophone. The wailing, honking, screaming saxophone, blown at full volume, had been the blues singer's alter ego since the days of the big Midwest blues bands, often taking a complete chorus after the singer had sufficiently established the mood. The saxophone was the instrumental counterpart, in tone, inflection, and style, to the blues singer's message, which itself had come to depend less upon words than upon conveyed emotion.

The electric guitar and bass as mainstay, a hard-driving drummer, a piano, and at least one saxophone—these were the main ingredients of the band backing the blues singers. If we add to this, in some cases, a small male or female vocal ensemble for the blues singer to "play" to, which gave the responses to his calls and echoed his key phrases, we have virtually complete the medium of the urban blues which, by the early 1950s, had been given the commercial designation "rhythm-and-blues."[22]

This rhythm-and-blues, especially as conventionalized by such entertainers as Chuck Berry and Bo Diddley, was still performed by black musicians for an almost exclusively black audience, reached either in person or via recordings—a market which rivaled that for the race recordings of city and country blues thirty years earlier. But it also unquestionably formed the basis for the music—rock 'n' roll—that won a vast young white audience from the mid-fifties on. So closely, in fact, did early rock 'n' roll performers imitate black models that the early recordings of the white singer Elvis Presley (who spent his adolescent years in the blues ambience of Memphis) sold primarily to black audiences. Rock 'n' roll itself and subsequently the more eclectic popular music designated simply as "rock," is dealt with in the next chapter.

The Potency of Black Musical Styles in American Popular Music

The derivation, within the past generation, of rock music from a species of black urban blues is but the most recent confirmation of a salient and perennial fact of American musical life: every vital new movement in our popular music has had its impetus from black musicians and black musical styles. The music of the minstrel show, ragtime, jazz, the blues in its many manifestations including boogie-woogie, and most recently rock—these are the really distinctive and important native developments in American popular music.

This perennial revitalization of our popular music by black musical styles is not, at present, a source of unmixed satisfaction to black musicians. Though it confirms the dominant role of black musical traditions and styles in American popular culture, the pattern of white imitation and appropriation of these successive musics is seen by some both as an exploitation of black music and an adoption, by the music industry and the populace generally, of its *manner* without its *substance*. Musical movements have appeared that have been, at least in part, both protests against the commercial appropriation of black styles and affirmations of black culture. Bop of the late forties was a kind of protest in the direction of increased complexity, virtuosity, and aloofness, while the raw, unrestrained emotionalism of the new black jazz of the sixties and the earthy regressiveness of the so-called funky jazz of the same period (which had marked blues characteristics) were both attempts, in a sense, to redefine a black musical character and to differentiate it strongly from the increasingly homogenized "mainstream" of popular music.

The "Soul" Synthesis

A broader synthesis of black musical styles, and one embodying many elements of the blues, is embraced in the concept of "soul," which also has distinctly racial connotations that go far beyond questions of musical style. It is for this reason difficult to define satisfactorily. Charles Keil writes: " 'Soul' may be partly defined as a mixture of ethnic essence, purity, sincerity, conviction, credibility, and just plain effort." He offers extensive documentation of the way in which those most caught up in the phenomenon express its essence.[23] The ethnic orientation of "soul" is clear; it began to evolve, as Keil points out, after the Supreme Court's school desegregation decision of 1954, one of the landmarks in a decade that saw the aspirations of African-Americans take a definite turn toward strengthening racial and cultural *identity*, rather than achieving integration per se.

As a concept, soul embraces a wide spectrum of life's aspects, from religion to sexuality to food; indeed, it emphasizes a kind of synthesis of everything, and the communication and sharing of experience and strong emotion.

Musically, soul is a synthesis as well—of blues, jazz, and gospel. It is represented by the work of such performers as Otis Redding, James Brown, Ray Charles, Aretha Franklin, and Ike and Tina Turner. Its chief musical characteristics are a relentless ostinato, often with a prominent "backbeat" (offbeat emphasis), and the use of a blues saxophone and a small vocal group to echo key phrases and sounds. Soul music is sometimes prone to use "camp" introductions.[24] Formally many of the pieces display a simple but effective buildup from a soft, underplayed beginning to a shouting, repetitive, near-hysterical catharsis, after which the intensity subsides.

As a commercial category the term "soul" has become so widespread that it bids fair to replace the older, narrower categories of "race" and "rhythm-

and-blues" as applying generally to the work of any black singer who is accepted by, and sings with conviction and commitment for, a primarily black audience.

The blues singers of the late 1980s, especially the men, have large followings, both for their records and for their personal appearances, which (like the appearances of rock singers) take on the aspects of elaborately staged rituals in which the audience plays an important part.[25] The singing involves an exaggeratedly stylized vocal delivery, with melismatic shouting and moaning. The guitar, when used, is played with a technique heavily dependent upon electronic amplification and manipulation, and the whole is usually accompanied by a fairly large band with characteristics of both rock and jazz. It includes a prominent rhythm section of drums, electric bass, piano, and often electric piano and organ. There are usually a number of supporting "horns" (saxophones, trumpets, trombones). A fairly consistent feature is the vocal ensemble already referred to, for responses and echoes. The more elaborate production numbers include strings as well.

Is the blues itself in a state of decline? This depends on one's point of view, of course. It is worth noting that in the case of any popular art still not too far removed from its folk roots, two contrasting attitudes eventually develop. On one hand there is the attitude of those who wish to see preserved the purity and integrity of a particular form of expression, as it evolved in a particular time, place, and set of circumstances. This attitude draws a circle around a specific corpus of music and performers, designating it as "authentic," and worthy of cultivation and study. Charles Seeger (writing of folk music proper) has characterized such an attitude as that of the *structuralists*.[26] He opposes to this the attitude of the *functionalists*, who regard the structuralists slightly as "purists" and characterize their outlook (in blues and jazz) with the term "moldy fig." The functionalists accept fully whatever happens to the music, which will, they feel, in all circumstances take whatever direction it *must* and, as a popular art form whose first laws are those of adaptation and survival, will appropriate to itself whatever seems to meet its needs at the moment.

Whichever view one takes, it must be recognized that there is a feeling among many African-Americans that the blues has outlived its time as a current form of communicative art; that its message is no longer relevant or appropriate; and that, indeed, it is too reminiscent of slavery and its residual consequences. And it is true that objective observation provides a good many indications to support the idea that the blues is in a state of decline. Except for revivalism and the conscious cultivation of traditional styles, the music, both vocal and instrumental, has entered a stage of exaggerated mannerism typical of any popular music that feels itself in intense competition for a large market. The highly conventionalized lyrics seem to have lost the breadth, immediacy, and inventiveness of traditional blues. Even the time-honored phrases and images, when they appear, seem, except in a very few hands, to have become clichés, delivered with showy stylization but without much conviction. Whether or not Paul Oliver, longtime observer of the blues, may be of the "moldy fig" school is an open question. But his summation of the situation in 1969 raised issues that may well be pondered in relation to any popular music but most unavoidably be dealt with in assessing what has happened to the blues.

> In the past, blues has shown a remarkable capacity for survival; its demise has been predicted often enough and it may still survive the successive competition of Rock 'n' Roll, Soul and whatever comes next. But it shows every sign of cultural decline; the ascendancy of formal mannerism over content, the rococo flourishes and extravagant posturings both physically and instrumentally are signs of an art form in its final stages. From direct and forthright origins as a functional art created of necessity, it has passed through the successive phases of development and maturity, the means evolving to meet the demands of meaning. As so often happens in an art form which has continued beyond its period of greatest value as expression and communication, it has reached a late stage of flamboyant embellishment. Not for a decade have lyrically significant blues appeared in any numbers, and its most meaningful expressions have been the tortured, impatient, openly aggressive abstractions of the playing of the music.[27]

Despite the currency of the perception that the blues has for some time been in a state of decline, to be cultivated only by revivalists, collected by aficionados, and studied by scholars, there is in the 1980s a generation of very able guitarist-vocalists, such as Albert Collins and Johnny Copeland, and the younger Robert Cray and Joe Louis Walker, who are effectively reaffirming the validity of blues technique, form, and feeling. As performers on the electric guitar, they are the heirs of men like Aaron "T-Bone" Walker, Jimi Hendrix, and B. B. King, their numbers consisting characteristically of vocals alternating with extended guitar solos.[28] Like earlier bluesmen, they travel extensively, and are taking the blues not only to Europe, but to Africa and Japan.

Whatever the present and future state of the blues, there can be no doubt of its importance up to this point. Oliver's summation concludes by calling it "one of the richest and most rewarding of popular arts and perhaps the last great folk music that the western world may produce."

Further Reading

The blues has, since mid-century, inspired more writing than nearly any other genre of American music. The following selective list does not include biographical works.

Baraka, Amiri. *Blues People.* New York: Morrow, 1963.
A survey by an eminent black writer, who uses music to illustrate and illuminate the history of his people in America.

Bastin, Bruce. *Red River Blues: The Blues Tradition in the Southeast.* Urbana: University of Illinois Press, 1986.
Well-researched and annotated regional study, part of the Music in American Life series.

———. "From the Medicine Show to the Stage: Some Influences upon the Development of a Blues Tradition in the Southeastern United States," *American Music,* vol. 2, no. 1 (Spring 1984)

Charters, Samuel. *The Bluesmen.* New York: Oak Publications, 1967.

———. *Sweet as the Showers of Rain.* New York: Oak Publications, 1977.
These two titles constitute a two-volume expansion of the author's earlier *The Country Blues* (New York: Rinehart, 1959).

Cook, Bruce. *Listen to the Blues.* New York: Scribner's, 1973.

Ferris, William, Jr. *Blues from the Delta.* New York: Da Capo, 1984 (reprint of 1979 ed.).

Garland, Phyl. *The Sound of Soul.* Chicago: Henry Regnery, 1969.

Gillett, Charlie. *The Sound of the City.* New York: Dell, 1970.

A history of rock 'n' roll, with a useful section on rhythm-and-blues.

Handy, W. C. *Father of the Blues.* New York: Macmillan, 1941.

In spite of the obvious kind of exaggeration implicit in its title, Handy's autobiography contains a wealth of background information, written from the standpoint of firsthand professional experience, on America's popular music business during the first four decades of this century.

———, ed. *Blues: An Anthology.* New York, 1926. Reprint, New York: Macmillan, 1972.

A famous collection of early published blues by Handy and others. A 1949 edition includes a rather extensive and valuable essay, "The Story of the Blues" by Abbe Niles. This is included in the most recent edition, which also incorporates additional blues, and guitar-chord symbols.

Keil, Charles. *Urban Blues.* Chicago: University of Chicago Press, 1966.

An indispensable study, and one of the few to deal adequately and from a variety of angles with the modern urban component of the blues. His annotated outlines of blues styles (Appendix C) is valuable.

Oliver, Paul. *The Meaning of the Blues.* New York: Macmillan, 1960. Paperback ed., Collier, 1963.

Possibly more relevant to Chapter 2, this also deserves inclusion here as an exhaustive and perceptive study of blues subjects and the milieu of its people, in the form of an extensive commentary of 350 blues texts, arranged according to subject.

———. *Songsters and Saints: Vocal Traditions on Race Records.* Cambridge: Cambridge University Press, 1984.

Well-illustrated and documented study of the blues, songs, ballads and sermons recorded in the 1920s.

———. *The Story of the Blues.* New York: Chilton, 1969.

A comprehensive study, profusely illustrated with photographs, this is a basic source, though concentrating mainly on the rural and "classic" blues. There is a fine bibliography and discography.

Oster, Harry. *Living Country Blues.* Detroit: Folklore Associates, 1969.

Redd, Lawrence H. *Rock Is Rhythm and Blues.* East Lansing: Michigan State University Press, 1974.

The first part of the book defends the thesis implicit in the title; the second is devoted to transcriptions of six interviews with Riley "B.B." King, Brownie McGhee, Arthur "Big Boy" Crudup, Jerry Butler, Dave Clark, and Jessie Whitaker.

Shaw, Arnold. *Black Popular Music in America.* New York: Schirmer Books, 1986.

———. *Honkers and Shouters: The Golden Years of Rhythm & Blues.* New York: Macmillan, 1978.

———. *The World of Soul: Black America's Contribution to the Pop Music Scene.* New York: Cowles, 1970.

Taft, Michael. *Blues Lyric Poetry: An Anthology.* New York: Garland, 1983.

Lyrics of more than two thousand blues songs, transcribed from reissue LPs. Published with a companion three-volume concordance.

Titon, Jeff Todd. *Early Downhome Blues: A Musical and Cultural Analysis.* Urbana: University of Illinois Press, 1977.

In addition to cultural background, photographs, and reproductions of contemporary advertisements, this study includes transcriptions from forty-eight blues recordings of the 1920s, with musical analysis, thus making it one of the most musically thorough and useful studies in the field.

See also various works in the reading lists for Chapter 2 (additional background on the folk phase) and Chapter 14 (jazz, especially the early jazz so closely related to blues).

Listening

Blues recordings, like those of jazz, have a history of over sixty years, and are available today in a bewildering array of issues and reissues. Discography in the field has become highly specialized as to both region and chronology. The following list is highly selective; for a far more extensive discography, and record source, consult specialty catalogs such as the current Blues and Gospel Catalog from Down Home Music, Inc.

General

The Story of the Blues, notes by Paul Oliver. 2 LPs. Columbia CG 30008.

"Classic" City Blues

Ma Rainey

Ma Rainey's Black Bottom. 7 LPs. Yazoo 1071.

Single LP reissues of Ma Rainey, of lesser quality, are:

Blues the World Forgot. Biograph BLP 12001.

Oh My Babe Blues. Biograph BLP 12011.

Queen of the Blues. Biograph BLP 12032.

Bessie Smith

Bessie Smith's entire recorded output for Columbia has been reissued in five 2-LP albums, under individual titles, as CG 33, 30126, 30450, 30818, and 31093. Her work is also represented in most jazz anthologies.

Also relevant:

Rare Recordings of the Twenties. 4 LPs. Columbia CBS-64218, 65379, 65380, 65421.
Part of the import series *Aimez-vous le jazz?,* these recordings feature Louis Armstrong playing with various blues singers such as Clara Smith, Sippie Wallace, Chippie Hill, and Victoria Spivey.

The Victoria Spivey Recorded Legacy of the Blues. Spivey 2001.

Stars of the Apollo Theatre. Columbia K-CG-30788.
Sheds additional light on the vaudeville phase of the classic blues.

Country Blues

The Rural Blues: A Study of Vocal and Instrumental Resources. Folkways RF-202.

The Country Blues, vols. 1 and 2. Folkways RF-1, RF-9.

Blues Roots/Mississippi. Folkways RF-14.

Roots of the Blues. NW-252.

Let's Get Loose: Folk and Popular Blues Styles from the Beginnings to the Early 1940's. NW-290.

Mississippi Blues, 1927–1941. Yazoo 1001.

Tex-Arkana-Louisiana Country. Yazoo 1004

See also the Listening section for Chapter 2. For further specialization by performer and geographical area, consult the catalogs of Down Home Music, Inc. and Arhoolie Records.

Piano Blues and Boogie-Woogie

Cuttin' the Boogie: Piano Blues and Boogie Woogie, 1926–1941. NW-259
The Boogie Woogie Masters. Affinity AFS 1005.
Boogie Woogie. 3 LPs. Murray Hill M 61358.

Magpie Records has issued 21 volumes of piano blues, 4401–21. Single tracks are included in most jazz anthologies.

Urban Blues and Soul Music

Blues Roots/Chicago—The 1930's. Folkways RF-16.
Roots: Rhythm and Blues. Folkways RF-20.
Straighten Up and Fly Right: Rhythm and Blues from the Close of the Swing Era to the Dawn of Rock 'n' Roll. NW-261.
Anthology of Rhythm and Blues, vol. 1, Columbia CS 9802.
Super Black Blues. Bluestime BT 29003. Includes "T-Bone" Walker, Joe Turner, Otis Spann, and others.

Also useful are some fairly representative collections by individual artists, which often go by such titles as "The Best of . . .", of which the following are merely samples. For more detailed discographies of individual performers, consult specialty catalogs such as the one noted above from Down Home Music.

The Best of Muddy Waters. Chess 9255.
The Best of B. B. King, vols. 1 and 2. Ace 198, 199.
T-Bone Walker Sings the Blues. Pathe 154 675-1.
John Lee Hooker Plays and Sings the Blues. Chess 9199.
Bobby "Blue" Bland: Foolin' with the Blues. Charly CRB 1049.
Ray Charles. Everest FS 244.
Aretha Franklin's Greatest Hits, vols. 1 and 2. Columbia CS 9473, 9601.

PROJECTS

1. Based on W. C. Handy's autobiography (and any other sources you can find) describe in a brief essay what life was like for a black musician in the Deep South in the first quarter of the twentieth century.
2. Make a further study, along the lines suggested in the chapter, of the relationship of early published blues to those that appear in the recordings of the 1920s.
3. Assemble a list of at least ten male and ten female blues singers who recorded between 1920 and 1930, with a brief biographical sketch of each. Cite at least one recording for each, and listen to as many others as you can.
4. Besides those listed in the chapter, find three examples of blues form and harmony in instrumental jazz. Try to select examples from different periods of jazz.
5. Make an annotated discography of at least ten entries by at least five different boogie-woogie pianists. Describe and classify as best you can the different styles that you hear. Select one or two examples, and analyze as best you can their relationship, in form and harmony, to the sung blues.
6. Compare three recordings of Mississippi delta blues performers with three recordings of Texas blues performers. Describe them, and determine to what extent they either support or contradict the stylistic generalizations made in the chapter.
7. Make a collection of urban blues lyrics since 1950 (including rhythm-and-blues and soul). Compare them, in scope and treatment, with those in Paul Oliver's study *The Meaning of the Blues,* which are predominantly rural and date from before 1950.
8. Assemble a list of at least five singers

from the rhythm-and-blues and soul categories whose work you feel still belongs to the authentic blues tradition, however you may interpret that. Cite examples, and explain what there is about their work that influences your choice.

9. Compile a short discography of two important blues saxophonists prominent since 1950. Describe their work, and include a brief biographical sketch.

10. Make a study of urban gospel music, and its relation to the urban blues.

11. Make a study of a commercial style such as the "Detroit sound" or "Motown" (as represented, say, by the Supremes). How much does it owe to the blues? Analyze the similarities and differences between such a stylization and the more mainstream blues tradition—the "blues continuum."

9

Rock

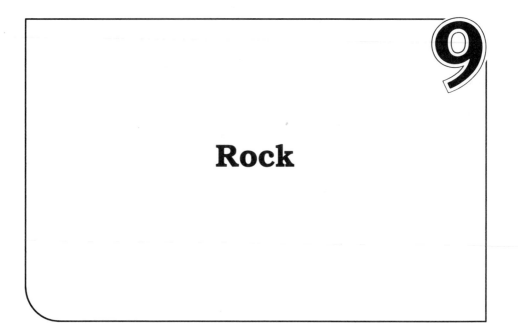

IN the quarter-century since its emergence, rock has become our dominant form of popular music. It differs significantly from previous forms of mass entertainment in being "goodtime" music that is also, to a greater extent than any popular music before it, an expression of revolt. It is also essentially the product and expression of urban culture—some have said of "street culture."[1] Although since the 1970s the true "street culture" has not been the natural home of rock performers or most of their devotees, rock is nevertheless as distinctly an outgrowth and expression of urban life and values as country music is of rural life and values. Traceable ultimately to common origins in the rural South, these two have grown apart, musically and socially (and one might almost say politically), and have become the musical property of two distinctly different constituencies that are still identifiable, in a cultural if not literal sense, as *city* and *country*.* Together they account for the major portion of our popular music.

For rock, as for all popular music, the recording has become the primary vehicle. Given the current state of technology, recordings can be made nearly anywhere, and recorded music can go anywhere, penetrating freely both national and cultural boundaries. It has been truly observed that rock has thus become the pervasive new *oral tradition* of mass culture. Purveying sound as content, it has become virtually the popular music of most of the world.

In approaching the consideration of rock, two things are clear at the outset: it is a music of *youth*; and it began, at least, as an *underground* music.

* Somewhat ironically, certain rock stars today, such as Bruce Springsteen, still cultivate a rural or a small-town image, but their music and lyrics are quite distinct from country music.

As David Pichaske put it, early rock "expressed a visceral impatience with socio-political norms."[2] Some startling paradoxes emerge, to be sure, from the enormous commercial success of this underground music, but its genesis as the music of the dispossessed, the dissatisfied, and the rebellious is periodically recalled by the appearance of such a phenomenon as punk rock, which announced itself unmistakably as both youth and underground.

The explosive emergence of rock, shortly after the middle of this century, to its position of nearly complete dominance of popular culture almost worldwide, is simply accepted by many as a symptom of our rapidly changing times. But thinkers are prone to seek connections–analogies to the past. To what can the phenomenal rise of rock be compared? *Are* there any analogies to it in cultural history? One writer has found a correspondence with tribal art, in terms of the element of participation.[3] The same writer sees an analogy to the age of Chaucer, "a more verbal era when poetry and music are back in the hands of the people."[4] Another writer has found a whole range of correspondences with nineteenth-century Romanticism.[5]

What is the fundamental nature of rock? How does it actually function in our culture? Is it really popular music, pure and simple? Is it in reality a folk music, as Carl Belz suggests?[6] Is it an unacknowledged form of art music? Individual answers will vary greatly, but they are best based on an examination of the music itself, and it is to this that we now turn.

Characteristics of the Music

The Basic Makeup of the Rock Band

Like the blues, rock was, and indeed still is, music for the *singer* (in contrast to the more instrumental jazz), backed up by an ensemble dominated by one or more guitars, a bass, and often, though not always, a piano or other keyboard instrument, all driven by a strong and relentless beat from the drummer. Typically all of the instruments are now electric, and the keyboard and drums are often synthesized. The common practices of adding a saxophone (usually the husky-voiced tenor) and a backup vocal group came directly from rhythm-and-blues. All other additions (from sitar to symphony orchestra) are peripheral to these irreducible ingredients of the rock band.

Style Traits

Rhythm

The most basic and obligatory element of rock is the *beat*, as maintained by the drummer and the bass player, sometimes with the assistance of the rhythm guitarist and the keyboard player. Forthright, loud, and insistent, the beat usually incorporates a simple melodic figure in the bass, which is obsessively repeated in an *ostinato* that shows rock's strong relationship to boogie-woogie. This is apt to be most noticeable in the music of those black artists whose work shows a relationship to rhythm-and-blues, from Chuck Berry in the 1950s to Prince in the 1980s.[7] Another rhythmic feature of rock that is close to its roots is the prominent "backbeat"—the strongly marked offbeat *reaction* to the basic pulse that is so typical a feature of black music-making, where the drummer has simply picked up and imitated the hand-clapping, for example, of black congregations, sacred and secular.[8] But the rock beat can become more highly developed, showing its derivation from a combination of the boogie-woogie bass,[9] as noted above, and the rhythms of the Latin band.[10] With the combination of drum set, bass, guitar, and supplementary percussion, the rock beat can evolve at times into an intricate combination of rhythms. This has been especially true of jazz-influenced rock.

Color and texture

Arnold Shaw has characterized rock as being, *for its mass audience*, music of "energy, volume, distortion, and rebellion."[11] This is at least an accurate description of "hard" rock (as opposed to "soft" or "pop" rock), which is a sound of hard-driving energy, high decibel level, and a tone quality deliberately distorted by the high amplification needed to produce that high volume level. Conditioned since its inception by its nearly total commitment to electric instruments, rock is, with rare exceptions, inherently an amplified electric sound. The texture of rock is that of most accompanied song in African and African-influenced Western music: melody, interrupted by breaks (giving opportunity for "responses" by a vocal group, saxophone, or the like), with an accompaniment of persistent and repetitious rhythm.

Since rock has evolved in so many different directions, and developed so many sub-styles, with varying degrees of popular acceptance and commercial viability, this basic color and texture is subject to a great deal of modification through eclectic influences. Thus "folk-rock," for example, will revert to acoustic stringed instruments; "jazz-rock" will introduce the saxophones and brass of the jazz band, with improvised solos; "raga rock" will use sitars or other Eastern instruments, "baroque rock" the harpsichord, and so on.

Melody, harmony, and tonality

In terms of melody, rock reveals its roots in both the blues and country music. It is *singers'* music; furthermore, its tunes are well suited to the relatively untrained and unskilled voices associated with the vernacular traditions from which it sprang. In range, melodic structure, and available pitch material (scales), rock melody is characterized by folklike simplicity. Indeed, the degree of sophistication typical of the products of Broadway or Tin Pan Alley would be false to its very nature. Nevertheless, that its elemental resources can be used with extraordinary subtlety by gifted song composers is seen, for example, in the works of Dylan or the Beatles.

This simplicity of melody dictates a corresponding simplicity in tonality and the selection of supporting chords; a single key prevails, and the choice of chords is extremely limited.

In its pitch material, rock presents an interesting synthesis of the blues scale(s) and the modes of Anglo-Celtic (Appalachian) folk music; some inter-

Example 9–1 Anglo- and African-American Scales Compared

Scales frequently used for Anglo–American folk music

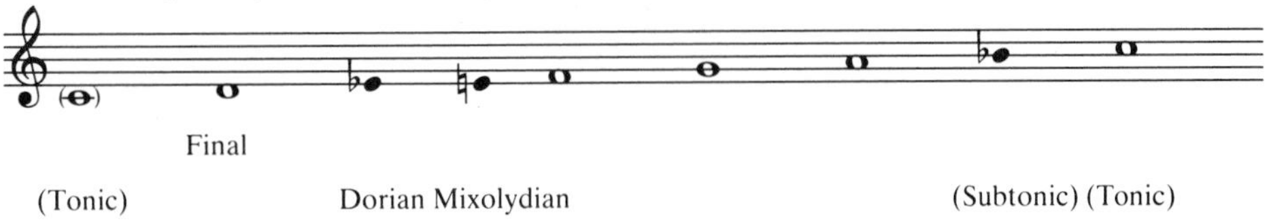

African–American blues scale

esting similarities between these two traditions may be seen in Example 9–1.*

This tendency away from the standard major or minor scale is especially apparent in the use, both harmonically and melodically, of the *subtonic* note—the pitch a whole step below the tonic, as illustrated in Example 9–1. This results in a corresponding de-emphasis of the *leading tone* as a melodic tone and of the whole family of *dominant* chords (so important in the popular music of Tin Pan Alley) as harmonic entities. Interesting inferences could be drawn here; what we are actually dealing with is the contrast between the cultivated harmonic tradition of European classical music, which our sophisticated pre-rock popular music inherited, and the vernacular traditions of both African-American and Anglo-American folk music. In terms of the performing media that generated each, it must also be remembered that Tin Pan Alley music is piano-based, whereas rock, like the folk music from which it came, is guitar-based. It is risky to oversimplify the matter, but contrasting a single pair of examples may at least serve to illustrate the point.

Example 9–2 shows, in their simplest form, the harmonies of the most important strains of each song. In each there are only five chords used; four of these are common to both songs. (Rock inherited the chords of European harmony as well as the inflections of the blues and folk music.) The great difference is in their usage—a difference that becomes audibly apparent when Example 9–2 is played. It is most striking in the final phrase of each; the Tin Pan Alley song confirms its comfortable conventionality by stating the time-honored dominant-to-tonic cadential progression three times, while the rock song, which never uses that progression at all, ends on a quite different kind of cadence, preceding the final tonic with the subtonic chord, a chord prevalent in both folk music and the blues. Also significant is the fact that the Tin Pan

* For a fuller treatment of the blues scale, see Chapter 2 and Example 2-3.

Example 9–2 Tin Pan Alley and Rock Harmonies Compared

"Daisy Bell" (Harry Dacre, 1892) *chorus strain*

"The Wind Cries Mary" (Jimi Hendrix, 1967) *principal strain*

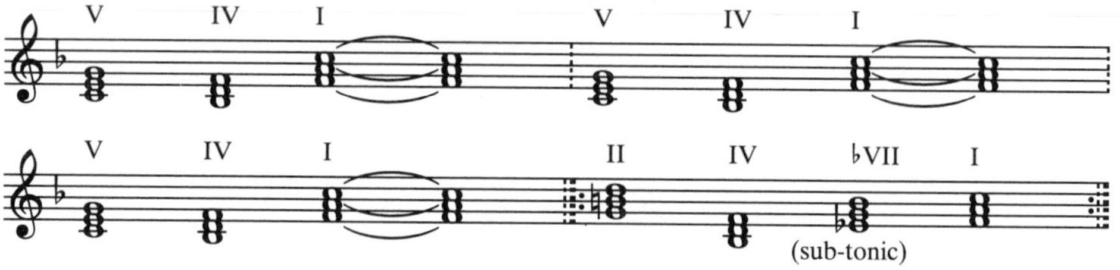

Alley song changes key at the end of the second phrase (typically, to the dominant), while the rock song not only stays in the same key throughout but uses the same chord progression for the first three phrases. Its most striking harmonies are saved for the last phrase, which is repeated to accommodate the title line.[12]

Form

The unit of rock is the song; the form derives from the lyrics themselves. Adopting the strophic form from the blues and the ballad, a rock song usually has more verses, and is therefore more extensive, than a Tin Pan Alley popular song. As in folk music, the use of a refrain is very common.

Extending form beyond the strophic song and building larger-scale works through the juxtaposition of successive sections, which present contrasts in musical material, tempo, texture, and tonality, are not fundamentally suited to rock. Rock's ventures into larger forms (opera, for example) still exhibit a structure consisting of a series of shorter "numbers." Where the basic unit, the song, is extended, this is often done by a means of a long concluding section based on the repetition of material previously heard (perhaps a single word, or exclamation)—a section that builds in an ecstatic and orgiastic *crescendo* of power and intensity, often ending quietly in a mood of momentary exhaustion and satiation. While this sort of climactic catharsis can be found in the extended and improvisatory blues of performers such as B. B. King, it is fundamentally an inheritance from black gospel music. In rock numbers of the 1980s, these free-form *codas* tend to become quite long, may be heavily orchestrated, and display an eclectic "grafting" of diverse sound effects.[13]

Vocal styles

The heritage of the blues is again apparent in the vocal styles used in rock; the shout, the cry, the groan (of either pain or ecstasy), use of falsetto, the mumbled slur deliberately "throwing away" portions of the lyrics—all these have their roots in blues singing (and, it should be noted, in gospel singing as well), and have become basic resources of the rock singer.[14]

Given this influence from the blues, it is also true that vocal styles in popular music tend to be highly individual; tone quality, inflection of the voice, manner of delivery, even accent, become identifying "trademarks" of a particular singer. The highly individualized styles of extremely popular leading singers become prototypes, imitated by those who follow. Black blues singers such as Joe Turner, Muddy Waters, and John Lee Hooker were influential on early rock 'n' roll vocalists; there developed subsequently a Bob Dylan type of delivery, a Beatles style of singing and inflection, a David Byrne manner of monotone half-recitation, and so on.

Style Traits Summarized: The Typical Successful Album of the 1980s

Listening to a typical successful album of the 1980s, we are conscious first of being immersed in a sound-world of intricately layered electronic glitter, as much the product of the studio and the engineer as of the composer and the performers. Since the 1960s, rock musicians and producers have taken full advantage of a continually evolving technology in the production of the basic vehicle of rock, the sound recording. Synthesized sounds, complex echo and reverberation effects, and the multiplying of layers of sound through overdubbing have become commonplace and indeed obligatory ingredients of the music, and effects not easily duplicated in live performances are taken for granted on recordings. The sound studio has become itself a sound resource.

The enrichment of the sound through the addition of instrumental colors borrowed from jazz or classical music (horns, strings, etc.) has become typical of the successful recording. Whether recorded by live musicians or synthesized, these additions are usually achieved by overdubbing; that is, these elements of the texture are added in successive layers after the basic recording of the song itself is completed.

The backup vocal group, an inheritance from rhythm-and-blues, is still much in evidence in the rock album of the 1980s; most often the vocal group emphasizes fragments of the lyrics by repetition, although in some more sophisticated albums by groups such as Talking Heads the vocal group has its own material, sometimes creating a kind of counterpoint in which solo singer and vocal group or groups sing contrasting material simultaneously.[15]

But all of this—the synthesized sound, the complex layering of overdubbed voices and instruments—is perceived as packaging for the "star," the solo singer who gives identity to the album, and whose vehicle the album is. (Less frequently than in previous decades is there a *group* identity.) The message of the star, and hence of the song, may be aggressive and threatening (somewhat less so in the 1980s than in the previous decade), intimate and insistently seductive, lonesome and lamenting, ironic (as a commentary on some aspect of contemporary life), or (less often) joyous and carefree. If the lyrics are sometimes deliberately obscure, the message is usually clear in the sound itself. At times the very sound may in fact overwhelm the lyrics, which can be reduced to elemental fragments or vocal ejaculations, building, as described above, to an intense climax. Very often part of the message is that the sound *does not stop*—hence its implied continuation in the still very frequent fade-out ending.

The technology of the 1980s has added another dimension to the range of rock's stimuli through the medium of the *video*. In terms of technical possibilities, it supersedes the live performance visually, just as the studio recording had superseded it in the dimension of sound.

Characteristics of the Words

There are rock fans who say that they never pay attention to the words, and it is true, as we have noted, that the *sound* of rock is the emotive *message* of rock. Nevertheless rock, like country music, and like the folk music that was the source of them both, is fundamentally word-oriented; its vehicle is the song, not, as in jazz, the instrumental number. This has given rise to the close scrutiny of rock lyrics, considered by some as poetry in their own right. We shall now turn our attention to some of the characteristics of these lyrics.

Rock Lyrics and the Blues

Early rock 'n' roll, coming as it did directly out of rhythm-and-blues, naturally reflected this in its lyrics. From Roy Brown's "Good Rockin' Tonight," as recorded by Wynonie Harris in 1947, to Chuck Berry's "Rock 'n' Roll Music" a decade later, the family likeness is clear: a celebration of energy, of vitality, of movement, of sex, of dancing, of the very act of making the music itself. Like rhythm-and-blues, it was music to dance to. The classical blues form itself (*aab*) did appear in rock 'n' roll, as it had in rhythm-and-blues; its emphasis, by repetition, of a single line, followed by a concluding line, can be found as a kind of relic of classical blues in the choruses of such early rock 'n' roll songs as "I Can't Go On," "Good Golly, Miss Molly," and "Maybellene."[16]

But the broader range of blues lyrics was missing from early rock 'n' roll, which was *little else* than music to dance to. In general, the growing popularization of rock 'n' roll, and the subsequent evolution of rock, created a widening separation from blues lyrics in both form and content. This can be summed up by saying that rock lyrics have an adolescent orientation, while blues lyrics have an adult orientation.

Rock Subject Matter

Sex

Folk blues, as we have seen in the previous chapter, treated sexual themes in a frank, matter-of-fact way; rhythm-and-blues tended to do the same. When this music began to reach a wider young public, it encountered heated opposition from the older generation in general, and from parents in particular. Those interested in producing it on a commercially profitable scale began to censor—by disguising or transmuting—references to sex, often in metaphors such as dancing or automobile driving—images common enough in the cultures, to be sure. This is especially apparent in the "cover" versions of black rhythm-and-blues songs.[17] Though rock 'n' roll seemed, in comparison with the Tin Pan Alley products of the time, to be earthy, Pichaske has called its earthiness "a debased, adolescent form of R&B [rhythm-and-blues]."[18]

The gradual emergence of more overt references to sex in later rock again reveal the music's parentage in the blues. The young British groups that emerged in the 1960s were greatly influenced by American blues singers such as Howlin' Wolf, Muddy Waters, and Bo Diddley. The new groups, best typified in this regard by the Rolling Stones, introduced a more direct treatment of sex into rock; in particular, the aggressiveness and bravado illustrated, for example, by Muddy Waters's "Hoochie Coochie Man"[19] was reflected in such Stones songs as "Satisfaction," "Parachute Woman," and "Play With Fire," and the early (1964) "I'm a King Bee" was a reworking of an actual blues number.[20]

As rock 'n' roll broadened its range, and became known simply as "rock," obsessive preoccupation with sex became a somewhat less prominent feature, although—as in its ultimate parent, the blues—sex is frequently present just below the surface. In the 1980s, overt sexual themes reappear in the lyrics of such super-pop, and primarily teen-age-oriented, stars as Prince (Rogers Nelson).[21] (A segment of the underground punk rock movement of the 1980s has continued to put out quasi-pornographic recordings, adding fuel to the fires of controversy over censorship.)

Dissent

Rock was *born* as an underground form, with origins in the "outcast" rhythm-and-blues. When it was popularized and adopted by the mass of youth as "rock 'n' roll," its threatening aspects diminished. But its identity as an underground genre was reasserted in the troubled decade that followed its birth. The 1960s saw a new infusion of folkness into rock, which became, in the hands of Bob Dylan and others, a vehicle for protest—for dissent. New songs appeared that had a bitterly serious purpose, a cutting edge. They were no longer good-time music; the term "rock 'n' roll" was no longer appropriate. Entertainment, even sex, became subordinated to expressions of outrage—at times ironic, at times threatening. We need only compare the relatively good-natured anti-parental satire of "Yakety-Yak" of the 1950s (in which youth objects to having to do household chores in order to receive an allowance)[22] with the far more sober and bitter "Subterranean Homesick Blues" of the 1960s by Bob Dylan:

> Twenty years of schoolin'
> And they put you on the day shift
> Look out kid they keep it all hid.[23]

to get a feel for the depth of the new social-consciousness themes. There was "extroverted" dissent, often couched in pungent irony, and focusing on specific issues, often political:

> Come on all of you big strong men,
> Uncle Sam needs your help again.
> He's got himself in a terrible jam,
> Way down yonder in Vietnam.
> So put down your books and pick up a gun;
> We're gonna have a whole lotta fun.[24]

Bob Dylan's songs of the 1960s expressed outrage over social issues such as racism ("Oxford Town");[25] they also dealt with the perceived generation gap ("The Times They Are a-Changing' ")[26] and with a particular perception of "establishment" religion ("With God on Our Side").[27]

Or the lyrics can simply express an identification with the outcast, the underdog, the "common man," perceived as hapless, helpless, confused, and victimized—doomed to ride on a "down-bound train."[28]

Another kind of dissent appears in rock lyrics that might be called "introverted", expressing resignation, self-deprecation, a kind of desperate and nihilistic malaise.[29]

While dissent in rock lyrics may have been less prominent in some periods than in others, it has by no means disappeared as a theme of both lyrics and sound,[30] nor as a *stance* of the performers. Having attained the status of a new worldwide oral tradition in popular culture, rock may be expected periodically to manifest dissent in one form or another.

The psychedelic and the surreal

When rock left the realm of simple good-time music in the 1950s and confronted the troubled 1960s with increased sophistication, the imagery of its lyrics became, in the hands of some artists, less direct, less rooted in the obvious realities of a tangible, everyday world, and more given to the exploration of the visionary and the surreal, as experienced in a subjective mental state denoted by the term "psychedelic." Rock lyrics found their way into paths explored by poetry and painting three-quarters of a century earlier, creating and juxtaposing fantastic images with obscure or subliminal significance—a carefree life beneath the waves in a yellow submarine; a dreamworld of ambulatory chessmen and a smoking caterpillar which we enter by falling down a rabbit hole (one mapped out for us a century ago by Lewis Carroll); a courtroom scene in which an electric guitar, victim of a highway accident, is brought before a jury.[31]

The psychedelic mental state has always been associated with the creative impetus. From the earliest recorded times chemical inducements of this state have been known and used; from mushrooms and peyote to opium, mescaline, and LSD, technology has merely updated the means available. Though the rock ambience of the 1960s began to include (and indeed to imply) the widespread use of drugs everywhere, it was the street and drug culture of San Francisco that most explicitly expressed and came to typify it. There can be no reasonable doubt that drug use was alluded to in the coded references of "acid rock," just as metaphors for sex had been used earlier.[32]

This is not to imply that all psychedelic images or mental states in rock lyrics refer to the use of drugs. The drug image still clings to most people's perception of rock, however; as the staggering costs in human terms of these dangerous chemical shortcuts to the psychedelic state of mind have become increasingly apparent, rock musicians and promoters themselves have taken steps to counteract this negative association. Campaigns such as Danny Goldberg's Rock Against Drugs and Bill Graham's Crack Down are representative.[33]

Love-as-distinguished-from-sex, and the new altruism

If rock 'n' roll began as dance music in the 1950s, with relatively inconsequential lyrics, it had considerably broadened by the 1960s, and no single characterization, not even that of socially conscious protest music, could include all of it. The lyrics of popular music have always had as their main subject the human love relationship; rock has never been an exception. What we notice by the time of rock's maturity in the 1960s, however, is the appearance of songs that treat the human love relationship in aspects other than purely (or mainly) sexual.[34]

There is another class of lyrics that go still farther, and treat love as a more universal and at the same time more subjective feeling—love of fellow beings, love of the earth, love of life itself. Perhaps a manifestation of the same impulses that motivated the "flower children," and closely related to anti-violence, anti-discrimination, and anti-war sentiments, these songs have come from a wide range of authors.[35]

Along these same lines, a new altruism has manifested itself, addressing humanitarian issues such as hunger in a positive, rather than ironically negative, manner. This has been associated with the production of large-scale benefit concerts and recordings; the 1985 superstar album *We Are the World* is perhaps the most celebrated example. Produced as a project to raise money for the relief of hunger in Africa, it included thirty-six stars in its roster of performers.

The Rural Image in Rock

There was a time when the term "folk" meant "rural," and in spite of rock's identity as the "sound of the city" (to quote the title of an early book) part of the *folkness* of rock is still expressed, paradoxically, in terms of a persistent rural or small-town image. It is significant that, reflecting rock's origins, the most characteristic accent and vocal inflection of rock singers is that of the rural South; that is, the part of the United States that made up the old Confederacy. This is assumed and maintained regardless of the origin and background of particular performers themselves. The rural or small-town image is expressed in peripheral ways as well—it appears on the album covers, for example, of artists as diverse as Jimi Hendrix, Bob Dylan, Kenny Loggins, and Bruce Springsteen.[36]

Rock Lyrics As Poetry; Rock As Art

To what extent has some rock music assumed the status and function of *high art*, as opposed to commercially produced entertainment (*popular art*) or the distinctive expression of a certain community, however defined, by members of that community (*folk art*)? This question has been debated since the 1960s. It can be misleading and falsifying to separate the *words* of rock from the *music*; their close relationship cannot be too strongly insisted on, and it is even debatable whether lyrics separated from music should be considered as poetry at all. Nevertheless, rock's identity as *art* has tended to focus on its lyrics.[37]

The perception of rock as art seemed to make its first appearance in two nearly simultaneous forms, in relation to two diametrically opposed styles—the heightened folklike imagery of Bob Dylan, with its incisive, ironic, and often oblique references to the issues of our times, and the more lighthearted, polished eclecticism of the Beatles (beginning with the uniquely unified album *Sgt. Pepper's Lonely Hearts Club Band* of 1967), which still conveyed to many an equally ironic commentary perhaps more subtle and varied than Dylan's, though not as direct or emotive.

The claims of rock lyrics as poetry may be made on three levels. The first is simply the level of higher standards of craftsmanship—of increased polish and sophistication in the lyrics. (While perhaps a debatable criterion for ranking in terms of poetry, it is at least evidence of increased skill and versatility in verse-making.) The work of the Beatles, beginning with the *Sgt. Pepper* album, may be taken as representative, in terms of greater variety of meters, more sophisticated rhyme schemes, the use of internal rhyme ("I get by . . . I get high . . . Gonna try . . ." and "if I'm wrong I'm right where I belong I'm right"), and a richer and more free-associating imagery ("marmalade skies . . . kaleidoscope eyes . . . plasticine porters with looking-glass ties").[38] It should be emphasized that what is meant here has nothing to do with simply using longer, or more conventionally "poetic," words or constructions; it is the more imaginative and evocative use of ordinary words and phrases, in ways that make the listener pay attention to them.

On another level, there has been a notable broadening of rock's frame of reference—a greater awareness of other poetry, and of some of the commanding figures in art, literature, and history. This is best illustrated by the richer fabric of allusions that we find in rock since the 1960s. Some of Bob Dylan's lyrics show the influence of Biblical imagery, phraseology, and poetic form (compare, for example, "I Pity the Poor Immigrant" with passages from Ecclesiastes), as well as the heritage of the Anglo-Celtic ballad ("A Hard Rain's a-Gonna Fall" is the paraphrase of "Lord Randall"). Biblical allusions may, in fact, be found in a broad range of rock lyrics, including those of the Beatles ("Within You and Without You") and Leonard Cohen ("Last Year's Man"). The Doors, as the name of a group, is a reference to William Blake and Aldous Huxley;* there are allusions to Descartes (Phil Ochs, "I Kill Therefore I am"), Edgar Allan Poe (Phil Ochs, "The Bells"), Frank Lloyd Wright (Paul Simon), A. A. Milne (Jefferson Airplane, "Pooniel"), Edward Arlington Robinson (Paul

* Blake's phrase "the doors of perception" was adopted by Huxley to refer to drug-induced experience.

Simon, "Richard Cory"), James Joyce (Jefferson Airplane, "Rejoyce"), and so on. What all of this shows is an increased awareness on the part of rock composers and lyricists of an artistic and historical *context* for their work.

The third level on which rock lyrics aspire to poetry is a more difficult one to define; it has to do with rock lyrics adopting what we might call the *stance* of high art. The artist becomes an observer, rather than a protagonist, creating a measure of *detachment* from the subject—establishing what is known as "aesthetic distance". The direct expression of emotion is replaced by detached observation and commentary—the goal is more aesthetic than rhetorical.

What this entails is in fact a renunciation of "folkness," a loss of artistic innocence. It sacrifices that directness of approach to a subject—that complete lack of *art-consciousness*—that is the very attribute by which we recognize folk art. It is the difference between the unabashed, unreflective, sensual exuberance of Roy Brown's "Good Rockin' tonight"[39] and the obscure, ambiguous introversion of David Byrne's "Memories Can't Wait."[40]

In fact, it is precisely this obscurity and ambiguity, this avoidance of strictly literal meaning, this use of enigmatic metaphor, these multiple levels of possible meanings, paralleling developments in serious poetry since the end of the nineteenth century, that rock lyrics offer as credentials for their consideration as poetry. Artfulness has replaced folkness.

Since rock has its very roots in folkness, this artfulness presents an interesting paradox. Simon Frith has noted: "The irony was that it was on the basis of its folk conventions that rock developed its claims as a 'high art' form."[41]

A Brief History of Rock's Times and Styles

In treating popular culture, the most concrete, manageable, and easily verifiable aspect is the historical one: who did what, and where and when it was done. It is not surprising, then, that while thoughtful critical and analytical essays on rock are still comparatively rare, its history has been written up extensively. A summary overview here will therefore suffice to recall a sequence of events, artists, and styles already well known to many readers.

Roots in Black Music

We have already noted that the most significant innovations in our vernacular music, from minstrelsy to jazz, originated in the music of African-Americans. The same is no less true of rock. There is no question but that the so-called rhythm-and-blues, discussed in Chapter 8, was the taproot of rock. The term (itself a trade designation, but more accurately descriptive than most) indicated a somewhat commercialized form of urban blues, in which either a single blues singer or a highly polished vocal ensemble was accompanied by a fairly small blues band, including a strongly marked rhythm section and usually at least one blues saxophonist.[42]

Rhythm-and-blues recordings had, in the early 1950s, a somewhat narrow market, largely racially defined; it was music by black performers for black listeners. As such, it was a direct descendant of the previously described "race records." Black folk elements were unmistakably present: the content, delivery, and hoarse tone-quality of the blues; the saxophone "responses"; the "backbeat" (offbeats strongly marked in the drums, a direct legacy of the offbeat hand-clapping so often associated with black music-making); and the frank and unself-conscious treatment of sexual themes and lyrics.

On the other hand, there was already evident the influence of popularization, even of Tin Pan Alley—as indicated, for instance, in the adaptation of old "standards" from popular music, such as "Blueberry Hill" or "Blue Moon," without regard for the somewhat incongruous effect produced by the juxtaposition of cliché "pop" lyrics with the earthier musical style of the blues. The stylized, polished vocal ensembles point to the same influence, as does the unmistakable tendency toward the trivialization of themes and lyrics in a music intended primarily for dancing.

Had this music remained, as it began, nearly the exclusive province of a young black audience, the whole history of American popular music would have been vastly different. As it happened, black rhythm-and-blues, played on black radio stations in the large cities (a new phenomenon in the late 1940s and early 1950s) and recorded and sold through outlets primarily intended for the black public, began to be listened to and become popular with an increasingly large group of white youth. This coincided with a period of low inventiveness and pallid offerings from the established white popular music industry, and of increased independence and dissatisfaction with conventionality on the part of many young whites.

It was a disc jockey on a Cleveland radio station, Alan Freed, who first realized the potential inherent in the popularity of black rhythm-and-blues among white adolescents. In 1951 he began programming the music extensively. (It is probably true that he invented the name "rock 'n' roll": his early radio program was called "Moondog's Rock and Roll Party.") He also arranged live stage shows of black rhythm-and-blues performers for predominantly white audiences. In 1954 he moved to New York as disc jockey for WINS, which quickly became the city's leading popular music station. His activities, not only as disc jockey but as concert promoter, writer, and dedicated partisan, did much to publicize and advance rock 'n' roll in its early stages.

By 1954 white groups were "covering" (recording their own versions of) popular black rhythm-and-blues recordings; Bill Haley's "Shake, Rattle, and Roll" of that year, a version of an earlier recording by the blues singer Joe Turner, was among the first of the very popular "covers." Freed himself played, and championed, the original black versions. But rock 'n' roll, as a new form of white popular music based on black rhythm-and-blues, began to evolve as a distinct music, and the black artists who were among the most popular with the growing constituency of whites were those whose styles were closest to the new idiom—Chuck Berry (b. 1926), Bo Diddley (Elias McDaniel, b. 1928), Fats Domino (b. 1928), and Little Richard (Richard Penniman, b. 1935). Conversely, rock 'n' roll as a primarily white phenomenon began with those white performers who most closely patterned their work on black models—men such as Bill Haley (1925–81), whose "Rock Around the Clock" (1955) has been recognized as the first white rock 'n' roll hit, and Elvis Presley (1935–77), who was strongly imprinted with the blues ambience of Memphis. It was Presley (whose coming was presaged, as we have noted, by his early producer's search for a "white boy who could sing colored") who most forcefully exemplified the combination of black and white influences that constituted early rock. His famous "Heartbreak Hotel" (1956) accomplished the symbolic feat of achieving popularity in both black (rhythm-and-blues) and white (country-and-western) markets.

White Country Music and Early Rock

If black rhythm-and-blues was the taproot of rock, it was not its *only* root; white country music also played an important role. As noted in Chapter 7, white country music (or country-and-western, to use the trade term) had evolved out of folk roots as a traditional and conservative regional music. By the 1950s, however, its public was no longer so narrowly limited, thanks to the broad cultural mixing produced by the war years, and the popularity of western movies and movie stars.

When we recall that there was already a strong blues strain in country music, its part in the formation of rock can more easily be accounted for. The electric guitar had long been used in country music, and the singing guitarist, as basic to white country music as to black country blues, became the mainstay of the early rock ensemble, as typified by performers like Bill Haley, Elvis Presley, Carl Perkins (b. 1932), and Buddy Holly (1936–59), all of whom were identified with *rockabilly* (see Chapter 7, p. 188).

The country music style with the closest affinity to the urban blues style was honky-tonk, which, as noted earlier, used a piano and was strongly influence by boogie-woogie. This early style, with its distinctly adult themes and lyrics, was cultivated by such performers as Jerry Lee Lewis, and some of the music was scarcely distinguishable from that of the black musicians on which it was based. But at the same time, country-influenced rock was moving in another direction—toward pop and the growing teenage audience. The themes reflected the concerns and conflicts of adolescents ("Peggy Sue"; "Wake Up, Little Susie") and also a tendency toward exaggeration, cliché, and trivia in the lyrics ("Blue Suede Shoes").

The Impact of Rock on the Recording Industry

It was in the mid-1950s that rock began to overturn the popular music recording industry. Prior to this time, the pop music field, representing the declining stages of Tin Pan Alley, had been dominated by a few major recording companies and was fairly stable, with its "hits" remaining at the top of the popularity charts for an average of five or six months. But given the new technology that allowed recordings to be produced nearly anywhere in the country, this situation was ripe for change, and the new idiom of rock, at first rejected and opposed by the major companies, was what brought this change about. Small independent record companies (the "indies"), which had been mainly responsible for supplying the hitherto limited black rhythm-and-blues market, now expanded and multiplied to meet the new demand for rhythm-and-blues and rock 'n' roll. Early rock thus belonged to the independents. The major companies, representing the conservative Tin Pan Alley tradition, found themselves left out of an increasingly large and volatile part of the market. Hits would zoom into prominence overnight, and disappear almost as fast. As in the early publishing days of Tin Pan Alley, a single hit would be enough to establish a company. In an effort to gain a position in the new pop arena, the major companies issued their own cover versions of popular rock hits—cleaning and polishing them up but depriving them of their immediacy, and so misunderstanding that it was the rough edges engendered by its spontaneity and sheer energy that gave rock its appeal.

At the same time, rock itself, as it evolved, owed a great deal to commercial pop music in the matter of lyrics and themes, especially as it diverged from the more adult rhythm-and-blues and began to adapt itself to the increasingly active teenage market.

Commercialization and Dilution: The Teen Market

The shift away from the adult orientation of rhythm-and-blues in one area of "country rock" in the late fifties had become typical of rock generally by the early sixties, as the vast teenage market began to be catered to. The preoccupation with cars, for example, was reflected in any number of "hot rod" songs, such as "Little Deuce Coupe," which, in a manner curiously typical of folk art, combines vernacular expressions with oddly technical descriptions of the car's mechanical features. From California came surfing songs (best represented, probably, by the highly successful and polished recordings of the Beach Boys). These, along with the entire surfing cult, spread rapidly throughout the country, having little to do, ultimately, with the actual practice of the sport: as Belz remarks, "the surf itself had been obviated as an essential ingredient."[43]

In a class of songs given over largely to a rather literal treatment of external things and concerns, there arose at this time a peculiar phenomenon—songs about death ("Teen Angel" is perhaps the best-known representative). Set in familiar adolescent surroundings and circumstances, they perhaps represented an attempt (however seldom it transcended the mawkish) to confront at least one of the most obvious themes associated with real poetry.[44]

New Infusions of the 1960s

The British influence

The state of rock music as the mid-sixties approached has been at least hinted at; its essential flavor and folklike spontaneity had been dissipated in imitation, and in adaptation to the demands of a nearly all-devouring commercialism. At this point developments in England become a part of our picture, since it was from this source that the revitalization of American rock came.

This development was not as strange as it might at first appear, when one considers the long interdependence of British and American popular music. In one direction, English ballad opera was a staple here in Colonial times; the English music hall provided songs and a song style for our musical comedy in the nineteenth century; and Gilbert and Sullivan has been almost as popular and perennially successful here as in England. Most important, British folk music, a subtly pervasive presence in nearly all English music, was a source of one of America's most important strains of folk music. In the other direction, our blackface comedy, ragtime, blues, and jazz were each, in their heyday, exports that were much in demand. A broad segment of the younger British public has always followed avidly developments in American popular music—especially the fruits of our black popular culture.[45] There have been times when the devotion to some particular phase was stronger in England than in America generally. The sixties was such a time. It was then that, illustrating the folklorists' theory of "marginal survival" (according to which items of folklore will survive on the distant margins of a culture after they have ceased to become important at its core), the earthier manifestations of the blues, which no longer enjoyed very wide popularity here, were being assiduously cultivated by a segment of British youth. Big Bill Broonzy, Howlin' Wolf, Sonny Terry, and Brownie McGhee were known in England not only from their recordings but from personal tours. As adherents of a later style, such men as Chuck Berry and Bo Diddley were well known and influential in England after they had been largely supplanted here.[46]

Young British groups developed their own kind of expression of the essential rhythm-and-blues ingredients, and though it was never more than an imitation, it showed in many cases a surprising mastery of the externals, at least. Thus, what the English groups gave back to America, when they were "discovered" and began to export their records and themselves, turned out to be America's own black rhythm-and-blues, filtered through the temperament and experience of British youth, and giving off echoes, when the beat was a little less relentless, of the music hall and, further in the background, of English folk music.

Some of these groups never went much beyond the somewhat limited range staked out by the shouting, "bragging" blues. A good example is the enormously influential Rolling Stones, who produced efficiently aggressive statements (and became efficiently aggressive personal symbols) of revolt, nihilism, and sexual bravado.

One group, however, succeeded amazingly well in transcending these limitations. The Beatles (John Lennon, 1940–80; Paul McCartney, b. 1942; George Harrison, b. 1943; and Ringo Starr [Richard Starkey], b. 1940), born into the British equivalent of rhythm-and-blues, as were all the other groups, began their meteoric journey across the mid-century skies of popular culture by a reintroduction of innocence—an infectious pleasure in music-making akin to what was felt in the folklike singing and playing of early black rock 'n' roll artists like Chuck Berry, and of white rockabilly singers.

This innocence proved to be the quality that opened the way to a much broader range of expression for the Beatles, which their collective talent enabled them to explore. In the process came inevitably sophistication, but also genuine musical and poetic development. Their work, from folk beginnings, gradually came to acquire that aesthetic distancing from its subject that gave it a genuine *art*-stance. The *Sgt. Pepper's Lonely Hearts Club Band* album (1967), in its entirety, probably best signaled that development, of which even segments of the world of fine-art music had to take notice. Writing from the vantage point of this world, musicologists such as Wilfred Mellers and composers such as Ned Rorem could regard the Beatles' work as almost pointing the way towards a kind of salvation for fine-art music, or at least one avenue of escape from its paralyzing dilemma of noncommunication.

The inevitable eclecticism that the Beatles' work came to embody (running the gamut from synthesized sound to Renaissance music and Indian ragas) was widely imitated, of course, and has become endemic in much rock music from that point on. Having traversed, presumably, all the ground they could as a group, the Beatles broke up; whatever the immediate causes, this was inevitable. Their influence, especially here in America, was enormous.

In fact, from the mid-sixties on, so interwoven are the stories of British and American rock that it is impossible to trace native rock music without nearly constant references to what British groups were doing. They have continued to be a creative and innovative force, especially in the integration of rock with certain aspects of European fine-art music, a development that will be discussed in due course.

Folk influence, and rock as a vehicle for dissent

That phenomenon known as the urban folk movement—which transplanted homegrown folk music, its anxious concerns, and even some of the folk musicians themselves from the Mississippi delta, the Oklahoma Dust Bowl, and the Kentucky coal mines to the coffeehouses of Greenwich Village, and ultimately to the tour circuit and the LP record—has been chronicled in Chapter 4.

Folk music as popular entertainment flourished briefly in the late fifties and early sixties, as purveyed by groups like the Kingston Trio and Peter, Paul, and Mary, and by Joan Baez. Yet neither the urban folk movement nor popular folk music had any impact on rock itself until the mid-sixties, and this impact was initially produced largely by one man, Bob Dylan. Emerging with acoustic guitar, harmonica, and social-significance songs from the Greenwich Village scene in 1962, Dylan, who was never comfortably classifiable as either a pure folklorist or a protest singer, made his controversial switch to a rock style and approach (with electric guitars and hard-driving rhythm section) in 1965. This cross-fertilization of folk-oriented subject matter and approach with rock musical style had an influence at the time second only to that of the Beatles. It infused rock with a new element of conscious social comment: satirical, often bitter and angry. This has remained a consistently identifying aspect of rock ever since. Though more prevalent in some periods than in others, social criticism and dissent have never been completely absent, and in the 1980s the songs of stars such as Bruce Springsteen show this continuing identification.

Bob Dylan's work, especially in relation to the urban folk song movement, was discussed in Chapter 4. He has been a perennial and influential presence in American vernacular music for a quarter of a century, with a succession of styles and stances that have given the appearance, at least, of some rather widely vacillating swings: from rock back to ballad-type allegorical folk (*John Wesley Harding*, 1968), to lighter, more easygoing country (*Nashville Skyline*, 1968–69), back to a hard-rock ballad style (*Desire*, 1975), to a phase that has been labeled in an oversimplification, "religious"* (*Saved*, 1980; *Shot of Love*, 1981), and, in the mid-eighties, to a musical style both retrospective and conventional, with lyrics clearly showing a desire to disclaim the role of prophet (*Empire Burlesque*, 1985).

Other alumni of the Greenwich Village coffeehouses, such as Paul Simon (b. 1941) and John Sebastian (b. 1944), moved at least onto the fringes of rock, helping to define what became known as folk-rock, and contributing some memorable songs. Solo singers in the folk genre who have also written their own songs, such as Judy Collins (b. 1939), Joni Mitchell (b. 1943), and Leonard Cohen (b. 1935), have employed rock idioms; their work has added another dimension to the enormous breadth of popular music, and pointed up the difficulties inherent in trying to fashion and use labels.

Uptown Rhythm-and-Blues: Rock on the Production Line

Rock by the 1960s, in a position of hitherto unimaginable affluence and influence, had attracted to its production an almost unlimited supply of inventiveness and trained skill, and had at its disposal all that recording technology could offer. The work of Phil Spector, who in a very literal sense "produced" such groups as the Crystals, the Ronnettes, and the Righteous Brothers, using a studio orchestra and the full capacity of the studio to manipulate sound in recording, was representative. This trend was even more fully realized in the work of the so-called Motown groups: the Miracles, the Temptations, the Four Tops, and, best known, the Supremes. In other words, the 1960s ushered in an era of studio-produced sound, wherein the sound studio itself, with the engineer at the control panel, became almost the most important instrument. Effects were developed that were impossible to duplicate in live performance; as Carl Belz pointed out, the recording itself became the "original."[47]

Rock and Satire

An indication of rock's degree of sophistication by the sixties was an increased propensity for the wildest satire—satire of pop culture and pop music, including rock itself. When an art form, either popular or folk, has evolved to a certain stage, it begins to satirize itself; restless and inventive minds *within* the tradition begin to use its conventions as raw material, to make commentaries on it. Rock became, in the hands of such clever and inventive talents as Frank Zappa (b. 1940) and the Mothers of Invention, a kind of expressive game. The poses, the theatrics, the put-ons intentionally made it difficult to determine whether the game was being played seriously. An elaborately staged contempt for the audience and for the conventional assumptions on which the live concert is based became a mannerism. This had its parallel in the actions of the bebop musicians of two decades before, and of the punk rockers since, but there was also a remarkable resemblance, in attitude and even in action, to

* Even without considering the moral and ethical orientation of his songs, the relationship of Dylan's lyrics in *all* periods both to the heritage of gospel language and rhetoric and to Biblical imagery and poetic form has been largely overlooked.

some of the staged "happenings" of the avant-garde fine-art scene. But while the fringes of the fine-art avant-garde *seemed* at least to be always in dead earnest, performers like Zappa, in spite of some occasionally very lucid statements made in interviews,[48] were able successfully to keep their public sufficiently in doubt about their intentions to create a considerable degree of tension and interest. The Mothers of Invention exemplified a tidal drift of many young, talented, and intelligent musicians to rock, beginning in the 1960s, and illustrated the breadth of styles and resources they brought to it. Zappa himself, the first court jester of rock, has since turned his attention to the avant-garde fringes of fine-art music.

Eclecticism and Fusion

Jazz-rock

In the late 1960s there began a process of fusion in American popular music that has been going on ever since. Rock began to absorb influences from other kinds of music, and to permeate in turn other genres, such as popular musical theater.* The fusion with jazz has been the most successful; perhaps the relationship of both to the blues is what makes this work. It has taken place chiefly at the hands of a new breed of young musicians whose talent and exposure to music are extensive enough for them to play with facility in a number of different styles. Most noteworthy in this regard was the group Blood, Sweat and Tears, which produced in the years 1968–70 three very successful albums fusing jazz and rock styles; along with the group Chicago, also important in its early stages, they virtually defined jazz-rock.

In terms of instrumentation, jazz-rock consists of a rock band to which brass and saxophones are added. In terms of musical style, jazz-rock involves the combining of an incessant rock beat with jazz solos that are freer rhythmically. The rhythmic structure of the beat itself is based on a duple division of the pulse, rather than the characteristic triple division of the more relaxed swing jazz (see Chapter 14). It is thus related, in its duple division and its repetitiousness, to the *clave* of Latin music (see Chapter 3, especially Examples 3–9 and 3–10). As played by a rhythm section consisting of electric guitar, electric bass, and several drums, it has a machine-like precision and drive. It is often quite complex. Example 9–3 shows such a beat, as transcribed from the playing of the rhythm section in "Beginnings," a jazz-rock number by the group Chicago. (The composite cymbal, drum, and tom-tom part, played by a single drummer, changes somewhat from measure to measure; what is given is a sample.) The metronomically precise and insistent beat of jazz-rock is one of its most salient features.

Occasionally, as in Chicago's "Does Anybody Really Know What Time It Is?"[49] there is a dabbling in the asymmetric meters that preoccupied so-called progressive jazz for a time. By virtue of the jazz-derived improvisations, jazz-rock pieces are apt to be quite extended in length. Combining the elements

* See Chapter 11.

Example 9–3

of two very popular modes of expression, jazz-rock very often verges on pop, and is extraordinarily vulnerable to commercialization.

From the other side, as we shall see in Chapter 14, many jazz musicians, including Miles Davis, John McLaughlin, Joe Zawinul, Chick Corea, and Herbie Hancock have absorbed rock influences. This persistent cross-fertilization, now so much a feature of American music of all kinds, makes it difficult always to distinguish with certainty, in *instrumentally* dominated popular music of the 1970s and 1980s, between jazz and rock.

Classical and Eastern music

The attempted synthesis of rock with classical music has been described by Shaw as "an occasional fusion of disparate elements,"[50] rather than an identifiable movement or a distinct style. There are interesting parallels between this phenomenon and the kind of synthesis of jazz with symphonic music that was essayed earlier in the century. In both cases the attempt was made from both sides, so to speak. In the 1920s some serious composers took notice of jazz—in Europe, Stravinsky and the French; in America, John Alden Carpenter and Aaron Copland, among others. In the same way, in the 1960s and 1970s some serious composers have taken note of rock and its ambience, as illustrated by Leonard Bernstein's *Mass* (written for the opening of the Kennedy Center for the Performing Arts in Washington, DC, in 1971), which was subtitled "A Theater Piece for Singers, Players and Dancers." From the entertainment world, on the other hand, we find musicians (jazz-oriented in the 1920s and 1930s and rock-oriented in the 1960s and 1970s) similarly interested in such a synthesis—seeking to transcend somewhat the limitations of their genre, or seeking a degree of permanence, significance, or intellectual respectability. Young British musicians were attempting this in the sixties and seventies; for example, Keith Emerson, with the Nice, performed his *Five Bridges Suite* with symphony orchestra in Croydon in 1969.[51] It represents a serious attempt to integrate media and styles: Edwardian English symphonic music, mid-century jazz piano style, neo-baroque fugal piano style (somewhat in the manner of Dave Brubeck), virtuosic rock organ playing, rock song fragments with run-of-the-mill lyrics, and a jazz-rock finale that, as usual in these essays, manages somehow to leave the symphony orchestra far behind. The "bridges" of the title have reference, among other things, to the building of "bridges to those musical shores which seem determined to remain apart."[52]

Other British groups to make use of the sounds and forms of classical music (including full symphony orchestra) were the Bee Gees, Procul Harum, and Deep Purple.[53]

While the Beatles (and especially George Harrison) were probably the first to incorporate elements of Asian (in their case Indian) music into their work, beginning in the mid-1960s,[54] the influence of Asian music (including musical themes, scales, forms, and instruments) on many aspects of American music is probably both a symptom and a by-product of the increasing attention given to Asian culture generally, including music, philosophy, and religion, in the West since mid-century. It is another manifestation of the enormous wealth of music and musical traditions readily accessible today.

Other groups and artists reflecting the influence of India, especially, have been the Incredible String Band (Scottish) and John McLaughlin (English).

Punk and New Wave

The "folk" *function* of rock has been most evident since 1975 in the underground music of the period: *punk* rock, merging into *new wave*.* It may be termed folk in the sense of the spontaneity of its origins, of the immediacy of its concerns with its own "community" (those who see themselves as the rejected and dispossessed of society), and of its pronounced anti-art and anti-commercial stance. If to the average fan rock is (in Shaw's phrase) "music of energy, volume, distortion, and rebellion," the "rebellion" aspect has come to be most conspicuously represented, in this period, by this underground music. Its rebellion is twofold: against the norms of society in general, and against the rock "establishment" in particular, which is seen as having betrayed its origins and become a vast commercial monolith.

Aside from the Rolling Stones (sometimes considered the original, prototypical punk group, with their emphasis on revolt, aggressiveness, and sexual bravado), the punk movement itself began in New York City (Patti Smith, the Ramones, the Velvet Underground), spread to London (the Sex Pistols), and then to Los Angeles (Wierdos, Circle Jerks) and San Francisco (the Lewd, the Avengers). These four cities are still the epicenters of this underground phase of rock, but groups of its fans and followers may be found in virtually any urban center today, identifiable as much by the characteristic dress and hairstyle as by their music.

* New wave, as a movement, is subject to various interpretations. To some it is merely punk that has adopted a new name to avoid negative associations and evade censure; to others it is punk that has "sold out" and become pop. To the latter, the "true faith" of punk is being preserved in "hardcore," described below.

Shaw has characterized punk as a "rallying point of rebellion against authority and aggression against respectable society."[55] Nowhere is this "nihilistic punk metabolism" (to use Belsito and Davis's terms[56]) more evident than in the names of the groups, which call up images normally considered aberrant or repulsive (the Mutants, the Ghouls, Flesheaters, Twisted Sister), destructive (Crime, Damage, Slash, Search and Destroy, Black Flag [a poison], Destroy All Music), or tastelessly offensive to normal sensibilities (Dead Kennedys).

Yet it is precisely "normal sensibilities" that punk/new wave is committed, by its very nature, to offend, and in this there is a consistency, even a *purity* of dedication that admits of no compromise. There is a pronounced anticommercial stance; unskilled devotees sometimes perform with the groups, and those who begin to "make it," in the terms in which success is defined in popular music, are ostracized. And as with any dedicated underground movement, an intuitive but uncannily precise distinction is made between casual masqueraders and the committed; poseurs are harshly separated from the genuinely "possessed." There is a constantly updated faddism, and an instant though unspoken consensus on what (and who) is "in," with an utter contempt for what (and who) is not.

That shock and violence seemed unavoidably endemic to the punk (if less so to the new wave) movement, and indeed became identifying characteristics, has attracted notice and concern. At performances, destruction of the premises was (and often still is) the norm. Fights were routine, and performers threw themselves at the audience, threw food at the audience, vomited on the audience.[57] That the violence among these "tormented, obsessed people" reached the limits of self-destruction is seen in a number of suicides, as for instance that of Bobby Pyn.

The 1980s have brought changes to the underground scene, as punk has evolved in different directions. While there are still groups such as Suicidal Tendencies producing material that is destructive, nihilistic, and revolting to normal sensitivities, a turning toward more constructive attitudes can be noted in so-called "hardcore," a movement that can be seen as either a sequel to punk or its continuation in the late 1980s. While still expressing dissent in a rough-edged and largely unimaginative musical style that is the epitome of *hard rock* ("loud, fast, and angry" according to one writer), songs have appeared that focus on specific issues, rather than anger for its own sake. Lyrics (typically so difficult to understand in performance that they are published on lyric sheets which accompany the records, or in fan magazines known as "fanzines") can be found that now deal, for example, with the use of live animals in scientific experiments ("Mad Scientists' Ball" by Dead Silence), with the environment ("Progress" by Clown Alley), and with tyranny and oppression ("Dr. Harley" by Rhythm Pigs). In a still more positive vein is the work of groups such as 7 Seconds, producing songs that perceptively address real human issues:

> I'm not a "punker," just a human being, with this urge to exercise
> What's in my heart and mind . . .
> We could be the new wind . . . [58]

Rock and Avant-Garde Classical Music

In our century both underground and mass cultures have held a certain fascination for devotees of avant-garde "high" culture; this was true of jazz in the 1920s (then perceived as an underground genre of music), which was fervently embraced in literary and artistic circles, especially in France. (From the other side, jazz a little later began to see itself as art music, and became "bohemianized" in the bebop era.) In the 1960s, the hippies became the bohemians* of the mass media. Mass culture also yielded subject matter for avant-garde artists. "Pop art" was but one manifestation of this; still more interesting was the tendency for the stars of popular culture to be adopted as icons of high art (as illustrated, for example, by Andy Warhol's famous treatment of Marilyn Monroe). In fact, as Bernard Gendron has observed, in the postmodern era the boundaries between mass culture and high culture are withering away.[59]

Rock has become bohemianized as well. Frank Zappa's entrance into the ranks of the avant-garde has been confirmed by the fact that his works have been conducted and recorded by the archpriest himself, Pierre Boulez. (Gendron has dubbed this an example of "celebrity-interchange.") And David Byrne (b. 1952) has widened his range from that of singer-guitarist-composer for a band with quasi-punk beginnings to being film director, actor, designer, photographer, and writer.

These developments inevitably attract the attention of the mass media. Byrne, for example, has been titled "rock's hip Renaissance man" by *Time* magazine, which bestowed the ultimate and symbolic *imprimatur* on this culture merger by granting Byrne a *Time* cover (which he was allowed to design himself), and a feature article in which his position was summed up as follows: "Merging high cult and mass culture, Byrne is spearheading the invasion of Manhattan's avant-garde scene into Middle America's consciousness."[60]

Peripheral and Regional Phenomena

The stripping of rock to the bare essentials needed for dancing is a functional description of *disco* music. The term came from the French *discothèque*, a type of cabaret in France in the 1960s in which records were played for dancing in place of live music—a practice that soon became common in dance halls in the United States. The type of music known as disco appeared in the mid-1970s, and was subsequently popularized by the film *Saturday Night Fever.* It is characterized by a strongly marked beat, four-to-the-bar, obsessively prominent in the drums, at a tempo that varies remarkably little from a speed of 120 to the minute; the lyrics are highly emotive, and minimal in content. The impoverishment of musical resources in disco led to its rapid decline in

* It must be remembered that living and acting "with disregard for conventional rules of behavior" is only *part* of the definition of *bohemian*; it is the presence of "real or pretended artistic or intellectual aspirations" that is the key to understanding this interesting relationship between high culture and underground or mass culture. See *The Random House Dictionary of the English Language.*

popularity as early as the end of the 1970s. An interesting peripheral phenomenon associated with disco was the practice of adapting certain popular "classics" (such as the first movement of Beethoven's Fifth Symphony, or Mussorgsky's *Night on Bald Mountain*) to the disco beat and format—a practice reminiscent of what some commercializing big bands were doing in the 1940s.

Reggae is a regional genre originating in Jamaica in the 1960s, an adaptation of an earlier type of music known as "ska". The rhythm of reggae, like that of Calypso music from another part of the West Indies (Trinidad), is strongly Caribbean in its syncopation. Reggae tends to de-emphasize the strong beat, and ornament the offbeats with a complex overlaying of cross-rhythms, performed with a variety of Latin percussion sounds, either acoustic or synthesized. Reggae is distinctly ethnic—a Caribbean appropriation of an African original. To understand its frame of reference and its undercurrents, one must understand Rastafarianism (a millenial faith that revered the late Haile Selassie, emperor of Ethiopia, as a savior who would lead black people to freedom) and the "Back to Africa" movement of Marcus Garvey. The lyrics of many of the songs, such as Bob Marley's "Get Up Stand Up," have political or religious content, in a positive and often mystical way. Bob Marley, who died in 1981, was the reggae musician best known in the United States. Although not as popular here as in Europe (or of course in Jamaica), reggae has had an understandable influence on black American rhythm-and-blues and soul performers.

Rap music, like reggae, is both regional and ethnic. Its immediate origin is in the black street culture of the South Bronx, in New York City, and its principal characteristic is rapid-fire talking (not singing) over a basic rock background—"rhymed street slang delivered at breakneck speed" is Shaw's apt definition.[61] The content is usually strongly social or political. The style originated with black disk jockeys, "MCing" or "rapping" over the music. But the roots go far deeper in black culture, and analogies with this phenomenal impromptu verbal and versifying facility can be found in black preaching, in the "talking blues," in the "dirty dozens" of American street culture, in Calypso, and even in the role of professional minstrels in African courts.[62]

The overwhelming importance of broadcasting and recordings as the disseminating media for popular music has long made the role of the disk jockey pivotal. In addition to being instrumental in both disco and rap music, the disk jockey was also responsible for the development of another 1980s offshoot of rock. For dancing, what was needed was long segments of music, free of intros and tags, and free of the distraction of lyrics. Disk jockeys therefore began to create their own taped sequences by chaining together suitable *parts* of a number of records—the long instrumental "breaks." From this there developed not only *break music*, but *break dancing* as well.

The Pluralism of the 1980s

We can well end this brief historical survey of rock with the observation that we are in an age of pluralism, not only in rock but in all music. It is an age in which there is *much* going on and in which there is a great deal of diversity and decentralization, and consequently it is an age in which we can really only be sure of two things: nothing lasts very long; and overall trends are very difficult to identify. This is a timely warning against oversimplification, and against the belief that *any* survey of the field (this one included) can hope to account for all that has been happening, or be up to date even as it is being written.

Some Final Considerations

We turn in conclusion to a consideration of a few of the issues raised by the rock phenomenon, coming full circle to include issues suggested, but not explored, in the introduction to this chapter.

Rock and Youth

It is in its relation to the young that rock seems most obviously to function as a kind of folk music. Its vast "community," to and of which it speaks unmistakably, is youth worldwide. Like any authentic folk music, it reinforces the sense of *identity* of the members of that community—their distinctness, their "separateness" from others (in this case, from older generations). It can be (and has been) justly compared to tribal music. In this sense, it means both *more* and *less* than music has come to mean generally in Western culture: less, in that to the average member of its community, a rock song is not an external, objectified piece of art to which one consciously pays close attention; more, in that it is a mood-manipulator, a complete *ambience,* which not only reinforces identity but serves to defines one's "space." We need cite but one manifestation of this, familiar in this country: rock is not only music to drive the car to or relax on the beach with; it allows one to claim as one's space everything within the audible range of the car stereo or the "boom box."

The Phenomenon of the Star, and Its Paradoxes

If youth is the vast "community" of rock, the progressive isolation of the rock musician from this community (both physically and in terms of values) which inevitably becomes more pronounced the closer the musician approaches star status, presents an interesting paradox. The star system, in fact, challenges, rock's essential "folkness"—its identity and lineage as an underground form. Rock is supposed to speak not only *to* but *for* its audience—it must maintain the illusion that its performers are of the same background, have the same problems, concerns, etc. The greater the star status, the less this can be true, obviously, regardless of the star's origins. Simon Frith has observed: "Rock musicians . . . began their careers by expressing the interests of a real community, and the problem of their authenticity only emerges later, when they are recording stars."

The basic truth here is that the performer inevitably lives in a different world from that of his or her audience; the more popular the performer, the more this is true. Both the demands and the material rewards of being a star performer, in other words, subordinate all other concerns. Frith, a sympathetic but clear-eyed observer, writes: "There is, in short, a contradiction between rock musicians' communal claims and their private life-styles."[63]

This life-style, based on material wealth and fame, can be and often is expressed in behavior that contemptuously ignores normal values. The destructive excesses of punk, for example, seemed to epitomize this visibly negative aspect of rock: the abrasive, antisocial behavior *potentially* engendered by the star status of its most successful practitioners, and the overwhelming demand for their product.[64] The deep imprint of this image of the rock musician, and the fact that this behavior is expected, is illustrated, ironically, by the problems encountered by those who do not exhibit it.[65] The fact of the matter is that stardom, with its sudden conferring of hitherto unimaginable money and power, is a burden that not all of us are equipped to carry well.

Rock As a Journalistic Oral Tradition

Rock, as we mentioned in the beginning of this chapter, is the *new* oral tradition, crossing easily both political and cultural boundaries worldwide. It is essentially a *journalistic* oral tradition. Hit songs, and even *styles* of songs, are broadly and almost instantly disseminated, and as quickly superseded by the next hit or style. Each is strongly associated with what has been termed its "historical moment"; as the song or style *of that moment* it has an exceedingly short life. If it is later recalled, it is as an exercise in nostalgia—a re-creation, not so much of the song, but of its historical moment. This distinguishes what might be called authentic rock (with its functional "folkness") from so-called "easy listening" music—music that is in touch with no particular historical moment. The significance of the steady growth in the audience for such "easy listening" music (now called in the trade "adult contemporary") has only been partly explored as yet.[66]

The Problems of Evaluation

We come finally to the problem not only of reporting, but of trying to *evaluate*, new developments in the evolution of rock. The problems are identical in nature to those confronted in the study of any phase of popular culture; there is a strong tendency to study it strictly *in terms of* its popularity. Modern scholarship in the field of popular culture, in fact, encourages this approach: categorizing music in terms of economics is seen to offer certain advantages, not the least of which is that it removes from the study all considerations of *taste*.[67] Thus the history of rock, as it is most frequently told, becomes the history of what the "charts" tell us about it.

The charts do indeed gives us "facts" that are undeniably both tangible and relevant. What is to be sought beyond this weekly deluge of facts is perhaps not so much evaluation, in terms of fixed criteria, as a sense of *context*, in which developments can be seen in relation to the larger panorama of popular music, and of all American music. But getting beyond the charts takes time. A noted authority has said, "I personally believe five to ten years must elapse before the significance of a rock group or individual can be assessed."[68] This is typical of the approach from which the most valuable writing on rock has issued. We live in a period when facts are easy to come by; it is the acquisition of *perspective* that takes thought—and time.

Further Reading

"Rockwrite" has produced almost numberless books (some eighty on Elvis Presley alone through 1983, according to Peter Gammond), as well as single articles in books of essays and in periodicals. Much of the writing is about single figures. It is undeniably good for promotion to have a "biography" of a rising star in print, and unfortunately for the serious reader, many of the books have little to offer but what Gammond has called "the nauseous claptrap of the pop publicist." Well-executed historical writing is rare; serious critical writing still rarer. Reference works date rapidly but are useful. This list begins with two of the best of these, then proceeds to historical and critical writing.

Reference Works

Shaw, Arnold, ed. *Dictionary of American Pop/Rock.* New York: Schirmer Books, 1982.

Helander, Brock. *The Rock Who's Who.* New York: Schirmer Books, 1982.

Historical and Critical Writing

Bangs, Lester. *Psychotic Reactions and Carburetor Dung: An Anthology.* ed. Greil Marcus. New York: Knopf, 1987.

Belz, Carl. *The Story of Rock.* 2d ed. New York: Oxford University Press, 1972.

Bergman, Billy. *Recombinant do re mi: Frontiers of the Rock Era.* New York: Quill, 1985.

Denisoff, R. Serge. *Sing Me A Song of Social Significance.* 2d ed. Bowling Green, OH: Bowling Green State University Press, 1984.
See comment at end of Chapter 4.

Frith, Simon. *Sound Effects: Youth, Leisure, and the Politics of Rock 'n' Roll.* New York: Pantheon, 1981.

Gillett, Charlie. *The Sound of the City.* Rev. ed. New York: Pantheon, 1984.

Marcus, Greil. *Mystery Train: Images of America in Rock 'n' roll Music.* New York: Dutton, 1982.

Middleton, Richard, and David Horn, eds. *Popular Music* (an ongoing series, which began as an annual but from vol. 5 on is published as a journal in three issues per year). Cambridge: Cambridge University Press, 1981– .
The themes of the first volumes are:
1: *Folk or Popular? Distinctions, Influences, Continuities*
2. *Theory and Method*
3. *Producers and Markets*
4. *Performers and Audiences*
5. *Continuity and Change*

Miller, Jim, ed. *The Rolling Stone Illustrated History of Rock & Roll.* New York: Rolling Stone, ca. 1980.

Rimler, Walter. *Not Fade Away: A Comparison of Jazz Age with Rock Era Pop Song Composers.* Ann Arbor, MI: Pierian Press, 1984.

Rockwell, John. *All American Music.* New York: Knopf, 1983.
Includes interesting chapters on Neil Young and Talking Heads.

Whitcomb, Ian. *After the Ball: Pop Music from Rag to Rock.* New York: Simon & Schuster, 1973.

Periodicals

Rolling Stone. Bi-weekly (New York).
This has become a general-interest periodical, with a special emphasis on popular music but with articles on American culture, politics, and art.

Creem. Monthly (Los Angeles).
Retaining an underground, street-culture stance, this is a "rock and roll magazine which covers pop culture from an iconoclastic and irreverent point of view" (*Standard Periodical Dictionary*).

Listening

Recordings have been the basic vehicle of rock, and they have been produced in unprecedented quantities from an enormous number of broadly dispersed companies, many of them small and short-lived. Thus the problems of compiling discographies, which in any case date very rapidly, are immense. Furthermore, unlike jazz, rock has had the benefit of very few well-edited anthologies of the quality, for example, of the Smithsonian collections of classic jazz, big band music, or country music. Three known exceptions, one by a commercial company, are listed below. There are also a few mammoth reissue series by such firms as Rhino and Savoy, and occasional reissues by British, German, and Japanese firms. Otherwise, the nearest approximation to anthologies are commercial reissues of single artists or groups under such titles as "The Best of . . .", "Greatest Hits of . . .", or ". . .'s Golden Hits." There are specialized discographies of stars such as Presley and Dylan. Most general reference works include some form of discography; a model for clarity and completeness in this regard is Brock Helander's *The Rock Who's Who*; though dating from 1982, it is still a valuable reference for general rock discography. A basic, and hopefully representative, selection follows.

Annotated Anthologies

Atlantic Rhythm & Blues: 1947–1974. A 14-LP set. 14-Atlantic 81299-1.

Straighten Up and Fly Right: Rhythm and Blues from the Close of the Swing Era to the Dawn of Rock 'n' Roll. NW-261.

Shake, Rattle & Roll: Rock 'n' Roll in the 1950's. NW-249.

Single Artists

These representative commercial reissues are arranged alphabetically by artist or group.

The Beatles/1962–1966. 2 LPs. Apple/Capitol SKBO 3403.

The Beatles/1967–1970. 2 LPs. Apple/Capitol SKBO 3404.

Sgt. Pepper's Lonely Hearts Club Band [Beatles]. Capitol/Apple SMAS 2653.

Saturday Night Fever, movie sound track [BeeGees/disco]. RSO 2-4001.

Chuck Berry's Greatest Hits. Archive of Folk & Jazz Music 321.

Blood, Sweat & Tears Greatest Hits. Columbia PC-31170.

Bob Dylan Biograph. Columbia C5X 38830.
A 5-LP set, with material ranging from 1962 to 1981.

Grandmaster Flash & The Furious Five: Greatest Messages [rap music]. Sugarhill SH 9121.

What a Long, Strange Trip It's Been: The Best of the Grateful Dead. 2 LPs. Warner Brothers 2W 3091.

The Jimi Hendrix Experience: Smash Hits. Reprise MSK 2276.

Michael Jackson—Anthology, November 1986. 2 LPs. Motown MODT2-6195.

Surrealistic Pillow [Jefferson Airplane]. RCA AYL1 3738.

Earth [Jefferson Starship]. Grunt BXLI 2515.

Legend: The Best of Bob Marley & the Wailers [reggae]. Island 90169.

Elvis Presley: Pure Gold. RCA AYL1 3732.

The Rolling Stones: Hot Rocks 1964–1971. 2 LPs. London 2PS 606/7.

Diana Ross and the Supremes Greatest Hits. 2 LPs. Motown 2-663.

Simon and Garfunkel Greatest Hits. Columbia JC-31350.

Bruce Springsteen and the E Street Band: Live 1975–1985. 5 LPs. Columbia C5X 40558.

PROJECTS

1. Find and listen to two early "covers" (recordings by white musicians derived from earlier recordings by black musicians) from the 1950s, and their original versions. Write a descriptive comparison, trying to account for the differences.

2. If you have access (through friends, libraries, or a local radio station) to fairly representative record collections of both early rock and country music of the 1950s, document the relationship of the two in that period. As background, read chapter 8 of *Country Music, U.S.A.*, either 1st or 2nd edition, by Bill Malone.

3. Do a taped essay on the role of the disc jockey in modern popular music, beginning with Alan Freed. Include taped excerpts of several current disc jockeys, with a brief commentary on their delivery, content, and style.

4. Interview a local disc jockey, and produce a paper profiling the job (both positive and negative aspects), and recording his or her opinions or current trends in popular music, the influence and responsibilities of the disc jockey, etc.

5. Interview the manager, or a knowledgeable employee, of a local record store, and produce a paper on a topic such as (1) the buying habits of the local publics (e.g. percentages for rock, for country, for classical, for folk, for soul, for "underground," etc.); (2) any recognizable characteristics (e.g. apparent age, occupation, dress, behavior, etc.) of the various publics; (3) the store's handling of "underground" recordings; (4) the effect of rock videos on the sales of specific albums; (5) their experiences in the handling of hit albums (the predictability of hits, the buying rush—how strong and how *long*, etc.); or make up your own approach.

6. Describe the work of four British rock groups besides the Beatles and the Rolling Stones that have been influential in the United States, detailing this influence.

7. If you have had recent firsthand experience in a foreign country, other than Canada or Britain, describe the popular music there, and its relationship to American rock or to popular music generally in the United States.

8. Make a study of the complex array of popularity charts in *Billboard* magazine, the trade journal of American popular music.

9. Do a brief study contrasting rock drumming with jazz drumming.

10. If you have some background or interest in English literature, assemble a small collection of rock lyrics from the 1980s and try to confront the question of rock "poetry"—the quality and consistency of the imagery, the extent to which it can stand on its own as poetry, and so forth.

11. Describe and analyze the theatrical aspects of a live rock concert you have attended.

12. Write a paper entitled "The Rock Video as Synthesized Theater."

13. Describe in as much detail as possible a recent synthesis of rock and symphonic music—on records or, preferably, in a live performance. Comment on its effectiveness.

14. Make a study of the modern sound recording studio and its equipment, and illustrate some of its impact on modern pop and rock recordings.

15. Document a recent altruistic or humanitarian effort (such as a benefit recording or concert, or a significant antidrug effort) undertaken by a rock artist or group since the appearance of *We Are the World*.

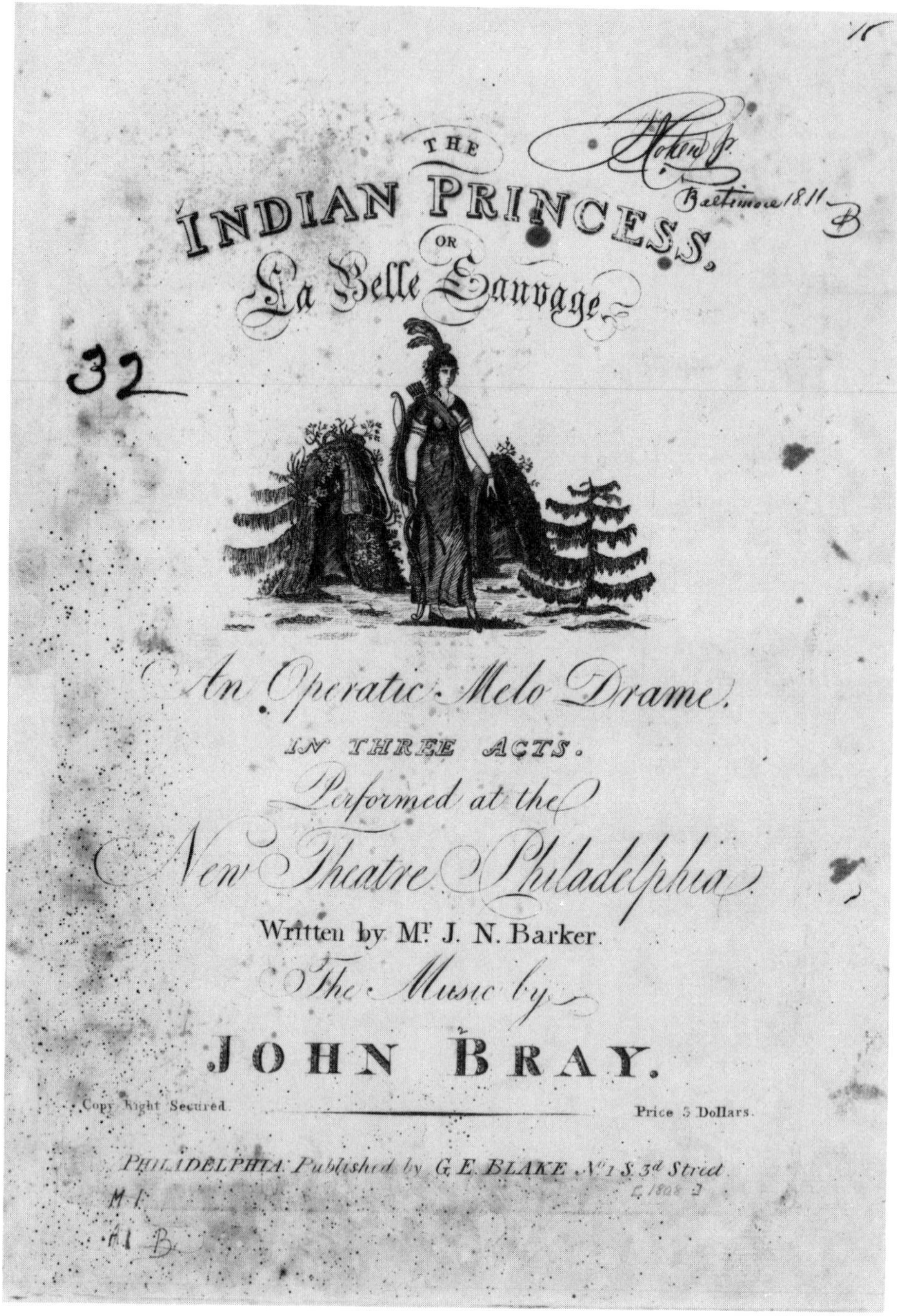
THE
INDIAN PRINCESS,
OR
La Belle Sauvage
An Operatic Melo Drame
IN THREE ACTS.
Performed at the
New Theatre Philadelphia
Written by Mr. J. N. Barker.
The Music by
JOHN BRAY.
Copy Right Secured.
Price 5 Dollars.
PHILADELPHIA: Published by G. E. BLAKE No. 1 S. 3d Street

Photo from the collections of the Library of Congress

PART FOUR

Popular Secular Music

A by-product of the growth of cities, and the consequent specialization of human endeavor, is always the evolution of a popular culture (produced for the masses by specialists) as distinct from a folk culture (made for people in smaller groups, or cultural "villages," by people who are themselves members of the village). If we illustrate this by an analogy with the production of another commodity we consume in great quantities—our daily bread—a first stage in this evolution is reached when the home-baked is replaced by the store-bought. A second stage is reached when that baked in the neighborhood bakery is replaced by the mass-produced plastic-wrapped article for sale in the supermarket; large, efficient baking plants serve huge areas, and the bread looks and tastes about the same whether we buy it in Arizona or Rhode Island.

Popular music requires a certain critical mass of population to support the commercial process devoted to its production. It will emerge whenever sufficient numbers of people are willing to pay for an art that has the look or sound of the familiar (it almost always has some points of resemblance either with folk art or with the well-accepted fine art that people know), that is made easily available by the mechanisms of its commercial distribution, and that adds something desirable and even necessary to their lives without being too difficult to understand. Its primary purpose is to entertain.

In America, popular music in Colonial and Federal times was largely an importation of the thriving broadside and ballad opera business in England. We did not begin to make our own distinctive kind (unless one considers as popular music the products of the Yankee singing-school composers) until the Jacksonian era—an era of cultural as well as political populism. It was not until the end of the nineteenth century that the making of popular music became an industry—an industry in which the United States has for a century been the undisputed leader.

Popular art is no longer ignored by scholars and observers of culture. Popular music (as a component of popular culture) is an extremely sensitive indicator of the temperament and preoccupations of a people. Nor is popular art ignored any longer by "serious" artists. It has become subject matter itself. We have seen this come about fairly recently in the visual arts, but Charles Ives was already composing music that was "about" popular music in the first two decades of this century.

We have characterized above the commercial process by which popular music is disseminated. But that tells us nothing about its inherent quality. Because of the vast market, those who can successfully create this kind of music are naturally very well paid for it. But the gift of creating something that many people will regard as memorable, and that will be immediately and widely in demand, is mysterious and rare, and there are never very many around at any given time who can do it extremely well.

It should be clear that the distinctions made between popular music and folk, ethnic, or fine-art music are distinctions of *function*, not of quality or ultimate value. The superlative popular song, the "evergreen," the one song in perhaps a hundred thousand that transcends the ephemeral nature of the genre, and has that imponderable property of resonating in the memory and feelings of generation after generation, is surely one of the glories of American music.

10

Secular Music in the Cities from Colonial Times to the Jacksonian Era

MUSICAL life in the largest American cities (Philadelphia, New York, Boston, Charleston, and Baltimore) during the Colonial and Federal periods was by no means primitive or dull. Music historians, together with performers specializing in the re-creation of early music, have illuminated the existence of a lively and varied musical culture in our growing urban centers. It will be the purpose of this chapter to survey this interesting period and put it into some perspective.

Treating all of our early secular musical activities together in the section devoted to popular music may seem arbitrary. But it is difficult to disentangle "classical" from "popular" in this early period; furthermore, to try and do so would falsify the picture that these times present. As Julian Mates has written, "The eighteenth century managed to thoroughly blur the distinction between serious music and light music."[1] While it is true that the beginnings of classical music in America, along with the emergence of attitudes and conventions associated with the European tradition, can certainly be identified here in the eighteenth century, it must be realized that even in Europe—with few exceptions the source of our music and our musical conventions during this era—the distinction between "classical" and "popular" was not nearly as clear-cut as it was to become with the advent of Romanticism. Indeed, the terms as we know and use them would not have been used or understood then. In America, especially, the period saw little difference in basic musical language between songs, dances, or marches on the one hand and keyboard sonatas, theater overtures, and music for masques or pantomimes on the other. Only gradually did distinctions in musical sophistication and context of performance begin to create the gulf (with its attendant social connotations) that has become so familiar to us, and the divide did not really become a salient fact of cultural life until about the 1830s, the beginning of the age of Jackson. Although exceptions will be noted in due course, music in our cities prior to this can be said to have been basically popular in nature and appeal. Even the institution that came later to epitomize classical music, the "concert of vocal and instrumental music," typically had a variety unusual in later periods, and was presented with the clear intent of entertaining and diverting those who came to hear it. As an advertisement for a concert in 1791 in Charleston expressed it, "the endeavors of the performers will be exercised in selecting those pieces best calculated to please the audience."[2]

Concerts and Dances

The giving of public concerts for which people pay admission presupposes a certain "critical mass" of population that will include enough people with the means, the leisure, and the inclination to support such endeavors. For the first hundred years of eastern seaboard settlement this was not the case. But by the middle of the eighteenth century, public concerts were being given fairly regularly in at least the four major cities, Philadelphia, New York, Boston, and Charleston. (Oscar Sonneck determined that the first "concert of music on sundry instruments" was given in Boston in 1731.)

What were these concerts like? Many of the early ones would hardly fit our notion of a formal concert of classical music; their character as essentially popular entertainment is illustrated by the fact that, in addition to the music itself (which, as we shall see, was quite varied), they could include other elements as well—dramatic recitations, card tricks, balancing acts ("a dance upon wire"), and other "Manly Feats of Activity."

Another pleasurable aspect of concert life was the outdoor concert in the summer months, modeled after English practice. (Even the names of the "gardens" built for this type of entertainment were borrowed from famous originals in London: New York had its Ranelagh Gardens, and there were Vauxhall Gardens in Charleston, Philadelphia, and New York.) Two attractions existed then that have been familiar to patrons of outdoor summer concerts ever since—fireworks and ice cream!

Dancing in the Eighteenth and Early Nineteenth Centuries

That the range of pleasures offered by these events (a range that has since been severely narrowed by the strict conventions of the "classical" concert) was agreeably broad is demonstrated by the fact that the concert proper was nearly always followed by "proper music . . . to wait upon such ladies and gentlemen, as may choose to dance." "The concert will terminate by a ball" was the pleasant and in fact nearly obligatory promise put forth in most advertisements for concerts. The kinds of dancing that would have gone on at these balls must have varied with time and place. In Colonial times, especially among the landed gentry of the southern colonies, it is likely that the elegant *minuet*, and possibly also the more intricate *gavotte*, would be danced. After the Revolution, these dances, with their suggestions of monarchy and aristocracy, fell out of favor. The *country dances*, on the other hand, enjoyed the widest popularity throughout the period. Of English origin, they were done in all the colonies and states, by all classes of society, in urban as well as rural settings. A French importation, the *cotillion*, became the *quadrille* (which in time gave rise to the more typically rural *square dance*). Both the country dance, with its typical lining up of dancers in opposing rows (as in the later *Virginia reel*), and the quadrille, with its square set of eight dancers, were social dances, as contrasted with later couples dances such as the *waltz* and the *galop*. The music for country dances came from a variety of sources—as Ruth Mack Wilson has put it, "from the same fund of melodic material drawn upon for ballad operas, topical songs, military marches, and ballads."[3] Fortunately some of it has been preserved in manuscript books, mainly for the use of the fifers and fiddlers who played for dancing. Many tunes used for eighteenth-century dancing are still familiar to us today, including "The Rakes of Mallow", "The Irish Washerwoman", "Soldier's Joy" (which in its countless variants became a staple in the fiddler's repertory), and "The College Hornpipe" (Example 10–1)[4] (better known to us today as "The Sailor's Hornpipe").

Example 10–1 THE COLLEGE HORNPIPE

It is possible that the instrumentalists assembled for early "Concerts of Musick" also provided the dance music for the balls that followed; if so, they would constitute dance orchestras a good deal larger than those that would have been available to accompany most dancing. For this purpose the fiddle was the single most common instrument used.

It is known that a great many African-Americans were accomplished musicians, and played for dances in the northern as well the southern colonies and states. Some of the scant information we have on this subject comes from contemporary newspapers, in advertisements about slaves—either "for sale" or "runaway." These indicate that the most common instrument played was the fiddle, but the fife, drum, flute, banjo, and French horn also appear in the lists.[5]

Musical Societies

Musical societies began to be formed in the cities in the latter half of the eighteenth century. The St. Cecilia Society in Charleston, South Carolina, founded in 1762, is famous for being the first of proven record, but such societies could be found in every major city well before 1800. Their principal function was to present a series of concerts during a season, with tickets sold by subscription. These societies tended to come and go—to form and then disappear from notice. There were lean years and fat years, as the ebb and flow of concert life was affected by war, epidemics, or fires. But musical societies tended to give some stability and continuity to the musical life of the cities. Though most of them were short-lived, some few did endure; no doubt the most famous and august of these was one that came into being late in the period, in 1815 in Boston—the Handel and Haydn Society, still active today.

In addition to the single concert or the concert as part of a subscription series, a familiar institution was the *benefit* concert. One type of benefit concert used the term in a now long-forgotten sense—it was a benefit for the musician giving the concert, who, after paying expenses, would pocket the hoped-for profits. He or she was a professional relying on music for a livelihood; often in straitened circumstances, and having contributed services more or less generously to the community and to similar benefits for other musicians, the performer giving the "benefit" was in turn asking for some tangible (and often sorely needed) reward. All too often the results were disappointing.

But the term *benefit* was also used in the sense in which we understand it today—a concert to benefit a charity (Sonneck reports on a mammoth concert in Philadelphia in 1786 to benefit the "Pennsylvania Hospital, the Philadelphia Dispensary, and the Poor"[6]), or refugees like those who flocked to this country from the West Indies following uprisings there, and from France after the French Revolution.

Despite the popularity that certain events generated, the public, then as now, was fickle, and support for concerts was apt to be sporadic and unpredictable. The records abound with instances in which concerts were either postponed or canceled because advance ticket sales, or "subscriptions," were too meager, and many benefit concerts failed even to meet expenses.

The Performers

Who were the musicians that furnished the music for the first hundred years of our urban musical life? Records of our early concert life show many of them (other than "gentlemen," who were clearly not dependent upon music for a livelihood) to have been of a hardy, resourceful, and versatile breed. In addition to being music masters, many were also dancing masters and fencing masters; they were thus equipped to minister to more than one need of the polished aristocrat of the day, especially in the southern colonies. Many also offered a variety of musical instruments for sale—as well as tobacco and other sundries. Only later was there full-time employment for those who plied only musical trades; many of these, in addition to being performers and composers, were also publishers of music, impresarios, and, then as now, church organists.

The child prodigy was evidently a great attraction at concerts, promoted by parents who were professional performers, and who seized the opportunity to capitalize on an unsophisticated public's curiosity and eagerness to be amazed. The ages of such children were naturally featured in their announcements. A concert by "P. Lewis, Professor of Music," who presented an entire program in Boston in 1819 in which his children—aged eight, seven, and four—were the sole performers, was exceptional only because the children were so young—and so numerous. There are records of musical midgets being similarly exploited, and, in a later period, blind performers such as the black pianist Blind Tom.

The century 1730–1830 was a period of gradual transition from the amateur to the professional. The distinction had existed from the very beginning; though the word "amateur" does not appear at first, his identity was made plain by the use of the word "gentleman," as distinguished from the professional, who was designated as "professor." By this the "gentleman amateur" not only maintained his distinction of class, but insulated himself from judgment by professional standards. An advertisement of a concert in Charleston in 1772 makes both these points all too plain: "The vocal part by a gentleman, who does it merely to oblige on this occasion."[7] The distinction was further maintained by the practice of having the "gentleman" performer remain anonymous, in contrast to the professional, whose very career depended on the prominence of his or her name. Toward the end of the century, the word "amateur" began to appear, with the same differentiation of social status; a benefit concert in Baltimore in 1793 announced the aid of "a number of respectable gentlemen amateurs, who will render this concert pleasing and universally satisfactory."[8]

After the privations of the Revolution had passed, the flow of professional immigrants increased, mostly on account of the increased appetite for musical theater in the cities. As Richard Crawford has pointed out, this resulted in the gradual reduction of the amateur, "gentleman" or not, to a distinctly subordinate role in the growing musical life of the cities.[9] Thus was begun a pattern that has repeated itself in the history of evolving communities ever since.

The Composers

Who were the composers of this music? Late in the eighteenth century it began to be common to print programs, especially in the newspapers, and from these we can get some idea of who the most frequently performed composers were. Even printed programs do not always yield conclusive information, however; often the composer was not listed, and when we read, for example, "Concerto Clarinet . . . Mr. Henry" it is not at all clear whether Mr. Henry was the composer, the performer, or both. Where composers were clearly indicated we find, as might be expected, they were mostly European; Haydn, Pleyel, Handel, Stamitz, and Corelli appear frequently. After the Revolution, with the coming into prominence of the professional musician, we find the names of those, either immigrants or native-born, who must be recognized as our first American composers. Most were either performers, impresarios, compilers, or publishers as well. Little known as they may be today, even by most musicians, they are important enough to warrant individual mention here, though the following expandable list is necessarily arbitrary:

Native-born musicians (in approximately chronological order)

Francis Hopkinson: born in Philadelphia 1737; composer, poet, inventor, statesman, signer of the Declaration of Independence; active in Philadelphia; died there 1791.

William Billings: born in Boston 1746; best known for sacred choral compositions (see Chapter 5), but his topical patriotic anthems were popular in the cities for a brief time; active in Boston; died there 1800.

Samuel Holyoke: born in Boxford, Massachusetts, 1762; composer of both secular and sacred music, bandmaster, teacher; active in Boston and Essex County, Massachusetts; died in East Concord, New Hampshire, 1820.

Oliver Shaw: born in Middleborough, Massachusetts, 1779; blind composer, singer, publisher; active in Boston and in Providence, Rhode Island; died in Providence 1848.

Foreign-born professional musicians (in order of arrival in America)

Alexander Reinagle: born in England ca. 1756; arrived in America 1786; composer, teacher, pianist, impresario; active mostly in Philadelphia and Baltimore; died in Baltimore 1809.

James Hewitt: born in England 1770; arrived in America 1792; composer, conductor, publisher; active in New York and Boston; died in Boston 1827.

Victor Pelissier: born in France ca. 1740–50; arrived in America ca. 1792; composer, arranger, French horn player; active mostly in Philadelphia and New York, composing and arranging for the theaters; died in New Jersey ca. 1820.

Rayner Taylor: born in England 1747; arrived in America 1792; composer, organist, teacher, music director; active mostly in Philadelphia; died there 1825.

Benjamin Carr: born in England 1768; arrived in America 1793; composer, singer, music publisher, organist; active in New York and Philadelphia; died in Philadelphia 1831.

Concert Music

What music was played at these concerts? The programs were much more varied than we are accustomed to; as the frequent appearance of the phrase "Concert [earlier spelled "Consort"] of Vocal and Instrumental Musick" indicates, songs were nearly always included. The songs might be taken from popular operas of the day, but often they were individual songs of indeterminate authorship or origin, most of which have not survived. (Songs from the theater and popular patriotic songs are dealt with later.) The instrumental pieces were overtures, symphonies (not usually performed in their entirety, as later audiences would come to expect), sonatas, and concertos or solos for various instruments. Popular solo instruments were the violin, the guitar, the "German flute" (the contemporary name for the transverse flute, in contrast to the recorder), the French horn, and the harp.

Programmatic pieces intended to depict momentous events (usually battles, but sometimes travels by sea or land, which in those days were also momentous and could be equally hazardous) began to appear toward the end of the eighteenth century. *The Battle of Prague*, by the Bohemian-born František Kočzwara (or in its Germanized form Franz Kotzwara), showed up on numerous programs for half a century, and was a kind of prototype. American contributions to the genre were represented by *The Battle of Trenton*, a pastiche arranged from various sources by James Hewitt,* and, after the French Revolution, *The Demolition of the Bastille*, by John Berkenhead. These programmatic pieces persisted well into the nineteenth century, as we shall see.[10]

Orchestral ensembles were associated at first with theaters, and began to exist separately only late in the period. (The Philharmonic Society in Boston, formed about 1809, was probably the most noteworthy independent orchestra before 1830.) Orchestras assembled for the performance of symphonies included the full complement of strings and winds common in Europe at the time, though the number of stringed instruments used was considerably smaller than we are accustomed to. For keyboard instruments, this was a transitional period, in which the piano (usually known by its full name "pianoforte") was replacing the harpsichord. Organs were to be found in most urban churches after the Revolution, and many musicians, then as now, earned a portion of their livelihood playing in churches. The organ concert, as compared to the use of the organ in the services, was practically unknown. Public concerts devoted exclusively to sacred choral music (as distinct from church services, or the more modest performances of the singing-schools) were apparently rare, and the popularity among urban concertgoers of such American "originals" as William Billings (described in Chapter 5) was brief indeed, and by the 1790s was supplanted by the combination of the professional solo performer and the musical theater.[11]

The Audiences

What were the audiences for these concerts like? For one thing, they could be noisy, though probably not nearly as noisy as theater audiences. Nevertheless, the admonition by the performer who "finds himself obliged to request that silence may be observed during his performance" was not unusual. They could even be rowdy; one concertgoer wrote to a newspaper complaining of behavior "more suited to a *broglio* than a musical entertainment," and one concert manager advertised that "every possible precaution will be used to prevent

* When French titles became popular, this or a similarly inspired piece appeared on programs as *La Bataille de Trenton*.

disorder and irregularity," while another promised that a "number of constables will attend to preserve order."[12]

Beyond the question of decorum, there are observations to be made concerning the predominant social makeup of concert audiences. There is little doubt that they did not represent the broad spectrum of the populace at large—an advertisement in Charleston in 1799 makes it clear that "persons of color" will not be admitted, for example. And from the same city in 1782 we find an announcement to the effect that "gentlemen of the navy, army [referring to officers during the British occupation of the city] and the most respectable part of town" would be admitted. That the gentry would have servants (or slaves) to perform such services as going early to secure "particular rooms, boxes or situations in the gardens" was taken for granted.[13] To sum up, it is clear that concerts, at least in the early part of the period, were primarily for "gentlemen." (It is an indication of the times that "ladies" typically were admitted on the "gentleman" 's ticket, sometimes two for each.)

Before the end of the eighteenth century, we find here and there interesting hints foreshadowing an attitude toward music that later became pronounced among those in the nineteenth century who saw the arts as instruments for improvement and reform. An observer in Philadelphia in 1792 wrote of concerts as bringing about "a gradual improvement in the national taste," while another (in the same city in 1790) wrote of music that its "powers are so great, as in a high degree to influence the national character."[14] This view, that there were not only *aesthetic* but indeed *moral* dimensions to music, is essentially the view of Romanticism. It became increasingly apparent in Boston in the second and third decades of the nineteenth century, and can be seen in two related cultural impulses of the time in this "Athens of America": the desire for "better," more "scientific" music (which meant European music), and the cleavage between "art" and "entertainment." A symbol of this was the previously mentioned Handel and Haydn Society, founded "for the purpose of improving the style of performing sacred music, and introducing into more general use the works of Handel and Haydn and other eminent composers."[15] The serious-minded Society eschewed "lighter" music (glees and popular or operatic songs and choruses) and for years devoted most of its efforts to practicing and performing those two mainstays in the repertoire of serious singing societies to this day—Handel's *Messiah* and Haydn's *The Creation*. Visiting artists who brought to Boston the more varied, more popular, and less sophisticated programs typical of an earlier day were either ignored or treated with patronizing contempt by the proponents of a more cultivated type of music. We see here then the beginnings of the distinction, for better or for worse, between "classical" and "popular."

Bands and Military Music

The wind instrument band has a long association with American music, going back well into the eighteenth century. Its subsequent development will be treated in Chapter 12; but so closely intertwined were all aspects of music in the cities in the period under consideration in this chapter that we need to note here the role of the bands that existed, and of military music.

The music of drums and wind instruments, their portability and their tonal carrying power so well suited to the outdoors, has had an association with the military going far back into history. The functions of military music have been manifold: to dignify ceremonial functions, to lift morale, to enable soldiers to march in step together, and, of supreme practical importance, to convey signals and commands. The last two needs, essential but utilitarian, were met by the simplest means—that which has long been known as *field music*. For eighteenth-century foot soldiers this meant drums and fifes, which were incorporated into each company unit. The fifers were often young boys. Collections of music for the fife existed in print and manuscript in the eighteenth century, and the tunes were often those of songs or dances of the period. "Lady Hope's Reel" was one such tune. It is shown in the first two lines of Example 10–2 as it was written down by a fifer in the Revolutionary War, Giles Gibbs, Jr., who was seventeen years old when he copied out these tunes in the summer of 1777. He was captured and killed by a British raiding party in 1780. Gibbs probably copied the tune merely for his own use, to jog his memory, and notated it without bar lines. The second part of the tune is obviously somewhat garbled, and the title as he wrote it ("Ladies hope Reele") is at variance with, and has an entirely different connotation from, the generic family of titles generally assigned to it in contemporary collections—another illustration of oral tradition at work. Example 10–3 presents the tune as edited, with reference to other sources, for a modern edition of *Giles Gibbs, Jr.: His Book for the Fife*.[16]

For mounted units, the trumpet was used. Knowledge of the calls and signals used, and proficiency in their performance, were essential to the army's

Example 10–2

Example 10–3 LADY HOPE'S REEL

success, and contemporary accounts show the attention given to the training of field musicians in the Continental Army under George Washington.[17]

To fulfill more elaborate functions, larger ensembles, known as *bands of music*, were formed. (The alternative German term *Harmoniemusik* was also applied both to the ensemble and to the music it performed.) The basic makeup was a pair of oboes, a pair of French horns, and one or two bassoons, often with a pair of clarinets either replacing or supplementing the oboes. This was a kind of ensemble well known in Europe, and masters such as Haydn and Mozart wrote a considerable amount of what was basically outdoor music for this ensemble, or augmented versions of it. "Bands of music" were usually employed by the regimental officers themselves, and were used on social as well as military occasions. Made up of fairly skilled musicians, who often played stringed instruments as well, they came to play a rather prominent role in the musical life of the times, especially during the time of the Revolution, which, in the cities (especially those occupied by the British), was not always marked by great austerity. The *Harmoniemusik* played for military ceremonies and parades, at which the public were often spectators. They also played for dances for the officers and their ladies, and even gave public concerts, and on occasion played in the theaters. In the days before orchestras were firmly established, much of the ensemble music of the time (when specifics of instrumentation were not so rigidly insisted upon as was the case later) was furnished by the bands of music, with their versatile players capable of "doubling" on several instruments. This was certainly true of outdoor summer concerts in the "pleasure gardens." Thus we see the American band tradition already firmly established at the time of the Revolution.

Musical Theater

The musical theater, in its many varied forms, was the institution upon which most of the musical life in the cities centered in this period, especially after the Revolution. It was usually the theater that employed those professional musicians who were active here, and that attracted performers, composers, and impresarios from Europe (mostly from England).

In the eighteenth century, music was a nearly universal accompaniment to theatrical performances of all kinds; even what we would regard today as straight drama (the plays of Shakespeare, for example) were usually presented with interpolated songs, dances, and incidental music. What is generally regarded as the first theater in the colonies was built in Williamsburg, Virginia, in 1716, and there is evidence that musicians were employed in this enterprise from the very beginning.[18] Furthermore, it has been shown that the majority of stage works produced here were actually "musicals"—belonging to one of the many various, confusing, and overlapping types that will be alluded to presently.

But if music was nearly always present in the theater, and its presence taken for granted, it was the most ephemeral ingredient of any production, and its providers were subordinate and often anonymous. The music for operas, or related musical genres, was often appropriated from other sources to begin with; it was also frequently changed from production to production, and from city to city, as the show traveled. The music was frequently not published (in contrast to the libretto or text, which was frequently on sale to the public in advance of the production), and it was subsequently often lost altogether. From the truly impressive number of musical stage works presented here in the century between 1730 and 1830 a disappointingly small amount of the actual music has survived, especially from the earlier part of the period.

Genres

The main line of development

There existed in this period a vast array of entertainments in which music was a major ingredient. Some of these fascinating variants will be dealt with presently, but we shall first focus our attention on what would be regarded as the main line of development. The forms we would most recognize today as "musicals" were the famous ballad opera and its often less precisely defined successors, the pastiche opera and the comic opera. (Unfortunately, we do not find the terms, then or now, used consistently; the multitude of forms the popular musical theater has assumed have always eluded precise definition.) What ballad opera, pastiche opera, and comic opera had in common was spoken dialogue, which was interspersed with songs, and sometimes with dances and choruses. The music was in a style familiar to its public, which included, as we shall see, a broad cross-section of city-dwellers of the time. For the most part the characters and situations were drawn from everyday life, or from current or well-known historical events or people. That the popular musical stage was in tune with the concerns of the times in America is illustrated by the fact that at least three contemporary operas were based on the story of William Tell—a Swiss hero in his country's struggle for freedom.

Ballad opera is a term that has been incorrectly applied to all popular musicals of the period that originated in England or were based on English models. Correctly used, the designation refers to a musical entertainment in which the tunes used are those of ballads or popular songs (one writer has described them as "popular ditties of the street-ballad type") which were already well known by the audience. Musically, then, ballad opera is a form based on *parody*—an unfailingly effective device for popular entertainment. The original was the famous *The Beggar's Opera*, first performed in London in

1728. With its already-popular tunes, its memorable low-life characters, and its satirization of the conventions of the imported upper-class Italian opera of its day (which it nearly put out of business for a time), it was an instant success, and was soon widely imitated. In its original form, the opera had nearly seventy songs and at least three dances. Though the initial intensity of its popularity, and the heyday of ballad opera in general, was over in London in a decade or so, a certain few operas of this genre proved to be amazingly long-lived, especially in America. *The Beggar's Opera* itself was performed in Providence, Rhode Island, by a "Sett of Inhabitants" (amateurs) at least as early as 1746, and by a professional company in New York by 1750.[19] Julian Mates has written that "it was *The Beggar's Opera*, in most places, which introduced the musical to America."[20] It was a staple of the repertory through the remainder of the eighteenth century, and has been revived, in various forms, ever since.

It was another ballad opera, reduced to a one-act farce called *Flora, or the Hob in the Well*, that is generally considered to be the first *documented* performance of an opera (so-called) in America; this took place in Charleston, South Carolina, in 1732. *Flora* continued to appear on programs right up to the end of the century, as did other ballad operas such as *Damon and Phillida*, *The Honest Yorkshireman*, and *The Mock Doctor*, a farce adapted from Molière. An early, and thought to be the first, ballad opera by an American, *The Disappointment: or, the Force of Credulity*, written in 1767 by "Andrew Barton" (probably a pseudonym), had its first performance in this century, in 1937; thereby hangs a fascinating tale too long to be recounted here.[21]

In the second half of the eighteenth century, ballad opera was gradually replaced by *comic opera*, as the role of the composer became more important, and the music became more fully developed and demanding and more closely related to the plot. An intermediate stage, called *pastiche opera* or *pasticcio*, has been identified, in which the songs, while still not original to the opera, were borrowed from more sophisticated sources, were better suited to the story, and were given more elaborate accompaniments. *Love in a Village* was of this type: the well-known English composer Thomas Arne provided the music, some of which was original. It was first performed in London in 1762; reaching America at least by 1767, the piece was performed almost continuously in the major cities for the rest of the century.

The next development was what is properly known as *comic opera* itself, in which the music is written specifically for a particular play, by a single composer.* *The Padlock*, a short comic opera performed in London in 1768 and brought to America the following year, was an early example. It was composed by the English composer-performer Charles Dibdin, and was famous for its black character Mungo, portrayed by Dibdin himself. After the Revolution, American composers, most of them professional immigrants, were composing comic operas. *The Archers, or Mountaineers of Switzerland*, based on the story of William Tell, was the first opera in which both text (by William Dunlap) and

* Although the practice of having a single composer compose all the music for a given play has come to be regarded as the norm, there have been exceptions to this right into the twentieth century. As late as 1927, Jerome Kern included the Tin Pan Alley song "After the Ball," then thirty years old, in the score of *Show Boat*.

music (by Benjamin Carr) were by Americans. It was first performed in New York in 1796; as too often happened, most of the music was lost. A later American opera that has survived is *The Indian Princess, or La Belle Sauvage*, with text by James Nelson Barker and music by John Bray, first performed in Philadelphia in 1808. It is based on an American subject—the story of Captain John Smith and Pocahontas. Called "An Operatic Melo-Drame," it includes "action music," after the manner of the later *melodrama*, to accompany such stage actions as "Indian Girls arranging Flowers," "Pocahontas enters from the woods," "Indians stealing after Smith," and "Indians fighting with Smith." This musical play was probably the first to reverse the pattern of nearly a century by crossing the Atlantic in the opposite direction: it was produced in London, in a pirated version, in 1820.[22]

Political independence of the colonies from England was declared in 1776, and confirmed by treaty six years later, but cultural independence evolved much more slowly. For three-quarters of a century more, the legacy of English comic opera, with its comic characters, its homely but pungent satire, and its popular, folklike songs, was entertaining Americans, if not continuously in the large cities of the eastern seaboard, then in crude, sparsely documented, but keenly enjoyed performances in frontier towns and cities. The tenacity of the pieces themselves was amazing. An example is *The Poor Soldier* (a favorite of George Washington), written by an Irish playright, John O'Keeffe, and first performed in London in 1783. William Shield provided the music, some of it composed, and some adapted from folk and other sources. It reached the United States in 1785, and after a successful New York "run" of nineteen performances by the famous Old American Company, it was taken on the road by that company. Thereafter, until the end of the eighteenth century, hardly a year went by without a performance of *The Poor Soldier* somewhere, by some company (usually as an afterpiece to another work). It was to last well into the nineteenth century as well; in 1801 it was done in Cincinnati—the first play performed in the Northwest Territory—and continued to be played throughout the Ohio Valley for twenty years. It played in New Orleans forty times between 1806 and 1842. *The Poor Soldier* was part of the American theatrical scene in one form or another almost until the Civil War; the same was true of *Love in a Village*, both thriving alongside the circus and the minstrel show. An extremely popular song from *The Poor Soldier* was "A Rose Tree" (Example 10–4). It is an indication of its popularity that words of the song, detached from the opera, appeared in later songsters, while the tune, detached from its words, was found in copybooks of airs and dance tunes.[23]

Other theatrical entertainments with music

In addition to the comic operas, there was a bewildering variety of theatrical entertainments, all of which employed music in some form. The shorter afterpieces that followed the main play or opera (a theatrical presentation hardly ever consisted of just a single play, and could go on for four or five hours!) were sometimes composed originally for this function. But they were also sometimes condensed and degraded or burlesqued versions of what had originally been full-length operas—*Flora, or the Hob in the Well*, the first opera of legend to be performed in America, is an example. For this type of

Example 10–4 A ROSE TREE

A__ rose tree in full bear - ing had sweet flow - ers__
fair to see; One__ rose be - yond com - par - ing for
beau - ty__ at - trac - ted me. Though_ ea - ger then to win it,
love - ly, bloom - ing fresh and gay, I____ find a can - ker
in it, and now throw_ it____ far a - way.

piece the term *ballad farce*, or simply *farce*, was often used. *Interludes* were even slighter pieces that went between the acts of longer works.

An important independent form was the *pantomime*, in which stage action and speech were accompanied by wordless music. The eighteenth-century pantomime so popular in America often featured the old stock comic figures of the *commedia dell'arte*, especially that of Harlequin, whose humorous antics were backed up by what Anne Shapiro has so aptly termed "action music."[24] The name of Harlequin appears in the titles of many of these pieces—"Harlequin Doctor," "Harlequin Barber," "Harlequin Balloonist," "Harlequin Pastry-cook." American composers such as Hewitt and Reinagle contributed music to pantomimes, very little of which has survived. In the nineteenth century the device of accompanying stage action with purely instrumental music, descriptive of the situation in a conventional way, was a feature of *melodrama*. As we noted earlier, the musical play *The Indian Princess*, of 1808, had elements of both opera and melodrama. The technique of melodrama (action accompanied by wordless music) was adapted in the early twentieth century to the silent film.

Dance was inevitably a part of pantomime, and began to be a prominent element in "ballet pantomimes" toward the end of the eighteenth century—a pioneering introduction of ballet to this country.

The *masque* was an older form, related to the pantomime, which was serious in intent and dealt with historical or mythological figures treated in an allegorical way. The *circus* originated in the eighteenth century as an exhibition of feats of horsemanship, and gradually acquired elements of pantomime (the circus clown is a close relative of Harlequin) and even of comic opera. It was enormously popular in America during this period, and was serious competition for the theater of the day. The *extravaganza* was an entertainment that relied heavily on elaborate scenic effects. The *olio* was a real potpourri of songs, duets, instrumental numbers, recitations, and short musical burlesques, which anticipated the first half of the minstrel show, and the later musical *revue*. Rayner Taylor became known for his "burlesque olios." Many of these various and variegated forms of entertainment, which involved music of some kind, included kinds of acts that would be found later in vaudeville, such as rope dancing, dancing over eggs, etc.[25]

The Actor-Singer, the Theatrical Company, and the Composer

Versatility was the rule in the early musical theater; specialization had not entered the picture. Given the nature of English comic opera, all actors had to be singers, to a degree, and vice versa. Managers and impresarios also had roles to play on stage; Lewis Hallam and Thomas Wignell, two of the most important theatrical entrepreneurs of the time, were both noted comic actors. There were a number of producing companies in existence, all of which spent at least part of their time touring. It is enough to identify one: the famous Old American Company arrived in Williamsburg from England in 1752 as Hallam's London Company of Comedians, but changed its name to the American Company. During the Revolutionary War, due to the ban on theatrical entertainments,* the company retired to Jamaica, but it returned in 1785 as the Old American Company, a name pointing proudly to its longevity in the field in which it was to be preeminent for half a century. Its huge repertory over the years, of which over half were said to be musicals, included all the popular comic operas.

After the privations of the war passed, the demand for theatrical entertainment in the new country drew many trained musicians here, as we have noted. While the presence of professional musicians contributed greatly to the concert life of the cities, it was the theaters that gave them steady employment at good pay. Those who were orchestra leaders, like Alexander Reinagle and James Hewitt, had to act as composers on occasion. But the role of the composer in the early American theater was minor; a quantity of music was needed, and consumed, but most of it was simply borrowed and arranged from already existing sources. At the turn of the century this changed, and American composers began to write complete scores for musicals; Benjamin Carr's *The Archers*, produced in 1796, was a landmark in this regard.

Theater Orchestras

The eighteenth century saw the instrumental accompaniment for theatrical production grow from a single performer on the harpsichord (aided perhaps

* In October 1778 the Continental Congress enacted a ban on "Play Houses and theatrical entertainments," on the basis that frequenting them "has a fatal tendency to divert the minds of the people from a due attention to the means necessary for the defence of their country and preservation of their liberties." The Pennsylvania Legislature enacted an even more stringent ban. Though far from being strictly enforced, it remained on the books for a decade.

by a single violinist) to a full-sized orchestra of perhaps twelve to fifteen musicians in the largest theaters. By 1760 most cities had theater orchestras; by the end of the century, several had more than one. Size and makeup could vary considerably, and precise information is lacking, but the instrumentation was probably as complete as in European theaters, and would include a keyboard instrument (harpsichord or, later, piano), the full range of strings, and French horns, oboes, flutes, clarinets, and bassoons, with many of the woodwind players playing more than one instrument. Leadership, as in Europe at the same time, was divided between the keyboard player and the leader of the violins; the modern conductor had not yet emerged. In the larger theaters the playing was probably quite good; at the end of the century, the orchestra in Wignell's and Reinagle's company in Philadelphia, under the leadership of Alexander Reinagle himself, set new standards for theater orchestra performance (as did the orchestra of Victor Herbert in New York a century later.)

Before the war, theater orchestras were filled out with "gentlemen amateurs," who were not paid but were probably quite good players, for the most part, and whose presence added prestige to the theater. After the war, their places were largely taken over by professionals. During the 1790s, as we have noted, there was an influx of French musicians—refugees from the French Revolution, and from the uprisings and turmoil in the West Indies.

Theaters and Audiences

The first theatrical performances in the colonies were given in buildings made for other purposes—often in taverns or warehouses (though not, of course, in churches). The first musical in America, in 1732, was given in the Courtroom in Charleston, South Carolina. By mid-century, theaters had been built in most cities. The space for the audience, according to a plan which remained basically unaltered to the twentieth century, was divided into three distinct parts: at the bottom level was the "pit" (now called the "orchestra"); above this, in a horseshoe shape around the walls, were one or more tiers of boxes; and above the boxes was the gallery. The distribution of the audience was rigidly defined: "ladies and gentlemen in the boxes, the pit occupied almost entirely by unattached gentlemen, and the gallery 'reserved for the rabble.' "[26] An announcement of 1759 quotes the following prices: "Box, 8 shillings. Pit, 5 shillings. Gallery, 2 shillings."[27]

The behavior of audiences was, by our standards, notoriously bad. There was loud talking and often card playing in the boxes, and coming and going, with the slamming of doors. Prostitutes, who used the theater (in Sonneck's words) "as a kind of stock exchange,"[28] were by custom assigned the upper boxes. Liquor was served to the "unattached gentlemen" in the pit; some attempt at control was evident in an announcement that "the managers respectfully hope the Gentlemen will not call for any till the conclusion of the first piece." It was not until the end of the century that the custom of allowing some of the audience to sit on the stage during the performance was abolished. But the greatest disturbances came from the gallery. It was customary for people in the gallery to interrupt the orchestra's performance by shouting down requests for popular tunes—requests which, if not complied with to their satisfaction, would result in loud demonstrations. A letter to a New York newspaper as late as 1802 describes the behavior of the gallery "gods": "The mode by which they issue their mandates is stamping, hissing, roaring, whistling; and, when the musicians are refractory, groaning in cadence." The habit of the gallery's throwing objects at the orchestra, and into the pit, was notorious. "As soon as the curtain was down, the *gods* in the galleries would throw apples, nuts, bottles and glasses on the stage and into the orchestra." Mates quotes a report of a performance in 1794 "when half the instruments in the orchestra were broken by missiles from the upper reaches of the theater."[29] Thieves and pickpockets in the theaters were common. In addition, feelings (often motivated by the volatile political issues of the day) ran high, especially in the Federal era and after the French Revolution; certain tunes were associated with certain factions (pro- or anti-Federalist, pro- or anti-French, and so on), so that managers and orchestra leaders had to be extremely judicious in the choice of music, in order not to provoke the riots that were all too common in the theaters of the day—riots that could, of course, be incited by more trivial likes and dislikes as well.

Popular Song

Popular song—enjoyed by the general populace, marketed for a wide public, and not connected with the stage or the concert hall—is at once the most widespread kind of music-making and the most difficult to chronicle. Secular songs were not published complete with lyrics and music together until the last decade of the eighteenth century. Before that time, popular songs were disseminated in print for the most part by the publication of the words alone. This implies the existence of a body of tunes in oral tradition—in other words, an early example of the kind of overlapping with folk tradition so characteristic of American music. Historians' efforts to find out exactly what people were singing by matching tune to lyrics are beset by many difficulties: often the tune was not specified; even where a popular title was given, accuracy is often still elusive owing to the fact that not only did the same tune go by a number of different names, but the same name was sometimes used for completely different tunes![30]

The words alone to popular songs were distributed by the practice, already two hundred years old in England, of publishing *broadsides*—single sheets, with words alone, cheaply printed, and sold in shops or in the streets.[31] The ballad tradition, possibly revitalized on both sides of the Atlantic by the tremendous popularity of *The Beggar's Opera*, was strong throughout the eighteenth century, and has never completely died out, as we saw in Chapter 4. Another way of disseminating lyrics was in *songsters*, booklets containing the words alone to a number of ballads or songs; these became very numerous in the nineteenth century.

By the time of the Revolution, newspapers, of which there were a great many in the colonies, had become another medium for the publication of lyrics, especially topical verses dealing with the patriotic and political matters that were of so much concern at the time.[32] It is not possible to determine now whether all of these versifications (often crude by literary standards) were in fact meant to be sung, but the strength of the ballad tradition, the number of tunes known to be in wide circulation, and the fact that in many cases the names of the tunes were given justify our including this vast output in our consideration of popular song. Many patriotic songs, including "Yankee Doodle" and the many sets of words associated with it, were first disseminated in this manner. Fortunately many spirited, if not highly polished, songs from this quasi-oral tradition are now available in print and on recordings.[33]

One very popular song that was parodied in broadsides of the time was "The Dusky Night" or "A-Hunting We Will Go." The tune is given in Example 10–5 as it appeared in a copybook of 1797.[34]

Example 10–5

The first version of the song, as used in a revival of *The Beggar's Opera* in England, is:

> The Dusky Night rides down the Sky,
> When wakes the Rosey Morn,
> The Hounds all join the Jovial cry, (2x)
> The Huntsman winds his Horn. (2x)
>
> (*Chorus*)
> Then a Hunting let us go. (4x)

The broadside parody, attacking the British desire to raise more revenue from the colonies, appeared in journals of the day in New York and Philadelphia. It substitutes "A-taxing we will go" for the original words of the chorus. (The text was quoted in Chapter 4, page 86, as an example of an early American propaganda song.)

This chapter is concerned primarily with secular music, but there was no very clear dividing line between sacred and secular in this period, and religion was often invoked in political and military struggles. There was some crossover, therefore, between hymns and patriotic songs, and the best example of this can be seen in William Billings's "Chester," especially with the updated topical verses added for its second version of 1778.* It is said to have been the most popular song of the Revolutionary War.

After the war, songs began to be printed with a skeletal keyboard part included. The first, published in 1788, were *Seven Songs for the Harpsichord*

* Both the music and the words of "Chester" are quoted in Chapter 5, Example 5–5.

(dedicated to George Washington) by the American-born statesman, inventor, poet, and composer Francis Hopkinson, of Philadelphia.[35] Immigrant composers soon thereafter began to publish collections of songs. Benjamin Carr, a prolific composer who enjoyed considerable success, composed mostly for the theater, but published many songs, both individually and in sets, between 1794 and 1830.[36] Victor Pelissier published *Pelissier's Columbian Melodies* by subscription, beginning in 1812; these were mostly songs he had written for the theater, but included was his "Ode on the Passions," an interesting example of music to accompany recitation, reminding us of the taste for melodrama that was emerging in the nineteenth century.[37]

The turn of the century saw the beginnings of changes, large and small, tangible and intangible, gradual but significant. The role of the composer was becoming more important (it was typical of new practices in both performance and composition, for example, that the Carr and Pelissier songs had, for the most part, completely written-out keyboard parts, instead of the older skeletal parts that left much more to the performer's discretion and skill). In terms of the medium of dissemination, the publishing of songs individually, rather than in sets, marked the beginning of *sheet music*, which became, during the nineteenth century, the basis for the entire popular music industry, known later as Tin Pan Alley. In the first quarter of the nineteenth century the growth in sheer volume of music published was in marked contrast to the last quarter of the eighteenth; in the period 1801–25 nearly ten thousand titles appeared of secular music alone.[38] The range, in terms of songs, was broad—from topical songs on political or patriotic themes, crude but timely, to settings of the poetry of Shakespeare, Sir Walter Scott, or Thomas Moore. This very breadth was symptomatic of a divergence of taste that was to lead, as the century progressed, to the fragmentation of our musical culture.

Further Reading

Books, General, Regional, and Specialized

Camus, Raoul F. *Military Music of the American Revolution*. Chapel Hill: University of North Carolina Press, 1976. Basic work by a leading authority.

Hamm, Charles. *Yesterdays: Popular Song in America*. New York: W. W. Norton, 1979.
The first five chapters deal with this period.

Johnson, H. Earle. *Hallelujah, Amen!: The Story of the Handel and Haydn Society of Boston*. Boston: Bruce Humphries, 1965.

———. *Musical Interludes in Boston, 1795–1830*. New York: AMS Press, 1967. Reprint of 1943 pub.
A regional study based on Sonneck's model (see *Early Concert-Life in America*, below) of a painstaking search of contemporary periodicals.

Keller, Kate Van Winkle, and Carolyn Rabson. *The National Tune Index*. New York: University Music Editions, 1980. Not a book, but a valuable research tool available in many libraries. Microfiche index to 38,500 eighteenth-century secular tunes from 520 sources, with cross indexes. Accompanied by a printed *User's Guide*.

Lambert, Barbara, ed. *Music in Colonial Massachusetts. 1630–1820*. 2 vols. I: *Music in Public Places*. II. *Music in Homes and in Churches*. Charlottesville: University Press of Virginia, 1980, 1985.

Laws, G. Malcolm, Jr. *American Balladry*

from British Broadsides. Philadelphia: American Folklore Society, 1957.

———. *Native American Balladry*. Philadelphia: American Folklore Society, 1964.

Lowens, Irving. *Music and Musicians in Early America*. New York: W. W. Norton, 1964.
Articles on various topics, from the seventeenth century to the mid-nineteenth, by an important authority and scholar.

Mates, Julian. *The American Musical Stage Before 1800*. New Brunswick, NJ: Rutgers University Press, 1962.
Popularly written, readable, with copious documentation.

Sonneck, Oscar George. *Early Concert-Life in America* (1731–1800) New York: Musurgia, 1949. Reprint of 1906 ed.
An important work by a pioneering scholar in American music. A narrative study based on contemporary periodicals, this is still a basic source, and a model for subsequent studies.

———. *Early Opera in America*. New York: Benjamin Blom, 1963. Reprint of 1915 ed.

———. *Francis Hopkinson and James Lyon*. New York: Da Capo, 1967. Reprint of 1905 ed.

Music in Facsimile Reprints

American Musical Miscellany (1798). New York: Da Capo, 1975.
A collection of songs with tunes and bass lines.

The Beggar's Opera (1728). New York: Dover, 1973

Hopkinson, Francis. *Seven Songs for the Harpsichord or Forte Piano* (1788). Philadelphia: Musical Americana, 1954

The Indian Princess (1808). New York: Da Capo, 1972.
Text by James Barker, and music by John Bray, printed separately, as they were originally.

Rubsamen, Walter, ed. *The Ballad Opera: A Collection of 191 Original Texts of Musical Plays Printed in Photo-facsimile*. 13 vols. New York: Garland, 1974.

Works by a Single Composer in Modern Editions

Barton, Andrew. *Disappointment: or, The Force of Credulity* (1767). Jerald C. Grave and Judith Layng, eds. Recent Researches in American Music, vols. 3 and 4. Madison, WI: A-R Editions, 1976.
Modern reconstructed performing edition of famous ballad opera not performed until 1937! Preface has extensive commentary.

Carr, Benjamin. *Selected Secular and Sacred Songs*. Recent Researches in American Music, vol. 15. Madison WI: A-R Editions, 1986.
Preface has extensive commentary.

Gibbs, Giles, Jr. *Giles Gibbs, Jr.: His Book for the Fife*. Kate Van Winkle Keller, ed. Hartford: Connecticut Historical Society, 1974.

Pelissier, Victor. *Pelissier's Columbian Melodies* (1812). Recent Researches in American Music, vols. 13 and 14. Madison, WI: A-R Editions, 1984.
Mostly theater music with some independent songs and instrumental pieces. Preface by Karl Kroeger has extensive commentary.

Shield, William. *The Poor Soldier* (1783). Brasmer and Osborne, eds. Recent Researches in American Music, vol. 6. Madison, WI: A-R Editions, 1978.
John O'Keeffe wrote the play. Preface of this edition has considerable commentary.

Modern Collections or Anthologies

Anderson, Gillian, comp. and ed. *Freedom's Voice in Poetry and Song*. Wilmington, DE: Scholarly Resources, 1977.

This compendious "inventory of political and patriotic lyrics in colonial American newspapers" concludes with a songbook with 92 songs and 8 poems.

Keller, Kate Van Winkle, and Ralph Sweet, eds. *A Choice Selection of American Country Dances of the Revolutionary Era, 1775–1795.* New York: Country Dance and Song Society of America, 1976.
Twenty-nine dance tunes on single staff, with directions for performing the dances.

Marrocco, W. Thomas, and Harold Gleason, comps. and eds. *Music in America.* New York: W. W. Norton, 1964.
Includes thirteen relevant compositions by Reinagle, Taylor, Carr, Hewitt, and others.

Rabson, Carolyn, comp. and ed. *Songbook of the American Revolution.* Peaks Island, ME: NEO Press, 1974.
Single-staff tunes, with suggested chords; annotations and sources.

Silber, Irwin, comp. and ed. *Songs of Independence.* Harrisburg, PA: Stackpole Books, 1973.
Single-staff tunes, with suggested chords, copious annotations and sources.

Articles in American Music *by subject*

Theater

"The First Hundred Years of American Lyric Theater" by Julian Mates, vol. 1, no. 2 (Summer 1983).

"Music in Eighteenth-Century American Theater" by Cynthia Adams Hoover, vol. 2, no. 4 (Winter 1984).

"*Pocahontas*: Her Life and Times" by William Brooks, vol. 2, no. 4 (Winter 1984).

"Origin of Species: Conflicting Views of American Musical Theater History" by Edith Borroff, vol. 2, no. 4 (Winter 1984).

"Action Music in American Pantomime and Melodrama, 1730–1913" by Anne Dhu Shapiro, vol. 2, no. 4 (Winter 1984).

"Opera in Colonial Boston" by David McKay, vol. 3, no. 2 (Summer 1985).

"English-American Interaction in American Musical Theater at the Turn of the Nineteenth Century" by Susan L. Porter, vol. 4, no. 1 (Spring 1986).

"*Disappointment* Revisited: Unweaving the Tangled Web" by Carolyn Rabson, vol. 1, no. 1 (Spring 1983), and vol. 2, no. 1 (Spring 1984).
Fascinating tale of the "first American opera," composed in 1767 but not performed until 1937.

Individual musicians

"Alexander Reinagle, His Family Background and Early Professional Career" by Anne McClenny Krauss, vol. 4, no. 4 (Winter 1986).

"Rayner Taylor" by Victor Fell Yellin, vol. 1, no. 3 (Fall 1983).

"Rayner Taylor's Music for *The Æthiop*," parts I and II, by Victor Fell Yellin, vol. 4, no. 3 (Fall 1986), and vol. 5, no. 1 (Spring 1987).

Regional

"New York City Concert Life, 1801–5" by John W. Wagner, vol. 2, no. 2 (Summer 1984).

Listening

Songs and Choral Music

The Birth of Liberty: Music of the American Revolution. NW-276.
Includes topical songs and choruses, including Billings's "Lamentation Over Boston" and "Independence."

The Flowering of Vocal Music in America, vol. 2. NW-231.
Solo vocal and ensemble music by Benjamin Carr, Oliver Shaw, and George K. Jackson.

Hopkinson, Francis. *America Independent; or, The Temple of Minerva.* Musical Heritage Society MHS 3684.

Music of the Federal Era. NW-299.
Solo songs, one trio, and chorus.

Songs from a Colonial Tavern as performed by Tayler Vrooman in Colonial Williamsburg (Colonial Williamsburg series). MCA 228.
Includes ballads, catches, and popular songs.

The Williamsburg Singers (Colonial Williamsburg series) WS102.
Part-songs by English, and two American, composers.

Instrumental Concert and Dance Music

Come and Trip It: Instrumental Dance Music 1780's–1920's. NW-293.
The only relevant tracks are one piece by Reinagle, and six country dances.

Music of the Federal Era. NW-299.
Music of Samuel Holyoke, Rayner Taylor, Benjamin Carr, and Oliver Shaw, plus an excerpt from the notorious *The Battle of Prague.*

Two albums from the Colonial Williamsburg series, *A Williamsburg Candlelight Concert* (WS100) and *An Evening of Music at Carter's Grove Plantation* (WS103), are relevant, though they consist entirely of European music.

Band and Military Music

The Birth of Liberty: Music of the American Revolution. NW-276.
Includes a variety of fife tunes and marches.

Music of the Federal Era. NW-299.
Various marches, including *The President's March* (*Hail Columbia*), and *Gov. Arnold's March,* with a terrific solo on the serpent!

Theater Music

Bray, John. *The Indian Princess,* excerpts. NW-232.
Notes by Victor Fell Yellin.

Music of the Federal Era. NW-299.
Includes excerpts from Pelissier's *The Voice of Nature* and the anonymous *Alknomook, or The Death Song of the Cherokee Indians.*

Taylor, Rayner. *The Ethiop,* excerpts. NW-232.
Notes by Victor Fell Yellin.

PROJECTS

1. If you are a country dance enthusiast, write a paper on the eighteenth-century forebears of either the "square dances" or the "line dances" that are popular today.

2. Assemble an up-to-date bibliography on black musicians in America in the eighteenth century, and summarize some of the latest findings in this difficult-to-research field.

3. As noted in the chapter, in eighteenth-century American cities the "amateur" musician was gradually replaced by the "professional" as the mainstay of public music-making. This pattern of evolution has repeated itself in growing communities ever since. Investigate your own community, and write a paper assessing the relative roles of amateurs and professionals at the present stage of its development. Are the major public musical events performed by amateurs or professionals? What proportion of all musical events is presented by each group? What types of productions are associated with each?

4. As revealed in the chapter, audiences in the eighteenth century were often inconsiderate and ill-behaved. From personal observation, write a paper on the behavior of present-day audiences for a variety of events in a variety of locations: a classical concert, a jazz concert, a rock concert, a concert of folk music, and so on. To what would you attribute the differences, both between the eighteenth and the twentieth centuries, and between various kinds of contemporary events?

5. As a group project, work up the presentation of a scene from an eighteenth-century ballad opera. Include some of the songs if possible, although the spoken dialogue of the printed texts alone will make a comprehensible scene. A copious source, available in larger libraries, is W. Rubsamen, ed., *The Ballad Opera: A Collection of 191 Original Texts of Musical Plays Printed in Photo-Facsimile.* (New York: Garland, 1974).

6. Sketch a plot and scenario for a modern-day "ballad opera," dealing in a comical and even satirical way with some current issue or event. Read the texts of several ballad operas in preparation for this (see project 5 above for a source); the scenes should be short and the characters few, and allowance should be made for the inclusion of "airs," which can be parodies of existing popular songs.

7. Write a paper on the history of *The Beggar's Opera,* including such twentieth-century reincarnations as the Brecht/Weill *Threepenny Opera.*

8. If you are a singer, prepare for performance a group of three or four American patriotic songs from the eighteenth century, and present them with verbal program notes. Unaccompanied singing, or use of a guitar accompaniment, is a satisfactory alternative to the use of the piano, especially where no written-out accompaniment exists. Consult the reading list for this chapter for sources.

9. Reread the material in this chapter on eighteenth-century "concerts of music"—events that often included rhetorical, visual, dramatic, and even acrobatic elements as well. Supplement this with some reading in Sonneck, *Early Concert-Life in America* (New York: Musurgia, 1949). Then write a paper comparing these eighteenth-century concerts with the "performance art" of our own time (see Chapter 18). In what ways are they similar, in terms of the use of "mixed media" and different levels of appeal? In what ways are they different?

10. Study the modern edition of *Disappointment: or, The Force of Credulity* (Madison, WI: A-R Editions, 1976), and read the two articles on the subject by Carolyn Rabson in American Music (vol. 1, no. 1 [Spring 1983], pp. 12ff, and vol. 2, no. 1 [Spring 1984], pp. 1ff). Write an article, in a lively journalist style, describing the piece and its history.

11

Popular Musical Theater from the Jacksonian Era to the Present

THE age of Jackson, characterized by westward expansion and a new degree of political populism, marked the beginning of a new era of *cultural* populism as well. One useful yardstick of this new populism was the music publishing industry, which was expanding rapidly and catering to a much broader segment of the people. New methods of lithography made possible the use of black-and-white illustrations in sheet music in the late 1820s, and colored illustrations in the 1840s[1]—developments that were clearly linked to a growing popular market, as can be seen in the popular nature and appeal of illustrated sheet music published in the 1820s and 1830s. Thus the period from 1820 to 1840, which saw the admission of three new western states into the union (Missouri, Arkansas, and Michigan), the opening of the Erie Canal, and the construction of the Baltimore and Ohio Railroad to carry paying passengers as far west as Harpers Ferry, West Virginia, also saw the mass publication of sentimental popular favorites such as "Woodman! Spare That Tree!"—and also, for less genteel tastes, "Massee Georgee Washington and General Lafayette," "My Long-Tail Blue," "Jim Crow," and "Zip Coon"—all illustrated with blackface figures with exaggerated features, dress, and poses.[2]

As the country was expanding westward, so were its cities growing rapidly, both on the more settled eastern seaboard and in the Ohio and Mississippi valleys. And as the cities grew, so did the number and size of the theaters, and the audience for the vast array of theatrical entertainments that we noted in the last chapter—comic operas, farces, pantomimes, and melodramas. Two forms in particular—the *olio,* a kind of variety show that predated vaudeville, and the *circus,* which had incorporated comic song-and-dance acts into its original format—prepared the way for the first of a succession of truly indigenous forms of popular musical entertainment.

Minstrelsy and Musical Entertainment Before the Civil War

The first of these indigenous forms, and one that swept the country by mid-century, was the blackface minstrel show. It was based on what had become by then a common source of entertainment among the broader masses, both in America and in England: the exaggerated portrayal of any exotic people—rural people, Irish people, German people, Jewish people and, as early as the eighteenth century, African people.

Since the earliest days of their presence here, black people had displayed their native talents as musicians, dancers, and entertainers both among themselves and for the benefit of the whites who made use of them in this capacity. Many African-Americans, for example, had considerable reputations as fiddlers, and were much in demand to furnish music for dancing for both blacks and whites. Their faculty for spontaneous song and dance, and for unbridled comedy, was also well known. Lewis Paine, spending some time in Georgia in the 1840s, comments as follows in describing the festivities after a corn shucking:

> The fiddler walks out, and strikes up a tune; and at it they go in a regular tear-down dance; for here they are at home. . . . I never saw a slave in my life but would stop as if he were shot at the sound of a fiddle; and if he has a load of two hundred pounds on his head, he will begin to dance. One would think they had steam engines inside of them, to jerk them about with so much power; for they go through more motions in a minute, than you could shake two sticks at in a month; and of all comic actions, ludicrous sights, and laughable jokes, and truly comic songs, there is no match for them. It is useless to talk about Fellows' Minstrels, or any other band of merely artificial "Ethiopians"; for they will bear no comparison with the plantation negroes.[3]

It is clear from this that there was abundant material here for imitation by white entertainers, once they saw its potential. The original black minstrelsy was an informal, spontaneous, and exuberant affair of the plantation. But its reputation spread. Thus it came about that the native songs, dances, and comedy of the slaves first reached the general American public in the form of parodies by white entertainers.

The Beginnings of Minstrelsy

Impersonations on the stage of the black man by the white were already taking place in the eighteenth century, both here and in England. Indicative of the close relationship of the English and American stages is the fact that the first actors to exploit the caricature of black people as a source of entertainment were English. Charles Dibdin, it will be remembered, had created the part of the black character Mungo, which he played himself with great success, in the comic opera *The Padlock* in 1768. In the 1820s, the English actor Charles Mathews, while on tour here, painstakingly noted down the contents and patterns of black speech, which he later used in such caricatures as that of Agamemnon, a runaway slave.[4] Two American entertainers, George Washington Dixon (1808–61) and Thomas Dartmouth "Daddy" Rice (1808–60), were doing blackface song-and-dance routines in the 1820s and 1830s. Dixon introduced the songs "Long Tail Blue" (referring to the blue swallowtail coat associated with the black urban dandy) and "Coal Black Rose." Rice was famous for his song-and-dance routine "Jim Crow," which he introduced in 1832 and which, according to a well-known story, he adapted from the singing and movements of a black man he encountered in Cincinnati.[5]

Familiar and very popular as single acts in olios and circuses, the impersonation of blacks had, by the 1830s, evolved into two stage types. One, typified by Gumbo Chaff or Jim Crow himself, portrayed the ragged plantation or riverboat hand, joyous, reckless, uncouth. The other, typified by Zip Coon or Dandy Jim, was a citified northern dandy, with exaggeratedly elegant clothes and manners. Incidentally, the extent to which some songs of the minstrel period have entered into the great body of perennial American tunes is illustrated by the fact that the tune of "Zip Coon" has been perpetuated since the Civil War as "Turkey in the Straw."

The minstrel show itself was put together in the early 1840s. It consisted of songs (both solo and "full chorus"), dances, jokes, conundrums, satirical speeches, and skits. The performers, only four in number at first, seated themselves in a rough semicircle on the stage. The word "seated" may be misleading, however—they were much of the time dancing and cavorting around the stage, and even when in contact with the chairs they would be constantly in motion, executing the most comical gyrations and contortions. In the middle were the banjo player and the fiddle player (the instrument was played like a country fiddle, held against the chest). The two "end-men" played the tambourine and the bones, and these, along with the inevitable foot-tapping of the banjo player, provided a kind of primitive "rhythm section." It was the end-men who indulged in the most outrageous horseplay. The bones, which were in the beginning actually just that, were held one pair in each hand and rattled together. The fiddle played the tune more or less straight, while the banjo played an ornamented version of it, so that their roles must have been somewhat analogous to those of the cornet and clarinet in early jazz, with the resulting heterophony. It is interesting to note that the banjo did not strum chords, as it would in the later jazz band, but played an actual melodic line, on one string at a time. Since the banjo music was eventually written down and published, along with method books for the instrument, we know the kind of music that must have been played on it, and it presupposes a good deal of agility.

What did the early minstrel band actually sound like? Hans Nathan, in his *Dan Emmett and the Rise of Early Negro Minstrelsy*, has this to say:

> The volume of the minstrel band was quite lean, yet anything but delicate. The tones of the banjo died away quickly and therefore could not serve as a solid foundation in the ensemble. On top was the squeaky, carelessly tuned fiddle. Add the dry, "ra, raka, taka, tak" of the bones and the tambourine's dull thumps and

ceaseless jingling to the twang of the banjo and the flat tone of the fiddle, and the sound of the band is approximated: it was scratchy, tinkling, cackling, and humorously incongruous.[6]

The minstrel show held the public's attention in the large cities for some time before it was superseded by the early variety shows and musicals, but it was in the smaller cities and the rural towns that it found its real public. There it proved to have remarkable vitality and staying power, and well into this century minstrel troupes were still touring in rural America. There the coming of the minstrel show was as eagerly anticipated as the coming of the circus, with which it had a good deal in common. The troupe's arrival was signaled by the inevitable parade through town, winding up at the theater where the evening performance was to be given. At this performance the public's expectations of an evening of vivid and diverting entertainment were seldom disappointed; they laughed hard at the comic songs, repartee, conundrums, and grotesque antics of the end-men, and the skits and parodies that made up the second half of the show. But there also may have been some moist eyes in the crowd at the close of the sentimental songs, ranging from "Old Black Joe" and "My Old Kentucky Home" to such later (and less slave-oriented) songs as "She May Have Seen Better Days" or "Just Tell Them That You Saw Me."[7]

Dan Emmett

Daniel Decatur Emmett (1815–1904) was a pioneer performer in minstrelsy, and one of the most important composers and authors of its early folkish and rough-hewn material. Born in a small Ohio town just emerging from the backwoods, Emmett grew up in a frontier society similar to that in which Lincoln was raised, with all its virtues and vices—its examples of courage and fierce independence, its violence and prejudices, and, above all, its rough-and-ready humor. Dan Emmett learned the printing trade, and began making up verses to be sung to popular tunes, in accordance with a prevalent custom of the times. At eighteen he enlisted in the army, where he mastered the drum and fife. In the late 1830s he began appearing in circuses, singing and playing the drums, and later the banjo and the fiddle.

Blackface singing and dancing with banjo accompaniment was by this time common in the circus; of the four performers who formed the original Virginia Minstrels in New York City in 1843 (Dan Emmett, Frank Brower, William Whitlock, and Richard Pelham), at least three had had experience in touring circuses. The Virginia Minstrels, the first group to use the classic instrumentation discussed above (fiddle, banjo, tambourine, and bones), and the first to put together a whole evening of minstrel music, dancing, and skits, caught on with both public and press in New York and Boston. A tour of the British Isles later that same year (1843) was less successful, and it was there that the original company broke up. But the popularity of this entertainment in the United States was so great that many imitators and competitors soon appeared—E. P. Christy and his troupe among them. Emmett, upon his return to this country in 1844, soon reestablished himself as an "Ethiopian" performer, working in urban theaters in the winter and touring with circuses in the summer, until the middle 1850s, when he tried several theatrical ventures in the Midwest. He had meanwhile composed many songs, some of which had been published as early as 1843. Returning to New York in 1858, he worked with Bryant's Minstrels, by then the foremost minstrel troupe, until 1866—as performer and as composer-author of songs and skits, especially for the shows' finales, the "walk-arounds."

It was for Bryant's Minstrels that Dan Emmett wrote "Dixie" (full title, "I Wish I Was in Dixie's Land") in 1859. Perhaps the most phenomenally popular song of the nineteenth century, it was minstrelsy's greatest single legacy to American music. It soon acquired a significance entirely unintended and even resented by its composer, when it was adopted by the Confederacy at the outbreak of the Civil War.

After the war, as we shall see, minstrelsy lost much of its original flavor and character, becoming, as Nathan has said, "an efficient large-scale variety show which favored less and less the dry, tough humor of Emmett's texts and tunes and the primitive style of his performances."[8] With this development, Emmett's career in minstrelsy was virtually over; he went to live in Chicago, barely averting extreme poverty by working at various jobs, musical and otherwise. In the 1880s, the entertainment profession came to his aid, with various benefit performances and two touring engagements with minstrel companies, during which he appeared on the stage, usually to sing or fiddle "Dixie" to tumultuous applause. In 1888 he returned to the town of his birth—Mount Vernon, Ohio—where, except for a "farewell tour" in 1895, he lived simply until his death in 1904.

Stephen Foster and Minstrelsy

Stephen Collins Foster (1826–64) will be considered more fully in the next chapter, in connection with American popular song. But since he was minstrelsy's best-known composer, it is in this connection that we make his acquaintance here. He was not, like Emmett, a minstrel performer himself, but in 1845 he began writing "Ethiopian songs" at first for the enjoyment of a group of friends. In Cincinnati he met a member of a professional minstrel troupe (the Sable Harmonists) who introduced his "Old Uncle Ned" in one of their programs. In 1848 he wrote "Oh! Susanna," selling it outright to a Pittsburgh publisher for $100. It became enormously popular. The next year he signed a contract with the leading New York publisher, First, Pond & Co., and committed himself to a songwriting career. In 1852 he made a brief steamboat trip down the Ohio and Mississippi to New Orleans—his only visit to the South.

While Foster's minstrel songs represent only a portion of his output, they represent, with few exceptions, his best. His minstrel songs belong to the two types then common: the fast tunes, often comic ("The Glendy Burke," "Camptown Races," "Nelly Bly," and of course "Oh! Susanna"), and the slow, sentimental songs ("Massa's in de Cold Ground," "My Old Kentucky Home," "Old Black Joe," and "Old Folks at Home"). The dialect so typical of minstrel material was used in Foster's early songs ("My Brudder Gum," "Ring de Banjo"), but he dropped this mannerism in his later songs, rightly thinking that it would restrict the universality of their appeal.

Zenith and Decline

The minstrel show reached its zenith in the years just prior to the Civil War. After that it began to lose its original flavor; with larger bands and casts and more varied fare, it increasingly resembled the variety show, which indeed did replace the minstrel show almost completely in New York in the 1860s. But the latter continued strong in smaller centers of population, as we have noted. After the Civil War, Negro musicians and entertainers themselves began to participate, and all-black minstrel companies toured for another half-century or so. Minstrelsy thus became both a training ground and a source of employment for many black musicians who later branched out in the direction of blues or jazz. W. C. Handy was one, as was "Ma" Rainey, who toured widely in the South with various minstrel shows and circuses in the first two decades of this century. Other jazz figures who played for a time in minstrel bands include Bunk Johnson, Lester Young, and Jelly Roll Morton.[9]

After the Civil War, blackface comedy done mostly by white performers continued to entertain audiences outside of the format of the minstrel show itself. Blackface acts, modeled after minstrel songs, dances, and skits, were a staple of vaudeville after the decline of genuine minstrelsy; according to one authority, a majority of the acts in vaudeville in the 1880s were in fact blackface.[10] Black impersonations, of course, persisted right down through the first three or four decades of this century, through the heyday of singers like Al Jolson (1886–1950), and Eddie Cantor (1892–1964), who got their start in the last waning epoch of vaudeville.

But the majority of touring minstrel companies after the Civil War consisted of black performers. All-black troupes such as the Georgia Minstrels, the Original Black Diamonds (of Boston), Haverly's Genuine Colored Minstrels, and W. S. Cleveland's Colossal Colored Carnival Minstrels toured the United States, with occasional trips abroad, mostly to England, until the end of the century. Despite the (nominally) free status of blacks, and the drastically changed social and economic conditions in the South after the Civil War, the basic content and characterization of black people in postwar minstrel songs remained virtually the same as during slavery, with continued nostalgic references to idyllic plantation life—and these were performed, and often also composed, by blacks themselves. The songs of James Bland (1854–1911), the best-known black songwriter for the minstrel stage, are typical in this regard. "Oh, Dem Golden Slippers," "In the Evening by the Moonlight," and "Carry Me Back to Old Virginny"[11] were all composed about 1880; in terms of their characterization of black people and depiction of conditions in the South, they could have been written thirty years earlier. But the nostalgically clothed stereotype was what audiences continued to want to hear.

Less than a generation later, there were the beginnings of change. Around the turn of the century, performers such as the team of Bert Williams (1874–1922) and George Walker (ca. 1872–1911) black singers-comedians who also wore blackface makeup, helped to bring new standards of integrity to the stage portrayal of the black man. As George Walker said in 1906,

> The one hope of the colored performer must be in making a radical departure from the old "darkie" style of singing and dancing. . . . There is an artistic side to the

> black race, and if it could be properly developed on the stage, I believe the theatergoing public would profit much by it. . . . My idea was always to impersonate my race just as they are. The colored man has never successfully taken off his own humorous characteristics, and the white impersonator often overdoes the matter.[12]

Playing eventually in shows such as *In Dahomey* (1902) and *In Bandana Land* (1907), Williams and Walker were part of the first wave of black shows with black performers at the turn of the century—a development treated more fully later. The shadow of minstrelsy still lingers over some aspects of these shows, even as late as the 1921 *Shuffle Along* of Eubie Blake and Noble Sissle.[13]

Musical Characteristics and Contributions of the Minstrel Show

The instrumentation and sound of the early minstrel band have already been described in discussing its origins. The melodies of minstrelsy were very like those of the folk music of the time, except that they were almost exclusively in the major mode. Many of the earlier minstrel tunes, especially the lively ones (the walk-arounds and banjo tunes), are purely pentatonic, or nearly so.* They also tend to the repetition of short motives, usually a measure in length. Dan Emmett's "De Boatman's Dance," of 1843, illustrates both of these characteristics (Example 11–1).[14]

Minstrel tunes, like those of the march and the later ragtime, were almost invariably in duple meter. Their rhythm, especially that of the dances and banjo tunes, is of particular interest, because it bears an embryonic relationship to that of ragtime and jazz. The African-American elements in minstrel music, however diluted, constituted the only widely popular manifestation of these traits before ragtime and blues. In the minstrel show we find that the "buck and wing dance" and the later "cakewalk," especially, exhibited inherently jazzy rhythms. Directing our attention specifically to the banjo, we find that against the steady jingling of the tambourine and the probably constant beat of the performers' feet on the floor (effectively taking over the rule of the drums, which were lacking in early minstrel bands), the banjo player, judging from early printed versions of banjo tunes, must have been playing lively and often syncopated rhythms similar to those that would appear later in ragtime. A comparison of the rhythm of the opening measures of Scott Joplin's *Maple Leaf Rag* (1899) with that of a minstrel banjo tune by Dan Emmett, "Nigger on de Wood Pile" (1845),[15] shows this relationship, especially at the places where identical or nearly identical rhythmic figures are marked (Example 11–2).

Fortunately, at least one commendably authentic re-creation of the sounds, and a few of the songs, of the early minstrel show have been recorded, by Robert Winans and his collaborators,[16] so that our acquaintance with this rough-and-ready popular entertainment need not be based solely on verbal descriptions and on the printed music of the songs and banjo tunes. As for the songs themselves, we all know a great many: "Dixie," "Turkey in the Straw," "Oh! Susanna" (and many others by Foster), "Buffalo Gals" (and its descen-

* See Chapter 1, with Examples 1–6 and 1–7, for a discussion and illustrations of the pentatonic scale. The pentatonic nature of some of Stephen Foster's minstrel songs was alluded to there.

Example 11–1 DE BOATMAN'S DANCE

dant, "Dance with a Dolly"), "Jordan Is a Hard Road to Travel" (popular in early hillbilly music), "Oh, Dem Golden Slippers," and "Carry Me Back to Old Virginny." These and others give us the flavor of the minstrel legacy that has become woven into the common heritage of American song.

Other Musical Entertainments

Aside from the enormously popular minstrel show, the vernacular musical stage evolved but little between the gradual demise of the various forms related to the ballad opera and the rise of more sophisticated kinds of entertainment that began to attract a large public in New York immediately after the Civil War. The pantomime, with its stock *commedia dell'arte* characters, no longer flourished, although a French offshoot, the ballet-pantomime, held the stage in the 1830s and 1840s, most notably as performed by the Ravel family. Their presentations included, in addition to actual ballet, farces, rope-dances,

Example 11–2

Joplin (1899)

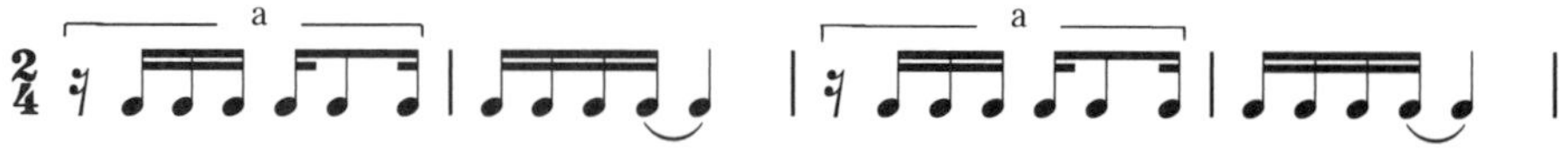

Emmett (1845)

Joplin

Emmett

gymnastics, comic pantomimes, and spectacles known as "tableaux vivants." The heterogeneous nature of the entertainment, with its obvious attempt to appeal to a broad range of tastes, was typical of the period. The extravaganza was based largely on spectacle, and was often topical. The traveling Ronzani troupe from Europe presented in New York an extravaganza titled "Novelty, with the Laying of the Atlantic Cable" in 1857. Another popular form was the burlesque, which then was a humorous and satirical parody on a well-known play or story. A burlesque on Shakespeare's *Hamlet* appeared in 1828; the first on an American subject was *Pocahontas* in 1855, followed the next year by a sequel, *Hiawatha*. (Only after the Civil War did the term gradually shift in meaning, to that of a show whose essential attraction was the display of the female form.)

The blackface minstrel show actually appropriated many of the elements of pantomime, farce, extravaganza (in its more lavish productions), and especially (in its original sense) burlesque. Surviving texts show that minstrelsy was full of satirical parodies of other stage forms. If the upper classes patronized Italian and French opera and scorned the minstrel show as lowbrow and vulgar entertainment, the minstrels in their turn made fun of these elite forms, in pointed satire.*

* *La Belle L.N.* and *Grand Dutch S.* were minstrel parodies of well-known Offenbach comic operas, as was pointed out by Deane Root and John Graziano. See *The New Grove Dictionary of American Music*, vol. 1, p. 327.

From the Civil War Through the Turn of the Century

Immediately after the searing and costly War between the States, the popular musical stage entered a period of exuberant growth, characterized by foreign importation, outright imitation, and native experimentation. A new and energetic era was beginning—with great leaps in industry and transportation, and the heterogeneous, enriching inflow of immigrants. Above all, the cities grew, and with them the wealth and expectations of all but the poorest of their inhabitants. In an era of affluence and expansion the public was in the market for—and got—new theatrical diversions.

The New York Stage in the 1860s

New York City's dominance as America's entertainment capital was well established by the mid-nineteenth century. It was the first stop for touring artists and companies from Europe, and the magnet toward which all native talent was drawn. For a century and a half the most diverse of American cities, it has been, if not always the *originator*, certainly the great *assimilator* of culture—and the ultimate testing ground and marketplace for innovations from everywhere else in the country. Talent and ideas can come from anywhere, but in musical theater it has been New York that has set the fashions.

Let us pay our respects to *The Black Crook*, a heterogeneous extravaganza that is unfailingly mentioned as the precursor of the American musical. Produced in 1866 in Niblo's Garden, the best-appointed theater in New York, with its stage completely rebuilt for the occasion, the original production lasted five and a half hours, and was a spectacle lavish beyond anything that had been seen previously. Its thin, derivative melodramatic plot was overwhelmed by huge ensemble numbers, costumes, extremely elaborate scenic effects and changes, and, as a significant ingredient, the dancing of no fewer than two hundred French ballet dancers in "immodest dress . . . the flesh-colored tights, imitating nature so well that the illusion is complete. . . arms and neck apparently bare, and bodice so cut as to show off every inch and outline of the body above the waist," as reported by one disapproving clergyman.* As Cecil Smith adds, after quoting this report: "This description, if widely circulated, must have been a source of incalculable satisfaction to Wheatley [the producer] and his partners."[17] For in fact *The Black Crook*, running for sixteen months and grossing more than a million dollars, became an American institution; it toured extensively and was revived eight times in New York. In the twentieth century it was revived as late as 1929, and subsequently the cir-

* The lore of *The Black Crook* includes the attractive legend that the French dancing girls were part of a ballet troupe that was stranded here when the Academy of Music, in which they were originally brought over to appear, burned down before their performance, and that the producer of *The Black Crook*, fortuitously seizing the opportunity to put them in his show, thereby added a subsequently essential ingredient to musical comedy by accident. Deane Root and Stanley Green have shown this to be an apocryphal embellishment; the French troupe was brought here solely to appear in *The Black Crook*—three months after the Academy burned. See notes to the LP, *"I Wants to Be a Actor Lady,"* which includes two excerpts from later productions of this legendary show.

cumstances of its origin became the basis for Sigmund Romberg's last musical (unfortunately not successful), *The Girl in Pink Tights* (1954).

The Black Crook has been called the starting point of American musical comedy. But this is inaccurate, for, as Cecil Smith has pointed out, real musical comedy was not to appear for another generation, and *The Black Crook*, with its dated plot and its emphasis on stage spectacle, looked more to the past than to the future.[18] None of its ingredients were new, nor did any *one* of them—the ballet, the glorification of the female figure, the spectacular staging—prove to be an indispensable ingredient of the later musical, though all of them reappear consistently as elements. What was new was not only their combination but the prodigally lavish scale of the production (said to have cost more than $35,000, a record, and an astounding outlay for the time), and the fact that its long run (474 performances) established a new pattern that subsequent producers aimed to duplicate. It was the first real Broadway "hit."

After the impetus of *The Black Crook*, the New York stage became the arena for continued experiment on a new scale. Imports were periodically popular. Old concepts—such as the pantomime, the burlesque (with its "trousers" roles as a convenient institution for getting the female figure onstage in tights), and the extravaganza—were refurbished and combined in new ways. One form emerged that was to become a prominent and typically American entertainment for half a century—vaudeville. Its antecedents were to be found in the minstrel theater, the English music hall, and, more immediately, the lowbrow entertainments offered in beer halls and saloons to which the name "burlesque" had come to be applied. But in the 1880s Tony Pastor, called the "father" of vaudeville, successfully turned it into clean, family entertainment. Vaudeville typically was a succession of individual acts, including dancers, acrobats, jugglers, magicians, and animal acts, usually headlined by a well-known comedian or singer.

After the turn of the century booking agencies made vaudeville acts available to thousands of theaters throughout the country. Vaudeville was at its most flourishing stage in the first two decades of this century; as it waned, it tended to merge with those forms that were replacing it. Live vaudeville acts shared the evenings with films in the larger theaters, and many vaudeville performers found themselves in demand to fill the considerable "on air" time of the new media—radio in the 1930s, and television in the 1950s. Vaudeville is an interesting component of the American entertainment scene partly for the great number of performers who began their careers on its stages, and who subsequently became well known—even stars—on the Broadway stage, in radio, in films, and on television. Among these were Lillian Russell, Sophie Tucker, George M. Cohan, Al Jolson, Eddie Cantor, Jimmy Durante, Ed Wynn, Jack Benny, and the durable George Burns.[19] As to the role of music in vaudeville, it occupied much the same necessary but ephemeral and anonymous position that it had in the eighteenth-century theatrical productions that were examined in the previous chapter. John Graziano has said that while "music was central to the success of a vaudeville show, its originality was not a paramount consideration."[20] Unlike the minstrel show, vaudeville in and of itself left us no discernible body of music; many of the songs heard on its stages will be considered in the next chapter.

Importations from London, Paris, and Vienna

The American popular stage languished musically until the importation of comic opera of exceptionally high quality from London, Paris, and Vienna beginning in the last quarter of the century. This may be regarded as a mixed blessing, of course, depending upon one's viewpoint. Possibly it delayed the development of a truly indigenous popular musical theater; certainly it imprinted on the American musical a European stamp that was still visible (in some quarters) well into the twentieth century. But at the same time it introduced new standards of quality to the popular stage—quality of both ideas and craftsmanship, without which the American musical could never have reached its own level of competence and sophistication so soon.

W. S. Gilbert and Arthur Sullivan in London, Jacques Offenbach in Paris, Johann Strauss, Jr., in Vienna—each of these represented a peak of achievement in English, French, and German comic opera, all coming at about the same time. It was an unprecedented era of concentrated brilliance, which was bound to cast a few beams on this side of the Atlantic as well.

As far as the general public was concerned, the London "invasion" came first; *H.M.S. Pinafore* was heard (in a stolen version) in Boston in 1878, and became prodigiously popular at once. (The dismal story of the way Gilbert and Sullivan's comic operas were pirated here reflects little credit on the status of international copyright agreements or the ethics of American theatrical producers.) After *Pinafore*, there followed in short order *The Pirates of Penzance* (premiered in New York by the author's own company, to protect their rights), and then *Iolanthe*, *The Sorcerer*, and *Princess Ida*, climaxed by the phenomenal success of *The Mikado* in 1885. Well-knit comic plots, songs that grow naturally out of comic or romantic situations on the stage, well-crafted lyrics that make their points deftly, and memorable tunes that still never get in the way of the lyrics—these are some of the qualities that have made Gilbert and Sullivan continuously popular on both sides of the Atlantic for a century and more. Furthermore, as both consumers and producers here recognized at once, these were precisely the qualities that musical comedy needed and had been lacking. It is not that musical comedy was henceforth to evolve precisely along the rather stylized lines of Gilbert and Sullivan; literal imitation, particularly of a foreign genre, is a peculiarly futile artistic exercise. But a new example of superior craftsmanship had been shown, and it was to help usher in a new era of competence on the American musical stage.

Both French *opéra bouffe* and Viennese operetta had been known in the United States in the 1860s and 1870s, but for the most part in their original languages and therefore not accessible to wide audiences. (Both Johann Strauss, Jr., and Offenbach had visited America in the 1870s, primarily as orchestral conductors.) The new popularity of English comic opera created a popular audience for other European light operas as well, and many were presented in English translations.*

* In order not to leave the reader with too simple a picture of the tastes of the time, however, it is necessary to note that the works of Richard Genée and François Chassaigne were more popular at the time than those of their respective countrymen, Strauss and Offenbach. In any era, the siftings of public taste require time.

After a lull in the nineties, Viennese operetta again enjoyed a great period of popularity here with the advent of *The Merry Widow* by Franz Lehar in 1907, and *The Chocolate Soldier* by Oskar Straus in 1909. A host of operettas more or less on the Viennese model were subsequently produced by our immigrant composers, as we shall see. Vienna itself, and the atmosphere of the Viennese operetta, still haunts the American musical stage from time to time; in 1934, for example, there appeared a show ostensibly about the Johann Strausses, senior and junior, with a musical score from their waltzes and the appropriate title *The Great Waltz*.

The Americanization of the Musical

While these foreign importations were enjoying their popularity, there was gradually emerging a more native kind of musical show. The Harrigan and Hart comedies of the period represented an important early step toward the Americanization of the musical. These plays with interpolated songs were the first to discover New York itself as a promising setting for a musical, and thus tap a vein that from *The Belle of New York* to *Wonderful Town* has yielded attractive pay dirt. Portraying with accuracy and humor the Irish, the blacks, and the Germans in believable comic situations growing out of the everyday lives of everyday people, they were an immediate success. The first was *The Mulligan Guard Ball* (1879), and this was followed by many Mulligan Guard sequels with the same characters, much in the manner of a television situation-comedy series. The songs, all by David Braham (1834–1905), a London-born musician who came here at the age of fifteen, became popular at the time in their own right and were sometimes borrowed for other shows. Some songs, such as "The Widow Nolan's Goat" from *Squatters' Sovereignty*, brought a true Irish folk flavor to the musical stage.[21]

The movement toward the Americanization of the musical comedy of this period culminated in the shows and songs of George M. Cohan (1878–1942), an energetic and ambitious showman who came up from vaudeville to become an author, composer, stage director, and performer who well-nigh dominated the musical stage in the first two decades of this century. In describing Cohan, the one word inevitably used by writers is "brash." The directness of his style, his informality, and above all his fast pace (Heywood Broun described him as "a disciple of perpetual motion") brought new vitality to the theater. Cohan was right for his time, and fittingly marked the last stage in the adolescence of our popular musical theater, sounding a decisive note of independence from Europe. His three most important and characteristic shows came early in the century: *Little Johnny Jones* in 1904, and *Forty-five Minutes from Broadway* and *George Washington, Jr.*, in 1906. (*The Little Millionaire*, the last of this genre, came in 1911.) Of the first three, each has its American hero (a jockey, a reformed gambler, a young super-patriot), and the three shows together contain the best of Cohan's show tunes.

Cohan could write a good moderate-tempo tune (e.g., "Mary's a Good Old Name," with its echoes of ragtime and barbershop harmony) and an American-sounding waltz ("Forty-five Minutes from Broadway"), but his most characteristic songs were his snappy up-tempo show tunes, in which he invariably made the most of the kind of rudimentary syncopation found in the chorus of

"Dixie" (e.g., "Give My Regards to Broadway," "Yankee Doodle Boy," "You're a Grand Old Flag," and one of his few non-show songs, "Over There," the most popular song to emerge from World War I). His lyrics could be good, or at times appallingly inept, yet he could come up with a surefire catch-phrase, and much of the effectiveness of his songs is due to his ability to find just the right musical setting for those phrases, which were often the titles as well: "Give my regards to Broadway"; "You're a grand old flag"; "Over there"; "So long, Mary"; "I was born in Virginia" (this last was the closest in rhythm to ragtime that Cohan got). Cohan's quotations from other songs ("Yankee Doodle," "Dixie," "The Girl I Left Behind Me," "The Star-Spangled Banner," "Marching Through Georgia," "Auld Lang Syne") were an odd but characteristic quirk in his patriotic numbers.

George M. Cohan was a phenomenal success in his day, but given his limitations it was inevitable that his material, his approach, and even his songs should become dated, and the American musical theater passed him by in the 1920s. He continued his career as an actor; he was a success in *Ah! Wilderness*, and was cast as President Franklin D. Roosevelt in the musical *I'd Rather Be Right*. Before his death, his career was dramatized on the screen in *Yankee Doodle Dandy*, with James Cagney, and his music was recently back on Broadway in the nostalgic reconstruction *George M!* (1968).[22]

The First Half of the Twentieth Century

We now approach the period of greatest success, influence, and achievement for the American popular musical stage—the time when it played its most significant role, not only as a medium for entertainment, but as an expression of, and contribution to, American life and culture for the broadest range of American people. Allowing a few years' extension at either end, this period coincided roughly with the first half of the twentieth century. It was a period of variety as well as vitality; we shall now take up several of its aspects in turn, leading finally to the consideration of the American musical in its most mature and significant phase.

Black Musicians on Broadway: The Emergence from Minstrelsy

Late in the nineteenth century it began to be apparent that the contributions of black musicians to America's popular musical stage need not—in fact *could* not—be forever limited to the caricatured renditions of the minstrel stage. (The minstrel show was by the end of the century more the province of blacks than of whites as performers, but the stereotypes remained the same.) Change, however, was painfully slow, as we shall see.

It should be clear that there were two aspects to the contributions of black musicians. The first was the talent that black professional writers and composers placed at the service of prevalent white theatrical styles; the second was the infusion of styles that were essentially of black origin into the music of the popular stage—at first ragtime, later blues and jazz, and ultimately rhythm-and-blues. The first kind of black participation has gone on more or less continuously since the turn of the century. For example, Robert Cole (1863–1911) and the brothers J. Rosamund Johnson (1873–1954) and James Weldon Johnson (1871–1938) were professional songwriters for the Broadway stage around 1900; their song "The Maid with the Dreamy Eyes," for instance, was written especially for Anna Held in *The Little Duchess* of 1901.[23] Later, Noble Sissle (1889–1975) and Eubie Blake (1883–1983) wrote "You Were Meant for Me" for Gertrude Lawrence and Noel Coward.

As for the infusion of musical elements of African-American origin, ragtime had reached Broadway in the 1890s; or actually it is more accurate to say that attenuated whiffs of ragtime reached Broadway, in the form of ragtime songs. Songs of this type were "Mister Johnson, Turn Me Loose," by the white ragtime composer and sometime minstrel performer Ben Harney, and "All Coons Look Alike to Me," by the black songwriter Ernest Hogan. Both songs were incorporated into *Courted into Court* in 1896 by May Irwin, a popular white singing comedienne who was famous for her renditions of "coon songs."[24] The ragtime song soon became disreputable (Hogan suffered acutely for his contribution, mostly on account of its title, during his lifetime), but it was the form in which at least the flavor of ragtime was first brought to the predominantly white audiences of the time, even before the appearance of shows such as *Clorindy*. Outside the theater, songs by both black and white composers showing similar ragtime influence were making their way on Tin Pan Alley, as we shall see in the next chapter.

What of the appearance of black artists on the Broadway stage itself? The great difficulty these performers faced, as we have noted, was the image of the minstrel show, which cast a long shadow. Harrigan and Hart pioneered as early as 1883 in using a group of black dancers in one of the last of their white comedies, *Cordelia's Aspirations*, but the title of their number, "Sam Johnson's Cakewalk," suggests strong minstrel influence still. An important step was the appearance in the 1890s of shows featuring beautiful black women (*The Creole Show*, 1890; *The Octoroons*, 1895). *Oriental America* (1896) was the first Broadway show with an all-black cast, and it broke significantly with minstrel tradition.

Two important landmarks came in 1898. Robert Cole produced the first full-length all-black musical show, *A Trip to Coontown*. But more successful and memorable was an all-black musical comedy sketch, *Clorindy, the Origin of the Cakewalk*, with music by the talented and thoroughly trained musician Will Marion Cook (1869–1944). This show, with its characteristic music, dancing, and choral singing, created a sensation and opened the doors for black music and musicians on the Broadway stage, performing for predominantly white audiences. The first wave of black musicals followed. Will Marion Cook himself wrote a succession of shows; the next three were unsuccessful, but *In Dahomey* (1902), satirizing the scheme to colonize American blacks in Africa; *In Abyssinia* (1906), an extravaganza laid in Africa; and *In Bandana Land* (1908), set in the American South, were all hits.[25] The team of Cole and the Johnson brothers (already mentioned) wrote two musicals, *The Shoo-Fly Regiment* (1906) and *The Red Moon* (1908), and J. Rosamund Johnson wrote the music for *Mr. Lode of Koal* (or Kole), of 1909. Thus the first period of activity of the black musical lasted for a decade.

After a lull during the second decade of this century, a second era of black musical shows was inaugurated in 1921 by the famous *Shuffle Along*, with lyrics by Noble Sissle and music by Eubie Blake. It was essentially a revue. Some of its fast numbers (of which "I'm Just Wild About Harry" was the most famous) are imbued with the ebullient but easygoing momentum of ragtime and early jazz; some (such as "Bandana Days") are almost pure George M. Cohan. Of its slow songs, some are in the style of the standard sentimental show tune ("Love Will Find a Way"), which the authors feared, needlessly, might not be accepted by a white audience from black singing actors; other slow tunes are close to the blues ("Daddy, Won't You Please Come Home"). A recent reconstruction of some of the show's numbers from contemporary recordings shows that the instrumental playing gave a fairly authentic flavor of ragtime and early jazz, while the singing represented the kind of compromise with currently popular show singing that attenuated its own essential qualities.[26] This hybridization of styles is especially noticeable in the blues numbers, and is also a mark of the first actual blues recordings made about the same time, which were sung by show singers and not blues singers.

Shuffle Along brought together some distinguished black talent. In addition to Sissle as singer and Blake as both pianist and orchestra leader, Josephine Baker, Florence Mills, and Paul Robeson sang; in the orchestra pit, Hall Johnson played the viola and William Grant Still the oboe. The show is credited with helping to initiate the Harlem Renaissance of the 1920s—a period of unprecedented cultural activity and rising intellectual and artistic self-esteem among American urban blacks. From that time until the Depression many all-black shows played Broadway. Blake and Sissle wrote three more, and among others of note were *Keep Shuffling* (1928) and *Hot Chocolates* (1929), with music by Thomas "Fats" Waller (1904–1943).

Shows for all-black casts were written by whites as well; *Blackbirds of 1928*, with music by Jimmy McHugh (which included "I Can't Give You Anything but Love, Baby"), introduced the tap dancer Bill "Bojangles" Robinson to the Broadway stage. Later Oscar Hammerstein II brought out a very successful adaptation from the realm of classical opera (Bizet's *Carmen*) in the all-black *Carmen Jones* (1943). And this is perhaps the place to mention the fact that two important American operas appearing in the 1930s had all-black casts: Virgil Thomson's *Four Saints in Three Acts* (1934), and (except for one small part for a white man) George Gershwin's *Porgy and Bess* (1935).

A more recent black idiom, rhythm-and-blues, was brought to Broadway in a lavishly staged black adaptation of a classic (*The Wizard of Oz*) called *The Wiz* (1975).

Operetta, and Three Immigrant Composers

Building on the basic style, form, and approach of operetta, three immigrant composers brought a consistently high level of competence to the popular musical stage. During the forty years from Victor Herbert's first success, *The Wizard of the Nile* (1895), to Sigmund Romberg's last Viennese piece, *May Wine* (1935), there was hardly a time when there was not an American operetta on the Broadway stage. What were the distinguishing features of the operetta? After briefly tracing this adopted form through its generation of popularity, we shall perhaps arrive at a rough-and-ready description that will differentiate it from the other types of shows competing for the public's attention.

Its three great American exponents were Victor Herbert, Rudolf Friml, and Sigmund Romberg. All three were European-born, and all received there a thorough musical training (though Romberg's was more practical than formal, gained by hanging around the very epicenter of German-language operetta, the Theater-an-der-Wien in Vienna). All came to America, thus fully trained and equipped, in their twenties. Although there is no question that they fully adopted and were adopted by America, and that their work belongs in any account of American music, it nevertheless remained basically European in style and approach, in contrast with the work of Cohan, Berlin, Gershwin, and Rodgers.[27]

Victor Herbert (1859–1924) had the broadest musical experience and competence of the three, with a versatility seldom encountered. He was a virtuoso cellist (premiering two cello concertos of his own composition here), a symphony conductor (of the Pittsburgh Symphony for five seasons), a bandmaster, and a composer of symphonic music and opera. He entered the field of the popular musical show at the relatively late age of thirty-five, but once in, he knew that the theater was his métier. He was extraordinarily facile; the shows that he wrote or contributed music to number in the dozens. With his thorough knowledge of the orchestra, he was one of the first popular composers to write his own orchestrations, thus improving enormously the quality of the sounds that emanated from the orchestra pit and bringing new high standards to this craft.

Herbert continued to write musicals right up until his death, but his major contributions were made in the two decades between *The Wizard of the Nile* (1895) and *Eileen* (1917), and included *The Fortune Teller* (1898), *Babes in Toyland* (1903), *Mlle. Modiste* (1905), *The Red Mill* (1906), *Naughty Marietta* (1910), and *Sweethearts* (1913). In addition to his gift for producing a memorable melody (surely a sine qua non in the business, in any period but the most moribund), Herbert's virtuosity as a composer enabled him to handle ensemble and choral scenes (e.g., the opening scene of *Naughty Marietta*, with its street cries) with a skill and inventiveness heretofore associated only with opera. He could produce telling variations (as in the theme piece in *The Serenade*) and stylistic parodies (his extended number "If I Were on the Stage" from *Mlle. Modiste* contains an evocation of *Die Fledermaus*, a polonaise, and one of his most famous waltzes, "Kiss Me Again").[28] He could produce a rousing march ("Tramp, Tramp, Tramp," in *Naughty Marietta*) or an authentic-sounding Hungarian czardas ("Romany Life," in *The Fortune Teller*). In short, the musical stage had in Victor Herbert a gifted, competent, and prolific composer.

Rudolf Friml (1879–1972), born in Prague, was another thoroughly schooled musician, who was in his early years a concert pianist. His range was somewhat narrower, but between 1912 (*The Firefly*) and 1928 (*The Three Musketeers*) he produced some enduring operettas, including *Rose Marie* (1924) and *The Vagabond King* (1925).

Sigmund Romberg (1887–1951) was more versatile than Friml. He identified himself completely with the popular musical theater, writing music for numerous revues for the Shuberts and others, including annual "editions" of

The Passing Show between 1914 and 1924. But his forte was operetta, with a pronounced Viennese flavor, and his main contributions were *Maytime* (1917), *The Student Prince* (1924), *The Desert Song* (1926), *The New Moon* (1928), and *May Wine* (1935).

From the major works of these three composers, we can arrive at a working definition of that form so popular in America from the Gay Nineties to the Depression—the operetta, or "light opera." Its setting was exotic, belonging to another place and time: perhaps Vienna itself (Romberg's *The Blue Paradise, Blossom Time,* or *May Wine*) or Heidelberg (Romberg's *The Student Prince*) or Hungary (Herbert's *The Fortune Teller*), but Paris would do (Herbert's *Mlle. Modiste,* or, in a late medieval setting, Friml's *The Vagabond King*). A New World setting could be made to work, if it was remote enough from the urban or rural humdrum in place and time. Eighteenth-century New Orleans was ideal (Herbert's *Naughty Marietta* and Romberg's *The New Moon*). The Canadian Rockies was a daring departure, but with Friml's *Rose Marie* it succeeded (a near-duplicate setting, the Colorado Rockies, was chosen for a witty but slight satire of the genre in Rick Besoyan's *Little Mary Sunshine,* 1959). Romberg's late treatment of a New York setting (*Up in Central Park*) dealt, characteristically, with a time remote enough to be romanticized (the 1870s era of Boss Tweed) and given an appropriate Currier and Ives atmosphere.

The characters often included royalty or nobility, frequently incognito (*Mlle. Modiste, The New Moon, Sweethearts*), but gypsies, brigands, and opera singers were favorites. The plot usually involved either concealed identity or concealed fortune (*The Red Mill, Naughty Marietta, The Student Prince, The Desert Song*), and the hoary theatrical device of look-alikes was employed (*The Fortune Teller, It Happened in Nordland*).

The music was tuneful, often memorably so, and showed a craftsmanship far better than average. Like its Viennese counterpart, it placed its greatest faith in its waltzes, which really epitomized the genre, and we could do worse than to close our brief survey of a form once so popular with a litany of a few of its greatest waltzes, of which nearly every show had at least one: "The Absinthe Frappé" (Herbert's *It Happened In Nordland*); "Kiss Me Again" (Herbert's *Mlle. Modiste*); "The Streets of New York" (Herbert's *The Red Mill*); "I'm Falling in Love with Someone" (Herbert's *Naughty Marietta*); "Sympathy" (Friml's *The Firefly*); "Will You Remember?" known also as "Sweetheart Waltz" (Romberg's *Maytime*).

The Revue from the Gay Nineties to the Advent of Television

Thriving during the same period as the operetta was an even lighter form of entertainment, usually associated with the late spring or summer portion of the season, which could name among its humbler ancestors, if it chose, the olio, the minstrel show, and vaudeville, and among its more sophisticated and risqué the type of Parisian show from which it took its generic name—the *revue.* The "trade" names were many: "passing show," "follies," "scandals," "vanities." It was a succession of single acts, usually lacking even a pretense of dramatic thread or interest. Into it went the ancient elements of song-and-dance, burlesque, spectacle, and of course the display of feminine beauty. Of such elements (except spectacle) vaudeville and the older burlesque had been constituted. But the revue, brought "uptown" from the vaudeville theaters, was produced with a lavishness and sophistication that made it appeal to the Broadway theater public. In short, it had "class." It concerns us in passing, only for the few good scores and songs to come out of this type of show, when gifted composers were called upon to write for it.

The revue as we know it began with *The Passing Show of 1894*, which was musically undistinguished but established the potential popularity of the genre. The pattern of shows with yearly editions was begun in 1907 with the famous *Ziegfeld Follies*, which with few exceptions were produced each year by the great show business entrepreneur Florenz Ziegfeld, until his death in 1932. (Three more *Ziegfeld Follies* were produced after his death, the last in 1943.) The productions set new standards for opulence, for the beauty of the girls, and for the quality of talent presented, a roster of which reads like a list of the greats of the entertainment world during the generation the shows encompassed: Anna Held (Ziegfeld's first wife), Fanny Brice, Sophie Tucker, W. C. Fields, Will Rogers, Eddie Cantor, Ed Wynn. Both Victor Herbert and Irving Berlin provided music on occasion; songs to come out of the *Ziegfeld Follies* included "Shine On, Harvest Moon" (1908) and Irving Berlin's "A Pretty Girl Is Like a Melody" (1919), which, like many of the hit songs in these shows, was made into a lavish production number.

Ziegfeld's main competition was *The Passing Show* (reviving the title of the prototype of the form), whose editions ran from 1912 through 1924—for the last ten years with music by Sigmund Romberg. Its 1918 version introduced Fred and Adele Astaire, and two songs, "Smiles" and "I'm Forever Blowing Bubbles," that were not by Romberg. *George White's Scandals* ran from 1919 to 1939; these are worthy of note mostly because George Gershwin wrote all the music for the five shows of 1920–24, including "Somebody Loves Me." Irving Berlin's *Music Box Revues*, 1921–24, brought out his "Say It with Music."

The revue furnished a welcome pattern for the musicals that, as we shall see, were in demand as soon as sound was added to motion pictures. The form continues to exist, and many "book" shows (that is, musical comedies with ostensible plots) continue to be only one small step away from the revue (*Hair*, for example, in 1968), as indeed many always have been, with a continual freshening of topical material. But the heyday of the extravaganza type of revue ended with World War II. Changing tastes, and television spectaculars reaching millions instead of the stage show's thousands, are two factors in its decline.[29]

The Musical in Its Maturity: Show Boat *to* West Side Story

The musical show had its period of greatest achievement in the thirty years that began with *Show Boat* (1927) and ended with *West Side Story* (1957). (By the time *Pal Joey* came along, midway between those two, the term "musical *comedy*" was no longer appropriate.) Naturally allowance must be made for the risks of trying to define an era precisely, but the point is that during this time the musical had set itself new musical-dramatic problems, and had solved them, without ceasing to captivate and entertain its audience. *Carousel*,

Kiss Me, Kate, Guys and Dolls, and *My Fair Lady* came very close to perfection in the form. It was a period of sustained creation by major writers devoting their talents principally to the live musical stage, and it was, moreover, a period when the popular stage still had its audience. Broadway was in a clear position of leadership, and supplied America (and much of the world) with its best popular music.

Show Boat, long an acknowledged landmark, marks a fairly clear beginning of the era. Operetta had had its last spurt of great productions in the year or two previous. Jerome Kern, a veteran at forty-two, had been writing for Broadway for nearly a quarter-century; but this was clearly a new departure, and it set its sights on new territory for the musical to explore. The end of the era is more difficult to establish precisely, but by the time of *West Side Story* the new ground that the musical had staked out had been rather thoroughly cultivated, and the work of the major writers and teams that had given their stamp to the period was concluded, or nearly so; the two subsequent and last collaborations of Richard Rodgers and Oscar Hammerstein II (*Flower Drum Song*, 1958, and *The Sound of Music*, 1959), and the last collaboration of Frederick Loewe and Alan Jay Lerner (*Camelot*, 1960), while successful, were by no means their best. New creators, new types of shows, and new patterns of entertainment were on the way.

A glance at the thirty years under consideration reveals the domination of five superbly equipped and successful composers: Jerome Kern (1885–1945), Irving Berlin (1888–1989), George Gershwin (1898–1937), Richard Rodgers (1902–79), and Cole Porter (1891–1964), each of whom wrote music for a least a dozen shows (of which some fall outside the limits of our period). Four others also made important contributions: Kurt Weill (1900–50), and near the end of the period, Frederick Loewe (1901–88), Frank Loesser (1910–69), and Leonard Bernstein (b. 1918). During these thirty years, only one year passed without the appearance of a new show by at least one of these nine composers; in most years there were two or three. Their shows and the best-known of their hundreds of songs are so familiar that a mere listing would be pointless. It will be more profitable here to consider certain aspects of the musical itself—areas in which innovation and evolution occurred during its era of greatest achievement.

The evolution of dramatic values

During this period there was a great widening and deepening of the dramatic dimensions of the musical—a gain in both range and verisimilitude, without compromising the musical's essential nature as entertainment. Subject matter, plot, characterization, and range of emotion were all broadened. A brief look at eleven shows of the era should substantiate this.

Show Boat (1927: music by Jerome Kern, books and lyrics by Oscar Hammerstein II), our point of departure, clearly stood out as being of more substantial stuff, dramatically, than its forebears. Adapted from Edna Ferber's novel, it put real characters in valid situations—Magnolia, the sheltered daughter of the Mississippi show boat's owner, who survives a broken marriage with a riverboat gambler to make her way to the top as a musical comedy star; the half-caste Julie, singing two love songs that shattered the conventional sentimental mold, "Can't Help Lovin' Dat Man" and "Bill" ("an ordinary boy"). Also worthy of note was the realistic and sympathetic portrayal of blacks on the stage—in this case, as stevedores on the levee. "Old Man River" is not, and should not be confused with, a real African-American song, but it is a superb theatrical song, right in its context.

Gershwin's *Porgy and Bess* (1935) had impressive dramatic dimensions, but since it was a venture into the realm of opera itself, it will be considered as such in Chapter 16. Apart from this, satire and social comment absorbed a good deal of the musical theater's energies in the 1930s. After this preoccupation (which will be dealt with below), the musical made new dramatic strides in the 1940s.

Pal Joey (1940: music by Richard Rodgers, lyrics by Lorenz Hart, book by John O'Hara) was again of real dramatic substance, based on O'Hara's stories, which the author himself had suggested as a framework for a musical. It is strongest in characterization: the hero is a crass, selfish opportunist, finally abandoned by the two women who have, each in her own way, been used by him. The shoddy nightclub milieu of Chicago marked a new venture into the seamier aspects of realism. Vera's unsentimental love song to a heel, "Bewitched, Bothered, and Bewildered," which gained musical force through a characteristic Rodgers device of the almost obsessive development of a small melodic motive, carried its dramatic theme a step further than had Julie's two songs in *Show Boat*. So novel for 1940 were the elements thus introduced into a Broadway musical that *Pal Joey* did not succeed with the public until its revival twelve years later.

Lady in the Dark (1941: music by Kurt Weill, lyrics by Ira Gershwin, book by Moss Hart) plunges us into the realm of psychosis and the dream fantasy. As foreign as this theme may seem to musical comedy, it was not new; Rodgers and Hart had explored it in 1926 in *Peggy-Ann*, and Romberg's *May Wine* (1935), with book by Frank Mandel based on a novel, dealt with a psychiatrist who was himself the victim of a delusion. But *Lady in the Dark* presents an almost clinical treatment of the subject, as the heroine, Liza, undergoes psychoanalysis. The dream sequences, more than mere surrealistic burlesque, have a genuine bearing on the heroine's problems, and the three men among whom she must choose are real, three-dimensional characters. The dramatic resolution is neatly paralleled by a musical one; the mysterious tune Liza remembers from childhood, which has haunted the play as a fragmentary motive, appears at the end, completed and harmonized, as "My Ship."

From the psychiatrist's couch to an Oklahoma cornfield on a summer morning—the musical show was ranging far. *Oklahoma!* (1943: music by Richard Rodgers, lyrics and book by Oscar Hammerstein II, based on a play by Lynn Riggs, *Green Grow the Lilacs*) broadened this range, and posed the problem of a sophisticated medium dealing with a folk subject and setting. The treatment was sympathetic and did not stoop to burlesque or caricature, nor did the music descend in sophistication to the imitation of folk music. "Oh, What a Beautiful Mornin'," for all the ingenuousness of its sentiments (sentiments basically foreign to folk music itself), is, melodically and harmonically, a quite sophisticated song. The plot has a classic design—two love triangles. The songs grow naturally out of the situations, which permit the introduction of a wide range of unconventional songs, from the refreshingly homely description of "The Surrey with the Fringe on Top" to the bizarre fantasy of "Pore Jud." Even the love song, "People Will Say We're in Love," has a fresh approach.

Carousel (1945: music by Richard Rodgers, lyrics and book by Oscar Hammerstein II, based on the play *Liliom* by the Hungarian playwright Ferenc Molnar) has elements of tragedy and symbolic fantasy, with a finale built on the age-old theme of redemption—heavy fare for a musical show. The hero is an outcast who must conceal his tenderness beneath a bullying, swaggering exterior. Thus he cannot, in life, communicate his love to Julie, nor can she to him—"*If* I loved you" is as much as they can ever say to one another. His suicide brings an opportunity for redemption; stealing a star that he gives to the daughter he has never seen in life, he conquers, for them both, the alienation that was threatening to warp her existence as it had his. Music has an ample role; the entire prelude is pantomimed to a carousel waltz, and there is a ballet-pantomime sequence in the second act.

In a period of such vitality and productivity, it was inevitable that some shows would be less successful in their attempts to extend the boundaries of the musical. *Allegro* (1947: music by Richard Rodgers, lyrics and book by Oscar Hammerstein II) was such a show. But even the relative failures of the period are interesting when they are inventive. The chorus, used effectively in the dream sequences of *Lady in the Dark*, has here a much more expanded role; it is used, in the words of the authors, "to interpret the mental and emotional reactions of the principal characters, after the manner of a Greek chorus." It has somewhat the role of the Stage Manager in Thornton Wilder's play *Our Town* of 1938, with which the first part of *Allegro* has some points in common. The life of the son of a small-town doctor, who also becomes a doctor, is traced from birth to the time when, fed up with the compromises, intrigues, and general vacuity of his lucrative city practice, he returns home to work with his father. But thirty-five years of biography is difficult to stage with dramatic intensity, even with characters more interesting and vividly drawn than Joseph Taylor, Jr., and Jenny Brinker.

Street Scene (1947: subtitled in the score "An American Opera," music by Kurt Weill, lyrics by Langston Hughes, book by Elmer Rice, based on his play of the same title) is a slice of New York City tenement life. The starkness of its story, compressed within less than twenty-four hours and seen from a single vantage point, gives it some of the aspects of Greek tragedy, fundamentally unrelieved. As its subtitle indicates, it is very close to opera. Music has a dominant role and is present most of the time, often underscoring dialogue and action, while the "songs" (some of which are subtitled "aria") emerge from a more or less continuous musical texture, instead of being set apart. Especially noteworthy are the ensembles. Duets and trios (fairly rare in the conventional musical) emerge naturally out of the dramatic context. The trio with Rose and her father and mother ("There'll Be Trouble") climaxes a scene that is operatic in conception and execution. Ensembles such as the Ice Cream Sextet (one of the few lighter moments) brought to the musical stage the unusual sound of a complex contrapuntal texture of interweaving voices.

Two more Rodgers and Hammerstein collaborations brought innovations in theme and setting. *South Pacific* (1949), one of the best-crafted musicals of the period, was able to deal in song with one of the play's basic themes, interracial marriage, in "You've Got to Be Taught" ("to hate and fear"). These virtuosos of the form were able next to execute the remarkable feat of bringing an exotic Oriental setting to the stage (*The King and I*, 1951) and treating it tastefully, without resorting either to crude spectacle or to caricature, and without subjecting the audience to imitations of Oriental music. They also showed the extent to which sentimental convention could be discarded by authors with sufficient talent and daring, in depicting a relationship between two principals in which the love interest is present only by muted implication. (Five years later the authors of *My Fair Lady*, an otherwise nearly perfect piece, felt obliged to make a concession to conventional sentimentality—even more persistent than "middle-class morality," it seems—in bringing Eliza back to Henry Higgins in a dénouement that is weak and unconvincing dramatically, and that George Bernard Shaw had specifically ruled out in the preface to a play written after his *Pygmalion*, on which *My Fair Lady* was based.)

The Most Happy Fella (1956; music, lyrics, and book by Frank Loesser, based on the play *The Knew What They Wanted* by Sidney Howard) explores new dramatic depths for the Broadway stage while retaining its idiom and approach. This is manifested in the growth we see in an older man—Tony, the wine grower—up to the point where he has the capacity to forgive the young Rosabella (whom he has wooed by mail and brought to be his bride) her infidelity. A pervading theme is that of loneliness seeking companionship. A full and rich score, with music present most of the time, emphasizes the characterization or furthers the action in a variety of forms, from recitative and song to large ensemble and choral numbers or instrumental interludes.

Satire and "social significance"

In the troubled political and economic climate of the 1930s, the theater did what it has always done in such times—it assumed the role of commentator, satirist, and gadfly. What was new was the fact that the musical show, hitherto the realm of entertainment, fantasy, and escape, began to get itself involved to an extent previously unknown. It is not that political satire had ever been completely absent from musical comedy, here or abroad, as a close look at Gilbert and Sullivan reveals. But it now became more pointed and overt. A trend was established, and the orbit of politics furnished a setting for shows from *Strike Up the Band* (1930) to *Louisiana Purchase* (1940).

The treatment given this theme represented a rather wide spectrum of approaches. Three shows by the team of George Gershwin (music), Ira Gershwin (lyrics), and George S. Kaufman and Morrie Ryskind (book) were brilliantly acidic and made use of outrageous fantasy. The first was *Strike Up the Band* (1930), followed by *Of Thee I Sing* (1931). The latter—with its right combination of the fantastic (a beauty contest to determine who is to be the new First Lady, "Miss White House"), good show songs, and genuinely humorous satire (the vice-president is such an anonymous figure that he cannot join the public library because he cannot produce two references)—was the most successful of the three, and the first musical to win the Pulitzer Prize. The third, *Let 'Em Eat Cake* (1933), not only suffered the disadvantages of being a sequel, but carried its fantasy to the extremes of revolution and dictatorship, and failed.

Two shows of this period had an even more conscious emphasis on "social significance." *Pins and Needles* (1937) was a very successful revue produced by the garment workers' union; an amateur show, with emphasis on overt propaganda, it was nevertheless very successful, and ran (with updating) for three years. It marked composer Harold Rome's entrance into the field of popular music. *The Cradle Will Rock* (1938: music, lyrics, and book by Marc Blitzstein), another timely propaganda piece, will be dealt with in connection with American opera, in Chapter 16.

At the other end of the spectrum were shows that treated their themes with a lighter touch—musicals making use of satire, rather than satire taking the form of musicals. The veteran Irving Berlin wrote the music and lyrics for *Face the Music* (1932) and *As Thousands Cheer* (1933), both with books by Moss Hart, and *Louisiana Purchase* (1940), with book by Morrie Ryskind. All were in the nature of conventional musical comedy, with elements of the revue to allow for the incorporation of the satirical sketches. Rodgers and Hart's one venture into this field was *I'd Rather Be Right* (1937). Cole Porter successfully satirized not only American politics but the Soviet Union in *Leave It to Me* (1938). The hit of the show was the very nonpolitical "My Heart Belongs to Daddy," which brilliantly etched one of Cole Porter's favorite hard-bitten female types. Porter returned to political satire, again of the Soviet Union, in *Silk Stockings* (1955), of which the hit song was the politically neutral (if sexually partisan) "All of You."

Increased sophistication of musical resources

During the period under consideraticn the Broadway show utilized more fully and freely the musical means that had long been at the disposal of opera—that is, all the resources European art music had so painstakingly evolved since the Middle Ages. Melody and harmony had already been absorbed; Herbert, Friml, and Romberg were of course thoroughly and classically schooled musicians. And the works of Jerome Kern and George Gershwin, even in the early songs, show them to have mastered thoroughly the craft of handling fairly complex chromatic harmonies. Kern showed that with skill it was possible to introduce into the limited dimensions of the popular song (which he, like Irving Berlin, completely accepted) rather startling juxtapositions of fairly remote tonalities, as he so deftly illustrated in "Smoke Gets in Your Eyes" (1933) and "Long Ago and Far Away" (1944: from a film score). This example was not lost on subsequent composers; Leonard Bernstein used it effectively in "Tonight," from *West Side Story* (1957).

Counterpoint (the sounding together of two or more melodies) is by nature an undramatic device, in a form where words are important, and where the attention, for greatest dramatic effect, should be focused on only one thing at a time. But carefully introduced, it can be effective, if only as a foil for the otherwise constant monody. This is the basis for the ensemble number, which may involve, for example, two characters ("Marry the Man Today" from *Guys and Dolls* is a superb and witty illustration, incorporating a quasi-canonic echoing effect between the voices); or the kind of integration of many parts that takes place in the *Street Scene* Ice Cream Sextet; or the superbly crafted ensemble near the end of the first act of *West Side Story*, when five characters present three different interpretations of what "tonight" means to them. Occasionally even imitative counterpoint has its place: Kern included a fugue in *The Cat and the Fiddle* as early as 1931, and the "Fugue for Tin Horns" (actually a three-part canon) in *Guys and Dolls* is one of the most effective opening numbers in any musical. As background for the dance sequence "Cool," Bernstein used a fugue effectively in *West Side Story*.

The dimensions of the song itself—still the basic unit of popular music—were enlarged. The usual 32-bar format was discarded as early as 1932 in Cole Porter's "Night and Day" (from *The Gay Divorce*), which is built along ampler lines with a 48-bar chorus, and a verse so important in setting the mood that it can hardly be omitted.

Recitative (intoned speech, with the overwhelming emphasis on the words) had long been integral to opera, where everything is sung, but found its way into the musical as well, as in the introduction to the duet that is the title song in *Guys and Dolls*. A still more striking use of the recitative concept is shown in the opening scene of *The Music Man* (1957), when the rhythmically spoken chatter of the salesmen imitates the chugging of a train as it picks up speed.

Above and beyond an increased broadening and sophistication of technique, the musical during this period came gradually to assign a far greater role to music itself; there was more of it, and it was given more work to do. Instead of being called upon only when it was time for a song or dance, it underscored dialogue, accomplished transitions, or arranged itself in a sequence of movements that became the equivalent of the operatic scene. Furthermore, in the best musicals the entire score had a unity to it. Jerome Kern took a large step in this direction in the score of *Show Boat* when he employed a few key motives, associated with certain characters, at appropriate moments in the background. This was a technique long known to opera, but new to the musical.

Increased importance of the dance

Another evolutionary development that helped bring the musical to its high point in this period was the increased attention lavished on the dance. Song and dance had always gone together on the entertainment stage, and ballet was actually introduced into the musical with the coming of *The Black Crook* in 1866. But a new era was begun when George Balanchine, noted Russian-born choreographer and ballet-master who had come to the United States in 1933, was called upon to create a special jazz ballet for the Rodgers and Hart show *On Your Toes* (1936). The result was the famous "Slaughter on Tenth Avenue," an extended "story" ballet sequence within the musical. After its considerable success two more collaborations of Balanchine with Rodgers and Hart ensued, *I Married an Angel* and *The Boys from Syracuse* (both 1938). From that time forward, choreography and dance, in whatever style is appropriate, have become basic integrated ingredients in the best musicals, especially telling in drama and fantasy sequences, as in *Carousel* and *Allegro*. For *Oklahoma!* (1943) a new orientation for the dance was required, and Agnes De Mille created what were essentially folk-ballet sequences. The musical *On the Town* (1944), with score by Leonard Bernstein, had actually originated as a ballet, *Fancy Free,* by the same composer, with choreography by Jerome Robbins. Robbins also contrived the dance and movement for *West Side Story,* in which it played an important role in the unfolding of the action—indeed that was one of the few musicals conceived and directed by a choreographer. The score itself is nearly a succession of dances, with dance rhythms underlying even the love song. The two contrasting types (jazz-rock and Latin) in juxtaposition express the essential conflict that is the basis of the modern urban plot derived from Shakespeare's *Romeo and Juliet.*

The Musical Since the Advent of Rock

Another thirty years, and more, have passed since *West Side Story,* and these decades have wrought profound changes in the American popular musical stage. Late in the 1950s, Broadway began to lose the ear of its hitherto large public—an ear it had been able to take for granted in the three decades we have just been considering, when the best of America's popular tunes were from Broadway shows. Partly to blame was the decline of the big bands, which were no longer there to function as a medium for the dissemination of these tunes. The "hit parade" was over. Partly it was the fact that Broadway itself was in something of a slump—a dry transitional period, when the great composers were gone or were past their most productive period, and the new talent had not yet matured. (When a new generation did arrive, it would strike out in dramatically new directions.) But for the most part, it was the fact that receptiveness to show tunes, and to the whole ambience of the musical, was narrowing, especially among younger people, as the new and affluent youth market turned to rock 'n' roll, no longer interested in the wares of Broadway. Radio first, and eventually the record industry, followed the market; a gulf began to open up between the musical and the broad public.

Change is never abrupt; some continuity was indeed provided by the sustained activity of composers whose best works belong to the thirty-year period we have just considered. Thus Frank Loesser produced *Greenwillow* (1960) and *How to Succeed in Business Without Really Trying* (1961); Frederick Loewe and Alan Jay Lerner wrote *Camelot* (1960); and Richard Rodgers, who pioneered so many new departures in the musical theater, for the first time provided his own lyrics with *No Strings* (1962), a show that was venturesome in many respects. But in no case do these shows represent the best work of their composers. After this, the musical seemed to go in two different directions.

The Musical Evolving Toward Greater Sophistication

As the musical continued to evolve, the music itself acquired, at the hands of some composers, more sophistication and polish. It embraced a wider range of styles, of expressive possibilities, and of techniques, which enabled it better to adapt to, and express, the dramatic situation. Of the many aspects of the music that could be examined, two will serve to illustrate this greater sophistication: the more supple handling of form, and the more consistent and effective use of ensembles (duets, trios, and so on).

Many of our most memorable show tunes have managed very well to say what they had to say within the 32-bar form that was standard for popular songs: four phrases of 8 bars each, usually in the melodic pattern *aaba*, with *b* constituting a phrase of contrast—the "bridge" to the return of *a*. This basic pattern, preceded by an introduction and some kind of prefatory (and often narrative) "verse", and then repeated in some fashion, has been the ground plan for that basic unit of the musical—the "number." But since mid-century, innovative composers have not been content to accept that pattern, and have introduced calculated surprises into the "number" (which still remains, for the most part, the basic unit of the musical). An interesting example is Stephen Sondheim's best-known song, "Send in the Clowns." Even where, as here, the composer starts from a basic four-phrase pattern, which also assumes the shape *aaba* (with the addition of a final two phrases of *a*, only one of which is sung), irregularities have been introduced. The measures are longer, fewer, and not all the same length (each phrase has at least one "short" measure of three instead of four beats). The bridge has been extended, so that the entire number is an asymmetric succession of phrases of unequal length: 6 + 6 + 9 + 7, with an added repetition of 5 + 7 measures. Even without verifying the arithmetic by counting out the measures, we *feel* the asymmetry as part of the expression; the characters involved are hardly the kind of people most of us meet every day, nor is theirs an everyday situation.

The busy, babbling chorus "Company," which introduces Sondheim's musical of that title, is of exceptional length, and is again a succession of asymmetric units, which assumes the shape *aa'bc*: in this case (excluding the introduction) 12 + 8 + 15 + 32 bars. The whole is then repeated, with the *b* and *c* segments extended and a 12-bar coda added. Again, the run-on form, in which there are many people talking at once and there seems to be always something more to say, fits the "company" exactly.

This opening chorus is illustrative of the increased and effective use of ensembles in the musical. The use of counterpoint (having people singing different things at the same time) was the exception before *West Side Story*, though we noted a few earlier examples from Weill's *Street Scene* (1947) and Loesser's *Guys and Dolls* (1950). But more widespread facility in the use of ensembles, and skill in adapting them to the stage situation, were additional indications of increased technical savoir-faire in the musical after mid-century. By way of examples, in Sondheim's *Company* (1970) there is (in addition to the opening chorus) "Poor Baby"; in his *A Little Night Music* (1972) "Soon," and the brief "Perpetual Anticipation"; and in Marvin Hamlisch's *A Chorus Line* (1975) the "Montage" numbers.

Other aspects as well showed the increased musical sophistication of the Broadway show: evidence of a new boldness in harmony, tonality, and orchestration, for example, and a capacity for integrating into the whole a greater variety of musical styles. But with all these "advances," it was paradoxical that, in the musical after mid-century, the *music itself* mattered less in the whole scheme of things. It was no longer the single most significant ingredient, especially in terms of what had formerly been the most memorable part of the earlier musicals—the singable, hummable song. There might actually be more music (it is practically continuous in *Sweeney Todd* and *Dreamgirls*), but it is subservient to other aspects. On the decline of the overall role of music, and hence of the composer, observers are generally in agreement.

Gerald Bordman has written: "Emphasis on composers in earlier shows has now passed to librettists, directors, and choreographers."[30]

Accompanying this decline in the role of the song was an equally noticeable de-emphasis on plot in the musical. Story and song both lost their essential function. What replaced them? For one thing, the musical built on a "concept," rather than a story.* The concept could be the tangled relationships of sex, love, and marriage (*Company*, 1970); it could be the trauma of dancers desperately trying to be hired for shows (*A Chorus Line*, 1975); it could be the painter and his painting, and hence the relationship of art to life (*Sunday in the Park with George*, 1984). At its simplest, it could be the circus (*Barnum*, 1980), or, as the British writer-composer Andrew Lloyd Webber has shown, it could simply be the elaborately costumed setting of a series of descriptive verses by a well-known poet about a well-known domestic animal (*Cats*, 1981).

Text is important to the conceptual musical; lyrics have acquired new brilliance, wit, and sophistication. Penetrating and urbane, at times earthy, the best are replete with clever rhymes, especially internal ones. In our time, the worthiest successor to Ira Gershwin as a lyricist has been Stephen Sondheim (b. 1930). An example of exceptional intricacy of both meter and rhyme scheme is found in his "Beautiful Girls," the opening number of *Follies*. While each chorus (there is no verse) adds up to a standard 32 bars (with a customary extension at the end) made up of 4-bar phrases, the lyrics are highly asymmetric as to the number of syllables per phrase, varying from seven to seventeen. The rhyme scheme is one of elegant complexity, with no less than four different rhyming "distances" used simultaneously. As Example 11–3 shows, the widest distance is one of 16 measures of music. Most striking are the internal rhymes—those at a distance of less than the standard 4-measure phrase. Of these there are three kinds: five at 2 measures, two at 1 measure, and two ear-catching rhymes at a half-measure.

The entire song is worth a close look, as a vivid illustration of the way in which the sophisticated musical can sound catchy and familiar, and yet embody the most subtle intricacies in musical form, prosody, and rhyme.

Elaborate scenic and stage effects have become an integral (and expensive) ingredient in the musical, often assuming a higher priority than song or story. Almost any contemporary musical is an example; shows such as *The Wiz* (taking us from Kansas to the fantasy land of Oz), *Sweeney Todd* (with its overwhelming portraying of London at its seamiest), and *Barnum* (putting us *in* the circus) were notable for their stunning visual elements. By the time we get to *Sunday in the Park with George* (where an artist's painting is assembled in its brilliant color before our eyes), so far had staging preempted the song that one critic mused that the audience might well leave the theater "humming the scenery."[31]†

* Who first applied the term is not certain, but at least three writers have noted the existence of the "conceptual" or "conceptualized" musical: Stanley Green, Gerald Bordman, and Andrew Lamb (see the endnotes to this chapter).

† As well might one hum the entire array of elaborate stage effects in more recent spectacle musicals such as *Phantom of the Opera* and *Les Misérables*. Here, just as in the nineteenth century beginning with *The Black Crook*, the element of spectacle has been largely responsible for making these musicals so successful that they overlap into the next section in their appeal to a larger audience.

Example 11–3

Beautiful Girls

Hats off, here they come, those Beautiful girls.
That's what you've been waiting for.
Nature never fashioned a flower so fair. 2
No rose can compare,
Nothing respectable 1 16
Half so delectable.
16
Cheer them in their glory, diamonds and pearls,
Dazzling jewels by the score.
This is what beauty can be,
Beauty celestial, ½ 2
The best, you'll
agree:
All for you, these beautiful girls!

Careful, here's the home of Beautiful girls,
Where your reason is undone.
Beauty can't be hindered from taking its toll. 2
You may lose control.
Faced with these Loreleis, 1 16
What man can moralize?
16
Caution, on your guard with Beautiful girls,
Flawless charmers every one.
This is how Samson was shorn:
Each in her style a ½ 2
Delilah
reborn,
Each a gem,
A beautiful diadem 2
of beautiful—welcome them,
These beautiful girls!

The person who has tended to replace composer, lyricist, and librettist has been the director or the choreographer (often one and the same). Bordman has identified a genre he calls "director's musicals," among which he counts *On the Town* (1944, Jerome Robbins), *Sweet Charity* and *Chicago* (1966 and 1975, Bob Fosse), and *A Chorus Line* (1975, Michael Bennett). "In a sense, these director's shows were a throwback to the sort of musicals written before the advent of the great composers, lyricists, and librettists." They were, he continues, "star vehicles: the star was the director-choreographer."[32]

Not only has there been a steadily widening range of subject matter and setting (from the New Testament to the comic strip), but *themes* new to the popular musical stage have been introduced in the past decade: homosexual love in *La Cage aux Folles* (1983); onstage horror and bloodthirstiness in *Sweeney Todd* (a counterpart, as has been suggested, of the onstage horror shows of rock groups such as Kiss and Alice Cooper?).

This line of evolution of the musical has led to its increasing estrangement from the broad public that it could at one time call its own. As Andrew Lamb has said, "artistic development no longer walks comfortably hand in hand with popular taste."[33] Did the musical lose its public because it abandoned story and song, in the traditional sense? Or did it develop in some of the directions we have just indicated because it had already lost its public (to rock, to TV, to films)? Whatever the answers, composers, lyricists, librettists, and directors began to cultivate a more experienced and knowledgeable, and therefore somewhat elite, public.

No one better illustrates this trend than Stephen Sondheim. Detached from the larger public (his shows have generally been lauded by critics and sophisticated theatergoers and bypassed by the populace), he has been concerned with either developing new forms or dramatically reinterpreting traditional ones. The following brief survey is not complete, but may be taken as representative of his development, and with it that of the sophisticated, "adult" musical. In *Anyone Can Whistle* (1964), an odd failure, he delved heavily into psychoanalysis (who and what is sane and who and what is not) and first revealed his obsession with ambiguity. *Company* (1970), already dealt with in some detail, was a study in "relationships." *A Little Night Music* (1972), his most successful musical (perhaps, as Lamb suggests, because it contains his most popular song, "Send in the Clowns"), exists in an atmosphere of old-world decadence, jadedness, and malaise, whose musical symbol is the waltz. *Sweeney Todd* (1979) is theatrical horror of near-operatic proportions. In *Sunday in the Park with George* (1984) Sondheim in effect "staged" a painting, using it to comment on the relationship of the artist to life. The second-act "sequel," while dramatically inconclusive and ambiguous (a Sondheim trait), contains a cynical and telling commentary on the condition of art in our time. In *Into the Woods* (1988) he explored the dark underside of familiar fairy tales, revealing the bitter reality that may follow the illusionistic "happily ever after."

Bordman, before the appearance of *Sunday in the Park*, wrote: "there is an underlying misanthropy and disillusionment permeating virtually everything Sondheim and his associates have put their hand to. A Sondheim show is rarely comfortable or comforting."[34] It has been suggested that the subject of *Sunday in the Park*, the painter Georges Seurat (1859–91), who advanced modern art but never sold a painting, is, in his portrayed aloofness and isolation, a "stand-in" for Sondheim himself.

The Musical Playing to a Larger Audience

In spite of its lesser role in popular culture, the musical has continued, if not to thrive, at least to survive. Its survival is mainly attributable to types of shows that have earned less critical acclaim but relatively more popularity, despite the fact many (though not all) have been derivative, second-rate, and short-lived.

The musical stage has always reflected, with greater or lesser distinctness, the culture of its times. The repertory of the American musical since 1960 contains pieces that reflect in a variety of ways the impact of the dominant youth culture, including rock. A sampling will suggest this variety, as heterogeneous in approach as is popular music itself in this age. *Bye Bye, Birdie* (1960: music by Charles Strouse, lyrics by Lee Adams) is simply a more or less conventional musical comedy that uses the phenomenon of the early rock star (Elvis Presley is the prototype) as material for rather good-natured satire. *Hair* (1967: music by Galt MacDermot, lyrics and book by Gerome Ragni and James Rado) appears to look not *at* but *out from* the youth culture. Themes of youth's concerns are treated with a light touch. The music eschews the harder, more aggressive style of rock, and the show, reverting basically to the format of the revue, includes some well-crafted and expressive songs reflecting both the degree of sophistication that had been achieved with the material of the new popular music and its eclecticism: the subjects range from a comment on environmental deterioration ("Air") to an adaptation from Shakespeare ("What a Piece of Work Is Man").

The following year there appeared an entire show based loosely on Shakespeare's *Twelfth Night*, called *Your Own Thing*, with music and lyrics by Hal Hester and Danny Apolinar. We have already noted the close relationship between the English and American popular musical theaters. *Jesus Christ Superstar* (1971) by the British composer Andrew Lloyd Webber and lyricist Tim Rice, had originally come into existence in recorded form, in 1969. In spite of the unconventionality of the subject for the popular musical stage, it is commercial popular entertainment in every sense, with songs in a slightly sophisticated version of contemporary popular idiom, plus witty, up-to-date dialogue and technological spectacle. Such controversy as the show aroused centered on the treatment of the subject matter rather than on the music itself, which, to the extent that it was rock at all, was so attenuated as to be nearly pure pop. *Godspell* (1971: lyrics and music by Stephen Schwartz, book by John-Michael Tebelak), somewhat less pretentious and perhaps more consistent dramatically, followed in 1971. *Grease* (1972: music, lyrics, and book by Jim Jacobs and Warren Casey), a piece about high school kids in the rock 'n' roll era of the 1950s, was clearly geared to its own audience of those who grew up in that milieu. After the early 1970s, rock musicals, never a major part of the repertoire, faded from Broadway.

Meanwhile, Broadway was seeking to cater to its traditional audience, in more or less traditional ways. There were musicals based on very familiar books, such as *Man of La Mancha* (1965), with music by Mitch Leigh, based on *Don Quixote*; and more recently *Big River* (1985), with music by Roger Miller, based on *Huckleberry Finn* (Kurt Weill was at work on a musical on the same subject at the time of his death in 1950).[35] There were musicals on familiar figures or periods in American history, such as *1776* (1969) with music by Sherman Edwards, *Chicago* (1975) with music by John Kander (based on the gangster era), and the previously mentioned *Barnum* (1980) with music by Cy Coleman.

Beginning in the 1960s there has been a special reliance on the show built around a striking female personality (whether real or fictional), and often designed as a vehicle for one star. *Call Me Madam* (1950, Irving Berlin), based on the political hostess Mrs. Perle Mesta, and a vehicle for Ethel Merman, was a prototype and was ahead of its time. *Gypsy* (1959, Jule Styne), based on the career of Gypsy Rose Lee, was a special case in that the star, again Ethel Merman, did not play the title role. Subsequently there appeared *Funny Girl* (1964, Jule Styne), based on Fanny Brice, with Barbra Streisand as the star; *Hello Dolly!* (1964, Jerry Herman), starring Carol Channing, and in a later black version Pearl Bailey; *Mame* (1966, Jerry Herman), with Angela Lansbury; *Applause* (1970, Charles Strouse), for Lauren Bacall, adapted from the 1950 movie *All About Eve*, in which Bette Davis starred as an aging Broadway star; the British import *Evita* (1978, Andrew Lloyd Webber), based on the life of Eva Peron; and *Woman of the Year* (1981, John Kander), for Lauren Bacall, an updated version of the Katherine Hepburn–Spencer Tracy movie of 1942.*

Show business itself (often in portrayals of the more selfish, ruthless, insensitive, and pathetic side of what goes on behind the scenes) has been a favorite subject; among such shows are *Gypsy*, *A Chorus Line*, two shows by Sondheim, *Follies* (1971) and *Merrily We Roll Along* (1980), *Dreamgirls* (1981, with music by Henry Krieger, its subject a female Motown group much resembling the Supremes), and *Harrigan 'n' Hart* (1985). Related to this genre are musicals based on older forms of entertainment. Burlesque is treated in *Sugar Babies* (1979: a vehicle this time for a male star, Mickey Rooney), and radio in *The 1940's Radio Hour* (1979). Older films are resurrected in *42nd Street* (1980: based on the 1933 film), and the already-mentioned *Applause* (1970) and *Woman of the Year* (1981). The comic strip furnished the subjects for *Li'l Abner* (1956), *Annie* (1977), and, reflecting more recent tastes, *You're a Good Man, Charlie Brown* (1967: based on the durable and long-lived *Peanuts*, by Charles Schultz), and *Doonesbury* (1983: the script was written by Gary Trudeau, the creator of the original comic strip).

The revue, which virtually died out during the heyday of the story musical, has again been cultivated, mostly as a retrospective of the work of a single composer. Thus we have *Side by Side by Sondheim* (1977), *Ain't Misbehavin'* (1978: on the jazz pianist Fats Waller), *Eubie!* (1978: on the ragtime pianist and songwriter Eubie Blake), *Sophisticated Ladies* (1981: on Duke Ellington), and *Star Dust* (1986: this time based on the work of a lyricist, Mitchell Parish, who wrote the words of the title song).

Our picture of Broadway seeking a larger audience is rounded out by a rather extraordinary series of revivals in the 1980s. For the younger generation (to the extent that they go at all), the revivals cater to a newly acquired taste; for those who got to know these shows and their songs in the years when they first appeared, they cater to nostalgia, of course, but they also demonstrate

* Tess, the heroine of *Woman of the Year*, became a TV journalist in the 1981 musical. None of the critics, at the opening, failed to comment on the resemblance to Barbara Walters.

that there is still an audience for the song-and-story musical of what we have identified as its most flourishing period. Cued by the revival of *Oklahoma!* in 1979, there were in the next decade revivals on Broadway of at least eight shows by the major figures: *The King and I* and *South Pacific* (Richard Rodgers); *My Fair Lady*, *Camelot*, and *Brigadoon* (Frederick Loewe—*Brigadoon* had *two* revivals, in 1980 and 1986); *Show Boat* (Jerome Kern); *Can-Can* (Cole Porter); and *West Side Story* (Leonard Bernstein); in addition there have been numerous reconstructions and revivals of early shows by Gershwin. Reaching back to a still more distant era have been the revivals of such operettas as *Naughty Marietta*, *The Desert Song*, and *The New Moon*. Of course, these shows had never been absent from theaters in other cities throughout the country, nor from the stages of college and community theaters—perhaps, after all, more accurate indicators of American taste at large in any period than what occupies the more fashionable and trendier stages of Manhattan.

The Film Musical

While heavily dependent for most of its history upon the live stage (which after all had a head start of over half a century in developing the musical), the film musical nevertheless evolved rather quickly into a distinct genre, with a style and mode of treatment of its own. It has in fact contributed some memorable shows, independent of Broadway originals—movie musicals such as *42nd Street*; *High, Wide, and Handsome*; *The Wizard of Oz*; the animated *Pinocchio*; *Singin' in the Rain*; *A Star Is Born*; *Gigi* (derived from a Broadway straight play, not a musical); and *Mary Poppins*.*

Techniques for adding sound to films were developed in the 1920s, and a pioneering film with operatic music, *Don Juan* (appropriately starring John Barrymore), was presented in New York in 1926. The introduction of popular music to films was not far behind. When the four Warner brothers, in Hollywood, were looking for the right talent to introduce popular song into the movies, they picked two seasoned Broadway singing actors who had come up through vaudeville, Al Jolson and Fanny Brice. The first films were not "all-talking" pictures, but they made their point, and before 1930 silence, in the movies, was at an end.† Jolson's first vehicle, *The Jazz Singer*, with five songs including Irving Berlin's "Blue Skies," had its historic premiere on October 6, 1927. The next year Jolson did *The Singing Fool*, which included his well-known "Sonny Boy," and the same year Fanny Brice did *My Man*, with *her* famous "Second-Hand Rose."[36] After this, things developed rapidly, and the movie musical was truly on its way with the first "all-talking–all-singing–all-dancing" film, *The Broadway Melody*, of 1929.

Within the next few years, a precociously successful Hollywood attracted

* In recent years, as we have seen, there have been examples of a reverse flow of ideas, with earlier movies furnishing the material for Broadway shows such as *Applause*, *42nd Street*, and *Woman of the Year*.

† The whole story of the live music that accompanied silent films in many theaters, from a single piano or organ to full orchestra, is a fascinating study in itself, though not relevant to the film musical.

much of the best Broadway talent—singers, dancers, choreographers, and directors—and composers and lyricists were engaged not only to adapt existing works but to write new musicals. As early as 1930 Sigmund Romberg and Oscar Hammerstein II wrote music and lyrics for *Viennese Nights*; the next year George and Ira Gershwin wrote *Delicious*, and Rodgers and Hart did *The Hot Heiress*, the first of their many films in the 1930s. Other Broadway songwriters who wrote early for films included Irving Berlin, Vincent Youmans, and Cole Porter, and (slightly later) Harold Arlen, Arthur Schwartz, and Jimmy McHugh. Jerome Kern, many of whose shows had been adapted for film (including a partially silent, patchwork *Show Boat* in 1929, the first of three film versions), did not begin to write original film scores until 1935, but after that time he wrote almost exclusively for Hollywood. For many Broadway composers, the era of commuting began, and for the next quarter-century American popular music turned on a Broadway-Hollywood axis.

After an initial period of experimentation, the film musical sorted itself out into several fairly well-defined genres, and it will be easiest to trace its progress during its greatest period of the 1930s, 40s, and 50s by looking briefly at each of these.

The Revue and the Backstage Musical

It was natural that movie producers, scrambling to find out just what a film musical should or could be, would rely heavily at first on that most flexible of forms, the revue, and its close relative, the show about show business itself—the "backstager." Both could easily accommodate within their fairly loose structure nearly anything entertaining, and a show that proved successful could always be followed by a sequel. What Ziegfeld did on Broadway in the teens and twenties with his "follies" was imitated by Hollywood in the 1930s. After *The Broadway Melody* (1929, with sequels in 1936 and 1940), there was *The Gold Diggers of Broadway* (1929, followed by *Gold Diggers of 1933, 1935*, and *1937*), *Footlight Parade* (1933), and *Fashions of 1934*; in 1946, after wartime revues such as *Stage Door Canteen* and *Thousands Cheer* (both 1943), there appeared the nostalgic *Ziegfeld Follies*. In 1952, we were taken backstage to the early days of film-making itself in *Singin' in the Rain*, with its title song by one of the earliest "native" Hollywood composers, Nacio Herb Brown. More recent films such as *All That Jazz*, *Fame*, and *The Rose* (1979) have given us updated backstage "revelations."*

Among the host of backstage films, some have stood out as exceptional. *42nd Street* (1933) established a precedent for its tough look at the behind-the-scenes Broadway of its day, and for its multitude of talent, which included Bebe Daniels, Ginger Rogers, Una Merkel, Ruby Keeler, Warner Baxter, Dick Powell, and Ned Sparks, with Busby Berkeley as the choreographer for the opulent stage scenes. *42nd Street* was one of the first of the great film musicals; two decades later, just before its decline, came another musical show about

* As one writer has remarked, "Nowadays the characters have more to reveal: *Fame* takes in child molestation, porno film, gay shame, abortion (which earlier backstagers couldn't show) and even failure (which earlier musicals didn't believe in)." Ethan Mordden, *The Hollywood Musical* (New York: St. Martin's, 1981), p. 226.

show business, the remade *A Star Is Born* (1954) with music by Harold Arlen and lyrics by Ira Gershwin—noteworthy as one of Judy Garland's most impressive vehicles.

The Dance Musical

Closely related to the backstage musical was the dance musical. Both involved lavish production numbers, and since the dance musical was usually about a dancer, it furnished yet another glimpse of show business. Fred Astaire, who went to Hollywood in 1933, virtually created the genre, with his versatile talents as singer and actor, as well as dancer. In that same year he and Ginger Rogers danced in secondary roles in *Flying Down to Rio*, with music by Vincent Youmans. So successful were they as a team that the next year they starred in *The Gay Divorcée*, with songs by Cole Porter, which included "The Continental" and "Night and Day." The lavish production number, with elaborate sets and a large corps of dancers to augment the stars, became a hallmark of the dance musical; the one for "The Continental" lasted seventeen minutes, and set a standard for all that were to follow. Ginger Rogers and Fred Astaire starred in a total of nine dance musicals (all but one in the 1930s); most of them had music by either Jerome Kern or Irving Berlin.[37] Kern, who had settled in Hollywood by 1935, when the next Astaire-Rogers film, *Roberta*, was made, added "Lovely to Look At" for the film version of the original Broadway show, which had introduced "Smoke Gets in Your Eyes." The films of this pair, major entertainment events of the 1930s, were among the most popular and influential in the history of the film musical. In the 1940s Astaire went on to dance in movies with Eleanor Powell, Rita Hayworth, and Bing Crosby. The 1940s saw the rise to prominence of another dancer, actor, and choreographer, Gene Kelly, who also came to Hollywood by way of Broadway, having starred in the original production of Rodgers and Hart's *Pal Joey* in 1940. Kelly's dance musicals with Judy Garland, *For Me and My Gal* (1942) and *The Pirate* (1948: with music by Cole Porter), as well as *On the Town* (1949), *An American in Paris* (1951), and *Singin' in the Rain* (1952), were noteworthy.

Operetta and the Singer's Musical

Another genre that matured in the 1930s was the musical featuring the singing star(s). From the operatic stage came singers John McCormack (the earliest, to make *Son o' My Heart* in 1930), Lily Pons (for whom Jerome Kern wrote *I Dream Too Much* in 1935), Grace Moore, Lawrence Tibbett, and Gladys Swarthout, who all made musicals in the 1930s.[38] But the most successful actor-singers of this genre were the team of Jeannette MacDonald and Nelson Eddy. Beginning with *Naughty Marietta* in 1935 (an adaptation of a Victor Herbert musical of 1910), the eight musicals they made together between then and 1942 virtually defined the film operetta. Typical of the genre was its reliance on adaptations of earlier operettas in middle-European style, principally those by Sigmund Romberg (*Maytime* and *The New Moon*) and Rudolf Friml (*Rose-Marie* and *The Firefly*).

Black Musical Styles As the Basis for Film Musicals

Jazz, which had never really been used undiluted in the Broadway musical in its heyday (Jerome Kern, for one, actively disliked it), became a subject for movie musicals, mostly because of the opportunities it gave to film the bands while playing, but also because of its "backstage" possibilities. *The King of Jazz* was made as early as 1930, with Paul Whiteman and Bing Crosby. Later came *Blues in the Night* (1941: with music by Harold Arlen, including the title song), and, in the same year, *Birth of the Blues*, with Crosby, Mary Martin, and Jack Teagarden. This film was notable for its recognition of the role of black musicians, in the number "The Waiter and the Porter and the Upstairs Maid." In 1943 appeared the all-black musical *Stormy Weather*, which starred Bill "Bojangles" Robinson as the central figure, and included Lena Horne, Fats Waller, and Cab Calloway.[39]

Two non-jazz black musicals are worthy of note. One was the very early *Hallelujah* (1929), directed by King Vidor: not so much a musical as an honest, realistic film about black life in the South, which inevitably involved music (including two songs by Irving Berlin). *Cabin in the Sky* (1943) was a folk-tale fantasy about redemption; Ethel Waters was outstanding in a cast that also included Lena Horne and Eddie Anderson, with Duke Ellington and his band as an added attraction.[40]

Other Genres

The film musical includes other specialized genres. Comedy musicals began with teams like the Marx Brothers (*Duck Soup*, 1933, is representative) and George Burns and Gracie Allen, or with single stars such as Eddie Cantor or Mae West. World War II produced a demand for lighthearted comedy; it was during this time that the trio of Bing Crosby, Bob Hope, and Dorothy Lamour produced most of their *Road to* series, beginning with *Road to Singapore* (1940), and the versatile comic Danny Kaye starred in three films, *Up in Arms* (1944), *Wonder Man* (1945), and *The Kid from Brooklyn* (1946).[41]

Shirley Temple, the most phenomenally successful child singer-dancer-actress Hollywood has known, defined the child musical in the twenty-seven feature films she made (in sixteen of which she was the central figure) between the ages of six and twelve (1934–40), with a veritable galaxy of other stars in "supporting" roles. Hollywood similarly created the "skating" musical around three-time Olympic winner Sonja Henie in the late 1930s. Other minor forms were the radio musical (the *Big Broadcast* series of the 1930s was really another form of the backstage musical) and the college musical.

Walt Disney developed a unique form of musical in the feature-length animated cartoon. Beginning with *Snow White and the Seven Dwarfs* (1938), a series of children's classics appeared, the best of which was probably *Pinocchio* (1940). If the animated musicals lacked human stars, the best of them had one essential ingredient, the hit song: "Some Day My Prince Will Come," "Whistle While You Work" (from *Snow White*), and especially "When You Wish Upon a Star" (from *Pinocchio*) certainly entered the canon of American popular song of the prewar years.

Ripe for exploitation as subjects for film musicals were the famous composers and singers of musical comedy themselves. Musical biographies were thus a prolific genre, though generally inferior in quality and displaying a crass distortion of the truth. From *The Great Waltz* (1939, on Victor Herbert) and *Swanee River* (1940, on Stephen Foster) through *Lady Sings the Blues* (1972, on Billie Holiday), hardly any major composer or performer has escaped being the subject of a (usually) second- or third-rate film musical.

Film Versions of Broadway Musicals

Finally, we come to that genre to which the major portion of film musicals belong—the movie version of a Broadway show. The film musical, as we have seen, began by being heavily dependent on the vehicles of the live stage. And although film evolved some notably independent genres (of which the dance musical, as typified by the works of Fred Astaire, is probably the most distinctive), reliance on the live musical as a source continued, and since 1950 has been stronger than ever, to the point where a film version of a successful stage musical is a foregone conclusion. These adaptations are too numerous to list. Still, they are *adaptations*, and the basic differences between stage and screen prevented the movie versions from being simply duplicates. There was the question of length; movies had to be considerably shorter than stage shows. There was the question of realism; interpolated song and dance had more of a tendency to "stick out" in the greater realism of film. (This partly accounts for the extensive reliance on the backstage musical, of whatever genre—in other words, films that were *about* performers, since singing and dancing is what singers and dancers do.) Then there were the visual aspects, film being much more flexible. In the presence of live performers, the limitations of the proscenium are accepted, but in film, the camera must not be static; it must range, in its mobility, from the full-screen close-up to the long shot that takes in a whole city; it must use to the fullest extent its capacity for special effects, such as panning, fading, and combining multiple images. (It was the dance musical that first exploited cinematic possibilities; it could show us more dancers, in more expanded and elaborate settings, and from many more angles of vision, than would be possible on the live stage.)

What happens to musicals in film adaptations? They are obviously cut, both in overall length, and in the number of songs, which might be a third to a half of those used in stage versions. Often new songs are needed. Occasionally, the film version has been able to profit from the collaboration of the same songwriter; when Jerome Kern moved to Hollywood, for example, he often furnished new songs for movie adaptations of his Broadway shows. And very frequently the cast is changed, even when the movie version follows closely on the heels of the stage version.

Conclusion

The period of the movie musical's greatest flowering was from the 1930s to the mid-1950s (a far shorter period of effulgence than that of the stage musical), and what is left of it is possibly more dependent than ever on the Broadway musical (which *has* somehow managed to survive). Ethan Mordden has summed up the reasons:

> No matter how the musical's confused present develops, it is undebatable that the form has been running down since the 1950's. We know the reasons—inflation has made the middle-budget musical unworkable; rock doesn't work well for most stories; the current generation of moviemakers doesn't know how to make a musical; and the intense naturalism of contemporary film makes anything but a backstager unthinkably quaint.[42]

With this long postscript on the film musical, we bring to a close our attempt to trace just the barest outlines of a vast, sprawling, and vital scene, the last century and a half of American popular musical theater—theater which, in all its various forms, has furnished such a significant part of our entertainment, and contributed so many of our popular songs.

It is to another vast body of popular song, that whose domain was essentially outside of the theater, that we turn next.

Further Reading

Books

Biographical works on individual composers are too numerous to list here; they vary greatly in quality, as works on popular figures tend to. Among those that may be cited as setting a standard for the best are Gerald Bordman's *Jerome Kern: His Life and Music* (New York: Oxford University Press, 1980) and Douglas Jarman's *Kurt Weill: An Illustrated Biography* (Bloomington: Indiana University Press, 1982). Also not included are the "books" (complete texts, i.e. libretti) to individual musicals, many of which are available.

Reference works

Bloom, Ken, ed. *American Song: The Complete Musical Theatre Companion*. New York: Facts-on-File, 1985.
Extensive two-volume work. Vol. 1 has entries, by show, on over 3000 productions; vol. 2 has indexes by songs, people, and year of production.

Green, Stanley, ed. *Encyclopedia of the Musical Theatre*. New York: Dodd, Mead, 1976. Reprint, Da Capo, 1980.
Useful single-volume work, 492 pp. Entries by name, song, and show, with brief commentary on each show, and appendices on awards and prizes, and long runs.

———. *Encyclopedia of the Musical Film*. New York: Oxford University Press, 1981.
Same Organization and format as the preceding.

———. *Broadway Musicals Show by Show*. Milwaukee, WI: Hal Leonard, 1985.

The nineteenth century

Nathan, Hans. *Dan Emmett and the Rise of Early Negro Minstrelsy*. Norman: University of Oklahoma Press, 1962.
A most important study of the early minstrel show, as well as of Emmett himself. Nearly half the work consists of a valuable anthology of all types of minstrel material by Emmett and others, including, for example, the complete text of a skit or "extravaganza."

Root, Deane L. *American Popular Stage Music, 1860–1880*. Ann Arbor, MI: UMI Research Press, 1981.

Saxton, Alexander. "Blackface Minstrelsy and Jacksonian Ideology," *American Quarterly*, vol. 27 (1975), pp. 3–28.

Toll, Robert C. *Blacking Up: The Minstrel Show in Nineteenth Century America*. New York: Oxford University Press, 1974.

The twentieth century

Bordman, Gerald. *American Musical Theatre: A Chronicle*. New York: Oxford University Press, 1978.

———. *American Operetta: From* H.M.S. Pinafore *to* Sweeney Todd. New York: Oxford University Press, 1981.

———. *American Musical Comedy: From* Adonis *to* Dreamgirls. New York: Oxford University Press, 1982.

———. *American Musical Revue: From* The Passing Show *to* Sugar Babies. New York: Oxford University Press, 1985.

Green, Stanley, *Ring Bells! Sing Songs!: Broadway Musicals of the 1930s*. New Rochelle, NY: Arlington House, 1971. Detailed study, with photos, integrated with news of the day.

Mates, Julian. *America's Musical Stage: Two Hundred Years of Musical Theatre*. Westport, CT: Greenwood, 1985. Main emphasis on the earlier period.

Mordden, Ethan. *Better Foot Forward: The History of the American Musical Theater*. New York: Grossman (Viking Press), 1976.

———. *The Hollywood Musical*. New York: St. Martin's, 1981.

Sampson, Henry T. *Blacks in Blackface: A Source Book on Early Black Musical Shows*. Metuchen, NJ: Scarecrow Press, 1980.

Sennett, Ted. *Hollywood Musicals*. New York: Harry N. Abrams, 1981. Opulent photo-display book, with text.

Music

Piano-vocal scores are not included, since they are available for practically all of the important musicals of the twentieth century, beginning with Victor Herbert. Three useful collections of mostly earlier material are:

Appelbaum, Stanley, ed. *Show Songs from "The Black Crook" to "The Red Mill."* New York: Dover, 1974. Includes sixty songs from fifty shows, with commentary by the editor, and illustrations.

Jackson, Richard, ed. *Stephen Foster Song Book*. New York: Dover, 1974. Forty of Foster's songs in their original published versions, with original sheet music covers and notes on the songs by the editor. All the important minstrel songs are included.

Great Songs of Broadway. New York: Quadrangle/New York Times, 1973. Seventy-four songs from sixty-three shows, from 1901 to 1971. General introductions by Alan Jay Lerner and Jule Styne, but no introductions to individual songs or shows.

Articles (*in chronological order by subject*)

Mahar, William J. " 'Backside Albany' and Early Blackface Minstrelsy: A Contextual Study of America's First Blackface Song," *American Music*, vol. 6, no. 1 (Spring 1988).

Shout, John D. "The Musical Theater of Mark Blitzstein," *American Music*, vol. 3, no.4 (Winter 1985).

Bristow, Eugene K., and J. Kevin Butler. "*Company*, About Face! The Show that Revolutionized the American Musical," *American Music*, vol. 5, no. 3 (Fall 1987).

Listening

Single, or in a few cases double, LPs are available for most of the successful Broadway shows and film musicals, which include the better-known songs, often sung by the original cast. Occasionally (*Evita*, *Sweeney Todd*) the lyrics or even the complete libretto may be included. Some less readily available early material is found in the following:

The Early Minstrel Show. NW-338.
Commendably authentic reconstruction of material from pre–Civil War minstrelsy.

Don't Give the Name a Bad Place: Types and Stereotypes in American Musical Theater 1870–1900. NW-265.

"I Wants to Be a Actor Lady" and Other Hits from Early Musical Comedies. NW-221.

The Vintage Irving Berlin. NW-238.
Archival recordings from 1919 to 1942.

Follies, Scandals, and Other Diversions from Ziegfeld to the Shuberts. NW-215.
Archival recordings from 1919 to 1942.

Shuffle Along. NW-260.
"An archival re-creation of the 1921 production featuring members of the original cast."

. . . and then we wrote . . . : American Composers and Lyricists Sing, Play, and Conduct Their Own Songs. NW-272.
Fifteen rarities, from Victor Herbert to Stephen Sondheim.

Where Have We Met Before? Forgotten Songs from Broadway, Hollywood, and Tin Pan Alley. NW-240.
Fourteen more rarities.

Smithsonian Collection of American Popular Song.
LPs of archival recordings. Most of the collection is more relevant to the next chapter, but it includes a considerable amount of show material.

PROJECTS

1. Make a study of the early circus in America, and its relation to other forms of popular musical theater.

2. Make a study of the old-time minstrel skit with music known as "The Arkansas Traveler." For a start, consult the versions in *The New Lost City Ramblers Song Book* (see the reading list for Chapter 7), and in Carl Sandburg's *Folk-Say*.

3. Compare "Jordan Is a Hard Road to Travel" (in Nathan, *Dan Emmett*, p. 335) with "The Other Side of Jordan" (as found in *The New Lost City Ramblers Song Book*, and based on performances by Uncle Dave Macon, recorded on *Uncle Dave Macon*, Folkways RBF-51). Find out as much as you can about the survival of such minstrel songs in traditional country music.

4. Compare the use of dialect in the minstrel songs of Dan Emmett, Stephen Foster, and James Bland.

5. Read, and write a brief review of, Jacques Offenbach's diary of his visit to America in the 1870s (published as *Orpheus in America* [Bloomington: Indiana University Press, 1957]).

6. Trace and identify quotations of other popular songs in George M. Cohan's "Yankee Doodle Boy." Find at least four additional songs of the same general period that themselves contain snatches of other popular songs, and identify these.

7. Compare the text of an original play with the "book," or libretto, of a musical show based on that play. Note technical changes and changes of plot, emphasis, and characterization. What do you think were the reasons for the changes? (Examples would be *Oklahoma!* vis-à-vis *Green Grow the Lilacs*; *Carousel* vis-à-vis *Liliom;* *The Most Happy Fella* vis-à-vis *They Knew What They Wanted*; and *My Fair Lady* vis-à-vis *Pygmalion*.)

8. Make a brief study of the use of the popular musical theater as an instrument of propaganda, in any given age.

9. If you are sufficiently knowledgeable musically, make a study of remote key relationships in the songs of Jerome Kern or the popular songs of Leonard Bernstein.

10. If you have some background or training in music, select two songs by Jerome Kern and two songs by Stephen Sondheim, and compare them as to *form.*

11. If you are knowledgeable in the field of dance, make a study of the contributions of George Balanchine, Agnes De Mille, Jerome Robbins, Bob Fosse, or Michael Bennett to the popular musical stage.

12. Attend a performance, and do a careful review, of a musical show written since 1970. Assess such things as dramatic verisimilitude, depth of characterization (do the characters seem "real," believable, three-dimensional?), appropriateness of the songs to the situations in which they are sung, and distinctiveness and quality of the songs. Include a brief account of the breadth of your own acquaintance with musical comedy.

13. Select two show songs of the 1920s or 1930s and two show songs of the 1970s or 1980s, and do a comparative study of their lyrics; include a comparison of their language and subject, as well as of their form, prosody, rhyme scheme, etc.

14. If you are a jazz fan, find at least three jazz versions apiece of two different Broadway or Tin Pan Alley standards; identify the composer and the year of composition, and compare the versions.

12

Popular Song, Dance, and March Music from the Jacksonian Era to the Advent of Rock

OVER forty years ago, when little serious attention was given to the study of popular culture, a writer began his history of popular music with the assertion that it "is an index to the life and history of a nation."[1] Since then, the intensive research that has been devoted to popular music has confirmed this, and has shown that by studying the nature of what is genuinely popular in a given era, it is possible to gain a vivid picture not only of the life and history, but also of the attitudes, feelings, motivations, prejudices, mores—in fact, the dominant *world view*—of that era. The songs that are enjoyed and sung by a broad segment of the populace fulfill this role even better than does the popular musical stage, which we examined in the last chapter. Musical theater, for all of its popularity, could not possibly reach and be enjoyed by the masses to the extent that popular song could. An age that numbered its theatergoers in the tens of thousands would number in the millions those who sang its songs.

Popular Song from the 1830s Through the Civil War

Chapter 10 ended with a consideration of our popular song before 1830, and at the beginning of Chapter 11 we noted the changes that were then under way in American social, political, and cultural life, and the developments in music printing that went hand in hand with the growth of a mass market for sheet music. The growth of this market, however, and with it the birth of distinctively American song, was related to far more than technology. Nicholas Tawa begins his book *A Music for the Millions* by observing:

> A turbulent era in American history opened with Andrew Jackson's election to the presidency and his passionate attack on privilege. It closed with Lincoln's election and the onset of the Civil War. From 1828 to 1861, new democratic beliefs and practices interspersed themselves aggressively among older aristocratic ways of thinking. . . . This was a critical time for the American people; a time of confusion, of conflict between old and new ways of living, thinking, and believing. . . . Inevitably, music reflected the social, economic, and political upheaval of these years. The once-dominant European-derived composition mirroring a narrow, leisured constituency was soon overwhelmed by a different type of musical work, one imbued with ideas favored by the common citizenry and exposed in the simplest verbal and melodic terms—the American popular song.[2]

The Parlor Song

The basic and most flourishing genre of the period was what has become known as the parlor song. These songs were purchased by, and sung in the living rooms of, the rapidly expanding numbers of middle-class families in cities and towns—to the accompaniment of the piano, the harmonium (reed organ), or the guitar. They were also sung in public by touring professional singers, who were often the composers as well. In keeping with the modest musical skills of the singers for whom they were intended, and with a view to their popular appeal, the tunes were simple—moderate in range, clear and predictable in form; practically all were in the major mode, even the sad songs. The accompaniments were easy enough to be played by those with the most rudimentary keyboard techniques, involving usually only the three basic chords in the major mode, and so simple in texture as to be always subordinate to the melody sung by the voice.[3] Indeed, simplicity and directness of expression were values that were prized in these songs, even when they were performed by professionals.

Melodies from Italian operas, principally those of Rossini (1792–1868), Donizetti (1797–1848), and Bellini (1801–35), were in circulation here with English words, and were better known and more popular in America in the antebellum period than is generally supposed. Italianate influence can be found even in some of the songs of Stephen Foster.[4] But the basic models for the new popular song are to be found much closer to oral tradition. Irish folk melodies, especially as adapted and given new words by the Irish poet Thomas Moore (1779–1852), were popular here throughout the nineteenth century, beginning with the first printing of Moore's famous collection *Irish Melodies* in 1808.[5] Of course, the long history of immigration from Ireland was at least a partial basis for their popularity, but the unadorned attractiveness and accessibility of the melodies (some of which are clearly related to dance tunes) helped win them wide acceptance. Then, too, Moore's new words often struck a note of melancholy and nostalgia—having to do with parting, with death, and with looking back on a past that was better than the present—which somehow, paradoxically for a new country with ever-widening possibilities, seemed in accord with nineteenth-century sentiments. Much of Moore's large collection is unfamiliar today, but a few of the songs have entered permanently into the body of American song, including "Believe Me, if All Those Endearing Young Charms," "The Minstrel Boy," "The Last Rose of Summer," and "The Harp that Once Through Tara's Halls."

Other imports from the British Isles were popular here, and helped set the American parlor song on its course. "Home, Sweet Home," with its melody (probably original) by the English composer Henry Bishop and words by the American John Howard Payne, was introduced in an opera by Bishop in London in 1823, and immediately achieved phenomenal and lasting success—probably more so in this country than in England. A decade later another nostalgic song, "Long, Long Ago," by the Englishman Thomas Haynes Bayly, entered the canon of perennial American songs, and in 1841 appeared the pathetic song of parting "Kathleen Mavourneen," by F. N. Crouch, called an "Irish Ballad."[6]

Among native American songs that were sentimental or nostalgic in tone—often having to do with separation, usually by death—the following (in chronological order) are representative: "Flow Gently, Sweet Afton" (1838), with music by the American J. E. Spilman on a poem by the great Scottish poet Robert Burns;[7] "Near the Lake There Drooped the Willow" (1839), with music by Charles Horn, to words by the popular journalist and poet George P. Morris;[8] "Ben Bolt" (1848), with tune (possibly not original) by Nelson Kneass to words by Thomas Dunn English;[9] and "The Ocean Burial" (1850) a "favorite and touching ballad" with music by George N. Allen to words by Rev. Edwin H. Chapin.[10] The words to "The Ocean Burial," which begin "O! bury me not in the deep, deep sea," were later brought ashore and transformed into the text for one of the most popular of all cowboy songs, "O Bury Me Not on the Lone Prairie." George Frederick Root (of whom more will be heard in Chapter 15) wrote such sentimental songs on the subject of death as "The Hazel Dell" (1853) and "Rosalie, the Prairie Flower" (1855).[11] The best-known of the sentimental songs of love, separation, and death by Stephen Foster began to appear in the 1850s, including "The Village Maiden" (1855), "Gentle Annie" (1856), and, perhaps his most famous song in this vein, "Jeanie with the Light Brown Hair" (1854).[12]

Religious sentiments are sometimes encountered in these sentimental songs; "Rock'd in the Cradle of the Deep" (1840) is an example that was very popular. Nicholas Tawa has pointed out the intertwining of sacred and secular in the nineteenth-century parlor song, and the difficulty of making a clear distinction between the parlor song with religious sentiments and the hymn.[13]

Related to the song with religious sentiments was the song that espoused an attitude or pointed a moral. The attitude might be pessimistic ("Love Not!" 1833), questioning ("Ah! May the Red Rose Live Always!" 1850, by Stephen Foster, with the lines "Why should the beautiful ever weep? /Why should the beautiful die?"), exhortative ("Be Kind to the Loved Ones at Home," 1847 by Isaac B. Woodbury), or patently optimistic ("There's a Good Time Coming," 1846, a setting by Stephen Foster of verses by Charles Mackay, taken from a London newspaper).[14]

In the realm of what Tawa calls the "unillusioned song" was the comic piece. "Old Rosin the Beau"[15] (probably first published here in 1838) has a devil-may-care attitude to approaching death, set to a rollicking pentatonic Irish tune. Many of the comic songs published in sheet music form came from minstrelsy; Foster's "Oh! Susanna" (1848), with its comic paradoxes ("It rain'd all night the day I left, /The weather it was dry"), is no doubt the best known. Foster's post-minstrel humorous songs ("There Are Plenty of Fish in the Sea," 1862; "My Wife Is a Most Knowing Woman," 1863; "If You've Only Got a Moustache," 1864)[16] lack the characteristic tang and bite of minstrelsy, and draw on that perennial fund of comic material based on the pitfalls of courtship and marriage.

Diametrically opposed to temperance songs, which we will encounter later, were the songs of conviviality and drink. "Old Rosin the Beau" is certainly in this category, which also includes such songs as "We Won't Go Home Till Morning" (1842) and "Vive la Compagnie" (1844).[17]

Touring Professionals: Henry Russell and the Hutchinson Family

Parlor songs were not confined to the parlor; in the period before the Civil War professional singers were on the road, giving concerts in New York, Boston, and Philadelphia, as well as in smaller cities and towns. Professional performers played an important role in shaping public taste, in acquainting the public with new songs, and in promoting them. That even songs for the "parlor" could profit by such promotion is shown by the sheet music covers, which frequently advertised songs as having been "sung by," or even "sung with distinguished applause by," some popular singer.

One of the most successful and influential of these was the Englishman Henry Russell (1812–1900 or 1901). The impression that his example made on our subsequent composers and performers (including Stephen Foster and the Hutchinsons), the popularity of many of his songs, and the ground he broke for future artists who toured the United States were out of all proportion to the brevity of his stay here; Russell was in the United States only from 1836 to 1841 (or 1842), and again in 1843–44. A most effective singer who also played his own piano accompaniments, he pioneered as a "one-man show" at a time when few other performers could hold the interest of an audience for an entire evening by themselves. His style and his material (he performed mostly his own songs) were designed to be spellbinding. His diction was such that every word was understood; it is significant that two men who influenced him greatly were an actor (the Englishman Edmund Kean) and an orator (the American Henry Clay). Thus he was eminently fitted for popularity at a time when the main purpose of both singer and song was to arouse the emotions.

His songs tell us much about what was popular with antebellum audiences. Of his sentimental songs the best-known are "The Old Arm Chair" (1840) and "Woodman! Spare That Tree!" (1837). Both have as their basis a special kind of sentimentality prevalent in the nineteenth century—sentimental attachment to a particular object.* More overtly dramatic were such extended scenic monologues as "The Ship on Fire" and "The Maniac." Real spellbinders that depended for their effect on acting ability as well as singing, these were almost like one-man operatic scenes. They were taken up with great success by American singers such as the Hutchinsons.[18]

Many of Russell's songs espoused social causes; the emotions so effectively aroused in his hearers were meant to be directed toward the alleviation

* This kind of sentimentality has survived in American popular culture and is frequently found in country music, as shown in songs such as "Picture on the Wall" (possibly identical with an 1864 song by Henry Clay Work) and "Send Me the Pillow that You Dream On."

of some current evil. This accorded with a prevalent view of the time as to the *moral* function of art, and especially of song. "The Maniac" was not merely a melodramatic scene; it called attention to the wretched conditions in the mental asylums of his day. "The Dream of the Reveller" (1843) dealt with the evils of alcohol abuse, and after his return to England Russell wrote many antislavery songs. Thus, what Russell's compatriot Charles Dickens was aiming to do by literary means (and it is interesting to note that Russell set at least one of Dickens's poems, though a nondidactic one) Russell aimed to do with song.

Among the foremost American performer-composers to follow Henry Russell's example were the Hutchinson Family Singers. From a rural New England background of strong convictions, they composed and sang songs supporting many of the causes in which they so firmly believed. The earliest of these causes, in which they always took an active part, was that of temperance; their song "King Alcohol" appeared frequently on their programs. After mid-century, when the group had already begun to disband, some of the Hutchinsons worked and sang in the cause of women's rights, including universal suffrage. Through the years, various members of the family sang campaign songs for presidential candidates from William Henry Harrison (1840) to Rutherford B. Hayes (1876), including many songs about Lincoln. But the cause that most absorbed them during the 1840s, their period of greatest activity, was the abolition of slavery. They sang frequently at antislavery meetings and rallies, appearing with the most radical abolitionists of the time, Wendell Phillips and William Lloyd Garrison. They participated in street marches, and on their tours they refused to sing in halls that would not admit blacks. They were well acquainted with Frederick Douglass, the escaped slave who settled in Lynn, Massachusetts, and became a campaigner against slavery, and they traveled with him to England. Abolition was by no means a universally popular cause, even in the North, and the Hutchinsons were hissed on occasion when they sang songs deemed "political." Their most famous abolitionist song, "Get Off the Track," was often sung to mixed reactions; it inspired wild enthusiasm among abolitionist sympathizers, and abuse, vocal and sometimes physical, from others.*

The Hutchinson Family was, at the height of its success in the 1840s, a quartet consisting of three brothers—Judson, John, and Asa—and their sister Abby. Although the entire family was more or less musical (there were thirteen children who lived to maturity), it was the three brothers, later joined by their sister, who were encouraged to form a professional family group by the example of popular Swiss singers and instrumentalists, the Rainer Family, who toured New England around 1840. In 1842 they set off on an initial tour of New Hampshire (their native state), Vermont, and upstate New York. Later that year they appeared successfully in Boston, and the next year in New York. Ultimately, before the group began to break up in 1849, they became the most successful and popular family group in America, and were soon widely imitated by other ensembles of "family singers." Their concert fare was by no

* "Get Off the Track" was an adaptation of the popular minstrel song "Old Dan Tucker"! While this may strike us as paradoxical today, it is simply evidence of the broad popularity of blackface minstrel songs in the 1840s.

means all "protest" songs; in fact, these permeated their programs only gradually from 1844 on. Their basic repertoire was made up of glees, comic songs, Scottish songs, patriotic songs, and sentimental ballads, including those of Stephen Foster. Their stock of more extended melodramatic pieces included "The Maniac" and "The Ship on Fire" by Henry Russell.

A consistent feature of performances of the Hutchinson Family was the blend of their voices—a feature that Dale Cockrell notes as having an influence on commercially popular vocal groups well into this century. He writes:

> In fact, the Hutchinsons in the long run are probably most responsible for taking the SATB blend and bringing it into the mainstream of American popular song. Not only is the format of the various "family," "brother" and "sister" acts of the last fifty years—the Osmonds, the Brothers Four, the Andrew Sisters—beholden to them but also, very likely, a sweet sound, one based on a rich vocal blend.[19]

A significant part of the appeal of the Hutchinson Family was the fact that as "native-born Yankee singers," with their "fresh and unsophisticated nature," their clarity of enunciation which made them easily understood, and their simplicity of style, they embodied all that was "truly American." Dale Cockrell quotes a Baltimore reviewer of 1844 as saying:

> Their songs are so truly American, the love of country and of home is so alive and so real with them, that we catch from them the very spirit of patriotism.[20]

It would appear, then, that in the arena of popular music the Hutchinson Family was working toward the same ends that Anthony Philip Heinrich and William Henry Fry (as we shall see in Chapter 15) were trying to promote in the more circumscribed arena of classical music—"Americanism."

Stephen Foster

Without doubt the best-known and most popular composer of the entire century was Stephen Collins Foster (1826–64). No other American composer has been so romanticized, or has inspired, unwittingly, such an indelible image in the popular mind—an image based both on the wide and enduring currency of his songs, and also on the undoubtedly sad circumstances that attended the last years of his short life. The comparison with the Austrian composer Franz Schubert (1797–1828), who also wrote many imperishable songs and died young, has tempted some. But although Foster was no "American Schubert" (for one thing, they cannot be compared in terms of the sheer breadth of the genres in which they worked), and although the popular Foster image is based on a good deal of misinformation and misinterpretation, the facts, insofar as modern objective scholarship can determine them, are more interesting than the fiction, and his accomplishments, his legacy, and his influence are undeniably impressive.

The events of Foster's life have been extensively documented. He was born as the ninth child into a fairly prosperous family in Pittsburgh. He was evidently of a reflective and sensitive temperament and showed an early interest in and aptitude for music; it was not to be expected, either of his family or of the mercantile environment of Pittsburgh in the 1830s, that this aptitude would be especially encouraged. Pursuing music in spite of this, Foster achieved enough success with some of his songs in the late 1840s (notably "Oh! Susanna") to induce him to sign contracts with publishers in New York and Baltimore. He actually became a professional songwriter in the 1850s and was able, for a time, to support himself in this way. His contracts, in fact, were somewhat unusual for the time in providing that the composer receive not a one-time payment but continuing royalties on sales: in 1853, these were raised to 10 percent—potentially a very favorable arrangement. In 1852 he and his wife, Jane, made a trip (his only one) to the part of the country that served as the romanticized locale for so many of his songs, when they traveled on his brother's steamboat down the Mississippi to New Orleans. But by the mid-1850s, serious problems began to surface, as manifested in his being persistently in debt (mostly to his brothers); in periodic, and ultimately prolonged, separations from his family; in a failure to manage prudently such resources as he had (he began to be overdrawn with his publishers, and in 1857 in order to secure cash he sold, for the first but not the last time, all future rights to the songs already published); and finally, in the alcoholism that defeated him in his last years in New York—years in which he struggled to turn out enough songs (few or none of which were among his best) to maintain a meager income.

Foster's output of songs can be divided roughly into two categories: parlor songs, and songs for the minstrel stage. The parlor songs are of two kinds, sentimental (with the characteristics already described above) and comic. Among the sentimental songs are "Open Thy Lattice, Love" his first published song (1844), "Jeanie with the Light Brown Hair" (1854), "Gentle Annie" (1856), and "Beautiful Dreamer" (published posthumously in 1864, but not necessarily "the last song ever written," as advertised on the cover).[21] The non-minstrel comic songs, already dealt with, belong mostly to his last years, and are not especially distinguished.

The songs Foster wrote for the minstrel stage (described variously on their covers—"plantation melody," "plantation song," "Ethiopian melody") are with few exceptions his most enduring. The comic songs, with their inherent rhythmic vitality (achieved partly through the repetition of distinctive rhythmic fragments, together with the occasional use of syncopation) and their simple but catchy melodic lines, show, of all his output, the closest relationship to the rough-hewn folk songs, sacred and secular, of the antebellum frontier. To cite but one example of this relationship, Foster's tunes sometimes draw on what was evidently a common fund of musical motives—familiar patterns for phrase beginnings and endings. The recurring cadence in "Oh! Susanna," for example (to the words "Susanna, don't you cry") is also prominent in a tune from the shape-note tradition, which is called "Tennessee" in William Walker's *Southern Harmony* of 1844. And the beginning of the chorus of "Camptown Races" ("Gwine to run all night!") is identical with the beginning of the chorus of the black spiritual "Roll, Jordan, Roll." (Foster's song, first published in 1850, may well have influenced the spiritual, rather than the other way around.) These exuberant, high-spirited songs for the minstrel stage include "Oh! Susanna" (1848), "Camptown Races" (1850),

"Nelly Bly" (1850), "Way Down in Ca-i-ro" (1850, with its original piano part marked "a la banjo"), "Ring, Ring de Banjo" (1851), and "The Glendy Burk" (1860).

The sentimental minstrel songs (Foster himself used the word "pathetic", in the sense of evoking pathos) include songs, such as "Old Folks at Home," that are among the best-known and at the same time the most controversial from our perspective of over a century later. Unlike the comic songs, they portray blacks with a profound sympathy, as human beings capable of feeling deeply the pain of separation, and the unending weariness of a life of servitude—a weariness to be relieved only by an often welcome death. The grief of separation—whether from loved ones or from an irrevocable past—is uppermost in the three best-known "pathetic plantation" songs: "Old Folks at Home," "My Old Kentucky Home," and "Old Black Joe." Significantly, Foster abandoned dialect ("de" for "the," "dis" for "this," etc.) in the latter two songs. Aided by the absence of a localizing vernacular, the "old Kentucky home" could be anyone's longed-for home, in a longed-for past; the "darkies" and the "little cabin floor" become merely incidental. (William Austin has said of this song that it "uses the black mask to intensify the pathos.")[22] In "Old Black Joe," we are reminded by the word "black" and the reference to "cotton fields" that the subject is indeed a black man, but the weariness and the longing to be reunited with those "departed long ago" are conceivably universal. Thus the nostalgia and the world-weariness accorded well with sentiments frequently expressed in popular song of the period generally, including the non-minstrel songs of Foster himself.

But if the pathetic plantation songs portray blacks in sympathetic terms, they tend, at the same time, to romanticize plantation (i.e. slave) life; hence their controversial status today. Nowhere is this more apparent than in the portrayed love of slave for master, as expressed in "Massa's in de Cold Ground." While it would be unreasonable to deny categorically that genuine sentiments of this kind ever existed at any time, there is a deep undercurrent of irony associated with their conventional expression.[23]

A consideration of Foster's "pathetic plantation songs" would be incomplete without taking account of the highly significant appearance in 1852 of Harriet Beecher Stowe's novel *Uncle Tom's Cabin,* the central theme of which is slavery. The novel achieved instant popularity, and was almost immediately adapted for the stage; William Austin writes that nine versions of it were produced in New York before the end of 1852. Foster originally conceived "My Old Kentucky Home," with the play in mind, though he changed his final version, deleting the name Uncle Tom. At one time or another, however, at least four of his plantation songs—"Old Folks at Home," "My Old Kentucky Home," "Massa's in de Cold Ground" (sung by chorus), and "Old Black Joe"—were sung in stage versions of *Uncle Tom's Cabin.**

In spite of the unevenness of his output, and the fact that both his life and

* William Austin has thoroughly explored Foster's relation to the Stowe novel, and the plays that were made from it, in his *"Susanna," "Jeanie," and "The Old Folks at Home": The Songs of Stephen Foster from His Time to Ours.* In this book, indispensable to a deeper understanding of the meaning of Foster's songs, Austin traces the preoccupation with these songs on the part of an impressive array of musicians, from Antonín Dvořák and Charles Ives to Pete Seeger, Ray Charles, and Ornette Coleman.

his work have been misunderstood and misrepresented, Stephen Foster's place as one of our greatest songwriters is certainly more secure now than ever. If his total output of songs is examined, it becomes clear that his range is broader than has been commonly realized. Yet when all is said, of all his output it is the "pathetic plantation songs" that penetrate deepest. Perhaps this is partly because, in Austin's words, they are "so densely ambiguous." It is their melodies, of course, that assure their currency and their staying power. Yet once we have heard the words, the tunes "mean what their words mean," and the implications of their meaning, with all the attendant ambiguity would soon be seared into the American consciousness by the momentous events that accompanied the last years of Stephen Foster's life.

Songs of the Civil War

Uncle Tom's Cabin was only one of many portents of the tragedy of epic proportions that America was to live through in the next decade. Our greatest national trauma (more lives were lost in the Civil War than in all of America's other wars combined) left an indelible mark on all aspects of our culture. Popular song was, as could be expected, the quickest to mirror the war's events, its ideals, its motivations, its slogans, and, of course, its anguish. By the time of the Civil War, the popular music publishing industry was in place and functioning. It was able to get songs to the public with an immediacy that rivaled that of the newspapers. Within a few days of the Confederate bombardment of Fort Sumter, which began the war, George F. Root's "The First Gun is Fired!"[24] was in print. More than in any other period in our history, popular song was the journalism of the emotions.

The songs of the period are of several distinct types. There are patriotic rallying songs, sung by both North and South—often to the same tune. Somewhat related to these are songs about specific events, battles, campaigns. More poignant personal expressions are the plaintive songs of soldiers in the field, thinking of home, and at home those of wives, mothers, and families, waiting, hoping, and praying for the safe return of, or grieving for the loss of, their fathers, sons, brothers, and husbands away at war. These songs grew in numbers and importance as the war, supposed at first to last a few weeks (Lincoln's first call for volunteers was for a period of ninety days), dragged on and took its increasing toll year after year. Inevitably there were comic songs. Of the hundreds of songs written, a few that somehow lasted will, in our brief survey, have to represent the many.

Although songs relating to the issues of the fatally looming conflict were in circulation before the war, the actual outbreak of hostilities created an immediate need for songs, and both sides rushed to fit new words to existing tunes—a time-honored practice. New verses to "The Star-Spangled Banner" were attempted by both sides, and there were both northern and southern versions of "La Marseillaise," a stirring tune borrowed from the French Revolution, which had figured prominently in American politics since soon after our own War for Independence. "The Yellow Rose of Texas"[25] became "The Song of the Texas Rangers," and Henry Russell's famous "Woodman! Spare that Tree! (touch not a single bough)" became "Traitor! Spare that Flag! (touch not a single star)."[26] The ambivalence of Maryland as a border state was illustrated by the fact that both sides converted the German song "O Tannenbaum" into "Maryland, My Maryland," but with two sets of words urging diametrically opposed loyalties. James Ryder Randall, a poet whose sympathies were with the South, urged his "Mother state" to join the Confederacy:

Dear Mother, burst the tyrant's chain,
  Maryland! My Maryland!
Virginia should not call in vain!
  Maryland! My Maryland!

The North answered with a version with words by William H. C. Hosmer:

One sword-strike for the good old flag,
  Maryland, my Maryland!
Down with secession's shameless rag,
  Maryland, our Maryland![27]

"Dixie" (originally "I Wish I Was in Dixie's Land") was a song written for Bryant's Minstrels by the Ohioan (and Union sympathizer) Dan Emmett. Its use in a show in New Orleans (with no credit given in the version published there to Emmett as the composer) at a crucial time, when secessionist feelings were running high, caused it to spread rapidly throughout the South, where it became virtually the musical symbol of the Confederacy. Many different sets of words were put to the tune, and it was not exclusively the property of the South; it could be found, with appropriate words, in virtually every state. The lively tune defied attempts to make it convey lofty sentiments, but as a rallying song it had no equal.[28]

The other song most often associated with the Civil War is "The Battle Hymn of the Republic." It made its way, by gradual transformation, from a camp-meeting song with the words, "Say, brothers, will you meet us on Canaan's happy shore?" to a marching song used by Union regiments, growing out of that famous incident at Harpers Ferry in 1859, with the somewhat crude words (which still have a good deal of currency, especially in parodies) "John Brown's body lies a-mouldering in the grave," to the loftier hymn, with words by Julia Ward Howe, that we know today.[29] Two more rallying songs, one for each side, need to be mentioned. The South had "The Bonnie Blue Flag" (1861), a "southern patriotic song" with an Irish lilt, by Harry Macarthy.[30] The North had George F. Root's "The Battle Cry of Freedom," an immensely popular song, the verse of which is shown in Example 12–1.

On the printed sheet music of another of Root's songs, "Just Before the Battle, Mother," there appears this note: "In the Army of the Cumberland, the Soldiers sing the Battle-Cry when going into action, by order of the Commanding general." The tune of this stirring song was quoted more than once by Charles Ives, whose father, as we shall see, had been a Civil War bandmaster.

As the war dragged on and hopes for an early end were cruelly disappointed, the tenor of the new songs that appeared began to change. Lincoln's call in 1862 for more volunteers brought the response "We Are Coming, Father

Example 12–1 THE BATTLE CRY OF FREEDOM

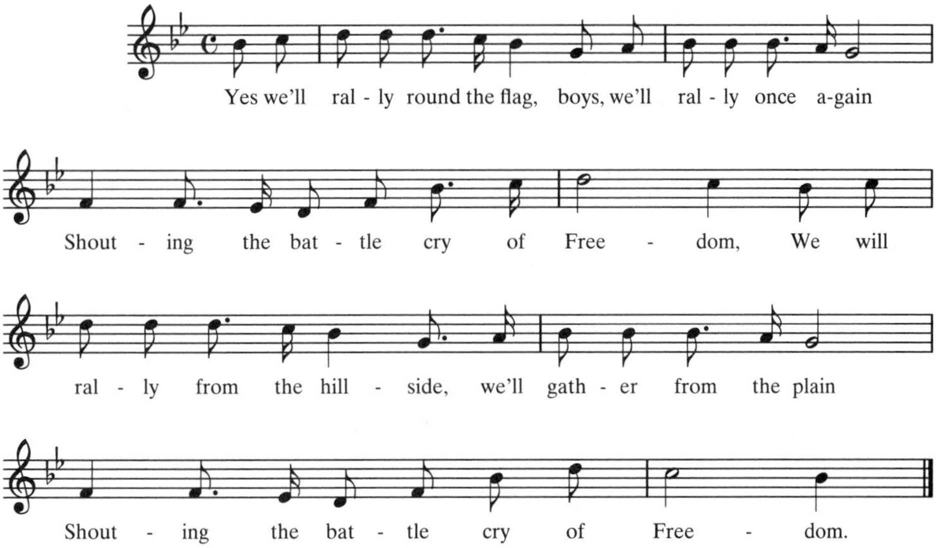
Yes we'll ral - ly round the flag, boys, we'll ral - ly once a-gain
Shout - ing the bat - tle cry of Free - dom, We will
ral - ly from the hill - side, we'll gath - er from the plain
Shout - ing the bat - tle cry of Free - dom.

Abraam, 300,000 More," a poem set by many different composers; Stephen Foster's setting was not the first, but it was probably his best war song.[31] "Tramp! Tramp! Tramp! (the boys are marching)" (1864) by Root,[32] coming late in the conflict, is actually a song put into the mouths of prisoners of war looking forward to release. "When Johnny Comes Marching Home" (1863, dedicated "To the Army and Navy of the Union") looks forward optimistically to war's end. Supposedly composed by the noted Civil War bandmaster Patrick Gilmore (under the pseudonym Louis Lambert), the rollicking tune has pronounced Irish folk characteristics, and is unusual in being a spirited tune in the minor mode, in a period when practically all popular melodies, even those to sad words, were in major.[33] The soberer "Tenting on the Old Camp Ground" (1864) by Walter Kittredge (a friend of the Hutchinsons) looks back on a prolonged conflict, with its chorus:

> Many are the hearts which are weary tonight,
> Wishing for the war to cease;
> Many are the hearts looking for the right
> To see the dawn of peace.

This song was sung by a surviving branch of the Hutchinson Family (the "tribe of Asa"), and remained popular for years after the war at the reunions of veterans.[34]

Among other sober songs put into the mouths of soldiers in the field are "Just Before the Battle, Mother," by the Northern composer George F. Root (whose publishing firm of Root & Cady, in Chicago, brought out many war songs),[35] and another by one of the best composers who cast in their lot with the South, John Hill Hewitt. Setting a poem by a northern woman, Ethel Lynn

Beers, of Goshen, New York, Hewitt produced in "All Quiet Along the Potomac Tonight" a song that transcended sectionalism and treated with a combination of sympathy and irony the death of a lone soldier on guard duty.

> "All quiet along the Potomac tonight,"
> Except here and there a stray picket
> Is shot as he walks on his beat to and fro,
> By a rifleman hid in the thicket;
> 'Tis nothing! a private or two now and then,
> Will not count in the news of the battle,
> Not an officer lost! only one of the men
> Moaning out all alone the death rattle.[36]

The death in battle of very young boys, many of whom enlisted as drummers (some as young as thirteen) was the subject of several songs; probably best-known is "The Drummer Boy of Shiloh."[37]

Many of the sentimental songs were sung in both the North and the South, with the occasional alteration of a verse or two. One of the most popular was "Weeping, Sad and Lonely; or, When This Cruel War Is Over" (1863), which, according to the authors of *The Singing Sixties*, was "a ballad so mournful that generals were forced to forbid their troops to sing it, yet so popular that its sale approached a million copies."[38] Mournful it is indeed, and reminiscent in some ways of the host of mournful songs that we encountered in Chapter 7, which emerged a generation or two later from the rural South with hillbilly (later called country) music.

Humor was a necessary and inevitable accompaniment to hardship and danger, and comic songs abounded among the soldiers. They were most often parodies of other songs: both "The Army Bean" and "Army Bugs" (lice) were sung to the tune of "In the Sweet By and By," and these insects were also the subject of "The Greybacks So Tenderly Clinging," sung to the tune of "Marching Through Georgia."[39] Food was the subject of "Goober Peas"[40] (peanuts), as well as of "The Army Bean." Humor on the home front frequently involved the use of dialect—a stock in trade of the popular musical stage in the nineteenth century, as we saw in the last chapter. The dialect may be a kind of generic vernacular, as in "Abraham's Daughter; or, Raw Recruits," by Septimus Winner;[41] rural New England ("Yankee Robinson at Bull Run");[42] Irish ("They've Grafted Him into the Army");[43] or German ("I Goes to Fight mit Sigel").[44]

A subject only recently explored is the attitude toward blacks portrayed in popular songs of the time. One researcher, Caroline Moseley, has found it mostly negative, even in the Unionist and abolitionist songs of the North, and has written: "One would expect that antislavery songs would present a positive view of black people. There is, in fact, little in any abolitionist song which relates meaningfully to blacks."[45]

The attitudes of black people themselves toward the war and ultimate emancipation was of course inferred and expressed in songs written by white songwriters. "We Are Coming from the Cotton Fields" expressed without dialect the African-Americans' eagerness to fight in the Union cause. The very popular "Kingdom Coming" (1862), a dialect song by Henry Clay Work, couched in jubilant terms the anticipation of freedom. The chorus goes:

> De massa run? ha, ha!
> De darkey stay? ho, ho!
> It mus' be now de kingdom comin'
> An' de year ob Jubilo![46]

The song was indeed written by a white man (one whose father had been jailed in Illinois for his activities in helping runaway slaves to escape) and was introduced, following an intensive promotional campaign, by Christy's Minstrels in Chicago. But it is also known to have enjoyed wide currency among blacks; entering oral tradition, it achieved something of the status of a folk song, along with "Steal Away" and other songs that had specific reference to freedom in this present life.

The "millennial" view of emancipation represented in "Kingdom Coming" was common to many songs. Emancipation was too often viewed, by even the most fervent abolitionists, as an end in itself; there was little grasp of the severe and persistent problems that would follow in its wake. But given the circumstances, such understanding would have been a great deal to expect of even the most enlightened and farsighted thinkers, much less of popular song, which mirrors only the most immediate feelings and concerns of the day.

If this section seems to have dwelt at considerable length on the popular songs associated with a chronologically brief period, let it be said, for one thing, that these songs reflected events and issues that have loomed large and cast long shadows on the American scene—shadows that are still with us today.* Secondly, in no other period of crisis has popular song been so important, as mirror, as symbol, and as catalyst, than in the period surrounding the American Civil War.

Popular Song from the Civil War Through the Ragtime Era

The half-century between the Civil War and World War I witnessed not only profound change, but also an acceleration in the *rate* of change that marks it as the beginning of the modern age. As such it presents contradictory images, and calls forth contradictory responses. Westward expansion, epitomized by the completion of the transcontinental railroad in 1869, a scant four years after Lee's surrender at Appomattox, was perceived as progress; yet it was accomplished at the shameful cost of killing off many of the original inhabitants who had lived on the land for centuries, and destroying the survivors' way of life. Industry and invention flourished, manufacturing and selling goods undreamed of in any previous time, and raising the material standard of living (for most) far above what it had been; this was perceived as progress, and was celebrated in the many fairs and expositions that were held. Yet it was achieved only with a frightful waste of natural resources; and in many cases

* In considering the question of race in America, Austin's work on the many-faceted meanings of the songs of Stephen Foster has probably only scratched the surface.

workers who produced the goods were exploited beyond the point of endurance, and strife between management ("the bosses") and the newly formed and struggling labor unions reached shockingly bloody proportions. Cities grew and prospered, as did the nation overall; yet corruption among those who governed was all too common. Immigrants poured into the country from both Europe and Asia; their hopes and prospects for a better life were on the whole justified, yet discrimination, and worse, degraded many and worked against their entering the "mainstream" of American life.

The Gilded Age (to use Mark Twain's famous term) has been given many interpretations. For all its excesses—it's "crass materialism" and flagrant examples of corruption and waste—the age of "rowdy adolescence" was also a time of solid accomplishments as well; schools, colleges, and libraries were built as well as bridges and railroads, and there was Chautauqua as well as burlesque. Let us try now to see what popular music was like during this period of ambivalence and change.

Popular Song Before Tin Pan Alley

Popular song, which had itself become an industry by the end of the century, did not mirror the full range of the contradictory images described above. The songs that were most widely sold and sung purveyed for the most part what popular song has always purveyed—romantic love, nostalgia, some humor, and some moralizing. The most popular topical songs were those that presented the positive aspects of events; Henry Clay Work's enthusiastic tribute to progress "Crossing the Great Sierra" (published in 1869 after the completion of the railroad) was more successful than his sympathetic and prophetic lament "The Song of the Red Man" (1868), which has the following lines:

> Driven westward we came, but the paleface was here,
> With his sharp axe and death-flashing gun;
> And his great Iron Horse now is rumbling in the rear
> *O my brave men!* your journey is done.[47]

A few well-established songwriters wrote songs about social issues. Work, the composer of "The Song of the Red Man," also wrote one of the most popular temperance songs, "Come Home, Father" (1864). George Frederick Root wrote "The Hand That Holds the Bread" in 1874, in support of the Grange movement rallying farmers against middlemen and monopolists. Septimus Winner wrote "Out of Work" in 1877, reflecting one of the frequent depressions of the period. But except for a few of the temperance songs, songs of social comment were not big items in the general marketplace. Songs such as "No Irish Need Apply," "Drill, Ye Tarriers, Drill," "The Farmer Is the Man Who Feeds Them All," and "The Dodger," all from this period, have survived doggedly in the special anthologies of their constituencies, and in the quasi-oral tradition described in Chapter 4.[48]

The Civil War left a legacy of bitterness; seldom has any song expressed such hatred as "I'm a Good Old Rebel," published in 1866.[49] More widespread were feelings of war-weariness, sorrow, and a general depletion of spirit. Charles Hamm comments on the lack of "force" in the songs of the period, and says: "Poets and songwriters were quite content to turn out songs of romantic love and nostalgia, many of them reminiscent of the sentiments so popular in American songs of the 1820's and 1830's."[50] Songs of gentle sentiment were popular. "Whispering Hope (Oh how welcome thy voice)" (1868, by Septimus Winner) speaks of comfort after sorrow—a mellifluous duet in waltz time, anticipating the popular waltz songs of the 1890s. There was a preoccupation with growing old; three typical songs of love and remembrance in old age are all still well-known: "When You and I Were Young, Maggie" (1866), "Sweet Genevieve" (1869), and "Silver Threads Among the Gold" (1873). Both retain the four-part choruses of the earlier period. Another popular song about aging was "Grandfather's Clock" (1876), by Henry Clay Work. And an enormously popular song from the same year dealt with homesickness: "I'll Take You Home Again, Kathleen." Even the waltzing exuberance of "The Flying Trapeze" (1868), with its gracefully arching melody expressive of the swings of the aerialist, and its ruefully comic final verses, is tinged with the sadness and hopelessness of lost love:

> Once I was happy, but now I'm forlorn,
> Like an old coat that is tattered and torn.[51]

In many ways the popular song of the period was linked more to the past than to the future. There was (relatively) an innocence, a sincerity, a concern with "causes" (as expressed in the songs in support of temperance, woman suffrage, better treatment of immigrants,[52] etc.), and, above all, an artistic and commercial climate in which the individual could still count—could still succeed—which was largely displaced with the coming of the "marvelous hit-making machine," to use Russell Sanjek's colorful phrase.[53] Charles Hamm reports that Thomas Westendorf, who wrote the highly successful song "I'll Take You Home Again, Kathleen" about 1875 in Plainfield, Indiana, was later sent a check for $50 each month for many years "in gratitude" by the publisher, who, having bought the song outright, was under no contractual obligation to do so. (The publisher, John Church & Co., was based not in New York, but in Cincinnati.) The whole story (beginning with a "hit" coming out of Plainfield, Indiana!) would have been, if not unthinkable, at least highly unlikely two decades later.[54]

Tin Pan Alley: Popular Music Publishing Becomes an Industry

As American cities became larger, wealthier, and more sophisticated in the last two decades of the nineteenth century, two things happened that affected popular music. One was the increased vitality, and ultimately the Americanization, of the popular musical stage, as we saw in the last chapter. The other was the gradual emergence of a centralized industry for the publication and promotion of American popular songs. Both phenomena were centered on New York City. A leading city for entertainment since the middle of the nineteenth century, New York assumed absolute dominance in the fields of both popular musical theater and popular song publishing in the last two decades of that century.

Broadway and Tin Pan Alley were interrelated in complex ways, but were never one and the same. Tin Pan Alley publishers did publish the most popular show songs as sheet music—songs by Victor Herbert and George M. Cohan, to cite examples from the era we are here considering. (Show tunes have for the most part been left out of consideration in this chapter, since considerable space is devoted to the popular musical theater in Chapter 11.) It is also true that successful Tin Pan Alley songs (those not written for shows) were frequently incorporated into stage productions, especially those with a more or less plotless revue format which allowed for interpolation. The very loosely plotted show *A Trip to Chinatown* of 1892, for example used many interpolations during its run of 650 performances, including the ubiquitous "After the Ball," written the same year by the arch-entrepreneur Charles K. Harris. (Thirty-five years later, the same song was used in Jerome Kern's *Show Boat!)*

Broadway and Tin Pan Alley (neither term has ever defined with much accuracy a geographical location) cohabited the same area in the beginning—what was then the theater district of East 14th Street in Manhattan, where Tony Pastor's famous Opera House, the home of vaudeville, was located.* But the close relationship exemplified in this proximity grew looser over time, and as the musical theater developed, under the powerful influence of the great show composers of the new century, the *stratification* of American popular song, as noted by many observers, took place. In terms of craftsmanship and sophistication, Broadway show songs, from Victor Herbert to Jerome Kern and George Gershwin, were at the top. As Nat Shapiro has written, "The Broadway musical is traditionally the the primary source of superior popular music in this country."[55] Beginning in the 1890s, theater songs dominate the great canon of American popular song, which includes most of the "evergreens" such as "Smoke Gets in Your Eyes." Slightly below the theater songs is a class of songs that began to appear in the 1930s, the movie songs. This category also includes a number of evergreens: "The Way You Look Tonight," "You'd Be So Nice to Come Home to," "Over the Rainbow," and "Laura" are among them.

Beyond theater songs and movie songs was that vast category of songs purveyed by what James Maher has called "the marketplace-oriented music publishing companies known collectively as Tin Pan Alley." Its songs issued forth in prodigious quantities, only the tiniest fraction of which attained "hit" status. Most of them were short-lived, manufactured to conform to the passing fashions of the year, the season, the month. Yet here too, as we shall see, were some "evergreens"—in the prodigious output of Tin Pan Alley some few songs that have had the enduring qualities to make them "standards."†

* The general location of both "Broadway" and "Tin Pan Alley" moved gradually uptown—the latter to 28th Street (its most renowned location in its heyday, and its home at the time it got its name), then to 42nd Street, and finally to 47th Street and the Brill Building, its last stronghold.

† While it was not too uncommon to find composers contributing to two of the three strata here defined, Irving Berlin was virtually the only songwriter to contribute to all three—composing extensively and successfully for Broadway, Hollywood, and Tin Pan Alley.

New York's dominance in popular song publishing was not achieved at the hands of the old-line publishers—certainly not at the hands of publishers who would send monthly checks to songwriters out of sheer gratitude. As Sanjek has put it,

> Much as would the post–World War II music houses when faced with the annoying presence of hillbilly and race music, the established arts- and parlor-music publishers failed to perceive the future. It was in the hands of music publishers specializing in new popular American music—first formed around 1885, whose founders . . . were, as one of them, Isidore Witmark, remembered, "youngsters who had caught on and had a fair notion of the direction in which they were headed. What they knew least about was music and words, what they cared about least might be answered in the same phrase. They discovered that there was money in popular song."[56]

The basic vehicle for the dissemination of the popular song, and therefore the basic commodity of the industry, continued until the 1920s to be sheet music. The money in popular song, it was realized by these new entrepreneurs, was in songs that sold not in thousands of copies, but in millions. In the 1880s sales began to climb toward this goal, and in 1892 the song that perhaps more than any other symbolizes the era—"After the Ball," by Charles K. Harris—sold over two million copies in its first few years. In order to ensure himself a large share of the profits, Harris (who only a few years before had hung out his sign in Milwaukee advertising "Charles K. Harris/Banjoist and Song Writer/ Songs Written to Order") had formed his own company, an example that many other songwriters were soon to follow.

In the first years of this century sheet music sold for as little as ten cents a copy; occasionally it might be unloaded for as little as two cents. But the average was around fifty cents. Sales figures, post–"After the Ball," could easily top the million mark for very successful songs. George M. Cohan's "Over There" (1917) sold two million copies; Jean Schwartz's "Bedelia" (1903), three million; and "The Rosary" (1898) by Ethelbert Nevin (not a religious song), four million. But "After the Ball" was still the champion; it is said to have sold eventually over ten million. "On a Sunday Afternoon," by another prominent composer-entrepreneur, Harry von Tilzer, sold 10,000 copies in a single day in a New York department store in 1902.

For a song to reach anything even approaching this volume of sales (few did, and most barely paid for their printing costs), of course it had to be publicized, and this became a profession in itself, in which ingenuity and brashness paid off. Song "pluggers" were at work in music stores and department stores, playing and singing songs for prospective customers. Irving Berlin, Jerome Kern, George Gershwin, and Vincent Youmans all got started in the profession this way. But this in itself was not enough; a larger public had to be reached. In the days before radio and the sound movie, vaudeville and the revue, with their loose formats that allowed for the interpolation of songs, were the best media for this. Earlier generations had certainly been aware of the performer's role in promoting a song; we have noted the "as sung by" billing given to popular singers on the covers of sheet music as early as the Jacksonian era. But a whole new order of "persuasion" was applied to prominent vaudeville performers beginning in the 1890s, including outright payment (a form of subsidy that vaudeville circuit managers tried to stop, but that was merely circumvented), or the more circuitous methods of offering a share of the profits, credit as co-author of the song, or headline billing, with picture, on the sheet music itself.* The practice of listing the singer who introduced the song as co-author (he or she *might* have contributed some extra verses) also assured the performer a share of the profits, while confusing, for uninitiated future generations, the real authorship of the song.

But securing the services of a prominent singer was not necessarily where promotional endeavors ended. The professional song plugger was limited only by the extent of his ingenuity and daring, and with the example of P. T. Barnum's publicity exploits behind him, he was alert to all possibilities. Amateur singers would be paid to sing the publisher's merchandise on the popular amateur-night programs that were given in many vaudeville theaters; the tunes were ensconced in the street organs leased to immigrant organ grinders by an Italian *padrone*, with whom the song pluggers made it their business to maintain "close communication." In the early freewheeling days, still more ingenious schemes were carried out. An anonymous "boomer" (a plugger who also sang) left this account from the early 1900s:

> I'm a song promoter. I'm the man who makes popular songs popular. I earn big money and I've grown into a necessity to the music publishing house that employs me. . . . Maybe I go to the swellest theater in town Monday night and sit in a lower box, in my evening clothes, like an ordinary patron. During the daytime I will have fixed the orchestra and had the music run over. Between the first and second act, perhaps, I stand up in my box and start singing. The audience is startled. Ushers run through the aisles. A policeman comes in and walks toward the box. About the time the policeman is where he can be seen by all the audience I step out on to the stage in front of the curtain and begin the chorus, with the orchestra playing and the audience, that is now onto the game, clapping so hard it almost blisters its hands.[57]

The World's Fairs of Chicago (1893) and St. Louis (1904) offered large-scale opportunities for plugging. "After the Ball" was essentially "made" at the former. The novelist Theodore Dreiser (whose brother, as Paul Dresser, had a fairly successful career as a songwriter, best known for "My Gal Sal") left a valuable account of how the whole process worked in a magazine article written in 1898.[58]

As to the songs themselves, many are still well known nearly a century later, and have become the symbols of the era of Tin Pan Alley's first flowering, the "Gay Nineties." The squarer 4/4 meter of the typical antebellum song had given way to 3/4; the waltz-song dominated the field. To name but a few of the more familiar ones (in addition to "After the Ball") there was "Daisy Bell," better known as "A Bicycle Built for Two" (1892, by Harry Dacre); "The Bowery" (also 1892, by Percy Gaunt—this song is said to have slashed the value of real estate along this lower Manhattan street); "The Sidewalks of New York"

* A singer with the reputation of an Al Jolson could demand "all of the above." A publisher recalled many years later that "Jolson was best 'influenced' by getting a piece of a song, a byline as co-author and his name and photo on the title page." See Sanjek, *From Print to Plastic*, p. 12.

(1894, by Charles B. Lawlor and James W. Blake); "The Band Played On" (1895, by Charles Ward); and "Meet Me in St. Louis" (1904, by Kerry Mills). As the variety show, with its solo performer, had replaced the minstrel show, with its onstage chorus, so in popular songs the earlier four-part chorus was replaced by the solo "chorus" (the older name stuck, though it was no longer literally accurate). From then on, in the conventional Tin Pan Alley song, it was the "chorus" that had the identifiable "tune"; the "verse," with its lead-in narration, was the part hardly anyone remembered, and it was frequently omitted, especially when the tunes were later used as jazz "standards." In other musical respects as well, conventionality was the rule: the 32-bar form, for both verse and chorus, was invariable; the major mode predominated; and the harmonies were the basic I, IV and V7 chords, with the addition typically of the embellishing, secondary V7s (a feature of concurrent "barbershop" harmony).[59]

A perusal of a collection such as *Favorite Songs of the Nineties*, with its eighty-nine songs published between 1884 and 1906, reveals a somewhat broader range of subject matter and treatment than might be expected. There are, of course, songs of romantic love, usually on the less serious side (most are waltzes) and often with a humorous twist. These would include such songs as "Daisy Bell" (1892), "The Band Played On" (1895), "On a Sunday Afternoon" (1902), and "Wait 'till the Sun Shines, Nellie" (1905). Even more lighthearted were such comic, or near-comic, songs as "The Cat Came Back" (1893), "Everybody Works but Father" (1905, written for Lew Dockstader's minstrel company), or "Waltz Me Around Again, Willie" (1906); or such topical songs as "In My Merry Oldsmobile" (1905), or "Meet Me in St. Louis" (1904, a promotional song for the world's fair of that year).

There was a broad range of songs that played quite deliberately on the sentiments, written out of sincere feelings (here we think of Paul Dresser) or out of shrewd calculation as to what would sell (and here we think of Charles K. Harris), or, as is more likely in most cases, a combination of the two. Perhaps, as has been suggested, these songs offered an opportunity for emotional release, even if vicarious, at a time when the outward display of emotion was not acceptable in Protestant middle-class society. Prominent in this genre were the songs about women either bought or betrayed—women not as objects of romance, but as objects of pity. So much have these songs been associated with the period that their very titles have entered the language as phrases symbolic of the late Victorian age: "She May Have Seen Better Days" (1894), "Mother Was a Lady" (1896), "Take Back Your Gold" (1897), "She Is More to Be Pitied Than Censured" (1898), "Only a Bird in a Gilded Cage" (1900).* Songs about separation by death were numerous; familiar are "My Gal Sal" (Paul Dresser's most famous song, of 1905) and "Dear Old Girl" (1903). Many a song that is actually about death reveals the fact only in the verse, as Charles Hamm has pointed out; the better-known chorus has more general sentiments. Examples are "'When You Were Sweet Sixteen" (1898), "You Tell Me Your

* It should be noted that the lighter songs of the period have also contributed phrases to our vernacular speech, such as "the lovelight in her eyes," "the only pebble on the beach," or "pin a rose on me." It is possible, of course, that such phrases were already current and were simply picked up by songwriters.

Dream, I'll Tell You Mine" (1899), and "In the Shade of the Old Apple Tree" (1905). More blatantly pathetic "tearjerkers" are represented by "In the Baggage Coach Ahead" (where "baby's cries can't waken her"), published in 1896, and composed by Gussie Davis, who was (according to Eileen Southern) the first black songwriter to succeed in Tin Pan Alley.[60]*

One of the ethnic groups most often portrayed on the late nineteenth-century musical stage was the Irish, as we noted in the last chapter; they were also favorite subjects in popular song. Comic songs included "Down Went McGinty" (1889), "Who Threw the Overalls in Mistress Murphy's Chowder" (1898), and "Bedelia" ("I want to steal ye") of 1903—the latter advertised, to appeal to as many constituencies as possible, as an "Irish coon song serenade"! The sentimental Irish songs are even better known: "Sweet Rosie O'Grady" (1896), "My Wild Irish Rose" (1899), and "Where the River Shannon Flows" (1905, advertised as "The Irish Swanee River").[61]

The Ragtime Song

The nature and origins of ragtime, whose brief but intense flowering began in the 1890s and was over before 1920, will be considered in the next chapter. Ragtime, in its revival, has come to be regarded as essentially music for solo piano. In its day, however, ragtime had a far broader meaning. The ragtime or "coon" song we tend now to see as a vulgarized offshoot of pure ragtime, with its essential characteristics diluted. In its day, however, the ragtime song was an important, and popular, manifestation of the "'ragtime craze." With all its vulgarity, it brought a new dimension to American popular song. Ben Harney's "You've Been a Good Old Wagon, but You've Done Broke Down," with its distinct folk flavor and its touch of ragtime rhythm, was a significant departure for published songs of the era. Written in 1894, it was published first in 1895, not in New York but in Louisville, Kentucky. Bought by the Alley firm of Witmark, it was published the next year in New York, with great success. (The first actual piano rags were not published until 1897.) This success was partly due to the fact that May Irwin, a white singer of "coon songs" and evidently one of the first of the "red-hot mamas," had introduced the song and also Harney's "Mister Johnson, Turn Me Loose" on the stage; it was also partly due to the fact that Harney himself was performing in New York by this time, and achieving notoriety with (according to a reviewer) "his genuinely clever plantation Negro imitations and excellent piano playing"—which must have been ragtime, but ragtime played, as Eubie Blake has said, "like white people played it."[62]

Ragtime songs began to appear as sheet music, and to be incorporated into stage shows. The white composer Frederick Allen ("Kerry") Mills produced a memorable little "ragtime cakewalk" called "At a Georgia Camp Meeting," published in 1897 as a piano piece, and in 1899 as a song. The tune, with its ragtime syncopations, became very popular, and was much associated with the craze for a dance called the cakewalk that swept America and even

* The cover of this famous example gives a picture and byline to Imogene Comer, "Queen of Descriptive Vocalists," while at the same time taking opportunistic advantage of the scenario to advertise "The Empire State Express of the New York Central . . . Fastest Train in the World."

invaded Europe. The cakewalk, originally a plantation slave dance, had appeared in exaggerated form as the minstrel show "walk-around" for years. Other notable ragtime songs to stand out from the run-of-the-mill in the next few years were "Bill Bailey, Won't You Please Come Home" (1902, Hughie Cannon) and "Waiting for the Robert E. Lee" (1911, Lewis Muir), by white composers, and "My Ragtime Baby" (1898, by Fred Stone), "Under the Bamboo Tree" (1902, by Robert Cole and the Johnson Brothers, interpolated in the show *Sally in Our Alley*), and, at a fairly late date, to go with a popular dance of the time, "Balling the Jack" (1914, by Cris Smith), by black composers.[63]

Some of ragtime's most elemental syncopations (of the type found in pre-rag minstrel tunes like "Dixie") enlivened many Tin Pan Alley songs that were otherwise simply fairly peppy tunes in duple meter. One such tune (labeled a march-schottische) is "Hot Time in the Old Town" (1896, Theo. A. Metz), said to have been based on a song heard in a famous St. Louis bordello. Interestingly enough, a slightly earlier song of the same type and origin, "Ta-Ra-Ra Boom-De-Ay!" (1891, credited to Henry Sayers on the sheet music), shows none of the same ragtime influence. A later song by the famous Tin Pan Alley entrepreneur Harry von Tilzer shows the same faint imprint of ragtime syncopation—"Wait 'Till the Sun Shines Nellie" (1905). One of Von Tilzer's song pluggers, and an ardent admirer of his, the young Irving Berlin, had his first great success with "Alexander's Ragtime Band" (1911), which was still basically a march. This style of peppy tune with rudimentary dashes of syncopation was noticeable in many of George M. Cohan's songs, as we have seen, and appeared sporadically in hit tunes right up through the twenties: "Ja-Da" (1918, Bob Carleton), "'Way Down Yonder in New Orleans" (1922, Henry Creamer and Turner Layton, black composers), "If You Knew Susie" (1925, Buddy De Sylva), and "Yes, Sir, That's My Baby" (1925, Walter Donaldson).

The shadow of blackface minstrelsy was long indeed, lasting well into the twentieth century. So persistent, and evidently popular, was the "darky" image in song that it was present even in songs whose well-known *choruses* gave little hint of it. "Ida! Sweet as Apple Cider" (1903) and "Coax Me" (1904) have faint traces of dialect, and references to a "dusky maid" and "dusky lovers" in their verses. Even the well-known "Mighty Lak' a Rose" (1901, by Ethelbert Nevin—a song that did not come out of Tin Pan Alley), in spite of the "eyes so shiny blue," has dialect (including the endearing term "Mammy") that shows a clear relationship to the long tradition of black dialect songs reaching back to the 1840s and before.[64]

We have briefly sketched the rich mix that was popular song in the two decades surrounding the turn of the century—years when the "marvelous hit-machine" was being built. Before we follow popular song farther into the twentieth century, let us look at another important ingredient in our popular musical culture: the American Band.

The Band in America After the Jacksonian Era

Bands and Band Music to the Time of Sousa

As was noted in Chapter 10, the wind band was an important part of the American musical scene in the Colonial and Federal periods; "bands of music" (then dominated by the woodwind instruments) served both military and civilian functions, and were popular providers of concert music, as well as music for dancing and marching. During the first half of the nineteenth century European experiment and invention resulted in improvements in brass instruments, making them more flexible and capable of producing a complete chromatic scale easily. The fairly large family of keyed bugles came first, later to be replaced by the saxhorns and their descendants, the alto, tenor, and baritone horns, and that famous solo instrument the cornet. These improvements, as well as the greater durability and carrying power of brass instruments (important for outdoor functions) led to the gradual elimination of clarinets, oboes, and bassoons, and the rise of the *brass band*, which dominated the scene until well after the Civil War. There were bands noted for their excellence in many cities by the 1830s, including the Boston Brass Band, the Providence Brass Band, and the Dodworth Band in New York. By the late 1850s, bands such as the Dodworth in New York, and that of Patrick S. Gilmore (1829–92) in Boston, were playing summer outdoor concerts, and indoor promenade concerts in the winter, as well as providing smaller groups for dances, dinners, and other functions.[65] A sampling of the music played by these bands includes quicksteps, polkas, schottisches, and waltzes—a fair reflection of the dances that were popular at the time.

With the coming of the Civil War came also the need for brass bands in ever-greater numbers. Often existing bands enlisted *in toto* to be attached to the newly forming and growing regiments that were going to war. Prominent bandmasters such as Gilmore in Massachusetts and Harvey Dodworth in New York trained bands and bandmasters (as John Philip Sousa was to do during World War I).

The standard Civil War band was small by present-day standards, consisting of a dozen brass players and five drummers. But even before hostilities ceased, there was a portent of things to come. When Patrick Gilmore, then in New Orleans, was asked by General Banks to provide music for the inauguration of the new governor there, he assembled a band of five hundred and a chorus of six thousand (including schoolchildren), and put on the first of his many mammoth concerts, climaxed by the firing of fifty cannon (electrically controlled from the podium), and the ringing of all the church bells in the city.

After the war, Gilmore expanded on the concept of the concert event of huge proportions. In Boston in 1869 he put together an orchestra of a thousand players and choruses totaling ten thousand singers for a five-day National Peace Jubilee, for which a special coliseum with a large organ were constructed. In 1872, for a World Peace Jubilee, he doubled his forces again, assembling two thousand instrumentalists and choruses of twenty thousand in another specially built coliseum that seated a hundred thousand. This Jubilee lasted eighteen days, and to augment the entertainment, Gilmore invited bands from England, France, and Germany, as well as Johann Strauss and his orchestra from Vienna. Patrick Gilmore never again assembled anything on this scale (proportionally equivalent, in complexity and the sheer numbers involved, to the modern Olympic Games), but the "jubilee" concept—under the more modern designation "festival"—is still a related cultural phenomenon worldwide; and the assembling of large instrumental forces survives in the "massed bands" heard today wherever school bands and bandsmen gather.

Less spectacular but ultimately more significant was the work that Gilmore did beginning in 1873 in developing his 22nd Regimental Band in New York into a combination concert and touring band.* He was to establish a pattern for bands which lasted half a century—a pattern that many tried to emulate, though few succeeded. He played summer concerts at Manhattan Beach, and winter concerts in Gilmore's Garden (this establishment, originally P. T. Barnum's Hippodrome, ultimately became Madison Square Garden, and under that name moved later to a succession of new locations). In the spring and fall, Gilmore's band toured, going as far west as St. Louis in 1875, and in the following year to Salt Lake City, San Francisco, and Chicago, and then to Philadelphia for the centennial celebrations. In 1878, Gilmore took his band to Europe, where it compared favorably with the best. This kind of schedule Gilmore maintained until his death in 1892. As we shall see in Chapter 15, American symphony orchestras, led by the example of another immigrant musician, Theodore Thomas, were establishing a similar pattern, combining concert-giving in their home city with touring.

A typical band program of the late nineteenth century would show a judicious mixing of classical favorites, numbers by featured "headline" soloists, and popular songs and hymns. The classical ingredient consisted of transcriptions from the orchestral repertoire, mostly operatic overtures. This was modeled on European practice; on an earlier trip to Europe Gilmore had heard leading bands there performing much of the orchestral literature, and instituted the custom here—it was later followed by Sousa, and persisted well into this century. Classical selections were always balanced by popular numbers; the soprano soloists who appeared with the bands might sing operatic excerpts, but would be sure to include songs such as "Silver Threads Among the Gold," and even popular hymns such as "Nearer My God to Thee." Touring concert bands like Gilmore's, and later Sousa's, played much the same role in the dissemination of popular songs as did the big dance bands of the 1930s and 1940s. Featured instrumental soloists were big attractions; these included accomplished performers on the saxophone, baritone horn, and trombone—the best-known of the latter, Arthur Pryor (1870–1942), played with Sousa and later formed his own band. But by far the most popular "stars" with the bands were the cornet soloists. The cornet had developed into an extremely facile virtuoso instrument, which was to the band what the violin as a solo instrument was to the orchestra. The succession of legendary cornet virtuosos who played with Gilmore from the 1870s to the 1890s included Matthew Arbuckle, Jules Levy, Alessandro Liberati, and Herbert L. Clarke (1867–1945), who later played with Sousa. These men either composed or had written for them elaborate solos (often variations on popular or operatic tunes), and were just

* Gilmore's 22nd Regimental Band came ultimately to have very little connection with military functions and duties, but so strong was the association of bands with the military that even John Philip Sousa, when he formed his own independent "business" band in 1892, capitalized on this association, as well as on the reputation he had gained for the U.S. Marine Band, by calling it "Sousa's New Marine Band."

as much the idols of aspiring young cornetists in cities and towns everywhere as were the Fritz Kreislers and Jascha Heifetzes to young violinists a generation or two later.*

Gilmore tempered the sound of the brass band with the gradual reintroduction of woodwind instruments, which in time became numerically dominant, until by the end of the century the concert band consisted, in rough proportion, of one-third clarinets (the equivalent of the orchestra's violins), one-third other woodwinds, and one-third brass; the percussion section was somewhat smaller in proportion than in the brass band days. Under Gilmore and Sousa, who were both very discriminating and demanding musicians, the professional concert touring band developed into an ensemble that in terms of dynamic range, tone quality, blend, phrasing, and precision was certainly the equal of the best orchestras of its day.

John Philip Sousa (1854–1932) and the Band from the 1890s On

The man who is universally recognized as the most important single figure in the development of the American band and its music began his independent professional career as an orchestral violinist (he played under the popular French composer and conductor Jacques Offenbach in Philadelphia in 1876) and a conductor with traveling musical shows. In 1880 he was invited to direct the U.S. Marine Band, an organization in which he had served a seven-year apprenticeship beginning at age thirteen. By this time he had heard, and been impressed by, Gilmore's band, and he perceived the potential of the wind band. He reorganized the Marine Band and its repertoire thoroughly, and raised it to a position of excellence and renown, even securing permission to take it on tour. In 1892 he formed his own independent band, which he conducted, except for an interval of training bands for the Navy during World War I, until his death in 1932. Thus he assumed the mantle of Patrick Gilmore in the very year of Gilmore's death.

Paying and treating his musicians well, Sousa at the same time made of his band a profitable business, with stockholders. It was essentially a touring ensemble, and except for a very few regular engagements (such as those at Manhattan Beach, New York, and Willow Grove, Pennsylvania) the band was on the road a great deal. In contrast to Theodore Thomas (see Chapter 15), Sousa never thought of himself as an educator of the public, but rather as an entertainer, though the quality of his ensemble and the breadth of his repertoire undoubtedly did accomplish a good deal of education. He followed Gilmore's example in balancing his programs between popular and classical selections; furthermore, he kept up with the times in terms of popular music. His solo trombonist, Arthur Pryor, was from Missouri, the cradle of ragtime, and he arranged and taught the band to play this new music. (Pryor's composition *Lassus Trombone*, in this vein, was long a popular band number,

* It must be noted that W. C. Handy also began his career as a performer on the cornet and the trumpet, enjoying a considerable reputation as a virtuoso soloist on the latter, along with his better-known activities as a bandmaster.

especially with trombonists.) Sousa's band took ragtime to Europe in 1900, and his turn-of-the-century programs, with their "plantation songs and dances" and "coon songs," show that contemporary popular derivatives of black American music had a place on his programs. He later incorporated some form of jazz into his programs.

Considering his active public life, Sousa's creative output was phenomenal. He completed twelve operettas, eleven suites, seventy songs, nearly a hundred other instrumental pieces of various kinds, and over two hundred arrangements and transcriptions, as well as three novels and an autobiography. But he is best known for his marches. Between 1877 and 1931 he composed 136 of them, an imposing proportion of which (one could cite *Semper Fidelis, The Thunderer, The Washington Post, The Liberty Bell, King Cotton, El Capitan,* and *The Stars and Stripes Forever*) have, along with some of the songs of Stephen Foster, entered the domain of our permanent national music. Nor is their popularity limited to America; like the Foster songs and the waltzes of Johann Strauss, Jr., they have become part of a world music.[66]

Sousa had a flourishing grass-roots tradition on which to build. The 1890s, when his own band was touring and establishing its reputation, was the great era of American bands, especially in the towns and small cities in the Midwest. Town bands furnished music both functional and entertaining, and they were a strong focus of community pride. Before the advent of movies and later of radio, it was town bands, along with singing and theatrical groups, that accounted for most of what local entertainment and culture existed; these attractions were augmented by such traveling entertainments as circuses, minstrel shows, lecturers and performers on the Chautauqua circuit, and occasional visits by the bands of Alessandro Liberati, Frederick Innes, Thomas Brooke, Patrick Gilmore, and even Sousa himself.[67]

Although the decline of the professional concert/touring band, which can be placed at about the time of Sousa's death in 1932, takes us beyond the immediate era under consideration, this is perhaps the moment to trace briefly the subsequent story of the American wind band. There were two significant developments. The first was the passing of leadership to the *academic* band movement; college and university bands developed significantly, in size, in excellence, and in general esteem, especially in the Midwest. The second development was related to this, but was also the outgrowth of the work of Edwin Franko Goldman (1878–1956) whose professional band countered the general trend of decline. The Goldman Band performed continuously from 1918 to 1979; after Edwin Franko Goldman's death in 1956, it continued under the direction of his son, Richard Franko Goldman (1910–80). Both father and son were interested in augmenting the band's repertoire, and in the 1950s Richard Franko Goldman began to commission new works. Thus it was that works for the newly developed "symphonic band," or "symphonic wind ensemble" began to come from established composers, many of them on commissions. This flow of new works for band reached its peak in the 1950s and 1960s; there was hardly a major American composer of the time who did not contribute at least one work for band, including Virgil Thomson, William Schuman, Walter Piston, Peter Mennin, Vincent Persichetti, Howard Hanson, Paul Creston, and Ross Lee Finney.[68]

Popular Song from Ragtime to Rock

We now return to popular song where we last left it, at the close of the ragtime era, in order to describe the three decades between 1920 and 1950—decades that have generally been regarded as the "golden years" of Tin Pan Alley.

The Major Media Shift and the Role of the Big Bands

These "golden years" began with three developments that drastically changed the *media* by which popular song reached the public, and thus brought fundamental changes to the entire industry. The phonograph recording became a significant factor after the turn of the century, radio in 1922, and the sound movie in 1929. Russell Sanjek has given succinct descriptions of each of these developments:

> Million-copy sales of sheet music came to an end in 1920. . . . Almost overnight, in 1921 the American public turned from sheet-songs to phonograph records for its music.
>
> Almost from the start of commercial broadcasting, radio's potential as a new promotional medium for popular music was self-evident. Publishers in the cities with new radio stations immediately went to work to win the friendship of radio performers. Beginning in 1922, when the number of active stations jumped from 28 in January to 570 in December and broadcasters (who were essentially technicians at the time) attempted to cope with programming, the major houses sent their songpluggers to "assist" the new industry with subsidized musical entertainment.
>
> When the talking-picture makers learned that popular music attracted people into movie houses to a far larger extent than the silent-picture "theme songs," a grand exodus of the most productive songwriters followed as the motion-picture industry literally bought up Tin Pan Alley and moved it to the Coast. . . . In all, 320 songwriters and composers were working on sound-picture lots in the summer of 1929.[69]

What was taking place after 1920, then, was a gradual shift in the consuming public from an active to a passive role, as the phonograph and the radio replaced the parlor piano as a source of music in the home. Even that intermediate stage represented by the player piano ("canned" music produced by a "live" instrument), was edged out, sales of player pianos having reached their peak in 1923.

As the Depression arrived in the early 1930s, radio and the new talking pictures became the dominant media, dealing a severe blow to the phonograph, which did not really recover its position until the end of the decade, with recordings of the popular swing bands. Radio thus became a prime means for the dissemination and plugging of songs, as it has remained to this day (in changed form, and with a more specialized audience and material). Many of the prominent bands performed on weekly broadcasts in the 1930s, either from a permanent base or by remote hookup while on tour. Singers with the bands became increasingly important as purveyors of new popular songs. Some bandleaders were themselves composers, and a few of the best songs in this period came from the bands. These tended to be basically instrumental in conception, range, and design, and the words were incidental. Exceptionally, Isham Jones produced two notable songs in 1924 that were really vocal in nature, and have become standards: "It Had to Be You" and "I'll See You in My Dreams." Duke Ellington contributed many, most of which are decidedly instrumental in character: "Mood Indigo" (1931), "Sophisticated Lady" (1933), "Solitude" (1934), and "Do Nothing Till You Hear from Me" (1943) are a few. "Caravan" (1937) was written with Juan Tizol, and the very instrumental "Take the 'A' Train" (1941) was by Ellington's arranger, Billy Strayhorn. The important subject of the whole relationship of jazz to Tin Pan Alley will be dealt with presently.

Stability and Pluralism in Popular Music Between the Wars

While the big technological media shifts had profound effects on the popular music industry, the nature and style of popular song itself changed little in this period. Many of the songs from as early as the teens—songs such as "Some of These Days" (1910, by the black songwriter Shelton Brooks), "My Melancholy Baby" (1911, by Ernest Burnett), "I Ain't Got Nobody" (1915, by another black songwriter and jazzman, Spencer Williams), and that surprisingly early "standard" by Jerome Kern, "They Didn't Believe Me" (1914) have the sound of the best Tin Pan Alley songs of the "golden years," especially in their choruses. Songs written twenty or thirty years later, such as "You Go to My Head" (1938, by J. Fred Coots) or "Long Ago and Far Away" (1944, by Jerome Kern), do not differ essentially. Charles Hamm has collected considerable evidence to illustrate this "continuity of musical style" in the output of Tin Pan Alley between the wars, including the listing of several songs written in the teens that became hits in the 1930s, the 1940s, and even the early 1950s, up to the very advent of rock.[70]

The evolutionary changes that did take place in popular song during this period were significant but subtle, mostly in terms of a greater adventurousness in harmony and form. Kern's far-reaching key relationships in the bridge; Gershwin's chromatically driven harmonic progressions and chord choices; the stretching of the standard 32-bar form by Harold Arlen and Cole Porter—these developments were picked up by musicians, especially jazz players and arrangers, but would seldom be consciously noticed by the general public. By this time the verse had been largely discarded by singers and dance band arrangers alike, so in many songs composers and lyricists did without the verse altogether, launching immediately into the catchy and often familiar chorus.

The subject matter of the lyrics remained essentially unchanged as well; popular song was committed to entertaining and providing escape. "Brother, Can You Spare a Dime" (1932, with lyrics by E. Y. Harburg and music by Jay Gorney) was an anomaly.[71] Only the advent of World War II brought some change, in the form of war songs, but with rare exceptions like "The Last Time I Saw Paris" (1940, by Jerome Kern) and "Rodger Young" (1945, by Frank Loesser) few were worthy of survival. Topical song remained in the domain of blues, hillbilly music, and radical folk music until these more or less underground currents erupted into popular and commercial notice with the coming of rock.

But if popular song was essentially static during this period, it was also pluralistic in a way that we might easily overlook in viewing this relatively stable period. The notion that there was but a single popular music in America until the explosive advent of rock 'n' roll is false. The stratification referred to earlier in relation to the beginnings of Tin Pan Alley was a fact of our cultural life throughout this period. There were show songs—those for Broadway being somewhat more sophisticated than those for Hollywood. Beyond them lay the vast output of more or less run-of-the-mill popular songs—songs that responded quickly to fad or fashion, and had a very high mortality rate. Sanjek points up this cleavage in taste—this pluralism—in describing the policies of Tin Pan Alley publishers in the 1930s:

> Well-written songs possessing any poetic qualities were rejected immediately, because it was the general Tin Pan Alley feeling that true sheet-music buyers had little or no interest in them and therefore they were "not commercial." Those "great" songs of the 1930s, beloved by cultural elitists and social historians, were well known only to a minority of Americans—those who were better educated and more affluent than the average radio "fan" and who had access to the Broadway stage and other sophisticated entertainment.[72]

Though this view is perhaps open to debate, it does seem to be borne out by a few statistics. Hamm has compiled a list of the "top forty" songs between 1900 and 1950—in terms of those most often recorded. Of these, only twelve (30%) are from plotted Broadway shows, another six (15%) are from revues (a form descended from vaudeville), and the other twenty-two (55%) are non-show Tin Pan Alley songs.[73]

A panoramic glance at these Tin Pan Alley songs of 1920–50 is instructive. In the early years we find the occasional anachronistic song that belongs to an earlier period; "Three o'Clock in the Morning" (1922, Julian Robeldo) is a waltz-song that could have been written in the Gay Nineties. There are the fundamentally instrumental big band songs, of which the Ellington examples represent the best. A few topical songs appear, such as the previously mentioned "Brother, Can You Spare a Dime?" (1932, Jay Gorney) or "The White Cliffs of Dover" (1941, Walter Kent; one of the better specimens in a spate of songs relating to the war). At the lowest level of sophistication were inanities such as "The Music Goes 'Round and 'Round" (1935), "A-Tisket, A-Tasket" (1938), "Open the Door, Richard" (1947), and "Rudolph, the Red-Nosed Reindeer" (1949). Equally ephemeral was the brief fad of adapting melodies of nineteenth-century composers (chiefly Tchaikovsky) and fitting them with lyrics ("Moon Love" and "Our Love," 1939; "Tonight We Love," 1941). Prophetic of developments to come was the general popularity achieved by a few country songs before mid-century. "The Last Round-up" (by the New York composer Billy Hill) and "Tumbling Tumbleweeds" (by the Canadian Bob Nolan) were synthetic western songs, riding on the popularity of western movies (Hollywood westerns used almost no authentic regional music). But the appearances of "San Antonio Rose" (1940, Bob Wills) and "The Tennessee Waltz" (1948, Pee Wee King) as nationally rather than regionally popular songs were straws in the wind. By the time Hank Williams's "Cold, Cold Heart" (1951) and "Your Cheatin' Heart" (1952) had similarly taken hold nationally, the trend that shifted a large segment of the popular music industry to Nashville had been established. This story, and what led up to it, has been treated much more fully in Chapter 7.

The Latin American influence on American popular music has been treated rather extensively in Chapter 3; we can simply note here some early Spanish-language songs that became popular. They included José Padilla's "La Violetera" ("Who'll Buy My Violets?" 1923) and "Valencia" (1926); Maria Grever's "Cuando vuelva a tu lado" ("What a Diff'rence a Day Made," 1934) and "Ti-Pi-Tin" (1938); and Emilio Uranga's "Alla en el Rancho Grande" (1934). Portuguese influence (by way of Brazil) was represented by songs like Zequinha Abreu's "Tico-Tico" (1943) and Antonio Carlos Jobim's "Garota de Ipanema" ("The Girl from Ipanema," 1964).

But these song types were really peripheral to the mainstay of Tin Pan Alley in this period—the ballad. This basic type of love song provided most of the "standards," those few songs that in quality and appeal transcended the quantities of ephemera produced. As illustration of the best the Alley had to offer in these three decades (again excluding show and movie tunes), here is a select list of a dozen independent songs: "I Cried for You" (1923, Arthur Freed, Gus Arnheim, Abe Lyman); "Blue Skies" (1927, Irving Berlin); "I'll Get By" (1928, Fred Ahlert); "Star Dust" (1929; Hoagy Carmichael; this perennial, one of the most frequently recorded of all popular songs, began as a quasi-ragtime piano piece, which was later slowed down and given lyrics by Mitchell Parish); "Mean to Me" (1929, Fred Ahlert); "Sweet and Lovely" (1931, Gus Arnheim, Harry Tobias, Jules Lemare); "I'm Gettin' Sentimental over You" (1932, George Bassman); "Stormy Weather" (1933, Harold Arlen; written by this veteran Broadway composer for Harlem's Cotton Club, where it was introduced by Ethel Waters); "Deep Purple" (1934, Peter de Rose; another song that originated as a piano solo, words being added in 1939); "You Go to My Head;" (1938, J. Fred Coots); "The Last Time I Saw Paris" (1940, Jerome Kern; this topical piece originated as an independent song, one of Kern's few, for which lyricist Oscar Hammerstein dictated the words over the telephone; it was later incorporated into a movie, and won an Academy Award); "I'll Remember April" (1941, Gene de Paul).

Tin Pan Alley and Its Relation to Jazz and Black Vernacular Music

It is generally true that the typical popular song between the wars (whether from Broadway, Hollywood, or Tin Pan Alley) had little actual relationship to jazz or other black vernacular music. The period's inherent conservatism has been noted, and the successful white songwriters—New York Jewish composers such as Irving Berlin, Jerome Kern, George Gershwin, and Harold Arlen—were talented men who succeeded in meeting the demands of a broad public, many of whom knew black music not at all or only in modified and diluted form. This is not to deny that many of the songwriters themselves—notably Gershwin and Arlen—had a familiarity with black musical styles that did emerge in some of their songs, as we shall see. But the prevailing style of popular song showed little evidence of this influence, and even such black songwriters as Shelton Brooks and Spencer Williams, and later Duke Ellington, wrote songs in the commercially popular generic Tin Pan Alley style.

The one exception to this was the blues. There were a few white composers whose songs reflected the influence of black idioms to a greater than usual extent, of these George Gershwin and Harold Arlen were perhaps the most significant. Gershwin was not a jazz composer, but his rhythms, especially in up-tempo songs like "I Got Rhythm" (which became a jazz standard), certainly suggested those of the more popularized forms of jazz, and he made more use of blue notes and blues harmonies than any other Tin Pan Alley composer, with the possible exception of Harold Arlen. Arlen was perhaps the closest to jazz and blues of any of the major songwriters of this period. As Alec Wilder has written, "He, more than any of his contemporaries, plunged himself into the heartbeat of the popular music of his youth, the dance band." Wilder goes on to show how Arlen's "don't-worry-about-the-mud-on-your-shoes attitude," characteristic of blues and jazz, is illustrated in songs like "Sweet and Hot" (1930), "Between the Devil and the Deep Blue Sea" (1931), "I Gotta Right to Sing the Blues" (1932), "That Old Black Magic" (1942), and especially the memorable "Blues in the Night" (1941).[74]

The relation of jazz itself to popular music was in this period a symbiotic one, each contributing to the other. Jazz was heavily indebted to Broadway, Hollywood, and Tin Pan Alley for its basic material—the songs whose melodies and chord progressions became the basis for its arrangements and improvisations. Jazz has certainly brought forth its own composers, but since the fundamental genius of jazz is elaboration rather than composition, the popular song and its characteristic harmonic and melodic progressions have never been completely replaced as a basis for jazz pieces. Consider jazz without the hundreds of renditions of "Star Dust," without Coleman Hawkins's "Body and Soul," without Charlie Parker's "Embraceable You," and without the score of bebop versions of "How High the Moon."

For its part, popular music was indebted to jazz for a continuously revitalized rhythmic basis, and for the jazz arrangements by popular hot bands that contributed their flavor to, and helped promote, the songs. The versions of popular songs preserved in a current anthology of American popular song make this point convincingly.[75] Performances by such singers as Bing Crosby, Ethel Waters, Mildred Bailey, Jack Teagarden, Billie Holiday, Lena Horne, Sarah Vaughan, and Ella Fitzgerald, backed up by bands such as those of Benny Goodman, Teddy Wilson, Artie Shaw, Harry James, and Duke Ellington, impart, through interpretation, a jazz or blues flavor to songs that do not necessarily possess it inherently.

Finally, the relation of black vernacular dance to popular music in this period is crucial. Since the turn of the century, innumerable vernacular dances have entered the mainstream of popular dance. The Charleston, the Shimmy, the Black Bottom, and various "animal dances," such as the Turkey Trot, the Grizzly Bear, and the Bunny Hug, began, despite opposition, to coexist with and gradually replace the older polkas, schottisches, and waltzes. (One animal dance—possibly "made up" by the popular and influential team of Vernon and Irene Castle before World War I—was the Fox Trot, which became respectable and survived well into the period under consideration.) The Toddle was danced to Dixieland jazz. But the dance that became indelibly associated with swing jazz came out of places like the Savoy Ballroom in Harlem in the late 1920s (the home ground of many of the hottest bands). First known as the Lindy Hop (after Charles Lindbergh's famous flight), it became more broadly familiar as the Jitterbug. Although most of the young could and did do it, when performed by accomplished jitterbuggers in its more flamboyant and elaborate form it was a dance to watch as well. It was the dance symbol of hot jazz, and the interaction and mutual stimulus between a hard-driving swing band and a group of equally hard-dancing, frenzied jitterbuggers on the dance floor were undeniable.

The relationship between popular song and popular dance has been rarely and probably inadequately observed. After jazz had become, with bop, music for listening rather than dancing, it was the young audience's demand for a strongly pulsed music to dance to that contributed as much as anything to the popularity of rock 'n' roll, and the subsequent decline of both jazz and Tin Pan Alley.

The Decline of Tin Pan Alley and the Dispersion of the Popular Music Industry

After mid-century, an upheaval in the popular music industry, leading to its dispersion and decentralization, began in the "provinces," far removed from the creaking but still functioning Broadway-Hollywood axis. Regional and ethnic musics began to account for significantly larger shares of the market. Coming out of teeming and troubled urban areas like Chicago, Detroit, and Philadelphia was black rhythm-and-blues; from the South and West came white hillbilly music, given the trade name country-and-western. As an offspring of both came rock 'n' roll.

There is an interesting parallel between this development and the beginnings, half a century earlier, of Tin Pan Alley, the collective name for the then-new "marketplace oriented music publishing companies." Although the birth of Tin Pan Alley was marked by the centralization of the industry, and the rock era by its decentralization, there is a sense in which the advent of rock marks the completion of another cycle in the periodic *democratization* of American popular music. It was with the beginning of another such cycle, in the Jacksonian era of a century and a half ago, that we began the long story that this chapter has attempted to tell.

Further Reading

Reference

Kinkle, Roger. *The Complete Encyclopedia of Popular Music and Jazz, 1900–1950*. 4 vols. New Rochelle, NY: Arlington House, 1974.

Shapiro, Nat, and Bruce Pollock. *Popular Music: An Annotated Index of American Popular Songs*. 10 vols. Vols 1–6, New York: Adrian Press, 1964–73; vols. 7–10, Detroit: Gale, 1984–86. Entries are arranged by year, and within each year alphabetically by title, with notes on the composers, lyricists, and publishers.

———*Popular Music, 1920–1979: A Revised Cumulation*. Detroit: Gale, 1985. A three-volume rearrangement of the above, with a single alphabetical sequence and unified indexes.

General

Hamm, Charles. *Yesterdays: Popular Song in America.* New York: W. W. Norton, 1979.

This well-documented work has chapters relevant to nearly every aspect of the present chapter.

Spaeth, Sigmund. *A History of Popular Music in America.* New York: Random House, 1948.

Despite its being out of date, and anecdotal in its approach, this is still a useful book, if only for its extensive annotated citations and of songs and songwriters, mostly by decade.

The 1830s Through the Civil War

Books and articles

Austin, William W. *"Susanna," "Jeannie," and "The Old Folks at Home": The Songs of Stephen Foster from His Time to Ours.* New York: Macmillan, 1975.

A perceptive study of the complex array of meanings that Foster's songs have had in a variety of contexts.

Brink, Carol. *Harps in the Wind: The Story of the Singing Hutchinsons.* New York: Macmillan, 1947. Reprint, New York: Da Capo, 1980.

Cockrell, Dale. "The Hutchinson Family, 1841–45; or, The Origins of Some Yankee Doodles," *I.S.A.M. Newsletter,* vol. 12, no. 2 (November 1982).

Heaps, Willard A. and Porter W. *The Singing Sixties: The Spirit of Civil War Days Drawn from the Music of the Times.* Norman. University of Oklahoma Press, 1960.

A copious source of information on the songs in their context.

Howard, John Tasker. *Stephen Foster, America's Trobadour.* New York: Crowell, 1934. New ed, New York: Crowell, 1953.

Still the standard Foster biography.

Lawrence, Vera Brodsky. *Music for Patriots, Politicians, and Presidents: Harmonies and Discords of the First Hundred Years.* New York: Macmillan, 1975.

A handsome large-scale book, with commentary, song texts, and profuse facsimile reprints of the covers and some of the music itself.

Levy, Lester S. *Grace Notes in American History: Popular Sheet Music from 1820 to 1900.* Norman: University of Oklahoma Press, 1967.

Arranged by topic, with background for each of the songs. Includes single-line tunes, and photo reprints of covers.

Moseley, Caroline. " 'When Will Dis Cruel War Be Ober?' Attitudes Toward Blacks in Popular Song of the Civil War," *American Music,* vol. 2, no. 3 (Fall 1984).

Tawa, Nicholas. *Sweet Songs for Gentle Americans: The Parlor Song in America, 1790–1860.* Bowling Green, OH: Bowling Green University Popular Press, 1980.

Includes music to many songs.

———*A Music for Millions: Antebellum Democratic Attitudes and the Birth of American Popular Music.* New York: Pendragon, 1984.

Editions of music

These are collections of facsimile reprints of the original sheet music publications, usually including the covers, with notes by the editors.

Crawford, Richard, ed. *The Civil War Songbook: Complete Original Sheet Music for 37 songs.* New York: Dover, 1976.

Jackson, Richard, ed. *Popular Songs of Nineteenth Century America.* New York: Dover, 1976.

Contains sixty-four songs.

———*Stephen Foster Song Book.* New York: Dover, 1974.

Contains forty songs.

From the Civil War Through the Ragtime Era

Books and articles

Bierley, Paul E. *John Philip Sousa: American Phenomenon.* New York: Appleton-Century-Crofts, 1973.

Goldberg, Isaac. *Tin Pan Alley: A Chronicle of American Popular Music.* New York: Frederick Ungar, 1961.

Includes introduction by George Gershwin, and supplement "From Sweet and Swing to Rock 'n' Roll" by Edward Jablonski.

Levy, Lester S. *Grace Notes in American History: Popular Sheet Music from 1820 to 1900* (see above).

Morgan, H. Wayne, ed. *The Gilded Age: A Reappraisal.* Syracuse, NY: Syracuse University Press, 1963.

A collection of articles dealing with various aspects of the period; especially relevant is the chapter "Gilt, Gingerbread, and Realism: The Public and Its Taste."

Schwartz, H. W. *Bands of America.* Garden City, NY: Doubleday, 1957. Reprint, New York: Da Capo, 1975.

Sousa, John Philip. *Marching Along.* Boston: Hale, Cushman & Flint, 1928.

Editions of music

Fremont, Robert A., ed. *Favorite Songs of the Nineties: Complete Original Sheet Music for 89 Songs.* New York: Dover, 1973.

Jackson, Richard, Ed. *Popular Songs of Nineteenth-Century America* (see above).

Levy, Lester S., ed. *Sousa's Great Marches in Piano Transcription.* New York: Dover, 1976.

Tawa, Nicholas. *Sweet Songs for Gentle Americans: The Parlor Song in America, 1790–1980.*

See entry above.

From Ragtime to Rock: Books and Articles

American Popular Song. Washington, DC: Smithsonian Institution Press, 1984.

James R. Morris's 28-page introductory essay to this 7-LP recorded anthology, and biographical material and notes on the individual songs by Morris and others, make this a useful resource.

Fox, Ted. *Showtime at the Apollo.* New York: Holt, Rinehart & Winston, 1983. This famous Harlem theater, its performers, and its audience, were crucial to developments in American popular music of this period.

Levy, Lester S. *Give Me Yesterday: American History in Song, 1890–1920.* Norman: University of Oklahoma Press, 1975.

Pessen, Edward. "The Great Songwriters of Tin Pan Alley's Golden Age: A Social, Occupational, and Aesthetic Inquiry," *American Music,* vol. 3, no. 2. (Summer 1985)

Sanjek, Russell. *American Popular Music and Its Business.* 3 vols. New York: Oxford University Press, 1988.

———. *From Print to Plastic: Publishing and Promoting America's Popular Music (1900–1980).* I.S.A.M. Monograph no. 20. Brooklyn: Institute for Studies in American Music. 1983.

Stearns, Marshall and Jean. *Jazz Dance: The Story of American Vernacular Dance.* New York: Macmillan, 1968. Reprint, New York: Schirmer Books, 1979.

This exemplary study fills a need, as an awareness of vernacular dance is indispensable to an adequate understanding of the popular music of the period.

Wilder, Alec. *American Popular Song: The Great Innovators 1900–1950.* New York: Oxford University Press, 1972.

This subjective but highly respected book by a songwriter-author treats in considerable detail a great number of songs by all of the significant songwriters of the period.

Listening

Entries are arranged in approximate chronological order according to the earliest material that they include. Those selected as examples of the music before the advent of recording are mostly re-creations from original editions.

Come and Trip It: Instrumental Dance Music 1780s–1920s. NW-293.

An Evening with Henry Russell. Nonesuch 71338.

Includes complete texts, and extensive notes by Charles Hamm.

There's a Good Time Coming: Songs by the Hutchinson Family. Smithsonian Collection N020.

Songs of the Civil War. NW-202.

Notes by Charles Hamm.

The Yankee Brass Band: Music from Mid-Nineteenth Century America. NW-312.

Includes extensive notes by Jon Newsom, with descriptions and pictures of the original instruments used.

The Hand That Holds the Bread: Progress and Protest in the Gilded Age/Songs from the Civil War to the Columbian Exposition. NW-267.

Notes by William Brooks.

"Angels' Visits" and Other Vocal Gems of Victorian America. NW-220.

Notes by Richard Jackson.

Where Home Is: Life in Nineteenth-Century America/Crossroads of the East and West. NW-251.

The Sousa and Pryor Bands: Original Recordings 1901–1926. NW-282.

Notes by James R. Smart.

The Pride of America: The Golden Age of the American March. NW-266.

Recordings by the Goldman Band.

American Popular Song. (From the Smithsonian Collection of Recordings.)

A 7-LP archival anthology, with copious notes. (See above under "Books and articles.")

Come Josephine in My Flying Machine: Inventions and Topics in Popular Song 1910–1929. NW-233.

Praise the Lord and Pass the Ammunition: Songs of World Wars I and II. NW-222.

The Vintage Irving Berlin. NW-238.

The Golden Years of Tin Pan Alley: 1920–1929. NW-279.

The Golden Years of Tin Pan Alley: 1930–1939. NW-248.

Brother, Can You Spare a Dime: American Song During the Great Depression. NW-270.

Where Have We Met Before? Forgotten Songs from Broadway, Hollywood and Tin Pan Alley. NW-240.

PROJECTS

1. Sigmund Spaeth restated a thought expressed many times when he wrote that our popular song "captures the civilization of each period far more accurately than do many of the supposedly more important arts." Taking any decade in our history, make a survey of its popular songs, and assess the extent to which this statement applies, and how it applies.

2. If you are a singer, plan a group of Irish songs to add to your repertoire. The group could consist of some of the lesser-known songs from Thomas Moore's *Irish Melodies*; alternatively, it could be a selection of Irish songs from various periods, from Thomas Moore to "My Wild Irish Rose."

3. Make a study of the player piano in relation to American popular music.

4. Make a study of the popular dances of any given period, relating them to the popular music of that time. (Examples would be the relation of the two-step to the Sousa march, the cakewalk to ragtime, the Charleston to the music of the 1920s, the jitterbug to swing jazz.)

5. If you have access to a library with large nineteenth-century periodical holdings, make a study of the music, especially songs, that appeared in nineteenth-century magazines such as *Godey's Ladies' Book.*

6. Are there any folk or rock groups to which you could compare the Hutchinson Singers, in terms of their use of topical, political, or protest material? Research the question, and do a brief but well-documented paper on it, bringing out contrasts as well as any similarities you might see, in terms both of the groups and of the times.

7. Nicholas Tawa has referred to the "unillusioned song" of pre–Civil War days. Taking the songs from *any* given period, discuss the nature of *illusion* in popular song and the reasons for its presence.

8. After reading *"Susanna," "Jeannie," and "The Old Folks at Home"* by William W. Austin, recall and recount your own experiences with the songs of Stephen Foster. Include your first impressions of them, and then any subsequent experiences with the songs. Were you aware of any change in your perception of the "pathetic plantation songs," for example? Do they seem to you "densely ambiguous"? Examine them again in the light of your own possibly changing perceptions—and American society's changed perceptions—of race, and of the long episode of slavery, Emancipation, and the subsequent struggle for equality.

9. After listening to a collection such as *Songs of the Civil War* (NW-202) make an inventory of the songs by category (i.e., patriotic, comic, nostalgic, songs for the home front, etc.), and write a commentary on the many kinds of songs that came out of the Civil War, and the point of view of each.

10. Songs about separation by death were common in the nineteenth century. They have always been a staple of country music (which inherited some of its songs from the sentimental repertory of the nineteenth century), and made a brief appearance in the teen-age death songs of early rock 'n' roll. But such songs were almost totally absent from the output of Tin Pan Alley during its "golden years." Putting together what you know, write a paper discussing possible reasons for this.

11. Political campaign songs have always constituted a special genre of popular song. Before the advent of the television commercial, these songs were important carriers of partisan themes (and partisan slander). If recent political campaigns on all levels have seemed to descend to new depths of acrimony, it is sobering to examine the campaign songs of the period with which this chapter is concerned (1828 to roughly 1952). With the aid of such collections as *Music for Patriots, Politicians, and Presidents* for the first hundred years, and anthologies of the second hundred years as they become available, make a study of some aspect of American political campaign songs. (Many libraries and local and regional historical societies have collections of sheet music relevant to this and other genre studies.)

12. If you come from a relatively small community in which a town or city band has been an important entity, assemble some recollections (either your own, or those of relatives or acquaintances) of the band's activities and significance in the life of the community.

13. Interview the director of a local high school, college, or community band. Any aspect of the band's function and its music may be the focus; one possibility is the changes in the band's literature and repertoire that have occurred in the last half-century. The content of a typical band concert of today might be compared to that of a concert of twenty, thirty, or forty years ago.

14. Jerome Kern's "Smoke Gets in Your Eyes" (1933) is famous for having its "bridge" (its third 8-bar phrase) begin in a distant key. If you have sufficient musical training, plot the key relationship of the bridge to the rest of the song in at least ten other popular songs of the period 1920–50, and write up a summary of your findings.

15. If you have access to a record collection of the Tin Pan Alley "golden years," or a recorded anthology such as the Smithsonian *American Popular Song,* make a comparison study of the interpretations of five of the great song "stylists" of the era—female singers such as Marion Harris,

Ethel Waters, Mildred Bailey, Frances Langford, Billie Holiday, Lena Horne, Judy Garland, Jo Stafford, Sarah Vaughan, and Ella Fitzgerald, and male singers such as Fred Astaire, Bing Crosby, Nat "King" Cole, Frank Sinatra, Perry Como, Johnny Mathis, and Tony Bennett. Where possible, compare differing interpretations and styles as applied to a single song.

Photo from the Frank Driggs Collection

PART FIVE

Jazz and Its Forerunners

JAZZ occupies a unique and not easily classifiable position in the panorama of American music. If it has been widely considered to be popular music (which in a strict sense it has hardly, if ever, been), the terms "folk" and "classical" have also been used in trying to place it in the larger picture of American music. It does not fit well under any of these verbal umbrellas.

Jazz, beginning (like the blues) as unmistakably the music of black musicians, still has a clear and persistent, though nowadays by no means exclusive, racial identity. It is also thought by many to be the single most distinctive American music—indeed, *the* American music. This perception, even if exaggerated, is all the more remarkable in that of the six streams we have chosen to identify, jazz, though approaching its century mark, is still the newest.

Jazz and classical music have come to be our two most "serious" forms of music-making—serious in terms of their sophistication, in terms of the intellectual as well as musical qualifications demanded in their practice, and in terms of the low priority that their most dedicated practitioners assign to the profit motive—hence the survival of both genres largely independent of mass appeal, and their inherent resistance to being commercialized. Virgil Thomson's characterization of jazz as a "persecuted chamber music" makes the point deftly.

If jazz and classical music have this much in common, it is natural that there should have been many serious attempts to fuse them—attempts that have yielded interesting if not ultimately satisfactory results. For the ways in which they differ are also fundamental. Although there have been classical improvisers (a few) and jazz composers (many), the most basic difference is that classical music is a comprehensive manifestation of the art of the composer, and jazz a stylistically unique manifestation of the art of the improvising performer.

13

Ragtime and Pre-Jazz

IT can fairly be contended that every new development in American popular music for a century and a half can be traced directly or indirectly to some form of music made by black Americans. This influence is a thread, seen or unseen, acknowledged or unacknowledged, in nearly every discussion of what constitutes the distinctive properties of American popular music, and what their source is.

Although there is much common ground and mutual influence between them, there are two discernible traditions of black music—vocal and instrumental. The vocal tradition has a sacred aspect, running from the spiritual and the shout through the modern gospel song, and a secular aspect, which includes the work song and the blues, culminating in the vocal-plus-instrumental manifestations of rhythm-and-blues and soul.* The sharing of musical characteristics between sacred and secular has already been noted as typical of black music.

The instrumental tradition of black music, less well documented in the beginning than the vocal, begins with music-making among the slaves—banjo playing, fiddle playing, and the use of drums (or drum substitutes) and other percussion instruments such as the bones. These features were picked up and imitated in the minstrel show, in which blacks themselves participated after the Civil War, as we have seen. Black instrumental music had its first brief flowering in ragtime (in all its phases), and its second, more extensive and enduring, manifestation in jazz. The two cannot be separated entirely, and it is the ragtime-jazz *continuum* that is the subject of the fifth section of this book.

* The vocal tradition of black music has been explored in Chapters 2, 6, 8, and 9.

The Context of Ragtime from Its Origins to Its Zenith

It will help our understanding of both ragtime and jazz if we realize that in the beginning *both* terms had broader and looser definitions than the more purist ones we find applied today. In dealing with ragtime, for example, we find that our idea of it as exclusively solo piano music is somewhat at variance with its contemporary perception. The dominant form of American popular music has always been the song, and as Edward Berlin has pointed out, it was the ragtime songs—songs such as "You've Been a Good Old Wagon But You've Done Broke Down" (1895), "A Hot Time in the Old Town" (1896), "Mister Johnson, Turn Me Loose" (1896), "All Coons Look Alike to Me" (1896), "At a Georgia Campmeeting" (in its version as a song, 1899), "Hello! Ma Baby" (1899), and "Waiting for the Robert E. Lee" (1912)—that were more often recognized as "ragtime," in their day, than the now-familiar piano pieces. This even raises the possibility that the piano versions of these ragtime songs played some part in the evolution and popularization of piano ragtime itself.[1]

The Origins of Ragtime

The roots of ragtime are broader than has generally been supposed. Its most easily identifiable feature—a syncopated melody against a steady marchlike bass in duple meter*—can certainly be found in music published, in the 1880's, not in the middle Mississippi Valley (generally considered to be the cradle of ragtime), but in New York. And the distinctive rhythmic features of banjo tunes of the early minstrel show (see chapter 11) were not only present but had appeared in print before the Civil War.[2]

Both the songs and the dances of the period had their role in the development of ragtime. The ragtime song, or "coon song," discussed in Chapter 12, began as a self-deprecating kind of song in the 1880s. Both in the crudity of its words and in the grotesque caricatures of its sheet music covers, the coon song was grossly insulting to black people; at least some of the many objections to ragtime itself can be traced to these associations. But many of its musical characteristics (and it must be remembered that coon songs were written and sung by black as well as white performers) were essentially those of ragtime as we know it, and the songs certainly popularized ragtime ingredients. As Arnold Shaw has said, "Coon songs were an infusion into the pop music scene of high spirits, revelry, and rhythmic drive, much as Rhythm and Blues was later in the 1950s," and he also makes the point that, as in the case of rhythm-and-blues half a century later, the coon song was as much a style of singing as it was a type of song.[3] The lineage of the female "coon shouter" starts perhaps with Mama Lou, in Babe Connors's St. Louis brothel, who, according to Shaw, may have been the writer of "Ta-Ra-Ra Boom-De-Ay" and "The Bully," songs that were later popularized on the New York stage by the white singer May Irwin (1862–1938).† The lineage continues with the white singer Sophie Tucker (1884–1966), and the singing style, at least, is represented more recently by the black singer Willie Mae "Big Mama" Thornton (1926–84).

* The musical characteristics of ragtime, including syncopation, will be examined in due course.

† See Chapter 12, p 332.

Dance was crucial in the development of ragtime. The earliest known ragtime instruction book, written in 1897 as the ragtime craze was just beginning, gives an alternative name for "RAG TIME" as "Negro Dance time," and for the next two decades the names of specific dances were associated with published rags.[4] The *march* could be used as dance music; many early rags include the terms "march" or "two-step" or both in their titles or subtitles. The rag, as we shall see, took its formal organization directly from that of the march. A specialty dance that also contributed to ragtime was the *cakewalk*. A march involving an exaggerated kind of strutting, it presumably originated on the plantations, with slave couples competing for the prize of a cake. It was taken over into the minstrel show, and was on Broadway by the 1870s; by the 1890s it had become a popular, though strenuous and exacting, dance for the general public.[5] Many early rags also incorporated the term "cakewalk" in their titles.

Caribbean dance rhythms—rhythms of the danza, the habanera, or the seguidilla—have been cited as one of the sources of ragtime rhythms. Louis Moreau Gottschalk (1829–69), a Louisiana-born pianist of international stature, incorporated these rhythms into most of his piano pieces with West Indian associations, including his *Danza* (1857), *La Gallina* (copyright 1869), and *Ojos Criollos* (no copyright date), the latter two of which carry the subtitle "Danse cubaine." The earliest collections of Creole songs from Louisiana also contain syncopations identical to those found in ragtime.[6] The actual extent to which this music could have influenced ragtime itself is debatable, however. The whole question of Latin American influence (principally rhythmic) on the origins of both ragtime and jazz is often overlooked and is in need of more investigation—investigation that might convince us, for example, that a piece like Joplin's *Solace* (1909, subtitled "A Mexican Serenade"), an exquisite example of a rag with a habanera bass, is not the isolated anomaly that it may appear to be.

Ragtime As Piano Music and the Work of Scott Joplin

Despite the breadth of interpretations given the term "ragtime," it was as music for solo piano that it ultimately achieved significance, and endured. The dissemination of piano ragtime is widely thought to have been given considerable impetus by the gathering of ragtime pianists (before the term had been applied to the genre) at the World's Columbian Exposition in Chicago in 1893. There, according to Blesh and Janis, "hundreds of the itinerant piano clan had gathered" (including Scott Joplin, 1868–1917, and Ben Harney, 1871–1938), presumably to be heard on the "Midway" and in the red-light district; but more informative documentation as to what music was played will probably never come to light.[7] Not long afterward—in the same year (1896) in which Ben Harney moved to New York from his native Louisville, and began introducing ragtime through his highly successful playing and singing—Scott Joplin moved to Sedalia, Missouri, where for the next five years he composed, played, and published the first of the approximately three dozen piano pieces that he and his publisher referred to as "classic rags." Thus Ben Harney, the white Brooklynite Joseph Lamb (1877–1960), and others in New York, and Scott Joplin, Tom Turpin (1873–1922), Arthur Marshall (1881–1968), Scott Hayden

(1882–1915), James Scott (1886–1938), and others in the Midwest, helped to launch ragtime as we know it into what became, in the next two decades, a national craze.

Ragtime for the piano assumed in its initial stages three forms: piano renditions of ragtime songs; the "ragging" of unsyncopated music; and, thirdly, what we think of as ragtime today, original compositions for the piano. The latter began to be published in 1897–William Krell's *The Mississippi Rag* was possibly the first, with *Harlem Rag* by the St. Louis composer Tom Turpin coming out the same year. It is probable that at least three thousand rags were published between 1897 and 1920; estimates have run as high as ten thousand. As could be expected most of these were mediocre musically, and were simplified in their published versions to be more suited to the modest pianistic abilities of the many who bought them and attempted to play them at home. What are today regarded as the masterpieces of piano ragtime were not necessarily best-sellers; Scott Joplin's most famous work, *Maple Leaf Rag* (1899), was virtually the only one of his works to become widely popular in his lifetime, and it was the work that justified his being heralded on sheet music covers as "the king of ragtime writers."

Scott Joplin has emerged as the single most important ragtime composer of the period. A versatile musician (he played the cornet and piano and led a band) with high musical standards and determined ambition, he lavished a great deal of effort and resources on composing and producing large-scale works for the stage, none of which were successful in his lifetime. (His opera *Treemonisha* was elaborately staged and recorded in the 1970s, and he was awarded a Pulitzer prize posthumously in 1976.) But his most enduring and influential works are his rags, whose musical inventiveness and craftmanship set a standard against which others are measured, and validate the term that he and his publisher applied to them—"classic."

The association of the piano with the ragtime era is no coincidence; figures show that the sales of pianos rose sharply after 1890, and declined just as steeply in the 1920s. But a modified form of the piano, the mechanical player piano, was also an important feature of the era; after 1900, player piano sales also rose steeply, reaching a peak before the ragtime era was completely over.[8] Thus a great deal of ragtime (as did its successor, "novelty" piano music) came into American homes in the form of piano rolls. These rolls could be either "hand-played," often by the composer himself, or "arranged" by the calculated punching of the paper rolls.* In fact, many rags, including one by Joplin himself, appeared only in piano rolls, and were never published in sheet music form. Thanks to the interest generated by the ragtime revival, there has also been a revival of the player piano and its rolls—enhanced by computer technology![9]

Those who bought the sheet music, however, intent on playing it at home, soon discovered that ragtime is not easy to play. To aid the learner and cash in on the boom, instruction books in ragtime began to appear—the earliest by Harney himself in 1897. One truly valuable document is an all-too-brief set of

* For an interesting application in contemporary music of the technique of "arranging" piano rolls by calculated punching, see the discussion of the work of Conlon Nancarrow in Chapter 17.

six exercises by Scott Joplin himself, published as *School of Ragtime* in 1908, with accompanying explanations and admonitions. (Joplin concentrates most on accurate rendering of the rhythm, and warns the performer, as he was to do over and over again in his published rags: "Never play ragtime fast at any time.") To provide personal instruction, studios were opened to accept pupils—and, yes, the first advertisement for "Ragtime Taught in Ten Lessons" appeared in Chicago in 1903.

The term "ragtime" (alternatively "rag time" or "rag-time") itself did not appear until the 1890s. Its origin is still in dispute, but seems most likely to have to do with references to the syncopation as "ragged" time. Once its popularity was well under way, in the first decades of this century, the term was applied to any popular music that was played fairly fast and had strongly marked rhythm, regardless of whether it employed any of the syncopations of real ragtime. This development was epitomized by Irving Berlin's first great hit song, "Alexander's Ragtime Band" (1911), which is not ragtime at all, though as a result of its tremendous popularity its composer was even hailed as a key figure in the history of ragtime! It is indicative of the fluid state of perception of our black-derived popular music that only a few years later the terms "ragtime," "blues," and "jazz" were being used almost interchangeably.

In its heyday the creation and publication of ragtime was not, like Tin Pan Alley and the popular song industry, concentrated in New York City. The mid–Mississippi Valley and the Ohio Valley were strong areas for ragtime, and an examination of sheet music shows that rags were published not only in St. Louis, Kansas City, Columbia, and Sedalia, Missouri (the latter the home for a while of Scott Joplin and of his publisher John Stark), but also in Indianapolis, Cincinnati, Memphis, Nashville, Chicago, Detroit, New Orleans, Dallas, and San Francisco, and even in such places as Temple, Texas (for early Joplin pieces); Moline, Illinois; New Albany, Indiana; Kiowa, Kansas; and Oskaloosa, Iowa. John Hasse, who has been both a researcher into and a performer of Indiana ragtime, has termed the ragtime era "the golden age of local and regional music publishing."[10] Piano ragtime was also a genre to which women composers contributed significantly; May Aufderheide (1890–1972), of Indianapolis, was only the best known among many.[11]

Ensemble Ragtime

The performance of ragtime was not limited either to the solo piano version or the song; as soon as it became popular, this music began to be played by many different kinds of ensembles, including brass bands, concert bands, dance bands and orchestras, and smaller groups that included mandolins, guitars, and banjos. "Stock" arrangements for bands and orchestras (mostly for dancing) were issued by publishers; and sheet music publications of rags for piano often advertised versions of the same piece "published for band, orchestra, mandolin, guitar, etc." As was noted in the preceding chapter, John Philip Sousa was quick to recognize the popularity of ragtime. He began to program it in the 1890s, and on his first tour of Europe in1900 he gave most of his audiences there their first taste of ragtime, with arrangements of such pieces as *Smoky Mokes* and *Bunch o' Blackberries.*[12]

The Musical Characteristics of Ragtime

Ragtime Rhythm

The rhythmic basis of ragtime is the combination of a steady beat in the bass—which ragtime shares with the march (on the piano, this is provided by the left hand)—and a melody above that features the contradictory accentuation provided by syncopation. Since the "ragging" is in the rhythm, let us look more closely at this element and see how ragtime composers used the device of musical *syncopation*. Syncopation is so basic to the rhythmic life of much American music that it will be worthwhile to devote some time to an examination of it as it occurs in ragtime, as a basis for understanding it as encountered elsewhere. Syncopation is the displacing of accents from their normal position in the musical measure, so that they contradict the underlying meter.[13] Syncopation assumes a steady beat, stated or implied, and cannot be said to exist without it. This is normally supplied in ragtime by the "oom-pa" of the left hand, while the right hand has the melody, with its characteristically displaced accents. How does the right hand accomplish this syncopation, or displacing of accents? In ragtime it is done simply by arranging the succession of long and short notes to make *some* of the longer notes begin at rhythmically weak spots in the metric continuum, so that the accent they create at the moment of their attack serves to contradict rather than reinforce the prevailing background meter.

Some examples will illustrate how this works. Example 13–1 is the

Example 13–1

rhythm of the first two measures of the fiddler's tune "Turkey in the Straw." Here all the notes except the last are the same length, so that there can be no accents by virtue of note length, and hence no syncopation. The running notes constitute a continuous background made up of what might be called the "lowest common denominator" of durations, since they are the shortest notes used. They occur in groups of four to a beat. This is exactly the same metric background that is used in ragtime—hence the "squareness" of its rhythmic figures, as compared to later swing-jazz.

Let us observe the ways in which longer notes can be superimposed on this background. If we want a longer note to reinforce the meter, it will do this most strongly if its beginning coincides with the first note of a rhythmic subdivision. (Example 13–2)

Example 13–2

This is the normal position of the lowest, and hence the "'heaviest," of the left-hand bass notes. Somewhat weaker, and in fact creating a mild contradiction, or syncopation, would be a note beginning on the third of the sixteenth notes of our background. (Example 13–3).

Example 13–3

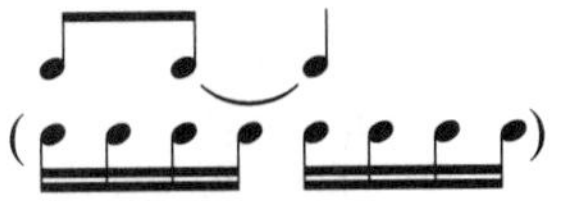

This mild syncopation, called by Berlin "augmented syncopation,"[14] had been in wide use in American popular song since the earliest days of the minstrel show. It is the only type of syncopation found in "Dixie," for example; and it is found in a number of other songs of the same genre, such as "Camptown Races" and "The Yellow Rose of Texas." It persisted to the end of the nineteenth century, and was a feature of many of the ragtime songs described above (including "A Hot Time in the Old Town" and "Hello! Ma Baby"). It flavored some Sousa marches of the 1890s, such as *High School Cadets* and *Manhattan Beach,* and in the early years of the twentieth century it was characteristic of some of the peppier songs (for example) George M. Cohan including "Yankee Doodle Boy" and "Over There."

But this mild form of syncopation was never an important feature of ragtime itself, which characteristically used the still livelier and jauntier kind of syncopation created by having longer notes beginning on either the second or the fourth of the background sixteenths (Example 13–4).

Example 13–4

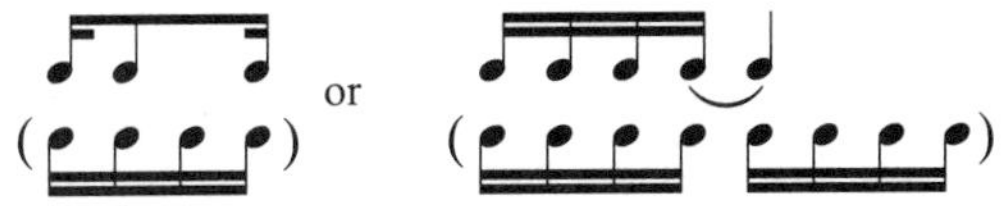

These, or variants of these, are the typical syncopations that may be found on every page of ragtime.*

If we now observe the way these syncopations are placed in genuine ragtime, we get an idea of the fine balance the best composers achieved between contradiction and affirmation of the meter within the phrase. Example 13–5 from the first strain of Scott Joplin's *The Entertainer* (1902), the contradictions, or syncopations, are marked with an S. This well-known rag shows a typical number and distribution of syncopations. Rags of what might be called the classic period usually have between two and four to a phrase, fairly evenly distributed.

It will be readily apparent that given the subdivision of the beat into four parts, the variety of syncopated figures available to the composer is rather

* Edward Berlin makes a distinction between the two forms in Example 13-4. The first he calls "untied" syncopation, and he notes that it was more typical of earlier ragtime; the second, which he calls "tied" syncopation, seems to appear with greater frequency in the more mature phase of ragtime. It must be understood, of course, that in the somewhat rarer cases in which ragtime was notated with the half note (rather than the quarter note) as the basic beat value, the note values in the examples just cited would be doubled.

Example 13–5

limited, and that rhythmically ragtime can all too easily take on the character of a series of clichés. This was undoubtedly one of its most severe limitations, which only the most gifted composers could transcend. As ragtime strove to evolve, there was a tendency in some works of the middle and late periods to crowd more syncopations into the phrase. Some of Joseph Lamb's compositions reveal this, such as Example 13–6, from the first strain of his *American*

Example 13–6

Beauty Rag (1913). Here there are seven syncopations in the first phrase—six of them within the first two measures, including four in immediate succession. When we listen to the actual music, it is apparent that Lamb uses these syncopations with ease and grace, but there is a certain air of ripeness about it that suggests a genre that has almost reached the limits of its refinement.

A rhythmic feature to appear in late ragtime (Berlin places it about 1911) is the dotted rhythm in Example 13–7, which actually amounts in perfor-

Example 13–7

mance to an unevenness in playing the lowest-common-denominator durations, with the first of each pair being longer than the second (though not, in actual practice, three times as long, as a strict interpretation of the rhythm as written would indicate). This unevenness was a performance practice that would later, after the advent of jazz, be applied to the performance of earlier ragtime; a comparison between Scott Joplin's performance, on a piano roll, of his *Maple Leaf Rag* in 1916 with an interpretation of the same piece by Jelly Roll Morton in 1938 shows this clearly.[15] The relation of the uneven performance of background notes to the "swung" eighths of swing jazz is evident; the appearance of dotted rhythms in ragtime pieces of the teens may be an indication that the practice of swing had earlier precedents than has been generally assumed.*

Ragtime Form

It is in its standardized form that ragtime shows most clearly its relation to the march, which is based on a succession of musically independent "strains" of

* See Chapter 14, pp. 381–384, for a treatment of the swing era.

uniform length (16 measures), most of which are repeated. An introduction is optional; Joplin, except in his most famous rag, almost invariably uses one. In the most typical pattern for ragtime, after the introduction two or three strains in the main key are followed by two strains (called the "trio" in the march) in the related key of the subdominant. Often the first strain, unrepeated, is brought back just before the trio. There are variants, but a typical rag would have the form *aabb a ccdd*, with each letter representing a 16-bar strain. Sometimes the final strain returns to the principal key; more often (as in the march) the rag ends in a different key from that in which it began. Joplin, in his late rags, tried a somewhat more expanded form.[16]

The Mingling of African-American and European-American Traits in Ragtime

Ragtime represents an interesting intersection of musical traits that can be identified as European and African in origin and approach. Its rhythm, as has been pointed out, is derived from African-American sources. On the other hand, ragtime form, melody (except for syncopation), and harmony are clearly related to those of the American popular song and dance music of the time—European-derived, by way of Tin Pan Alley. The harmonies, where they depart from the basic three chords, employ for the most part the familiar "barbershop" type of chromaticism. A rare intersection of African-Americanism and European-Americanism is found in the first trio (subdominant) strain of Joplin's *Pine Apple Rag* (Example 13–8), where the quintessential blues harmony (the subdominant chord with a flatted seventh) appears in the same phrase with a conventional modulation to the mediant key (this rag was copyrighted in 1908, four years before the first published blues appeared).

Example 13–8

Ragtime represents an even more interesting intersection of the two cultures in terms of performance practice. European music is basically a written tradition—one, that is, of fidelity to a piece of music as written in notation by the composer. African-American music—and this includes jazz—is largely an aural tradition, with all the latitude this gives the performer in re-creating individual works. Unlike jazz, ragtime had a written tradition from the very beginning. The question then arises: How faithful to the written and published versions of rags were contemporary performances? Or, put the other way around, how much do the printed versions convey of the way ragtime was actually played by its leading performers, including the composers themselves? We do know that publishers pressured composers to simplify their rags for publication, so as not to discourage sales among a not too highly skilled public. And performances recorded (by Jelly Roll Morton, for example, as noted above), after the heyday of ragtime had passed show pianists taking considerable liberties with the printed versions, which in some cases they may not even have seen. On the other hand, there is considerable evidence that many of the best-known composers of classic ragtime (including Tom Turpin, Scott Joplin, Arthur Matthews, and Joseph Lamb) played their music essentially as they had written it, and desired other performers to do the same. Ragtime, passing the peak of its popularity before the advent of recordings or radio, reached its vast public essentially by means of printed music—in this, it was unique among African-American-derived musics.[17]

The Decline and Metamorphosis of Ragtime

Ragtime's original heyday was brief, in retrospect; scarcely a generation had elapsed between its full-fledged appearance in the 1890s and its decline and metamorphosis into other styles. Recognizing the dual forms, vocal and instrumental, that ragtime assumed, Berlin has noted that by the mid-1910s vocal ragtime (as the ragtime song) "merged with the mainstream of popular music, while piano ragtime inclined toward what became known as jazz."[18]

Piano ragtime, in its dispersion, assumed several forms, and affected several distinct genres. Foremost, of course, was its merging with jazz. We have already noted that in its early stages the term "jazz," like "ragtime" itself, had a much broader and looser meaning than we apply today, and that, for a time, the two terms were used almost interchangeably.

Jelly Roll Morton

Ferdinand Joseph ("Jelly Roll") Morton (1890–1941), a New Orleans–born pianist and bandleader, was a key figure in this transition. His own works (variously and somewhat imprecisely titled "rags," "blues," and "stomps," among other designations) date mostly from the post-ragtime era. In these we can see that Morton's own style had superseded classic ragtime, while reinterpreting some of its elements. Morton's identity as a bandleader is also evident; not only did many of the pieces exist as band numbers, but Morton often wanted his piano itself to "sound as much like a band as possible." Nevertheless, he drew a clear distinction between the new jazz and older ragtime, which he had grown up with and knew thoroughly. His historic recordings, with commentary, made for Alan Lomax at the Library of Congress in the late 1930s, illustrate these distinctions, and are a valuable source of information about the transition from ragtime to jazz.[19] Though Morton makes his first appearance in our panoramic survey in connection with ragtime, it is really for his work in the formative stages of jazz that he is most important. After extensive traveling from 1904 to 1922, he went to Chicago, where he recorded, both as piano soloist and bandleader, the works by which he is known. We shall return to him in the next chapter as our first real jazz composer.

Two Offshoots of Ragtime: Stride Piano and Novelty Piano

As classic piano ragtime itself declined, two other offshoots appeared—descendants of the parent form, but not to be confused with it. One was the largely New York phenomenon of "stride piano," also known as "Harlem piano." This genre, cultivated by James P. Johnson (1894–1955) and Fats Waller (1904–43) in the 1920s and 1930s, retains some of ragtime's characteristics, most notably a steady left-hand rhythmic pulse (expanded to wide-reaching "strides" between low bass notes and mid-range offbeat chords), with syncopated right-hand figuration. Basically a virtuoso form developed by pianists with phenomenal facility, stride piano is faster than ragtime, with a driving beat and very elaborate melodic line; we shall encounter it again in the next chapter.

Another offshoot of ragtime was the so-called "novelty piano" music of the early 1920s; anyone familiar with such pieces as *Nola, Canadian Capers, Kitten on the Keys,* or *Dizzy Fingers* knows the style. A "show-off" kind of piano music (carefully made to sound more difficult than it actually is), it has been described by Ronald Riddle as "a refined, white suburban extension of ragtime."[20] The "novelty" itself was an attraction in tune with the times; such words as "tricky," "sparkling," and "scintillating" were used to describe and sell it. It was ideal for the medium of the player piano during the last few years of that instrument's popularity; before being replaced by the phonograph and the radio, the player piano made this novelty music accessible to people without the technical ability to play it themselves. But the sheet music itself also sold extremely well; Zez Confrey's *Kitten on the Keys* (which first appeared as a piano roll played by the composer) outsold *Maple Leaf Rag* when it was issued as sheet music in 1921. Musically, novelty piano shared the basic underlying features of ragtime, but emphasized greater speed, an obviously exhibitionist kind of virtuosity, and a particular species of syncopation known as "secondary rag," in which the regular quadruple subdivisions of the basic pulse are grouped in threes (Example 13–9).

Example 13–9

Early appearances of the ingredients of novelty piano came at the very end of the ragtime era, with Henry Cohen's *Canadian Capers* in 1915, Felix Arndt's ubiquitous *Nola* in 1916, and George Gershwin and Will Donaldson's

Rialto Ripples in 1917. But the composer most closely associated with the genre was Edward E. "Zez" Confrey (1895–1971). After *Kitten on the Keys* (1921) appeared *Dizzy Fingers*, *Stumbling* (originally a song), *Coaxing the Piano*, *Smart Alec*, and *You Tell 'Em, Ivories*. Titles were important to the "novelty"—*Kitten on the Keys* was followed by *Dog on the Piano* and *Mouse's Hooves*, while *Dizzy Fingers* spawned *Fancy Fingers*, *Feather Fingers*, and *Hot Fingers*. As Ronald Riddle has pointed out, the "verbal high jinks are in accord with the flashy legerdemain of the style."

Novelty piano, for all of its short-lived superficiality, had in its technical aspects—especially its secondary rag—an unmistakable influence on certain piano music of the 1920s and 1930s, especially that of George Gershwin. Riddle has mentioned Confrey's influence via the popular *Kitten on the Keys*, on Gershwin's *Rhapsody in Blue* (Confrey played in the same famous Aeolian Hall concert that introduced the *Rhapsody* in 1924!) He has also pointed out its influence on European composers such as Ravel and Martinů, when they wrote in an obviously "jazzy" style; in fact, some aspects of novelty piano were taken by outsiders to be synonymous with jazz at the time. Riddle's excellent article on the subject closes with the observation that "in the end, the piano novelty suffered a sad but predictable fate: it lost its novelty. While it lasted it was great fun . . . but it was too hot *not* to cool down."

Ragtime in Relation to Blues and Country Music

The relationship of the blues to ragtime is an interesting one. Ragtime, in its classic form, was a fusion of African-American rhythmic traits (mainly syncopation) with European harmony (mainly dominant and diminished seventh chords) and form (derived from the march, with its invariably regular 16-bar strains). Existing as an essentially *written* form of music, it was only slightly influenced by what was, prior to 1912, the essentially *aural* tradition of the blues. Nevertheless, there are interesting traces of blues to be found in ragtime before 1912. This is not surprising, since blues and ragtime emerged from the same social, cultural, and even geographical milieu—the music of itinerant black musicians on or near the Mississippi—with ragtime more prevalent in the middle Mississippi Valley and blues more prevalent in the lower. (Memphis can well be designated as the meeting point of the two.) As Edward Berlin has pointed out, the use of blue notes was fairly common, even in classic ragtime; the principal one was the flat third of the major scale (in ragtime most often appearing as the raised second degree, since it usually progresses up to the unaltered third degree). This is very noticeable in Scott Joplin's first published rag, *Original Rags*, in the introduction and the second and last strains; we have already noted Joplin's use, in his *Pine Apple Rag* of 1908, not only of the "blue" third of the scale but also of the blues harmony associated with this note. And in terms of blues form, Berlin has pointed out what amounts to a 12-bar blues chorus in a rag published in 1904![21]

With the appearance of published blues in 1912, blues influences in ragtime became more pronounced. At the same time, the blues themselves as published had definite ragtime characteristics. There was crossover and confusion in both musical features and names, and we enter a period, in the late

1910s, when the terms "rag" and "blues" (and "fox trot" as well) came to be used almost interchangeably. The term "jazz," when it appeared slightly later, was used just as indiscriminately. By this time ragtime was well on its way to losing its distinctiveness, its characteristics dispersed and altered.

Although there is much apparent evidence of the influence of ragtime on early country music, the evidence is based almost entirely on recordings made, with one exception, no earlier than 1924—at least a decade after ragtime had begun its decline and metamorphosis. We can hardly expect to find, then, the characteristics of classic ragtime in undiluted and unaltered form in pieces *called* rags in country music recordings of the 1920s and 1930s. In the white country tradition the much-recorded *Dill Pickles Rag,* for example, has little ragtime syncopation, but exhibits some of the late ragtime characteristics found in "novelty piano" (which may have been a far stronger influence than classic ragtime)—characteristics such as secondary rag, and uneven playing of dotted rhythms. (It also shows the typical tendency of hillbilly musicians to add beats to the phrases.)[22] The so-called "rags" of black rural groups, as exemplified by the Dallas String Band in its recordings of *Dallas Rag* in the late 1920s, show a similar distancing from classic ragtime, which was typical of the era. Rags by black guitarists and pianists such as Blind Blake, Blind Boy Fuller, Blind Willie McTell, and Cow Cow Davenport used ragtime syncopations, but these were often combined with blues, "talking blues," and even boogie-woogie traits. In other words, the term "rag," which may often have simply been used to take advantage of its popularity and boost record sales, had come to be interpreted very broadly. To further confuse the issue, there was a popular dance in the twenties and thirties *called* the "rag." And in many cases a rag was simply "a snappy little ditty that an instrumentalist plays to show off his ability to play."[23]

The Ragtime Revival

In a sense it was only in revival that ragtime regained its integrity and distinctiveness. The revival of ragtime, which began about mid-century, has now lasted far longer than did the ragtime era itself. It has been a selective revival, focusing almost exclusively on piano rags—thus giving a more narrowly purist definition of the genre, half a century after the fact.

The revival of traditional jazz, under the umbrella name of "Dixieland," began, as we shall see in the next chapter, in the 1940s. Working backwards chronologically, the next step, given the obvious relationship of ragtime to early jazz, was the rediscovery and study of ragtime itself, which was then generally viewed as a quite dated and old-fashioned precursor of jazz. Rudi Blesh followed this path; his early history of traditional jazz, *Shining Trumpets,* was published in 1946, and he and Harriet Janis went on to produce *They All Played Ragtime,* the first important study of the form, in 1950. In the late 1950s the performer, entertainer, and scholar Max Morath began his series of ragtime programs both live and televised, his recordings, and his writings on the period. A renewed interest in ragtime that began in sheer enjoyment of and enthusiasm for the music (in the case of Blesh and Morath) soon began to discover in the best of the piano rags musical excellences that had largely escaped the public in the ragtime era itself. Versatile musicians such as William Bolcom, Joshua Rifkin, and Gunther Schuller became interested in ragtime. Rifkin made studio-quality recordings, on a concert grand piano, of the rags of Scott Joplin in 1970; from his first best-selling record he separated ragtime from its association with the tinny, out-of-tune barroom piano and its accompanying stereotypical milieu, and focused on its musical values. This and other performances, and the critical acclaim they attracted, helped to foster the perception of ragtime as an American classical music, and introduce it to the concert hall. Ironically, this had the effect of validating, more than half a century later, the conviction that Scott Joplin, his publisher John Stark, and a very few others had held about the "classic" rags at the time they were written.

Music scholarship and editorship followed this interest, and *The Collected Works of Scott Joplin*, edited by Vera Brodsky Lawrence, was issued in 1971. In 1972 Gunther Schuller reinstated instrumental ragtime when he refurbished old stock arrangements (notably those found in the famous "Red Back Book"), and founded and rehearsed the New England Conservatory Ragtime Ensemble, dedicated to the high-quality performance of ensemble ragtime by skilled musicians. William Bolcom and John Hasse are among those who have not only continued to perform and record piano ragtime, but have composed rags of their own. This renewed attention to the musical aspects of ragtime has made the works of some of the early composers of what has now become known as "classic" ragtime (a term that still has no satisfactorily rigorous definition)—especially Scott Joplin, James Scott, and Joseph Lamb—stand out in perspective against the mass of mediocrity perpetrated in the ragtime era itself. Thus a few dozen rags emerge as small gems, illustrative of the potential for investing miniature and highly circumscribed forms such as the rag with refinement, craftmanship, and vitality.

Pre-Jazz

Minstrelsy, ragtime, and the blues were only the most public and audible forms of black (or black-derived) music that came before jazz. Behind them, mostly unheard and unheeded by white Americans, were all the varied musical manifestations of what has been called the "black experience": the music of West Africa itself, and on this continent the ecstatic responsory cries and shouts of worshipers in meeting houses and at outdoor revivals, the work songs, the lonely field hollers, the hypnotic drumming of Caribbean cults and ceremonies.

Where and when, from all this background, did actual jazz begin to emerge? This is a complex question, the first part of which cannot be adequately answered with the single place name New Orleans, important as its role was. It will be necessary to take a broader look geographically, for there were musical developments in all the cities and towns of the South, and in the larger cities of the North (in other words, wherever there was a sizable black population) that set the stage for the emergence of jazz.

Broadway, "Black Bohemia," and Black Bands at Home and Abroad

An important forerunner of jazz in New York was orchestral ragtime, which from the late 1890s until after the first World War was heard both in stage shows and as played by black dance orchestras. In the series of successful variety shows with all-black casts, beginning about the turn of the century (described in Chapter 11), available examples show that the music was essentially vocal and instrumental ragtime.[24]

In many parts of the country it had long been the role of black musicians to furnish music for dancing. As Eileen Southern has said: "In many places the profession of dance musicians was reserved by custom for Negroes, just as was, for example, the occupation of barber. Consequently, black dance orchestras held widespread monopolies on jobs for a long period in the nation's history—even after World War I."[25]

In the early 1900s New York's Black Bohemia (an area in West Manhattan around 53rd Street) furnished the "syncopated dance orchestras" that were much in demand for all occasions. Such an orchestra gave a public concert in 1905, and by 1910 James Reese Europe (1881–1919) had founded the famous Clef Club, whose orchestra gave public concerts, including a famous and highly successful one at Carnegie Hall in 1912. James Weldon Johnson, the well-known black poet, wrote of this concert: "New York had not yet become accustomed to jazz; so when the Clef Club opened its concert with a syncopated march, playing it with a biting attack and an infectious rhythm, and on the finale bursting into singing, the effect can be imagined. The applause became a tumult!"[26]

With the entry of the United States into World War I in 1917, African-Americans joined the armed forces in large numbers, and bands were formed of black musicians whose services were much in demand. The most famous of these bands was formed and led by James Reese Europe himself. When this band went to France it was enormously popular, not only with the American troops but with the French as well.[27] Was Europe's band playing jazz? Probably not in the strict sense, since he laid great stress on its reading the music accurately. But read his own description of the band's playing:

> We accent strongly . . . the notes which originally would be without accent. It is natural for us to do this; it is, indeed, a racial musical characteristic. I have to call a daily rehearsal of my band to prevent the musicians from adding to their music more than I wish them to. Whenever possible they all embroider their parts in order to produce new, peculiar sounds.[28]

This is a revealing hint of the practice of improvisation, here kept in check, but so important a part of jazz performance.

After the war both James Reese Europe and Will Marion Cook made European tours, with groups recruited from the best black musicians to be found in America; several members of these groups, such as Sidney Bechet (1897–1959), later became famous jazz musicians. What one would give to have a recording, for example, of Bechet playing "The Characteristic Blues" with Cook's ensemble, as he did for King George V in a command performance at Buckingham Palace in 1919!

Brass Bands

More famous as precursors of jazz were the black brass bands that took part in the nationwide flourishing of bands that we saw in Chapter 12. New Orleans, possibly owing to French influence, had an exceptional number of bands, as well as dance orchestras. The French interest in the military, or brass, band goes back to Napoleonic times. There were also trained musicians playing in the French Opera House who regularly taught the instruments.

The bands were not large by present standards, consisting of only ten or twelve pieces, including trumpets or cornets, alto and baritone horns, trombones, tuba, clarinets, and drums. They could furnish music for concerts as well as parades; in addition, there was often a smaller group affiliated with the band that played for dances, since many of the men doubled on stringed instruments. The repertoire of both groups had of necessity to be broad, and by no means consisted entirely of the new ragtime (which was frowned upon by many of their patrons). They played marches and two-steps, of course—this was the very matrix of ragtime, and of much early jazz—but they also played quadrilles, polkas, waltzes, and mazurkas.

It was for their parade music that black bandsmen in the South ultimately became most famous, and not the least important job of these bands was playing for funerals. The lodge or secret society (often more than one) to which the deceased belonged would engage the band. In the legendary and often-described scene, the band would march solemnly to the graveyard, playing hymns such as "Nearer My God to Thee" or "Come Ye Disconsolate," or "any 4/4 played very slow." After the burial the band would re-form outside the cemetery and march away to the beat of the snare drum only. After it was a block or two away from the graveyard, it would burst into ragtime—"Didn't He Ramble," or a "ragged" version of a hymn or spiritual. It was then that the "second line" of fans and enthusiastic dancing bystanders would fall in behind the band.[29] No better evidence exists of the close relationship between early jazz and the march. It is interesting to compare an early "jazzed" march such as "High Society," with its famous clarinet obbligato in the trio section (an obbligato solo, incidentally, that established the reputation of its earliest "jazz" performer, Alphonse Picou), with a march accepted as "'standard," such as a Sousa piece of about the same time.

The Excelsior and the Onward were the most famous bands. No recordings exist, of course, of these bands in the formative period of jazz around the turn of the century (though it is frustrating for the student of jazz to realize that there *might* have been some; Sousa's band was recording before 1890). But a recording of the surviving Eureka Brass Band (an organization dating from the 1920s), which was made in the 1950s, gives some idea of the sound.[30]

There was keen competition among the bands, and "cutting" or "bucking" contests were common. A few legendary names emerge from this period—none larger than that of Charles "Buddy" Bolden (1877–1931), the New Orleans trumpet player. He was a versatile musician, reading music when necessary but preferring to play by ear. (The "uptown" New Orleans musicians, playing for the high-paying bordellos, were notable exceptions to the general practice among bandsmen of the period; these players for the most part prided themselves on being *unable* to read, feeling that it would inhibit their style.) Bolden played "sweet" music for the general public and "hot" music for the "district" and its patrons. It was for the latter that he became most famous, introducing his "hot blues" about 1894. Was Buddy playing jazz, that far back? Ear-witnesses like Bunk Johnson (1889–1949) say that he was. It is certain that he was heavily imbued with the blues. The New Orleans bass player "Pops" Foster has written of him: "He played nothing but blues, and all that stink music, and he played it very loud."[31] Thus there was ample evidence at an early date of the perennial and symbiotic relationship between blues and jazz.

Romantic legend has given New Orleans the reputation of being almost solely responsible for the birth of jazz. It is possible that the claim may be found to be somewhat exaggerated, as we learn more of the prehistory of this important genre. But there is no doubt that this unique city, with its rich blend of traditions, played an important part. In any event, that part was largely over by the end of World War I, and certainly by the advent of the first recordings. In the next chapter we shall deal with the development of jazz itself, as we can trace it from the time of its earliest actual surviving recorded sounds.

Further Reading

Books

Berlin, Edward A. *Ragtime: A Musical and Cultural History*. Berkeley: University of California Press, 1980.
An excellent study, with probably the best analysis of the musical elements of ragtime.

Blesh, Rudi, and Harriett Janis. *They All Played Ragtime*. 4th ed. New York: Oak Publications, 1971.
The first book on the subject, and still the source of a wealth of information.

Hasse, John, ed. *Ragtime: Its History, Composers, and Music*. New York: Schirmer Books, 1985.
A valuable collection of articles on various aspects, including some by Hasse himself. Extensive bibliography and discography, well organized.

Lomax, Alan. *Mister Jelly Roll: The Fortunes of Jelly Roll Morton, New Orleans Creole and "Inventor of Jazz."* 2nd ed. Berkeley: University of California Press, 1973.
Morton's memoirs as told in the famous Library of Congress sessions in 1938, with some interludes by Lomax.

Schafer, William J., and Johannes Riedel. *The Art of Ragtime: Form and Meaning of an Original Black American Art*. Baton-Rouge: Louisiana State University Press, 1973.

Schafer, William J. *Brass Bands and New Orleans Jazz*. Baton Rouge: Louisiana State University Press, c.1977.

Schuller, Gunther. *Early Jazz: Its Roots and Musical Development*. New York: Oxford University Press, 1968.
See chapter 2, "The Beginnings."

Shaw, Arnold. *Black Popular Music in America*. New York: Schirmer Books, 1986.
See especially chapter 3, "My Ragtime Baby."

Southern, Eileen. *The Music of Black Americans: A History*. 2d ed. New York: W. W. Norton, 1983.
When the first edition was published in 1971, it was the first comprehensive his-

tory of the entire field of African-American music; as revised and updated, it is still more valuable.

———,ed. *Readings in Black American Music*. 2d ed. New York. W. W. Norton, 1983.

Stearns, Marshall. *The Story of Jazz*. New York: Oxford University Press, 1956; reprint, 1974.
This standard work has excellent chapters on "Ragtime," "The New Orleans Background," and "The Transition to Jazz."

Collections of Music, with Commentary

The Collected Works of Scott Joplin, edited by Vera Brodsky Lawrence, with an essay by Rudi Blesh. New York: New York Public Library, 1971.
Vol. 1 consists of works for the piano; vol. 2, works for voice.

Classic Piano Rags: Complete Original Music for 81 Piano Rags. Selected and with an introduction by Rudi Blesh. New York: Dover, 1973.

Ragtime Rarities: Complete Original Music for 63 Piano Rags. Selected and with an introduction by Trebor Jay Tichenor. New York: Dover, 1975.

Ragtime Rediscoveries: 64 Works from the Golden Age of Rag. Selected and with an introduction by Trebor Jay Tichenor. New York: Dover, 1979.

Ferdinand "Jelly Roll" Morton: The Collected Piano Music. Transcribed, edited, and with extensive commentary by James Dapogny. Washington, DC: Smithsonian Institution Press, 1982.
A prodigious undertaking, this volume, in the words of its editor,"contains a version of every piece Jelly Roll Morton ever published or recorded as a piano solo." It includes editions of published works, transcriptions of piano rolls, and (the largest single group) transcriptions of recorded piano performances.

Listening

Ragtime

The wealth of ragtime available on records falls into three categories: (1) realizations of old piano rolls (the only kind of documentation we have from the ragtime era itself); (2) archival recordings from the 1920s and 30s, after the heyday of ragtime had passed; and (3) modern recordings.

(1) Biograph has issued a number of albums of player piano recordings, both "hand-played" (sometimes by the composer himself) and "arranged"—that is, made by punching holes in the roll without actually playing the piece. Of these *Scott Joplin—1916: Classic Solos Played by the King of Ragtime Writers and Others from Rare Piano Rolls* (Biograph 1006Q) and *Jelly Roll Morton—Rare Piano Rolls, 1924–1926* (Biograph 1004Q) are probably the most important.
(2) Of archival recordings, among the most interesting and significant are:

Ragtime, 1: The city (*Banjos, Brass Bands, & Nickel Pianos*) Compiled and annotated by Samuel Charters. Folkways RBF 17.

Ragtime 2: The Country (*Mandolins, Fiddles, & Guitars*) Compiled and edited by Samuel Charters. Folkways RBF 18.

Maple Leaf Rag: Ragtime in Rural America. NW-235

Indiana Ragtime: A Documentary Album. Produced and annotated by John Edward Hasse and Frank J. Gillis. Indiana Historical Society.

2 LPs and an informative booklet, documenting regional ragtime.

Joseph Lamb: A Study in Classic Ragtime. Folkways 3562.

Zez Confrey: Creator of the Novelty Rag. Folkways RF-28.
Both piano rolls and recordings.

(3) Among the more significant modern performances are:

Piano Rags, vols. 1–3. Performed by Joshua Rifkin. Nonesuch 71248, 71264, 71305.

Heliotrope Bouquet: Piano Rags. Performed by William Bolcom. Nonesuch 71257.

Scott Joplin: The Complete Works for Piano. 5 LPs. Performed by Dick Hyman. RCA CRL S-1106.

Kitten on the Keys: The Music of Zez Confrey. Performed by Dick Hyman. RCA XRLI-4746.

Joplin: The Red Back Book. New England Conservatory Ragtime Ensemble, Gunther Schuller, conductor. Angel S-36060.

Piano Music of Ferdinand "Jelly Roll" Morton. Performances by James Dapogny. Smithsonian 1003.

Classic Rags and Ragtime Songs. Smithsonian 1001.

Pre-Jazz

The Music of New Orleans, vol. 2: *Music of the Eureka Brass Band.* Folkways FA-2462.

The Music of New Orleans. vol. 3: *Music of the Dance Halls.* Folkways FA-2463.

The Music of New Orleans. vol. 4: *The Birth of Jazz.* Folkways FA-2464.

The Music of New Orleans. vol. 5: *The Flowering.* Folkways FA-2465.
This series consists of recordings, made in New Orleans in the 1950s, of performances reminiscent of the old styles.

A History of Jazz: The New York Scene. Folkways RF-3.
Includes a recording by James Reese Europe's Society Orchestra of 1914, and *Sensation Rag* by the Original Dixieland Jazz Band of 1917.

Steppin' on the Gas: Rags to Jazz 1913–1927. NW-269
Includes four recordings by James Europe's band in the 1910s.

PROJECTS

1. Write a paragraph, a page, or several pages, giving your own personal perception of the contribution of black music to American popular music. After you have written this, read Arnold Shaw's introduction to his *Black Popular Music in America.* Add another paragraph, or page, commenting on the extent to which Shaw's assessment of the situation confirms or contradicts your own. Does Shaw seem to present a reasonable, well-documented, balanced view? Does his introduction support the rejection of extremist views on *either* side of the question? How?

2. A broad and general sensitivity to the feelings of any group perceived as a minority (whether defined in terms of race, color, religion, or any other basis) is fairly recent and still imperfect, as our jokes and our songs reveal. The study of popular art is a study not of what later periods may select, but of what is actually popular in contemporary culture, and therefore revealing of its nature. This precept leads a scholar like Vera Brodsky Lawrence to include sheet music covers in her edition of the works of Scott Joplin, and Edward Berlin and Arnold Shaw to discuss the "coon song" in their treatises. If you were doing an illustrated lecture on American popular culture since the Jacksonian era, think about how you would treat the minstrel skit, the coon song, the Irish (or Jewish, or Chinese) song, the Polish (or Italian, or Catholic, or Mormon) joke. Discuss your views in a paper. Is censorship justifiable, and under what circumstances?

3. Write a paper comparing the role of women in ragtime (you could begin with Max Morath's article "May Aufderheide and the Ragtime Women" in Hasse, *Ragtime: Its History, Composers, and Music*) with the role of women in jazz (consulting such works as *American Women in Jazz, 1900 to the Present: Their Words, Lives, and Music* by S. Placksin or *Stormy Weather: The Music and Lives of a Century of Jazz Women* by L. Dahl [New York: Pantheon, 1984]).

4. The musical relationship between blues and ragtime was, in the classic period of ragtime, somewhat noticeable but not great. Investigate the relationship between the *texts* of ragtime songs (such as those mentioned in the chapter) and those of early blues. For ragtime songs, consult Edward Berlin's chapter "Ragtime Songs" in Hasse, *Ragtime: Its History, Composers, and Music*; Blesh and Janis's *They All Played Ragtime*; and song collections such as *Favorite Songs of the Nineties* (see the previous chapter). For blues lyrics, see Chapter 8, and such sources as the W. C. Handy anthology and Paul Oliver's *The Meaning of the Blues.*

5. Study Scott Joplin's brief *School of Ragtime* (included in the Collected Works, and available in most libraries). Find examples in actual rags of the rhythmic figures Joplin presents as teaching examples. If you are a pianist, work up a demonstration of these on the piano.

6. Make a study of Scott Joplin's opera *Treemonisha* (the vocal score is included in the Collected Works, and the work has been recorded). How much of it is ragtime? Include critical comments (reviews, etc.), and information about recent performances if possible.

7. Investigate the life and works of one or two of the lesser-known composers of ragtime—composers not mentioned in this chapter. For a start, consult Blesh and Janis, *They All Played Ragtime.* Listen to as many of their rags as you can, and assemble a discography.

8. Write a paper on the player piano—its history, how it worked, its revival (including the present-day computerized version), and its literature, including ragtime.

9. "Has the importance of New Orleans in the early development of jazz been overestimated in most standard books?" Taking either the negative or the positive side of this question, prepare a well-substantiated summary of your case.

10. Make a brief study of jazz and pre-jazz on the New York scene prior to 1925. Crucial to your task will be *Jazz: A History of the New York Scene* by Samuel B. Charters and Leonard Kunstadt, 1962 (reprint, New York: Da Capo, 1981), and the Folkways record RF-3, cited in the Listening section of this chapter.

14

Jazz

BEFORE the actual sounds of jazz began to be captured and preserved, however unsatisfactorily at first, by the phonograph, we can only speculate as to what this music really sounded like. We do have some re-creations, years after the fact, by a few of its musicians. What little has survived in notation gives no very accurate idea of a music that existed largely without being written down. And verbal descriptions, together with some knowledge of what instruments were used and under what conditions they were played, furnish imprecise clues at best. In the previous chapter we considered jazz before the advent of recordings—"primitive" jazz, according to the chronology of one prominent writer, André Hodeir.[1] We now pick it up with the first preserved sounds.

The New Orleans Style: The Traditional Jazz of the Early Recordings

Although jazz was first recorded in 1917, the most readily available early recordings date from about 1923, by which time the style generally known as "traditional" jazz was well under way. Because these early performances, by Freddie Keppard (cornetist, 1889–1933), King Oliver (cornetist and bandleader, 1885–1938), Jelly Roll Morton (pianist, bandleader, and composer, 1890–1941), Kid Ory (trombonist and bandleader, 1886–1973), Louis Armstrong (cornetist, trumpeter, and singer, 1898–1971), and others, were so important in defining what jazz was, and laying the groundwork for what it was to become, we shall begin by examining one in some detail, using this as a point of departure for a brief description of the basic nature and structure of jazz.

Traditional Jazz as Illustrative of Jazz Method and Structure

In its essence and in its historical genesis, jazz is basically a *way* of playing and singing—a style of performance. This style is defined by many aspects—texture, tone color, phrasing, the choice of instruments, the freedom to "bend" both pitch and rhythm, and the freedom of the individual player to improvise within certain clearly understood limits. (In addition, no one doubts the existence of less tangible approaches and attitudes that are essential to defining the authentic "feel" of jazz, but we will confine ourselves here to its tangible elements.) There have from the very beginning been original jazz compositions, and composer-performers—Jelly Roll Morton, in the first three decades of the century, and Duke Ellington, beginning in the 1920s, are but two of the best known. But the very essence of jazz remains its manner of performance, and the mainstay of jazz repertoire has traditionally been the jazz interpretation of "standards." These may be either standard popular songs, or, more simply, the standard "ground plan" of the blues, as outlined in Chapter 2. Thus the basic procedure of traditional jazz (a procedure that was still in use well into the bop era of the 1940s and 1950s) was to produce a series of what are called *variations* on a standard formal or harmonic plan.

For an example let us return to the famous "Dippermouth Blues" referred to briefly in Chapter 8. The original recording of 1923 is readily accessible, and in instrumentation, style, and form, it is representative of the traditional, or New Orleans, style.[2]

The instrumentation is two cornets, one clarinet, one trombone, and a "rhythm section" of piano, banjo, and drums. Except for the addition of a second cornet, innovative for its time, this is a typical makeup for traditional jazz. (The cornets, played by King Oliver and Louis Armstrong, sound quite different from trumpets, which came into use in jazz later.) In describing the texture we can make an analogy with the earlier ragtime. The "front line" instruments (in this case, the cornets, clarinet, and trombone) correspond to the right hand, to which is entrusted the melody, or the simultaneous overlayering of melodies. The rhythm section (in this case, the piano, drums, and banjo) corresponds to the left hand, which has the job of keeping the beat going, and of outlining the harmonies. If we grasp this division of function between front line and rhythm section it will serve us well in understanding jazz texture throughout the decades to follow. The front line will later increase, in the big band, to complete sections of saxophones, trumpets, trombones, plus whatever additional melody instruments may be employed; the rhythm section will drop the antiquated banjo, add string bass (later in its electric version), switch to electric piano or synthesizer, and even electrify the drums. In very small combos, the rhythm section will be reduced to piano and drums, or simply drums—the drum set being the irreducible representative of the rhythm section which jazz can hardly do without. But the two functions, those of melody and rhythm, remain in any music that can be called jazz.

Ragtime, as a solo piano form, had a single melody (at most, lightly harmonized) in the right hand. Traditional jazz, on the other hand, exhibits in its most typical choruses a complex layering of melodic lines, with the cornet(s) in the middle, the trombone below, and the clarinet adding a more ornate and decorative line on top of it all. "Dippermouth Blues" shows this texture in all but a few of the choruses, in which the clarinet and later the first cornet emerge as soloists.

In its form, "Dippermouth Blues" is an apt illustration of the fundamental variation technique of jazz. After the 4-bar introduction, each of the nine choruses is an exposition of the 12-bar blues form. Close listening, however, discloses subtle variations in the harmony from chorus to chorus. It appears in its simplest, most standard form (as set forth in Chapter 2) in the sixth chorus (the first solo chorus by King Oliver on cornet):

phrase 1:	I	—	—	I7
phrase 2:	IV7	—	I	—
phrase 3:	V7	—	I	—

The first two choruses of the piece show the kind of embellishing of the harmony that is typical of jazz versions of the blues—embellishments that, in the second and third phrases, show the influence of the European-based harmonies of ragtime:

phrase 1:	I	IV	I	I7
phrase 2:	IV	#ivd7	I	VI7
phrase 3:	II7	V7	I	—

Countless other blues are variations on some version of this basic blues pattern. But the blues as performed is more than simply a formal and harmonic plan; a manner of performance is implied that includes the inflection of certain notes—the blue notes, as described in Chapter 2. Listen to King Oliver's lowered thirds of the scale at the beginning of his solos, and clarinetist Johnny Dodds's blues sevenths at the beginning of his.

Another vital ingredient of jazz method is improvisation. Upon a formal and harmonic ground plan such as the one illustrated above the musicians are free to invent, in an appropriate jazz style, their own melodic lines that fit with, and express, that harmony and that form. Ideally, as improvisation, it never sounds exactly the same way twice. Depending upon the talent and mood of the performer, the improvisation can be fresh, spontaneous, and loaded with new ideas, or it can follow patterns already established in previous performances or by other performers. But good jazz improvisation is never a matter of "anything goes." It is a product (as is all good art) of a fine balance between discipline and freedom—in the case of the jazz solo, between the discipline imposed by the preset form and harmony and the freedom to create within these limitations. This balance is the real essence of jazz performance.

To see this basic method of improvisation—the balance between discipline and freedom—still at work in the jazz of a quarter of a century later, a brief digression from our chronological survey for a moment may be suggested. Familiarize yourself with the popular song "Embraceable You," by George Gershwin, and then listen to alto saxophonist Charlie Parker's highly inventive 1947 improvisations on the tune, with a rhythm section of just piano, bass, and drums.[3]

Louis Armstrong has been deemed the first great improvising soloist in jazz, establishing a high standard for generations to come. He was one of the performers who defined the "hot" style of playing in the 1920s, and was an early master of "swing." Swing is not easily described, but all of its elements amount to contradictions or dislocations, in one way or another, of a regular metric pattern—playing pairs of shorter notes unequally within a beat so as to give more length and stress to the first, displacing accents, or playing notes slightly behind or ahead of the beat. His solos, with their melodic inventiveness, rhythmic drive, and variety of tonal color, especially during the period from the 1920s through the late 1930s, were models that had a great influence on the course of jazz as it moved out of the traditional period.[4]

Dissemination and Change: The Pre-Swing Era

Chicago

It is important to realize that jazz, by the time we encounter it on recordings, was already in a state of change. Where was it coming from, and what was its environment? New Orleans had put its stamp and name on it. But the recordings of this period were not made in New Orleans; they were made in Chicago, in New York, in Richmond, Indiana. Jazz had spread to the upper Midwest and to the East Coast, and its first great wave of popularity was beginning. New Orleans jazzmen had emigrated to the south side of Chicago, to New York, and to other urban centers. Musicians, both black and white, who had never been within a thousand miles of New Orleans were playing jazz. Considering the impact of its increasing popularity, and the numbers of new players that were taking it up, changes were inevitable, and gradually the traditional freewheeling, relaxed, improvised style was lost. We can sense this in some of the recordings made by younger musicians in the so-called Chicago style. It was transitional; the white musicians were all, to a greater or lesser extent, learning from the blacks—and, because of the attitudes and conditions of the time, whites were reaping a disproportionate share of the economic gains. The Chicago style shows jazz in a kind of adolescence between the carefree youth of the traditional stage and the maturity of the big-band stage, with its more sophisticated craftmanship. It can be heard in the famous "Royal Garden Blues" with Bix Beiderbecke (1903–31) and the Wolverines, and in both "Jazz Me Blues" and "There'll Be Some Changes Made" with the Chicago Rhythm Kings.[5] It is a sort of derivative New Orleans style, but lacking some of the spontaneity, and it actually sounds more dated than earlier New Orleans jazz.

What was the milieu of jazz in the 1920s? Musicians played a great deal for and among themselves, after hours, but for the paying public (a rapidly growing constituency) its home was the nightclub and its orbit of related establishments. This was to constitute its basic environment, physically and economically, for years to come. One effect of Prohibition was to relegate the public dispensing of liquor to the tough guy—the mobster who could either dictate to the law or take it into his own hands. Consequently, especially in places like Chicago, jazz came under the aegis of the gangster.[6] For a fuller understanding of jazz, its environment must be kept in mind, in terms not only of its effects on the lives of its musicians, but of the whole set of prejudices that grew up around it. The nightclub and its milieu is still basic to the day-by-day support of a sizable segment of jazz and the vast core of players who earn wages playing it.

With isolated exceptions, usually for recordings, the bands of this period were racially segregated. This led to what might be thought of as two parallel traditions in jazz. Although the color line began to be broken in the 1930s (often at high personal cost to those courageous enough to pioneer in this direction) and mixed bands eventually became fairly common, the jazz scene even today is still not free of vestiges of this unfortunate dichotomy along racial lines, as we shall see.

Three New York Developments

New York became the scene of intense jazz activity in the 1920s. But the stage was set for this activity long before, and any notion that jazz was imported wholesale from New Orleans and was sprung full-blown on a public totally unprepared for such novel music is false. As we have noted in the previous chapter, all-black musicals and extravaganzas had been produced in Brooklyn and on Broadway before the turn of the century, and while they did not incorporate what would be called jazz, we know enough of the impression made at the time to sense that some of the authentic elements of jazz must have been present. Ragtime was already very well known in New York in the first decade of this century. Black Bohemia had flourished as early as 1900, furnishing dance orchestras and musicians whose services were much in demand. James Reese Europe had given a concert with his Clef Club orchestra in Carnegie Hall in 1912, in collaboration with Will Marion Cook; again, what the audience heard must have been at least a foretaste of jazz.[7] The all-white Original Dixieland Jazz Band had played in New York as early as 1917. So the ground was prepared.

Harlem piano

Three important developments began to emerge in New York before 1930. The first was a solo piano style, outgrowth of ragtime, that was mentioned in Chapter 13. "Rent-party," "parlor-social," "Harlem," "stride"—these names all describe, in terms of economics, geography, or left-hand agility, a solo piano idiom best illustrated in the work of its recognized founder, James P. Johnson (1894–1955). To get the flavor of his rollicking piano style, listen to his "Carolina Shout" (1921), "You Can't Do What My Last Man Did" (1923), "You've Got to Be Modernistic" (1929), or "What Is This Thing Called Love?" (1930).[8] The atmosphere and function of the Harlem rent party of the twenties and thirties is succinctly described by Marshall Stearns when he calls it "an unstable social phenomenon that was stimulated by Prohibition and made necessary by the Depression." He continues: "The object of such a party is to raise the rent, and anybody who can pay a quarter admission is cordially invited. The core of the party usually centers around a pianist whose style was shaped by many similar situations: he plays very loud and very rhythmically."[9]

It should be noted that the work of Johnson, Fats Waller (1904–43), and others far transcended the limited and highly functional milieu of the rent party, and became influential in the mainstream of jazz itself.

Jazz and the wider public

A second development on the New York scene in the twenties, though somewhat peripheral to jazz itself, is interesting because it shows both the tremendous impact that jazz had by this time and the way in which the American penchant for assimilation was being indulged. New York, as the capital of the American entertainment business, has historically been not only the Great Marketplace but the Great Assimilator. Jazz was becoming enormously popular—a new force to be reckoned with in American music. As is usual, those *outside* the tradition itself saw it as "raw material"—vital and interesting, to be sure, but needing to be "worked over." (Somewhat in the same vein, European composers in the nineteenth century had started the practice of working over folk music.) Of course, there was a broad spectrum of reaction to jazz as raw material, with mixed and complex motives. Some were merely interested in "selling" it. For some this motive was mingled with a sincere desire to educate the public to its unique qualities. Some saw it as providing the basis for a new kind of concert, or fine-art, music. But almost all actual treatments of jazz involved setting it in a context that, while extending its temporal dimensions, diluted its essential "hot" quality. Paul Whiteman (1890–1967), whose work can be thought of as usually embodying all these motives, assembled a large orchestra of extremely able concert musicians and then employed a few genuine jazz players to impart to the ensemble the rhythm and flavor of jazz. The resulting "sweet" jazz thus became more acceptable to a broader segment of the public, many of whom may have thought that indeed what they were hearing *was* jazz.

Carrying assimilation a step further, this period saw the composition of extended works intended for the environment and the audience of the formal concert, and using ensembles often approaching symphonic makeup and proportions. Of all such works of this period, probably the most successful was the famous *Rhapsody in Blue*, for piano and large ensemble (though in its original conception the ensemble was smaller and more jazz-oriented than the full symphony orchestra now used to perform the piece). The *Rhapsody* was written by George Gershwin for the now-memorable concert given by Paul Whiteman in Aeolian Hall, New York, in 1924.[10] This work, which has not lost its freshness even today, is one of the best to come out of that first period of groping toward a successful amalgamation of jazz and concert music. The period was marked by the production of concertos, symphonies, and ballets strongly influenced by the jazz idiom. It also coincided with a period of great jazz popularity in Europe and jazz influence on prominent European composers of the time, such as Maurice Ravel, Igor Stravinsky, and Darius Milhaud. While jazz here was attaining a rather slow and very reserved acceptance on the part of many Americans (on racial grounds as well as on grounds of its origins and environment), it was welcomed with open arms in Europe, especially in France and Germany. Accounts of the reception of American jazz musicians abroad from the 1920s to the 1970s make enlightening reading indeed, as they sound a consistent theme of enthusiastic, even worshipful, acceptance.

Early steps in the evolution of the big band

The third development in the New York scene at this time was squarely in the mainstream of jazz: the evolution of the big band. This led directly into the period of jazz's greatest stability, popularity, and economic security—an era that lasted until the end of World War II, and that has been designated by some (including Hodeir) as the classical era of jazz. New York can claim no monopoly in the development of the big bands.[11] But it did serve as a magnet to draw talented musicians from New Orleans (often by way of Chicago), from Chicago itself, from Kansas City, and elsewhere—musicians who helped forge the new institution that was to carry jazz to every part of the land and, ultimately, of the world.

The term "big band" may be misleading. Compared with a full orchestra, the bands were still small—scarcely more that about fifteen musicians (Figure 14-1). But this was twice the size of a New Orleans–style band, and many players and jazz fans considered the "big" bands a betrayal of the very essence of jazz. We can see the big bands today as a pragmatic solution to the problem of balancing the demand for a fuller, larger, and more varied sound with the need to retain the *sine qua non* of jazz—improvisational freedom, and the elusive hot quality that goes with it.

We have examined "Dippermouth Blues" as recorded by King Oliver's Creole Jazz Band. Though recorded in Chicago, it was played in authentic New Orleans style, with only seven musicians. Fletcher Henderson (1897–1952), a pianist and leader-arranger from Georgia, recorded the same piece, with slight additions, in New York in 1925, calling it "Sugar Foot Stomp."[12] The differences constitute an interesting documentation of the beginnings of the big band. There are now eleven musicians, the most significant addition being two saxophones. The individual hot solos are still there, the most memorable being the choruses played by Louis Armstrong himself, who plays essentially the same solos as in the earlier King Oliver version. But the new trend toward *arranged* jazz is apparent in the way the instruments play predetermined figures together at the "breaks" (the fill-in passages at the ends of the phrases), in the tightly disciplined and rehearsed (if not written-down) clarinet ensemble playing, and especially in the almost chorale-like presentation of the blues progression twice near the end. Another Fletcher Henderson piece, "The Stampede," arranged by Don Redman (1900–64) and recorded in 1926, shows the trend carried further by using a still greater proportion of arranged ensemble effects, while still allowing for individual improvisation.[13]

Duke Ellington

Of all the jazz musicians who came into prominence with the big band, none had a longer or more influential career than Edward Kennedy "Duke" Ellington (1899–1974), whose creative activity spanned half a century. He was a pianist, but he never pushed himself to the forefront as a soloist; his medium

Figure 14.1. The Jazz Band: Its Growth and Evolution

	RHYTHM					MELODY								
						Brass				Reeds				
King Oliver (1923)	Piano		Banjo	Drum set		Cornet, Cornet	Trombone			Clarinet				
Duke Ellington (1927)	Piano	Acoustic bass	Banjo	Drum set		Trumpet, Trumpet	Trombone			Alto sax [Soprano sax, Baritone sax]*		Tenor sax [Clarinet]		Baritone sax [Alto sax, Clarinet]
Duke Ellington (1940)	Piano	Acoustic bass	Guitar	Drum set		Trumpet, Trumpet, Cornet	Trombone, Trombone, Valve trombone			Alto sax	Alto sax	Tenor sax	Tenor sax	Baritone sax
Stan Kenton (1958)	Piano	Acoustic base		Drum set		Trumpet, Trumpet, Trumpet, Trumpet, Trumpet	Trombone, Trombone, Trombone, Trombone, Trombone		French horn, French horn	Alto sax	Alto sax	Tenor sax		Baritone sax
Gil Evans (1973)	Piano [Electric piano]	Electric bass	Guitar	Drum set	Symphonic percussion, Synthesizer	Trumpet, Trumpet, Flugelhorn	Trombone [Tuba]	Tuba	French horn, French horn	Alto sax		Tenor sax [Flute]	Baritone sax	Baritone sax [Soprano sax, Flute]
American Jazz Orchestra (1989)	Piano	Acoustic bass	Guitar	Drum set		Trumpet, Trumpet, Trumpet, Trumpet	Trombone, Trombone, Trombone, Bass trombone			Alto sax	Alto sax [Clarinet, Flute]	Tenor sax	Tenor sax [Clarinet]	Baritone sax [Clarinet, Flute, Bass clarinet]

*Reed doublings are common, but not standardized, and will vary over time, from band to band, and even from one piece to another.

of expression was the band itself, and as leader, arranger, and composer he made music with a group that held together with exceptional consistency and continuity throughout the years. A famous piece coming out of the very beginnings of his work with the big band medium is "East St. Louis Toodle-Oo".[14] Though the extremely early version first recorded is not to be compared with his mature work of a dozen or so years later, it shows already the smooth and disciplined playing that were evident even in his fast numbers, and the use of instrumental effects and colors typical of Ellington's essentially orchestral approach to jazz.

The Ellington band's unique use of instrumental color is the product of two factors: the imagination of Ellington himself (joined, from 1938 on, by his arranger Billy Strayhorn), and a succession of remarkable players that Ellington had in his band. Trumpet players Bubber Miley, Cootie Williams, and Ray Nance; trombonists Joe Nanton, and Juan Tizol; clarinetist Barney Bigard; and saxophonists Johnny Hodges (soprano and alto), Ben Webster (tenor), and Harry Carney (baritone) are a few whose expansion of the tonal possibilities of their instruments, together with Ellington's use of these new possibilities, contributed to the Ellington sound. To gain a proper sense of the range and variety of this sound, the listener needs to hear more than just a few pieces. "East St. Louis Toodle-Oo," cited above, is only a beginning. To cite works from the peak period of the late 1930s and early 1940s, the use of color in the slow "Blue Serge" (1941), the moderate-paced "Ko-ko" (1940), "Concerto for Cootie" (1940, later becoming the basis for the song "Do Nothing Till You Hear from Me"), and the up-tempo "Main Stem" (1942, a hard-driving piece with a remarkable variety of color in the Kansas City style) are suggested. Especially noteworthy among the shorter works for its pictorial sense and use of color is a train piece that also incorporates the blues, "Happy Go Lucky Local" (1946).[15]

As a composer, Duke Ellington had a broad range. He was primarily an instrumental composer, writing for his band, but he also was responsible for a fairly large output of songs—some of which began as such, and some of which resulted from words being put to his band numbers. He pioneered in writing more extended works for jazz ensemble, beginning as early as 1931 with *Creole Rhapsody* (which filled two sides of a ten-inch 78-rpm record), and including *Black, Brown and Beige* (1943, a multi-movement commentary on the history of black people in America),[16] and many suites, from the *Deep South Suite* of 1946 to the *Togo Brava Suite* of 1971. He also wrote musicals, film scores, a ballet, incidental music to a Shakespeare play, and, in the late 1960s and early 1970s, a series of *Sacred Concerts.*

The Swing Era and the Big Bands

The big band style, as it evolved in the East, drew on the New Orleans archetypal style, either directly or by way of Chicago. There had to be adjustments, as we have seen. But before the big band style could reach its full development, there was another part of the country to be heard from. This was "the West" to easterners, but it was actually the heartland—specifically Kansas City. In the days before mass media threatened to blanket the whole country and induce a homogenized culture suffocating to regional artistic identity, it was possible for different areas to develop artistic dialects as distinctive as their speech. What we are calling attention to here may seem like a fine distinction to the beginning listener to jazz, but listen to the hard-driving beat—"jump," it was called, or "four heavy beats to a bar, and no cheating" (to quote Count Basie)—of Bennie Moten's "Toby" or "Moten Swing" (both 1932), or Count Basie's "Roseland Shuffle" (1937), "Every Tub" (1938), or, in a more understated vein, "Dickie's Dream" (1939).[17] You will then get a notion of that "Kansas City" ingredient that went into big band jazz after the arrival in the East of Bennie Moten (1894–1935), William "Count" Basie (1904–84), Lester Young (1909–1959), and a host of other players from "the West." It was closely akin, actually, to the drive of boogie-woogie, which had come from the same part of the country.

The so-called swing era, virtually synonymous with the heyday of the big bands, is usually thought to have come to full flower about 1935, and to have bloomed gloriously for nearly a decade. This was the period of jazz's broadest popularity. By this time, after the repeal of Prohibition and partial recovery from the Depression, the mob-controlled nightclubs no longer constituted the nearly exclusive support and environment for jazz. Dance halls, which by the mid-thirties grew into large, well-appointed, and well-attended ballrooms, gave jazz a new forum and a broader popular base. The big "name" bands toured these, as well as giving stage shows in theaters. Recordings, of course, sold extremely well by this time, and could be heard on phonographs at home, in the jukeboxes that soon provided a ubiquitous accompaniment to nearly all public eating and drinking in the land, or on the new popular mass medium of the day, radio. The disc jockey, with his enormous influence, came into being. There were also weekly broadcasts of live bands. Movies featured jazz bands. This was unquestionably the period when jazz enjoyed its widest public.

Big Band Music and Musicians

What was the jazz of this period like? Anyone born before 1925 can call up a litany of the big bands, a very few of which survived into the 1970s. We have already considered in some detail the band of Duke Ellington, and mentioned another of the most influential band leaders of the period, Count Basie. An important white musician of the swing era was Benny Goodman (1909–86), clarinetest and bandleader. His highly skilled band of fourteen to sixteen musicians played an essentially hot style closely derived from that of black jazz artists of the time. Goodman acknowledged this heritage, using arrangements written for him by Fletcher Henderson, some of which were based on traditional New Orleans originals by King Oliver or Jelly Roll Morton. In addition, Goodman was one of the first to incorporate black musicians into his ensembles, using them at first as featured performers in his trio, quartet, and sextet. The disciplined but driving swing of his band helped to bring jazz to a new plateau of popularity and acceptance as dance music. This was dramatized by a famous breakthrough at the Palomar Ballroom in Los Angeles in 1935, where Goodman established that a tremendous audience, especially among younger people, existed for the hotter swing, alongside the more staid "sweet" jazz.[18] A series of recordings and broadcasts ensued in the later thirties, characterized by the hot solos of Goodman, trumpeter Harry James, and drummer Gene Krupa. Typical of this Goodman swing style are the Fletcher Henderson arrangements of Handy's "St. Louis Blues" or Oliver's "Sugar Foot Stomp."[19] The latter is especially interesting for two reasons: first, because of the comparison it affords with two earlier versions of the work already cited, and second, because it was one of the Henderson arrangements that helped to accomplish the historic breakthrough for swing in 1935.

In considering Goodman's contributions, it may be noted further that the small jazz combo that played in conjunction with the larger band, consisting of clarinet, piano, and drums, occasionally augmented by vibraphone or guitar, was ahead of its time in concept and style, and forecast the sounds and approach of postwar "cool" jazz. Goodman was also one of the first jazz musicians who had been thoroughly schooled in classical music as well, performing and recording music by Mozart, Brahms, Bartók, and Stravinsky—the latter two contemporary composers, indeed, wrote works especially for him. Goodman thus forecast a catholicity of approach to music that is typical of many talented younger musicians from the 1960s on.

To mention some bands is to leave out many more. Our purpose here, however, is not to present a catalog of the bands, but to try to characterize the sounds of the period and the milieu in which they flourished, and to trace the processes of change constantly at work on both.[20]

Latin influence

Before we move out of the swing era, we should note three other important aspects of the scene. The first is the work of the Latin bands popular at the time (the "Latin tinge," often underestimated in American music, has been discussed in Chapter 3). The rumba craze was no less intense than that of the tango earlier, or the mambo, samba, or cha-cha subsequently. What the purely Latin bands played was not jazz, of course, but it illustrates and reminds us of the perennial Latin presence and influence in American music. Jazz was by no means unaffected by it, and Latin drummers were soon to be incorporated into jazz ensembles (as were those from Africa, which has quite a different tradition, albeit with similar instruments). An interesting example, from somewhat later, of this Latin assimilation is "Tin Tin Deo" (1948), with the celebrated Cuban drummer Chano Pozo.[21]

The small combo

The second aspect is the simultaneous cultivation of the small ensemble in the era of the big band. This was no longer the old-time jazz ensemble (which did indeed enjoy a revival) but the intimate group of three to seven players that was the vehicle for developing some of the newest ideas in jazz. Its commercial aspect was represented by the "cocktail combo" playing in small bars, but there were important artistic dimensions to the small combo as well. The Benny Goodman Sextet's recording of "I Found a New Baby" (1941) furnishes a good example.[22] Actually the small combo has always been present at every phase in jazz evolution; it was not an invention of the post–World War II "cool" or "progressive" schools. Louis Armstrong had recorded with from two to six musicians in the twenties.[23] The solo pianist also flourished; Jelly Roll Morton, Earl Hines (1903–83), Fats Waller, Art Tatum (1909–56), Bud Powell (1924–66), and Erroll Garner (1921–77) were leading figures.

The traditional revival

The third aspect to be considered before leaving this period is the persistent vitality of the traditional (often called New Orleans) style of jazz. It has never wholly died out. An early copy of New Orleans style (mostly white and more or less New York–oriented), known generally as "Dixieland," was translated into big band terms in the work of such white bandleaders Bob Crosby ("South Rampart Street Parade," 1937) and Eddie Condon ("Somebody Loves Me," 1944).[24] But a real revival of the older style was one of the landmarks of the 1940s as well. In an episode in American music replete with both nostalgia and human interest, players who had been active in the very early days of jazz (some of whom had never before been recorded) were located, sometimes with considerable difficulty, and reinstated with honors in the kingdom of jazz, for the purpose of re-creating the authentic traditions and music of the long-gone New Orleans beginnings. How authentic such re-creations can be in an art so basically improvisational, and so dependent upon the player's subjective impressions of a *total* environment, may be open to question. But the documents are there now, recorded a generation after the fact, for all time. For examples, listen to Bunk Johnson, legendary symbol of this revival, in "Down by the River" (1942) or "Make Me a Pallet on the Floor" (1945)[25] or Kid Ory, in any number of revival recordings. Younger musicians also became interested in the old style, and the work of Lu Watters and Turk Murphy may be referred to in this regard.

Wartime and the Seeds of Change

With the entry of the United States into World War II there came, on one level, a kind of freezing of the status quo. In times of prolonged major crisis, especially war, we find certain kinds of art supported and indulged, both as a necessary release and for the sense of stability they afford. Such times are not hospitable to changes and evolutions in art, which are apt to be disturbing. The feeling of security that a repetition of the accustomed can give is what is needed—and sought. During the war people flocked to ballrooms to hear the name bands and bought the latest records; and overseas soldiers, sailors, airmen, and marines heard the same bands and the same pieces. (This is not to say that wartime hardships, including shortages of gasoline for touring, did not take their toll among the bands, some of which disbanded even before the war was over.) Meanwhile, underneath the desperately needed continuity of the surface, changes were being wrought that would profoundly alter the jazz scene once the war was over.

The Emergence of Modern Jazz: Bop as a Turning Point

In the decades since the end of World War II the whole fabric of Occidental music has frayed into so many different strands that it has become a daunting task to try to keep track of them, or form any sort of overall picture. Jazz has been no exception to this; beginning in the 1940s a combination of factors wrought evolutionary changes in jazz that brought a whole new set of leaders to the fore and made significant alterations, not only in the music itself, but in the function of jazz, in its audience, and in the way it was perceived. From the beginning of the 1930s through the end of World War II, there had been, for most fans, one kind of jazz—that of the big bands. The best-known names were Benny Goodman, Glenn Miller, Artie Shaw, Tommy Dorsey, Harry James, and the like.* Jazz, however attenuated by the popular bands in the minds of its devotees, came as close in this period to being synonymous with America's popular music as it has ever been or is ever likely to be again. After the war, all was different. At about mid-century, the place of jazz in our culture changed. For one thing, it lost such mass following as it had possessed, especially among the young, who have shown repeatedly that what they really like most is music with a strong beat that they can dance to (a need that was soon to be met by black rhythm-and-blues, and white rock 'n' roll). At the same time jazz began, for the first time, to be considered seriously as *art* music, not only by its fans and critics, but by some of its practitioners as well. Jazz became bohemianized.

It began with *bop*. It has been customary to call the advent of bop (the term is a shortening of "rebop" or "bebop") a revolution in jazz—a revolt against, variously, the big bands; the restrictive harmonic framework of the jazz playing then in style; commercialism; and, above all, racial injustice. There is certainly some truth in each of these perceptions—the last one even though by this time there was at least some breaking down of the color bar. Bop *can* be seen in this light as a "black backlash" to the "white synthesis."[26]

In terms of the music itself, however, it distorts a clear picture of the origins of this crucial development to ignore its *evolutionary* aspects. Bop had, in fact, its antecedents across a fairly broad spectrum of the jazz of the 1940s, including some of the innovative playing and arranging going on in a few of the big bands themselves, notably those of Count Basie (especially the rhythm section) and Earl Hines. Other big bands that were playing convincingly in bop style before the end of the forties were those of Billy Eckstine, Boyd Raeburn, Claude Thornhill, and Woody Herman. John Birks "Dizzy" Gillespie (b. 1917), a pioneer in the development of bop, played with both the Eckstine and Raeburn bands, wrote several numbers for Woody Herman's, and soon formed his own band, as big as the biggest.[27]

Bebop's musical ingredients had their precedents in the work of individual players as well, and bop certainly could not have assumed the sound it did had it not been for the playing of such important jazz figures as Art Tatum, Lester Young, and Roy Eldridge. What gave it the aspect of revolution was that, in the case of bop, a unique set of circumstances both speeded up the evolutionary process and hid it from public view until the new style was well established.

* White bandleaders all, to be sure. Even then, the bands of Duke Ellington, Count Basie, Billy Eckstine, Lionel Hampton, Jimmie Lunceford, and other black jazzmen, who were regarded by aficionados as playing "real jazz," had a smaller public.

The most compelling musical circumstance attending the evolution of bop was simply the proximity and mutual influence of a number of very gifted musicians who were also highly innovative, who were not content to play the same things in the same way, who thought a lot about new musical ideas, and who spent long hours searching for them, and practicing and perfecting them when they hit upon them. Added to the racial feelings mentioned above, a restlessness, a ripeness for change, was felt by a number of talented, inventive black musicians at about the same time and in the same place—in New York City in the early 1940s.

The first outstanding exponents of the new style were the trumpeter Dizzy Gillespie and the alto saxophonist Charlie Parker (1920–55), together with pianist Thelonious Monk (1917–82) and drummer Kenny Clarke (1914–85). Gillespie and Parker both had keenly creative minds, as well as extremely facile technique on their respective instruments. Bop then developed as the first jazz to demand an entire ensemble of virtuoso performers.* Not surprisingly, the ensemble was characteristically small—a quintet or sextet made up of a rhythm section (piano, bass, and drums) and a "front line" of just two or three instrumentalists. In addition to an astounding virtuosity, there was an obscuring of the familiar melodies jazz fans had grown accustomed to hearing. Bop continued to use the harmonic basis (the "changes") of certain jazz "standards" (Gershwin's "I Got Rhythm" was a favorite), but free, elaborate, and very difficult new melodic variations were invented on the original harmonies, often overlapping phrase endings. Frequently the harmonic plan itself, the very basis of jazz, would be changed through the use of substitute chords. Tempos were usually very fast. To accompany all this, the supporting rhythm section became much lighter. The cymbal, with its bright, insinuating tone, and the string bass, now "walking" at a fast pace, together took over from the drums the job of keeping the beat, and the drums could now be used both less frequently and more effectively for accentuation, or for the superimposing of cross-rhythms that made the rhythmic texture more complex and tended at times to obscure the beat. From then on the jazz rhythm section was permanently transformed in color, density and complexity, in an evolutionary development that would outlast bop itself. This lightening and obscuring of the beat, together with the fast tempos, discouraged dancing to bebop; it became instead a music for *listeners*, and this encouraged its being perceived as an *art* music.

At first few listeners could follow the new music, and it is still true that very few musicians can successfully imitate it. Bop became controversial, even among jazz musicians, and its followers, whether or not they grasped the music, quickly formed a cult based on appearances that *could* very easily be grasped—dark glasses, berets, goatees, cultish "hip" language, a disdain for the non-hip public as outsiders (a disdain not necessarily typical of all of the bop musicians themselves).

Early bop was not well documented in commercial recordings. This was partly owing to the famous ban on recording that was imposed by the Amer-

* In this sense, bop bore the same relationship to swing jazz that bluegrass did to country music.

ican Federation of Musicians in August 1942.* The presence of other factors, however, is indicated by the fact that bop was sufficiently developed before the ban so that recordings could have been made. But for whatever combination of reasons, bop was a fait accompli by the time recording was resumed in 1944; its circle of performers had widened, and it was sprung more or less full blown on a largely unsuspecting public. Thus our recordings pick it up already well along, and after its influence among jazz players had spread to a considerable extent. Listen to "Shaw 'Nuff" (1945), with Gillespie and Parker performing with just piano, bass, and drums, or "KoKo," of the same year, with just four performers (Gillespie himself doubles on piano), for the essence of the style.[28] Note the unison passages used to open and close the pieces. (These passages possibly had their origins in the rigorous practice sessions Parker and Gillespie had together in the early days, playing etudes in unison in all keys as fast as they could.) The unisons were new to jazz, and were a contradiction of the old spirit of heterophony and polyphony that underlay the traditional jazz of the twenties and thirties. The unison lines became in turn a tradition that stuck, reappearing in post-bop works.

In due course bop was translated into big band terms, just as traditional jazz had been before it. In "Oop-Pap-a-Da" (1947) Gillespie records with a band of seventeen pieces (large even for the big band era) a work that not only transfers to the large ensemble the drive and virtuosity of bop, but shows another characteristic, vocalizing on nonsense syllables (which incidentally provided titles for many of these pieces).[29] The singing exhibits the same fluidity and virtuosity that we hear in the instrumental solos. ("Scat" singing, as this is called, was not new to jazz; Louis Armstrong was doing it in the 1920s.)

There were many other very able jazz musicians playing in the bop style or in bop combos in the 1940s and 1950s. That the list (which would include such eminent performers as trumpeters Fats Navarro, Clifford Brown, and Miles Davis; saxophonists Dexter Gordon, Sonny Rollins, Stan Getz, and Gerry Mulligan; pianists Bud Powell, John Lewis, George Shearing, Tadd Dameron, and Oscar Peterson; drummers Max Roach and Art Blakey; and vibraphonist Milt Jackson) contains the names of so many who went on to participate in and influence subsequent styles is testimony to the very seminal nature of bop. As a turning point in the history of jazz it was comparable to the earlier emergence of swing, which took jazz out of its ragtime rhythmic mold, and to the later influence of rock, which again profoundly affected the rhythmic basis of jazz.

Another important legacy of bop is the increased importance of the composer-performer. Before bop, jazz composers such as Ellington were exceptional, for jazz was almost exclusively a performer's art, based on the elaboration of "standards" (mostly popular songs). With bop, the inventiveness of many of its performers crossed that elusive line between creating ever more elaborate variations on standard "changes" (a practice that in itself

* Some private recordings, made with portable equipment, did chronicle its evolutionary stages. See "Bebop and the Recording Industry: the 1942 AFM Recording Ban Reconsidered" by Scott DeVeaux in the *Journal of the American Musicological Society*, vol. 41, no. 1 (Spring 1988).

would have been entitled to be considered "composing" in previous periods of musical history) into full-fledged free composition. Composer-performer heirs of the bop era, many of whom actually started out playing in bebop combos, would include Thelonious Monk, Miles Davis (b. 1926), Charles Mingus (1927–79), John Coltrane (1926–67), and Ornette Coleman (b. 1930), many of whom will be considered again later in this chapter.

The Progeny of Bop

Although bop itself is often said to have ended with the early death of Charlie Parker in 1955, there is a subsequent continuity both of styles and performers that constitutes a lineage reaching well into the last quarter of the twentieth century.

Cool jazz

What has become known as "cool" jazz followed so closely on the heels of bop that it can almost be regarded as the other side of the same coin—the same dispassionate objectivity (symbolized, one could say, by the typical avoidance of instrumental vibrato), the same underlying complexity, the same careful avoidance of the obvious that almost tends to obscurity. But now these features were exhibited in a music of understatement, of restraint, of leanness. What had been interpreted by some as an attitude of disdain in bop became in cool jazz one of detachment. Virtuosity was at times refined into preciosity.

The rapidity of change of identifiable artistic movements in our time is illustrated by the fact that many of the same musicians played both bop and cool, and a definite lineage can be established. An early example, in a kind of transitional stage between the two styles is "Boplicity" (1949), with Miles Davis (trumpet), J. J. Johnson, (trombone), and Kenny Clarke (drums)—all of whom were influential in the development and spread of bop.[30] The tempo has been slowed somewhat, but otherwise many bop characteristics remain: the light style of drumming, with the emphasis on the cymbal; the important role of the bass in keeping the beat; and, an important trademark of bop, the unison playing at the beginning of the piece (in this case harmonized by the arranger, Gil Evans).

"Criss-Cross" (1951), by Thelonious Monk, reveals more characteristics of the cool trend.[31] The vibraphone appears, here played by Milt Jackson (b. 1923). The tone of the "vibes"—warmed somewhat by its mechanical vibrato, but still restrained and detached—made it almost a symbol of cool jazz. There are only two other melody instruments, piano and alto saxophone, and a rhythm section of just bass and drums. The unison lines in the opening are still there from bop, and a penchant for quotation found in both styles. Here, for example, we hear fragments of "Every little breeze seems to whisper Louise" as the alto saxophone enters for its solo.

Mention of the vibraphone leads to a consideration of one of the most influential small combos in this style, the Modern Jazz Quartet, with piano (John Lewis, also a composer), vibes (Milt Jackson, heard in "Criss-Cross," as noted above), bass (Percy Heath), and drums (Connie Kay). With no wind instruments (in fact this entire ensemble is really a rhythm section, so to speak), their small combo epitomized the restrained understatement toward which cool jazz tended. "Django" (1960), is an example of the extended form some jazz had achieved by this time.[32] The series of short choruses that had characterized jazz form even through the big band era was now replaced at the hands of innovative musicians by longer lines, and sections of greater dimensions.

Slimly represented in discographies and anthologies, because he performed and recorded relatively little, is the pianist and composer Lennie Tristano (1919–78), who was making in the late 1940s a complex, restrained, and lean music, with emphasis on contrapuntal lines and a corresponding de-emphasis on the rhythm section. Somewhat outside the direct lineage of bop, he nevertheless influenced players such as Lee Konitz and Billy Bauer, forecast many of the developments of the "third stream," and contributed a distinctly individual voice to the complex picture of postwar jazz.[33]

"Cool" jazz dominated what was *new* in the jazz of the 1950s—not what was popular. Its adherents were most apt to be found in intellectual circles—on college campuses, among both students and professors. There was an intellectual ferment about jazz that affected critics, fans, and some composer-performers themselves. If jazz was *art*, then there was no reason why it shouldn't appropriate whatever it took a fancy to in fine-art music, learning and borrowing from both the forms and the technical procedures of European or European-derived classical music. For example, John Lewis, whose Modern Jazz Quartet represented the quintessence of "cool" jazz, in the late 1950s became interested in the music of the Italian Renaissance and the *commedia dell'arte*.[34] Such evolutionary steps, which are rather far removed from the direct heritage of bop itself, are dealt with below among the developments that ran parallel to bop.

Hard bop and funk

Evolving directly from bop in the 1950s and 1960s, and often regarded as a reaction to the restraint and intellectualism of cool jazz, was a development known as *hard bop*. It represented a pull back toward the roots of jazz, especially its roots in black gospel music. This is displayed at its most obvious in such pieces as "The Preacher" (1954), or "Nica's Dream" (1956),[35] by the pianist and composer Horace Silver (b. 1928), who, with drummer Art Blakey (b. 1919), was a leader in the evolution of hard bop. Many of the features of bop are present (the texture of the rhythm section, the unison or homophonic openings and closings); that it was indeed an evolution directly from bop is illustrated by Silver's "Stop Time."[36] But hard bop tended to relax the frenetic tempos of bop, and the rhythmic basis of the newer *funky* jazz, as it was called, often showed a return to the characteristically black "backbeat", or to a Latin beat as in "Nica's Dream." There was a preference for darker, "earthier" tone colors; for this reason the huskier tenor saxophone was preferred over the lighter alto (as had been the case also in the visceral rhythm-and-blues). Of the many tenor players associated with the style a significant few, including Sonny Rollins, John Coltrane, and Wayne Shorter, went on to figure prominently in the development of later styles; this was true as well of the Austrian-born pianist-composer Joe Zawinul. Jazz after mid-century never regained the broad popularity it had previously enjoyed. In spite of its return to its "roots," funky jazz did not have a large audience; the college set (both students and their professors) were more intrigued with what Dave Brubeck and others of the West Coast school were doing, and the mass of youth had found rock 'n' roll.

Modal jazz

Another successor to bop in which many of the same musicians were involved has been called *modal jazz*. It represented a new venture for jazz both harmonically and structurally, in that it no longer used the chord progressions of standard tunes as the basis for improvisation; what replaced these was simply a succession of scales on which the performer improvised. Most of these scales corresponded to the *modes* of folk music (Dorian, Phrygian, and so on—see Chapter 1), hence the name; but other scales (the so-called synthetic scales, not encompassed by the traditional system of key signatures) were available as well to venturesome composers and performers. One very seminal set of pieces that set a precedent for jazz in this direction were those on the 1959 album *Kind of Blue*.[37] The trumpeter Miles Davis, who had a hand in influencing new developments and indicating new trends in jazz for more than three decades, beginning in the late 1940s, was the leader and stimulator of the small combo that produced this album, but some of the other musicians (notably Bill Evans, piano; John Coltrane, tenor saxophone; and Julian Adderley, alto saxophone) contributed significantly to the realization of its concepts, and went on to develop the style further. Bill Evans's notes to the album are indicative of the new directions jazz was taking:

> As the painter needs his framework of parchment, the improvising musical group needs its framework in time. Miles Davis presents here frameworks which are exquisite in their simplicity and yet contain all that is necessary to stimulate performance with a sure reference to the primary conception. . . . Miles conceived these settings only hours before the recording dates and arrived with sketches which indicated to the group what was to be played.

This conception of jazz (the term *modal* is actually too restrictive in its connotations) was carried further by Evans himself, by Eric Dolphy, by McCoy Tyner, and most notably by John Coltrane. It combines the presence of a "framework" of some sort (to use Evans's excellent term), with a liberal amount of freedom for the performer.

John Coltrane was a crucially important voice in the jazz of the decade 1955–65. A commanding player technically, he was also one of the most serious-minded composer-performers in jazz. The expressive potential of what we have chosen to call *modal jazz* is summed up in the intense earnestness of his "Alabama" of 1963,[38] with its slow, thoughtful opening and closing sections, emphasizing spare, drone-like open fifths. The innovative compositional aspects of those on the leading edge of jazz in the 1960s is illustrated in the treatment given a standard song such as Richard Rodger's "My Favorite Things," from the popular musical *The Sound of Music;* using variation techniques akin to those of classical composers, Coltrane concentrates on exploring extensively the implications of just the first few measures of this lilting, lighthearted waltz.[39]

Free jazz

A small proportion of Coltrane's later work fell into the category of one of the most extreme, least understood, and least popular movements in jazz history—so-called *free jazz*. Ornette Coleman's album *Free Jazz* of 1960 gave the concept its name, and was as seminal in this regard as Miles Davis's *Birth of the Cool* (1949–50) had been for that genre, and as his *Milestones* (1958) and *Kind of Blue* (1959) were for so-called modal jazz. Free jazz usually exhibits one or more of the following characteristics: (1) collective improvisation; (2) freedom from preset chord progressions and/or established tonality; (3) extension of the sonorous range of instruments (especially the saxophone) by playing extremely high pitches, or making the instruments squeal, shriek, or groan; (4) playing deliberately "out of tune" in relation to conventional intonation; (5) expansion of form, by creating pieces in which the length of the sections, and hence the overall length, is not predetermined, and which may thus be quite extensive (*Free Jazz* lasts thirty-six minutes, Coltrane's *Ascension* nearly forty, Cecil Taylor's *3 Phasis* nearly an hour); (6) the occasional use of a fairly large ensemble (*Free Jazz* uses eight players, *Ascension* eleven); (7) the occasional omission of the piano from the ensemble (by Coleman, Coltrane, and the Art Ensemble of Chicago, among others).

So-called free jazz includes a wide range of individual styles. Representative names and works have been cited above: Ornette Coleman's *Free Jazz* (1960), the earliest, contains sections with a distinct jazz beat and bop-like solos; John Coltrane's *Ascension* (1965) also has sections with a definite beat, but the solos tend to include more of the extreme tonal characteristics enumerated under (2)–(4) above; the Art Ensemble of Chicago's *Certain Blacks* (early 1970s), with its spoken or chanted additions, is typical of the more theatrical, satirical, and racially specific aspects of the genre. (This group's incorporation of spoken poetry, in the form of chanted verbal graffiti, became the prototype for later multi-media "poet bands.")[40]

Fitting approximately into the category of free jazz is the work of Cecil Taylor (b. 1933) which in many ways is in a class by itself. Taylor's extensive background includes early training in percussion as well as piano, an intense interest in literature, poetry, and dance (he collaborated in 1979 with the noted Russian dancer Mikhail Baryshnikov), and study at the New England Conservatory of Music. A gifted absorber of many musical influences, including the whole range of jazz styles, he has stated a desire to *use* European influences, rather than try futilely to reject them. In collaboration with a small ensemble, known as the Cecil Taylor Unit, he has produced music of exceptionally high intensity, energy, and turbulence, characterized by long periods of unrelieved tension. A musician with an impressive command of his instrument, Taylor leads the ensemble by cueing from the piano, following a loosely structured plan that includes some notated elements. Abandoning (except in isolated sections) the most enduring and pervasive identifying characteristic of jazz—the steady beat—Taylor's music, retaining only the instrumentation of the jazz combo (plus violin), comes very close in sound to the music of the European-influenced avant-garde, but with far more sustained energy for the most part. His work seems more concerned with the flow and juxtaposition of textures and densities than with melody, harmony, or even rhythm. In terms of the expressive exploitation of tonal color as a resource, his best work* is on a par with anything done by the avante-gardists. Taylor's *3 Phasis*,[41] of 1978, is one of the few so-called "free jazz" works of extensive length that seem able to sustain interest for their full duration—this in a genre of pieces that are listened to *in their entirety* probably only by the very devoted few.

Free jazz was hailed as innovative by the critics, while enjoying very little popularity with the broad public. In this respect its composer-performers found themselves in a situation comparable to that of avante-garde classical composers of the same era. Indeed, the 1960s was a time when "free form" music, influenced by the ideas of John Cage and others, was in vogue in a certain part of the world of experimental art music; composers were occupied in concocting various schemes to achieve group improvisations, and unpredictability characterized many of the art "happenings" of the time.

The parallels between free jazz and avant-garde classical music are not complete, however. The electronic manipulation of sounds, and even the electronic amplification of individual instruments with its inherent alteration of the acoustic tone, was largely avoided in free jazz.† Also avoided was the use of timbres and textures associated with the more or less intellectually oriented "cool" jazz. The choice of instruments and their manipulation were governed by a desire for a freer expression of *emotion*—hence the preference for instrumental timbres closely related to the human voice. The analogy with the ways in which traditional blues singers manipulated both their voices and their instruments is clear; the paradox here is that in free jazz it was a case of highly sophisticated and versatile performers—the avante-garde of jazz—reaching back to the "roots" of the genre, in terms of emotional expressiveness. As Albert Ayler said, "It's not about notes anymore. It's about feelings!"

That these feelings had in some measure to do with race and the desire to define and strengthen the sense of black cultural identity cannot be doubted. The relationship of all the jazz of the 1960s in which black musicians played a leading role (hard bop, modal jazz, free jazz, and so on) to the social turmoil of the times has been emphasized by some writers who also point out the identification of many of the young black jazz musicians such as Albert Ayler (1936–70) and Archie Shepp (b. 1937) with one aspect or another of the black nationalism movement.[42]

The combination of a determination to stress black cultural identity and the lack of any sizable public for avant-garde jazz led several composer-performers to band together and form musical cooperatives. The best-known example is the Association for the Advancement of Creative Musicians in Chicago; the Art Ensemble of Chicago was one of the performing groups that came out of this association. Their work typically emphasized both black

* Supported in its execution, of course, by such able musicians as saxophonist Jimmy Lyons, trumpeters Eddie Gale Stevens and Raphe Malik, drummers Andrew Cyrille and Ronald Shammon Jackson, and violinist Ramsey Ameen.

† Ramsey Ameen, a musician who recorded with Cecil Taylor, explained his refusal to use an electric pickup on his violin by saying that his instrument "refuses to talk to him on the telephone" (liner notes to NW-201 and 303).

culture and free jazz. By the early 1970s the group had become quite eclectic, embracing by turns such disparate stylistic elements as the use of exotic percussion instruments, the use of such "classical" instruments as flutes and oboes, a rock beat over which free jazz solos were improvised, funky recollections of rhythm-and-blues, and echoes of minimalism (discussed in Chapter 18) in terms of harmony and rhythm.

A turning away from extremism and experimentalism, and a reaching out to a larger audience, began to occur in both jazz and classical music in the 1970s, as we shall note in due course. The overtly and even militantly racial overtones that characterized some black jazz of the 1960s abated in the 1970s, and many of its proponents, for various reasons, began to adopt (or re-adopt) more accessible and popular styles such as rhythm-and-blues.

Labels and categories are of limited use at best, and can be particularly misleading in jazz. Movements such as free jazz have never been more than loosely defined, and any attempt at definition must include a variety of personal styles and approaches. Indeed, there is much to be said for viewing jazz since bop without labels, by tracing the individual creative adventures of a few crucial musicians such as Miles Davis, Charles Mingus, John Coltrane, Cecil Taylor, and Ornette Coleman, all of whom have gone through various phases relating to more than one of the so-called "movements" we are attempting to delineate in this chapter.

The "Third Stream" and Other Developments Parallel to Bop

Bop and its successor styles, as outlined in the preceding pages, constitute a singularly consistent lineage in terms of the composer-performers involved, over the span of four decades: from Dizzie Gillespie, Charlie Parker, and Thelonious Monk, through Miles Davis, John Lewis, Horace Silver, Art Blakey, Julian Adderley, Joe Zawinul, Sonny Rollins, to Charles Mingus, John Coltrane, Bill Evans, McCoy Tyner, Ornette Coleman, and Cecil Taylor—we encounter again and again the same musicians, involved at different stages of their careers with different styles developing from the mid-century turning point that was bop. Sidemen becoming leaders, and groups forming and disbanding, to re-form later with changes in personnel—this is the typical way in which the jazz torch has been passed for three-quarters of a century.

Parallel to this lineage, and not unconnected with it, were certain related developments that deserve attention. What these developments had in common was the incorporation of musical elements, procedures, and actual instruments (violins, cellos, flutes, and French horns, for example) that had hitherto been considered foreign to jazz. The term "third stream" was invented and applied by Gunther Schuller (b. 1925) shortly after mid-century to the merging of elements from the jazz and "classical," or European, traditions to form a new "stream" in music.[43]

The first of these developments involved a few big bands, innovative survivors of that era from the 1920s to the 1950s. The adventurous Duke Ellington and Woody Herman were leaders. Ellington had pioneered in the expansion of jazz form through the use of symphonic devices, as in his *Black, Brown and Beige* of 1943; and his remarkable short piece "The Clothed Woman," of 1947, shows in its opening and closing sections harmonic and coloristic procedures that venture far beyond the resources of the jazz of his time. In 1945 Stravinsky wrote his *Ebony Concerto* for Woody Herman's band, and in 1946 Herman recorded the multi-movement *Summer Sequence,* by his pianist-arranger Ralph Burns. Stan Kenton (1911–79), active as a bandleader from the 1940s to the 1970s, became known for a sound that has been described as "massive," and featured a brass section that was large even by big band standards. The popularity of his biggest hits was often attended by a certain overblown pretentiousness that was particularly evident when he attempted to adopt titles, and even actual pieces, from the classical literature (as in Concerto to End All Concertos," his trademark piece "Artistry in Rhythm," or his actual transcriptions of works by that other master of the "wow" technique, Richard Wagner). But it was precisely Kenton's commercial success that allowed him to pioneer as he did in certain directions: he enlarged the big band concept, assembling for a brief period one of nearly orchestral proportions (forty-three players, including strings), and he performed arrangements and compositions by innovative young arrangers such as Pete Rugolo (whose "Mirage" of 1950 was a truly remarkable piece to have been written for a group known basically as a jazz orchestra), Bill Holman, and Bob Graettinger (noted for his multi-movement work *City of Glass*).* He also gave many gifted young players their start, and he and his promotional and publishing organization were extensively involved in educational projects, especially in colleges and universities.[44]

Small combos playing a species of "cool" jazz also began to incorporate materials derived from the European classical tradition. The so-called "West Coast" school of jazz (mostly white performers, including such men as Dave Brubeck (b. 1920), Paul Desmond, Gerry Mulligan, Chet Baker, Bob Brookmeyer, and Shorty Rogers) is illustrative of this.

One aspect of these explorations was rhythmic innovations that took jazz out of the duple or quadruple grouping of pulses (expressed by the meters 2/4 and 4/4) that had characterized it since its earliest associations with the march and two-step. The first change in this direction was the introduction of triple meter, typified by the waltz.[45] Then followed so-called asymmetrical meters in which groupings of two, three, and four pulses were mixed in recurring sequence. A well-known piece involving asymmetrical meter is "Take Five," by Paul Desmond in which the pulses are grouped as in Example 14–1.

Example 14–1

Dave Brubeck's "Unsquare Dance" and "Tears of Joy" by Don Ellis (1934–78) both use an asymmetrical grouping of seven pulses. (Example 14–2). Such meters are not usual in Occidental music, though exceptions can readily be found in the folk music of certain areas in southeastern Europe. The rumba,

* To label this type of big band excursion "progressive jazz" is to adopt Kenton's own trade designation for it; nevertheless, this label, more broadly applied, has found a certain degree of acceptance.

Example 14–2

of Latin origin, is an interesting case of an asymmetrical grouping of eight pulses that is written, with deceptive simplicity, in 4/4 (Example 14–3).

Example 14–3

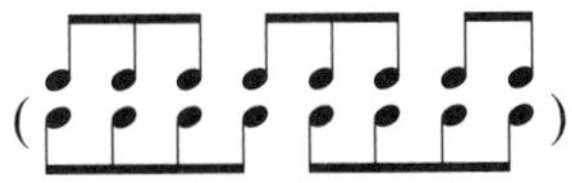

Brubeck's "Blue Rondo A La Turk" groups nine pulses asymmetrically, against which, later in the piece, can be heard the more usual triplet grouping (shown in parentheses in Example 14–4).[46]

Example 14–4

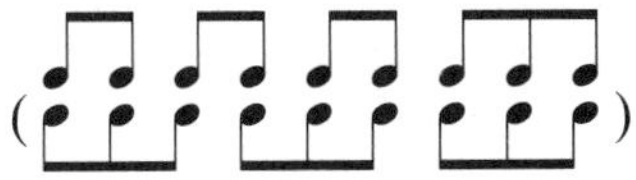

In the late 1950s, other small combos were exploring different musical resources more or less new to jazz. The work of John Lewis and the Modern Jazz Quartet has been alluded to above. George Russell, concerned with structure and tonal organization, propounded his theory of the "Lydian chromatic concept," and wrote pieces reflecting this concern.[47] Gunther Schuller himself worked toward a synthesis of avant-garde European procedures and sounds (including twelve-tone technique) with jazz styles and improvisation, over a considerable period of time between the late 1940s and the early 1960s; several of his resulting compositions were included in the album *Jazz Abstractions*.[48]

Fusions, Eclecticism, and the Pluralism of the 1970s and 1980s

As a strategically important point of departure for comprehending the fusions and pluralism of the 1970s and 1980s, it will be useful to examine what was happening in the bands that Miles Davis assembled during the late 1960s.* From *Nefertiti* of 1967 to the landmark *Bitches Brew* of 1969, a fairly rapid and direct transition can be observed. In *Nefertiti* Davis uses a conventional quintet of all acoustic instruments, with trumpet and tenor saxophone as "front line," employing much of the unison playing that was a legacy of bop, against which is some highly individualistic playing on piano and drums. The interesting

* In doing this, we are in a sense picking up the line of descent from bop to free jazz that was traced earlier in this chapter.

transitional *Filles de Kilimanjaro* (1968) shows a greater degree of eclecticism; current avant-garde influences are evident in the fragmented pointillism of the rather extended improvisations, and there are subtle suggestions of funk in "Mademoiselle Mabry," but even more striking is the palpable influence of rock. This is obvious in the gradual trend toward electrification—acoustic and electric versions of both piano and bass are used.

Still more significant is the change in the *rhythmic* basis of the music—always an indicator of major developments in jazz. From ragtime-oriented traditional jazz to swing in the late 1920s, to bop in the 1950s, and in the late 1960s to rock-influenced jazz, it is the nature of the underlying beat that has most affected the music. In *Bitches Brew* the rhythmic basis and the new role and sound of the rhythm section for jazz-rock are established. The enlarging of the ensemble from five to eleven players takes place mostly in the rhythm section; there are now three drummers and an additional percussionist, playing mostly Latin instruments, and two electric pianos. The beat is now distinctly the "square" beat of rock (that is, with evenly spaced subdivisions), ornamented with Latin embellishments; with no "swing" to it, it lacks the relaxed, forward-propelling character of the swing or bop beat. Further, the electric bass lays down the familiar, insistent, highly repetitious *ostinato* of rock.

The transition to jazz-rock is also marked by the complete adoption of the electric versions of piano, bass, and guitar, and the use of devices such as echo effects, born in the recording studio.

Many of the players on these Davis recordings of the late 1960s were to become important in further developments in the jazz-rock fusion of the 1970s, including pianists Herbie Hancock, Chick Corea, and Joe Zawinul, guitarist John McLaughlin, and saxophonist Wayne Shorter.

The Electric Jazz of the 1970s

The group Weather Report, formed in 1971 by Josef Zawinul (b. 1932), reflected with a high degree of competence a broad range of trends and influences. Indeed, their work can serve as a kind of index of the ingredients of much of what has been called *electric jazz*, or the fusion music of the 1970s. The sound is indeed mostly electronic, either in its source or in its manipulation; increasingly divorced from live acoustic sound, it is thus alien to the familiar image of "real" performers playing "real" instruments. So versatile in fact had electronic sound technology become by this time that it is often difficult for those uninitiated in studio techniques to identify a given sound source. What is heard is an intricate collage of sounds, synthesized or electronically manipulated, mingled with the occasional sound of acoustic instruments. Rhythmically, the music uses for the most part a highly elaborated rock beat.* Weather Report achieves highly inventive textures; the ostinatos associated with rock undergo change in the course of a piece, appearing in metamorphosed forms or in alternating sequence, and are not confined to the bass, appearing sometimes in upper voices. The residual jazz ingredient is most

* See Chapter 9, Example 9-3.

palpable in the solos, and in the fact that the group's music was, in the 1970s, still almost totally instrumental.

The music was, in fact, eclectic. Much of what Weather Report did, for example, is not easily classifiable as either jazz or rock. Typical of the times was the influence of ethnic—and specifically third-world—music, especially that of Africa and India.[49]

Jazz-rock fusion, influenced at least in concept by third-world music, is heard in highly distilled form in the early 1970s work of John McLaughlin (another former Miles Davis sideman) and his Mahavishnu Orchestra. *Birds of Fire*, of 1973, is representative. There are obvious references to Hindu religion and poetry, but except for the trancelike moods produced (which it had in common with much other so-called "fusion" music of the time), the music itself owed comparatively little to traditional Indian music. It was a virtuoso synthesis of rock and jazz influences: rock timbres (mostly electric); jazz-like solos in a non-swinging rock metric scheme, superimposed on rock ostinatos and rock harmonic patterns; and interesting asymmetric meters.*

Pianist Herbie Hancock (b. 1940) an alumnus of the Miles Davis group of the 1960s, cultivated in the 1970s and 1980s a species of music closely resembling that popular with the mass audience of rock, especially in its commitment to electronics and the technology of the recording studio. The very popular "Chameleon" of 1973 had a predominantly electric sound; in "Rockit," of ten years later, which was No. 1 on the pop chart, Hancock dispensed with horns entirely and, with the aid of very complex electronic technology, produced a piece that represented the extreme of electrification. Significantly, its promotional video was enormously popular. Other cuts on the same album (*Future Shock*), using Motown-style background vocals and a pronounced backbeat, combined disco and gospel influences and departed from the realm of jazz altogether for what could be described as electric funk.†

Chick Corea (b. 1941), another alumnus of the Miles Davis bands, on the other hand maintained even in the 1970s a blend of electric and acoustic sound. His work with electric keyboards showed their potential as distinctly solo instruments. But he never dispensed with wind instruments, and his collaborations with Joe Farrell and later Steve Kujala, both eminent performers on flutes as well as saxophones, were noteworthy. A pronounced Latin influence pervades much of Corea's work.[50]

Jazz-Funk As "Wordless Rock": A Summation

Much of 1970s jazz, verging as it did so closely on rock, threatened for a time either to confirm (in the minds of some) the death of jazz itself, or to render a distinction between the two outdated. Nevertheless, even in this period the

* Meters such as 3+3+4 (used in "Celestial Terrestrial Commuters"), native to southeastern Europe, had been explored, as we noted earlier in this chapter, in the cool jazz epoch by Brubeck and Ellis.

† But Hancock's credentials as an authentic jazz pianist were reasserted in this same period by his work, for example, on the first album of the young trumpeter Wynton Marsalis, and his jazz score for the film *'Round Midnight*, starring Dexter Gordon.

distinctions between jazz-rock, as it was called, and rock itself were both obvious and decisive. Improvisation, often at very great length (a characteristic noted above in modal jazz), was still an important ingredient. Extended works in the jazz-rock genre tended to juxtapose sections of contrasting tempos and moods. Cross-rhythms, foreign to most rock, were still occasionally employed by drummers. But, most important of all, jazz-rock retained its identity as decidedly *instrumental* music, whereas rock has remained throughout its history primarily *vocal* music, with the song as the medium and the singer as the star.[51]

As an example of the so-called fusion movement, a piece such as John McLaughlin's "One Word"[52] of 1972 is virtually "wordless rock"; as such, it distills the essence of what has been called "fusion music." But the distinctions are typical, and decisive. The McLaughlin piece displays an instrumental virtuosity and a purely musical imagination that, except in the case of artists like Jimi Hendrix, are seldom heard in essentially blues-derived and hence song-and-message-oriented rock itself. Rather than a fusion of jazz and rock, much of the music suggests an *absorption* and *development*, in purely instrumental terms, of rock's modal harmonic language, its ostinato/minimalist formal procedures, and its electric timbres. While fusion music has been the most popular jazz style since the big band era, its purely instrumental nature—its very "wordlessness"—broadened by making less explicit the range of interpretations that could be put on it. In the sense, then, of being more abstract than rock, it remained true to the nature of jazz in at least one of its aspects; hence it failed to capture much of the mass audience at which at least some of it was surely aimed.

This attempt at fusion had been approached from both sides, so to speak; we noted in Chapter 9 the incorporation of certain jazz elements (primarily those belonging more specifically to blues bands) in the work of such rock groups as Chicago or Blood, Sweat and Tears. But observers well grounded in jazz are reluctant to regard those groups' music as a genuine fusion, pointing out its basic nature as rock with added saxophones and horns, incorporating traits that had long been present in rhythm-and-blues.

The judgments of critical observers have varied. Mark Gridley has termed jazz-rock "the first jazz style to attain widespread popularity since the swing era."[53] James Lincoln Collier has seen jazz-rock as simply "another of those popular musics derived from jazz . . . rather than as part of the main line of development of jazz itself."[54] The very popularity of rock may be supposed to have exerted a significant influence on some jazz musicians, struggling to maintain both themselves and their art in a climate of a steadily dwindling public for what might be (deceptively) termed "mainstream" jazz. John Rockwell, dealing with the question of "selling out," gives evidence for both the defense and the prosecution:

> Charitably considered, jazz musicians perceived an energy and a direct vitality in the best rock and saw a way to make a new, different, clean-lined, fresher music than they had within the confines of jazz. Uncharitably, they sold out, as fast and ignominiously as they could, by abandoning artistic conscience, distorting the pure acoustic sound of their instruments in favor of electronic alternatives or cultivating a glutinous, amplified texture that buried the individuality of whatever acoustic instruments remained.[55]

That electric jazz has remained a component in the pluralism of the 1980s is demonstrated in the work of Weather Report, a group exhibiting a singular continuity of concept. After fifteen years, Weather Report (essentially Joe Zawinul and Wayne Shorter), in its 1986 *This Is This*, continued to purvey a highly sophisticated and inventive kind of electric fusion music, whose jazz characteristics are to be found in its basically instrumental nature, its improvisatory solos, and its references to earlier styles.[56]

Other Fusions, and the Third Stream Again

The 1970s and 1980s have been marked by further explorations in the interconnections between jazz and Western fine-art music, especially that of the avant-garde. Ornette Coleman, noted for his explorations in free jazz, produced a large-scale piece for jazz ensemble and symphony orchestra called *Skies of America*, recorded in 1972. Pianist Keith Jarrett (b. 1945; interestingly, yet another pianist who played with Miles Davis in the late 1960s) was a prodigy who began with classical training and experience. He moved into the world of jazz in the 1960s, without abandoning the world of classical music, which he continued to perform. By the 1970s he was performing and recording a kind of music that was labeled jazz but that enjoyed wide popularity, incorporating elements of nineteenth-century Romanticism, twentieth-century minimalism, and various ethnic musics, as well as jazz styles as diverse as bop and boogie-woogie—all informed by a kind of personal and artistic mysticism that found a certain resonance in late twentieth-century culture.* Worthy of note is Jarrett's complete commitment, after leaving the Davis band, to acoustic instruments; in this he anticipated an important trend of the 1980s.

In a more lighthearted vein, Chick Corea produced his "concept album" *The Mad Hatter* in 1978, which uses Alice (of Wonderland) and Humpty Dumpty as points of reference for a quasi-cantata involving a wide variety of styles, from mildly avant-garde classical (with string quartet) to nineteenth-century Romantic, to bop, to pop.

More serious, and self-consciously avant-garde, is some of recent work of Anthony Braxton (b. 1945), a saxophonist who came out of the highly venturesome background of the Chicago Association for the Advancement of Creative Music, the cooperative that gave birth to the Art Ensemble of Chicago (mentioned earlier). Braxton's music for quartet (reeds, piano, bass, percussion but no drums) consists of complex, dense contrapuntal textures, from which emerge occasionally bop-like unisons between the wind instrument and the piano. Of interest is "pulse track" music, in which the continually changing tempo (described by the composer as "an accordion sound space context that stretches and contracts the sound space"), challenges one of the basic assumptions of jazz, the steady beat. The influence of minimalism is occasionally apparent. The recordings are accompanied by notes at times even more extravagantly abstruse than those that accompanied some classical avant-garde recordings of the 1970s.

* One of his compositions, "Runes," was dedicated "to the unknown," while another, "Solara March," was dedicated "to Pablo Casals and the sun."

> The concept of pulse tracks in this context refers to the use of extended structural devices (moments) that are approached as fixed metric sound events in the same sense as in vertical harmony (i.e. be-bop)—but directed instead at the "forward space" of the music—that being structural events which are positioned into the space of the music—to be repeated as a continuum that supports (and defines) the nature of the unfolding invention (music).[57]

We have already noted the influence of third-world musics on the jazz of the 1970s. This is hardly surprising when we consider that a greatly increased awareness of Asian and African culture was a feature of the social and philosophical upheavals of the 1960s. In that decade aspects of Indian music had begun to find their way both into rock (via George Harrison and the Beatles) and into Western classical music (as illustrated by the collaborations between the violinist Yehudi Menuhin and the Indian musician Ravi Shankar). By the 1980s Gunther Schuller himself had redefined and broadened his concept of "third stream" to include "various ethnic or vernacular musics,"[58] and it is now clear that—given our increased access to, wider knowledge of, and greater esteem for, the world's ethnic and traditional musics—cross-cultural influences, and the breaking down of conventional cultural barriers and categories, will be very much a part of the future of *all* American music.

Revivalism

Yet another aspect of the pluralism of the 1970s and 1980s is revivalism—the conscious cultivation of older styles, and re-creation of older pieces. So-called "Dixieland" jazz (a term originally applied to renditions of traditional jazz by early white performers, but later broadened to include *all* re-creations of the New Orleans style) was, as we have already noted, the first jazz style to undergo revival, in the 1940s. The enthusiasm for Dixieland has never abated and has, in fact, spread worldwide. As reinterpreted in the 1970s and 1980s, it has become a "festival" genre—the basis for numerous annual events that draw performers, many of them amateur enthusiasts, from many parts of the world, and attract large audiences.[59] The jazz heard at these events is an interesting sort of heterogeneous species, displaying regional and contemporary graftings onto the stock of traditional jazz.

A similar metamorphosis has accompanied a revived interest in big bands in the 1970s and 80s; ensembles like those assembled by Jaco Pastorius and Toshiko Akiyoshi have reinterpreted a variety of past styles in contemporary terms, with varying degrees of artistic success. And the numerous school workshops and clinics conducted by leaders such as Stan Kenton and Maynard Ferguson, who never abandoned the concept of arranged jazz for big band, have helped to make jazz programs in schools and colleges effective conservators of the big band tradition.

Another factor in the revival and conservation of jazz, especially big band jazz, is the growing concept of *repertoire bands*—bands whose function it is to re-create specific pieces, just as a symphony orchestra re-creates a Beethoven symphony. This represents an attempt to maintain jazz from the past as a living repertoire, instead of having its existence limited to documentary recordings. This is of course a contradiction of the perception that the basic nature of jazz is that it is *improvisatory*—the product of th musician, and the milieu, and hence so ephemeral that it exists on as soon as the sound is gone. (Purists who hold this view in the ex even objected to the recording of jazz in the first place.*) On the ot supporters of the repertoire concept hold that jazz, in addition to bein of making music, is also a body of music literature (as much as is, say sixteenth-century madrigal or the eighteenth-century string quartet), and such should constitute a repertoire that can, in the hands of capable musician *educated* to its nuances, be re-created in a valid way. The debate over this goes on; indeed, it is a debate that arises over the re-creation (after the irretrievable moment of its creation has gone by) of any improvisatory music, which does not exist (at least initially) in written form, and in which the *performer* has the dominant role. In our time, this evidently applies mainly, and in America almost exclusively, to vernacular music—folk music, ethnic music, and jazz.[60]

New Virtuosos and the Return of Acoustic Jazz

One of the most significant developments in the 1980s has been the post-rock resumption of the acoustic jazz tradition. Like the bebop of forty years before, with which it has certain parallels, this new resurgence has been led by a new generation of virtuosos—highly skilled performers who are also composers, and who in addition have a thorough understanding of jazz traditions.† Gunther Schuller "discovered" and sponsored one such performer in the young Ricky Ford. Jaco Pastorius is another —an alumnus of Weather Report who has helped raise the electric bass to the status of a jazz solo instrument. Perhaps best known is the young trumpeter Wynton Marsalis (b. 1961), who has demonstrated a remarkable fluency in both jazz and classical music—a flexibility and catholicity not uncommon among today's young musicians.

In terms of the reinterpretation of older styles, almost everything (with the notable exception of the now widely popularized Dixieland) appears, transformed, in the new post-rock acoustic jazz. There can be found 12-bar blues, rhythm-and-blues, standards such as Ellington's "Sophisticated Lady" and Coltrane's "Giant Steps," Gillespie-like trumpet solos with embedded quotes, Davis-like cool playing, and occasional hints of "free jazz" in some solos.

Most notable, as might be expected, is a resurgence—a reinterpretation—of bebop, to the extent that the term "neo-bop" has, unsurprisingly, been applied to this current stage of jazz. The unison openings and closings are there, and as an occasional alternative to the prevailing small combo, "big bands" (big in sound, at least) have been formed, made up of virtuoso performers throughout, and reminiscent of the Gillespie bands of the 1940s. In

* The objection of the purists, of course, is to the very attempt to capture, and in so doing ossify, the spontaneous artistic moment that is a jazz performance. In partial defense of their position, it can be pointed out, for example, that the early recordings, with their three-minute time limit, *did* falsify by severely truncating the live performances.

† The phenomenon of virtuoso performers taking the lead in the revitalization of a particular genre (as was the case with bop) is also very much a part of the avant-garde classical scene of the 1970s and 80s. See Chapter 18.

some cases, tempos that are fast even by the standards of bop in the 1940s and 50s make the term "super-bop" appropriate; perhaps the stretching of the limits of human capacity, so pervasive in athletics, is a characteristic of our times.[61]

But the new post-rock acoustic jazz is not revivalism; new aspects, new additions, new influences are evident. The palette of instrumental color has been expanded; Jaco Pastorius (b. 1951), for example, in addition to presenting the electric bass as a jazz solo instrument (a troublesome exception, perhaps, to labeling this development acoustic jazz), has also introduced virtuoso harmonica (as played by "Toots" Thielemans), and virtuoso steel drum (as played by Othello Molineaux) with his band World of Mouth, in *Invitation* (1983). Although players can still find interesting things to do with the chord progression of "I Got Rhythm" (as Marsalis does in "Hesitation," on his first album), the choice of harmonic basis is much wider than it was in the bop of mid-century. Irregular phrase lengths and more sophisticated formal schemes, including the use of a succession of different tempos, meters, and styles in the same piece, have been employed. From the avant-garde, echoes of minimalism can be found. In the matter of rhythm, perhaps the most crucial element of jazz, cross-rhythms are often superimposed that can confound the sense of the prevailing meter for measures at a time. In "Skain's Domain,"[62] for example, there is a basic relaxed bop beat of about 230 per minute, which, even as the ear tries to follow and grasp its organization, shifts tantalizingly back and forth between groupings of four and three (expressible as 4/4 and 3/4 respectively). Superimposed on these fluctuations are cross-rhythms of a different order, based on a triple grouping of the shorter values (expressible as 3/8, 6/8, 12/8, and so on)—Example 14–5. All of this is done with an ease and fluency that dazzles the ear even as it mystifies it.

Example 14–5

Jazz As an International Music

The facts of musical life in the 1980s indicate a new degree of internationalism for *all* music. Jazz, which is no exception, has had a long history of acceptance and appreciation abroad. Both in Britain and in France, beginning after World War I, there was an avid interest in American jazz, even if its public was at first limited. France, ever since important jazz writing and scholarship began to emanate from there in the 1930s, has been a special place for both the music and the musicians, many of whom have lived and worked there for considerable periods.* But the appreciation and performance of jazz has long since spread worldwide; Holland, Scandinavia, West Germany, and Japan may be cited especially, but there is hardly any area of the globe—first, second, or third world—in which there is not some knowledge and appreciation of jazz.

Appreciation and knowledge are one thing; significant contribution in terms of performance and composition is another. It is easy for Americans to view jazz as being not only American in origin (which is indisputable) but *exclusively* American (which is not), and to regard foreign brands of jazz (until the last quarter of this century these were mostly European) as pallid, inferior copies of American "originals." Even further, there has been a conviction, even if largely unspoken, that non-Americans were forever barred, by birth and geography, from conceiving, composing, or playing "real" jazz, whatever that might mean or however it might be defined.† While the judgment as to the originality of foreign-made jazz might have constituted a fairly just assessment until the last decade or so, we have now arrived at a point in the history of jazz in which the conviction as to its quality or merit will have to be seriously questioned. As John Rockwell has put it,

> Since the Second World War, the growth of European jazz has been so rapid as to call into question the assumption that jazz is an inherently American music. Jazz by this time is no more exclusively American than it is exclusively black.[63]

We can only briefly here document this in terms of specific performers. The Belgian gypsy guitarist Django Reinhardt (1910–53) and the French violinist Stephane Grapelli (b. 1908) made early and well-known contributions to jazz. More recently, the Swedish saxophonist Arne Domnerus, the German trombonist Albert Mangelsdorff, and the French pianist Martial Solal should be noted; the work of the Austrian pianist Joe Zawinul in the group Weather Report has already been dealt with. There is evidence that European groups are now making "the jazz language work for them in their own accents," to quote Gary Giddin's apt phrase.[64]

It is apparent that jazz in our time has become, in the same way as the sixteenth-century sacred polyphony of Palestrina or the eighteenth-century classicism of Mozart, an international music. Jazz is about to begin its second century; as this approaches, Americans should perhaps recognize that while they will not necessarily be *giving up* the lead in jazz, they will certainly at least be *sharing* it with the world.

* The reception of American jazz and jazz musicians in France is a topic that is ripe for extensive documentation.

† A parallel conviction, that only blacks could play "real" jazz, has been voiced periodically. While it is abundantly clear that black musicians have been largely responsible for most of the important developments in the evolution of jazz (and indeed, of American popular music itself for over a century), the notion that non-blacks are forever *outsiders*, incapable of making real contributions to jazz, has been rather thoroughly discredited in the history of jazz, most of all by jazz musicians themselves, and is a view held only by polemicists whose primary concerns often do not have to do with the music itself.

Further Reading

Jazz has stimulated the production of an enormous volume of written material, which runs the gamut from sound, well-informed studies by competent musicians and scholars (too few) to the kind of press-agent-inspired writing typical of many (but not all) record-jacket notes. There are biographical and autobiographical works (some of considerable value), there are pictorial studies, and there are works written with a pronounced racial, social, or musical bias. The discerning student will soon become discriminating and find what is most informative and individually helpful in this vast array of printed matter. The very numerous biographical works on single jazz figures are not included in the following, which is necessarily a highly selective basic reading list.

Comprehensive General Works Published Since 1975

Collier, James Lincoln. *The Making of Jazz.* Boston: Houghton Mifflin, 1978.

Gridley, Mark C. *Jazz Styles: History and Analysis.* 2d ed. Englewood Cliffs, NJ: Prentice-Hall, 1985.
Instructor's Manual and Discography published separately.

Kennington, Donald, and Danny L. Read. *The Literature of Jazz: A Critical Guide.* 2d ed. Chicago: American Library Association, 1981.
A well-reviewed bibliography, well indexed.

Shaw, Arnold. *Black Popular Music in America.* New York: Schirmer Books, 1986.
Though dealing with a subject broader than jazz itself, this is invaluable in placing jazz in the context of black contributions to American popular music.

Tirro, Frank. *Jazz: A History.* New York: W. W. Norton, 1977.
Although this work was reviewed unfavorably by some, it is useful in that its examples are keyed to the *Smithsonian Collection of Classic Jazz*; it also includes transcriptions of pieces from that collection. A "Synoptic Table" relates jazz developments to other arts and to history.

Respected Older Works that Are Still Valuable

Hodeir, André. *Jazz: Its Evolution and Essence.* Trans. David Noakes. New York: Grove Press, 1956.

Sargeant, Winthrop. *Jazz: A History.* Rev. ed. New York: McGraw-Hill, 1964.

Stearns, Marshall. *The Story of Jazz.* New York: Oxford University Press 1956; reprint, 1974.
Highly recommended, especially for its treatment of the beginnings of jazz.

Williams, Martin, ed. *The Art of Jazz.* New York: Da Capo, 1981 (reprint of 1959 ed.).

Collections of Essays and Interviews

Giddins, Gary. *Riding on a Blue Note: Jazz and American Pop.* New York: Oxford University Press, 1981.

Shapiro, Nat, and Nat Hentoff. *Hear Me Talkin' to Ya.* New York: Rinehart, 1955. Reprint, New York: Dover, 1966.
Quotations from more than 150 jazz musicians, arranged to shed light from firsthand sources on nearly every aspect of jazz.

Williams, Martin. *The Jazz Tradition.* Rev. ed. New York: Oxford University Press, 1983.

Period Studies, in Approximate Chronological Order

Lomax, Alan. *Mister Jelly Roll: The Fortunes of Jelly Roll Morton, New Orleans Creole and "Inventor of Jazz."* 2d ed. Berkeley: University of California Press, 1973.

Based on an extensive series of interviews recorded at the Library of Congress.

Schuller, Gunther. *Early Jazz: Its Roots and Musical Development.* New York: Oxford University Press, 1968.

Deals with the beginnings through early Ellington and early big bands, with emphasis on Armstrong, Morton, and Ellington. Important for its attention to and analysis of the music itself.

———. *The Swing Era: The Development of Jazz 1933–1945.* New York: Oxford University Press, 1988.

Hadlock, Richard. *Jazz Masters of the Twenties.* New York: Macmillan, 1965.

Stewart, Rex. *Jazz Masters of the Thirties.* New York: Macmillan, 1972.

Gitler, Ira. *Jazz Masters of the Forties.* New York: Macmillan, 1966.

———. *Swing to Bop: An Oral History of the Transition in Jazz in the 1940s.* New York: Oxford University Press, 1985.

Goldberg, Joe. *Jazz Masters in Transition, 1957–1969.* New York: Macmillan, 1970.

Shaw, Arnold. *52nd Street: The Street of Jazz.* New York: Da Capo, 1977.

Spellman, A. B. *Four Lives in the Bebop Business.* New York: Limelight, 1985.

Budds, Michael J. *Jazz in the Sixties.* Iowa City: University of Iowa Press. 1978.

Giddins, Gary. *Rhythm-a-ning: Jazz Tradition and Innovation in the '80s.* New York: Oxford University Press, 1985.

Regional or Specialized Studies

Williams, Martin, ed. *Jazz Masters of New Orleans.* New York: Macmillan, 1967.

Rose, Al, and Edmond Souchon. *New Orleans Jazz.* 3d ed. Baton Rouge: Louisiana State University Press, 1984.

Charters, Samuel B., and Leonard Kunstadt. *Jazz: A History of the New York Scene.* New York: Da Capo, 1981 (reprint of original 1962 ed.)

Illustrated by a recording with the same title, Folkways RF-3.

Dahl, Linda. *Stormy Weather: The Music and Lives of a Century of Jazzwomen.* New York: Pantheon, 1984.

Roberts, John Storm. *The Latin Tinge: The Impact of Latin American Music in the United States.* New York: Oxford University Press. 1979.

This book, also cited in Chapter 3, deals with a frequently overlooked and inadequately studied aspect of jazz as well.

Pearson, Nathan W., Jr. *Goin' to Kansas City.* Urbana: University of Illinois Press, 1988.

Russell, Ross. *Jazz Style in Kansas City and the Southwest.* Berkeley: University of California Press, 1971.

Useful Annotation to Record Anthologies

Smithsonian Collection of Classic Jazz. Notes by Martin Williams.

Smithsonian Collection of Big Band Jazz: From the Beginnings to the Fifties. Notes by Gunther Schuller and Martin Williams.

Periodicals

Down Beat. Monthly (Chicago).

Popularly written periodical which now includes blues, rock, and popular music.

Journal of Jazz Studies. Semi-annual, 1973–81; annual since 1982 as *Annual Review of Jazz Studies* (New Brunswick, NJ).
Devoted to serious studies in jazz.

Listening

Jazz discographies date rapidly. Historically there has hardly been a commodity more ephemeral and capricious in its availability than the popular music recording. A recent trend mitigating this capriciousness, however, has been the compilation of genuine anthologies, with documentation as to recording dates and personnel, and often with extensive notes. Seven of these anthologies are listed below. While each anthology has somewhat different limits and emphasis, there is also some overlapping. Because these anthologies are basic to any record library, recorded examples cited in this chapter have been drawn from them as far as possible.

The Smithsonian Collection of Classic Jazz, 1st ed.
A 6-LP set (86 tracks), with an extensive booklet of notes by Martin Williams. Recordings span 1916–66. Though superseded by the following, it is still found in many libraries.

The Smithsonian Collection of Classic Jazz, rev. ed.
An enlarged edition, expanded to 7 LPs, and 95 selections.

The Smithsonian Collection of Big Band Jazz.
6 LPs, with a 52-page booklet of notes by Gunther Schuller and Martin Williams. Recordings span 1924–1956.

The Folkways History of Jazz Series.
11 separately jacketed LPs, each with a booklet of notes. More emphasis on roots and earlier music; stops about 1940.

Encyclopedia of Jazz on Records, ed. Leonard Feather. MCA 4061–63.
3 sets of 2 LPs each, spanning the 1920s through the 1960s.

New World Recorded Anthology of American Music.
This anthology (over 160 LPs to date) has many relevant recordings; the first 100 albums are indexed in Elizabeth A. Davis, *An Index to the New World Anthology of American Music* (New York: W. W. Norton, 1981). Since New World's editorial policy seems to be to avoid extensive treatment of groups and performers already well represented elsewhere, this anthology is most useful as a well-annotated supplement, valuable for the additional (and sometimes different) light it throws on certain areas.

Also Useful

Atlantic Jazz. Atlantic 81700–11, complete set Atlantic 81712.
A 15-LP set, in 3 double and 9 single albums, compiled according to styles and movements, from New Orleans to fusion.

More Specialized Anthologies Issued by Smithsonian

Singers and Soloists of the Swing Bands. 6-LP set.

Duke Ellington 1938; Duke Ellington 1939; Duke Ellington 1940; Duke Ellington 1941. Four 2-LP sets, #2003, 2010, 2015, 2027.

Dizzy Gillespie: The Development of an American Artist. 2 LPs, #2004.

An Experiment in Modern Music: Paul Whiteman at Aeolian Hall. 2 LPs, #2028.

The Legendary Freddie Keppard. (Earliest of the New Orleans trumpet-cornet artists to record). 1 LP, #2020.

Louis Armstrong and Earl Hines, 1928. 2 LPs, #2002.

Fletcher Henderson: Developing an American Orchestra, 1923–1937. 2 LPs, #2006.
Music of Fats Waller & James P. Johnson. 1 LP, #1021.
Teddy Wilson: Statements and Improvisations 1934–1942. 1 LP, #2005.
Art Tatum: Pieces of Eight. 1 LP.

PROJECTS

1. Make an assessment of jazz in your local area. Is there music being played that is recognizably jazz, as distinct from rock or merely pop music? Where is it being played, and for whom? What styles can one hear—are there bands playing in a revival of the big band style? of traditional (Dixieland) jazz? of cool?
2. Keep a diary of jazz listening for a month, noting pieces and artists heard, and making some general comments on the music and where it fits into the overall panorama of jazz outlined in this chapter. Make it a point to listen to at least 25 pieces during this time, and include as great a variety of styles and periods as you can.
3. If the calendar of musical events in your area allows, or your travel capabilities permit, attend three separate live jazz performances. Try for a variety of experiences. Write a commentary on the music of each, placing it in the general framework of contemporary jazz as outlined in this chapter.
4. Investigate and write on the jam session in jazz—from the legendary "cutting contests" in New Orleans to the staged jam sessions of today's jazz festivals.
5. If you feel qualified to accept the challenge, make a beginning study of the use of quotation in the jazz of the last thirty years. Some mention of it has been made in the text; it is a fertile field for exploration, beginning with bop.
6. If you have access to a library with good periodical holdings, make a comparative study of two or three periodicals devoted more or less exclusively to jazz. For example, choose from *Down Beat; Jazz; Jazz Report; Journal* (or *Annual Review*) *of Jazz Studies; Jazz Journal* (London); or back volumes of *Metronome* (no longer published).
7. Using as references newspapers such as the *New York Times* or the *Christian Science Monitor,* or general magazines such as *The New Republic* or *Saturday Review,* or music magazines such as *Etude,* compare the coverage of jazz, and the attitude displayed toward it, in two one-year periods spaced fairly far apart.
8. The culture, and the music in particular, of black Americans has gone through periods of discovery or rediscovery by white Americans. Study any one of the following, or make a comparative study of more than one, or all of them: (*a*) discovery and popularization of African-American music in the minstrel show; (*b*) popularization of the African American spiritual after the Civil War; (*c*) the "Harlem Renaissance" of the 1920s; (*d*) the adoption and adaptation of rhythm-and-blues in the 1950s. Have other similar phenomena occurred?
9. Assemble a brief documentary description of jazz in Chicago as it existed under the rule (and patronage) of the gangsters of the 1920s and early 1930s. Ronald Morris's *Wait Until Dark* (Bowling Green, OH: Bowling Green University Popular Press, 1980) would be a logical starting place, but consult also firsthand accounts found in Mezz Mezzrow's *Really the Blues* and Shapiro and Hentoff's *Hear Me Talkin' to Ya.*
10. Make a brief survey of the history of jazz in any foreign country.
11. Make a brief survey of the current state of jazz in any foreign country.
12. Interview at least five people (you may include yourself) on the subject "Electric vs. Acoustic Jazz: Which Do You Prefer, and Why?" and write up the results in a brief paper.
13. If your area has a radio show devoted to jazz (on a public radio station, for example), interview the commentator or disk jockey on one of the following topics:

(*a*) his or her assessment of the current trends in jazz; (*b*) what mail or telephone responses tell about local tastes in jazz; (*c*) his or her own list of the five best new releases of the past year or so, with reasons for the choice; or (*d*) a topic of your own invention.

14. If there is a retired jazz musician in your community, interview him/her about his/her experiences, recollections of noted jazz figures, working conditions, comparisons of jazz *now* with jazz *then*, etc.

Photo by Jim Steere, courtesy the Chicago Symphony Orchestra.

PART SIX

Classical Music

THE pursuit of fine art in America, in terms of classical music, had a prehistory marked by European domination (at first British and then German), with now and then a voice in the wilderness protesting the state of affairs but with only a few hints that a distinctive national music was appearing. This prehistory came to an end after World War I. Since then, things have happened swiftly: a decade now may witness as much evolutionary change as did a half-century previously. Our classical music emerged from adolescence into strong-featured adulthood between the wars, finding its own mature voice. In the third quarter of the century it became polarized. The ground broken in the second quarter, especially in the "definitive decade" of the 1930s, continued to be cultivated by some, who showed that it was capable of yielding new and fresh crops. At the hands of others, pursuing technical innovations and new aesthetic concepts, our classical music, effacing its national character, merged its identity to a degree into that of a new international music—though there are those who maintain that even under these circumstances, American music inevitably still possessed a character of its own. In fact, the embracing of the "new internationalism" is viewed by some as being in itself a manifestation of a very American ideal—that of the "melting pot." The last quarter of this century seems to be characterized by reconciliation, by a decline of the dogmatisms of "modernism," and by the acceptance, and even the enjoyment and celebration, of eclecticism, pluralism, and diversity in our classical music.

Unfortunately, the barriers to understanding and acceptance that hedge about classical music have nowhere been more pronounced than in America, where the gulf between fine art and popular art began to appear in the Jacksonian era of populism and expansion, and grew perceptibly wider in the period of industrialization after the Civil War. It was at this time that aspirations to culture began to be manifested by the new middle and upper classes. Thus the actual and inherent distinction between popular and fine art became obscured, and a false distinction began to appear, based on the social stratification that was becoming so pronounced in this period. To this was added the stratification of gender. It was largely the business of women to support classical music; they were the teachers, the arrangers of concerts, the fund-raisers, the patronesses. To the common man, then, classical music became either "highbrow" or "sissy," or both. The devastating effect of this on a young man with musical talent and the drive to develop it is dramatically illustrated in the case of Charles Ives. Though this set of attitudes toward classical music has fortunately waned, vestiges of it remain.

The very existence of this gulf—a gulf troublingly inconsistent with democratic concepts—seemed to give rise to an almost idealistic yearning to bridge the gap either by bringing classical music to the masses or by amalgamating "mass" art and "elite" art so as to nullify the distinction between them. The visionary Arthur Farwell, as we shall see, took the first approach, arranging concerts to bring music to the people of crowded urban areas in natural outdoor surroundings. George Gershwin and Aaron Copland in the 1920s took the second, each attempting to bridge the gap from his own side of it with symphonic works employing the idioms of popular music and jazz. Similar attempts have subsequently appeared from time to time, showing that the urge toward some sort of reconciliation, whether idealistically or opportunistically motivated, is still there; "third stream" music and "symphonic rock" are manifestations of this.

Whatever may be the precise nature of future attempts to achieve a cross-fertilization between our various musics, it is true that the genre we know as classical music is the most comprehensive one, in its capacity to assimilate the materials and modes of expression of folk music, ethnic music, popular music, jazz, or any other kind of music. Much of what is new comes from this sector of art, which maintains at most times a lively research department and experimental wing.

In the chapters that follow, we shall explore in five stages (corresponding roughly with the five developmental stages outlined in the first paragraph above) the complex picture of American classical music.

15

Laying the Foundation: Accomplishments from the Jacksonian Era to World War I

WHEN in 1828 General Andrew Jackson was swept by a substantial majority into the presidency—the first president from west of the Appalachians—he was riding the combined wave of two related movements that were to bring fundamental changes to American politics and society, and ultimately to American music. These were the rise of political populism, and the increasing importance of the West.

The soldier-politician who has given his name to the era was not himself so much the instrument as the symbol of these related movements of geographical expansion and an increased degree of political democracy.* Jackson's place of birth, where North Carolina met what was then the wilderness; the success of his military adventures on the western frontier, against three of those regarded as the infant nation's traditional enemies (the Indians, the British, and the Spaniards); his limited education, combined with his lack of inherited social position; the base of his political support in the more equalitarian West; and the stand he took against "the rich and powerful" in his opposition to the Bank of the United States—all these factors contributed to his image as a hero of the "plain people." The campaign of 1828 was the first one based on an appeal to the broad mass of voters (an appeal that had its negative side in the introduction of a hitherto unprecedented level of personal slander).

The relationship of American democracy to American music—a relation-

* As an indication of how geographical expansion coincided with increased political democracy, between the battle of New Orleans in 1815 (in which Jackson's frontier militia defeated the British regulars) and Jackson's election in 1828, the union admitted six new states, five of which granted the vote to all adult males.

ship that will have considerable relevance to this chapter—has been commented on by Irving Lowens, who has pointed out that it is the interaction of two tendencies, equalitarianism on the one hand and libertarianism on the other, that defines American democracy. He further writes:

> It is my contention that the past history of the United States has demonstrated a certain correlation between the dominance of the equalitarian urge and the vitality of popular music, and a similar correlation between the dominance of the libertarian urge and the vitality of fine-art ["classical"] music.[1]

It is Lowens's general observation that there was a balance between the two up to about 1830 (and we have seen that the distinction between classical and popular music was not firmly drawn in this period), that equalitarianism was dominant from the Jacksonian era to the Civil War (a fact accompanied by the vitality of popular music in this period), and that libertarianism dominated between the Civil War and World War I (accompanied by a corresponding vitality of classical music).

There can be little doubt of the equalitarian urge of the age of Jackson, and we have already observed in Chapters 11 and 12 the growth and vigor of what has been called our "vernacular" music. This musical populism was represented in sacred music by the products of the singing-school, which were supplanted in the cities, as we have seen, but were still vigorous on the frontier. In secular music, it was represented by developments in popular song and theater—especially, beginning in the 1840s, by the minstrel show.

As a kind of counterbalance to this musical populism (typified for many by the lowbrow "minstrel ditties"), voices had begun to be raised, even earlier in the century, on behalf of reform, of education, of the propagation of "good music" as being morally and spiritually uplifting. A distinction, indeed a cleavage, between "good music" and popular entertainment began to be more clearly evident. It would never have occurred to earlier professionals, such as Rayner Taylor or Alexander Reinagle, to think in these terms. The perceived gulf between the two, which has begun to narrow only in the twentieth century, was distinctly a product of the nineteenth century. Nor was this growing cleavage between "classical" and "popular" uniquely an American phenomenon; it was happening in Europe as well, when the advent of what we have come to call the Romantic era brought with it idealistic conceptions about the role of art and the artist. Should music (and with it all art) *improve, educate,* and *enlighten* us, or is it enough that it merely *entertain* us? These were fundamental questions that arose in the nineteenth century—and that still arise. It is on these lines that the boundaries of the categories *classical* and *popular* were set.*

1830–1865: Education and Reform in a Time of Expansion

The movement to reform and improve American music, and to harness what was seen as its great potential for educational and moral benefit, began in the

* It is interesting to note that musicians such as Louis Moreau Gottschalk and John Philip Sousa—both of whom did compose and perform some classical music, but who sought to entertain their public with hardly a thought of educating them—are difficult to categorize in this period.

domain of religious music, and is epitomized in developments in New England during this period. The leading figures all came out of the background of the singing-school, but sought to improve on what they saw as the naive crudities of the anthems and fuging tunes of such earlier singing-school masters as William Billings (see Chapters 5 and 6). A transitional figure was the blind singer-composer-teacher Oliver Shaw (1779–1848; see Chapter 10). Shaw studied with two European immigrant musicians then resident in New England, and he soon determined to help improve, as he saw it, the church music of his time. As early as 1810 he was a leader in establishing the Psallonian Society in Providence, Rhode Island—created, its founders said, "for the purpose of improving themselves in the knowledge and practice of sacred music and inculcating a more correct taste in the choice and performance of it."[2] The phrase "a more correct taste" is worthy of note; taste and correctness became cardinal concerns of the reformers, and it is directly relevant that Oliver Shaw also took an active role in the founding, five years later, of the Boston Handel and Haydn Society, which had similar goals (see Chapter 10), and that he was an early teacher of Lowell Mason.[3]

Mason, Johnson, and Root: Three Pioneer Believers in the Place of Music in Education

We have already encountered Lowell Mason in Chapter 6, as compiler of *The Boston Handel and Haydn Society Collection of Church Music* of 1822, which introduced the practice of adapting melodies by European masters for use as hymn tunes. With Oliver Shaw and others, Mason was instrumental in driving a native, folk-oriented religious tradition out of the cities. Yet, in the large view, his work can be seen as a continuation of a New England cultural tradition; it is not so surprising that Bostonians, who took the lead in teaching people to read music in the eighteenth century, were the first to make music a regular part of public school education in the nineteenth.

Lowell Mason (1792–1872), born in a village southwest of Boston, went to a singing-school at the age of thirteen. His grandfather had been a singing-master; Lowell himself taught singing-schools, led the parish choir, organized and led instrumental groups, and composed at least one anthem before he was twenty. He was a voracious learner, and made himself proficient at all the instruments he could lay his hands on.

His period of preparation for what he then little suspected would be his life's work was passed in Savannah, Georgia, from the time he was twenty until he was thirty-five. While working there as a banker, he studied harmony and composition with a competent "scientific" (German) musician, held a post as organist and choirmaster, and was superintendent of one of the first Sunday schools in the country—significant in view of his later concern with teaching music to children.

When Mason moved to Boston in 1827, his life work gradually but surely unfolded. His first accomplishments were in the field of church music; his church choirs attracted notice far and wide for their excellence. But, more important, his developing interest in teaching children to sing soon bore fruit. Mason was convinced that nearly all children could be taught to sing, if it was done in the right way. He began extensive teaching under the auspices of his church (the Bowdoin Street Church of the Rev. Lyman Beecher), and his classes ultimately became very large. The public concerts he gave with his children's choirs proved his point, and attracted wide and favorable attention. Today we take pretty much for granted the fact that children are taught to sing; it is hard to realize that formerly the musical capacities of the average child (like so many inborn abilities of children) were undernourished or ignored completely.

The movement for music in education began in the churches, but ultimately found its way into the schools. The Boston Academy of Music that Mason founded was a means to this end. It was established in 1833 after the performances by his singing classes for children had aroused community interest. A private organization, it did not have to wait for official school board action, but set about at once to teach vocal music to children, both at the Academy itself and in the schools—a few private ones at first. Mason himself did this teaching single-handedly in the beginning, but soon he was joined by George J. Webb, an organist who had emigrated from England, and by A. N. Johnson and George Frederick Root. The Academy itself offered both juvenile and adult classes, as well as private instruction. Children were accepted into singing classes Wednesday and Saturday afternoons free of charge, provided they would promise to attend for at least a year.

The activities of the Academy were in fact broad, and its goals embraced the improvement of church music and the training of music teachers, as well as what appears to have been the primary one: "to introduce vocal music into schools, by the aid of such teachers as the Academy may be able to employ." When, in 1837, Boston's school committee adopted resolutions recommending that music be introduced experimentally in four public schools but failed (as such bodies often do) to get funds from the city council, Mason offered to teach in one of the schools without pay. The offer was accepted, and this was the beginning. His impressive results led, the next year, to the adoption of resolutions authorizing the introduction of music as a branch of popular education into the public schools of Boston—a step the Boston Academy termed the "magna charta of musical education." This time funds were forthcoming, and Mason became the country's first "supervisor of public school music." The traditional goals of public school music were established—not to produce trained musicians, but to give all students "the power of understanding and appreciating Music."

Still another venture in which Mason pioneered was the editing and publication of music especially suited for use in the teaching of children. Beginning with the *Juvenile Psalmist* in 1829 (for church use) and the secular *Juvenile Lyre* in 1831 (for school use), Mason produced a number of songbooks for this purpose, culminating in a three-volume graded music series, the first representative of a type of publication now legion.

Mason's gifts as a composer were modest, but he seldom essayed what he knew to be beyond his powers; he knew what he could do, and for whom he was composing. Among his many hymn tunes, his "Missionary Hymn" ("From Greenland's icy mountains") and "Nearer, My God, to Thee" have become part of the common store of American religious music.

A. N. Johnson (1817–92) was active in Boston until the Civil War in music teaching, editing, and publishing, part of that time in association with Mason and Root. By mid-century he and Lowell Mason had parted ways. Johnson had developed his own choral methods, but, more important, Johnson promoted American music and composers in his publications, in contrast to Mason's reliance on European music; his voice thus was one of the few raised in this period on behalf of "nativism" (a subject about which we shall say more presently). In the 1860s the focus of his activities moved west; he pioneered in founding no fewer than eight music schools and conservatories, in Pennsylvania, Ohio, Indiana, and western New York state.

George Frederick Root (1820–95) was first a student and then a partner of A. N. Johnson in Boston, and he worked closely with Lowell Mason, whose methods he introduced in New York. He is known for his popular songs,* especially Civil War songs such as "The Vacant Chair," "Just Before the Battle, Mother," and "Tramp! Tramp! Tramp!" He also composed several works in the then-popular genre of the cantata. These were extended compositions on both sacred and secular subjects, consisting of separate numbers for chorus and solo voices with simple accompaniments, written for singers with modest skills. *The Haymakers* (1857), an unpretentious but charming secular piece, deals in a naive and idyllic way with one episode of farm life—a life that Root knew well from his personal background, and one that has seldom been dealt with or romanticized in American music. While Root grew up with the strong opposition to the theater on moral grounds still prevalent in New England in his time, he did call *The Haymakers* "An Operatic Cantata," and included directions for simple staging. The second part of it has been recorded.[4]

Lowell Mason, A. N. Johnson, and George Frederick Root are representative of the movement toward the betterment and reform of American music, and toward its wider use in education. Their efforts began with, and focused on, church music. All three were teachers; Mason and Johnson founded schools. All were concerned almost exclusively with music for persons of modest musical abilities, including children. This accounts in large part for their success. All were involved in the *business* of music, as school administrators, traveling lecturers and conductors, editors and compilers, but especially as publishers. Mason in particular became very wealthy, and he incidentally founded a musical dynasty that lasted well into the twentieth century.[5]

Heinrich, Fry, and Bristow: Three Outspoken "Nativists"

Given the cultural background of the adolescent nation, it was understandable, even inevitable, that most of those concerned with improvement, education, and reform in music should turn for their source to "the courtly muses of Europe" (to use Emerson's 1837 phrase).[6] There was, especially in intellectually and culturally sophisticated circles in Boston, New York, and Philadelphia, an increased regard for Europe as the fount of all art, including music.

* That he published some of his songs under the pseudonym G. Friedrich Wurzel, the German translation of his name, is an indication of the German hegemony in all things musical at the time—the very thing that men such as A. N. Johnson and William Henry Fry were each in their own way going against the current to oppose.

However, a few voices of the time, in harmony with Emerson's views, were heard in support of at least the *ideal* of self-reliance in American music. The extent to which this ideal was capable of realization, particularly in the period before the Civil War, made its advocacy all too ironic, to be sure. But the debate between the two points of view that Betty Chmaj has termed the "nativist" and the "expatriate," which has been a central issue in American music, began to be joined in earnest in this period.[7] Heinrich, Fry, and Bristow, as composers, were among our most outspoken "nativists"—those who wanted to see flourish a distinctive American music, written by American composers and, equally important, actually *performed* for American audiences. The "expatriates"—skeptical if not openly scornful of our native product, and espousing a more cosmopolitan view—were represented by writers and critics such as the New Yorker Richard Storrs Willis and the Bostonian Transcendentalist John Sullivan Dwight.

Anthony Philip Heinrich (1781–1861) arrived in Philadelphia from his native Bohemia in 1810. He was both a businessman and an amateur musician. The heir to substantial wealth and to a thriving wholesale mercantile business, he took over the musical direction of the Southwark Theater, working without pay. The Napoleonic wars and their aftermath wiped out both business and fortune the year after he arrived. Outward circumstances seemed to confirm his inward desires, and he thenceforward committed himself wholly to music. Living and working here, except for some fairly extended visits to Europe, for the next fifty years he pursued with fanatical zeal his ideal of making his adopted country a musical nation. Unlike other immigrant musicians, he came here as an "amateur" but, by dint of extraordinary labor and sacrifice, became a "professor."

In 1817 Heinrich went from Philadelphia to Pittsburgh expecting to become musical director of the one theater there. Now a poor man, he walked the entire distance. When the Pittsburgh job failed to materialize, he went on down the Ohio River and into Kentucky, arriving at Lexington the same year, and giving concerts in that small but prosperous city on the route of westward migration.[8] Not long after, worn out and ill, he went to live in a log house in Bardstown, Kentucky. Here, in the relative wilderness, at nearly forty years of age, he began to write music. This now became his ruling passion, and the environment in which he started to compose furnished the stuff of romantic legend, which Heinrich never lost an opportunity to foster. For the rest of his life he referred to himself by such titles as "The Wildwood Troubadour," "Minstrel of the Western Wilds," or, more concretely, "The Loghouse Composer of Kentucky."

A scant two years after his wilderness experience of self-discovery the industrious Heinrich produced his first published work, with the elaborate title *The Dawning of Music in Kentucky, or The Pleasures of Harmony in the Solitudes of Nature* (1820). In the preface he makes one of the earliest pleas for the cause of the "nativist" in his adopted country:

> The many and severe animadversions, so long and repeatedly cast on the talent for Music in this Country, has been one of the chief motives of the Author, in the exercise of his abilities; and should he be able, by his effort, to create but one single

> *Star* in the *West,* no one could ever be more proud than himself, to be called an *American Musician.*[9]

The Dawning of Music in Kentucky consists mostly of short pieces—songs, dances, and variations on familiar tunes—for various combinations of piano and voice or voices, with the occasional inclusion of other instruments such as violin or flute.

A short supplement, *The Western Minstrel,* contains a descriptive piece of the type then much in vogue. Depicting the journey Heinrich had made himself, it is titled *The Minstrel's March, or Road to Kentucky.* There are landmarks identified in the score, from the opening "A Tempo Giusto da Filadelfia" to the final enigmatic "Sign of the Harp" (an inn?) reached after "Landing and Cheers." After the opening call of the post horn, a descending scale depicts the "Market Street hill." The Alleghenies are traversed in nine difficult measures; "Passage on the Ohio" begins *dolce,* but "The Rapids" (agitated passage for left hand) are encountered before the final "Standing in for Port" and "Casting Anchors." Heinrich carried programmaticism to extremes, even for the nineteenth century; he seldom wrote anything without some extramusical reference. Very often the allusion was topical, even if only in the title (*Tyler's Grand Veto Quick Step* is a singular example). Such programmaticism was, as we have seen, typical of the time; the reader will recall the "battle" pieces of the eighteenth century (see Chapter 10), which had their descendants as late as the Civil War (*The Battle of Manassas* by Blind Tom is an example).

Another aspect of Romanticism was the glorification of Nature; Heinrich, possibly influenced both by his wilderness experience and by his long friendship with John James Audubon, expressed this in many works. Audubon comes to mind particularly in two of these. The first is titled *The Columbiad; or, Migration of American Wild Passenger Pigeons.* The program furnishes an interesting artistic record of the once-familiar sight of these birds, now gone forever from the American scene, and is worth quoting in full as an example of the extreme detail of the programmaticism of the era, and also of the Romantic view of nature, with its hints of the pathetic fallacy:

> Introduction. A Mysterious Woodland Scene, the assembling of the wild passenger pigeons in the "far west" for their grand flight of migration.
>
> I. Andante de Allegro. The flitting of birds and thunderlike flappings of a passing phalanx of American wild pigeons.
> II. The aerial armies alight on the primeval forest trees, which bend and crash beneath their weight.
> III. Andante ed Andantino. A twilight scene. The cooing of the doves previous to their nightly repose.
> IV. Allegro Mosso. With Aurora comes the conflict of the Beechnuts.
> V. Adagio ed Allegretto Cantabile. The vast conclave in grand council resolve to migrate elsewhere.
> VI. Molto Animato, Sudden rise and flight of the myriad winged emigrants.
> VII. Piu mosso. The alarm of hunters' rifles startles the multitude. The wounded and dying birds sink tumultuously earthward.

VIII. Allegro Agitato. In Brooding agitation the columbines continue their flight, darkening the welkin as they utter their aerial requiem, but passing onward, ever onward to the goal of their nomadic wandering, the green savannas of the New World.

IX. Finale. *The Columbiad.* Marcia grande ed a passo doppio. American folk tunes: *Hail Columbia* and *Yankee Doodle.*

The second bird piece is a work for full orchestra that went through many versions (Heinrich reworked many of his pieces); in its final form it bears the fanciful title *The Ornithological Combat of Kings; or, the Condor of the Andes and the Eagle of the Cordilleras.* Fortunately, the twenty-five-minute piece has been recorded, allowing us to hear this "Grand Symphony," which Heinrich considered his best work, and on which he labored, off and on, for twenty years—the last revisions are dated 1856.[10]

Heinrich, the "Loghouse Composer of Kentucky," had left Kentucky for good by 1823. After some years of moving around, he settled in New York in 1837, and he spent most of the rest of his life there. It is important to realize that, as eccentric as Heinrich appears to us today, he was recognized as a leading American composer in his time, and that he fully immersed himself in the musical life of that time. We find him, for example, presiding at the historic meeting (to be discussed below) that led to the founding of the Philharmonic Society of New York in 1842. He was an indefatigable and disarmingly ingenuous promoter of his own music,* but his best efforts to secure even barely adequate performances of his works were frustrated by the fact that they were inordinately difficult and complex. "Scientific" and "German" (terms taken to be virtually synonymous) were frequently applied to his music, both by those who intended to compliment and those who intended to criticize it. Anthony Philip Heinrich's relationship to what might be termed the populist "mainstream" of American culture of his time is poignantly summed up in an account of his playing at the White House for President John Tyler; we see the enraptured, perspiring artist playing one of his most flamboyantly idealistic and patriotic compositions for the practical politician, who ends the session abruptly and prematurely by saying to the composer: "That may all be very fine, sir, but can't you play us a good old Virginia reel."[11]

Meanwhile, there were other American composers also engaged in the struggle for the performance and acceptance of American works. William Henry Fry (1813–64) was a practicing journalist, from a well-to-do Philadelphia newspaper family, who was also a composer. Opera was his great love, and with his second complete opera, *Leonora,* he sought to pioneer in the composition of serious opera in the English language—something he felt had not been done up to that time, either by English or American composers.[12] *Leonora,* given a lavish production in Philadelphia in 1845 at the composer's expense, was a success with the public, but not with the critics, who found too much of Italian opera (especially Bellini) in it.

Fry subsequently spent six years in Europe as a journalist. His attempt

* Heinrich was a compulsive letter-writer. Often, after the manner of composers, he wrote offering to write or dedicate works, or seeking to secure performances. Among letters not answered, as far as we know, were those to Jenny Lind, Paganini, and Queen Victoria.

to secure even a rehearsal of *Leonora* in Paris—a rehearsal for which he was willing to pay all expenses himself—was met with refusal based on an all-too-familiar prejudice, as stated by the director of the operahouse: "In Europe we look upon America as an industrial country—excellent for electric telegraphs, but not for art."[13] Upon Fry's return to America in 1852, he found American prejudice against American music, and in favor of European, no less in evidence, and, in his view, much less tolerable in his native land. While still working for the *New York Tribune,* he set out to do something about it. He was then fairly prominent on the musical scene, through the performance of a number of his works by—ironically—a French conductor, Louis Antoine Jullien. Fry proceeded to give, at his own expense, a series of lectures on musical subjects, illustrated by vocal soloists, a large chorus and orchestra, and military band! Fry was well informed, and was a witty and highly effective—if bold and unconventional—speaker.* His lectures must have been well worth hearing—the nineteenth-century equivalents, perhaps, of Leonard Bernstein's series of television programs with the New York Philharmonic providing illustrations. In the climactic last lecture Fry delivered another deeply felt plea for America's development and acceptance of its own music, and an American "Declaration of Independence" from European domination. Coming a generation after that of Heinrich, it was not to be the last:

> Until this Declaration of Independence in Art shall be made—until American composers shall discard their foreign liveries and found an American School—and until the American public shall learn to support American artists, Art will not become indigenous to this country, but will only exist as a feeble exotic, and we shall continue to be provincial in Art. The American composer should not allow the name of Beethoven, or Handel or Mozart to prove an eternal bugbear to him, nor should he pay them reverence; he should only reverence his Art, and strike out manfully and independently into untrodden realms, just as his nature and inspirations may invite him, else he can never achieve lasting renown.[14]

There were to come those who would more effectively "strike out manfully and independently into untrodden realms" in terms of their musical output—we shall encounter some of them in Chapter 17. But Fry will be remembered for his ringing call for independence on behalf of American music, issued a mere fifteen years after Emerson had sounded a similar call on behalf of American letters in "The American Scholar."

George Frederick Bristow (1825–98), "serious, industrious, and unassuming"—a competent, versatile, thoroughgoing professional musician, was born in New York, spent his entire life in and around that city, and died there. The son of a professional musician, he early learned the violin, piano, and organ. The choice of a career was never in doubt; he was playing violin in a theater orchestra at the age of eleven, and for over sixty years he was involved in every phase of New York's musical life at the period when it was attaining the position of dominance and influence in American music that it holds to this day. We find Bristow's name cropping up again and again in musical annals—the busy, on-the-spot professional—and through a glance at some episodes of

* One critic likened his mind to "an eagle, [that] seems to soar, untrammelled—but wayward and uncertain," and his genius to a "splendid frigate at sea without a helm."

his long career we can form a good picture of the musical life of our cities beginning in the 1840s.

In 1842 a meeting was called to discuss the formation of a symphony orchestra in New York. Orchestras had come and gone in our three largest cities since the turn of the century; what makes this meeting momentous in retrospect was that it resulted in the formation of the Philharmonic Society of New York, the nation's oldest orchestra still in continuous existence. Its first concert was given that same year. The musicians themselves saw to the preliminary advertising, took tickets at the door, acted as ushers, and played the concert. Out of the income from ticket sales, and from dues and fines for absences that members assessed themselves, they paid themselves modest fees for playing, and divided the profits at the end of each season; these dividends varied throughout the nineteenth century from a low of $17.50 to a high of $225. George Frederick Bristow was a member of the New York Philharmonic at its founding, and continued so for forty years.

The mid-nineteenth century was the heyday of the great showman and entrepreneur P. T. Barnum. He had hitherto made his reputation through the display of such sensational items as the body of a mermaid, an aged black woman reputed to have been George Washington's nurse, and, of course, "General" Tom Thumb. Out of the desire to elevate his image somewhat, he sent an agent to Europe to put the great Swedish singer Jenny Lind under contract for an American tour. The result was one of the most fascinating triumphs of show business in nineteenth-century America, grossing over $700,000 in ninety-three concerts in nineteen cities. The success of the venture was the product of thorough advance planning and shrewd marketing. Jenny Lind's arrival in New York was preceded by what was probably the most extensive advertising campaign ever mounted in the history of show business up to that time. By the time she arrived in triumph in 1850, Barnum had virtually all of New York at her feet. For her opening concert at Castle Garden the first ticket, sold at auction, went for $225. (For succeeding concerts, some were to bring as much as $650.) The first concert was a memorable triumph—apparently artistically as well as financially, though we have harder evidence for the latter than for the former. At any rate, the impact on New York's concert life was tremendous. George Frederick Bristow was a member of the orchestra.

During the season of 1853–54 another brilliant showman made his appearance on the New York scene. Louis Antoine Jullien was a flamboyant French conductor and impresario who fully grasped the need for theatricalism as an ingredient for successful concert-giving in the mid-nineteenth century, and was ready to supply it, with boldness and ingenuity. Having been forced to flee France because of his debts, Jullien spent some very uneven years in England before deciding to try his luck in the New World. An indication of his style may be gained from his opening bit of stage business: he customarily strode to the podium with white gloves on, followed by a page bearing his silver baton on a velvet-covered tray. He then elegantly shed the gloves and picked up the baton.*

* Jullien somewhat anticipated the "cult of the conductor" which, after the advent of Wagner, swept Europe and America toward the end of the nineteenth century—a cult that, no less than Jullien's shallower pretensions and antics, had much of its *raison d'être* in the box office.

Jullien's programs included, along with the usual popular polkas, schottisches, galops, and so on, the most outrageous novelties. The famous *Fireman's Quadrille,* in the course of which three companies of New York firemen came charging down the aisles toward the stage with buckets and ladders, was almost too sensational. But the orchestral discipline was apparently superb, furnishing an example Americans could well profit from. And some of the classics were performed along with the lighter fare. Perhaps most noteworthy is the fact that, presumably in the novelty department, Jullien did perform works by American composers—his record on this score seems to have been better than that of the New York Philharmonic Society at the time. Pieces with detailed programs, such as those of Heinrich that we have encountered, were of course grist for his mill. Jullien performed several works of William Henry Fry (it cannot be overlooked that Fry was at that time in a highly influential position as music critic for the *New York Tribune*!), including his *Santa Claus Symphony,* complete with snowstorms and sleigh bells. As a violinist in the Jullien orchestra we find—needless to say—George Frederick Bristow.

The significance of Bristow's career is not, of course, defined merely by his participation in these colorful mid-century musical events. He was also a church organist, for eleven years conducted the Harmonic Society (a choral organization), and from 1854 until his death was visiting teacher of music in the New York public schools; the pioneering work of Lowell Mason and others had borne fruit in our largest metropolis, although music did not become established as a regular part of the curriculum until 1898. But Bristow's most significant accomplishments were as a composer. The work for which he became best known is his full-length opera, the first on an American subject by an American composer. *Rip Van Winkle,* based on Washington Irving's story, was produced in 1855 at Niblo's Garden, the scene of many mid-nineteenth-century musical and theatrical attractions. The composer himself conducted, showing yet another side of his versatility. The opera ran for seventeen performances, with satisfactory box-office results—no mean accomplishment.

Bristow wrote orchestral music as well, including at least four symphonies, with another titled *Niagara* in progress at his death. The New York Philharmonic performed his first symphony at a public rehearsal in 1845, and programmed his *Concert Overture* in 1847. But despite these early gestures, and spurred perhaps by the fact that Jullien, a foreign conductor, had played more American works, dissatisfaction with the treatment of American composers at the hands of the New York Philharmonic surfaced in 1853, in a published letter by William Henry Fry, which charged the Philharmonic with being "an incubus on art." At this point Bristow also stood up for the "nativists" in a letter of his own, in which he said:

> During the eleven years the Philharmonic Society has been in operation in this city, it played once, either by mistake or accident, one single American composition, an overture of mine. As one exception makes a rule stronger, so this single stray fact shows that the Philharmonic Society has been as anti-American as if it had been located in London during the Revolutionary War, and composed of native-born British tories.[15]

Bristow resigned (briefly, as it turned out) from the orchestra. The situation did apparently improve somewhat subsequently; at least Bristow himself could have had little cause to complain, since as far as we can tell the Philharmonic Society eventually performed all of Bristow's completed symphonies. Three of them were recorded in the 1960s, including the *Arcadian Symphony* (*"The Pioneer"*), the last movement of which is subtitled "Indian War Dance."[16] Like programmatic works with references to American Indians by other composers of the time, it betrays no acquaintance with actual Indian music (it was too early for that), and sounds in fact suspiciously like French ballet music, of which Bristow would have heard and played a good deal.

In summary, Bristow's compositions stand today as landmarks left by one of our first composers to deal competently with the larger forms of music. Perhaps just as significant, his accomplishments were those of a musician trained entirely in America. Bristow never went to Europe to study—an example that was to become, later in the century, something of an exception.

We have just examined the careers and works of three composers who, different as they were, all stood up for a "nativist" view—that there should evolve a distinctively American music, developing a life of its own not in the shadow of European tradition, together with an audience to appreciate and support such music. There were critics, however, who took an opposite view, a view expressed in the ideals of the Handel and Haydn Society. These critics were imbued with an almost reverential attitude toward those European masters—mainly Germanic—whose music was just beginning to be performed and heard in the culturally adolescent republic. Handel, Mozart, Beethoven: these were the composers who inspired them, and by whose standard they believed *all* music, American or not, should be measured. They urged a cosmopolitan, universal view of music. As Richard Storrs Willis wrote in 1854, addressing Fry, "The Temple of Art is a *universal* temple, and that you are an American is no reason that you should have free admission there." The use of the word "Temple," capitalized, brings the whole issue neatly into focus, as it is symptomatic of the reverential attitude of the "expatriate" view. The works of Beethoven in particular, especially the idealism of the Ninth Symphony, were held to represent the highest achievements in Art.[17]

John Sullivan Dwight (1813–93) was the leading spokesman for this view. He was a New England Transcendentalist—a member of a small, loosely knit group of thinkers and writers, including Emerson and Thoreau, who took an active role in the intellectual life of America at this time. Though not a musician himself, Dwight was the man who interpreted the philosophy as it applied to music. In 1852 he began publishing his *Journal of Music,* which for nearly thirty years was the most influential music periodical in the country. Dwight expressed disdain for what he called "mere musical trifles"; it was his conviction that "Music stands for the highest outward symbol of what is most deep and holy."

In our intellectual life, the decades before the Civil War constituted an arena of conflicting views on many issues, including music. An idealistic dedication to the cosmopolitan, the universal, the expression that seeks to transcend place and time, competed with an equally idealistic desire to express the national, the specific, the unique sense of *this* place and *this* time.*

This competition of ideas was played out against the background of our

* The debate between these two views, as Betty Chmaj aptly points out, is perennial.

period of greatest national expansion, between the Louisiana Purchase and the Civil War, including the controversial (then as now) Mexican War, with the territorial acquisitions that followed it. It was a time of fierce national pride; "Manifest Destiny" was its appropriate motto. Observers have pointed out two prevalent and related characteristics of the American temperament in this period: an intense desire for cultural independence from Europe—for a literature, architecture, and art of their own that Americans could take pride in—and a marked sensitivity to criticism from Europeans who were scornful not only of America's cultural achievements but of the very *capacity* of Americans to achieve in this department of life.*

The unfortunate truth is that there was at this time very little evidence in terms of extant works to refute this European view of America—the view shared by anti-nativist critics here. It is indeed ironic that those very composers who spoke most feelingly on behalf of an American music that could stand on its own feet (most notably Heinrich, Fry, and Bristow) produced music that was itself highly imitative of—indeed virtually indistinguishable from—the European music of the time (Italianate in the case of Fry, Germanic in the case of Heinrich and Bristow). The *idea,* justifiable as it was, was premature in terms of the talent, skill, and originality that America had in its service at the time.

We have yet to consider the most gifted musician of the era. He encountered in his career the contradictory currents we have been describing: the widening gulf between classical and popular music—between music as entertainment and music as an educating and elevating moral force—and the issue of "nativism" vs. "expatriatism" in American art. Both as a composer and as a virtuoso performer, he found himself caught between two audiences, neither of which he could wholly satisfy.

Louis Moreau Gottschalk and the Virtuoso in Nineteenth-Century America

In 1853 there appeared on the New York scene, just arrived from Europe, one of the most brilliant pianists of the age. He had recently completed a triumphant concert tour of Spain, where the queen had made him a Cavalier of the Order of Isabella the Catholic; Chopin had predicted a great future for him; the great French composer Hector Berlioz was his friend and mentor. Louis Moreau Gottschalk would have been an outstanding figure whatever his origin, but his importance is all the greater because he was an American. He was, in fact, the first American musician to rank unquestionably with the greatest in Europe in his time—there is abundant documentation for this. As a pianist, he must have been superb, especially in the performance of his own works; as a composer, he has left some colorful piano pieces based on the folk music of Louisiana and the West Indies that will continue to hold their place in the world's piano music; as a diarist, he has left some brilliant, witty, and highly

* The categorical and humiliating rejection, on grounds of nationality, that both Fry and Gottschalk experienced in Paris in the 1840s (described in this chapter) was a typical expression of this attitude.

perceptive observations of the United States, the West Indies, and South America during eleven years of travel and concertizing. Proud of being an American, he was an ardent patriot, but also a keen and critical observer. The circumstances of his life were such that he spent more than half of it outside his native land.

Louis Moreau Gottschalk (1829–69) was born in New Orleans, the oldest of seven children. His father (probably at least partly of Jewish extraction), a well-educated gentleman, had emigrated from London. His mother, Aimée de Bruslé, was a Creole, a cultured woman of French extraction whose parents were both refugees from bloody slave insurrections on the island of Santo Domingo in the West Indies. Gottschalk's father, Edward, became a successful businessman, and was able to provide for his family all the cultural advantages that New Orleans offered at the time.

New Orleans in the 1830s was a cultural melting pot in which relatively new American influence, a generation after the Louisiana Purchase, vied with the established French. The St. Charles Theater gave performances in English (and in Italian, by visiting Italian opera companies); the Théâtre d'Orléans, with its orchestra and opera troupe, was the focal point of French culture. Of considerable significance also was that colorful mixture of the African, the West Indian, and the Hispanic that constituted the folk ambience dealt with in Chapter 20.

It was into this multicolored and multi-cultural world that Louis Moreau Gottschalk was born. He soon showed the unmistakable signs of musical precocity—picking out on the piano, at the age of three, tunes his mother (an accomplished singer) had sung; beginning lessons in piano and sight-singing with the director of music at the St. Louis Cathedral soon afterward; substituting as organist at the cathedral at the age of seven; playing from memory melodies that he heard from operas given at the St. Charles Theater and the Théâtre d'Orléans; and playing the piano regularly in public beginning at the age of nine. By the time he was eleven, his teacher was saying that there was nothing more he could learn from any musician in New Orleans; when he was thirteen, his parents sent him to Paris to study.

The young American prodigy's reception by the director of piano classes at the Paris Conservatoire in 1842 is significant to our story of American music—he rejected him without even hearing him play, because, in his opinion "l'Amérique n'était qu'un pays de machines à vapeur" ("America was nothing but a country of steam engines"). That Gottschalk, seven years later at the age of twenty, was invited to sit as a judge at examinations at this same conservatory is a fitting sequel, and suggests how rapidly he took his place among the leading young pianists of the day. Not only musically but socially, he was soon in the most exalted company. We have noted his acquaintance with Berlioz and Chopin; among the younger musicians, his contemporaries, he was the friend of Jacques Offenbach, Georges Bizet, and Camille Saint-Saëns. Among writers who knew and admired his playing were Victor Hugo, Alexandre Dumas *père,* and Alphonse de Lamartine. His remarkable appearance, stage presence, and charm were universally commented upon throughout his life; he was to become, in effect, one of the first "matinee idols."

The closing highlight of his eleven-year European sojourn, first as student and then as concert artist, was his triumphal tour of Spain. Made under the direct patronage of the queen herself, it was rich with characteristic incident, including Gottschalk's adoption of a homeless Andalusian waif, and a severe injury to his hand (from which he fortunately recovered completely) inflicted by a jealous court pianist.

By the time Gottschalk went to Spain he had already established himself as a composer. Especially popular were three piano pieces he had written when still in his teens in Paris, based on folk tunes of the Louisiana blacks that he remembered from his childhood—*Bamboula: Danse des Nègres* (which, with foresight, he dedicated to the queen of Spain on its publication), *Le Bananier: Chanson nègre,* and *La Savane: Ballade créole.* Responding to the demand for musical "acrobatics" (especially in Spain), he began writing pieces such as his brilliant paraphrase on *The Carnival of Venice,* his Spanish-flavored etude *Manchega,* and his caprice on three Spanish dance tunes, *Souvenirs d'Andalousie.* And in response to the popularity of programmatic pieces he produced a *Grande Symphonie* for ten pianos, *El Sitio de Zaragoza* ("The Siege of Zaragoza"). This "symphony," of which a popular fragment (*La Jota Aragonesa*) has survived, exhibits another phase of nineteenth-century concert-giving that was by no means an exclusively American phenomenon—the multiple-piano piece. (A concert of Gottschalk's in San Francisco thirteen years later included a piece for fourteen pianos and gave rise to a bizarrely humorous anecdote that he recorded in his *Notes of a Pianist.*)[18]

Gottschalk's initial concerts in New York appeared to have been carefully planned by his advance agent, who may have profited in a more dignified way from the example set by Barnum in his advance campaign for Jenny Lind's New York appearances three years before. It is interesting to look at the program for Gottschalk's opening concert—a relatively intimate one given at Niblo's Salon on February 11, 1853. It was the usual medley, consisting of songs, a flute and piano duet, duets for two pianos, and piano solos performed by Gottschalk that included two operatic transcriptions and three "poetic caprices" (one was *Le Bananier*), ending with his *Carnival of Venice.* We look in vain on concert programs of the day for Beethoven sonatas, Bach preludes and fugues, or even the works of Chopin. These Gottschalk knew and loved, playing them for his friends, but to play them at public concerts would have been out of the question.

Gottschalk's large concert followed in Niblo's Garden six days later. There a full orchestra accompanied him in Carl Maria von Weber's *Concertstück;* he also played solos and shared the program with a second pianist and with two singers. The concerts, though they cost Gottschalk more than $2,000, were an unquestioned success with the public and paved the way for his subsequent career in America. Following the second concert, P. T. Barnum offered Gottschalk a contract for a two- or three-year tour; Gottschalk, on the advice of his father, turned it down, on the grounds that Barnum's price was too low and that he was a vulgar showman who would do more harm than good to his career.

Gottschalk went to Philadelphia, where he played to enthusiastic response a reworked version of *The Siege of Zaragoza* that included "Yankee Doodle," "Hail Columbia," "The Star-Spangled Banner," "Oh, Susanna," and "Old Folks at Home" in place of the Spanish tunes. Gottschalk played in Louisville, and then boarded a river steamer for the return to his native New

Orleans. (On board the steamer, he is said to have asked permission to play daily for the slaves below decks, who were bound for the New Orleans slave market. The captain refused. The incident is thoroughly characteristic of Gottschalk.) After a tremendous reception and round of concerts in the city of his birth, he set out once more. His life continued to be one of almost constant travel and concert-giving.

His years in the United States were twice interrupted by sojourns in the West Indies. The second of these, beginning in 1857, lasted five years—years in which Gottschalk virtually dropped out of sight. He himself describes them as

> years foolishly spent, thrown to the wind, as if life were infinite, and youth eternal; six years, during which I have roamed at random under the blue skies of the tropics, indolently permitting myself to be carried away by chance, giving a concert wherever I found a piano, sleeping wherever the night overtook me—on the grass of the savanna, or under the palm-leaf roof of a *veguero* (a tobacco-grower) with whom I partook of a tortilla, coffee, and banana, which I paid for on leaving in the morning, with *"Dios se lo pague"* (God repay you); to which he responded with a *"Vaya usted con Dios"* (God go with you)—these two formularies constituting in this savage country, the operation so ingeniously perfected among civilized people, that is called "settling the hotel bill."[19]

Much as he loved the United States (to which he formally declared allegiance in Havana before returning to his war-torn country in 1862), there is no question that he felt more at home in Latin America, that he was better understood there, and that his receptions there were more spontaneous and enthusiastic.

The lines quoted above are from the important journal that Gottschalk began the year he embarked upon his long West Indian rambling. Published as *Notes of a Pianist,* they cover the nearly twelve years from that time until the year before his death. The are brilliantly written (in French), and are reminiscent of the essays and memoirs of his older mentor Berlioz in their wit and insight. As valuable descriptions and commentaries on American life of the time, they rank with the journals and writings of Frances Kemble, Frederick Law Olmsted, and Alexis de Tocqueville. Who knew better, for example, or could better have expressed, the American state of mind with regard to the fine arts a century ago than Gottschalk, writing in 1862?

> There is no doubt that there are immense lacunæ in certain details of our civilization. Our appreciation of the *beaux-arts* is not always enlightened, and we treat them like parasites occupying a usurped place. The wheels of our government are, like our managers, too new not to grate upon the ear sometimes. We perhaps worship a little too much the golden calf, and do not kill the fatted calf often enough to feast the elect of thought. Each of us thinks himself as good as (if not better than) any other man—an excellent faith that engenders self-respect but often leads us to wish to reduce to our own level those to whose level we cannot attain. These little faults happily are not national traits; they appertain to all young societies. We are, in a word, like the beautiful children of whom Montaigne speaks, who bite the nurse's breast, and whom the exuberance of health sometimes renders turbulent.[20]

It is characteristic that Gottschalk, who had suffered much at the hands of the rude and boorish among his countrymen, should still have been able to write so understandingly of the young America's "turbulence," even as he wrote sympathetically of the plight of the slaves, although it was rebellious slaves who had killed his maternal relatives in Santo Domingo.

When Gottschalk did return for the last time to the United States, it was to undertake a nearly killing schedule of concerts that took him, in three and a half years, to every large city in the wartime United States (he did not travel into the Confederacy) and to many of its smaller towns. He played many concerts in New York, Philadelphia, Boston, and the beleaguered nation's capital, where Lincoln was once in the audience. He played in Portland, Maine, and Peoria, Illinois; in Harrisburg, Pennsylvania, his concert was canceled because the Confederate army was too close; Gottschalk records vividly the chaos that reigned there two weeks before the Battle of Gettysburg. He played for benefits for wounded soldiers and wrote feelingly of the tragedies of war. Of the rigors of the traveling concert artist he wrote:

> I have just finished (it is hardly two hours since I have arrived in New York) my last tour of concerts for this season. I have given eighty-five concerts in four months and a half. I have traveled fifteen thousand miles by train. At St. Louis I gave seven concerts in six days; at Chicago, five in four days. A few weeks more in this way and I would have become an idiot! Eighteen hours a day on the railroad! Arrive at seven o'clock in the evening, eat with all speed, appear at eight o'clock before the public. The last note finished, rush quickly for my luggage, and en route until next day, always to the same thing. . . . The sight of a piano sets my hair on end like the victim in the presence of the wheel on which he is about to be tortured.[21]

Finally, in April 1865, he left for California via the Isthmus of Panama. He played numerous concerts in San Francisco and the towns of northern California and Nevada. Then, in September 1865, disaster struck; it was apparently Gottschalk's enemies who seized upon the late return of two young women students to the Oakland Female Seminary after a Sunday afternoon carriage drive with Gottschalk and an acquaintance, and succeeded in blowing it up into a scandal of such menacing proportions that Gottschalk had to be smuggled secretly onto a boat bound for Panama.

He spent the remaining four years of his life in South America, concertizing and arranging huge festivals that often involved the entire resources of a community, choral and instrumental. It was Berlioz, in Europe, who had first promoted and directed this kind of mammoth musical event; Gottschalk may even have helped him with some of the rehearsals. They were very popular in South America, where the entire city felt itself involved in the excitement. It meant a tremendous amount of work for the director, of course—writing or adapting special music, supervising the copying, and then directing countless hours of rehearsals. It was during one of these mammoth festivals in Rio de Janeiro that Gottschalk collapsed. He died less than a month later.

Gottschalk's compositions have already been discussed in part. The overwhelming majority, like those of Chopin, are for piano solo. In accord with Gottschalk's needs as a concert artist in the nineteenth century, these compositions fall into three main categories. First, there are the folk-tune-based ethnic pieces, such as *Bamboula*. These distillations of folk dances and songs, in the tradition of Chopin's mazurkas and Liszt's Hungarian Rhapsodies, were always popular—as much in Europe as in America. With the Creole pieces should be included some pieces based on Spanish dances, and some of West Indian origin. A second class of compositions is the virtuoso concert pieces, or "paraphrases," consisting of medleys of operatic airs, or popular tunes that were often patriotic. *The Union*, for example, so popular during the Civil War, includes "The Star-Spangled Banner," "Hail Columbia," and, as a final tour de force, "Hail Columbia" and "Yankee Doodle" played at the same time. This seldom failed to bring down the house. A third class is the so-called salon pieces. These Gottschalk liked the least, but as a popular artist and "matinee idol" he had to write, play, and publish them. They are sentimental creations, with titles such as *The Dying Poet*. The most famous of these is *The Last Hope: Religious Meditation*. Published, it sold extremely well, and was found on many a parlor piano. Young ladies who played the piece, attending his concerts, would invariably ask Gottschalk to play it; it became almost a ritual for him to end his concerts with it, head bowed and eyes closed. (The main theme from *The Last Hope* lives on in a different guise. Almost two decades after Gottschalk's death, a Congregational minister put sacred words to it, and it has since led an independent existence as the hymn tune "Mercy.")

Gottschalk also wrote songs, a few works for multiple pianos, a small amount of chamber music, some works for piano and orchestra, two symphonies, and three operas. A great deal of the music he is known to have written cannot be found.

As a performer, Gottschalk made an indelible impression in the United States as undoubtedly our greatest nineteenth-century virtuoso. Yet he did not have an easy time of it. He had to play for an extremely varied audience, in a time of transition. Actually, he was caught between two publics, and neither was large enough for a professional concert artist to cater to exclusively. On the one hand were those so unsophisticated musically that even his most obvious crowd-pleasers were beyond them. On the other were those who thought Gottschalk's music too light—who wanted the "classics." In the realm of fine-art music, America was rapidly becoming increasingly dominated by German music. Gottschalk could play the "classics," but they were not what he did best, and he knew better than to try to build a career on performing them publicly. He saw his mission as entertaining, and on occasion consoling, his fellow human beings, individually or in assembled multitudes; this he did, by all accounts, superbly well.

After the Civil War: The Pursuit of Culture in a Time of Industrialization

After the trauma of the Civil War, the patterns of American life changed. Expansion of our physical borders was succeeded by the westward movement of a substantial portion of the population, by settlement and cultivation of the land, by the building of towns and cities, by the exploitation of natural resources, and by industrialization. The telegraph was quickly followed by the railroad in linking east and west. Great wealth began to accrue to a new class of men—the builders of a new industrial society, entrepreneurs in growing new enterprises: coal and iron mining, steelmaking, railroad building, engineering, construction, manufacturing, and the extracting and refining of petroleum.

With this new wealth came the desire to advance education and culture. Educational and cultural enterprises conceived in the earlier part of the century, which hitherto had led a struggling existence, now prospered on a scale impossible before the industrial age. Colleges and universities were founded and endowed, as were libraries and art museums. In the larger cities, the two most expensive forms of music-making—opera and the symphony orchestra—began to flourish conspicuously.

The Symphony Orchestra and Theodore Thomas

Culture, and with it "high art" and its artifacts, began to be in more demand, and in the nineteenth century there seemed only one place to go for them. Thus in this period of cultural growth our dependence on Europe increased rather than decreased. Interestingly, however, there was one area of music in which the United States, with its energy, vitality, and thirst for accomplishment, actually forged ahead of Europe: in the development of the symphony orchestra. It will be appropriate to begin our consideration of this by recounting the collaborations of two of the most able musicians here at the time of the Civil War.

In 1862, when Gottschalk returned from the West Indies to begin anew his concertizing in the United States, he invited to appear with him one of New York's leading violinists, the twenty-seven-year-old Theodore Thomas. Three years later, Thomas, who was just beginning his innovative career as a conductor, returned the favor, and Gottschalk appeared as both performer and composer on the first of a new series of "symphony soirees" with Thomas's own orchestra. The next week Gottschalk again appeared as soloist and composer in a version of *The Union* for piano and orchestra. Thus the orbits of two of America's most celebrated musicians intersected briefly. The contrast between the two men is interesting. Gottschalk, the Creole, the mercurial virtuoso, French in temperament and musical taste, sought to entertain his public. Thomas, the German, the thoroughgoing farsighted planner—convinced, like Lowell Mason, of the moral value of music—sought to elevate and educate his. Following Thomas's lead and responding to his tireless and meticulous labors, American orchestral music was to develop, through the next fifty years, along the lines of the German tradition.*

Theodore Thomas (1835–1905) was born in a small town in north Germany, where his father was a town musician (*Stadtpfeifer*). The family emigrated to America when Theodore was ten, settling in New York. The boy, already an accomplished violinist, found employment where he could, playing in theater orchestras of course, but also for dancing schools. At fifteen he set out alone on a tour of the South, giving solo recitals in hotel dining halls. He

* Of course this was not solely due to Thomas's influence; the influx of German musicians to this country in the latter half of the nineteenth century was a significant factor. The identification of orchestral music as a largely German tradition in American life persisted until well into this century; when Leopold Stokowski took over the Philadelphia Orchestra in 1912, he found that rehearsals were still being conducted in German.

would put up his own posters (billing himself as "Master T. T."), collect the money at the door, and then unpack his violin and play the concert. This episode shows the youth's boldness and initiative; in a daguerreotype of him at that age he looks the picture of complete self-possession and confidence. When he returned to New York he got a job as a leading violinist in the new German theater there. With complete candor he wrote later of himself at that period: "I played everywhere, in opera and concerts, and was very popular."

In 1860 came a singular opportunity to conduct (though not Thomas's first conducting experience, as research has shown); as is often the case, it was suddenly thrust upon him by the illness of the regular opera conductor, and Thomas stepped in, conducting at sight an opera he had never played or seen. He must have done well, for he was then and there engaged as regular conductor for the opera. The experience convinced him that this was where his life's work lay.

In 1862 he assembled the first of his own orchestras; in 1864 it was formally organized as the Theodore Thomas Orchestra, and it was to remain in virtually continual existence for twenty-four years. Although during that quarter-century Thomas also conducted the Brooklyn Philharmonic, the New York Philharmonic, and the ill-fated American Opera Company, and founded the Cincinnati Festival, his own orchestra was the main vehicle for his accomplishments. After it finally disbanded in 1888, Thomas's attention shifted to the Midwest, which was coming of age culturally. In 1889 a Chicago businessman, Charles Norman Fay, undertook to secure enough guarantors among the business community to found a permanent orchestra in that city expressly for Theodore Thomas. He was successful, and in 1891 the Chicago Symphony gave its first concert under Thomas's direction. This orchestra became the second principal vehicle for Thomas's realization of his orchestral ambition; he conducted the Chicago Symphony until his death in 1905.

Thomas worked and planned tirelessly, in the face of apathy, opposition, and calamity (the Chicago fire of 1871 nearly ruined one of his earlier ventures), to establish the symphony orchestra and its repertory firmly in American musical life. To a great extent he succeeded. His achievements were fourfold:

1. He raised the standard of orchestral playing in the United States with his uncompromising policy of hiring only the best players available, and his insistence upon thorough rehearsals and strict orchestral discipline. The Theodore Thomas Orchestra soon had an enviable reputation in Europe as well as in America; on a trip there in 1867, Thomas satisfied himself that his American orchestra was already rivaling the best orchestras in Europe.

2. He toured widely with his own orchestra. This was necessary in order for the orchestra to play enough concerts to survive, but it had benefits beyond those of offering fairly secure employment to his musicians—it gave many communities their first sight and sound of a symphony orchestra. This was seed work, inspiring musical enthusiasts in cities without orchestras to form them. The past century has seen a phenomenal growth of orchestras throughout the country. Opera (whose time may now be coming, as the signs show) could be rather accurately regarded until very recently as an immigrant. Not so the symphony orchestra; since the time of Theodore Thomas America has

been a country of orchestras, their numbers unequaled and the quality of the best ones unsurpassed.

3. By 1867 a judicious combination of summer outdoor concerts, tours, and regular concerts enabled Thomas to take the bold step of offering a full season's engagement to his musicians. Thomas lived up to his contracts, even though it meant going into debt personally on occasion. Even now, comparatively few orchestras offer full-time employment; in Thomas's day, before the advent of recordings, which now account for a large share of the income of our major orchestras, it was a monumental undertaking.

4. Thomas became famous for his meticulous programming strategy, which was designed to offer some of what the audience knew and liked while carefully introducing longer, more involved, and less familiar works; eventually he presented complete symphonies. His early programs show a carefully balanced mixture of arias, polkas, and waltzes with overtures and the movements of symphonies. The care he lavished upon the details of such programming extended even to selecting, for a given program, a piece of light dance music that had a tune similar to the theme of a symphony he was going to introduce. His programming shows a steady progression over the years, so that concerts of the later years in Chicago resemble those of today, except in their somewhat greater length. But this type of programming at the beginning of Thomas's career would have meant playing to virtually empty halls. With his uncanny skill, he *led* his audiences, which for symphony orchestra concerts were consistently large. He was uncompromising in his dedication to quality in performance, but he never believed that symphonic music was for the elite.

The subsequent history of the symphony orchestra in America shows that the seed work began to yield results even in his lifetime. In Boston, where the Theodore Thomas Orchestra had often played, Major Henry Lee Higginson founded an orchestra in 1881, saying later that "Theodore Thomas made the Boston Symphony Orchestra possible." The St. Louis Symphony was founded the same year, followed by the Pittsburgh Symphony in 1895, the Cincinnati Symphony in 1896, the Los Angeles Symphony (later to become the Los Angeles Philharmonic) in 1897, and the Philadelphia Orchestra in 1900. Today there are more than a thousand orchestras in cities throughout the United States, including not only major professional orchestras but semiprofessional, community, and college orchestras. The place of the symphony orchestra in American musical life is secure.

Black Performers and Composers

Sometime in 1876 in New York there appeared as soloist with Theodore Thomas's orchestra a Cuban violinist of African parentage, José White.[22] White was trained in Paris and was recognized in Europe as a distinguished violinist and composer. While not an American, his accomplishments, and those of others of African descent who had succeeded in Europe, could not but have been an inspiration to black musicians here. Not until quite recently has there been a general awareness of the activities of these musicians in American concert life following the Civil War. In the days of slavery the musical talent of many blacks, and the value placed upon this talent (not to say its exploitation in many cases) by whites, has been noted; many slaves as well as "free persons of color" were skilled instrumentalists. After Emancipation, the scope of their activities increased, as did the difficulties they encountered in a society that had nominally freed them while retaining, by and large, its notion that their race was inherently inferior.

The best-known of these musicians was the phenomenal Thomas Greene Bethune, known universally in his lifetime (1849–1908) as "Blind Tom." Born in slavery on a plantation near Columbus, in Harris County, Georgia, his extraordinary musical abilities were recognized when he was four by the Columbus journalist-politician James Bethune, who had purchased him in 1850. He began to be taken on tours and "exhibited" as early as 1857. After the Civil War the Bethune family continued to manage and control Tom's professional career, both in America and in Europe, and their exploitation of his talent has been documented.[23] He appeared last on the Keith Circuit, as a vaudeville attraction, in 1905. He had a phenomenal memory for both words and music; he could play long and difficult pieces after a single hearing, and recite lengthy poems and orations. It is said that he had seven hundred pieces in his repertory, any of which he could play on demand. He played works by Bach, Beethoven, Mendelssohn, Chopin, and other European composers; played improvisations and fantasies on operatic tunes and popular songs; sang and did imitations; and also composed and played his own works, which numbered at least one hundred, including another in the long line of "battle pieces," *The Battle of Manassas*, composed when he was seven. (*The Rainstorm* had been written a year earlier.)

John William Boone, known as "Blind Boone" (1864–1927), another outstanding black pianist and composer, was more fortunate than Blind Tom in having a black manager who was also a devoted friend. He wrote a great deal of brilliant and difficult piano music, some of which incorporated African-American themes.[24] The work of many other black concert artists of the nineteenth century is now becoming better known.[25]

The Issue of a "National" Music Again

The half-century between the end of the Civil War and our entry into World War I saw a great increase in both the number and the level of training and technical competence of American composers. We find that the issue of nationality and "nativism" raised by the forerunners of these later composers—men such as Heinrich, Fry, and Bristow—was not eclipsed by the increased cultivation of American music, but was raised anew in this period. Henry F. Gilbert's tastes were broad, including popular and folk music, and his inclinations were fundamentally "nativist"; Arthur Farwell worked tirelessly in behalf of his vision of a distinctly American music. Edward MacDowell, on the other hand, declared that "purely national music has no place in art," and most of the composers we are about to consider below as belonging to the Second New England School, given their Germanic training with its dedication to "universal" values, would have agreed. But the issue was raised without any simplistic taking up of positions along "battle lines." For an authentic picture, we must examine the composers themselves, and their music.

The Second New England School[26]

Boston, the hub of New England life, has always been an important cultural center, but it occupied an especially commanding position of leadership from the mid-nineteenth century to World War I. Including in its orbit Cambridge and nearby Concord, its intellectual life had already, by the time of the Civil War, been marked by the great literary and philosophical tradition that included Emerson, Hawthorne, Longfellow, Whittier, and Thoreau. Musically the ground had been cultivated by the formation of the Handel and Haydn Society in 1815; the Boston Academy of Music, founded under the aegis of Lowell Mason in 1833; and the Harvard Musical Association, established in 1837. From 1840 on, orchestral and chamber music concerts were fairly regular occurrences. In 1862 lectures in music were instituted at Harvard; in 1867 the New England Conservatory (today one of our leading music schools) was founded; and in 1881 the Boston Symphony Orchestra was formed, partly thanks to the example of Theodore Thomas. It was a time of great patrons and patronesses. The two most notable were Henry Lee Higginson, who founded and supported (for long nearly single-handedly) the Boston Symphony and built Symphony Hall for it in 1900, and Mrs. Isabella Stewart Gardner, a colorful and generous patroness who surrounded herself with a large circle of artists and musicians to whom she gave help. She provided composers with places to work and assured them performances, engaging musicians to give chamber music concerts, orchestral concerts, and even operas at her two successive palatial Boston establishments, 152 Beacon Street and the even more sumptuous Fenway Court.[27]

It is not surprising, then, that Boston should have nurtured during this fifty-year period a tradition of musical composition and a group of composers who are often (conveniently, though somewhat inaccurately) considered together as a "school." Actually, what these composers had in common was a dedication to excellence of musical craftsmanship and to the highest ideals of "serious" composition as they saw them. In both instances this meant looking to Germany, and to German teachers and composers. Many of the New England composers went to Germany to study almost as a matter of course.

Notwithstanding the stimulating cultural climate generally, it was not an easy time for American composers. To go into the music profession, especially for an educated person of some means who obviously had alternatives, was considered a dubious step. Some of the New England composers made the decision fairly late. George Chadwick, until he was twenty-one, was slated for a career in his father's business; Arthur Foote at the same age was a Harvard graduate and had not yet decided to devote himself to music. And even after they had become trained and productive composers, performances were not always easy to secure—conductors and the public generally balked at the idea of an American composer's name on the program. The battle for the American composer, joined in the 1850s by William Henry Fry and George Frederick Bristow, did not really show significant results until the third decade of this century.

The musicians of the Second New England School broke ground for the American composer, helped to establish the place of music in our colleges and universities, and left behind an impressive body of music. Because he came earliest on the scene, and was gifted with tenacity and a sense of purpose, to John Knowles Paine (1839–1906), competent and dedicated, though not the most talented composer among the New Englanders, fell the role of pioneer. Born in Portland, Maine, he was the grandson of an organ builder and the son of a bandmaster. At nineteen, Paine, already an accomplished organist, was giving subscription organ concerts to raise money for study in Europe. He soon succeeded and went to Berlin, where he studied organ and concertized, returning to the United States in 1861. In the next year he began the association with Harvard that was eventually to entail his most important life work. He was first engaged as chapel organist and choirmaster, but, convinced that music should have a regular place in the college curriculum, he offered to give a course of lectures on musical form. Against opposition he was allowed to do so—without extra remuneration and with no credit given his students towards a degree. Courses in harmony and counterpoint were subsequently added; and recognition finally came in 1873, when he was given the rank of assistant professor, and in 1875, when he received the first full professorship of music at Harvard—and the first in the United States. Thus our oldest college became also the first one to establish courses in music as a regular part of its curriculum. Eventually other colleges followed suit; Harvard's curriculum became a model, and Paine was a leader in doing for music in the colleges what Lowell Mason in the earlier part of the century had done for it in the public elementary and high schools—also in New England.

Paine was an important leader in another way, in that he began to attract serious students; among them Arthur Foote, Daniel Gregory Mason, and John Alden Carpenter became important American composers of the next two generations.

Another New England pioneer, George Chadwick (1854–1931), was brought up in a typical Yankee musical atmosphere: his father, in his spare time from his varied pursuits, taught singing-schools and organized a community chorus and orchestra. George, who had learned the piano and organ, decided at twenty-one to go into music. After some study at the New England Conservatory and a year's teaching at a college in Michigan, he went to Germany at the age of twenty-three for three years of study. Soon after his return he joined the faculty of the New England Conservatory, beginning an affiliation that was to last nearly fifty years. In 1897 he became its director, a post he occupied until his death. Among his students were many important American composers: Horatio Parker, Edward Burlingame Hill, Henry Hadley, Frederick Converse, Daniel Gregory Mason, and William Grant Still.

The range of Chadwick's compositions was broad. In addition to symphonies, choral works, and chamber music he wrote overtures with classical allusions (*Thalia, Melpomene, Adonais, Euterpe*), a symphonic ballad based on Robert Burns's *Tam o' Shanter,* serious operas (among them *Judith* and *The Padrone,* the latter on the realistic native subject of the Italian immigrant and the political boss or *padrone*),* and comic operas, of which *Tabasco* was the best known. His works exhibit qualities of exuberance, vitality, and humor, reflecting his energy and the breadth of his interests and perceptions. Perhaps his best (and best-known) work is a suite for orchestra entitled *Symphonic*

* See note 38 to this chapter.

Sketches: four separate pieces (*Jubilee, Noël, Hobgoblin, A Vagrom Ballad*) written between 1895 and 1904. With its humorous incongruities, flashes of satire, and pervading good spirits (except for an enigmatic episode of rather somber and even bitter reflection just before the end of the last piece), it is perhaps the most "American"-sounding work to come out of the New England group of composers.

Horatio Parker (1863–1919), after suddenly taking an interest in music in his teens, made such rapid progress in learning piano and organ (his mother being his first teacher) that at sixteen he was a church organist—a calling shared by many of our New England composers, as we have seen. He studied with Chadwick, and at the age of nineteen went to Germany for three years of further study. On his return he settled in New York as organist and teacher. In 1894 he became professor of music at Yale University, and from then on was active not only in New Haven (where in addition to teaching he formed the New Haven Symphony) but in New York and Philadelphia also.

He is noted chiefly today for his choral works and for two operas, the first of which, *Mona*, was produced at the Metropolitan Opera House in 1912. His best-known work is the cantata *Hora Novissima*, a setting of portions of a twelfth-century satirical poem in Latin. With this work he achieved great success, not only in this country (it was first performed in New York in 1893) but in England as well. For England, a country devoted to choral music and great choral festivals since the days of Handel, Parker wrote two more works, for the Hereford and Norwich festivals. *Hora Novissima* is still performed occasionally; it was given a Carnegie Hall performance forty-four years after its premiere, at which time, the *New York Times* critic Olin Downes described it as "irretrievably old-fashioned and genuine, glorious music."

One of the most precocious, talented, and energetic composers of this time and place was also our first prominent woman composer, Amy Marcy Beach (1867–1944)—long known by the name she herself used professionally, Mrs. H. H. A. Beach. She was composing piano pieces at the age of four, playing public recitals at seven, and performing as soloist with the Boston Symphony Orchestra before she was eighteen. Her musical training, including subjects she taught herself, was accomplished entirely in Boston. During the years of her marriage to Dr. Beach (from 1885 until his death in 1910) she concentrated on composition, writing many songs and piano pieces, as well as chamber music, choral music, and larger works that included a piano concerto, an opera, and the splendid *Gaelic Symphony* (1894). It was only after her husband's death, when she was in her early forties, that she went to Europe, to further her career both as composer and as performer. Persistent and resourceful in securing performances of her own works, she was also generous in helping young musicians, and assumed leadership in many musical organizations, including the co-founding of the American Association of Women Composers in 1926. There has been a recent revival of interest in her work, and some recordings are now available, as reference to the discography will show. Except for some rather interesting late works such as her *Five Improvisations* for piano, her musical ideas are expressed in the full-bodied Romantic language associated with, say, Brahms.

There is always a problem of whom to leave out in an introductory survey of this kind, which aims not so much at comprehensiveness as at giving the reader a sampling, and a feel for the meaning, of significant trends. Some composers who belong spiritually and stylistically to the "Boston school"—the third generation, one might say—were active until well into the twentieth century. Daniel Gregory Mason (last scion of the notable American musical dynasty founded by Lowell Mason) wrote his best-known work, *Chanticleer*, as late as 1929. But by the twenties American music had come under other influences (the German, already on the wane, had been dealt a severe blow by World War I), was moving in other directions, and had acquired a new sound.

Nevertheless, the music of the nineteenth-century New Englanders represented an important cultural flowering. That it not only was but remains a viable part of our repertory is demonstrated by the renewed interest in it shown in the number of new performances and recordings (see the Listening section following this chapter). The music of Paine, Chadwick, Parker, and others, has been dismissed as "genteel," "Germanic," and "academic"; such characterizations of its origins and its cultural milieu are now coming to matter less than the music itself. Works such as Paine's Mass in D, Chadwick's *Symphonic Sketches*, Parker's *Hora Novissima*, Beach's *Gaelic Symphony*, and Arthur Foote's E Major Suite are assets of undeniable value to American music.

Opera, an Unassimilated Alien

The symphony orchestra, as has been noted, became a fully "naturalized" American institution in this period; our orchestras achieved excellence and status, and works by American composers were a noticeable, if not large, part of their repertory. Opera, on the other hand (as distinct from the lighter form of operetta, with spoken dialogue, described in Chapter 11), could well be described throughout this period as an exotic import—an immigrant form, which few American composers were successful in cultivating, and which failed to assume any distinctively American characteristics until well into the twentieth century. Fry's and Bristow's brief successes did not establish a pattern; until 1910 performances of operas by American composers were rare. The story of opera was a story of a succession of waves of French, Italian and German operas produced here. French opera was established early in the nineteenth century in New Orleans, and was intermittently popular in New York and other major East Coast cities. Italian opera had a better reception in the East, reaching New York in its original language in 1825. It dominated opera life in the eastern cities until after the Civil War, when there was a seesawing in popularity between German opera (which had been introduced about 1850 in German) and Italian opera.

It is interesting to note that, possibly because of the popularity of English comic opera in the early nineteenth century (as noted in Chapter 10), both Italian and German opera were first introduced here in adapted versions sung in English. However, by mid-century, opera was heard almost exclusively in a foreign language, though curiously enough not necessarily in the language in which the work was written. (It will be remembered that the second production of Fry's *Leonora*, the first "grand opera" by an American, was in Italian!) This situation, odd as it seems, was probably owing to the almost exclusive reliance on imported singers at this time. During the nineteenth century, directors and companies were generally identified as either Italian or

German. So strong was the commitment to the language that the Italian companies gave German operas in Italian, and the German companies Italian operas in German. Touring companies did present opera in English outside of the large cities, but in the urban centers such performances became rare in the late nineteenth century—the few attempts to present opera in the language of its audience (a practice long established in Europe) met with failure until well into the twentieth century, when the influence of the popular musical stage began to be significant.

Opera, then as now the most expensive of all musical forms, required a degree of patronage and subsidy that tended to identify its support—and hence the form itself—with the wealthier classes. Its identity, to many, as the ultimate cultural adornment of society served to segregate it decisively from popular entertainment. There were other factors contributing to this segregation as well, of course; the following description of the perceived place of opera in American culture in the nineteenth century is an apt one:

> A combination of the unintelligibility of its texts, the complexity of its vocal style, and the unacceptability of its scenarios (which often dealt with illicit erotic love, diabolism, and mythology) conspired to isolate "grand opera" from mainstream American culture. As a result it came to be considered by many somewhat suspect entertainment for the élite.[28]

So late did the "Americanization" of opera begin, with significant performances of American operas at the Metropolitan under the new leadership of Giulio Gatti-Casazza in the second decade of the twentieth century, that it belongs in the next chapter.

MacDowell, Loeffler, Gilbert, and Griffes: Four Individual Voices Around the Turn of the Century

These four composers have little in common but the fact that each had a highly individual background and artistic stance. MacDowell was the most "expatriate"; at one time he took up what he thought would be permanent residence in Germany. Loeffler, on the other hand, was an immigrant, who was impressed with musical opportunities in his adopted country. Gilbert had broad "nativist" tastes; while Griffes, in his brief career, responded to a variety of exotic influences.

In terms of producing a composer of truly international recognition, America had its first success story in the career of Edward MacDowell (1860–1908). His native land not only accepted but encouraged him—and heaped praise upon him, often so extravagantly as to put his sensitive nature ill at ease. Practically everything that he desired to preserve was published during his lifetime, in most cases immediately after its composition; some works were published in Europe while he was still there as a young man. His music was performed by our leading orchestras. He was also recognized in Europe, especially in Germany. The changing European attitude toward American music is illustrated by the fact that a rather famous "American concert" was given at the Paris Exposition in 1889: MacDowell himself performed his own Second Piano Concerto, and the concert also included works by Paine, Foote, and Chadwick. The notion, voiced about half a century earlier, that America was nothing but a country of steam engines was beginning to fade.

MacDowell was endowed artistically with a broad range of sensitivities, abilities, and interests. With his gift for drawing, he might have become a successful artist. (He was offered what amounted to a handsome art scholarship as a young man in Paris.) He was widely read, with a particular penchant for medieval lore and poetry, and felt a lifelong affinity for the Celtic culture of his background. After his boyhood in New York City, his brief career of scarcely thirty years divides itself into three well-defined periods: a lengthy European sojourn, during which he completed his education and established a reputation as a pianist, composer, and teacher; his "Boston" period, when he concertized, wrote, and had his largest and most significant works performed; and finally, the period of his professorship at Columbia, when he seldom played in public and, although he composed steadily, produced only shorter works.

At fifteen, MacDowell went to Europe to study, first in France and then in Germany. While still in his twenties he became a successful pianist, teacher, and composer, and a protégé of the great Franz Liszt. MacDowell had virtually settled in Germany (he and his American wife, a former pupil, had bought a house in Wiesbaden) when he was persuaded to return to the United States and take an active part in our rapidly developing musical life. By the time he came back and settled in Boston in 1888 (at that time the city was enjoying a great epoch of cultural activity, as we have noted) he had spent nearly half his life in Europe. During the next eight years he concertized, composed, and had his works widely performed. After his trip to Paris to play his concerto in 1889, his reputation became even more firmly established. From this period come many songs; many solo piano pieces, including the famous *Woodland Sketches;* and some of his most important orchestral compositions, including the *Indian Suite,* published in 1897.

MacDowell's use of genuine Indian themes in this suite represents one of the earliest, and perhaps most successful, attempts to use material of this kind in a symphonic composition. The songs (of Iroquois, Chippewa, and Kiowa origin) were taken from a collection made by a young German musicologist. MacDowell altered the material somewhat, and used it on his own terms. The themes retain some of their character when first presented, but are soon absorbed and transmuted in symphonic expansion and development, a trait typical of the way indigenous musical material was treated in this period. The *Indian Suite* is one of MacDowell's strongest works, ranking with the best American orchestral music of the nineteenth century.

It might seem natural that our leading composer of the time (and as such he was generally recognized) should write music using native melodies. Actually this was somewhat untypical of MacDowell, who otherwise (except for a few piano pieces) did not make use of folk material; who declared in a lecture, "Folk-Song in Its Relation to Nationalism in Music," that "purely national music has no place in art"; and who disparaged as "childish" what he regarded as artificial "means of 'creating' a national music." MacDowell was no "nativist."

In 1896 he took what was to be a decisive and even fateful step: he accepted a newly created professorship of music at Columbia University. This meant curtailing drastically his concertizing, and to a certain extent his composing, for MacDowell was far from regarding his new duties as perfunctory. He conceived ambitious plans for instruction at the university that reflected the breadth of his own artistic concerns and were to embrace both the technical and cultural aspects of music—in other words, the curriculum of both the conservatory and the liberal arts college. As MacDowell himself expressed his aims, they were "First, to teach music scientifically and technically, with a view to training musicians who shall be competent to teach and compose. Second, to treat music historically and aesthetically as an element of liberal culture." In connection with the second aim, he laid great stress on the importance of the musician's understanding the other arts.

MacDowell took a sabbatical leave in 1902–3, touring and playing concerts in Europe and America. Returning in the fall of 1903 to Columbia, he found a new administration unsympathetic to his ideas, and he resigned early in 1904. A year later began an increasingly debilitating mental collapse; he died early in 1908.

MacDowell's legacy—five orchestral works, two piano concertos, some choral works, forty songs, four piano sonatas, and numerous short piano pieces, mostly arranged in groups—was not large or really varied. His range of expression we can now see to have been rather narrow. Perhaps his talent for art gives us a clue to his musical nature; he was fundamentally a pictorialist, and furthermore one who was most at home in miniature forms. An America still attuned to the muses of Europe called him her "greatest composer"; that he was indeed distinguished there is no doubt, but it was the last era in which a composer of his range, temperament, and inclination could have been so called.

An enduring legacy that the MacDowells left for American composers, writers, and artists is the MacDowell Colony at Peterborough, New Hampshire. In 1896 MacDowell purchased a farm there, as a summer retreat for composing. After her husband's death, Mrs. MacDowell worked to establish a center where other artists could find the same peace and freedom from interruption that he had enjoyed. The original 50-acre farm has now grown to 450 acres, with thirty-one studios where individual artists, writers, and composers may work. The MacDowell Colony, prototype of several others, is an institution well known and significant to the arts in America.

Charles Martin Loeffler (1861–1935) was born either in Berlin or in Alsace, and came to America as an accomplished violinist in 1881. He soon settled in Boston, and was second concertmaster of the Boston Symphony Orchestra for over twenty years, as well as appearing frequently as soloist. His principal contribution, however, was as a composer. Trained in composition in Europe before his arrival, he wrote a large number of works here that reflected his broad interests, especially in literature. His music reveals an awareness of Russian and especially French music of the time. Although overt "Americanism" in his music is practically confined to one movement of his *Partita for Violin and Piano,* he had a little-known but genuine enthusiasm for jazz.[29] He was self-critical, revised his works extensively, and did not release many for publication. A widely read man who was esteemed in intellectual as well as artistic circles, Loeffler was often a beneficiary of the unique patronage of Mrs. Isabella Stewart Gardner of Boston.[30] Among works of his currently available, the moody and exotic *La Mort de Tintagiles,* completed in 1897, is representative of his forward-looking harmonic language and use of orchestral color. Based on a macabre and decadent marionette play by the Belgian Symbolist poet Maurice Maeterlinck, it employs as a solo instrument the comparatively rare viola d'amore (which Loeffler characterized as "the only instrument capable of expressing the spirit and mood of the doomed").[31] His songs include many settings of French and Irish poems. Representative of his chamber music are the beautiful and somewhat programmatic *Deux Rhapsodies* for oboe, viola, and piano, which are adaptations of earlier songs.

Henry F. Gilbert (1868–1928), like Loeffler, had a broad range of tastes (they shared an interest in French literature), but Gilbert's leanings were distinctly nativist. He incorporated African-American melodies, Indian melodies, and ragtime into his compositions. Impressed with the work of the photographer Edward S. Curtis and his pioneering studies of American Indians, Gilbert transcribed phonograph recordings Curtis had collected in the field, and wrote a score, performed by an orchestra of twenty-two musicians, to accompany Curtis's photographic presentation "The Story of a Vanishing Race," which opened at Carnegie Hall in 1911. Gilbert gave full rein to his impulsive curiosity, traveling to Chicago to hear exotic music at the Columbian Exposition of 1893, and taking a freighter to Europe just to attend the premiere of the opera *Louise* by a French composer whom he admired (Gustave Charpentier). Appropriately, much of his music was published by the Wa-Wan Press, a unique publishing venture about which we shall hear more presently. Illustrative of Gilbert's interest in America's vernacular musical sources is his eleven-minute symphonic poem *The Dance in Place Congo,* composed 1906–8. The setting, the tunes, and the title are taken from George Washington Cable's 1886 articles on African-American music-making in New Orleans during the Reconstruction era. The principal tune is the one Gottschalk had also used a half-century earlier as the basis for one of his best-known piano works, *Bamboula.*[32]

Charles Tomlinson Griffes (1884–1920), in a productive period as a composer that lasted a bare thirteen years, managed to create an amazingly large body of works, many of which have increased in stature and significance with the passage of time. Griffes's brief career as a composer, which began, along with a position as director of music in a prestigious boys' school outside of New York City, in 1907, was preceded by four years of study in Berlin in both piano and composition. His early works reflected the influence of German Romanticism; later he produced some remarkable pieces that have become the prime American examples of Impressionism, including *Roman Sketches* and *The White Peacock* for piano, the latter piece well-known in its orchestral version, which Griffes himself made. It was premiered by Leopold Stokowski in 1919, and used as a ballet the same year. Toward the end of his life Griffes produced a group of "Oriental" works, including *The Pleasure-Dome of Kubla Khan,* based on the poem by Coleridge; like *The White Peacock,* this is best known in its colorful version for orchestra. That his further development as a composer might have taken him into still other realms of expression is shown by his striking Piano Sonata of 1917–18, which is forward-looking in its dissonance and its neoclassical avoidance of any programmatic associations.

Arthur Farwell, Idealistic Promoter of a Native Music

At the same time that MacDowell and the Boston classicists were at their honorable work of cultivating in America what were basically European musical forms and modes of expression, there were other musical winds stirring in the land. To understand these, it is necessary to recall a few things that had happened meanwhile on the broad musical scene. In the 1870s the Fisk Jubilee Singers (followed soon by other groups) had begun to open up a reservoir of African-American musical culture vastly different from the popular caricatures of the minstrel stage. In the 1880s American Indian music was beginning to be seriously collected and studied. On the popular musical stage at about the same time, Harrigan and Hart were presenting plays with music that dealt with a cross-section of the everyday life of the people of New York. Ragtime arrived from the Midwest in the 1890s. From 1892 to 1895 the great Czech composer Antonin Dvořák (1841–1904) was in America as director of the National Conservatory in New York. His black student Harry Thacker Burleigh (1866–1949), later to become a prominent composer, arranger, and concert singer, was a frequent visitor to his New York apartment, and repeatedly sang spirituals for him. He heard the songs of Stephen Foster; he spent summers in Iowa, where he heard Indian music. Dvořák issued what was in effect a challenge to American composers, to look to their own native music as a foundation on which to establish in America what he termed "a great and noble school of music." And there were composers of the time who were more than ready to accept this challenge. A spirit of ferment and optimism accompanied the advent of the new century, which seemed to portend a new era. One pioneer composer, writing in 1903, addressed himself to "all composers who feel the pulse of new life that marks the beginning of an era in American music," inviting them to join those workers who had been striving

> to draw out of the dawning, though widely distributed realities and possibilities of American musical life, the elements and forces necessary to form a definite movement which shall make for the untrammeled growth of a genuine Art of Music. Such an art will not be a mere echo of other lands and times, but shall have a vital meaning for us, in our circumstances, here and now. While it will take the worthier traditions of the past for its point of departure, it will derive its convincing qualities of color, form, and spirit from our nature-world and our humanity.[33]

So wrote Arthur Farwell (1872–1952), a man of his time, whose initiative, enterprise, and integrity of ideals made him a leader and a mover. Coming out of the Midwest (he was born in St. Paul, Minnesota), he was headed for a career in electrical engineering, and earned an S.B. degree from the Massachusetts Institute of Technology in 1893. However, his attention had meanwhile been turned to music. He studied in Boston, got some help and encouragement from MacDowell, and then went to Germany and France for further study. He returned in 1899, accepted a lectureship at Cornell, and at this time began the study of Indian music. In 1901, his family having resettled in Newton Center, Massachusetts, Farwell returned there, and entered upon one of the most important ventures of his life—and the most significant for American music.

Having tried unsuccessfully to get his *American Indian Melodies* published, and having met other American composers who suffered similar rejections, he resolved to try to overcome the resistance to American music, and to create for himself and other American composers an outlet for their works. What he did was to found a composers' press: the Wa-Wan Press, of Newton Center, Massachusetts, came into being late in 1901, and two publications were issued that same year, the second being Farwell's *American Indian Melodies.* (The name "Wa-Wan" is that of an Omaha Indian ceremony of peace and brotherhood.) Issues were sold by subscription, but some pieces were published separately as sheet music. The emphasis was on quality—quality not only of the music chosen but of design and typography as well. In this Farwell was inspired by the examples of such predecessors as William Blake and William Morris. A glance at the complete output of the Wa-Wan Press (reprinted in five volumes by the Arno Press and the *New York Times* in 1970), shows that it maintained exceptional standards of workmanship and appearance.

The press was in existence for ten years, during all of which time it remained Farwell's venture. His lecture tours helped to support it, since the subscriptions did not always cover the costs. After he moved to New York in 1909 to take a job as staff writer for *Musical America,* issues dwindled; the last came out in 1911. A pioneering venture was over. But during the decade of its existence it published the work of thirty-six American composers, including nine women. Indian music (set by Farwell and others) formed an important but by no means exclusive part of it. Farwell himself did most of the editorial writing—stating, restating, and amplifying the cause for which the publication stood.

The aims of the Wa-Wan Press, as Farwell set them forth, were twofold. The first was "to promote by publication and public hearings, the most progressive, characteristic, and serious works of American composers, known or unknown." This meant, by and large, the younger, more "radical" composers, who could not get publication or a hearing elsewhere. Farwell insisted on quality, however (to the best of his ability to determine it), and the adjective "serious," referring to seriousness of *intent,* was important. Like William Morris before him, whose ideals partly inspired the enterprise, he completely eschewed commercialism, being likewise aware of the extent to which it could perpetuate and surround peoples' lives with shabbiness and mediocrity. For this reason, Farwell's work has special meaning for today.

The second aim of the Wa-Wan Press, and of Farwell himself, is less easily stated, but it had to do with developing an American music more in touch with American life. "It must have an American flavor," he wrote. "It must be recognizably American, as Russian music is Russian, and French music, French." He even suggested some of the ingredients: "ragtime, Negro songs, Indian songs, Cowboy songs, and, of the utmost importance, new and daring expressions of our own composers, sound-speech previously unheard." In this he showed his full awareness of, and appreciation for, the folk and popular currents that had surfaced, as we noted, in the last quarter of the nineteenth century. He spoke out boldly against German influence in particular, and recommended as an antidote more attention to the music of France and Russia, countries that, he said in 1903, "lead the world today in musical invention." Yet he never stooped to the narrow chauvinism and wholesale condemnation indulged in by the lesser minds. "The German masterpieces are unapproachable," he wrote, adding: "All that we do toward imitating them must necessarily be weak and apologetic." Of the role of European influence generally, he made one of the fairest and most perceptive assessments:

> It was natural that as the conditions for peaceful life were being wrung, step by step, from the land, there should follow the standards and the enjoyment of European culture. During this period it was the destiny of American musical activity to perpetuate the fundamental principles of the musical aspects of that culture in the New World. This accomplished simultaneously several important things. It gave crude America a general view of the spirit and form of European music. Through its own unavoidable crudeness it cleared that music of the ultra-refinement appropriate to an alien and venerable art evolution, but without meaning for pioneers about to face the task of expressing the broader feelings of a new and vast land, innocent of culture ideals. Moreover, it secured the distribution of trained musicians throughout the land, and thus provided a tolerably complete outfit of musical machinery, ready to be set into more purposeful operation when the right time and the right controlling minds should appear.

"But," he continued, "to-day this is past history."

> The swiftly increasing group of American composers of the present generation has tasted of the regenerative sunlight flooding the wide stretches of our land, has caught glimpses of the wealth of poetic lore in the traditions of Negroes and Indians, and seen that justice must be done at last to the myriad sights and sounds of our own country. Europe will never respect America artistically, until she sees the results of this rebirth. And American composers are pressing to the mark.[34]

The Wa-Wan Press, then, was more than just a publishing venture; it was the embodiment of an ideal—an ideal held with tenacity and vision by one man above all in his time. Arthur Farwell sounded for American music the same note that Emerson, two generations earlier, had sounded for American literature: first, find your own voice, cultivate your own field; second, do not divorce art from life.

It should not disillusion us to realize that the actual music published by the Wa-Wan Press, including that of Farwell, is in general less impressive than are Farwell's optimistic and inspiring pronouncements. His ideals *were* in time fulfilled, but it took another generation. The age and the people that perceived the need were not capable, at the same time, of substantially filling that need. Like Moses, they could show the way prophetically to the promised land, but they were not destined (or equipped) to enter it.

But we are not yet done with the remarkable Arthur Farwell. Let us follow a little further his career and interests. In addition to his many other concerns, he was active as a composer throughout his adult life, as his catalog of 168 compositions, extending from 1893 to 1950, shows.[35] These cover a far broader range than compositions on Indian themes. One of his most important orchestral works was a suite made from incidental music to Lord Dunsany's fantasy-play *The Gods of the Mountain* (1928).[36] Many of his works were written for special occasions, such as music for the *Pilgrimage Play* produced at the Hollywood Bowl in 1921, and *Grail Song*, a masque for community singing, dancing, and acting (1925).

Farwell's concern with making music an active part of the lives of the great mass of the people expressed itself in many novel ideas, which his abilities as a leader and organizer enabled him to bring to fruition. While working in New York, he organized with Harry Barnhart the New York Community Chorus, which eventually grew to 800 singers. In 1916, using this chorus, he collaborated in the production of a Song and Light Festival on the shores of a lake in Central Park. The lighting effects, spectacular for their day, were described in a contemporary account:

> One-half million candle power of illumination shining through hundreds of artistic panels and huge globes gave the lake at the end of the Mall a fantastic aspect of colorful fairyland. No two of the colored panels were alike. The reflections of delicate red, blue, green and gold shades twinkled in the water, which was dotted with gray boats carrying passengers through the festival of song and light.[37]

An orchestra and the 800-voice chorus performed some standard works by Handel, Wagner, and others, but integrated with these were songs such as "Old Black Joe" and "Nearer, My God, to Thee," in which the entire assembled audience of 25,000 gathered on the opposite shore of the lake, participated. The total effect must have been truly moving. Farwell later incorporated audience participation into his *Symphonic Song on "Old Black Joe."* Interestingly enough, the Swiss-born immigrant composer Ernest Bloch (1880–1959) did the same thing in his "epic rhapsody in three parts for orchestra" entitled *America* (1927), at the final climax of which the audience is to rise and sing the anthem that the composer has included in the score. And it was Roy Harris, a pupil of Farwell's, who composed a *Folk Song Symphony* for chorus and orchestra, utilizing American folk tunes and written with the express purpose of bringing about "a cultural cooperation and understanding between the high school, college and community choruses of our cities with their symphonic orchestras."

In California, where Arthur Farwell lived and worked from 1918 to 1927, he was connected with many projects for involving people more directly with music than the conventional concert format would allow, often in an outdoor setting. While teaching at the University of California in Berkeley he wrote *California,* a masque of song, given in the Greek Theater with audience participation; later, in southern California, he was instrumental in the establishment of the Hollywood Bowl, and he wrote music for *La Primavera,* a "Community Music Drama" produced in Santa Barbara in 1920. In 1925 he organized a series of outdoor concerts in a natural amphitheater that he named The Theater of the Stars, near Big Bear Lake, in the mountains of southern California.

Arthur Farwell's music may not impress us today as being his most important contribution (though it has been unduly neglected), but many of his ideas, as he eloquently expressed them, and the example of his accomplishments, are relevant in today's world and amply repay an acquaintance.

Conclusion

The period of nearly a hundred years with which this chapter has been concerned represents a great deal of ground covered. It began in an ebullient age of expansion and democratization, of fierce and sensitive national pride—an age of artistic innocence in which Heinrich, the "Loghouse Composer," could be dubbed "the Beethoven of America." It closes on the eve of a cataclysmic war involving profound changes in the order of a world more tightly bound together—an age of closer ties with the Europe from which American composers, caught in the tensions of what Chmaj has called the "double attraction," felt compelled to seek both *guidance* and *independence.* To use Blake's pair of terms, in art we have traversed the ground from "innocence" to "experience"—from Heinrich's idyllic *The Dawning of Music in Kentucky* to the dissonant Piano Sonata of Griffes, and the realistic *The Padrone* of Chadwick.[38]

At this point we, and American music, advance not simply to a new chapter, but to a series of parallel chapters, depicting the parallel progress of tradition and innovation.

Further Reading

Musicians are listed in the order of their treatment in the chapter. Consult also entries in *The New Grove Dictionary of American Music.*

Books and Articles

Lowell Mason

Rich, Arthur L. *Lowell Mason.* Chapel Hill: University of North Carolina Press, 1946.

A. N. Johnson

Stopp, Jacklin Bolton. "A. N. Johnson, Out of Oblivion," *American Music,* vol. 3, no. 2 (Summer 1985).

George Frederick Root

Epstein, Dena. "*The Haymakers* and George F. Root." Notes to NW-234.

Anthony Philip Heinrich

Barron, David. Notes to *The Ornithological Combat of Kings,* NW-208.

Heinrich, A. P. Preface to *The Dawning of Music in Kentucky,* and a letter, both reprinted in Gilbert Chase, ed., *The American Composer Speaks.* Baton Rouge: Louisiana State University Press, 1966.

Lowens, Irving. "The Triumph of Anthony Philip Heinrich" in *Music and Musicians in Early America.* New York: W. W. Norton, 1964.

Upton, William Treat. *Anthony Philip Heinrich.* New York: AMS Press, 1967.

William Henry Fry

Chmaj, Betty. "Fry versus Dwight: American Music's Debate over Nationality," *American Music,* vol. 3, no 1 (Spring 1985).

Lowens, Irving. "William Henry Fry: American Nationalist" in *Music and Musicians in Early America* (cited above).

Fry, W. H. "Prefatory Remarks to *Leonora*" in Chase, *The American Composer Speaks* (cited above).

Upton, William Treat. *William Henry Fry: American Journalist and Composer-Critic of Music.* New York, 1954. Reprint, New York: Da Capo, 1974.

John Sullivan Dwight

Cooke, George Willis. *John Sullivan Dwight: Brook-Farmer, Editor, and Critic of Music.* Hartford, CT: Transcendental Books, 1973.

Louis Moreau Gottschalk

Gottschalk, L. M. *Notes of a Pianist.* New ed., translated and with notes by Jeanne Behrend. New York: Knopf, 1964.
One of the most perceptive and brilliant documents that we have of nineteenth-century American life as seen by a musician.

Loggins, Vernon. *Where the Word Ends: The Life of Louis Moreau Gottschalk.* Baton Rouge, Louisiana State University Press, 1958.

Lowens, Irving. "Our First Matinee Idol: Louis Moreau Gottschalk" in *Music and Musicians in Early America* (cited above).

Theodore Thomas and the symphony orchestra in America

Thomas, Theodore. *Theodore Thomas: A Musical Autobiography.* Edited by George P. Upton. 2 vols. Chicago, 1905. Reprint of vol. 1, New York: Da Capo, 1964. Complete reprint, Grosse Pointe, MI: Scholarly Press, 1974.

Shanet, Howard. *Philharmonic: A History of New York's Orchestra.* Garden City, NY: Doubleday, 1975

Thomas, Greene Bethune (Blind Tom) and other black concert artists

Keck, George, ed. *Feel the Spirit: Essays in 19th Century Afro-American Music.* Westport, CT: Greenwood, 1988.
Includes material on Blind Tom and Blind Boone, with musical examples, by Ann Sears.

Southall, Geneva Handy. *Blind Tom: The Post-Civil War Enslavement of a Black Musical Genius.* Minneapolis: Challenge Productions, 1979.

———. *The Continuing "Enslavement" of Blind Tom, the Black Pianist-Composer (1865–1887).* Minneapolis: Challenge Productions, 1983.
These are two volumes of a planned three-volume series. A note of caution must be sounded: the works are poorly edited, and the accuracy of some of the extensive documentation has been questioned.

John Knowles Paine

Jackson, Richard. "Paine & Company." Notes to NW-206.

Schmidt, John C. *The Life and Works of John Knowles Paine.* Ann Arbor, MI: UMI Research Press, 1980.

Stone, Peter Eliot. Notes to *John Knowles Paine: Mass in D,* NW-262 and 263.

George Chadwick

Ledbetter, Steven. Notes to NW-339.

Horatio Parker

Kearns, William K. *Horatio Parker: His Life, Music, and Ideas.* Metuchen, NJ: Scarecrow Press, 1988.

Arthur Foote

Foote, Arthur. *Arthur Foote: An Autobiography.* Reprint, New York: Da Capo, 1978 (with introduction by Wilma Reid Cipolla).

Edward MacDowell

Gilman, Lawrence. *Edward MacDowell: A Study.* Reprint, New York: Da Capo, 1969 (with introduction by Margery L. Morgan).

MacDowell, Edward. *Critical and Historical Essays.* Reprint, New York: Da Capo, 1969 (with introduction by Irving Lowens).

Henry F. Gilbert

Darrell, R. D. Notes to NW-228.

Charles Tomlinson Griffes

Anderson, Donna K. Notes to NW-273.

Maisel, Edward, *Charles T. Griffes: The Life of an American Composer.* Reprint, New York: Da Capo, 1972 (with introduction by Donna K. Anderson).

———. Notes to NW-310 and 311.

Arthur Farwell

Culbertson, Evelyn Davis. "Arthur Farwell's Early Efforts on Behalf of American Music, 1889–1921," *American Music,* vol. 5, no 2 (Summer 1987).

Farwell, Arthur, ed. *The Wa-Wan Press.* Newton Center, MA: 1901–11. Reprint (in 5 vols., prepared by Vera Brodsky Lawrence, with an essay by Gilbert Chase), New York: Arno Press / New York Times, 1970.
An invaluable republishing venture for American music, this incorporates Farwell's considerable editorial writing.

Farwell, Brice, ed. *A Guide to the Music of Arthur Farwell.* Briarcliff Manor, NY: Privately printed, 1972 (distributed by the author).
"A centennial commemoration prepared by his children," this guide includes a chronological list of Farwell's compositions, a list of his writings, reprints of some of his later music, various articles, and other miscellany.

On "nativism" in American Music

Chmaj, Betty E. "Fry versus Dwight: American Music's Debate over Nationality," *American Music,* vol. 3, no. 1 (Spring 1985), p. 63.

Levy, Alan Howard. "The Search for Identity in American Music, 1890–1920," *American Music,* vol. 2, no. 2 (Summer 1984), p. 70.

Zuck, Barbara A. *A History of Musical Americanism.* Ann Arbor, MI: UMI Research Press, 1980.
A general work, with much interesting information. For an extensive and equally interesting dissenting opinion on this book see the review by Victor Fell Yellin, *American Music,* vol.1, no. 1 (Spring 1983), p. 70.

Additional relevant material

Mazzola, Sandy R. "Bands and Orchestras at the World's Columbian Exposition," *American Music,* vol. 4, no. 4 (Winter 1986).

Lawrence, Vera Brodsky. *Strong on Music: The New York Music Scene in the Days of George Templeton Strong, 1836–1875*, vol. 1: *Resonances*. New York: Oxford University Press, 1988.
The first volume (up to 1850) of a three-volume history of the concert life of New York as seen through the diaries of an inveterate concertgoer.

Music

Entries are given only for earlier and less generally accessible music, or for otherwise significant editions.

George Frederick Root

The Haymakers. 1857. Dennis R. Martin, ed. Recent Researches in American Music, vols. 9 and 10. Madison, WI: A-R Editions, 1984.

Anthony Philip Heinrich

The Dawning of Music in Kentucky and *The Western Minstrel*. Philadelphia, 1820. Combined reprint, New York: Da Capo, 1972.
This bit of early Americana has to be seen to be appreciated.

Yankeedoodle in W. Thomas Marrocco and Harold Gleason, eds., *Music in America*. New York: W. W. Norton, 1964.

William Henry Fry

Two arias from *Leonora* in Marrocco and Gleason, *Music in America* (cited above).

George Frederick Bristow

Two arias from *Rip Van Winkle* in Marrocco and Gleason, *Music in America* (cited above).

Louis Moreau Gottschalk

The Piano Works of Louis Moreau Gottschalk, edited by Vera Brodsky Lawrence, with essay by Robert Offergeld. 5 vols. New York: Arno Press, 1969.
The most complete and authoritative edition.

Piano Music of Louis Moreau Gottschalk, edited by Richard Jackson. New York: Dover, 1973.
A useful collection of twenty-six pieces.

John Knowles Paine

J. K. Paine: Complete Piano Music. New York: J. C. Schmidt, 1984.

Symphony No. 1. Reprint, New York: Da Capo (Earlier American Music series), 1972.

Arthur Farwell, Henry F. Gilbert, and others

Farwell, ed., *The Wa-Wan Press* (cited above).

Listening

Composers are listed in order of their appearance in the chapter. Entries are given only for earlier and less readily available music, or for otherwise noteworthy recordings. Otherwise consult, by way of its index (W. W. Norton, 1981) the New World *Recorded Anthology of American Music* series, the earlier *Music in America* recordings (now out of print, but available in many music department libraries), and the current Schwann catalog.

George Frederick Root

The Haymakers: An Operatic Cantata, part II. NW-234.

Anthony Philip Heinrich

The Dawning of Music in Kentucky. Vanguard 71178.

The Ornithological Combat of Kings. NW-208.

Laurel Waltz. NW-257.

William Henry Fry

Overture to *Macbeth.* MIA 132.

Adieu. NW-257.

George Frederick Bristow

Arcadian Symphony. MIA 135.

Symphony No. 2. MIA 143.

Symphony in F-sharp Minor. MIA 144.

Dream Land. NW-257.

Louis Moreau Gottschalk

A wide selection of Gottschalk's music is now available on recordings. *Night in the Tropics* in a two-piano version is on NW-208, and shorter pieces are on NW-257 and NW-282.

John Knowles Paine

Mass in D. NW-262 and 263.

Symphony No. 2 in A, Op. 34 (Im Frühling). NW-350.

George Chadwick

Symphony No. 2. NW-339.

Horatio Parker

A Northern Ballad. NW-339.

Charles Tomlinson Griffes

"By a Lonely Forest Pathway." NW-247.

The Pleasure-Dome of Kubla Khan, twelve songs and three chamber works. NW-273.

Collected works for piano. NW-310 and 311.

Arthur Farwell

The Gods of the Mountain. MIA 128.

Various Indian-inspired songs, choral pieces, and piano pieces are included on NW-213, with notes by Gilbert Chase on the "Indianist" movement.

PROJECTS

1. In this chapter the nineteenth century has been identified as the age in which, for a variety of reasons, the cleavage between classical and popular music became most pronounced. Considering the phenomena of "third stream" music, "minimalism," and the current concern with "accessibility" in classical music circles, has this cleavage grown less in our time? Has it become irrelevant? Give your considered views in a brief but well-documented paper.

2. Investigate the teaching of vocal music to elementary school children in your own community today. Compare this with the opportunities for learning to sing that were available to the children of Boston, first, before Lowell Mason opened the Boston Academy of Music, and then, after the Academy was in full operation, around 1840.

3. Compare the two approaches to nature illustrated by George Frederick Root's *The Haymakers* (1857, NW-234) and Anthony Philip Heinrich's *The Ornithological Combat of Kings* (1836–56, NW 208). Which shows a more realistic view, and which a more romanticized view of nature? How does this relate to the background of the two composers? Compare also the sophistication of musical means used.

4. Describe in a paper P. T. Barnum's enterprise of bringing the Swedish singer Jenny Lind over to America for a concert tour. For a start you can refer to *Barnum's Own Story* (New York: Dover, 1961), an engrossing autobiography, even if not to be taken altogether literally. Check this against *P. T. Barnum Presents Jenny Lind: The American Tour of the Swedish Nightingale* by W. Porter Ware and Thaddeus C. Lockard, Jr. (Baton Rouge: Louisiana State University Press, 1980). A further source is Max Maretzek's *Revelations of an Opera Manager in Nineteenth-Century America* (combined reprint of two books, published in 1855–1890, New York: Dover, 1968).

5. Describe present-day parallels to the kind of showmanship mixed with musicianship that Louis Antoine Jullien displayed. For more information on Jullien, consult the article and bibliography in *The New Grove Dictionary of American Music,* and John Tasker Howard and George K. Bellows, *A Short History of Music in America* (New York: Crowell, 1972), pp. 120–21.

6. John Sullivan Dwight, a controversial music critic in nineteenth-century Boston, has been called "the keenest critical intelligence on the entire American scene" (Irving Lowens) and "the archetypal dilettante critic who does not really *hear* music at all" (Robert Offergeld). After reading Lowens's "Music and American Transcendentalism" (*Music and Musicians in Early America*), Offergeld's notes to NW-257, and Betty Chmaj's "Fry versus Dwight: American Music's Debate over Nationality" (*American Music*), as well as delving into George Willis Cooke's biography of Dwight and, if possible, into the 1968 reprint of *Dwight's Journal of Music,* write a brief paper giving your own assessment of John Sullivan Dwight, his views on music, and the relevance they may have to the question of *art* versus *entertainment* in today's world.

7. Sample the coverage given the arts in a local newspaper for a period of several weeks. Observe the proportion of space given to local artists and local live performances, as compared with space devoted to "name" artists or stars, whose work is accessible mostly through the media of records, films, or television. Write a paper on how your findings relate to the "nativist" versus "expatriate" controversy dealt with in this chapter.

8. Read Louis Moreau Gottschalk's *Notes of a Pianist,* and write a paper on any of a number of subjects suggested by this brilliant diary—e.g., "The Life of a Concert Artist in Mid-Nineteenth-Century America" or "Music in the Mining Towns of the West."

9. Try to locate, through the facilities of a large library, vol. 2 of Theodore Thomas's autobiography (*Theodore Thomas: A Musical Autobiography* [Chicago: A. C. McClurg, 1905, 2 vols.]; this interesting volume, consisting of "Concert Programmes, 1855–1905," was omitted from the 1964 reprint of the autobiography, cited in Further Reading in this chapter). Consult it to compare samplings of early, middle, and late programs during this fifty-year period; comment on the changes made, and on Thomas's own "system of programme-making" as he sets it forth.

10. Write a paper on black musicians (other than Blind Tom) who were active in American classical musical life between the Civil War and World War I. Consult, as starting point, Eileen Southern, *The Music of Black Americans.*

11. Many composers of the Second New England School, composing between 1875 and 1925, wrote programmatic pieces—pieces with extramusical associations, such as John Knowles Paine's *As You Like It* or Arthur Foote's symphonic prologue *Francesca da Rimini.* Make a survey of programmatic works written during this half-century, and summarize the kind and variety of literary influences on composers of this period. Would your results justify its designation as the "American Romantic Period"?

12. Referring to MacDowell's *Critical and Historical Essays* and other sources, summarize his views about the place of music in "liberal culture," and specifically the directions in which he wished to ultimately develop the music department at Columbia University. Include his thoughts on the relation of music to the "sister arts."

13. Write a paper on the gigantic music festivals held in nineteenth-century America, using as a prototype those produced by Patrick Gilmore in Boston in 1869 and 1872. For a start, see Howard and Bellows, *A Short History of Music in America,* pp. 137–38, and Nicolas Slonimsky, "The Plush Era in American Concert Life," in Paul Henry Lang, ed., *One Hundred Years of Music in America* (reprint, New York: Da Capo, 1984).

14. Write a short paper on Sidney Lanier, American poet and musician.

15. Write a paper on opera in nineteenth-century America, expanding on the brief treatment in this chapter, through readings in Chase, *America's Music;* Howard, *Our American Music;* Howard and Bellows, *A Short History of Music in America;* and Lang, *One Hundred Years of Music in America.* For an interesting personal account read Max Maretzek's *Revelations of an Opera Manager in Nineteenth-Century America* (cited above).

16

Traditionally Evolving Classical Music After World War I

THE last chapter concluded with a reference to the parallel progress of tradition and innovation. It is true that to the listener in the adventurous period that began in the 1920s, *all* American art music seemed new, and stirred interest and controversy. It is only from the vantage point of a later time that we can see how tradition and innovation were being cultivated simultaneously. For example, *Intégrales* by Edgar Varèse, the *Symphony for Organ and Orchestra* by Aaron Copland, and *Rhapsody in Blue* by George Gershwin were all premiered in New York in 1924–25; each was perceived as *new* music, yet each bore quite a different relationship to the current state of musical evolution. What was most readily accepted and absorbed during this period was the music that was evolving along traditional lines. Indeed, the rare phenomenon of a group of serious composers of classical music producing works that appealed to a public of considerable size (not only in the concert hall, but through the media of film, ballet, and opera) caused some to call the period of American music between the wars a "Golden Age," referring to works such as Virgil Thomson's score for the film *The Plow that Broke the Plains,* Samuel Barber's *Adagio for Strings* (originally the middle movement of his First String Quartet), Aaron Copland's score to the ballet *Billy the Kid,* or Roy Harris's Third Symphony. It is with this music, and the continuation of its lineage into the postwar era, that this chapter will be concerned. The more individualistic and less readily approachable innovations of the twentieth century will be treated in the two chapters following.

Some Background for the "Fervent Years"

In dealing with our relatively popular and accessible music since 1920 we must avoid, as Virgil Thomson once cautioned the author, the tempting use of the term "mainstream," which in any period is usually a simplistic and deceptive abstraction, but is especially inapplicable to as complex and diverse a phenomenon as twentieth-century American music. There were simultaneous countercurrents, even in the "Golden Age" itself, and dissenting opinions on the part of those who sincerely held to a more elitist view of what serious music should be. The charge of "selling out" was leveled at Copland for using cowboy tunes, and Carl Ruggles was suspicious and displeased when audiences for contemporary music concerts actually *increased,* taking it as a sign that serious art was being compromised.

But the qualities that did unmistakably characterize the period were enthusiasm, energy, and optimism. As David Owens has put it, "America was taking stock, really for the first time, of its cultural assets, and it can be said that nothing before or after in the country's aesthetic history has exhilarated it to such a degree."[1] World War I did indeed mark a kind of watershed in American music. In the peace that followed, temporary and illusory though it proved to be, exciting things happened here artistically. "It was an adventurous time," as Aaron Copland put it. For it was then that an indigenous fine-art music, the coming of which had been prophesied—and in part made possible—by so many of the pioneers we encountered in the last chapter, began to flourish. The two decades between the wars, especially, were years of ferment and change—"fervent years," as they have been called. They were years of optimism and productivity. A perhaps comparable "Americanization" had happened earlier in the more immediately responsive field of popular music, but these were the years when American "serious" composers really began to find (or make) their place in American life, and to find an audience.

Partly this was the result of the existence of a group of young musicians of considerable talent who, fairly early in their lives and at that time unknown to each other, made the irrevocable decision to become composers, and who dedicated themselves fully and knowledgeably to preparing themselves for productive careers. (Roger Sessions, born in 1896, had already decided by the time he was thirteen that he was going to be a composer; Aaron Copland, born in 1900, reached the same decision by the time he was fifteen. Virgil Thomson, born in 1896, and Roy Harris, born in 1898, each came to this point at about the age of twenty-four.) That composing hardly existed at the time as a profession in America, and that the audience for American art music was practically nonexistent, did not daunt them. They managed to acquire the preparation they needed, they found out (by ingenuity, persistence, and trial and error) how to establish themselves as professional composers, and they set about building an audience. As Roger Sessions put it:

> The striking fact is that those who aspired to genuine and serious achievement, no longer a handful of ambitious individuals who remained essentially isolated, were young Americans who had begun to learn what serious accomplishment involved. They were determined to find their way to it. Such seeking had not

occurred before in the United States, but they did not find what they sought within the then existing framework of American music life.[2]

Americans in Paris

Not finding "what they sought within the then existing framework of American music life," most did turn once more to Europe. Postwar Europe, then, was by no means without influence during this period, but it was a different Europe and a different sort of influence. It was not merely that the war and its aftermath somewhat weakened German dominance—it was also that more venturesome things, visibly, at least, were taking place elsewhere. Arthur Farwell had already noted, two decades earlier, the greater musical inventiveness of France and Russia. By the third decade of this century the Russian Revolution had created a climate that was not particularly inviting to most American composers, and that hid from Western view (until half a century later) what Russian composers themselves (those who had not already left Russia for the West) were actually doing. France was in all ways more hospitable, and France, specifically in Paris, fostered an atmosphere of fervent concern for music (and for the arts generally) that was evidenced in a burst of new music being performed (some of it written during the war years) and in new artistic movements (Dada, for example, as a rejection of artistic formalism and rationality). This ferment attracted younger composers. The young French group of *Les Six*—Darius Milhaud, Francis Poulenc, Arthur Honegger, Georges Auric, Louis Durey, and Germaine Tailleferre—in the artistic company of the older iconoclast Eric Satie, held together and motivated by the writer Jean Cocteau, was making itself heard. But there was also important music by non-French composers: Igor Stravinsky, Arnold Schoenberg, Paul Hindemith, Béla Bartók, Serge Prokofiev. Serge Koussevitzky (1874–1951), noted Russian conductor, began in 1921 in Paris the "Concerts Koussevitzky," at which many new works were performed.

And among the young émigrés American composers formed a particular contingent. In the same year that Koussevitzky began his celebrated concerts, a music school for Americans was established in the palace at Fontainebleau. Although Paul Vidal of the Paris Conservatory was the composition teacher, it was an exceptional woman in her thirties, Nadia Boulanger (1887–1979)—an organist and a teacher of harmony, counterpoint, and composition—who was destined to have the most influence on a host of American composers who came to her for instruction, guidance, and encouragement throughout the twenties and thirties. A list of these young "Americans in Paris" who studied at least for a time with Mlle. Boulanger, gaining not only perceptive criticism but the confidence to find and strike out on their own paths, would include many of the most important American composers of the past fifty years: Virgil Thomson, Aaron Copland, Walter Piston, Roy Harris, Douglas Moore, Marion Bauer, Bernard Rogers, Robert Russell Bennett, Elliott Carter, Ross Lee Finney, David Diamond, Arthur Berger, Irving Fine, Theodore Chanler, Richard Franko Goldman, and Easley Blackwood.

A European composer who became an enthusiastic adoptive American, and who was also responsible for teaching and guiding many young American composers during this period, was the Swiss-born Ernest Bloch (1880–1959), who taught in New York, Cleveland, and San Francisco between 1917 and 1930.

Americans Back Home

American composers returning from Europe in the 1920s found reasons for both pessimism and optimism. Certainly there was as yet no great audience creating a demand for the music of American composers, and many could justifiably join H. L. Mencken in condemning our tendency to shallow materialism and our lack of interest in, or understanding of, the arts. Some of the young émigrés therefore stayed away for good; but many composers did not. As Copland, with characteristic optimism, has pointed out, positive forces (mostly generated by the composers themselves) were at work, and things were happening. The International Composers' Guild and its offshoot, the League of Composers, were active, and gave concerts of new music. In 1924 Serge Koussevitzky, whose celebrated concerts in Paris had introduced many new works, was appointed conductor of the Boston Symphony, beginning a long tenure during which he not only played many new American works but was often responsible, through commissions, for their creation. From 1928 to 1931 the Copland-Sessions Concerts, a collaborative venture on the part of two of our leading composers, was also a forum for the presentation of new works. The decade before the Stock Market crash of 1929 was a time of opulence in American life, and patrons of the arts were available. In the mid-twenties the Guggenheim Memorial Foundation was established, and Aaron Copland was given the first fellowship awarded to a composer. When in 1929 the RCA Victor Company offered an unprecedented award of $25,000 for a symphonic work, the competition was such that the prize had to be split five ways. American "serious" music, it seemed, was finally under way.

In the 1920s, catching the spirit of Paris at the time, there was a preoccupation with "modernism"—the thrill of the new. These were what Claire Reis (1888–1978), an indefatigable and indispensable supporter of new music in this period, called the "crusading days." At first the "crusading" was not merely, or even especially, done on behalf of what was *American,* but on behalf of what was *new.* Virgil Thomson has identified five composer "commandos"* (note the use by both Reis and Thomson of military terms!) who were, with a camaraderie born of combat that momentarily submerged their differences, fighting to establish a "beachhead" both for American composers and for new music in general. Igor Stravinsky, the anti-Romantic Russian émigré then in Paris, was a considerable influence on the group. The "modernism" of the period was typified by such works as George Antheil's "futurist" *Airplane Sonata* or his *Ballet mécanique,* by Virgil Thomson's un-"church"-like *Sonata da chiesa,* or by such dissonant works for piano as Copland's *Piano Variations* or Sessions's Piano Sonata No. 1.

Though frequent transatlantic travel kept developments coordinated (there were Copland-Sessions concerts both in New York and in Europe, for example), many of the leading "crusaders" in fact spent most of their time in

* Aaron Copland (b. 1900), Roger Sessions (1896–1985), Roy Harris (1898–1979), Walter Piston (1894–1976), and Thomson himself (1896–1989).

the 1920s and early 30s in Europe, carrying out their parts of the campaigns from abroad. Roger Sessions was much of the time in Germany and Italy, Virgil Thomson was in Paris, and New Jersey–born George Antheil (1900–59), the self-styled "bad boy of music," wrote all of his modernist works in Berlin, Paris, and Vienna.

The 1930s brought change, with the advent of fascist dictatorships in Italy and, especially, in Germany, economic depression here, and a consequent growth of interest in left-wing, if not communist, causes and philosophies. There was an ever-increasing flow of musicians from Europe—Americans returning, and Europeans escaping, especially from Germany and Austria. "Modernism" for its own sake gave way to more serious concerns, often political and social. In leftist musical-intellectual circles, "music for the people" was almost as much a concern as it was at the same time among folk musicians (as described in Chapter 4). Of course the idea of "music for the people" was utterly without interest for some composers, and was interpreted by others in ways that varied widely. Marc Blitzstein (1905–64) produced the most enduring social-political piece of the period in his opera *The Cradle Will Rock;* Aaron Copland wrote one "agitprop" song, "Into the Streets May First!" for the Composers Collective of New York,* and never again essayed a political song.[3] Nevertheless, it is undoubtedly true that the political, social, and economic moods and events of the 1930s were in some measure responsible both for the approachability of the music of the "Golden Age" and for its concern with "Americanism."

The Drive Toward an "American" Music

Since "Americanism" (or what was referred to in the last chapter as "nativism") acquired new meaning and force in American music in the 1930s, we have reached a point where it is necessary to deal directly with a distinction that was only implied in describing what led up to this period. This is the distinction between what Barbara Zuck calls "conceptual" Americanism, which she defines as "a pro-American-music stance expressed in lectures and writings or through activities in behalf of American music," and "compositional" Americanism, defined as "the musical use of native elements."[4] It is absolutely necessary to keep this distinction in mind as we encounter the question of "Americanism." To illustrate, Heinrich and Fry, in the nineteenth century, were "conceptual" Americanists in their advocacy of American music and American composers, but were not for the most part "compositional" Americanists, since their works were hardly distinguishable in style from the works of European composers of the time. Aaron Copland has been all his life a "conceptual" Americanist; he was a "compositional" Americanist in *Billy the Kid* but not, arguably, in his *Connotations for Orchestra*. But contradiction and ambiguity lurk behind every assertion, and the question is not as simple as it may appear. For example, Copland's *Piano Variations,* of 1930, is as "abstract" and "internationalist" as anything he has written, in the sense of being innocent of any perceptible use of native musical idioms; yet the composer has said

* The song drew from Charles Seeger the good-natured but frank comment "But do you think it will ever be sung in a picket line?"

that the work came out of a concern to write music "which would be recognizably American in quality."[5]

However they might interpret the term, it was natural that composers of the time should be seeking to write music that was "recognizably American." In this they were responding to the same urges that had been expressed two and three decades earlier by Farwell, Gilbert, and others. As Roger Sessions has stated,

> The principal concern of music in the twenties was the idea of a national or "typically American" school or style and, eventually, a tradition which would draw to a focus the musical energies of our country which, as Rosenfeld once said to Aaron Copland and the author, would "affirm America."[6]

For the new generation of composers who took the business of writing music with intense seriousness, it was no longer a matter of simply incorporating folk material into compositions or using it as a basis for symphonic elaborations, although both of these practices were and still are followed, and remain valid in themselves. But, as Copland put it,

> Our concern was not with the quotable hymn or spiritual: we wanted to find a music that would speak of universal things in a vernacular of American speech rhythms. We wanted to write music on a level that left popular music far behind—music with a largeness of utterance wholly representative of the country that Whitman had envisaged.[7]

There was much experimentation in this search for "a music that would speak of universal things in a vernacular of American speech rhythms." It was natural, for example, that as earlier composers had looked to American Indian music, African-American spirituals, and minstrel tunes, composers in the third decade of the twentieth century should look to jazz, and the attendant popular music influenced by it.

The generation that preceded the young "commandos" had not all left the scene, and John Alden Carpenter (1876–1951) was one of the older composers who made use of the idioms of the "Jazz Age" in some of his works. He had studied with John Knowles Paine at Harvard before the turn of the century, but his major work was done in the period now under consideration. His "jazz pantomime" *Krazy Kat*,[8] based on the George Herriman comic-strip character, was first performed as a ballet-pantomime in New York in 1922, when Copland and others were still learning their trade. Its success led the Russian impresario Diaghilev to commission another work, *Skyscrapers*. It is subtitled "a ballet of modern American life," and its scenes alternate between depictions of "work" and "play." Produced in New York in 1926, it was something of a landmark in its treatment of modern urban life in terms of ballet.* Carpenter's music was not limited to evocations of jazz and popular music, however; like Loeffler, he had a broad range of interests. His early humorous suite for orchestra *Adventures in a Perambulator* (1914) depicts the world as seen by a

* Ballet has been the vehicle for many important musical developments in the twentieth century, including the ballet scores of Stravinsky and Ravel, and later ones by Thomson, Copland, and Sessions.

child, and his *Sea Drift* (1933) is an impressionistic symphonic piece inspired by Walt Whitman's group of sea poems of that title. His songs are an enduring part of American song repertoire. Carpenter, like his contemporary Charles Ives, combined business and art; from 1909 to 1936 he was vice president of his father's shipping firm in Chicago.

Neither Carpenter nor Ives (who will be treated in considerable detail in the next chapter) were particularly "conceptual" Americanists; both were on occasion "compositional" Americanists in their use of vernacular idioms. For the younger generation of American composers inclined to compositional Americanism (and obviously not all of them were), the choice among musical Americanisms was easy; it was the newly emerging and popular jazz that appealed to them, partly because it was American and partly because it was, at the time, new.* On Koussevitsky's suggestion the League of Composers commissioned an orchestral work from Aaron Copland. He responded with his jazz-based *Music for the Theater* in 1925, and the next year utilized jazz motifs again in his Concerto for Piano and Orchestra. George Gershwin's *Rhapsody in Blue,* Piano Concerto in F, and *An American in Paris* (the latter two commissioned by Walter Damrosch for the New York Symphony)—pieces intended for the concert hall by a composer already firmly established as a writer of popular songs and musical comedies—date from this period also. But after the 1920s, the tendency to turn to jazz as a stylistic source for American classical music waned; from then on, as jazz embarked on successive stages of expansion and development, the borrowing was more in the other direction, with jazz incorporating harmonic, melodic, and formal ideas that had been evolved in the art music of both Europe and America.

The American Composer Finds a Public

With the onset of the Depression decade before World War II, American fine-art music entered a period in which it became noticeably more functional, possibly more so than in any other period before or since. American composers had a public, and there was an actual need for their music. Copland has written:

> In all the arts the Depression had aroused a wave of sympathy for and identification with the plight of the common man. In music this was combined with the heady wine of suddenly feeling ourselves—the composers, that is—needed as never before. Previously our works had been largely self-engendered: no one asked for them; we simply wrote them out of our own need. Now, suddenly, functional music was in demand as never before in the experience of our serious composers. Motion-picture and ballet companies, radio stations and schools, film and theater producers discovered us. . . . No wonder we were pleased to find ourselves sought after and were ready to compose in a manner that would satisfy both our collaborators and ourselves.[9]

Though accused by some, as we have noted, of courting popularity—of "selling out"—many American composers responded to this new and broader

* It is interesting to note that the quest both for what was new and for what was American was not confined to Americans; many European composers were also fascinated with jazz at this time. Darius Milhaud's famous jazz-influenced ballet *La Création du monde,* for example, was presented in Paris in 1923.

public by writing works that were "compositionally" American. For a time, now that the American composer was recognized and his works were being accepted, "conceptual" Americanism was no longer an issue.

This new practical direction for American classical music tended to take the form of linking music functionally with other arts: film, dance, drama, and poetry. As an introduction to the traditionally evolving classical music after World War I, we shall consider each of these, and then turn to the more "abstract" forms of composition—the sonata, the quartet, the symphony—which also flourished and had a considerable public.

Music with Film

It is from this period, and from works written for the medium of the sound film, which was so largely an American development, that we choose the first of the works to be considered in some detail. Sound had been added to movies before 1930, and we have already encountered the rash of musicals that were rushed into production to fill the instant demand, as more and more theaters became equipped to show "talkies." After 1930 Broadway composers went in increasing numbers to Hollywood to work in films, but their contributions generally consisted of writing individual songs. The 1930s also saw the rise of the so-called symphonic film score, with lush orchestral music mostly by European composers brought up in the European symphonic-operatic tradition. These were extremely talented and facile composers; they moved to Hollywood and became specialists in the new craft, adapting their talents to the requirements of the industry and turning out many scores a year. Among them were Max Steiner (1888–1971), a Viennese composer, who arrived in Hollywood in1929; Erich Wolfgang Korngold (1897–1957), another Austrian, who came to Hollywood in 1934; and Franz Waxman (1906–67), born in Poland and trained in Berlin, who wrote his first film score in 1933.

Film scoring rapidly became a very specialized job. The relation to the film industry of those who have established themselves as composers in more or less autonomous media (symphonic and chamber music, opera) has in this country been from the beginning rather tenuous and spasmodic. Not until 1936 did one of our major composers write film music, and then it was in the field of the documentary, a genre that is independent of the pressures of the entertainment industry.

A Realistic Film of the American West

In the middle thirties, the Resettlement Administration, a United States government agency, wanted a documentary film to propagandize on behalf of its program to aid farm families driven out of drought-stricken areas—mainly the Dust Bowl of the Southwest. Pare Lorentz, a film reviewer turned filmmaker, was engaged to make this, his first movie. The result was a powerful and even dramatic documentary called *The Plow That Broke the Plains.*

The film still makes a stunning visual impact today, with its expressive footage of prairie grasslands; devastated, dust-blown farms; and hard-hit, long-suffering farm families; and its visual analogies, as for example between military tanks and mammoth harvesters, or between a collapsed tickertape machine and bleached bones on the plowed-over, denuded land.

Virgil Thomson (1896–1989), an individualistic composer and highly influential writer and critic during this entire period of our musical history, was engaged to write music for the film. The score, completed in 1936, showed what could be done by an experienced composer thoroughly acquainted with our indigenous music and able to manipulate its varied materials in an original, effective manner to emphasize the film's message. Both Thomson and Lorentz felt the rightness of "rendering landscape through the music of its people," as the composer has put it. The music therefore integrates material representative of the vastness and variety of American vernacular music, including a Calvinist psalm tune, cowboy songs (with their strong suggestions of Irish origin), African-American blues, and war songs of the early twentieth century.

The film itself, twenty-seven minutes long, is still available. Even more readily available is the music, in the form of a fifteen-minute suite for orchestra fashioned by the composer himself. The music is quite effective apart from the film (in which it is actually covered at times by the narration), and in fact John Cage has written: "Unless Muzak-inclined, one would do better to hear *The Plow* accompanied by pictures of one's own invention, which, thanks to the composer's faithfulness to those of Lorentz, may well resemble them."[10]

The "Prelude" is an austere evocation of the virgin prairie (which now exists only in the imagination—and in music like this), and it incorporates the first two phrases of the psalm tune "Old 100th" in a setting in which it manages to sound perfectly natural.

"Pastorale (Grass)" is a short movement making much of canonic imitation (in the manner of a round). The theme, related to that of the first movement, is here vaguely reminiscent in its opening notes of the Lutheran chorale tune "How Brightly Shines the Morning Star."

The two middle movements, rather symmetrically framed by the outer movements, as we shall see, are the ones in this documentary of the Plains landscape that are most clearly related to the "music of its people." "Cattle" blends in an appropriate setting reminiscences of three authentic cowboy tunes. The first one recalled is "I Ride an Old Paint," which appears in Carl Sandburg's *The American Songbag* (Example 16–1).

Example 16–1

Original a fourth lower

Thomson's version of the tune is polyrhythmic—that is, it superimposes on the waltz (or Irish jig) rhythm of the tune itself a slower, broader waltz rhythm as accompaniment (Example 16–2).

Example 16–2

This treatment is extended to the second tune as well, "The Cowboy's Lament," shown in Example 16–3 as found in Vance Randolph and Floyd Shoemaker's *Ozark Folksongs.*

Example 16–3

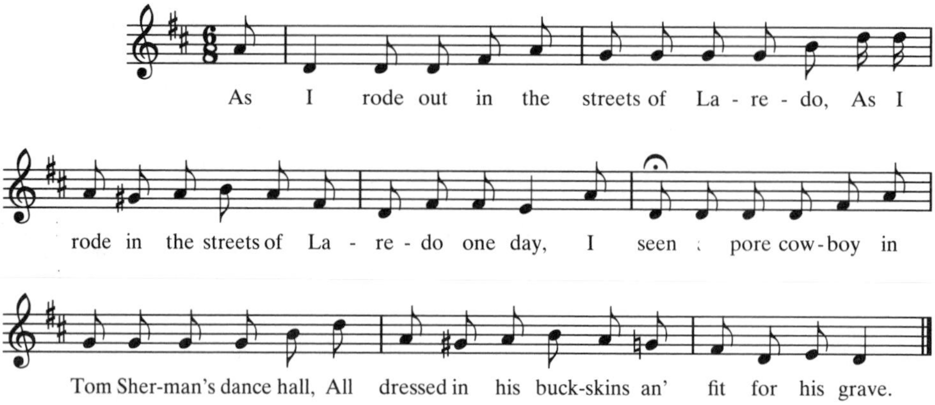

The third is a brief recollection of "Whoopee Ti Yi Yo, Git Along, Little Dogies," shown in Example 16–4 as it appears in John Lomax's *Cowboy Songs and Other Frontier Ballads,* juxtaposed with Thomson's quotation.[11] It is interesting to compare Thomson's treatment of this tune, with Copland's very different usage in *Billy the Kid* (see Example 16–8, below).

Example 16–4

Original a third lower in Lomax

The fourth movement of the suite is "Blues," appropriately conventionalized and urbanized in the style of 1920s commercial jazz, to underscore the brash and ruinous exploitation of the land. Toward the end the music becomes progressively more dissonant (it is marked "Rough and violent"), and the themes more and more incoherent, climaxed by a final jangling chord that has as its underpinning, appropriately, the diminished triad.

With singular appropriateness, "Drought," the fifth movement, is a shorter, more somber version, in the minor mode, of the "Pastorale (Grass)" canon.

The sixth and last movement "Devastation," brings back the material of the first, to complete the archlike structure. It goes on to include a complete fugue (which, in the film, is also a part of "Prelude"), and ends this documentation of "the most tragic chapter in American agriculture" with a gigantic tango on a stretched-out version of the fugue theme.

In 1937, the year after *The Plow That Broke the Plains* was finished, Thomson collaborated with Pare Lorentz on another documentary, *The River,* also for the United States government. Thomson again used folk material—this time delving into southern shape-note folk hymnody (described in Chapter 6).

Two Films About the Small Town and the Big City

In the 1930s, when a major American composer devoted attention to film music, it was most often for a documentary. In 1939 and 1940, however, Aaron Copland (who had scored one documentary, *The City,* in 1939) wrote two film scores for the "industry"—both for stories of exceptional quality by eminent American writers. The first was John Steinbeck's *Of Mice and Men,* and the second Thornton Wilder's *Our Town.*

When our established fine-art composers did work on feature films in the thirties and forties (which happened far less frequently in this country than in Europe), certain standard industry concepts—such as the "symphonic score," with its consistent reliance on rich, thick orchestral sonorities and its debt to older European styles, and the "assembly line" method whereby the composer's music is clothed in its final orchestral garb by someone else—were abandoned. Thus the collaboration of composers of independent stature on films generally had the effect of *simplifying* the music, in texture and orchestration, rather than making it more complex, and this slimming down, letting light and air into the score, managed in itself to give the music a more American character.

This is nowhere more evident than in Copland's score for *Our Town,* Thornton Wilder's play about life and death, the commonplace and the universal, dramatized in episodes in the lives of two families in a small New England town. As with the Thomson film scores, the music is more readily available in the form of an orchestral piece called simply *Our Town: Music from the Film Score.* Copland's concert version seems to lean on the movie's scenario more than does Thomson's suite from *The Plow.* Without reference to the play, it would be difficult to see the reason for ten minutes of calm, slow, elegaic music; knowing the play, and its extraordinarily deliberate pace, one is able to restage it in one's own imagination. For if the magic of Thornton Wilder's drama comes off, the calm and quiet of the commonplace gradually and subtly become the calm and quiet of the whole star-inhabited universe; and Grover's Corners, New Hampshire, is a window on that austere, lovely, lonely universe.

Quite different from the music for *Our Town* is the score Leonard Bernstein created for the Elia Kazan film *On the Waterfront* (1954). This film is about a longshoreman who is possessed of a degree of sensitivity and moral integrity that seems irreconcilably at odds with the harsh, brutal world of the waterfront in which he has always lived. The quiet opening melody, unaccompanied (one of the main themes of the score), has a spacious diatonic simplicity about it, until the introduction of the one "blue note" (a master stroke of inflection and timing) at once affects the whole feel of the music. For all the spareness of its opening, and its references to jazz (appropriate to the urban setting and the theme of alienation), it is soon apparent that this is a "symphonic film score," basically of the older vintage, with well-crafted orchestral effects and the piling of statement upon statement of its motives to build its climaxes. In its themes, and especially in their development, the score owes as much to Broadway (and to Richard Strauss and Gustav Mahler) as to jazz. Like much of Bernstein's music, it is inherently choreographic. The score has also been made into a symphonic suite.

Music with Dance

The 1930s was a vital period of new beginnings for ballet, as well as for film. It was in 1936, we recall, that George Balanchine was called upon to create the first jazz ballet sequence. (*Slaughter on 10th Avenue*) by a "serious" choreographer to go into a musical show, setting new standards for dance routines on the popular musical stage. But ballet itself began looking for new material and fresh approaches; its real "Americanization" began at this time (taking into account earlier venturesome essays, such as Diaghilev's production of *Skyscrapers,* with a score by John Alden Carpenter, in 1926). In 1937 Lincoln Kirstein commissioned for his Ballet Caravan the ballet *Filling Station,* with music by Virgil Thomson—a score consisting of twelve numbers, with copious references to popular dances (the waltz, the tango, the Big Apple) and other Americana, "all aimed," as Thomson has written, "to evoke roadside America as pop art."

Billy the Kid

The next year Kirstein again commissioned a ballet score from an American composer, and brought into being the first "western" ballet: Copland's *Billy the Kid.* A more unequivocally "American" theme could hardly be imagined. (Musical comedy did not take up the American West until five years later, with *Oklahoma!*) Kirstein himself devised the scenario, around the short career of the legendary William Bonney (1859–81).

The scenario is given in the score as follows:

> The action begins and closes on the open prairie. The central portion of the ballet concerns itself with significant moments in the life of Billy the Kid. The first scene is a street in a frontier town. Familiar figures amble by. Cowboys saunter into town, some on horseback, others with their lassoes. Some Mexican women do a Jarabe which is interrupted by a fight between two drunks. Attracted by the gathering crowd, Billy is seen for the first time as a boy of twelve with his mother.

The brawl turns ugly, guns are drawn, and in some unaccountable way, Billy's mother is killed. Without an instant's hesitation, in cold fury, Billy draws a knife from a cowhand's sheath and stabs his mother's slayers. His short but famous career had begun. In swift succession we see episodes in Billy's later life. At night, under the stars, in a quiet card game with his outlaw friends. Hunted by a posse led by his former friend Pat Garrett, Billy is pursued. A running gun battle ensues. Billy is captured. A drunken celebration takes place. Billy in prison is, of course, followed by one of Billy's legendary escapes. Tired and worn in the desert, Billy rests with his girl. (Pas de deux.) Starting from a deep sleep, he senses movement in the shadows. The posse has finally caught up with him. It is the end.

A suite was made from the ballet score, and it is more readily available than the complete work both in score and on records (though it does omit music important to the action). The following description refers to the music of the suite.

The introduction, subtitled "The Open Prairie" in the score, is an evocation of the loneliness of the vast arid plains; if the "rightness" of this music is remarkable in a composer born in Brooklyn, and, as Arthur Berger points out, a "thorough-going New Yorker," he goes on to remind us of the psychologically not-so-different solitude and aridness of the teeming city streets. This same "openness" (achieved partly through the use of bare open consonances) can be heard in many other works of Copland as well. The prologue of *Billy the Kind* also has a vast static quality about it—if it can be called a dance, it is a lean, somewhat harsh, but majestic sarabande, a huge dilation upon its rhythmic motive (Example 16–5) that dwarfs merely human figures.

Example 16–5

When human figures do appear, in the first scene, their smallness is emphasized by the slightness and fragility of the little tune given to the solo piccolo (Example 16–6).

Example 16–6

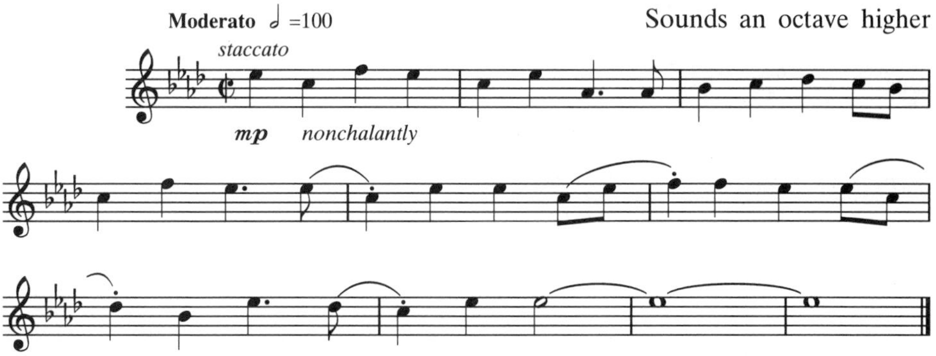

The tune is based on the folk song "Great Granddad" (Example 16–7).

Example 16–7

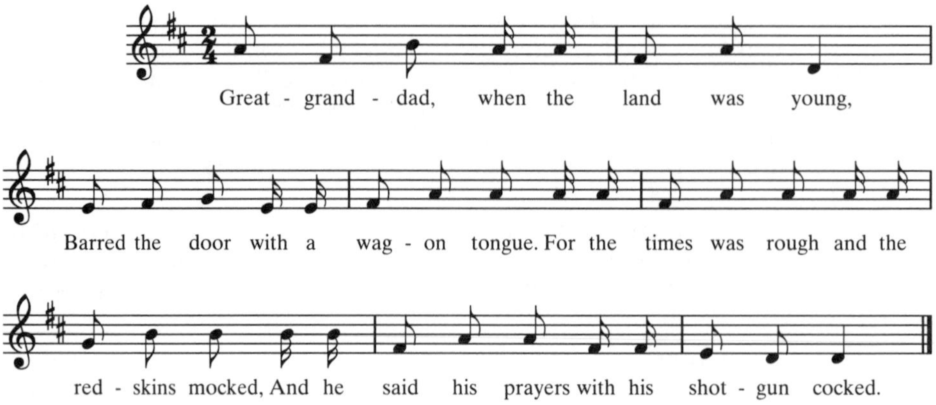

A careful comparison, however, reveals that Copland is not merely quoting: whereas the folk tune, after a promising start, goes flat in its second half, Copland's tune, using the folk tune as a point of departure, introduces changes (beginning with a simple one-note substitution to fix the weakness of the fourth bar) that keep the tune interesting to the end.

The street scene is in fact a collage of derivatives of actual cowboy tunes. There appears presently a distillation of "Git Along, Little Dogies," which alternates with phrases of "Great Granddad." The rough-edged, drunken effect is enhanced by occasional disagreements among the instruments as to what the right notes of the tune are, and by the hiccuping grace notes (Example 16–8). (This is quite different from Virgil Thomson's version of the same tune. For that, and the original cowboy song, see (Example 16–4, above.)

Example 16–8

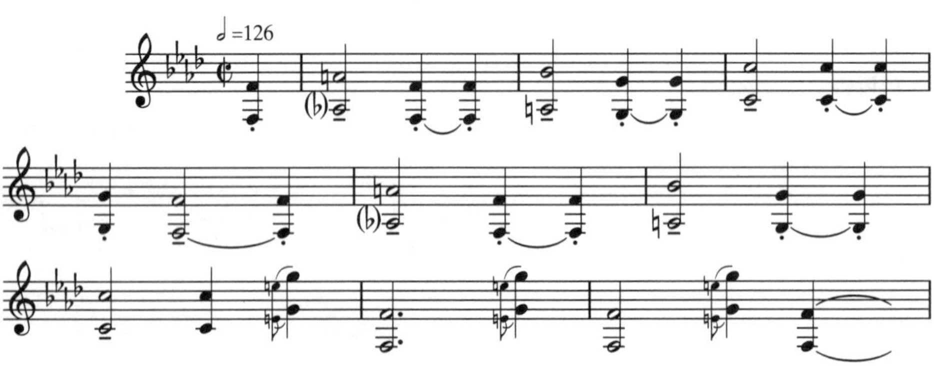

The effect of tipsy clumsiness is further engendered by the incongruous intrusion of a halting waltz rhythm, which contradicts the basically square duple meter of the simple cowboy tune so persistently as to bring the whole musical proceedings nearly to a halt. Duple meter reasserts itself strongly, however, and there appears next "The Old Chisholm Trail," with the first two lines of the song (Example 16–9) becoming Example 16–10 in the orchestra.

Example 16–9

Come a - long, boys, and lis - ten to my tale, I'll
tell you of my troub - les on the old Chis - holm trail.

Example 16–10

Soon there appears an adapted version of the verse of "Good-bye, Old Paint," and the first two tunes reappear. A raucous version of "Come Wrangle Your Bronco" appears in a giddily lurching 5/8 meter (Example 16–11).

Example 16–11

This gives way to a long variation on the familiar "Good-bye, Old Paint," beginning with the chorus portion (Example 16–12).

The next section ("at night, under the stars") is a quiet movement based on "Oh, Bury Me Not on the Lone Prairie." Except for an expressive lengthening of the stressed notes, it is very faithful to the original (Example 16–13).[12]

There follows in the suite the music for the gun battle, and then the drunken celebration scene after Billy is captured. In the latter, the garish little tune is made to sound still more tipsy by having its bass sound a half-step too high (Example 16–14).

After this extended sequence, the music of the suite omits the escape scene, the music of the lovers pas de deux in the desert, and the death of Billy at the hands of the posse, and goes directly to the recapitulation of the impressive "open prairie" music.

Billy the Kid is in a sense an American *Petrouchka,* on an appropriately simpler scale, with the detached artistic stance and even some of the same techniques of the Russian master. Like Stravinsky's masterpiece, it uses in-

Example 16–12

Example 16–13

digenous material, often in collage fashion (for crowd scenes), with expressive "distortions," all in neoclassic style. Like *Petrouchka,* Copland's *Billy* (both as ballet and as orchestral suite) has become firmly established in the repertory.

Copland followed this up four years later (1942) with another "western" ballet, *Rodeo,* a slight but attractive work for Agnes De Mille and the Ballets Russes de Monte Carlo. Another masterpiece, whose music is as well known as that of *Billy the Kid,* is Copland's ballet *Appalachian Spring,* written for Martha Graham in 1944. A pastoral ballet, focusing on a newly wedded farm couple in the Pennsylvania hill country, it is not so much a dance-drama as a dance-celebration, of spring, of love, and of life. The one folk tune used by Copland is that of the Shaker song "Simple Gifts," already quoted in Chapter 5 (Example 5–8); in the ballet score it becomes the subject of a rather elaborate set of variations.

Example 16–14

The whole question of what the composer does *with* or *for* folk material is of some interest here. With characteristic but reasoned perverseness, Oscar Wilde once turned around the old saw "Art imitates nature" by declaring that "Nature imitates art," supporting this by claiming that, for example, no one had ever really *seen* vivid sunsets until Turner began painting them. In other words, the observant, selective eye of the artist is capable of revealing beauties in nature that would escape the notice of the average eye. So it is often with the composer and folk music: his highly selective ear reveals and points up for us (sometimes by making seemingly slight but significant changes) beauty and character in folk music that may have lain fallow, or might forever have gone unnoticed by the average ear. This has been the case with both Thomson and Copland, who after Ives were our first major composers to deal successfully with folk music, revealing the beauty inherent in at least a few of its rough gems. Who would have seen, for example, what a little masterpiece was "Simple Gifts" had Copland not made so much of it in his ballet score *Appalachian Spring*? Arthur Berger, another highly literate composer, has written: "It might even be said, with a certain irony, to be sure, that Copland has had more influence on American folk music than it has had on him."[13] This is *almost* the equivalent of Wilde's dictum. If future observers cannot say that "American folk music has imitated Ives, Thomson, and Copland," at least their role in bringing it to our attention, and revealing its essence, must be taken into account.

A Circus and a Ballad in Dance Form

For further exploration of American music for the dance from this period, two other ballet scores are suggested. The first, *The Incredible Flutist,* is by another major American composer, the New Englander Walter Piston. Piston (1894–1976), another of the young "commandos" of the 1920s, was almost exclusively a composer of instrumental music. His ballet, making its appearance in May 1938—after Thomson's *Filling Station* and before Copland's *Billy the Kid*—has, by contrast, an Old World village setting, strongly suggestive of Mediterranean

Spain, and concerns the visit of a small traveling circus troupe with its wonder-working flutist, who transforms the village. An orchestral suite has been drawn from the score, which includes as its hit tune a ravishing tango in quintuple meter.

A second ballet score from the same period is an unusual one based on a popular native ballad. *Frankie and Johnny* was composed by Brooklyn-born Jerome Moross. It is based on jazz, blues, and ragtime idioms, and makes considerable use of folk tunes. An unusual feature is the use of women singers, costumed as Salvation Army workers, who interject portions of the ballad as commentary.

Musical Drama

In the last chapter we left opera still an "unassimilated alien." Its "Americanization" did not begin until the second decade of the twentieth century. When the Metropolitan Opera of New York, already the nation's leading company, acquired a new general manager in 1908—the Italian Giulio Gatti-Casazza—his enlightened idea of a proper repertory embraced a blend of the old and the new, including new operas by native composers. In 1910 he produced the first American opera that the Metropolitan, already more than a quarter of a century old, had ever performed: *The Pipe of Desire,* by Frederick Converse. Before Gatti-Casazza left in 1935 he had produced a total of sixteen American operas in twenty-seven seasons.* Noteworthy among these were *Natoma* (1911), on an American Indian theme, by Victor Herbert (well known for his musical comedies), *Mona* (1912) by Horatio Parker, *Shanewis* (1918), another Indian opera, by Charles Cadman, and *The King's Henchmen* (1927) and *Peter Ibbetson* (1931), two operas by Deems Taylor that had considerable success. Louis Gruenberg's *The Emperor Jones* (1933), as appropriate to its subject (it is based on the play by Eugene O'Neill), uses African-American musical elements, a resource Gruenberg had explored earlier in his *Daniel Jazz. Merry Mount* (1934), an opera by Howard Hanson after a story by Hawthorne, set in Puritan New England, was the last American opera of the Gatti-Casazza regime.[14]

These operas were, most of them, worthy forerunners of what was to come in the "definitive decade" of the 1930s, a decade that left innovative landmarks in the progress "toward an American opera" (to use Patrick Smith's phrase). These innovations were decidedly not happening at the Metropolitan, nor at any other major opera house. We will examine here four very different operas; one was premiered in Hartford, Connecticut, one in Boston, and one in a Broadway theater without scenery or costumes.

Four Operatic Landmarks of the 1930s

In 1934, the same year that Howard Hanson's *Merry Mount* was performed at the Met, a new opera was premiered in Hartford, Connecticut, that in at least

* The quarter-century 1910–35, under Gatti-Casazza, were the best years for American opera for the nation's highest-budgeted opera company; in the thirty-eight years following, under the next three managers, the number of American operas produced fell to a mere nine!

two respects opened up new possibilities for American opera: it dispensed with plot in the conventional sense in favor of atmosphere, achieved through a series of "imaginary but characteristic incidents," and it established a new standard for setting the American language to music on the stage. This was Virgil Thomson's *Four Saints in Three Acts.* The text is by Gertrude Stein, a formidable talent of forceful originality in the use of language.[15] The opera has been described as a "deeply fanciful work." It is set in Spain, and its principal characters are Saint Teresa and Saint Ignatius. Literal expectations must be laid aside; there are actually fifteen saints in all, in four acts, and one of the saints is represented by two singers identically dressed. The text, simply and beautifully set by Thomson so that every word can be heard and understood, often defies understanding in the literal sense. (It was Thomson's idea, daring in its day, that an all-black cast of singers could best interpret the words and music.) The work resists any sort of "interpretation"—religious, mythical, psychological, or otherwise. Yet it is more than mere playing with words and sounds; it creates its own atmosphere, and given a fair hearing, and a setting in which to work its magic (the memorable sets for the first production were of draped cellophane), it transports us into a saintly world of innocence and bliss.

It is quite a different world that we enter in George Gershwin's *Porgy and Bess,* premiered in 1935. In Charleston, South Carolina, in the early part of this century there was a crippled black beggar named Samuel Smalls who got himself around by means of a cart pulled by a goat, and thus acquired the name of Goat-Sammy. A white Charleston writer, Du Bose Heyward, wrote a short novel—his first—based on this character, whom he renamed Porgy. He set the story in Catfish Row (originally Cabbage Row), a large ancient mansion with a courtyard that had become a black tenement. By means of his knowledge of his city and its black people, he surrounded Porgy with thoroughly believable characters, and spun a tale of humor, foreboding, violence, brief joy, and desolation. The novel appeared in 1926. George Gershwin read it, liked it, and wrote to the author proposing that they collaborate in making an opera out of it. (Heyward was at the time working with his wife on a play adaptation, which was staged in 1927. The play, in turn, *nearly* became a musical produced by Al Jolson, with music by Jerome Kern.) Gershwin had many commitments at this time; after many delays, there was a period of intensive effort. Gershwin went to Charleston during the winter of 1934, and spent the summer of that year on one of the Sea Islands off its coast—composing, observing, and absorbing all he could of the atmosphere and the black people's music, with which he felt a great affinity. By August 1935 the opera was completed, and its first performance was in Boston in September of that year, with the New York opening the following month.

For those acquainted only with some of the superb songs of the opera (and who does not know "I Got Plenty o' Nothin' "; "Bess, You Is My Woman Now"; "It Ain't Necessarily So"; and, above all, "Summertime"?) the experience of the opera as a whole must come as something of a revelation. *Porgy and Bess* is a full-fledged, full-scale opera, in the realistic tradition. The story has been transformed into a tightly knit tragedy, though not without elements of joy, optimism, and especially (a thing Gershwin insisted upon) humor. The volatile central figure is Bess, around whom the action revolves.

Although Gershwin used no actual black folk music, there are touches of unmistakable realism and authenticity in the music. Among these are the complex six-voiced prayer set against a hummed drone, with which the storm scene opens and closes (this was inspired by what Gershwin heard while standing outside a black church in Hendersonville, South Carolina); almost all of the mourning scene, with its solo and response section ("Gone, gone, gone"), its spiritual-like "Overflow," and Porgy's preacher-like exhortations with their ejaculatory responses; Serena's prayer for Bess in act 2, scene 3; the fishermen's rowing song ("It takes a long pull to get there") from act 2, scene 1; the African-like drumming at the beginning of the picnic scene; and, an especially authentic touch, the street cries of act 2, scene 3 (those of the Strawberry Woman, the Honey Man, and the Crab Man).

Gershwin thoroughly immersed himself in the musical ambience of the South Carolina blacks, as we have noted—an ambience he found thoroughly compatible with his own, which is not surprising in view of the fact that the American popular music with which Gershwin grew up was based so largely on African-American musical style. Du Bose Heyward has described how, on a visit to a meeting of the Gullah blacks on a remote Carolina Sea Island, Gershwin joined wholeheartedly in the "shouting." Of his whole South Carolina experience Heyward said, "To George it was more like a homecoming than an exploration." Perhaps that accounts for the extraordinary success of this unique opera.

Because of Gershwin's identification with, and formidable success in, the world of popular music, the opera was not accepted unreservedly into the world of "grand opera." Nor was the composer himself accepted unreservedly into the world of the young avant-garde, though he certainly had his admirers among individual composers.* In recent years, *Porgy and Bess* has again met with rejection, but on other grounds—it is felt to be racially exploitative and demeaning. But the opera lives on, and continues to be produced—usually with all-black casts.

As we have noted, leftist movements in the 1930s, allied with the struggle of organized labor, attracted the support of artists and intellectuals of the time. Marc Blitzstein's opera *The Cradle Will Rock,* produced in 1937, was one of the most durable expressions of this support. Set in "Steeltown, U.S.A.," the opera is the story of the ultimately successful struggle of workers to organize. Thomson has called it a "political-tract *singspiel*"; its use of spoken dialogue does make it resemble the popular musical comedy, from which, in its day, it was distinguished chiefly by its subject matter, its use of symbolic characters (Reverend Salvation, Editor Daily, President Prexy, and the villain, Mr. Mister), and the fact that its satire, unlike that of "political" musicals such as *Of Thee I Sing,* went beyond entertainment to advocacy. Orson Welles had designed an elaborate production (in the climactic finale, the entire stage was supposed to rock!) under the auspices of the WPA Federal Theater Project. But a last-minute closing of the theater by the authorities (on account of budget cuts and not, as has generally been said, on account of the controversial nature

* Charles Martin Loeffler, for example (see the previous chapter). Copland, in his "jazz years," was often compared to Gershwin, but curiously they had little contact and, when they finally met, had little to say to each other. See Copland and Perlis, *Copland*, p. 130.

of the play) forced a dramatic change of venue; a new theater was found, and the opera had its premiere on a bare stage, without sets or costumes. In spite of its topical nature, the opera has survived and has had at least four subsequent New York productions, three of which involved Blitzstein's close friend Leonard Bernstein.[16] Blitzstein's influence on Bernstein, in works such as the latter's *Trouble in Tahiti* of 1951 and *Mass* of 1971, has been pointed out by Dietz and Gordon.[17]

Gershwin called *Porgy and Bess* a "folk opera." Douglas Moore (1893–1969) applied the same term to his radically different opera *The Devil and Daniel Webster*, although neither work incorporates actual folk music. Moore's opera, premiered in 1939, is set in New Hampshire; it is an operatic version of the fanciful short story of the same title by the Americanist writer Stephen Vincent Benét. In the climactic scene, the two protagonists of the title have a legal battle, before a jury of notorious American villains, over the soul of the farmer Jabez Stone, who is comforted and supported by his new bride, Mary. With its attractive and accessible music based on folk idioms, and its use of legendarily American settings and characters, the opera was the first of many such "Americanist" operas, including *The Jumping Frog of Calaveras County* (Lukas Foss, 1950), *The Mighty Casey* (William Schuman, 1953), *The Tender Land* (Copland, 1954), and *Susannah* (Carlisle Floyd, 1955). Douglas Moore himself continued this succession of longer and more serious operas on American characters with *The Ballad of Baby Doe* (1958) and *Carry Nation* (1966).

Opera After the 1930s

Probably the best-known American opera composer, and certainly the most successful in terms of performances, is Gian Carlo Menotti (b. 1911 in Cadegliano, Italy), who has cultivated the form for over half a century (he had written two operas by the time he was thirteen). He represents a reversal of the usual twentieth-century pattern in that he came to America to study, at the age of seventeen, and has lived mostly here ever since. Gifted with an instinct for effective popular drama, Menotti has always written his own texts. His first notable success was written in Italian—a comic opera, *Amelia al ballo*. In an English translation (as *Amelia Goes to the Ball*) it was so successful that it was performed at the Metropolitan in 1938.

One of Menotti's most-performed works is the melodrama *The Medium*, first performed at Columbia University, which had commissioned it, in 1946. That it is gripping and suspenseful theater is demonstrated by its successful run on Broadway the next year, together with its companion curtain-raiser comedy, *The Telephone*. *The Medium* is a compact thriller in two acts. Baba (also known as Madame Flora), an aging medium, holds faked séances, aided by her daughter Monica and by Toby, a mute boy whom Baba picked up as a destitute gypsy on the streets of Budapest. As the opera progresses, Baba herself falls victim to the very illusions she has peddled for so long to her clients. Finally, demoralized, tortured by fear and uncertainty, she kills Toby inadvertently. Menotti's gift for tense, realistic tragedy is further shown in *The Consul* (1950), which is set in a police state.

Menotti has always been ready to extend the media by which opera reaches the public. His early comedy *The Old Maid and the Thief*, of 1939, was written and produced as a radio opera, and in 1951 he wrote the first opera for television, *Amahl and the Night Visitors,* which has become a Christmas perennial. He has written in related forms such as the cantata (*The Death of the Bishop of Brindisi*) and the church opera (*Martin's Lie* and *The Egg*), and invented a form that he called a "madrigal-ballet" (*The Unicorn, the Gorgon, and the Manticore*). In recent years he has been interested in children's operas (*The Egg,* 1976; *The Trial of the Gypsy,* 1978; *Chip and His Dog,* 1979; *A Bride from Pluto,* 1982; *The Boy Who Grew Too Fast,* 1982). In 1958 he founded what has endured as one of the most important of today's music festivals, the Spoleto Festival of Two Worlds (shared between Spoleto, Italy, and Charleston, South Carolina), symbolizing Menotti's dual nationality, and reflecting the two greatest influences on his career and his music—the Italian love of the human voice and of effective theater, and the adventurous stimulus and enterprise of America.

In the next generation, Carlisle Floyd (b. 1926 in Latta, South Carolina) is an opera composer who, like Menotti, has written his own texts. He is more of an Americanist than Menotti, however; his most successful operas have had American settings, have been adapted from the works of American authors, or have been about prominent American figures. *Susannah* (1955), his most popular opera, transfers the Apocryphal story of Susannah and the Elders to rural Tennessee. The drama is thus played out in a setting of rural and primitive southern orthodoxy—stern, intolerant, and hypocritical. *Of Mice and Men* (1970) is a dramatically effective setting of the novel by John Steinbeck. The more recent *Willie Stark* (1981) is an adaptation of the novel *All the King's Men* by Robert Penn Warren, based on the career of the legendary Louisiana politician Huey Long.

If this chapter has devoted so much space to opera, it is because of its increasing cultivation, and the innovations that have been brought to it in the fifty years since the "definitive decade" of the 1930s. (We shall turn in Chapter 18 to some more radical innovations.) From an "unassimilated alien" it has become, at the hands of those with the talent and instinct to mold it into an expression of American speech and life, a form to be reckoned with. As a combination of vocal, musical, dramatic, and visual arts, opera is the most expensive and risky of all musical genres. But when it "comes off," as it has done in the case of many of the works cited above, it creates an overall artistic impression comparable to that of no other art form—hence its fascination for innumerable American composers (the author included). In spite of the high risks—of failure or simply of nonperformance—it has exercised an irresistible attraction. There has been scarcely a major composer, with the exception of purely instrumental composers such as Walter Piston and Roy Harris, who has not tried his hand at it. "One-or-two-opera" composers have been Aaron Copland (*The Second Hurricane,* a school play-opera, and *The Tender Land*), Roger Sessions (*The Trial of Lucullus,* and the complex and long-gestated *Montezuma*), William Schuman (*The Mighty Casey*), Samuel Barber (*Vanessa, Antony and Cleopatra*), and Gunther Schuller (*The Visitation,* after Kafka). Others have been or become more or less specialists, as were many European composers in the nineteenth century: this group includes Menotti, Floyd, Hugo Weisgall, Jack Beeson, and, more recently, Lee Hoiby, Dominick Argento, and Thomas Pasatieri.

Opera, since its "naturalization," has become not only more innovative but also more accessible in terms of production venues. The New York City Opera, since its founding in 1943 as the City Center Opera Company, has produced more American opera, including many premieres, than any other major company, though recently its emphasis has shifted to musical shows (many of which in the 1970s and 1980s have taken on some of the characteristics of opera). But more important, ultimately, than what is happening in just the few major houses is the activity at the grass roots. Community opera companies, and especially college and university opera departments and opera "workshops," have become not only laboratories for experimentation and bringing out new works, but also hosts for what amounts to a genuine American opera repertory—a repertory that would certainly include (in order of age) *Amelia Goes to the Ball* and *The Old Maid and the Thief* (Menotti), *The Devil and Daniel Webster* (Moore), *The Medium* (Menotti), *The Mother of Us All* (Thomson), *The Jumping Frog of Calaveras County* (Foss), *Amahl and the Night Visitors* (Menotti), *Trouble in Tahiti* (Bernstein), and *Susannah* (Floyd).

Music with Poetry

Music for Solo Voice

The song for a single voice with accompaniment has been an important form of musical expression since the Middle Ages. In America the art song, as it is called, has developed parallel to our vigorous popular song tradition, described in Chapter 11. The distinction is not one of quality, but of the level of sophistication. The art song is not bound by the conventions that have long dictated to popular song its form, its degree of difficulty, its subject matter, and, above all, its *approach* to that subject matter (though many of these conventions became less rigid from the time of the Beatles). Art songs have generally been written with the capabilities of the trained singer in mind; indeed, many have been written for specific singers. The accompaniment is more independent of the vocal line than in the popular song (it does not usually incorporate, or *double,* the voice part); it is more developed musically; and, most important, it is fully written out by the composer. In the case of the popular song, only the tune—and *sometimes* the harmony—is traceable to the composer; all the other aspects of a given performance as we hear it, including accompaniment, instrumentation, tempo, and even harmony, are determined by the singer and the arranger. In the art song, the composer is much more in control of every aspect of the song. Finally, the art-song composer usually works with a text that is more sophisticated and developed *as poetry;* often the works of recognized if not always major poets are set to music. Thus American composers have set verses by Walt Whitman (one of the most frequently used poets), Sara Teasdale, Vachel Lindsay, Edwin Arlington Robinson, Archibald MacLeish, E. E. Cummings, Emily Dickinson, Tennessee Williams, Mark Van Doren, Wallace Stevens, Paul Goodman, and James Agee, as well as many other English-language poets including William Blake (a great favorite), Robert Browning, Rudyard Kipling, and James Joyce. Occasionally a composer has been gifted enough to write his or her own texts successfully, but this is far less common than it is in the field of popular music.

American art song may be said to have begun in the Colonial period, when some of our earliest composers (of whom Francis Hopkinson is the best known) wrote songs, or "airs," in the English mold. In the nineteenth century the popular "parlor song" (treated at considerable length in Chapter 12), in a sentimental or melodramatic vein, was the dominant form of American song. At the very end of the nineteenth century, and during the first two decades of the twentieth, some songs were written that clearly began to transcend former limitations and to lay the foundations for a mature American art song, even though (like much American music of the time) they showed, in most cases, strong German or French influence. Among these were songs by Edward MacDowell, George Chadwick, Horatio Parker, John Alden Carpenter, Charles Wakefield Cadman, and Charles Griffes.[18] (The many songs of Charles Ives are surely very important in any consideration of American art song, but since his work as a whole belongs with an examination of musical innovation, it will be discussed in the next chapter.)

Some American songs

Songs tend to be composed in groups, most often to poems by the same author or from the same source, and less often on the same subject. From the wealth of American songs, four such groups are suggested as an introduction. The first is *Four Poems by Edwin Arlington Robinson,* a series of settings by John Duke (1899–1984) of some of the concise and sometimes cryptic verse portraits of that American poet (1869–1935). "Richard Cory" is from Robinson's *Children of the Night,* written before the turn of the century. In Duke's setting, as Ruth Friedburg has pointed out, until the climax the piano moves in an elegantly tripping rhythm (6/8), expressive of the hero's glitter and grace, while the singer, as narrator, sets forth the tale in a more pedestrian meter (2/4) appropriate to the townspeople.[19]

Richard Cory

Whenever Richard Cory went down town,
We people on the pavement looked at him:
He was a gentleman from sole to crown,
Clean favored, and imperially slim.

And he was always quietly arrayed,
And he was always human when he talked;
But still he fluttered pulses when he said,
"Good-morning," and he glittered when he walked.

And he was rich—yes, richer than a king—
And admirably schooled in every grace:
In fine, we thought that he was everything
To make us wish that we were in his place.

So on we worked, and waited for the light,
and went without the meat, and cursed the bread;
And Richard Cory, one calm summer night,
Went home and put a bullet through his head.

(An interesting reinterpretation of the *theme* of "Richard Cory," without using the actual text, is Paul Simon's song of the same title. Done in terms of contemporary pop-rock, its lyrics specify a somewhat conventionalized first-person narrator—"I work in his factory"—in a repeated chorus that blurs the sharp focus of Robinson's poem.)[20]

Others in the set of Robinson poems set by Duke are "Miniver Cheevy" (another sharply etched portrait), "Luke Havergal," and "Calvary."[21]

More terse as quick-sketch portraits are those that make up the *Eight Epitaphs* set to music by Theodore Chanler (1902–61) on texts by Walter de la Mare.[22] The last two songs, "Ann Poverty" and "Be Very Quiet Now," one only 6 measures long and the other 14, are extraordinary examples of conciseness in both words and music. The third and fourth song groups suggested as an introduction are by two major American composers: *Twelve Poems of Emily Dickinson* by Aaron Copland, and the ten *Hermit Songs,* on anonymous medieval Irish texts, by Samuel Barber.

Knoxville: Summer of 1915

In more extended compositions for a single voice and orchestra, the larger canvas demands poems of correspondingly greater length and compass. Because of the greater resources involved and the corresponding infrequency of performances, this medium is much less often used by composers. One outstanding example will suffice here—an American masterpiece that represents a rare coincidence of gifted poet and first-rate composer, each at the height of his powers. This is the hauntingly beautiful *Knoxville: Summer of 1915* by Samuel Barber, on a text by James Agee. The text, a fragment of the prologue to Agee's novel *A Death in the Family,* consists of the wonder-filled observations, through the eyes of childhood, of an uneventful summer evening. Barber, a composer noted for his lyricism, manages, in one of his greatest scores, to evoke an innocence and nostalgia that perfectly complement the text.[23]

After a brief orchestral opening, a gently rocking, singsong-like theme carries the first portion of the text (Example 16–15).

Example 16–15

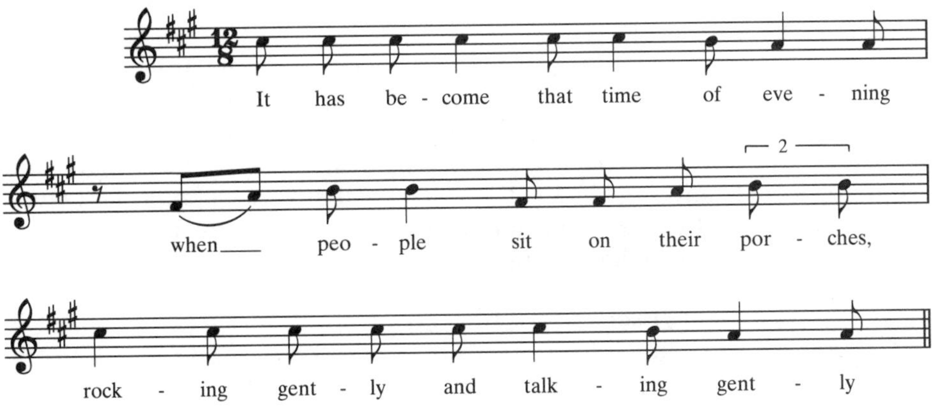

The passing of the streetcar becomes a major musical event in this setting, and a descriptive orchestral passage makes much of it. When it is past, the singer calls it forgotten; the orchestra, however, cannot forget it so easily, but mulls over the streetcar theme, ever more faintly, even after the singer has returned to the night that is "one blue dew." Upward-tending figures bring us back to the "rocking" theme once more, as our attention is drawn again to "parents on porches." The "dry and exalted noise of the locusts" is suggested fleetingly, and then there is a change of scene, to the "rough wet grass of the back yard." The woodwinds anticipate a new theme at this point—one based on a simple three-note motive that has a quality of "nothing in particular" and is repeated over and over, becoming the main building block of this section (Example 16–16).

Example 16–16

This innocent motive, stretched and intensified, carries us to the emotional climax of the work—even as an intensified and purified observation of the simple things around us leads inevitably to a realization of the untellable "sorrow of being on this earth . . . among the sounds of the night."

The benediction "May God bless my people . . ." is accompanied by a return to the music of the opening bars. Finally the rocking theme returns for the third time as the boy is taken in to be put to bed. The boy's unsatisfied quest to find out "who I am" is voiced calmly, in a high, detached *pianissimo,* whereupon the orchestra finishes softly with a final statement of the rocking theme.

Music for Chorus

As a nation we have grown up with choral singing. Psalm tunes were sung by whites and blacks both; the singing-schools early implanted among us a vigorous tradition of part-singing and fostered a native school of choral music that we are only now fully rediscovering and learning to value; the urban singing societies of the nineteenth century saw to it that the major works of the cultivated tradition were heard; the singing of the Fisk Jubilee Singers and similar groups from other black colleges started the choral singing of spirituals among blacks and whites alike, and introduced a new dimension to choral music; and by 1900 we had begun to compose our own large choral works, created mostly by New England organist-choirmaster-composers beginning with Dudley Buck (1839–1909) and including Horatio Parker (see Chapter 15), whose *Hora Novissima* (1891–92) for orchestra, chorus, and soloists has become a standard repertory work.

Two contrasting works are suggested as an introduction to American choral music of the last half-century. The first is *The Peaceable Kingdom* by

Randall Thompson, a sequence of choruses for unaccompanied mixed voices on Biblical texts from Isaiah. The title is that of a famous piece of folk art by the American painter and Quaker preacher Edward Hicks (1780–1849), illustrating the millennial text of Isaiah 11: 6–9, which begins, "The wolf also shall dwell with the lamb, and the leopard shall lie down with the kid; and the calf and the young lion and the fatling together; and a little child shall lead them." Thompson's procession of eight choruses (the verses illustrated in the painting are not actually sung in the composition it inspired) are settings of text that contrast the prophecies of woe and destruction to the wicked with the beautifully reassuring prophecies of joy to the righteous. The music shows a mastery of choral writing and exhibits a wide range of textures and devices, including the biting dissonance of "their faces shall be as flames," the quiet desolation of "the paper reeds by the brooks," the delicious word-painting of "the trees of the field shall clap their hands," and the exuberant polyphony of "as when one goeth with a pipe to come into the mountain of the Lord."

A more recent significant choral work of utterly different character is a setting by Roger Sessions of Walt Whitman's poem *When Lilacs Last in the Dooryard Bloom'd.* Described as a cantata for soprano, contralto, baritone, mixed chorus, and orchestra, it was commissioned by the University of California and completed in 1970.[24] Whitman's poem is a dirge on the death of Lincoln. The cantata is thus both a comment on the death of public figures (it is inscribed "To the memory of Martin Luther King, Jr., and Robert F. Kennedy") and, more broadly, a commentary on death itself.

Sessions shortened the long poem by only a dozen lines or so, and arranged its sixteen irregular-length stanzas into three parts. The first four stanzas form a kind of prologue, introducing Whitman's "trinity" of "Lilac blooming perennial and drooping star in the west,/ And thought of him I love." It also introduces the symbol of the mourning bird—a symbol Whitman had earlier used so effectively in his *Out of the Cradle Endlessly Rocking.* The second section describes the procession of the coffin, and the tribute of the poet: the sprig of lilac, the perfume ("sea-winds") for the grave, and the pictures—broad Whitmanesque scenes with people—to adorn the burial-house. The third section is the bird's carol of death ("dark mother," "strong deliveress"), Whitman's retrospective view of a Civil War battlefield, and a final passing beyond and leave-taking.

As would be expected in a dirge, the colors are basically somber, and the underlying movement, despite occasional rapid coloratura figuration, is slow-paced. A certain repeated "lamenting" rhythmic figure (occurring at the opening and in all sections) is prominent (Example 16–17).

Example 16–17

Also noteworthy, as a kind of associational word-painting, is the call of the bird (the hermit-thrush), shown in Example 16–18.

Roger Sessions was, of all the "commandos" of that generation, the least

Example 16–18

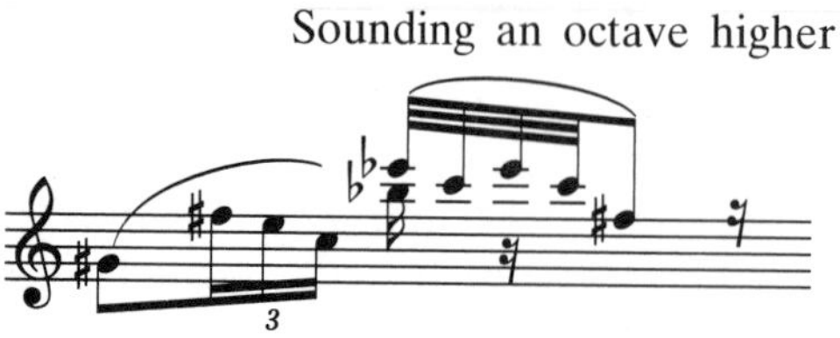

Roger Sessions, *When Lilacs Last in the Dooryard Bloomed.* Copyright © 1974 Merion Music, Inc. Used by permission.

inclined to "compositional Americanism." His musical language in this work, as elsewhere, tends to be complex and dissonant, but it is a complexity and dissonance arrived at with the most purposeful care.

Music Independent of Film, Dance, Drama, or Poetry

In the associative music we have examined so far, music is linked with one or more of the other arts. But the American classical music that has evolved along traditional lines since the 1920s has also embraced a great deal of so-called absolute music, independent of text or of any visual or dramatic component. Here compositional Americanism can still be found, as in Virgil Thomson's *Symphony on a Hymn Tune,* or the *Folk Song Symphony* of Roy Harris—the latter a conscious attempt to write "useful" music, as on occasion Harris's early mentor Arthur Farwell did. But for the most part the nativism, where it is deemed to exist, is more a matter of subjective feeling. It is difficult to support with analysis how or to what extent an instrumental piece "affirms America," or in what way it announces that it could have been written nowhere else. Nevertheless, it cannot be denied that we do make these judgments, which are often supported with a surprising consensus. In the rest of this chapter we shall sample some of the traditional repertoire of American "abstract" music composed since the 1920s.

Music for Solo Piano

We begin with three sets of short piano pieces by George Gershwin, Aaron Copland, and Samuel Barber. All three sets relate to American popular idioms, but show an interesting gradation in their progressively more subtle degrees of compositional Americanism.

Gershwin: Preludes for piano

George Gershwin composed five piano Preludes in 1926, to be played by himself as part of a concert (later taken on tour) with the Peruvian singer Marguerite d'Alvarez, who sang Gershwin's songs with the composer himself at the piano. Of the five, three were published the next year[25]—two bright movements, both marked "Allegro ben ritmato e deciso," flanking a central blues-like "Andante con moto e poco rubato," the best-known of the three. The first Prelude uses the jazz-Latin rhythm of the Charleston (very close to a speeded-up tango) with variants (Example 16–19). The catchy asymmetry of its rhythms is matched by simultaneous cross-relations in the chords (e.g., A-natural against A-flat), which constitute realizations in piano terms of the blue notes of the scale.

Example 16–19

The second Prelude is a blues with a piano texture akin to that of a Chopin nocturne. The accompaniment of the first and last sections uses a familiar Gershwinesque chromatic undulation, which seems to bespeak the combined influence of African-American and Jewish musical mannerisms, expressed here as the continuous vacillation between major and minor.

The third Prelude, "well-rhythmed and decisive," is somewhat closer to Broadway, and might be characterized as up-tempo ragtime—including pianistic "breaks"—interpreted with Gershwin's unique harmonic and melodic sense.

Copland: *Four Piano Blues*

The first of Copland's *Four Piano Blues*[26] (written in 1947) is almost a meditation on the theme of Gershwin's second Prelude. Marked "freely poetic," it is spare music, its blues harmonies transmuted, and its apparently free "rubato" is, in fact, immutably fixed in measures of 5/8, 7/8, and 8/8. The second, "soft and languid," dates from 1934. It is sophisticated play, with piquant poly-harmonies (in the first section) against stylized blues sonorities. The second section (marked "graceful, flowing") introduces a theme somewhat more French than bluesy, which Copland wittily combines with the opening material in the last section. The third piece (1948), marked "muted and sensuous," is a play of sonorities and lines, its rubato and improvisatory nuances again fixed in carefully notated rhythm, as in the opening bars and in the 7/8 measures. The last of the group is the earliest (1926). Marked "with bounce," it has an infectious lilt in its syncopation, and its seemingly impulsive stops and starts are carefully calculated.

Barber: *Excursions for the Piano*

On the flyleaf of Samuel Barber's *Excursions for the Piano,*[27] written in 1945, appears the following note: "These are 'Excursions' in small classical forms into regional American idioms. Their rhythmic characteristics, as well as their source in folk material and their scoring, reminiscent of local instruments, are easily recognized."

They each capture the features of their respective "regional American idioms" with an unerring ear, yet maintain, in their elegance, an aesthetic distance from their "subjects" that is even greater than in the Copland pieces. The first is an excursion into the realm of boogie-woogie in a small rondo form (*abaca,* with the returns defined chiefly in terms of tonality). The second is a slow, restrained blues, in four variations on the classic 12-bar form (with some extensions and contractions). The third evokes a cowboy ballad sung to a "guitar" accompaniment, and is a set of twelve variations on a 4-bar *ground,* with interspersed "vamp" sections as prelude, interlude, and postlude. (It is actually quite reminiscent of the *diferencias* of Renaissance Spain, cradle of the classical guitar and its literature.) The fourth is an excursion into the realm of the hoedown—a lively evocation of fiddle and banjo figuration. It is interesting to compare this with Louis Moreau Gottschalk's *The Banjo,* a similarly polished "translation" of banjo idioms into a piece for the concert hall a century earlier.

The piano sonata

In addition to writing small pieces for piano, American composers have not been reluctant to essay the large gesture as well—the serious work of extended proportions that, out of an intense awareness of tradition, is still most often given the name *sonata.* Thus we have piano sonatas by, among others, Samuel Barber, Ernest Bloch, Elliott Carter, Aaron Copland, Charles Tomlinson Griffes (although Griffes died in 1920, his piano sonata, one of his last works, belongs to the mature period of this chapter), Leon Kirchner, Peter Mennin, Roger Sessions, and Virgil Thomson. It is significant that with the exception of Sessions (who has written three) and Thomson (who has written four short ones) these composers have, to date, written only one piano sonata apiece; presumably, having once fought their way through to say what they had to say in this monochromatic and somewhat recalcitrant medium, they have been disinclined to return to it, whereas the composition of a string quartet or a symphony has usually proved to be habit-forming.

Chamber Music: The String Quartet

The string quartet acquired at the hands of Joseph Haydn (who wrote over sixty quartets) in the mature classic period a prestige that it has never since lost. The "commando" generation of American composers began to work in the string quartet medium as early as the 1920s, Howard Hanson writing his quartet in 1923,Roy Harris his first two before 1930, and Aaron Copland his *Two Pieces for String Quartet* in 1928. The 1930s saw the production of two quartets by Virgil Thomson, one by Samuel Barber, a third by Roy Harris, two by Walter Piston, one by Roger Sessions, and three by William Schuman. Since then the string quartet has been cultivated, not often, but with particular care, by nearly every important American composer. Of the eldest generation, Wallingford Riegger, Roger Sessions, and Walter Piston continued to write them; of the next-to-eldest, Ross Lee Finney, Elliott Carter, William Schuman, David Diamond, and Leon Kirchner; and of the composers born in the 1920s,

Lukas Foss, Peter Mennin, Andrew Imbrie, and Gunther Schuller, among others.

The newcomer to the string quartet might wish to begin his or her acquaintance with its less intensely serious side—through the pleasantly soporific eleven-minute *Lullaby* of George Gershwin (written about 1920, but not performed in its original form until nearly half a century later) or the graceful four-minute waltz that is the second movement of Virgil Thomson's String Quartet No. 2, composed in 1932.[28] The entire four-movement Thomson work is a clear, melodious, and unproblematic neoclassical / romantic quartet, with long arches of singing lines.

Schuman: String Quartet No. 3

A serious and energetic American quartet from the late 1930s is William Schuman's String Quartet No. 3 (1939).[29] This twenty-three-minute three-movement work illustrates two potent influences at work in tradition-oriented American music of the time—classicism and Americanism. The classical (or neoclassical) bent is shown in Schuman's choice of eighteenth-century forms—a double fugue in the first movement, and in the last movement a combination of two of the most prevalent formal procedures of classicism, the rondo and the variation. It is American in its rhythmic momentum and drive—a forceful, determined, and sometimes frenetic energy that seems very much in keeping with its New York City genesis.*

Yet another Americanism can be heard in the pitch relations, which show, both melodically and harmonically, a consistent preoccupation (not necessarily conscious) with the tension between the major and minor triad. This can be heard melodically in the principal fugue theme in the first movement (Example 16–20), in the secondary fugue theme (which is actually developed first) (Example 16–21), and in the principal theme of the third movement (Example 16–22). It appears harmonically at a climactic point in the first movement introduction (Example 16–23).

Example 16–20

* The same hard-driving rhythmic vigor can be heard in the Quartet No. 2, from 1951, by another New Yorker, Peter Mennin. Both Mennin and Schuman were, in addition to being gifted musically, highly efficient and well-organized men, who made their way rapidly to the top. It is hard to imagine this kind of rhythmically high-pressured music being composed by anyone who had not succeeded superbly in the high-pressure milieu of the "world music center," New York City.

Example 16–21

Example 16–22

Example 16–23

We can only speculate as to whether there is any relationship, conscious or unconscious, between this characteristically American ambiguity or tension about the major/minor third and its undeniable presence in American blues,* but it is a trait found not infrequently in our more conservative twentieth-century music. We shall presently encounter it again in the music of Roy Harris; perhaps it is significant that Schuman studied with Harris during the 1930s.

Chamber Music for Winds

With the advent of the new era in music that began in the 1920s, the wind instruments assumed a more important role in chamber music. This may have been due partly to the influence of French music—the French had cultivated the woodwinds with special care for more than a century, and the new generation of French composers, influenced some of the time by American jazz, were writing music that featured winds.

It is also true that the wind instruments, with their "cooler," more objective sound, their capacity for expressing both the sardonic and the whimsical, and their suitability to the "light touch," accorded well with the musical aesthetics of the age and the sounds of the new neoclassicism. This movement rejected the emotional involvement, the profound seriousness, and the complex chromaticism and "expressiveness" of post-romanticism (as exemplified

* See Chapter 2, Example 2–3.

by composers like Gustav Mahler, Richard Strauss, and Arnold Schoenberg) in favor of a more detached stance, tending toward the ironical, and a return to classical and contrapuntal forms and the diatonic scale (without renouncing dissonance). This new stance and this new sound, relying heavily on wind instruments, were epitomized by Igor Stravinsky's very influential Octet for flute, clarinet, two bassoons, two trumpets, and two trombones, written in 1923. Virgil Thomson produced an American neoclassical work (or "neo-baroque," as he has called it) in his *Sonata da chiesa* of 1926, written and first performed in Paris. Instrumentally it involves a quintet of seemingly disparate instruments (significantly including only one member of the string family): a viola, a small clarinet (in E-flat), a small trumpet (in D), a French horn, and a trombone. A "church sonata" that includes not only a chorale and a double fugue but also a tango, it does indeed, as its composer has said, make "funny noises."

We now examine two contrasting works for wind instruments from the 1950s—works that demonstrate yet again the variety of styles and sounds that existed even within what we have chosen to call the "traditionally evolving classical music" of the period. The first is representative of the conservative, neoromantic strain; the second is a blend of the neoclassical with some of the procedures of the American avant-garde of the time.

Barber: *Summer Music*

The standard "woodwind quintet" consists of flute, oboe, clarinet, bassoon, and one brass instrument, the French horn. This combination was first used in Europe at the end of the eighteenth century, but it has really come into its own, with significant repertory being written for it, in the twentieth. American composers in particular have been attracted to it.

Samuel Barber's *Summer Music* for woodwind quintet[30] (first performed in 1956) consists of a single uninterrupted movement. It evokes the feeling of summer with an opening marked "Slow and indolent" (Example 16–24).

Example 16–24

The first half of the piece is in the form of an arch, which moves, in contrasting tempos and themes, from the initial "Slow and indolent" through "A little motion," with its languidly graceful theme (Example 16–25), to "Faster," with its rhythmic chords (Example 16–26), to "Lively, still faster," with its light, rapid chattering (Example 16–27), and then, by reverse progression, back to "Slow and indolent" again.

Example 16–25

Example 16–26

Example 16–27

The second half concerns itself mainly with a theme of relaxed gaiety, which jogs along pleasantly in a vaguely ragtimey way (Example 16–28) and which reminds us of Barber's facility for subtle allusion, demonstrated in the earlier *Excursions for the Piano.*

Example 16–28

There are two more brief suggestions of the slowness and indolence of the opening, and an intense and sweeping interlude marked "Joyous and flowing"; and the work ends with the bassoon toying playfully once more with the little ragtime theme.

Riegger: Concerto for Piano and Woodwind Quintet

A return to the domain of neoclassicism is represented by the austere but impressive Concerto for Piano and Woodwind Quintet by Wallingford Riegger, composed in 1953.[31] The seeming austerity of the work can be attributed to its lean texture, its dissonance (consistently avoiding consonant triads and lush sonorities), its wide melodic intervals (the diminished octave is prominent), the rhythmic abruptness of some of the themes, and, finally, the wide spacings that often occur between the instruments, emphasizing the disparity of their tone colors (the piccolo, for example, is answered by the bassoon in an imitative passage in the first movement).

It is a piece firm in its musical logic, and of great power. For all of its craggy and forbidding visage on first acquaintance, it is a highly expressive piece once one is familiar with its materials and accepts its premises. It is one of the most original chamber works for winds by any American composer.

The work is in three movements. In the first, the main theme is announced at once by the piano alone (Example 16–29); its doubling by the left hand two octaves away gives it a hollow, arresting color.

Example 16–29

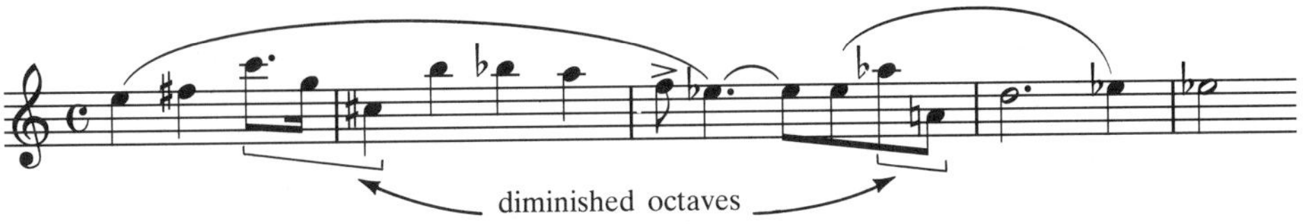

This fourteen-note theme contains all twelve tones of the octave, with two duplications. In this regard it resembles the musical materials used in the twelve-tone serial technique, a compositional technique in which the musical pitches must always appear in a prescribed serial order, according to various series that are derived from a prototypical original "row" of tones, which remains the same for an entire composition. This technique was developed by the great Viennese composer and teacher Arnold Schoenberg, who came to this country in 1933, and taught and composed here (mostly in Los Angeles) until his death in 1951. Schoenberg and his method were highly influential, and there developed an American school of twelve-tone composers. Many Americans who used serialism adapted it liberally for their own needs. This is true of Riegger's use of his material in the first movement of this concerto; he develops extensively certain intervals, and certain cell-like groups of notes, which may serve melodically or become the basis for chords.

This is not the place for a detailed analysis of this movement; suffice it to say that if you can become familiar with the basic theme, you will gradually become aware that this series of notes forms the basis of virtually the entire first movement. It appears right side up, upside down, and in imitation, and fragments of it generate both melody and harmony.

The concerto has its ingratiating moments, such as the duet between the flute and the bassoon that opens the second movement; it reappears in its original form near the end, and with different scoring near the beginning. It shares this movement with a more dynamic and abrupt kind of material, which culminates in a passage in imitative counterpoint—almost a trademark of neoclassicism. The main theme of the first movement is heard near the end.

The last movement is one of great originality and daring, partly because, in accord with a typically American non-doctrinaire approach to matters of this kind, it rejects serial chromaticism and expresses a tonal center unequivocally—in fact, hammers away at it with Beethovenian insistence. But it is also daring in its relentless unfolding of its initial marchlike theme, which only gradually gathers strength and momentum from its fragmentary opening. Presently winds and piano are answering each other. There follows next a passage that is distinctively American in conception, and is written from a precise "metronome sense." The unit of rhythm suddenly becomes the twice-as-fast eighth note, and we have a series of asymmetric measures containing, successively, six, seven, six, four, and five of these units. The steady-quarter-note march returns, and this time an insistent, singing, diatonic tune appears as a countermelody—similar in feel to the kind one finds in the trio of a good march by Sousa (Example 16–30).

Example 16–30

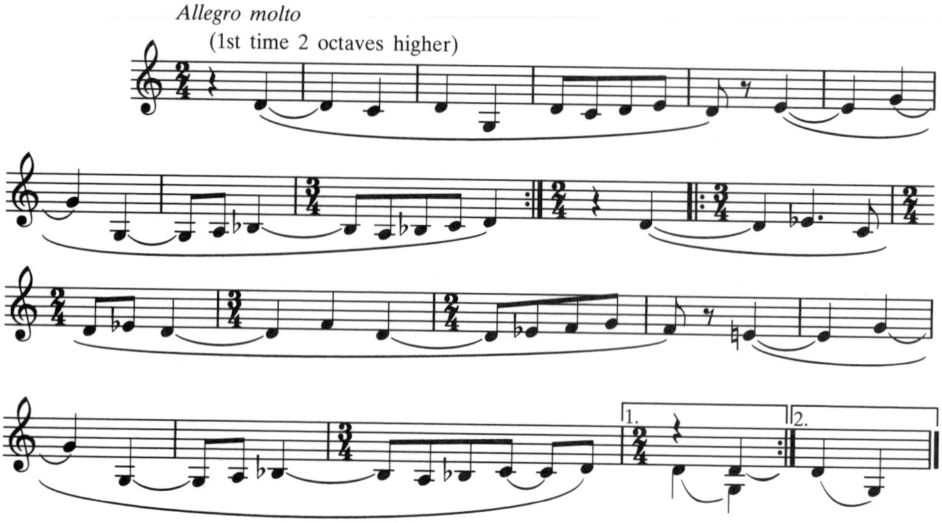

With these materials the movement sweeps along to a stirring climax, after which the main theme of the first movement returns to conclude the concerto in a soft, fading-away manner.

The Symphony

Like the string quartet, the symphony evolved as an important musical form in the eighteenth century, and by the death of Beethoven (1827) it had come to represent the ultimate vehicle for the expression of serious musical thought in terms of "absolute" or "pure" music. But Beethoven had already planted the seeds of programmaticism in the field of the symphony: his sixth (which has been nicknamed "Pastoral") was frankly descriptive of the countryside, and of feelings evoked by the countryside; and the ninth used voices, in a setting of Schiller's "Ode to Joy." The century that followed proceeded to view the symphony two ways: as a form of absolute music (used as such by Bruckner, Brahms, Dvořák, and Sibelius) and as program music (used as such by Berlioz,

Liszt, and Mahler). Early American symphonists, writing between 1850 and 1925—such as George Frederick Bristow, John Knowles Paine, and George Chadwick—mostly adopted the more classical, non-programmatic view of the symphony, though this did not prevent them from sometimes attaching programmatic titles to their works; examples would include Bristow's *Arcadian Symphony* and Amy Beach's *Gaelic Symphony*. More explicit programmaticism was indulged by some; one of the more extravagant examples was William Henry Fry's *Santa Claus Symphony* (c. 1853), alluded to in the preceding chapter.

The new generation of American composers, writing from the 1920s on, regarded the symphony in its classical sense, and the typical American symphony since then has been a non-programmatic work, generally in several independent movements, and usually regarded as a vehicle for the composer's most serious musical thoughts. Not all composers have become writers of symphonies, however; there tends to be a rough division, based on interests and temperament, between symphonists and non-symphonists. Confirmed symphonists have been Roy Harris (thirteen), Roger Sessions (eight), Henry Cowell (nineteen completed), William Schuman (ten to date), David Diamond (nine to date), Peter Mennin (nine) and Walter Piston (eight), and Alan Hovhaness (fifty-six, not all for full-sized orchestra). Those who have become involved only peripherally (two or three at the most, and mostly early works) are Virgil Thomson, Aaron Copland, Elliott Carter, and Samuel Barber.

Harris: Third Symphony

In Roy Harris (1898–1979) we confront once more the question of Americanism, both conceptual and compositional. Harris, the last to be considered here of the five "commandos" active since the 1920s, tended to be a peripatetic loner, imbued with a sense of his own destiny to express "the American spirit" and, like the poet Robert Frost, caught up in his own legend: that of a man close to the soil (for Frost, New England; for Harris, the Plains).* Harris was certainly a conceptual Americanist; his writings convey this, and of his symphonies, for example, the Sixth (1944) is based on Lincoln's Gettysburg Address, and the Ninth (1963) uses the preamble of the United States Constitution. In an overt way he was also a compositional Americanist, as his *Folk Song Symphony* (1940) demonstrates. But the mere incorporation of folk songs and national texts is a fairly trivial matter, as far as a style is concerned; there are more intrinsic ways in which Harris's music has been *felt* by many to express "the American spirit." Our consideration of the Third Symphony will perhaps be suggestive of some of these ways. His music was most in tune with the times, and most enthusiastically received, in the 1930s and 1940s; after World War II, interest in it waned, and he tended to repeat himself. His undoubted gifts and his authentic contribution are best represented by his Third Symphony (1939), one of the strongest and most compact of American symphonies.[32]

Seventeen minutes in length, it is in one continuous movement, though

* Roy Harris was indeed born in a log cabin in Lincoln County, Oklahoma, on Lincoln's birthday, but he moved to California at the age of five.

divided rather clearly into sections, as Harris has outlined for us.

I. Tragic—low string sonorities
II. Lyric—strings, horns, woodwinds (score p. 14, measure 139; ca. 5′)
III. Pastoral—woodwinds with a polytonal string background (p. 23, measure 209, ca. 7′)
IV. Fugue—dramatic
  A. Brass and percussion predominating (p. 57, measure 416, ca. 10′)
  B. Canonic development of materials from Section II constituting background for further development of Fugue (p. 72, measure 505, ca. 12′)
V. Dramatic—tragic
  A. Restatement of violin theme of Section I: tutti strings in canon with tutti woodwinds against brass and percussion developing rhythmic motif from climax of Section IV (p. 82, measure 567, ca. 13½′)
  B. Coda—development of materials from Sections I and II over pedal tympani (p. 93, measure 634, ca. 14½′)

The symphony is not programmatic in a very literal sense, but it will be noted that Harris has attached to each section a word whose significance goes beyond the purely musical. Like Arthur Farwell, who was one of Harris's early teachers and in a sense his "discoverer," Roy Harris has consistently and consciously sought the expression of human states of mind and even cultural values, especially those belonging to what he calls "the American spirit," according to his credo that the "creative impulse is a desire to capture and communicate feeling."

To become receptive to the unique qualities of this symphony, and indeed of Harris's work as a whole, you would do well to purge your ears of complex sounds and sensitize yourself to the drama inherent in the simple but basic conflict between the major and the minor triad (Example 16–31).

Example 16–31

We have already noted the exploration of this tension as a recurring trait of American music, in considering William Schuman's Third String Quartet. Harris makes much of it, changing through the movement of one voice (that entrusted with the third of the chord, the harmonic "coloring agent") the inflection of the entire chord (Example 16–32),

Example 16–32

or else sounding successively two versions of an implied chord third in a melodic line (Example 16–33).

Example 16–33

Sometimes he will allow both coloring agents to sound together momentarily (Example 16–34).

Example 16–34

Harris has, in fact, developed a theory of light and dark in musical sonority based on the "coloring" of chords and entire scales through these inflections.

Another Harris device to be seen in Example 16–34 is the juxtaposition of distantly related simple chords, illustrated again in Example 16–35, a more extended passage from near the climactic end of the symphony.

Example 16–35

Harris in this work is primarily a harmonist; that is, harmony appears to be a prime motivating element of the music. For the most part the melodies themselves appear to grow out of basic chords with a few embellishing tones, as can be seen in the opening tune that the cellos play (Example 16–36);

Example 16–36

or the melodic idea of the sound ("Lyric") section, which assumes a number of forms but appears first as in Example 16–37;

Example 16–37

or the woodwind solos of the third ("Pastoral") section, sounding over the multi-layered chordal background that Harris labels "polytonal" (Example 16–38).

Example 16–38

Even the energetic fugue subject (Example 16–39) has as its skeleton a simple chord with embellishing subordinate harmonies, implying nothing beyond the basic three chords of D major known to every beginning folk guitarist.

The form of the work, according to Harris's own description, is sufficiently clear to allow the listener to follow the unfolding of its essential musical

Example 16–39

drama, even on first hearing. It has been, and continues to be, widely performed; Virgil Thomson has called it "to this day America's most convincing product in that form."

Two Other Contrasting American Symphonies

For further acquaintance, two other American symphonies are suggested. Here again we confront the contrast, as in the two pieces for winds previously discussed, between two modes of expression within the same broad tradition and in the same general period. The first is a fairly early work, the Symphony No. 2 (*Romantic*) by Howard Hanson. Hanson (1896–1981) was a staunch conceptual Americanist all his life; as composer, teacher (he was director of the Eastman School of Music from 1924 to 1964), and conductor he vigorously championed American music and the American composer, though not operating in the New York circles of the "commandos." As the subtitle of his Second Symphony implies, this ever-popular work is warmhearted, large of gesture in the Romantic manner, and opulent in harmony and orchestration. Written in 1930, it was a virtual manifesto by its composer, intended in his words to be "lyrical and romantic in temperament," as opposed to what he saw as the tendency toward "cerebral" music.

The next work, chronologically, is another Second Symphony—that of Roger Sessions, dating from 1946. Because the death of Franklin Delano Roosevelt occurred while the work was being composed, it was dedicated to his memory. Two more different symphonies could hardly be found coming from a single country in a single era than the second symphonies of Hanson and Sessions, a fact that demonstrates the breadth of the American tradition—even of the tradition that might be designated, with perilous inexactitude, as "mainstream." The Sessions work is dense, complex, and dissonant; it fits the classic notion of "modern music," and the adjectives called up to describe it might well have been applied more than thirty years earlier to Stravinsky's *The Rite of Spring*. Indeed, it bears an odd resemblance at times to that now-familiar but still bewitching dragon of modernity, not in structure or technique, but in the sheer sound-image it creates. It is "modern music" in the good old-fashioned scandal-creating sense—the kind that used to cause riots among audiences in the days when concertgoers were less inhibited. Yet this four-movement work has strength, expressiveness, moments of fascinating, beguiling sound, and a "difficult" kind of beauty that is more apt to make its greatest impression in retrospect—after the sounds themselves have died away.

The perennial dichotomy invoked by Hanson (which one can hear debated at almost any period in the history of music) between music of the intellect ("cerebral") and music of the emotions can easily lead us astray if we try to apply it concretely to specific works and composers, since any music worth consideration has both aspects, and the mix is not easy to determine. If Hanson and Harris are taken as representing the view that music is a matter primarily of the feelings, is it a fair assumption that Roger Sessions, our most respected "difficult" composer, may be taken as representing the view that music is primarily a matter of the intellect? This is a highly questionable assumption. Listen to Sessions himself, in his comments on his Second Symphony: "My music is always expressive in intent, and often has very concrete associations for me." He goes on to qualify this: "In composing, however, I follow not the associations, but the impulsion of the musical ideas themselves in terms of melody, rhythm, and harmony. . . . The hearer must therefore get from the music whatever it may have for him."[33]

The Concerto

The concerto, as a work for solo instrument (or instruments) and orchestra, takes on a different character from that of the symphony, a character dictated by the presence of the solo performer. It is a dialogue. It also can hardly avoid being to some extent a display piece, very often composed for a specific performer. It was quite usual in the past for a composer to write a concerto for himself as performer. This was the origin of most of the piano concertos of Mozart and Beethoven; in this country MacDowell wrote his piano concertos for himself, and Copland appeared as soloist in his own early piano concerto. But the increasingly rigorous demands of the separate professions of composer and concert performer have rendered this practice rare in our time. Many concertos in the twentieth century have their genesis in a commission from a concert artist himself, or on his behalf.

In the 1920s the concerto for piano and orchestra was a natural vehicle for the incorporation of idioms from jazz and popular music into symphonic works, because the piano had established itself as a jazz instrument. Gershwin's popular Concerto in F, written in 1925, has become a standard repertory work—probably the best in this vein. It can form an ideal introduction, for many, to the twentieth-century American concerto. Also employing jazz idioms is the one-movement Concerto for Piano and Orchestra by Aaron Copland, first performed in 1927. A more highly distilled and sophisticated work than the Gershwin, it has not found as firm a place in the repertory. Another concerto that employs jazz idioms, using an instrument that is at home in jazz, is the difficult Concerto for Clarinet (with strings, harp, and piano) that Aaron Copland wrote for Benny Goodman in 1948. Written more than twenty years after the Piano Concerto, this is Copland's only other concerto, and was something of an anomaly at a time when the period of substantial interest in "symphonic jazz" was over.

After the passing of the "Jazz Age," American composers turned in the 1930s to the writing of concertos largely in the neoclassical or neoromantic vein; compact works such as the Concertino for Piano and Orchestra (1937) by Walter Piston and the sonorously romantic Concerto for Violin and Orchestra (1939) by Samuel Barber are typical. An exception to this, and to the generally conservative tendency of the times, was the composition of the large-scale four-movement Concerto for Violin and Orchestra by Roger Sessions in 1935. This difficult piece of "modern music" was considered unplayable by some violinists at the time—as quite a few new concertos have been when they first appeared. It was not performed with orchestra until 1940. It is actually a very lyrical work, and the unusual instrumentation—no orchestral violins, but a large wind section that includes alto flute, two English horns, a basset horn (a clarinet pitched between the normal-sized one and the bass clarinet), and a contrabassoon—yields some very interesting and attractive sounds.

Since the "definitive decade" of the 1930s the concerto has continued to be cultivated, and as twentieth-century American music has gained more of a foothold in the concert field, more works, and more extended works, have been written. The classic three-movement form—consisting of a fairly expansive and varied first movement, moderate to fast in tempo; a slow, expressive middle movement; and a brilliant, virtuosic, fast finale—has been the rule. The concerto, by virtue of its position in the economic and artistic scheme of things (where it gets played, and by whom), tends to be the most conservative of musical forms. Professional concert soloists must of necessity confine themselves to a fairly small and highly traditional list of works geared both to the tastes of paying concert audiences and to the number of new works they can learn and add to their own active repertory. The piano concerto, like the piano sonata, has proved to be a one-time venture for most American composers. In chronological order George Gershwin (1925), Walter Piston (1937), William Schuman (1942), Howard Hanson (1948), David Diamond (1949), Roger Sessions (1956), Peter Mennin (1957), Samuel Barber (1961), and Elliott Carter (1966) have each, to date, produced one piano concerto.

The piano and the violin have continued to dominate the concerto field, as they have since the eighteenth century, with the cello a rather distant third but coming up fast. Notable American contributions to the literature for cello and orchestra are concertos by David Diamond (1938), Samuel Barber (1945), Virgil Thomson (1950), and Peter Mennin (1956), and the somewhat unusual *A Song of Orpheus* (1961) by William Schuman, an expansion for solo cello and orchestra of a song to a text from Shakespeare's *Henry VIII*.

Concertos for other instruments, such as the viola, flute, clarinet, saxophone, and percussion instruments, are rarer but appear occasionally; Ross Lee Finney's Concerto for Alto Saxophone and Orchestra of Wind Instruments is a noteworthy example.[34] The concerto for multiple soloists harks back to an earlier concept of the concerto—one belonging to the late seventeenth and early eighteenth centuries, known as the baroque period. Such works, partly because they are usually conceived on a smaller scale, and partly to avoid needless complexity and confusion in the sound, usually use a smaller orchestra, often just strings. Samuel Barber's *Capricorn Concerto* (1944) for flute, oboe, trumpet, and strings is of this type. The seventeenth-century Italian term "concerto grosso" is sometimes applied to these twentieth-century works.

Still another type is the "concerto for orchestra." This seemingly contradictory term usually denotes a work that treats the various instruments of the orchestra itself in a soloistic fashion, as typified by the early and compact Concerto for Orchestra (1934) by Walter Piston, and the more recent work with the same title by Elliott Carter (1970).

Carter: Double Concerto for Harpsichord and Piano with Two Chamber Orchestras

On September 6, 1961, at a meeting of the Eighth Congress of the International Musicological Society in New York City, in the presence of nearly a thousand musicians and scholars from around the globe, there was performed for the first time Elliott Carter's impressive Double Concerto for Harpsichord and Piano with Two Chamber Orchestras.[35] It was an entirely fitting audience to witness the premiere of this work, which represented the most advanced level of complexity, sophistication, and virtuosity yet attained by music that was still derived and conceived in the evolving line of tradition.

Elliott Carter (b. 1908), a man with a remarkable breadth of intellectual background, wrote some vocal works and works for the stage early in his career, but since the composition of his Piano Sonata (1945–46), which was something of a landmark, he has concentrated almost exclusively on the production of chamber and orchestral music—music without text or programmatic associations.

The piano and its historical predecessor the harpsichord have tone qualities and basic modes of tone production that are usually regarded as incompatible. Carter has enlarged upon this incompatibility, and made it a basic structural feature of the work. The instrumental forces involved are divided into two small groups of equal size, one associated with each solo instrument, and placed as far away from each other as possible on the stage. A seating plan is given in the score. (Recordings of the concerto, like some sophisticated rock recordings, thus make very functional and structural use of stereophonic playback capabilities.) As the composer explains in his notes to the Nonesuch recording,

> The harpsichord is associated with an ensemble of flute, horn, trumpet, trombone, viola, contrabass and percussion (largely metallophones and ligniphones) while the piano is joined by an ensemble of oboe, clarinet, bassoon, horn, violin, cello, and percussion (largely membranophones).* In addition to being isolated in space and timbre, the antiphonal groups are partially separated musically by the fact that each emphasizes its own repertory of melodic and harmonic intervals. . . . The motion of the work is from comparative unity with slight character differences to greater and greater diversity of material and character and a return to unity. The form is that of confrontations of diversified action-patterns and a presentation of their mutual interreactions, conflicts and resolutions, their growth and decay over various stretches of time

The work is in one continuous movement lasting approximately twenty-three minutes, but as the composer has stated, it "falls into seven large

* Carter uses technical instrument terminology to differentiate types of percussion instruments: metallophones are sounded by striking a solid piece of metal (such as a triangle), lignophones by striking solid wood (as in a xylophone), membranophones by striking a stretched surface (e.g., a drumhead).

interconnected sections," which include written-out cadenzas for the soloists. The notated score is extremely detailed and complex, but as in much contemporary music, its sound paradoxically resembles sounds achieved through improvisation. As Eric Salzman, who reviewed the premiere for the *New York Times,* wrote, "In a larger sense the entire work is a cadenza."

Our survey of traditionally evolving classical music existing independent of the other parts began with the George Gershwin *Preludes for Piano,* and has ended with the Elliott Carter Double Concerto—a considerable journey showing the range of American music between two extremes of technical difficulty, accessibility, and compositional Americanism. The Gershwin speaks to us with wit, in an urbane and colloquial accent; the Carter, devoid of any conscious regionalism or nativism, brings us into the rarefied atmosphere of the avant-garde that is our next concern. Backing up somewhat in time so as to follow the developments of our experimental and innovative wing through the twentieth century to date, we enter the restless, challenging arena—sometimes harsh, sometimes quixotic, but nearly always stimulating—of individualism and exploration that is the subject of the next two chapters.

Further Reading

General Background

Copland, Aaron. *The New Music: 1900–1960.* New York: W. W. Norton, 1968.
A revised and enlarged edition of the 1941 original. An essential book, it includes material beyond the scope of this chapter.

Reis, Claire R. *Composers, Conductors and Critics.* New York, 1955. Reprint (with new introduction by the author and preface by Aaron Copland), Detroit: Detroit Reprints in Music, 1974.
Another essential book; largely a personal account (the author was director of the influential League of Composers for twenty-five years).

Rosenfeld, Paul. *Musical Impressions: Selections from Paul Rosenfeld's Criticism.* Edited and with an introduction by Herbert Leibowitz. New York: Hill & Wang, 1969.
A reprinting of some important and flamboyantly written essays by this controversial critic and enthusiastic supporter of new music.

Tawa, Nicholas E. *Serenading the Reluctant Eagle.* New York: Schirmer Books, 1984.
Perceptive and detailed overview of the period, including attention to the audiences for American music.

Thomson, Virgil. *American Music Since 1910.* New York: Holt, Rinehart & Winston, 1970.
Another essential book by a well-known participant and observer of the period.

Modern Music (1924–46).
This periodical, published by the League of Composers, with contributions from many of the important figures of the period, is an invaluable source; it is available (in a reprint) in many libraries.

Specific Genres, Issues, or Institutions

Carman, Judith, et al. *Art-Song in the United States: An Annotated Bibliography.* New York: National Association of Teachers of Singing, 1976.
A monumental bibliography of 1400 songs, listed by composer and indexed by "subject," poet, and title. Though the annotations are chiefly of interest to

singers, the mere compilation of such a list, with dates and publishers, makes it a valuable reference work.

Drummond, Andrew. *American Opera Librettos.* Metuchen, NJ: Scarecrow Press, 1973.
A study of the librettos of forty American operas performed 1948–71, with copious bibliography.

Hamm, Charles. "Opera and the American Composer" in Chase, *The American Composer Speaks* (cited below), pp. 285–97.
Written in 1961, this is a somewhat dated indictment of American opera composers, but its points are worth consideration.

Lederman, Minna. *The Life and Death of a Small Magazine (Modern Music, 1924–1946).* I.S.A.M. Monograph no. 18. Brooklyn: Institute for Studies in American Music, 1983.
Valuable monograph on the important periodical *Modern Music* by its long-time editor. Includes copious excerpts.

Leichtentritt, Hugo. *Serge Koussevitzky: The Boston Symphony and the New American Music.* Cambridge, MA: Harvard University Press, 1946.
Documentation of an important era and figure.

Levy, Alan Howard. *Musical Nationalism: American Composers' Search for Identity.* Westport, CT: Greenwood, 1983.
Developments and figures of the period seen in relation to one crucial issue.

———. "The Search for Identity in American Music, 1890–1920," *American Music,* vol. 2, no. 2 (Summer 1984).
Background to the same issue, treating the period immediately preceding that covered in the book.

Limbacher, James L., comp. *Film Music: From Violins to Video.* Metuchen, NJ: Scarecrow Press, 1974.
A collection of articles on many aspects of film music, and a reference work on film composers and their music.

Meckna, Michael. "Copland, Sessions, and *Modern Music:* The Rise of the Composer Critic in America," *American Music,* vol. 3, no. 2 (Summer 1985).

Moore, MacDonald Smith. *Yankee Blues: Musical Culture and American Identity.* Bloomington: Indiana University Press, 1985.
"Americanism" again, this time treated from a more narrowly racial standpoint, as can be deduced from the titles of the two main sections: "New England's Musical Mission" and "Ethnic Dissonance." This polarized perception ("Yankees, Negroes, and Jews") makes it a more limited treatment of the perennial theme of "Americanism" in music.

Potter, Hugh M. *False Dawn: Paul Rosenfeld and Art in America 1916–1946.* Published for the University of New Hampshire. Ann Arbor, MI: University Microfilms International 1980.
Furnishes broader background on an important figure.

Thomas, Tony. *Music for the Movies.* South Brunswick, NJ: Barnes, 1973.
Gives attention to individual film composers and their work, including Thomson and Copland.

Siegel, Marcia B. *The Shapes of Change: Images of American Dance.* Boston: Houghton Mifflin, 1979.

Zuck, Barbara. *A History of Musical Americanism.* Ann Arbor, MI: UMI Research Press, 1980.
For a critical review, see Victor Fell Yellin in *American Music,* vol. 1, no. 1 (Spring 1983), pp. 70–76.

Collections of Essays by a Single Composer

Bernstein, Leonard. *Findings.* New York: Simon & Schuster, 1982.

Carter, Elliott. *The Writings of Elliott Carter.* Compiled, edited, and annotated by Else Stone and Kurt Stone. Bloomington: Indiana University Press, 1977.

Copland, Aaron. *Copland on Music.* Garden City, NY: Doubleday, 1960.

———. *Music and Imagination: The Charles Eliot Norton Lectures, 1951–1952.* Cambridge, MA: Harvard University Press, 1952.

Sessions, Roger. *Roger Sessions on Music: Collected Essays*. Princeton, NJ: Princeton University Press, 1979.

Thomson, Virgil. *The State of Music*. 2d ed. New York: Random House, 1962.

———. *A Virgil Thomson Reader*. Introduction by John Rockwell. Boston: Houghton Mifflin, 1981.

Collections of Essays by Various Authors, Mostly Composers

Boretz, Benjamin, and Edward T. Cone, eds. *Perspectives on American Composers*. New York: W. W. Norton, 1971. See Further Reading for Chapter 18.

Chase, Gilbert, ed. *The American Composer Speaks: A Historical Anthology, 1770–1965*. Baton Rouge: Louisiana State University Press, 1966.
Includes essays relevant to this chapter (see also Further Reading for Chapter 17).

Cowell, Henry, ed. *American Composers on American Music: A Symposium*. Palo Alto, CA 1933. Paperback reprint (with new introduction), New York: Frederick Ungar, 1962.
An essential collection: see also Further Reading for Chapter 17.

Works Primarily About Individual Composers

Copland, Aaron, and Vivian Perlis. *Copland: 1900–1942*. New York: St. Martin's, 1984.
This is the first of two collaborative volumes that will probably form the definitive study of Copland's life and music; it illuminates the period as well.

Edwards, Allen. *Flawed Words and Stubborn Sounds: A Conversation with Elliott Carter*. New York: W. W. Norton, 1971.

Gruen, J. *Menotti: A Biography*. New York: Macmillan, 1978.

Hennessee, Don A. *Samuel Barber: A Bio-bibliography*. Westport, CT: Greenwood, 1985.

Hoover, Kathleen, and John Cage. *Virgil Thomson: His Life and Music*. New York: T. Yoseloff, 1959.

Olmstead, A. *Roger Sessions and His Music*. Ann Arbor, MI: UMI Research Press, 1985.

Pollack, Howard. *Walter Piston*. Ann Arbor, MI: UMI Research Press, 1981.

Schiff, D. *The Music of Elliott Carter*. New York: Da Capo, 1983.

Stehman, Dan. *Roy Harris: An American Musical Pioneer*. Boston: Twayne, 1984.

Thomson, Virgil. *Virgil Thomson*. New York, 1967. Reprint, New York: Da Capo, n.d.
Consult also entries in *The New Grove Dictionary of American Music*.

Listening

Much of the music discussed in this chapter is available on commercial recordings. Therefore only recordings of special interest or those that might otherwise escape notice are included here. Consult the index (W. W. Norton, 1981) to the New World *Recorded Anthology of American Music*, and the current Schwann catalog.

American String Quartets, vol. 2: *1900–1950*. Vox SVBX 5305.
Includes quartets by Copland, Piston, Gershwin, Thomson, Schuman, Sessions, Hanson, Mennin, Ives.

The Art Song in America. 2 LPs. Duke University Press, Durham, NC.

But Yesterday Is Not Today. NW-243.
Art Songs 1930–60, with notes by Ned Rorem.

Songs by American Composers. Desto DST 6411-12.

Toward an American Opera. NW-241.

When I Have Sung My Songs: The American Art Song 1900–1940. NW-247.

PROJECTS

1. Read Irving Lowens's perceptive essay, "American Democracy and American Music (1830–1914)" in his *Music and Musicians in Early America* (New York: W. W. Norton, 1964). He describes American democracy as having two important components, equalitarianism and libertarianism, and American music as also being made up of two components, a popular music and a fine-art music. He sees, furthermore, "a certain correlation between the dominance of the equalitarian urge and the vitality of popular music, and a similar correlation between the dominance of the libertarian urge and the vitality of fine-art music." He declines, however, to comment on whether this correlation exists past the time of World War I. After careful reading and thought, arrive at your own assessment of the situation in America, either between the World Wars or since World War II. Does such a correlation exist, and if so, how it could be be illustrated? If it does not, what factors make it no longer applicable?

2. Read a story or a play that has been made into an opera by an American composer, comparing the original with the opera. Note the changes that have been made, and try to account for them in terms of the requirements of opera. (Examples would be Du Bose Heyward's novel *Porgy,* or the play adapted by the author and his wife, vis-à-vis the opera *Porgy and Bess;* Emily Brontë's *Wuthering Heights* vis-à-vis Carlisle Floyd's opera of the same title; or Arthur Miller's play *The Crucible* vis-à-vis the opera of the same title by Robert Ward.)

3. Listen to Samuel Barber's short opera *A Hand of Bridge.* Compare the different musical characterizations of the four players, whose unspoken thoughts are sung as the game goes on perfunctorily.

4. Douglas Moore's opera *The Ballad of Baby Doe* and Meredith Willson's musical *The Unsinkable Molly Brown* both have the same setting (Colorado), and both deal with actual historical figures, women who faced the challenges of the mining-camp era of the West. Compare these two works, as a means of pointing out some of the differences—musical, dramatic, and in overall approach—between opera and the musical show.

5. Write a short paper on American poets (or one American poet) whose poems have been set to music by American composers. You could summarize a survey of the field or could concentrate on a single poet and compare settings by various composers. Carman's *Art-Song in the United States: An Annotated Bibliography* would be an invaluable—almost indispensable—help.

6. Interview a composer in your community who has written music for a film or a ballet, concerning the problems peculiar to the medium, and the methods used to solve them.

7. Interview a concert pianist on the subject of American piano sonatas and concertos in the active repertory. Prepare by becoming acquainted with at least three of each. (There are many touring artists, as well as artists-in-residence at colleges and universities. Advance planning, through consulting the offerings of local concert series and contacting the artist's management well ahead of time, will make this go more smoothly and be more productive.)

8. Interview a member of a professional string quartet on the subject of American string quartets in the active repertory. Prepare by becoming acquainted with at least four quartets by different composers. (There are several quartets that tour regularly, and quite a few attached as quartets-in-residence to some of the larger universities and music schools.)

9. Attend a concert that includes the performance of an American symphony.

Write a brief essay on any aspect or aspects of it that you wish. Your own observations and impressions are important. As supporting material, you may find it possible (if it is a local orchestra) to interview the conductor with regard to why he or she chose the particular symphony, some of the problems involved in its preparation, and the place of the American symphony (in general) in the active repertory of our symphony orchestras.

10. If there is a symphony orchestra in your community (a college or university orchestra, an amateur community orchestra, or a professional or semiprofessional orchestra), survey the entire season's programs; report on the percentage of American works included, and their type and vintage. You may want to include an interview with the orchestra's musical director on the subject of programming American music.

11. In past ages composers have not been notably literate, or prone to express themselves in writing, except in letters. This has changed in the twentieth century, and nowhere more noticeably than in the United States. Textbooks aside, Leonard Bernstein, Aaron Copland, Ned Rorem, Roger Sessions, and Virgil Thomson have several books each to their credit, not to mention numerous articles and essays by these and other composers. Read three books by three American composers, and write a brief paper with some such title as "The American Composer as Author."

12. Write a brief paper with the title "American Composers Write About Each Other's Music." In it, for example, you might review in juxtaposition Virgil Thomson's chapter on Aaron Copland in Thomson's *American Music Since 1910* and Copland's chapter on Thomson in Copland's *The New Music 1900–1960;* or John Cage's analysis and assessment of Thomson's music in Hoover and Cage, *Virgil Thomson: His Life and Music* and Thomson's chapter "Cage and the Collage of Noises" in *American Music Since 1910.*

13. Paul Rosenfeld was a perceptive commentator on the arts (not only music) in the period covered by this chapter; though controversial, he now seems to have been almost prophetic in his ability to identify artists who later became important. Do a paper on some aspect of his artistic criticism, using as a point of departure the material in the reading list above.

14. George Antheil was a controversial maverick of music in the 1920s and 1930s. Assessments of his importance vary widely; on the one hand we have his own view in his autobiography *Bad Boy of Music,* and at the other extreme an evaluation such as Alan Howard Levy makes in his book *Musical Nationalism.* After doing some reading, and listening to his music, write a paper surveying the gamut of opinions on Antheil, and include your own assessment.

15. Consulting biographical and other material, and listening to recordings, do a brief essay on an American composer who, because of limitations of space, has had to be omitted from the preceding chapter or mentioned only briefly. Such composers, in alphabetical order (a list still arbitrarily limited) might include: Ernst Bacon, Marion Bauer, William Bergsma, Paul Creston, Ingolf Dahl, Norman Dello Joio, David Diamond, Irving Fine, Ross Lee Finney, Lukas Foss, Howard Hanson, Alan Hovhaness, Andrew Imbrie, Leon Kirchner, Peter Mennin, Daniel Pinkham, Quincy Porter, Bernard Rogers, Arthur Shepherd, Elie Siegmeister, Leo Sowerby, William Grant Still, Howard Swanson, and Robert Ward.

17

Exploration and Experiment, I: New Ways with Old Tools

"TO experiment and to explore has never been revolutionary for an American; he is unaffectedly at home in the unregulated and the untried." So wrote Henry and Sidney Cowell in the first chapter of their influential book on Charles Ives.[1]

We have already encountered this unorthodoxy—a confident "tinkering" spirit in the arts, infused with a strong sense of self-reliance and independence of conventionality, and combined with a pronounced bent for the practical—manifested in the work of William Billings, who said that "every composer should be his own Carver" (and showed how to make a practical metronome to help singers keep time); in the writing of a string quartet, presumably by Benjamin Franklin, with tunings that allow it to be played on the open strings only; and in the invention of shape notes to facilitate learning to read music.

Yet for all their interest as signposts, these were limited ventures; they did not deal with the basic question of what music is or should be, and they did not extend any musical horizons. Our genuine exploratory and experimental tradition begins with George and Charles Ives, whose work really did push back our horizons, suggesting areas of musical experience that are still being explored.

In this chapter and the next we shall try to trace this tradition of exploration and experiment from the Iveses, father and son, to the present—a span of nearly a century. The first of these two chapters will deal with expanded concepts as they have been applied to the traditional means of writing and making music. Thus "new ways with old tools" refers to music written largely in traditional notation, re-created by musicians playing traditional instruments more or less in the way they were built to be played. Chapter 18 then deals with the new means of synthesizing and manipulating sound that expanding technology has made available, and with more radically different aesthetic concepts of the nature and function of music, and of art in general. The work of some practitioners belongs in both chapters, of course: Edgar Varèse and John Cage both began their explorations (in quite different directions) before the advent of electronics, but remained on the scene long enough to utilize new technology in their music making. Harry Partch is well-nigh unclassifiable, but his chronology, his aesthetic premises, and his return to monophony and pure intonation all seem to place him in this chapter, in spite of his brand-new and beautiful instruments. Otherwise, the main line of demarcation between the chapters should be clear.

Charles Ives (1874–1954)

In 1947, when the composer Henry Cowell and his wife, Sidney, were planning their book on Charles Ives, Mrs. Harmony Ives wrote to Sidney Cowell: "How he is going to get Charlie into a book I don't know." Indeed, the multifaceted Charles Ives does defy being put into any sort of book, as he defies being looked at from any single point of view. Every approach to him soon suggests others, and leads one off in many directions—as does listening to his music or reading his *Essays Before a Sonata.* (One has much the same experience in reading the essays of his spiritual mentor, Ralph Waldo Emerson.) Perhaps it is nearer the truth to say that every approach leads us around, or *through,* the career or the music to the ideas that animated and infused both. For it is the ideas, when all is said and done, that account for the man's increasing stature today. We go to Ives not so much for a crystallized corpus of well-ordered works as for a pandemonium of interrelated ideas. It is an interesting and perhaps significant commentary that in a comparatively young culture such as that of America, which has heretofore placed such value on tangible activity and its fruits (including technology), a man whose life was outwardly so uneventful (like that of Henry David Thoreau), and whose importance rests so largely on the ideas and ethical principles that both his career and his music embody, should be emerging as one of our major American heroes—of already legendary proportions. Henry Cowell, who knew him as well as any other musician did, anticipated the current assessment nearly fifty years ago when he wrote: "Ives is independent, and is truly great; both in invention and in spirit he is one of the leading men America has produced."[2]

Though it is impossible to "get Charlie into a book" (or to get anyone into a book, for that matter), we can perhaps give some help to the reader interested in making Ives's acquaintance by organizing our approaches to him along three main lines: first, the life; second, the music, together with the issues and ideas suggested by it; and, third, some account of the reception accorded the music over the past half-century, the assessments made of it, and the impact of Ives's music and ideas on our intellectual and cultural life.

The Life and Career

A brief treatment of Ives's life and career is essential, not only for its intrinsic interest, but because for all of what appears to us as his modernity, and for all the freshness and relevance of many of his ideas and his music today, it is nonetheless true that his world was quite a different one from ours, and he cannot be fairly understood without reference to that world. Philosophically and musically, as well as chronologically, his world was that of nineteenth-century America, which can be thought of as lasting into the first two decades of the twentieth century and ending with World War I, a cataclysm that dealt Ives a crushing blow and indirectly, at least, brought his composing career to a close.

Charles Edward Ives, the older of two boys in his family, was born October 20, 1874, in Danbury, Connecticut, a growing manufacturing town in the southwestern corner of the state. His boyhood in Danbury, where he spent his first nineteen years, was of exceptional significance to his work; he drew upon its impressions throughout the whole of his fairly short creative life.

Pervading nearly all these impressions, according to Ives himself, was the extraordinary figure of his father. George Ives (1845–1894) had an exceptional breadth of interest in, and knowledge of, music for his time and place, a forever curious and inquiring mind, and the spirit of an explorer, especially in musical acoustics. He had been the youngest—and reputedly the best—bandmaster in the Union army during the Civil War.[3] Returning to Danbury, he became virtually the town musician, playing the piano, organ, violin, and cornet, directing the music at the Methodist church, leading the Danbury Band, leading the singing at the camp meetings, organizing and leading chamber music groups, and arranging music for his many and varied ensembles. Yet Danbury, a microcosm of growing industrial America, held these musical activities in very low esteem. Music, except for the most popular, earthy variety (such as country fiddling), was an effeminate pursuit and no fit profession for a man—this was the prevailing attitude in nineteenth-century middle-class America. It was the burden of this attitude, with its subtle influences on George Ives's attitudes and behavior, that Charles had to bear all his life.[4] If his father was not exactly a black sheep, he was certainly not considered a very illustrious member of his prominent Danbury family of bankers, businessmen, and fairly substantial property owners.

If his regular musical pursuits were not recognized in the community, there was still less understanding and approval of his really venturesome experiments in music and musical sound, such as experimentation with musical intervals smaller than the half steps on the piano (quarter-tones, and smaller) through the tuning of glasses, and even through the invention of a special contraption, strung with twenty-four or more violin strings, built to play scales and tunes in these small intervals; or the tuning of a piano to the actual acoustical partials of a given fundamental; or the attempt to duplicate the complex sound of a church bell on the piano (one of Charles's earliest memories, and a crucial experiment that led to many of the others). There was exploration in the realm of conventional tuning as well—exercises imposed on Charles and other members of the family to "stretch the ears," which included playing or singing a tune in one key while playing the accompaniment in another.[5]

One instance of the simultaneity of musical sounds made a lasting impression on Charles. It has not been established whether this particular effect was deliberately planned or not, but on one occasion two bands, his father's and another, marched past each other in opposite directions around the park in Danbury, each playing a different tune, in a different key, and at a different tempo. The effect produced fascinated both father and son; Charles re-created it years later in an orchestral piece called *Putnam's Camp*. Another experiment carried out by his father dealt with the factors of space and distance as they affected the sounds of music. It is best described in Charles Ives's own recollection:

> The writer remembers hearing, when a boy, the music of a band in which the players were arranged in two or three groups around the town square. The main group in the bandstand at the center usually played the themes, while the others, from the neighboring roofs and verandas, played the variations, refrains, etc. . . . The bandmaster told of a man who, living near the variations, insisted that they were the real music and it was more beautiful to hear the hymn come sifting through them than the other way around. Others, walking around the square, were surprised at the different and interesting effects they got as they changed position. . . . The writer remembers, as a deep impression, the echo part from the roofs played by a chorus of violins and voices.[6]

The account would seem to invite us to revise somewhat our opinion of the musical receptiveness and curiosity of at least *some* of Danbury's inhabitants in the 1880s; it seems that there was even some kind of vote taken on the effectiveness of the experiment. Ives made use of the spatial dimension, including the effect of distant sounds (which he justly observes as being quite different in *quality* from sounds produced softly at close range), in his later works. This kind of distance perspective can be heard in his famous orchestral piece *The Unanswered Question.*

The experiments of George Ives are worth treating in some detail for at least two reasons. They show him to have been a man with a lively curiosity and rare ingenuity, and worthy of note in his own right; some of the ideas he tried out in rough form were devices that sophisticated avant-garde composers hit upon three-quarters of a century later. And they also show the kind of stimulation and example Charles was exposed to as a boy. Of all the influences on him, Charles Ives always took pains to place foremost that of his father. George Ives composed little or no music himself, but Henry and Sidney Cowell have written, "it is not too much to say that the son has written his father's music for him."

It should be made clear, however, that there were two complementary sides to Charles Ives's early musical background, and his father showed rare wisdom in insisting on a balance between them. On one hand there was the curiosity, the open-mindedness toward tinkering and experimentation, of which his father set such a remarkable example. On the other hand there was the solid grounding in musical rudiments that the boy received from his father and from others. He was taught the drums, the violin, the cornet, the piano, and the organ. His father also taught him sight-reading, harmony, and counterpoint. He began early to compose, and at thirteen wrote a piece, *Holiday Quickstep*, that his father's band played.[7] Ives's earliest extant song, found years later in the cellar by his mother, dates from his fourteenth year and is a dirge for the family dog.

The same year he began playing the organ occasionally in church, and at fourteen he got his first permanent job as church organist—a kind of work he did steadily for the next fourteen years in Danbury, New Haven, and New York City. He also gave organ recitals; one at the age of fifteen included the *William Tell* Overture, a Bach toccata, and a Mendelssohn sonata. All this is cited to dispel the notion that Ives was a musical amateur, a dilettante, or some sort of "primitive." Nothing could be further from the truth. His innovative and experimental tendencies showed up early (as in his *Variations on "America"* for organ, which he wrote in 1891, with touches of polytonality and plenty of tongue-in-cheek humor), but his father insisted that this sort of thing be supported by an underpinning of solid knowledge and technique. As he told him on one occasion, "Charlie, it will be time enough to write an improper fugue and do it well when you can write a proper fugue and do *that* well."

At twenty Ives entered Yale. His record shows that he was not a particularly good student, except in music. He studied with the renowned composer Horatio Parker. Parker, a strict taskmaster and academician, is conventionally disparaged as being intent on stifling Ives's creative impulses through his insistence on formally "correct" music. Though Ives soon gave up showing Parker his more adventurous essays, he admired and respected Parker and most of his music, which (Ives later said) "was seldom trivial," and Parker's importance to Ives's musical training was, until the 1980s, considerably underestimated.

While at Yale, Ives had an important church job. Being sociable and well liked, he joined several clubs and wrote music for fraternity shows. He substituted occasionally at the piano in the Hyperion Theater orchestra, and it was with this orchestra that he began to have some of his own music tried out. We have already had occasion to note the importance of theater orchestras in American music. Ives liked these small orchestras and the musicians who played in them, and he wrote or rearranged many of his pieces for them.

When Ives graduated from Yale in 1898, he decided, for reasons that will be explored later, to go into business, thus initiating one of the most astounding aspects of his career. For the next twenty years he was to pursue under full steam two careers at once: that of business executive and that of composer. The business he chose was life insurance. It was for him a dynamic and idealistic field. In brief, he threw himself as fully into his chosen business profession as he had into his music; his creative and humane approach (he pioneered in the field of estate planning and the training of insurance agents) made him and his partnership (Ives and Myrick) enormously successful, and when he finally retired in 1930 because of ill health, he could have been many times a millionaire. Instead, in accord with his principles, he took out of the business only enough to provide comfortably but modestly for himself and his family, and to set up a fund for the promulgation of his (and others') music.

The period of two decades between 1898 (when Ives first went into business) and 1918 was one of furious and unrelenting productivity. Ives literally led a double life, giving full attention to the business on weekdays and composing at night, on weekends, and during summer vacation. His output during this time would have been impressive for a full-time composer; considering the conditions under which he worked, it was prodigious.* There was a simultaneity in his composing methods that corresponded to the simultaneity in the music itself; he would usually be working on many pieces at once. During the very active five-year period 1911–16, for instance, he was composing some of his most important songs, the third and fourth violin sonatas, the Second String Quartet, the *Concord* Sonata, the orchestral *Three Places in New England,* the *Second Orchestral Set, Four New England Holidays,* the huge Fourth Symphony, and the gigantically conceived *Universe Symphony* that was never to be finished. Working often at a white heat, he would throw sheets of sketched notes over his shoulder as he finished them, to be gathered up and sorted later. Naturally many works remained in an unfinished or semifinished state. At his death, some sketch sheets (his music manuscript was extremely difficult to decipher) remained still unsorted, piled in drawers in his West Redding barn, some thirty or forty years after they had been written. Ives did make some attempts, between 1910 and 1915, to have some of his music played over; these attempts were mostly disastrous, and left the sensitive composer scarred and embittered—determined to continue writing but with virtually no thought of performance, an action of which only an extremely strong and determined will is capable. But it was not to be for long.

In 1917 came the onset of radical and tragic change. The entry of the United States into the First World War was a severe blow to Ives. He was unreservedly opposed to war, but once his country was in, he worked in very practical ways (as was characteristic of him) for the war effort—selling bonds (he advocated a new small-denomination bond of $50 so that more people could participate, in accord with his philosophy of involving the masses of common people, whether in art, politics, or business)—and making a gift to the government of two completely equipped ambulances. His increased activity meant the end of composing.

In 1918 his health broke severely. He recovered somewhat in 1919, but never resumed his former prodigious productivity. The short burst of new music that appeared in 1921 represented, with few exceptions, the completion of works previously under way—mostly songs. Before he was fifty, his career as a composer was over. By 1927 his business career was practically over, too; he formally retired in 1930. That he was able to live on, vitally interested in new music and in larger human concerns generally, for another quarter of a century, leading a carefully secluded but by no means unhappy existence, is due in large measure to the care and devotion of his wife, Harmony Twichell Ives, whom he had married in 1908.

As early as 1919, sensing and accepting the change in his life, Ives began to make plans for the future of some of his most cherished compositions. He finished the important *Concord* Sonata (which had been composed mostly in 1909 and 1910) and had it published at his own expense. To accompany the sonata he wrote a prologue, four essays (on Emerson, Hawthorne, the Alcotts,

* Confusion concerning the actual dates of composition of many of Ives's works—confusion to which he himself evidently contributed substantially—has led to the speculation that both his "modernism" and his period of most intense activity as a composer belong to the period *after* he left his business. But the precise dating of Ives's compositions is as yet far from conclusive. See the article by Maynard Solomon cited in the Further Reading section of this chapter.

Thoreau), and a lengthy epilogue. Since these texts proved too long to be printed with the sonata, they were published separately in 1920, as *Essays Before a Sonata*. The *Essays* are a kind of artistic and philosophical manifesto, and constitute the single most valuable documentation of Ives's thought. The sonata itself was ready for distribution in 1921. Copies of both were sent free of charge to friends and interested parties; there was a time when almost anyone requesting a copy of either from Ives himself would receive them. (John Kirkpatrick, the first interpreter of the sonata, received his first copy from Ives in this way, having chanced to see a copy of it in Paris.) Shortly afterward, he prepared an edition of *114 Songs*, again published at his own expense and distributed free of charge. The songs, a rich and varied collection, were again accompanied by some of Ives's voluble and brash prose in a "postface" (like a preface, but at the end!).

Ives was far from idle in his long retirement, nor did he withdraw completely from the world of music and musicians. He supported attempts to get his work, and that of other composers of "new music," before the public by subsidizing concerts and by financially supporting ventures such as the periodical *New Music*, launched in 1927. He supervised the editing of his own music by other devoted musicians (a task his frail health did not allow him to do himself), and it is thanks to their intensive and exhausting labors that much of Ives's music has reached the public. These people include Elliott Carter, Henry and Sidney Cowell, Lou Harrison, John Becker, Nicolas Slonimsky, and John Kirkpatrick. Ives was all his life determined to receive no money from his compositions. When some of his works were printed by *New Music* in the 1920s and 1930s, he insisted on paying the costs. He disdained the copyrighting of his music, and exclaimed, in connection with the publication of part of his Fourth Symphony, "If anyone wants to copy or reprint these pieces, that's FINE! This music is not to make money but to be known and heard. Why should I interfere with its life by hanging on to some sort of personal legal right in it?"[8] In later years, royalty checks were returned, or given away. When he received the Pulitzer Prize for his Third Symphony (written mostly in 1904; first performed in 1947), it is said that he told the committee, "Prizes are for boys. I'm grown up," and gave the money away.

The Music

Ives's range as revealed in the songs

Ives wrote nearly a hundred and fifty songs, his output spanning his entire creative career. The earliest songs were composed before he left Danbury for Yale, and the latest in 1923. The songs, in addition to forming a rich repertory in themselves, are an excellent introduction to the music of Ives. Their range is large—musically, from the simple to the complex and dissonant, and textually, over nearly every aspect of human experience. Romantic love (staple fare of the popular song) is the only significant area of experience not represented; possibly Ives's New England reticence accounts for this. The songs resulting from what he did choose to set have the universality that can come only from vivid impressions and feelings. Nine songs, arranged in approximate order of difficulty and dimension, are suggested as a beginning.

The easy songs show Ives using the simplest of means. *A Christmas Carol* (1897) has an unforgettable charm, and the unexpected rhythms at the ends of the phrases are entirely unconventional. *At the River* (1916), one of four songs based on hymn-tune themes published in the *114* collection, shows Ives reworking some of the musical material he likes best. The hymn by Robert Lowry is seen as it passes through the prism of Ives's unique musical imagination; it emerges fractured and colored with unusual harmonies. For a fuller Ivesian treatment, listen to the last movement of the Fourth Violin Sonata; this song was made out of the last portion of it. Ives had a habit of transferring his ideas from one medium to another (all composers do it to a certain extent); thus many of his songs have their counterparts in choral or instrumental works.

Some songs—growing out of, or depicting, some vivid human scene—have a little more of the Ivesian complexity about them. The text for *The Greatest Man* (1921) Ives found, as often happened, in a newspaper. It was a poem by Anne Timoney Collins, which told "in a half boasting and half wistful way" (to quote from the score) of a boy's pride in his father. Ives's setting captures both the spirit and the speech patterns. Like Modest Mussorgsky, he had a gift for musical realism in his songs. *Tom Sails Away* (1917) has a prose text by Ives himself:

> Scenes from my childhood are with me, I'm in the lot behind our house upon the hill, a spring day's sun is setting, mother with Tom in her arms is coming towards the garden; the lettuce rows are showing green. Thinner grows the smoke o'er the town, stronger comes the breeze from the ridge, 'Tis after six, the whistles have blown, the milk train's gone down the valley. Daddy is coming up the hill from the mill. We run down the lane to meet him. But today! In freedom's cause Tom sailed away for over there, over there, over there! Scenes from my childhood are floating before my eyes.

The song is set in Ives's more expansive and dissonant "prose" style. One of three war songs in the *114*, it includes a quote from George M. Cohan's "Over There" in the vocal line, while the piano quotes a tune apparently always in the back of Ives's mind when it turned (as it so often did) to thoughts of his country—David Shaw's "The Red White and Blue" ("O Columbia, the Gem of the Ocean").

Some of the songs make a more philosophical comment on the human condition. In *The Cage* (1906) the voice intones Ives's short prose text, using mostly the noncommittal whole-tone scale, while the piano, in a rhythmically independent part, uses severe sonorities based on the interval of the perfect fourth, to depict the restless pacing of the leopard in the cage (Example 17–1).

> A leopard went around his cage from one
> side back to the other side; he
> stopped only when the keeper came
> around with meat;
> A boy who had been there three hours began
> to wonder, "Is life anything like that?"

Several songs reflect Ives's social idealism. Of these, *West London* (1921), to a sonnet by Matthew Arnold, is one of the most successful, possibly since it

Example 17–1

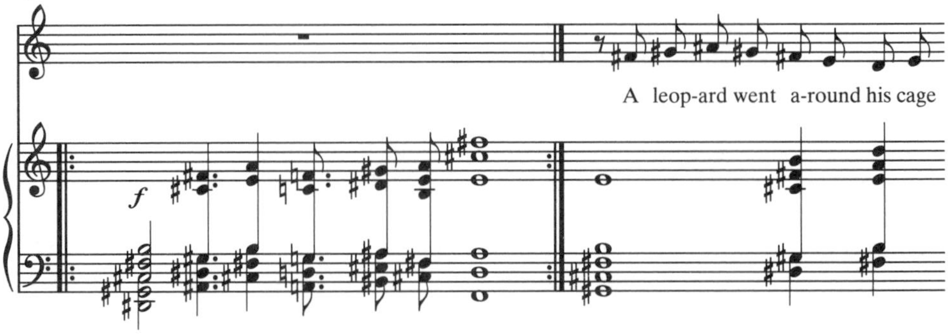
A leop-ard went a-round his cage

has as its basis a concrete scene of vivid realism. Less concrete is the song Ives placed first in the *114,* a startling work, big in conception, which he titled *Majority* or *The Masses* (1914). The text, by Ives, expresses one aspect of his complex and sometimes contradictory idealism—a deep faith in democracy.

> The Masses! The Masses! The Masses have toiled,
> Behold the works of the World!
> The Masses are thinking,
> Whence comes the thought of the World!
> The Masses are singing, are singing, singing,
> Whence comes the Art of the World!
> The Masses are yearning, are yearning, are yearn-
> ing.
> Whence comes the hope of the world.
> The Masses are dreaming, dreaming,
> The Masses are dreaming,
> Whence come the visions of God!
> God's in His Heaven,
> All will be well with the World!

Ives himself noted on the music, "Preferably for unison chorus; it is almost impossible for a single voice to hold the part against the score." *Majority* is a thesaurus of Ives's harmonic vocabulary; in addition to a few plain triads it uses extended chords built in thirds, fourths, and fifths, and also—possibly with programmatic connotations—appropriately massive, all-embracing tone "clusters" (chords built in seconds), two octaves in extent, combinations that strike not only the ear but the eye (Example 17–2). Two stanzas were omitted from the version in the *114;* to one of these stanzas, Ives wrote music in 1914 that anticipated the twelve-tone row technique later developed by the Viennese composer Arnold Schoenberg.[9]

It is possible that many of the recipients of the *114 Songs* were put off, or at least puzzled, by this opening song, with its strident dissonances. (The album was the butt of many contemporary jokes.) The fact is that Ives, for perhaps a variety of reasons, felt very strongly about the use of dissonance. It was, in a way, an indication for him of *manliness* in music. He complained

Example 17–2

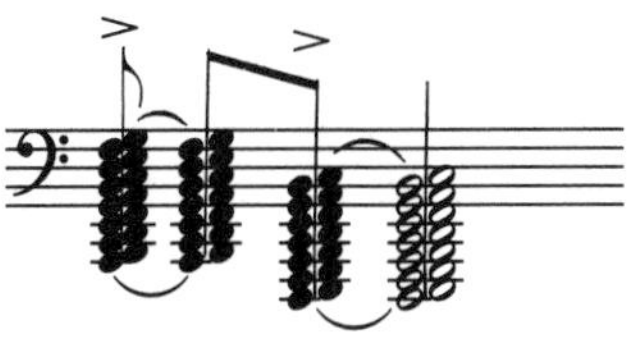

vociferously about the "sissies, that couldn't stand up and take the full force of dissonance like a man." Ives was, by all accounts, a master of the art of cussing, but the most damning adjective in his vocabulary was "nice." Recalling his boyhood, and the traumatic conflict between his natural bent for music (a form of activity dominated by "nice ladies") and his love of sports and natural honest regard for his peers (among whom music was a "sissy" thing to be spending one's time on), we can begin to understand at least one of the possible sources of Ives's whole set of attitudes on the emasculation of art. (Ives was not the only American artist to suffer from this conflict and the consequent obsessive need to assert "manliness"; among others may be mentioned Roy Harris and Ernest Hemingway.)

But Ives was far from being a simple man, and dissonance had other shades of meaning for him as well. For one thing, he felt the need to use whatever suited the expressive purpose at hand, which might in one instance be a crashing chord with ten or twelve different pitches in it, and in another an uncomplicated C major triad. There is also a sense for Ives in which dissonance, if used in the service of an art that emphasizes "substance" rather than "manner" (a favorite Ivesian polarity), can be virtuous. In his *Essays Before a Sonata* he wrote, "Beauty in music is too often confused with something that lets the ears lie back in an easy chair." Ives was always contemptuous of any "easy way." He continued the essay:

> Many sounds that we are used to do not bother us, and for that reason we are inclined to call them beautiful. Frequently—possibly almost invariably—analytical and impersonal tests will show, we believe, that when a new or unfamiliar work is accepted as beautiful on its first hearing, its fundamental quality is one that tends to put the mind to sleep. A narcotic is not always unnecessary, but it is seldom a basis of progress—that is, wholesome evolution in any creative experience.[10]

Earlier in the *Essays* his lack of regard for what is merely superficially or conventionally appealing in music provoked him to an even more vehement and epigrammatic outburst: "My God! What has sound got to do with music!" Here we catch a glimpse of Ives the Transcendentalist.

A brief survey cannot hope to touch on all the kinds of songs we find in Ives. We shall suggest here only one more type: the longer narrative songs, which have their roots in the vernacular. There are two of these that are noteworthy, and they are among his best songs. *Charlie Rutlage* (1920 or 1921) is a cowboy ballad. The text appeared in John Lomax's *Cowboy Songs,* without music, printed at first as anonymous folk poetry but later attributed to D. J. "Kid" O'Malley. Ives takes as his point of departure for the first and last verses a popular ballad style, which he transmutes with a few characteristic touches (such as the rhythmic displacements in the second line of each of the stanzas, and word-repetitions on "the golden gate," "in eternity," and "the shining throne"). In the middle three stanzas, the narrative itself, he reverts to melodrama; behind the recitation of the singer, the piano works up bits and pieces of "The Old Chisholm Trail" and other cowboy tunes, to a frenzied climax on the words "fell with him." This is followed by a memorably apt setting of "beneath, poor Charlie died" as a retransition to the final stanza, with its pointing up of the colloquial accentuation: "His *ree*lations in Texas." The whole is one of the gems of American song.

> Another good cow-puncher has gone to meet his fate,
> I hope he'll find a resting place within the golden gate.
> Another place is vacant on the ranch of the X I T,
> 'Twill be hard to find another that's liked as well as he.
>
> The first that died was Kid White, a man both tough and brave,
> While Charlie Rutlage makes the third to be sent to his grave,
> Caused by a cow-horse falling while running after stock;
> 'Twas on the spring round-up—a place where death men mock.
>
> He went forward one morning on a circle through the hills,
> He was gay and full of glee, and free from earthly ills;
> But when it came to finish up the work on which he went,
> Nothing came back from him; for his time on earth was spent.
>
> 'Twas as he rode the round-up, an X I T turned back to the herd;
> Poor Charlie shoved him in again, his cutting horse he spurred;
> Another turned; at that moment his horse the creature spied
> And turned and fell with him, and, beneath, poor Charlie died.
>
> His relations in Texas his face nevermore will see,
> But I hope he'll meet his loved ones beyond in eternity.
> I hope he'll meet his parents, will meet them face to face,
> And that they'll grasp him by the right hand at the shining throne of grace.

*General William Booth Enters Into Heaven** (1914) is perhaps Ives's best-known song, and justly so. The text is a portion of Vachel Lindsay's poem (minus six lines), which Ives read in a review. The drama and imagery of the imaginary scene put into play all of Ives's powers of musical characterization. Lindsay evidently conceived the poem to be sung with instruments—a bass drum in one spot, banjos in another, and in another "sweet flute music." His opening alliteration, "Booth led boldly with his big bass drum," furnishes Ives with a motive that begins the piece (Example 17–3) and also frames it; the

* General William Booth (1829–1912) was the founder, in England in 1878, of the Salvation Army, a religious philanthropic organization that officially began operations in the United States in 1880. As a means of reaching and helping the poor and downtrodden, the Salvation Army made considerable use of its uniformed street bands, which became a familiar sight and sound in American cities.

Example 17–3

ending is a faint dying away of the drumbeats in the distance. (One cannot help remembering here that Ives as a boy had played the drum parts in his father's band on the piano during their practices.) Vachel Lindsay had noted (with complex irony) that his poem was "to be sung to the tune of 'The Blood of the Lamb,' " but Ives chose instead a tune called "Fountain" ("There is a fountain filled with blood"), by Lowell Mason (see Chapter 6), whose hymn tunes he recalled frequently in his music (Example 17–4).

Example 17–4

The tune is overtly present only at the very end, the verse being quoted fully over the resumed bass-drum beat beginning with the words "marched on spotless," as Lindsay's phrases are made to overlap those of Mason's tune. Prior to this, the hymn tune is a kind of shadowy presence—Ives's settings of "Are you washed in the blood of the Lamb?" are based on a derivative of the tune, which is also present, unobtrusively, in the piano left hand under the words "Jesus came from the courthouse door." Other touches of text-painting are evident: the "banging banjo" tune, the trumpets, the memorable treatment of "round and round and round and round." The nearest that Ives comes to negating a tonal center is in the section beginning "Ev'ry slum had sent its half-a-score"; here he uses polychords in the piano (Example 17–5), and as often happens in this type of context, a whole-tone scale for the voice (cf. *The Cage*). *General William Booth* is a vivid musical drama in miniature on the theme of salvation, as is Schubert's *The Erl King* on the theme of death.

Example 17–5

Booth led boldly with his big bass drum
(Are you washed in the blood of the Lamb?
Are you washed in the blood of the Lamb, of the Lamb?)
Hallelujah
Saints smiled gravely and they said "He's come."

(Washed in the blood of the Lamb? The blood of the Lamb?)
Walking lepers followed rank on rank,
Lurching bravoes from the ditches dank.
Drabs from the alleyways and drug fiends pale—
Minds still passion-ridden, soul powers frail:—
Vermin-eaten saints with mouldy breath,
Unwashed legions with the ways of Death
(Are you washed in the blood of the Lamb?
Are you washed in the blood of the Lamb?)

Ev'ry slum had sent its half-a-score
The round world over. (Booth had groaned for more).
Ev'ry banner that the wide world flies,
Bloomed with glory and transcendent dyes.
Big-voiced lassies made their banjos bang, bang, bang, made their banjos,—
Tranced, fanatical, they shrieked and sang—They shrieked and sang: "Are you?
Are you washed in the blood?
In the blood of the Lamb—of the Lamb? Hallelujah!
Hallelujah, Hallelujah, Lord, Hallelujah, Lord, Hallelujah!"
It was queer to see
Bull-necked convicts, bull-necked convicts with that land make free.
Loons with trumpets blowed a blare,
On, on, upward thro' the golden air!
(Are you washed in the blood, in the blood of the Lamb,
in the blood of the Lamb, the Lamb, of the Lamb, the Lamb?) . . .

Jesus came from the courthouse door,
Stretched his hands above the passing poor.
Booth saw not, but led his queer ones,
Round and round, round and round and round and round and round and round and round and round—
Yet! in an instant all that blear review
Marched on, marched on marched on marched on marched on marched on marched on spotless, clad in raiment new.
The lame were straightened, withered limbs uncurled
And blind eyes opened on a new sweet world.
Are you washed in the blood of the Lamb?
Are you washed in the blood of the Lamb?

Ives and Programmaticism

That Ives was fundamentally a composer of program music can hardly be questioned; even his "pure" works—his sonatas and symphonies—at least have (except for the very early ones) programmatic titles, and in many cases the references go further than that. Much of his music bristles with quotations, tunes that either are familiar or are unfamiliar but have a familiar ring to them, and in most cases one is aware that a deliberate reference is intended.

One can hear Ives concurring with Emerson: "Borrowing can come of magnanimity and stoutness. . . . You do not quote, but recognize your own."

Perhaps it is Ives's nearly constant reference to a larger framework that at least partly accounts for his increased appeal today. Ives is coming into his own at a time when we are witnessing a resurgence of program music—music that, even if only by virtue of a title (and it can hardly be denied that an engaging title has been an important attribute of a composition since 1960), invokes something outside itself. The quotation, in advanced jazz as well as in concert music, is a frequent mannerism; and the montage, with its implicit capacity for commentary, is as frequently used in music as it is in art. All this Ives was doing more than fifty years ago.

If Ives is a programmatic composer he is also an impressionist, and the impressions he develops his pieces from are always vivid and keenly felt. *The Housatonic at Stockbridge* is an excellent place to start with in examining Ives the impressionist. Written before 1911, it forms the last movement of his *First Orchestral Set,* better known as *Three Places in New England.* Ives's own account of what suggested the piece gives us a point of departure; rarely is he so explicit about the genesis of a work.

> The last movement, *The Housatonic at Stockbridge,* was suggested by a Sunday morning walk that Mrs. Ives and I took near Stockbridge [in western Massachusetts] the summer after we were married. We walked in the meadows along the River and heard the distant singing from the Church across the River. The mist had not entirely left the river bed, and the colors, the running water, the banks and trees were something that one would always remember.[11]

Yet with Ives nothing is ever simple, and though the above might seem to be sufficient to account for this short and lovely piece, there is another influence at work as well—a poem by Robert Underwood Johnson (with the same title as Ives's piece), which begins "Contented river! in thy dreamy realm . . ."; personifies the river as having "grown human laboring with men"; and ends with the poet's restless determination to accompany the river "by fall and shallow to the adventurous sea." It is this final call to movement and action in the poem, rather than the passive impression of the Sunday morning walk, that best explains the accelerating, eddying turbulence of the last section of the piece—turbulence that subsides with utter suddenness, leaving a soft string sound and one of Ives's inconclusive, questioning subdominant endings. At least ten years after the composition of the orchestral piece Ives made a song out of it, incorporating selections from Johnson's text. The vocal line, with its fragment of Heinrich Zeuner's "Missionary Chant" (presumably the distant singing from the church to which Ives referred), can be traced note-for-note in the orchestral version, mostly in the French horns and English horns, until at last it is lost in the complex texture of the final rush to the sea.

The first two movements of *Three Places in New England* show Ives's impressionability to scenes from American history. *The "St. Gaudens" in Boston Common* (ca. 1911), subtitled *Col. Shaw and His Colored Regiment,* evokes the Civil War. Again there are two layers of reference: to the black regiment under Col. Robert Gould Shaw, that fought in the Civil War, and to the bronze relief by Augustus Saint-Gaudens, unveiled on Boston Common in

1897, which memorialized it. Ives's piece, a ghostly sort of march, evokes the marching regiment as the sculptor caught it. There are impressionistic echoes of the songs from the era, such as Stephen Foster's "Old Black Joe" and Henry Clay Work's "Marching Through Georgia." The piece furnishes an interesting example of the way Ives distills the essence of his tunes and allows their motives to suffuse his works. The interval of a minor third is important throughout *The "St. Gaudens"*; it is presented at once in the flute and piano (Example 17–6). This same minor third is common to the choruses of both songs—a kind of hidden link (Example 17–7) shows it first in "Old Black Joe" and then in "Marching Through Georgia"). The associational process is so subtle as to appear almost subconscious.

Example 17–6

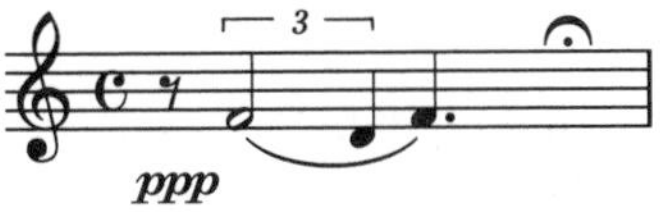

Example 17–7

Putnam's Camp, Redding, Connecticut (ca. 1912), the second of the *Three Places in New England,* harks back to the Revolution, and the tunes used are "The British Grenadiers," a snatch of "Yankee Doodle," and a march tune (Example 17–8) that Ives had used in his rollicking *Country Band March* nearly ten years earlier. (The same tune appears in the *Hawthorne* movement of the *Concord* Sonata and the second movement of the Fourth Symphony.)

Example 17–8

Ives's rather elaborate program depicts a child wandering away from a Fourth of July picnic at the site of the Revolutionary War encampment, falling asleep, and seeing the old soldiers marching out of camp with fife and drum, with Major General Israel Putnam himself coming over the hill. Ives's use of two different march tempos simultaneously will be discussed a little later.

A longer set of compositions, finished about the same time, further illustrates Ives's programmaticism. This is the "symphony" labeled *Four New England Holidays.* It consists of four movements, which may be played as separate pieces. In addition to treating specific holidays, there are references to the four seasons; each begins with an impressionistic evocation of its season and then proceeds to the celebration. Ives has described the pieces as "attempts to make pictures in music of common events in the lives of common people (that is, of fine people), mostly of the rural communities." Of the four movements—*Washington's Birthday* (winter), *Decoration Day* (spring), *The Fourth of July* (summer), and *Thanksgiving* (autumn)—we shall take a closer look at the third.

For *The Fourth of July* (summer), we have Ives's own description:

> It's a boy's '4th. . . . His festivities start in the quiet of midnight before, and grow raucous with the sun. Everybody knows what it's like—if everybody doesn't—Cannon on the Green, Village Band on Main Street, fire crackers, shanks mixed on cornets, strings around big toes, torpedoes, Church bells, lost finger, fifes, clam-chowder, a prize-fight, drum-corps, burnt shins, parades (in and out of step), saloons all closed (more drunks than usual), baseball game (Danbury All-Stars vs Beaver Brook Boys), pistols, mobbed umpire, Red, White and Blue, runaway horse—and the day ends with the sky-rocket over the Church-steeple, just after the annual explosion sets the Town-Hall on fire. All this is not in the music—not now.[12]

The multitude of impressions, seemingly random, crowding each other, superimposing themselves—all this is startlingly parallel to Ives's musical composition. Everywhere he looks there is something to record; he cannot get it all down. "All this is not in the music,—not now."

But what *is* in the music is a good deal. There is a quiet opening in which the violins and string basses begin "Columbia, the Gem of the Ocean," a great favorite of Ives's and the tune that is to be the mainstay of the movement. There is a gradual gain of momentum, as bits and pieces of a dozen other tunes are heard; there is an explosion of fireworks; the band finally comes on with a great tumultuous rendition of the main theme, wrong notes, missed beats and all; there is a final explosion—and again quietness. The sound of the band in full swing in this movement is one of the most vividly realized moments in all of Ives's music: the tunes ("Columbia, the Gem of the Ocean," "The Battle Hymn of the Republic," and "Yankee Doodle" all at once), recklessly off key, are heard through the buzz and roar of the crowd noises. Ives has built up a musical equivalent of the scene he saw and felt so vividly. A look at the score conveys the same sense of exuberant detail (especially in the explosion) that one hears in the sounds. Originally thought possibly unplayable, even by Ives himself, these are some of his grandest and most successful pages.

Simultaneity and perspective

You will encounter many manifestations of simultaneity in Ives's music. His impressionistic bent—his fidelity to his model, which was life itself as experienced—led him to try to render the sense of two or more things going on at the same time. Though his works are full of this, one famous example will suffice by way of illustration. In *Putnam's Camp* (the second of *Three Places in New England*) we hear one march beat established, and presently another—in a different tempo, marked "as a distant drum beat"—is heard superimposed. The rhythms are shown in Example 17–9.

Example 17–9

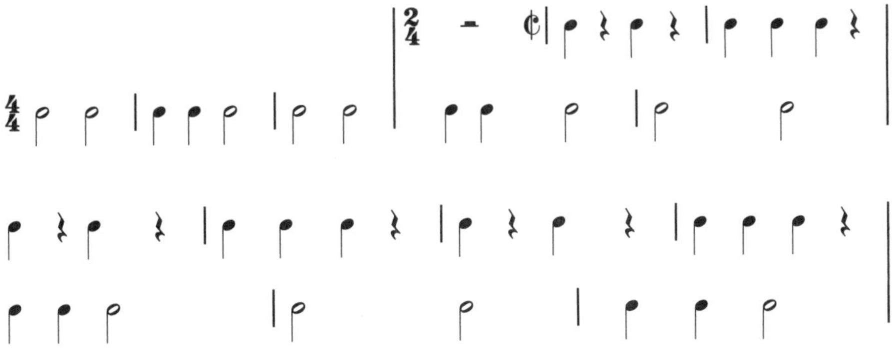

There are many examples of even more complex simultaneous meters in Ives's music, but this one is particularly clear, and has a direct relationship to the boyhood experience described earlier of hearing the two bands marching around the park. Such a representation in music was not entirely without precedent; Mozart, the superb dramatist (whom Ives, sharing the view of many modernists in his time, grossly underestimated), had put three dance orchestras on the stage in *Don Giovanni,* each playing a different dance in a different tempo. Mozart's orchestras harmonize, however; Ives was after a more clashing effect.

The concept of *perspective* finds its way into Ives's work as well—a sense of relative nearness and distance. His father had studied the differences in *quality* between a sound and its echo, and between a distant sound and a sound played softly at close range. Ives himself wrote: "As the distant hills, in a landscape, row upon row, grow gradually into the horizon, so there may be something corresponding to this in the presentation of music." This spatial sense can be heard in two works, both of which have philosophical connotations.

Some time before June 1908, Ives composed a short work he called *The Unanswered Question, A Cosmic Landscape.* It has become one of his most famous pieces. As Cowell describes it,

> The orchestra is divided, the strings playing very softly throughout offstage, representing the silence of the seers who, even if they have an answer, cannot reply; the wind group, on stage, is dominated by the trumpet, which asks the Perennial Question of Existence over and over in the same way, while "the Fighting Answerers (flutes and other people)" run about trying in vain to discover the invisible, unattainable reply to the trumpet. When they finally surrender the search they mock the trumpet's reiteration and depart. The Question is then

> asked again, for the last time, and the "silence" sounds from a distance undisturbed.[13]

The piece, as usually performed, requires two conductors; the sense of perspective is enhanced if the strings play offstage, or behind a curtain.

Not all the explorations of Ives's far-ranging musical mind can be traced here—his work with the twelve tones of the chromatic scale used in series, for example, and his work with quarter-tones, represented by three pieces for two pianos tuned a quarter-tone apart. Much of his work appeared to anticipate, or at least be concurrent with, the work of major European innovators such as Schoenberg—a fact to which he was apparently indifferent. Ives's denial in the 1930s, however, of *any* influence by European composers, and his disparagement of them, shows him as having adopted a somewhat exaggeratedly independent stance in this regard—a stance perhaps understandable in that it was in accord with the prevailing iconoclastic views held generally by the American avant-garde of that time.*

Ives's Humor

There are few composers with as demonstrably keen a sense of humor as Ives. It is obvious from his writings (in which a heated intensity and occasional acidity are nearly always counterbalanced by some remark of humorous detachment), from the marginal notes penned in his scores (mostly to "Rollo," his name for the unimaginative musician or listener who has to have everything according to the rules, and to what he is familiar with), and from the accounts of all those who knew him in life. The important thing to consider here is that it shows up in his music as well. It may show itself in just a sudden gesture, as in his thumbing-the-nose ending of the Second Symphony with a loud dissonance. It may appear in the crafting of an entire fantasy-comedy piece, such as the *Hawthorne* movement in the *Concord* Sonata or the vastly complex second movement of the Fourth Symphony, which is related to it—a piece of Falstaffian proportions in which he uses once again part of the *Country Band March* he wrote years before. Many of the short pieces he called *Cartoons* or *Take-offs* show a keen sense of humor.

The songs show several aspects of Ives's humor. He can use epigrammatical and witty texts, as in *Ann Street,* or a song to words he wrote himself, called *1, 2, 3*:

> Why doesn't one, two, three seem to appeal
> to a Yankee as much as one, two!

(This was from an early sketch, from Ives's bachelor days with his companions in Poverty Flat, entitled *Rube trying to walk 2 to 3!*—"written as a joke, and sounds like one! Watty McCormick only one to see it! and Harry Farrar! at 2:45 A.M.") Some songs describe a comic situation, as in the first of the two *Memories*

* See note 2 of this chapter.

songs ("sitting in the opera house—waiting for the curtain to rise") or *The Circus Band:*

> Where is the lady all in pink?
> Last year she waved to me I think;
> Can she have died? Can! that! rot!
> She is passing but she sees me not!

Ives makes humorous allusions in the music itself. In the otherwise serious *On the Antipodes,*

> Sometimes Nature's nice and sweet, as a little pansy, and
> Sometimes "it ain't."

is set with the expected "nice" saccharine sounds on the first line, followed by crashing dissonances on the second. Finally, an instance of rarefied, sophisticated humor is to be found in a song called *The Side Show.* The stumbling of an old lame horse that turns the merry-go-round is imitated by an uneven rhythm of five beats that Ives says makes the carousel tune sound "a bit like a Russian dance," at which point he quotes two bars of Tchaikovsky's famous 5/4 waltz from the *Pathétique* Symphony!

The sources of Ives's musical language

Although Ives's music has an unmistakable and distinctive sound, which has begun to influence other American music to a certain extent, it is difficult to define an Ives *style,* since he wrote in so many diverse ways. The sources of his musical language are his own inventive imagination with tones—and the music he heard and played in Danbury and New Haven before he was twenty-five. As the Cowells have written, "Ives' music had its roots in the church, stage, parlor, and dance music of a small American town—the popular music of his time, in short. . . . He was the first composer in the United States to commit himself unreservedly to the vernacular for the grammar of a new symphonic speech."[14]

Of course there are pages and pages in works such as the *Concord* Sonata and the Second String Quartet, and passages even in the songs, in which it would be farfetched to try to detect any relationship to popular music. But whenever Ives needs a musical *subject,* it is almost invariably to the popular sources that he turns. In 1917 he wrote a song (both words and music) called *The Things Our Fathers Loved:* with appropriately evocative music, it is in effect a short ode to Ives's musical roots.

> I think there must be a place in the soul all made of tunes, of tunes
> of long ago;
> I hear the organ on the Main Street corner,
> Aunt Sarah humming gospels;
> Summer evenings,
> The village cornet band, playing in the square.
> The town's Red, White and Blue, all Red, White and Blue

Now! Hear the songs!
I know not what are the words
But they sing in my soul of the things our Fathers loved.

Ives's attitude toward the performance of his music

We can be sure that Charles Ives had, at least as a young man, the normal composer's desire to hear his works realized in performance. The piano and organ works he could, of course, play himself; he once wrote, "There is nothing that I have ever written for a piano that I haven't been able to play."[15] It is likely that a good many of the germinal ideas to be more fully realized in later works were first played on the organ, and that some were even tried out on unsuspecting congregations until Ives finally gave up his church job in 1902, feeling that it was unfair to inflict his explorations on "captive" listeners. But it was at least possible for him to hear ideas for this medium. With the instrumental and orchestral works, it was different. Until about 1915 he made efforts to secure performances, or at least to hear some of his works. He occasionally hired individual performers to play with him, and groups of musicians from theater orchestras. The latter he had great respect for; and little could he have realized at the time that these informal readings were the nearest thing to performances of some of his works that he was to hear until after he had stopped composing. When the musicians really tried, he was respectful of their efforts; years later he declined to allow the premiere of a work to be billed as a "first performance," feeling it would not be fair to "those old fellers" who had done their best with his music in the early days.

So there is no doubt that in the beginning he wished, and even expected, to hear his works. As time went on, however, and after some bitter and humiliating experiences with performances and readings, his attitude toward performance seemed gradually to change. His music itself became less and less geared to actual realization in sound—less in touch with the practical problems.

As evidence of this we have the music's difficulties and enormous complexities—about which Ives manifested a curiously dualistic attitude. On one hand, he sometimes freely castigated the laziness, indifference, and lack of ability of performers who would not come to grips with the difficulties of new or hard music, including but not limited to his own. He described, for example, his own successful efforts to master complex simultaneous rhythms: "I have with much practice been able to keep five, and even six, rhythms going in my mind at once, so that I can hear each one naturally, by leaning toward it." On the other hand, at times he seemed quite ready to acknowledge that some of his music was possibly unplayable. Of the *Fourth of July* movement he wrote: "I did what I wanted to, quite sure that the thing would never be played, and probably *could* never be played." In the postface to the *114 Songs* he wrote: "Some of the songs in this book, particularly among the later ones, cannot be sung, and if they could, might perhaps prefer, if they had a say, to remain as they are; that is, 'in the leaf'—and that they will remain in this peaceful state is more than presumable." It will be noted that the idea that the music was unperformable—an idea proved wrong by more recent higher standards of musicianship—is linked with a certain half-bitter resignation traceable to the neglect, indifference, hostility, and ridicule he experienced.

Another evidence of his growing remoteness from the realistic arena of performance is seen in his apparent casualness with regard to the resources called for in a particular piece. He suddenly wants a flute in a piano sonata, or an organ pedal tone in a song (*On the Antipodes*). In another song, he writes at one point: "These four measures sound better sung with string quartet if one is available." It is true that many of these indications are marked *ad libitum,* that Ives was in later years notoriously and often exasperatingly permissive with regard to the details of performance of his works, and that these indications often seem to spring from an imaginative sense very akin to his sense of humor. Though these seeming caprices may be justified purely from the standpoint of the composer's imagination, and though they may sometimes be given a philosophical garb ("Why can't a musical thought be presented as it is born—perchance a 'bastard of the slums,' or a 'daughter of a bishop'—and if it happens to go better later on a bass-drum than upon a harp, get a good bass-drummer"), they nevertheless betray Ives's detachment from the professional world of music and the realities of performance. Bernard Herrmann, a practical professional musician, for years a conductor with CBS radio, who devoted a great deal of time and care to bringing out performances of Ives's music, said: "Ives, after all, was a very impractical man when it came to performances of music. By not being a professional musician in the sense that he did not have to make a living of music, he entered into an abstraction of music. Because it was an abstraction, it didn't deal with any of the realistic problems."[16]

This detachment took on at times the aspect of dealing with a reality of music that transcended any actual realization in sound, a realization that he seemed actually to disdain at times. His famous "My God! What has sound got to do with music!" is his most succinct and often-quoted statement of this attitude. He continues cogently:

> The waiter brings the only fresh egg he has, but the man at breakfast sends it back because it doesn't fit his eggcup. Why can't music go out in the same way it comes in to a man, without having to crawl over a fence of sounds, thoraxes, catguts, wire, wood, and brass?[17]

Beethoven, it may be remembered, voiced a similar impatience with the mechanism of performance—even before total deafness removed him, too, from the more mundane realms of music.

This sense of the unimportance of actual performance showed itself in another trait occasionally found in composers, even sometimes among those who are much more in touch with the world of performance—the disinclination to regard works as *finished,* or in final form. All his creative life Ives was rearranging his musical ideas—transforming them from one medium to another. The *Emerson* movement of the *Concord* Sonata he kept continually working at, changing bits here and there, cutting out or elaborating ("I may always have the pleasure of not finishing it"). This became also for him a philosophical question, and its most striking manifestation is in the *Universe Symphony.* A plan for this exists:

I. (Past) Formation of waters and mountains.
II. (Present) Earth, evolution in nature and humanity.
III. (Future) Heaven, the rise of all to the spiritual.

There are also some sketches and fairly explicit notes, which are fascinating, and have to do with the matters of perspective and simultaneity previously discussed. Ives did work on the *Universe Symphony* from time to time, even as late as 1951, but it is possible that it was conceived as a work never to be finished.

Idealism versus professionalism in music

Of the many aspects of Ives's idealism regarding art that might be explored, a central one, which eventually involves all the others, is his attitude toward professionalism, and what it does to an artist's independence and self-reliance. Ives was one of the last of our "amateur" composers (in the sense of not depending upon music for a living), and he was certainly a uniquely rugged individualist in the matter of the principle involved in deriving any income from his music. Ives himself spoke to the point as follows:

> We hear that Mr. Smith or Mr. Morgan, etc., et al., design to establish a "course at Rome," to raise the standard of American music (or the standard of American composers—which is it?); but possibly the more our composer accepts from his patrons *"et al.,"* the less he will accept *from himself.* It may be possible that a day in a "Kansas wheat field" will do more for him than three years in Rome. . . . If for every thousand-dollar prize a potato field be substituted, so that these candidates of Clio can dig a little in real life, perhaps dig up a natural inspiration, art's air might be a little clearer.

And again, in a strong statement that summarizes his attitude:

> Perhaps the birth of art will take place at the moment in which the last man who is willing to make a living out of art is gone and gone forever.[18]

Whether these are Ives's rationalizations for his early insight that he could not expect any degree of success, monetary or otherwise, from the only kind of music he was interested in writing is beside the point. The fact is that he made an early decision to go into business, so that his family (which he did not yet have) would not be forced to "starve on his dissonances." He apparently never regretted his decision, but saw a relationship between his daily work in the world and his art that tended to develop a "spiritual sturdiness" which showed itself in "a close union between spiritual life and the ordinary business of life." Emerson said: "There is virtue yet in the hoe and the spade, for learned as well as for unlearned hands." Ives said:

> I have experienced a great fulness of life in business. The fabric of existence weaves itself whole. You cannot set an art off in the corner and hope for it to have vitality, reality and substance. There can be nothing *exclusive* about a substantial art. It comes directly out of the heart of experience of life and thinking about life

and living life. My work in music helped my business and work in business helped my music.[19]

Ives's Music and the World

We have surveyed rather painstakingly the career, the music, and the ideas of Charles Ives, out of the conviction that Ives is one of the central figures in our story. It now remains to trace very briefly the story of the acceptance of his music, and to survey contemporary assessments of it.

Charles Ives's music was not suddenly discovered after his death, nor did he emerge dramatically from obscurity, Minerva-like, a full-grown hero made to order for the adulation of a new generation in the 1970s, the decade of his centennial (though one would think so to peruse some latter-day writing). The truth is more complicated, and as usual more interesting, for the list of hard-working and courageous protagonists in "the Ives case" is rather long and distinguished. After the discouragements of the teens, some recognition came as early as the 1920s. The poet Henry Bellamann, a lifelong friend of Ives after their first meeting, wrote and spoke in his behalf, and arranged performances of the *Concord* Sonata (one movement at a time) as early as 1920. A Town Hall concert in New York by the venturesome Pro-Musica group presented two movements of the Fourth Symphony, with Eugene Goosens conducting, in 1927.

As the Cowells have pointed out, the thirties was a time when it was mostly composers, and a few critics, who championed Ives's music. Henry Cowell had introduced Ives to Nicolas Slonimsky, a Russian-born composer, conductor, and writer who must have a significant place in any recounting of the story of American music beginning in the 1920s, when he came to America as an opera coach and, later, as Koussevitzky's assistant. Slonimsky conducted *Three Places in New England* in Boston in 1930, and *Decoration Day* in San Francisco in 1932. He also conducted Ives's music in Europe about the same time, with considerable success. It was, in fact, the acceptance of the music in Europe that had a lot to do with its being taken more seriously in America at this time—evidence that the influence of European taste and opinion was still strong here. Around 1930 the critic Paul Rosenfeld wrote enthusiastically about Ives, as did Aaron Copland, with some reservations, in 1933. Copland arranged for some of the earliest public performances of the songs.

The 1940s, as the Cowells have noted, was the time when Ives's music began to be championed by important performers. A landmark event, touching off much of the success of the forties, was the first complete public performance of the *Concord* Sonata in 1939 by John Kirkpatrick. (Kirkpatrick, who had discovered the sonata in 1927, subsequently became a leading Ives interpreter, scholar, and authority, and curator of the Ives collection at Yale University.) This performance in New York's Town Hall, which had to be repeated, marked the beginning of widespread favorable critical acclaim of Ives's music; Lawrence Gilman called the *Concord* Sonata "the greatest music composed by an American." Thus the stage was set for important performances in the next decade. The violin virtuoso Joseph Szigeti put the Fourth Violin Sonata in his repertory, and in 1944 the influential Los Angeles Evenings-on-the-Roof concerts, under Peter Yates, honored jointly Charles Ives and Arnold Schoenberg, both then seventy. In 1946 the West Coast composer and conductor Lou Harrison premiered the Third Symphony; the next year it was awarded the Pulitzer Prize. The first performance of the Second Symphony took place under Leonard Bernstein in 1951.

By this time Ives's music was well on its way, and the 1950s saw its acceptance and acclaim by a far greater segment of the general musical public, who now had a chance to hear a fair amount of it. (Ives himself, who died in 1954, heard very little; he had virtually stopped going to concerts after the 1920s and is said to have owned neither a radio nor a phonograph.) The principal barrier to the performance of Ives's music (except for the comparatively few published works) for the last thirty years has not been hostility or indifference to it, but the extreme difficulties of making performable editions out of the chaotic and jumbled manuscripts. It was for this reason that the Fourth Symphony had to wait until 1965 for its first complete performance. After Ives's death, much care was lavished on sorting out, cataloguing, and photostating the manuscripts. As has been noted, only the painstaking efforts through the years of such people as Henry and Sidney Cowell, John Kirkpatrick, Elliott Carter, Lou Harrison, and Bernard Herrmann have made much of Ives's music accessible at all.

For Ives the man there is no lack of admiration; his idealism, his grit, his humor, and his generosity have fired the imagination of succeeding generations. For the music there is admiration and love—tempered, for many who know it well, with certain reservations. Copland has pointed out the deleterious effect on Ives's music of his having worked in virtual isolation—"cut off from the vitalizing contact of an audience." We have already noted some of the musical consequences of this loss of contact. Elliott Carter points to the "large amounts of indifferentiated confusion," and is forced, reluctantly, to the conclusion that Ives's work often "falls short of his intentions." And, as Virgil Thomson has reminded us in connection with Ives, "Intentions are no guarantee of quality." He goes on to point out the need to distinguish purely musical quality from the wealth of not-strictly-musical associations that have grown up around Ives's work: "When time shall have dissolved away his nostalgias and ethical aspirations, as they have largely done for Beethoven and for Bach and even for the descriptive leitmotifs of Wagner, what sheer musical reality will remain in Ives's larger works?" Then there are the reservations engendered by the unevenness of his large output, much of it left in rough state. It is certainly inevitable that, given the pace at which Ives worked during the period of his "double life," he could hardly have achieved a very complete realization of all his ideas, or a very conclusive form for all his works. In the early years, the free rein he gave his imagination channeled all his energies into a kind of furious sketching approach to composition. One has the impression that his ideas were too profuse, and tumbled in upon him too fast, for many of them to be fully realized.

Yet there is enough. Ives's most cogent, most nearly perfect realizations—many of the songs, *The Unanswered Question, The Housatonic at Stockbridge,* practically all the *Holidays*—have been indispensable to our music. Virgil Thomson, speaking for all subsequent composers, hailed Charles Ives as "whether we knew it or not, the father of us all."

Carl Ruggles (1876–1971)

The picture most of us have of Carl Ruggles is that of a craggy New England nonagenarian who worked in a remodeled schoolhouse in Vermont, and whose entire output (those works he allowed to survive) consists of fewer than a dozen pieces: music of consistently high integrity, density, and dissonance. And this is one artist about whom the first impression—and the legend—is essentially accurate. Further investigation, as we shall see, will reveal that nothing about the legend needs revising, only filling out.

Ruggles is often mentioned with Ives. Indeed, they had much in common; they were nearly exact contemporaries, and both were New Englanders of a highly independent spirit and temperament. Although they did not meet until 1930, when both were over fifty (Ruggles was involved at the time with a particular New York wing of the avant-garde that held a disparaging view of Ives), they immediately became fast friends and great admirers of each other's music.

There are further points of similarity in career and attitude. Both had early practical acquaintance with music (Ruggles studied violin as a child; he once played for President Grover Cleveland!). Both received academic training from the best that the New England musical "establishment" had to offer (Ives from Horatio Parker of Yale, and Ruggles from John Knowles Paine at Harvard). Both were uncompromising idealists in music and indifferent to popularity, and when each struck out to find new paths, these paths (though quite dissimilar) both led into the domain of dissonant and "difficult" musical utterance.

Unlike Ives, however, Ruggles had an extremely small output, and the individual pieces themselves are compact. His orchestral "symphonic poem" *Sun Treader,* which was six years in the making, is, at seventeen and a half minutes, one of Ruggles's longest pieces. His complete surviving works could be performed in a single program of less than two hours. They are remarkably consistent, and each is honed to an amazing degree of perfection. There is no nostalgic or impressionistic display of Americana; in fact, Ruggles's music has no discernible relationship to American popular music, and very little to any other music. Ruggles was a most meticulous craftsman. But he was also not in a hurry. With the support of a patron and in good health, he was able to work in his forty-foot-square studio in Vermont, dividing his time between painting (his abstract canvases have been exhibited in several museums), composing (he often covered the walls like a mural with his music, written with different-colored crayons on huge staff paper, so that he could see an entire section at once), and entertaining a vast range of friends, treating them to samples of his skill as a raconteur. Unlike Ives, Ruggles seldom expressed himself in writing, but he was known for his voluble, opinionated talk—laced with salty profanity. (For once the cliché is apt: Ruggles descended from a seafaring family, grew up on Cape Cod, and went to Boston originally to study ship design.)

Also unlike Ives, Ruggles did involve himself in the working world of music. At the age of thirty-six he went out to Winona, Minnesota, where he taught in a conservatory and, most important, founded an orchestra and conducted opera and symphony concerts. When he returned to New York

(1917), he was over forty. It was about that time that he found his patron, but he continued to involve himself in the promotion of new music in New York, first with the International Composers' Guild with Edgar Varèse (1923–27) and then with the Pan-American Association of Composers (1927–33). Later in the thirties he taught seminars in modern composition at the University of Miami, Florida.

The Minnesota years seem to have been his last years of apprenticeship; when they were over, he began writing the music we know today. He allowed nothing he wrote before 1919 to survive. (He also destroyed an unfinished opera, *The Sunken Bell,* based on a German play.)

Ruggles has left only two works for voice: the early *Toys,* a song for voice and piano, and *Vox Clamans in Deserta* for voice and orchestra. *Angels* (rearranged in 1938 from an earlier work called *Men and Angels*) is for four muted trumpets and two muted trombones. For piano solo he wrote a group of pieces called *Evocations,* and for three pianos a piece called *Polyphonic Composition.* The rest are for larger forces. *Men and Mountains* (1924) consists of three movements: *Men* (for strings), *Lilacs* (also for strings, and frequently played alone), and *Marching Mountains* (for orchestra). *Portals,* for string orchestra, dates originally from 1926, but was revised several times. His two works for large orchestra are *Sun Treader* (1932, the title from a line in Browning) and *Organum* (1945).

Unlike Ives, a musical impressionist who sometimes did his tone-painting in a remarkably photographic way, Ruggles did his only painting on canvas, and even there he dealt with abstractions. His music never overtly reflects outward scenes. His melodies are often long, sweeping lines, gathering in intensity and covering a great range. He is usually very careful not to repeat a note too soon. The opening melody of *Portals* (Example 17–10) shows these features.

Example 17–10

His texture is usually contrapuntal, but he doubles parts extensively, and unlike Ives he seldom has more than three real parts going at once. When he pauses on a chord, on the other hand, it is often complex. Of the two sonorities in *Portals* shown in Example 17–11, the first has seven tones and the second eleven; in each there is only one tone doubled.

Ruggles's music is never dancelike or marchlike; there are no strong recurring accents. Even the prominent drumbeats in *Sun Treader* are accelerated, so that they establish no steady pulse. The form, like the rhythm, is rhapsodic, and virtually seamless.

Example 17–11

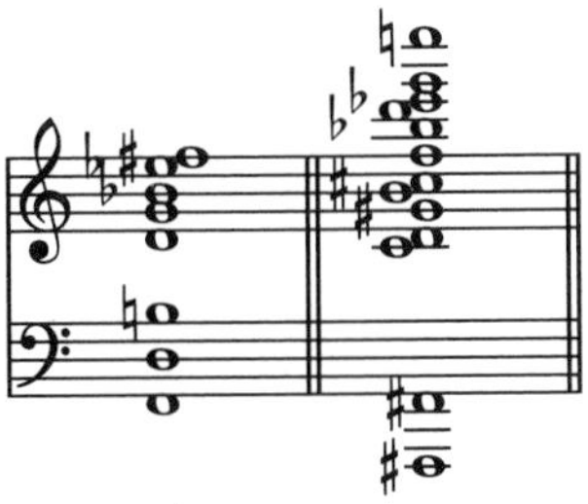

Ruggles is not apt to produce a detachable "tune" that one remembers, and he never quotes. Still, his music, in terms of its sound and, even more important, in terms of its *gesture,* leaves an unmistakable impression. It is dissonant and often dense, but it sings in a way much dissonant music does not, and it never seems to falter or lose its way.[20]

Though the sounds, to Ruggles's first audiences, were new, the aesthetic is old. Ruggles believed in a quality in art he called "the sublime." To him the greatest composers were Bach and Handel (and the greatest living composer was Charles Ives). Charles Seeger, in a 1932 article that still gives us the most well-rounded picture of the man and his music, referred to Carl Ruggles's work as a "distinct type of artistic effort—the attempt to convey the most approved ideal by the least approved means."[21]

"The American Five" and One Remarkable Woman

Five composers have been grouped together as representing the early-twentieth-century avant-garde of American music: Charles Ives, Carl Ruggles, Henry Cowell (with whom we shall deal presently), and two others, John J. Becker and Wallingford Riegger.* Becker (1886–1961) was the only one of the "five" from the Midwest. Though mid-America remained his territory (he held various teaching posts there for forty years), he was in close touch with Ives and Cowell, and became an energetic and uncompromising battler for the cause of new music. (One often finds the term "crusader" applied to Becker.) Beginning in the late 1920s he composed music that is often forceful and highly dissonant, and is characterized by an interest in contrapuntal forms such as canon and fugue. Of the music of the "five," Becker's comparatively small body of works are the least known and least performed.

Wallingford Riegger (1885–1961), a nearly exact contemporary of Becker, has already been encountered in the previous chapter as the composer of the striking Concerto for Piano and Woodwind Quintet. Though a lifelong advocate of new music, Riegger himself wrote in many styles, and some of his most accessible works (such as the often-performed *Dance Rhythms*) are re-

* The "American Five" form a kind of "far-out" complement to Virgil Thomson's five "commandos" (Thomson, Copland, Sessions, Piston, and Harris) who, for all of their innovation and modernity, were closer to the musical "center," and less avowedly devoted to the new and the experimental.

lated to and were in fact written for the dance. His credentials for inclusion in the "five" of the American avant-garde are represented by such works as the early *Study in Sonority* (1927) and *Dichotomy* (1932).

Ruth Crawford (Seeger) (1901–53) was a gifted composer whose breadth of interests and abilities resulted in her leaving, at her early death, a fairly small but important body of original compositions. Like Becker she was a midwesterner by birth, but she left for New York in 1929, and soon became a part of the avant-garde musical scene there, in association with Henry Cowell (who befriended and aided her, as he did so many), Carl Ruggles, and Edgar Varèse. Her early String Quartet (1931) is a remarkable work deserving of attention. A short work in four sections lasting barely ten minutes, the quartet is prophetic of later developments in its rhapsodic quality and in the rugged independence of its individual voices in the first section, the pointillistic scherzo character of the second, and the fascinatingly original contrapuntal dialogue and rhythmic relationship between the first violin and the other instruments in the last. In terms of sheer sound and texture, the most remarkable is the slow third section. Melody in the usual sense does not exist; our attention is held instead by what has replaced it: surging dynamic accents, and harmonies, mostly dissonant, that are constantly shifting in register and color. It would not sound out of place had it been composed fifty years later.[22]

Ruth Crawford Seeger's work in advanced idioms of the time is also well represented by her remarkable *Three Songs* (1930–33) to poems of Carl Sandburg. Ruth Crawford became a close friend of Sandburg's (initially through teaching piano to his daughters), and Sandburg's involvement with American folk music probably contributed to making this another of Crawford's avid interests. She made many transcriptions and arrangements of folk songs, including some for children. One of Crawford's teachers was Charles Seeger (1886–1979), whose perceptive mind and broad range of interests made him one of the most articulate and influential teachers, writers, and musicologists of this century in America. Ruth Crawford became Seeger's second wife, and their shared interest in folk music has been carried on by her stepson Pete, and by her own children Mike and Peggy.

Henry Cowell (1897–1965)

Henry Cowell came into the world gifted with the kind of observant, eagerly absorbing mentality that was able to reap the full benefit of growing up in the richly polyglot atmosphere of the San Francisco Bay area just after the turn of the century—the same milieu that a generation earlier had nurtured Jack London and Gertrude Stein. Unencumbered by even modest means, and free of any predetermined set of cultural values, Cowell was free to accept his musical stimulus where he found it—in Irish folk tunes (from his family), Gregorian chant (from a neighbor), Oriental music, and rural American hymnody (from early sojourns in Kansas and Oklahoma). In San Francisco, young Cowell heard Chinese opera more frequently than Italian. At five he started studying the violin, giving it up at eight. When he got hold of a battered old upright piano, he soon found he had an instrument that would open up new possibilities, and he began experimenting. In 1912, at the age of fifteen, he played in public in San Francisco a piece called *The Tides of Manaunaun;* it was a prelude to an opera he was writing based on Irish mythology. Manaunaun was the maker of great tides that swept through the universe; to convey the sense of this vast motion, Cowell, interestingly enough, hit upon the same device that Ives, on the other side of the continent and at about the same time, was using to convey the sense of the masses in *Majority*—huge groups of tones sounded together that could only be played with the entire forearm. These were soon to become known as "tone clusters." Cowell used them in many of his piano works—became notorious for them, in fact—but nowhere more effectively than in this very early piece (Example 17–12).[23]

Example 17–12

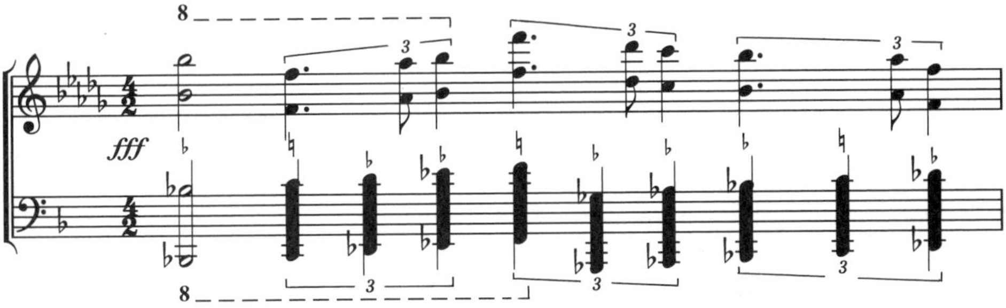

This would seem quite a start for a boy just turned fifteen, but Cowell had been composing since he was eleven, and there was much more to come. By the time he was twenty, he had composed 199 pieces, including an opera and a symphony. By then he had become convinced of the value of some systematic study, and found an ideal person to supervise it in Charles Seeger, then teaching at the University of California. Cowell's formal education had ended with the third grade, but he was a voracious learner: at the age of twenty he was seeing Seeger for lessons in music every morning in Berkeley, studying English with Samuel Seward every afternoon at Stanford, working at night as a janitor—and writing a book! Cowell went east to New York for further study, and began appearing in concerts playing his own works on the piano. Between 1923 and 1933 he made five important tours of Europe (including a trip in 1928 to the Soviet Union, which he was the first American composer to visit); his new music stimulated interest, not only in and of itself, but in new American music generally.

When he was not traveling abroad, Cowell divided his time for the next thirty years between teaching and lecturing (mostly at New York's New School for Social Research, where he was director of music, but also at Columbia and Stanford universities; Mills, Bennington, and Adelphi colleges; and the Peabody Conservatory), editing, writing, championing the new music of others, and of course continuing to compose a prodigious amount of music himself.

There are many sides to Cowell's work. There is Henry Cowell the teacher—one of our best, and an important influence on such composers as Lou Harrison, John Cage, and other free spirits of the musical "left wing."

There is Henry Cowell the tireless worker for new music, and new ideas in music. In 1927 he founded the important periodical *New Music Quarterly*, which published a great many new scores (though not a note of his own). It was through this that he met Charles Ives, becoming his first important discoverer, his lifelong promoter, with his wife Sidney Cowell his first biographer, and after Ives's death his musical executor.

There is Henry Cowell the imaginative theorist and inventor. The book he had virtually finished when he was twenty-two (not published until eleven years later, in 1930) was a slim but important volume called *New Musical Resources*. In it he sets forth the possibilities for new relationships between tones (including the dissonant counterpoint that was to become a familiar feature of new music); for an expanded rhythmic system, using regularly the less accustomed divisions of five, seven, and so on simultaneously with the more usual two, three, and four (Ives was doing this also, but Cowell even invented a new rhythmic notation and nomenclature to encompass it); and for new ways of building chords (in fourths and seconds in addition to the more usual thirds—his clusters he came to call *secundal* chords). An interesting, if somewhat speculative, feature of his work is his scheme of associating the frequency ratios of pitch intervals with rhythmic ratios. According to Cowell, an analogy could be established, for example, between the major triad, with its three pitches in the ratio of 3:4:5 (Example 17–13), and a rhythmic relation of three parts having the same ratios (Example 17–14). This integration of rhythm and pitch he sought to illustrate in two early quartets called the *Romantic* and the *Euphometric*.[24]

Example 17–13

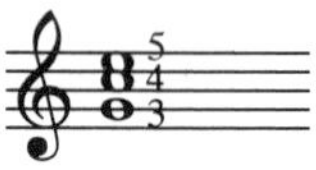

Example 17–14

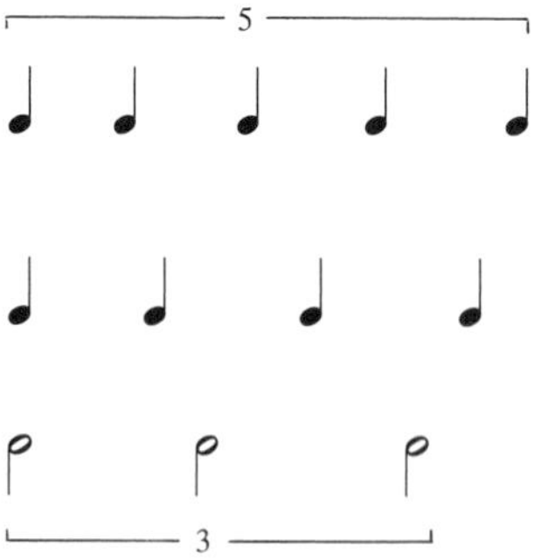

Cowell the inventor collaborated with Professor Léon Thérémin to produce, about 1931, an instrument called the "Rhythmicon," capable of rendering the rhythms of complex ratios. It was never widely used, but it made its point; what it did can now be more easily done by electronic means.

There is also Henry Cowell the student of a worldwide range of musical cultures. In 1931–32 he studied comparative musicology in Berlin with Professor Eric Moritz von Hornbostel. Oriental music he had already heard a great deal of in his youth. His works subsequently bore witness to the detailed study of musical cultures as widely separated as those of Japan, Persia, and Iceland.

And finally there is, as our major concern, Henry Cowell the prolific composer. We left him as the fifteen-year-old composer of a remarkable piano piece. What of his subsequent output?

It is, of course, as varied as the interests of the man himself. The experimental works—those that place him in this chapter as one of our innovators—were for the most part early works. Of these, the short works for piano are the most accessible and open up the most interesting possibilities.

Cowell used tone clusters for their descriptive appropriateness in other short works after *The Tides of Manaunaun.* About 1914 he wrote *Amiable Conversation,* a kind of dialogue between a low-pitched voice and a high-pitched one. It was suggested by an argument he overheard in a Chinese laundry; not understanding the words, he was free to listen to the voices simply as sounds that fluctuated in pitch and intensity as the conversation proceeded. Another early work of about the same vintage is *Advertisement,* in which small clusters are struck with the fist. Cowell describes it as a "humorous impression of the repetitive advertising in the flashing lights of Times Square." He gives the performer the option of repeating one section as many times as desired "to emphasize the absurdity."

About 1923 Cowell began to produce works calling for the performer to play directly on the strings of the piano. (A grand piano is required for these.) In *Aeolian Harp* (named after a small "harp" whose silk strings are played upon by the wind) the performer silently depresses the keys of the successive chords, releasing their dampers; the strings are then swept with the other hand (somewhat in the manner of the autoharp), sometimes with the fingers and sometimes with the thumbnail. They are also plucked. Another small descriptive piece using this technique is *The Fairy Answer:* chords played normally are "echoed" (slightly changed, to identify it as the work of the fairies) by strings swept by hand. In *The Banshee* (ca. 1923) the dampers are all released, and the performer, standing in the crook of the piano, plays directly upon the strings—at times sweeping across them in various ways, at times sweeping lengthwise on one or more strings, at times plucking them. This remarkable piece consists of sounds the farthest removed (until John Cage began playing on the outside of the piano) from the normal ones a piano makes—sounds that gave a significant foretaste of those that were to be produced electronically a quarter of a century later.

Still other possibilities were explored in a piece written about 1930, when Cowell was nearly finished with his experiments on the piano (he was completing his Piano Concerto) and was ready to turn to other matters. The piano piece in question is called *Sinister Resonance.* It involves further direct manipulation of the strings; playing several pitches on one string by "stopping" the string; "muting" strings with the hand; and playing harmonics by lightly touching the strings at the midpoint while they are played from the keyboard.[25]

Cowell's restless inventiveness often suggested areas of exploration that he himself made only a few sallies into, before turning to something else. He never followed up consistently or to any great depth the means suggested in his *New Musical Resources*, nor was it ever his intention to do so. Of the early piano pieces, *The Banshee* and *Sinister Resonance* proved to be the most prophetic. Both suggested a practice that became a trademark of the mildly avant-garde in the fifties and sixties—producing sounds on traditional instruments in ways other than those for which they were designed: blowing air through mouthpiece-less brass instruments, clicking the keys on woodwind instruments, or thumping on the bodies of string instruments. Cowell himself directs players to "tap back of instrument with padded drum stick" in his *United Quartet* (after the early years he was singularly prosaic in his choice of titles), but adds the thoughtful if unnecessary precaution "not hard enough to injure." The muted, damped, and otherwise manipulated sounds of the piano strings in *Sinister Resonance* also led directly into the sounds of the "prepared piano" of John Cage, the device that, more than any other single idea, launched Cage's career. Indeed, Cowell had himself experimented with using various mechanical objects to damp or mute the strings.

After the 1930s Cowell's experimentation with new musical resources began to give place to his eclecticism. He sought to apply the compositional processes appropriate for the writing of longer, more complex works to the musical materials (ethnic, folk, and traditional) of cultures in which the aims and aesthetics of fine art were unknown.

Around 1940 he discovered (as had Virgil Thomson before him) the tradition of native religious music, which began with the New England singing-school masters and continued into the rural South and Midwest in shape-note music—the tradition described in Chapter 6. This interest resulted in a series of compositions known by the title *Hymn and Fuguing Tune*, written for various combinations. They are greatly enlarged elaborations of the basic binary plan of the old *fuging tunes* of Billings and company; there is a first section, primarily chordal, emphasizing open consonances and consonant triads, and a second "fuguing" section, contrapuntal but still fundamentally consonant. Cowell used this material as a point of departure in other works of the period as well, from his Fourth Symphony (1946) to his Tenth Symphony (1953), both of which have hymn and fuguing sections, as well as Irish jigs, a Celtic kind of music-making that greatly appealed to Cowell.

In 1956–57 Cowell went on a world tour, sponsored in part by the Rockefeller Foundation and the United States government. He spent a considerable amount of time in Iran and in Japan, both studying their music and bringing a knowledge of our music to them. This marked the beginning of a series of works based on Persian music (*Persian Set*, 1957, and *Homage to Iran*, 1959) and Japanese music (*Ongaku* for orchestra, 1957). Later his interest expanded to include the music of Iceland; his Symphony No. 16 (1962) is subtitled *Icelandic*. In these works, as in the works inspired by American and Celtic music, Cowell only rarely uses traditional tunes, but writes his *own* Persian, Japanese, or Icelandic music. Always skillfully scored, even to suggesting the timbres of national instruments or the voicing of national choral singing, it nevertheless has a flavor of pleasant musical tourism, of the same type that issued forth in the nineteenth century when Russian and French composers were writing Spanish music.

Henry Cowell's mind was inventive, but quite literal, at times almost childlike. He worked prodigiously at a complicated craft in an uncomplicated way. It was his role to suggest new sound resources without troubling deeper musical waters. But because of his relentless efforts in so many directions (as composer, publisher, editor, impresario, teacher, propagandist, and traveling ambassador) American music and American composers are much in his debt.

Conlon Nancarrow and the Player Piano

Some of the innovators treated in this chapter have functioned more or less actively in the musical life of their times: composers such as Henry Cowell, Carl Ruggles, Edgar Varèse, Lou Harrison, and John Cage (see below) not only took part in but were often founders and leaders of various movements and organizations associated with "advanced" music of their times. But there have also been more or less solitary pioneers—those who, for one reason or another, have been "loners." By no means necessarily misanthropic, they have simply found that the thing *they* had to do with music could be done best (or perhaps *only*) by working alone, in relative isolation and solitude. Charles Ives and Harry Partch were among these. Another composer, whose peaceful and solitary working life in Mexico has been increasingly interrupted by the attention devoted to his music in the 1980s, is Conlon Nancarrow.

Conlon Nancarrow (b. 1912 in Texarkana, Arkansas) is a highly individual composer who ultimately committed himself to the exclusive and intensive cultivation of one singular sound resource (which happened also to have been one suggested by Henry Cowell)—the player piano.

In the early 1930s Nancarrow did study with Nicolas Slonimsky, Walter Piston, and Roger Sessions, but these studies were neither prolonged nor particularly satisfactory. Nancarrow has agreed with one interviewer's conclusion that he learned most from two sources—playing jazz trumpet in his youth, and what he later taught himself.[26] He did in fact take some small part in the 1930s New York musical scene, writing reviews for *Modern Music*. The short pieces he composed then (three of which were published in Henry Cowell's *New Music Quarterly* in 1938, after he had gone to Spain) Nancarrow has not disowned; he is simply no longer interested in them.

Like many artists and intellectuals of the time, Nancarrow was involved in radical left-wing causes.* He went to Spain in 1937–39, fighting in the Lincoln Brigade against Franco's fascists. After his return, when he was determined to leave the country again, he was denied a passport; the only options that were left to him were Canada and Mexico, and he chose Mexico, where he has lived since 1940. It was here, in relative solitude and isolation, that he gradually came to the conclusion that his musical ideas could best be realized on the player piano—an instrument that had actually fascinated him from his youth.

Is the player piano an "old tool," as the term applies to the innovators

* In the 1930s Nancarrow helped organize a Lenin Memorial Concert that took place in the improbably staid venue of Symphony Hall in Boston. One of Nancarrow's teachers, Walter Piston of Harvard, was an unlikely fellow-participant, for he was anything but a radical, and Nancarrow expressed his admiration of Piston's courage. See Gagne and Caras, *Soundpieces*, p. 284.

encountered in this chapter? The history of automatic instruments, which can be programmed to "play themselves" without the participation of a human performer, goes back to antiquity. In more recent times, the music box can be traced to the eighteenth century, and experiments with mechanical pianos began in the second half of the nineteenth century. By the early 1900s, the player piano as we know it was popular, and in full production. The way it worked was that a roll of paper with holes punched in it would pass over a "tracker bar," which resembled an elongated harmonica, with each hole representing a specific piano key. When a vacuum was created within the mechanism, each punched hole in the roll would allow air into the corresponding hole in the tracker bar (as with the harmonica), which would then force the hammer to strike the corresponding string. Thus was an already familiar and ubiquitous parlor instrument converted into an automaton that could execute, without a performer, anything available on commercial piano rolls, from popular songs to the most difficult solos in the repertory.

With a little thought it becomes evident that the holes on the roll not only can be punched to reproduce preexisting music (the original aim of the inventors), but can be punched in such a way as to allow for *any* combination of pitches and rhythms, including combinations that could not possibly be performed by a live pianist. Henry Cowell, in his highly interesting book *New Musical Resources* (1930), had suggested the possibility of using a player piano to achieve hitherto unheard-of effects, but had not himself undertaken any work on the idea.[27] It was Nancarrow who seized upon the possibilities, and who began in the 1940s actually to "compose" for the instrument, by punching out the rolls in accordance with a preconceived plan.

It is clear that when the purely physical limitations of the human pianist are removed, numerous possibilities exist, including very rapid passages, many simultaneous notes (far more than the pianist's ten fingers could reach), wide leaps, and complex rhythmic organization. Though he has explored and used all of these possibilities, it has been evolution in the temporal domain that has most interested Nancarrow. His modestly titled Studies for player piano, on which he has been working in relative seclusion in Mexico City for over forty years, now number over forty.

In spite of the limited tone color of the Studies (limited not only to the piano, but to one of only two pianos in existence), and their limited duration (they cannot exceed the limits prescribed by the length of a piano roll—the longest is about ten minutes and some are as short as one minute), they cover a wide range of expression. The early ones (the five parts of Study No. 3, for example) are clearly related to jazz and the blues; the first and last of this set are superhuman boogie-woogie which has to be heard to be appreciated. Study No. 6, with its *habanera* rhythm, has an obviously and delightfully Spanish frame of reference.[28]

Nancarrow's work soon took him into more musically abstract realms, however. His interest in the dimension of *tempo* has led him to develop pieces in which there are two or more tempos going on simultaneously. This idea is reminiscent of some of Ives's works; but Nancarrow, freed of the limitations of human performers, has been able to go much farther in the direction of complex relationships. The *ratio* of tempos can vary from fairly simple (4:5, for example) to complex and irrational relationships such as $2:\sqrt{2}$. For this superposition of tempos Nancarrow uses the term "temporal dissonance"; as with harmonic dissonance, the degree of dissonance varies with the degree of complexity of the relationship. Nancarrow's admittedly narrow concern with the aspect of tempo has resulted in a deliberate simplification of other aspects that to him are less important. For Nancarrow melody and harmony are secondary; in his words, "the melodic line is simply a crutch in order to realize certain temporal ideas."[29] In his later studies, he further simplified the elements of harmony and melody by using the musical device of *canon,* so that each separate "voice" contributing to the total texture has the same harmonic and melodic material. The complexity then arises from the varying rates of speed at which they progress, even to the point where individual voices will themselves speed up and slow down at varying rates. This is quite evident in Study No. 22 and, a little less overtly, in Study No. 36. Study No. 27 is one of the longer studies; it is based on a very obvious and unrelenting *ostinato* in the middle register, against which other parts come and go, in canon, at various tempos, speeding up and slowing down, the whole building to an enormous climax. Study No. 41a–b–c is noteworthy in that two individual studies (41a and b) are combined in 41c into one of Nancarrow's few attempts to compose for two pianos.[30]

Like Harry Partch, another solitary worker with whom we shall deal presently, Nancarrow has chosen to work in a medium that requires a unique set of conditions for its live performance. Nancarrow has modified his own two player pianos so thoroughly that it would require an enormous amount of time and effort to prepare other instruments to play the music in the way he has conceived it. Add to this the fact that, physically, each of his pieces exists in the form of a single roll of paper,[31] and we see that, as in the case of Partch, his art cannot survive in live form the inevitable decay and destruction to which physical objects are prey; in this it resembles the artifacts of the visual artist. Its dissemination to a broader public and its ultimate preservation depend upon the medium of recordings made in his studio; fortunately, there have been a number of these to date. Like the works of Partch, those of Nancarrow will eventually, with the deterioration of the unique instruments for which they were created, exist only in their recorded versions.

Lou Harrison and John Cage

Henry Cowell was the first American composer to remind us that the West Coast of the United States is, culturally as well as geographically, farther from Europe, and closer to Asia, than New York is. The orientation of our East Coast to Europe continues to survive our Colonial period (which lasted much longer culturally than politically); our West Coast, with more tenuous European ties and a greater variety of influences, has been more open to choices. In music, this openness to a vocabulary of sounds larger than that inherited from the European fine-art tradition, which we first noted in Cowell, has been carried further, in terms of both exploration and refinement, by two composers, both of whom were at one time students of Cowell.

One of these composers, Lou Harrison (b. 1917 in Portland, Oregon), went east in the 1940s to become, for a time, an important part of the New York musical scene. (It will be recalled that in 1947 he conducted the first performance of Ives's Third Symphony.) But he has always remained a West Coast man in his independence of "establishment" music and thinking (including that of the avant-garde establishment), in his concern with the music of the entire vast Pacific basin, and in the liberal breadth of his outlook. Concerned with plants and animals, Harrison has been a florist. (It is interesting to note that Cowell at one time made his living collecting wild plants, and that John Cage, the third of our freewheeling Pacific Coast composers, is an avid collector of mushrooms.) Harrison has also been a dancer, painter, playwright, conductor, and maker of musical instruments. He acknowledged and partook of the European twentieth-century tradition, as evidenced by his studies with the émigré Viennese composer and teacher Arnold Schoenberg, who settled in Los Angeles in the mid-thirties and became the center of a circle of students and devotees. This phase of Harrison's work is represented by a few twelve-tone works (not necessarily atonal) such as the largely proportioned *Symphony on G.* (Harrison also found an alternative way of organizing highly chromatic music, through controlling the number and kind of melodic intervals used, as he did in his Concerto for Violin and Percussion Orchestra, 1940–59.) His interest in a return to the pure intonation of just intervals* is exemplified in his *Four Strict Songs for Eight Baritones and Orchestra,* on his own text, patterned after the "making-things-right-and-good-again songs of the Navaho." The orchestra consists of a specially tuned piano, harp, percussion, and such other conventional orchestral instruments as can adjust to the pure tunings—i.e., strings and trombones. Harrison's interest in pre-tonal music (both medieval and Renaissance) is evidenced in works such as his *Mass* (1954) and his Suite for Symphonic Strings (1961). His abiding preoccupation with percussion sounds is apparent in many works, including several *Canticles,* a Suite for Percussion, and concertos for flute and for violin with percussion orchestra. Finally, his knowledge of, and love for, the music of the Orient is evident in many works, including *Solstice* (1950) for gamelan (a Javanese orchestra of percussion instruments), *Concerto in Slendro for Violin,* and most notably, *Pacifika Rondo,* a piece in seven movements for an orchestra of both Western and Oriental instruments.[32]

Another of Cowell's students, John Cage (b. 1912 in Los Angeles), is a West Coast composer who went east permanently when he was thirty. In his early years he combined the need to impose a systematic organization on his materials (which would be natural in one who studied under Schoenberg) with a love of percussion sounds, particularly those of an Oriental character. His *Construction in Metal* (1937), one of his earliest works available on recordings, shows clearly these two concerns. The rhythmic structure is of a rigidly predetermined type that Cage used until he turned to indeterminacy and electronics in the early 1950s. It partakes of Schoenbergian determinism but is also, in Cage's words, "analogous to Indian *tala* (rhythmic method)." As he explains it, "The whole has as many parts as each unit has small parts, and these, large and small, are in the same proportion." Thus the 16-measure units have an internal arrangement of 4 + 3 + 2 + 3 + 4, and there are sixteen of these 16-measure units, grouped similarly, with a 12-measure coda added as a

* See the discussion of pure intonation later in this chapter.

concession to the "Western" need for an ending. The West Coast–Oriental aspect of the work is evident in the use of gamelan and of Japanese temple gongs, while the eclectic noise preferences are seen in the use of brake drums and anvils.

Cage also formed an early attachment to the dance, which came about partly because some of his earliest jobs consisted of playing for dance classes and partly because he soon discovered that in the 1930s, when it was difficult otherwise to find an audience for percussion music, dancers were eager for new sounds to accompany their new choreographic creations. About 1936 Cage went to Seattle, where he was on the faculty of the Cornish School, as composer-accompanist for the dance group. It was there that he first hit upon the idea of the "prepared piano." A dancer had requested a score for a new ballet, *Bacchanale,* to emphasize percussion. Since the company could not afford a whole percussion orchestra, Cage (who was the son of an inventor) followed up on some of Cowell's experiments and modified the sound of a grand piano by muting or damping the strings with various objects, thereby in effect creating a percussion orchestra inside the piano, at the control of a single player. This was in 1938, and it was followed by many works for prepared piano, mostly for the dance. Cage then turned to other things, but in 1946–48, after he had moved to New York, he returned to the prepared piano, writing the well-known Sonatas and Interludes for Prepared Piano. There are sixteen sonatas and four interludes; the sonatas are in the short binary form, with each of the two parts repeated—a common form in the eighteenth century. This short form is appropriate, since each of the sonatas and interludes reveals its musical essence rather quickly and there is little change or development. Cage was at this time becoming interested in Oriental teachings, and these pieces represented an attempt to express, in terms of his gamelan-like instrument, the "permanent emotions" of the Indian tradition: the heroic, the erotic, the wondrous, the mirthful, the sorrowful, the fearful, the angry, and the odious.

Cage's tenuous Concerto for Prepared Piano and Orchestra (1951), based on a strictly ordered rhythmic structure that incorporates silences, is a kind of culmination of this aspect of his endeavors. From that point on, electronics, with its new sound sources, engaged him. (Here it must be noted that he had already delved into this realm, as far as the technology of the time would allow, in his *Imaginary Landscape No. 1* of 1939.) Also, Oriental teachings, as he understood and interpreted them, were leading him in the direction of indeterminacy as to musical results, and an abdication of the role of composer. These developments belong to the next chapter.

Harry Partch (1901–74)

There was another westerner, born at the turn of the century, who also struck out on his own—the embodiment, as a musician, of Blake's dictum "I must create a system, or be enslaved by another man's." Harry Partch, working for years alone and virtually unknown, rejected three of the most basic elements of his immediate musical heritage: conventional instruments, a scale of twelve equidistant notes to an octave, and counterpoint. His musical influences, as he himself listed them, are, like Cowell's, varied and typical of the West: "Christian hymns, Chinese lullabyes, Yaqui Indian ritual, Congo puberty ritual, Cantonese music hall, and Okies in California vineyards." Yet Partch did not become a "collector," either of exotic instruments or exotic systems. Instead, he found what he needed as a base for his own music in two ancient ideas that had become eclipsed in Western music: purely tuned intervals and monophony (the harmonized singing or reciting of a single voice). And he soon saw that his return to pure intervals would draw him into another endeavor—that of building his own instruments.

Harry Partch, the son of apostate former missionaries to China, was born in Oakland, California, but soon moved with his family into the southwestern desert area of Arizona and New Mexico, where he grew up. His father, who understood Mandarin Chinese, worked for the immigration service, moving frequently from one small railroad-junction town near the Mexican border to another. Thus the boy grew up, lonely and largely self-educated, among the polyglot people of "the declining years of the Old West," as he puts it—including the Yaqui Indians, the Chinese, and the hoboes and prostitutes his father and mother occasionally brought home. Young Harry Partch read a great deal, enjoying Greek mythology especially; and musical instruments, obtained by mail order, were in the household. At fourteen Partch began to compose seriously. A few years later he began to have doubts about accepting both the intonational system and the concert system of European-derived music. At twenty-one he found Hermann von Helmholtz's famous book on musical acoustics, *On the Sensations of Tone,* and began writing works using pure, or "just," intonation. At around twenty-six he wrote the first draft of his own treatise and manifesto, *Genesis of a Music.* At twenty-eight he burned, in a big iron stove, all the music he had written up to that time, and set out with determination and (as he describes it) "exhilaration" on new paths.

His first works of the early thirties were for Intoning Voice and Adapted Viola—a viola to which has been attached a longer cello fingerboard, marked so as to facilitate playing the smaller just intervals. These early works had texts from Chinese poetry, the Psalms, and Shakespeare. After much experimentation, other instruments were added: an Adapted Guitar, a Chromelodeon (an adapted reed organ), and a Kithara (a lyre-shaped plucked-string instrument with movable bridges, allowing for a sliding tone). Using these instruments, Partch wrote his first major work, *U.S. Highball.*[33] "A hobo's account of a trip from San Francisco to Chicago," with an adagio dishwashing interlude at Little America, Wyoming, it is to a great extent autobiographical, for Partch's life between 1935 and 1943 consisted in large measure of hoboing, dishwashing, WPA jobs, and wandering. This phase of his life came to an end only with the award of a Guggenheim Fellowship; his first work completed under this was *U.S. Highball,* which was premiered in New York in 1944.

U.S. Highball has a Subjective Voice (the protagonist) and several Objective Voices, whose words consist of "fragments of conversations, writings on the sides of boxcars, signs in havens for derelicts, hitchhikers' inscriptions"—all of which Partch had recorded in a notebook he always carried during his wanderings.

In succeeding years Partch built many new instruments, and rebuilt many earlier ones. The "string and voice" instruments eventually came to include, in addition to those mentioned above, Harmonic Canons (zither-like instruments with movable bridges for tuning, played with a pick), a retuned Koto, a bellows-operated Bloboy, consisting of auto horns and organ pipes, and a Crychord, with which sliding pitches are attained by changing the string tension with a lever. The percussion instruments feature various Marimbas. The Marimba Eroica is the largest; its lowest tone, below any of the notes on the piano, is produced by a Sitka spruce plank more than seven feet long suspended over a resonator eight feet long and four feet high. Many of the Marimbas are made of bamboo. The smallest and softest is the Mazda Marimba, made of twenty-four light bulbs "with their viscera removed," yielding a sound, according to Partch, like the "bubbling of a coffee percolator." Other percussion include a Gourd Tree, Cone Gongs, and the bell-like Cloud-Chamber Bowls—the tops and bottoms of twelve-gallon glass carboys suspended.[34]

Appealing in sound, his instruments, especially as he redesigned them, came to have a great visual appeal as well; they are very much "part of the set" of a Partch performance, which, in accord with the composer's ideas of corporeal music, has always, and increasingly in the later works, a strong element of theater in it. The players themselves (who must be specially trained) are also aware at all times that they are "on stage."

Major compositions since *U.S. Highball* have been *Plectra and Percussion Dances* (1949–52, a three-part work that includes *Castor and Pollux); Oedipus—A Music-Dance Drama* (1951); *The Bewitched—A Dance Satire* (1955); *Revelation in the Courthouse Park* (1960); *And on the Seventh Day Petals Fell in Petaluma* (1963–64); and Partch's last large work, *Delusion of the Fury* (1963–69).

In the 1940s, Partch thought of the realization of his works in terms of recordings (recordings he himself, for a time, issued under his own Gate 5 label). Thereafter, beginning approximately with *Oedipus,* they were conceived more and more as theatrical works, with set (including, of course, the instruments), costumes, dancers, singers, and actors; the players themselves, costumed, often serve as a chorus or take part in the action. Greek legend and drama and Japanese and African tales figure as sources for the larger works.

Partch's *Genesis of a Music* (first published, after many drafts, in 1947, with a revised and enlarged second edition completed in 1972) is, as has been noted, both manifesto and treatise. Unlike Cowell's earlier and comparable smaller work, *New Musical Resources,* it is not a suggestion of what *might* be done but a painstakingly thorough description of what Partch spent a lifetime doing—together with his reasons for doing so. The theoretical portions include, in terms of the *ratios* which Partch used to express intervals, a complete description and derivation of his scale of forty-three tones to the octave.

It takes a bold, energetic, and singularly dedicated and single-minded composer to develop and commit himself to a system of intonation impossible to produce on existing instruments; to build new instruments to the new specifications; and then to create new works exploiting the resources of both the intonation and the instruments.

Partch's music does not, of course, exhaust or even begin to explore significantly the vast implications of his system. His is largely a music in which instrumental color, especially that of percussion, plays a dominant role. The consequently lesser role that melody and harmony play, together with his penchant for sliding tones, which blur the sense of finely tuned pitch, do not allow for much exploration, from the standpoint of what the listener can perceive, of the resources of his elaborate forty-three-tone pitch system. Then, too, without the visual impact of a stage presentation, the music alone, after one gets used to the sounds, does not always seem to sustain interest over long periods. (Several of the major works last more than an hour.) Yet the sounds themselves are often very arresting and very beautiful. There are inevitable limitations in what Partch did, but considering the task he set himself, he certainly achieved all any creator could in one lifetime.

The most poignant limitation in such a lifework is that Partch's music can be performed only by specially trained performers, and only on his own instruments—one of a kind, and difficult and expensive just to maintain, let alone duplicate. It is not certain, following his death in 1974, what the future of his music—*live*—will be. But it is likely that this was of little concern to Harry Partch. He had done his work. In 1972 he wrote:

> I am not trying to institute a movement in any crypto-religious sense. If I were, *idea* would soon turn into something called form, and the world is already plagued with its ephemera. . . . [The pathbreaker's] path cannot be retraced, because each of us is an original being.[35]

Pure Intonation: A Postscript

It is interesting to note that three of the individualists treated in this chapter were concerned with pure, or just, intonation—that is, with the musical intervals resulting from simple and rational mathematical frequency ratios, in contrast with the irrational ratios and the "clouding" of all intervals except the octave that result from the compromise of twelve equal-tempered semitones to the octave. Cowell dealt theoretically with the concept in his *New Musical Resources*. Lou Harrison has written music to be played in pure intonation, and Partch committed himself to it wholly. There are others who have further explored it, including Ben Johnston, who studied with Partch. His String Quartet No. 2 (1964) combines just intonation (in a fifty-three-tone scale) with, oddly enough, the very serialization of both pitch and duration that has been so characteristic of the twelve-tone composers who have been utterly committed to equal temperament. Johnston's Sonata for Microtonal Piano (first performed in 1965) uses a piano specially tuned to a complex scale of eight-one different pitches, only seven of which appear in octave duplications.[36] Still others have been at work (necessarily building or modifying their own instruments) exploring the ramifications of a return to purely tuned intervals.

Edgar Varèse (1883–1965)

In the matter of putting genuinely new sounds and sound sources at the disposal of an expressive purpose, Harry Partch and Edgar(d) Varèse have been our two most original composers. They worked in very different ways, yet neither regarded sounds (as does John Cage) as ends in themselves. Both were dissatisfied with traditional instruments and with the tempered scale of twelve equal half steps to the octave (Partch rejected these instruments outright, while Varèse, whose ties to European tradition were stronger, used both while awaiting the development of technology that would furnish him with new sound sources). Both men, interestingly enough, felt the need of sounds of flowing, sliding pitch; Partch achieved this through the use of movable bridges on his stringed instruments, while Varèse at first did so with sirens (*Amériques, Hyperprism,* and *Ionisation*) and later used electronic means. Both began composing afresh in their thirties, their earlier output having been destroyed—Partch's deliberately, and Varèse's probably at least partly so. There were fundamental differences, of course. Partch was committed to a very "corporeal" concept of music; the presence of a musician performing was a vital part of the artistic transaction, which always took place in terms of something staged. Varèse conceived of his music as structures in sound; the human performer was dispensable.

In terms of the man himself and his milieu, Edgar Varèse could hardly present a greater contrast to Harry Partch. Parisian-born, and educated there and in Italy, Varèse acknowledged his roots in the European tradition, which he knew thoroughly. He knew and associated with many of the great European musicians of his time, especially Claude Debussy and Ferruccio Busoni, whose advanced ideas, contained in his *Sketch for a New Aesthetic of Music,* had a considerable influence on Varèse. Whereas Partch was a lone worker, in the manner of the frontiersman, building his instruments, writing his music, and working out his theories almost totally on his own, Varèse was immersed in the up-to-date urban world of his time (he loved cities, especially New York)—musical, literary, artistic, and political. During the European years he lived in Paris and later in Berlin. He was helped by Jules Massenet and Richard Strauss; he also knew Ravel, Picasso, and Lenin, and the writers Jean Cocteau, Hugo von Hofmannsthal, and Romain Rolland. Both in Europe and America he conducted concerts, and was a leader and co-founder of organizations devoted to furthering the cause of new music.

Varèse did not come to America until 1915, after the outbreak of World War I (he had served in the French army and been discharged because of ill health); he was then thirty-two. He is almost universally considered an American composer, however. He started composing anew here, taking his music in new directions; and his important—in fact, his entire surviving—output was composed after he arrived in his enthusiastically adopted land. His *Amériques* (1918–22), the first important piece written here, is a vast work, the significance of which (as Varèse wrote) is not "purely geographic, but as symbolic of discoveries—new worlds on earth, in the sky, or in the minds of men."[37]

Once established in America, for the last half-century of his life Varèse directed his enormous energies in several directions at various times. In addition to composing (with which he was always, of course, preoccupied, although new completed works appeared comparatively infrequently and at irregular intervals), he was a conductor, an organizer for new music, a researcher into new controllable sound sources, and a teacher, lecturer, and writer.

Varèse's Conceptions of Music

To prepare us for examining his music, it will be useful to let Varèse himself, through his writings, describe some of his conceptions of music. When he was about twenty, Varèse discovered a definition of music that fired his imagination, to which he kept returning again and again throughout his life—the definition of music by the Polish philosopher Hoëne Wronsky as "the corporealization of the intelligence that is in sounds."

This concern for "the intelligence that is in sounds" was indicative of the importance Varèse always gave to the study of acoustics. The son of an engineer, and destined as a boy for the same career, he early acquired (even though he was severely and permanently estranged from his dictatorial father) a taste for science. He regarded music as an "art-science," and pointed out that medieval philosophers had associated it with mathematics, geometry, and astronomy. He strongly advocated composers' making use of the latest scientific developments.

> We all think it very sensible that tools that have become outmoded should be replaced by the very newest thing in "efficiency." . . . Composers like anyone else today are delighted to use the many gadgets continually put on the market for our daily comfort. But when they hear the sounds that no violins, wind instruments, or percussions of the orchestra can produce, it does not occur to them to demand those sounds of science. Yet science is even now equipped to give them everything they may require. . . . If you are curious to know what . . . a machine could do that the orchestra with its man-powered instruments cannot do, I shall try briefly to tell you: whatever I write, whatever my message, it will reach the listener unadulterated by "interpretation." It will work something like this: after a composer has set down his score on paper by means of a new graphic, similar in principle to a seismographic or oscillographic notation, he will then, with the collaboration of a sound engineer, transfer the score directly to this electric machine. After that anyone will be able to press a button to release the music exactly as the composer wrote it—exactly like opening a book.[38]

This remarkable forecast of electronic-tape music was written in 1939. Twenty years later, Varèse qualified and clarified somewhat his apparent rejection of the performer.

> Because for so many years I crusaded for new instruments with what may have seemed fanatical zeal, I have been accused of desiring nothing less than the destruction of all musical instruments and even of all performers. This is, to say the least, an exaggeration. Our new liberating medium—the electronic—is not meant to replace the old musical instruments, which composers, including myself, will continue to use. Electronics is an additive, not a destructive, factor in the art and science of music.[39]

Varèse conceived of music as spatial, and of musical sounds as analogous to masses in space, with quasi-geometrical characteristics. He used sirens in some early scores to achieve what he called "parabolic and hyperbolic trajectories of sound."

In a lecture given as early as 1936 in Santa Fe he described his projected "corporealization" of music in a startling illustrative paragraph worth quoting in full.

> When new instruments will allow me to write music as I conceive it, the movement of sound-masses, of shifting planes, will be clearly perceived in my work, taking the place of linear counterpoint. When these sound-masses collide, the phenomena of penetration or repulsion will seem to occur. Certain transmutations taking place on certain planes will seem to be projected onto other planes, moving at different speeds and at different angles. There will no longer be the old conception of melody or interplay of melodies. The entire work will be a melodic totality. The entire work will flow as a river flows.[40]

Varèse had to wait another twenty years before he heard his music literally "projected into space." But his music had inspired a writer as early as 1925 to write of "great masses in astral space." Let us now examine some of the music of a composer who has been described as "the first astronaut."

The Music of Varèse

The music of Edgar Varèse falls clearly into three chronological groups. First are the early works, all written in Europe before World War I, and all lost or deliberately destroyed. (These included a symphony, *Bourgogne;* a symphonic poem, *Gargantua;* and an uncompleted opera *Ödipus und die Sphinx,* on which he was collaborating with Richard Strauss's librettist Hugo von Hofmannsthal.) The second group includes the nine works written in America between 1918 and 1936. (Varèse is surpassed in the sparseness of his output only by Ruggles.) He was an extremely careful workman; often years would elapse between the initial conception of a work and its appearance in final form. Beginning in the mid-1930s there was a fifteen-year hiatus in his composing; whether this was because he did not wish to write for conventional instruments and had no sophisticated electronic ones at his disposal, or because of his own depressed feelings and the lack of acceptance of his music, is not certain. He lived in the West for a while, returned to New York for the war years, and did do some work on a vast project called *Espace* ("Space"). In theme it was the counterpart of Beethoven's Ninth Symphony, or Ives's *Majority* ("Theme: TODAY, the world awake! Humanity on the march. . . . Millions of feet endlessly tramping, treading, pounding, striding, leaping.") In scope it was to be a kind of counterpart to Ives's *Universe Symphony;* Varèse at one time imagined a performance of it broadcast simultaneously from all the capitals of the world, with a choir in each singing in its own language! Like the *Universe Symphony,* it was never finished.

The third group of Varèse works are those few written between 1949 and 1960: *Déserts* for orchestra with electronic-tape interludes; organized sound (electronic) for a sequence, *Good Friday Procession in Verges,* in a film called *Around and About Joan Miró; La Poème électronique;* and two unfinished works, *Nocturnal*[41] and *Nuit,* both on texts from Anaïs Nin's *The House of Incest.*

It will be useful now to treat several significant works of Varèse briefly in the order in which they were composed.

Hyperprism (1922–23)

Even among Varèse's works, which tend not to be long, *Hyperprism* is the shortest—only four minutes. "Little *Hyperprism,*" as his wife called it, nevertheless caused a riot at its first performance, at an International Composers' Guild concert in 1923 with Varèse conducting. For this work he arrived at a type of instrumentation well suited to his ideas, and one he was to use, with various additions, in three more works (*Intégrales, Ecuatorial, Déserts*)—an orchestra of eight to a dozen wind instruments and a large percussion section of four to six players playing many different instruments. For *Hyperprism* these include a siren and a string drum, or "lion roar," which makes a unique and quite audible effect. As Varèse describes it in another score, it is "a single-headed drum; a piece of heavy twine is attached to the center of the membrane. The sound, approximating a lion's roar, is produced by drawing a piece of leather or canvas along the string, causing the membrane to vibrate."

Intégrales (1924–25)

In *Intégrales* Varèse further explored the ground he had broken in *Hyperprism,* enlarging his wind section and expanding the work to three times the length of the earlier one. Robert Craft, who has conducted and recorded most of Varèse's music, has called attention to the "repeated one-note rhythmic figure with interrupting appoggiaturas, that is a kind of germinal figure throughout Varèse's music."[42] This trait is nowhere more apparent than in *Intégrales;* at the beginning, for example, one note—the B-flat above the treble staff—persists, on various instruments, through seven pages.

It is possibly in *Intégrales,* as a matter of fact, that we find the majority of Varèse's characteristic musical traits most fully exemplified. When all is said and done, the kinds of sounds a composer chooses to make music with form a revealing common denominator in all of his or her works. With Varèse one hears, first of all and a good deal of the time, *sustained* sounds—extremely low, extremely high, getting louder, getting softer (this less often), and frequently articulated in repeated notes, as Craft has pointed out. One hears sliding sounds: a trombone *glissando,* a siren, a lion roar—later he will make more of these with electronics. And one hears certain favorite percussion sounds: a snare drummer executing rudimentary flams and rolls (which somehow inject a disturbingly mundane element into the music), little scraping noises, various noises of rattles and ratchets, the sounds of small hollowish wooden objects being hit (castanets, wood blocks, Chinese temple blocks, coconut shells), and of course cymbals and gongs. These are the most salient elements of Varèse's vocabulary.

Interestingly enough, they have their close counterparts in the later purely electronic music of *La Poème électronique* and the organized-sound interpolations of *Déserts.* Varèse makes music with tone color and rhythm. Harmony has been replaced by a sense of the mass and density of sounds. (He can make a "chord" out of several percussion instruments sounding together, as he shows us in *Hyperprism* and *Ionisation.*) His counterpoint is the juxtaposition of sound masses. By the time he wrote *Hyperprism,* he seemed to have succeeded more than any other composer of his era in dispensing with melody.

Even small fragments of melody (such as the quasi-jazzy bits in the middle of *Intégrales,* the oboe cadenzas in the same piece, or the curious, almost Ivesian, little high woodwind tune in *Arcana*) sound out of place by this point in Varèse's career. Only when the human voice sings (as in the incantation-like *Ecuatorial*) does melody still seem to fit this kind of "organized sound," as Varèse himself called his music.

Ionisation (1930–31)

Varèse's output became more sparse after he completed *Arcana* in 1927. In 1928 he went to France for five years, during which time he completed only one work, the famous *Ionisation.* For this five-minute work he used nothing but percussion—an orchestra of thirteen percussionists playing thirty-seven instruments (though not all at once). It was premiered in New York in 1933 by Nicolas Slonimsky. As the creation of a composer working in what could be considered the mainstream of Occidental music, it was epoch-making; however, percussion instruments had surely come to the height of fashion in any case, owing more than is generally realized to the Latin-African music of the Caribbean. The Cuban composer Amadeo Roldán, for example, had written six *Ritmicas* for percussion orchestra in 1930.

Déserts (1949–54)

After Varèse's long hiatus, he produced *Déserts,* for much the same kind of instrumental forces he had used before—twelve winds and a large assortment of percussion—but with the important addition of ten minutes' worth of electronic-tape sounds interpolated at three points into the thirteen and a half minutes of live instrumental music. This makes *Déserts,* at twenty-three and a half minutes, one of Varèse's longer works, although he indicated that the electronic interpolations could be dispensed with; there is some evidence that the decision to include them came fairly late. The genesis of the work is interesting. Varèse had evidently first conceived of the music as associated with a film that was to be made *afterwards*—a film that would show "the deserts of earth (sand, snow); the deserts of the sea; the deserts of outer space (galaxies, nebulae, etc.); but particularly the deserts in the mind of man."[43] The film was never made, but the conception was realized musically in this piece. All the characteristics of Varèse's vocabulary previously noted are present; *Déserts* is, if possible, an even more severely refined music of pure timbre and rhythm.

La Poème électronique (1957–58)

Varèse's eagerly awaited liberation, which he had long asked of science, from the limitations of the human performer and traditional acoustical instruments came with the opportunity to create eight minutes of sound to be projected literally *in space* through the medium of 425 loudspeakers in the Philips Pavilion designed by Le Corbusier for the Brussels International Exposition in 1958. (*La Poème électronique* was actually the title of the entire concept, which included visual projects designed by Le Corbusier; the pavilion was simply the "vessel" to contain both.) Here the sound masses (a montage made up of a combination of manipulated "real" and synthesized sound carefully assembled by Varèse, who worked for six to eight months in the Philips laboratory in Eindhoven, Holland) could literally move in space, thanks to a three-track tape and an elaborate "routing" of the sound channels through the maze of speakers installed in the roof of the pavilion.

Some of the components of this achievement Varèse had envisioned forty years before. (In 1916 he had said, "We . . . need new instruments very badly," and in 1922, "The composer and the electrician will have to labor together.") He had participated in and encouraged actual research for thirty years before. The technology that finally made *La Poème électronique* possible had already, in the post–World War II years, added a lively new electronic wing to the edifice of music, from which much was hoped for by many. It is to these developments, together with some contemporaneous new aesthetic concepts, that we now turn.

Further Reading

General

Lederman, Minna. *The Life and Death of a Small Magazine* (*Modern Music, 1924–1946*). I.S.A.M. Monograph no. 18. Brooklyn: Institute for Studies in American Music, 1983.
Valuable record of a periodical important to American music between the wars; the index makes it a useful reference work.

Mead, Rita. *Henry Cowell's New Music 1925–1936: The Society, the Music Editions, and the Recordings*. Ann Arbor, MI: UMI Research Press, 1981.
An invaluable documentation of the impressive activities of Cowell and others, so crucial to the experimental wing of American music at this time.

Mellers, Wilfred. *Music in a New Found Land: Themes and Developments in the History of American Music*. New York: Knopf, 1965.
An English musicologist views American music; all the composers in this chapter are given interesting and rather extensive treatment—Ives "as American hero," Ruggles "as American mystic," etc.

Reis, Claire R. *Composers, Conductors and Critics*. New York, 1955; reprint (with new introduction by the author and preface by Aaron Copland), Detroit: Detroit Reprints in Music, 1974.
Important as a source of information about the influential League of Composers (begun as an offshoot of Varèse's International Composers' Guild), written by the woman who was its director for twenty-five years.

Rosenfeld, Paul. *Musical Impressions: Selections from Paul Rosenfeld's Criticism*. Edited and with introduction by Herbert Leibowitz. New York: Hill & Wang, 1969.
Includes early critical assessment of Ives (1936), Ruggles (1928), and Varèse (1929).

Thomson, Virgil. *American Music Since 1910*. New York: Holt, Rinehart & Winston, 1970; paperback ed., 1972.
In addition to supplying insightful background, this work has summaries and assessments of Ives, Ruggles, Varèse, and Cage.

Yates, Peter. *Twentieth-Century Music: Its Evolution from the End of the Harmonic Era into the Present Era of Sound*. New York: Random House, 1967.
A readable and perceptive introduction to his subject by a Los Angeles author, lecturer, and critic who has produced

concerts of new music and written regularly for *Arts and Architecture* and other periodicals. Relevant are chapters on Ives and Cage, and two on "The American Experimental Tradition."

Collections of Writings by or Interviews with Composers

Chase, Gilbert, ed. *The American Composer Speaks*. Baton Rouge: Louisiana State University Press, 1966.
Excerpted writings of composers covering a 200-year span, from William Billings to Earle Brown. Included are pieces by Ives, Cowell, Cage, Partch, and Varèse.

Cowell, Henry, ed. *American Composers on American Music: A Symposium*. Palo Alto, CA, 1933; paperback reprint (with new introduction), New York: Frederick Ungar, 1962.
The prototype of such collections, this excellent "symposium" of the early thirties, focusing on the contemporary scene, includes thirty-one articles on American composers and on general tendencies.

Gagne, Cole, and Tracy Caras, eds. *Soundpieces: Interviews with American Composers*. Metuchen, NJ: Scarecrow Press, 1982.

Schwartz, Elliott, and Barney Childs, eds. *Contemporary Composers on Contemporary Music*. New York: Holt, Rinehart & Winston, 1967.
This collection covers the European scene as well, but Part 2 deals with "Experimental Music and Recent American Developments." There is some inevitable overlap between this collection and Chase, *The American Composer Speaks*.

Individual Composers

Charles Ives

Burkholder, J. Peter. *Charles Ives: The Ideas Behind the Music*. New Haven: Yale University Press, 1985.

———. "Charles Ives and His Fathers: A Response to Maynard Solomon." *Institute for Studies in American Music Newsletter*, vol. 18, no. 1 (November 1988).
A commentary on, and further exploration of, the questions of veracity raised in the Solomon article cited below.

Cowell, Henry and Sidney. *Charles Ives and His Music*. New York: Oxford University Press, 1955; rev. ed. (paperback), 1969.
Always valuable as the first biography (the section written by Sidney Cowell) and the first important study of the music (written by Henry Cowell), this is an excellent introduction to both, by an eminent composer and his wife who knew Ives personally and helped to bring his music before the public over a period of many years.

Hitchcock, H. Wiley. *Ives: A Survey of the Music*. I.S.A.M. Monograph no. 19. Brooklyn: Institute for Studies in American Music, 1977.
For those interested in the music itself, this brief survey is an excellent place to start.

———, and Vivian Perlis, eds. *An Ives Celebration*. Urbana: University of Illinois Press, 1977.
A collection of essays growing out of an Ives Festival-Conference in 1974, the year of the Ives centennial.

Ives, Charles, *Essays Before a Sonata, and Other Writings*. New York: W. W. Norton, 1961; paperback, 1964.

———. *Charles E. Ives: Memos*. Edited by John Kirkpatrick. New York: W. W. Norton, 1972.
These two books may be considered well-nigh indispensable primary sources for Ives's life, work, and, most important, thought. With some regrettable exceptions (such as the "Conduc-

tor's Note" to the Fourth Symphony) they contain nearly everything Ives wrote. The *Memos,* in addition, carefully and knowledgeably edited, contain some almost equally valuable appendices, including an annotated list of all Ives's compositions.

Perlis, Vivian, ed. *Charles Ives Remembered: An Oral History.* New Haven: Yale University Press, 1974.
Evidence of the new wave of interest in Ives, this consists of transcripts of recorded reminiscences by many who knew him: family members, business associates, friends, neighbors, and of course musicians, many of them well known. There are many photos, and reproductions of manuscript pages and programs. The actual voices of some of the contributors may be heard in excerpts from this oral history in the album *Charles Ives: The 100th Anniversary* (Columbia M4-32504).

Rossiter, Frank R. *Charles Ives and His America.* New York: Liveright, 1975.
An up-to-date and well-researched biography—and more; it also examines the issues faced, and raised, by Ives as an artist in early-twentieth-century America. Rossiter writes: "I became more and more convinced that the Ives Legend which has grown up around him gives a very imperfect picture of the man. I think that the key to an understanding of his place in American culture lies in his extreme artistic isolation."

Solomon, Maynard. "Charles Ives: Some Questions of Veracity." *Journal of the American Musicological Society,* vol. 40,. no. 3 (Fall 1987).
The "questions" this stir-creating article investigates have to do with images Ives allegedly went to some lengths to maintain. The first is about his father, as both an innovator and a predominant influence on his son's music; this perhaps exaggerated image is explored from the standpoint of modern psychology. The second is the image of his being free from the influence of other composers, especially those he so virulently denounced in *Memos,* cited above, from the 1930s. The third, and related, image, is that of himself as "the unrivalled inventor-creator"—an image he allegedly tried to support both by rather ingenuously falsifying the dating of his compositions, and by adding dissonances when revising works, for performance or publication, years after their initial composition.

Carl Ruggles

Harrison, Lou. *About Carl Ruggles.* Yonkers, NY: Oscar Baradinsky at the Alicat Bookshop, 1946.
This slim volume is the only book known, to date, devoted exclusively to Ruggles. It is written by an eminent, widely knowledgeable composer, who greatly admires Ruggles's music and sees in it a renewal of the tradition of serious contrapuntal music represented by Bach and Handel.

Seeger, Charles. "Carl Ruggles" in Cowell, *American Composers on American Music* (cited above).

John J. Becker, Wallingford Riegger, Ruth Crawford (Seeger), and Charles Seeger

Cowell, Henry, ed. *American Composers on American Music* (cited above).
Includes individual articles on all four.

Frankenstein, Alfred. Notes to New World recording NW-285, which includes music by Riegger, Becker, and Crawford.

Gaume, Matilde. *Ruth Crawford Seeger: Memoirs, Memories, Music.* Metuchen, NJ: Scarecrow Press, 1986.

———. "Ruth Crawford: A Promising Young Composer in New York, 1929–30," *American Music,* vol. 5, no. 1 (Spring 1987).

Henry Cowell

Cowell, Henry. *New Musical Resources.* New York, 1930; new ed. (with preface and notes by Joscelyn Godwin), New York: Something Else Press, 1969.
The importance of this youthful treatise, at times penetrating and prophetic and at times naive, has been discussed in the chapter.

Lichtenwanger, William. *The Music of Henry Cowell: A Descriptive Catalog.* I.S.A.M. Monograph no. 23. Brooklyn: Institute for Studies in American Music, 1986.

Manion, Martha L. *Writings about Henry Cowell: An Annotated Bibliography.* I.S.A.M. Monograph no. 16. Brooklyn: Institute for Studies in American Music, 1982.

Mead, Rita H. "The Amazing Mr. Cowell," *American Music,* vol. 1, no. 4 (Winter 1983).

———. *Henry Cowell's New Music* (see General Works, above).

Saylor, Bruce. *The Writings of Henry Cowell: A Descriptive Bibliography.* I.S.A.M. Monograph no. 7. Brooklyn: Institute for Studies in American Music, 1977.

Conlon Nancarrow

Gagne, Cole, and Tracy Caras, eds. *Soundpieces* (see above), pp. 281ff.

Reynolds, Roger. "Conlon Nancarrow: Interviews in Mexico City and San Francisco," *American Music,* vol. 2, no. 2 (Summer 1984).

Lou Harrison

Harrison, Lou. *Music Primer: Various Items about Music to 1970.* New York: C. F. Peters, 1971.

John Cage

Cage, John. *Silence.* Middletown, CT: Wesleyan University Press, 1961; paperback, Cambridge, MA: MIT Press, 1966.
The best single source of Cage's writing and lectures, including material from 1939 to 1961.

Gagne, Cole, and Tracy Caras, eds. *Soundpieces* (see above), pp. 70–81.

For additional material on Cage's later work see Chapter 18.

Harry Partch

Partch, Harry. *Genesis of a Music.* 2d ed. New York: Da Capo, 1974.
In this 500-page volume Partch sets forth the aesthetic and acoustical basis of his work, and describes his instruments (which are illustrated by photographs) and his compositions. Aside from his music and his instruments, this book is Partch's major work. He worked on it for twenty years before the first edition was published in 1947. The second edition is enlarged by a new preface; by chapters on new instruments built after 1947 and on the background of six of his major works; by some important appendices listing all the music; and by a chronology of the instruments.

Edgar Varèse

Ouellette, Fernand. *Edgard Varèse.* Translated by Derek Coltman. New York: Orion Press, 1968.
A biography that takes up the works in the context of Varèse's life. With its list of works and very extensive bibliography, which includes a great number of periodical articles and interviews, this "first biography" is informative despite its effusively worshipful tone.

Varèse, Louise. *Varèse: A Looking-Glass Diary,* vol. 1: 1883–1928. New York: W. W. Norton, 1972.
Rich in detail as in insight, this account by Varèse's wife is far more objective than the Ouellette biography.

Listening

Current Schwann catalogs indicate a rather wide selection of available recordings of works by composers treated in this chapter. The Ives list grows continuously; all of Varèse is available, and most of Ruggles and Partch; Cowell, Harrison, and Cage, with their relatively large output, are nevertheless fairly well represented. It only remains to suggest a few individual albums of some particular usefulness or significance.

Charles Ives

Charles Ives: The 100th Anniversary. Columbia M4-32504.
This 4-LP set consists of a sampling of the music, but also includes two sides of Ives playing his own music, and a "bonus" record of excerpts from the interviews that make up the oral history project *Charles Ives Remembered* (see Further Reading). A lengthy illustrated booklet is included.

Old Songs Deranged: Charles Ives, Music for Theater Orchestra. Columbia M-32969.
This interesting recording by the Yale Theater Orchestra contains some rarities, such as the *Holiday Quickstep* written for his father's Danbury band; it also reminds us of Ives's fondness for the theater orchestras of his own time, in which he occasionally played while at Yale, and with which he tried out some of his music.

Nine Songs by Charles Ives. NW-300.
The selection of Ives songs occupying the first side of this LP (the second is devoted to the songs of more recent American composers) is noteworthy for its rarities, including four French songs.

John J. Becker, Wallingford Riegger, and Ruth Crawford

Quartet Romantic. NW-285.
This collection, with notes by Alfred Frankenstein, includes short pieces by each composer, and additional discography not available in the Schwann catalog.

Henry Cowell

The Piano Music of Henry Cowell. Folkways FM-3349.
This consists of twenty pieces played by the composer himself, including all the ones treated in this chapter, with Cowell's own verbal annotations.

Quartet Euphometric. NW-218.

Quartet Romantic. NW-285.
This album also includes work relevant to this chapter by Wallingford Riegger, John J. Becker, and Ruth Crawford Seeger.

Conlon Nancarrow

Complete Studies for Player Piano: Conlon Nancarrow. 1750 Arch Records S-1768, S-1777.
This ambitious undertaking, of which three volumes have come out to date, is the best representation of Nancarrow's work, and has his emphatic approval.

Sound Forms for Piano. NW-203.
This record includes Studies Nos. 1, 27, and 36. This and the following do not have Nancarrow's approval (he refers to them as "terrible") but they are likely to be the only sources available in many places.

Conlon Nancarrow: Studies for Player Piano. Columbia MS 7222.
See note above.

John Cage

The 25-Year Retrospective Concert of the Music of John Cage. Produced by George Avakian, 10 West 33rd St., New York, N.Y. 10001.
A recording of a live performance at Town Hall, New York, in May 1958, this 3-LP album, with extensive notes and sample pages of the scores, is a good survey of Cage's work up to that time.

Also of Interest

Nicolas Slonimsky: Historic Premieres. Orion 7150.
An interesting documentary recording of Slonimsky conducting four pieces he had premiered: Ives, *Barn Dance* (from *Washington's Birthday*) and *In the Night;* Ruggles, *Lilacs;* and Varèse, *Ionisation*.

Sound Forms for Piano. NW-203.
This recording of experimental music includes Cowell, *The Banshee, Aeolian Harp*, and *Piano Piece* (*Paris 1924*); excerpts from Cage, Sonatas and Interludes for Prepared Piano; Ben Johnston, *Sonata for Microtonal Piano;* and three of Conlon Nancarrow's studies for player piano.

PROJECTS

1. Frank Rossiter, in *Charles Ives and His America*, quotes the American conductor Walter Damrosch as having written in 1923: "I do not think there has ever been a country whose musical development has been fostered so almost exclusively by women as America." Read Rossiter's book, with special attention to the first chapter, and comment in a brief talk or essay on the reflection of this observation in Charles Ives's attitudes and writings. Conclude with any observations you may have from your own experience, either past or present, and an assessment of the situation today.
2. If you play the guitar, banjo, or dulcimer, use one of these instruments to demonstrate quarter-tone tuning, devising some simple melodies using such a tuning.
3. Contrive a series of "ear-stretching" experiences similar to those of George Ives, in which a melody is sung or played in one key, and the accompaniment in another.
4. Devise and put on a simple music performance demonstrating the spatial element in music—similar to, but less elaborate than, the experimental performance devised by George Ives in Danbury, described on pp. 506–507.
5. Write a brief paper on Charles Ives as business executive, including an account of his important contributions to the life insurance business. Refer to his innovative concepts and his writings (such as his pamphlet *The Amount to Carry—Measuring the Prospect*).
6. From the approximately 120 songs by Charles Ives, most of which are available in print and many of which are recorded, make up a list of twelve (excluding the ones treated in this chapter) and write program notes for a hypothetical perfor-

mance of them, "cataloguing" them in some manner similar to that used in this chapter.

7. Write original program notes for two or three of the following Ives compositions: *Central Park in the Dark,* String Quartet no. 2, *Hallowe'en, Calcium Night Light, The Pond.* Comment upon the programmaticism involved.

8. After a careful study of the sources of Ives's musical language, and his use of quotation, write a brief essay assessing to what extent his work *is,* and to what extent it is *not,* "pop art."

9. Review thoughtfully Ives's statements about "idealism versus professionalism in music" in the section so labeled in this chapter, and read Ives more fully in this regard (starting with the complete Epilogue of the *Essays*). In what ways do you agree or disagree with his stance? Is this stance possible today? Make this the subject of a brief talk or paper.

10. The French-born Americanized composer Dane Rudhyar wrote in the early 1930s a very brief, nonspecific article titled "Oriental Influence in American Music." (It is printed in Cowell, *American Composers on American Music.*) His last paragraph reads: "The gateway to the Orient is through Occidental America. It is therefore natural to assume that it will be through America that the influence of Oriental music will first be felt in the Occident." To what extent has this happened in the half-century since that was written? Explore the topic from any aspect you choose, and write a brief but more specific essay with the same title as Rudhyar's.

11. Henry Cowell and Harry Partch both began fairly early to write treatises on their conceptions of the directions and resources required of the "new music"—Cowell in *New Musical Resources,* and Partch in *Genesis of a Music.* Make a brief comparative study of these.

12. John Cage's "Four Statements on the Dance" (four articles written between 1939 and 1957, included in his *Silence*) allude to the correlation of new sounds (especially percussion) with modern dance. If you have the opportunity, attend a performance of "modern dance" (now frequently incorporated into ballet itself) that uses new sounds, percussive or electronic, and review the program and its impact, including references to the Cage articles.

13. Interest in Conlon Nancarrow continues to grow, and writings and recordings continue to appear, and will after this edition goes to press. Assemble from various sources (reference works, periodical indexes, record catalogs, etc.) an up-to-date list of writings and recordings on Nancarrow, and conclude with your own personal view of his music, its influence, and its likely place in the history of American music.

14. In his *Genesis of a Music,* p. 9, Harry Partch clarifies his distinction between Corporeal and Abstract music, giving instances of each from a broad range of music. Read this and the material leading up to it, ponder this distinction, and think about your own listening habits and preferences. Of which type is the music that most (and least) appeals to you? Make an annotated diary of the music you listen to for a week or a month, describing the degree of Corporeality or Abstractness of each piece, giving your reasons for making the distinction, and describing your reaction to the music in terms of this distinction.

15. Harry Partch has called *U.S. Highball—A Musical Account of a Transcontinental Hobo Trip* "the most creative piece of work I have ever done." It is autobiographical, and Partch explains at some length its genesis and why, in his view, it "suggests epic feelings." (See *Genesis of a Music,* pp. 322–23.) Listen carefully to the work (issued on Gate 5 Records—as of this writing unfortunately out of print, but available in many library collections). Compare it to other works based upon some aspect of American experience, works that you believe similarly suggest "epic feelings" (the Dust Bowl Ballads of Woody Guthrie?).

16. Edgar Varèse said: "Science is the poetry of today." Comment on both the truths and fallacies implicit in this, and on the ways in which whatever Varèse meant by this was reflected in his music.

17. John Cage wrote a two-page article on Varèse, which is printed in his *Silence.* Using this as a point of departure (but acquainting yourself further with the ideas and music of both men), contrast the views of each on the use of sounds in music.

18

Exploration and Experiment, II: The Impact of Technology and New Aesthetic Concepts

IT is possible to become acquainted with that radically new music that was propagated after the middle of our century—to explore what Paul Griffiths so aptly called "the current tangle of endeavors"—by way of at least two possible approaches. One is through reading about it. No other period has inspired such a volume of writing about new music, in the form of books, articles (indeed, whole periodicals), printed lectures, record liner notes, and so on. Indeed the very novelty of many of these musical manifestations *invited* writing—both at the superficial level of mere reportage (there was a high curiosity quotient in many of the "happenings" of the avant-garde), and at the more thoughtful level of explaining and justifying the rationales behind the endeavors. Composers themselves, it must be said, have not been reticent in taking to pen and lectern, and with varying results have either reduced or further deepened the mystification of the public as to what was going on.

The other approach is through simply listening to the sounds themselves. Although the genetic aspects of the works cannot be left out of account altogether for a sympathetic appreciation of this music (and we shall deal with them in due course), a first approach through attention to the actual sounds has much to recommend it. As Roger Sessions, a composer who long championed the avant-garde, has written,

> One cannot insist too strongly or too frequently that, in the arts generally and in music in particular, it is only productions that really count, and that only in these—music, written or performed—are to be found the criteria by which ideas about music, as well as music itself, must finally stand or fall: not the converse.[1]

To the listener who approaches the music through the sounds themselves the whole picture of mid-century modernism is somewhat less obscure than it would appear from reading about it. It was, in fact, less revolutionary than evolutionary. One can observe a fairly consistent overall stylistic progression in the sound patterns of the new music—the evolution of a vocabulary of sound types and sound gestures. That this vocabulary is to a remarkable degree independent of the philosophies, systems, and rationales behind the music, and even to an extent independent of whether the sounds are produced electronically or by live performers,* shows the extent to which the *styles* of modernism, quite apart from its *ideas*, have asserted an autonomous existence. Thus it is possible (with due regard for the dangers of oversimplification) to characterize in a general way both the sounds themselves and the way in which they are used. Much of the new music in fact invites this approach—confining one's attention purely to the aural surface. If we take John Cage, the genial guru of modernism, at his word, "nothing takes the place but the sounds." Unlike Ives's ideal music, for the listener what it sounds like *is* what it is.

The Surface Features of Mid-Century Modernism

One consistent characteristic of the sounds is that they tend to avoid the middle portion of what had previously been the usual range in any parameter. Thus, in pitch they are often either very high or very low; in volume, either very soft (as in the case of many of Morton Feldman's compositions throughout) or very loud (George Crumb has specified that the dynamic level of his electrified string instruments in *Black Angels* be "on the threshold of pain"); and in duration either very short (often so short that their tone quality hardly registers with the listener) or very long indeed, avoiding the medium-length durations upon which traditional music is based.

Rhythmic complexity (engendered by the consistent use of a complicated and nonrepeating series of durations) is a crucial characteristic. This complexity is of the type used by Ives, as shown in the rhythmic pattern from *In the Night* reproduced in Example 18–1—considered unplayable by most performers in his day.

Example 18–1

With the advent of electronic music, it became possible to realize such complexities in the laboratory, so to speak. But there has arisen a new generation of virtuoso performers (challenged, like the John Henry of the ballad, to compete with the machine) who can execute these rhythms manually, and

* No better example of the interchangeability, in terms of style, of live and electronic music can be cited than the two alternative realizations of Milton Babbitt's *Phonemena* of 1974, available on NW-209.

these performers are now given complex series of durations to realize, such as Example 18–2, from Elliott Carter's Double Concerto. Rhythmic complexity has obscured, or entirely eliminated, the sense of *pulse* in this music—a feature both broadly typical and of the most decisive importance to its basic nature.

Example 18–2

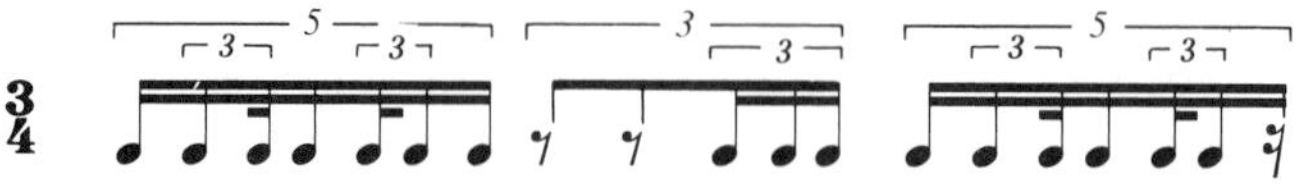

One aspect of music to which a great deal of attention has been paid in avoiding the unusual is tone quality. The search for new *sounds* has been an evident concern in most avant-garde music since mid-century, and this search has added to the tonal palette sounds that range from extended possibilities with traditional instruments, through electronically generated and/or processed sound, to the admission of any sound whatever (noise) as raw material for composition.

New Sounds and New Sound Sources

The quest for new sounds did not of course begin in the mid-twentieth century, and many of the special effects on traditional instruments, especially stringed instruments, were in use in the nineteenth-century. These include the use of harmonics (clear, high-pitched sounds produced by causing the string to vibrate in longitudinal segments); *col legno* (playing so that the wood of the bow instead of the hair makes contact with the string) *sul ponticello* (bowing far up on the string, very near the bridge, to produce an eerily rasping sound); or playing without the usual vibrato. To these effects were added the sounds produced by playing with excessive bow pressure (resulting in an excruciating beginner-like sound); bowing the strings on the opposite side of the bridge (resulting in high sounds of unpredictable pitch); and simply tapping or thumping on the body of the instrument—a resource used on the harp and the guitar, as well as on the bowed instruments. Sliding sounds are easy to achieve on stringed instruments, especially those that are bowed; this effect, removing the customary reference points of a stable set of pitches, is as disorienting to the ear as an earth tremor is to one's sense of balance.*

In the case of the woodwind instruments, new "multiphonic" effects (sounding more than a single pitch at once: achieved by the use of special fingerings and embouchure adjustments) were sought after and used, as were simpler effects such as clicking the keys. Brass players could be called upon to blow through their horns without forming the usual embouchure with their lips, producing thereby a windy amplification of the sound of their breath. As to the piano, we have already encountered modifications of piano tone in the music of Cowell and Cage; more recent works such as *Makrokosmos I* and *II*[2] (1972 and 1973) for amplified piano by George Crumb, and *Ni Bruit Ni Vitesse*[3]

* It is interesting to note that when Edgar Varèse used mechanical means to achieve sliding sounds (sirens) in his scores, he further heightened the impact of this effect by incorporating a sound that had very specific and decidedly threatening connotations outside of the realm of music.

(1972) by Lukas Foss, were successors to the early Cowell and Cage pieces, and showed a continuing exploration of the tonal possibilities of the grand piano. (Crucial limitations inevitably arise in using an instrument in a way it was not designed to be used; most of the novel piano effects, for example, are possible only on a grand piano.) We have already noted the increased importance in the twentieth century of the percussion section, and its open-ended potential for new sounds has made percussion virtually indispensable to contemporary music.

Other sources of new sounds are of course new instruments. On one hand we find increased use of instruments from non-Western cultures, principally Asian and African; Lou Harrison's felicitous incorporation of Indonesian gamelan instruments into some of his works is representative.[4] On the other hand, we find the invention and construction of new instruments, such as those built by Harry Partch, treated in the previous chapter. (It should be noted that a great many "new" instruments, though original, have predecessors in the instruments of some traditional culture.)

Another sound source has been the use in new ways of the oldest instrument of all, the human voice. The techniques of vocal production that for centuries have been used with the aim of producing sounds considered "beautiful" or "expressive," or both, as defined by a particular culture, have been extended to enable the human voice to produce, with practice, new sounds—sounds with two discernible pitches, for example, or very low sounds. (Many of these so-called "extended vocal techniques" require electronic amplification.) Other approaches have been to use electronic devices to slow down, speed up, or dissect and dismember ordinary speech or song, so that the meaning and identity of words are obliterated, and sheer vocal sounds, or phonemes, are left. (Slowing down is the basis for pieces such as Robert Ashley's *She Was a Visitor,* while dismemberment is the basis for the vocal part of Milton Babbitt's *Phonemena,* mentioned earlier.) Still another approach, leading often to humorous results, is the use of non-speech vocal sounds—hisses, clucks, lip-pops, tongue-clicks, and so on; this is the basis for a piece such as *Sound Patterns* by Pauline Oliveros.[5]

New modes of simultaneity have also produced new sounds. The combining of a few tones in dissonant relationships has been extended to the practice of heaping together a great many pitches—often all of the available pitches in a certain range. This is a further development of the "cluster" chords of Ives and Cowell that we encountered in the last chapter. The perception of dissonance, especially at soft dynamic levels, is replaced by what has been described as a *sound mass.* European composers such as György Ligeti (in *Atmospheres*) and Krzysztof Penderecki (in *Threnody for the Victims of Hiroshima*) were responsible in the 1960s for some of the most familiar examples of sound mass as extended to large orchestral ensembles, but earlier American composers including Edgar Varèse, John Becker, and Wallingford Riegger were using ultra-dissonant sound-mass techniques in the 1930s and 1940s, and David Cope has called attention to their more recent use by the Czech-born American composer Karel Husa in his work for band, *The Apotheosis of This Earth* (1971).[6]

Another option, of course, is *no* sound. Silence is indeed an important element—a more pronounced structural feature than in traditional music. The silences are apt to be longer in a work by Cage or one of the circle of composers he has most directly encouraged or influenced, such as Morton Feldman, Earle Brown, and especially Christian Wolff. As early as 1952 Cage himself preempted the ultimate position in the use of silence with his famous piece *4′ 33″*, in which no intended sounds whatever are produced, and which may therefore be performed by "any instrument or combination of instruments."

The more extreme of the sounds described in this section—extreme in terms of their remoteness from traditional musical tone—could well be called "noise." Indeed, as early as the turn of the century noise had been organized and incorporated into compositions. The isolated and radical European movements *futurismo* (Italian) and *bruitisme* (French) were early if unsuccessful predecessors, but the American composer George Antheil picked up on futurist ideas, and in his *Ballet mécanique*[7] (premiered in 1926), one of the most famous of the "noise pieces," he used a large percussion section that included electric bells, siren, and three airplane propellers. John Alden Carpenter, in his *Skyscrapers*,[8] premiered the same year, used a typewriter (and, as a visual symbol of "modernity," traffic lights). The selection of noises employed tends to be a function of the technology of the age: in the 1920s sirens, typewriters, and airplane propellers were appropriated "live"; after mid-century, the noises tended to be those rendered accessible and amplified by modern recording techniques—human brain waves, for example.[9] Moral and ethical concerns are also reflected in the choice of "noises." The new compelling environmental awareness, for example, has found expression in the increased use of the sounds of nature, such as the fascinating "songs" of the humpback whale, used by composers in various ways. Technology is giving us access to worlds of ever-tinier sounds; "plant music," for example, already exists.[10] As for future developments, John Cage, an accomplished mycologist, has declared his desire to "hear the mushroom itself, and that could be done with very fine technology, because they are dropping spores, and those spores are hitting surfaces."[11] This use of technology to render natural sounds usable in composition is an extension of *musique concrête,* which will be considered in due course, as will the philosophical implications of using any noise as a "found object" in art, and the substitution of "organized sound" for the concept of music as it has been known (Varèse), or the conscious abandonment altogether of the attempt to organize sound (Cage).

Finally, there has been a concern with the spatial aspects of sound—specifically, in the musical effects created by separating sound sources and placing them in various ways in the performance space. The reader will recall Ives's experiments with this; among many examples of a continuing interest in this spatial dimension, with live performers, could be cited Donald Erb's short *Spatial Fanfare for Brass and Percussion*[12] and the final movement of John Corigliano's Concerto for Clarinet and Orchestra (1977).[13] Tape music especially invites exploitation of the spatial dimension; Varèse's *Poème électronique,* with its 425 loudspeakers, was an elaborate prototype.

New Approaches to the Ordering of Sounds

In addition to the newness of the sounds themselves, the listener will be aware of a departure from traditional music in the way they have been used. Not only has there been a new and extended vocabulary of sounds; a new way of making sentences and paragraphs with this vocabulary is evident as well. Whatever the rationale behind the ordering of the sounds, or the category of the piece in terms of a "school," there has been a discernible tendency away from what was perceived in more traditional music as coherent (and therefore somewhat predictable) structure—away from the perception of a musical passage, apprehended as some kind of moving line (a melody perhaps) progressing toward some kind of goal or climax. Replacing the sense of movement or progression, we find a sense either that the music is static—resembling an unchanging field, or a stationary object—or that the music consists of a succession of individual *moments*, not perceptibly connected with one another. The composer Ralph Shapey has said, "The 'image' must create and sustain the unforgettable moment, and it is a series of such moments that result in a dynamic, unforgettable experience."[14] Jonathan Kramer has gone so far as to describe what he aptly calls "moment form." He writes:

> Because moment forms verticalize time, render every moment a Now, avoid functional implications between moments, and avoid climaxes, they are not beginning-middle-end forms. Although the piece must start for simple practical reasons, it may not begin; it must stop, but it may not end.[15]

As Kramer points out, this discontinuity is congruent with, and was very probably influenced by, two technological media developments: film and tape. In both of these media the *splice* has made the instant juxtaposition of discontinuous "moments" possible, and this proved to be a pervasive mode of organization for much of the new music since mid-century.

We have listed certain more or less *generic* surface features of the new music. The recognition of the new sounds, and the new ways of ordering these sounds, will serve as a kind of initiation for the listener, replacing a sense of strangeness and even hostility with at least a modicum of acquaintance. A desire to "understand" the new music is frequently expressed. There is no one satisfactory definition of what it means to "understand" *any* music, but the key to at least reducing the misunderstanding of the products of modernism is being ready to alter one's expectations of them as music.

The Two Dominant Rationales of Mid-Century Modernism

If the surface of mid-century modern music, as the ear alone perceived it, gave the impression of having simply appropriated more sounds into its vocabulary and devised new ways of relating them to each other, the situation in the 1950s and 1960s was far less simple from the composer's point of view. He or she had, as never before, to *rationalize*. Innocence was no longer possible; the new "advanced" composer knew too much. Even the decision *not* to rationalize had to be rationalized. There lay in wait for the serious young aspiring composer a maze of ideas, ideologies, methods, dogmas, and intellectual abstractions and justifications. The European intellectual climate had made European composers more prone to rationalization, but American composers had also become involved, despite a certain ineradicable residue of independence and distrust of hierarchical system. Among composers dedicated to advanced music, a fortunate few, such as Morton Feldman, succeeded in extricating themselves and confronting autonomously once more the basic function of the composer—to make music. Feldman himself said in the late 1960s, "Unfortunately for most people who pursue art, ideas become their opium. The sickness that you feel about the situation today is a piling up of multitudinous suggestions and multitudinous misconceptions, each tumbling over the other. There is no security to be one's self."[16]

A sign of the times was the extent to which these "multitudinous suggestions" were verbalized in the abundant writing about contemporary music. A few samples will convey the sense of the terms in which composers understood what composition was—or in which observers *presumed* composers understood it. The well-worn "time and space" theme, reverted to again and again, furnishes some typical examples.

> music as an object in Time and Space . . .

> In my music, the initial space-time image generates through expansions of *itself* all textures and a structural totality. Through permutations of this image I continue, rather than destroy, its state of being.[17]

> Sounds do not progress, but merely heap up and accumulate in the same place. . . . This blurs and obliterates the past, and obliterating it, removes the possibility of a future. . . . What is offered is not just music in time, but a new idea of time.[18]

In terms of rationale and method, the paths that composers took varied in detail with each individual, but two fairly clear general routes were followed—routes that diverged widely. Cage, in an address given in 1957, pointed up the difference rather clearly in terms of the amount of *rational* control exercised by the composer over the aural result: the production.

> Again there is a parting of the ways. One has a choice. If he does not wish to give up his attempts to control sound, he may complicate his musical technique towards an approximation of the new possibilities and awareness. (I use the word "approximation" because a measuring mind can never finally measure nature.) Or, as before, one may give up the desire to control sound, clear his mind of music, and set about discovering means to let sounds be themselves rather than vehicles for man-made theories or expressions of human sentiments.[19]

The almost diametrically opposed positions represented by the ideal of maximum rational control on the one hand (Milton Babbitt: "I believe in cerebral music, and I never choose a note unless I know why I want it there")[20] and a minimum of such control on the other (John Cage: "Discovering means to let sounds be themselves") polarized the new music in the 1950s and 1960s to the extent that the two approaches were given separate labels: *avant-garde* for the first and *experimental* for the second. Let us now examine briefly some of the premises and the manifestations of each.

Toward Maximum Rational Control by the Composer

The trend toward ever-greater control over the end result of musical composition was manifested in two distinct but related areas. The first was the control over every aspect of performance, going beyond the historically basic specifications of pitch, rhythm, and tempo (the composer's specification of which evolved in that order) to include the most detailed instructions regarding tone color and dynamic nuance. Increasing control is a process that has been going on progressively ever since clearly defined instrumentation and the use of instrumental effects began to be called for by composers of the Renaissance. Its ultimate realization, naturally, is the composition directly on tape (electronic music), which eliminates the performer entirely. This technological development will be dealt with more fully in due course.

A second, and more fundamentally crucial, area of increased control was that governing the myriad of choices the composer makes in writing the piece to begin with. In this century the greatest degree of predetermined control of choices has been represented by the technique of *serial organization,* a mode of organization already described in Chapter 16 in connection with the Concerto for Piano and Wind Quintet by Wallingford Riegger. "Classical" serial technique, applied to pitches alone, has been used by many American composers, including Milton Babbitt, Ben Weber, George Perle, Ross Lee Finney, until the late 1960s George Rochberg, and in some works Aaron Copland.

The serial organization of pitch alone has a history of more than half a century. After a decline in its influence, the resurgence of serialism, followed by its further evolution and extension, was primarily a European development, epitomized by the annual summer gatherings in the 1950s of the leaders of the movement in Darmstadt—a small German town that Paul Griffiths has called the "citadel of serialism."[21] But American composers such as Milton Babbitt and George Perle were pursuing serialism independently, and this pursuit took many forms and went in many directions. Ultimately, on both sides of the Atlantic, the move was taken toward subjecting the *total* aural result of a composition to the intellectual predetermination of serial procedures. What has become popularly known as *total serialization* involves, ideally, a procedure by which the ordering of all the other measurable dimensions of sound—duration, intensity, timbre, and register—is serially determined. This procedure results in a composition that has been called "the unpremeditated result of comprehensive premeditation."[22] The idea itself has become well known, although actual pieces in which all the so-called parameters of music (a term borrowed, significantly, from mathematics) have been serially predetermined are relatively rare. One such piece is Milton Babbitt's *Three Compositions for Piano,*[23] in which dynamics, rhythm, and pitch are serialized. The early date (1947) is testimony to the independent leadership of American composers in this field.[24]

Serialism continues to be cultivated; the convoluted and self-multiplying ramifications of serial organization have given rise to technical terms such as "nests" and "trees"—terms borrowed, curiously and paradoxically, from organic nature. The fact that the universities tend to be the centers for its cultivation, often pursued with the aid of foundation grants, has helped to foster the analogy of this type of composition to pure scientific research. Around this kind of music, and the theorizing that goes with it, a rarefied atmosphere is created in which the layman is made to feel not only uncomfortable but unwelcome and inferior. The pronouncements of some composers are not calculated to dispel this. Charles Wuorinen has said, "Composers have always been 'intellectuals' and this stance is absolutely unavoidable today, for music has grown too rich and complex to be handled by the illiterate."[25]

Today it is not only the layman who might conceivably feel "illiterate"; the researches and writings of Milton Babbitt, for example, are largely a closed book to any musician, and even to any composer, who has not become familiar with the mathematical terms and concepts that have been adopted by this branch of composition. The role of the researcher who works without consideration of any broader "practical" applications—or any "public," for that matter—is claimed for the composer of advanced music. This view is cogently expressed by Milton Babbitt himself in a now-famous article, circulated under the title "Who Cares If You Listen?"* Written for a magazine with broad circulation (*High Fidelity*), and in this case in terms any intelligent layman can understand, it is recommended as one of the most lucid and unequivocal statements of the viewpoint of the composer-as-research-specialist.[26]

The composer's attempt (usually by means of serialism) to achieve total rational control has acknowledged limitations. Of these, two became especially evident. The first stems from the basic premise of serialism that all the pitches, durations, intensities, and other properties constituting the predetermined series must be heard before any can be repeated. Thus the incessant change dictated by the constant and inexorable rotation through the series means that the whole gamut of sound material must be, in practical terms, nearly constantly present to the ear. But, as the proverb has it, the more things change, the more they are the same, and the aural result of this constant change is often actually a kind of *static* quality—a limitation difficult to overcome even in music using older procedures in which only pitch is serialized. As the German avant-gardist Karlheinz Stockhausen has put it, "If from one sound to the next, pitch, duration, timbre and intensity change . . . one is constantly traversing the entire realm of experience in a very short time, and thus one finds oneself in a state of suspended animation, the music 'stands still.' "[27]

A second limitation, which has already been hinted at, is the built-in tendency of serialism to defeat the avowed purpose of those adopting it as a means of achieving totally predetermined control; the music comes to resemble, to a remarkable degree, that generated by opposite procedures of deliberate randomness. As Křenek has said of serialism, "It is reasonable to assume that in pursuing this concept beyond certain limits one would reach a point of diminishing returns, for the internal organization of the final product would become so complicated that its outward appearance would be hardly distinguishable from that of organized chaos."[28]

The paradoxical similarity between the results of procedures designed to give the composer maximum control and those designed to give him minimum control have been noted by many observers,† and leads us to the consideration of the other dominant rationale of mid-century modernism.

* The title is the source of gross popular misunderstanding, since it was chosen not by Babbitt but by the magazine's editor, who was unwilling to change it at the author's request, and therefore chose to misrepresent, for popular consumption, Babbitt's carefully stated position.

† In explaining the phenomenon of maximum order resembling disorder, George Rochberg has invoked the aid of the physical concept of *entropy*, "the measure of the tendency of nature toward disorder, non-differentiation, and a final state of static equilibrium," in a fascinating essay too

Toward Minimum Rational Control by the Composer

The second path of the new music after mid-century was that of progressive relinquishment of rational control by the composer. Here, as at the opposite extreme of serialism, the musical result cannot be envisioned in full, but for a different reason—the composer has deliberately willed it so. Increasingly, aspects of the whole result are left either to the performer or to the operation, in some form or other, of chance.

Improvisation

A certain degree of planned relinquishment of control to the performer (quite aside from the ever-present element of interpretation) has existed from time to time, principally in the realm of improvisation. This specialized art (native in one particular form to jazz) virtually died out in European music in the early nineteenth century, but it has been revived in the new music of the last half of the twentieth, with new "rules of the game." The work of the Improvisation Chamber Ensemble, a small group founded by Lukas Foss in 1957, consisting of piano, clarinet, cello, and percussion, set high standards for this new kind of improvisation. In the interludes to Foss's *Time Cycle,* and in various other pieces, we hear skilled and disciplined artists who, after long practice together, produce highly integrated compositions, the outlines of which are carefully planned, but the actual details of which are spontaneous and differ with each performance.[29] Of the Ensemble's methods, Foss and Richard Dufallo, clarinetist and Ensemble member, have written:

> A specific formal or textural musical vision is committed to paper. . . . The musicians, as they play, translate the symbols into sound. They do not stake their hope on the element of chance and its capacity for yielding interesting musical results—they do not put their trust into the order, the system, which coordinates chance happenings. System and chance form the basis for ensemble improvisation, but the *performer holds the reins.* He does not passively translate his symbols into sound, he listens critically, and plays accordingly. . . . He corrects chance rather than surrenders to chance—chance controlled rather than chance in control.[30]

Limited indeterminacy

Improvisation is, of course, a form of indeterminacy, in that the details of the result are purposely not planned in advance. Improvisation in the strict sense, as exemplified in the work of Foss's Ensemble, involves wide performer choices within a carefully planned structure, and the interaction of players who are highly skilled, experienced in this type of performance, and used to working together. It is therefore rare. Furthermore, as in the case of improvisation in jazz, the effective scope of improvisation is inversely proportional to the size of the group. Therefore composers, in view of the limitations of true

---

long to quote from effectively. See "Indeterminacy in the New Music" in Rochberg, *The Aesthetics of Survival.*

improvisation, have sought other related means of applying indeterminacy within controlled limits.

Indeterminate notation is one means used, supplying performers with a basic idea of the sound intended, and specifying certain guides and limitations to its production. Graph notation, for instance, an early idea that survives in various forms, was used by Morton Feldman in the early 1950s to produce such works as *Projection 4 for Violin and Piano* (1951) and *Intersection 3* (1953), the latter having been realized on both piano and pipe organ. Indeterminate notation has since moved varying degrees of distance away from traditional notation and, more important, has given the player varying degrees of latitude in interpreting it. While a certain degree of standardization is beginning to evolve, most indeterminate notation must continue to rely heavily upon explanatory directions, which are sometimes as lengthy as the notation itself.[31]

Closely related to indeterminate notation is the practice of giving the performers (including the conductor) certain choices in the performance—choices relating to the order of musical events (including how many of all those possible are to be performed at all) and to the duration of these events. Earle Brown's *Available Forms I* (1961) furnishes an example of this procedure. This is a work for chamber ensemble in which the conductor moves at will from one to another of six "events," the notations for all of which are available to all the performers at all times. To such procedures Brown has given a name: "open form."*

Unlimited indeterminacy

The progression toward a minimization of control by the composer may be thought of as a continuum, beginning with improvisation. Further along, in the limited indeterminacy we have described, certain freedoms of a somewhat different character have been given the performer, and no two realizations of a work can be the same. It is important to recognize, however, that this is still indeterminacy in the service of the composer's initial vision, or image, of a piece. As we move further along the continuum in the direction of ever-decreasing control over the realized sound itself, we become involved with significant changes in the aesthetic concepts of what constitutes the essence and function of music, and of art in general. With Cage's "my purpose is to remove purpose," we encounter at once a fundamentally different attitude and a fundamentally different aesthetic. The listener who brings some intellectual background to highly indeterminate music has already been warned of the nature of the realm he or she is entering, in departing from the fairly uncomplicated stance of perceiving a work purely in terms of its sounds and stepping into the maze of the composer's methods and rationale. As David Cope has pointed out, the listener's reactions and judgments are apt to be profoundly affected as he or she enters this maze:

* It is significant that Brown was influenced by the work of the sculptor Alexander Calder. There is a certain correspondence between *open form* in music and the *mobile* in art; in both, the individual components are predetermined by the artist, but their relationship at any given moment (or in any given performance) is unpredictable.

> If the listener is unaware of the compositional process (in this case "chance") he will tend to judge the composition more or less as any other, depending upon background and experience. On the other hand, if he is aware of the act of indeterminacy his whole set of aesthetics is jarred and judgment is tied to a completely different set of aesthetics according to personal bias.[32]

This listener enters the realm of art as *process*, rather than finished product—a realm glimpsed already in some of the ideas of Charles Ives. (Feldman: "Down with the masterpiece—up with art.")

Although the extramusical accident has always been *one factor* in the composition of music, the listener encounters here the almost surgical isolation of chance, and its elevation to a position in which it replaces altogether what has been called imagination, intuition, inspiration. In this he encounters once again (as with indeterminacy's complementary opposite, total organization) the goal of removing artistic decisions from the domain of human memory, experience, and intuition, the effects of which are to be expurgated much as (in another context) would be the consequences of "original sin."

John Cage's *Music of Changes* (a piano piece written in 1951, lasting forty-three minutes) furnishes a useful early example of this, having been arrived at through an elaborate process of using charts and coin tosses in accord with the Chinese oracular book of wisdom *I Ching* ("Book of Changes"). Cage described in some detail his method of making the piece, and summed it up with this statement:

> It is thus possible to make a musical composition the continuity of which is free of individual taste and memory (psychology) and also of the literature and "traditions" of the art. The sounds enter the time-space centered within themselves, unimpeded by service to any abstraction, their 360 degrees of circumference free for an infinite play of interpenetration.[33]

With this type of new music, the scope of the composer in determining the actual sounds decreased; his role became more and more circumscribed by the relinquishment of more and more parameters to chance or to the performer, until it was reduced to that of merely setting up systems, or arranging for the unpredictable to happen. As this occurred—as compositional possibilities became narrowed and exhausted—there was a corresponding and compensatory widening of the *arena* of composer involvement into the visual, the spatial, the theatrical realm. Cage foresaw this when he said in 1957, "where do we go from here? Towards theatre."[34]*

The work of the Cagean wing of experimental music has suggested the concept of art as *therapy*—for the individual and for society. The silences in the works (by which is meant the lack of planned or intended sounds) condition us to listen carefully to the sounds of the environment wherever the concert may be taking place, much as the windows and other openings in modern architecture make the surroundings a part of the structure. Thus we are encouraged, through art, to listen more attentively to the sounds that surround us constantly. The same is true of theater; as Cage says, "Theatre takes place all the time wherever one is and art simply facilitates persuading one this is

* The extension of the new music into theater will be explored below.

the case." This view certainly has contributions to make to the richness and variety of our perceptions in the last half of the twentieth century. The problem lies in the fact that while many are ready to grant that this increased awareness of sounds (and of sights, and of "theatre") is beneficial, and can have a considerable aesthetic dimension, they are not so sure they want to pay for a slice of life, as it were, served up to them as art. For whether it is or is not art, it is something anyone can do for himself, and do-it-yourself art reduces the role of the specialist composer to zero and quickly puts him out of business. Cage himself, in a one-man dialogue, asked himself the ultimate question—"Why bother, since, as you have pointed out, sounds are continually happening whether you produce them or not?"[35]—but avoided answering it.

New Technology and the New Music

Technology in the most general sense has never been divorced from the practice of music; its application to the making of musical instruments is obvious. Before the turn of the century technology was harnessed for a new task—that of recording sound itself (hence music) to make it reproducible. This crucial development had two important consequences: it created a new medium of access for music, and it made possible a degree of permanence for the specific performance, hitherto so ephemeral. These two consequences revolutionized the music *industry*, but did little to change the nature of music itself. It is clearly, then, neither the technology of instrument making per se, nor that of recording music per se that is meant when we speak of its impact on mid-twentieth-century music; rather, it is the technology that introduced radically different ways in which music was made—the technology that made possible both the electronic synthesis of sound and the manipulation and transformation of natural or synthesized sound.

Although some work was done along these lines before World War II, the real breakthrough came as a spin-off of wartime research, especially the research that led to the development of sound recording on magnetic tape, and to the development of the digital computer. Without going into technical detail, from the listener's point of view the present sophisticated state of electroacoustic music can be understood as a composite of the following capabilities: (1) the ability to record any occurring sound or succession of sounds, (2) the ability to synthesize (to build up from the electronic scratch of the basic sine tone, as it were) any imaginable sound or succession of sounds, and (3) the ability to manipulate sounds obtained from either of these two processes in various ways, including slowing them down or speeding them up, reversing their direction in time, changing their timbre by filtering out certain frequencies, combining any number of them simultaneously, introducing echo effects, making them endlessly repeat, and juxtaposing them in any way by splicing.

Thus was born, around mid-century, the vast array of sounds and procedures known by the catchall term "electronic music." In the early years a distinction was drawn between the products that used as raw material "live" acoustic sound (a flute, a piano, a human voice, bird calls) and those that used purely synthesized tones. (*Musique concrète* was the term for the former, and simply *electronic music* for the latter.) But both procedures are now so widely used and intermingled that the distinction is no longer a useful one. In addition, it is further blurred by the fact that modern digital equipment can "listen to" and analyze the timbre of any live sound, and then synthesize and manipulate it in any way desired.

Historically the craft of the electronic composer has evolved from the "classical" studio techniques of manually cutting and splicing tape to produce a composition (a procedure that takes far longer than the listener might imagine!) to the use of sophisticated techniques of computer generation and manipulation.

But of far more concern to us here is the evolution of electroacoustic music from the listener's point of view. In its first stages (roughly the 1950s) nearly all efforts were directed toward the production of the sound on tape as the sole end product, self-contained and complete without live performers. To attend a "performance," all you did was be in the presence of loudspeakers (in number anywhere from one to four hundred) and listen. The first program of such music in the United States was given at the Museum of Modern Art in New York in 1952, and was the work of two of the pioneers of electroacoustic music, Otto Luening and Vladimir Ussachevsky.[36] Other composers such as Milton Babbitt and John Cage were also working in this medium at the time. Because of the amount and cost of the equipment involved, universities were both the centers and the patrons of its development—at first Columbia and Princeton, later joined by the Universities of Michigan and Illinois, and Stanford University.

From the beginning both "live" and synthesized tones were used as raw material. For a description of the material, procedures, notation, and formal organization of an early tape piece (1955), it is interesting to read Ussachevsky's "Notes on *A Piece for Tape Recorder*," and then listen to the piece itself.[37] Performerless tape music has continued to be cultivated; *La Poème électronique* (1958) by Edgar Varèse, mentioned in the last chapter, was a landmark. Subsequent carefully crafted compositions—some of them large-scale, and by no means inexpressive—by Luening and Ussachevsky, and after them Mario Davidovsky, Mel Powell, Kenneth Gaburo, Charles Wuorinen (whose *Time's Encomium*[38] of 1969 won the Pulitzer Prize), and Morton Subotnick, give indications of what is possible.*

But by and large the elimination of the performer did not prove to be the altogether worthwhile liberating advance it was at first thought to be. For one thing, for all the inventiveness that was applied, there seemed to be still a pervasive *sameness* to electronic sounds—the result of what Mel Powell described as tape music's "perilously limited array of options." Probably a more decisive limiting factor was the absence of a human performer—a vital ingredient to the essentially human transaction that is live musical performance. As early as 1953 Luening and Ussachevsky were combining live performers and tape sounds, and they produced two works for orchestra and

* Since it soon became evident that the recording, playable at home, and not the public "concert," was the important mode of dissemination for this music, it is not surprising that in the 1960s record companies themselves were commissioning electronic works (e.g., Subotnick's *Silver Apples of the Moon* and *The Wild Bull*, commissioned by Nonesuch, the latter still in print as 71208).

tape the next year (*Rhapsodic Variations*[39] and *A Poem in Cycles and Bells*[40]).

This has proven to be the most prevalent use of electronic music, and works for tape and a single performer or small group of performers are very numerous. The degree to which live performers must synchronize with the tape varies considerably, from situations in which they are completely independent (John Cage's *Aria with Fontana Mix*) to pieces in which the interaction is highly organized, as in Mario Davidovsky's various pieces appropriately called *Synchronisms.*

The most striking of the pieces for tape and a single performer are those that verge on "performance art," and capitalize on the dramatic potential of "man vs. the machine" in some form, involving the performer as actor. Jacob Druckman's *Animus* pieces (numbered I through IV, and composed 1966–77) are representative. Often in such pieces the very act of playing a musical instrument, with its all-too-human opportunities for mishap, becomes the subject matter, with the performer at once performing and acting out a commentary on performing. Thus the human dimension reasserts itself in terms of humanity in *conflict* with the technology of our time.

Electronic sound manipulation has been combined with live performance in very diverse ways. The most usual of these, as indicated above, is for the human performer to synchronize with a prerecorded tape which, though some of its ingredients may include sounds produced earlier by the same performer in the studio, is nonetheless implacably constant. But there has gradually evolved a genre known as "live electronic" music, based on an actual interaction between performer and machine. There is a great variety of ways in which this can be carried out. The performer can actually "play" a synthesizer designed for the purpose; instruments such as the early Synket and the more recent Synclavier are typical. More promising have been the possibilities opened up in the way of having the live sounds of traditional instruments manipulated on the spot during the performance. This can take the form of a delayed playback of the live sound, resulting in an "echo" effect that can be endlessly compounded, or the electronic distortion of the live sound, or a combination of these. Gordon Mumma's *Hornpipe* (1967), which involves an elaborate interaction between a solo French horn player, a "cybersonic console," and the acoustics of the performance space, is an example.[41] To cope with situations in which the performer is interactively involved with the electronics, a new kind of virtuoso performer has emerged—one who can produce a variety of live sounds (using the voice as well as the instrument) while at the same time controlling (often by the use of foot pedals) the electronic manipulation of these live sounds. The concertizing trombonist Miles Anderson is one such virtuoso.

The computer, with its ability to manipulate, at the speed of light, vast quantities of digital data (in which all "information" is handled in terms of numbers) began to find a variety of applications in the new music in the 1950s. The term "artificial intelligence," as applied to the computer, has led to misleading assumptions as to its role in music (and in other areas as well). Projects have been undertaken in which the computer has been able to "compose" music, using its capacity to generate random numbers, and selecting and manipulating the numbers generated in accordance with instructions encoded by the programmer (i.e., a human being). The most famous such work was the

Illiac Suite for String Quartet produced at the University of Illinois by Lejaren Hiller and Leonard Isaacson in 1957, and subsequently performed by a string quartet of human performers.

While this kind of experiment has yielded useful information, the results have never been taken very seriously artistically, and they do not represent the way computers have actually been used subsequently in new music. What *has* been exploited is the capability of the computer (in combination with other equipment such as converters, filters, and so on) to generate and store on tape sequences of sounds that can be very precisely specified by the computer as to pitch, timbre, duration, volume, and volume change ("envelope"). The computer and its satellite equipment can also "listen to," and take samples of, live sounds, which can then be stored and made available for manipulation and use in composition. To cite one (quite limited) example, the application of this capacity to the sounds of human speech is strikingly illustrated in works that Charles Dodge was creating in the early 1970s: *Speech Songs* (1973), *The Story of Our Lives* (1974), and *In Celebration* (1975).[42] Here spoken poetry was recorded and analyzed digitally, and the results were subjected to extensive manipulation, through changes in pitch, speed, and timbre and through simultaneous "layering," to produce a complex juxtaposition of sounds in which the words nevertheless remain intelligible.

The application of computer technology to music is naturally continually evolving, and in many directions. The flexibility, and ever-increasing capacity, and above all the *speed* of computer operations has enabled the computer to take on much of the labor of the "classical" studio techniques of cutting and splicing described earlier. Large universities, on account of their resources and their basic research function, have remained the centers for this kind of work; that of John Chowning and Leland Smith at Stanford is representative and prominent.

Other Aspects of Mid-Century Modernism

Toward Theater and the Combination with Other Media

The tendency of many of the endeavors in modernism's "tangle" was toward the involvement of other senses than the auditory, and hence other media. The extension of the new music into the "multi-media" realm is actually a fairly complex subject, for the heading embraces many essentially different kinds of endeavors. The preoccupation with combining multiple media did not at first involve working in the traditional composite forms of opera or ballet—opera, so termed, has only recently been cultivated by the avant-garde. The multi-media movement, rather, seemed to come out of two related impulses—either the need to have something visual going on during otherwise static performances of electronic music, or the desire to "theatricalize" the basic concert situation. (The ease with which a quasi-dramatic situation suggests itself in works for performer and tape has already been noted.)

Making "theater" out of a concert situation makes actors out of the performers. The late works of Harry Partch illustrated this; to his visually intriguing original instruments was added the dimension of the performers themselves, who, according to Partch's own instructions, were to be "on stage," as it were—a situation that readily invited the use of film to capture the totality of the works.[43] A more passive kind of theatricalism is represented by a piece such as *Vox balaenae* (*Voice of the Whale*) (1971)[44] by George Crumb, wherein three musicians playing electrified instruments (flute, cello, and piano) and making music "inspired by the singing of the humpback whale," are directed to wear masks and to play in a deep blue light. In this case, the music clearly exists independent of the visual setting, which merely adds an atmospheric dimension to the live performance.

As performance practices in contemporary music departed more and more from the traditional ways of playing instruments, there developed to a very limited extent a type of "instrumental theater" (cultivated more in Europe than in America) based on establishing a pseudo-theatrical relationship, occasionally erotic, between performer and instrument.[45]

A more recent and far more popular theatricalism, using a mixture of media, is the somewhat faddish "performance art" of the 1980s, centered on a solo performer who plays, sings, and speaks, aided by a battery of visual displays and props. Laurie Anderson is perhaps the best-known performer in this vein. "Performance art" is apt to verge on pop, the music partaking of rock and minimalism, and its visual aspect related to the video. It remains to be seen what a host of new artists launching what amount to one-man (or, more often, one-woman) shows will make of it.

The desire to make "theater" out of a basic concert situation, with the aim of either enhancing it artistically or popularizing it, is of course not new, and such ventures continue, involving stage setting, lighting, costuming the performers, and projecting the score so that it is visible to the audience.[46] But for a time the pursuit of combined media was a fashion, indulged out of a conviction that the concert situation *itself* was altogether outmoded and must be superseded, and that an art that addresses only one sense alone (the auditory) was simply behind the times. Richard Maxfield has written, "I view as irrelevant the repetitious sawing on strings and baton-wielding spectacle we focus our eyes upon during a conventional concert. Much more sensible either no visual counterpart or one more imaginatively selected such as lighting, cinema, choreography, fireworks, trees . . ."[47] But an extremist statement like this implies either a lack of awareness, or a denial, of the satisfaction that audiences have for many centuries derived from simply being in the presence of performers playing music. When all is said and done, the art of music is the art of sound; and while it is certainly necessary to give attention to pleasing, and even teasing, the other senses during its performance, the idea of the "relevance" of "what we focus our eyes upon" is itself basically irrelevant, as far as music is concerned.

There were other multi-media ventures that were not simply attempts to theatricalize the basic concert situation. Serious, and often very elaborate, attempts were made in the late 1960s and early 1970s to create whole artistic "environments." The extent to which visual (and other) components were coordinated with sound varied widely. A short environmental piece, *Souvenir* (1970) by Donald Erb, presented close coordination of the aural, visual, and tactile components in a "happy" and "non-neurotic" (in the composer's words) piece for dancers, instrumental ensemble of winds and percussion, electronic tape, projections, and "props" that include weather balloons (bounced around in the hall by the audience), and Ping-Pong balls, which the audience afterwards carries away as "souvenirs."[48]

An early multi-media "environment" in which there was no attempt to coordinate the aural and visual was *La Poème électronique* (1958) by Edgar Varèse, described in the previous chapter. Here, inside the pavilion especially designed by the architect Le Corbusier, there were visual projections that were chosen independently of Varèse's auditory electronic poem, which was simultaneously emanating from 425 loudspeakers placed throughout the interior.

Once the traditional concert situation was superseded, the temptation to expand multi-media works to gargantuan proportions proved irresistible to some. Robert Moran's "city pieces" involving "audiences" in their realization are representative; his *39 Minutes for 39 Autos*, done in San Francisco in 1969, involved a "potential of 100,000 performers, using auto horns, auto lights, skyscrapers, a TV station, dancers, theater groups, spotlights, and airplanes, besides a small synthesizer ensemble." Such mammoth one-time happenings have their counterpart in the visual arts in the works of Boris Christo, with his wrapped buildings, his forty-mile-long running fence, and his project to put umbrellas over huge areas in Japan and California simultaneously. In the realm of music they have antecedents in Varèse's *Espace* (which was to be broadcast simultaneously from all the capitals of the world), and Charles Ives's projected *Universe Symphony*. They verge on "concept art."

Multi-media works in which there was little or no coordination between the elements were usually the conscious by-products of indeterminacy, and were best described in their heyday as "happenings," a large portion of which were the result of chance operations of one kind or another. With John Cage and his followers and collaborators in the 1960s, the combination of multi-media experiments and indeterminacy led to the production of happenings (such as the four-hour *HPSCHD* described below) that were both lengthy and complex.

Cage's *Variations IV* (1964), for example, was "performed" in an art gallery in Los Angeles, and involved a collage of many sound sources (radio broadcasts, electronic sounds, street noises outside the gallery, and various sounds made by the "audience" itself as the people went through the gallery) combined with lights and other visual phenomena. *HPSCHD*, by Cage and Lejaren Hiller, was an even more complex effort. The sound alone was a dense overlaying of fifty-two electronic sound tapes and seven amplified harpsichords played by five live performers. The basic source material for the harpsichordists was *Introduction to the Composition of Waltzes by Means of Dice*, attributed to Mozart (the witty diversion of a genius at play, which has been cited again and again with singular seriousness by theorists of twentieth-century indeterminacy in search of antecedents). The choice of nearly all the sound material, live and electronic, was controlled by chance—in this case, by a computerized version of *I Ching*. The whole performance (which took place in the huge Assembly Hall of the University of Illinois in 1969, and lasted four and a half hours) was accompanied by visual projections from sixty-four slide projectors and eight movie projectors going simultaneously, as well as miscellaneous light beams and the reflected light from spinning mirrored balls—a manufactured "kinetic environment," and the most complex embodiment up to that time of Cage's dictum that "the more things there are, as is said, the merrier."[49]

A composer of Cage's reputation (he functions as a kind of dean of the experimental school) was able to command the forces necessary to produce the kind of new-music extravaganza represented by *HPSCHD*. Otherwise, such theatrical pieces have largely passed out of the picture, unable to match, in sheer resources available for visual and aural impact, the ultimate pop multimedia form: the live rock performance, with its elaborate light shows and other visual paraphernalia.

Opera, which along with ballet had been the conventional multi-media form for music, was inhospitable to the traditional atonal avant-garde; full-scale operas by such composers as Roger Sessions (*Montezuma*, produced in 1964) and Andrew Imbrie (*Angle of Repose*, produced in1976) are rare, and their productions have been infrequent. Since the mid-1970s, opera has been adopted and reinterpreted by the younger avant-garde, mostly of the minimalist school (see below). With Philip Glass's *Einstein on the Beach* (1976)[50] as an extremely popular opener, a type of opera has developed in accord with what Glass has termed "nonliterary theater," realized in terms of the "moment form" previously described, and accompanied by highly repetitive music. On a smaller scale, a "video opera" by Robert Ashley, *Perfect Lives* (*Private Parts*),[51] appeared after a long period of gestation (1977–83): it is a collaborative effort combining speech, song, and instrumental music (akin to minimalist rock) in a fragmented, episodic form that John Rockwell aptly calls "post-narrative theater"—another name for nonliterary theater.

Anti-Art, and the Confusion of Art with Life

The restlessly experimental fever among the indeterminacy wing of the avant-garde during its most active phase, in the 1960s, led some composers on the fringes to adopt a quasi-philosophical stance, and to direct their energies to exercises whose aim seemed to be to question the nature and function of music itself, and to undermine the assumptions and the *modus operandi* on which it is based. The ideas of John Cage appeared to provide the cues for much of this. Cage himself, while working with craftsmanlike diligence in realizing his own "happenings," as a leader hardly went beyond being a genial, witty, and provocative questioner and storyteller. But there were those in the next generation who took Cage's "purpose . . . to remove purpose" with intense earnestness (at least for a time). The rigorous application of indeterminacy had already denied the composer a good deal of his or her discretionary role in making a piece. Increased renunciation of the role of composer, and of the craft of composition, began to show itself in various manifestations.

One was the conscious use of human responses normally unrelated to the perception of art as the basis for a "composition." *Boredom*, for example (the very thing that all but the most doggedly experimental artists seek to avoid), was studied and exploited by Cage and others. La Monte Young's *Composition 1960 No. 7* consists of two notes forming the interval of a perfect fifth, to be held a "long time"; Philip Corner's *The Barcelona Cathedral* consists of the loud clang of ten metallic percussion instruments being sounded together every few seconds, for half an hour. Minimalism, treated below, grows out of this domain. Another human response unrelated to art that was exploited was the response to danger, real or imagined. So-called "danger music" introduces into the performance elements of real danger, sometimes in terms of potential damage to hearing from very loud sounds. Robert Ashley's *Wolfman* (1964) requires that feedback in a sound system be "played at the highest possible volume level."

"Concept" music consists merely of *ideas* for "pieces," or "happenings," the actual realization of which would be either impossible or, as expressions of the philosophy motivating them, ambiguous or manifestly pointless. Of the first type would be pieces that would take several hundred years to perform, for example, or that would involve an entire large city in their performance; of the second type George Brecht's *Drip Music* ("A source of dripping water and an empty vessel are arranged so that the water falls into the vessel") would be representative, as would La Monte Young's *Composition 1960 No. 9*, which, in his words, "consists of a straight line drawn on a piece of paper. It is to be performed and comes with no instructions."

The "pieces" often consisted *merely* of instructions ("word-scores"), some of which were gentle invitations to become aware of the beauties of the environment, or to relinquish some of the egotism of the "performer." Pauline Oliveros's *Sonic Meditations* include instructions to "Take a walk at night. Walk so silently that the bottoms of your feet become ears" and "Become performers by not performing." But if everything of which we are aware is art, then nothing is art, and art is nothing; and this anti-art stance, whether violent or gentle, was generally related to a confusion of art with life itself. Cage recognizes that this is what art (at least *some* kinds of art) has been up to, but insists on the confusion: "Art's obscured the difference between art and life. Now let life obscure the difference between life and art."[52]

Minimal Music: A Reaction to Modernism

Minimal music—perhaps better described as repetitive music—is by now very familiar as a kind of musical texture in which short, simple patterns are repeated for long periods of time, either without variation, or subjected to subtle changes that gradually alter the melodic, rhythmic, or timbral content. Early minimalist works (Satie's *Vexations*, from the last decade of the nineteenth century, had the performer play a simple 32-bar piece very slowly and softly 840 times) involved unrelieved repetition, with no subtle changes; they represented experiments in boredom and the hypnotic effects of repetition, and at the same time were, in effect, satires on the conventional concert situation. But minimalism as a serious way of making music began to appear prominently in the 1960s. It was associated with two trends of the times: one was an increased interest in Asian and African music, in which repetition plays a very significant role;* the other was the beginnings of a reaction to mid-

* Much Asian and African music that involves repetition exists for a purpose fundamentally different from that of Western music: namely, to produce in its listeners altered states of consciousness. This function of music has, like elements of Eastern philosophy and religion, been adopted by some Western composers. The need, in our time, to understand more about Asian and African music is clear, but is beyond the scope of this book.

century modernism itself, especially the serialism of the dominant academic East Coast—European "establishment."

La Monte Young (b. 1935), in his work with long sustained sounds (either acoustic or electronic) dating from the late 1950s, was an early influence on minimalism. (The cross-cultural aspect of minimalism, and its curious juxtaposition of mysticism and technology, is projected in the flavor of such titles as La Monte Young's *The Tortoise Recalling the Drone of the Holy Numbers as They Were Revealed in the Dreams of the Whirlwind and the Obsidian Gong and Illuminated by the Sawmill, the Green Sawtooth Ocelot and the High-Tension Line Stepdown Transformer,* of 1964.) Composers contemporary with Young who have become better known as proponents of minimalism are Terry Riley (b. 1935), Steve Reich (b. 1936), and Philip Glass (b. 1937). As Ruth Dreier has pointed out, they have many things in common. After a more or less traditional musical education, each became disillusioned with the serial avant-garde; each discovered and studied Asian or African music; each became interested in exploring the physical properties of sound; each was involved with other arts in addition to music; and each founded his own performing group.[53] In addition, each uses or has used electronic means (synthesizers and/or tape).

Riley's *In C*[54] (1964) was something of a landmark work. It partakes of indeterminacy in that the number and type of instruments is optional, as is the total length (the first performance, in San Francisco, lasted over an hour and a half). There is a single tempo, governed by the steady repetition of a "C" two octaves above middle C on the piano throughout. Each performer plays his or her way through a sequence of fifty-three musical fragments, precisely notated, repeating each as many times as desired before going on to the next. When all the performers have gone through all the fragments, the piece is over. The total aural result is that of a rhythmically active, relatively consonant sound mass, constantly changing in its details.

Most composers of repetitive music have tended to avoid indeterminacy, preferring to give the performers directions, in standard notation, as to exactly what they want. Certain particular procedures have been associated with individual composers; Steve Reich, for example, was concerned in his early works with "phasing," a procedure whereby two instruments play the same short phrase together to start with, and then, by a very gradual divergence in speed, move out of phase. This difficult maneuver is done in *Violin Phase* (1967) by having a live player perform "against" his or her own prerecorded tape.[55]

Although the concepts of trance-music, as it is sometimes called, partook in the beginning somewhat of the ideas of Cage and Satie, minimalism has far outstripped the experimental avant-garde in one surprising aspect—its popularity! Beginning as a radical movement, it has become an effective reactionary force to what has been perceived as the complexity, intellectualism, obscurity, and basic unattractiveness of mid-century modernism, of both the determinate and indeterminate schools. There are several obvious reasons for this, which can be summed up by noting that its pitch materials are simple (usually tonal diatonic fragments and simple chords), its sonorities are attractive, it has strongly marked rhythm, and its formal method (repetition with very gradual variation) is readily grasped. These features, especially its repetitiveness and its frequent use of synthesizers, in fact give it a surface akin to that of rock, much of which has been influenced by minimalist procedures (and possibly the other way around). Minimalist composers such as Glass, Reich, and John Adams are the new "stars" of so-called serious music. The basic method of pure repetitive music soon wears thin, of course. Fundamentally and purposely simplistic, and based on a kind of trance-producing *manipulation* of its listeners, it has always been held in disdain by composers and others who demand of music more development, variety, and expressiveness, as traditionally defined. Indeed, most minimalists in the 1980s have tended to incorporate more of precisely these features into their music—it is no longer as minimal as it was. But with all its limitations, the accessibility of minimalist music, with its significant crossover audience, has played a part in the movement of "classical" music beyond the ever-narrowing restrictions of mid-century modernism, and into the realms to be explored in the next chapter.

Further Reading

Books

General

Cope, David H. *New Directions in Music.* 4th ed. Dubuque, IA: William C. Brown, 1984.
A most useful book, full of examples and references.

Griffiths, Paul. *Modern Music: The Avant-Garde since 1945.* New York: George Braziller, 1981.
Some of the best writing on the subject, especially in conveying the historical perspective. Though much space is devoted to European developments, it is valuable in showing the relationship between the European and American avant-garde.

Rochberg, George. *The Aesthetics of Survival: A Composer's View of Twentieth-Century Music.* Ann Arbor: University of Michigan Press, 1984.
A thoughtful critique of modernism.

Rockwell, John. *All American Music: Composition in the Late Twentieth Century.* New York: Knopf, 1983.
Includes perceptive individual chapters on Babbitt, Cage, Rzewski, Ashley, Glass, and others.

Tawa, Nicholas. *A Most Wondrous Babble: American Composers, Their Music, and the American Scene, 1950–1985.* Westport, CT: Greenwood, 1987.

Vinton, John, ed. *Dictionary of Contemporary Music.* New York: E. P. Dutton, 1971.

Yates, Peter. *Twentieth Century Music: Its Evolution from the End of the Harmonic Era into the Present Era of Sound.* New York: Pantheon, 1967.
Though more relevant to the previous chapter, this book (now more than twenty years old) contains well-written introductions to Cage, electronic and computer music, and "Theatrical-Performance Music."

Broadly inclusive collections of essays and interviews

Battcock, Gregory, ed. *Breaking the Sound Barrier: A Critical Anthology of the New Music.* New York: E. P. Dutton, 1981.

Gagne, Cole, and Tracy Caras, eds. *Soundpieces: Interviews with American Composers.* Metuchen, NJ: Scarecrow Press, 1982.

Lang, Paul Henry, ed. *Problems of Modern Music.* New York: W. W. Norton, 1962.
Though over a quarter-century old, this

collection includes several articles that are still valuable.

Schwartz, Elliott, and Barney Childs, eds. *Contemporary Composers on Contemporary Music.* New York: Holt, Rinehart & Winston, 1967.

The serial wing of the avant-garde

Boretz, Benjamin, and Edward T. Cone, eds. *Perspectives on Contemporary Music Theory.* New York: W. W. Norton, 1972.
Selections, mostly from the periodical *Perspectives of New Music;* an instructive sampling of writings from the standpoint of the composer-as-research-specialist.

———. *Perspective on American Composers.* New York: W. W. Norton, 1971.
Broader in scope than the preceding, this takes in Ives, Varèse, Sessions, Copland, Piston, Carter, Berger, and Finney.

John Cage and the experimental wing of the avant-garde

Cage, John. *Silence.* Cambridge, MA: MIT Press, 1966.
This remains the most important single source of Cage's own expressions of his ideas.

Griffiths, Paul. *Cage.* Oxford: Oxford University Press, 1981.

Husarik, Stephen. "John Cage and Lejaren Hiller: *HPSCHD,* 1969," *American Music,* vol. 1, no. 2 (Summer 1983).

Kostelanetz, Richard. *John Cage.* New York: Praeger, 1970.

Montague, Stephen. "John Cage at Seventy: An Interview," *American Music,* vol. 3, no. 2 (Summer 1985).

Nyman, Michael. *Experimental Music: Cage and Beyond.* New York: Schirmer Books, 1974.
Good treatment, with many examples, of the indeterminacy-to-minimalism branch of the avant-garde, up to the early 1970s.

Thomson, Virgil. "Cage and the Collage of Noises" in *American Music Since 1910.* New York: Holt, Rinehart & Winston, 1970; paperback ed., 1972.

Electroacoustic and computer music

Much of the writing on this subject is understandably highly technical; the following are relatively accessible to the general reader.

Ernst, D. *The Evolution of Electronic Music.* New York: Schirmer Books, 1977.

Schwartz, Elliott. *Electronic Music: A Listener's Guide.* New York: Praeger, 1975.
A well-written introduction by a composer, it includes contributed observations by a number of other composers.

Wells, Thomas. *The Technique of Electronic Music.* New York: Schirmer Books, 1981.
Though highly technical, this book is recommended for its organization, its lucid explanations, and its copious references to sources.

Minimal music

Reich, Steve. *Writings about Music.* New York: New York University Press, 1974.

Periodicals

Perspectives of New Music, since 1962 (Seattle, WA).
More or less the official organ of the academic serial wing, with highly prestigious contributors and editorial board.

Source: Music of the Avant-Garde, 1967–72.
Published in its brief history a number of scores and articles, mostly of the indeterminacy wing.

Ear, since 1973 (New York).
More or less the organ of the opposition to academic serialism, it has published articles and scores of the Cagean-to-minimalist persuasion, with a growing cross-cultural emphasis.

Listening

A broad selection of modernist music is available on commercial recordings, including most of the pieces mentioned in the chapter. Issues by CRI, Nonesuch, and New World Records account for much of it.

PROJECTS

1. Collect five samples of writing about specific pieces of modern music—pieces that are available for you to listen to. (Record liner notes are probably the best source.) Rate each sample on a scale of +5 to −5, according to how much the writing enhances for you the experience of listening to the piece—increases your perception or "understanding" of the music. Annotate each rating briefly, quoting relevant passages to reinforce your assessment.

2. Write a well-reasoned critique of Milton Babbitt's important essay "Who Cares If You Listen?" (reprinted in both Chase, *The American Composer Speaks*, and Schwartz and Childs, *Contemporary Composers*). Deal with as many of its implications as you can fathom. For example, what do you think would happen if all "advanced" composers of "specialized" music withdrew in isolation from the "public life of unprofessional compromise and exhibitionism"? Or, related to this, what would be the ramifications of the "complete elimination of the public and social aspects of musical composition"?

3. If you have a fairly extensive background in mathematics, study a technical and mathematically oriented article on the new music, such as Milton Babbitt's "Twelve-Tone Invariants as Compositional Determinants" in Lang, *Problems of Modern Music;* or Babbitt's "Set Structure as a Compositional Determinant" or his "Twelve-Tone Rhythmic Structure and the Electronic Medium," both in Boretz and Cone, *Perspectives on Contemporary Music Theory*. Interpret for the layman, in a lecture, as much of the mathematics involved as you can.

4. Interview a performer who has worked out a piece written in indeterminate notation: what are the problems, challenges, and rewards? (In addition to touring organizations performing new music, there are new-music groups at most colleges and universities that have a sizable number of music students.) Recapitulate the essence of the interview—with comments, background, and illustrations of the notation, if possible—either orally or in a paper.

5. Assemble examples of at least five different methods of achieving indeterminacy in new music (either in composition or in performance). Describe the methods in detail. In the case of compositions indeterminate as to performance, compare if possible two (necessarily different) realizations of the same composition.

6. The most efficient piece of indeterminacy yet designed was a "composition" consisting of one word: "LISTEN." (See Nyman, *Experimental Music*, p. 88, for a reference to this, and a description of how this "piece" was "realized" through field trips to sound environments such as power stations.) Write a brief paper discussing this ultimate renunciation of the function of the artist in selecting and transforming his material, and discuss the concept of art as a kind of therapy, to "make us conscious of the life and sounds outside the accepted musical-social environment."

7. Taking a periodical such as *Time* magazine as a source, write a summary of, and commentary on, the pieces and programs of new music reviewed in any twelve-month period since 1980.

8. The critic Michael Walsh has written: "The injection of overtly theatrical elements into the concert world is one of the significant developments of post-war music. No longer can performers be content to sit poker-faced over their scores, playing the notes to the best of their ability and letting the emotional chips fall where they may. Musicians are now called upon to make eye contact (and sometimes more) with the audience, to wear costumes, to speak, to *act*—all in addition to negotiating the difficult techniques and vivid, unorthodox notation that mark new music" (from notes to NW-357). If you can arrange to attend a concert of new music in which the players wear costumes, speak, or act as well as play, write a brief commentary on Walsh's statement. Indicate whether it is valid for you; give your own views as to whether the costuming, speaking, or acting of players adds to, detracts from, or has no effect on the quality of your experience with the music.

9. Devise a two-minute piece for a group of performers (not necessarily musicians—perhaps a class) that consists entirely of speech (whispered, spoken, shouted) or other non-singing vocal sounds (laughing, crying, sustained humming, hissing, clucking, etc.). The piece should have an overall design, and the performance should be directed in some way, but it may involve a good deal of latitude for performer choice (a form of indeterminacy). It may involve two or more things going on at the same time. Have it performed, and get three critiques of the performance—one by yourself, one by a participant, and one by someone who acts as audience.

10. Listen to a fairly extended minimalist piece (perhaps, but not necessarily, one mentioned in the chapter) and write a brief paper examining your own reactions, both as you listen and afterwards. Could they best be described in terms of "boredom," "restless annoyance," "trance," or some other? Did they change as you listened? Was there another distinct reaction when the piece was over?

11. Write a brief essay setting forth your views on the role of any or all of the following in art: chance, boredom, psychological manipulation (e.g., inducing a trancelike state), collage (in the sense of the incorporation or juxtaposition of disparate elements, such as "noise" in music), or the presentation of a "found" or "observed object" as art.

12. If you have some knowledge of and familiarity with any of the other arts (poetry, painting, sculpture, drama, dance), describe any parallels you see in one or another of these arts with some of the aspects of modernism in music, such as mathematical determinism, indeterminacy (including the operations of chance), the use of new technology, or the use of repetition to a marked or extreme degree (as in minimalism).

19

Beyond Modernism: Autonomy, Assimilation, and Accessibility

IT is generally accepted that "classical" music has moved a stage beyond the mid-century modernism described in the previous chapter. Three manifestations attest to this: there is greater *autonomy* for the composer (who no longer feels an outsider if not fully committed to one of two highly exclusive schools, serialism and experimentalism); the music has *assimilated* more from a wide range of sources, including older European music, ethnic musics from around the world, popular and folk musics, and indeed modernism itself; and the music is more *accessible*—that is, capable of being enjoyed by a broader audience. The first highly visible break away from modernism came with minimal music, which began as a radical "movement" itself, in part as a defection from the serial establishment, and in part as a result of the influence of aspects of Asian and African musics. The move beyond modernism, however, has since become apparent along a broad front, and cannot be defined in terms of a single approach or style. Moreover, the freedom to compose music that might be described by any of a number of terms such as individualistic, eclectic, accessible, expressive, or romantic had been exercised by some composers all along. Thus the existence of possibilities beyond modernism was not so much *invented* as *revealed*, as the floods of dogmatism and extremism began to recede.

The New Autonomy

What has emerged, and what is being described in this chapter, is the reinstatement of freedom of choice—freedom from dogmas, fads, and systems, musical or philosophical, and a return of that "security to be one's self," the lack of which Morton Feldman saw as plaguing composers at the flood stage of modernism. As William Bolcom put it,

> We are in the 1980s, and it is generally accepted among most artists that modernism is on the wane. What is happening now is less a new movement—although critics have been quick to name it postmodernism—than it is a movement away from movements, those schools and isms that have bedeviled art and led towards its current sclerotic selfconsciousness.[1]

Thus a label such as "New Romanticism," for example, current in New York and elsewhere during the 1980s, itself connotes a fashion, and at best can characterize only a portion of the phenomenon. The situation is better described as Michael Walsh has done:

> During the 1960s the horizons of American music suddenly expanded. . . . The decline of Darmstadtism freed composers once again to give voice to individual modes of expression; while initial reactions were tentative and uncertain, within fifteen years a thousand flowers had bloomed.[2]

Of course among the thousand flowers, serialist and experimentalist blossoms are also available choices. In nearly any current issue of *Perspectives of New Music* (the scholarly and prestigious "uptown" journal of serialism) one can still see copious graphs and charts accompanying explanations, in mathematical terms, of ever more arcane ramifications of set theory. And a glance at *Ear* magazine (the tabloid-style "downtown" journal of experimental music) will show that there are still those who are interested in doing things like swinging loudspeakers, lasso-style, on 25-foot ropes. But it is symptomatic of the times that *Perspectives* now gives some coverage to the progeny of experimentalism as well, and even to those whose view looks past modernism itself, while *Ear* devotes considerable space to subjects such as jazz, ethnic music, and film music.

Assimilation and Re-Connection

Re-Connection with the Past

That "the past is dead and must be buried" has been identified as "the chief tenet of modernism."[3] But as modernism has receded, there has emerged a marked tendency for music to reestablish connections with the past. The composer Billy Jim Layton wrote, as long ago as 1965,

> The best hope for the world today, the direction, I am fully confident, of the important, vital music to be written, is that of a responsive and enlightened liberalism. . . . Today there is need for a new, rich, meaningful, varied, understandable and vital music which maintains contact with the great central tradition of humanism in the West.[4]

George Rochberg has said, "If it appears that a large part of the music of the twentieth century was a *music of forgetting*, the music of the end of the century and beyond must become a music of remembering."[5] This "remembering" takes many forms.

The first is outright quotation. Charles Ives, pioneer that he was, forecast what has become a salient characteristic of American music by his use of quotations—in his own case, the quotation of hymn tunes and popular songs (see Chapter 17). What kept the resulting works from falling to the superficial level of either mere pastiches or conscious attempts at "local color" was Ives's strong sense of identity with these tunes, and the depth of their meaning for him. We hear them altered, metamorphosed—as filtered through his temperament. It is not that the new music to emerge beyond modernism sounds like Ives's music, but it has again taken to quoting at the Ivesian level of identification, in the sense that Emerson meant when he said that "You do not quote, but recognize [in past works by other masters] your own."

Quotation in the new music is of course handled in highly individual ways, and varies greatly in extensiveness. It can be obscure and fragmentary, as in *Contra Mortem et Tempus* (1965)[6] by George Rochberg, an early work to employ quotation, which the composer describes as "a 'collage' or 'assemblage' of scraps and bits from the music of other composers (as well as an earlier work of my own) . . ." Similarly, in the first movement of his Piano Quartet (1976),[7] William Bolcom makes a very oblique reference to the music of Chopin in a movement that embraces widely contrasting styles. Less obscure is the type of quotation in which recognizable phrases of older music appear. In *Ancient Voices of Children* (1970)[8] by George Crumb, a toy piano plays a portion of a phrase from the eighteenth-century Anna Magdalena Bach Notebook, which slows to a stop before its end, "like clockwork . . . running down." A similar feeling is evoked in Crumb's *Black Angels* (also 1970)[9] for electronic string quartet, which quotes eleven measures of Schubert's *Death and the Maiden* as "a fragile echo of an ancient music." A somewhat different effect is achieved in *Prism* (1980)[10] by Jacob Druckman, in which recognizable snatches of older music are interrupted or overlaid with dissonant and/or atonal material. This is best illustrated in the second movement, which is based on a movement from a seventeenth-century opera by Francesco Cavalli.* What is exceptional in this is the quotation of such an extended amount of music. In the second of the three "acts" of *Music for the Magic Theater* (1967)[11] George Rochberg quotes an entire Adagio of Mozart, reworking it only in terms of instrumental color.

Another way in which a re-connection with the past is manifested is in the writing of original music essentially in a particular *style* of the past. A much rarer practice than outright quotation, it runs the risk of being mistaken for mere anachronism, to which the response is apt to be "This is music that has already been written." It would appear that only a composer with credentials as strong as George Rochberg's can pull it off with reasonable safety, as he has

* Similar tendencies exist in the other arts. A precisely parallel example of such "quotation" in the visual realm can be seen in the work of Doug and Mike Starn (b. 1961), who, in *The Christ Series*, have produced a great number of pieces based on reworked photographic images of *The Dead Christ*, a painting done by Philippe de Champagne about 1650 (exactly the period of the Cavalli opera quoted by Druckman). No doubt other examples could be cited.

done in his pivotal String Quartet No. 3 (1972),[12] a long work in which the entire middle portion is a set of variations which, in his words, "are clearly and unambiguously tonal (in A major) and embrace the harmonic/polyphonic palette of the Classical and Romantic traditions." Similarly the third movement of William Bolcom's Piano Quartet (1976) is not the traditional minuet or scherzo but an original waltz in a clearly tonal and quasi-popular idiom. The pronounced eclecticism of our time, and with it the acceptance of more than one style in a single piece, is what seems to make the adoption of a musical language of the past—a practice formerly so implacably condemned—at least conditionally, if somewhat uneasily, acceptable.

Another re-connection with the past is the return to the use of traditional media and traditional forms. The symphony orchestra and the string quartet, for example, are viable media for the newest of the new music; they have not been "starved" out of existence for want of new works, as one avant-gardist in the 1960s recommended, nor consigned exclusively to a repertoire at least septuagenarian (though it is unfortunately true that a disproportionate amount of their active repertoire *is* in fact this old). Furthermore, new life has been breathed into traditional forms that had been pronounced dead; composers are again writing symphonies, concertos, and string quartets, so labeled. And opera is no longer necessarily a non-narrative "moment" form, as has been shown by the reception accorded *Nixon in China* (1986) by John Adams.

Eclecticism and the Assimilation of Other Musics

Looking at the "third stream" from the other bank, as it were (see Chapter 14), we see that the eclecticism that has pervaded both jazz and rock is also a feature of the new classical music. Elements of jazz have been assimilated anew into symphonic music in pieces such as *Déjà Vu* (1977)[13] by Michael Colgrass (essentially a concerto for percussion and orchestra) and the last movement of John Harbison's Symphony No. 1 (1980–83).[14] Ragtime has again been cultivated, by composers such as William Bolcom, William Albright, and John Hasse. Other indigenous American music has been assimilated as well.[15]

The notable increase in the last fifty years in Americans' knowledge of and access to world musics has been a great stimulus to eclecticism, and has added enormously to the resources available for assimilation. Pioneers such as Henry Cowell, Colin McPhee, and Lou Harrison (the latter still active) led the way, especially in the case of musics from the Pacific basin. Later, as we saw in the last chapter, minimalist composers, including Terry Riley and Philip Glass, studied Indian or African music, and the differing *concepts* of music (if not the actual sounds) encountered there were reflected in their music. Steve Reich, as a drummer, was especially drawn to the music of Africa, and this influence is especially apparent in his ninety-minute-long *Drumming* (1971).[16]

The new autonomy is also manifested in assimilations from modernism itself. Thus some of the vocabulary described in the preceding chapter (atonality, sound mass, sliding tones, pointillism, "moment" form) are apt to be found coexisting in the new music with tonality, structural coherence, and references to the music of the past. Similarly, new technical means have been assimilated, including electronically generated sound (William Bolcom uses electronic tape in his *Black Host for Organ, Percussion, and Tape,*[17] as does William Albright in "Last Rites," from his *Organbook II*[18] of 1971), electric instruments (Druckman uses an electronic harpsichord in his *Prism* of 1980), and extended instrumental techniques (John Corigliano's Concerto for Clarinet and Orchestra, 1977,[19] would not sound the same without these). As Billy Jim Layton has expressed it,

> There is not the slightest reason to reject any particular technical device—electronic means, chance methods, anything—merely because it was invented or employed for aesthetic ends with which we are not much in sympathy. The true liberal will accept whatever in his judgment is useful and necessary to him, whether of the past or the present.[20]

Music of Association and the New Accessibility

Music with Associative Connotations

While the term "program music" is not in favor, and most composers tend to take pains to deny its application to their music, it is nonetheless true that there has been a resurgence of music that has, in one way or another, associations beyond the music itself.* The very use of a title for a work (a practice now increasingly common) suggests the desire to communicate something more than can be done by the generic term "quartet" or "symphony," or made-up clinical titles such as *Synchronism* or *Phonemena.* In an age of sophistication, titles may be indirect in their significance; as George Crumb has said in one case, they are "metaphors chosen more for poetic values rather than for specific meanings."

A text of course constitutes a strong associational element. In the new music, there is a notable return to practices of word-setting that are more lyrical than the jagged and fragmented lines of modernism, and show attention to natural word rhythms and inflections and a concern to let the words be understood. Composers have in fact shown a deeper concern and commitment to the poetry they choose to set. Rather than setting a text for a single work and letting it go at that, some composers have apparently developed more profound relationships with the works of particular literary figures, extending over a considerable period of time and encompassing a series of works. This has been the case with George Crumb and the works of Frederico García Lorca, with David Del Tredici and the *Alice* books of Lewis Carroll, and with Stephen Albert and the works of James Joyce.[21]

In the case of music without text (the domain of traditional program music) composers have in some instances made public the extramusical associations attached to their works, thereby validating them for the listener. Mysticism in various forms has been the point of departure for many of George Crumb's purely instrumental works: numerology, for example, in the case of

* As a significant sampling of works, approximately half of the compositions awarded the Pulitzer Prize in the 1970s and 1980s show some extramusical impetus or association.

Black Angels (completed on Friday the 13th, 1970); astrology and the zodiac for *Makrokosmos I* (1974).[22] Christian mysticism is the impetus for *Black Host* (1967) for organ by William Bolcom, based on the occult "black mass." Buddhist concepts of earth, man, and heaven are the stimuli for each of the three movements of the Piano Concerto of Peter Lieberson.[23] Dreams, or the state of dreaming, may be taken into account, according to the composers themselves, by listeners who seek an explanation of the nature and form of George Rochberg's *Music for the Magic Theater* (1966) and William Bolcom's *Whisper Moon* (1971).[24] All of this can be interpreted as evidence of composers seeking, and indeed needing, to relate their music, and art itself, to larger issues of life—neither (in Rochberg's words) "to seal art off from life," nor to *confuse* art with life, as some of the experimentalists had done. As Rochberg wrote of his *Contra Mortem et Tempus* (1965), composed after the death of his son,

> It . . . became clearer than ever before that the only justification for claiming one was engaged in the artistic act was to open one's art completely to life and its entire gamut of terror and joys (real and imagined); and to find, if one could, new ways to transmute these into whatever magic one was capable of.[25]

The New Relationship to the Public

The following statements by two composers of the same generation (John Corigliano, b. 1938; David Del Tredici, b. 1937) represent the new attitude toward the audience, and the reassessed view of the function of the composer:

> I don't understand composers with what I call an eternity complex, people who ignore today's audiences and think of themselves as misunderstood prophets whose masterpieces will be seen as such in a century or so. That, I think, reveals a basic contempt for audiences. . . . I wish to be *understood,* and I think it is the job of every composer to reach out to his audience with all means at his disposal. Communication should always be a primary goal.[26]

> Composers now are beginning to realize that if a piece excites an audience, *that doesn't mean it's terrible.* For my generation, it is considered vulgar to have an audience really, *really* like a piece on a first hearing. But why are we writing music except to move people and to be expressive?[27]

Specifically, the new accessibility is manifested (1) in a new freedom to write music that is tonal, though not necessarily according to older usage; (2) in music that has a discernible rhythmic pulse; (3) in music with a feeling of continuity, superseding the "moment" form described in the last chapter; and (4) in music that is eclectic, and thus apt to show a variety of influences and styles in a single work. These characteristics can coincide in interesting ways; tonality, for example, can be a function of eclecticism, when the influence is non-Western music. As John Rockwell has pointed out,

> Third-world music may not always be "tonal" in the strict Western sense, but for the most part it rests firmly on a home note, building upward from there in intervals based on the overtone series. Composers who allow themselves to be

influenced by such traditions may write music that sounds comfortably "tonal" to the lay public, yet retains its vitality and originality.[28]

The new accessibility and commitment to *communication*, however interpreted, has with some composers taken the form of *music as social statement*. Steve Reich's *Come Out* (1966) is a tape composition based on the recorded statement of a black man injured by the police. Christian Wolff, an early associate of John Cage and Morton Feldman, has since his *Changing the System* (1972–73) turned his attention mostly to political subjects, using labor and protest songs as material; examples of his work in this vein are his *Wobbly Music* (1975–76), *The Death of Mother Jones* (1977), and *Peace Marches 1, 2,* and *3* (1983–84). An eclectic composer who has turned to social statement is the pianist Frederic Rzewski, who has, in the course of his career, composed in a number of different styles. *Coming Together* and *Attica* (1972)[29] both had as their source and inspiration a letter from an inmate at the New York state prison in Attica, at the time of the prison uprising there. Best known is his *The People United Will Never Be Defeated!*, a long set of variations for piano on a leftist Chilean song. In this turning to social statement on the part of some, associated with the general move toward greater accessibility, there is an interesting parallel with the folk-protest movement of the 1930s and 1940s described in Chapter 4. Both movements suffered from the same kind of limitation: that of using (in Rockwell's words) "an idiom that speaks to a far different social and racial group than the victims of the oppression that is being protested."

Conclusion

The late 1980s in American classical music is a time of the full blooming of the "thousand flowers"—a time of unprecedented diversity and contrast. If the new autonomy, the new "freedom to be one's self," does not itself harden into dogma, this blossoming could well characterize American music well into the twenty-first century. Possibly the greatest risk is that the "movement away from movements" may lapse (as did experimentalism and indeterminacy) into an "anything goes" atmosphere, confusing the issue and encouraging the acceptance of mediocrity. There is no substitute for strong, individual, well-made works of art that, as David Del Tredici put it in the passage quoted above, can be found "to move people and to be expressive." In this regard it will be appropriate to close this chapter by returning to Roger Sessions's admonition quoted at the beginning of the preceding chapter:

> One cannot insist too strongly or too frequently that, in the arts generally and in music in particular, it is only productions that really count, and that only in these—music, written or performed—are to be found the criteria by which ideas about music, as well as music itself, must finally stand or fall: not the converse.[30]

Further Reading

Blaustein, Susan. "The Survival of Aesthetics: Books by Boulez, DeLio, Rochberg," *Perspectives of New Music*, vol. 27, no. 1 (Winter 1989), pp. 272–303.

Rochberg, George. *The Aesthetics of Survival: A Composer's View of Twentieth-Century Music.* Ann Arbor: University of Michigan Press, 1984.

Rockwell, John. *All American Music: Composition in the Late Twentieth Century.* New York: Knopf, 1983.
This incisive and readable book by an eminent critic covers many areas; chapters 6 and 7 are especially relevant to this chapter.

Rothstein, Edward. "The Return of Romanticism," *The New Republic,* August 27, 1984.

Tawa, Nicholas. *A Most Wondrous Babble: American Composers, Their Music, and the American Scene, 1950–1985.* Westport, CT: Greenwood, 1987.
See especially chapter 8, "Reconciliations," and its many notes and references.

Listening

Nearly thirty works currently available on records are cited in this chapter, with discographical references in the endnotes. This constitutes a significant and varied body of music illustrative of the trends described in this chapter. In addition, the following are suggested:

Adams, John. *Harmonielehre* (1985). Nonesuch 79115.

———. *Shaker Loops* (1978, rev. 1983). Philips 412214-1PH.

———. *Nixon in China* (opera, 1987). Nonesuch 79177.

Bolcom, William. Symphony No. 4 (1987); with *Session I.* NW-356.

Harbison, John. *Five Songs of Experience on Poems of William Blake* (1971). CRI S-313.

Rochberg, George. Concerto for Oboe and Orchestra (1984). NW-335.

———. Violin Concerto (1974). Columbia M35149.

Schwantner, Joseph. *Wind, Willow, Whisper . . .* (1980). CRI S-441.

Talma, Louise. *Diadem, for Tenor and Instruments* (1979). NW-317.

———. *Full Circle,* for orchestra (1985); with *The Ambient Air, for Flute, Violin, Cello, and Piano* (1980–83), and *Lament for Cello and Piano* (1980). CRI SD-549.

Zwilich, Ellen Taaffe. Symphony No. 1 (1982); *Celebration* (1984); *Prologue and Variations* (1984). NW-336.

PROJECTS

1. Listen to a piece of music written in the 1980s by one of the "minimalist" composers (Riley, Reich, Adams, Glass, et al.), and compare it with an earlier work by the same composer. Is the later work less or more "minimal" or "repetitive"?

2. If you are acquainted with contemporary developments in one of the other arts, write a brief paper comparing its current state with that of music, as described in this chapter. Has there been a move "beyond modernism"?

3. Eclecticism is a prominent feature of the new classical music, but it is also found in popular music as well. Assemble a list of five examples drawn from popular music which show assimilation of other musics (classical, avant-garde, non-Western, etc.), describe the examples, and compare them with some of the examples from classical music cited in this chapter.

4. Explore further the use of quotation in twentieth-century classical music. For example, how does obvious quotation (of either substance or style) affect your perception of a piece of music? (George Rochberg's *Music for the Magic Theater,* for substance, or his String Quartet No. 3, for style, might be usable points of departure.) If you were called upon to suggest possible reasons *why* quotation has figured significantly in twentieth-century American music, what would you say?

5. Write a brief paper on the use of titles in contemporary music. Include examples of composers who use them, and composers who don't. Does a title alter your expectations of a piece of music? Consider your perception, for example, of George Crumb's *A Haunted Landscape* (NW-326) if it were simply known as *Piece for Orchestra;* or of George Rochberg's Concerto for Oboe and Orchestra (NW-335) if it were called *A Haunted Landscape.*

6. Does it bother you to hear a piece by a contemporary composer that might possibly be mistaken for the music of some previous century? Why? Write a brief but well-thought-out essay on this.

7. Does it bother you to hear a number of different styles in a single piece? Why? Think about this, and write a brief essay on it.

8. The composer Carl Ruggles became concerned when audiences at contemporary music concerts in New York earlier in the century actually increased, viewing it as a sign that contemporary music was "selling out." And Milton Babbitt, in his famous (and mistitled) article "Who Cares If You Listen?" of 1958, suggested the "very real possibility of complete elimination of the public and social aspects of musical composition." On the other hand, John Corigliano, as quoted in this chapter, says that he does not "understand composers . . . who ignore today's audiences and think of themselves as misunderstood prophets." Write a brief essay explaining where you stand on this issue, and why.

Photo by Elemore Morgan, Jr.

PART SEVEN

Regionalism and Diversity

IT is fitting that a work that has set about to describe the vast panorama of American music close with a tangible reminder of its diversity—a diversity that has characterized America from the very beginning. This diversity has much to do with the regional differences inherent in the sheer physical extent of the country, and the complexity of its geography and its history. The mass media of today, fed by the popular music industry with its mega-marketing machine, may have submerged regionalism, but they have not succeeded in eradicating it. Look carefully under the veneer of a homogenized and ubiquitous popular culture, and you will find a variety of musics that derive their nature from a sense of *place* and of *ethos*.

This regional diversity assumes two forms. In certain areas it takes the form of an indigenous music, long rooted in the region, its recognizable characteristics surviving gradual change. The Cajun music of southern Louisiana, the *norteña* music of the lower Rio Grande Valley, and the Scandinavian dance music of the upper Midwest are examples of this.

In other areas, diversity consists in the presence of a number of relatively small, self-sufficient cultural communities, whose members continue to cultivate music and customs that originated elsewhere—in Latin America, in Europe, or in Asia. These cultural pockets, the existence of which is often virtually unknown to those of the cultural "mainstream," are found most often in, or on the fringes of, huge urban areas. New York City, with its large ethnic enclaves—villages, towns, and cities within the super-city—is the most outstanding example of this, but these pockets can be found in any of our metropolises. They are also typical of areas that have received substantial refugee populations, or that have drawn workers by virtue of powerful but capricious economic magnets such as mining. These pockets can occur in rural as well as urban areas. California is a well-known example, but an amazing amount of cultural diversity, under the surface, can be found even in states such as Wyoming.

Regions that in the recent past have drawn immigrants in large numbers often do not have a single easily identifiable *indigenous* music (such as might be found in the Appalachians, or southwestern Louisiana, for example) but tend, like New York City, to be great meeting-grounds for a multitude of cultures.

In the chapter that follows we shall look briefly at three places in the United States that are quite far apart geographically. This is no more than a sampling, of course; its main purpose is to encourage interested observers and students simply to look around, wherever they may be, in order to find and experience the diversity present in their own region.

20

Three Regional Samplings

THIS chapter looks at three diverse, geographically distinct regions in the United States, examining the music indigenous to each area and the ways it has been affected and altered by complex forces of migration and cultural interaction.

Louisiana and the French Influence

Louisiana, a land of sultry climate, dominated largely by the complex outflow, through shifting channels and bayous, of one of the largest river systems in the world, has a complex cultural pattern as well—albeit one that is fairly stable, the main ingredients of its mix having been established for over a century. To an indigenous Indian population was added that of French colonizers and settlers beginning in the early eighteenth century (thus establishing early the dominant cultural pattern), followed by scant Spanish immigration during the period of Spanish rule (1764–1800). A very important factor in the cultural mix of Louisiana was the dramatic rise in the black population, coming mostly from the West Indies, at the end of the eighteenth century; black people were brought to Louisiana in significant numbers by planters escaping the revolution in Haiti in the 1790s. (The cultural ties of Louisiana with the West Indies, especially Haiti, have been important ever since.) After the Louisiana Purchase in 1803, American influence and immigration naturally increased, and the substantial black population made possible, in part, the rapid growth of the sugar plantations. Italians, Hungarians, Slovenians, Germans, and Irish have since been added to the mix in smaller numbers.

The dominant cultural (and therefore musical) patterns of Louisiana, however, are the result of a complex interaction between those of French and African descent.

The Louisiana-French

French people began settling Louisiana early in the eighteenth century, as we have noted, some coming directly from France, and others arriving after a stopover of a few generations in the West Indies. Many were families of means and belonged to the aristocracy, and they soon constituted a wealthy planter class. Their cultural inclinations were urban and sophisticated; this was manifested in the fact that French opera was established in New Orleans as early as the 1790s.

At the other end of the economic scale was the French-descended refugee population that came to Louisiana from Acadia (now Nova Scotia) in the latter part of the eighteenth-century. A few of these Acadians had reached Louisiana before the Expulsion, but the great flow took place after 1755, when the victorious English, in a cruel episode known as the Dérangement, began to expel all Acadians who would not take an oath of allegiance to the British crown. The Acadians began arriving in Louisiana some ten years later, after stopovers in France and in the American colonies. These people, mostly farmers and fishermen whose families had come from Brittany and Normandy, were regarded with contempt by the upper-class French, who excluded them from New Orleans but allowed them to settle upstream, along a stretch of the right bank of the Mississippi that became known as the "Acadian coast." Though the " 'Cajuns" were regarded as inferior (an attitude that persists even today, and can be found, for example, among the proud descendants of the "free persons of color" who were an important part of the social and economic structure of eighteenth-century Louisiana), the colony nevertheless benefited from the presence of these industrious people, in their raising of crops and livestock to feed New Orleans, and their ability to construct the all-important dikes to control the rivers and bayous.

The Cajuns suffered a "second expulsion" after the Purchase and the coming of the Americans, when it was found that the land they occupied was ideal for raising sugar. They moved further south and west, into the bayous and swamps of the coastal regions, and the prairies of the west. Thus they came to occupy the "French triangle," with its base along the Gulf coast, and its apex around Alexandria. Tracing their lineage back two centuries to the first Acadian families (the Moutons, the Arceneaux, the Bernards, the Broussards, the Guidrys), they occupy the largest area of French-derived culture and language in the United States. There are now approximately one million people, roughly a quarter of the population of Louisiana, who identify themselves as Cajuns.

People of African descent have played a major role in Louisiana history and culture. Like the French, they have observed a complex ranking of caste and lineage. High in the social order were the "gens de couleur libre" ("free persons of color"), of whose presence in Louisiana there are records from the early eighteenth century. From 1725 on they either entered free, were freed in recognition of merit and loyalty, were given their freedom by a white parent or lover, or purchased their own freedom. (American Indians also had the status of "free persons of color.") Many became wealthy and influential, owning land and slaves. At the other end of the social scale (though not as low as the Cajuns!) were the black slaves from Africa or the West Indies.

Cajun Music

Despite a distinction made by an early collector between "Louisiana-French" folk songs and "Cajun" folk songs,[1] there is for our purposes little practical differentiation between them, beyond the use of continental French versus Cajun French for the words. In general usage, we find that French-derived white folk songs are designated "Cajun," while French-derived black folk songs are designated "Creole."[2]

There are some charming French songs and ballads that have been recovered in versions close to very old ones found in Europe. The famous "Malbrough s'en va-t-en guerre" was a satirical song aimed at the victorious Duke of Marlborough by the French in 1709, and its ubiquitous tune (familiar as "For He's a Jolly Good Fellow") may be far older than its association with its oldest known text. Among old ballads (possibly medieval) that have been recovered are "Le plus jeune des trois" and "Sept ans sur mer."[3]

The fiddle was the basic Cajun instrument from the earliest times, being used for the pastime of dancing, which to this day has never lost its great popularity—a dance lasting late into the night, to which the children were brought and bedded down, being known as a *fais do-do.* Dennis McGee and Sady Courville are the acknowledged masters of old-time Cajun fiddling style and repertoire, and have influenced younger fiddlers such as Dewey Balfa and Michael Doucet. In the 1920s the accordion (possibly making its way into the area via German settlers) began to be adopted, as it was farther west in the *musica norteña* of the Texas-Mexican border.* From the time (about 1926) when the Cajun accordionist Joseph Falcon and his wife, née Cleoma Breaux, recorded "Allons à Lafayette," the accordion had become an integral part of the Cajun band, which consisted in addition of fiddle, guitar, and, in the early days, triangle, or " 'tit fer." In a later period Ambrose Thibodeaux and Nathan Abshire emerged as legendary Cajun accordionists. Listening to early recorded sources, we find a music that is lighthearted in mood and theme, with a marked predilection for love songs, and a repertory consisting mostly of waltzes, pieces in duple meter related to hoedown music, and pieces related to the blues. The vocal style is unique and unmistakable, though difficult to describe. Vocal tone is somewhat flat and nasal, at times only approximately the pitch, with frequently interjected yells and wails.

The rhythmic vitality of some of this traditional music can be illustrated by the delightful folk song "Les clefs de la prison," with its lively syncopations. (This song was used by the American composer Virgil Thomson in his suite *Acadian Songs and Dances,* adapted from his film score for *Louisiana Story.*) A similar tendency toward syncopation in the vocal line can be heard in some of the early recordings, such as "La femme qui jovait les cartes."[4]

Cajun music, as we noted above, began to be recorded in the late 1920s, at the same time that regional music was being marketed within many other

* See Chapter 3.

folk communities. Traditional folk songs do appear, of which "J'ai passé devant la porte" seems to be an example, apparently very well known; but since it did not appear in a folk music collection until after the first commercial recording, it is difficult to tell what relationship this has to its existence in oral tradition.[5]

Cajun musicians, though managing to retain a distinct regional identity in their music, have in true folk fashion appropriated for their use whatever appealed to them and their patrons outside of their own tradition. This early absorption of other music is shown in a rather amusing "Cajunizing" of "Home, Sweet Home" (it becomes a waltz), and an appropriation of the tune of the popular ballad "Casey Jones."[6]

In the late 1930s and the 1940s, with the expansion of the oil industry and the influx of workers from the rural Southeast, Cajun music lost many of its earlier distinctive characteristics, and was nearly swamped in the flood of country-and-western music. It was about this time, for example, that the Hawaiian steel guitar, which had recently become popular in country music, joined the Cajun band. And one hears in "Le côte farouche de la vic" a Cajun adaptation of the country music song "It Wasn't God Who Made Honky-Tonk Angels."* Many of the recordings of this period take on the character of hillbilly music sung in patois.

There have been other influences as well. Harry Choates, recording in the late 1940s, was known as the "Fiddle King of Cajun Swing," and more recently groups such as Coteau are making a fusion of Cajun music with rock.

However, since the 1950s there has also been a resurgence of the older styles; the accordion is back, and so are some of the older songs. In fact, with musicians such as Michael Doucet (who has revived Cajun fiddle playing) and his group Beausoleil, Cajun music has undergone a full-fledged revival, and re-connection with its traditions.

Zydeco: Cajun Rhythm-and-Blues

The presence of black musicians in Cajun territory has resulted in a rhythm-and-blues translation of Cajun music known as *zydeco* (or *zodico* or *zarico*).[7] Zydeco† music retains and features the accordion, but adds to the band the piano, electric guitar, electric bass, drums, and sometimes saxophones, usually leaves out the fiddle, often adds a characteristic "rub-board" (which has the function and sound of the washboard of the early jug and blues bands), and has a strong rhythm-and-blues flavor. Clifton Chenier (1925–87), the "king of zydeco" (he had many publicity photos taken wearing an actual crown), was a versatile musician who in the 1960s and 1970s performed both zydeco, singing in Cajun-French, and out-and-out Gulf Coast rhythm-and-blues, which he sang in English.[8] Important performers of zydeco in an older style, closer to Cajun music, are the accordionists Freeman Fontenot and Alphonse "Bois-sec" Ardoin, and the fiddler Canray Fontenot. The newer style, closer to rhythm-and-blues, is represented by accordionists John Delafose, Rocking

* See Chapter 7.

† On the Louisiana-Texas Gulf Coast the term "zydeco" can also refer to a party like the *fais do-do*, or to a gumbo dish.

Dopsie, Rocking Sidney, Stanley "Buckwheat" Dural, and Doozoo Chavez. White musicians such as Wayne Toups and Zachary Richard are also performing zydeco.[9]

Creole Music

There is ample evidence of black music-making in and around New Orleans in the nineteenth century. Seven "Creole" songs, in dialect French, were included at the end of the famous *Slave Songs of the United States* published in 1867. Place Congo, opposite the Vieux Carré (and on the present-day site of Louis "Satchmo" Armstrong Park), was the scene of weekly black festivities and ceremonies, from which whites were traditionally excluded. As was true in Africa itself, there was (and is) a nearly inseparable association of music and dance. The *bamboula,* the *counjaille,* the *calinda,* the *habanera*—these were types of songs, but they were also dances. The *bamboula,* for example, was named for a small drum made from a section of the huge bamboo that grows in the West Indies; the drum accompanied both song and dance. The dance itself was vividly described in a much-quoted article by George Washington Cable, which included the music (Example 20–1).[10]

Example 20–1

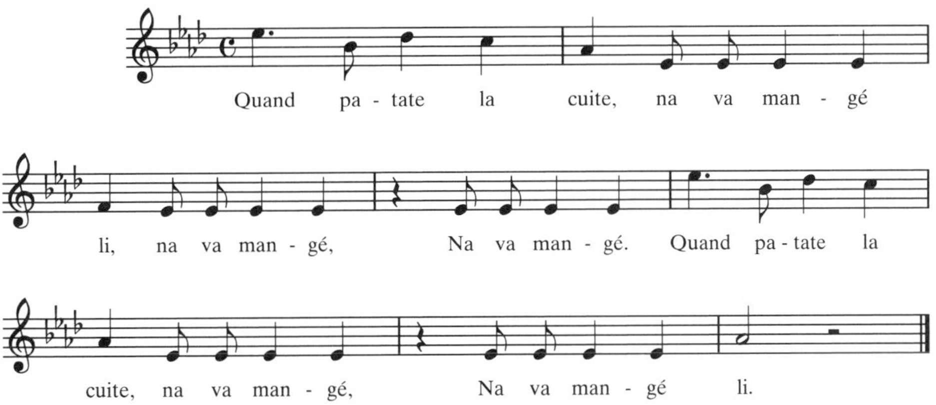

The song was heard as early as the 1830s by the great Louisiana-born composer and pianist Louis Moreau Gottschalk, whom we encountered in Chapter 15. He used it as the basis of one of his most popular piano pieces, *Bamboula.* The first measure has a rhythm basic to much Latin American music—and, via New Orleans, presumably, to much American black music as well—that of the *habanera* or *danza,* which could be either song or dance.

The *calinda* was a satirical song/dance, and as such was the heir to a considerable tradition in the West Indies and in Africa. Cable describes it as "a grossly personal satirical ballad . . . a dance of multitude, a sort of vehement cotillion." Example 20–2 shows one calinda that Cable describes as "still familiar to all Creole ears; it has long been a vehicle for the white Creole's satire; for generations the man of municipal politics was fortunate who escaped entirely a lampooning set to its air."[11]

Example 20–2

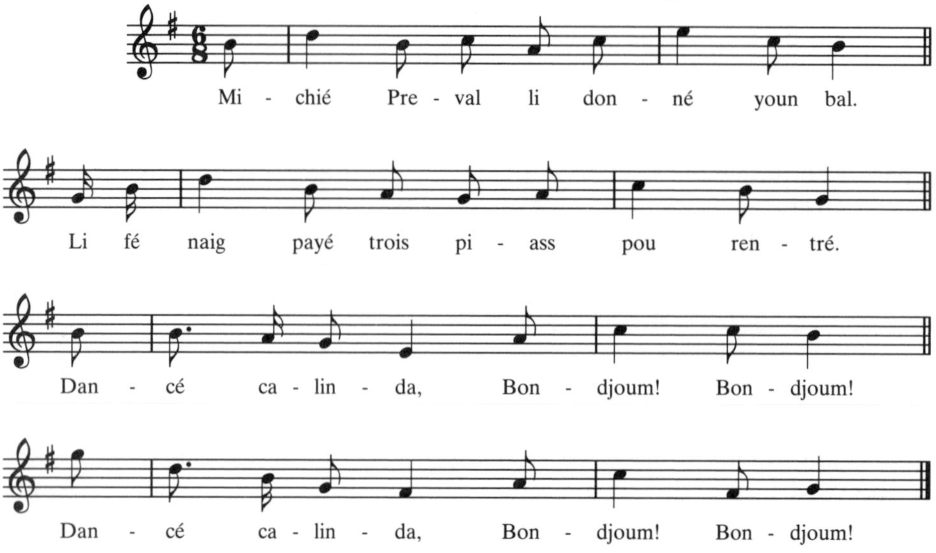

Monsieur Preval gave a big ball,
He made the blacks pay to dance.
Dance the Calinda, bondjoum, bondjoum
Dance the Calinda, bondjoum, bondjoum.

There were numberless stanzas, of course, and new ones were fashioned to fit new occasions. Krehbiel gives the story of the original, insofar as it could be pieced together.[12]

There is a marked and interesting resemblance between the first part of the tune of this satirical song and that of the well-known Cajun "Saute crapaud," which is, according to Whitfield, "one of the best known of the French folk songs of our state" (Example 20–3).[13] The enigmatic words—"Jump, toad, your tail will burn;/ Take courage, another will grow"—suggest that this, too, may once have been a satire of some kind. Nothing seems to be known of the origin of either song.

A pervading influence among the blacks of French Louisiana—and not

Example 20–3

unknown among whites, as well—was *voodoo,* known in New Orleans as *hoodoo.* Originating principally among the Dahomeans in Africa, voodoo had become intermingled with the liturgy and ritual of Roman Catholicism (despite the general opposition of the Church) among the blacks of the French West Indies, especially San Domingo and Martinique. From there it traveled to New Orleans, which became the capital of hoodooism in the United States. Attempts were made to outlaw its practice, and from time to time, before the Louisiana Purchase, the importation of slaves from the French-speaking parts of the Caribbean was banned in order to combat its growth. Hoodoo ceremonies were marked by rhythmic drumming, chanting, and dancing. Both the calinda and the bamboula were associated with it. The goal seemed to be a kind of ecstatic possession by one of the hoodoo deities. According to eyewitness accounts, this possession was not unlike that to be seen at primitive revival meetings.*

Much of the Creole music we have just described contained some of the important seeds of jazz, and it was jazz that was the culminating musical form to be developed by black musicians from the rich variety of influences present in turn-of-the-century New Orleans.[14]

The Upper Midwest and the Scandinavian Influence

We have examined briefly the French-Iberian-African culture at the mouth of the Mississippi. At the source of this great river, and across the upper Midwest, we find a land that in its climate, its topography, and the ethnic background of its people is in utter contrast. In the geological day-before-yesterday the land was scoured by glaciers, which left behind many lakes and a rich glacial soil, supporting vegetation that varied from prairie in the south to dense forest in the north. It lies right in the center of the North American continent, and while its early Scandinavian settlers (especially the Swedes and Finns) found the topography similar to that of their homeland, the Norwegians in particular found the harsh continental climate much more extreme. As a Norwegian immigrant wrote home from Wisconsin in 1857, "The winter here is shorter than in Norway, but it is usually much colder, and when the summer comes, that in turn is much warmer. . . . Many people not adjusted to the climate break down."[15]

The first inhabitants encountered by the Europeans were the Chippewa and the Dakota Sioux. Throughout the seventeenth, eighteenth, and early nineteenth centuries a tenuous white presence was maintained by the successive establishment of forts and trading posts by first the French, then the English, and finally the Americans, all of whom were interested primarily in furs. But the beginning of permanent settlement had taken place well before the Civil War, by which time a series of land-grabbing treaties and military operations had practically driven out the Indians, to make way for a rapid influx of prospective farmers.

* One subject that has yet to be thoroughly explored is the common thread of "possession" that manifests itself in hoodoo, in Shaker ritual, in revivalism, in gospel music (via the Holiness churches), in reggae, and in jazz.

Scandinavian immigrants began settling in Wisconsin in the 1840s, and in Minnesota in the 1850s. The Swedes, the most numerous group, began as farmers, but later moved to the cities, to be outnumbered in farming by the Norwegians, the next most numerous. The Norwegian immigrant man, bringing with him a strong attachment to the land, would characteristically progress from hired hand to shareman to landowning farmer. Other immigrant peoples, also from northern or central Europe, were the Germans (notably in Wisconsin), the Danes, the Finns, the Poles, and the Czechs. But by the last quarter of the century it was the Scandinavians whose presence was decisive in determining the cultural makeup of the upper Midwest.

It is the largely rural and conservative Norwegians who have striven most consciously to preserve their language and their culture. This has led to the establishment of staunchly nationalistic organizations such as the Sons of Norway (which until 1942 published its official organ in Norwegian). The highly convivial social activities of these clubs were often looked upon with disapproval by that other strong influence on Norwegian life, the Lutheran Church, especially as represented by its more strictly puritanical and pietistic adherents and congregations. Thus the Norwegians had for a long time to live with a deep-seated ambivalence in their culture toward two things that were of crucial importance to the social existence of many of them—dancing and the fiddle. This ambivalence was perhaps not always as simply resolved as in an incident that occurred many yeas ago in Spring Grove, Minnesota. On one occasion the pastor there unaccountably showed up at a Saturday night dance, whereupon the fiddler "laid his violin down and went over to him and shook his hand and said, 'Well now pastor, we love you as a pastor, and all this and that, but we don't think it's right that you should come to our dances.' "[16]

Scandinavian-American Music in the Upper Midwest

The chief focus of our brief survey will be the kind of regional music one would be most apt to find in this area—music for dancing. The music, the instruments, and the dances themselves occur in layers, based on their antiquity. The oldest dances from Norway, such as the *halling* (in which the dancer kicks a hat off of a vertically held pole), the *springer*, or the *gangar*, belong to a bygone era, and are encountered only in deliberate and costumed revivals. The same is true of the instruments that were brought direct from Norway, and were associated with the old dances. Chief among these was the Hardanger fiddle (*Hardangfele*), an instrument that has, beneath the four strings played with the bow, a set of sympathetic strings that vibrate in resonance with the bowed strings. Its widespread use died out during the early years of this century, but there are now a few musicians who have revived the playing of the Hardanger fiddle, and it is valued as a tangible symbol of that cherished "Norwegian-ness."[17]

As the old dances and the old instruments went out of general use, they were replaced by the three dances most popular among Scandinavian-Americans today—the waltz, the schottische, and the polka. The most popular instruments for dances are now the regular fiddle and the accordion, accompanied by guitar, piano, pump organ, or banjo, as available. In rural areas, dances took place at house parties in homes, or in the cleared-out second-floor lofts of roomy barns. (More recently, barns that have never housed hay or cattle have been built especially for "barn dances.") In the towns and cities, public dances are held in various social halls.

In the first years of this century commercial recordings of Scandinavian music began to be made by professional and semiprofessional bands.[18] As early as 1915 the Swedish immigrant musician and entertainer Hjalmar Peterson (who adopted the stage name "Olle i Skratthult") recorded his love song "Nikolina," which was to become immensely popular in succeeding years, and was performed in many variants both as a song and an instrumental piece (Example 20–4). Its use of mixed meter is exceptional in a musical tradition that, being so closely related to the dance, is fundamentally extremely predictable in terms of meter, phrase, length, and form.[19]

Example 20–4 NIKOLINA

When you're in love you're in an awful torture,
Who ever has tried it will not disagree,
I was so very fond of Nikolina
And Nikolina was as fond of me.

The impact of recordings, radio, the jukebox, traveling vaudeville (Olle i Skratthult himself was "on the road" for years with his band of entertainers), and movies was to force changes in Scandinavian-American music, and a decline in home music-making. This has been a familiar pattern everywhere. But it was, ironically, through the very medium of the old recordings that the "old-time" styles of the early twentieth century were ultimately preserved. It is also in keeping with the pattern observed elsewhere that there has recently been a revival of old-time music. State agencies and programs such as the Folk Arts Program of the Minnesota State Arts Board are engaged in actively encouraging the documentation and preservation of "people's arts."* Closely

* At this time most of the fifty states have such programs, under various titles.

related to this preservation movement are ethnic gatherings such as the annual Nordic Fest in Decorah, Iowa, and widespread celebrations of Syttende Mai (May 17, Norwegian Independence Day).*

The work of LeRoy Larson, folklorist, scholar, banjo player, and record producer, together with his Minnesota Scandinavian Ensemble, typifies what is being done in the way of contemporary live performance. His work, like that of Michael Doucet in Louisiana, John Nielson and Justin Bishop in Colorado, and many others, is not simply to preserve, but to re-create, to reinterpret, and to create anew in traditional styles, and thus to demonstrate their vitality and validity as an effective alternative to the progressive homogenization of American culture. Were it not for them, and people like them in virtually every state, this chapter would have been confined to simply chronicling the decline and death of regional musics in this country.

The Sacramento Valley: A Rich Mix of Cultures

The Sacramento Valley of California is a broad alluvial valley between two mountain ranges—a low coastal range to the west, and the Sierra Nevada to the east. From the high, snow-trapping barrier range of the Sierra flow down into the valley a series of tumultuous rivers which, until barely a century ago, spread wide out of their banks in the spring, flooding the valley, depositing rich alluvial soils and clays, and filling the huge old basins with half a million acres of water from January to May. Tamed now by scores of dams and hundreds of miles of levees, they furnish the water that allows a multitude of crops to grow through the long hot season from May to October, when no rain falls.

Unlike Louisiana and the upper Midwest—longer-settled regions whose cultural identity, bearing the characteristics of a few dominant immigrant groups, has been established for well over a century—the Sacramento Valley presents a picture of a complex "cross-bedding" of successive migrations from many directions, which has left a rich mix of cultures, many of them still distinct and unassimilated. The phase of greatest influx is so recent that the sense of transiency has still not been replaced by one of settled permanency, and there is nothing that can be identified as a single distinctive regional culture. Each wave of newcomers has come with its own culture, in its own time, and for its own reasons. Trappers, mission founders, would-be empire builders, gold seekers, agricultural barons, land speculators, laborers imported en masse for railroad building or harvesting, networks of immigrants bringing relatives from foreign countries, military, defense, and government workers, wealthy entrepreneurs, and refugee populations—all have formed part of the picture.

A Thumbnail Cultural Chronology of the Valley

A peaceful Indian population with a culture singularly well adapted to the unique region were the original inhabitants; they and their way of life have

* Practically all ethnic groups everywhere in America have similar gatherings to celebrate their original national holidays—the Mexican "Cinco de Mayo" is another example.

been all but gone for a century. The Spaniards scarcely penetrated the valley to any extent, and the Mexican government, heir to Spain's territorial claim in 1822, could exercise only a tenuous hold on an area where American trappers and adventurers roamed freely. (The significant Mexican influence and presence was destined to come much later.) The discovery of gold in the Sierra foothills in 1848 brought sudden, irreversible, and drastic change. With the rapid influx of easterners (accompanied by significant immigration from Europe), acquisition by the United States and statehood (in 1850) were inevitable. The population soared, and when the easily obtainable placer gold ran out (about 1853), large corporations took over the mining, and individual miners left or went into farming, which was destined to become the fertile valley's major industry. Railroad building in the 1860s brought in the first of the great laborer populations, the Chinese; as an immigrant labor population the Chinese were replaced by the Japanese beginning about 1900.

From 1900 to 1920 was the time of the great land boom, and the period saw further diversification of the Valley's population. Land companies bought up large tracts (many upon the dissolution of the huge holdings that had originally been Mexican land grants) and advertised heavily in the East. Colonization projects brought more immigrants.

As agriculture in the Valley changed from the growing of wheat, which could easily be harvested mechanically, to fruit and vegetable crops, which required hand picking, the need for seasonal labor grew, and this has made a large transient population of farm workers, with the social problems attendant on it, a part of the Sacramento Valley scene since very early in this century. Since as early as 1919, Mexicans have been coming to do this work.

The Depression and drought of the 1930s brought many from the Dust Bowl areas of Texas, Oklahoma, and Kansas (thus adding to the constituency for country music, which became especially strong in the adjoining San Joaquin Valley to the south). World War II brought further shifts in population throughout the nation; many who came to the Valley during the war stayed or returned to it, thus beginning another period of population growth, which is still going on. Significant recent additions are large refugee populations from southeast Asia.

An Incomplete Cultural and Musical Inventory of the Sacramento Valley

Among the American Indians there is, as described in Chapter 3, a new movement under way to restore and revitalize their native dance, music, crafts, and culture. This movement is strong in the Sacramento Valley, despite the fact that few of the Indians there may be descended from the original tribes. There are frequent intertribal powwows, often under the auspices of a college or university. There is considerable mutual cooperation and support between the native American and the Chicano movements.*

Many Chinese came to the Valley and worked as miners during the gold

* See Chapter 3, especially n. 30.

rush, until driven out of this occupation by the Americans. Many more were brought in in the ensuing decade to build the railroad. Hardworking, canny, thrifty, keeping to themselves and to their own traditions, they were the object of scorn and persecution. Their numbers in the Valley declined after 1890. In the decades since World War II, many Chinese have become fully integrated into the social, economic, and cultural life of the Valley, and only small groups of mostly elderly Chinese still clung to Chinese culture, language, and music.[20] Beginning in the 1960s the influx of Chinese as refugees from Vietnam and other parts of southeast Asia increased dramatically.

Another early immigrant group was the Portuguese, who were among the first Europeans to settle in the Sacramento area, some arriving with the gold rush. Coming mostly from the Azores, they established small family farms. Following a familiar pattern, the immigrants, once established, encouraged others from the same areas to come, and provided for them upon their arrival. The Portuguese tended to form tightly knit communities, their social activities centering around the Church (St. Elizabeth's in Sacramento still celebrates a Portuguese Mass) and its Holy Days. The *festas* are colorful celebrations, including a procession with music, followed by a feast. For years there were radio programs with a live band playing Portuguese music. Portuguese dances and songs are performed in the social halls in the community, accompanied by traditional *violas de arames, violãos,* and *guitarras.* A popular folk song from the Azores known and sung by the Portuguese in Sacramento is "Lira" (Example 20–5).

Example 20–5 LIRA

A shepherd came down from the hills
And knocked on my door.
He brought a sealed letter [with the news]
That my Lira was dead.

The Japanese began immigrating in significant numbers around the turn of the century, many coming from Hawaii after its annexation by the United States. Replacing the Chinese as a source of labor, they too were targets of persecution and mistrust until after World War II. Members today of a highly visible and well integrated component of Valley population, a few older Japanese are now making conscious efforts to keep alive their own rich traditions of music, dance, and drama; there is one group in Sacramento that rehearses and performs regularly.

Another Asian group to establish itself early in this century in the Sacramento Valley were the Sikhs. They began arriving between 1904 and 1908, settling in Sutter County, which they found similar in its physical characteristics to their native Punjab, in northern India. An agricultural people, they have, with the loosening of legal restrictions, acquired a great deal of productive land, and have become an important part of the region's economy, especially in the growing of fruit. A close-knit community, whose ethos is continually reinforced by new arrivals from India, they have carefully preserved their culture, customs, religion, and music. As in many older cultures, a firm distinction exists between religious music, which carries with it a venerable weight of tradition and is wholly dedicated to the service of worship, and various types of vernacular music, which are less formal. The sacred music of the Sikhs (the various forms of which are called *Kirtan*) derives from the earlier Hindu tradition based on the *ragas*.[21] This music is performed in the Sutter County community to the accompaniment of the harmonium, with drums and other percussion instruments, and may be heard in the services in the *Gurdwaras*, or temples, which anyone may attend. The songs and dances of the more informal folk music, on the other hand, may be performed in the celebration of weddings, births, harvest, and so on, or on still more spontaneous occasions. While this music has a certain weight of tradition behind it, it is naturally far more vulnerable to the influence of popular music, and more susceptible to change, than the religious music. Recent investigations show that this music is in a continual state of transition under the impact of the popular music not only of the United States, but of India as well, especially as disseminated by the products of the flourishing Indian movie industry.[22]

A small colony of Russians settled in Bryte (just across the Sacramento River from Sacramento) in 1912; their numbers increased after the Russian Revolution, and there are several other small Russian communities in the Valley and in the foothills to the east, each with its Russian Orthodox Church. The average age of members of these communities is advancing; the *balalaika* can no longer be heard in Russian restaurants, which have had to close down, and the only Russian music that can be heard in public is liturgical chant in the Orthodox churches.

The major influx of Mexicans, and their considerable contribution to the cultural mix, is fairly recent, beginning with the harvests of the early 1920s.

Their music today is mainly of the *musica norteña* tradition described in Chapter 3, with strong Chicano overtones.

Immigrants from Greece, coming primarily from Peloponnesus, began arriving in the early 1900s, and built their first church in Sacramento in 1921. Though the Greeks are thoroughly integrated into the community, they have preserved a good deal of their culture, focused on the Greek Orthodox Church. Since the 1950s and 1960s there has been a renaissance of Byzantine liturgical music in California, with a return to the old modal style, reinterpreted and harmonized, and a growth in the number and excellence of the choirs in churches. This was followed in the 1970s and 1980s by a renewed interest in Greek folk dance and costumes, and consequently in authentic Greek folk music, with regional distinctions preserved. Folk dance festivals, in which many young people take part, are frequent events. Several Greek bands are active, playing popular American as well as traditional Greek music. The traditional *klarino* (a type of clarinet) is no longer much used in the bands in Sacramento, but the *bouzóuki,* a fretted lute-like instrument with a long neck, has appeared in ensembles with greater frequency since the popularity of the film *Zorba the Greek.* It keeps company in the bands with electric guitar, drums, and electric keyboards. Greek music is flourishing but adapting—or, rather, flourishing *by* adapting.

Conclusion

In this final chapter we have concluded our sweeping glance over the panorama of American music by trying to convey a sense of one of its most characteristic attributes—diversity. As this is written, the author senses a renewed concern on the part of many, both in and out of arts councils, commissions, and boards—a concern that could be only sparsely documented here—for the health of our culture. He senses an awareness of the impoverishment that would come with the loss of regional and traditional musics through their complete absorption in mass culture, and he finds generous-minded patrons, producers, scholars, and performers working to see that this does not happen. The economics of the entertainment industry—the great "hit machine"—does indeed depend upon the mass production and marketing of a technically perfect, homogenized product devoid of regional eccentricities, and upon a public devoted to consumption rather than participation. But what the hit machine cannot do is to reflect, to serve, or to place value on our diversity, our eccentricity—the very things that give us individuality. As Woody Guthrie sang, looking out from the sixty-fifth floor of one of the mass culture machine's chic and insulated bastions,[23]

> It's a long way's from here to th'U.S.A.

To lessen this distance and bring th'U.S.A. and its far-flung and diverse musics into sharper focus has been the goal of this book.

Further Reading

Louisiana

Allen, William Francis, Charles Ware, and Lucy McKim Garrison, eds. *Slave Songs of the United States*. New York, 1867. Paperback reprint, New York: Oak Publications, 1969.
Seven Louisiana songs in patois are included in this famous early collection.

Ancelet, Barry Jean. *The Makers of Cajun Music*. Québec: Presses de l'Université du Québec, 1984.
A beautifully prepared treatise, in both English and French, with many fine color photos.

Berry, Jason, Jonathan Foose, and Tad Jones. *Up from the Cradle of Jazz: New Orleans Music Since World War II*. Athens: University of Georgia Press, 1986.

Broven, John. *South to Louisiana: The Music of the Cajun Bayous*. Gretna, LA: Pelican, 1983.

———. *Rhythm and Blues in New Orleans*. Gretna, LA: Pelican, 1983.

Cable, George Washington. "The Dance in Place Congo"; "Creole Slave Songs." Reprinted in Bernard Katz, ed., *The Social Implications of Early Negro Music in the United States*. New York: Arno, 1969.
The importance of these articles, and the music they include, has been indicated in this chapter.

Desdunes, Rodolphe Lucien. *Our People and Our History*. Trans. Sister Dorothea Olga McCants, Baton Rouge: Louisiana State University Press, 1973.
Published in Montreal in French in 1911, this is a classic in the history of Louisiana's "Creoles of color."

Krehbiel, Henry Edward. *Afro-American Folksongs: A Study in Racial and National Music*. New York: Frederick Ungar, 1914; reprint, 1962.
Krehbiel collaborated with Cable and with Lafcadio Hearn in collecting and studying black folk music in Louisiana in the nineteenth century. Chapters 9, 10, and 11, on "Creole" music, are the results of this collaboration.

Lomax, John A. and Alan. *Our Singing Country*. New York: Macmillan, 1949.
This section "French Songs and Ballads from Southwestern Louisiana" contains seven complete songs collected there in 1934, including three of the songs mentioned in this chapter.

Mills, Gary B. *The Forgotten People: Cane River's Creoles of Color*. Baton Rouge: Louisiana State University Press, 1977.

Post, Lauren C. *Cajun Sketches*. Baton Rouge: Louisiana State University Press, 1962.
Deals with the geography, economics, traditions, and music of the region.

Rushton, William Faulkner. *The Cajuns: From Acadia to Louisiana*. New York: Farrar, Straus & Giroux, 1979.

Savoy, Ann Allen. *Cajun Music: A Reflection of a People*, vol. 1. Eunice, LA: Bluebird Press, 1985.

Whitfield, Irène Thérèse. *Louisiana French Folk Songs*. Baton Rouge, LA: 1939. Enlarged paperback ed., New York: Dover, 1969.
An important collection in this area. Because of its uniqueness, its few weaknesses are all the more unfortunate: The musical transcriptions are, it must be suspected, not always trustworthy, and there is a lack of uniform documentation as to where, and especially when, the songs were collected. There are translations of the texts into standard French, but not into English.

The Upper Midwest

Bergmann, Leola Nelson. *Americans from Norway*. Philadelphia: Lippincott, 1950.

Larson, Leroy Wilbur. "Scandinavian-American Folk Music of the Norwegians in Minnesota." Ph.D. Thesis, University of Minnesota, 1975.

———, ed. *Scandinavian Old Time Music*

Book 1 & 2. Minneapolis, MN: Banjar Publications, ca. 1980, 1984.

Leary, James P. "Old Time Music in Northern Wisconsin," *American Music,* vol. 2. no. 1 (Spring 1984).
A valuable documentation of the current state of old-time music in the Chequamegon Bay area, a region of rich ethnic diversity.

The Sacramento Valley

McGowan, Joseph A. *History of the Sacramento Valley.* 2 vols. New York and West Palm Beach: Lewis Historical Publishing, 1961.
While not up to date, this is an extensive survey of the first century and more of the Valley's history.

Listening

Louisiana

Bahaman Songs, French Ballads and Dance Tunes, Spanish Religious Songs and Game Songs. AAFS L-5.
It is unfortunate that this catchall album does not contain more of the French music, but the examples it does give are all valuable.

Street Cries and Creole Songs of New Orleans. Folkways 2202.

Arhoolie Records has a large catalog of Cajun and zydeco music, of which the following is only a sample:

Folksongs of the Louisiana Acadians, vols. 1 and 2. Arhoolie 5009, 5015.

Louisiana Cajun Music. 5 vols.
Vol. 1: *The 1920s: First Recordings.* Old Timey 108.
Vol. 2: *The Early 30s.* Old Timey 109.
Vol. 3: *The String Bands of the 30s.* Old Timey 110.
Vol. 4: *From the 30s into the 50s.* Old Timey 111.
Vol. 5: *The Early Years: 1928–1938.* Old Timey 114.

Michael Doucet: Dit Beausoleil. Arhoolie 5025.
Doucet is an outstanding reinterpreter of traditional styles, especially as a fiddler player.

Clifton Chenier: Louisiana Blues and Zydeco. Arhoolie F 1024.

Zydeco Live. 2 vols. Rounder 2069–70.

The Upper Midwest

The most comprehensive catalog at present is that of Banjar Records. The following is a sampling of available albums.

Early Scandinavian Bands and Entertainers. BR 1840.
Reissues of old 78s.

Scandinavian-American Folk Dance Music, vols. 1 and 2. BR 1825, 1830.

The Hills of Old Wisconsin: Leonard Finseth, fiddle. BR 1842.

New Sweden '88: Old Time Swedish Favorites. BR 1638.

I'll Be Home for Lefse. The Minnesota Scandinavian Ensemble. BR 1844. A mix of old pieces and new ones in traditional style.

The Sacramento Valley

José-Luis Orozco canta 160 Años del Corrido Mexicano y Chicano. Bilingual Media Productions BMP JL-10.

Chicano Music All Day: El Trio Casindio and the Royal Chicano Air Force. Centro de Artistas Chicanos. Nonántzin C/S284.

PROJECTS

1. Look around in your own community and make an inventory of the various cultures that are not in the "mainstream," that have retained their culture and perhaps their language as well, and that have their own distinctive and identifiable music and musical tradition.

2. Pick one culture in your own community that fits the description in project 1 above, and make a study (through interviews, attendance at social and religious events, etc.) of their music, and the way it functions in their culture.

3. Find out about any national holidays that are celebrated by ethnic groups in your community, and attend and report on them. These are usually celebrations of national independence, like the American Fourth of July; Mexicans, for example, celebrate *Cinco de Mayo* (May 5), and Norwegians *Syttende Mai* (May 17).

4. Find out about and report on the support your own state government gives to folk, ethnic, or regional arts, through a state folklorist, or a state arts board or arts council.

NOTES

The following abbreviations of record collections or anthologies are used throughout these notes:

AAFS Library of Congress Archive of American Folk Song
FAAFM Folkways *Anthology of American Folk Music,* a 3-LP set (2951–53).
FHJ Folkways History of Jazz, an 11-LP set (2801–11).
MIA *Music in America,* a series no longer in print but available in many record libraries.
NW *Recorded Anthology of American Music,* produced by New World Records, a series still in progress at over 160 LPs. Many issues are available in record stores. Elizabeth A. Davis, *An Index to the New World Recorded Anthology of American Music* (New York: W. W. Norton, 1981) covers the first 100 issues.
SmCAPS *Smithsonian Collection of American Popular Song,* a 7-LP anthology. Also on cassettes.
SmCBBJ *Smithsonian Collection of Big Band Jazz,* a 6-LP anthology. Also on cassettes.
SmCCCM *Smithsonian Collection of Classic Country Music,* an 8-LP anthology.
SmCCJo *Smithsonian Collection of Classic Jazz,* original edition; a 6-LP anthology. Superseded by the following, but already in many libraries.
SmCCJr *Smithsonian Collection of Classic Jazz,* revised edition; a 7-LP anthology. Also on cassettes.

Chapter 1: The British-American Tradition

1. A sampling of recordings of *Barbara Allen:* in *Folk Songs of the Old World—The Roger Wagner Chorale* (Capitol S-345); *Joan Baez*, vol. 2 (Vanguard 2097); *Anglo-American Ballads*, (AAFS: L-1).

2. On AAFS: L-1.

3. Jean Ritchie, *Singing Family of the Cumberlands* (New York: Oak Publications, 1963), p. 17.

4. Charles Seeger, notes to *Versions and Variants of Barbara Allen* (AAFS: L-54): see below, note 20.

5. See Roger D. Abrahams and George Foss, *Anglo-American Folksong Style* (Englewood Cliffs, NJ: Prentice-Hall, 1968), p. 29.

6. See Bertrand Harris Bronson, *The Traditional Tunes of the Child Ballads*, vol. 1 (Princeton, NJ: Princeton University Press, 1959), pp. 9–33.

7. The word *antine* here invites an interesting study. There is no such word in English usage. Baring-Gould, collector of the first of these versions using it, postulates that it is a corruption of the French *antienne*, which means "antiphon." Since an antiphon is a piece of liturgical music, the image of every grove ringing "with a merry antine" is a plausible and indeed a rather happy one. The second version, collected in California in 1938, shows a further step in the process of change through misunderstanding, since the sense of *antine* as music, even in the corrupted form of the word, has now been lost, and the refrain reverts once more to the "plant" motif, carrying with it the euphonious but by now completely meaningless word.

8. Evelyn Wells, *The Ballad Tree* (New York: Ronald Press, 1950), p. 97.

9. One example will illustrate this. "The Grey Cock" exists in a complete traditional text (only recently rediscovered) in which the lover, hurrying at night to the house of his beloved, has to cross a burning river. He finally arrives and is let in, and they spend the night together, in the course of which it is revealed that the lover is really a ghost, his earthly form having presumably perished in the fire. Knowing that the dead must return to the grave before the cock crows, the beloved offers bribes to the bird not to crow before daylight. The cock, however, crows prematurely, and the lovers must part forever. In most current versions the supernatural element has been eliminated, the lover remains an ordinary mortal, the crowing of the cock is simply a conventional announcement of the coming of day, and the whole ballad has become merely a commonplace tale of a night visit from a lover. Five versions of this ballad appear in the excellent recorded collection *The Long Harvest* (Argo [Z] DA-66-75), complete with texts and notes. See the Listening section at the end of this chapter.

10. As Abrahams and Foss have written, "It is considerably easier to observe and analyze a tradition which is 'uncontaminated' by print, but there is a real question whether any such tradition has ever existed." *Anglo-American Folksong Style*, p. 35.

11. Some of these survived to become venerable folk songs; see the reference to "Captain Kidd" on page 138.

12. See Jean Thomas, *Ballad Makin' in the Mountains of Kentucky* (New York: Oak Publications, 1964), pp. 136–38, and G. Malcolm Laws, Jr., *Native American Balladry* (Philadelphia: American Folklore Society, 1964), pp. 44–45.

13. See John Cohen and Mike Seeger, *Old-Time String Band Song Book* (New York: Oak Publications, 1976), p. 27.

14. Francis James Child, *The English and Scottish Popular Ballads*, a multi-volume work currently available in several editions.

15. See Laws, *Native American Balladry*, pp. 79–82 and 134. A facsimile reprint of "The Ocean Burial" is included in Richard Jackson, ed., *Popular Songs of Nineteenth-Century America* (New York: Dover, 1976).

16. See Laws, op. cit., p. 126. A portion of "The Drummer Boy of Shiloh" is included in Charles Hamm, *Yesterdays: Popular Song in America* (New York: W. W. Norton, 1979), p. 252.

17. Laws, *Native American Balladry*, pp. 51 and 223–24.
18. Ibid., pp. 47–48.
19. Ibid., p. 111.
20. Bronson, in his monumental *Traditional Tunes of the Child Ballads*, vol. 2, actually identifies four tune groups for this ballad, for which he prints 191 variants altogether, with seven additional "sports." Not all four tune types have wide currency in America, however. Charles Seeger, in his article "Versions and Variants of the Tunes of Barbara Allen," treats extensively the two versions that he recognizes as current in America, which are here represented in Examples 1–1 and 1–2. This fascinating article was first printed in *Selected Reports*, vol. 1, no. 1 (Los Angeles: Institute of Ethnomusicology, University of California, 1966) and reprinted as notes to *Versions and Variants of Barbara Allen* (AAFS: L-54).
21. Seeger, op. cit., p. 122.
22. Bronson, *Traditional Tunes of the Child Ballads*, vol. 1, p. 3.
23. The reader with some musical background and a curiosity about the subject may wish to consult Bertrand Bronson, "Folk Song and the Modes," *Musical Quarterly*, vol. 32, no. 1 (January 1946), pp. 37–49.
24. For an interesting comparison of an older and a newer tune side by side, listen to two adjacent bands on a record entitled *Oh, My Darling: Folk Song Types* (NW-245), part of the *Recorded Anthology of American Music*. "Sweet William," a Child ballad (Child 7), is sung unaccompanied to an old-type tune using the pentatonic scale. "The Lexington Murder" is sung to a more recent type of tune, with a guitar accompaniment that uses the familiar three basic chords; the tune follows the chords.
25. As an illustration of this, compare the written version of "Barbara Allen" as given in Example 1–2 with the performance from which it was derived, that of Mrs. Rebecca Tarwater, available on *Anglo-American Ballads* (AAFS: L-1).
26. For an interesting treatment of this whole question, see Alan Lomax, "Folk Song Style," *American Anthropologist*, vol. 61, no. 6 (December 1959), and also the introduction to *The Folk Songs of North America* by the same author (Garden City, NY: Doubleday, 1960).
27. Vance Randolph and Floyd C. Shoemaker have described the play-party as it existed in the Ozarks and reproduced some eighty play-party songs, with descriptions of the dances, in *Ozark Folksongs*, vol. 3 (Columbia: State Historical Society of Missouri, 1949). Some play-party games are also given in Cecil Sharp's *English Folk-Songs from the Southern Appalachians*, ed. Maud Karpeles, vol. 2 (London: Oxford University Press, 1932), pp. 367–83.
28. A representative selection of such songs may be heard on recordings such as *Old-Time Music at Clarence Ashley's* (Folkways 2355), which includes "Sally Ann," "The Old Man at the Mill," and "Pretty Little Pink"; or *Mountain Music of Kentucky* (Folkways 2317), which includes "Blackeyed Susie."
29. These lines as found on Folkways records 2355 and 2317, cited above; used by permission.
30. Printed versions of these appear in most collections, including those in the reading list at the end of this chapter. For recorded versions, consult the list of recordings given there also. Because of the increased interest in fiddling, and the corresponding increase in fiddling contests and fiddlers' conventions, it is now much easier to hear live performers of this music—always much more satisfactory.
31. See Hans Nathan, *Dan Emmett and the Rise of Early Negro Minstrelsy* (Norman: University of Oklahoma Press, 1962), p. 92, and Mark Twain, *Life on the Mississippi*, chapter 3.
32. Quote from Marion Thede, *The Fiddle Book* (New York: Oak Publications, 1967), p. 11.
33. Thede, *The Fiddle Book*, p. 26.
34. See the endpaper of R. P. Christeson's excellently printed collection *The Old-Time Fiddler's Repertory* (Columbia: University of Missouri Press, 1973).

Chapter 2: The African-American Tradition

1. "The Survival of African Music in America" was an important early study by Jeannette Robinson Murphy, published in *Appleton's Popular Science Monthly* in September 1899. It is reprinted in the notes of the Folkways album *Roots of Black Music in America,* 2694.

2. For further information on African survivals see Eileen Southern, *The Music of Black Americans* (2d ed.), and *Readings in Black American Music* (2d ed.), especially Readings 7, 8, and 9 (both New York: W. W. Norton,1983). See also Dena J. Epstein, *Sinful Tunes and Spirituals: Black Folk Music to the Civil War* (Urbana: University of Illinois Press, 1977), especially chapters 1 and 7; Maultsby, "West African Influences and Retentions in U.S. Black Music" in Irene Jackson ed., *More Than Dancing: Essays on Afro-American Music and Musicians* (Westport, Conn.: Greenwood Press, 1985); and Marshall Stearns *The Story of Jazz* (New York: Oxford University Press, 1956), chapters 1, 2, and 3.

3. Two permanently valuable documents to come out of this area are the *Slave Songs of the Georgia Sea Islands* by Lydia Parrish (New York, 1942; reprint, Hatboro, PA: Folklore Associates, 1965), and the recordings of *Animal Tales Told in the Gullah Dialect* by Albert Stoddard (AAFS: L-44, 45, 46). The Gullah dialect contains a high percentage of West African words, as was revealed in Lorenzo Turner's study *Africanisms in the Gullah Dialect* (Chicago: University of Chicago Press, 1949). A fine recording illustrating both the sacred and the secular music of the islands is *Georgia Sea Island Songs* (NW-278), recorded in 1960–61 by Alan Lomax, who also provided notes for the album.

4. Jazz, coming out of folk roots, is the American music that most obviously expresses this trait, but the spiritual, especially in its folk phase, also manifests it significantly. This may be heard in an example such as "Handwriting on the Wall" from *Afro-American Spirituals, Work Songs, and Ballads* (AAFS: L-3), or "Sheep, Sheep, Don't You Know the Road," from NW-278.

5. Any number of other examples might be substituted, of course, but of these the first may be found on *African Drums* (Folkways FE-4502), track 6, and the second on AAFS: L-3 (cited above). The entire album *Roots of Black Music in America* (Folkways 2694) is relevant and instructive.

6. For more information on this opposition, and some of the reasons for it, see Epstein, *Sinful Tunes and Spirituals,* pp. 192–97.

7. As quoted in Southern, *The Music of Black Americans,* pp. 38, 41, and 59.

8. See Southern, *The Music of Black Americans,* pp. 75–79 and *Readings in Black American Music,* pp. 52–61.

9. Both "The Song of the Contrabands" and the "Songs of the Freedmen of Port Royal" are reproduced in facsimile in Epstein's excellent *Sinful Tunes and Spirituals,* where they and their context are discussed at some length.

10. Among them James Miller McKim, as quoted in Miles Mark Fisher, *Negro Slave Songs in the United States* (Ithaca, NY: Cornell University Press, 1953), pp. 12–13. See also Murphy, "The Survival of African Music in America," reprinted in notes to *Roots of Black Music in America* (Folkways FA-2694).

11. William Francis Allen, in his preface to Allen et al., *Slave Songs of the United States* (reprint, New York: Oak Publications, 1965), pp. iv–vi.

12. For the reader interested in learning more about the controversy over the origin of the spiritual, the following are suggested: George Pullen Jackson presents the case for essentially (though not exclusively) white origin, especially in his *White and Negro Spirituals: Their Life Span and Kinship.* Dena Epstein presents a contrasting view in "A White Origin for the Black Spiritual? An Invalid Theory and How It Grew," *American Music,* vol. 1, no. 2 (Summer 1983), as does William Tallmadge in "The Black in Jackson's White Spirituals," *The Black Perspective in*

Music, no. 9 (1981). A well-balanced view is presented by John F. Garst in "Mutual Reinforcement and the Origins of Spirituals," *American Music*, vol. 4, no. 4 (Winter 1986). The latter two articles contain references to additional sources.

13. "Look How They Done My Lord," from *Spirituals with Dock Reed and Vera Hall Ward* (Folkways FA-2038); "Handwriting on the Wall," from *Afro-American Spirituals, Work Songs, and Ballads* (AAFS: L-3). Both of these appear in printed versions in Johnson, *The Books of Negro Spirituals* (New York: Viking, 1940). Other selections on the same recordings are also illustrative and valuable.

14. The variable seventh is especially clear in "Low Down the Chariot and Let Me Ride," on FA-2038 (cited above).

15. Both are included in the album *Negro Folk Music of Africa and America* (Folkways 4500). Excellent examples are also to be heard on *Georgia Sea Island Songs* (NW-278).

16. The most often recorded of the preachers was the Rev. J. M. Gates, some of whose sermons are included in the Riverside *History of Classic Jazz;* in the Folkways *History of Jazz* series, vol. 1, *The South* (2801); and in the *Anthology of American Folk Music*, vol. 2, *Social Music* (Folkways 2952).

17. An interesting example is a variant of "Do Lord Remember Me," recorded with banjo in 1936, found on *Negro Religious Songs and Services* (AAFS: L-10).

18. Recordings such as "He Got Better Things for You," made in 1929 by the Memphis Sanctified Singers (*Anthology of American Folk Music*, Folkways 2952), and "Precious Lord," made by the Gospel Keys probably in the early 1940s (*The Asch Recordings*, Folkways AA-1), illustrate this.

19. Listen to Sturdivant's famous "Ain't No Grave Can Hold My Body Down," recorded in 1942 (*Negro Religious Songs and Services*, AAFS: L-10); also "Since I Laid My Burden Down" (*Anthology of American Folk Music*, vol. 2, Folkways 2952).

20. "Lift Up a Standard for My King" (related to a traditional spiritual) and "I'm a Soldier in the Army of the Lord" (*Negro Blues and Hollers*, AAFS: L-59) illustrate this, as does *"I'm in the Battlefield for My Lord"* by the Rev. D. C. Rice and His Sanctified Congregation (*Anthology of American Folk Music*, vol. 2, Folkways 2952). The first two are field recordings from the early 1940s; the last was recorded commercially in 1929.

21. Many contemporary examples illustrate this; for one from the 1950s, listen to "He's a Friend of Mine," as performed by the Spirit of Memphis on *An Introduction to Gospel Song* (Folkways RF-5).

22. Quoted in Harold Courlander, *Negro Folk Music, U.S.A.* (New York: Columbia University Press, 1963), pp. 81–82.

23. *Negro Work Songs and Calls* (AAFS: L-8); *Negro Folk Music of Alabama*, vol. 1 (Folkways 4417). For transcriptions of some of the calls in this latter album, and an excellent treatment of the subject, see Courlander, *Negro Folk Music, U.S.A.*, chapter 4. Two rather extended street cries of Charleston are included on the first side of the Riverside *History of Classic Jazz* (see suggestions for listening, Chapter 12); a few more meager examples from New Orleans are included on *The Music of New Orleans*, vol. 1 (Folkways 2461).

24. Both may be heard on AAFS: L-8 (cited above), side 1. The first is track 7; the second, track 6. The importance of *hearing* the calls in conjunction with this exposition cannot be overemphasized; only in this way can the true musical "feel" of blue notes be experienced. In the transcriptions both have been transposed, for the sake of comparison.

25. This inflected dominant can be heard in the spiritual "Trouble So Hard" (*Afro-American Spirituals, Work Songs, and Ballads*, AAFS: L-3), and in a call recorded in *Negro Folk Music of Alabama*, vol. 1 (Folkways 4417) and transcribed in Courlander, *Negro Folk Music, U.S.A.*, p. 84. The flattened dominant became important in the jazz of the 1950s.

26. *Afro-American Blues and Game Songs* (AAFS: L-4).

27. *Negro Blues and Hollers* (AAFS: L-59, track A-2).

28. *Afro-American Blues and Game Songs* (AAFS: L-4).

29. Paul Oliver, *The Meaning of the Blues* (New York: Macmillan, 1960; paperback, Collier, 1963).
30. As quoted in Bruce Cook, *Listen to the Blues* (New York: Scribner's, 1973), p. 40.
31. Examples of these vocal styles have been conveniently assembled in *The Rural Blues*, ed. Samuel Charters (Folkways RF-202).
32. "Levee Camp Moan," performed by Texas Alexander (*The Country Blues*, vol. 2, Folkways RF-9), and "Special Rider Blues," performed by Son House (*Negro Blues and Hollers*, AAFS: L-59), illustrate this.
33. Amiri Baraki (LeRoi Jones), *Blues People* (New York: Morrow, 1963), pp. 81–82.
34. Perhaps the richest recorded collection is *Negro Prison Songs from the Mississippi State Penitentiary*, collected and annotated by Alan Lomax (Tradition TLP-1020). "Early in the Mornin'," from this record, is particularly fine. "Long John" (from *Afro-American Spirituals, Work Songs, and Ballads*, AAFS: L-3) and "Hammer, Ring" (from *Negro Work Songs and Calls*, AAFS: L-8) are also good examples.
35. Printed versions appear in a great number of collections. As for recordings by traditional singers, there are greatly truncated versions sung by Leadbelly (*History of Jazz*, vol. 1, Folkways 2801) and the Williamson brothers (*Anthology of American Folk Music*, vol. 1, Folkways 2951). A version in the manner of a work song is found on AAFS: L-3, cited above; and the derivative blues ("Spike Driver Blues"), as sung by Mississippi John Hurt, is in *Anthology of American Folk Music*, vol. 3 (Folkways 2953).
36. This is splendidly illustrated in the ballad "The Titanic," on *Georgia Sea Island Songs* (NW-278).

Chapter 3: American Indian and Hispanic Traditions

1. It is beyond the scope of this book to deal with the characteristics of the music of the various cultural areas; interested readers may consult *North American Indian Musical Styles* by Bruno Nettl (Philadelphia: American Folklore Society, 1954), as well as the article in *The New Grove Dictionary of American Music* by the same author (vol. 2, pp. 460–68).
2. Walter Collins O'Kane, *Sun in the Sky* (Norman: University of Oklahoma Press, 1950), pp. 186–91.
3. Frances Densmore, *The American Indians and Their Music* (New York: Women's Press, 1926), p. 63.
4. See *Songs of Love, Luck, Animals, and Magic*, NW-297.
5. Densmore, *The American Indians and Their Music*, p. 63.
6. This may be heard sung by Pigeon himself as "Pigeon's Dream Song" on *Songs of the Menominee, Mandan, and Hidatsa* (AAFS: L-33).
7. This may be heard on AAFS: L-33 (cited above), track B-7.
8. This may be heard on *Music of the American Indian: Sioux* (AAFS: L-40), track A-7; a sung version follows the flute performance.
9. A Chinook version of "Jesus Loves Me" can be heard on *Music of the American Indian: Northwest (Puget Sound)* (AAFS: L-34), and a Hopi version of "Dixie" on *Music of the American Indian: Pueblo: San Ildefonso, Zuni, Hopi* (AAFS: L-43).
10. This may be heard as performed by the Los Angeles Northern Singers on *Songs of Earth, Water, Fire and Sky* (NW-246). Willard Rhodes regarded this category of songs as "a passing fad or fashion which flourished because of novelty in uniting an Indian melody with English words" (Rhodes, "Acculturation in North American Indian Music" in *Acculturation in the Americas* [Chicago: University of Chicago Press, 1952]); but he may well not have been in a position to grasp the cultural significance of this special type of song.
11. Thus we have the songs and dances of "eastern Indians" (Cherokee and Creek) being recorded in Sequoyah County, Oklahoma: see NW-337.
12. Ghost Dance songs recorded among Great Basin and Plains tribes may be heard on the following recordings in the Library of Congress *Music of the American*

Indian series (AAFS): *Songs of the Pawnee and Northern Ute* (L-25), *Plains: Comanche, Cheyenne, Kiowa, Caddo, Wichita, Pawnee* (L-39), *Kiowa* (L-35), *Great Basin: Paiute, Washo, Ute, Bannock, Shoshone* (L-38), and *Sioux* (L-40).

13. There is no doubt about the acculturational influence on the peyote cult and music. Called the Native American Church, the cult has Christian overtones, and has adopted Christian symbols and words, which appear in many of the songs. An interesting example from the Sioux, in which "JESUS ONLY" is spelled out twice, can be heard on AAFS: L-40 (cited above). Other peyote songs can be heard on AAFS: L-35 and L-38 (cited above), and on *Delaware, Cherokee, Choctaw, Creek* (AAFS: L-37) and *Navajo* (AAFS: L-41).

14. David P. McAllester, *Peyote Music*, Viking Fund Publications in Anthropology, no. 13 (New York: Viking, 1949), p. 85.

15. For more information on the *matachines* dance, see "Matachines: A Midwinter Drama from Iberia" in *Music and Dance of the Tewa Pueblos* by Gertrude Prokosch Kurath (Santa Fe: Museum of New Mexico Press, 1970), and portions of her article in *The New Grove Dictionary of American Music* (vol. 2, pp. 477–78). See also "The Matachines Dance—A Ritual Folk Dance" by J. Donald Robb in *Western Folklore*, vol. 20, no. 2 (1961), pp. 87–101, as well as many references and examples of the music from the same author's *Hispanic Folk Music of New Mexico and the Southwest* (Norman: University of Oklahoma Press, 1980). The music of two matachines dances can be heard on the Folkways album *Spanish and Mexican Folk Music of New Mexico* (FE-4426), with notes by J. Donald Robb. Robb points out that at times these dances appear in two distinct versions: "a Spanish version with fiddle and guitar imported from a nearby Spanish village and an Indian version with Indian music, chorus, drums, and costuming, which nevertheless follows generally the plot, the dance evolutions, and other aspects of the traditional *matachines* dance" (*Hispanic Folk Music of New Mexico and the Southwest*, p. 6).

16. Examples of this music can be heard on *"Chicken Scratch": Popular Dance Music of the Indians of Southern Arizona*, Canyon Records C-6085, with notes by the collector, Robert Nuss. The *musica norteña* of the lower Rio Grande Valley will be discussed in the second part of this chapter, and Cajun and *zydeco* music in Chapter 20.

17. Alan Merriam, *Ethnomusicology of the Flathead Indians* (Chicago: Aldine, 1967), p. 147.

18. See *Powwow Songs: Music of the Plains Indians*, NW-343, with notes by Charlotte Heth.

19. Marta Weigle, as quoted in the notes to NW-292, *Dark and Light in Spanish New Mexico*. For more information on Los Penitentes see her *Brothers of Light, Brothers of Blood* (Albuquerque: University of New Mexico Press, 1976). For a sensitive eyewitness account of Penitentes rituals during Holy Week a half-century ago, see *Brothers of Light* by Alice Corbin Henderson (Chicago: Rio Grande Press, 1962), with illustrations by William Penhallow Henderson.

20. Joaquín Fernández, in a note to the author. Robert L. Vialpando, of Alcalde, New Mexico, is a collector and researcher of alabados.

21. See NW-292 (cited above). Side 1 is devoted to alabados sung by elderly members of the Penitentes who had belonged to the Brotherhood since the late nineteenth and early twentieth centuries. The pito is also heard. Robb's extensive *Hispanic Folk Music of New Mexico and the Southwest* includes many transcriptions of alabados, and one pito melody. The Penitente Manual, including the texts of the alabados, is painstakingly copied by hand by members of the Brotherhood; a sample page of such a copy is reproduced in Robb, op. cit., p. 619, and also in Bill Tate, *The Penitentes of the Sangre de Cristos*, (Truchas, NM: Tate Gallery, 1968), p. 33.

22. See *Music of the Spanish Folk Plays in New Mexico* by Richard B. Stark (Santa Fe: Museum of New Mexico Press, 1969), and *Hispanic Folk Songs of New Mexico* by John Donald Robb. A "Pedimento de las Posadas," recorded in a small town in south Texas in 1934, is included in the

catchall issue *Bahaman Songs, French Ballads and Dance Tunes, Spanish Religious Songs and Game Songs* (AAFS: L-5).

23. Robert Louis Stevenson, "The Old Pacific Capital," in *Across the Plains.* For a fuller account of California mission music see "The Rise and Fall of Indian Music in the California Missions" by Larry Warkentin, in *Latin American Music Review,* vol. 2, no. 1 (Spring–Summer 1981).

24. See *Mission Music of California* by Owen da Silva (Los Angeles: Warren Lewis, 1941). Two recordings are listed at the end of this chapter.

25. It has been estimated that in the seventeenth century, for example, there were more Africans than Spaniards in Mexico. See Robert Stevenson *Music in Aztec and Inca Territory: Contact and Acculturation Periods* (Berkeley: University of California Press, 1977), p. 231, to which Claes af Geijerstam makes reference in his *Popular Music in Mexico* (Albuquerque: University of New Mexico Press, 1976), p. 11.

26. The *corrido* is a descendant of the earlier *villancico* and the *jácara,* forms using the vernacular language, whose subject matter could originally be either sacred or secular—telling stories of saints or of revolutionary heroes. The villancico in Mexico reached a peak of development in the late seventeenth century. Spanish models for these and other adapted forms are treated in Gilbert Chase, *The Music of Spain,* 2d ed. (New York: Dover, 1959).

27. An excellent sampling may be heard on NW-292, *Dark and Light in Spanish New Mexico,* with notes by Richard Stark. A polka and a waltz may also be heard on *Spanish Mexican Folk Music of New Mexico,* Folkways P-426, with notes by John Donald Robb. Both the waltz and the quadrille (*las cuadrillas*) owe their presence in Mexico to French influence in the nineteenth century, especially during the French occupation of 1862–67.

28. It must not be assumed that these cultural mixings occurred only north of the Rio Grande. As Geijerstam has pointed out, the waltz, the polka, the mazurka, and the schottische were imported into Mexico itself in the nineteenth century, reaching Mexico City mostly from Paris. See *Popular Music in Mexico,* p. 16.

29. The term *charro* refers to the highly skilled rope artists in who performed in rodeos, or *chareadas.*

30. Making up an increasingly large percentage of the population of the United States, especially in the Southwest, people of Mexican descent constitute a rather complex cluster of three or four fairly distinct groups. *Mexican-Americans* are those who were born here or have lived here long, identify themselves most strongly as Americans, and have become thoroughly assimilated into what might be termed the mainstream of American life. Sometimes identified as a separate, and much smaller, group are *Hispanic-Americans,* whose ancestors settled in Texas, New Mexico, or California (the "Californios") before Anglo settlement and domination came to those areas. They may even regard their cultural heritage as coming more from Spain than from Mexico. A third group are *Chicanos,* whose identity as a cultural group was born in the 1960s. These tend to be young Mexican-Americans who have rediscovered and are celebrating their ethnic identity. In varying degrees activist and militant, they are impatient with what they see as discrimination against their race (La Raza) and may, in the extreme, look upon the United States as a country of oppression and racism. Their cultural focus tends to be definitely not Spanish (except in language), and not so much Mexican as pre-Columbian Indian, and even pre-Aztec. (The mythical Aztlán, placed somewhere in the American Southwest, is regarded as the birthplace of all native American races. According to this view, the migrations northward from Mexico in historical times are regarded as a *return* to a legendary homeland.) A fourth group are *Mexicanos,* or Mexican immigrants, both documented and undocumented. They form a fairly large and mobile population. Although many, if not most, of them do not intend to stay in this country and resist assimilation, they account for a significant part of the constant replenishment of Mexican culture that

comes through the continuous immigration from Mexico. See *Crossing: A Comparative Analysis of the Mexicano, Mexican-American and Chicano* (San Pedro, CA: International Universities Press, 1983) by Maximiliano Contreras. Much information was also derived from a paper "Mexicans and Mexican Americans in the United States—Past and Present" presented by Lawrence Cardoso at the Symposium "Ethnicity in American Culture" at the University of Wyoming in June 1985, and from a conversation with the musician-poet-painter José Montoya of Sacramento. See also "Unraveling America's Hispanic Past: Internal Stratification and Class Boundaries" by Ramón Gutiérrez, and "Mexicanos, Chicanos, Mexican-Americans, or Pochos . . . Qué somos? The Impact of Nativity on Ethnic Labelling" by Aída Hurtada and Carlos H. Arce, both in *Aztlán*, vol. 17, no. 1 (Spring 1986).

31. This variant is transcribed from the earliest version to appear on phonograph records, about 1929. It may be heard on *Texas-Mexican Border Music*, vol. 2 (Folklyric 9004); see the Listening list at the end of this chapter. The complete histories of the case and of the ballad are found in *"With His Pistol in His Hand"* by Americo Paredes (Austin: University of Texas Press, 1958).

32. See Dan William Dickey, *The Kennedy Corridos: A Study of the Ballads of a Mexican American Hero* (Austin: University of Texas Press, 1978).

33. Transcribed from Falcon FLP-2091 (record courtesy of Joaquín Fernández).

34. Robb, *Hispanic Folk Songs of New Mexico*, pp. 201–313. All four of the canciónes mentioned here ("Cielito Lindo," "La Golondrina," "La Cucaracha," and "La Adelita") have great meaning for Mexicans and Mexican-Americans alike; their interesting histories are unfortunately too long to be recounted here.

35. See " 'El Hijo del Pueblo': José Alfredo Jiménez and the Mexican *Canción Ranchera," Latin American Music Review*, vol. 2, no. 2 (Spring–Summer 1982), especially pp. 43–44.

36. These four songs are sung by Peter Hurd on *Spanish Folk Songs of New Mexico*, Folkways FA-2204.

37. John Storm Roberts, *The Latin Tinge* (New York: Oxford University Press, 1979), pp. 39–43.

38. Ibid., chapters 4 and 5.

39. Ibid., p. 57.

40. John Bennett, in *The New Ethnicity: Perspectives from Ethnology* (Proceedings of the American Ethnological Society), as quoted in Roberta Singer, "Tradition and Innovation in Contemporary Latin Popular Music in New York City," *Latin American Music Review*, vol. 4, no. 2 (Fall–Winter 1983), p. 183.

41. René López has said: "We consciously impart this whole sense of history to the people we come into contact with." See Singer, "Tradition and Innovation," cited above, from which this quote was taken. Roberta Singer is also co-author of the notes for NW-244 (see Listening for this chapter), which was produced by René López.

42. See notes by Roberta Singer and Robert Friedman on NW-244.

43. See Singer, "Tradition and Innovation," cited above. See also John Storm Roberts, *The Latin Tinge*, p. 223.

Chapter 4: Aspects of Folk Music in Twentieth-Century America

1. John Powell, in his preface to George Pullen Jackson, *Spiritual Folk-Songs of Early America* (reprint, New York: Dover, 1964).

2. See John Greenway, *American Folksongs of Protest* (Philadelphia: University of Pennsylvania Press, 1953; paperback reprint, New York: A. S. Barnes, 1960).

3. The tune is that of "A-Hunting We Will Go." The complete song is printed and recorded in *The Birth of Liberty*, NW-276. See p. 266 for facsimile.

4. D. K. Wilgus, *Anglo-American Folksong Scholarship Since 1898*, (New Brunswick, NJ: Rutgers University Press, 1959), p. 228.

5. R. Serge Denisoff, *Sing Me a Song of Social Significance*, 2d ed., (Bowling Green, OH: Bowling Green State University Press, 1983), p. 99.

6. R. Serge Denisoff, *Great Day Coming: Folk Music and the American Left* (Urbana: University of Illinois Press, 1970).

7. The entire text and tune are in Greenway, *American Folksongs of Protest*, p. 249. They appear with a tune variant, in *Hard-Hitting Songs for Hard-Hit People* (New York: Oak Publications, 1967). The ILD (International Labor Defense) sent lawyers into North Carolina to defend accused union leaders.

8. The complete text appears in Greenway, *American Folksongs of Protest*, pp. 269–70, and text and tune in *Hard-Hitting Songs*, p. 142. Aunt Molly's rendition of it is available on *Aunt Molly Jackson, Library of Congress Recordings* (Rounder 1002).

9. Quoted in Denisoff, *Great Day Coming*, p. 119.

10. Greenway, *American Folksongs of Protest*, p. 259.

11. Ibid., p. 115.

12. For a slightly fuller account of the composition of "The Sinking of the *Reuben James*" see David King Dunaway, *How Can I Keep from Singing: Pete Seeger* (New York: McGraw-Hill, 1981), pp. 97–98. The song is included in *The Woody Guthrie Songbook* (New York: Grosset & Dunlap, 1976). Seeger's performance of it is included in *The World of Pete Seeger* (Columbia CG-31949).

13. See *Ballads of Sacco & Vanzetti*, commissioned by Moses Asch in 1945, composed and sung by Woody Guthrie, Folkways FH-5485.

14. Greenway, *American Folksongs of Protest*, p. 275.

15. Charles Seeger, "The Folkness of the Non-Folk vs. the Non-Folkness of the Folk" in Bruce Jackson, ed., *Folklore and Society* (Hatboro, PA: Folklore Associates, 1966).

16. Pete Seeger, quoted in Denisoff, *Great Day Coming*, p. 119.

17. Ibid., p. 82.

18. Ibid., p. 86.

19. See Dunaway, *How Can I Keep from Singing: Pete Seeger*, chapter 1.

20. Music and text of all of the songs by Bob Dylan mentioned in the foregoing section except "Only a Pawn in Their Game," "Masters of War," "With God on Our Side," "North Country Blues," "A Hard Rain's A-Gonna Fall," "Who Killed Davy Moore?" and "I Pity the Poor Immigrant" are published in *Bob Dylan* (New York: Warner Bros., 1974). Dylan's performances of most of these songs are included on either *The Freewheelin' Bob Dylan* (Columbia PC-8786) or *The Times They Are A-Changin'* (Columbia PC-8905).

21. Guy and Candie Carawan, *We Shall Overcome: Songs of the Southern Freedom Movement*, (New York: Oak Publications, 1963), p. 7. For further background on the Carawans' work at Highlander Folk School, (now Highlander Center, in New Market, Tennessee) see Josh Dunson, *Freedom in the Air: Song Movements of the 60's*, (New York: International Publishers, 1965), pp. 37–43; and "Song Leaders for Social Change," *Christian Science Monitor*, September 2, 1982.

22. "We Shall Overcome" had been adapted from the religious song as early as 1945 by union workers in Charleston, South Carolina. It was the "theme song" of Highlander Folk School, from whence it was introduced into the Civil Rights movement.

23. All of these songs may be found in *We Shall Overcome: Songs of the Southern Freedom Movement* (cited above).

24. Songs such as "I'm On My Way to the Freedom Land;" "I'm So Glad," and "Certainly, Lord" illustrate, as do many others, this practice, which was so prominent a feature of the nineteenth-century African-American spiritual. For further amplification of the religious models for the protest song, see "Religious Roots of the Song of Persuasion" in Denisoff, *Sing Me a Song of Social Significance*, 2d ed., pp. 48–57.

25. Tom Paxton, telephone interview with Josh Dunson, quoted in Dunson, *Freedom in the Air*, p. 105–6.

26. For a fuller discussion, and more examples, of protest songs being altered for broader public consumption (including the subtle alteration of "Where Have All the Flowers Gone") see Denisoff, *Sing Me a Song of Social Significance*, pp. 33–34.

27. Local history records that Thomas Dula was hanged in 1868 for the murder of

Laura Foster in Wilkes County, North Carolina. A ballad on the subject was collected from oral tradition and published in a collection by Duke University Press in 1952. It is said, however, that the Kingston Trio got their version from a traditional singer, Frank Proffitt.

28. Both quotes are from "After Dormant Decade, Folk Music Blooms," by Catherine Foster in *The Christian Science Monitor*, December 31, 1986.

Chapter 5: Religious Music in Early America

1. David McKay and Richard Crawford, *William Billings of Boston* (Princeton, NJ: Princeton University Press, 1975), p. 8.

2. All the music of the Ainsworth Psalter is included in *The Music of Henry Ainsworth's Psalter* I.S.A.M. Monograph no. 15 (Brooklyn: Institute for Studies in American Music, 1975), as well as in the older *The Music of the Pilgrims* by Waldo Selden Pratt (Boston: Oliver Ditson, 1921).

3. Recordings of "Guide Me, O Thou Great Jehovah," "Amazing Grace," "Why Must I Wear This Shroud?" and "When Jesus Christ Was Here on Earth" as sung in rural Baptist churches in Kentucky furnish an illustration from living tradition of a practice that must be at least similar to the Usual Way of three hundred years ago, even to the lining out. These can be heard on *The Gospel Ship*, NW 294. A similar rendition of "Amazing Grace" can be heard on *Mountain Music of Kentucky*, Folkways FA-2317. Gaelic psalmody as practiced in the Free Church of Scotland, especially in the Outer Hebrides, is strikingly illustrative of this tradition. The cassette *Gaelic Psalmody Recital*, vols. 1 and 2, from Lewis Recordings in Scotland, is an excellent example of this type of traditional singing.

4. James Franklin, brother of Benjamin, indulged in some wild and humorous hyperbole on this point (which indeed must have had some basis in experience) when he wrote in the *New England Courant* in 1724: "I am credibly inform'd, that a certain Gentlewoman miscarry'd at the ungrateful and yelling Noise of a Deacon in reading the first Line of a Psalm; and methinks if there were no other Argument against this Practice (unless there were an absolute necessity for it) the Consideration of it's being a Procurer of Abortion, might prevail with us to lay it aside" (quoted in McKay and Crawford, *William Billings of Boston*, p. 14).

5. There is evidence that singing-masters sometimes took their pay in produce—Indian corn, for example. For this and many other interesting details of the New England singing-school tradition, see Alan Buechner, "Yankee Singing Schools and the Golden Age of Choral Music in New England: 1760–1800" (Ph.D. dissertation, Harvard University, 1960), and, based on this, his copious annotations to the recording *The New England Harmony* (Folkways FA-2377).

6. McKay and Crawford, *William Billings of Boston*, p. 23.

7. Gilbert Chase, *America's Music, From the Pilgrims to the Present*, 3d ed. (Urbana: University of Illinois Press, 1987), p. 113.

8. Fortunately, several of these books are now available in facsimile reprint form, including Lyon's *Urania*, Belcher's *Harmony of Maine*, and Billings's *Continental Harmony* and *Psalm-Singer's Amusement*. Consult the reading list.

9. This may be heard in *The New England Harmony* (Folkways FA-2377).

10. It is not clear in what circumstances and by whom Billings's Christmas pieces were sung, since the Puritans had suppressed traditional Christmas customs as "Prophane and Superstitious" in the seventeenth century, and this proscription was in effect until the mid-nineteenth century, at which time Christmas was still a regular working day in Boston. See McKay and Crawford, *William Billings of Boston*, p. 144–45.

11. This is on NW-276.

12. In spite of the new stirrings of cultural, as well as political, independence, the extent to which this flourishing of native activity built upon European tradi-

tions and sources, especially British, should be known and acknowledged. There was a parallel, and earlier, tradition in England, and much of the pedagogical material for the introductions came from British books such as William Tans'ur's *Royal Melody Complete.* A lot of the music, both tunes and settings, came from British and continental sources, especially after the turn of the century; it should also be noted that the fuging tune itself (or, to be more exact, the "fuging psalm-tune") was developed in England in the mid-eighteenth century. There is no art (or art form) without forebears.

13. The most comprehensive recordings available to date are *The New England Harmony,* cited above and NW-255. See also the suggestions for listening at the end of this chapter.

14. In 1956 the Moravian Music Foundation, with headquarters in Winston-Salem, was founded for the purpose of "research, publication, and education," having its basic resource the Peter Memorial Library, with over ten thousand manuscripts of early Moravian music. Through the efforts of the foundation, much of this music is now available in modern editions. The sacred songs and choruses are eminently useful and rewarding for church as well as concert performances. A representative sampling is available on records. Consult the reading and listening lists at the end of this chapter.

15. Donald M. McCorkle, *The Moravian Contribution to American Music* (Winston-Salem, NC: Moravian Music Foundation), p. 9.

16. As a matter of fact, many of the musical practices of the Shakers (if not the music itself) bear some resemblance to those of the Indians: the origins of songs in visions, the use of meaningless syllables, the concept of songs as "gifts," the use of song to accompany ritualistic movement.

17. This and the following Shaker song appear in *The Gift to Be Simple: Songs, Dances and Rituals of the American Shakers,* by Edward Deming Andrews (Locust Valley, NY, 1940; reprint, New York: Dover, 1962), p. 100. A version that differs only slightly is found in Daniel W. Patterson, *The Shaker Spiritual* (Princeton, NJ: Princeton University Press, 1979), p. 180.

18. In Andrews, *The Gift to Be Simple,* p. 136. A version that differs only slightly is found in Patterson, *The Shaker Spiritual,* p. 373.

19. Andrews, *The Gift to Be Simple,* pp. 7–8.

Chapter 6: Religious Music During and After the Time of Expansion

1. Quotes in this paragraph are from Robert Stevenson, *Protestant Church Music in America* (New York: W. W. Norton, 1966; paperback reprint, 1970).

2. Ibid., p. 85, n. 218.

3. Not long after the invention of the four-shape system, a system of seven shapes was devised, in 1832— one shape for each tone of the diatonic scale, and for each of the syllables used in continental European practice (do, re, mi, etc.) The seven-shape, seven-syllable system did become established in portions of the South. But although the seven-syllable system ultimately triumphed everywhere else in the English-speaking world, it did not succeed in dislodging the four-syllable (fa, sol, la, mi) practice from its stronghold in *Sacred Harp* circles—nor has it to this day.

4. George Pullen Jackson, *Down-East Spirituals and Others,* 2d ed. (New York: J. J. Augustin, 1953), p. 176.

5. The solemn chorale that figures so prominently in Bach's St. Matthew Passion, "O Haupt voll Blut und Wunden" ("O head, now bloody and wounded") was originally a Renaissance love song, "Mein G'muth ist mir verwirret, das macht ein Jungfrau zart" ("My mind is all in disarray; this is what a tender young maid has done").

6. There are numerous recordings of this well-known folk hymn—renditions in both the white and the black traditions. One of the most interesting is a

lined-out version on *The Gospel Ship* (NW-294).

7. Recorded on *White Spirituals from "The Sacred Harp"* (NW-205) and *Sacred Harp Singing* (AAFS: L-11).

8. For an interesting study of the persistence of this parallelism in rural church singing right down to our own time, see "Folk Organum: A Study of Origins" by William H. Tallmadge, *American Music,* vol. 2, no. 3 (Fall 1984).

9. From the autobiography of James B. Finley, quoted in Charles A. Johnson, *The Frontier Camp Meeting* (Dallas: SMU Press, 1955), pp. 64–65.

10. Johnson, *The Frontier Camp Meeting,* p. vii.

11. From a letter written in Kentucky in 1803, printed in the *Methodist Magazine,* London, that year. Quoted in Johnson, *The Frontier Camp Meeting,* p. 57.

12. Samuel E. Asbury, quoted in Gilbert Chase, *America's Music, From The Pilgrims to the Present,* 3d ed. (Urbana: University of Illinois Press,1987), p. 204.

13. See Jackson, *White and Negro Spirituals: Their Life Span and Kinship* (New York, 1944; reprint, New York: Da Capo, 1975), pp. 83–86, and the interesting collection of such wandering choruses and rhyme pairs in two appendices.

14. See William Tallmadge, "The Black in Jackson's White Spirituals," *The Black Perspective in Music,* no. 9 (1981); also John Garst, "Mutual Reinforcement and the Origins of Spirituals," *American Music,* vol. 4, no. 4 (Winter 1986).

15. As reprinted in Jackson, *White and Negro Spirituals,* the white hymn (with tune dated 1853) from McCurry's *Social Harp,* and the black spiritual from the Fisk *Jubilee Songs* of 1872. A performance of the black spiritual by the Fisk University Jubilee Quartet recorded about 1913 can be heard on *An Introduction to Gospel Song,* RBF 5, available from Folkways/Smithsonian. A substantially different version of "Roll, Jordan, Roll" appears in *Slave Songs of the United States,* 1867 (reprint, New York: Oak Publications, 1965).

16. The hymn tunes in Lowell Mason's *The Boston Handel and Haydn Society Collection of Church Music* (1822), which were made out of "beautiful extracts from the works of Haydn, Mozart, Beethoven and other eminent modern composers," were in most cases highly adapted from the original melodies. Many were taken from an English publication of 1812 by William Gardiner called *Sacred Melodies from Haydn, Mozart and Beethoven.* Gardiner's (and Mason's) borrowings can still be found in twentieth-century hymn collections. Some of the tunes still in use are "Sardis" and "Germany (Fulda)" by Beethoven, and "Austria" (the Austrian national hymn) by Haydn, though most have different names in the Mason collection.

17. As an illustration, one of the more popular hymns in this collection is "Safe in the Arms of Jesus," with words by Fanny Crosby. Fanny Jane Crosby (1820–1915), using hundreds of pen names in addition to her real name, worked for years under a contract that called for the production of three songs a week. How far she exceeded even this is indicated in her own statement: "I have often composed as many as six or seven hymns in one day." It is no wonder that her total output has been estimated at more than eight thousand hymns.

18. The term "gospel" seems first to have been applied to these songs in 1874, when P. P. Bliss published his *Gospel Songs, a Choice Collection of Hymns and Tunes New and Old for Gospel Meetings, Prayer Meetings, Sunday Schools, Etc.* This was a year before the famous Sankey-Bliss *Gospel Hymns* series began.

19. The major mode was thought to be more cheerful and optimistic, and reinforced better the millennial spirit of the revivalist preaching of the day, which replaced the grim pessimism and preoccupation with death and eternal judgment that had characterized antebellum "hellfire" preaching and the songs that went with it.

20. A similar chorus may be heard in "My Lord Keeps a Record," a gospel hymn rendered in traditional mountain style in Virginia on *The Gospel Ship* (NW-294).

21. Erik Routley, *The Music of Christian Hymnody,* quoted in Stevenson, *Protestant*

Church Music in America (cited above), p. 112.

22. "Brighten the Corner Where You Are" and "In the Garden" can be heard, as sung by Rodeheaver himself (assisted in the second song by Mrs. William Asher), on NW-224.

23. Appropriately, Ira Sankey's reed organ is now in the possession of the Billy Graham Evangelistic Association. George Beverly Shea, the musician for years most closely associated with Graham, can be heard singing one of Sankey's best-known songs, "The Ninety and Nine," accompanied by this organ, on NW-224.

24. The terms "Holiness," "Sanctified," and "Pentecostal" are sometimes used interchangeably to describe this general movement, which was actually made up of several distinct movements and many sects, as manifested in many practically independent denominations and churches. The term "Pentecostal" is not universally applicable to the movement as a whole, since it connotes a particular emphasis on the phenomenon of glossolalia, or "speaking in tongues," which not all Holiness churches or adherents practice. The terms "Apostolic" or "Church of God" (or "Church of God in Christ") are frequently encountered as names of the Holiness churches. The Holiness and Pentecostal denominations were frequently racially integrated early in this century but have since become largely segregated. See Robert Mapes Anderson, *Vision of the Disinherited: The Making of American Pentecostalism* (New York: Oxford University Press, 1979).

25. "The Royal Telephone" is given as found in *Favorite Songs and Hymns*, published by Stamps-Baxter in 1939. A close variant of this, called "Telephone to Glory," was recorded several times by black gospel singers in the 1920s: see Paul Oliver, *Songsters and Saints* (New York: Cambridge University Press, 1984), p. 205. The metaphor lives on: the Mighty Clouds of Joy, a present-day black gospel quartet, recorded a distant variant with the title "Call Him Up."

26. "Where We'll Never Grow Old," as recorded by Smith's Sacred Singers in 1926, is included in the *Smithsonian Collection of Classic Country Music* (cited hereafter as "SmCCCM"). So also is the Carter Family's 1935 recording of "Can the Circle Be Unbroken," with their inventive added verses that have since become traditional. Also in the same collection is "What Would You Give in Exchange for Your Soul" in a 1936 recording by the Monroe brothers. A recent performance in old time style of "He'll Set Your Fields on Fire" is included in *Favorite Gospel Songs*, as performed by Harry and Jeanie West (Folkways 2357). "Give the World a Smile," almost a theme song of the Stamps Quartet, can be heard as sung by them on the archival album with the same title (RCA Camden 2193). "If I Could Hear My Mother Pray Again" is included in *Roy Acuff's Greatest Hits* (Columbia CS 1034).

27. Examples of this "ruralizing" of nineteenth-century urban gospel hymns can be heard in "Going Down the Valley" (original "We Are Going Down the Valley," from about 1890), recorded by Ernest V. "Pop" Stoneman and his Dixie Mountaineers in 1926, on NW-235. "To the Work," another hymn from the Sankey collection, with words by Fanny Crosby and music by W. H. Doane, can be heard in a "southernized" version as a solo with guitar accompaniment on *Country Gospel Song* (Folkways RF-19). More recent performances in the old style of "Sweet By-and-By" and "Amazing Grace," both included in the Sankey *Gospel Hymns 1 through 6* (though "Amazing Grace" antedates this late nineteenth-century collection) can be heard on the album *Favorite Gospel Songs* (Folkways 2357).

28. Bill Malone, *Southern Music—American Music* (Lexington: University Press of Kentucky, 1979), p. 69.

29. Ibid., pp. 67–68.

30. J. Frank Smith and Smith's Sacred Singers can be heard in a 1926 recording of "Where We'll Never Grow Old" (1914) in SmCCCM. Ernest Phipps and his Holiness Singers can be heard in a 1930 recording of "Shine on Me" in the *Anthology of American Folk Music*, vol. 2 (Folkways 2952), in "I Know that Jesus Set Me Free"

and "Went Up in the Clouds of Heaven" in *Country Gospel Song* (Folkways RF-19), and in "If the Light Has Gone Out in Your Soul" on NW-245.

31. Bascom Lamar Lunsford, an Appalachian ballad singer, can be heard in a 1928 recording, with five-string banjo, of "Dry Bones" in the *Anthology of American Folk Music*, vol. 2 (Folkways 2952). An early gospel recording of Uncle Dave Macon singing "Jesus Lover of My Soul," a hymn from the Moody-Sankey collection, is included in *Country Gospel Song* (Folkways RF-19). The Stoneman Family recorded gospel music under the name of the Dixie Mountaineers; their 1926 recording of "Going Down the Valley" is the title song of NW-236. Recordings of the Carter Family are readily available in reissues today; their sacred songs are represented in anthologies by a 1932 recording of "Little Moses" in the Folkways anthology (2952) cited above, by the previously cited 1935 recording of "Can the Circle Be Unbroken" in SmCCCM, by "Lonesome Valley" and "The Little Black Train" in *Country Gospel Song* (Folkways RF-19).

32. The Chuck Wagon Gang is represented in anthologies by their 1941 recording of "Jesus Hold My Hand" in SmCCCM. A recently issued Columbia Historic Edition, *Chuck Wagon Gang*, includes sixteen pieces recorded between 1936 and 1960 (Columbia FC-40152).

33. Malone, *Southern Music—American Music*, p. 113.

34. See the Florida Boys' 1986 release *Together*, Canaan Records WR 8362.

35. One black Baptist lady, describing Holiness worship, said to Tony Heilbut, "To me, it's just like going to a movie; they *amazing*." In Heilbut, *The Gospel Sound* (New York: Simon & Schuster, 1971), p. 201.

36. William E. B. DuBois, *The Souls of Black Folk: Essays and Sketches* (Chicago: McClurg, 1903), chapter 10, as quoted in Oliver, *Songsters and Saints*, p. 140. On the capacity for *showmanship*, and even for "clowning," that was involved, see Heilbut, "The Secularization of Black Gospel Music" in William Ferris and Mary L. Hart, ed., *Folk Music and Modern Sound* (Jackson: University Press of Mississippi, 1982), p. 103.

37. Heilbut, *The Gospel Sound*, p. 103.

38. Folkways/Smithsonian issues offer a good selection. The *Anthology of American Folk Music*, vol. 2, includes two sermons by the Rev. Gates and one each by the Rev. McGee, the Rev. Moses Mason, and the Rev. D. C. Rice. *An Introduction to Gospel Song*, RF-5, has four more. All were recorded between 1927 and 1931.

39. Several early commercial recordings make this point very clearly, especially "I'm in the Battlefield for My Lord" (1929) with the Rev. D. C. Rice and his Sanctified Congregation (*Anthology of American Folk Music*, vol. 2, Folkways 2952). On the same record is "Fifty Miles of Elbow Room" (1931) with the Rev. F. W. McGee and congregation. Two other recordings with the Rev. McGee, "I Looked Down the Line and I Wondered" and "Jesus the Lord Is a Saviour," both from 1929, are included in *An Introduction to Gospel Song*, Folkways RF-5. Two field recordings made in 1940 illustrate the persistence of this practice: "Lift Up a Standard for My King" and "I'm a Soldier in the Army of the Lord," both on AAFS: L-59 (Library of Congress). All of these groups were connected with the Church of God in Christ, a Sanctified denomination.

40. NW-224 includes a 1949 recording of Rosetta Tharpe and her mother singing "Daniel in the Lion's Den" with piano, bass, and drums. *An Introduction to Gospel Song* (Folkways RF-5) and *The Asch Recordings* (Folkways AA-1/2) both include recordings of Sister Ernestine Washington singing with Bunk Johnson's band.

41. "God Moves on the Water" is included in *Country Gospel Song* (Folkways RF-19). A partial transcription of the text is in Oliver, *Songsters and Saints*, p. 224. Oliver points up an interesting contrast between the races in their responses to the Titanic disaster: for whites it could be accounted for by "human error or folly," while blacks attached far more metaphorical significance to it as "indicating the inevitability of God's judgment on the arro-

gance of those who believed themselves invincible" (ibid., p. 223).

42. Some blues singers did record gospel songs, usually under different names. Blind Lemon Jefferson's recording of "I Want to Be like Jesus in My Heart" was released under the name of Deacon L. J. Bates, and Charley Patton recorded gospel songs as Elder J. J. Hadley. There were token releases by other blues singers as well. See Oliver, *Songsters and Saints*, pp. 202–4.

43. "John the Revelator" is in the Folkways *Anthology*, vol. 2.

44. See Oliver, *Songsters and Saints*, pp. 195–96. "Since I Laid My Burden Down" and "He Got Better Things for You" are included in the Folkways *Anthology*, vol. 2.

45. Horace Clarence Boyer, "C. A. Tindley: Progenitor of Black-American Gospel Music," *Black Perspectives in Music*, vol. 11, no. 2 (Fall 1983), p. 113.

46. The Fisk University Jubilee Quartet and the Tuskegee Institute Singers can be heard in recordings from the 1910s in *An Introduction to Gospel Song*, Folkways RF-5.

47. Four male group recordings from 1944 to 1950 are included on NW-224. Horace Clarence Boyer's chronology of male gospel ensembles can be found in his article in *The New Grove Dictionary of American Music*, vol. 2, pp. 254–59. This can be compared with Heilbut's chronology in chapter 3 of *The Gospel Sound*.

48. "Lord, Send Me Down a Blessing" can be heard on the album *Sacramento Community Choir Live*, under the direction of Clarence Eggleton (Onyx R 3824).

49. "I Worship Thee," by John Kee, is included in the album *Show Me the Way* by the New Jerusalem Baptist Church Choir of Flint, Michigan, on Sound of Gospel SOG-2D160.

50. Heilbut, "The Secularization of Black Gospel Music," p. 113. Examples of contemporary gospel music may be heard in virtually any album by Andraé Crouch, the Winans, Al Green, or the Hawkins Family. "Contemporary" gospel is a product in which there is indeed a fine line, often subtly crossed, between the sacred and the secular. The secularization of which Heilbut speaks sometimes involves not only adopting the "highly complex recording techniques of a . . . Michael Jackson," but imitating, in a muted way, the latter's sex appeal as well, as album photos of Al Green or Edwin Hawkins, with open shirt and necklace, show.

51. Horace Clarence Boyer, "A Comparative Analysis of Traditional and Contemporary Gospel Music" in *More Than Dancing*, Irene Jackson, ed. (Westport, CT: Greenwood Press, 1985), p. 143.

52. "You Don't Have to Jump No Pews (I've been born again)" on the album *Autograph*, produced by Lexicon Music, Inc., SPCN-7U57-10740.

53. Sharon Stratton-Dobbins, as quoted in Romeo Eldridge Phillips, "Some Perceptions of Gospel Music," *Black Perspectives in Music*, vol. 10, no. 2 (Fall 1982).

Chapter 7: Country Music

1. It is interesting to note that the term "hillbilly" itself (like so many labels that have stuck in art generally) was originally somewhat derogatory. The first recorded use of the term appeared in a New York periodical in 1900, as follows: "A Hill-Billie is a free and untrammelled white citizen of Alabama, who lives in the hills, has no means to speak of, dresses as he can, talks as he pleases, drinks whiskey when he gets it, and fires off his revolver as the fancy takes him" (quoted by Archie Green in "Hillbilly Music: Source and Symbol," Journal of American Folklore, July–September 1965).

2. It would be interesting to speculate as to just what accounts for this popularity among those who feel strong ties to rural life and mores, wherever they happen to live, as well as for the scorn with which this music is regarded among those who belong culturally to the city and its milieu. It is perhaps not too great an oversimplification to state that the line between those who appreciate country music and those who hold it in contempt

may be drawn with fair accuracy on the basis of whether their background, attitudes, and values are basically rural or urban /suburban.

3. Bill Malone is of the opinion that this style of playing may well have been picked up from the instruction manuals that came with the instruments when they were purchased from the mail-order houses. (See his *Country Music, U.S.A.* 1st ed. [Austin: University of Texas Press, 1968], p. 126.)

4. From the American practice, now familiar, of adopting a brand name (e.g., Kleenex, Xerox) as a generic name for a product in common use. As such the word is now usually uncapitalized.

5. Dock Boggs's singing, especially in "Sugar Baby" (1928), illustrates this well: *Anthology of American Folk Music,* vol. 3 (Folkways 2953).

6. This trait can be heard in examples ranging from authentic folk renditions of "Amazing Grace" and "Wayfaring Stranger" on *Mountain Music of Kentucky* (Folkways 2317) to the singing of such country stars as Roy Acuff in "Great Speckle Bird," included on *Roy Acuff's Greatest Hits* (Columbia CS-1034), and Hank Williams in "I Saw the Light," included in the album of the same title (MGM SE-3331). For a study of singing styles as a crucial element of folk music, see Alan Lomax, "Folk Song Style," *American Anthropologist,* vol. 61, no. 6 (December 1959), and also his introduction to *The Folk Songs of North America* (Garden City, NY: Doubleday, 1960).

7. Riley Puckett, 1924, singing "Rock All Our Babies to Sleep," as noted in Malone, *Country Music, U.S.A.* 2d ed., p. 87.

8. Lomax, *The Folk Songs of North America,* p. 281.

9. Jimmie Rodgers's famous "Blue Yodel No. 1 (T for Texas)" is illustrative—found on *The Best of the Legendary Jimmie Rodgers* (RCA LSP-3315[e]). His "Blue Yodel No. 11" is found on *Country Music South and West* (NW-287).

10. Quoted in Malone, *Country Music, U.S.A.,* 2d ed., p. 242. For an anecdote on the relation between experience and sincerity see Maurice Zolotow, "Hillbilly Boom," *Saturday Evening Post,* quoted in Linnell Gentry, ed., *A History and Encyclopedia of Country, Western, and Gospel Music,* 2d ed. (Nashville, TN: Clairmont, 1969), pp. 60–61.

11. Clarence Ashley, an old-time musician, recorded almost as an afterthought during one session in 1930 his version of "The House Carpenter," a venerable English and Scotch ballad from the Child canon. It turned out to be one of his most memorable recordings. It can be heard in *Anthology of American Folk Music,* vol. 1 (Folkways 2951).

12. "Wildwood Flower," as recorded by the Carter Family, is SmCCCM, 2/7. (In this chapter the *Smithsonian Collection of Classic Country Music* will be cited in this short form—2/7 is band 7 on Side 2.)

13. "Wabash Cannon Ball," as made famous by Roy Acuff's singing of it, is SmCCCM 8/1.

14. D. K. Wilgus, "An Introduction to the Study of Hillbilly Music" in the *Journal of American Folklore,* reprinted in Gentry, *A History and Encyclopedia of Country, Western, and Gospel Music,* 2d ed., p. 229.

15. "Listen to the Mocking Bird," published in 1855, became a favorite with country fiddlers (see SmCCCM 3/1), and "Lorena," published in 1862 with guitar as well as piano accompaniment, has become a country standard. It can be heard as recorded by Johnny Cash in 1959, in a version somewhat altered from the original, on NW-207.

16. "Footprints in the Snow" can be heard on *Old Time Music at Clarence Ashley's* (Folkways 2355) and *Bill Monroe's Country Music Hall of Fame* (MCA-140). "Great Speckled Bird," one of Roy Acuff's most popular songs, can be heard in his version as SmCCCM 4/7. "It Wasn't God Who Made Honky-Tonk Angels" is SmCCCM 10/6. "Le cote farouche de la vic" is included in *Cajun Music: The Early 50's* (Arhoolie 5008).

17. "Old Man at the Mill" is on *Old Time Music at Clarence Ashley's* (Folkways 2355).

18. The same tune was later used by Woody Guthrie in his "Tom Joad," one of

his Dust Bowl Ballads based on John Steinbeck's *Grapes of Wrath.* Other Mixolydian tunes may be heard on NW-236: "I Truly Understand You Love Another Man," "Old Joe Clark," and "Little Maggie."

19. "Snow Dove," also known as "The Butcher Boy," on *Mountain Music Bluegrass Style* (Folkways FA-2318).

20. "Wreck on the Highway" may be heard on *Roy Acuff's Greatest Hits,* Columbia CS 1034.

21. For a provocative discussion of sentimentality as a characteristic attitude of the South, and some speculation as to its origins, see Wilbur J. Cash, *The Mind of the South,* (New York: Knopf, 1941), especially pp. 82–87, 126–130.

22. "No Letter in the Mail," as sung on *Mountain Music of Kentucky* (Folkways 2317).

23. As sung on *Mike Seeger's Old Time Country Music* (Folkways 2325).

24. "Katy Cline," as sung on *Mountain Music Bluegrass Style* (Folkways 2318).

25. "Little Black Train," as sung by Dock Boggs, in *Dock Boggs,* vol. 2 (Folkways 2392).

26. From "No Disappointment in Heaven," as sung by Dock Boggs, Folkways 2392 (cited above).

27. " 'Mid the Green Fields of Virginia," sung by the Carter Family, on the album of the same title (RCA ANL-1-1107[e]).

28. "New River Train," on *Mountain Music Bluegrass Style* (Folkways 2318).

29. "Rowan County Crew," as sung by Dock Boggs on *Dock Boggs,* vol. 1 (Folkways FA-2351).

30. Among these are "The Wagoner's Lad" in Cecil Sharp, *English Folk-Songs from the Southern Appalachians,* vol. 2 (London: Oxford University Press, 1932), p. 123, recorded in 1928 by Buell Kazee, on *Anthology of American Folk M,* vol. 1 (Folkways 2951); and "Sally Ann" (Sharp, p. 351), recorded by Clarence Ashley, on *Old-Time Music at Clarence Ashley's* (Folkways 2355).

31. Sharp, p. 35; recorded on Folkways 2951 (cited above).

32. See Doron Antrim, "Whoop-and-Holler Opera," reprinted in Gentry, *A History and Encyclopedia* (cited above), pp. 65–70.

33. For Clarence Ashley's fascinating accounts of this primitive but influential form of traveling show business, see the notes to *Old-Time Music at Clarence Ashley's* (Folkways FA-2355).

34. Malone, *Country Music, U.S.A.,* 2d ed., p. 39.

35. A. C. "Eck" Robertson and Henry Gilliland were the musicians. See Malone, *Country Music U.S.A.,* 2d ed., p. 35. Robertson's recording of the play-party tune "Sally Gooden" (see Chapter 1) is included as the first track on SmCCCM.

36. Fiddlin' John Carson's 1923 recording of "The Little Old Log Cabin in the Lane" is SmCCCM 1/2.

37. For examples illustrative of this phase of "old-time" music, an excellent and representative selection of material from the early recordings by such artists as Clarence Ashley, Buell Kazee, Uncle Dave Macon, Dock Boggs, the Stoneman Family, and the Carter Family is available in *Anthology of American Folk Music* (Folkways 2951–53).

38. Uncle Dave Macon's "Jordan is a Hard Road" (derived from an old minstrel song by Dan Emmett—see Chapter 11) is SmCCCM 1/4. Folkways RF-51, *Uncle Dave Macon,* includes sixteen of his recorded songs, and a discography. Two songs are included in *Anthology of American Folk Music,* nos. 78 and 79.

39. The Carter Family can be heard in SmCCCM (2/7 and 4/9) and on NW-287 (*Country Music South and West*). RCA has released *'Mid the Green Fields of Virginia* (the title song of which is a Tin Pan Alley song by Charles K. Harris) with sixteen of their songs. Gid Tanner and his Skillet Lickers can be heard in an early recording as SmCCCM 1/8.

40. Two of Vernon Dalhart's most successful recorded songs, "The Prisoner's Song" and "The Wreck of the Old 97" (the first of country music's legion of railroad songs), are SmCCCM 1/5 and 1/7.

41. See note 9 above. Recordings by Jimmie Rodgers are included in SmCCCM (2/8 and 2/9) and on NW-287 and NW-314–15. RCA reissues of his 78-rpm recordings

are still available and continue to sell well, demonstrating his popularity with succeeding generations.
42. All the musicians and groups mentioned in this paragraph are represented in SmCCCM, Roy Acuff by two of his best-known songs, "The Great Speckled Bird" and "Wabash Cannon Ball." Columbia has reissued fifteen of Acuff's songs on *Roy Acuff's Greatest Hits* (CS 1034). We shall be hearing more of Bill Monroe in connection with bluegrass music.
43. Charlie Seeman in "The American Cowboy: Image and Reality," notes to *Back in the Saddle Again*, NW-314–15.
44. *Songs of the Cowboys*, collected by Nathan Howard "Jack" Thorpe, was published in New Mexico in 1908, followed by *Cowboy Songs and Other Frontier Ballads*, collected by John Alan Lomax, in 1910.
45. Several of these are included in NW-314–15. One of the best-known of these, "When the Work's All Done This Fall" (on a poem by the cowboy poet D. J. O'Malley), is included, as recorded by Carl T. Sprague in 1925, both in NW-314–15 and in SmCCCM 2/5.
46. Gene Autry, Tex Ritter, Patsy Montana, and the Sons of the Pioneers are represented in SmCCCM, NW-287, and NW-314–15.
47. The vitality of cowboy poetry, always an important adjunct to cowboy song, is illustrated in the surprising growth of events such as the annual Cowboy Poetry Conference in Elko, Nevada, and its numerous progeny springing up elsewhere in the West.
48. Most of the songs and all of the artists mentioned in this paragraph are represented in SmCCCM or NW-207, *Country Music in the Modern Era*, which can be supplemented with the Ernest Tubb Decca reissues on *The Ernest Tubb Story*, MCA 2-4040.
49. Most of the songs mentioned in this paragraph are in SmCCCM, which can be supplemented with commercial issues such as *The Ernest Tubb Story* (MCA 2-4040).
50. Bob Wills and "western swing" are represented in SmCCCM (6/3 and 6/8), and NW-287 and NW-314–15, which can be supplemented with commercial anthologies such as *The Best of Bob Wills* (MCA 2-4092).
51. Hank Williams is represented by only two tracks in SmCCCM ("I'm So Lonesome I Could Cry" and "Lovesick Blues," 10/8 and 10/9), but there are continual reissues of his work by MGM.
52. Gary Giddins, in notes to NW-249, *Shake, Rattle & Roll: Rock 'n' Roll in the 1950's*.
53. Malone, *Country Music, U.S.A.*, 2d ed., p. 394. See also Reid, *The Improbable Rise of Redneck Rock* (Austin, TX: Heidelberg, 1974), for a personal, informative account of the Austin scene, and those who have had a part in it.
54. Willie Nelson's recording of "Blue Eyes Crying in the Rain," from his 1975 album *The Red-Headed Stranger*, is the last track of SmCCCM.
55. Malone, *Country Music, U.S.A.*, p. 369.
56. There is generous documentation of "classic" bluegrass music in SmCCCM sides 13 and 14, including Bill Monroe's "Muleskinner Blues" and tracks by all of the others mentioned in this paragraph. See also *Hills & Home: Thirty Years of Bluegrass* (NW-225).
57. The recording of "Bottom of the Glass" by Seldom Scene is SmCCCM 14/9, and that of "Rocky Top" by the Osborne Brothers is SmCCCM 13/7. Further examples of the eclecticism of "progressive" bluegrass or "newgrass" can be heard on *Progressive Bluegrass*, vols. 1 and 2 (Folkways 2371–72), and on tracks by the Osborne Brothers, the Newgrass Revival, and others on *Hills & Home: Thirty Years of Bluegrass* (NW-225).
58. See *New Lost City Ramblers*, vols. 1–5, (Folkways 2395–99). The songbook has been reissued as *The Old-Time String Band Songbook* (New York: Oak Publications, 1976).

Chapter 8: Blues: From Country to City

1. Bruce Cook, *Listen to the Blues* (New York: Scribner's, 1973), p. 122.
2. W. C. Handy, ed., *Blues: An Anthology,* first published in 1926 (reprint, New York: Macmillan, 1972), pp. 100–101.
3. Paramount 12384; reissued on *Ma Rainey,* vol. 2 (Biograph BLP 12011).
4. Handy, *Blues: An Anthology,* pp. 111–14.
5. One example of Ma Rainey's recordings is included in the Folkways *Anthology of American Folk Music.* Over thirty of her performances have been reissued by Biograph Records, (BLP 12001, 12011, 12032).
6. Bessie Smith is well represented by single selections in most comprehensive jazz anthologies, including the *Smithsonian Collection of Classic Jazz* (SmCCJ: see Chapter 14, note 2, on this collection). In addition, Columbia Records has reissued all 160 of the available Bessie Smith recordings, with the sound reprocessed to compensate for the weaknesses of early recording techniques.
7. "Countin' the Blues:" Ma Rainey, vocal; Louis Armstrong, cornet; Buster Bailey, clarinet; Charlie Green, trombone; Fletcher Henderson, piano, with banjo and drums (1924), on *Ma Rainey,* vol. 2 (Biograph BLP-12011). Examples of Armstrong's work with other singers of the period may be heard on Columbia's imported *Rare Recordings of the Twenties,* on 4 LPs, CBS-64218, 65379, 65380, 65421. Single examples are included in most jazz anthologies.
8. "Dippermouth Blues," King Oliver's Creole Jazz Band, SmCCJ; also on Folkways History of Jazz (cited hereafter as "FHJ") vol. 3. The typical blues harmonic pattern is outlined in Chapter 2, p. 46.
9. "Ko-ko," Duke Ellington, SmCCJ.
10. "Parker's Mood," Charlie Parker, SmCCJ.
11. "Honky-Tonk Train," Meade "Lux" Lewis, SmCCJ, FHJ vol. 10, or NW-259.
12. "Yancey Stomp," FHJ vol. 10; "How Long Blues," FHJ vol. 2.
13. Keil, *Urban Blues* (Chicago: University of Chicago Press, 1966), Appendix C.
14. *Mississippi Blues, 1927–41* (Yazoo 1001) is a good introduction. Tracks by some of the individuals referred to may be found in the collections listed at the end of the chapter; in addition, there are many albums devoted to these single performers.
15. *Tex-Arkana-Louisiana Country* (Yazoo 1004) is a good introduction. As with the delta style, tracks by some of the individuals referred to may be found in the collections listed at the end of the chapter; in addition, there are many albums devoted to these single performers.
16. See tracks by individuals in listed collections, and albums devoted to single performers.
17. It was from this same Angola prison farm that the blues singer Robert Pete Williams was released twenty-five years later, again through the offices of a folklorist, Harry Oster.
18. Great Bluesmen /Newport (Vanguard VSD 77/78) illustrates this.
19. Amiri Baraka, *Blues People* (New York: Morrow, 1963), p. 168. Joe Turner's version of "Shake, Rattle and Roll" (NW-249) and Wynonie Harris's "Good Rockin' Tonight" are readily accessible examples.
20. Baraka, *Blues People,* pp. 171–72.
21. The best single collection documenting this phase is *Blues Roots/Chicago—the 1930's* (Folkways RF 16). Carr and Blackwell can be heard on NW-290, and on *The Story of the Blues* (Columbia CG 30008).
22. Rhythm-and-blues, like the earlier race records, is a vast commercial category. Charlie Gillett has written: "As a market category . . . 'rhythm and blues' was simply a signal that the singer was black, and recording for a black audience." The album *Straighten Up and Fly Right: Rhythm and Blues from the Close of the Swing Era to the Dawn of Rock 'n' Roll* (NW-261) gives a broad sampling of styles from the 1940s and early 1950s, with excellent notes. For other sources, see the suggestions for listening at the end of this chapter.
23. Keil, *Urban Blues,* especially chapter

7, "Soul and Solidarity." The quote above appears on p. 160.

24. These often consist of exaggeratedly "straight" music rendered with a satirical irony. Otis Redding's album *Try a Little Tenderness* (Atco SD-33-261) is an example. The same thing can be observed in "new wave" jazz, discussed in Chapter 14.

25. Keil, in his valuable *Urban Blues*, includes a rather detailed description and analysis of a complete stage appearance, in chapter 5, "Big Bobby Blue Bland on Stage."

26. Seeger, "The Folkness of the Non-Folk vs. the Non-Folkness of the Folk," in *Folklore and Society*, ed. Bruce Jackson (Hatboro, PA: Folklore Associates, 1966).

27. Oliver, *The Story of the Blues* (New York: Chilton, 1969), p. 168.

28. The 1985 album *Showdown*, with Albert Collins, Johnny Copeland, and Robert Cray (Alligator AL 4743), is illustrative.

Chapter 9: Rock

1. The titles of two fairly early books on rock, both dating from the early 1970s, express this. George Melly's *Revolt into Style* (Garden City, NY: Anchor/Doubleday, 1971) deals primarily with the British scene, but takes its title from a comment that Elvis Presley had turned "revolt into a style." Charlie Gillett's *The Sound of the City*, 1st ed. (New York: Dell, 1970) begins with an introduction subtitled "Dancing in the Street," wherein he writes that "Rock and roll was perhaps the first form of popular culture to celebrate without reservation characteristics of city life that had been among the most criticized. In rock and roll, the strident, repetitive sounds of city life were, in effect, reproduced as melody and rhythm" (p. 1). Simon Frith, however, writes: "Rock 'n' Roll . . . has celebrated street culture both for its participants and for its suburban observers, and by the mid-1960s such a celebration meant more to the latter group" (in *Popular Music, 1: Folk or Popular? Distinctions, Influences, Continuities*, ed. Richard Middleton and David Horn [Cambridge: Cambridge University Press, 1987], p. 168).

2. Pichaske, *The Poetry of Rock* (Peoria, IL: Ellis Press, 1981), p. 2.

3. Jonathan Eisen, ed., *The Age of Rock* (New York: Random House/Vintage, 1969), p. xiii.

4. Eisen, *The Age of Rock*, p. xii.

5. Wil Greckel, "Rock and Nineteenth-Century Romanticism: Social and Cultural Parallels," *Journal of Musicological Research*, vol. 3 (1979), pp. 177–202.

6. Belz, *The Story of Rock* (New York: Oxford University Press, 1972), chapter 1.

7. An example from the 1980s is "Purple Rain" by Prince.

8. The backbeat is very evident in the prototypical "Shake, Rattle and Roll," which is actually a rhythm-and-blues number (NW-249). It can also be heard in "Maybellene," and other selections from the same album. For an example from the 1980s, listen to Bruce Springsteen's "Born in the USA."

9. The link with boogie-woogie (see Chapter 8) is shown clearly in such numbers as Lloyd Price's "Mailman Blues" (NW-249), but it is also in Little Richard's "Every Hour" on the same album. Both are in the classical 12-bar blues form.

10. The Latin beat is clearly illustrated in Leiber and Stoller's "What About Us?" written for the Coasters—in 1959 this was perhaps rock 'n' roll's first protest song (NW-249). An interesting mixture of Latin and African rhythms can be heard in "New Orleans," on the same album.

11. Arnold Shaw, in a talk before the International Association for the Study of Popular Music, New York City, October, 1985.

12. The tune of "Daisy Bell" is easily recalled by the words of its final phrase: "a bicycle built for two." The Hendrix song may be heard on *Are You Experienced* (Reprise RS 6261) or *Smash Hits* (Reprise MSK 2276).

13. A recent example may be found in "Purple Rain," by Prince (WAR 25110–1).

14. For an interesting compilation of

eighteen annotated examples of various vocal styles in the rural blues, see *The Rural Blues: A Study of the Vocal and Instrumental Resources,* compiled by Samuel B. Charters (Folkways RF202).

15. As for example in "The Great Curve" by David Byrne and Brian Eno, from *Remain in Light* (SIRE SRK 6095).

16. "Maybellene" can be heard on NW-249.

17. The much-cited example of successive versions of Hank Ballard's "Work with Me, Annie" make this point. The original, from 1954, had a blues form with a strong backbeat. Its code phrase, "work with me," was thereafter laundered to "rolling with me" (as sung by Etta James), and then to "dancing with me" (as sung by Georgia Gibbs).

It is regrettable that the complex tangle of copyright ownership in popular music and the single-minded profit orientation of the industry effectively preclude the fuller quotation of music or lyrics.

18. Pichaske, *The Poetry of Rock,* p. 13.

19. NW-261.

20. The lyrics are printed in Pichaske, *The Poetry of Rock,* p. 65; the music is on *The Rolling Stones* (London PS-375), June 1964.

21. For examples, "Temptation" from *Around the World in a Day,* and "Nicky" from *Purple Rain.* See the article by Mark Tucker in *IASPM Newsletter,* November 1984.

22. "Yakety-Yak" by Jerry Leiber and Mike Stoller: lyrics printed in Richard Goldstein, *The Poetry of Rock* (New York: Bantam, 1968), p. 28.

23. Bob Dylan, "Subterranean Homesick Blues" (1965): music and lyrics are in *Bob Dylan* (New York: M. Witmark, 1965), pp. 90–92. Dylan's performance can be heard on *Bringing It All Back Home* (Columbia CS 9128).

24. Joe MacDonald, "I-Feel-Like-I'm-Fixin'-to-Die Rag" (Vanguard VSD 79266).

25. Bob Dylan, "Oxford Town": music and lyrics are in *Bob Dylan,* cited above. Dylan's performance can be heard on *The Freewheelin' Bob Dylan* (Columbia 8786).

26. Bob Dylan, "The Times They Are a-Changin' ": music and lyrics are in *Bob Dylan,* cited above. Dylan's performance is on the album of the same title (Columbia KCS 8905, CL 2105).

27. Bob Dylan, "With God on Our Side" can be heard on *The Times They Are a-Changin',* cited above.

28. Bruce Springsteen, from the album *Born in the USA* (Columbia QC 38653).

29. For one example, see "Blank Generation" by Richard Hell: the lyrics are quoted in *Best of New Wave Rock* (New York: Warner Bros., ca. 1978), p. 51.

30. Bruce Springsteen's "Born in the USA," cited above, is a recent example.

31. See "Yellow Submarine," by Lennon and McCartney for the Beatles (Capitol SW 153); "White Rabbit," by Grace Slick for the Jefferson Airplane; (RCA LSP 3766) and "Electric Guitar," by David Byrne for the Talking Heads (SIRE SRK 6076).

32. It was probably the Byrds, not the Beatles, who produced the first psychedelic song relating to LSD, in their "Eight Miles High" of 1966 (*Fifth Dimension,* (Columbia CS 9349).

33. See "Music Community Fighting Drugs, Censorship," *International Musician,* October 1986.

34. For an example see Paul Simon, "Kathy's Song," from *Sounds of Silence* (Columbia PC 9269).

35. For examples see "Mother Nature's Son," by the Beatles, and "One Love," by Bob Marley.

36. The image persists into the 1980s in the works of such artists as Bruce Springsteen, whose "Born in the USA," (cited above), with its lyrics of dissent, presents the small-town image in a negative way.

37. At least two books, in two different decades, appeared under the title *The Poetry of Rock:* Richard Goldstein's in 1968 and David Pichaske's in 1981. Both focus almost entirely on the lyrics, which are quoted extensively.

38. "With a Little Help from My Friends," "Fixing a Hole," and "Lucy in the Sky with Diamonds," all from the *Sgt. Pepper* album (Capitol SMAS 2653).

39. Roy Brown, "Good Rockin' Tonight"

(copyright 1948): Wynonie "Blues" Harris's 1947 recording of the rhythm-and-blues classic is on NW-261, which reprints the lyrics.
40. David Byrne, "Memories Can't Wait," from *Fear of Music* (1979).
41. Simon Frith, *Sound Effects: Youth, Leisure, and the Politics of Rock 'n' Roll* (New York: Pantheon, 1981), p. 30.
42. The best-known representatives, from the late 1940s and early 1950s, include Joe Turner, Wynonie "Blues" Harris, Louis Jordan, Aaron "T-Bone" Walker, McKinley Morganfield ("Muddy Waters"), Hank Ballard and the Midnighters, LaVern Baker, and the Chords. See NW-261, *Straighten Up and Fly Right: Rhythm and Blues from the Close of the Swing Era to the Dawn of Rock 'n' Roll.* For an interesting documentation of more regional sounds of the period, closer to the folk tradition, see *Roots: Rhythm and Blues* (Folkways RBF-20) and *Roots: The Rock and Roll Sound of Louisiana and Mississippi* (Folkways FJ-2865).
43. Beltz, *The Story of Rock*, p. 97.
44. For a more sociological interpretation of the death songs, or "coffin songs," see R. Serge Denisoff, *Sing Me A Song of Social Significance* (Bowling Green, OH: Bowling Green State University Press, 1983), pp. 171ff.
45. It is perhaps indicative of this that one of the most perceptive and readable histories of American pop music, *After the Ball*, came from a young British author: Ian Whitcomb wrote the book at the conclusion of his own brief career as a rock star both in England and America. See Further Reading for this chapter.
46. As Muddy Waters said to an American college audience, "I had to come to you behind the Rolling Stones and the Beatles. I had to go England to get here!" Quoted in Arnold Shaw, *Honkers and Shouters* (New York: Macmillan, 1978), p. 526.
47. Belz, *The Story of Rock.*
48. See, for example, the interview with Frank Zappa by Frank Kofsky in *Jazz and Pop*, reprinted in Eisen, *The Age of Rock*, p. 254.
49. On *Chicago Transit Authority*, GP 8 (1969).
50. Arnold Shaw, *Dictionary of American Pop/Rock* (New York: Schirmer Books, 1982), p. 76.
51. As has already been noted, the British and American rock scenes have been almost inextricably interwoven from the mid-1960s on, with British developments often slightly in the lead. Commuting is commonplace, as illustrated by the fact that the album in which Emerson's piece appears (*Five Bridges*) was recorded half in England and half in New York.
52. From the liner notes to *Five Bridges* (Mercury SR-61295).
53. See especially Procul Harum's *Live (with the Edmonton Symphony Orchestra)* (A&M SP-4335).
54. See "Norwegian Wood," on the album *Rubber Soul* (Capitol /Apple SW-2442).
55. Shaw, *Dictionary of American Pop/Rock*, p. 293.
56. Peter Belsito and Bob Davis, *Hardcore California: A History of Punk and New Wave* (Berkeley, CA: The Last Gasp of San Francisco, ca. 1983).
57. Of the singer Rozz it was written: "His very first gesture on the first night as the first chord was struck was to run full speed off the stage, land on the tops of the front tables, grab drinks out of people's hands, throw them down on the floor, and kick the chairs over" (Belsito and Davis, *Hardcore California*).
58. "New Wind," from the 7 Seconds album *New Wind*, by Kevin Seconds (Positive Force #8/Better Youth Records). For an introduction to this material the author is indebted to Chris Espinoza, and her paper "Alternative Rock: The Evolution of Punk," written for one of his classes at California State University, Sacramento.
59. Bernard Gendron, "New York: Rock Meets the Avant-Garde," a paper given at a meeting of the International Association for the Study of Popular Music, New York City, October 1985.
60. *Time*, October 27, 1986.
61. Shaw, *Dictionary of American Pop/Rock*, p. 301.

62. *Greatest Message's* by Grandmaster Flash and the Furious Five (SH 9121) may be taken as representative.
63. Both quotes in this section are from Frith, *Sound Effects*, pp. 75 and 79. The entire section "Musicians and the Audience" is a well-thought-out treatment of this apparent paradox.
64. Two quotes are illustrative: " 'Fantasy [Studios in Berkeley] is a very pristine studio' Leonard reports. 'No one ever trashed it before. They used to have three expensive designer lamps. Now they have only two because we decided to play baseball with apples and Phil hit a home run. They also had a few more bar stools until we realized that bar stool legs make better bats than drum sticks.

" 'During an afternoon off, the band decides to see what a fire extinguisher looks like when it hits the ground from 21 floors up. Well, they found out! It blew out the glass doors and windows . . . We all went into our rooms, folded our hands on our laps, and watched the Waltons [a significant choice as a symbol of respectability], just in case they came looking for us' remembers Leonard." Leonard, of Y&T, as reported in "Summer '85 Concert Calendar," *Aardvark*.
65. "The group finds that being so normal can get them into trouble. Says lead singer Katrina Leskenich, 'People in the business can't get used to the idea that we're decent and friendly' " (ibid.).
66. Charles Hamm has traced the evolution of this growing audience in his well-documented article "The Fourth Audience" in *Popular Music*, 1, pp. 123–41.
67. For an interesting article on this subject see "On Being Tasteless" by William Brooks, in *Popular Music, 2: Theory and Method*, ed. Richard Middleton and David Horn (Cambridge: Cambridge University Press, 1982), pp. 9–10.
68. Brock Helander, in a letter to the author.

Chapter 10: Secular Music in the Cities from Colonial Times to the Jacksonian Era

1. Julian Mates, *The American Musical Stage Before 1800* (New Brunswick, NJ: Rutgers University Press, 1962), p. 16.
2. Quoted in Oscar Sonneck, *Early Concert-Life in America, 1731–1800* (New York: Musurgia Press, 1949), p. 27. For much of the information on the concert life of this period I am indebted to Sonneck, who pioneered the serious and systematic study of American music, for the work that resulted in the book cited above. His painstaking study of contemporary newspapers up to 1800, is being expanded in a project being carried out by the society that bears his name; it can be supplemented, but never superseded.
3. Ruth Mack Wilson, *Connecticut's Music in the Revolutionary Era* (Hartford, CT: American Revolution Bicentennial Commission of Connecticut, 1979), p. 31.
4. "The College Hornpipe" is given as it appears in *Henry Beck's Flute Book*, a copybook containing instructions for the German flute, and 314 airs and dance and march tunes. The original is in the Library of Congress. Another version of "The College Hornpipe" is found in *A Choice Selection of American Country Dances of the Revolutionary Era, 1775–1795*, by Kate Van Winkle Keller and Ralph Sweet, 2d ed. (New York: Country Dance and Song Society of America, 1976). This little booklet is a treasure-trove of music and dance steps for eighteenth-century country dancing.
5. See Eileen Southern, *The Music of Black Americans*, 2d ed. (New York: W. W. Norton, 1983), chapters 2 and 3.
6. Sonneck, *Early Concert-Life in America*, p. 108ff.
7. Quoted ibid., p. 21.
8. Ibid., p. 48.
9. The circumstances attending, and contributing to, replacement of the amateur by the professional musician are treated with sympathy and perception by Richard Crawford in his notes to NW-299, *Music of the Federal Era*.
10. The best single sampling of concert music of the period is to be found on NW-

299, which treats both vocal and instrumental music, including an excerpt from the ubiquitous *The Battle of Prague.* It does not accurately reflect the *proportion* of American music on concert programs of the Colonial period, which were dominated by European music.

11. Sonneck sums up this development, and the reasons for it, in *Early Concert-Life in America,* pp. 121–22.

12. Ibid., pp. 20, 165, 168, 54.

13. Ibid., p. 54.

14. Ibid., pp. 88, 100.

15. From the preamble to the constitution of the Handel and Haydn Society, as quoted by Charles C. Perkins in *History of the Handel and Haydn Society* (New York: Da Capo, 1977), p. 39. A periodical article of 1815 further elucidates: "It is contemplated to practise the compositions of such European masters as have been most eminently great in their works of sacred music" (ibid., pp. 39–40).

16. The original manuscript of the Gibbs fife book is in the possession of the Connecticut Historical Society. The edited version is given as published in *Giles Gibbs, Jr.: His Book for the Fife,* edited by Kate Van Winkle Keller (Hartford: Connecticut Historical Society, 1974). This tune, which was also a fiddle and dance tune, can be heard, excellently played, on NW-276, along with three other such tunes.

17. Raoul Camus, in *Military Music of the Revolution* (Chapel Hill: University of North Carolina Press, 1976), provides a wealth of interesting detail as to the various calls or "beats," with musical examples, especially in chapter 4.

18. See Mates, *The American Musical Stage Before 1800,* p. 40.

19. See David McKay, "Opera in Colonial Boston," *American Music,* vol. 3, no. 2 (Summer 1985), p. 140, and O. G. Sonneck, *Early Opera in America* (New York: Benjamin Blom, 1963), p. 15.

20. Mates, *The American Musical Stage Before 1800,* p. 142.

21. See *"Disappointment* Revisited: Unweaving the Tangled Web" by Carolyn Rabson in *American Music,* vol. 1, no. 1 (Spring 1983), and vol. 2, no. 1 (Spring 1984), for details of the original, and of the three re-creations of the work in this century, the most recent of which was published, in full score with commentary, as vols. 3 and 4 of Recent Researches in American Music (Madison, WI: A-R Editions, 1976).

22. Both text and music of *The Indian Princess* were published in New York by Da Capo, 1972. Excerpts from the music are on NW-232.

23. "A Rose Tree" is included in the modern edition of *The Poor Soldier,* Recent Researches in American Music, vol. 6 (Madison, WI: A-R Editions, 1978).

24. See Anne Dhu Shapiro, "Action Music in American Pantomime and Melodrama, 1730–1913," *American Music,* vol. 2, no. 4 (Winter 1984).

25. Mates describes some of these in *The American Musical Stage Before 1800,* pp. 164ff.

26. Ibid., p. 64.

27. Quoted in Sonneck, *Early Opera in America,* p. 26.

28. Ibid., p. 121.

29. Mates, *The American Musical Stage Before 1800,* p. 73.

30. For samples of the detective work involved in matching tune to lyrics in eighteenth-century songs, see Carolyn Rabson's *Songbook of the American Revolution* (Peaks Island, ME: NEO Press, 1974), and Gillian Anderson's *Freedom's Voice in Poetry and Song* (Wilmington, DE: Scholarly Resources, 1977). Solving some of these fascinating problems has now been made easier by the publication of *The National Tune Index* (New York: University Music Editions, 1980).

31. In spite of competition from songsters, periodicals, and sheet music, the printing of ballads continued well beyond the eighteenth century; Malcolm Laws lists twenty-six nineteenth-century ballad printers in his *American Balladry from British Broadsides* (Philadelphia: American Folklore Society, 1957).

32. Gillian Anderson, examining issues of 126 newspapers, found nearly 1500 such lyrics printed during the ten-year period 1783–93. See her *Freedom's Voice in Poetry and Song.*

33. See Anderson, *Freedom's Voice in Poetry and Song*, and Rabson, *Songbook of the America Revolution*. NW 276 includes no fewer than six of these songs, the words of which were published in contemporary newspapers: "A Song on Liberty," to the tune of "The British Grenadiers"; "Junto Song," to the tune of "A-Hunting We Will Go"; "American Vicar of Bray," to the tune of "Country Gardens"; "Liberty Song" and "Come Shake Your Dull Noddles" (giving both the American and British sides of the issue), both to the tune of "Heart of Oak"; and "The King's Own Regulars," to the tune "An Old Courtier of the Queen's."

34. From *Eleazar Cary's Book*, in the collection of the Connecticut Historical Society. The tune also appears in *The American Musical Miscellany* of 1798 (reprint, New York: Da Capo, 1972). As indicated in the preceding note, the song in its parody version may be heard on NW-276.

35. The music as published consisted of a melody on one staff, under which the text for the singer was printed, and a bass line below on another staff. The keyboard player, according to long-established custom, would fill out the harmony in performance. The facsimile edition of Hopkinson's *Seven Songs for the Harpsichord* (Philadelphia: Musical Americana, 1954) shows this, as do individual pages reproduced in Hamm's *Yesterdays: Popular Songs in America* (New York: W. W. Norton, 1979) and the A-R editions of Benjamin Carr's music (cited below) and *The Poor Soldier* in Recent Researches in American Music, vol. 6 (Madison, WI: A-R Editions, 1978).

36. See Benjamin Carr, *Selected Secular and Sacred Songs*, Recent Researches in American Music, vol. 15 (Madison, WI: A-R Editions, 1986.)

37. See *Pelissier's Columbian Melodies*, Recent Researches in American Music, vols. 13 and 14 (Madison, WI: A-R Editions, 1978).

38. See Richard J. Wolfe, *Secular Music in America, 1801–1825: A Bibliography*. (New York: New York Public Library, 1964.)

Chapter 11: Popular Musical Theater from the Jacksonian Era to the Present

1. See D. W. Krummel's article "Publishing and Printing of Music" in *The New Grove Dictionary of American Music*, vol. 3, p. 652.

2. See Hans Nathan, *Dan Emmett and the Rise of Early Negro Minstrelsy* (Norman: University of Oklahoma Press, 1962), pp. 35–58.

3. Lewis W. Paine, in *Six Years in a Georgia Prison* (New York, 1851), quoted in Eileen Southern, ed., *Readings in Black American Music*, 2d ed. (New York: W. W. Norton, 1983), p. 91. Paine, a white man from Rhode Island, went to the South for an extended stay on business and was sentenced to prison there for helping a slave to escape.

4. See Nathan, *Dan Emmett*, pp. 44–49.

5. See Nathan, *Dan Emmett*, pp. 50–52. For the full story, as told in the *Atlantic Monthly*, see Charles Hamm, *Yesterdays: Popular Song in America* (New York: W. W. Norton, 1979), pp. 118–21.

6. Nathan, *Dan Emmett*, p. 128.

7. W. C. Handy gives a vivid account of the last heyday of the touring minstrel companies around the turn of the century (most of them by this time consisting entirely of black performers) in his autobiography *Father of the Blues* (New York: Macmillan, 1941), chapters 4 and 5.

8. Nathan, *Dan Emmett*, p. 276.

9. See Marshall Stearns, *The Story of Jazz* (New York: Oxford University Press, 1956), chapter 11.

10. See Douglas Gilbert, *American Vaudeville: Its Life and Times* (reprint of 1940 ed., New York: Dover, 1963), pp. 78–79.

11. Facsimile reprints of the original sheet music of all three of these James Bland songs, including the rather shocking caricatures on their covers, are found in Richard Jackson, ed., *Popular Songs of Nineteenth-Century America* (New York: Dover, 1976).

12. Gilbert, *American Vaudeville*, p. 284.

13. An archival re-creation of the 1921 production of *Shuffle Along* is available as NW-260. Of special relevance here is the minstrel-like skit "The Fight" on Side 2.
14. The complete song, with piano reduction, is reproduced in Nathan, *Dan Emmett*, pp. 320–23. It may be heard on NW-338.
15. Quoted in Nathan, *Dan Emmett*, p. 340. An explanation of syncopation, and some further examples, will be found in the treatment of ragtime in Chapter 13.
16. NW-338, *The Early Minstrel Show*. At least five of the songs and instrumental numbers quoted by Nathan in *Dan Emmett*, are included on this record.
17. Cecil Smith, *Musical Comedy in America* (New York: Theatre Arts, 1950), p. 16.
18. A single song, possibly borrowed from the repertory of the English music hall as an interpolation, is reprinted in Stanley Appelbaum, ed., *Show Songs from "The Black Crook" to "The Red Mill"* (New York: Dover, 1974).
19. A fleeting and fragmentary remnant of the songs, and the singing of some of the stars, of the heyday of vaudeville is conveyed in some of the early archival recordings in the *Smithsonian Collection of American Popular Song*, which includes recordings of Sophie Tucker from 1910, of Billy Murray from 1914, and of Al Jolson from 1921. Some useful re-creations (the style is principally Jolson's) are those of Don Meehan in the album *Song and Dance Man* (Folkways 3858).
20. John Graziano, from the excellent article on vaudeville in *The New Grove Dictionary of American Music*, vol. 4, p. 452.
21. A number of Braham's songs for the Harrigan and Hart shows are included in NW-265, and five of the songs are reprinted in Applebaum, *Show Songs* (cited above).
22. An assortment of Cohan's songs are found in Appelbaum, *Show Songs*, and in Robert Fremont, ed., *Favorite Songs of the Nineties* (New York: Dover, 1973). "The Yankee Doodle Boy" is included on NW-221.
23. "The Maid with the Dreamy Eyes" is included in Appelbaum, *Show Songs*.
24. "Mister Johnson, Turn Me Loose" and "May Irwin's Bully Song" are included in Appelbaum, *Show Songs*. A recording of "May Irwin's Bully Song" is included in NW-221. Two other songs of this genre, "Kentucky Babe" (subtitled "A Plantation Lullaby") and "Under the Bamboo Tree" (by Cole and Johnson, interpolated into the show *Sally in Our Alley*), are found in Fremont's anthology *Favorite Songs of the Nineties* (cited above).
25. A recording of Cook's "Darktown Is Out Tonight," from *In Dahomey*, is on NW-265. The sheet music for "I'm a Jonah Man," a song not by Cook, but interpolated into *In Dahomey* for the black comedian Bert Williams, is included in Appelbaum, *Show Songs*.
26. The archival recording of *Shuffle Along* is NW-260.
27. Jerome Kern, given his early experience in England, was to an extent cosmopolitan in this regard; and it must be said that Romberg, musically the most adaptable of the three immigrants, could on occasion write a tune as American in feel as any—as he showed, for example, in the lovely "Softly, as in a Morning Sunrise."
28. The entire number "If I Were on the Stage" is reprinted in Fremont, *Favorite Songs of the Nineties;* several other Herbert songs are found in Appelbaum, *Show Songs*.
29. An excellent sampling of this genre, with notes by George Oppenheimer, is NW-215, titled *Follies, Scandals, and Other Diversions: From Ziegfeld to the Shuberts*.
30. Gerald Bordman, *American Musical Comedy from "Adonis" to "Dreamgirls"* (New York: Oxford University Press, 1982), p. 189.
31. Douglas Watt, *New York Daily News*, May 3, 1984.
32. Bordman, *American Musical Comedy*, p. 186.
33. Andrew Lamb, in his article on the musical in *The New Grove Dictionary of American Music*, vol. 3, p. 295.
34. Bordman, *American Musical Comedy*, p. 188.
35. Musicals on American subjects greatly interested the German émigré

composer Kurt Weill in the late 1940s. His biographer Douglas Jarman has written: "During the last five years of his life Weill seems to have been more and more consciously attempting to create an indigenous operatic tradition based on the classics of American literature. . . . Lotte Lenya [Weill's widow] remembers finding on his desk a list of equally 'classic' subjects including *Gone with the Wind* and Melville's *Moby Dick* that Weill was considering using as the bases of future works" (from *Kurt Weill: An Illustrated Biography* by Douglas Jarman [Bloomington, Indiana University Press, 1982], p. 137). Clearly the American musical theater suffered a great loss in Weill's death.

There have been at least two other attempts to put Huck Finn on the musical stage— one in 1902, and *Huck and Jim on the Mississippi* in 1983, with songs by Bruce Pomahac and lyrics by Joshua Logan, which never reached Broadway.

36. Fannie Brice's singing of "Second-Hand Rose", which she did originally in *Ziegfeld Follies of 1921*, is included in NW-215. Al Jolson's singing of "Let Me Sing and I'm Happy" from the 1930 film *Mammy* can be heard on NW-238.

37. Ginger Rogers's singing of Berlin's "Cheek to Cheek," from the film *Top Hat,* is available on NW-238. Several examples of Fred Astaire's singing from the 1930s are included in the *Smithsonian Collection of American Popular Song.*

38. Grace Moore's singing of "Rock-a-Bye-Baby," from the 1925 *Music Box Revue,* is on NW-238.

39. Bill Robinson can be heard in a 1932 recording on NW-215, and Lena Horne, singing the title song "Stormy Weather," in the *Smithsonian Collection of American Popular Song.*

40. Ethel Waters can be heard on NW-238, and in 1925 recordings in the *Smithsonian Collection of American Popular Song.*

41. Danny Kaye can be heard in a 1942 recording on NW-215.

42. Mordden, *The Hollywood Musical* (New York: St. Martin's Press, 1981), p. 224.

Chapter 12: Popular Song, Dance, and March Music from the Jacksonian Era to the Advent of Rock

1. Sigmund Spaeth, *A History of Popular Music in America* (New York: Random House, 1948), p. 3.

2. Tawa, *A Music for the Millions* (New York: Pendragon, 1984), p. 1.

3. A perusal of the original published versions of these songs, facsimiles of which are in collections such as *Popular Songs of Nineteenth-Century America,* edited by Richard Jackson (New York: Dover, 1976), will verify this general description. The keyboard parts do tend to get a little more pianistic in the introductions and the rare interludes, but these could always be omitted.

4. Stephen Foster's "Ah! May the Red Rose Live Alway" (1850) shows the influence of Italian opera, in the introduction and postlude, and especially in the fermatas, which invite and even demand some kind of ornamentation. The song can be found in the *Stephen Foster Song Book,* edited by Richard Jackson (New York: Dover, 1974). Charles Hamm, in *Yesterdays: Popular Song in America* (New York: W. W. Norton, 1979), delineates the Italian influence in chapter 4, subtitled "Bel Canto Comes to America—Italian Opera as Popular Song."

5. See Hamm, *Yesterdays,* chapter 3.

6. Most of the songs cited in this section of the chapter have been selected with a view to their availability in facsimile reprints of the original antebellum sheet music editions. An early American edition (perhaps the first) of "Home, Sweet Home" (1823) is reprinted in Jackson, *Popular Songs.* "Long, Long, Ago" (1833) is also reprinted in *Popular Songs,* as well as in *Sweet Songs for Gentle Americans,* edited by Nicholas Tawa (Bowling Green, OH: Bowling Green University Popular Press, 1980). "Kathleen Mavourneen" is also in *Sweet Songs.*

7. "Flow Gently, Sweet Afton" is in *Sweet Songs.* Scottish influence on the

American parlor song was significant—probably second only to that of Ireland. The dates given for all songs in this chapter are the dates of the earliest known publication.

8. "Near the Lake" in *Sweet Songs.* The weeping willow was a much-used symbol of death.

9. "Ben Bolt" is in *Popular Songs.*

10. "The Ocean Burial" is in *Popular Songs.*

11. "The Hazel Dell" and "Rosalie, the Prairie Flower" are in *Sweet Songs.*

12. All of these Foster songs are reprinted from early editions, in *Stephen Foster Song Book.*

13. "Rock'd in the Cradle of the Deep" is in *Popular Songs.* Nicholas Tawa contributes this insight into the often-blurred distinction in the nineteenth century between the sacred and the secular in popular song, and between the sacred parlor song and the hymn: "Some sacred works are in the form of a prayer and therefore difficult to distinguish from contemporary hymns. The difficulty is compounded because hymns like Lowell Mason's 'Watchman Tell Us of the Night' (Boston, 1830) were also published for solo voice with piano accompaniment. Hymn settings in this format were purchased by the same Americans who enjoyed sacred and other parlor songs. . . . the line dividing sacred song and hymn is impossible to draw since both are stylistically so similar. Hymns were freely sung by soloists in concert and at home; sacred parlor songs were included in church services" (Tawa, *Sweet Songs for Gentle Americans,* p. 144).

14. "Love Not!" and "Be Kind to the Loved Ones at Home," with their diametrically conflicting advice, are both in *Sweet Songs.* "Ah! May the Red Rose Live Alway!" and "There's a Good Time Coming" are both in *Stephen Foster Song Book.*

15. "Old Rosin the Beau" (with its variant text, "Rosin the *Bow*") is in *Popular Songs.*

16. All the Foster songs mentioned in this paragraph are in *Stephen Foster Song Book.*

17. Both in *Popular Songs.* The dates given are merely those of the first known publications in America; the tunes, at least, of both songs are far older, and "We Won't Go Home Till Morning" has had many different sets of words. It was familiar in eighteenth-century France, and nineteenth-century Louisiana, with a satirical text beginning "Malbrough s'en va-t-en guerre" (see also Chapter 20, n. 3). Its best-known words, "For He's a Jolly Good Fellow," came from England later in the nineteenth century, according to Richard Jackson (see notes to *Popular Songs*).

18. All four of the songs mentioned in this paragraph are on the excellent album *An Evening with Henry Russell* (Nonesuch 71338), with notes by Charles Hamm.

19. Dale Cockrell, "The Hutchinson Family, 1841–45; or, the Origins of Some Yankee Doodles," *Newsletter of the Institute for Studies of American Music,* vol. 12, no. 1 (November 1982), p. 14.

20. Ibid., p. 13.

21. All the Stephen Foster songs cited in this chapter are included, in facsimiles of the original editions, in *Stephen Foster Song Book.*

22. William W. Austin, *"Susanna," "Jeanie," and "Old Folks at Home"; The Songs of Stephen C. Foster from His Time to Ours* (New York: Macmillan, 1975), p. 233.

23. See the quotation from Lewis Clarke's *Narrative,* in Austin, op. cit., p. 244.

24. "The First Gun is Fired! 'May God Protect the Right!' " is in *The Singing Sixties: The Spirit of Civil War Days Drawn from the Music of the Times* by Willard A. and Porter W. Heaps (Norman: University of Oklahoma Press, 1960), p. 18; its opening phrase shows an obvious indebtedness to Beethoven.

25. The fascinating story of "The Yellow Rose of Texas," a durable (though lately controversial) song that apparently originated during the Mexican War, is told in the monograph *The Yellow Rose of Texas: The Story of a Song* by Martha Anne Turner (El Paso: Texas Western Press of the University of Texas Press at El Paso, 1971).

26. I am indebted for much of the information in this section to Heaps, *The Singing Sixties* (cited above), and to the

extensive research that went into its preparation.

27. The tune and the Confederate text of "Maryland, My Maryland" are in *Popular Songs*. For a fuller account of the struggle for Maryland, with quotations from both versions, see *The Singing Sixties*, pp. 26–32.

28. The first published version of "I Wish I Was in Dixie's Land" is in *Popular Songs* and in *The Civil War Songbook: Complete Original Sheet Music for 37 Songs*, edited by Richard Crawford (New York: Dover, 1976); it can be heard on NW-202.

29. An excellent capsule history of "The Battle Hymn of the Republic," including excerpts from several different texts, is found in *The Singing Sixties*, pp. 50–54. A facsimile of the first published version is in *Popular Songs*.

30. Both "The Bonnie Blue Flag" and "The Battle Cry of Freedom" are in *Popular Songs*.

31. Stephen Foster's setting of "We Are Coming, Father Abraam" is in *Stephen Foster Song Book*. The earliest setting, by Luther O. Emerson, is in *The Civil War Songbook*, and may be heard on NW-202.

32. "Tramp! Tramp! Tramp!" is in *Popular Songs*.

33. "When Johnny Comes Marching Home" is in both *Popular Songs* and *The Civil War Songbook*. It may be heard in its original version on NW-202.

34. "Tenting on the Old Camp Ground" may be found in the same sources as "When Johnny Comes Marching Home" cited above.

35. "Just Before the Battle, Mother" is in *Popular Songs*.

36. "All Quiet Along the Potomac Tonight" is in both *Popular Songs* and *The Civil War Songbook*, and is on NW-202.

37. "The Drummer Boy of Shiloh" is in *The Civil War Songbook* and can be heard on NW-202; the tune and one verse are in Hamm, *Yesterdays*, p. 252.

38. "Weeping, Sad and Lonely" is in *The Civil War Songbook;* the text alone is in *The Singing Sixties*, p. 224. The song can be heard on NW-202.

39. The partial texts of these songs are found in *The Singing Sixties*, pp. 150–53.

40. Both the tune and words of "Goober Peas" appear in *Popular Songs*, and also in *The Singing Sixties*, pp. 136–37.

41. Words and music of "Abraham's Daughter" are in *The Singing Sixties*, pp. 81–83.

42. Ibid., p. 78.

43. The tune and one verse may be found in Hamm, *Yesterdays*, p. 251, and the full text in *The Singing Sixties*, p. 101–2.

44. The words of "I Goes to Fight mit Sigel" are in *The Singing Sixties*, p. 98.

45. Caroline Moseley, " 'When Will Dis Cruel War Be Ober?' Attitudes Toward Blacks in Popular Song of the Civil War," *American Music*, vol. 2, no. 3 (Fall 1984).

46. "We Are Coming from the Cotton Fields" is in *The Civil War Songbook* and is included on NW-202. "Kingdom Coming" is in both *Popular Songs* and *The Singing Sixties*, pp. 268–70.

47. "The Song of the Red Man" is included, with text and notes, in NW-267, *The Hand that Holds the Bread: Progress and Protest in the Gilded Age*. I am indebted to William Brooks, the annotator of this album, for the reference to these two songs, and for pointing out their interesting juxtaposition.

48. "The Hand That Holds the Bread," "Out of Work," "No Irish Need Apply," and "Drill, Ye Tarriers, Drill" can all be heard on NW-267. The last four songs mentioned in the paragraph are included in *Songs of Work and Protest* (New York: Dover, 1973).

49. "I'm a Good Old Rebel" may be heard on NW-202; words, music, and the highly graphic sheet music cover are in *Grace Notes in American History* (Norman: University of Oklahoma Press, 1967), p. 382–84.

50. Hamm, *Yesterdays*, p. 254.

51. All the songs mentioned in this paragraph, except "I'm a Good Old Rebel," are in *Popular Songs*.

52. For an example of a song urging tolerance and understanding for immigrants, see "Only an Immigrant" (1879) in *Grace Notes in American History*, p. 56–59.

53. See Russell Sanjek's highly informative monograph *From Print to Plastic: Publishing and Promoting America's Popular*

Music (1900–1980), I.S.A.M. Monograph no. 20 (Brooklyn: Institute for Studies in American Music, 1983). As Sanjek points out, there were monopolistic practices in the music publishing business, through the Board of Music Trade, beginning even before the Civil War, but no centralized dominance of the kind that later characterized Tin Pan Alley.

54. For the story of "I'll Take You Home Again, Kathleen" see Hamm, *Yesterdays*, pp. 262–64.

55. Alec Wilder has documented this extensively in *American Popular Song* (New York: Oxford University Press, 1972), which is organized along the lines of this stratification. George Gershwin noted the same thing early in his career; of his first acquaintance with the songs of Jerome Kern he wrote: "Kern was the first composer who made me conscious that most popular music was of inferior quality, and that musical-comedy music was made of better material."

56. Sanjek, *From Print to Plastic*, pp. 7–8.

57. Quoted in Isaac Goldberg, *Tin Pan Alley: A Chronicle of American Popular Music* (New York: Frederick Ungar, 1961), p. 207. An even more ingenious scheme for plugging a song called "Please Go 'Way and Let me Sleep" is also recounted.

58. Quoted in Goldberg, *Tin Pan Alley*, pp. 197–201.

59. The choruses of "After the Ball," "Daisy Bell," and "Forty-five Minutes from Broadway" illustrate all these rigorous conventions. All the songs cited in this paragraph are in *Favorite Songs of the Nineties*, edited by Robert Fremont (New York: Dover, 1973).

60. All the songs cited in this paragraph are in *Favorite Songs of the Nineties*.

61. All the songs cited in this paragraph are in *Favorite Songs of the Nineties;* "Bedelia" may be heard on *Song and Dance Man*, Folkways 3858.

62. Readers investigating this period are bound to encounter sooner or later the somewhat irrelevant controversy over Harney's race. While Eubie Blake has said that Ben Harney was black passing for white, more recent research has shown that Harney came from a white Kentucky family. See William Tallmadge's article on Harney in *The New Grove Dictionary of American Music*, vol. 2, p. 327.

63. Of the ragtime songs mentioned in this paragraph, "At a Georgia Camp Meeting" can be heard in a revised version as played by Sousa's band on NW-282; "Bill Bailey, Won't You Please Come Home" and "Under the Bamboo Tree," are in *Favorite Songs of the Nineties* (cited above); and "Waiting for the Robert E. Lee" can be heard on Folkways 3858, *Song and Dance Man*.

64. All the songs cited in this paragraph are in *Favorite Songs of the Nineties*.

65. See H. W. Schwartz, *Bands of America* (reprint, New York: Da Capo, 1975), p. 45. For an excellent sampling of the music of these brass bands of the 1860s, played on period instruments, see *The Yankee Brass Band: Music from Mid-Nineteenth Century America* (NW-312), which includes extensive notes, and pictures of the instruments.

66. Recordings of Sousa marches are of course numerous. Of particular interest are archival recordings on NW-282, *The Sousa and Pryor Bands*, which also has excellent notes. Also valuable is NW-266, *The Pride of America: The Golden Age of the American March*, with modern performances by the Goldman Band. A useful reminder that the Sousa marches were indeed *popular* music is the fact that they were published as sheet music, in piano transcriptions and sometimes even as songs supplied with words. A collection of twenty-three of these is published in facsimile, with their original covers, as *Sousa's Great Marches* (New York: Dover, 1975).

67. A lively and sympathetic description of the town bands of the period is given by Schwartz in *Bands of America*, pp. 170–76. Schwartz quotes ads placed in music papers and business magazines, for the purpose of attracting musicians to small communities that could offer them steady employment as well as a position in the local band. Of the twenty-three ads quoted, all but five are from towns in the Midwest.

68. NW-211, *Winds of Change*, documents

this development with notes, and with recordings, by the Northwestern University Symphonic Wind Ensemble, of five works for band from the 1950s and 1960s.

69. Sanjek, *From Print to Plastic*, pp. 13, 16.

70. Hamm, *Yesterdays*, pp. 337–39. Hamm gives two reasons for this continuity. One was economic, having to do with the dominance of ASCAP (the American Society of Composers, Authors and Publishers, founded in 1914), which served as a single source for songs in each of the new media. The other was artistic, and rests on the argument that the popular song style of the period, having been developed fairly recently, continued to meet relatively constant public needs during the entire period.

71. See NW-270, *American Song During the Great Depression*, for a sampling of topical and deliberately nontopical songs of the period.

72. Sanjek, *From Print to Plastic*, p. 19.

73. Hamm, *Yesterdays*, Appendix 5, pp. 487–88. Any list is apt to have its own self-contained bias, of course; a list of recorded songs may reflect the popularity of a particular dance band, or the popularity of their particular version of a song, as well as the inherent popularity of the song itself.

74. Wilder, *American Popular Song*, p. 254–74.

75. The anthology referred to is the 7-LP *American Popular Song*, one of the Smithsonian Collection of Recordings.

Chapter 13: Ragtime and Pre-Jazz

1. See Edward Berlin, *Ragtime: A Musical and Cultural History* (Berkeley: University of California Press, 1980), pp. 1–7.

2. For reference to a piano piece with ragtime syncopations published in 1886, see Berlin, *Ragtime*, pp. 107–8. For a discussion of the banjo's contribution to piano ragtime, see Lowell H. Schreyer, "The Banjo in Ragtime" in John Edward Hasse, ed., *Ragtime: Its History, Composers, and Music* (New York: Schirmer Books, 1985).

3. Arnold Shaw, *Black Popular Music in America* (New York: Schirmer Books, 1986), p. 42.

4. From *Ben Harney's Ragtime Instructor*, as quoted in Berlin, *Ragtime*, p. 115 (see also pp. 13–14).

5. See Shaw, *Black Popular Music*, pp. 43–44.

6. See for example "Miché Bainjo," in Allen, Ware, and Garrison, *Slave Songs of the United States*, 1867 (cited in the Further Reading section to Chapter 2).

7. See Rudi Blesh and Harriet Janis, *They All Played Ragtime*, 4th ed. (New York: Oak Publications, 1971), pp. 18 and 41.

8. This is graphically shown on a chart in Hasse, *Ragtime*, p. 15.

9. See "Ragtime on Piano Rolls" in Hasse, *Ragtime*.

10. See *Indiana Ragtime: A Documentary Album* in the Listening section at the end of this chapter.

11. See the article "May Aufderheide and the Ragtime Women" by Max Morath, in Hasse, *Ragtime* (cited earlier).

12. For an extensive treatment of ragtime arrangements see "Band and Orchestral Ragtime" by Thornton Hagert, in Hasse, *Ragtime*. Archival recordings of instrumental ragtime are rare, but a few examples are found in *The Sousa and Pryor Bands: Original Recordings 1901–1926* (NW-282); *Steppin' on the Gas: Rags to Jazz 1913–1927* (NW-269); *Ragtime*, I: *The City* (Folkways RBF 17); and *Ragtime* II: *The Country* (Folkways RBF 18). Some reconstructions by modern orchestras are heard on *Come and Trip It: Instrumental Dance Music 1780's–1920's* (NW-293).

13. A more genetic explanation of the syncopation of ragtime and jazz as survivals of the genuine polyrhythms of African music is put forward in Gunther Schuller's *Early Jazz: Its Roots and Musical Development* (New York: Oxford University Press, 1968), chapter 1, based on the research of A. M. Jones. However plausible and interesting this theory, a consideration of it is beyond the scope of this book. The explanation of syncopation (always a some-

what involved and risky undertaking!) presented here is intended to instill a workable understanding of it from the standpoint of the European-derived rhythmic basis (that of a single dominating pulse), which is the heritage and conditioning of most American listeners.

14. Berlin, in his *Ragtime,* pp. 82–89, includes a rather thorough treatment of ragtime syncopation that is consistent with the author's explanation.

15. These two performances of the *Maple Leave Rag* are the first two pieces in the *Smithsonian Collection of Classic Jazz.*

16. Berlin presents a succinct but fairly comprehensive treatment of ragtime form in his *Ragtime,* pp. 89–91. See also "Joplin's Late Rags: An Analysis" by Guy Waterman, in Hasse, *Ragtime.*

17. See "The Score versus Performance," pp. 76–78, in Berlin, *Ragtime.* See also "Jelly Roll Morton and Ragtime" by James Dapogny in Hasse, *Ragtime.*

18. Berlin, *Ragtime,* p. 61.

19. See *Mister Jelly Roll: The Fortunes of Jelly Roll Morton, New Orleans Creole and "Inventor of Jazz"* by Alan Lomax, 2d ed. (Berkeley: University of California Press, 1973) for the extensive transcription of Morton's reminiscences constituting his personal memoirs. His piano music has been painstakingly transcribed and edited by James Dapogny in *Ferdinand "Jelly Roll" Morton: The Collected Piano Music* (Washington, DC: Smithsonian Institution Press, 1982), which includes historical and textural annotations. See also "Jelly Roll Morton and Ragtime," also by Dapogny, in Hasse, *Ragtime.*

20. See Ronald Riddle's article "Novelty Piano Music" in Hasse, *Ragtime.*

21. James Chapman and Leroy Smith, *One o' Them Things?,* cited in Berlin, *Ragtime,* pp. 155–57.

22. The only readily available archival recording of *Dill Pickles Rag* is that made by the Kessinger Brothers in 1929, reissued on Folkways RBF-18, *Ragtime,* 2: *The Country.*

23. For further amplification of this subject, see the excellent article "Ragtime in Early Country Music" by Norm Cohen and David Cohen, in Hasse, *Ragtime,* a source for much of the information in this paragraph. Two relevant recordings, whose breadth of interpretation of the term "ragtime" serves to underscore the point made here, are *Ragtime,* 2: *The Country* (RBF 18) and *Maple Leaf Rag: Ragtime in Rural America* (NW-235).

24. "Darktown is Out Tonight" by Will Marion Cook, from the show *Clorindy* of 1898, is on NW-265. The music for "I'm a Jonah Man," by Alex Rogers, from the show *In Dahomey* of 1903, is in *Show Songs from the Black Crook to the Red Mill,* edited by Stanley Appelbaum, (New York: Dover, 1974).

25. Eileen Southern, *The Music of Black Americans,* 2d ed. (New York: W. W. Norton, 1983), p. 338.

26. Quoted ibid., p. 287. The sound of this orchestra may be heard on *A History of Jazz: The New York Scene 1914–1945* (Folkways RBF-3) and on *Steppin' on the Gas: Rags to Jazz 1913 to 1927* (NW-269).

27. An interesting account of the band's experiences is contained in *From Harlem to the Rhine,* by Arthur Little, who served as a captain in the regiment: excerpts are reprinted in Southern, *Readings in Black American Music,* 2d ed. (New York: W. W. Norton, 1983).

28. Quoted in Southern, *The Music of Black Americans,* p. 352.

29. Much of the foregoing is based on Bunk Johnson's description, as quoted in Marshall Stearns, *The Story of Jazz* (New York: Oxford University Press, 1956), pp. 50–51.

30. *The Music of New Orleans,* vol. 2; *Music of the Eureka Brass Band* (Folkways FA-2462).

31. From Foster's autobiography, quoted in Bruce Cook, *Listen to the Blues* (New York: Scribner's, 1973), p. 88.

Chapter 14: Jazz

1. André Hodeir, *Jazz: Its Evolution and Essence* (New York: Grove Press, 1956), chapter 2.

2. "Dippermouth Blues" is included in the *Smithsonian Collection of Classic Jazz* (this exists in an original edition, hereafter cited as "SmCCJo," and an enlarged revised edition, hereafter cited as "SmCCJr"; most pieces appear—as in the present case—in both editions, and for them the citation is "SmCCJ"). "Dippermouth Blues" is also in the Folkways History of Jazz (hereafter cited as "FHJ"), vol. 3. The fact that this New Orleans–based group actually made the recording in Chicago shows the state of dissemination and transition that jazz had already entered by 1923.

3. Charlie Parker's versions of "Embraceable You" are in SmCCJ.

4. Armstrong is well represented in most general anthologies, but note also the thirty-two selections in the Smithsonian's *Louis Armstrong and Earl Hines, 1928*. For additional examples of traditional jazz, beyond those found in general collections, see *The Legendary Freddie Keppard* (Smithsonian) and *Steppin' on the Gas: Rags to Jazz 1913–1927* (NW-269).

5. "Royal Garden Blues" is included in the Riverside History of Classic Jazz, no longer in print but still available in many libraries. "Jazz Me Blues" and "There'll Be Some Changes Made" are in FHJ, vol. 6. These last two recordings are interesting to listen to in connection with a rather illuminating critique of both by one of the musicians involved, Mezz Mezzrow. The first appendix of his *Really the Blues* (New York: Random House, 1946; paperback reprint, New York: Anchor, 1972) is a discussion of the whole relationship between the New Orleans and Chicago styles by a musician who speaks colorfully and lucidly from firsthand knowledge.

6. See Ronald L. Morris, *Wait Until Dark: Jazz and the Underworld 1880–1940* (Bowling Green, OH: Bowling Green University Popular Press, 1980). The subject is also treated in Mezzrow's *Really the Blues* (cited above).

7. See Chapter 13; also, Eileen Southern, *The Music of Black Americans*, 2d ed. (New York: W. W. Norton, 1983), chapter 12, and Southern, ed., *Readings in Black American Music*, 2d ed. (New York: W. W. Norton, 1983), chapter 8.

8. "Carolina Shout" is in SmCCJ; "You Can't Do What My Last Man Did" is in FHJ, vol. 7; "You've Got to be Modernistic" is in the *Encyclopedia of Jazz on Records*, vol. 1 (MCA 4061); "What Is This Thing Called Love?" is on NW-274. See also *Music of Fats Waller & James P. Johnson*, issued by Smithsonian.

9. Marshall Stearns, *The Story of Jazz* (New York: Oxford University Press, 1956; reprint, 1974), p. 122.

10. For an award-winning re-creation of this historic concert through the use of thirty-two archival recordings, accompanied by album notes, see the 2-LP set *An Experiment in Modern Music: Paul Whiteman at Aeolian Hall*, issued by Smithsonian. The original orchestration of *Rhapsody in Blue* was done by Ferde Grofé, and many subsequent orchestral versions have appeared, with varying degrees of authenticity.

11. For documentation of the development of the big bands elsewhere, notably in Chicago, St. Louis, Kansas City, and San Antonio, see *Big Bands and Territory Bands of the 1920s* and *Sweet and Low Blues: Big Bands and Territory Bands of the 1930s* (NW-256 and 217).

12. Fletcher Henderson's "Sugar Foot Stomp" is included in FHJ, vol. 7.

13. "The Stampede" is in SmCCJ. Five other Fletcher Henderson arrangements from the late 1920s and early 1930s are in the Smithsonian collection *Big Band Jazz* (SmCBBJ: see below, note 20).

14. "East St. Lous Toodle-Oo" is in SmCCJ in two versions, one from 1927 and the other from 1937. The title was evidently a misinterpretation of what Ellington actually called the piece—"East St. Louis *Todalo*." *Todalo* referred to a dance movement. See Chadwick Hansen, "Jenny's Toe Revisited: White Responses to Afro-American Shaking Dances,"

American Music, vol. 5, no. 1 (Spring 1987), p. 6. The entire article is an interesting exposition of the word in its many forms, and the movements to which it referred.

15. All the works mentioned in this paragraph are included in either SmCCJ or SmCBBJ. See also the Listening section at the end of this chapter.

16. Ellington's *Black, Brown and Beige* had its first complete performance since its 1943 Carnegie Hall premiere in a version Ellington had long envisioned, for big band and symphony orchestra, in Sacramento, California, in March 1988, as arranged by Randall Horton and performed by the Camellia Symphony.

17. "Toby" is in FHJ, vol. 10, on NW-217, and in SmCBBJ. "Moten Swing" is in both SmCCJ and SmCBBJ, and in the FHJ, vol. 8. "Every Tub" is on NW-274. "Dickie's Dream" is in FHJ, vol. 10. An early example is "There's a Squabblin' " by Walter Page's Blue Devils, with Count Basie on piano, from NW-256. Five more fine examples of the Basie band between 1937 and 1941 are included in SmCBBJ.

18. See Stearns, *The Story of Jazz,* pp. 149–50, and Nat Shapiro and Nat Hentoff, *Hear Me Talkin' to Ya* (reprint, New York: Dover, 1966), pp. 313–21.

19. Goodman's "St. Louis Blues" and "Sugar Foot Stomp" are included in *The King of Swing: Benny Goodman's Complete 1937–1938 Jazz Concert, No. 2* (Columbia S2-180).

20. The Smithsonian record collection *Big Band Jazz: From the Beginnings to the Fifties* (SmCBBJ) includes 52 pages of notes on the bands and the era.

21. "Tin Tin Deo" is included in *Three Decades of Jazz: 1939–1949* (Blue Note BST 89902).

22. "I Found a New Baby" is in SmCCJ and on NW-274.

23. SmCCJ includes several of these recordings; for a variety of small combos see NW-250.

24. "South Rampart Street Parade" and "Somebody Loves Me" are included in the *Encyclopedia of Jazz on Records,* MCA 4061–63.

25. "Down By the River" is in FHJ, vol. 3; "Make Me A Pallet on the Floor" is in the Riverside History of Classic Jazz (cited in note 5 above).

26. Arnold Shaw, *Black Popular Music in America* (New York: Schirmer Books, 1986), p. 162. For one view of the whole racial situation that prevailed in jazz in the 1930s and 1940s, see pp. 158–63.

27. Eckstine's "Good Jelly Blues" (1944) may be heard on NW-284; his "Cool Breeze" (1946) on SmCBBJ. Raeburn's "A Night in Tunisia" (1945, by Gillespie) and "Boyd Meets Stravinsky" (1946) are both in SmCBBJ. Thornhill's "Donna Lee" (1947, by Parker, arranged by Gil Evans) is on NW-284 and in SmCBBJ. Herman's "Apple Honey" (1945) is in SmCBBJ, and his "Lemon Drop" (1948) is on NW-271. Gillespie's own big band may be heard on both SmCBBJ and NW-271. Both Dan Morgenstern (in the notes to NW-271) and Mark Gridley (*Jazz Styles: History and Analysis,* 2d ed. [Englewood Cliffs, NJ: Prentice-Hall, 1985], pp. 143–44) caution against viewing bop as a revolt against the big bands, and stress its evolutionary rather than revolutionary origin.

28. "Shaw 'Nuff" and "KoKo" are in SmCCJ and in NW-271; the latter is devoted entirely to bop and has excellent notes.

29. "Oop-Pap-a-Da" is included in *The Bebop Era,* RCA Vintage LPV 519, no longer in print, but in many libraries.

30. "Boplicity" is in SmCCJ.

31. "Criss-Cross" is in SmCCJ.

32. "Django" is in SmCCJ. See also "Woody'n You," NW-242.

33. Tristano's work may be heard in SmCCJ and on NW-216.

34. See his suite *The Comedy,* excerpts from which have been published by MJQ Music. A single movement may be heard on NW-216.

35. Available, respectively, on *The Best of Horace Silver* (Blue Note BST 84325) and NW-242.

36. NW-271, *Bebop.*

37. *Kind of Blue:* Columbia PC 8163. For a rather extensive guide to and analysis of the pieces on this album, see Gridley, *Jazz Styles: History and Analysis,* 2d ed., pp. 216–23. "So What," from this album, can also be heard in SmCCJ.

38. "Alabama" is in SmCCJ; it can also be heard on the album *The Best of John Coltrane,* MCA2-4131.
39. "My Favorite Things" is on the album of the same title; it is also included in *The Best of John Coltrane* (cited above).
40. The Screaming Pygmy Orchestra of Sacramento is an example.
41. NW-201; another album from the same 1978 session is NW-303. Taylor's *Enter Evening,* of 1966, is in SmCCJ.
42. The seminal work in this regard is LeRoi Jones's book *Blues People* (New York: Morrow, 1963). Frank Kofsky, in *Black Nationalism and the Revolution in Music* (New York: Pathfinder Press, 1970), is concerned with political and social aspects, while John Storm Roberts, in *Black Music of Two Worlds* (New York: Praeger, 1972), explores the relation to Africa.
43. It is useful to consult Schuller's own writings on the subject, especially as in the 1980s he has broadened the meaning of the term "third stream" to include the synthesis of "the essential characteristics and techniques of contemporary Western art music and various ethnic or vernacular musics"—in other words, including other musics in addition to jazz. See his notes to NW-216; "Third Steam Revisited" in his *Musings* (New York: Oxford University Press, 1986); and his article "Third Stream" in *The New Grove Dictionary of American Music.*
44. *Summer Sequence,* "The Clothed Woman," and "Mirage" are all included in NW-216. More of the Kenton band's best work is represented in SmCBBJ by Bill Holman's arrangement of "What's New."
45. "The Jitterbug Waltz," as played by Fats Waller, was an early instance. Later examples include "It's a Raggy Waltz" and others by Dave Brubeck, found on *Adventures in Time* (Columbia G-30625).
46. "Tears of Joy" by Don Ellis is found in the album of the same title (Columbia KG 30927). All the other pieces referred to in this paragraph are on *Adventures in Time* (cited above).
47. Russell's "Concerto for Billy the Kid," composed for and recorded by Bill Evans in 1956, is on NW-216.
48. Schuller's "Transformation" is on NW-216.
49. The influence of third-world music is evident, for example, in "Second Sunday in August," where pedal point and the resultant static harmony show the influence of Indian music, and in the use of the African thumb piano in "Surucucu"; both are from the album *I Sing the Body Electric,* of 1971–72.
50. For illustrations of aspects of Corea's work referred to in this paragraph, see *Return to Forever* (ECM 1-1022) of 1972, and *Again and Again* (Elektra 60167) of a decade later.
51. Mark Gridley sets forth in some detail the distinctions between jazz itself and rock or jazz-rock, in *Jazz Styles,* 2d ed. pp. 312–17.
52. John McLaughlin, *Birds of Fire,* Columbia PC 31996.
53. Gridley, *Jazz Styles,* 2d ed., p. 312. On this and the following pages, he articulates with clarity the distinctions between jazz and rock.
54. Collier, *The New Grove Dictionary of American Music,* vol. 2, p. 558.
55. John Rockwell, *All American Music: Composition in the Late Twentieth Century* (New York: Knopf, 1983), p. 194.
56. Weather Report, *This Is This,* 1986 (Columbia FC 40280). "Update" is "electric bop," and "China Blues" is a one-chord piece, with extended melodic "play" on the traditional blue notes (the third, fifth, and occasionally seventh and second degrees of the scale).
57. Anthony Braxton, from notes to *Four Compositions* (*Quartet*) 1984 (BSR 0086), an album that illustrates the points made in the foregoing paragraph.
58. *The New Grove Dictionary of American Music,* vol. 4, p. 377. See also Schuller's brief, trenchant article "Third Stream Revisited" in *Musings* (cited above).
59. The Dixieland Jazz Festival in Sacramento, California, is an example; one of the nation's largest, it now draws groups from as far away as Poland and Russia.
60. The repertoire concept in jazz has been supported by such authorities as Martin Williams and Gunther Schuller. For an incisive statement in its favor, as

related especially to the works of Duke Ellington, see Schuller's article "The Case for Ellington's Music as Living Repertory," written originally for *High Fidelity* magazine, and reprinted in his *Musings*.

61. A comparison of tempos is interesting. Using the quarter note, typically defined in bop by the walking bass, as a basis, the up-tempo bop performances of the mid-1940s hovered around 300 to the minute. Gillespie and Parker's famous "Shaw 'Nuff" of 1945 (NW-271, SmCCJ) was played at 288; Parker pushed this to 312 in his "KoKo" of the same year (ibid.). The Gillespie band played "Things to Come" (NW-271, SmCBBJ), in 1946, at a frenetic 340, which was fast even for the up-tempo bop of the day, and the performance was not uniformly clean. By contrast, Ricky Ford's ensemble played his "One Up, One Down" (NW-204) in 1977 *cleanly* at 344. To set these tempos in context, the standard fast tempo numbers of the swing bands of the late 1930 were considerably slower; Benny Goodman played Fletcher Henderson's "Down South Camp Meeting" at 216 to the minute, and the Basie band performed "Doggin' Around" (SmCCJ) at 256. But even in the 1930s there were extraordinary precursors of bop tempos in the Midwest bands; Bennie Moten's famous "Toby" (NW-217, SmCBBJ, FHJ vol. 10) was played at an amazing 316 to the minute in 1932—faster than Parker's "KoKo"!

62. "Skain's Domain," on *J Mood* (Columbia FC 40308), 1985, with Wynton Marsalis, trumpet; Marcus Roberts, piano; Robert Leslie Hurst III, bass; and Jeff Watts, drums.

63. Rockwell, *All American Music*, p. 168.

64. "Breuker Battles the Bourgeoisie" in Giddins, *Riding on a Blue Note* (New York: Oxford University Press, 1981), pp. 205–10. A fairly detailed exposition of the music, the methods, and the aims—political, social, and aesthetic— of the Dutch saxophonist Willem Breuker and his group Kollektief (especially in the analogy between their work and that of the Chicago-born Association for the Advancement of Creative Musicians) is included in this 1979 article, which is an excellent introduction to the contemporary European jazz scene—a scene only sparsely represented by recordings available in this country.

Chapter 15: Laying the Foundation: Accomplishments from the Jacksonian Era to World War I

1. Irving Lowens, *Music and Musicians in Early America* (New York: W. W. Norton, 1964), p. 267.

2. As quoted by William Brooks in his notes to NW-231.

3. Oliver Shaw was a composer of songs, which he himself sang with great effectiveness. His "There's Nothing True but Heav'n," on a poem of Thomas Moore, is on NW-231.

4. NW-234.

5. William Mason (1829–1908), son of Lowell Mason, was a prominent pianist and teacher; Henry Mason (1831–90), another son of Lowell Mason, was an instrument builder, and co-founder of the Mason & Hamlin Piano Company; Daniel Gregory Mason (1873–1953), son of Henry Mason, was a prominent composer.

6. Ralph Waldo Emerson, "The American Scholar"; though his remarks referred to the activity of the scholar, and hence primarily to literature, his themes of embracing what is common and prizing what is at hand were later applied to music by one of his most fervent admirers, Charles Ives.

7. Betty Chmaj, in "Fry versus Dwight: American Music's Debate over Nationality" (*American Music*, vol. 3, no. 1 [Spring 1985], pp. 63ff), documents the two points of view as represented by Fry (the composer) versus Dwight (the critic), but the article involves many more figures, and the author presents what she calls the "double attraction" as a tension perennial in American art.

8. For an account of the early musical life of this frontier city, see Joy Carden, *Music in Lexington before 1840* (Lexing-

ton, KY: Lexington–Fayette County Historic Commission, 1980). In 1817, the year of Heinrich's arrival, a concert was given that included a performance of Beethoven's First Symphony.

9. The complete *The Dawning of Music in Kentucky* has been reprinted in facsimile (New York: Da Capo, 1972). The preface is reprinted in Gilbert Chase, ed., *The American Composer Speaks* (Baton Rouge: Louisiana State University Press, 1966).

10. NW-208.

11. The account, worth reading in full, is by John Hill Hewitt (son of the James Hewitt encountered in Chapter 10); it can be found in Chase, *The American Composer Speaks*, pp. 72–75.

12. Fry's comments on the potential of opera in English, and the preeminence of vocal dramatic music over any other kind, are set forth in his "Prefatory Remarks to Leonora," reprinted in Chase, *The American Composer Speaks*, pp. 47–52.

13. As quoted in Irving Lowens's excellent article "William Henry Fry: American Nationalist" in *Music and Musicians in Early America*.

14. Quoted in Lowens, *Music and Musicians in Early America*, pp. 217–18.

15. Quoted (drawing on John Tasker Howard, *Our American Music*) by Gilbert Chase, in *America's Music, From the Pilgrims to the Present*, 3d ed., (Urbana: University of Illinois Press, 1987), p. 308.

16. *Arcadian Symphony*, MIA 135; Symphony No. 2, MIA 143; Symphony in F-sharp Minor, MIA 144.

17. Margaret Fuller, an erudite and articulate member of Emerson's circle, wrote extensively on Beethoven.

18. Louis Moreau Gottschalk, *Notes of a Pianist*, transl. and ed. by Jeanne Behrend (New York: Knopf, 1964), pp. 300–303.

19. Ibid., pp. 39–40.

20. Ibid., p. 52.

21. Ibid., pp. 102–3.

22. Eileen Southern, *The Music of Black Americans: A History*, 2d ed. (New York: W. W. Norton, 1983), p. 250.

23. See Geneva Handy Southall, *Blind Tom: The Post–Civil War "Enslavement" of a Black Musical Genius* and *The Continuing Enslavement of Blind Tom, The Black Pianist-Composer (1865–1887)* (Minneapolis: Challenge Productions, 1979 and 1983). A third, concluding volume is in preparation.

24. See the material on both Blind Tom and Blind Boone, with musical examples, by Ann Sears in George Keck, ed., *Feel the Spirit: Essays in 19th Century Afro-American Music* (Westport, CT: Greenwood, 1988).

25. See Southern, *The Music of Black Americans.*

26. The First New England School is considered to be the eighteenth-century singing-school composers, including William Billings, Justin Morgan, Timothy Swan, Supply Belcher, and others. See Chapter 5.

27. See Herbert A. Kenny's notes to NW-268.

28. *The New Grove Dictionary of American Music*, vol. 3, p. 414, article by Maria F. Rich, Victor Fell Yellin, and H. Wiley Hitchcock.

29. See Ellen Knight, "Charles Martin Loeffler and George Gershwin: A Forgotten Friendship," *American Music*, vol. 3, no. 4 (Winter 1985), p. 452.

30. See note to NW-268 (cited above).

31. From the program notes for a 1933 performance, as quoted by Ellen Knight in notes for NW-332.

32. *The Dance in Place Congo* is on NW-228, which includes valuable notes (including a personal memoir of Gilbert) by David Baker. Cable's original articles have been reprinted in Bernard Katz, ed., *The Social Implications of Early Negro Music in the United States* (New York: Arno Press, 1969).

33. Arthur Farwell "A Letter to American Composers," *The Wa-Wan Press* (reprint, New York: Arno Press/New York Times, 1970), vol. 1, p. xvii.

34. Arthur Farwell, "An Affirmation of American Music" (1903), reprinted in Chase, *The American Composer Speaks*, pp. 91–93.

35. *A Guide to the Music of Arthur Farwell* has been privately printed; see Further Reading for this chapter. In many cases the same work was adapted for various

media (piano, chamber combination, chorus, orchestra).

36. See Listening list for this chapter; this is one of the few Farwell compositions that have been recorded.

37. *A Guide to the Music of Arthur Farwell,* p. 85.

38. *The Padrone,* a still-unperformed opera by George Chadwick, composed in 1912–13, is an operatic precursor of *The Godfather:* it "tells a realistic story of poor Italian immigrants whose lives are ruined by a small-time mafioso figure who controls them" (*The New Grove Dictionary of American Music,* vol. 1, p. 385, article by Steven Ledbetter and Victor Fell Yellin).

Chapter 16: Traditionally Evolving Classical Music After World War I

1. David Owens, "American Music's 'Golden Age' ", *The Christian Science Monitor,* May 12, 1982. Though Owens is not the only commentator to use the term "Golden Age," he has applied it consistently to the period 1929–55 in American music.

2. Roger Sessions, *Reflections on the Music Life in the United States* (New York: Merlin Press, 1956), p. 16.

3. See Aaron Copland and Vivian Perlis, *Copland: 1900–1942* (New York: St. Martin's, 1984), pp. 224–30.

4. Barbara Zuck, *A History of Musical Americanism* (Ann Arbor, MI: UMI Research Press, 1980), p. 8. Victor Fell Yellin, who takes issue with Zuck's work in a review (*American Music,* vol. 1, no. 1 [Spring 1983], pp. 70–76), suggests using "musical Americanism" for the advocacy, and "musical americanisms" for the use of specific musical ingredients.

5. From an open interview in 1979, as transcribed in the *Newsletter* of the Institute for Studies in American Music, November 1979.

6. Sessions, *Reflections,* p. 140. Paul Rosenfeld was an influential and controversial writer on the music of the time, enthusiastic about modern American music and active on its behalf. See Further Reading for this chapter.

7. Aaron Copland, *Music and Imagination* (Cambridge, MA: Harvard University Press, 1952), p. 104.

8. NW-228, with notes by R. D. Darrell.

9. Aaron Copland, *The New Music* (New York: W. W. Norton, 1968), pp. 161–62.

10. Kathleen Hoover and John Cage, *Virgil Thomson: His Life and Music* (New York: T. Yoseloff, 1959), pp. 177–78. The complete text of *The Plow that Broke the Plains* is included in the score of the orchestral suite, published by G. Schirmer (New York). The suite includes all of the music here discussed.

11. See Further Reading for Chapter 1 for bibliographical references for all three of these collections. Both Thomson and Copland consistently went to the most authoritative sources for their folk material.

12. All the cowboy songs used by Copland in *Billy the Kid* may be found in John and Alan Lomax's *Cowboy Songs and Other Frontier Ballads,* a basic collection first issued by John Lomax in 1910. All are reprinted by permission of The Macmillan Company.

13. Arthur Berger, *Aaron Copland* (New York: Oxford University Press, 1953), p. 93.

14. Excerpts from four of the American operas produced at the Metropolitan during this period, *Natoma, The King's Henchmen, The Emperor Jones,* and *Merry Mount* are found on NW-241, *Toward an America Opera,* with notes by Patrick J. Smith.

15. Victor Fell Yellin has pointed out interesting parallels, in terms of both text and text setting, between the work of Stein and Thomson and that of the nineteenth-century English team of Gilbert and Sullivan: "Virgil Thomson, Arthur Sullivan, Gertrude Stein, and William Gilbert," paper delivered at a meeting of the Sonneck Society in Lawrence, Kansas, April, 1982.

16. *The Cradle Will Rock* has been recorded (CRI SD 266).

17. See the article on Marc Blitzstein by Robert J. Dietz and Eric Gordon in *The*

New Grove Dictionary of American Music, vol. 1, p. 236.

18. An excellent sampling of American songs from this period is NW-247, with comprehensive notes by Philip Miller.

19. "Richard Cory" is included on NW-243. For an excellent brief study of Duke's songs see Ruth Friedburg, "The Songs of John Duke," *Bulletin of the National Association of Teachers of Singing,* May 1963.

20. "Richard Cory" on *Sounds of Silence,* Simon and Garfunkel (Columbia PC-9269).

21. "Luke Havergal" and "Miniver Cheevy" are also included on NW-243.

22. "Thomas Logge" from *Eight Epitaphs,* by Chanler, is included on NW-243.

23. The text by James Agee, omitted here for reasons of space, is included in the score published by G. Schirmer (New York), and with most recordings of the work; in its entirety (Barber did not use the entire text) it can be read in Agee's novel.

24. NW-296, with complete text, and notes by Michael Steinberg and Justin Kaplan.

25. Available in many recorded versions. Music published by New World Music (New York).

26. All four are on NW-277. Music published by Boosey & Hawkes (New York).

27. Available in several recorded versions. Music published by G. Schirmer (New York).

28. Both the Gershwin and the Thomson quartets are available in a useful 3-LP album of nine quartets issued as *American String Quartets,* vol. 2: *1900–1950* (Vox SVBX-5305).

29. Schuman's Quartet No. 3 is included in the Vox album cited in the preceding note. Score published by Theodore Presser (Bryn Mawr, PA).

30. Several recordings of Barber's *Summer Music* are available. Score published by G. Schirmer (New York).

31. Several recordings of Riegger's *Concerto for Piano and Woodwind Quintet* are available. Score published by Associated Music Publishers (New York).

32. Numerous recordings of Harris's Third Symphony are available. Score published by G. Schirmer (New York).

33. Roger Sessions, program notes, New York Philharmonic.

34. Ross Lee Finney's Concerto for Alto Saxophone is on NW-211.

35. Several recordings are available of the Elliott Carter Double Concerto. Score published by Associated Music Publishers (New York). The Nonesuch recording (H-71314) is the one that includes Carter's notes quoted subsequently in the chapter. These notes also appear in *The Writings of Elliott Carter* (see Further Reading list), pp. 326–30.

Chapter 17: Exploration and Experiment, I: New Ways with Old Tools

1. Cowell, Henry and Sidney, *Charles Ives and His Music,* rev. ed. (New York: Oxford University Press, 1969).

2. In *American Composers on American Music: A Symposium* (Palo Alto, CA, 1933; reprint, New York: Frederick Ungar, 1962). The Ives legend was subjected, in the late 1980s, to searching scrutiny—scrutiny that has had the effect of placing his work and his image in more accurate perspective, without diminishing his importance. See Maynard Solomon "Charles Ives: Some Questions of Veracity," *Journal of the American Musicological Society,* vol. 40, no. 3 (Fall 1987), pp. 443–70, and J. Peter Burkholder, "Charles Ives and His Fathers: A Response to Maynard Solomon," *Newsletter of the Institute for Studies in American Music,* vol. 18, no. 1 (November 1988).

3. For a famous and amusing anecdote concerning President Lincoln, General Grant, and George Ives's Brigade Band of the First Connecticut Heavy Artillery, see Cowell and Cowell, *Charles Ives and His Music,* p. 15.

4. For a rather full treatment of this theme, see Frank Rossiter, *Charles Ives*

and His America (New York: Liveright, 1975).

5. George Ives's copybook contains a version of "London Bridge" with the tune in G and the accompaniment in F-sharp. This was to prove a very seminal concept for Charles, as we shall see presently. While recent research (see note 2 above) has failed to find corroboration for George Ives's experimentation, it should be kept in mind that there is, on the other hand, no evidence to *disprove* it.

6. This description, together with other pregnant observations and speculations concerning the spatial element in music, is found in a rambling "Conductor's Note" published in 1929 with the Fourth Symphony (New York: Associated Music Publishers, 1965).

7. Included on *Old Songs Deranged: Charles Ives, Music for Theater Orchestra* (Columbia M-32969).

8. Cowell and Cowell, *Charles Ives and His Music*, p. 121.

9. For the partial text of an interesting penciled memo Ives wrote into the score concerning this plan of composing, see Charles Ives, *Charles E. Ives: Memos*, ed. John Kirkpatrick (New York: W. W. Norton, 1972), p. 164.

10. Charles Ives, *Essays Before a Sonata, and Other Writings* (New York: 1961; paperback reprint, 1964), pp. 97–98.

11. Ives, *Memos*, pp. 87–88.

12. Ibid., p. 104.

13. Cowell and Cowell, *Charles Ives and His Music*, pp. 176–77. For an interesting exposition of the way Ives introduced later changes into his works, see H. Wiley Hitchcock and Noel Zahler, "Just What *Is* Ives's Unanswered Question?," *Notes: The Quarterly Journal of the Music Library Association*, vol. 44, no. 3 (March 1988).

14. Ibid., pp. 4–5.

15. *Memos*, p. 142.

16. Cited in Vivian Perlis, ed., *Charles Ives Remembered* (New Haven: Yale University Press, 1974), p. 160.

17. Ives, *Essays Before a Sonata*, p. 84.

18. Ibid., pp. 88, 92–93.

19. Quoted in Cowell and Cowell, *Charles Ives and His Music*, p. 97.

20. Audience reaction to an early performance of Ruggles's music provoked a famous outburst from Charles Ives. He seldom went to concerts, but in 1931 he attended a Town Hall performance, under Slonimsky, which included *Men and Mountains*. In response to some hisses near him, Ives, according to his own account later, "jumped up and shouted 'You god damn sissy . . . when you hear strong masculine music like this, get up and use your ears like a man!' " (Ives, *Memos*, p. 141).

21. Charles Seeger, "Carl Ruggles," in *Musical Quarterly*, reprinted in Cowell, *American Composers on American Music*.

22. An excellent recording of Ruth Crawford Seeger's String Quartet is available (Nonesuch 71280). See Matilde Gaume, *Ruth Crawford Seeger: Memoirs, Memories, Music* (Metuchen, NJ: Scarecrow Press, 1986), and also "Ruth Crawford: A Promising Young Composer in New York, 1929–30," *American Music*, vol. 5, no. 1 (Spring 1987), by the same author.

23. Cowell's own performance of this and nineteen other of his piano compositions may be heard on *The Piano Music of Henry Cowell* (Folkways FM-3349).

24. These quartets were considered unplayable by Cowell himself at the time he wrote them (1915–19). Given the more highly developed technical skills of today's performers, this is no longer the case; Cowell's two-minute *Quartet Euphometric* has been recorded, and is available on *Chamber Works of Henry Cowell, Arthur Shepherd, and Roy Harris* (NW-218).

25. Most of these piano pieces are published (by Associated Music Publishers, New York), so that the notation is accessible for examination. All of this music may be heard in a recording as played by the composer himself (*The Piano Music of Henry Cowell*, Folkways FM-3349). Cowell performed these pieces for years on tour in the United States and abroad; his recorded renditions often differ significantly from the printed score. Nevertheless, the recording is a fascinating and well-nigh indispensable document, and includes the composer's spoken annotations.

26. Cole Gagne and Tracy Caras, eds.,

Soundpieces: Interviews with American Composers (Metuchen, NJ: Scarecrow Press, 1982), p. 283.

27. Henry Cowell, *New Musical Resources,* new ed. (New York: Something Else Press, 1969). See especially his section on "time," in which he says: "Some of the rhythms developed through the present acoustical investigation could not be played by any living performer; but these highly engrossing rhythmical complexes could easily be cut on a player-piano roll. This would give a real reason for writing music especially for player-piano" (pp. 64–65).

28. Study No. 3a–e and Study No. 6 are included in vols. 1 and 2, respectively, of the *Complete Studies for Player Piano,* 1750 Arch Records S-1768 and 1777.

29. Roger Reynolds, "Conlon Nancarrow: Interviews in Mexico City and San Francisco," *American Music,* vol. 2, no. 2 (Summer 1984), p. 6.

30. Study No. 22 is on 1750 Arch Records S-1777. Both Study No. 36 and Study No. 27 are on NW-203. Study No. 41 a–b–c is on 1750 Arch S-1768. (Though Nancarrow has called the New World recordings "terrible", they are cited because they are probably the most readily available examples of his music.)

31. Nancarrow himself devoted five years to making transcriptions in musical notation of a number of his Studies, some of which have been published in the periodical *Soundings.* However, in addition to being obviously unplayable, these are in many respects merely notational approximations of the original works' temporal relationships, and therefore do not constitute accurate archival documentation of the works as he conceived and executed them.

32. Recordings of most of the pieces mentioned are available; NW-281 includes a rather typical ten-minute chamber work, his Suite for Violoncello and Harp, on *Chamber Music by Lou Harrison, Ben Weber, Lukas Foss, and Ingolf Dahl.*

33. As Partch added more instruments to his collection, he rescored earlier works; thus the version of *U.S. Highball* recorded in Illinois in the late 1950s and issued by Gate 5 Records includes many more instruments than were used in the original version.

34. Partch's instruments are pictured and described in detail in his *Genesis of a Music,* 2d ed. (New York: Da Capo Press, 1974); their sound is demonstrated, with commentary by Partch himself, on a record that is included with the recording of his last large work, *Delusion of the Fury* (Columbia M2-30576).

35. Partch, *Genesis of a Music,* p. xi.

36. The Johnston String Quartet is available on Nonesuch H-71224, and the Sonata for Microtonal Piano on NW-203.

37. In a note to Odile Vivier, as quoted in Fernand Ouellette, *Edgard Varèse,* trans. Derek Coltman (New York: Orion Press, 1968), p. 56.

38. Varèse, "Freedom for Music," in Gilbert Chase, ed. *The American Composer Speaks* (Baton Rouge: Louisiana State University Press, 1966), pp. 190–91.

39. Varèse, from a lecture given at Princeton University, 1959; quoted in Elliott Schwartz and Barney Childs, eds., *Contemporary Composers on Contemporary Music* (New York: Holt, Rinehart, & Winston, 1967), p. 202.

40. Varèse, from a lecture, reprinted ibid., p. 197.

41. A first version of *Nocturnal* was performed in 1961, but he did not wish it performed again until he had revised it, a project he never completed.

42. Craft, jacket notes to Columbia ML-5478, which includes *Intégrales, Octandre,* and three other compositions of Varèse.

43. Ouellette, *Edgard Varèse,* p. 181.

Chapter 18: Exploration and Experiments, II: The Impact of Technology and New Aesthetic Concepts

1. Roger Sessions, "Problems and Issues Facing the Composer Today," in Paul Henry Lang, ed., *Problems of Modern Music* (New York: W. W. Norton, 1962), p. 24. Reprinted in *Roger Sessions on Music: Collected Essays* (Princeton, NJ:

Princeton University Press, 1979), pp. 71–87.

2. *Makrokosmos I* is available on Nonesuch 71293, and both *I* and *II* are on Attacca Records, Babel 8528-3.

3. Turnabout 34514.

4. See Lou Harrison, *Three Pieces for Gamelan with Soloists,* CRI 455, and *Double Concerto for Violin and Cello with Javanese Gamelan,* TR 109.

5. Both *She Was a Visitor* and *Sound Patterns* have been recorded on Odyssey 32160156 (now out of print).

6. Golden Crest CRS-4134.

7. Philips 6514254.

8. American Recording Society 37 (now out of print).

9. Alvin Lucier (b. 1931) based his *Music for Solo Performer* (1965, Davis, California) on the amplification of the alpha current, a low-voltage brain signal. David Rosenboom (b. 1947) has gone much further with this, and has produced recordings, and edited a publication *Biofeedback and the Arts: Results of Early Experimentation* (Vancouver: A.R.C., 1976).

10. See references in David Cope, *New Directions in Music,* 4th ed. (Dubuque, IA: William C. Brown, 1984), pp. 316–17.

11. John Cage, from David Cope, "An interview with John Cage," *The Composer,* vol. 10, no. 1 (1980), as quoted in Cope's *New Directions in Music,* p. 317.

12. Louisville Records 772.

13. NW-309.

14. Ralph Shapey, as quoted in notes to the recording of his *Evocation* (CRI 141).

15. Jonathan Kramer, "Moment Form in Twentieth Century Music," *Musical Quarterly,* vol. 64, no. 2 (April 1978); reprinted in Gregory Battcock, ed., *Breaking the Sound Barrier: A Critical Anthology of the New Music* (New York: E. P. Dutton, 1981).

16. Morton Feldman in an interview with Robert Ashley, in Elliott Schwartz and Barney Childs, eds., *Contemporary Composers on Contemporary Music* (New York: Holt, Rinehart & Winston, 1967), p. 365.

17. Ralph Shapey in notes about his own works, quoted on CRI 232 and 141.

18. Brian O'Doherty on the music of Morton Feldman, quoted on CRI 276.

19. John Cage, *Silence* (Cambridge, MA: MIT Press, 1966), p. 10. The notion of "letting sounds be themselves" is strikingly reminiscent of the Polish philosopher Wronsky's definition of music as "the corporealization of the intelligence that is in sounds"—a definition that greatly influenced Varèse.

20. Milton Babbitt, as quoted by Anthony Bruno in "Two American Twelve-Tone Composers," *Musical America,* vol.71, no. 3 (February 1951). See Gilbert Chase, *America's Music, From the Pilgrims to the Present,* 2d ed. (New York: McGraw-Hill, 1955), p. 618.

21. Paul Griffiths, *Modern Music: The Avant Garde Since 1945* (New York: George Braziller, 1981) p. 74. The entire book, though emphasizing European developments, is a lucid exposition of mid-century modernism.

22. Ernst Křenek, "Serialism," in John Vinton, ed., *Dictionary of Contemporary Music* (New York: E. P. Dutton, 1971), p. 673.

23. CRI S-461.

24. Milton Babbitt's *Three Compositions for Piano* (CRI S-461) is cited and analyzed by David Cope in *New Directions in Music,* 4th ed., pp. 42–44. Other available examples of total procedural control by Babbitt, who pioneered in this direction in this country, are *Post-Partitions* (NW-209) and two works on CRI SD-138, *Composition for Four Instruments* (1948) and *Composition for Viola and Piano* (1950).

25. Charles Wuorinen in an interview with Barney Childs, in *Contemporary Composers on Contemporary Music,* p. 375.

26. Milton Babbitt, "Who Cares If You Listen?" is reprinted both in Schwartz and Childs, *Contemporary Composers on Contemporary Music,* and in Gilbert Chase, ed., *The American Composer Speaks* (Baton Rouge: Louisiana State University Press, 1966).

27. Karlheinz Stockhausen, quoted in Michael Nyman, *Experimental Music: Cage and Beyond* (New York: Schirmer Books, 1974), p. 23.

28. Křenek, "Serialism" in Vinton, *Dictionary of Contemporary Music,* p. 673.

29. Foss's *Time Cycle* is available on CRS 8219. *Studies in Improvisation* is on RCA LM-2558 (currently out of print).
30. From notes to *Studies in Improvisation.*
31. John Cage, ed., *Notations* (New York: Something Else Press, 1969) reproduces a broad sampling of mid-twentieth-century notation.
32. David Cope, *New Music Composition* (New York: Schirmer Books, 1977), p. 116.
33. Cage, *Silence,* p. 59.
34. Ibid., p. 12.
35. Ibid., p. 59.
36. Some of the music heard at this landmark event can be heard on Desto 6466, *Tape Music: An Historic Concert.*
37. Ussachevsky, *A Piece for Tape Recorder.* The essay is reprinted in Lang, *Problems of Modern Music;* the piece is available on CRI SD-112 and Finnadar 9010.
38. Nonesuch 71225.
39. Louisville 5455.
40. CRI 112.
41. Gordon Mumma's *Hornpipe* is described at some length, with a picture and a diagram, in Cope, *New Directions in Music,* 4th ed. pp. 164–67.
42. All three of these compositions by Charles Dodge are available on CRI 348.
43. *The Dreamer That Remains: A Portrait of Harry Partch* is possibly the best of these, and is currently available, distributed by Films, Incorporated.
44. NW-357.
45. See Griffiths, *Modern Music,* pp. 126–28.
46. The Kronos Quartet, on the cutting edge of innovation in the field of chamber music, has "staged" such concerts.
47. From *An Anthology of Chance Operations;* quoted in Cope, *New Directions in Music,* 4th ed., p. 208.
48. *Souvenir,* by Donald Erb, is admirably described in Cope, *New Directions in Music,* 4th ed., pp. 232–35.
49. A recorded version of *HPSCHD,* reduced in forces, cut to twenty minutes in length, and of course lacking the excitement of the live visual element, was available on Nonesuch 71224 (now out of print).
50. CBS M4-38875.
51. Lovely Records LMC 4913.
52. John Cage, *A Year from Monday* (Middletown, CT: Wesleyan University Press, 1963), p. 19.
53. Ruth Dreier, "Minimalism" in *The New Grove Dictionary of American Music,* vol. 3, p. 240.
54. CBS MS-7178.
55. Steve Reich's simpler phase music includes *Clapping Music, Violin Phase,* and *Piano Phase;* no recordings of these are currently in print.

Chapter 19: Beyond Modernism: Autonomy, Assimilation, and Accessibility

1. William Bolcom, in the Introduction to *The Aesthetics of Survival* by George Rochberg (Ann Arbor: University of Michigan Press, 1984).
2. Michael Walsh, in notes to NW-335, which consists of music by George Rochberg and Jacob Druckman. It will be remembered that Darmstadt, Germany, host to annual summer convocations of the avant-garde after World War II, has been called the "citadel of serialism." In designating the 1960s as the watershed, Walsh thus assigns a fairly early date to the initial reactions to modernism, which points up the age of this trend, and the increasing overlapping of artistic trends in our time.
3. William Bolcom, in Rochberg, *The Aesthetics of Survival,* p. viii.
4. Billy Jim Layton, "The New Liberalism," *Perspectives of New Music,* vol. 3, no. 2 (Spring–Summer 1965).
5. George Rochberg in a 1981 paper, as quoted in John Rockwell, *All American Music: Composition in the Late Twentieth Century* (New York: Knopf, 1983), p. 87.
6. Available on CRI 231.
7. CRI 447.
8. Nonesuch 71255.

9. Available in several recorded versions.
10. NW-335.
11. Desto 6444.
12. Nonesuch 71283.
13. NW-318.
14. NW-331.
15. *The Hills of Mexico* (1984, Kicking Mule Records 340) by Daniel Kingman draws on the style (and the performers) of genuine traditional cowboy music, in creating a concerto grosso for fiddle, banjo, and orchestra; similarly, the same composer's *Living Fire* (1986) is an interpretation in symphonic terms of the idiom and the message of African-American gospel music.
16. DG 2740106.
17. Nonesuch 71260.
18. Both on Nonesuch 71260.
19. NW-309.
20. Layton, "The New Liberalism."
21. Among George Crumb's works using texts of Federico García Lorca are: *Ancient Voices of Children* (Nonesuch 71255); *Madrigals, Books I–IV, for Soprano and Instrumental Ensemble* (NW-357); *Night of the Four Moons* (CBS M-32739); *Songs, Drones and Refrains of Death* (Desto 7155); and *Night Music I* (CRI S-218). Two of David Del Tredici's "Alice" works available are: *In Memory of a Summer Day (1980) (Child Alice, Part I)* (Nonesuch 79043) and *Final Alice* (London LDR-71018). Two works of Stephen Albert on poems of James Joyce are *To Wake the Dead, for Soprano and Chamber Ensemble* (CRI S-420) and *Flower of the Mountain* (Nonesuch 79153). A third, *Treestone*, has not been commercially recorded as of this writing.
22. Nonesuch 79213.
23. NW-325.
24. Folkways 33903.
25. George Rochberg, quoted in notes to CRI 231, which includes *Contra Mortem et Tempus*.
26. John Corigliano, from an interview printed on the jacket of NW-309.
27. David Del Tredici, as quoted in Rockwell, *All American Music*, p. 83 (emphasis original).
28. Rockwell, *All American Music*, p. 77.
29. Both *Coming Together* and *Attica* are on Opus One 20.
30. Roger Sessions, "Problems and Issues Facing the Composer Today" in Paul Henry Lang, ed., *Problems of Modern Music* (New York: W. W. Norton, 1962), p. 24.

Chapter 20: Three Regional Samplings

1. See Irène Thérèse Whitfield, *Louisiana French Folk Songs* (New York: Dover 1969; reprint of 1939 ed.), which is still an important work in the field.

2. The term "Creole" can be a source of considerable confusion. It seems to have three distinct applications. The most generally accepted original meaning is that of a person of French, Spanish, or Portuguese descent born in the New World. But a parallel usage of "Creoles" refers to people of African descent born in the Western Hemisphere (as opposed to Africans, who were termed "bozoles"—both terms being derived from the Portuguese, and dating from the first slave importations by the Portuguese in the fifteenth century). A third, and informal, usage simply has the connotation of indigenous or "homemade" as applied to any food, furniture, customs, etc. of the Gulf states region.

3. "Malbrough s'en va-t-en guerre" is found in Whitfield, *Louisiana French Folk Songs*, p. 61 (concerning this song, see also Chapter 12, n. 17 above). Both "Le plus jeune des trois" and "Sept ans sur mer," as recorded in New Iberia, Louisiana, in 1934, are included in *Bahaman Songs, French Ballads and Dance Tunes, Spanish Religious Songs and Game Songs* (AAFS: L-5). Transcriptions are printed in John and Alan Lomax, *Our Singing Country* (New York: Macmillan, 1949).

4. "Les clefs de la prison" may be heard on AAFS L-5. "O chère 'tite fille," on the same album, was also used by Virgil Thomson, as was the Cajun song "Pas loin de chez moi," to be found in Whitfield,

Louisiana French Folk Songs, p. 108. "La femme qui jovait les cartes," a well-known Cajun song, has been reissued on *Louisiana Cajun Music: The Early 30's* (Old Timey 109).

5. "J'ai passé devant ta porte" is included in Old Timey 109 (cited above) under the title "Mon coeur t'appelle." Its printed version as a folk song appears in Whitfield, *Louisiana French Folk Song,* p. 88.

6. "Home, Sweet Home" may be heard in the *Anthology of American Folk Music* (Folkways 2952); the "Casey Jones" tune is found in Whitfield, *Louisiana French Folk Songs,* p. 114, as "Les filles de Mann Dugas."

7. The term is said to have originated in the words of a traditional song, "Les haricots sont pas sale" ("Beans are not salty")—*les haricots* being rendered in black Cajun dialect as *zarico* or, as usually found in print, *zydeco.*

8. The album *Clifton Chenier: Louisiana Blues and Zydeco* (Arhoolie F 1024), his first, gives a sampling of both his English-language rhythm-and-blues and Cajun-French zydeco repertoire. The Arhoolie catalog lists many more releases, by Chenier and other zydeco artists.

9. For a good sampler see *Zydeco Live,* on 2 LPs (Rounder 2069–70).

10. Two articles by Cable that included music, "The Dance in Place Congo" and "Creole Slave Songs," were printed in *The Century Magazine* in 1886, and are reprinted in Bernard Katz, ed., *The Social Implications of Early Negro Music in The United States* (New York: Arno, 1969).

11. Cable, "The Dance in Place Congo," in Katz, *Social Implications,* p. 42.

12. Henry Edward Krehbiel, *Afro-American Folksongs: A Study in Racial and National Music* (New York: Frederick Ungar, 1914; reprint, 1962), p. 151.

13. The music is from Whitfield, *Louisiana French Folk Songs.* An early commercial Cajun recording of it can be heard on *Anthology of American Folk Music* (Folkways 2952).

14. Some of the best treatment of black music in pre-twentieth-century New Orleans and the West Indies is found in Marshall Stearns, *The Story of Jazz* (New York: Oxford University Press, 1956): see especially chapters 3, 4, and 5. The author also wishes to acknowledge the assistance of the poet and researcher Brenda Marie Osbey of New Orleans.

15. Quoted in Leola Nelson Bergmann, *Americans from Norway* (Philadelphia: Lippincott, 1950), p. 52.

16. Quoted by LeRoy Larson in "Scandinavian-American Folk Dance Music of the Norwegians in Minnesota" (Ph.D. Thesis, University of Minnesota, 1975), p. 30. Larson devotes a chapter to "The Devil-Violin Belief in Minnesota and Scandinavia."

17. Andrea Een, a musician on the faculty of St. Olaf College in Northfield, Minnesota, performs the old repertoire on the Hardanger fiddle. Other performers, such as Archie Tiegan and Elmo Wick, play it in a style more like that of the regular fiddle. I am indebted to Philip Nusbaum, Folk Arts Program Associate of the Minnesota State Arts Board, for this information, and for samples of Hardanger fiddle playing.

18. See *Early Scandinavian Bands and Entertainers,* Banjar BR 1840.

19. This version of "Nikolina" is transcribed by the author from a 1930s recording reissued on the Banjar album just cited. Another version of it appears in *Scandinavian Old Time Music Book 2* (Minneapolis, MN: Banjar Publications, 1984), edited by LeRoy Larson.

20. Chinese in the Valley seeking to preserve their own musical traditions have been heavily dependent on San Francisco, with its large Chinese population. But Curtis Gaesser, a graduate student at California State University, Sacramento, witnessed and taped a performance by a group in Sacramento playing traditional Chinese instruments, under the leadership of Raymond Fong.

21. An accurate description of the Indian *raga* involves complex musical (in terms of scale and rhythm) combined with ethical concepts that are very imperfectly rendered by the single word "mode."

22. Joyce Middlebrook, a graduate student at California State University, Sacramento, has done a preliminary investigation of music in the culture of the Sikhs in Sutter County, and is at work on a master's thesis on one aspect of the subject.

23. Woody Guthrie, *Bound for Glory* (New York: E. P. Dutton, 1943), p. 293. Reprinted by kind permission.

The following have graciously granted permission to reprint copyrighted material:

Excerpt from "The False-Hearted Knight" from *British Ballads from Maine,* by Barry, Eckstorm, and Smyth (New Haven: Yale University Press, 1929). Reprinted by Permission.

Texts from Folkway Records Nos. 2317 and 2355. Reprinted by permission of Moses Asch, Folkway Records.

Excerpt from "Black Jack Davy" from *The Fiddle Book* by Marion Thede © 1967 by Music Sales Corporation, New York. Used by Permission.

Excerpt from "Black Jack Davie" from M.A. Thesis, "Some Representative Illinois Folk-Songs," David Seneff McIntosh, Iowa State University, 1935. Used by Permission.

Excerpt (2) from "Tom and Jerry" from *The Old-Time Fiddler's Repertory,* edited by R. P. Christeson, by permission of the editor and the University of Missouri Press. Copyright © 1973 by the Curators of the University of Missouri.

Excerpt (3) from "Tom and Jerry" from *The Fiddle Book* by Marion Thede © 1967 by Music Sales Corporation, New York. Used by Permission.

Excerpt from "Rabbit Dance" from the album notes to *Songs of Earth, Water, Fire, and Sky,* by Charlotte Heth. Recorded Anthology of American Music: NW-246.

"El Corrido Gregorio Cortez" from Folklyric LP 9004, Arhoolie Records, 10341 San Pablo Avenue, El Cerrito, CA 94530. Used by Permission.

"La Muerte de Martin Luther King" by Rafael Ramirez. Reprinted by Permission of RAMMS Music, A Division of House of Falcon, Inc.

Excerpts from *American Folksongs of Protest* by John Greenway. Reprinted by Permission of the University of Pennsylvania Press, Copyright © 1953.

"This Land Is Your Land," words and music by Woody Guthrie. © 1956 (renewed), 1958 (renewed), and 1970 Ludlow Music, Inc.

Excerpt from "Warm and Freedom Love," by Rev. Frederick Douglass Kirkpatrick; Copyright © 1968 by Rev. F. D. Kirkpatrick, 1978 by Sanga Music, Inc. Used by Permission. All rights reserved.

Excerpts from *The Gift to Be Simple* by Edward Deming Andrews. Reprinted by permission of J. J. Augustin Incorporated Publisher, Copyright © 1940.

Excerpt from *Down-East Spirituals* by George Pullen Jackson. Reprinted by permission of J. J. Augustin Incorporated Publisher.

Excerpt from "He Bore It All" by J. R. Baxter, Jr., and Virgil O. Stamps. © 1926 by Stamps-Baxter Music/BMI. All Rights Reserved. Used by permission of The Benson Co., Inc., Nashville, TN.

Excerpt from "Lord, Send Me Down a Blessing" by Willis Devone. © 1982 by Sure Been Good Music/BMI. All rights reserved. Used by permission of The Benson Co., Inc., Nashville, TN.

"I Worship Thee" ("You Taught Me How to Love") reproduced by permission of Bridgeport Music.

Excerpt from "You Don't Have to Jump No Pews" by Andrae Crouch. © 1979 by Communique Music (Administered by Copyright Management, Inc.). Reprinted by Permission.

"The Wabash Cannonball" adapted from Vance Randolph, *Ozark Folksongs,* edited and abridged by Norm Cohen (Urbana: University of Illinois Press, 1982). Used by Permission.

"Earl's Breakdown" © 1953 by Peer International Corporation. Copyright Renewed. International Copyright Secured. All Rights Reserved.

Excerpt from "The Hesitating Blues" by W. C. Handy. Reproduced by permission of Macmillan Publishing Company, A Division of Macmillan, Inc., from *Blues: An Anthology,* by W. C. Handy, edited by Jerry Silverman. © 1972, The Macmillan Company.

Excerpt from "Wall Street Blues" by W. C. Handy. Reproduced by permission of Macmillan Publishing Company, A Division of Macmillan, Inc., from *Blues: An Anthology,* by W. C. Handy, edited by Jerry Silverman. © 1972, The Macmillan Company.

Excerpt from "Subterranean Homesick Blues" by Bob Dylan. Copyright © Warner Bros. Inc. 1963. All Rights Reserved. Used by Permission.

Excerpt from "I-Feel-Like-I'm-Fixin'-to-Die-Rag." Copyright © 1965 Alkatraz Corner Music Co. Words and Music by Joe McDonald. All Rights Reserved. Used by Permission.

Excerpt from "I'm Not a Punker" by Kevin Seconds, reproduced by permission of Better Youth Publishing.

Excerpt from "Ladies Hope Reele," *His Fife Book,* Giles Gibbs, Jr. Facsimile Courtesy The Connecticut Historical Society.

Excerpt from "Lady Hope's Reel," *His Fife Book,* Giles Gibbs, Jr. Courtesy The Connecticut Historical Society.

Excerpt from "The Dusky Night," *Eleazar Cary's Book.* Photo by Robert J. Bitondi, Courtesy The Connecticut Historical Society.

Excerpt from "De Boatman's Dance," from *Dan Emmett and the Rise of Early Negro Minstrelsy* by Hans Nathan. Copyright © 1962 by the University of Oklahoma Press.

"Beautiful Girls" (Stephen Sondheim). © 1971 Range Road Music, Inc., Quartet Music Inc., Rilting Music, Inc., and Burthen Music Company, Inc. Used by permission. All rights reserved.

Excerpt from "I Ride an Old Paint" from *The American Songbag,* edited by Carl Sandburg. Reprinted by permission of Harcourt Brace Jovanovich. Copyright © 1927.

Excerpt from *Billy the Kid,* Aaron Copland. Copyright © 1946 by Aaron Copland; Renewed 1973. Reprinted by permission of Aaron Copland, Copyright Owner, and Boosey & Hawkes, Inc., Sole Publisher.

"Richard Cory" reprinted from *The Children of the Night,* by Edwin Arlington Robinson (New York: Scribner's, 1897).

Excerpts from *String Quartet III,* William Schuman. Copyright © 1942 by Merion Music, Inc. Used by Permission.

Text of *Tom Sails Away,* Charles Ives. Copyright © 1935 Merion Music, Inc. Used by Permission.

Excerpt from *The Cage,* Charles Ives. Copyright © 1955 by Peer International Corp. Used by Permission.

Excerpts from *Majority,* Charles Ives. Copyright © 1935 by Merion Music, Inc. Used by Permission.

Excerpts from *General William Booth Enters Into Heaven,* Charles Ives. Copyright © 1935 Merion Music, Inc. Used by Permission.

Excerpts from *Three Places in New England,* Charles Ives. Copyright © 1935 Mercury Music Corporation. Used by Permission.

Excerpt from *1, 2, 3,* Charles Ives. Copyright © 1935, Merion Music, Inc. Used by Permission.

Excerpt from *The Circus Band,* Charles Ives. Copyright © 1953 by Peer International Corp. Used by permission.

Text from *On the Antipodes,* Charles Ives. Copyright © 1935 Merion Music, Inc. Used by Permission.

Text of *Things Our Fathers Loved,* Charles Ives. Copyright © 1955 by Peer International Corp. Used by Permission.

Carl Ruggles: *Portals:* © 1930 American Music Editions, Theodore Presser Company.

Excerpt from "Bound for Glory," Woody Guthrie. Reprinted by permission of E. P. Dutton, Inc.

Index